OUTSIDE READINGS
IN
SOCIOLOGY

Outside
Readings in
SOCIOLOGY

EDGAR A. SCHULER
Department of Sociology and Anthropology
Wayne University

DUANE L. GIBSON
Department of Sociology and Anthropology
Michigan State College

MAUDE L. FIERO
Department of Sociology and Anthropology
Wayne University

WILBUR B. BROOKOVER
Departments of Social Science and of Sociology and Anthropology
Michigan State College

❦

THOMAS Y. CROWELL COMPANY

New York   1953

PREFACE

A DIFFICULT PROBLEM has arisen in recent years with respect to the use of college libraries for "outside reading" assignments by students in large classes, such as those in introductory sociology. A generation or two ago, with smaller classes and less crowded library conditions, all students could be required to supplement their professors' lectures and their adopted texts by going to the library. Today, however, the satisfactory use of this method has become all but impossible at most universities and colleges, especially with large, lower-division classes.

The present volume was prepared by the editors at the invitation of the publishers expressly to deal with this problem by making it possible for each student to enjoy the convenience of having his own copy of a comprehensive collection of carefully selected supplementary readings at an extremely low cost. In this connection it should be kept in mind that the editors consider that a book of readings should *complement* rather than *duplicate* the adopted text. Thus, the primary function of the textbook is to present the basic facts, concepts, and generalizations of a subject, whereas the role of the readings book is to encourage greater student interest, understanding, and motivation by illustrations and concrete examples.

The two most important criteria used by the editors were (1) Will this selection contribute to the student's clearer understanding of sociology? and (2) Is this selection readable? Before its inclusion every selection in this volume received a critical appraisal in the light of these criteria.

In order to provide reading material in the most useful and convenient form for students and teachers, the following features are included:

1. *Headnotes:* A short introductory statement appears at the beginning of each selection. In general, these provide brief introductions to the selections, call attention to certain inter-selection relationships not necessarily apparent from the table of contents, occasionally provide additional cues for possible multiple uses of specific selections, and sometimes generalize on the topic of the selection as it applies to the field of sociology.

2. *Biographical Notes:* The biographical notes, which appear as part of the bibliographical footnote on the opening page for each selection, have been prepared not only to document the scientific, scholarly, or artistic qualifications of the writers but to give some idea of the wealth and variety of experience they represent as a group.

3. *Correlation Table:* Suggestions for using the selections in the book with several leading recent textbooks in sociology are included in a correlation table at the back of the book.

4. *Index:* The index for this volume has been prepared so that the topics, as far as practicable, parallel those found in standard introductory sociology textbooks.

A final word should be said concerning some guiding principles that the editors have attempted to follow throughout the process of developing this work. They have tried to create a *balanced* book, of interest and value to college students of sociology generally, not primarily for students majoring in sociology, nor for the even more limited category of prospective professional sociologists. Nobody can fully please everybody—and the editors have not attempted by compromise to achieve the impossible. Believing in the possibility of genuine *liberal education,* they have sought to provide an orientation that will expand the reader's horizon and human concerns beyond his own immediate place and time; to inculcate a truly scientific humility in the face of diverse peoples, customs, and beliefs; and to affirm their own belief in the values of a maturing social science for our own democratic society, and for an increasingly rich and humane life for all peoples everywhere.

EDGAR A. SCHULER
DUANE L. GIBSON
MAUDE L. FIERO
WILBUR B. BROOKOVER

ACKNOWLEDGEMENTS

THE EDITORS wish to express their deep gratitude to all authors and publishers whose works were made available for inclusion in the present volume even though, in a few cases, last-minute changes in plans necessitated exclusion of selections whose reproduction had already been arranged. Special acknowledgement appears in connection with each selection.

The courtesy and helpfulness of several library staffs, together with the publications made available, were indispensable to the successful completion of this project. It is a distinct pleasure to acknowledge our indebtedness for such help to Wayne University Library; Michigan State College Library; Detroit Public Library, particularly the Social Sciences Department; and McGregor Library of Highland Park. The cordial assistance of Dr. Flint Purdy, Director of Libraries at Wayne University, at certain critical points is especially appreciated.

The editors also wish to acknowledge and express their deep appreciation for the assistance given them by others during their work on this project. Mrs. La May Adamson, a graduate student in the Department of Sociology and Anthropology, Wayne University, assembled with great resourcefulness the data on which the biographical notes are based. Miss Thelma Kostegian, first as student assistant and later as secretary to the Department of Sociology and Anthropology, Wayne University, has participated capably and conscientiously at every stage of the effort leading to this book. Likewise, a number of academic colleagues and administrative officials have encouraged the undertaking and have provided many helpful suggestions on selections and related matters. To all of these the editors extend their thanks.

Finally, the editors owe perhaps their greatest indebtedness to the members of their respective families and to Miss Lydia Holtman, who have ("practically" always) accepted uncomplainingly disrupted domestic living patterns "for the duration," and also have rendered substantial assistance in the later stages of the project.

CONTENTS

I: INTRODUCTION

II: ENVIRONMENT AND PRECONDITIONING FACTORS

III: PERSON AND GROUP

IV: SOCIAL ORGANIZATION: INTERPERSONAL RELATIONS AND UNIFORMITIES OF BEHAVIOR

V: SOCIAL ORGANIZATION: COLLECTIVE BEHAVIOR

VI: SOCIAL ORGANIZATION: STRATIFICATION AND MOBILITY

VII: SOCIAL ORGANIZATION: INSTITUTIONS AND INSTITUTIONALIZED BEHAVIOR

VIII: SOCIAL ORGANIZATION: ECOLOGICAL

IX: COMMUNICATON AND SOCIAL PROCESSES

X: SOCIAL AND CULTURAL CHANGE: DISORGANIZATION, PLANNING AND VALUES

APPENDIX: CAREER OPPORTUNITIES FOR PERSONS TRAINED IN SOCIOLOGY

CHAPTER I

INTRODUCTION

---

1. Can Science Be Explained? *

ACCORDING TO A SAYING traditional among students, "Sociology is a subject that deals with what everybody already knows in a way that nobody can understand." The idea behind the criticism implicit in this saying is a common one: science should be able to describe and explain "everyday things" in a way that a layman can easily grasp. A careful reading of this selection from a recent revolutionary book on writing style by Rudolf Flesch will, however, make clear why this simplicity and clarity cannot always be achieved for any audience.

Actually, says Flesch, there are *three* levels of scientific explanation. Two of these are for laymen, one of which discusses the operation, the other describes and explains the principle under consideration, and a third for scientists, which gives a technical description and analysis. The readings that appear in this book fit into the second or the third category. Most of them have been chosen because they illustrate concepts and principles employed in the science of sociology. They are expected to complement the more technical exposition of the standard introductory text.

* Rudolf Flesch, *The Art of Plain Talk* (New York, Harper & Bros., 1946), pp. 141-147. Reprinted by permission of the publisher and the author. Copyright, 1946, by Rudolf Flesch.

The author (b. 1911) is a lecturer at New York University, writer, and editorial consultant. Born in Vienna, he attended Columbia University on a refugee scholarship. Former Research Assistant, Association for American Adult Education; Columbia Broadcasting System, 1942-44; O.P.A. Information Specialist, 1944-46. Well known for his work on readability. *The Art of Plain Talk* sets forth his theories for the general public. His articles have appeared in *American Mercury*, *Harper's*, *Journal of Applied Psychology*, and *Public Administration Review*.

When people talk about something that's difficult to read, they are apt to say it's "too technical." The ordinary person, when he gets bogged down in a book or article, wouldn't think of saying, "The author of this can't write"; he will say, "A layman like me will never understand this" and let it go at that. In other words, most people think that some subjects are easy and some difficult and it hardly matters what language is used in explaining them.

I don't agree with those people. The principles of simple language are just as important, or maybe more so, in explaining, say, biochemistry, than they are for a news broadcast. The only difference is this: When you use simple language for anything that is not scientific or technical, you can explain it to anybody; but when you simplify science, you will find that only part of it will be understandable to the layman, and another part, however simply stated, will be clear only to people who have some training in that branch of science. There is no scientific discovery or theory that cannot be popularized—up to a point; the important thing is to know just what can be explained to the ordinary person and what can't.

Let me show you an example of what I mean: Some time ago Commander Howard S. Aiken of Harvard University developed a so-called mathematical robot, that is, an automatic calculator that can solve tremendous, otherwise insoluble mathematical problems. Now how can anybody explain this incredible machine to a layman? At first sight, you would think it's impossible; but that isn't so. In fact, the machine is being operated by laymen; they get a code book prepared by a mathematician and all they have to do is to follow the code and punch holes in a tape. So the operations of the machine can be explained very simply; the book probably says something like "First punch hole A6; then punch hole C31" and so on.

But you can also go one step further and explain to a layman what Commander Aiken was about when he was building that machine: you can tell what the problem was, for what purpose the machine was going to be used, what theory he had in mind and how he put it into practice, and finally what tests he used to be sure the monster-gadget worked. All this can be told in simple, ordinary language, and if it's properly dramatized and made interesting, it will go a long way toward explaining the meaning of this scientific development: not exactly what was done, but why and how it was done. It will give the layman an explanation he can understand, and usually that will be all he wants.

There is, of course, a third kind of explanation, a mathematical explanation of the machine for mathematicians. This, too, can be put in simple language, that is, short sentences, simple words and so on, and that will save mathematicians time and effort in reading their professional journals. But—let's face it—the layman will never understand the formulas and graphs. To understand exactly what Commander Aiken has done, you have to have so-and-so many years of higher mathematics, and that's that.

Or let's take another example that happens to be handy. How can the scientific yardstick formula of this book be explained? The answer is exactly the same. Again, there are three levels of explanation, two for laymen, one for scientists only. First, there is the *operation* of the formula: that can be explained by the simple set of directions which you will find in the back of the book. Second, there is the *meaning* of the formula: to explain that properly, I would have to go into the history of language simplifying, the relationship between language and understanding, the readability formulas that were developed by other researchers, the differences between those formulas and this one, and so on. Then I could dramatize the whole story and that would probably give most people all the explanation they want. However, there is still the third level, that of the *scientific* explanation; and here I would have to get into statistical regression formulas and multiple correlation and whatnot, and nobody who hasn't had a course in statistics would know what I am talking about.

Now let's see how the principles of language simplifying apply to these three types of scientific explanation. First, let's take a look at the language of operation sheets, directions, shop manuals, popular mechanics, the literature that tells how to do a technical job. Here is an example I picked at random from a book on papermaking:

In the event of there being more than one screen serving the machine (as is usually the case) it is necessary to watch carefully the operation of the screens with reference to the stock supplied them, and each valve should be opened or closed in proportion to the capacity of the screen it is feeding. If there is any difference in the capacities of the screens, it is probably due to the cams or toe-blocks being worn, or some other thing affecting the oscillation of the diaphragm.

Now obviously this is not very readable. But what are the obstacles the reader has to face? Certainly *not* the technical terms; in fact, any reader interested in papermaking machines is apt to know what a cam or a toe-block is, and if not, will have no trouble finding out. But that technical knowledge won't make it any easier for him to work his way through "in the event of there being" or "with reference to the stock supplied them" or "in proportion to the capacity." The simple fact is that people who know something about certain technical operations are usually those least equipped for writing about them or explaining what they know to somebody else.

Not so long ago a *New York Times* story described the excellent instruction manuals put out by Bell Telephone Laboratories for the Army and Navy. Let me quote one sentence: "The company has discovered that it is easier to hire a qualified editor and teach him what he needs to know about the technical terms involved than it would be to take a qualified engineer and teach him what he would need to know about the art of editing . . ."

If those papermakers had followed the same principle, our passage would probably read somewhat like this:

Usually the machine is served by more than one screen. If so, watch carefully how much stock goes through each. To keep the flow even, just open or close the valves. (If you want to make the screens work evenly, look first for worn cams or toe-blocks. Most often that's what makes the difference.)

In other words, all writing of the operation-sheet type should address the reader directly, and should tell him step by step what to do. It's as simple as that. Anybody who writes how-to-do prose should start off by reading a good cookbook; here, for instance, is a model paragraph from Fannie Farmer:

APPLE PIE
Line pie plate with pastry. Pare, core, and cut apples in eighths, put row around plate ½ inch from edge, and work towards center until plate is covered; then pile on remainder. Mix sugar, nutmeg, salt, lemon juice, and grated rind, and sprinkle over apples. Dot over with butter. Wet edges of undercrust, cover with upper crust, and press edges together. Prick several places with fork. Bake.

Anybody can understand that, and anybody can understand any kind of technical directions that are written in the same style.

When we come to the second level of scientific explanation, we find, oddly enough, that there is also one single standard formula. The reason is simple: Since the meaning of any modern scientific fact can only be explained by the method of its discovery, and since the scientific method is the same in all branches of science, any such explanation will be the story of a scientist, or several scientists, going through the classic four stages of modern scientific method: observation, hypothesis, deduction, and experimental verification. So this type of popularization will show how a scientist got curious about certain facts, thought up a theory to explain them, devised experiments to prove the theory, and finally tested it and found that it worked. If two scientists working on the same problem can be shown, so much the better: this will make the reader appreciate not only the scientific method, but also the fact that modern science is never a one-man affair.

Popular science written by this standard formula is probably the most educational type of writing there is: it's the only way of making laymen appreciate scientific method. But let's not get into this; let me rather show you a classic example. This is from a *Reader's Digest* article on penicillin by J. D. Ratcliff:

The story of penicillin begins in 1929, when Dr. Alexander Fleming . . . was examining a glass culture plate milky with millions of bacteria. His sharp eye detected something. There was a fleck of green mold on the plate, and around this fleck was a halo of clear fluid. *Something was destroying the bacteria!* A mold that had dropped in from the air was causing their sudden death on an unprecedented scale . . .

Dr. Fleming fished out the mold but research on it stood still for ten years . . . Then the sulfa drugs came along to reawaken interest in this field.

The sulfa drugs were amazing performers against some bacterial diseases; sorry failures against others. Something better was needed . . . Dr. Howard Florey of Oxford remembered Fleming's work. That green mold was poison to bacteria on culture plates. Might it not also work in the bodies of men?

Florey and his colleagues . . . decided to investigate . . . They set to work at the tedious task of growing the green mold in earthen-ware flasks. When the mold had grown into a hard, rubbery mat the chemists took over. Hidden somewhere in the mold was a bacteria killer.

By a slow process of elimination, the chemists discarded chemical components of the mold that had no antibacterial effect. In the end they turned up with the minutest pinch of a yellow-brown powdery stuff. This *might* be the bacteria murderer.

The first trials of the yellow powder were run in test tubes. It appeared that as little as one part in 160 million would slow the growth of bacteria! . . . This looked splendid. But there was still a big hurdle to overcome. The stuff somehow poisoned microbes. Might it not also poison men?

Florey and his helpers . . . shot huge doses of sure streptococcus death into 50 mice. Then the mice were divided into two groups of 25 each. One group would get no further attention; the other would get penicillin.

Within 17 hours all the unprotected mice were dead. . . . Hundreds of other mice trials followed, with similarly favorable results.

At last Florey was ready to carry his work from mice to men. . . .

And so on. This is science for laymen at its best, and it's written in typical *Reader's Digest* manner, so that an average person can understand it. But I hope you realize that it is a piece of what might be called science appreciation, not of scientific explanation. It does not even have the chemical formula for penicillin in it. In short, from a scientist's point of view, it offers no explanation at all.

To explain science fully, as I said before, you will have to use a third level of explanation, and this is where the layman will never be able to keep up with you. Suppose, for instance, you are asked for an explanation of what retene is, and the *Encyclopædia Britannica* gives you the following clue:

RETENE, an aromatic hydrocarbon occurring in wood tars and obtained by distilling resinous woods. It crystallises in colourless plates melting at 98.5° C and boiling at 394° C. Chronic acid oxidises the hydrocarbon to retene quinone (an *ortho*diketone) and permanganate oxidises the quinone to 3-hydroxy-*iso*propyldiphenyl—1:1':2'—tricarboxylic acid. These reactions show that retene is thyl-*iso*propylphenanthrene, $C_{18}H_{18}$, with the adjacent structural formula.

Plainly, there is no way of really telling a layman what retene is. To understand it, with or without simple language, you have to be a chemist, and that's that.

There is only one bit of advice I can offer in this business of giving laymen an exact scientific explanation: don't try. It is far better to be as frank as Bertrand Russell in his popular explanation of the relativity theory, who says at one point:

. . . this part can be expressed by the method of "tensors." The importance of this method can hardly be exaggerated; it is, however, quite impossible to explain it in non-mathematical terms.

Or, if you are unfortunate enough to be assigned to such an impossible job, you might add some sort of apology, the way Gove Hambidge did in the 1941 *Yearbook of Agriculture*:

. . . The editor would like to point out that to visualize even the more elementary aspects of atmospheric circulation over the earth is not easy, since you have to imagine that you are a mile or two up in the air, on your stomach with your head toward the North Pole, a clock nearby lying on its back so you can readily tell which is clockwise and which counter-clockwise rotation—also a mirror so you can see how everything would be reversed if you were in the Southern instead of the Northern Hemisphere, and you have to remember constantly that a south wind is a northward-moving wind, an east wind a westward-moving wind, and vice versa.

ᵕᦳᵕᦳᵕᦳᵕᦳᵕ

2. On the Relation of Pure to Applied Sociology *

THROUGHOUT THIS BOOK OF READINGS we are primarily concerned with illustrations of pure sociology; but the reader should never lose sight of the practical implications embodied in the works of pure science. In his book, *Applied Sociology*, Lester F. Ward clearly defines both pure and applied sociology, discusses their interrelationships, and shows how they differ from political and reform movements, such as socialism. More than fifty years ago Ward's sociological writings created such an intellectual stir in Russia that they were burned by order of the Imperial Council of Ministers. What probably most disturbed the reactionary Czarist officials was precisely the liberal ideas of applied sociology—"the conscious improvement of society by society"—found in this selection.

THE TERMS "PURE" AND "APPLIED" should be used in the same sense in social science as in all other sciences. Any apparent differences should be such only as grow out of the nature of social science as the most complex of all sciences, and hence the most difficult to reduce to exact formulas. It is important, therefore, to gain at the outset a clear conception of what is meant by these terms, and especially of the essential distinction between pure and applied sociology. Before proceeding, therefore, to set forth the principles of applied sociology at length, it may be well briefly to define the two branches with the special object of rendering this distinction clear.

PURE SOCIOLOGY

scientific inquiry into the actual condition of society

Pure sociology is simply a scientific inquiry into the actual condition of society. It alone can yield true social self-consciousness. It answers the questions What, Why, and How, by furnishing the facts, the causes, and the principles of sociology. It is a means of self-orientation. When men know what they are, what forces have molded them into

---

* Lester F. Ward, *Applied Sociology* (Ginn & Company, 1906), pp. 3-11. Reprinted by permission of the publisher.

The author (1841-1913), as one of the founders of sociology, ranks with Comte and Spencer. For forty years was with U. S. government in several scientific and research capacities. President of the Institut International de Sociologie, 1900-03. Professor of Sociology, Brown University, from 1906 until his death. First president of American Sociological Society, 1906-07. Widely known for research in paleobotany. *Dynamic Sociology* (1883) was his pioneer contribution to sociology. His books include *Sketch of Paleobotany*, *Psychic Factors of Civilization*, and *Pure Sociology*.

their present shape and character, and according to what principles of nature the creative and transforming processes have operated, they begin really to understand themselves.   Not only is a mantle of charity thrown over everything that exists, such as virtually to preclude all blame, but a rational basis is now for the first time furnished for considering to what extent and in what manner things that are not in all respects what they would like to have them may be put in the way of such modification as will bring them more into harmony with the desired state.   At least it thus, and only thus, becomes possible to distinguish between those social conditions which are susceptible of modification through human action and those that are practically unalterable or are beyond the reach of human agency.   In this way an enormous amount of energy otherwise wasted can be saved and concentrated upon the really feasible.

But by far the most important effect of the knowledge furnished by pure sociology is that of showing the difficulty of modifying certain conditions which are not absolutely unalterable, but which, without such knowledge, are supposed capable of easy alteration.   In most such cases those who imagine themselves to be sufferers from their presence believe that certain others have them under their control and might alter or abolish them if they were willing to do so.   This is the source of the greater part of the bitter class animosity in society.   In other words, the most important lesson that pure sociology teaches is that of the great stability of social structures.   But it also teaches that few if any social structures are wholly incapable of modification, and the further truth is revealed that in most cases such structures, though they cannot be changed by the direct methods usually applied, may be at least gradually transformed by indirect methods and the adoption of the appropriate means.

Applied sociology, therefore, rests upon pure sociology.   If it has any scientific character at all, it presupposes it and proceeds entirely from it.   In so far as the idea of reform inheres in applied sociology it can bear no fruit except it so proceeds.   Reform may be defined as the desirable modification of social structures.   Any attempt to do this must be based on a full knowledge of the nature of such structures, otherwise its failure is certain.   Such knowledge includes an acquaintance with the history of the structures to be affected.   This history must go back to a time when the structures were not injurious but useful. It must go back to the period of their development in response to external and internal stimuli.   Such a period there must have been in every case, otherwise the structures could never have come into existence.   In the prosecution of such a research it will not do to be deceived by names.   The names of institutions change, sometimes, after ceasing to be longer in harmony with social conditions, acquiring forms descriptive of their real or supposed evil character. Applied sociology looks beneath all this and learns from pure sociology what was their origin, what has been their complete history, and what is their true nature. With such data the question of their modification through the conscious action of society can be intelligently considered, and if, as is usually the case, they cannot be immediately abolished or abruptly changed, the way is made plain for the adoption of indirect means that will secure their gradual transformation and the elimination of their anti-social elements.

All this would mean a complete change in the whole method of reform. With the idea of reform has always thus far been associated that of heat rather than light. Reforms are supposed to emanate from the red end of the social spectrum and to be the product of its thermic and not of its luminous rays. But the method of passion and vituperation produces no effect. It is characteristic of the unscientific method to advocate and of the scientific method to investigate. However ardent the desire for reform may be, it can only be satisfied by dispassionate inquiry, and the realization of the warmest sentiments is only possible through the coldest logic. There either is or has been good in everything. No institution is an unmixed evil. Most of those (such as slavery, for example) that many would gladly see abolished entirely, are defended by some. But both the defenders and the assailants of such institutions usually neglect their history and the causes that created them. The hortatory method deals with theses and antitheses, while the scientific method deals with syntheses. Only by the latter method is it possible to arrive at the truth common to both. Only thus can a rational basis be reached for any effective action looking to the amelioration of social conditions.

APPLIED SOCIOLOGY

Just as pure sociology aims to answer the questions What, Why, and How, so applied sociology aims to answer the question What for. The former deals with facts, causes, and principles, the latter with the object, end, or purpose. The one treats the subject-matter of sociology, the other its use. However theoretical pure sociology may be in some of its aspects, applied sociology is essentially practical. It appeals directly to interest. It has to do with social ideals, with ethical considerations, with what ought to be. While pure sociology treats of the "spontaneous development of society," applied sociology "deals with artificial means of accelerating the spontaneous processes of nature." The subject-matter of pure sociology is achievement, that of applied sociology is improvement. The former relates to the past and the present, the latter to the future. Achievement is individual, improvement is social. Applied sociology takes account of artificial phenomena consciously and intentionally directed by society to bettering society. Improvement is social achievement. In pure sociology the point of view is wholly objective. It may be said to relate to social function. In applied sociology the point of view is subjective. It relates to feeling,—the collective well-being. In pure sociology the desires and wants of men are considered as the motor agencies of society. In applied sociology they are considered as sources of enjoyment through their satisfaction. The distinction is similar to that between production and consumption in economics. Indeed, applied sociology may be said to deal with social utility as measured by the satisfaction of desire.

In the analysis of a dynamic action . . . the only one of the three effects upon which it was found necessary to dwell was the direct effect of the action in transforming the environment. In applied sociology the only one of these effects considered is the one that was there put first, viz., that of satisfying the desire of the individual. In other words, while in pure sociology the constructive direct effects of human effort only were dealt with, in applied sociology it is the success of such efforts in supplying human wants that is taken into account.

All applied science is necessarily anthropocentric. Sociology is especially so. The old anthropocentric theory which taught that the universe was specially planned in the interest of man is not only false but pernicious in discouraging human effort. But true, scientific anthropocentrism is highly progressive, since it teaches that the universe, although very imperfectly adapted to man's interests, can be so adapted by man himself. Applied sociology is chiefly concerned with enforcing this truth. Throughout the theological and metaphysical stages of human thought philosophy was absorbed in the contemplation of the alleged author of nature. Pure science produced the first change of front, viz., from God to nature. Applied science constitutes a second change of front, viz., from nature to man. Nature is seen to embody utilities and effort is directed to the practical realization of these.

Applied sociology differs from the other applied sciences in embracing all men instead of a few. Most of the philosophy which claims to be scientific, if it is not actually pessimistic in denying the power of man to ameliorate his condition, is at least oligocentric in concentrating all effort on a few of the supposed élite of mankind and ignoring or despising the great mass that have not proved their inherent superiority. The question of superiority in general will be considered later, but it may be said here that from the standpoint of applied sociology all men are really equal. Nor is this in the Jeffersonian sense precisely, though it is a sense akin to that, viz., that, whatever may be the differences in their faculties, all men have an equal right to the exercise and enjoyment of the faculties that they have. Applied sociology is egalitarian to the extent of aiming to secure this right for all men equally. It is not only anthropocentric but pancentric.

With a few such exceptions, growing out of the nature of the science (and in this respect it does not differ from other sciences), applied sociology is entirely analogous to other applied sciences. No science can be applied unless it rests on exact mechanical principles. In Pure Sociology . . . it was shown that sociology does rest on such principles. Applied sociology assumes that these principles are true, and this work is therefore based on that one and cannot even be understood by one not acquainted with that. It does not, however, follow that the reader must accept as true all the principles laid down in that work. He may question their validity to any extent. But they may be clearly understood without being accepted, and all that is maintained here is that this work cannot be understood unless the principles set forth in that one are also understood.

Science is never exactly the same thing as art. Applied science is therefore not the same as art. If it is art it is not science. A science, whether pure or applied, is a discipline that can be taught more or less fully in a class-room, not necessarily from books, but from books, lectures, and object-lessons. In most sciences, even in the pure stage, field studies are of the highest importance, and in their applied stage it becomes almost essential for the student to apply the principles directly to nature, but this is almost always done in miniature, or on a small scale, for practice only, and without expectation of any practical result. In this way preparation may be made for all the practical arts. But the applied sciences thus taught are not the arts themselves. Applied mathematics is not mensuration, surveying, or engineering. Applied astronomy is not navigation. Applied physics is not manufacture. Applied chemistry is not agriculture. Applied biology leads to a great number of arts, some of which are of very recent origin.

Comte laid down two principles, which, however much they may fall short of universality, are well worthy of attention. One was that the practical applications of the sciences increase with their complexity. This was long rejected with disdain and the superior utility of the physical forces over any of the applications of vital phenomena was pointed to as its conclusive refutation. But are these forces more useful to man than those which have caused the earth to yield its cereals and fruits and have produced domestic animals?   And now, with the modern discoveries in bacteriology and kindred branches bringing their incalculable benefits to man, we may well doubt whether even electricity has proved a greater boon.

The other principle was that phenomena grow more susceptible to artificial modification with the increasing complexity of the phenomena. Comte did not illustrate this as fully as he should have done, but his main conclusion from it was that social phenomena are the most susceptible of all to modification.   Doubts as to the validity of this principle have been less freely expressed than in case of the one last considered.   But it seems to me that they are even more justifiable. Still, it depends here very much upon the point of view.   The modification of social phenomena has proved very difficult, while that of physical phenomena seems comparatively easy.   But this is a superficial view.   The real reason why attempts to modify social phenomena have so often failed is that the phenomena were not understood.   It is equally impossible to modify physical phenomena before they are understood.   Comte did not say that the complex sciences were more easily understood than the simple ones; on the contrary, he constantly insists on their greater difficulty of comprehension.   The principle under consideration, fully stated, would be that, assuming them equally well understood, the modifiability of phenomena is in direct proportion to their complexity.   Thus stated, it may be regarded as open to discussion.   No adequate attempt has yet been made either to confirm or to disprove it.   I am myself disposed to accept it with certain reserves; but this is not the place to discuss it in full.

But the degree to which the application of a science to human uses becomes possible, desirable, or prominent depends rather on the nature of the science than on its position in the hierarchy.   Sidereal astronomy has remained for the most part a science of pure contemplation, but there are great possibilities in astrophysics.   Nearly all branches of physics have proved useful, but until the discovery of the X-rays spectrum analysis remained a pure science.   Chemistry, though applicable to human uses in nearly all its departments, has probably thus far contributed less in this direction than has physics as a whole. Biology has already been mentioned, and its possibilities are immense, but the departments now found to be the most useful are the ones that were unknown a century ago, and long remained fields of mere idle curiosity, regarded as the farthest possible removed from any practical utility.   In this respect bacteriology may be compared to electricity.   Psychology is now almost exclusively a pure science, but no one dares to say that it will always remain such.   That sociology may become an applied science no one will dispute who believes that it is a science at all. And although its phenomena are the most complex of all and the most difficult fully to understand, when understood, if they ever are, the results their study promises in the direction of their modification in the interest of man are beyond calculation.

But applied sociology is not government or politics, nor civic or social reform. It does not itself apply sociological principles; it seeks only to show how they may be applied. It is a science, not an art. The most that it claims to do is to lay down certain general principles as guides to social and political action. But in this it must be exceedingly cautious. The principles can consist only of the highest generalizations. They can have only the most general bearing on current events and the popular or burning questions of the hour. The sociologist who undertakes to discuss these, especially to take sides on them, abandons his science and becomes a politician. A large part of Herbert Spencer's writings is of this character. Much of it is to be found even in his Synthetic Philosophy. It only reflects his prejudices and his feelings, and is not scientific. Moreover, as I have repeatedly shown, it is not in harmony with his system as a whole, but rather in conflict with it.

The same may of course be said of nearly the whole social reform movement embraced under the general term "socialism," and including the utopian schools as well as the practical ones—Fourier as well as Karl Marx. They all seek to bring about modifications in social structures. They would change human institutions more or less radically and abruptly. While the advocates themselves do not attempt, except in a few cases on a small scale, to produce these changes, they seek to create a public sentiment in favor of such changes sufficiently general to secure them through legislation. In so far as they actually succeed in this they accomplish their end. The changes are voted or decreed and the state strives to realize them. But often the institutions fail to yield even to the power of the state, and a long struggle follows, such as France is now having with the parochial schools. But all know in how few cases the social reform party acquires political control. This is on account of the stability of social structures. In old settled countries with definite class interests, prescriptive rights, and large vested interests, this is more clearly seen than in new countries, and hence it is in these latter that social reform movements are most successful. But the statistics show that the socialist vote is increasing in all countries where it is made a political issue, and the time may arrive when the party will come into power somewhat generally.

But all this is politics. It is art and not science. The sociologist has no more quarrel with any of these movements than he has with any other political parties,—Whig, Tory, Democrat, Republican. He observes them all, as he does all social phenomena, but they only constitute data for his science. All that he objects to is that any of these things be called sociology. Misarchism, anarchism, and socialism are programs of political action, negative or positive, and belong to the social art. They are not scientific theories or principles and do not belong to social science.

⋘⋙⋘⋙⋘⋙

3. The Transition to Science in Human Relations*

THE PRECEDING SELECTION (2, by Lester F. Ward) presents an early, classic discussion of the theoretical distinction between pure and applied sociology. The present selection is a contemporary treatment of many of these same ideas. In it George Lundberg sets forth the tremendous strides which have already been taken toward the application of science to human relations. He shows specific, present-day examples of this application and presents his ideas of the future steps which he feels must be taken if the social sciences are to assist in achieving more rational "management of social relations."

I

I HAVE EXPRESSED the view that the best hope for man in his present social predicament lies in a type of social science strictly comparable to the other natural sciences. We have reviewed some of the objections that have been urged both by physical and social scientists to this proposal. I am not under the illusion that my argument can be established conclusively in so brief a compass. Actually, of course, only time and future scientific development can finally demonstrate the validity of the position which I have outlined.

In the meantime, we are confronted with the necessity of proceeding

* George A. Lundberg, Can Science Save Us? (Longmans, Green & Co., Inc., 1947) pp. 35-42. Reprinted by permission of the publisher and the author.
The author (b. 1895) is Head, Department of Sociology, University of Washington. Research supervisor, Federal Emergency Relief Administration, 1934. Consultant, National Resources Planning Board, Washington, D. C. since 1942. Editor, Sociometry, 1941-45. Received University of Minnesota's Outstanding Achievement Award at the centennial celebration, 1951. His works include Foundations of Sociology, Social Research, and articles in American Sociological Review, Social Forces, Philosophy of Science, Harper's, and other magazines.

on some hypothesis as to the way out of our difficulties. It is generally agreed, even by those who differ most radically as to the proper approach, that our first need is a unified, coherent theory on which to proceed. A society cannot achieve its adjustments by mutually incompatible or contradictory behavior, any more than can an individual organism. However we may differ on details and on ends, we must agree on certain broad means, certain principles of action toward whatever ends we do agree upon.

In short, we all apparently agree with Comte's appraisal of the situation as he saw it almost a hundred years ago. Speaking of the theological, the metaphysical, and the positive scientific approaches, he said: "Any one of these might alone secure some sort of social order: but, while the three co-exist, it is impossible for us to understand one another upon any essential point whatever."

Of course there are some who find in our present predicament merely further evidence of the futility of the scientific approach in human affairs. They overlook the fact that, actually, science has as yet not been tried on social problems. Consequently, they advocate a return to theology, or "the" classics, either in their historic forms or in new versions in which the advocates of these approaches personally can play the role of major prophets. If I could see any chance of bringing about a return to theology or "the" classics, I might give it serious consideration, because any one unified approach might be better than two or more contradictory ones. But I see no such possibility in the long run. The commitments we have already made to science, chiefly in our technological culture, are of such character that we can neither go back nor stand still.

Our technological developments and our methods of communication have resulted in a fundamental interdependence which dominates our lives. This state of affairs requires, as we shall see, that we bring our social arrangements into line with this basic technological pattern, rather than vice versa. This basic technological pattern unquestionably rests upon natural science. On this ground, rather than on any assumption of absolute or intrinsic superiority of science as such, I think the following conclusion is inescapable: *In our time and for some centuries to come, for better or for worse, the sciences, physical and social, will be to an increasing degree the accepted point of reference with respect to which the validity (Truth) of all knowledge is gauged.*

If we accept this conclusion, then a number of questions arise. What are some examples of what the social sciences have done or might do in furthering sound and orderly adjustments in human relations? What, if anything, has been achieved in the social sciences to date? . . .

II

What are some examples of types of work by social scientists that are of vast importance in managing human relations?

The work of such agencies as the Census Bureau is known to all and is taken more or less for granted. Without the data and the analyses which it provides, the administration of public affairs would certainly dissolve in chaos and perhaps civil war. It is equally certain that no international organization can function without an elaborate organization of this kind to provide the essential facts regarding people and their characteristics and activities. Perhaps the most permanent contribution of the ill-fated League of Nations was the establishment of an international statistical bureau which still continues to function at Princeton University. The Office of Population Research of the same university is engaged in detailed studies of local population trends in Europe and elsewhere, including predictions of future areas of population pressure. This work would be of the utmost practical importance to the administration of any world organization. The Scripps Foundation, the Milbank Memorial Fund, and many others are engaged in similar or related work of a character that measures up very well to the standards of the physical sciences.

In the meantime anthropologists and sociologists have greatly extended our scientific knowledge of other peoples and cultures. This knowledge has in turn thrown a flood of light on our own civilization and permits the formulation at least of hypotheses regarding human behavior in general. The importance of this kind of knowledge in facilitating our contacts with other cultures during the recent war is too well known to require review. Is it not generally agreed that increasing contacts make the accumulation of such knowledge imperative in peace as well as in war?

We mentioned in the preceding chapter the importance of instruments and methods of observation and measurements in the social as well as in the physical sciences. Hundreds of such instruments have already been invented by means of which vocational aptitudes, success in college and other undertakings, and social behavior of great variety can be accurately measured and predicted. Perhaps the best known, but by no means the only one, of these devices is the public opinion poll. We have in this technique an illustration of how the development of the social sciences may be as significant for the future of social organization as many physical inventions have been in our industrial development.

The degree to which the public will can make itself reliably felt in government and in community action has always been in the foreground of political discussion. With the expansion of the areas within which public opinion must operate, many students of the problem have despaired of the capacity of the town meeting technique adequately to make operative the public will. In the face of this situation, social scientists have developed in recent years an instrument which cheaply and accurately permits us to learn the beliefs, the attitudes, and the wishes of the rank and file of the population. To be sure, the public opinion polls are at present thought of as interesting devices mainly for predicting the outcome of elections. But this is a very minor aspect of their full possible importance. These techniques also have been extensively used in the army and as a guide to the administration of liberated areas in Europe and elsewhere. Under the auspices of Allied Force Headquarters, Stuart C. Dodd developed a polling organization for determining in the invaded areas facts regarding the behavior and conditions of life as well as opinion regarding such subjects as public security, crime and the mores governing its control, the people's satisfaction with governing officials, attitudes toward co-belligerency, status of shelter and clothing, food supply and distribution, etc.

For example, complaints reached Allied authorities in Sicily regarding the malfunctioning of the rationing system. The local officials denied it and pointed to long lines of people ostensibly being served. A survey indicated that very few people had received their sugar ration for five months. Thereupon the local officials were confronted with these facts and were told to get busy. A follow-up survey in a week showed the situation greatly improved, and in two weeks practically corrected. Here we have a public which for the first time in years finds itself consulted on such matters and then observes that its complaints actually bring results. Experience of this kind probably goes farther than any propaganda for democracy that could be invented.

It may well be that in the perspective of history we have here a social invention—a technological device based on social science and on social research—which may rank in importance with gunpowder, telephone, or radio. It may be a device through which can be resolved the principal impasse of our age, namely, the apparent irreconcilability of authoritarian control on one hand and the public will on the other. It may be that through properly administered public opinion polls professionalized public officials can give us all the efficiency now claimed for authoritarian, centralized administration, and yet have that administration at all times subject to the dictates of a more delicate barometer of the people's will than is provided by all the technologically obsolete paraphernalia of traditional democratic processes. In short, it is not impossible that as advancing technology in one department of our lives leads to a threatened breakdown of democracy, so an improved social technology may restore and even increase the dominance of the people's voice in the control of human society.

I envision a time when the science of public opinion will be a science comparable to meteorology; when charts of all kinds of social weather, its movements and trends, whether it be anti-Semitism, anti-Negro sentiment, or mob-mindedness, will be at the disposal of the administrators of the people's will in every land. Dodd formulated and proposed to the United Nations plans for the establishment of a Barometer of International Security designed to detect authoritatively and early the tensions that lead to war. It is true that mere knowledge of these tensions does not automatically operate to alleviate them. But it is also true that a reliable diagnosis of the tension and an understanding of the sentiments that underlie it is essential for an intelligent approach to the problem. Right now it would be helpful to know exactly where are the pressure areas against Negroes and American-born Japanese. Is it not vitally important in postwar Europe to know where high and low pressure areas are in respect to the scores of minorities that must find their places in European society? We shall probably not hear anything more about the Barometer of International Security for the time being. The powers that be are obviously not interested in the wishes of the people who are being mercilessly bartered and moved about like so many pawns. But that does not affect the importance of the instrument as a technological achievement.

It would be easy to continue this recital of how developments in the social sciences already have ameliorated many social problems and have greatly facilitated public administration and policy. But the achievements are not merely in such obvious and practical fields as I have mentioned. The underlying theoretical and scientific knowledge upon which such practical devices rest must also be developed. As only one example of scientific work aiming directly at the construction and verification of scientific theory, I might call attention to Stouffer's study of the mobility habits of an urban population. Stouffer observed the apparently chaotic movements of the people of Cleveland in their frequent change of apartments. But isn't this much too complex for scientific study? Well, he considered various hypotheses which might constitute a generalized description of this behavior. He finally arrived at one hypothesis, which he states in rigorous mathematical terms. He then shows that a comprehensive study of the actual behavior of the people corresponds with remarkable accuracy to this hypothesis. The resulting generalization may be stated as follows: "The number of persons

going a given distance is directly proportional to the number of opportunities at that distance and inversely proportional to the number of
intervening opportunities." This law has subsequently been tested for
other cities and larger areas, and for at least one foreign country. It has
already been found to hold with certain modifications and under stated
conditions for the movements of the people of the United States as a
whole, and for Sweden.

We are not here interested primarily in the possible practical uses of
these findings. I cite the case rather as an illustration of the possibility
of arriving at scientific generalizations of social behavior essentially of
the same sort as those that, in their full development, have proved so
valuable in the physical sciences.

To those who constantly have their minds on quick and dramatic
solutions to the world's troubles this type of research is likely to seem
offensively trivial—a kind of fiddling while Rome burns. "Writers" are
fond of referring contemptuously to basic scientific work as an "ivory
tower" and as "lecturing on navigation while the ship sinks." Navigation today is what it is because some people were willing to study the
principles of their subject while their individual ships went down, instead of rushing about with half-baked advice as to how to save ships
that could not be saved, or were not worth saving anyway. As A. J.
Carlson has recently said: "The failure of bacteria to survive in close
proximity to certain moulds looked trivial at first, but few informed
people would label the discovery of that initial fact *trivial* today."

So much, then, for a few illustrations, rather than a summary, of the
the type of work that is being done and that needs to be done in the
social sciences. Is there enough of it being done? Clearly not, or we
would not need to flounder as we are in national and international
affairs, pursuing diametrically opposite courses within the same decade.
Can the social sciences ever hope to catch up with the other sciences,
the increasingly rapid advance of which constantly creates new social
problems? Certainly we can, if we devote ourselves to the business
with something like the seriousness, the money, and the equipment that
we have devoted to physical research. Consider how the physical scientists are today given vast resources to concentrate on the invention of a
new submarine detector or a new bomb, not to mention the peacetime
occupations of these scientists with penicillin and sulpha drugs. Obviously, I am not criticizing this action. On the contrary, it is the way
to proceed if you want results. Is there anything like that going on
regarding the world organization and its numerous subsidiary problems,
all of them important to peace and prosperity?

Comparatively speaking, there is almost nothing that could be called fundamental research into the basic nature of human relations. To be sure, there are endless petty projects, surveys, conferences, oratory, and arguments by representatives of pressure groups, as if argument ever settled any scientific questions. Of basic social research there is hardly anything. Why? . . . It is not yet realized that scientific knowledge is relevant to a successful world organization. We still think that common sense, good will, eloquent leaders, and pious hopes are sufficient when it comes to management of social relations.

❦❦❦❦

4. On the Concept of Function in Social Science *

SOCIOLOGICAL PHENOMENA can be analyzed both in terms of *structure* or form and in terms of *function*. Although this article by A. R. Radcliffe-Brown might be presumed, according to its title, to be addressed to a consideration solely of the latter term, it actually deals with the complex interrelationship of both concepts. The author spent many years studying primitive societies in Africa, Asia, Australia, and Oceania, convinced that such comparative materials were essential to the development of adequate generalizations about social structure and social function. The richness of ideas set forth in this article represent the product of long years of investigation by a distinguished anthropoligist.

THE CONCEPT OF FUNCTION applied to human societies is based on an analogy between social life and organic life. The recognition of the analogy and of some of its important implications is at least as old as Protagoras and Plato. In the nineteenth century the analogy, the concept of function, and the word itself appear frequently in social philosophy and sociology. So far as I know the first systematic formulation of the concept as applying to the strictly scientific study of society was that of Emile Durkheim in 1895.

* A. R. Radcliffe-Brown, *The American Anthropologist*, 27 (1935), 394-402; also included in his *Structure and Function in Primitive Society* (Glencoe, Illinois, 1952; London, Cohen & West Ltd., 1952). Reprinted by permission of the publisher and the author.

The author (b. 1881) is a British anthropologist. Emeritus Professor, Oxford University. Has had varied career as a Professor of Anthropology: Cape Town, Sydney, Chicago, Oxford. President Anthropological Institute, 1939-40. Member, Royal Academy of Sciences, Amsterdam. Author, *The Andaman Islanders, The Australian Aborigines, Taboo*. Editor, *African Systems of Kinship and Marriage* (with Daryll Forde).

Durkheim's definition is that the "function" of a social institution is the correspondence between it and the needs of the social organism. This definition requires some elaboration. In the first place, to avoid possible ambiguity and in particular the possibility of a teleological interpretation, I would like to substitute for the term "needs" the term "necessary conditions of existence," or, if the term "need" is used, it is to be understood only in this sense. It may here be noted, as a point to be returned to, that any attempt to apply this concept of function in social science involves the assumption that there are necessary conditions of existence for human societies just as there are for animal organisms, and that they can be discovered by the proper kind of scientific enquiry.

For the further elucidation of the concept it is convenient to use the analogy between social life and organic life. Like all analogies it has to be used with care. An animal organism is an agglomeration of cells and interstitial fluids arranged in relation to one another not as an aggregate but as an integrated whole. For the biochemist, it is a complexly integrated system of complex molecules. The system of relations by which these units are related is the organic structure. As the terms are here used the organism is not itself the structure; it is a collection of units (cells or molecules) arranged in a structure, i.e., in a set of relations; the organism has a structure. Two mature animals of the same species and sex consist of similar units combined in a similar structure. The structure is thus to be defined as a set of relations between the entities. The structure of a cell is in the same way a set of relations between complex molecules, and the structure of an atom is a set of relations between electrons and protons. As long as it lives the organism preserves a certain continuity of structure although it does not preserve the complete identity of its constituent parts. It loses some of its constituent molecules by respiration or excretion; it takes in others by respiration and alimentary absorption. Over a period its constituent cells do not remain the same. But the structural arrangement of the constituent units does remain similar. The process by which this structural continuity of the organism is maintained is called life. The life-process consists of the activities and interactions of the constituent units of the organism, the cells, and the organs into which the cells are united.

As the word function is here being used the life of an organism is conceived as the functioning of its structure. It is through and by the continuity of the functioning that the continuity of the structure is preserved. If we consider any recurrent part of the life-process, such as respiration, digestion, etc., its function is the part it plays in, the contribution it makes to, the life of the organism as a whole. As the terms are here being used a cell or an organ has an activity and that activity has a function. It is true that we commonly speak of the secretion of gastric fluid as a "function" of the stomach. As the words are here used we should say that this is an "activity" of the stomach, the "function" of which is to change the proteins of food into a form in which these are absorbed and distributed by the blood to the tissues. We may note that the function of a recurrent physiological process is thus a correspondence between it and the needs (i.e., necessary conditions of existence) of the organism.

If we set out upon a systematic investigation of the nature of organisms and organic life there are three sets of problems presented to us. (There are, in addition, certain other sets of problems concerning aspects or characteristics of organic life with which we are not here concerned.) One is that of morphology—what kinds of organic structures are there, what similarities and variations do they show, and how can they be classified? Second are the problems of physiology—how, in general, do organic structures function, what, therefore, is the nature of the life-process? Third are the problems of development—how do new types of organisms come into existence?

To turn from organic life to social life, if we examine such a community as an African or Australian tribe we can recognize the existence of a social structure. Individual human beings, the essential units in this instance, are connected by a definite set of social relations into an integrated whole. The continuity of the social structure, like that of an organic structure, is not destroyed by changes in the units. Individuals may leave the society, by death or otherwise; others may enter it. The continuity of structure is maintained by the process of social life, which consists of the activities and interactions of the individual human beings and of the organized groups into which they are united. The social life of the community is here defined as the functioning of the social structure. The function of any recurrent activity, such as the punishment of a crime, or a funeral ceremony, is the part it plays in the social life as a whole and therefore the contribution it makes to the maintenance of the structural continuity.

The concept of function as here defined thus involves the notion of a structure consisting of a set of relations amongst unit entities, the continuity of the structure being maintained by a life-process made up of the activities of the constituent units.

If, with these concepts in mind, we set out on a systematic investigation of the nature of human society and of social life, we find presented to us three sets of problems. First, the problems of social morphology

—what kinds of social structures are there, what are their similarities and differences, how are they to be classified? Second, the problems of social physiology—how do social structures function? Third, the problems of development—how do new types of social structure come into existence?

Two important points where the analogy between organism and society breaks down must be noted. In an animal organism it is possible to observe the organic structure to a large extent independently of its functioning. It is therefore possible to make a morphology which is independent of physiology. But in human society the social structure as a whole can only be observed in its functioning. Some of the features of social structure, such as the geographical distribution of individuals and groups can be directly observed, but most of the social relations which in their totality constitute the structure, such as relations of father and son, buyer and seller, ruler and subject, cannot be observed except in the social activities in which the relations are functioning. It follows that a social morphology cannot be established independently of a social physiology.

The second point is that an animal organism does not, in the course of its life, change its structural type. A pig does not become a hippopotamus. (The development of the animal from germination to maturity is not a change of type since the process in all its stages is typical for the species.) On the other hand a society in the course of its history can and does change its structural type without any breach of continuity.

By the definition here offered "function" is the contribution which a partial activity makes to the total activity of which it is a part. The function of a particular social usage is the contribution it makes to the total social life as the functioning of the total social system. Such a view implies that a social system (the total social structure of a society together with the totality of social usages, in which that structure appears and on which it depends for its continued existence) has a certain kind of unity, which we may speak of as a functional unity. We may define it as a condition in which all parts of the social system work together with a sufficient degree of harmony or internal coniistency, i.e., without producing persistent conflicts which can neither be resolved nor regulated.

This idea of the functional unity of a social system is, of course, a hypothesis. But it is one which, to the functionalist, it seems worth while to test by systematic examination of the facts. . . .

The concept of function as defined above constitutes a "working hypothesis" by which a number of problems are formulated for investigation. No scientific enquiry is possible without some such formulation of working hypotheses. Two remarks are necessary here. One is that the hypothesis does not require the dogmatic assertion that everything in the life of every community has a function. It only requires the assumption that it may have one, and that we are justified in seeking to discover it. The second is that what appears to be the same social usage in two societies may have different functions in the two. Thus the practice of celibacy in the Roman Catholic Church of to-day has very different functions from those of celibacy in the early Christian church. In other words, in order to define a social usage, and therefore in order to make valid comparisons between the usages of different peoples or periods it is necessary to consider not merely the form of the usage but also its function. On this basis, for example, belief in a Supreme Being in a simple society is something different from such a belief in a modern civilized community.

The acceptance of the functional hypothesis or point of view outlined above results in the recognition of a vast number of problems for the solution of which there are required wide comparative studies of societies of many diverse types and also intensive studies of as many single societies as possible. In field studies of the simpler peoples it leads, first of all, to a direct study of the social life of the community as the functioning of a social structure, and of this there are several examples in recent literature. Since the function of a social activity is to be found by examining its effects upon individuals, these are studied, either in the average individual or in both average and exceptional individuals. Further the hypothesis leads to attempts to investigate directly the functional consistency or unity of a social system and to determine as far as possible in each instance the nature of that unity. Such field studies will obviously be different in many ways from studies carried out from other points of view, e.g., the ethnological point of view that lays emphasis on diffusion. We do not have to say that one point of view is better than another, but only that they are different, and any particular piece of work should be judged in reference to what it aims to do. . . .

5. A Study of Attitudes *

SIGNIFICANT ADVANCES were made in the application of social science research to practical problems in human relations while our country was going through one of its most serious crises—World War II. This selection by Samuel A. Stouffer, war-time head of the professional staff of the Research Branch in the War Department's Information and Education Division, describes some of that group's research. The perspective of history may prove, as the author maintains, that the major development of social science research in World War II was in the area of *attitudes*, just as that of World War I was in the area of "*aptitudes*." Certainly, the uses of the findings he describes here appear to be manifold. This selection, like that by Professor Lundberg (3), should give the reader some "feeling" for the utility and worth-while applications of the scientific study of individual and group behavior in practical situations.

IN JULY, 1941, the Secretary of War issued an order prohibiting surveys of attitudes of enlisted men. If their attitudes were critical of the Army, the order said, a survey would be "destructive in its effect on a military organization where accepted responsibility on the part of every individual is fundamental."

Five months later, an exception to this rule was permitted. With the personal backing of Chief of Staff George C. Marshall, a group of psychologists and sociologists used anonymous questionnaires to sound out the attitudes of a representative cross section of 1,500 enlisted men in one infantry division in training. The study was made the day after Pearl Harbor. For the first time in any modern army, the new methods of social science research had a chance to show their power in comparison with the reports of visiting officers, who had to get their impressions from haphazard and biased samples of informants.

The report was critical, all right. Straight from the pencils of the men came frank and documented indictments of the training methods, the leadership system, and other activities of an army which was enmeshed in ancient tradition and only beginning to awake to the needs

* Samuel A. Stouffer, *Scientific American*, 180, No. 5 (May, 1949), 11-15. Copyright Scientific American, Inc. Reprinted by permission of the publisher and the author.

The author (b. 1900) is Professor of Sociology, Harvard University, and Director, Harvard Laboratory of Social Relations. With Information and Education Division of the War Department, 1941-46. His research papers apply quantitative methods in social science. Co-author (with Paul K. Lazarsfeld), *Research Memorandum on the Family in Depression.* Co-author, *The American Soldier.*

of modern mechanized war. The complaints were not just idle gossip and griping. For example, statistical tables and charts proved that the men were discriminating in their criticisms: some practices were condemned by nine out of 10; some were approved by almost as large a proportion.

General Marshall himself read the report on this division. So did many of the officers on the General Staff. One general started reading it at midnight and said the next day that it was so exciting and revealing that he did not put it down until three o'clock in the morning. A considerable number of changes were instituted as a result of that one study, including a revision of plans for the new Officers' Candidate Schools. Most important of all, the War Department put such research on a permanent basis. Between Pearl Harbor and the end of the war, the Research Branch of its Information and Education Division made more than 200 surveys of representative samples aggregating over half a million U. S. enlisted men and officers.

The Army had opened up a new channel of communication. The top command now could replace guesswork about some of the morale problems with evidence. To be sure, not all officers welcomed it. There was always opposition, but skepticism diminished as the war progressed. The standard argument that it would "upset a man's morale" to give him a chance to say frankly what he thought without fear of reprisal was easy to refute with evidence.

Moreover, it was possible to show that these surveys, using the best methods available to social science, got down to some solid realities. They proved to be of value in predicting the performance of groups of men in combat. For example, before the Normandy invasion all the enlisted men in the 108 rifle companies in four divisions were studied in England. An attitude or morale index was constructed for each company. After two months of fighting in Normandy, each company's record was compared with its pre-battle attitude index. The criterion of its behavior under the stress of combat was taken to be its noncombat casualty rate, because many if not most of the noncombat casualties at this period were psychiatric in character, and some companies had much higher noncombat casualty rates than others. Comparing the three rifle companies with the worst attitude index with the three rifle companies with the best index in each regiment, we found that on the average the companies with the worst indexes before combat had 60 per cent more nonbattle casualties in Normandy than the companies with the best.

The surveys were applied to hundreds of problems, many of which do not loom large in the perspective of total war, but were important at the time. Why did men in malarial regions fail to use Atabrine as regularly as they should? What attitudes and practices were associated with trench foot? Which of two kinds of huts did men in Alaska prefer? What were the favored types of winter clothing among front-line troops in Belgium, Luxemburg and Germany? What radio trans-scriptions did men want? What did they like most to read in Yank magazine? What about needs for athletic equipment? What could be done to improve a difficult laundry situation in Panama? What were the sources of difficulties in soldiers' relations with the French? Such inquiries were routine and were made in increasing numbers.

Some of the larger-scale enterprises were: Studies of soldiers' postwar plans, which provided a factual basis for drawing up the GI Bill of Rights; studies of psychiatric screening which led to the development by the Research Branch, in cooperation with the Surgeon General, of a test that was used routinely in all induction stations in the last year of the war; special surveys of the Air Forces and of other large components of the Army such as the infantry (the idea of the Combat Infantryman's Badge grew out of one of these studies); analyses of problems of occupying troops, which led to changes in occupation policy in Germany.

One of the most useful researches was the one that established the point system for demobilization at the end of the war. The President and the War Department decided that the order of demobilization should be determined in terms of what the soldiers themselves wanted. The idea of a point system was conceived in the Research Branch. Representative samples of men throughout the world were queried, and from their responses the variables of length of service, overseas duty, combat duty and parenthood emerged as most significant. The final weights assigned to these variables yielded point scores which had a close correspondence with the wishes of the maximum number of soldiers, even if they did not exactly reproduce these wishes. Studies of reactions to the point system showed that the response to it was remarkably favorable, except among minorities who felt they were personally most injured by it (for example, combat infantrymen). Even after many men became angered by the alleged slowness of demobilization, the majority, though hostile to many if not most Army policies, continued to approve the point system (which determined the order, not the rate, of demobilization). In view of the explosive tensions in the early demobilization period, historians may find that the establishment of an objective system whose justice was accepted by most men saved the country from what could have been a crisis seriously damaging to American prestige.

Plainly the findings and the experience gained from these many surveys are not limited to the military sphere or to wartime application. While these were all studies of men at war, they have implications of general social importance. For social scientists their chief present interest lies in the question of how the findings and techniques that were developed can be applied to civilian institutions.

One important problem to which they may be applied, for example, is that of increasing job satisfaction. In World War I psychologists first measured *aptitudes* on a large scale, with such crude devices as the Army Alpha test. Out of that work came hundreds of psychological studies in the years between the wars. By World War II psychology was ready with improved techniques of measurement and classification to aid in the selection of airplane pilots, navigators and bombardiers, and to assign soldiers generally on a basis that took account of their abilities. But satisfaction and efficiency on the job depend on more than aptitudes. They depend also on the interests and motivations of men.

In World War II the Research Branch found that aptitudes and attitudes were like the two blades of a pair of scissors. Men who got a chance to volunteer for their specific assignments were much better satisfied than those who never got a chance to choose, even though many of the latter actually were using their civilian skills. It would have been possible for the Army to extend the range of freedom of choice much further. In the future, in civilian industry as well as in the armed forces, it is likely that much more attention will be given to such attitudes. More can be done to glamorize unpopular jobs—the Navy may have shown how to do this with its Seabees.

One of the most important concepts used in the Research Branch was the principle of relative deprivation. This idea reconciled many otherwise paradoxical findings, not only in the field of job satisfaction but elsewhere. For example, two of the most extreme branches of the Army as far as promotion opportunities were concerned were the Air Forces and the Military Police. The Air Forces were full of sergeants and corporals. The MPs were mostly privates. Yet men in the Air Forces complained of lack of promotion opportunities more than did those in the Military Police. Why? The concept of relative deprivation led to an answer. Since most Air Forces men got promotions, those who did not tended to be personally aggrieved. Since few MPs got promotions, those who did not had so much company that they did not take it as a personal injustice. MPs who were promoted were so few that the promotion was a matter of exceptional pride. In other words, one's deprivation was always viewed relative to that of others, and the research problem was to find out who the "others" were.

Almost everyone expected that Northern Negro soldiers stationed in Southern camps would be more dissatisfied than those stationed in Northern camps. It is true that those sent South did complain, often bitterly, of Jim Crow regulations and of treatment by the local police. But in general their morale was as good as or better than that of Northern Negroes stationed in the North. Why? After elaborate cross-tabulations that eliminated education and other factors as the explanation, it finally appeared, as should have been seen earlier, that relative to civilian Negroes in the South the Negro soldier apparently perceived himself to be well treated. But when a Northern Negro at a Northern camp compared himself with civilian Negroes making big money in the war industries, he apparently felt himself not so fortunate.

In spite of intense eagerness to get home, the job satisfaction of soldiers in the rear areas of active theaters overseas was as high as or higher than that of men doing the same kinds of jobs in the U. S. Why? Part of the explanation, of course, was the sense of the importance of their overseas mission. But another significant aspect appears to be the fact that, relative to the combat troops they knew, the rear-area men had jobs which, though often unpleasant, tended to be safe. Very few were found who had the desire to change places with the combat men.

On the other hand, these rear-area troops and soldiers in overseas noncombat areas such as Panama, Alaska, Iran and most of India-Burma were the most vocal of all in their criticism of officers. Why? Analysis of many studies all over the world indicated that one of the basic factors in enlisted men's antipathy to officers related to the special privileges of rank, which involved many practices alien to American democratic traditions. If the supply of attractive women, liquor or entertainment was severely limited, as was often the case overseas, the problem of equitable distribution became acute. If, as was charged, the officers tended to monopolize such desired objects, the men's resentment is understandable. There was even greater scarcity of these attractions in the front lines, but there the officers and men shared the same deprivations. At camps in the U.S. there was less deprivation; therefore the so-called caste system, though productive of much irritation, was not as heavily criticized there as in places where the relative deprivation of enlisted men as compared with officers was greatest.

All this has significant implications for civilian life. In industry, or in the family, or wherever we are, satisfaction is a relative matter. The key to understanding a given attitude is to learn the context in which the attitude is expressed and the standards of comparison that exist in the given situation.

These studies also made clear the importance of studying what the sociologist calls informal social controls. Perhaps few organizations have more elaborate formal rules than the Army, but in the last analysis, in the Army as elsewhere, the most powerful control is that of one's own fellows. Some searching analyses were made of the process of "goldbricking"—that is, appearing to be busy without really accomplishing much of anything. Goldbricking, an older word for which, significantly, is "soldiering," sometimes was practiced with so hearty a group spirit that it represented high morale from the standpoint of the group—though not from the standpoint of the Army command. Studies showed that there were clear-cut codes about goldbricking. A soldier who refused to conform to the code was a target for scorn from his fellows; on the other hand, when the group felt that a given task was necessary or that the group would be punished if it were not fulfilled, then an individual goldbricker became an object of scorn.

A long series of studies of combat troops, based on thousands of systematic interviews and on personal front-line experiences of Research Branch members, emphasized the central importance of such informal controls, or group opinion, in stress situations. Compared with the feeling that one must not lose face in the eyes of one's fellows or let them down, patriotism, hatred of the enemy and other stereotyped explanations of what keeps a person going in combat seem to have been negligible factors.

One of the greatest weaknesses of social science has been the infrequency of its use of deliberately designed controlled experiments, which are the only sure method of determining whether a change in one variable actually will be followed by a change in another. From the beginning of the war the Research Branch recognized the need for such experiments. But neither the Army nor the U.S. public in general has been in the habit of asking for this kind of evidence from social scientists. Although the Army would not think of adopting a new weapon without exhaustive trials, it was not nearly as ready to try out a new social idea—such as a different personnel policy or a different training method—on a very limited scale, with careful controls to measure exactly what the effects would be.

There were instances in which the Research Branch was able to obtain a kind of experimental proof, even in situations that were not deliberately set up as controlled experiments. For example, the Army tried out in Europe the radical idea of placing an entire platoon of Negro volunteers in a white infantry combat company. This was done in several divisions, most of which saw several months of subsequent battle. At the end of the compaign interviewers polled sample groups of men in several divisions to find out how the attitudes of men who had served with Negroes compared with those of men who had not. In divisions that had no mixed companies, 62 per cent of the soldiers said they would dislike very much to serve in the same companies as Negroes. Of white infantrymen who had fought in the same divisions but not the same companies as Negroes, only 20 per cent said they would dislike it very much. And among white infantrymen who had actually been in the same companies as Negroes, only 7 per cent said they disliked it very much.

There was another very interesting finding. Two thirds of the white men in the mixed companies, when polled after the experience, said that they had been opposed to the scheme beforehand and had thought it would fail. This was almost exactly the same proportion of opponents as was found in divisions that had not experienced the plan; in other words, the retrospective answers about attitudes corresponded closely to those of groups reporting current attitudes, so one finding tended to confirm the other. The findings can therefore be considered, cautiously of course, to approach in reliability the result of a controlled experiment, although it falls far short of the ideal.

Early in the war the Research Branch sought a full-fledged opportunity to demonstrate the value of controlled experiments. This opportunity came in connection with the physical training program.

A committee of physical educators had proposed a new physical conditioning program for the Army, based on modern experience in training football players and other athletes. They believed that the traditional Army regimen of setting-up exercises and hikes was uninteresting to the men, time-consuming and generally inefficient. A Research Branch survey of samples of troops throughout the country, using tests of physical proficiency devised by the committee, confirmed the criticism. It showed that men who had been in the Army six months to a year and had been subjected to the old-fashioned conditioning system made little better scores on tests of strength or of stamina than did new recruits. That the tests were valid measures of physical condition was confirmed by the fact that paratroopers, initially selected for ruggedness and subjected to particularly rigorous physical training, were able to make high scores on them.

A controlled experiment was then set up. Two samples of new recruits, matched on initial proficiency tests, were selected. One sample was put through the conventional Army course of calisthenics and hikes. When retested the group showed only a slight improvement over its initial scores. The other group was given the rigorous new program of training. After six weeks its proficiency scores were far superior, almost as high as those of the paratroopers. Moreover, the men getting this training liked it better than did those in the traditional program. The results persuaded the Army to scrap its traditional procedures and introduce the new program on an Army-wide basis.

While the hopes that this demonstration would induce the Army to try other experiments in handling its human resources were not fully realized, the use of controlled experiments became an important part of the developmental work of the Information and Education Division. One of the functions of this Division was to make motion picture films to give the soldiers better orientation to the war. The "Why We Fight" series of films, produced under the direction of Colonel Frank Capra, was studied in detail. Analyses were made by the attitude-survey method of the effectiveness of the films in general, the differential effects on different types of soldiers and the impact of specific elements of film content.

Experimental studies also were of use in testing theories on propaganda techniques. For example, is propaganda more effective when it tries to present an opposing point of view and refute it than when it merely reiterates one's own position, à la Goebbels? Experimental studies made in the Research Branch suggest that the answer may be yes and no. Presenting both sides seemed to be more effective for winning the better-educated soldiers to the point of view wanted, but less effective among the less educated. The latter tended to get from the two-sided presentation doubts that they might not otherwise have had.

One of the chief obstacles to carrying out controlled experiments is the lack of good criteria of measurement. For example, the Research Branch made extensive studies of fear among soldiers. Thousands of combat men were interviewed. Some experiments were carried out, notably at the school for training paratroopers. But even at the end of the war there was no reliable answer to the following question: Is it better to scare combat soldiers badly from the beginning of their training, to lead them gradually into more and more frightening situations, or not to scare them at all? What complicates the problem is that fear may have either harmful or useful effects: It may freeze a person or cause him to act erratically or run away; on the other hand, it may make him more attentive to danger signals and selective of those to which he must respond in different ways. The trouble is that we have as yet no good criteria for measuring fear and evaluating its adaptive value.

A good case can be made for the hypothesis that this lack of measured criteria is one of the main reasons why experimentation in the social sciences is so rare as compared with the physical sciences, and why the social sciences have moved so slowly. Medical science made similarly slow progress until modern instruments of biological measurement were developed. The Research Branch made some new attacks on the measurement problem in social psychology and sociology, and a considerable part of its report is devoted to a fresh analysis of measurement theory which, it is hoped, will stimulate concerted efforts in this direction. Another decade or two of accumulated experience is likely to see great improvements in social science, particularly as more and more of the newer students get a hardheaded training in mathematics, statistics and the design of experiments.

≈§≈§≈§≈

6. What Do Attitude Surveys Tell Us? *

THE PRECEDING SELECTION (5, by Samuel A. Stouffer) summarized some of the findings of wartime attitude surveys. The postwar publication of these attitude surveys stimulated much evaluative discussion of such studies among social scientists. Paul Lazarsfeld wrote an extensive review of two of the volumes of this four-volume work, now known popularly as "The American Soldier Series." In his review, part of which is reproduced here, Lazarsfeld shows us what attitude surveys can do for sociology. In particular he uses striking examples that illustrate the dangers inherent in "common-sense" generalizations about attitudes and behavior.

IT WILL BE HELPFUL to consider the special role played by attitude surveys in contemporary social science. Although surveys are only one of the many techniques available, at the moment they undoubtedly constitute the most important and promising step forward that has been made in recent years.

* Paul F. Lazarsfeld, The Public Opinion Quarterly, 13, No. 3 (Fall, 1949), 378-380. Reprinted by permission of the publisher and the author.
     The author (b. 1901) is Chairman, Department of Sociology, Columbia University. Former Director of Bureau of Applied Social Research. Consultant on problems of communication (radio, magazines, newspapers). Born in Vienna. Social psychology studies for American business concerns and for U. S. government. Among his books are Radio and the Printed Page, Radio Research (with F. Stanton), The People Look at Radio. Co-author, Research Memorandum on the Family in Depression.

The limitations of survey methods are obvious. They do not use experimental techniques; they rely primarily on what people say, and rarely include objective observations; they deal with aggregates of individuals rather than with integrated communities; they are restricted to contemporary problems—history can be studied only by the use of documents remaining from earlier periods.

In spite of these limitations survey methods provide one of the foundations upon which social science is being built. The finding of regularities is the beginning of any science, and surveys can make an important contribution in this respect. For it is necessary that we know what people usually do under many and different circumstances if we are to develop theories explaining their behavior. Furthermore, before we can devise an experiment we must know what problems are worthwhile; which should be investigated in greater detail. Here again surveys can be of service.

Finding regularities and determining criteria of significance are concerns the social sciences have in common with the natural sciences. But there are crucial differences between the two fields of inquiry. The world of social events is much less "visible" than the realm of nature. That bodies fall to the ground, that things are hot or cold, that iron becomes rusty, are all immediately obvious. It is much more difficult to realize that ideas of right and wrong vary in different cultures; that customs may serve a different function from the one which the people practising them believe they are serving; that the same person may show marked contrasts in his behavior as a member of a family and as a member of an occupational group. The mere description of human behavior, of its variation from group to group and of its changes in different situations, is a vast and difficult undertaking. It is this task of describing, sifting and ferreting out interrelationships which surveys perform for us. And yet this very function often leads to serious misunderstandings. For it is hard to find a form of human behavior that has not already been observed somewhere. Consequently, if a study reports a prevailing regularity, many readers respond to it by thinking "of course that is the way things are." Thus, from time to time, the argument is advanced that surveys only put into complicated form observations which are already obvious to everyone.

Understanding the origin of this point of view is of importance far beyond the limits of the present discussion. The reader may be helped in recognizing this attitude if he looks over a few statements which are typical of many survey findings and carefully observes his own reaction. A short list of these, with brief interpretive comments, will be given here in order to bring into sharper focus probable reactions of many readers.

1. Better educated men showed more psycho-neurotic symptoms than those with less education. (The mental instability of the intellectual as compared to the more impassive psychology of the-man-in-the-street has often been commented on.)
2. Men from rural backgrounds were usually in better spirits during their Army life than soldiers from city backgrounds. (After all, they are more accustomed to hardships.)
3. Southern soldiers were better able to stand the climate in the hot South Sea Islands than Northern soldiers. (Of course, Southerners are more accustomed to hot weather.)
4. White privates were more eager to become non-coms than Negroes. (The lack of ambition among Negroes is almost proverbial.)
5. Southern Negroes preferred Southern to Northern white officers. (Isn't it well known that Southern whites have a more fatherly attitude toward their "darkies"?)
6. As long as the fighting continued, men were more eager to be returned to the States than they were after the German surrender. (You cannot blame people for not wanting to be killed.)

We have in these examples a sample list of the simplest type of inter-relationships which provide the "bricks" from which our empirical social science is being built. But why, since they are so obvious, is so much money and energy given to establish such findings? Would it not be wiser to take them for granted and proceed directly to a more sophisticated type of analysis? This might be so except for one interesting point about the list. *Every one of these statements is the direct opposite of what actually was found.* Poorly educated soldiers were more neurotic than those with high education; Southerners showed no greater ability than Northerners to adjust to a tropical climate; Negroes were more eager for promotion than whites; and so on.

If we had mentioned the actual results of the investigation first, the reader would have labelled these "obvious" also. Obviously something is wrong with the entire argument of "obviousness." It should really be turned on its head. Since every kind of human reaction is conceivable, it is of great importance to know which reactions actually occur most frequently and under what conditions; only then will a more advanced social science develop.

7. Recent Trends in Sociology *

IN THIS ARTICLE John Useem has outlined the trends in sociological research at mid-century. He also presents the historical perspective within which the achievements of sociology should be considered. The limitations of sociology are also recognized and to some extent explained. The background provided by this analysis will prove valuable in orienting the reader toward many of the other selections in this book.

ORIENTATION TO THE POSTWAR ERA

THE YEARS SINCE WORLD WAR II have been transitional ones for American sociology. While the traditional types of studies character-istic of the period between the two world wars have continued, new patterns of sociological research are coming into prominence. The latter do not represent an abrupt break with the past, but they do show alterations in structure, focus, and design in response to the nation's changing problems and as an outgrowth of scientific developments within sociology itself. The salient features of the emergent patterns may be briefly summed up and will serve as a useful guide for the in-terpretation of current sociological works.

The first trend concerns the *structural framework* within which sociological studies are pursued. Perhaps the most distinctive aspects of the postwar era are: (1) a convergence of sociological, anthropo-logical, and psychological approaches, thus making for an interdisci-plinary social science; (2) the establishment of large-scale research organizations in which research involves the cooperative efforts of many and concerns subject matter of considerable magnitude; (3) expansion of research services by governmental, military, civic, and commercial agencies in order to secure data essential for the making of policy decisions and the administration of programs (most notable addition is the sponsorship of world-wide studies by new international organiza-tions, particularly the United Nations); (4) increase in the number of trained persons, technical facilities, and financial resources available for sociological work (especially noteworthy are the substantial allocations

* John Useem, "Sociology: Recent Trends," *Social Education*, 14, No. 3 (March, 1950), 102-104. Reprinted by permission of the publisher and the author.

The author (b. 1911) is Professor of Sociology and Anthropology, Michigan State College. Visiting professor, Foreign Service Institute, U. S. Department of State, summer of 1951. Member, Board of Directors, Institute of Ethnic Affairs. Special field of interest is sociology of power in cross-cultural relationships. Author of numerous articles in journals of sociology and anthropology.

of funds by foundations and the revisions in academic training to meet the needs of the foregoing changes); and (5) the further growth of an applied social science to provide a special body of knowledge relevant to current issues plus the services of social science experts equipped to investigate acute problems.

The second change pertains to the shifting *foci of interest* among sociologists. No simple enumeration can depict adequately the scope and content of the newer type of interest. Several illustrations may be used to exemplify the nature of the nascent fields. The study of small-group social structure is attracting considerable attention in so-ciological circles. It is common knowledge that within every formal organization there function congeries of informal groupings which make up the immediate social world of the individual. They exist in the industrial plant, the armed forces, the community, and wherever per-manent social arrangements prevail. By close-range, intensive studies of these primary groups, we can obtain both exact and meaningful information on how people work out their social relationships in a complex civilization. The findings thus far have proved most instruc-tive. One specific instance will serve to indicate the value of such studies. Research into corner gangs in one city, *Street Corner Society*, disclosed that what had been conceived of as an area marked by social disorganization was actually a highly-organized and culturally-integrated social order with its own style of life and coherent values. Individuals raised in this environment are socialized and acquire their basic life habits within this social orbit. The gang serves as a culture filter for that which diffuses into the area from the larger society, sets the models of behavior, constructs the images of the outside world, provides the social atmosphere, and forms the basis of personal allegiances. The gangs, in turn, are incorporated into a larger social network within the community. Hence, knowledge of the gang configuration yields insight into the motives and conduct of its members in the total society. The same process of inquiry into the small groups of various social institu-tions is revealing some of the fundamental principles which govern human behavior. ·

Sociological explorations into another frontier of knowledge, human nature and the changing social order, is still in a pioneer stage but has already led to some major discoveries. We know very little as yet about how people successfully handle those problems which stem from the complexities and conflicting demands of modern life. Data about those who have experienced neuroses and psychoses are fairly extensive with respect to their numbers, distribution, and life histories. Studies are just beginning on the social strengths in mental health to supplement our knowledge of the areas of social weakness. The socialization process by which the newborn acquires the modes of behaving expected of members of society has been mapped out; researches are now underway to learn something about how persons adjust to their changing roles in life, such as the transition from middle to old age or from one status position to another. Sundry theories present many suggestive hypotheses on interpersonal relationships, the nature of conformism and deviancy to old and new group standards, and types of social participation in institutions. These are attracting a considerable amount of the serious attention of students who find them fruitful subjects of investigation.

Postwar conditions in the United States and world-wide crises have caused sociologists to begin the study of new types of phenomena. Thus since the last decade, interest has been redirected from men on relief to men in the armed forces; the housing shortage of the country has expanded a subject at one time confined to submarginal slum dwellers to its present form that encompasses the housing arrangements of the entire population. Similarly, World War II precipitated a major interest in areas of the world outside of the United States. The comparative study of societies was once a major theme in sociology. American sociology for a time turned inward to plot the national social scene; now it faces both ways. The world-wide struggle for dominance promises to keep the outward orientation conspicuous for many years. Out of this has already come research into the social character of nations, the social institutions of culture areas, and the interaction between societies with different ways of life.

These cases merely mirror the kinds of changes which are taking place in the foci of interest. It does not follow that sociology has become an up-to-date survey of the miscellaneous assortment of social changes, a technical science of human pathologies, or a composite portrait of the human race. The raw materials used, raw materials that are dictated by opportunity and demand, have changed but the basic objectives remain unaltered; namely, to learn the principles which govern social interaction, to find the determinants of man's social behavior, and to identify the types of social actors, social structures, and cultures.

• • • • • •

SOCIOLOGICAL DILEMMAS: OLD AND NEW

It probably is inevitable that the sociologist is a role-conscious professional, preoccupied with the scientific sufficiency and social utility of the field. The complex of reasons which have created this state of mind fall outside the scope of this discourse. Still the mental pattern in relationship to the present status of sociology in science and society merits some attention. The sociological literature today, as in the past, is replete with critiques accompanied by varied proposals for improving the discipline. One might liken the case to that of a robust child who becomes the object of numerous comments from relatives and friends on how he can attain adult respectability and, possibly, social distinction Anxious observers worry over flaws in character and training and pre scribe sundry corrective measures, eagerly acclaim each sign of growth, and wait with high expectations for the emergence of the successful adult who makes good in the world. Those who seek more details from a sympathetic friend who is sanguine, will find inspiring Chase's *The Proper Study of Mankind*, a glowing account of the application of scientific knowledge to human affairs. Readers desiring an account of the intimate details of current shortcomings from a critical, but no less optimistic, member of the family can turn to Shils' *The Present State of American Sociology*. As in all such cases it is well to remember that the diagnoses and remedies given represent opinions not shared by all concerned and reflect projected images of the ideal conceived by the authors.

It is premature to make an evaluation of the net gains or to forecast the ultimate patterns, for many of the sociological studies emanating from the new trends have appeared chiefly as brief reports of research projects underway. There are numerous real, unresolved dilemmas and the final test, actual accomplishments, will not be in full evidence for some time. The enthusiastic response to recent developments is sobered by a recognition of the obstacles which must be overcome before sociology fulfills its present expectations.

⋘⋙

CHAPTER II

ENVIRONMENT
AND PRECONDITIONING FACTORS

---

8. Geographical Environment and Culture *

A BASIC QUESTION for which an answer has always been sought is:
Why do people behave as they do?　One answer that has flourished
for a long time, and still exhibits considerable vitality, is that the way
people live is determined by their geographical environment.　In
this reading W. D. Wallis properly disposes of the idea that
"geography *determines* culture."　He also points out some of the
weaknesses of the even more moderate point of view that "geography *sets the stage* for culture."　His position is well expressed in this
poetically worded statement: "Geographical environment is the
cradle in which man's genius awaits the promptings of motives
which give him mastery over his fate."

THE VIEW THAT NATURE has made or has unmade man is suggested by
man's dependence upon nature.　He is a creature of the earth's surface.
Only by keeping touch with her can be maintain life.　Out of her womb
is he born, from her he receives nourishment, to her embrace he ultimately returns.　Yet her children have not received impartial treatment.
Some have nestled in favored spots where bounteous nature fills all
needs; others have been put down in hard places where life is a constant
struggle with environment, a niggardly provider from whom blessings

* W. D. Wallis, Social Forces, 4, No. 4 (June, 1926), 702-708.　Reprinted by
permission of the publisher and the author.
The author (b. 1886) is Professor of Anthropology, University of Minnesota.
Rhodes Scholar, Oxford University, 1907-10.　Among his books are Messiahs—
Christian and Pagan, Culture and Progress, The Canadian Dakotas.

are wrung with sweat of brow and horny hands, or sought under dangerous and precarious conditions.

Herodotus remarked that Egypt is the gift of the Nile. Though he meant geographical Egypt cultural Egypt was almost coterminous with it and the one could scarcely be separated even in thought from the other. Egyptian civilization depended upon the fertility of the land, a fertility attributable to inundations providing a constantly renewed alluvium, and to a warm and abundant sunlight. Wheat is native to the Mediterranean area. It is plausible that nature herself provided the wild seed, covered it with a rich soil, watered it, and by the warmth of a southern sun nurtured it into a grain whose rare virtues were manifest. Thus were offered to the natives who dwelt along the turgid Nile advantages not vouchsafed those inhabiting colder and less happy regions beyond the Mediterranean. Nature had been kinder to those who dwelt along the river bank than to those whose abode was in desert or on bleak mountain height. Bodin stressed the fact that civilization is limited by degrees of latitude and of longitude, and also by altitude, noting the superiority of plains and river valleys as seats of civilization. Inspired by Bodin, Montesquieu pointed to climatic zones as delimitations of culture. The natives in the tropics did not advance beyond savagery because heat was enervating and because every need was supplied by nature. Those living in frigid zones were equally unfortunate, nature in that region being as niggardly as in the tropics she was beneficent, the polar inhabitants being forced by the inclemency of the region to spend most of their time and energy in securing food and clothing. The temperate zones furnish the happy mean; here man's needs are not fully supplied by nature; he must exert himself in order to satisfy them; the requisite labor stimulates without exhausting his efforts and capacities. For proof of his assertion Montesquieu pointed to the geographical distribution of civilization. The centers of civilization lie within the temperate zone and diminish in quality as we proceed toward the tropics or toward the polar regions. In the present century the views of Bodin and of Montesquieu have been championed by Miss Semple and by Ellsworth Huntington, who describe the extent to which not only effort and ability but civilization as well are matters of climate.

The dependence of civilization upon geographical environment must be accepted. But these writers leave out of the reckoning factors which are an intimate part of the situation. However favorable the surroundings, the culture must have attained a certain advance or no advantage is taken of environment. The Nile doubtless had long been irrigating and enriching the soil of Egypt, scattering the land with wild grains out of which man was destined to make cultivated cereals.

Nature may give the blessing but it is not really a blessing until man accepts it and learns to utilize it. Whether he does one or both depends upon himself as well as upon nature. Lucky accidents are not lessons to those not already alert. While the effects of climatic conditions upon mentality and upon physical stamina are not to be underrated, the fact remains that climatic conditions act differently upon different individuals as well as upon different civilizations. The balmy climate of Southern California has acted in one way upon the early Mexican-Spanish population, in another way upon the later European-American. Within certain bounds, heat does not kill intellectual or physical effort but merely handicaps it.

Again, by the theory of Montesquieu and of Huntington it is difficult to explain the shiftings in the centers of civilization from millenium to millenium, or even from century to century. Races which in the last thousand years have achieved greatness in art, literature, and science, lie within the cooler temperate zones. But what shall we say of the preceding thousands of years?

Moreover, the shiftings of civilization within a given geographical area make it difficult to accept the hypothesis that the environment accounts for the civilization, since the same conditions yield widely different products. If the Nile made ancient Egyptian civilization, must we not say that it made the civilization of medieval times, and that of modern times? Yet these products are of the most varied character.

In explaining everything the environment explains nothing. We know that in some parts of the world the climate has remained constant throughout thousands of years, whereas the civilization in that area has undergone manifold change. Whether we speak of the valleys of the Nile, the Euphrates and Tigris, the Rhine, or the Po, contrasts in successive civilizations stand out against a background of a same geographical environment maintaining itself through kaleidoscopic changes in social life, religion, art, and science.

Huntington does not save the day by pointing to a change in climatic conditions in Palestine and Italy, changes which he assumes account for the shiftings of civilization in those areas. The climatic changes have been trivial compared with the momentous changes in civilization which those lands have witnessed in the past three thousand years. The attempts to show the direct effects of environment upon national character must be rated equally unsuccessful. Gomperz fails to convince us that the intellect of Greece was the outcome of a rugged interior and an indented coastline. His theory will not account for the fact that Greek civilization developed in the sixth and fifth centuries B.C., arts, sciences, and philosophies which culminated in a period of brilliancy never achieved previously nor subsequently. Geographical conditions in Greece have not changed in any noteworthy respect, if they have changed at all; meanwhile, in this land of brilliant sunshine, civilization has waxed and waned, has died and found new birth.

Nor can we accept Taine's view that the spirit of English literature has been dictated by the environment. If the fogs and bogs of the North made morose and phlegmatic Saxons and Danes, how could they make light-hearted and vivacious Celts? When Sir William Ramsay assures us that the rugged mountains of Anatolia could not fail to arouse the religious sense, and Draper and Miss Semple declare that the monotony of the desert inspires belief in monotheism, we can only conclude that they have not read the evidence aright, because they have not read all of it. Must they not first explain why Mohammed arose when he did, and why the same desert region produced monotheism in one century and polytheism in another? Must they not also demand that the deserts of China, of Australia, and of North and South America deliver up their secrets of a monotheistic faith? In a word, those who support the thesis that the geographical environment is responsible for culture show nothing more than that culture must subsist in an environment, and that, given the culture and the environment, a correlation between the two can be made.

The defenders of the view that geographical environment constitutes the determinants of culture have been loth to define the meaning which they attach to "geographical environment." Their use of the term shows that they employ it now in the sense of what exists for the culture in question, now in the sense of what exists for the civilized man but does not exist for the culture in question. The two meanings are not synonymous. Shall we say that the Alleghany Indian of two centuries ago lived in an environment of coal, or that he lived in an environment of a useless black substance which we call coal and which we recognize, but he did not, as a substance capable of giving light, heat, and power? Was aluminum a part of our environment fifty years ago? There seems but one answer: Coal, a substance capable of giving light, heat, and power, was no part of the environment of the Alleghany Indian, though, as we now know, it was all about him; aluminum, a useful metal, was no part of our environment fifty years ago, though the substance, unknown, was about us on every side awaiting discovery and utilization.

Civilization has created these portions of the environment.

By environment we mean those things and influences with which we come into contact directly or indirectly. Though Captain Kidd's treasure lies buried at my doorstep, so long as I am uninfluenced by its presence it can not be said to constitute a part of my environment. At some future date knowledge may make it such.

Some years ago, accompanied by a friend, I boarded a train at Bischofsheim, in southern Germany. We rode through a beautiful country romantic with historic associations. Our enjoyment of these was now and then interrupted by the conversation of two ladies from Iowa, mother and daughter. The burden of their talk was: What should they do with the chicken-house and the back porch when they returned to their Iowa home? They had no eye for scenery nor for historical associations. Our physical bodies passed through the same physical surroundings, but our environments were as far apart as mediaeval Germany and the hen-roost in Iowa.

America was no part of the environment of the ancient Roman nor of the mediaeval Londoner, but today America is part of the environment of the inhabitants of these cities. Civilization created this change in environment. The new environment of America gave us a new civilization, but the old civilization of Europe gave us the new environment, the Americas. The nature of the actual environment of a people can not be settled by the cartographer. How can he describe the environment of the New Yorker? The environment of some New Yorkers is the region of Long Island Sound and Hudson River. But many a New Yorker lives in an environment as large, almost, as the national boundaries. Not only do his wanderings make this actual: he may travel as far in a museum or with a book as others with an unlimited ticket. Nor do we forget the subtlety and indirectness of the geographical influences. These so-called influences, however, are merely the medium in which human forces and motives find resisting fulcrum.

By adapting itself to environmental influences human life shows its reasonableness, its balance, its ingenuity, its freedom. It makes the most of them in order that it may rise above their compulsions. Without geographical environment civilization is as impossible as war without gravitation, but environment does not explain nor cause civilization more than gravitation causes or explains war. The shiftings in the center of civilization from one region to another, and the various changes in civilization which a given geographical area witnesses can be explained only by reference to the human life there resident. This human life possesses cultural traits received from another geographical horizon which it will transmit to some further region. The environment which accounts for these shiftings is a culture environment overleaping geographical barriers or even annihilating them and setting up new ones.

At one time to some peoples rivers are a means of separation; at other times and to other peoples they are a means of communication. What the geographical environment signifies, which is almost equivalent to saying what the geographical environment is, depends upon the peoples concerned. They create it to a much larger extent than it creates them. Countries once the white man's grave have been made habitable. Mortality decreases as man remakes the environment. In regions where formerly environment had complete mastery of man he has subjected it to his will and now is its master. As Buffon expressed it: "The more, therefore, he observes and cultivates nature the more means he will find of making her subservient to him and of drawing new riches from her bosom without diminishing the treasures of her inexhaustible fecundity." To attribute social advance to geographical environment is to place ourselves by the side of the old lady who marvelled at the providential way in which big rivers were made to run past big towns. The teleology is inverted.

Man is not an automaton, but a creature with a will. As Kirchoff says:

The suggestions thrown out by the nature of his birthplace sometimes find him a docile, sometimes an indifferent pupil. What is now the world-harbor of New York once served the Indians as nothing but a hunting place for edible mollusks. On the same rock-bound coast that educated the Norwegians into intrepid sailors, the Lapps are at present eking out a paltry existence as fishermen. . . . If, however, man ventures to pit his strength against the elemental power of the sea; if he goes further and elects as his vocation the sailor's struggle with storm and seething breaker, then the poet's word in its full significance may be applied to him: "Man's stature grows with every higher aim." The mariner's trade steels muscle and nerve, it sharpens the senses, it cultivates presence of mind. With each triumph of human cleverness over the rude forces of nature it heightens the courageousness of well-considered, fearless action.

Geographical environment is the cradle in which man's genius awaits the promptings of motives which give him mastery over his fate.

In many ways he is and always has been dependent upon the geographical environment; he can no more escape it than he can dodge the forces of gravitation; the one as surely as the other fashions him and accounts for some of his characteristics. It may be that our arboreal ancestors,—if they were arboreal!—climbed down from the trees because the trees were degenerating in that area, forced to earth while our unfortunate, because too fortunate, simian cousins remained within their leafy bowers.

Man, possibly, is an example of the fact that unfavorable environment in the end may prove to be a favorable one, eliciting potencies which else lie dormant or atrophy in disuse. Conformity to environment can not guarantee survival, much less can it ensure progress. When one speaks in terms of conformity to environment one thinks of mollusks and the smaller parasites, admirably adapted to the environment. The failure or refusal of higher forms to conform closely with environment is a distinguishing trait. Or shall we say they conform to different environments, though these environments lie within the same latitudes and longitudes, as drawn by the cartographer? The oyster and man live in much the same environment if only they knew it, but knowing it or not knowing it is the element which makes the environment what it is. The dyne of selection is as important as the array of things upon which selection operates.

Rational selection of environment is taken for granted when it is alleged that environment is a determining factor in economic, social, or political life, that it makes or unmakes a people, determining whether a given tribe or nation is to rise to prominence in world affairs or is to sink into inoffensive and powerless rivalry for a place in the sun.

Undoubtedly certain environments are favorable and other environments are unfavorable; yet, the advantages they offer are conditional upon the response of the culture. Man can do well where conditions are unfavorable; he can do poorly where conditions are favorable. He is more than a creature of the environment, or he is no human being. The story of his conquest of nature and of his utilization of her forces is evidence that he is a creator as well as a creature of environment.

· · · · · ·

With advance in civilization man is able more and more to escape the exactions of the environment, to impose his will more masterfully upon nature, to conquer his conqueror. The correlation between man's economic life and his geographical environment is not evidence of the influence of physical environment. The correlation shows the extent to which man has adapted himself to the environment, the extent to which he has compelled it to minister to his needs, to serve his purposes, to respond to his will. We do not find canoes in the Sahara desert. If the converse of the picture is that the environment does not drive man to build canoes, the obverse is that enterprises other than canoe-building ensure salvation.

Moreover, where geographical conditions are the same or similar we do not find a same and often not a similar reaction.

The reaction to the geographical environment depends not so much upon the nature of the environment as upon the nature of the culture transplanted to the environment.

Adaptation to physical environment depends upon the will, the training, the social inheritance of those who inhabit a given locality. If we wish to predict what a people will do when they move into a new environment, it is more important to know the people than to know the place—or better, one must know both.

Nietzsche leaves out of the reckoning an important factor when he declares: "If thou knewest a people's need, its land, its sky, and its neighbor, then wouldst thou divine the law of its surmountings, and why it climbeth up that ladder to its hopes." The people themselves are one of the factors in their progress, and usually the most important of the factors. As Horace says, "They change their sky, not their spirit, those who travel across the seas."

Within limitations which shift with the civilization, almost any kind of culture can flourish in almost any kind of physical environment. But culture can not flourish independently of surrounding cultures. Savagery can not persist indefinitely when its neighbors are civilized peoples Civilization can not maintain itself in a sea of savagery, but ultimately will give way to savagery or bring savagery into line with civilization.

An analysis of the geographical environment does not afford as valuable insight into the culture of a people as does a knowledge of the culture of its neighbors. The distribution of cultures confirms this induction. There is a geography of culture as clearly marked, as distinct in demarcating outlines, as different in content, as is the physical geography.

The lines which mark out culture areas are not coterminous with those which delimit river, valley, mountain systems, plateaus, plains. Culture boundaries in some cases to an extent respect geographical lines, as, for example, in aboriginal North America; yet in the main, culture lines cross and interpenetrate geographical boundaries as though the latter did not exist. Where geographical features impose limitations the limitations are respected; but not until we know the culture do we know the limitations. Geographical features do not break up civilized America as they do, or did, aboriginal America.

To a forest-dwelling people the region of wood imposes limiting conditions upon the construction of houses; yet the Eskimo disregard such limiting conditions, finding at hand other materials out of which to make habitations.

Were the Eskimo isolated groups, not intermingling and not exchanging articles in trade, their isolation would be pointed to as imposed by environment. But they rise above these specious limitations and do trade, travel, visit, and intermingle. Were art wholly absent from their culture the lack of suitable materials for the operation of the artistic impulse would be pointed to as responsible for the absence of art. Here again they rise above our expectations, refuse to acknowledge obviously limiting conditions, are artists. The limiting conditions can not be inferred apart from the culture which inhabits a given environment. To this extent the poet is right: "In thine own breast stands the star of thy fate."

Physical environment is not a matter apart from social development, nor one to which the culture can be indifferent. The culture shows its wisdom by acquaintance with environment and by making the most of it. If "being influenced" by the environment means making the most of it, then it is the part of wisdom to be influenced. Adaptation to environment illustrates the freedom and rationality of the group. With advance in civilization man attains relative freedom from environment. He may acquire freedom by changing place of abode, escaping to regions where the preferred environment is to be found, though this at best usually is a matter of individual rather than one of group choice; or he may protect himself through his own devices from the inclemency and extremes of the environment.

Man learns to make nature do his bidding. Where there is dearth of rainfall he supplies rivers of irrigating canals. The water which will not come from the heavens shall be induced to come up through the earth. The wilderness and the desert are made to blossom like the rose; in the dreariest wastes man induces nature to be prodigal of her blessings. As man develops power, as his devices become more ingenious, environment is reinterpreted and remade.

In early stages of social development nature may determine man's activities; later he gives the emphasis to the environment. He no longer trembles at nature's threat for he can throttle the threat in its utterance. Sun, wind, and wave are made to generate power which man uses to his enhancement. As a factor in progress physical environment is important in the case of two peoples of the same level of culture, possessing the same handicrafts, the same mechanical ability. As between widely diverse cultures differences in environment do not much matter. The superior advantages of the physical environment of North America mean much to the culture of Canadians and to the peoples of the States; they mean much less to the Spanish in Mexico; they mean still less to unenlightened Indian tribes. The environment of Australia is a factor in the social evolution of Europeans who now govern that continent; it is a much weaker factor in the life of the aborigines. In one case the culture is able to utilize the environment, in the other it is not. The importance of physical environment to social evolution is in direct proportion to the advance of the culture. It is the lever as well as the fulcrum, but its leverage is determined by the civilization.

As Voltaire says, though climate has influence, government has a hundred times more, and religion in conjunction with government has still more.

◆§◆§◆§◆§◆

9. How Differences in Environment Affected Separated One-Egg Twins *

A LONG-STANDING CONTROVERSY in American social science concerns the relative importance of heredity and environment in the development of human personality: To what extent is human behavior the result of biological inheritance; how do culture, social experience, or learning influence behavior? One way to answer the question is to study the adult personalities of identical twins who were separated early in life. Since such one-egg twins have the same genetic origin, differences that are found in later life can be presumed to have resulted from differences in education, family relationships, and other social experiences. Analysis of such cases is difficult because few twins are separated in early years. The fundamental research summarized in this selection, therefore, resulted from a diligent search by the author, Horatio Newman. Although his study is based on relatively few cases, its findings provide some understanding of the influence of the socio-cultural environment on human behavior.

IN EACH OF THE TWENTY CASES of separated one-egg twins every effort was made to reconstruct the life experiences of the twins and to discover any differences in environment or experience that might have tended to produce differences in ability, personality or physical condition. We roughly subdivided environment into three categories: educational, social and physical-health.

* Horatio H. Newman, *Multiple Human Births* (Doubleday and Co., 1940), pp. 189-199. Copyright 1940 by H. H. Newman, reprinted by permission of the author and Doubleday and Co., Inc.

The author (b. 1875) was formerly Associate Professor Zoology, University of Chicago; Emeritus since 1940. Head of Instruction, Physiology, Marine Biological Lab., Woods Hole, Mass., 1909-12. Dean in the Colleges of Science, University of Chicago, 1915-22. His books include *The Physiology of Twinning, Evolution Yesterday and Today, The Phylum Chordata.* Editor and contributor, *The Nature of the World and of Man.*

It was found that whenever the educational experiences of a pair of twins differed to a marked extent the twin with the greater amount of education had a distinctly higher score on all ability and scholastic achievement tests, while in those cases where there was no difference in education, or only a small difference, the scores of the twins of a pair tended to be about as similar as the average of one-egg twins reared together. A few examples of this close correlation between differences in education and those in mental ability will make this important point clear.

THE EFFECTS OF DIFFERENCES IN EDUCATION

In the case of twins *Gladys* and *Helen*, Gladys stopped school after the third grade, while Helen went on through college and became a teacher. There was a difference of about thirteen years of formal schooling in favor of Helen. In the Stanford-Binet Test Helen's I.Q. was one hundred and sixteen (high normal) and Gladys' was ninety-two (low normal), a large difference of twenty-four points. On the Otis S.A.[1] Test Helen had an I.Q. of one hundred and six, Gladys ninety-four, a difference of twelve points. On the International Test Helen scored one hundred and eighty-eight points, Gladys one hundred and forty-three, a difference of forty-five points. On the Stanford Achievement Test Helen had a mental age of eighteen years ten months, Gladys a mental age of thirteen years and one month, a difference of sixty-nine months. It seems certain that in the case of Gladys the great deficiency in education had inhibited the development of the rather high grade of mental ability with which she was endowed by heredity and which was well developed in her twin sister.

In the second case, that of twins *James* and *Reece*, the differences in both education and ability were less striking but quite noteworthy. James completed grade and high school in a town of about two thousand inhabitants, while Reece attended a rural grade school in the mountains which was open only during five months in the year. He attended only when he felt like it and stopped at the eighth grade. On the Stanford-Binet Test James's I.Q. was ninety-six (almost up to average), while Reece's I.Q. was only seventy-seven (commonly regarded as bordering on the "dull and backward" classification), a difference of nineteen points. On the Otis S.A. Test James's I.Q. was one hundred and four (above average) and Reece's was eighty-four, a difference of twenty points. On the International Test James scored one hundred and twenty-four points, Reece eighty-nine, a difference of thirty-five points.

---

[1] Scholastic Achievement.

On the Stanford Achievement Test James had a mental age of sixteen years, Reece thirteen years, one month, a difference of thirty-five months.

In the third case, that of twins *Eleanore* and *Georgiana*, Eleanore stopped school at the end of the fifth grade, while Georgiana finished grade school and high school and then had three years at normal school, a difference in favor of Georgiana of ten years of schooling. In this case, though both girls were quite efficient as office assistants, their mental rating was considerably below the average. Nevertheless, Georgiana was consistently superior to Eleanore. Georgiana's I.Q. on the Stanford-Binet was seventy-eight, Eleanore's was only sixty-six, a difference of twelve points, but in a part of the scale where a few points are rather significant. On the Otis S.A. Test Georgiana's I.Q. was eighty-four and Eleanore's sixty-nine, a difference of fifteen points. On the International Test Georgiana scored ninety-eight points, Eleanore sixty-nine, a difference of twenty-nine points. On the Stanford Achievement Test Georgiana's mental age was fourteen years, one month, Eleanore's ten years, eleven months, a difference of twenty-eight months. This case shows that with a good education a poorly endowed person can improve his ability to a moderate degree but cannot reach the level of a potentially able but poorly educated person such as the twin Gladys of our first case. Some comment might be made here as to the minimal endowment necessary for successfully completing a course in some normal schools and qualifying as a teacher.

The fourth and last case where there was a considerable difference in education is that of twins *Mabel* and *Mary*. Mary was educated through grade school and three years of high school in a medium-sized city and finished her last year in the high school of a large city. Mabel finished the eighth grade in a small country school near her farm home. As is usually the case in country schools, the terms were short. The difference in years of education was actually about five. On the Stanford-Binet Test Mary had an I.Q. of one hundred and six, Mabel of eighty-nine, a difference of seventeen points. On the Otis S.A. Test Mary's I.Q. was one hundred and eleven and Mabel's ninety-seven, a difference of fourteen points. On the International Test Mary scored one hundred and four points, Mabel ninety-six, a difference of only eight points, but in the same direction as the other differences. On the Stanford Achievement Test Mary had a mental age of seventeen years, three months, Mable fourteen years, five months, a difference of thirty-four months.

Out of the twenty cases studied, these four cases were the only ones in which the differences in schooling between twins of a pair differed more than a year or two. It will be noted that in each of these four cases the better educated twin had a distinctly higher rating on all the tests. The consistency of the results on the various tests increases our confidence in the validity of the tests themselves and in the reality of the differences in mental ability of the twins examined. One can hardly question the conclusion that mental ability within certain limits can be improved by education or suffer for the lack of it. In each of these cases we must assume that the twin with the lower I.Q. had an inherited capacity to reach at least the rating of the twin partner with the higher I.Q. If the differences in education had been greater, presumably the differences in I.Q. would have been greater. One's I.Q., then, is not fixed by heredity alone but may be raised or lowered many points according to the type and amount of education the individual experiences.

Remarkably enough, however, the remaining sixteen cases of separated twins, in which differences in education had amounted to no more than a year or two, showed an average difference in I.Q. even slightly less than that of one-egg twins reared together. From this we may draw the conclusion that small differences in education do not appreciably affect ability, but that large differences in education may induce important differences in ability.

EFFECTS OF DIFFERENCES IN SOCIAL ENVIRONMENT

Differences in social environment are difficult to estimate in terms comparable to those in education. The method of estimating these differences was that of rating them by five independent judges and averaging their estimates. When these rated differences in social environment were compared with differences in scores on personality tests there was no reliable correlation of the group as a whole between differences in social environment and differences in personality traits. What is the explanation of this unexpected result? There seem to be two possible answers to this question. Either differences in social environment have no effect on personality traits or else the tests of personality do not bear any direct relation to our rather rough-and-ready estimates of differences in the total social environment. We regard the second answer as more probable than the first.

We find in some cases of separated twins that the chief difference in social environment is one between city life and country life. In other cases the difference is one between relative wealth and relative poverty. In still other cases the difference is mainly one of contacts with cultured as over against relatively uncultured family groups and associates. In one pair of twins one twin had led a respectable life and the other had

had a more or less lawless career. In another pair the life of one twin had been full of stimulating social contacts, while the other had led a decidedly sheltered and isolated existence without stimulating contacts of any sort. In another case one twin had a large family of children to whom she had devoted all her energy and affection, while the twin sister, though married, was childless and had followed a professional career. In still another case one twin girl had spent most of her life in London, England, while the other had, since eighteen months of age, lived in a small town in Ontario. These varied types of social environmental difference are so unrelated to each other that one would not expect any summation of such differences to be correlated with differences in scores made on any particular kind of personality test.

If, then, we are to discover any relation between differences in social environment and differences in personality we shall have to find them through the study of individual cases. When this was done we found clear evidence that differences in social experience actually do produce differences in personality.

Perhaps the most striking personality difference of all was that found between twins *Mildred* and *Ruth*. Mildred was the foster child of a banker who was also the mayor of a medium-sized city. He was a well-educated man whose home was a gathering place of interesting and cultured people. Mildred entered into all of these activities. Ruth, on the other hand, was the foster child of a man of little education who was a foreman of laborers. The foster mother disapproved of Ruth's normal associates and kept her at home after school hours, with dolls as her only companions. On all the personality tests Ruth showed an inhibited character, shy, diffident, silent, with lisping speech and an unhappy expression, while Mildred was much more confident, unembarrassed, talkative, happy in facial expression and spoke without a trace of lisping. Although both girls were high school seniors in two different cities and had had equal educational opportunities, Mildred's I.Q. on both the Stanford-Binet and the Otis S.A. tests was fifteen points higher than that of Ruth. From this it might be inferred that the cultured and stimulating home life of Mildred, as contrasted with the barren home life of Ruth, had made a difference in mental ability equal to that of several years of formal schooling in some of the other cases.

Another interesting case was that of *Mary* and *Mabel*. These twins, in addition to the educational differences already described, had lived very different lives. Mary had lived all her life in a town and had devoted herself to her studies and to music and music teaching. Mabel had lived on a large and prosperous farm, participating actively in all the work commonly done by an able-bodied farm woman. On all of the personality tests the scores of these twenty-nine-year-old women were among the most different of the whole twenty pairs. Mabel, the farm woman, was slow and phlegmatic; Mary was far more excitable and responsive, almost neurotic. On the other hand, Mabel was more aggressive and was evidently the leader and manager. She had fewer fears and was less readily shocked by unpleasant words and ideas. She walked about with a firm, almost masculine stride, in contrast with Mary's ladylike step and manner. The two women seemed totally unlike in overt behavior and gave the impression of having very different personalities.

The case of *Gladys* and *Helen,* who had the greatest difference in schooling, also illustrates the effects of social differences on personality. These social differences are inherent in the fact that Helen had gone through college and was a teacher, while Gladys had been an industrial worker most of her life. In some of the personality tests the scores were very similar; on others very different. It appears that these twins are alike in fundamental personality traits but differ greatly in their reactions to different social situations. The largest contrast was in overt behavior. Helen, the teacher, was much more suave and polished, was much more interested in her personal appearance and made more of an effort to produce a favorable personal impression. Gladys was all business, without social charm or concern about how she impressed others.

In contrast to these cases in which the differences in social environment seemed definitely to have produced appropriate differences in personality, was the case of twins *James* and *Reece.* James had always lived in town with his maternal grandparents. He had had a good high-school education and was engineer for a sand-and-gravel company. He was a steady, respected citizen. Reece, on the contrary, had lived the life of a mountaineer, had never worked steadily, had engaged in illegal pursuits characteristic of his environment and had been caught and punished several times. In spite of this great difference in social experience, these twins, who had never spent a night together since babyhood, were almost indistinguishable as to their behavior when with us. They made highly similar scores on all the personality tests. It appears that the differences in environment and experience have not modified their fundamental personality traits but have merely served to direct the primitive impulses, common to both, into modes of behavior in one case characteristic of a primitive environment and in the other case into those more in accord with the ideals of a higher level of civilized life. Neither of these men is criminalistic in character, but both are rather individualistic, rather stubborn and both tend to resist opposition vigorously. One expressed his strong character by primitive modes of action; the other restrained his primitive impulses in favor of actions which are more socially acceptable in a modern urban community.

EFFECTS OF DIFFERENCES IN PHYSICAL ENVIRONMENT

Under the head of physical environment we include differences in climate, housing, food, physical exercise, hygiene and disease. In no two pairs of separated twins did we find the same combination of these physical environmental differences. In some pairs one of these types of environmental difference was well marked; in others another type. Here again, as in the study of differences in social environment, the case-study method is more likely to reveal the effects of specific differences in the physical environment than is the statistical method.

There were two pairs of twins in which there was a great difference in health. The first of these is the case of twins Thelma and Zelma, twenty-nine-year-old married women. Thelma was a victim of advanced tuberculosis and was exceedingly frail, weighing only seventy-two pounds; while Zelma was quite healthy and weighed ninety-eight pounds, normal for such a small, delicately formed woman. Apart from this great difference in weight, Thelma was a sort of shrunken replica of Zelma. The second case where the health condition constituted the only marked environmental effect was the case of fifty-eight-year-old twins Ada and Ida. Ada was a robust and normally healthy woman, while Ida had an enormous goiter and showed very pronounced symptoms of goiter disease (thyroxin deficiency). Ada was vigorous and active, Ida easily fatigued and somewhat sluggish. Ada weighed two hundred and eight pounds, Ida two hundred and twenty-seven, the extra weight due to excess water in the tissues, a condition characteristic of goiter disease.

There were two cases of twins with pronounced difference in muscular development. The first is the case of Mabel and Mary, twice previously referred to in this chapter. Mable was a muscular farm worker and Mary a sedentary, ladylike music teacher and store clerk. Mabel weighed one hundred and thirty-eight pounds and was hard muscled; Mary weighed only one hundred and ten pounds and her muscles were soft and poorly developed. It is obvious that the great difference in the occupations of these two women was responsible for most of their difference in muscularity and weight. The second of these cases was that of the twins Paul O. and Paul C. Paul C. had been addicted to gymnastics and Paul O. had led a sedentary life. Paul C. was very well developed, muscularly, while Paul O. was much less so. The difference in weight was over ten pounds in favor of Paul C. and was due entirely to excess muscle.

There was one case of marked differences in the condition of the teeth. The twins *Edith* and *Fay* showed a striking contrast in this respect. Fay, at the age of thirty-eight years, had one of the most perfect sets of teeth I have examined, while Edith's teeth were in extremely bad condition, the incisors discolored and much worn and cheek teeth much decayed. It appears that Edith had had several children in rapid succession while she and her husband were trying to establish claim on a North Dakota farm. During this period food was scarce, especially those foods rich in tooth-building ingredients. It was during this period that Edith's potentially fine teeth deteriorated. Fay, who lived in a city and always had everything a prosperous husband could supply, took care of her teeth and was rewarded by having them in perfect condition.

STATISTICAL COMPARISONS

Comparisons were made between the fifty pairs of one-egg twins reared together and twenty pairs of one-egg twins reared apart. In these two sets of twins the only difference is in the environment. Let us see which characters are least affected and which are most affected by differences in environment.

The twins reared apart were, on the average, no more different than those reared together in measurable physical characters except for one character, body weight, which in twins is largely a measure of differences in food, health and physical exercise. The average difference in weight for twins reared apart was twice as great as that for twins reared together. In all other physical measurements, except those directly dependent on differences in weight, the average differences in the two sets of twins was almost exactly the same.

The situation is quite different when we come to deal with mental differences. The average difference in I.Q. of twins reared together was 5.3 points and for twins reared apart 8.2 points, an excess of nearly three points. This difference was almost entirely accounted for by the four cases in which there was a great difference in education.

The average difference in scholastic achievement for the twins reared apart was more than twice as great as for twins reared together, indicating that achievement tests register more accurately differences in schooling than do ability tests.

Since only one personality test was given to the twins reared together, it was not easy to compare the two sets of twins with respect to differences in personality, but there are many evidences that environmental differences have caused greater differences in personality than in any other traits.

In conclusion, we may fairly say that our researches have done at least two things: 1, they have shown conclusively that the human heredity-environment problem is extremely complex, that it is not one problem but many, that the problem differs with respect to every character studied and that there is therefore no general solution for the problem as a whole; 2, that solutions can be given only for well-defined heredity-environment setups, such as that for children in the same family reared together, and for a limited number of one-egg twins reared under a variety of different environmental conditions.

We realize that while we have helped to solve with some degree of success a few parts of the heredity-environment problem, there remains much to be done. We have at least untangled some of the threads in that very intricate mesh that constitutes the organism we call man.

⊷⧉⊷⧉⊷⧉⊷⧉⊷

10. The Concept of Culture *

THE BEGINNING STUDENT of sociology soon discovers that culture is one of the most significant concepts about which he will learn. At the same time he finds that his previous acquaintance with the variety of meanings popularly attached to the word tend to confuse his grasp of the special meaning given it by social scientists. Since the concept was originally used by the anthropologists, its explanation by one of them has particular validity. Clyde Kluckhohn here gives us a clear and readable description of culture. Further comprehension may be achieved by examining some patterns of culture from different societies. Specific illustrations of that aspect of culture concerned with family relations as it is manifested in various societies appear in selections 11, 19, 66, 67 and 87.

* Clyde Kluckhohn, *Mirror for Man* (New York: McGraw-Hill Book Co., 1949), pp. 17-36. Reprinted by permission of the publisher and the author.

The author (b. 1905) is Professor of Anthropology, Harvard University; Director of Russian Research Center. Authority on Navaho Indians. Co-chief of Joint Morale Survey, Military Intelligence, U.S.A. and O.W.I., 1944-45. Editor (with Henry Alexander Murray), *Personality in Nature.* Author of numerous articles in psychological, anthropological, and sociological publications. Co-author, *Navaho Means People.*

WHY DO THE Chinese dislike milk and milk products? Why would the Japanese die willingly in a Banzai charge that seemed senseless to Americans? Why do some nations trace descent through the father, others through the mother, still others through both parents? Not because different peoples have different instincts, not because they were destined by God or Fate to different habits, not because the weather is different in China and Japan and the United States. Sometimes shrewd common sense has an answer that is close to that of the anthropologist: "because they were brought up that way." By "culture" anthropology means the total life way of a people, the social legacy the individual acquires from his group. Or culture can be regarded as that part of the environment that is the creation of man.

This technical term has a wider meaning than the "culture" of history and literature. A humble cooking pot is as much a cultural product as is a Beethoven sonata. In ordinary speech a man of culture is a man who can speak languages other than his own, who is familiar with history, literature, philosophy, or the fine arts. In some cliques that definition is still narrower. The cultured person is one who can talk about James Joyce, Scarlatti, and Picasso. To the anthropologist, however, to be human is to be cultured. There is culture in general, and then there are the specific cultures such as Russian, American, British, Hottentot, Inca. The general abstract notion serves to remind us that we cannot explain acts solely in terms of the biological properties of the people concerned, their individual past experience, and the immediate situation. The past experience of other men in the form of culture enters into almost every event. Each specific culture constitutes a kind of blueprint for all of life's activities.

One of the interesting things about human beings is that they try to understand themselves and their own behavior. While this has been particularly true of Europeans in recent times, there is no group which has not developed a scheme or schemes to explain man's actions. To the insistent human query "why?" the most exciting illumination anthropology has to offer is that of the concept of culture. Its explanatory importance is comparable to categories such as evolution in biology, gravity in physics, disease in medicine. A good deal of human behavior can be understood, and indeed predicted, if we know a people's design for living. Many acts are neither accidental nor due to personal peculiarities nor caused by supernatural forces nor simply mysterious. Even those of us who pride ourselves on our individualism follow most of the time a pattern not of our own making. We brush our teeth on arising. We put on pants—not a loincloth or a grass skirt. We eat three meals a day—not four or five or two. We sleep in a bed—not in a hammock or on a sheep pelt. I do not have to know the individual and his life history to be able to predict these and countless other regularities, including many in the thinking process, of all Americans who are not incarcerated in jails or hospitals for the insane.

To the American woman a system of plural wives seems "instinctively" abhorrent. She cannot understand how any woman can fail to be jealous and uncomfortable if she must share her husband with other women. She feels it "unnatural" to accept such a situation. On the other hand, a Koryak woman of Siberia, for example, would find it hard to understand how a woman could be so selfish and so undesirous of feminine companionship in the home as to wish to restrict her husband to one mate.

Some years ago I met in New York City a young man who did not speak a word of English and was obviously bewildered by American ways. By "blood" he was as American as you or I, for his parents had gone from Indiana to China as missionaries. Orphaned in infancy, he was reared by a Chinese family in a remote village. All who met him found him more Chinese than American. The facts of his blue eyes and light hair were less impressive than a Chinese style of gait, Chinese arm and hand movements, Chinese facial expression, and Chinese modes of thought. The biological heritage was American, but the cultural training had been Chinese. He returned to China. Another example of another kind: I once knew a trader's wife in Arizona who took a somewhat devilish interest in producing a cultural reaction. Guests who came her way were often served delicious sandwiches filled with a meat that seemed to be neither chicken nor tuna fish yet was reminiscent of both. To queries she gave no reply until each had eaten his fill. She then explained that what they had eaten was not chicken, not tuna fish, but the rich, white flesh of freshly killed rattlesnakes. The response was instantaneous—vomiting, often violent vomiting. A biological process is caught in a cultural web.

A highly intelligent teacher with long and successful experience in the public schools of Chicago was finishing her first year in an Indian school. When asked how her Navaho pupils compared in intelligence with Chicago youngsters, she replied, "Well, I just don't know. Sometimes the Indians seem just as bright. At other times they just act like dumb animals. The other night we had a dance in the high school. I saw a boy who is one of the best students in my English class standing off by himself. So I took him over to a pretty girl and told them to dance. But they just stood there with their heads down. They wouldn't even say anything." I inquired if she knew whether or not they were members of the same clan. "What difference would that make?"

"How would you feel about getting into bed with your brother?"

The teacher walked off in a huff, but, actually, the two cases were quite comparable in principle. To the Indian the type of bodily contact involved in our social dancing has a directly sexual connotation. The incest taboos between members of the same clan are as severe as between true brothers and sisters. The shame of the Indians at the suggestion that a clan brother and sister should dance and the indignation of the white teacher at the idea that she should share a bed with an adult brother represent equally nonrational responses, culturally standardized unreason.

All this does not mean that there is no such thing as raw human nature. The very fact that certain of the same institutions are found in all known societies indicates that at bottom all human beings are very much alike. The files of the Cross-Cultural Survey at Yale University are organized according to categories such as "marriage ceremonies," "life crisis rites," "incest taboos." At least seventy-five of these categories are represented in every single one of the hundreds of cultures analyzed. This is hardly surprising. The members of all human groups have about the same biological equipment. All men undergo the same poignant life experiences such as birth, helplessness, illness, old age, and death. The biological potentialities of the species are the blocks with which cultures are built. Some patterns of every culture crystallize around focuses provided by the inevitables of biology: the difference between the sexes, the presence of persons of different ages, the varying physical strength and skill of individuals. The facts of nature also limit culture forms. No culture provides patterns for jumping over trees or for eating iron ore.

There is thus no "either-or" between nature and that special form of nurture called culture. Culture determinism is as one-sided as biological determinism. The two factors are interdependent. Culture arises out of human nature, and its forms are restricted both by man's biology and by natural laws. It is equally true that culture channels biological processes—vomiting, weeping, fainting, sneezing, the daily habits of food intake and waste elimination. When a man eats, he is reacting to an internal "drive," namely, hunger contractions consequent upon the lowering of blood sugar, but his precise reaction to these internal stimuli cannot be predicted by physiological knowledge alone. Whether a healthy adult feels hungry twice, three times, or four times a day and the hours at which this feeling recurs is a question of culture. What he eats is of course limited by availability, but is also partly regulated by culture. It is a biological fact that some types of berries are poisonous; it is a cultural fact that, a few generations ago, most Americans considered tomatoes to be poisonous and refused to eat them.

Such selective, discriminative use of the environment is characteristically cultural. In a still more general sense, too, the process of eating is channeled by culture. Whether a man eats to live, lives to eat, or merely eats and lives is only in part an individual matter, for there are also cultural trends. Emotions are physiological events. Certain situations will evoke fear in people from any culture. But sensations of pleasure, anger, and lust may be stimulated by cultural cues that would leave unmoved someone who has been reared in a different social tradition.

Except in the case of newborn babies and of individuals born with clear-cut structural or functional abnormalities we can observe innate endowments only as modified by cultural training. In a hospital in New Mexico where Zuñi Indian, Navaho Indian, and white American babies are born, it is possible to classify the newly arrived infants as unusually active, average, and quiet. Some babies from each "racial" group will fall into each category, though a higher proportion of the white babies will fall into the unusually active class. But if a Navaho baby, a Zuñi baby, and a white baby—all classified as unusually active at birth—are again observed at the age of two years, the Zuñi baby will no longer seem given to quick and restless activity—*as compared with the white child*—though he may seem so as compared with the other Zuñis of the same age. The Navaho child is likely to fall in between as contrasted with the Zuñi and the white, though he will probably still seem more active than the average Navaho youngster.

It was remarked by many observers in the Japanese relocation centers that Japanese who were born and brought up in this country, especially those who were reared apart from any large colony of Japanese, resemble in behavior their white neighbors much more closely than they do their own parents who were educated in Japan.

I have said "culture channels biological processes." It is more accurate to say "the biological functioning of individuals is modified if they have been trained in certain ways and not in others." Culture is not a disembodied force. It is created and transmitted by people. However, culture, like well-known concepts of the physical sciences, is a convenient abstraction. One never sees gravity. One sees bodies falling in regular ways. One never sees an electromagnetic field. Yet certain happenings that can be seen may be given a neat abstract formulation by assuming that the electromagnetic field exists. Similarly, one never sees culture as such. What is seen are regularities in the behavior or artifacts of a group that has adhered to a common tradition. The regularities in style and technique of ancient Inca tapestries or stone axes from Melanesian islands are due to the existence of mental blueprints for the group.

Culture is a way of thinking, feeling, believing. It is the group's knowledge stored up (in memories of men; in books and objects) for future use. We study the products of this "mental" activity: the overt behavior, the speech and gestures and activities of people, and the tangible results of these things such as tools, houses, cornfields, and what not. It has been customary in lists of "culture traits" to include such things as watches or lawbooks. This is a convenient way of thinking about them, but in the solution of any important problem we must remember that they, in themselves, are nothing but metals, paper, and ink. What is important is that some men know how to make them, others set a value on them, are unhappy without them, direct their activities in relation to them, or disregard them.

It is only a helpful shorthand when we say "The cultural patterns of the Zulu were resistant to Christianization." In the directly observable world of course, it was individual Zulus who resisted. Nevertheless, if we do not forget that we are speaking at a high level of abstraction, it is justifiable to speak of culture as a cause. One may compare the practice of saying "syphilis caused the extinction of the native population of the island." Was it "syphilis" or "syphilis germs" or "human beings who were carriers of syphilis?"

"Culture," then, is "a theory." But if a theory is not contradicted by any relevant fact and if it helps us to understand a mass of otherwise chaotic facts, it is useful. Darwin's contribution was much less the accumulation of new knowledge than the creation of a theory which put in order data already known. An accumulation of facts, however large, is no more a science than a pile of bricks is a house. Anthropology's demonstration that the most weird set of customs has a consistency and an order is comparable to modern psychiatry's showing that there is meaning and purpose in the apparently incoherent talk of the insane. In fact, the inability of the older psychologies and philosophies to account for the strange behavior of madmen and heathens was the principal factor that forced psychiatry and anthropology to develop theories of the unconscious and of culture.

Since culture is an abstraction, it is important not to confuse culture with society. A "society" refers to a group of people who interact more with each other than they do with other individuals—who cooperate with each other for the attainment of certain ends. You can see and indeed count the individuals who make up a society. A "culture" refers to the distinctive ways of life of such a group of people. Not all social events are culturally patterned. New types of circumstances arise for which no cultural solutions have as yet been devised.

A culture constitutes a storehouse of the pooled learning of the group. A rabbit starts life with some innate responses. He can learn from his own experience and perhaps from observing other rabbits. A human infant is born with fewer instincts and greater plasticity. His main task is to learn the answers that persons he will never see, persons long dead, have worked out. Once he has learned the formulas supplied by the culture of his group, most of his behavior becomes almost as automatic and unthinking as if it were instinctive. There is a tremendous amount of intelligence behind the making of a radio, but not much is required to learn to turn it on.

The members of all human societies face some of the same unavoidable dilemmas, posed by biology and other facts of the human situation. This is why the basic categories of all cultures are so similar. Human culture without language is unthinkable. No culture fails to provide for aesthetic expression and aesthetic delight. Every culture supplies standardized orientations toward the deeper problems, such as death. Every culture is designed to perpetuate the group and its solidarity, to meet the demands of individuals for an orderly way of life and for satisfaction of biological needs.

However, the variations on these basic themes are numberless. Some languages are built up out of twenty basic sounds, others out of forty. Nose plugs were considered beautiful by the predynastic Egyptians but are not by the modern French. Puberty is a biological fact. But one culture ignores it, another prescribes informal instructions about sex but no ceremony, a third has impressive rites for girls only, a fourth for boys and girls. In this culture, the first menstruation is welcomed as a happy, natural event; in that culture the atmosphere is full of dread and supernatural threat. Each culture dissects nature according to its own system of categories. The Navaho Indians apply the same word to the color of a robin's egg and to that of grass. A psychologist once assumed that this meant a difference in the sense organs, that Navahos didn't have the physiological equipment to distinguish "green" from "blue." However, when he showed them objects of the two colors and asked them if they were exactly the same colors, they looked at him with astonishment. His dream of discovering a new type of color blindness was shattered.

Every culture must deal with the sexual instinct. Some, however, seek to deny all sexual expression before marriage, whereas a Polynesian adolescent who was not promiscuous would be distinctly abnormal. Some cultures enforce lifelong monogamy, others, like our own, tolerate serial monogamy; in still other cultures, two or more women may be joined to one man or several men to a single woman. Homosexuality has been a permitted pattern in the Greco-Roman world, in parts of Islam, and in various primitive tribes. Large portions of the population of Tibet, and of Christendom at some places and periods, have practiced complete celibacy. To us marriage is first and foremost an arrangement between two individuals. In many more societies marriage is merely one facet of a complicated set of reciprocities, economic and otherwise, between two families or two clans.

The essence of the cultural process is selectivity. The selection is only exceptionally conscious and rational. Cultures are like Topsy. They just grew. Once, however, a way of handling a situation becomes institutionalized, there is ordinarily great resistance to change or deviation. When we speak of "our sacred beliefs," we mean of course that they are beyond criticism and that the person who suggests modification or abandonment must be punished. No person is emotionally indifferent to his culture. Certain cultural premises may become totally out of accord with a new factual situation. Leaders may recognize this and reject the old ways in theory. Yet their emotional loyalty continues in the face of reason because of the intimate conditionings of early childhood.

A culture is learned by individuals as the result of belonging to some particular group, and it constitutes that part of learned behavior which is shared with others. It is our social legacy, as contrasted with our organic heredity. It is one of the important factors which permits us to live together in an organized society, giving us ready-made solutions to our problems, helping us to predict the behavior of others, and permitting others to know what to expect of us.

Culture regulates our lives at every turn. From the moment we are born until we die there is, whether we are conscious of it or not, constant pressure upon us to follow certain types of behavior that other men have created for us. Some paths we follow willingly, others we follow because we know no other way, still others we deviate from or go back to most unwillingly. Mothers of small children know how unnaturally most of this comes to us—how little regard we have, until we are "culturalized," for the "proper" place, time, and manner for certain acts such as eating, excreting, sleeping, getting dirty, and making loud noises. But by more or less adhering to a system of related designs for carrying out all the acts of living, a group of men and women feel themselves linked together by a powerful chain of sentiments. Ruth Benedict gave an almost complete definition of the concept when she said, "Culture is that which binds men together."

It is true any culture is a set of techniques for adjusting both to the external environment and to other men. However, cultures create problems as well as solve them. If the lore of a people states that frogs are dangerous creatures, or that it is not safe to go about at night because of witches or ghosts, threats are posed which do not arise out of the inexorable facts of the external world. Cultures produce needs as well as provide a means of fulfilling them. There exist for every group cultur-ally defined, acquired drives that may be more powerful in ordinary daily life than the biologically inborn drives. Many Americans, for example, will work harder for "success" than they will for sexual satisfaction.

Most groups elaborate certain aspects of their culture far beyond maximum utility or survival value. In other words, not all culture promotes physical survival. At times, indeed, it does exactly the op-posite. Aspects of culture which once were adaptive may persist long after they have ceased to be useful. An analysis of any culture will disclose many features which cannot possibly be construed as adaptations to the total environment in which the group now finds itself. However, it is altogether likely that these apparently useless features represent survivals, with modifications through time, of cultural forms which were adaptive in one or another previous situation.

Any cultural practice must be functional or it will disappear before long. That is, it must somehow contribute to the survival of the society or to the adjustment of the individual. However, many cultural func-tions are not manifest but latent. A cowboy will walk three miles to catch a horse which he then rides one mile to the store. From the point of view of manifest function this is positively irrational. But the act has the latent function of maintaining the cowboy's prestige in the terms of his own subculture. One can instance the buttons on the sleeve of a man's coat, our absurd English spelling, the use of capital letters, and a host of other apparently nonfunctional customs. They serve mainly the latent function of assisting individuals to maintain their security by preserving continuity with the past and by making certain sectors of life familiar and predictable.

Every culture is a precipitate of history. In more than one sense history is a sieve. Each culture embraces those aspects of the past, which, usually in altered form and with altered meanings, live on in the present. Discoveries and inventions, both material and ideological, are constantly being made available to a group through its historical contacts with other peoples or being created by its own members. However, only those that fit the total immediate situation in meeting the group's needs for survival or in promoting the psychological adjustment of individuals will become part of the culture. The process of culture building may be regarded as an addition to man's innate biological capacities, an addition providing instruments which enlarge, or may even substitute for, biological functions, and to a degree compensating for biological limitations—as in ensuring that death does not always result in the loss to humanity of what the deceased has learned.

Culture is like a map. Just as a map isn't the territory but an abstract representation of a particular area, so also a culture is an abstract description of trends toward uniformity in the words, deeds, and artifacts of a human group. If a map is accurate and you can read it, you won't get lost; if you know a culture, you will know your way around in the life of a society.

Many educated people have the notion that culture applies only to exotic ways of life or to societies where relative simplicity and relative homogeneity prevail. Some sophisticated missionaries, for example, will use the anthropological conception in discussing the special modes of living of South Sea Islanders, but seem amazed at the idea that it could be applied equally to inhabitants of New York City. And social workers in Boston will talk about the culture of a colorful and well-knit immigrant group but boggle at applying it to the behavior of staff members in the social-service agency itself.

In the primitive society the correspondence between the habits of individuals and the customs of the community is ordinarily greater. There is probably some truth in what an old Indian once said, "In the old days there was no law; everybody did what was right." The primitive tends to find happiness in the fulfillment of intricately involuted cultural patterns; the modern more often tends to feel the pattern as repressive to his individuality. It is also true that in a complex stratified society there are numerous exceptions to generalizations made about the culture as a whole. It is necessary to study regional, class, and occupational subcultures. Primitive cultures have greater stability than modern cultures; they change—but less rapidly.

However, modern men also are creators and carriers of culture. Only in some respects are they influenced differently from primitives by culture. Moreover, there are such wide variations in primitive cultures that any black-and-white contrast between the primitive and the civilized is altogether fictitious. The distinction which is most generally true lies in the field of conscious philosophy.

The publication of Paul Radin's *Primitive Man as a Philosopher* did much toward destroying the myth that an abstract analysis of experience was a peculiarity of literate societies. Speculation and reflection upon the nature of the universe and of man's place in the total scheme of things have been carried out in every known culture. Every people has its characteristic set of "primitive postulates." It remains true that critical examination of basic premises and fully explicit systematization of philosophical concepts are seldom found at the nonliterate level. The written word is an almost essential condition for free and extended discussion of fundamental philosophic issues. Where dependence on memory exists, there seems to be an inevitable tendency to emphasize the correct perpetuation of the precious oral tradition. Similarly, while it is all too easy to underestimate the extent to which ideas spread without books, it is in general true that tribal or folk societies do not possess competing philosophical systems. The major exception to this statement is, of course, the case where part of the tribe becomes converted to one of the great proselytizing religions such as Christianity or Mohammedanism. Before contact with rich and powerful civilizations, primitive peoples seem to have absorbed new ideas piecemeal, slowly integrating them with the previously existing ideology. The abstract thought of nonliterate societies is ordinarily less self-critical, less systematic, nor so intricately elaborated in purely logical dimensions. Primitive thinking is more concrete, more implicit—perhaps more completely coherent than the philosophy of most individuals in larger societies which have been influenced over long periods by disparate intellectual currents.

No participant in any culture knows all the details of the cultural map. The statement frequently heard that St. Thomas Aquinas was the last man to master all the knowledge of his society is intrinsically absurd. St. Thomas would have been hard put to make a pane of cathedral glass or to act as a midwife. In every culture there are what Ralph Linton has called "universals, alternatives, and specialties." Every Christian in the thirteenth century knew that it was necessary to attend mass, to go to confession, to ask the Mother of God to intercede with her Son. There were many other universals in the Christian culture of Western Europe. However, there were also alternative cultural patterns even in the realm of religion. Each individual had his own patron saint, and different towns developed the cults of different saints. The thirteenth-century anthropologist could have discovered the rudiments of Christian practice by questioning and observing whomever he happened to meet in Germany, France, Italy, or England. But to find out the details of the ceremonials honoring St. Hubert or St. Bridget he would have had to seek out certain individuals or special localities where these alternative patterns were practiced. Similarly, he could not learn about weaving from a professional soldier or about canon law from a farmer. Such cultural knowledge belongs in the realm of the specialties, voluntarily chosen by the individual or ascribed to him by birth. Thus, part of a culture must be learned by everyone, part may be selected from alternative patterns, part applies only to those who perform the roles in the society for which these patterns are designed.

Many aspects of a culture are explicit. The explicit culture consists in those regularities in word and deed that may be generalized straight from the evidence of the ear and the eye. The recognition of these is like the recognition of style in the art of a particular place and epoch. If we have examined twenty specimens of the wooden saints' images made in the Taos valley of New Mexico in the late eighteenth century, we can predict that any new images from the same locality and period will in most respects exhibit the same techniques of carving, about the same use of colors and choice of woods, a similar quality of artistic conception. Similarly, if, in a society of 2,000 members, we record 100 marriages at random and find that in 30 cases a man has married the sister of his brother's wife, we can anticipate that an additional sample of 100 marriages will show roughly the same number of cases of this pattern.

The above is an instance of what anthropologists call a behavioral pattern, the practices as opposed to the rules of the culture. There are also, however, regularities in what people say they do or should do. They do tend in fact to prefer to marry into a family already connected with their own by marriage, but this is not necessarily part of the official code of conduct. No disapproval whatsoever is attached to those who make another sort of marriage. On the other hand, it is explicitly forbidden to marry a member of one's own clan even though no biological relationship is traceable. This is a regulatory pattern—a Thou Shalt or a Thou Shalt Not. Such patterns may be violated often, but their existence is nevertheless important. A people's standards for conduct and belief define the socially approved aims and the acceptable means of attaining them. When the discrepancy between the theory and the practice of a culture is exceptionally great, this indicates that the culture is undergoing rapid change. It does not prove that ideals are unimportant, for ideals are but one of a number of factors determining action.

Cultures do not manifest themselves solely in observable customs and artifacts. No amount of questioning of any save the most articulate in the most self-conscious cultures will bring out some of the basic attitudes common to the members of the group. This is because these basic assumptions are taken so for granted that they normally do not enter into consciousness. This part of the cultural map must be inferred by the observer on the basis of consistencies in thought and action. Missionaries in various societies are often disturbed or puzzled because the natives do not regard "morals" and "sex code" as almost synonymous. The natives seem to feel that morals are concerned with sex just about as much as with eating—no less and no more. No society fails to have some restrictions on sexual behavior, but sex activity outside of marriage need not necessarily be furtive or attended with guilt. The Christian tradition has tended to assume that sex is inherently nasty as well as dangerous. Other cultures assume that sex in itself is not only natural but one of the good things of life, even though sex acts with certain persons under certain circumstances are forbidden. This is implicit culture, for the natives do not announce their premises. The missionaries would get further if they said, in effect, "Look, our morality starts from different assumptions. Let's talk about those assumptions," rather than ranting about "immorality."

A factor implicit in a variety of diverse phenomena may be generalized as an underlying cultural principle. For example, the Navaho Indians always leave part of the design in a pot, a basket, or a blanket unfinished. When a medicine man instructs an apprentice he always leaves a little bit of the story untold. This "fear of closure" is a recurrent theme in Navaho culture. Its influence may be detected in many contexts that have no explicit connection.

If the observed cultural behavior is to be correctly understood, the categories and presuppositions constituting the implicit culture must be worked out. The "strain toward consistency" which Sumner noted in the folkways and mores of all groups cannot be accounted for unless one grants a set of systematically interrelated implicit themes. For example, in American culture the themes of "effort and optimism," "the common man," "technology," and "virtuous materialism" have a functional interdependence, the origin of which is historically known. The relationship between themes may be that of conflict. One may instance the competition between Jefferson's theory of democracy and Hamilton's "government by the rich, the wellborn, and the able." In other cases most themes may be integrated under a single dominant theme. In Negro cultures of West Africa the mainspring of social life is religion; in East Africa almost all cultural behavior seems to be oriented toward certain premises and categories centered on the cattle economy. If there be one master principle in the implicit culture, this is often called the "ethos" or Zeitgeist.

Every culture has organization as well as content. There is nothing mystical about this statement. One may compare ordinary experience. If I know that Smith, working alone, can shovel 10 cubic yards of dirt a day, Jones 12, and Brown 14, I would be foolish to predict that the three working together would move 36. The total might well be considerably more; it might be less. A whole is different from the sum of its parts. The same principle is familiar in athletic teams. A brilliant pitcher added to a nine may mean a pennant or may mean the cellar; it depends on how he fits in.

And so it is with cultures. A mere list of the behavioral and regulatory patterns and of the implicit themes and categories would be like a map on which all mountains, lakes, and rivers were included—but not in their actual relationship to one another. Two cultures could have almost identical inventories and still be extremely different. The full significance of any single element in a culture design will be seen only

when that element is viewed in the total matrix of its relationship to
other elements. Naturally, this includes accent or emphasis, as well
as position. Accent is manifested sometimes through frequency, sometimes through intensity. The indispensable importance of these questions of arrangement and emphasis may be driven home by an analogy.
Consider a musical sequence made up of three notes. If we are told
that the three notes in question are A, B, and G, we receive information
which is fundamental. But it will not enable us to predict the type of
sensation which the playing of this sequence is likely to evoke. We
need many different sorts of relationship data. Are the notes to be
played in that or some other order? What duration will each receive?
How will the emphasis, if any, be distributed? We also need, of course,
to know whether the instrument used is to be a piano or an accordion.

Cultures vary greatly in their degree of integration. Synthesis is
achieved partly through the overt statement of the dominant conceptions, assumptions, and aspirations of the group in its religious lore,
secular thought, and ethical code; partly through habitual but unconscious ways of looking at the stream of events, ways of begging certain
questions. To the naïve participant in the culture these modes of
categorizing, of dissecting experience along these planes and not others,
are as much "given" as the regular sequence of daylight and darkness
or the necessity of air, water, and food for life. Had Americans not
thought in terms of money and the market system during the depression
they would have distributed unsalable goods rather than destroyed them.

Every group's way of life, then, is a structure—not a haphazard collection of all the different physically possible and functionally effective
patterns of belief and action. A culture is an interdependent system
based upon linked premises and categories whose influence is greater,
rather than less, because they are seldom put in words. Some degree
of internal coherence which is felt rather than rationally constructed
seems to be demanded by most of the participants in any culture. As
Whitehead has remarked, "Human life is driven forward by its dim
apprehension of notions too general for its existing language."

In sum, the distinctive way of life that is handed down as the social
heritage of a people does more than supply a set of skills for making a
living and a set of blueprints for human relations. Each different way
of life makes its own assumptions about the ends and purposes of
human existence, about what human beings have a right to expect from
each other and the gods, about what constitutes fulfillment or frustration. Some of these assumptions are made explicit in the lore of the
folk; others are tacit premises which the observer must infer by finding
consistent trends in word and deed.

11. Taking One's Proper Station *

INABILITY OF AMERICANS to understand the "unexplainable" actions of the Japanese soldier was a serious obstacle in World War II. Ruth Benedict's *The Chrysanthemum And The Sword* is a major contribution to our understanding of the Japanese. In this selection she describes the codes and values that define many of the relationships between persons in a culture quite different from our own. One of the most effective ways of learning the meaning of the term culture is to compare the conceptions of proper behavior in different societies. Here Benedict describes how sex, age, position in the family, and other factors define the person's proper relations with the people in his circle of interaction. This not only helps us to appreciate Japanese behavior but by contrast provides a basis for understanding how American culture defines our own behavior.

JAPAN FOR ALL ITS RECENT WESTERNIZATION is still an aristocratic society. Every greeting, every contact must indicate the kind and degree of social distance between men. Every time a man says to another "Eat" or "Sit down" he uses different words if he is addressing someone familiarly or is speaking to an inferior or to a superior. There is a different "you" that must be used in each case and the verbs have different stems. The Japanese have, in other words, what is called a "respect language," as many other peoples do in the Pacific, and they accompany it with proper bows and kneelings. All such behavior is governed by meticulous rules and conventions; it is not merely necessary to know to whom one bows but it is necessary to know how much one bows. A bow that is right and proper to one host would be resented as an insult by another who stood in a slightly different relationship to the bower. And bows range all the way from kneeling with forehead lowered to the hands placed flat upon the floor, to the mere inclination of head and shoulders. One must learn, and learn early, how to suit the obeisance to each particular case.

It is not merely class differences which must be constantly recognized by appropriate behavior, though these are important. Sex and age,

* Ruth Benedict, *The Chrysanthemum and the Sword* (Boston: Houghton Mifflin Co., 1946), pp. 43-75. Reprinted by permission of the publisher.

The author (1887-1948) was an anthropologist, educator, poet (under the name Ann Singleton). Member of staff, Department of Anthropology, Columbia University. Researches guided Allied propaganda in World War II. Studied Mission, Blackfoot, Apache, Pueblo, and Pima Indians on location. Special studies of mythology, folklore and primitive religions. Among her books are *Patterns of Culture* and *Race, Science and Politics*.

family ties and previous dealings between two persons all enter into the necessary calculations. Even between the same two persons different degrees of respect will be called for on different occasions: a civilian may be on familiar terms with another and not bow to him at all, but when he wears a military uniform his friend in civilian clothes bows to him. Observance of hierarchy is an art which requires the balancing of innumerable factors, some of which in any particular case may cancel each other out and some of which may be additive.

There are of course persons between whom there is relatively little ceremony. In the United States these people are one's own family circle. We shed even the slight formalities of our etiquette when we come home to the bosom of our family. In Japan it is precisely in the family where respect rules are learned and meticulously observed. While the mother still carries the baby strapped to her back she will push his head down with her hand, and his first lessons as a toddler are to observe respect behavior to his father or older brother. The wife bows to her husband, the child bows to his father, younger brothers bow to elder brothers, the sister bows to all her brothers of whatever age. It is no empty gesture. It means that the one who bows acknowledges the right of the other to have his way in things he might well prefer to manage himself, and the one who receives the bow acknowledges in his turn certain responsibilities incumbent upon his station. Hierarchy based on sex and generation and primogeniture are part and parcel of family life.

Filial piety is, of course, a high ethical law which Japan shares with China, and Chinese formulations of it were early adopted in Japan along with Chinese Buddhism, Confucian ethics and secular Chinese culture in the sixth and seventh centuries A.D. The character of filial piety, however, was inevitably modified to suit the different structure of the family in Japan. In China, even today, one owes loyalty to one's vast extended clan. It may number tens of thousands of people over whom it has jurisdiction and from whom it receives support. Conditions differ in different parts of that vast country but in large parts of China all people in any village are members of the same clan. Among all of China's 450,000,000 inhabitants there are only 470 surnames and all people with the same surname count themselves in some degree clan-brothers. Over a whole area all people may be exclusively of one clan and, in addition, families living in far-away cities are their clan fellows. In populous areas like Kwangtung all the clan members unite in keeping up great clan-halls and on stated days they venerate as many as a thousand ancestral tablets of dead clan members stemming from a common forebear. Each clan owns property, lands and temples and has clan funds which are used to pay for the education of any promising clan son. It keeps track of dispersed members and publishes elaborate genealogies which are brought up to date every decade or so to show the names of those who have a right to share in its privileges. It has ancestral laws which might even forbid them to surrender family criminals to the State if the clan was not in agreement with the authorities. In Imperial times these great communities of semi-autonomous clans were governed in the name of the larger State as casually as possible by easygoing mandarinates headed by rotating State appointees who were foreigners in the area.

All this was different in Japan. Until the middle of the nineteenth century only noble families and warrior (samurai) families were allowed to use surnames. Surnames were fundamental in the Chinese clan system and without these, or some equivalent, clan organization cannot develop. One of these equivalents in some tribes is keeping a genealogy. But in Japan only the upper classes kept genealogies and even in these they kept the record, as Daughters of the American Revolution do in the United States, backward in time from the present living person, not downward in time to include every contemporary who stemmed from an original ancestor. It is a very different matter. Besides, Japan was a feudal country. Loyalty was due, not to a great group of relatives, but to a feudal lord. He was resident overlord, and the contrast with the temporary bureaucratic mandarins of China, who were always strangers in their districts, could not have been greater. What was important in Japan was that one was of the fief of Satsuma or the fief of Hizen. A man's ties were to his fief.

Another way of institutionalizing clans is through the worship of remote ancestors or of clan gods at shrines or holy places. This would have been possible for the Japanese "common people" even without surnames and genealogies. But in Japan there is no cult of veneration of remote ancestors and at the shrines where "common people" worship all villagers join together without having to prove their common ancestry. They are called the "children" of their shrine-god, but they are "children" because they live in his territory. Such village worshipers are of course related to each other as villagers in any part of the world are after generations of fixed residence but they are not a tight clan group descended from a common ancestor.

The reverence due to ancestors is paid at a quite different shrine in the family living room where only six or seven recent dead are honored. Among all classes in Japan obeisance is done daily before this shrine and food set out for parents and grandparents and close relatives remembered in the flesh, who are represented in the shrine by little miniature gravestones. Even in the cemetery the markers on the graves of great-grandparents are no longer relettered and the identity even of the third ancestral generation sinks rapidly into oblivion. Family ties in Japan are whittled down almost to Occidental proportions and the French family is perhaps the nearest equivalent.

"Filial piety" in Japan, therefore, is a matter within a limited face-to-face family. It means taking one's proper station according to generation, sex, and age within a group which includes hardly more than one's father and father's father, their brothers and their descendants. Even in important houses, where larger groups may be included, the family splits up into separate lines and younger sons establish branch families. Within this narrow face-to-face group the rules that regulate "proper station" are meticulous. There is strict subservience to elders until they elect to go into formal retirement (inkyo). Even today a father of grown sons, if his own father has not retired, puts through no transaction without having it approved by the old grandfather. Parents make and break their children's marriages even when the children are thirty and forty years old. The father as male head of the household is served first at meals, goes first to the family bath, and receives with a nod the deep bows of his family. There is a popular riddle in Japan which might be translated into our conundrum form: "Why is a son who wants to offer advice to his parents like a Buddhist priest who wants to have hair on the top of his head?" (Buddhist priests had a tonsure.) The answer is, "However much he wants to do it, he can't."

Proper station means not only differences of generation but differences of age. When the Japanese want to express utter confusion, they say that something is "neither elder brother nor young brother." It is like our saying that something is neither fish nor fowl, for to the Japanese a man should keep his character as elder brother as drastically as a fish should stay in water. The eldest son is the heir. Travelers speak of "that air of responsibility which the eldest son so early acquires in Japan." The eldest son shares to a high degree in the prerogatives of the father. In the old days his younger brother would have been inevitably dependent upon him in time; nowadays, especially in towns and villages, it is he who will stay at home in the old rut while his younger brothers will perhaps press forward and get more education and a better income. But old habits of hierarchy are strong.

Even in political commentary today the traditional prerogatives of elder brothers are vividly stated in discussions of Greater East Asia policy. In the spring of 1942 a Lieutenant Colonel, speaking for the War Office, said on the subject of the Co-prosperity Sphere: "Japan is their elder brother and they are Japan's younger brothers. This fact must be brought home to the inhabitants of the occupied territories. Too much consideration shown for the inhabitants might engender in their minds the tendency to presume on Japan's kindness with pernicious effects on Japanese rule." The elder brother, in other words, decides what is good for his younger brother and should not show "too much consideration" in enforcing it.

Whatever one's age, one's position in the hierarchy depends on whether one is male or female. The Japanese woman walks behind her husband and has a lower status. Even women who on occasions when they wear American clothes walk alongside and precede him through a door, again fall to the rear when they have donned their kimonos. The Japanese daughter of the family must get along as best she can while the presents, the attentions, and the money for education go to her brothers. Even when higher schools were established for young women the prescribed courses were heavily loaded with instruction in etiquette and bodily movement. Serious intellectual training was not on a par with boys', and one principal of such a school, advocating for his upper middle class students some instruction in European languages, based his recommendation on the desirability of their being able to put their husband's books back in the bookcase right side up after they had dusted them.

Nevertheless, the Japanese women have great freedom as compared to most other Asiatic countries and this is not just a phase of Westernization. There never was female foot-binding as in the Chinese upper classes, and Indian women today exclaim over Japanese women going in and out of shops, up and down the streets and never secreting themselves. Japanese wives do the family shopping and carry the family purse. If money fails, it is they who must select something from the household and carry it to the pawnshop. A woman runs her servants, has great say in her children's marriages, and when she is a mother-in-law commonly runs her household realm with as firm a hand as if she had never been, for half her life, a nodding violet.

The prerogatives of generation, sex, and age in Japan are great. But those who exercise these privileges act as trustees rather than as arbitrary autocrats. The father or the elder brother is responsible for the household, whether its members are living, dead, or yet unborn. He must make weighty decisions and see that they are carried out. He does not, however, have unconditional authority. He is expected to act responsibly for the honor of the house. He recalls to his son and younger brother the legacy of the family, both in material and in spiritual things, and he challenges them to be worthy. Even if he is a peasant he invokes *noblesse oblige* to the family forebears, and if he belongs to more exalted classes the weight of responsibility to the house becomes heavier and heavier. The claims of the family come before the claims of the individual.

In any affair of importance the head of a family of any standing calls a family council at which the matter is debated. For a conference on a betrothal, for instance, members of the family may come from distant parts of Japan. The process of coming to a decision involves all the imponderables of personality. A younger brother or a wife may sway the verdict. The master of the house saddles himself with great difficulties if he acts without regard for group opinion. Decisions, of course, may be desperately unwelcome to the individual whose fate is being settled. His elders, however, who have themselves submitted in their lifetimes to decisions of family councils, are impregnable in demanding of their juniors what they have bowed to in their day. The sanction behind their demand is very different from that which, both in law and in custom, gives the Prussian father arbitrary rights over his wife and children. What is demanded is not for this reason less exacting in Japan, but the effects are different. The Japanese do not learn in their home life to value arbitrary authority, and the habit of submitting to it easily is not fostered. Submission to the will of the family is demanded in the name of a supreme value in which, however onerous its requirements, all of them have a stake. It is demanded in the name of a common loyalty.

Every Japanese learns the habit of hierarchy first in the bosom of his family and what he learns there he applies in wider fields of economic life and of government. He learns that a person gives all deference to those who outrank him in assigned "proper place," no matter whether or not they are the really dominant persons in the group. Even a husband who is dominated by his wife, or an elder brother who is dominated by a younger brother, receives no less formal deference. Formal boundaries between prerogatives are not broken down just because some other person is operating behind the scenes. The façade is not changed to suit the facts of dominance. It remains inviolable. There is even a certain tactical advantage in operating without the trappings of formal status; one is in that case less vulnerable. The Japanese learn, too, in their family experience that the greatest weight that can be given to a decision comes from the family conviction that it maintains the family honor. The decision is not a decree enforced by an iron fist at the whim of a tyrant who happens to be head of the family. He is more nearly a trustee of a material and spiritual estate which is important to them all and which demands of them all that they subordinate their personal wills to its requirements. The Japanese repudiate the use of the mailed fist, but they do not for that reason subordinate themselves any the less to the demands of the family, nor do they for that reason give to those with assigned status any less extreme deference. Hierarchy in the family is maintained even though the family elders have little opportunity to be strong-armed autocrats.

Such a bald statement of hierarchy in the Japanese family does not, when Americans read it with their different standards of interpersonal behavior, do justice to the acceptance of strong and sanctioned emotional ties in Japanese families. There is very considerable solidarity in the household. . . . It is important in trying to understand their demand for hierarchy in the wider fields of government and economic life to recognize how thoroughly the habit is learned in the bosom of the family.

⋗⋚⋗⋚⋗⋚⋗

12. U.S. Population and National Welfare *

THE NUMBER, DISTRIBUTION, AND QUALITY of people in a society are factors to which sociologists are giving increasing consideration. In this article Frank W. Notestein uses data from the 1950 Census to provide up-to-date information on trends in numbers, regional distribution, age distribution, and rate of increase of the U.S. population as compared with other countries of the world. His main focus of attention, in presenting these demographic data, is the implications of the U.S. population structure for our future national welfare.

THE TENSE INTERNATIONAL SITUATION and our experience in Korea seem to have fostered many misconceptions about the power position of the U. S. We hear talk of our being hopelessly outnumbered in a struggle for survival with the rapidly increasing peoples of the Far East. This pessimistic account runs to the effect that our population is small, whereas the Far Eastern population is huge; that our numbers are not increasing, while unlimited reproduction is multiplying those in Asia; that our nation is no longer rich in young men, whereas China's popu-

* Frank W. Notestein, Scientific American, 185, No. 3 (September, 1951), 28-35. Reprinted with permission from Scientific American and the author.
The author (b. 1902) is Professor of Demography, Princeton University. United Nations population consultant. Co-editor, Population Index. Co-author, Controlled Fertility; The Future Population of Europe and the Soviet Union; Population Projections, 1940-1970.

lation is heavily loaded with youths. From these notions many draw the inference that our power is waning while that of the Far East is rising rapidly. Actually there are several errors in this picture.

It is true that the U. S. has a very small part of the world's two and a third billion people: in 1950 only six out of every 100 of the world's people lived within our continental boundaries. But our proportion of the world's population has been increasing, not falling. A hundred years ago the U. S. accounted for only two per cent of the world population, and 50 years ago only five per cent. Our population has increased more rapidly than that of the world in general or of the Far East in particular. It is increasing more rapidly now, and may well continue to do so for some time to come. Moreover, a larger proportion of our population is in the age groups from which the labor force is drawn, and we probably have even a larger proportion in the ages between 20 and 40 than China has.

Most important, we are much the healthiest and wealthiest of the world's great powers. Our influence and that of our friends in the Western world has never depended mainly on numbers; we always have been, and shall remain, a rather small minority of the world's people. The prosperity, prestige and power of the U. S. have been based largely on the rich natural resources at our command, our excellent health, our high skills and our effective political and economic organization. Taken together, these spell large per capita production. In agriculture we make more efficient use of our manpower than most other countries. Whereas in Asia three or four out of every five workers work on the land and produce only a meager per capita supply of food and fiber, in the U. S. our people are fed and clothed much better with only about one worker in every eight working on farms. This leaves the other seven of the eight available for nonagricultural pursuits. That circumstance, coupled with our high industrial efficiency, accounts for the fact that the U. S., with only about six per cent of the world's population, produces almost one half of the world's industrial goods.

The huge population of Asia (well over a billion) and its very high birth rates are not the threat to our leadership that they may seem. With the mass of the population living close to the margin of subsistence, the death rates in the Far East are tragically high, so the rate of population increase is in general rather low in spite of the high birth rates. Any substantial reduction of the death rates through improvement of the food supply would bring a rapid population increase, but the new mouths to feed would absorb most of the increased production; hence it will be extremely difficult to achieve sustained improvements in living conditions. For some decades to come the situation in Asia spells poverty and not power—except power to absorb suffering and punishment. The fact is that the Far East probably would be more prosperous and more powerful if it had half as many people as it has now.

It is not in the Far East but in Eastern Europe and the U.S.S.R. that the most significant new developments are occurring. This quarter of the world has a large population which until recently has been technologically backward. But these peoples are now rapidly acquiring the skills needed to turn their fairly abundant resources into economic products. Barring major catastrophes or the grossest sort of mismanagement, they should achieve rapid increases in per capita production and in population during the next few decades. In industrialization they should advance rapidly because they are moving along a path already well charted by the Western world. Their populations should grow swiftly because they are getting the knowledge and the production with which to reduce their high death rates. This segment of the human race is the one that would seem to have the best chance, among the hitherto backward peoples, of becoming a major new focus of political power in the world and of maintaining its position.

All this suggests two major guides to policy for the U. S.: 1) as a small minority people it will be well for us to gain and keep as many like-minded friends as possible; 2) as the more numerous peoples modernize themselves technologically, we shall be able to maintain our leadership in peace and war only by rapidly increasing our own efficiency. In other words, our leadership in the future, as in the past, must be based on quality of performance, not on the number of people. The task is not a simple one, for it requires ever-advancing innovation.

Let us look at our recent population trends to see in what directions they seem to be taking us. During the past 100 years the population of the U. S. increased more than sixfold, while the world's population only doubled; our average annual rate of increase was almost two per cent, in contrast with about three quarters of one per cent for the world as a whole. This increase was due only in relatively small part to immigration; most of the growth was accounted for by the native-born white population. But our rate of growth has been falling decade by decade. It dropped from three per cent a year between 1850 and 1860 to .7 per cent a year in the depression decade 1930-1940. In the 1940s there was a spectacular resurgence of growth; we added 19 million to our population and the average annual rate of increase was twice that in the 1930s. Whether this was a temporary spurt or a permanent change of trend remains to be seen; we shall return to that question later. First let us consider the changes in the composition of our population.

Between 1900 and 1950, when the total population almost doubled,

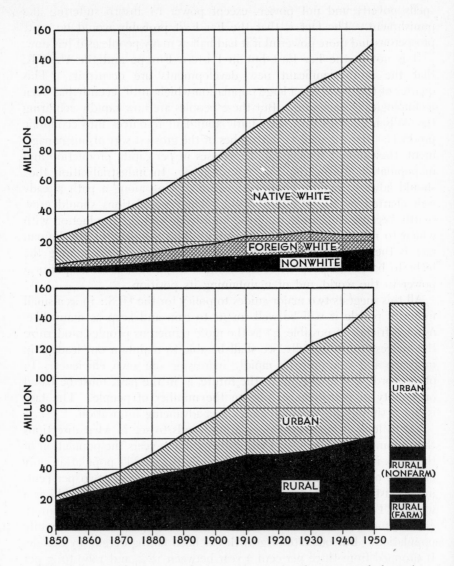

Size of the population went from 23,192,000 in 1850 to 150,696,000 in 1950. The diagram at the top of the page shows that the principal constituent of this growth was the multiplication of native whites. The diagram at the bottom of the page shows that the urban population grew at a much faster rate than the rural. In the column at the lower right a new set of definitions has been applied to our present population. This shows that the proportional decline of the farm population is even greater than that suggested by the decline of the rural.

the rural population increased by only a little more than one third. By 1950 the people living in rural areas, including unincorporated villages and towns, amounted to only 41 per cent of the total population. Those actually living on farms, not all of whom gained their livelihood from agriculture, constituted 16 per cent of the total. Thus in 1950 a farm population some millions smaller than that of 1900 was producing a more ample food supply for nearly twice as many people. The shrinkage of the farm population does not mean that it produced less than its share of the nation's natural increase. With its high birth rates and favorable death rates, it contributed more than its share to the growth of the population, but as job opportunities on the farm shrank, there was a huge and continuous movement of farm sons and daughters toward the cities. Farm families have done extraordinarily well in supplying the nation both with food and with the people to eat it.

During the past 50 years great changes also have occurred in the regional distribution of the population. The sections that have shown the most marked growth are the South, which had the largest absolute increase in numbers, and the West, which had the largest proportionate increase. The two regions achieved their increases in diametrically opposite fashions. The South has grown mainly because of a very high birth rate, which has more than offset the fact that more people have migrated away from the region than to it. The West, on the other hand, has had a comparatively low rate of natural increase, but it has grown prodigiously by attracting migrants from other regions. In general the highest natural increases have come in areas of low economic opportunity. The freedom of internal migration in the U. S. has been one of the sources of our great economic strength, for it has permitted the flexible adjustment of discrepancies between the rate of natural increase and economic opportunity in a region. People have been able to move easily to areas where economic expansion is taking place. Without such migration, the regional differences in the levels of living and per capita productivity would be very much greater than they are.

Another great element of strength in our demographic situation is the age composition of the population. In our population only a little more than one fourth are children under age 15, whereas in Asia, for example, about four persons of each ten are in that generally unproductive group. The rearing of children of course is the soundest investment that a nation can make, and in our case the investment is a particularly good one, for at current rates of survival more than 95 per cent of those born will live at least to age 15 and more than 60 per cent will live to age 65. But in the Far East the investment is much more precarious; a conservative estimate is that a smaller proportion of those born live to age 15 there than live to age 65 in the U. S. Probably more than 40 per cent of the children in the Far East never reach the productive years of life.

A hundred years ago our own age distribution was much like that of the Far East today. The median age of our population was only 18.8. Fifty years ago it had risen to 22.9. Since 1900 the picture has changed radically. At the turn of the century the age structure was represented by a pyramid that was broadest at the base (representing the number in the youngest age group) and narrowed in rather regular steps for each five-year age group from youth to old age (see page 83). This structure reflected the fact that both the birth rates and the death rates before 1900 had been high: each year's crop of babies was larger than that of the year before, and the older birth classes, besides being smaller to begin with, had tended to die at a relatively early age.

Now the way to produce an older population is to cut both the risks of death and the rate of expansion of the birth crops. Since 1900 the U. S. has done both, with the result that the median age of the population has risen to 30.1. By 1940 the base of the pyramid had been sharply narrowed, because of the decline in the number of births. At that time many demographers, including the writer, suggested that the U. S. might reach its maximum population in a few decades. But events in the 1940s upset these predictions. Death rates declined with unexpected speed, and birth rates rose spectacularly. The base of the age pyramid broadened again. The pyramid for 1950 in the illustration on page 83 clearly shows the extent of our error and should warn the reader that current predictions also may be invalidated by future events.

We had a dip in the number of births during the depression and a sharp rise during the 1940s. As a result there will be considerable swings in the next few years in the size of classes coming of age for school, military service, work and marriage. We have already felt the complications of these changes. At a time when the armament program and the new upsurge of population growth are creating inflationary pressures, the annual additions to the productive group are relatively small, because the people who are now moving into the military and working ages are the reduced birth classes of the depression years. The fluctuations in the size of the birth classes will, of course, be felt for many years, as wave following trough breaks on the schools, the labor market, the hospitals, the pension funds and the insurance systems.

Thus far, however, the recent swings in births have not changed the

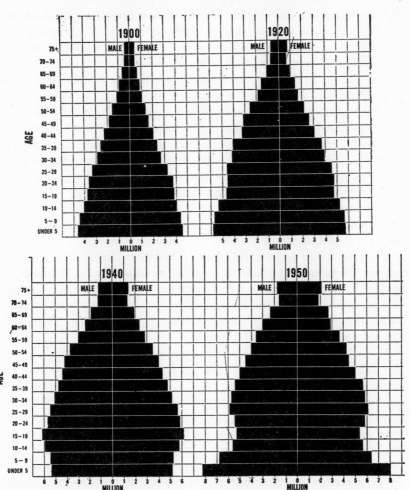

Age and sex distribution of the population notably shows the effects of the economic depression of the 1930s. These pyramids show the number of men and women in each age group in 1900, 1920, 1940, and 1950. The two upper pyramids are broadest at the base; the lower pyramids are notched by the declining birth rate of the 1930s. Now, however, the base of the pyramid has broadened again.

total picture much. In 1950, as in 1940, about 58 per cent of the population was of working age, as against 45 per cent in 1850. In the past 100 years the proportion of old dependents in the population has risen considerably, but the proportion of young dependents has declined sharply, the proportion of young workers has increased somewhat and the proportion of old workers has more than doubled. In short, from the point of view of economic productivity the age distribution of our population has been improving. If we make effective use of our older workers, in all probability that improvement will continue.

This brings us to the consideration of what the future trends in our population are likely to be. Predictions are risky, as we have seen, but we have some facts to go on and can examine the possibilities. We shall leave out of the discussion the uncertain factor of immigration, which has played an important, though not predominant, part in our population growth in the past. We might increase our numbers greatly by opening the doors again, for it is clear that so long as the U. S. remains free and wealthy in a poverty-stricken world, we can have as many newcomers as we care to accept. But this seems an unlikely event, and in any case immigration policy is a large subject of its own that is beyond the scope of this article.

The two major factors that shape population change in a nation are mortality and fertility. Let us consider mortality first. It can be said at once that the growth of our population would not be affected much by any further reductions in mortality rates, unless we lengthened life by reducing the mortality among oldsters (i.e., over 60). A statistical example will illustrate why this is so.

We shall consider a group of 1,000 live-born white girls. In 1901 the risks of death were such that barely more than half of the 1,000 could expect to live to the age of 60. In 1948 more than half would live to the age of 75, assuming that the death risks remained at the 1948 level. To put it another way, at the 1901 survival rate for white females 1,000 births a year would maintain a total population of 51,000 persons, while at the 1948 rate the same number of births would maintain a population of 71,000, with an average life-expectancy of 71 years. (In India, according to the most recent official life tables—for 1921-1931 —the death risks were so high that 1,000 female births a year would maintain a population of no more that 27,000.)

Now most of the gain in average life-expectancy in the U. S. between 1901 and 1948 was due to a spectacular reduction in the mortality of people under 45. There is relatively little further room for improvement in mortality rates below that age. Even if there were no deaths at all before the age of 45 among white females in the U. S., 1,000 births a year would support a population only six per cent larger than the 71,000 figure given above, assuming that the death rates of people above 45 were not reduced. This hypothetical maximum gain of six per cent is much less than the 30 per cent gain that was actually achieved by the reduction of mortality under 45 between 1901 and 1948. By eliminating or greatly reducing deaths before 45 among Negroes, whose mortality rates are still far higher than those of whites in spite of great improvement since 1901, we could add somewhat more to our population potential. But it remains true that the maximum mortality reduction we could achieve for people under 45, or even up to 60, would not greatly increase our population growth. There is, of course, no theoretical limit to the population increases that we might obtain by cutting mortality rates among people over 60; if no one ever died, a population recruited even by only one birth a year would grow indefinitely. Perhaps future advances in the control of the degenerative diseases of old age will have great effects on the size and character of our population, but such speculation seems futile at present. It seems safe to say that the growth of the U.S. population under 60 will not be influenced to any important extent by changes in mortality.

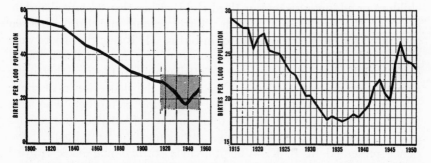

Fertility of the white population steadily decreased from the 1800s to the end of the 1930s. The diagram at the right shows in greater detail the area indicated by the gray rectangle on the diagram at the left.

Consequently the major determinant of our growth probably will be fertility, that is, the trend in the birth rate. The events of the past decade have made this very difficult to forecast. Until the early 1940s the direction of the trend seemed perfectly clear. There had been an almost unbroken decline in the birth rate since 1800. All available evidence seemed to point toward a continuation of that decline. The nation was rapidly adopting the small-family system, apparently in all strata of the population. There was ample evidence that the reductions in births were coming about mainly through the growing prevalence and increasing effectiveness of contraceptive practices. It seemed that the people, poor and well-to-do alike, wanted fewer children and were rapidly finding the means of fulfilling that want. Further declines in the birth rate could confidently be predicted.

So went the reasoning; the events took another course, as the charts on page 85 demonstrate. From a depression low of 2.3 million in 1933 the annual number of births rose to 3.9 million in 1947 and stayed at about 3.7 million through 1950. But it is far from certain that the birth boom of the 1940s foreshadows a continuation of high birth rates in the future. There are indications to the contrary in some of the characteristics of the boom.

For example, the increase in births has been most marked in those sectors of the population where fertility has been under the most effective control and is normally low—among city families, those living in the Northeast and those with college education. The groups that are usually the most fertile—farm families, those living in the South, those with the least education—had the smallest increases.

Moreover, the indications are that the huge increase in births during the 1940s was due mainly to the fact that more families were having children or adding a second or third child, rather than to any abandonment of the small-family system. First, second and third children accounted for most of the increases in births. It is true that there were also considerable increases in the numbers of families that had a fourth or fifth child, but this appears to be attributable to the fact that more women were exposed to that risk, because of the sharp rise in marriage rates in 1940 and 1941. The actual proportion of mothers who bore fourth and fifth children, of the total number of married women in a position to do so, probably declined throughout the baby boom. Evidence presented by P. K. Whelpton in a forthcoming book entitled *Cohort Fertility* indicates that similar factors also probably account for most of the increase in third births.

The increase in first and second children almost certainly has been due in part to the growing social disapproval of childless and one-child families. If this attitude continues, it will tend to produce a permanent increase in births. However, the increase seems to have been due in even larger part to the fact that people have been marrying at progressively younger ages, which has resulted in a very large increase in the number of marriages. This process cannot go on indefinitely. When the trend toward earlier and earlier marriage ages stops, the marriage rate will fall sharply, and if the marriage age should then rise, the drop in the number of marriages would be precipitous. That in turn, of course, would result in a sharp drop in the number of births.

These considerations lead us to wonder whether the baby boom of the past decade may not foreshadow a rather sharp decline in births during the next few years, instead of marking the beginning of an upward trend. To be sure, the fact that couples marry younger means that the

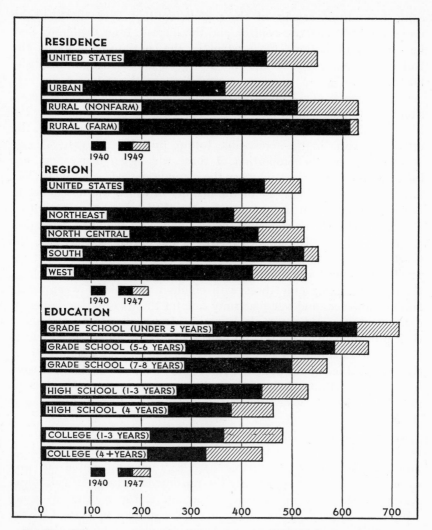

Fertility differences among various groups in the population are also in a state of change. The numbers at the bottom of this diagram represent children under 5 years per 1,000 married women between the ages of 15 and 49. Between 1940 and 1949, for example, the fertility of the rural population increased little and the fertility of the urban population a good deal.

wife is exposed to the possibility of having children for a larger part of the child-bearing period of her life, and the parents therefore have more chances of exceeding the number of children they want or more time to change their minds about wanting additional children. On the other hand there is every indication that the major part of the increase has come from those sectors of the population that have their fertility under the most effective control, and the increase from this group may be canceled to a considerable extent by the continued decline of the truly large families—a decline that has gone on throughout the baby boom.

On balance, it now seems that we should expect a considerable recession from the high birth rates of the 1940s before very long. It is unlikely, however, that we shall return to the low birth rates of the depression years in the foreseeable future, provided the marriage age stays young and the proportion of those who never marry does not increase. No one knows whether these conditions will continue. We have learned a good deal about the manner in which the resurgence in births developed, but we still know rather little about the motivating forces. Evidently the revival of the economy after the great depression released a backlog of postponed marriages and births. Clearly also, the Government strongly encouraged a rise in the birth rate, without explicitly planning to, first by exempting married men from conscription, then by exempting only those with children and finally by providing family allowances and free maternity care for the wives of the fathers it drafted. Veterans' benefits also contained family allowances, and under their provisions marriage was no longer a deterrent to advanced education. The expansion of social security, increases in tax exemptions for dependents, the current period of full employment—these, too, probably have had something to do with the increases in births. The present military service act, which defers the induction of fathers, adds a new stimulus to procreation.

Yet we do not really know what were the most important factors behind the baby boom; it is possible that less tangible causes, on which no systematic evidence is available, have been more influential than any we have mentioned. Apparently the wartime experience taught young America that it was fun to marry young and rear a small family, especially when it could be done with financial assistance from the Government. If this is so, and if new economic difficulties do not arise, we may expect the stream of births to be sustained well above that of the depression years, though below the current level.

Our population should therefore continue to grow, at a rate somewhat lower than that of the 1940s. But we are not in a position to make any precise estimates of our future size; there are too many unknown variables at work. The measure of that uncertainty can be seen in the fact that the most recent population projections by the Bureau of the Census for the year 1960 range from a low of 161 million to a high of 180 million.

It is by no means certain that it would be to the advantage of the nation to have a continuation of the recent high rate of population increase. Growth of the population reduces the amount of natural resources available per person, which means that the nation must turn to the use of inferior or substitute resources, and such uses generally entail higher costs. Technological advances may well cancel such added cost, but income used in canceling higher costs is not available for other uses. From the standpoint of the economic welfare of the population as a whole, the only economic advantage that comes from a large population as such lies in the economies it makes possible through specialization in production. It is not at all certain, however, that larger numbers would greatly increase such economies in the U. S.

Rapid growth undoubtedly supplies a kind of stimulus to the economy, making it more dynamic and flexible, but growth is only one of the ways of achieving this, and if the costs of the growth are high, it may not be the most efficient way. Precipitous changes in the rate of growth are troublesome. As we have seen, such changes introduce waves and troughs into the age distribution, and these require the nation to maintain more facilities to care for its population than it would if the same numbers were distributed more smoothly over the life span. School buildings are one striking example; they must be built to take care of peaks of population. The ebb and flow of births is, in the long run, a costly affair.

From the military point of view the matter of population size may have a somewhat different aspect. Even from this point of view, however, it is questionable whether the desirability of a larger population is as great as is commonly supposed. Since our population will in any case remain a relatively small one in world-wide terms, our main asset lies in our power to produce more material than we require to maintain ourselves. This asset can be retained only if we are able to invest heavily in the health and training of our youth, which involves retaining a high level of living. These considerations suggest that it is wise to avoid growth that presses on our resources, even when the object is to maximize national power. On the whole it seems to the writer that the nation is fortunate to have come through its period of rapid growth without generating a population that seriously strains our resources.

From the point of view of power and economic welfare the characteristics of the population may be more important than its size. One of our most important assets will continue to be the favorable distribution of the population between the working and the dependent ages. The value of this asset will depend to a considerable extent on the effectiveness with which we employ the older worker. The number of young workers will continue to grow, but the older workers will increase even more rapidly. The aged will increase most rapidly of all. The "problems of the aged" are difficult human and social problems, but these are minor liabilities of one of our most magnificent assets—the fact that relatively little of the life created in the U. S. is lost before it reaches the age when it can contribute to the social product.

If the strength of the nation lies less in numbers than in per capita productivity, then we need to place great and growing emphasis on the quality of the population. Here we have some disturbing problems. The uneducated and the poor continue to produce a disproportionate share of the nation's children, although the disparity has narrowed in recent years. While it seems likely that in all the principal groups in our population the majority are fairly sound stock, from the point of view of the nation's skills it is surely unfortunate that a disproportionately large share of the children are reared by parents with the least education and the least ability to provide for their children's education. Similarly, it is unfortunate that the states whose high birth rates produce the heaviest educational burdens are also the ones least able to carry the loads. If the leadership of the U. S. is to be maintained, in our increasingly complex world, it is essential that we develop the skills of all our people to the maximum of their inborn potential. This we have not done, and shall not do until the ability of the child replaces the income of the parents as the major criterion for educational opportunity.

If the population problems facing us in the future seem difficult, it may be pointed out that under peacetime conditions the problems ahead will be small compared with those already solved. Western civilization for the first time in man's long history has learned to substitute the control of fertility for death as a means of checking unlimited increase. Our reduction of peacetime mortality since 1900 has saved many more lives than have been lost in the wars of this century. With all our tragic failings we have become relatively efficient producers of life, and given peace and moderate wisdom we should continue to increase that efficiency.

❧❧❧

CHAPTER III

PERSON AND GROUP

---

13. Final Note on a Case of Extreme Isolation *

FOR CENTURIES there have been unverified tales and partially verified accounts of children who were raised by animals or in some
other way managed to live in complete isolation from human beings.
If such *feral* men were found, they would have great significance for
social science. They would provide a crucial means of determining
the nature and extent of social-cultural influence on human behavior. Since the earlier accounts were either mythical or largely
legendary, scientists have credited them with little validity. It is
highly doubtful if any child ever lived without at least some human
association, but in recent years a few verified cases have been reported in which relatively slight association occurred. In this
selection Kingsley Davis gives his final report on such a case and
makes some comparisons between the child, Anna, and another
child, Isabelle, who lived under similar circumstances.

One cannot be sure to what extent Anna's failure to achieve the
level of socialization of a normal 10-year-old was due to organic
deficiency. Clearly, however, a tremendous change took place in
her behavior after the isolation was ended. It seems certain that
many typically human behavior patterns were not achieved until
Anna was able to associate with other humans from whom she could
learn such behavior.

* Kingsley Davis, The American Journal of Sociology, 52, No. 5 (March, 1947),
432-437. Reprinted by permission of the University of Chicago Press and the author.
   The author (b. 1908) is Associate Professor of Sociology, formerly Director of
Bureau of Applied Social Research, Columbia University. Author, Youth in Depres-
sion, The Human Society, Modern American Society (with others.) Editor,
Population of India and Pakistan. Contributor to sociological journals, New York
Times Magazine, and Foreign Affairs.

EARLY IN 1940 there appeared . . . an account of a girl called Anna.[1] She had been deprived of normal contact and had received a minimum of human care for almost the whole of her first six years of life. At that time observations were not complete and the report had a tentative character. Now, however, the girl is dead, and, with more information available, it is possible to give a fuller and more definitive description of the case from a sociological point of view.

Anna's death, caused by hemorrhagic jaundice, occurred on August 6, 1942. Having been born on March 1 or 6, 1932, she was approximately ten and a half years of age when she died. The previous report covered her development up to the age of almost eight years; the present one recapitulates the earlier period on the basis of new evidence and then covers the last two and a half years of her life.

EARLY HISTORY

The first few days and weeks of Anna's life were complicated by frequent changes of domicile. It will be recalled that she was an illegitimate child, the second such child born to her mother, and that her grandfather, a widowed farmer in whose house her mother lived, strongly disapproved of this new evidence of the mother's indiscretion. This fact led to the baby's being shifted about.

Two weeks after being born in a nurse's private home, Anna was brought to the family farm, but the grandfather's antagonism was so great that she was shortly taken to the house of one of her mother's friends. At this time a local minister became interested in her and took her to his house with an idea of possible adoption. He decided against adoption, however, when he discovered that she had vaginitis. The infant was then taken to a children's home in the nearest large city. This agency found that at the age of only three weeks she was already in a miserable condition, being "terribly galled and otherwise in very bad shape." It did not regard her as a likely subject for adoption but took her in for a while anyway, hoping to benefit her. After Anna had spent nearly eight weeks in this place, the agency notified her mother to come to get her. The mother responded by sending a man and his wife to the children's home with a view to their adopting Anna, but they made such a poor impression on the agency that permission was refused. Later the mother came herself and took the child out of the home and then gave her to this couple. It was in the home of this pair that a social worker found the girl a short time thereafter. The

[1] Kingsley Davis, "Extreme Social Isolation of a Child," *American Journal of Sociology*, XLV (January, 1940), 554-65.

social worker went to the mother's home and pleaded with Anna's grandfather to allow the mother to bring the child home. In spite of threats, he refused. The child, by then more than four months old, was next taken to another children's home in a near-by town. A medical examination at this time revealed that she had impetigo, vaginitis, umbilical hernia, and a skin rash.

Anna remained in this second children's home for nearly three weeks, at the end of which time she was transferred to a private foster-home. Since, however, the grandfather would not, and the mother could not, pay for the child's care, she was finally taken back as a last resort to the grandfather's house (at the age of five and a half months). There she remained, kept on the second floor in an attic-like room because her mother hesitated to incur the grandfather's wrath by bringing her downstairs.

The mother, a sturdy woman weighing about 180 pounds, did a man's work on the farm. She engaged in heavy work such as milking cows and tending hogs and had little time for her children. Sometimes she went out at night, in which case Anna was left entirely without attention. Ordinarily, it seems, Anna received only enough care to keep her barely alive. She appears to have been seldom moved from one position to another. Her clothing and bedding were filthy. She apparently had no instruction, no friendly attention.

It is little wonder that, when finally found and removed from the room in the grandfather's house at the age of nearly six years, the child could not talk, walk, or do anything that showed intelligence. She was in an extremely emaciated and undernourished condition, with skeleton-like legs and a bloated abdomen. She had been fed on virtually nothing except cow's milk during the years under her mother's care.

Anna's condition when found, and her subsequent improvement, have been described in the previous report. It now remains to say what happened to her after that.

LATER HISTORY

In 1939, nearly two years after being discovered, Anna had progressed, as previously reported, to the point where she could walk, understand simple commands, feed herself, achieve some neatness, remember people, etc. But she still did not speak, and, though she was much more like a normal infant of something over one year of age in mentality, she was far from normal for her age.

On August 30, 1939, she was taken to a private home for retarded children, leaving the county home where she had been for more than a year and a half. In her new setting she made some further progress, but not a great deal. In a report of an examination made November 6 of the same year, the head of the institution pictured the child as follows:

Anna walks about aimlessly, makes periodic rhythmic motions of her hands, and, at intervals, makes guttural and sucking noises. She regards her hands as if she had seen them for the first time. It was impossible to hold her attention for more than a few seconds at a time—not because of distraction due to external stimuli but because of her inability to concentrate. She ignored the task in hand to gaze vacantly about the room. Speech is entirely lacking. Numerous unsuccessful attempts have been made with her in the hope of developing initial sounds. I do not believe that this failure is due to negativism or deafness but that she is not sufficiently developed to accept speech at this time. . . . The prognosis is not favorable. . . .

More than five months later, on April 25, 1940, a clinical psychologist, the late Professor Francis N. Maxfield, examined Anna and reported the following: large for her age; hearing "entirely normal"; vision apparently normal; able to climb stairs; speech in the "babbling stage" and "promise for developing intelligible speech later seems to be good." He said further that "on the Merrill-Palmer scale she made a mental score of 19 months. On the Vineland social maturity scale she made a score of 23 months."

Professor Maxfield very sensibly pointed out that prognosis is difficult in such cases of isolation. "It is very difficult to take scores on tests standardized under average conditions of environment and experience," he wrote, "and interpret them in a case where environment and experience have been so unusual." With this warning he gave it as his opinion at that time that Anna would eventually "attain an adult mental level of six or seven years."

The school for retarded children, on July 1, 1941, reported that Anna had reached 46 inches in height and weighed 60 pounds. She could bounce and catch a ball and was said to conform to group socialization, though as a follower rather than a leader. Toilet habits were firmly established. Food habits were normal, except that she still used a spoon as her sole implement. She could dress herself except for fastening her clothes. Most remarkable of all, she had finally begun to develop speech. She was characterized as being at about the two-year level in this regard. She could call attendants by name and bring in one when she was asked to. She had a few complete sentences to express her wants. The report concluded that there was nothing peculiar about her, except that she was feeble-minded—"probably congenital in type."

A final report from the school, made on June 22, 1942, and evidently the last report before the girl's death, pictured only a slight advance over that given above. It said that Anna could follow directions, string beads, identify a few colors, build with blocks, and differentiate between attractive and unattractive pictures. She had a good sense of rhythm and loved a doll. She talked mainly in phrases but would repeat words and try to carry on a conversation. She was clean about clothing. She habitually washed her hands and brushed her teeth. She would try to help other children. She walked well and could run fairly well, though clumsily. Although easily excited, she had a pleasant disposition.

INTERPRETATION

Such was Anna's condition just before her death. It may seem as if she had not made much progress, but one must remember the condition in which she had been found. One must recall that she had no glimmering of speech, absolutely no ability to walk, no sense of gesture, not the least capacity to feed herself even when the food was put in front of her, and no comprehension of cleanliness. She was so apathetic that it was hard to tell whether or not she could hear. And all this at the age of nearly six years. Compared with this condition, her capacities at the time of her death seem striking indeed, though they do not amount to much more than a two-and-a-half-year mental level. One conclusion therefore seems safe, namely, that her isolation prevented a considerable amount of mental development that was undoubtedly part of her capacity. Just what her original capacity was, of course, is hard to say; but her development after her period of confinement (including the ability to walk and run, to play, dress, fit into a social situation, and, above all, to speak) shows that she had at least this much capacity—capacity that never could have been realized in her original condition of isolation.

A further question is this: What would she have been like if she had received a normal upbringing from the moment of birth? A definitive answer would have been impossible in any case, but even an approximate answer is made difficult by her early death. If one assumes, as was tentatively surmised in the previous report, that it is "almost impossible for any child to learn to speak, think, and act like a normal person after a long period of early isolation," it seems likely that Anna might have had a normal or near-normal capacity, genetically speaking.

On the other hand, it was pointed out that Anna represented "a marginal case, [because] she was discovered before she had reached six years of age," an age "young enough to allow for some plasticity." While admitting, then, that Anna's isolation may have been the major cause (and was certainly a minor cause) of her lack of rapid mental progress during the four and a half years following her rescue from neglect, it is necessary to entertain the hypothesis that she was congenitally deficient.

In connection with this hypothesis, one suggestive though by no means conclusive circumstance needs consideration, namely, the mentality of Anna's forebears. Information on this subject is easier to obtain, as one might guess, on the mother's than on the father's side. Anna's maternal grandmother, for example, is said to have been college educated and wished to have her children receive a good education, but her husband, Anna's stern grandfather, apparently a shrewd, hard-driving, calculating farmowner, was so penurious that her ambitions in this direction were thwarted. Under the circumstances her daughter (Anna's mother) managed, despite having to do hard work on the farm, to complete the eighth grade in a country school. Even so, however, the daughter was evidently not very smart. "A schoolmate of [Anna's mother] stated that she was retarded in school work; was very gullible at this age; and that her morals even at this time were discussed by other students." Two tests administered to her on March 4, 1938, when she was thirty-two years of age, showed that she was mentally deficient. On the Stanford Revision of the Binet-Simon Scale her performance was equivalent to that of a child of eight years, giving her an I.Q. of 50 and indicating mental deficiency of "middle-grade moron type."

As to the identity of Anna's father, the most persistent theory holds that he was an old man about seventy-four years of age at the time of the girl's birth. If he was the one, there is no indication of mental or other biological deficiency, whatever one may think of his morals. However, someone else may actually have been the father.

To sum up: Anna's heredity is the kind that *might* have given rise to innate mental deficiency, though not necessarily.

COMPARISON WITH ANOTHER CASE

Perhaps more to the point than speculations about Anna's ancestry would be a case for comparison. If a child could be discovered who had been isolated about the same length of time as Anna but had achieved a much quicker recovery and a greater mental development, it would be a stronger indication that Anna was deficient to start with.

Such a case does exist. It is the case of a girl found at about the same time as Anna and under strikingly similar circumstances. A full description of the details of this case has not been published, but, in addition to newspaper reports, an excellent preliminary account by a speech specialist, Dr. Marie K. Mason, who played an important role in the handling of the child, has appeared. Also the late Dr. Francis N. Maxfield, clinical psychologist at Ohio State University, as was Dr. Mason, has written an as yet unpublished but penetrating analysis of the case. Some of his observations have been included in Professor Zingg's book on feral man. The following discussion is drawn mainly from these enlightening materials. The writer, through the kindness of Professors Mason and Maxfield, did have a chance to observe the girl in April, 1940, and to discuss the features of her case with them.

Born apparently one month later than Anna, the girl in question, who has been given the pseudonym Isabelle, was discovered in November, 1938, nine months after the discovery of Anna. At the time she was found she was approximately six and a half years of age. Like Anna, she was an illegitimate child and had been kept in seclusion for that reason. Her mother was a deaf-mute, having become so at the age of two, and it appears that she and Isabelle had spent most of their time together in a dark room shut off from the rest of the mother's family. As a result Isabelle had no chance to develop speech; when she communicated with her mother, it was by means of gestures. Lack of sunshine and inadequacy of diet had caused Isabelle to become rachitic. Her legs in particular were affected; they "were so bowed that as she stood erect the soles of her shoes came nearly flat together, and she got about with a skittering gait." Her behavior toward strangers, especially men, was almost that of a wild animal, manifesting much fear and hostility. In lieu of speech she made only a strange croaking sound. In many ways she acted like an infant. "She was apparently utterly unaware of relationships of any kind. When presented with a ball for the first time, she held it in the palm of her hand, then reached out and stroked my face with it. Such behavior is comparable to that of a child of six months." At first it was even hard to tell whether or not she could hear, so unused were her senses. Many of her actions resembled those of deaf children.

It is small wonder that, once it was established that she could hear, specialists working with her believed her to be feeble-minded. Even on nonverbal tests her performance was so low as to promise little for the future. Her first score on the Stanford-Binet was 19 months, practically at the zero point of the scale. On the Vineland social maturity scale her first score was 39, representing an age level of two and a half years. "The general impression was that she was wholly uneducable and that any attempt to teach her to speak, after so long a period of silence, would meet with failure."

In spite of this interpretation, the individuals in charge of Isabelle launched a systematic and skilful program of training. It seemed hopeless at first. The approach had to be through pantomime and dramatization, suitable to an infant. It required one week of intensive effort before she even made her first attempt at vocalization. Gradually she began to respond, however, and, after the first hurdles had at last been overcome, a curious thing happened. She went through the usual stages of learning characteristic of the years from one to six not only in proper succession but far more rapidly than normal. In a little over two months after her first vocalization she was putting sentences together. Nine months after that she could identify words and sentences on the printed page, could write well, could add to ten, and could retell a story after hearing it. Seven months beyond this point she had a vocabulary of 1,500-2,000 words and was asking complicated questions. Starting from an educational level of between one and three years (depending on what aspect one considers), she had reached a normal level by the time she was eight and a half years old. In short, she covered in two years the stages of learning that ordinarily require six. Or, to put it another way, her I.Q. trebled in a year and a half. The speed with which she reached the normal level of mental development seems analogous to the recovery of body weight in a growing child after an illness, the recovery being achieved by an extra fast rate of growth for a period after the illness until normal weight for the given age is again attained.

When the writer saw Isabelle a year and a half after her discovery, she gave him the impression of being a very bright, cheerful, energetic little girl. She spoke well, walked and ran without trouble, and sang with gusto and accuracy. Today she is over fourteen years old and has passed the sixth grade in a public school. Her teachers say that she participates in all school activities as normally as other children. Though older than her classmates, she has fortunately not physically matured too far beyond their level.

Clearly the history of Isabelle's development is different from that of Anna's. In both cases there was an exceedingly low, or rather blank, intellectual level to begin with. In both cases it seemed that the girl might be congenitally feeble-minded. In both a considerably higher level was reached later on. But the Ohio girl achieved a normal mentality within two years, whereas Anna was still markedly inadequate at the end of four and a half years. This difference in achievement may suggest that Anna had less initial capacity. But an alternative hypothesis is possible.

One should remember that Anna never received the prolonged and expert attention that Isabelle received. The result of such attention, in the case of the Ohio girl, was to give her speech at an early stage, and her subsequent rapid development seems to have been a consequence of that. "Until Isabelle's speech and language development, she had all the characteristics of a feeble-minded child." Had Anna, who, from the standpoint of psychometric tests and early history, closely resembled this girl at the start, been given a mastery of speech at an earlier point by intensive training, her subsequent development might have been much more rapid.

The hypothesis that Anna began with a sharply inferior mental capacity is therefore not established. Even if she were deficient to start with, we have no way of knowing how much so. Under ordinary conditions she might have been a dull normal or, like her mother, a moron. Even after the blight of her isolation, if she had lived to maturity, she might have finally reached virtually the full level of her capacity, whatever it may have been. That her isolation did have a profound effect upon her mentality, there can be no doubt. This is proved by the substantial degree of change during the four and a half years following her rescue.

Consideration of Isabelle's case serves to show, as Anna's case does not clearly show, that isolation up to the age of six, with failure to acquire any form of speech and hence failure to grasp nearly the whole world of cultural meaning, does not preclude the subsequent acquisition of these. Indeed, there seems to be a process of accelerated recovery in which the child goes through the mental stages at a more rapid rate than would be the case in normal development. Just what would be the maximum age at which a person could remain isolated and still retain the capacity for full cultural acquisition is hard to say. Almost certainly it would not be as high as age fifteen; it might possibly be as low as age ten. Undoubtedly various individuals would differ considerably as to the exact age.

Anna's is not an ideal case for showing the effects of extreme isolation, partly because she was possibly deficient to begin with, partly because she did not receive the best training available, and partly because she did not live long enough. Nevertheless, her case is instructive when placed in the record with numerous other cases of extreme isolation. This and the previous article about her are meant to place her in the record. It is to be hoped that other cases will be described in the scientific literature as they are discovered (as unfortunately they will be), for only in these rare cases of extreme isolation is it possible "to observe *concretely separated* two factors in the development of human personality which are always otherwise only analytically separated, the biogenic and the sociogenic factors."

❦❦❦

14. G. H. Mead's Theory of Individual and Society *

THE WORKS OF G. H. MEAD have been of great value because of their analysis of the relationship between the person and the group. Mead was a social philosopher who developed keen insight as an "armchair" analyst of social behavior. His "social behaviorism" emphasized the role of language in the development of human behavior and indicated that the human mind is a social phenomenon. After his death three volumes of his lectures and articles were published. Charles Morris, who edited the first volume, *Mind, Self and Society*—largely a compilation of his lectures—prepared an introduction to Mead's basic theory. The present selection, taken from this introduction, although hardly an adequate summary of Mead's "social behaviorism," presents some of the concepts that have had major impact on sociology.

THE TRANSFORMATION of the biologic individual to the minded organism or self takes place, on Mead's account, through the agency of language, while language in turn presupposes the existence of a certain kind of society and certain physiological capacities in the individual organisms.

The minimal society must be composed of biologic individuals participating in a social act and using the early stages of each other's actions as gestures, that is, as guides to the completion of the act. In the

* George Herbert Mead, *Mind, Self, and Society, from the standpoint of a social behaviorist* (Chicago: The University of Chicago Press, 1934), pp. xx-xxvi. Edited, with introduction, by Charles W. Morris. Reprinted by permission of the publisher.

The author (1863-1931) was an American philosopher and social psychologist. Career spent almost exclusively at University of Chicago as professor of philosophy. Followers of his teaching in social psychology are known as "social interactionists." Essays appeared in *International Journal of Ethics* and *Journal of Philosophy.* Writings, unpublished manuscripts, classnotes, edited under the following titles: *The Philosophy of the Act; Mind, Self, and Society; Movements of Thought in the Nineteenth Century.* The editor (b. 1901) is Lecturer in Philosophy, University of Chicago, Guest Lecturer, Institute of Design, Chicago, and New School for Social Research, New York. Author, *Six Theories of Mind; Logical Positivism, Pragmatism and Scientific Empiricism; The Open Self; Foundation of the Theory of Signs; Signs, Language and Behavior.*

"conversation of gestures" of the dog fight each dog determines his behavior in terms of what the other dog is beginning to do; and the same holds for the boxer, the fencer, and the chick which runs to the hen at the hen's cluck. Such action is a type of communication; in one sense the gestures are symbols, since they indicate, stand for, and cause action appropriate to the later stages of the act of which they are early fragments, and secondarily to the objects implicated in such acts. In the same sense, the gestures may be said to have meaning, namely, they mean the later stages of the oncoming act and, secondarily, the objects implicated: the clenched fist means the blow, the outstretched hand means the object being reached for. Such meanings are not subjective, not private, not mental, but are objectively there in the social situation.

Nevertheless, this type of communication is not language proper; the meanings are not yet "in mind"; the biologic individuals are not yet consciously communicating selves. For these results to transpire the symbols or gestures must become significant symbols or gestures. The individual must know what he is about; he himself, and not merely those who respond to him, must be able to interpret the meaning of his own gesture. Behavioristically, this is to say that the biologic individual must be able to call out in himself the response his gesture calls out in the other, and then utilize this response of the other for the control of his own further conduct. Such gestures are significant symbols. Through their use the individual is "taking the rôle of the other" in the regulation of his own conduct. Man is essentially the rôle-taking animal. The calling out of the same response in both the self and the other gives the common content necessary for community of meaning.

As an example of the significant symbol Mead uses the tendency to call out "Fire!" when smoke is seen in a crowded theater. The immediate utterance of the sound would simply be part of the initiated act, and would be at the best a non-significant symbol. But when the tendency to call out "Fire!" affects the individual as it affects others, and is itself controlled in terms of these effects, the vocal gesture has become a significant symbol; the individual is conscious of what he is about; he has reached the stage of genuine language instead of unconscious communication; he may now be said to use symbols and not merely respond to signs; he has now acquired a mind.

In looking for gestures capable of becoming significant symbols, and so of transforming the biologic individual into a minded organism, Mead comes upon the vocal gesture. No other gesture affects the individual himself so similarly as it affects others. We hear ourselves talk as others do, but we do not see our facial expressions, nor normally watch our own actions. For Mead, the vocal gesture is the actual fountainhead of language proper and all derivative forms of symbolism; and so of mind.

Mind is the presence in behavior of significant symbols. It is the internalization within the individual of the social process of communication in which meaning emerges. It is the ability to indicate to one's self the response (and implicated objects) that one's gesture indicates to others, and to control the response itself in these terms. The significant gesture, itself a part of a social process, internalizes and makes available to the component biologic individuals the meanings which have themselves emerged in the earlier, non-significant, stages of gestural communication. Instead of beginning with individual minds and working out to society, Mead starts with an objective social process and works inward through the importation of the social process of communication into the individual by the medium of the vocal gesture. The individual has then taken the social act into himself. Mind remains social; even in the inner forum so developed thought goes on by one's assuming the rôles of others and controlling one's behavior in terms of such rôle-taking. Since the isolation of the physical thing is for Mead dependent upon the ability to take the rôle of the other, and since thought about such objects involves taking their rôles, even the scientist's reflection about physical nature is a social process, though the objects thought about are no longer social.

•   •   •   •   •   •

It is the same agency of language which on this theory makes possible the appearance of the self. Indeed, the self, mind, "consciousness of," and the significant symbol are in a sense precipitated together. Mead finds the distinguishing trait of selfhood to reside in the capacity of the minded organism to be an object to itself. The mechanism by which this is possible on a behavioristic approach is found in the rôle-taking which is involved in the language symbol. In so far as one can take the rôle of the other, he can, as it were, look back at himself from (respond to himself from) that perspective, and so become an object to himself. Thus again, it is only in a social process that selves, as distinct from biological organisms, can arise—selves as beings that have become conscious of themselves.

Nor is it merely the process of being aware of one's self that is social: the self that one becomes conscious of in this manner is itself social in form, though not always in content. Mead stresses two stages in the development of the self: the stages of play and the game. In play the child simply assumes one rôle after another of persons and animals that have in some way or other entered into its life. One here sees, writ large as it were, the assumption of the attitudes of others through the self-stimulation of the vocal gesture, whereas later in life such attitudes are more abbreviated and harder to detect. In the game, however, one has become, as it were, all of the others implicated in the common activity—must have within one's self the whole organized activity in order to successfully play one's own part. The person here has not merely assumed the rôle of a specific other, but of any other participating in the common activity; he has generalized the attitude of rôle-taking. In one of Mead's happiest terms and most fertile concepts he has taken the attitude or rôle of the "generalized other."

* * * * * *

Through a social process, then, the biologic individual of proper organic stuff gets a mind and a self. Through society the impulsive animal becomes a rational animal, a man. In virtue of the internalization or importation of the social process of communication, the individual gains the mechanism of reflective thought (the ability to direct his action in terms of the foreseen consequences of alternative courses of action); acquires the ability to make himself an object to himself and to live in a common moral and scientific world; becomes a moral individual with impulsive ends transformed into the conscious pursuit of ends-in-view.

Because of the emergence of such an individual, society is in turn transformed. It receives through the reflective social self the organization distinctive of human society; instead of playing his social part through physiological differentiation (as in the case of the insect) or through the bare influence of gestures upon others, the human individual regulates his part in the social act through having within himself the rôles of the others implicated in the common activity. In attaining a new principle of social organization, society has gained a new technique of control, since it has now implanted itself within its component parts, and so regulates, to the degree that this is successfully done, the behavior of the individual in terms of the effect on others of his contemplated action.

❧❧❧❧

15. The Middle-Class Male Child and Neurosis *

THE PROCESS OF SOCIALIZATION—of learning to be a social being—takes place primarily within the family group. This process is carried on in ways that differ not only among societies but also between the strata and sub-cultures of a single society. Here Arnold W. Green discusses the socialization that the typical middle-class male undergoes in our society. Through his exposition he shows how and why the very nature of what might appear to be the most favorable surroundings may produce neurosis.

THE CLAIM HAS BEEN MADE that "lack of love" and "irrational authority" do not, in and of themselves, cause the development of neurotic symptoms. These phenomena do operate, however, in individual etiologies of neurosis, but only within a certain context. The term "personality absorption" has already been used. Personality absorption is the physical and emotional blanketing of the child, bringing about a slavish dependence upon the parents. It is personality absorption, in conjunction with factors other than lack of love or irrational authority, that produces a certain type of neurosis.

To delineate the kind of socialization which maximizes personality absorption, it will be necessary to conceive of a parental type which simultaneously occupies several population segments: native-white, Protestant urban, college-educated, middle-class. The training of children born to parents who can thus be characterized, is so experientially consistent it has a certain range of predictive value.

Now, how can we define the middle-class child's situation? It has already been said that his personality is "absorbed," and to the extent that it has been absorbed, he is in danger of developing neurotic symptoms. But why is it absorbed?

Perhaps the best way to view his social conditioning is to consider his parents, and their position in relation to him. The father's work takes him far from the place of residence, where most of his associates are only slightly less strangers to him than they are to his family. He is a white-collar worker. As a salesman, office worker, minor bureaucrat,

---

* Arnold W. Green, American Sociological Review, 11 (1946), 31-41. Reprinted by permission of the publisher and the author.

The author is Associate Professor of Sociology, Pennsylvania State College. Author, "The Sociological Analysis of Horney and Fromm," American Journal of Sociology; and Henry Charles Carey: Nineteenth-Century Sociologist. Co-author (with Eleanor Melnick), "What Has Happened to the Feminist Movement?" in Gouldner, Studies in Leadership.

or professional man, his job-techniques revolve around manipulating the personalities of others, instead of tools.   Since he has internalized the supreme middle-class value, individual success, he tries to use his associates as means to further his career; in fact, he has himself been conditioned to view his associates, education, hobbies, intellectual interests, in terms of their possible value to his career.   On the job he views himself not so much as functionally associated with others in a common purpose, as a self-contained unit establishing "contacts" with others.   His work relations are not defined in fixed terms of status and role to the extent that they were in the past, for he is on the move, or views himself in that way.   He has, then, a well-developed tendency to view his relations with others *in terms of what he, as a mobile, displaced person, can get out of them.*

Yet the modern middle-class father cannot use his *child* either in the new sense of manipulating others to his own advantage, nor, be it noted, in the ways available in the past.   In the old rural-familistic system, the child served well three predominant interests of the father: he would soon work on the farm, or during the earlier days of the industrial revolution, in the factory, become an economic asset to the father in other words; he would provide economic security in the father's old age; and finally, he would provide psychological security by preserving the family name, a form of this-worldly immortality in a society which made the family the primary repository of most social values.

In terms of dollars alone, the cost of raising a modern middle-class child represents a serious threat to the personal ambition of the father. At the very time when, in terms of his primary success-goal, he should have time and money available for further study if a professional man, money for clothes, entertaining, household furniture and an automobile for purposes of presenting a "front" in any event; at this time when his career is in its initial and hence its crucial stage, the presence of the child represents a diversion of energy and funds, so long, of course, as the career remains his primary goal.   A certain degree of ambivalence directed toward the child is inevitable.   Not the depth, but the present height of the middle-class birth-rate is the noteworthy phenomenon, indicating an amazing vitality of the old rural-familistic values which find little support in modern social structure.

With the advancing individuation of modern society, not only has individual success become a supreme value, but also individual, hedonistic enjoyment.   The child again presents an interference with most of the recreation available to the middle-class father, for whether commercialized (movies, sports events, plays) or social (golf, bridge, tennis, dinner parties), these are designed not for family-wide participation, but individual- or couple-participation.

In conjunction with the above factors, the growing middle-class emphasis upon "scientific child care" and the child's higher education, further increase the father's duties and obligations, while his rights steadily diminish. What emerges from his total situation is an ambivalence toward his child which is more or less widespread, though very rarely admitted, even with confidantes. Finally, children interfere with the companion and partner roles of husband and wife, which are more and more displacing the traditional patriarchal and housewife-and-mother roles.

And how about the mother? She enters marriage and perhaps bears a child with no definite role and series of functions, as formerly. Her old role within the patriarchal family, with its many functions, its economic and emotional security, its round of community participations, is lost, but no well-defined role has taken its place. She feels inferior to men because comparatively she has been and is more restricted. If she works after marriage she faces sex discrimination on the job and perhaps her husband's criticism if his traditional role of bread-winner is important to him.

Half-seriously she prepared for a career prior to marriage, half-seriously because a career is regarded by most middle-class girls as insurance against the grim possibility they will not be married; through a "good" marriage (the folk phrase "she married well" refers not to personality adjustment but to the bank balance and career prospects of the husband) the middle-class girl attains far more status than is possible through a career of her own. But the period of phantasy dalliance with a career, or an embarkation upon one, leave her ill-fitted for the drudgery of housecleaning, diapers, and the preparation of meals. The freedom which the urban apartment and modern household devices have brought the middle-class housewife has been commonly misinterpreted as well as exaggerated. While the Victorian housewife had more work to do, that work was part of a well-integrated system of household and community activities. While the modern middle-class housewife has more leisure-time than either her mother or grandmother, she must still work at a number of household jobs for which she has not been trained, which are usually not an essential part of her value-system, and which are isolated from her social activities. One sociologist has expressed this dilemma facetiously: half her working day is spent doing something she does not like, the rest is spent thinking up ways of getting even with her husband. The resulting boredom frequently leads to a period of indecision early in the marriage over whether to have children or resume the career. This internal conflict has been well-expressed by Thompson:

In the present economic situation in the United States increase of population is not desired. The fact that small families are the rule is one of the factors driving women out of the home. Now that they are not in the home a kind of vicious circle is formed, for it is no longer convenient to be occupied in the home by one or two children. Much conflict centers here, for it is one of the problems of the culture which as yet has no generally satisfactory solution. Individual women have worked out ways of having both children and a career, but most women still do one or the other; and in either case there are regrets and often neurotic discontent . . . the problem is not solved by going to the other extreme and trying to prove one's adequacy by having a child or two. The women of past generations had no choice but to bear children. Since their lives were organized around this concept of duty, they seldom became aware of dislike of the situation. . . . Nowadays, when women have a choice, the illusion is to the effect that unwanted children are less common, but women still from neurotic compulsion bear children they cannot love.

And so it is inevitable that the child shall be viewed with some degree of ambivalence by both father and mother, for he represents a direct interference with most of the dominant values and compulsions of the modern middle class: career, social and economic success, hedonistic enjoyment. There is some doubt that under modern middle-class conditions, children automatically bring husband and wife closer together.

To return to the consideration of the middle-class child. Personality absorption takes place against a background of parental ambivalence. The mother has little to do, in or out of the home; she is her single child's sole companion. Modern "scientific child care" enforces a constant supervision and diffused worrying over the child's health, eating spinach, and ego-development; this is complicated by the fact that much energy is spent forcing early walking, toilet-training, talking, because in an intensively competitive milieu middle-class parents from the day of birth on are constantly comparing their own child's development with that of the neighbors' children. The child must also be constantly guarded from the danger of contacting various electrical gadgets and from kicking valuable furniture. The middle-class child's discovery that the living-room furniture is more important to his mother than his impulse to crawl over it, unquestionably finds a place in the background of the etiology of a certain type of neurosis, however absurd it may appear.

Under constant supervision, with limited play-area in a house touching other homes on all sides, or in an apartment, and lacking companions, the child's physiological expansiveness, fed by his boredom, persists in getting him into trouble: screaming, running around the apartment, upsetting daddy's shaving mug, rending teddy-bear in two, emptying his milk on the rug to observe what pattern will be formed. This "trouble" is all a matter of definition. . . .

Already the parents have made "love" of supreme importance in their relation to the child, theirs for him and his for them, partly because of the love-complex of our time, which is particularly ramified within the middle class, and partly as a compensation for the many sacrifices they have made for the child, long debated before and after its arrival. *The child's need for love is experienced precisely because he has been conditioned to need it.* That the need is biological seems unlikely. Now, the more ambivalent the parents are toward the child, the more seriously is the "trouble" he causes them interpreted. He should not act in such a way because of the sacrifices they have made in his behalf, and the least he can do is show his gratitude by "loving" them in turn, *i.e.*, keeping out of "trouble." When the trouble inevitably occurs, *the most effective punishment imaginable is the threat to withdraw their love from him.* He "needs" that love because his personality has been absorbed by these two persons, because he has been conditioned to have a slavish-emotional dependence upon them. *Not the need for parental love, but the constant threat of its withdrawal after the child has been conditioned to the need, lies at the root of the most characteristic modern neurosis.* Mamma won't like you if you don't eat your spinach, or stop dribbling your milk, or get down from that davenport. To the extent that a child's personality has been absorbed, he will be thrown into a panic by this sort of treatment, and develop guilt-feelings to help prevent himself from getting into further trouble. In such a child a disapproving glance may produce more terror than a twenty-minute lashing. . . .

The threat of love-withdrawal is usually the mother's technique for controlling the child. At first the father may threaten to withdraw love, but as the child grows older the father finds a more subtle control —the expression of disapproval. The child is limited to his parents for modelling his behavior. While very young, he wants to set the table and sweep the floor "like mummy." In a few years standards of manly conduct are imposed and he wants to do things "like daddy." The father now controls him through the child's new self-conception, and it is not so much the use of "authority" as threatening the child's self-respect. The child is not a person who amounts to very much, how does he ever expect to get along when he gets old enough to go to school, or join the Boy Scouts, or go to college, or get a job? Again, to the extent that the child's personality has been absorbed, he will be made to feel small, insignificant, unworthy. And, feeling absorbed, caught and helpless, must propitiate these combined god-monsters that he needs so desperately. Hence anxiety, guilt-feelings, the sense of inferiority; seek security at all costs, for he is living alone and afraid, in a world he never made.

As for authority, its exercise generates neurotic symptoms only under two conditions, both of which must be present; close identification of the child with at least one parent; the effective blocking-off of all avenues of authority-avoidance for twenty-four hours of the day. . . .

The important differentiation is not between rational and irrational authority but the extent to which any parental authority succeeds in absorbing the child's personality, *which is itself dependent upon factors other than the imposition of arbitrary authority.*

Yet when we have used the term "personality absorption" we have not by any means explained a neurosis etiology. The personality of the middle-class girl of the late nineteenth century was "absorbed" by her parents, she was subjected to the demands of "love" and unquestioning obedience, at least ideally; nevertheless, the rate of neurosis under those conditions was probably not too high, as nearly as can be judged at this later date. Why? Because she was not faced with inconsistent expectations of conduct on the part of others and herself. Because love and obedience were integrated within a role which changed relatively slightly from childhood into adolescence, courtship, and finally into marriage. In other words, her initial goals and self-conceptions were constantly re-enforced with each new life experience.

The modern middle-class child on the other hand, particularly the boy, who has found surcease from anxiety and guilt by blind obedience and "love" for his parents, is not allowed to stabilize his relationships with others on that basis. His play-group, which may be denied him until he has reached school age, makes him feel a certain shame and inadequacy in attempting to approach its members with familiar techniques. He also early discovers that he is involved in competition with others, as an individual with his contemporaries, and as a representative of his family unit with other families.

If the abstraction "ours is a competitive society" is translated into terms of what happens to the child born to modern middle-class parents, it becomes quite relevant to the present discussion. Before the child has developed a real self-awareness he becomes part of a process of invidious comparison with other families: he uttered his first word two months earlier than the Jones' boy; he weighed so many pounds at the end of his first year. At Sunday School he received the Bible for perfect attendance; at public school his grades in arithmetic were higher than two-thirds of the other members of the class. He may take piano lessons in view of the day when Mrs. Smythe's pupils will be on public exhibition before the parents of the neighborhood. Everything he accomplishes or fails to accomplish becomes an inevitable part of the family's attempt to maintain or improve its standing in the community.

But effective competition demands a certain degree of independence, firmness of purpose, perhaps aggressiveness. Even for the "normal" middle-class child the transition from submission to some degree of independent behavior is made difficult. And for the child whose personality has been absorbed, an especially exacerbated conflict arises. He is expected to "do things," to accomplish, perhaps to lead in some endeavor, like other children, but his earliest social conditioning was dependence, submission, inferiority; his accomplishments, if any, are on a god-scale—in phantasy. He is desperately attempting to stabilize all later relationships on the basis of his earliest conditioning. Any pressure to compete only exaggerates his anxiety, guilt, and feelings of inadequacy. Life in the modern middle-class home insures that he shall feel that pressure.

There are, then, three elements in the etiology of what has been called the most characteristic neurosis of modern society; personality absorption; the reiterated threat to withdraw a love which has been made of paramount importance; a conflict between the resulting initial adjustment of submissive propitiation and the later assumption of goals of achievement and roles of independent action.

The child is not able to establish an integrated self-conception. Propitiation has meant obedience and "love" for the parents, leading to a compulsive repression of self-will. But he soon discovers that propitiation, in the sense of meeting new parental expectancies, means exhibiting independence, self-assertiveness, aggressiveness, outside the home. The father, as the child's mediator of the outside male world, rather than the mother, makes this demand uncompromisingly which may, incidentally, be one of the unsuspected sources of the so-called Oedipus complex. This seems more than likely since male neurotics often recall facing the father's ridicule of their first fumbling efforts to meet the father's expectations of "manly" conduct.

With the new conflicting expectations, on the part of parents and contemporaries, the child's anxiety reaches new heights, a *double set of guilt-feelings appear where previously there was only one*: at first he felt guilty only if he failed to love and obey, and this guilt could be assuaged by the propitiation of submission; now, however, the god-monsters will be appeased only by a combination of submission in his role of child-in-family, and assertiveness in his play-group, school-pupil, and other roles enacted outside of home. An integration of these conflicting roles is impossible. His conception of himself becomes one of abject failure. Any striving is painful for it violates the initial submissive adjustment. But he feels equally guilty for not making the effort to achieve. This is a key to much of his contradictory and self-blocking behavior: his desire to be the last man in the last regiment and his desire to conquer the world; his demand that everyone shall love him, and his settled conviction that no one could love a person as base as he; his inability to erect a hierarchy of values; his endless debate over the value of his own goals. He is damned if he does and damned if he doesn't. He is embraced by a psychological Iron Maiden: any lunge forward or backward only impales him more securely on the spikes.

~~~

16. Portrait of the Authoritarian Man *

ANALYSIS OF THE FACTORS involved in personality formation is a major problem in social science. One of the basic theories of personality development, originating with Sigmund Freud, considers early childhood experience all-important in determining adult modes of behavior. Using this theory as a point of departure, a group of social psychologists developed the concept "authoritarian personality—a person whose family background and social environment have made him peculiarly attuned to anti-democratic beliefs—" and conducted extensive research on the subject. In this article Samuel H. Flowerman summarizes some of their conclusions about this type of personality and the means through which may be developed democratic men and women rather than authoritarian personalities. Although many sociologists would question some phases of this research, it has had a significant impact on sociological research dealing with personality development.

* Samuel H. Flowerman, The New York Times Magazine (April 23, 1950), pp. 9, 28-31. Reprinted by permission of the publisher and the author.
The author (b. 1912) is Visiting Professor of Education, Teachers College, Columbia University; Staff Lecturer, Postgraduate Center for Psychotherapy, New York; and consulting psychologist. Co-editor of a five-volume series (published by Harper, sponsored by the American Jewish Committee) that includes "The Authoritarian Personality." Author of numerous articles in sociological and anthropological journals.

FINDINGS OF RECENT scientific investigations reveal that the real menace
to democracy is not the brutal dictator but the anonymous man-in-the-
crowd on whose support the dictator depends for power. Social scientists have found that this nameless individual is not a creation of the
dictator but a ready-made "authoritarian personality"—a person whose
family background and social environment have made him peculiarly
attuned to anti-democratic beliefs. It requires authoritative personalities
to take hold of authoritarian ideals; it takes authoritarian personalties
—thousands and even millions of them—to build an authoritarian state.

Concern about authority and the relationship between the ruler and
the ruled is not new. It runs through the fabric of recorded history
of civilization. Philosophers and poets—from at least as far back as
ancient Egypt and Greece to present-day Existentialists—have wrestled
with the dilemma of how to attain the highest level of development of
the individual within some system of order governing man's relation to
man. In the United States a spate of studies about various aspects
of personality development has been going forward for several decades.
And research workers, most of them trained here, have been conducting
studies in post-war Germany in an effort to understand why a people
will produce, nurture and follow a dictator. The bulk of these inquiries
tend to yield somewhat consistent results: there is something special,
something different about the "authoritarian man."

Perhaps the most detailed study of all time in this field was made
by a team of social psychologists in California, working for almost five
years. They recently completed an investigation of the democratic and
anti-democratic ideas and attitudes of the American man-in-the-crowd,
seeking keys to their origin. Teams from other parts of the country
have added to their findings. The California group—T. W. Adorno,
Else Frenkel-Brunswik, Max Horkheimer, Daniel Levinson and R. Nevitt
Sanford—interviewed and tested more than two thousand persons in the
San Francisco Bay area, Los Angeles, Portland, Ore., and Washington, D. C.

Among the groups tested were factory workers, officer candidates in a
maritime training school, veterans, members of service clubs (Rotarians
and Kiwanis), office workers, male inmates of a prison, members of
parent-teacher associations, out-patients in a psychiatric clinic, church
groups and college students.

While the California study is not a statistical study but rather examines various groups psychologically, it was found that authoritarian
men did exist in many groups and in many places. Based on the California study and other readings and observations over a number of years,
social scientists feel that it can be said that about 10 per cent of the

population of the United States probably consists of "authoritarian men and women" while as many as another 20 per cent have within them the seeds that can grow into authoritarianism.

Lest the conclusion be drawn that there are only two kinds of people, authoritarians and anti-authoritarians, it should be said that the social scientists' findings rate persons on a scale from very low to very high, as regards their authoritarian tendencies, with perhaps the bulk of the population clustered around the middle.

From the findings of the California study has emerged this composite psychological portrait of the Authoritarian Man:

He is a supreme conformist. The Authoritarian Man conforms to the nth degree to middle-class ideas and ideals and to authority. But conforming is no voluntary act for him; it is compulsive and irrational. It is an attempt to find security by merging with the herd, by submitting to some higher power or authority. Not only does he feel compelled to submit; he wants others to submit, too. He cannot run the risk of being different and cannot tolerate difference in anyone else.

In a mild form, such compulsive submission to authority may find a Casper Milquetoast chewing each mouthful of food thirty times because some bogus health expert has said he should. In its extreme form it finds people reduced to sheep, herded into marking "yes" on ballots that do not have "no," bleating "Heil!" to the commands of a Hitler, and doing his bidding even when it means oppressing, even killing, other people.

Authoritarians see the world and its inhabitants as menacing and unfriendly. Being so threatened, so anxiety ridden, they must seek security somehow, somewhere. The best security for the authoritarian is to surrender to a powerful authority. He agrees, for example, that "What the world needs is a strong leader"; and "There are two kinds of people, the weak and the strong."

To him, life is a power system into which he must fit. He doesn't have to wield the power himself so long as he can be near power, sharing it vicariously. It is this latter tendency which makes the authoritarian such a good camp-follower.

But the authoritarian is a loyal camp-follower only so long as the leader remains strong. Let the leader falter, let him be defeated; then, "Down with the old, up with the new."

So today in Germany many people agree that Hitler was bad, but only because he was unsuccessful in the long run; their basic way of life is still authoritarian—they simply await a new, stronger, more powerful leader.

He is rigid and shows limited imagination. He is a mechanical man, a kind of robot who reacts to only a limited number of ideas and can't be budged out of the channels in which he has been conditioned to operate. This doesn't mean that the Authoritarian Man is a person of low intelligence; but it does mean that his personality restricts his intelligence and imagination. He is generally incapable of figuring out alternate solutions to problems.

The extent to which this rigidity operates was demonstrated by Dr. Milton Rokeach, a junior member of the California team and now at Michigan State College. Dr. Rokeach worked out a series of simple problems in arithmetic and map reading. He presented these problems to groups of adults and children whose authoritarianism had already been determined. All the people in the experiment were taught to solve the problems by using a complicated method, but nothing was said about other, easier, solutions; they were simply instructed to get the right answers. As Dr. Rokeach's guinea pigs continued to work down the list of problems they soon reached a series of examples that could be solved either the hard way or very simply. Authoritarians continued to solve the problems the hard way. The non-authoritarians shifted readily to the easy solutions—they were able to use more channels.

He is herd-minded. And to be herd-minded—"ethnocentric," is the scientists' term—implies being prejudiced. To the authoritarian, people who are—or seem to be—different are strange, uncanny and threatening, although they may be few in number and unimportant in influence. He tends to exalt his own group and reject members of other groups. (To be sure, there are some exceptions to this praise of one's own group. Sometimes members of minority groups take over the prejudices of the majority groups and engage in what psychologists call "self-hate.")

The person who dislikes one "out-group" generally dislikes many other "out-groups." In this respect he is like the hay-fever victim, who is usually allergic to more than one kind of pollen.

The authoritarian puts neat—and often false—labels on people. In his group he may see individuals; outside his own group he sees only masses or types. So he will frequently say of members of "minority" groups that "that kind" is "lazy," "sex-crazy," "dishonest in business," "money-mad," "smelly," and so on. What is more, he tends to see "them" everywhere.

He is a phony conservative. He waves the flag, he sounds like a patriot, but at heart hates the very traditions and institutions he professes to love. In his most rabid form the phony conservative is the anti-democratic agitator who is more destructively radical than the radicals he claims he is attacking.

The California team distinguishes between the true conservative and the phony conservative. The true conservative may be patriotic, believe in American traditions and institutions and support their continued existence; he may also believe in a laissez-faire economy. But he is also for giving every individual an equal "break" regardless of his group membership. And it is in regard to this last point that the true conservative can be distinguished from the counterfeit flag-waver.

He is a moral purist. The authoritarian frowns on sensuality, a trait he is ready to find in members of other groups. He regards his own group as morally pure. Authoritarian men—and women—tend to agree, for example, that no "decent man" would marry an unchaste woman. Even male prisoners jailed for sex crimes support statements condemning sex crimes; and they are also more conforming, more anti-Semitic, more anti-Negro, and more pseudo-conservative than their fellow-prisoners.

It would be a grave mistake to regard the authoritarian as a lunatic or freak, although doubtless there are such extreme cases. If anything, the democratic person may appear outwardly to be less well-adjusted because he "internalizes" his problems to a greater degree and blames himself for many of his difficulties. The authoritarian "externalizes" his problems and blames other people and other forces. On the surface, the authoritarian may seem to be less troubled, but this is often because he has buried his smoldering resentment and hostility within himself.

By contrast with his opposite the extremely democratic personality is a man with a mind of his own; he is a flexible individual, adjusting readily to new situations. He is sensitive to the part he plays in conflicting situations and he is ready to take responsibility for his own behavior.

The model anti-authoritarian tends to like all sorts of people regardless of whether they are members of his group. He is without prejudice against religious or racial minorities. He regards persons as individuals, not types. Nor is he inclined to judge the moral standards of others. It is easy for him to see some good in the world and some hope for its future. Most important, he refuses to surrender his individuality to a "big shot," although he may submit to rational authority by choice when he believes that such authority is based upon equality, superior ability, and cooperation, and that it is subject to dismissal for a job badly done.

The findings of these studies suggest that people are not deliberately and systematically taught the ABC's of authoritarianism. Authoritarianism is a term which describes personality; and personality is developed in the crucible of inter-personal relationships, the most important of which is the relationship between parent and child.

As a child the typical authoritarian was usually subjected to harsh discipline and was given little affection in a home in which the father was a tough boss. In such a home children must "knuckle under" and submit. There is little opportunity to disagree and to act as an individual. Fear rules, and parents and other figures of authority are regarded as menacing, punitive and overpowering. This fear, based on the inability to disagree, is carried over into adult life; when the opportunity to assert one's self occurs, it is seized by way of compensation. The slave of one generation becomes the domineering master of the next generation.

On the other hand, as a child the democratic individual most often grew up in a home where the mother had much to say. Children in these families knew affection and had a feeling that they counted as individuals. They exercised the right to disagree, although often not without conflict and guilt. As adults they regard their parents as flesh-and-blood characters with the traits of real people. In childhood, the democratic person was able to choose equality and independence instead of blind, passive submission. As an adult, the democratic person is not so easily pushed around because he has no compulsive need, based on fear, to submit to the authority of the "big shot."

To be sure, there are reasons for the development of authoritarian personalities which are not to be found in the home. There are the major environmental upheavals—depressions and unemployment, inflations, wars, earthquakes, revolutions, floods—which alter ways of living and believing. There are also the chance experiences which an individual encounters in a lifetime. Sometimes the harshness of a child's home may be offset by kindly teachers, decent playmates, and other significant figures who treat the child affectionately as an individual. Sometimes a child grows up in such a way as to be able to throw off the effects of his slavery.

But these rebels are perhaps the exception, whereas the slave personality occurs more often when childhood has been spent in an authoritarian home. Certainly research findings indicate that so far the key to the difference between the authoritarian and democratic personalities lies in the relationship between parents and children. Learning to disagree with one's parents may be the capstone of a democratic personality.

How great is the threat of authoritarian development in this country? There are several deeply ingrained trends in American culture which probably offset to a considerable degree the spread of authoritarianism.

Americans traditionally scoff at authority. An American President reads a State of the Union message before Congress and is heckled, only to answer right back. Prizefight referees are booed when they award unfair decisions against Negro boxers in favor of white boxers. Players and spectators "razz" baseball umpires. Radio programs and movies make fun of cops, school teachers and principals, and especially fathers.

American homes are mother-oriented—and if anything—child-dominated. Women control the family purse strings of America, handle immediate problems of discipline, and are favored by over-sentimentality in a Victorian sense.

We have an American creed of fair play, of equality, and of upward mobility among social and economic classes. We are an individualistic, freedom-loving, rational, practical people. Americans are suspicious of flag-waving and of military authority.

Yet there are those who note that our American creed is "honored more in the breach than in the observance." Wide gaps separate what we claim to believe and what we feel and do. Like any national group, we are susceptible to anti-democratic ideologies; we have authoritarian personalities among us.

To develop freer personalities—personalities less susceptible to authoritarian ideas—we must learn how to select better teachers and to train them better; we must see them as engineers of human relations instead of instructors of arithmetic and spelling. We must reach parents so that they can learn the importance of affection and equality in the home. Mental health programs must be developed to help people become better parents. And laws, as social controls, can serve the useful purpose of limiting the effects of bigots and bringing the force of authority—which they frequently fear and have to submit to— to bear upon them.

Another source of enlightenment is to be found in our colleges and universities. Stimulated by the studies of authoritarian personality, scores of graduate students all over the country are pursuing research projects in human relations. Already the knowledge which comes from such research is reaching students in schools and colleges throughout the United States, and is beginning to reach scholars and students in France, England, Belgium and Italy.

There are many healthy signs in America today. Love has chased the behaviorists from the nursery; modern parents are less ashamed of loving their children. We regard juvenile delinquency as a social problem rather than an ordinary crime. Alcoholism has been the subject of research and humane treatment. Colleges turn down large bequests containing discriminatory clauses. Movies about such social problems as prejudice have increased in number and improved in quality (and have made money at the box office). Eight states have laws barring discrimination in employment. Three states bar discrimination in higher education.

These signs herald a future in which there may be fewer authoritarians, for they tend to check the authoritarian personality at its source and aim to make the American background more fruitful for the development of its antagonist, the democratic man and woman.

❧❧❧❧

17. Status and Role *

As a member of various groups the person acquires *statuses* and performs certain *roles*. Ralph Linton's discussion of these two concepts has become a classic in sociological and anthropological literature. He examines the theory of status and role with illustrations from both primitive and civilized societies. The concepts are further illustrated by the five following selections (18-22), each of which analyzes in some detail the nature of a certain specific role.

The term *status*, like the term *culture*, has come to be used with a double significance. A *status*, in the abstract, is a position in a particular pattern. It is thus quite correct to speak of each individual as having many statuses, since each individual participates in the expression of a number of patterns. However, unless the term is qualified in some way, *the status* of any individual means the sum total of all the statuses which he occupies. It represents his position with relation to the total society. Thus the status of Mr. Jones as a member of his community derives from a combination of all the statuses which he holds as a

* Ralph Linton, The Study of Man, pp. 113-121. Copyright 1936 by D. Appleton-Century Company. Reprinted by permission of the publishers, Appleton-Century-Crofts, Inc., and the author.

The author (b. 1893) is Sterling Professor of Anthropology at Yale University. Was Assistant Curator of North American Ethnology, Field Museum of Natural History. Excavation expeditions to New Mexico, Guatemala, Marquesas, Taumotus, Tahiti. His books include The Tanala, A Hill Tribe of Madagascar; Acculturation in Seven American Indian Tribes; The Cultural Background of Personality; Arts of the South Seas; Most of the World: the Peoples of Africa, Latin America, and the East Today; Halloween through Twenty Centuries (with Adelin Linton).

citizen, as an attorney, as a Mason, as a Methodist, as Mrs. Jones's husband, and so on.

A status, as distinct from the individual who may occupy it, is simply a collection of rights and duties. Since these rights and duties can find expression only through the medium of individuals, it is extremely hard for us to maintain a distinction in our thinking between statuses and the people who hold them and exercise the rights and duties which constitute them. The relation between any individual and any status he holds is somewhat like that between the driver of an automobile and the driver's place in the machine. The driver's seat with its steering wheel, accelerator, and other controls is a constant with ever-present potentialities for action and control, while the driver may be any member of the family and may exercise these potentialities very well or very badly.

A rôle represents the dynamic aspect of a status. The individual is socially assigned to a status and occupies it with relation to other statuses. When he puts the rights and duties which constitute the status into effect, he is performing a rôle. Rôle and status are quite inseparable, and the distinction between them is of only academic interest. There are no rôles without statuses or statuses without rôles. Just as in the case of *status*, the term *rôle* is used with a double significance. Every individual has a series of rôles deriving from the various patterns in which he participates and at the same time a *rôle*, general, which represents the sum total of these rôles and determines what he does for his society and what he can expect from it.

Although all statuses and rôles derive from social patterns and are integral parts of patterns, they have an independent function with relation to the individuals who occupy particular statuses and exercise their rôles. To such individuals the combined status and rôle represent the minimum of attitudes and behavior which he must assume if he is to participate in the overt expression of the pattern. Status and rôle serve to reduce the ideal patterns for social life to individual terms. They become models for organizing the attitudes and behavior of the individual so that these will be congruous with those of the other individuals participating in the expression of the pattern. Thus if we are studying football teams in the abstract, the position of quarterback is meaningless except in relation to the other positions. From the point of view of the quarterback himself it is a distinct and important entity. It determines where he shall take his place in the line-up and what he shall do in various plays. His assignment to this position at once limits and defines his activities and establishes a minimum of things which he must learn. Similarly, in a social pattern such as tha·

for the employer-employee relationship the statuses of employer and employee define what each has to know and do to put the pattern into operation. The employer does not need to know the techniques involved in the employee's labor, and the employee does not need to know the techniques for marketing or accounting.

It is obvious that, as long as there is no interference from external sources, the more perfectly the members of any society are adjusted to their statuses and rôles the more smoothly the society will function. In its attempts to bring about such adjustments every society finds itself caught on the horns of a dilemma. The individual's formation of habits and attitudes begins at birth, and, other things being equal, the earlier his training for a status can begin the more successful it is likely to be. At the same time, no two individuals are alike, and a status which will be congenial to one may be quite uncongenial to another. Also, there are in all social systems certain rôles which require more than training for their successful performance. Perfect technique does not make a great violinist, nor a thorough book knowledge of tactics an efficient general. The utilization of the special gifts of individuals may be highly important to society, as in the case of the general, yet these gifts usually show themselves rather late, and to wait upon their manifestation for the assignment of statuses would be to forfeit the advantages to be derived from commencing training early.

Fortunately, human beings are so mutable that almost any normal individual can be trained to the adequate performance of almost any rôle. Most of the business of living can be conducted on a basis of habit, with little need for intelligence and none for special gifts. Societies have met the dilemma by developing two types of statuses, the ascribed and the achieved. Ascribed statuses are those which are assigned to individuals without reference to their innate differences or abilities. They can be predicted and trained for from the moment of birth. The achieved statuses are, as a minimum, those requiring special qualities, although they are not necessarily limited to these. They are not assigned to individuals from birth but are left open to be filled through competition and individual effort. The majority of the statuses in all social systems are of the ascribed type and those which take care of the ordinary day-to-day business of living are practically always of this type.

In all societies certain things are selected as reference points for the ascription of status. The things chosen for this purpose are always of such a nature that they are ascertainable at birth, making it possible to begin the training of the individual for his potential statuses and rôles at once. The simplest and most universally used of these reference

points is sex. Age is used with nearly equal frequency, since all individuals pass through the same cycle of growth, maturity, and decline,
and the statuses whose occupation will be determined by age can be
forecast and trained for with accuracy. Family relationships, the simplest and most obvious being that of the child to its mother, are also
used in all societies as reference points for the establishment of a whole
series of statuses. Lastly, there is the matter of birth into a particular
socially established group, such as a class or caste. The use of this type
of reference is common but not universal. In all societies the actual
ascription of statuses to the individual is controlled by a series of these
reference points which together serve to delimit the field of his future
participation in the life of the group.

The division and ascription of statuses with relation to sex seems to
be basic in all social systems. All societies prescribe different attitudes
and activities to men and to women. Most of them try to rationalize
these prescriptions in terms of the physiological differences between the
sexes or their different rôles in reproduction. However, a comparative
study of the statuses ascribed to women and men in different cultures
seems to show that while such factors may have served as a starting point
for the development of a division the actual ascriptions are almost
entirely determined by culture. Even the psychological characteristics
ascribed to men and women in different societies vary so much that
they can have little physiological basis. Our own idea of women as
ministering angels contrasts sharply with the ingenuity of women as
torturers among the Iroquois and the sadistic delight they took in the
process. Even the last two generations have seen a sharp change in the
psychological patterns for women in our own society. The delicate,
fainting lady of the middle eighteen-hundreds is as extinct as the dodo.

When it comes to the ascription of occupations, which is after all an
integral part of status, we find the differences in various societies even
more marked. Arapesh women regularly carry heavier loads than men
"because their heads are so much harder and stronger." In some societies women do most of the manual labor; in others, as in the
Marquesas, even cooking, housekeeping, and baby-tending are proper
male occupations, and women spend most of their time primping.
Even the general rule that women's handicap through pregnancy and
nursing indicates the more active occupations as male and the less
active ones as female has many exceptions. Thus among the Tas-
manians seal-hunting was women's work. They swam out to the seal
rocks, stalked the animals, and clubbed them. Tasmanian women also
hunted opossums, which required the climbing of large trees.

Although the actual ascription of occupations along sex lines is highly variable, the pattern of sex division is constant. There are very few societies in which every important activity has not been definitely assigned to men or to women. Even when the two sexes coöperate in a particular occupation, the field of each is usually clearly delimited. Thus in Madagascar rice culture the men make the seed beds and terraces and prepare the fields for transplanting. The women do the work of transplanting, which is hard and back-breaking. The women weed the crop, but the men harvest it. The women then carry it to the threshing floors, where the men thresh it while the women winnow it. Lastly, the women pound the grain in mortars and cook it.

When a society takes over a new industry, there is often a period of uncertainty during which the work may be done by either sex, but it soon falls into the province of one or the other. In Madagascar, pottery is made by men in some tribes and by women in others. The only tribe in which it is made by both men and women is one into which the art has been introduced within the last sixty years. I was told that during the fifteen years preceding my visit there had been a marked decrease in the number of male potters, many men who had once practised the art having given it up. The factor of lowered wages, usually advanced as the reason for men leaving one of our own occupations when women enter it in force, certainly was not operative here. The field was not overcrowded, and the prices for men's and women's products were the same. Most of the men who had given up the trade were vague as to their reasons, but a few said frankly that they did not like to compete with women. Apparently the entry of women into the occupation had robbed it of a certain amount of prestige. It was no longer quite the thing for a man to be a potter, even though he was a very good one.

The use of age as a reference point for establishing status is as universal as the use of sex. All societies recognize three age groupings as a minimum: child, adult, and old. Certain societies have emphasized age as a basis for assigning status and have greatly amplified the divisions. Thus in certain African tribes the whole male population is divided into units composed of those born in the same years or within two- or three-year intervals. However, such extreme attention to age is unusual, and we need not discuss it here.

The physical differences between child and adult are easily recognizable, and the passage from childhood to maturity is marked by physiological events which make it possible to date it exactly for girls and within a few weeks or months for boys. However, the physical passage from childhood to maturity does not necessarily coincide with the social transfer of the individual from one category to the other.

Thus in our own society both men and women remain legally children until long after they are physically adult. In most societies this difference between the physical and social transfer is more clearly marked than in our own. The child becomes a man not when he is physically mature but when he is formally recognized as a man by his society. This recognition is almost always given ceremonial expression in what are technically known as puberty rites. The most important element in these rites is not the determination of physical maturity but that of social maturity. Whether a boy is able to breed is less vital to his society than whether he is able to do a man's work and has a man's knowledge. Actually, most puberty ceremonies include tests of the boy's learning and fortitude, and if the aspirants are unable to pass these they are left in the child status until they can. For those who pass the tests, the ceremonies usually culminate in the transfer to them of certain secrets which the men guard from women and children.

The passage of individuals from adult to aged is harder to perceive. There is no clear physiological line for men, while even women may retain their full physical vigor and their ability to carry on all the activities of the adult status for several years after the menopause. The social transfer of men from the adult to the aged group is given ceremonial recognition in a few cultures, as when a father formally surrenders his official position and titles to his son, but such recognition is rare. As for women, there appears to be no society in which the menopause is given ceremonial recognition, although there are a few societies in which it does alter the individual's status. Thus Comanche women, after the menopause, were released from their disabilities with regard to the supernatural. They could handle sacred objects, obtain power through dreams and practise as shamans, all things forbidden to women of bearing age.

The general tendency for societies to emphasize the individual's first change in age status and largely ignore the second is no doubt due in part to the difficulty of determining the onset of old age. However, there are also psychological factors involved. The boy or girl is usually anxious to grow up, and this eagerness is heightened by the exclusion of children from certain activities and knowledge. Also, society welcomes new additions to the most active division of the group, that which contributes most to its perpetuation and well-being. Conversely, the individual who enjoys the thought of growing old is atypical in all societies. Even when age brings respect and a new measure of influence, it means the relinquishment of much that is pleasant. We can see among ourselves that the aging usually refuse to recognize the change until long after it has happened.

In the case of age, as in that of sex, the biological factors involved appear to be secondary to the cultural ones in determining the content of status.   There are certain activities which cannot be ascribed to children because children either lack the necessary strength or have not had time to acquire the necessary technical skills.   However, the attitudes between parent and child and the importance given to the child in the family structure vary enormously from one culture to another. The status of the child among our Puritan ancestors, where he was seen and not heard and ate at the second table, represents one extreme.   At the other might be placed the status of the eldest son of a Polynesian chief.   All the *mana* (supernatural power) of the royal line converged upon such a child.   He was socially superior to his own father and mother, and any attempt to discipline him would have been little short of sacrilege.   I once visited the hereditary chief of a Marquesan tribe and found the whole family camping uncomfortably in their own front yard, although they had a good house built on European lines.   Their eldest son, aged nine, had had a dispute with his father a few days before and had tabooed the house by naming it after his head.   The family had thus been compelled to move out and could not use it again until he relented and lifted the taboo.   As he could use the house himself and eat anywhere in the village, he was getting along quite well and seemed to enjoy the situation thoroughly.

The statuses ascribed to the old in various societies vary even more than those ascribed to children.   In some cases they are relieved of all heavy labor and can settle back comfortably to live off their children. In others they perform most of the hard and monotonous tasks which do not require great physical strength, such as the gathering of firewood. In many societies the old women, in particular, take over most of the care of the younger children, leaving the younger women free to enjoy themselves.   In some places the old are treated with consideration and respect; in others they are considered a useless incumbrance and removed as soon as they are incapable of heavy labor.   In most societies their advice is sought even when little attention is paid to their wishes. This custom has a sound practical basis, for the individual who contrives to live to old age in an uncivilized group has usually been a person of ability and his memory constitutes a sort of reference library to which one can turn for help under all sorts of circumstances.

In certain societies the change from the adult to the old status is made more difficult for the individual by the fact that the patterns for these statuses ascribe different types of personality to each.   This was the case among the Comanche, as it seems to have been among most of the Plains tribes.   The adult male was a warrior, vigorous, self-reliant, and pushing. Most of his social relationships were phrased in terms of competition. He took what he could get and held what he had without regard to any abstract rights of those weaker than himself. Any willingness to arbitrate differences or to ignore slights was a sign of weakness resulting in loss of prestige. The old man, on the other hand, was expected to be wise and gentle, willing to overlook slights and, if need be, to endure abuse. It was his task to work for the welfare of the tribe, giving sound advice, settling feuds between the warriors, and even preventing his tribe from making new enemies. Young men strove for war and honor, old men strove for peace and tranquillity. There is abundant evidence that among the Comanche the transition was often a difficult one for the individual. Warriors did not prepare for old age, thinking it a better fate to be killed in action. When waning physical powers forced them to assume the new rôle, many of them did so grudgingly, and those who had strong magic would go on trying to enforce the rights which belonged to the younger status. Such bad old men were a peril to young ones beginning their careers, for they were jealous of them simply because they were young and strong and admired by the women. The medicine power of these young men was still weak, and the old men could and did kill them by malevolent magic. It is significant that although benevolent medicine men might be of any age in Comanche folklore, malevolent ones were always old.

❦❦❦

18. What Women Want *

THE PREVIOUS SELECTION (17, by Ralph Linton), represents an analysis, largely theoretical, of the concepts of *status* and *role*. This selection, by the outstanding anthropologist, Margaret Mead, considers one broad status position, the American woman. Writing in a popular vein, but attacking the subject with skill and thoroughness, she presents the ill-defined and contradictory situation that faces many women in our society.

* Margaret Mead. Reprinted from the December, 1946, issue of *Fortune*, pp. 172-224, by Special Permission of the Editors. Copyright 1946 Time, Inc.

The author (b. 1901) is the foremost woman anthropologist in America. Associate Curator of Ethnology, American Museum of Natural History. Wrote O.W.I. pamphlets during World War II. Has studied primitive groups for twenty-five years. Among her books are *Coming of Age in Samoa*, *Male and Female*, *The School in American Culture*, *Soviet Attitudes toward Authority*.

MORE THAN A QUARTER of the women in the U. S. are disturbed, articulately, definitely disturbed about their lot—as women. A large proportion of these are the pace setters of the country, the college graduates, the middle-class women, the women with well-equipped houses and few children, and the women, accordingly, who have time to express their discontent and make it felt. Another large percentage of the discontented are the women who have to work because they are widowed or divorced or single, but who have no real interest in their jobs, who can't take the same pride in having a job that men can take because having a job is still regarded as second best for a woman. They express their discontent in various ways, some by wishing they could be born again as men, others by antagonism toward other women, by antagonism toward men, by excessive demands on their children for whom they have "given up everything." These are the actively discontented. The passive kind merely show apathy; they are "the girls without any ambition," the women who are content with stopgap jobs, and the women who "let themselves go" at home, and spend their lives in shapeless dressing gowns. Both kinds of women, the women who feel that life has offered them a second-rate deal and the women who simply feel no challenge, no urgency, no reason for either doing a better job or cooking a better dinner, play a significant and a destructive part in American life.

•   •   •   •   •   •

Now of what does this female discontent consist? American women are better fed and better sheltered than almost any other women in the world. By and large their husbands seldom beat them. They are free to go almost anywhere in public life; they walk with faces uncovered, yet unexposed to disapproving comment or molestation. They can go to school just as their brothers can, and in fact often have a chance at a more modern education because it has seemed safer on the whole to do our experimenting on our daughters rather than on our sons. They can hold jobs, join unions, own businesses, sign checks, run for office, wear pants in public places. In most states their property is their own, and the worst limitations on their freedom are a few laws designed to protect their potential or actual maternity. If we were to go back and look over the issues raised by earlier generations of feminists, it would look as if a very large part of the battle that they fought has been won.

And yet persistent fact is that the most articulate, the best-educated, the most mobile group of American women is disturbed. Roughly, this disturbance takes two forms, discontent with the present conditions of homemaking for the woman with children, and confusion about how a woman is to look at herself: should she see herself as a person or primarily as a woman? If we consider the complaints about homemaking, the chief complaint might be identified as isolation. Men have left the home, children have left the home, grandparents and maiden aunts and widowed cousins no longer live together in the same home—and the wife remains at home all alone. This exodus from the home is relatively new. True, there are primitive tribes in the South Seas where women are supposed to be so magically potent—and inimical to hunting or fishing or warmaking—that the grown men have to sleep together in a men's house most of the time, and perhaps only come home to breakfast. But they don't come home to lonely individual women sitting listening to a daytime serial but to whole groups of women having a pretty jolly time of it, eating a feast of their own making, and gaily tailoring each other's colored grass skirts. There are also primitive peoples in New Guinea who are so suspicious of each other that each little family lives to itself, never sharing food with a neighbor, and with someone always presiding over the cook pot for fear a passerby may pop a bit of poison in. But in such a suspicious society as this, husbands are so wary that they stay at home—to watch their wives. In the great families of China and in the women's quarters of India, groups of women and children ate and slept and gossiped and worked together. On the lonely farms of the early U.S., men and women, parents and children, shared the same kind of life together. (And the exacting nature of homemaking isn't so conspicuous on a farm, for although mother may have to get up often with the baby, father has to get up often with the calf.) Thus in primitive, in Oriental, and in our own historically past society, people worked in some sort of group, together, and enjoyed the companionship that accompanied the work.

Women in our society complain of the lack of stimulation, of the loneliness, of the dullness of staying at home. Little babies are poor conversationalists, husbands come home tired and sit reading the paper, and women who used to pride themselves on their ability to talk find on the rare evening they can go out that their words clot on their tongues. As the children go to school, the mother is left to the companionship of the Frigidaire and the washing machine. Yet she can't go out because the delivery man might come, or a child might be sent home sick from school. The boredom of long hours of solitary one-sided communication with things, no matter how shining and stream-lined and new, descends upon her. Moreover, the conditions of modern life, apartment living, and especially the enormous amount of moving about during the war, all serve to rob women of neighborhood ties. The better her electric equipment, the better she organizes her ordering, the less reason she has to run out for a bit of gossipy shopping at the corner store. The department stores and the moving-picture houses cater to women—alone—on their few hours out. Meanwhile efficient mending services and cheap ready-made clothes have taken most sensible busy work out of women's hands and left women—still at home—listening to the radio.

This boredom and loneliness of doing alone the jobs that were once done either in chattering groups of women or by a whole family working together is one thread that runs through women's discontent. The other is the enormous contradiction between the way girls are brought up and the life they will have to lead, between what we teach girls and what we expect of a girl. In school, in the papers, from books and films and radio, boys and girls learn to value the same things, to ask of life the same rewards: variety, choice, freedom. Whether it is men speaking or women, whether they are talking about men's work or about women's, the same comments are made over and over again. The thing that matters about the way you spend your time is whether it is interesting, varied, full of contacts with other people, and whether you are free, know your hours, can depend upon time off. American boys are taught that they will be able to choose their jobs (that this is often not true, and certainly not true in a depression, doesn't alter the fact that that is what they are taught) and choose their girls, both. They choose their jobs for one set of reasons, and their girls for another. They are free— so they are taught. But while girls are taught that they will choose their jobs in the same way as boys and choose their husbands as boys will choose their wives (because they prefer them as human beings), they can't choose their work after marriage. If you are a man, your way of making a living is still a matter of choice; if you are a girl, it ultimately isn't. Good cooks, poor cooks, and no cooks at all, girls who from childhood have been "baby-carriage peekers" and girls who shudder at the sound of a child's shriek as if it were chalk squeaking on a blackboard, girls who enjoy responding to other people's demands and girls who want to pursue a single purpose of their own—all are expected, because they fall in love and want to be married, to want also to be homemakers and to enjoy the routine of bringing up children.

Not so long ago, in most countries of the world, men were given as little choice. Even today, on the island of Bali, men plow the land and plant the rice, transplant and weed and harvest it whether or not they like agriculture. Only the very exceptional and gifted escape some time spent on the basic activity of farming. On the great plains of China, men with a vocation for farming, and men without any such vocation,

farm; and women with and without special vocation cook and clean
the house and rear the children. The idea of choice doesn't arise.
But the U.S. (in 1946) is not China or Bali or a peasant community
in Europe. It is a society with a universal public-school education and
great mass-communication chains, where the value of choice and of
freedom is played up in every conceivable way. As women have demanded and received the right to vote, to own property, to practice
professions (all on the grounds that they should be treated as the same
kind of people as men, not as a special class of biologically determined
defectives), it is only another step for them to demand the same degree
of choice about the way they work to make a living. If a man's choice
of a girl doesn't carry with it a compulsory sort of job, why should a
girl's choice of a man prescribe a compulsory job for the next thirty
years? That is the question that lurks, unformulated, behind the formulated protests of women. Married women often say they had to "give
up everything" to marry. Still it may be observed that many men and
unmarried women feel that married women have given up very little.
They feel that the matrons have exchanged the very uncareer-like
exactions of some dull job for the potential variety in homemaking, with
its thousand different tasks. It is not so much what women have given
up for marriage but the fact that they had no choice between career and
housekeeping that is so irksome to them.

Some new solutions of this discontent are imminent. They will
depend in great part, of course, on such matters as full employment or
depression, on whether the world is able to prepare for peace or must
devote itself to preparing for war. But if we were to have in America
many years of developing order and prosperity, what form could these
solutions take? If we have to make some adjustments so that women
will feel that they have as much choice as men, and if, given choice,
many of them elect to work outside the home at least part of the time,
what will happen to the home? Will it become so difficult to bring up
children to be full human beings that outraged voices will sound
throughout society and shout women back into the home again?

If we look at history, present and past, and at the position of women
all over the world, among savage and civilized peoples, we find that it is
possible for society to do almost anything with the relationships between
men and women. There are cultures where women are dominating
and men responsive, where women manage the finances and men
wheedle pocket money out of them and spend their time daydreaming
of forgery and alchemy, where women initiate the love affairs and no
man would be so foolhardy as to make the first advances, where both
men and women enjoy and rear the children; cultures where fathers are

indulgent and loving and mothers stern disciplinarians, where girls grow up envying boys and wishing they had been born boys, and cultures where boys grow up envying girls, wishing they had been born girls. Human beings are exceedingly plastic, and the relationship of men and women to each other is a very flexible thing.

If in assaying our own society we find that we have educated women to want to act in terms of their full individuality, and not as members of the sex that bears children, and that this education isn't working very well, what alternatives can we consider? There are scientists—especially from the fields of biology, medicine, and psychiatry—who feel the answer would be to re-emphasize women's biological role: bearing and feeding children. They would recommend educating girls, not to be persons first and women second, but to be women primarily, women who will see the only choice they want to make as a choice among potential fathers of their children. They point to the neurosis from which childless women suffer, and conclude that although human beings are very flexible, they are not so flexible that we can ignore the fact that woman was born to reproduce the race.

These exponents of a biological rather than a social outlook make a plausible argument, supported by many case histories of maladjusted women. American culture may in time return to a respect for the biological realities, but at present that is not our direction. We are not likely to abandon coeducation and bring up children from infancy with different toys and different kinds of exercise in order to limit the horizon of girls and so condition them to their biological role. The whole trend in the U.S. is away from every sort of biological limitation on human activity and achievement.

•   •   •   •   •   •

If a return to a stronger social emphasis on women's biological role is therefore unlikely in the U.S., what are the other possible solutions? There are many who will press for the diffusion of homemaking among a mass of community agencies, nursery schools, day-care centers, laundries, diaper services, play schools, and infirmaries. Women who work outside the home because they must thus will no longer carry the impossible double burden they carry now, and women who work outside the home because they elect that way of life can have their children adequately cared for. There is no doubt that we need many more of such resources to care for the children of working mothers, to get rid of door-key children playing in the streets because there is no one at home, and also to remove from the home a lot of useless drudgery that is out of line with our standards of efficiency. But, if we really take out of the home everything that the woman as homemaker is supposed to do in it, it is questionable whether we shall have homes at all. This solution has been tried, in wartime, in almost every large country. Child specialists have studied children who grow up in institutions, and the results are discouraging. Unless all the institutions where the children are taken care of in droves are staffed by a very large number of women and men to replace the missing parents, the children don't come out human. They don't know how to fall in love, marry, and have children —to say nothing of their becoming responsible, self-initiating human beings.

To get the kind of human beings on which a society like America depends (individuals with enterprise, self-starters able to form a committee and tackle any problem at the drop of a hat) we need to bring up our children in homes—and in homes where mothers have as high a position as fathers. . . .

If we can't go back to treating women as special child-bearing creatures but must treat them as persons, and yet can't give up the home for a lot of institutions that aren't able to develop children's personalities, there is at least one other possible solution. We can meet women's demand for choice and for work that brings them out of their isolated houses and flats if at the same time that we make it possible for the married woman to get out of the home we also encourage the married man to take some share in it. This is not a plea for getting fathers to wash dishes. There is no proof at all that children's personalities are dependent upon anybody's washing dishes. The Samoans eat off leaves, the Eskimos pass a large hunk of meat from hand to hand, the Malays cook rice in green bamboo, crack the bamboo, and throw it away. The only possible connection between housekeeping and bringing up children is that while an adult is doing something with the hands, it is easy to watch and talk with a child. But cleaning the car is equally suitable, or planting the garden, or feeding the goldfish, for that matter. The best fathers and the best mothers probably do some physical things— walk, skate, climb, swim, whittle, build models, shine the silver—with their children. But there is no reason why most of the present drudgery of housekeeping, the sort of drudgery that takes up the hours that might be spent in some different surroundings, shouldn't go out of the home altogether. Then groups of women will work in canning factories, instead of each one canning at home, and those who like laundries will work together in laundries, as the women of Europe once laughed and gossiped as they washed their clothes on the riverbanks. What would remain in the home would be shared living, a family eating, sleeping, and playing together. It is actually the arranging of this shared living that keeps the middle-class woman tied to her house—no matter how many frozen vegetables she is able to buy—and keeps the woman who works sagged and tired from trying to coordinate her home activities and work hours. . . . When men take a greater part in these activities that we call living, as opposed to making a living, we shall approach again the sort of balance between the sexes that we had in early America, on our American farms, when both worked together at the same tasks, often within earshot of each other.

WOMAN'S CHOICE

Letting men into the home and giving them a greater share in making choices about the way in which life is to be enjoyed would probably not effect a great revolution in American social life. A large proportion of women would probably elect homemaking—without outside work—as a full-time occupation for generations to come, unless war or new forms of political organization compelled them to do otherwise. Given freedom of choice, given the possibility of a marriage in which bringing up children and holding a job or pursuing a career do not present an impossible combination, most women will find one reason for their discontent removed and continue to give their time to homemaking. That is what their mothers did, and that is the basic picture of home life that they absorbed as small children. But such a pattern of life would include choice. Young people consider whether they will get a car and a smaller house, or a larger house and wait for the car, or whether they will build a shack at the seashore or go somewhere different each summer. They might also come to consider how the work is to be divided. Shall they both work and share the expense of getting the drudgery out of the house, and share also the task of keeping life going at home, or shall the girl elect to spend her full time at home, even if it means some drudgery because they won't be able to afford laundry service and precooked foods?

The position of women in America at present is explosive and potentially harmful. It keeps a great number of employed women working unhappily, troubled and anxious about the homes they also have to manage somehow. It makes a great number of educated women feel they are faced with an unbearable choice and leaves them correspondingly unhappy whichever choice they make. It produces many maladjusted children who reflect their mothers' discontent. It makes for a general uneasiness in society. Once the vote was an issue. Yet, when women were given the vote, it was found that the vote—such a terrible issue when they were denied it—became a mild enough routine of life.

Only a few women went into politics, only a few became active party workers.   But a disturbed area of life, a sense of festering injustice, was removed.   The participation of women as citizens was improved, and life went back on a more even keel.   A climate of opinion that ceases to regard married women as if they were inherently different from other human beings, that regards marriage as the privilege of all human beings and homemaking as a job for any pair of parents who take it on, would have the same stabilizing effect on women's present confused discontent.

❦❧☙❦

19. Cultural Contradictions and Sex Roles *

As THE PRECEDING ARTICLE (18, by Margaret Mead) indicates, American women are subject to conflicting definitions of the roles they should play.   These contradictions may be even more serious for college women than for others.   Every college co-ed who reads this article will recognize many of the problems reported by Mirra Komarovsky.   They are dilemmas that impinge on the individual in our changing contemporary society when the norms for each status and role are not clearly defined. `

PROFOUND CHANGES in the roles of women during the past century have been accompanied by innumerable contradictions and inconsistencies. With our rapidly changing and highly differentiated culture, with migrations and multiplied social contacts, the stage is set for myriads of combinations of incongruous elements. Cultural norms are often functionally unsuited to the social situations to which they apply.   Thus they may deter an individual from a course of action which would serve his own, and society's, interests best.   Or, if behavior contrary to the norm is engaged in, the individual may suffer from guilt over violating mores which no longer serve any socially useful end.   Sometimes culturally defined roles are adhered to in the face of new conditions without a conscious realization of the discrepancies involved.   The reciprocal actions dictated by the roles may be at variance with those demanded

* Mirra Komarovsky, *American Journal of Sociology*, 52, No. 3 (November, 1946), 184-189.   Reprinted by permission of the University of Chicago Press and the author.

The author (b. 1906) is Chairman, Department of Sociology, Barnard College. Formerly Research Associate, Council Research Social Sciences, Columbia University, 1931-35.   Author, *The Unemployed Man and His Family*.   Her articles have appeared in various journals.

by the actual situation. This may result in an imbalance of privileges and obligations or in some frustration of basic interests.

Again, problems arise because changes in the mode of life have created new situations which have not as yet been defined by culture. Individuals left thus without social guidance tend to act in terms of egotistic or "short-run hedonistic" motives which at times defeat their own long-term interests or create conflict with others. The precise obligation of a gainfully employed wife toward the support of the family is one such undefined situation.

Finally, a third mode of discrepancy arises in the existence of incompatible cultural definitions of the same social situation, such as the clash of "old-fashioned" and "radical" mores, of religion and law, of norms of economic and familial institutions.

The problems raised by these discrepancies are social problems in the sense that they engender mental conflict or social conflict or otherwise frustrate some basic interest of large segments of the population.

This article sets forth in detail the nature of certain incompatible sex roles imposed by our society upon the college woman. It is based on data collected in 1942 and 1943. Members of an undergraduate course on the family were asked for two successive years to submit autobiographical documents focused on the topic; 73 were collected. In addition, 80 interviews, lasting about an hour each, were conducted with every member of a course in social psychology of the same institution— making a total of 153 documents ranging from a minimum of five to a maximum of thirty typewritten pages.

The generalization emerging from these documents is the existence of serious contradictions between two roles present in the social environment of the college woman. The goals set by each role are mutually exclusive, and the fundamental personality traits each evokes are at points diametrically opposed, so that what are assets for one become liabilities for the other, and the full realization of one role threatens defeat in the other.

One of these roles may be termed the "feminine" role. While there are a number of permissive variants of the feminine role for women of college age (the "good sport," the "glamour girl," the "young lady," the domestic "home girl," etc.), they have a common core of attributes defining the proper attitudes to men, family, work, love, etc., and a set of personality traits often described with reference to the male sex role as "not as dominant, or aggressive as men" or "more emotional, sympathetic."

The other and more recent role is, in a sense, no sex role at all, because it partly obliterates the differentiation in sex. It demands of the women much the same virtues, patterns of behavior, and attitude that it does of the men of a corresponding age. We shall refer to this as the "modern" role.

Both roles are present in the social environment of these women throughout their lives, though, as the precise content of each sex role varies with age, so does the nature of their clashes change from one stage to another. In the period under discussion the conflict between the two roles apparently centers about academic work, social life, vocational plans, excellence in specific fields of endeavor, and a number of personality traits.

One manifestation of the problem is in the inconsistency of the goals set for the girl by her family.

Forty, or 26 per cent, of the respondents expressed some grievance against their families for failure to confront them with clearcut and consistent goals. The majority, 74 per cent, denied having had such experiences. One student writes:

How am I to pursue any course single-mindedly when some way along the line a person I respect is sure to say, "You are on the wrong track and are wasting your time." Uncle John telephones every Sunday morning. His first question is: "Did you go out last night?" He would think me a "grind" if I were to stay home Saturday night to finish a term paper. My father expects me to get an "A" in every subject and is disappointed by a "B." He says I have plenty of time for social life. Mother says, "That 'A' in Philosophy is very nice dear. But please don't become so deep that no man will be good enough for you." And, finally, Aunt Mary's line is careers for women. "Prepare yourself for some profession. This is the only way to insure yourself independence and an interesting life. You have plenty of time to marry."

A Senior writes:

I get a letter from my mother at least three times a week. One week her letters will say, "Remember that this is your last year at college. Subordinate everything to your studies. You must have a good record to secure a job." The next week her letters are full of wedding news. This friend of mine got married; that one is engaged; my young cousin's wedding is only a week off. When, my mother wonders, will I make up my mind? Surely, I wouldn't want to be the only unmarried one in my group. It is high time, she feels, that I give some thought to it.

A student reminisces:

All through high school my family urged me to work hard because they wished me to enter a first-rate college. At the same time they were always

raving about a girl schoolmate who lived next door to us.   How pretty and
sweet she was, how popular, and what taste in clothes!   Couldn't I also
pay more attention to my appearance and to social life?   They were overlooking the fact that this carefree friend of mine had little time left for
school work and had failed several subjects.   It seemed that my family had
expected me to become Eve Curie and Hedy Lamarr wrapped up in one.

Another comments:

My mother thinks that it is very nice to be smart in college but only if it
doesn't take too much effort.   She always tells me not to be too intellectual
on dates, to be clever in a light sort of way.   My father, on the other hand,
wants me to study law.   He thinks that if I applied myself I could make
an excellent lawyer and keeps telling me that I am better fitted for this
profession than my brother.

Another writes:

One of my two brothers writes: "Cover up that high forehead and act
a little dumb once in a while"; while the other always urges upon me the
importance of rigorous scholarship.

The students testified to a certain bewilderment and confusion caused
by the failure on the part of the family to smooth the passage from one
role to another, especially when the roles involved were contradictory.
It seemed to some of them that they had awakened one morning to find
their world upside down: what had hitherto evoked praise and rewards
from relatives, now suddenly aroused censure.   A student recollects:

I could match my older brother in skating, sledding, riflery, ball, and many
of the other games we played.   He enjoyed teaching me and took great
pride in my accomplishments.   Then one day it all changed.   He must
have suddenly become conscious of the fact that girls ought to be feminine.
I was walking with him, proud to be able to make long strides and keep
up with his long-legged steps when he turned to me in annoyance, "Can't
you walk like a lady?"   I still remember feeling hurt and bewildered by
his scorn, when I had been led to expect approval.

Once during her freshman year in college, after a delightful date, a
student wrote her brother with great elation:

"What a wonderful evening at ———— fraternity house!   You would
be proud of me, Johnny!   I won all ping-pong games but one!"
"For heaven's sake," came the reply, "when will you grow up?   Don't

you know that a boy likes to think he is better than a girl?   Give him a little competition, sure, but miss a few serves in the end.   Should you join the Debate Club?   By all means, but don't practice too much on the boys." Believe me I was stunned by this letter but then I saw that he was right. To be a success in the dorms one must date, to date one must not win too many ping-pong games.   At first I resented this bitterly.   But now I am more or less used to it and live in hope of one day meeting a man who is my superior so that I may be my natural self.

It is the parents and not the older sibling who reversed their expectations in the following excerpt:

All through grammar school and high school my parents led me to feel that to do well in school was my chief responsibility.   A good report card, an election to student office, these were the news Mother bragged about in telephone conversations with her friends.   But recently they suddenly got worried about me: I don't pay enough attention to social life, a woman needs some education but not that much.   They are disturbed by my determination to go to the School of Social Work.   Why my ambitions should surprise them after they have exposed me for four years to some of the most inspired and stimulating social scientists in the country, I can't imagine. They have some mighty strong arguments on their side.   What is the use, they say, of investing years in training for a profession, only to drop it in a few years?   Chances of meeting men are slim in this profession. Besides, I may become so preoccupied with it as to sacrifice social life. The next few years are, after all, the proper time to find a mate.   But the urge to apply what I have learned, and the challenge of this profession is so strong that I shall go on despite the family opposition.

The final excerpt illustrates both the sudden transition of roles and the ambiguity of standards:

I major in English composition.   This is not a completely "approved" field for girls so I usually just say "English."   An English Literature major is quite liked and approved by boys.   Somehow it is lumped with all the other arts and even has a little glamour.   But a composition major is a girl to beware of because she supposedly will notice all your grammar mistakes, look at your letters too critically, and consider your ordinary speech and conversation as too crude.

I also work for a big metropolitan daily as a correspondent in the city room.   I am well liked there and may possibly stay as a reporter after graduation in February.   I have had several spreads [stories running to more than eight or ten inches of space], and this is considered pretty good for a college correspondent.   Naturally, I was elated and pleased at such breaks, and as far as the city room is concerned I'm off to a very good start on a career that is hard for a man to achieve and even harder for a woman. General reporting is still a man's work in the opinion of most people. I have a lot of acclaim but also criticism, and I find it confusing and difficult to be praised for being clever and working hard and then, when my efforts promise to be successful, to be condemned and criticized for being unfeminine and ambitious.

Here are a few of these reactions:

My father: "I don't like this newspaper set-up at all. The people you meet are making you less interested in marriage than ever. You're getting too educated and intellectual to be attractive to men."

My mother: "I don't like your attitude toward people. The paper is making you too analytical and calculating. Above all, you shouldn't sac-rifice your education and career for marriage."

A lieutenant with two years of college: "It pleased me greatly to heal about your news assignment—good girl."

A Navy pilot with one year of college: "Undoubtedly, I'm old-fashioned, but I could never expect or feel right about a girl giving up a very promising or interesting future to hang around waiting for me to finish college. Nevertheless, congratulations on your job on the paper. Where in the world do you get that wonderful energy? Anyway I know you were thrilled at getting it and feel very glad for you. I've an idea that it means the same to you as that letter saying 'report for active duty' meant to me."

A graduate metallurgist now a private in the Army: "It was good to hear that you got that break with the paper. I am sure that talent will prove itself and that you will go far. But not too far, as I don't think you should become a career woman. You'll get repressed and not be interested enough in having fun if you keep after that career."

A lieutenant with a year and a half of college: "All this career business is nonsense. A woman belongs in the home and absolutely no place else. My wife will have to stay home. That should keep her happy. Men are just superior in everything, and women have no right to expect to compete with them. They should do just what will keep their husbands happy."

A graduate engineer—my fiancé: "Go right ahead and get as far as you can in your field. I am glad you are ambitious and clever, and I'm as anxious to see you happily successful as I am myself. It is a shame to let all those brains go to waste over just dusting and washing dishes. I think the usual home life and children are small sacrifices to make if a career will keep you happy. But I'd rather see you in radio because I am a bit wary of the effect upon our marriage of the way of life you will have around the newspaper."

Sixty-one, or 40 per cent, of the students indicated that they have occasionally "played dumb" on dates, that is, concealed some academic honor, pretended ignorance of some subject, or allowed the man the last word in an intellectual discussion. Among these were women who "threw games" and in general played down certain skills in obedience to the unwritten law that men must possess these skills to a superior degree. At the same time, in other areas of life, social pressures were being exerted upon these women to "play to win," to compete to the utmost of their abilities for intellectual distinction and academic honors. One student writes:

I was glad to transfer to a women's college. The two years at the co-ed university produced a constant strain. I am a good student; my family expects me to get good marks. At the same time I am normal enough to want to be invited to the Saturday night dance. Well, everyone knew that on that campus a reputation of a "brain" killed a girl socially. I was always fearful lest I say too much in class or answer a question which the boys I dated couldn't answer.

Here are some significant remarks made from the interviews:

When a girl asks me what marks I got last semester I answer, "Not so good—only one 'A'." When a boy asks the same question, I say very brightly with a note of surprise, "Imagine, I got an 'A!'"

I am engaged to a southern boy who doesn't think too much of the woman's intellect. In spite of myself, I play up to his theories because the less one knows and does, the more he does for you and thinks you "cute" into the bargain. . . . I allow him to explain things to me in great detail and to treat me as a child in financial matters.

One of the nicest techniques is to spell long words incorrectly once in a while. My boy-friend seems to get a great kick out of it and writes back, "Honey, you certainly don't know how to spell."

When my date said that he considers Ravel's *Bolero* the greatest piece of music ever written, I changed the subject because I knew I would talk down to him.

A boy advised me not to tell of my proficiency in math and not to talk of my plans to study medicine unless I knew my date well.

My fiancé didn't go to college. I intend to finish college and work hard at it, but in talking to him I make college appear a kind of a game.

Once I went sailing with a man who so obviously enjoyed the role of a protector that I told him I didn't know how to sail. As it turned out he didn't either. We got into a tough spot, and I was torn between a desire to get a hold of the boat and a fear to reveal that I had lied to him.

It embarrassed me that my "steady" in high school got worse marks than I. A boy should naturally do better in school. I would never tell him my marks and would often ask him to help me with my homework.

I am better in math than my fiancé. But while I let him explain politics to me, we never talk about math even though, being a math major, I could tell him some interesting things.

Mother used to tell me to lay off the brains on dates because glasses make me look too intellectual anyhow.

I was once at a work camp. The girls did the same work as the boys. If some girls worked better, the boys resented it fiercely. The director told one capable girl to slow down to keep peace in the group.

How to do the job and remain popular was a tough task. If you worked your best, the boys resented the competition; if you acted feminine, they complained that you were clumsy.

On dates I always go through the "I-don't-care-anything-you-want-to-do" routine. It gets monotonous but boys fear girls who make decisions. They think such girls would make nagging wives.

I am a natural leader and, when in the company of girls, usually take the lead. That is why I am so active in college activities. But I know that men fear bossy women, and I always have to watch myself on dates not to assume the "executive" role. Once a boy walking to the theater with me took the wrong street. I knew a short cut but kept quiet.

I let my fiancé make most of the decisions when we are out. It annoys me, but he prefers it.

I sometimes "play dumb" on dates, but it leaves a bad taste. The emotions are complicated. Part of me enjoys "putting something over" on the unsuspecting male. But this sense of superiority over him is mixed with feeling of guilt for my hypocrisy. Toward the "date" I feel some contempt because he is "taken in" by my technique, or if I like the boy, a kind of a maternal condescension. At times I resent him! Why isn't he my superior in all ways in which a man should excel so that I could be my natural self? What am I doing here with him, anyhow? Slumming?

And the funny part of it is that the man, I think, is not always so unsuspecting. He may sense the truth and become uneasy in the relation. "Where do I stand? Is she laughing up her sleeve or did she mean this praise? Was she really impressed with that little speech of mine or did she only pretend to know nothing about politics?" And once or twice I felt that the joke was on me: the boy saw through my wiles and felt contempt for me for stooping to such tricks.

Another aspect of the problem is the conflict between the psychogenetic personality of the girl and the cultural role foisted upon her by the milieu. ˏ At times it is the girl with "masculine" interests and personality traits who chafes under the pressure to conform to the "feminine" pattern. At other times it is the family and the college who thrust upon the reluctant girl the "modern" role.

While, historically, the "modern" role is the most recent one, ontogenetically it is the one emphasized earlier in the education of the college girl, if these 153 documents are representative. Society confronts the girl with powerful challenges and strong pressure to excel in certain competitive lines of endeavor and to develop certain techniques of adaptation very similar to those expected of her brothers. But, then, quite suddenly as it appears to these girls, the very success in meeting these challenges begins to cause anxiety. It is precisely those most successful in the earlier role who are now penalized.

It is not only the passage from age to age but the moving to another region or type of campus which may create for the girl similar problems. The precise content of sex roles, or, to put it in another way, the degree of their differentiation, varies with regional class, nativity, and other subcultures.

Whenever individuals show differences in response to some social situation, as have our 153 respondents, the question naturally arises as to the causes. It will be remembered that 40 per cent admitted some difficulties in personal relations with men due to conflicting sex roles but that 60 per cent said that they had no such problems. Inconsistency of parental expectations troubled 26 per cent of the students.

To account for individual differences would require another study, involving a classification of personalities in relation to the peculiar social environments of each. Generally speaking, it would seem that it is the girl with a "middle-of-the-road personality" who is most happily adjusted to the present historical moment. She is not a perfect incarnation of either role but is flexible enough to play both. She is a girl who is intelligent enough to do well in school but not so brilliant as to "get all 'A's"; informed and alert but not consumed by an intellectual passion; capable but not talented in areas relatively new to women; able to stand on her own feet and to earn a living but not so good a living as to compete with men; capable of doing some job well (in case she does not marry or, otherwise, has to work) but not so identified with a profession as to need it for her happiness.

A search for less immediate causes of individual reactions would lead us further back to the study of genesis of the personality differences found relevant to the problem. One of the clues will certainly be provided by the relation of the child to the parent of the same and of the opposite sex. This relation affects the conception of self and the inclination for a particular sex role.   •

The problems set forth in this article will persist, in the opinion of the writer, until the adult sex roles of women are redefined in greater harmony with the socioeconomic and ideological character of modern society. Until then neither the formal education nor the unverbalized sex roles of the adolescent woman can be cleared of intrinsic contradictions.

◦§◦◦§§◦§◦

20. The Social Role of the Stranger *

THE CONCEPT OF "SOCIAL MOBILITY" is today a common one in introductory sociology. Not so common, however, is a systematic study of one of the "roles" resulting from social mobility—that of "the stranger." Here it is done by Simmel, an outstanding German theorist of an earlier period. His analysis of the social role of the stranger is typical of his sociological insight. The reader may grasp Simmel's generalizations more easily if he bears in mind, while reading them, his own experiences as a stranger.

IF WANDERING IS THE LIBERATION from every given point in space, and thus the conceptional opposite to fixation at such a point, the sociological form of the "stranger" presents the unity, as it were, of these two characteristics. This phenomenon too, however, reveals that spatial relations are only the condition, on the one hand, and the symbol, on the other, of human relations. The stranger is thus being discussed here, not in the sense often touched upon in the past, as the wanderer

* Reprinted from The Sociology of Georg Simmel (translated and edited by Kurt H. Wolff), pp. 402-408, by permission of The Free Press, Glencoe, Illinois. Copyright 1950.

The author (1858-1918) was a German philosopher and sociologist; lecturer at University of Berlin, then professor at Strasbourg. His subjects covered a wide range; his contributions to the sociological conceptions of superordination, subordination, conflict, and the stranger are significant. Between 1893 and 1910, translations of his writings by Albion W. Small appeared in American sociology journals.

who comes today and goes tomorrow, but rather as the person who comes today and stays tomorrow. He is, so to speak, the *potential* wanderer: although he has not moved on, he has not quite overcome the freedom of coming and going. He is fixed within a particular spatial group, or within a group whose boundaries are similar to spatial boundaries. But his position in this group is determined, essentially, by the fact that he has not belonged to it from the beginning, that he imports qualities into it, which do not and cannot stem from the group itself.

The unity of nearness and remoteness involved in every human relation is organized, in the phenomenon of the stranger, in a way which may be most briefly formulated by saying that in the relationship to him, distance means that he, who is close by, is far, and strangeness means that he, who also is far, is actually near. For, to be a stranger is naturally a very positive relation; it is a specific form of interaction. The inhabitants of Sirius are not really strangers to us, at least not in any sociologically relevant sense: they do not exist for us at all; they are beyond far and near. The stranger, like the poor and like sundry "inner enemies," is an element of the group itself. His position as a full-fledged member involves both being outside it and confronting it. The following statements, which are by no means intended as exhaustive, indicate how elements which increase distance and repel, in the relations of and with the stranger produce a pattern of coordination and consistent interaction.

Throughout the history of economics the stranger everywhere appears as the trader, or the trader as stranger. As long as economy is essentially self-sufficient, or products are exchanged within a spatially narrow group, it needs no middle-man: a trader is only required for products that originate outside the group. Insofar as members do not leave the circle in order to buy these necessities—in which case *they* are the "strange" merchants in that outside territory—the trader *must* be a stranger, since nobody else has a chance to make a living.

This position of the stranger stands out more sharply if he settles down in the place of his activity, instead of leaving it again: in innumerable cases even this is possible only if he can live by intermediate trade. Once an economy is somehow closed, the land is divided up, and handicrafts are established that satisfy the demand for them, the trader, too, can find his existence. For in trade, which alone makes possible unlimited combinations, intelligence always finds expansions and new territories, an achievement which is very difficult to attain for the original producer with his lesser mobility and his dependence upon a circle of customers that can be increased only slowly. Trade can always absorb more people than primary production; it is, therefore, the sphere indicated for the stranger, who intrudes as a supernumerary, so to speak, into a group in which the economic positions are actually occupied—the classical example is the history of European Jews. The stranger is by nature no "owner of soil"—soil not only in the physical, but also in the figurative sense of a life-substance which is fixed, if not in a point in space, at least in an ideal point of the social environment. Although in more intimate relations, he may develop all kinds of charm and significance, as long as he is considered a stranger in the eyes of the others, he is not an "owner of soil." Restriction to intermediary trade, and often (as though sublimated from it) to pure finance, gives him the specific character of *mobility*. If mobility takes place within a closed group, it embodies that synthesis of nearness and distance which constitutes the formal position of the stranger. For, the fundamentally mobile person comes in contact, at one time or another, with every individual, but is not organically connected, through established ties of kinship, locality, and occupation, with any single one.

Another expression of this constellation lies in the objectivity of the stranger. He is not radically committed to the unique ingredients and peculiar tendencies of the group, and therefore approaches them with the specific attitude of "objectivity." But objectivity does not simply involve passivity and detachment; it is a particular structure composed of distance and nearness, indifference and involvement. I refer to the discussion . . . of the dominating position of the person who is a stranger in the group; its most typical instance was the practice of those Italian cities to call their judges from the outside, because no native was free from entanglement in family and party interests.

With the objectivity of the stranger is connected, also, the phenomenon touched upon above, although it is chiefly (but not exclusively) true of the stranger who moves on. This is the fact that he often receives the most surprising openness—confidences which sometimes have the character of a confessional and which would be carefully withheld from a more closely related person. Objectivity is by no means non-participation (which is altogether outside both subjective and objective interaction), but a positive and specific kind of participation—just as the objectivity of a theoretical observation does not refer to the mind as a passive *tabula rasa* on which things inscribe their qualities, but on the contrary, to its full activity that operates according to its own laws, and to the elimination, thereby, of accidental dislocations and emphases, whose individual and subjective differences would produce different pictures of the same object.

Objectivity may also be defined as freedom: the objective individual is bound by no commitments which could prejudice his perception, understanding, and evaluation of the given. The freedom, however, which allows the stranger to experience and treat even his close relationships as though from a bird's-eye view, contains many dangerous possibilities. In uprisings of all sorts, the party attacked has claimed, from the beginning of things, that provocation has come from the outside, through emissaries and instigators. Insofar as this is true, it is an exaggeration of the specific role of the stranger: he is freer, practically and theoretically; he surveys conditions with less prejudice; his criteria for them are more general and more objective ideals; he is not tied down in his action by habit, piety, and precedent.

Finally, the proportion of nearness and remoteness which gives the stranger the character of objectivity, also finds practical expression in the more *abstract nature* of the relation to him. That is, with the stranger one has only certain *more general* qualities in common, whereas the relation to more organically connected persons is based on the commonness of specific differences from merely general features. In fact, all somehow personal relations follow this scheme in various patterns. They are determined not only by the circumstance that certain common features exist among the individuals, along with individual differences, which either influence the relationship or remain outside of it. For, the common features themselves are basically determined in their effect upon the relation by the question whether they exist only between the participants in this particular relationship, and thus are quite general in regard to this relation, but are specific and incomparable in regard to everything outside of it—or whether the participants feel that these features are common to them because they are common to a group, a type, or mankind in general. In the case of the second alternative, the effectiveness of the common features becomes diluted in proportion to the size of the group composed of members who are similar in this sense. Although the commonness functions as their unifying basis, it does not make *these* particular persons interdependent on one another, because it could as easily connect everyone of them with all kinds of individuals other than the members of his group. This too, evidently, is a way in which a relationship includes both nearness and distance at the same time: to the extent to which the common features are general, they add, to the warmth of the relation founded on them, an element of coolness, a feeling of the contingency of precisely *this* relation—the connecting forces have lost their specific and centripetal character.

In the relation to the stranger, it seems to me, this constellation has an extraordinary and basic preponderance over the individual elements that are exclusive with the particular relationship. The stranger is close to us, insofar as we feel between him and ourselves common features of a national, social, occupational, or generally human, nature. He is far from us, insofar as these common features extend beyond him or us, and connect us only because they connect a great many people.

A trace of strangeness in this sense easily enters even the most intimate relationships. In the stage of first passion, erotic relations strongly reject any thought of generalization: the lovers think that there has never been a love like theirs; that nothing can be compared either to the person loved or to the feelings for that person. An estrangement—whether as cause or as consequence it is difficult to decide—usually comes at the moment when this feeling of uniqueness vanishes from the relationship. A certain skepticism in regard to its value, in itself and for them, attaches to the very thought that in their relation, after all, they carry out only a generally human destiny; that they experience an experience that has occurred a thousand times before; that, had they not accidentally met their particular partner, they would have found the same significance in another person.

Something of this feeling is probably not absent in any relation, however close, because what is common to two is never common to them alone, but is subsumed under a general idea which includes much else besides, many *possibilities* of commonness. No matter how little these possibilities become real and how often we forget them, here and there, nevertheless, they thrust themselves between us like shadows, like a mist which escapes every word noted, but which must coagulate into a solid bodily form before it can be called jealousy. In some cases, perhaps the more general, at least the more unsurmountable, strangeness is not due to different and ununderstandable matters. It is rather caused by the fact that similarity, harmony, and nearness are accompanied by the feeling that they are not really the unique property of this particular relationship: they are something more general, something which potentially prevails between the partners and an indeterminate number of others, and therefore gives the relation, which alone was realized, no inner and exclusive necessity.

On the other hand, there is a kind of "strangeness" that rejects the very commonness based on something more general which embraces the parties. The relation of the Greeks to the Barbarians is perhaps typical here, as are all cases in which it is precisely general attributes, felt to be specifically and purely human, that are disallowed to the other. But "stranger," here, has no positive meaning; the relation to him is a non-relation; he is not what is relevant here, a member of the group itself.

As a group member, rather, he is near and far *at the same time*, as is characteristic of relations founded only on generally human common-ness. But between nearness and distance, there arises a specific tension when the consciousness that only the quite general is common, stresses that which is not common. In the case of the person who is a stranger to the country, the city, the race, etc., however, this non-common element is once more nothing individual, but merely the strangeness of origin, which is or could be common to many strangers. For this reason, strangers are not really conceived as individuals, but as strangers of a particular type: the element of distance is no less general in regard to them than the element of nearness.

This form is the basis of such a special case, for instance, as the tax levied in Frankfort and elsewhere upon medieval Jews. Whereas the Beede [tax] paid by the Christian citizen changed with the changes of his fortune, it was fixed once for all for every single Jew. This fixity rested on the fact that the Jew had his social position as a *Jew*, not as the individual bearer of certain objective contents. Every other citizen was the owner of a particular amount of property, and his tax followed its fluctuations. But the Jew as a taxpayer was, in the first place, a Jew, and thus his tax situation had an invariable element. This same position appears most strongly, of course, once even these individual characterizations (limited though they were by rigid invariance) are omitted, and all strangers pay an altogether equal head-tax.

In spite of being inorganically appended to it, the stranger is yet an organic member of the group. Its uniform life includes the specific conditions of this element. Only we do not know how to designate the peculiar unity of this position other than by saying that it is composed of certain measures of nearness and distance. Although some quantities of them characterize all relationships, a *special* proportion and reciprocal tension produce the particular, formal relation to the "stranger."

❦❦❦

21. The Teacher's Roles*

EVERY PERSON plays numerous roles in each of the various groups of which he is a member. In our society occupation is one of the

---

* Willard W. Waller in J. S. Roucek and Associates, *Sociological Foundations of Education* (New York: Thomas Y. Crowell Company, 1942), pp. 204-211. Reprinted by permission of the publisher.
The author (1899-1945) was a sociologist. Has been called "provocative, original,

more important group situations within which one learns roles and acquires statuses. In this article Willard Waller analyzes the occupational roles of the school teacher with special attention to the teacher's relations with students. Since the article was written several years ago, the teacher roles described by Waller may be somewhat different from those observed by the reader. However, much of his analysis applies to contemporary American teachers. It thus illustrates how the roles of this occupational group are prescribed by the institutional structure.

THE PROBLEM OF DEALING with other human beings is mainly that of finding the role one is to play in a social situation and then adapting it to the needs of the occasion. Obviously the teacher's job is to help young children to develop. It is his task to awaken their interests and encourage potentialities of growth, to leave them free and yet to acquaint them with those disciplined procedures without which we cannot live, to make them feel secure, happy, and friendly, in short, to help them to a fuller life. If the teacher can do these things, if he is successful in the human relations of his job, all other good things will be added to him. His students will learn eagerly, he will be the idol of principals and supervisors, and even parents will probably like him. Obviously, then, the human relations of the teacher are much more important than mere technical skill or knowledge of his subject.

The roles played by the teacher in the classroom and the community have received little consideration by students of education. Their thinking on the subject is almost as much dominated by conventional fictions and stereotypes as is that of the mythical man on the street. The teacher stereotype in its usual form is a sort of caricature of the teacher personality. It represents the teacher as a cranky, irritable despot ruling over the small concerns of children; it makes him a creature hardly fit to live in society and at the same time endows him with attributes of purity and high-mindedness far beyond those of ordinary mortals. The fictions to which we refer are even current in the teaching profession itself; they are idealized conceptions of the teacher and his work aimed at helping him solve his ego problems. Of course, there is an element of truth in these stereotypes and fictions, and the subsequent discussion will perhaps reveal this, but our fundamental task is to cut through them to the hard core of reality.

_____

and unorthodox" in his teaching and writing. Some of his books are *The Sociology of Teaching*, *War In The Twentieth Century*, *The Veteran Comes Back*, *The Family* (revised by Reuben Hill, 1951).

THE TEACHER'S CLASSROOM ROLES

We have often heard it said that an institution is the lengthened shadow of a man, but it is more often true that a man is the shortened shadow of an institution. In the case of the teacher we can make this observation quite often. His classroom roles revolve around his fundamental task. The school has specialized in the inculcation of certain bodies of facts and skills which young pupils are sometimes reluctant to master. Consequently the teacher must somehow induce his pupils to learn these things. However, in order to induce students to learn, he must at the same time impose upon himself a set of roles which involve iron compression of his own personality and those of his pupils. This compression, or repression, never quite succeeds—in fact, if it did succeed completely, it would be fatal to the school. Actually, therefore, other aspects of the teacher's personality constantly intrude themselves into classroom interaction. Thus he plays a variety of roles in his relations with his students.

The teacher must dominate the classroom situation. His will to impart information must overcome the will of the student not to receive it. Perhaps we do not ordinarily realize how completely the child is frustrated in the ordinary school and the ordinary classroom. When he enters the school, he must leave nine-tenths of his personality outside it. He must subordinate nearly all of his self to the demands of an institution. He cannot move about freely. He cannot converse with his friends. He must give his attention to the task at hand as determined by the teacher; he must learn what he tells him to learn when he tells him to learn it. He must learn multiplication tables, and a thousand times overlearn them, when he very much desires to go outside and play football. He must study history when his heart aches for the old swimming hole. He must devote his attention to the intricacies of English grammar when he is spontaneously most interested in the girl who sits next to him. Put all of these frustrations together and add them up and you will understand why the student does not always cooperate whole-heartedly with school authorities in his own education.

It is true, no doubt, that the program of the school considers only the child's own interest, and the child himself may give his conscious assent to this dogma. Nevertheless, there will always be a part of him which opposes the teacher and the teacher-dominated social order. To be sure, the restrictions of the school have sense in them; for if a number of people are to work together in a plant of limited size, their life must be regimented, and similarly, every child must be reasonably quiet if other children are to learn. However, these are things which children have a tendency to forget. Most of them, it is true, have a will to learn, but they have also somewhere in their psyche a will to resist the frustrating regimen of the school, something which we may as well call "a will not to learn."

Compare, for example, a boy's eager acceptance of information as to just how he should hold a baseball in order to throw an out-drop with the manner in which he receives enlightenment concerning the industries of Siam. Or compare the girl's retentive memory for compliments, proposals, and invitations to the Yale prom with the sieve-like affair to which she consigns the campaign issues which presumably brought John Quincy Adams to the Presidency. How glad the boy is to learn about baseball or the girl about dancing! How long and arduously they will practice for a small improvement! And if someone compliments them on their skill, they will remember those golden words forever. It is not so with spelling and arithmetic. Youngsters must learn them a thousand times, and do them over a thousand times, to gain even a precarious hold upon them, not merely because those are not things which students spontaneously want to learn, but also because a part of the student resists such learning to the death. This is the will not to learn.

In this psychic atmosphere the teacher lives and does his work. He must make the students learn, and therefore he must dominate them. He must be able to present a topic in such a way as to elicit as much spontaneous interest as he can. When the attention of the class wanders, he must be able to bring it back to the subject in hand, by persuasion if possible, by force if necessary. If the ever-present covert resentment of school routine breaks out into open rebellion, the teacher must know how to quell it. In short, he must know how to play the role of domination.

TEACHER'S LEADERSHIP

This domination, however, is of a peculiar kind. It is not mere personal ascendency, although there is always an element of such personal domination in it. Neither can it ever be a purely formal exercise of authority, such as might obtain in the relationships of officers and privates in the army. The formal, institutional, authoritative aspect of the teacher's domination must always, however, play a large part in his ascendency over his students. Only very gifted teachers can afford to depend to any degree upon personal leadership. For personal leadership is something that must be recreated every hour; it must be won over and over again. Thus, such leadership does not accord well with the institutional sort of domination.

The paradox of the teacher's institutional leadership may be illustrated by the following example: A certain girl has distinguished herself in no way in college. Her grades are only fair; her lessons are moderately prepared; her contributions to classroom discussions are few and not unusually brilliant. In her entire life she has shown few or no tendencies to personal aggression. She did not take much part in extra-curricular activities nor was she ever elected president of anything. We take such a girl upon graduation from college, place her behind a desk in front of a group of children, and say to her, "You are now a leader. You must lead these children and educate them." The fact is that just such a girl not infrequently succeeds under just such circumstances! Her personality is colorless, and therefore she fits perfectly into her institutional role. Moreover, she probably enjoys the experience of obtaining as a symbol of authority the respect which she could never gain as a person. And this case has its opposite number in the student who is an excellent natural leader but turns out to be a poor teacher because he intrudes his own personality into the classroom to too great a degree.

The teacher's leadership is a highly patterned form of leadership. There is a ritual which goes with it, and any element of personal ascendency must be filtered through that ritual. The teacher's major social role is embodied in the ritual of the classroom. He is himself as much subordinated to that role as are his students. And when he steps outside it, he does so at his peril.

The teacher's institutional leadership demands that he keep a high degree of social distance between himself and his students. The concept of social distance implies that a person may be physically quite near to another but psychically or socially inaccessible. Officer and man may share the hardships of a campaign to the last detail, but there is always a sort of social gulf between them. Likewise the teacher must always hold himself aloof and hide most of his characteristics as a person from his students.

It is well enough to say to the beginning teacher, as almost every supervisor does, "You must keep your distance," but it is quite another thing for such a teacher actually to keep it. The beginning teacher, moreover, rarely knows in any concrete way what keeping one's distance means. To maintain distance one must somehow convince the other person that one belongs to a different world. Thus, the teacher must never talk about his own concerns, and as far as possible he must hide them from his students. He must be coolly impersonal at all times. He must give his commands and instructions without allowing any of his quite personal fears or hostilities to enter into them. He must not be too much the human being, lest this interfere with his efficiency as a symbol of authority. He must always remember that when one is an institutional leader that sort of familiarity which comes from intimate association does in fact breed contempt.

It is tempting to speculate as to just why the teacher's domination is bearable to his students. One reason is that students consent to it with their conscious minds, although not, as we have shown, without some hidden and submerged rebellion. This consent is conditional, of course, upon the teacher's continuing to play his institutional role. As long, therefore, as he keeps the classroom interaction in the well-beaten institutional tracks, as long as he does nothing to stir up the slumbering demons in the inner recesses of the student mind, as long as he plays the role of the teacher, so long will the students accept his authority.

TEACHER'S PRESTIGE

A further factor affecting the teacher's domination is that of prestige. Prestige is the halo which we put about the leader's head. It is an imaginary quality with which we endow him in our own minds and hearts. Prestige is derived from our tendency to perceive other human beings in more or less complete configurations. Even if we know but little about another person, we incline, if he is a person who affects us at all, to form some kind of picture of his total personality. We are avid in our curiosity concerning his private life, and we devour details with appetite; we want to know whether he smokes cigarettes, and is kind to children, what he likes to eat for breakfast, and whether he wears socks when he goes to bed. And even if we fail to get any of this information, we are still not completely and finally frustrated, because we supply these missing details in our own imaginations.

The teacher is a person who plays a great role in the child's life, and the child is certain to be very curious about him. However, as he keeps himself a great distance from his pupil the latter is forced to rely upon his imagination to form a picture of the teacher's total personality. By interposing a great distance between him and his student, by displaying to the child only that segment of himself which pertains to his institutional character, the teacher endows himself with vast prestige in the child's mind. He thus creates the familiar "halo effect" of the psychologist, but enhanced and enlarged by the operation of social distance. This is in fact the fundamental reason for social distance. Familiarity breeds contempt not because the qualities revealed by familiarity are necessarily contemptible, but because any familiar knowledge of the teacher shatters the picture in the child's mind of the teacher as an institutional leader. Carefully regulated unfamiliarity contributes to that picture and keeps it inviolate. That is why the teacher must keep [his distance] in order to control.

We have oversimplified the problem of the teacher's role in order to bring out its dominance aspect. The fact is that the teacher has other roles which are dynamically related to the authority role, and which in turn help to make the teacher's authority acceptable. There are, of course, occasional teachers who are all authority, who in fact conform fairly closely to the pattern which we have described. However, while all teachers must know how to play this role in fact, many also know how to supplement it with other supplementary roles and to put such a pleasant face upon authority as to make the teacher-pupil relationship pleasant and rewarding.

◆◆◆◆◆

22. The Fool as a Social Type *

In this, the last of the selections concerned with the concepts of role and status, Orrin E. Klapp discusses the role of that unique individual—the fool. He says, "Our problem here is to define the fool as a social type. What is the role of the fool? What situations make fools, and what are the status and function of the fool in social organization?" The reader will find this an interesting analysis as well as a useful one. Klapp discusses the process by which an individual comes "to play the fool" and the possibilities of escaping the role. This analysis should be compared with the role-analysis of less deviant positions—the stranger, the teacher, and the college co-ed—in the preceding selections. Here one sees that the author has analyzed what might at first glance appear to be an absurd personal role and shown that the fool actually performs a significant social function.

Among the collective labels which have an unusual power of assigning status is the epithet of "the fool." The fool represents a collective

---

* Orrin E. Klapp, The American Journal of Sociology, 55, No. 2 (September, 1949), 157-162. Reprinted by permission of the author and the University of Chicago Press.

The author (b. 1915) is Assistant Professor of Sociology, San Diego State College. His Ph.D. thesis at the University of Chicago in 1948 was "The Hero As a Social Type."

concept of a kind of person or conduct peculiarly ridiculous and inferior. Despite his low status, however, the fool is a symbol of fundamental importance, representing a role especially valued by the group. The fool is a social type found widely in folklore, literature, and drama. The role of the fool is institutionalized in comedy and in the professions of the clown and jester. Everyone plays the fool at some time; fool-making is a continual social process; it is safe to say that every group must have a fool. Moreover, there is a tendency to dramatize social forces as a conflict of heroes and villains. In this human drama the fool also plays a part. Whereas the hero represents the victory of good over evil, the fool represents values which are rejected by the group: causes that are lost, incompetence, failure, and fiasco. So that, in a sense, fool-making might be called a process of history. Public figures who becomes classified as fools lose their chance of leadership. The label of "the fool" is, therefore, a propaganda device of special significance.

Our problem here is to define the fool as a social type. What is the role of the fool, what situations make fools, and what are the status and function of the fool in social organization? As a social type the fool has certain definable characteristics, as to both personal traits and roles. The creation of a fool is accomplished by ascribing characteristics of the fool to a person through situations which "make a fool" of somebody or popular definitions which impute the character of a fool, that is, jokes and epithets. For purposes of investigation a fool is defined here as a person, real or imaginary, who is generally ridiculed and who occupies a distinctive status because of this.

TYPES OF FOOLS

The fool is distinguished from the normal group member by a deviation in person or conduct which is regarded as ludicrous and improper. He is usually defined as a person lacking in judgment, who behaves absurdly or stupidly. The antics of the fool, his ugliness, gracelessness, senselessness, or possible deformity of body represent departures from corresponding group norms of propriety. The fool is the antithesis of decorum, beauty, grace, intelligence, strength, and other virtues embodied in heroes; and, therefore, as a type is antiheroic. The deviation of the fool from the normal has three characteristics: It is an extreme exaggeration or deficiency; it is an evidence of weakness or irresponsibility; and it is an offense against propriety rather than against mores. With regard to the first of these, as the following examples will show, the role of the fool involves a striking exhibition of some incongruity or shortcoming. With respect to the second, the role of the fool inherently involves failure, weakness, or comic frustration. Because of his ineffectuality, the fool is regarded as incompetent and irresponsible. Despite his shortcomings, therefore, he is distinguished from the villain by the fact that his pranks involve no evil intent or are too stupid to be taken seriously. The fool is thus tolerated and is regarded with amusement rather than being punished. The types of fools described below are distinguished by the particular way in which they depart from group norms, whether by an excess or by a deficiency in respect to some virtue: (1) the antic fool, (2) the comic rogue, (3) the rash fool, (4) the clumsy fool, (5) the deformed fool, (6) the simple fool, (7) the weak fool, (8) the comic butt, (9) the pompous fool, and (10) the mock hero.

The first three types deviate through excesses of conduct. The antic fool departs from decorum through impulsive or playful behavior, e.g., pranks, leaps, undignified postures, grimaces, mimicry, and other capers. He is the "cutup" or "life of the party." In the theatrical profession some of the epithets given to this role are "clowning" or "mugging." The comic rogue, or "scamp," is different from the antic fool in that his conduct departs from propriety specifically in the direction of forbidden behavior: "mischief" or criminality, e.g., impudent gestures, liberties, obscenities, or preposterous, burlesque villainies. His ineffectualness, lack of serious intent, or other weakness, however, prevents the group from taking him seriously. The rash fool, on the other hand, is characterized by immoderate extremes or lack of judgment in directions ordinarily approved by the group. His enthusiasm, however, is "recklessness"; his daring is "foolhardiness"; his bravery is "bravado." The rash fool is found in our society in the roles of the daredevil, the flagpole-sitter, the stunt flyer, and the youth with the "hot-rod" racer. He is found also in the prodigal or wastrel, the person given to ruinous extremes in life or business. Finally, the rash fool is seen in the leader who gets "too far ahead of his time."

Other fool types depart from group norms through a deficiency in person or conduct. The clumsy fool shows a lack of grace or proficiency in situations requiring expertness and decorum, e.g., one who slips or falls into an awkward posture on a public occasion. The person who hobbles, limps, or is physically awkward more easily acquires this role. The deformed fool deviates in appearance from group norms of beauty, stature, posture, health, etc. He may be ugly, dwarfed, crippled, gigantic, animal-like, or subhuman in appearance. Deformity has the symbolic capacity to suggest various inappropriate roles of the fool. Artificial distortions through make-up are used to suggest the deformities of the fool, as, for instance, the large feet and bulbous nose of the clown. Any person who departs markedly from group norms of appearance is easily cast in the role of the fool. On the other hand, a demonstration of deficiency of intelligence or wit places a person in the category of the simple fool. He is classed as naïve, senseless, backward, or rustic. Among the roles which create the simple fool are ludicrous failure, comic frustration, unintelligible behavior or utterances, and the quality of being easily taken advantage of. Another type of deficiency is found in the weak fool, the person lacking in aggressiveness, strength, or courage, e.g., the "sissy." Oversubmissive and overprotected personality types are caught in this appellation. So also is the person whose moral code, dress, background, etc., render him "too nice" for the world of practical affairs. The weak or oversubmissive fool, when his conduct becomes of serious consequence to the group, is called a coward, a type marginal to the villian or traitor.

The role of the comic butt is played particularly by deformed, weak, and simple fools. This may be defined as the regular recipience of group derision and abuse. The butt is persecuted because his appearance constantly draws derision or because he is too stupid, submissive, or cowardly to fight back. In appearance he may be bedraggled, drooping, forlorn, in patches, or he may present a picture of battered dignity, e.g., the comedy type of the hobo. As in the case of the comic-strip character, "Sad Sack," "everything happens to him." Despite his misfortunes, the comic butt is apparently indestructible. He survives blows, falls, and insults; and the onlookers laugh rather than pity.

Two fool roles are distinguished which involve pose or pretense to status. The great or pompous fool deviates from group standards through an excess of pride or presumption and a lack of competence. Persons of rank, age, or great size are particularly vulnerable to this role. They are deflated or "shown up" by revelation of pretense, defeat by a lesser rival, or a mistake, and thus made fools. Another pretender fool is found in the mock hero, a device commonly used in satirical literature. A mock hero is made by casting an ineffective person in the role or pose of the hero, e.g., by epithets applied to an ordinary person, such as "Crusader," "Sir Galahad," "Superman." Various devices reveal that the supposed hero is really a fool: he performs the gestures of the hero, but his weaknesses are apparent through his armor.

FOOL-MAKING SITUATIONS AND PROCESSES

As has been stated, certain collective processes and situations make fools. Fool-making situations are so constantly presented to the average person that he may be unable to avoid occasionally falling into the role. Life is a continual process of fool-making. Popular humor, derision, and belittlement are constantly assigning this role. Consequently, because fool-ascription is a status descent, social relations are continually rendered unstable by fool-making. These processes and situations are of interest to those desirous of stabilizing or controlling political structure, e.g., through leadership or propaganda.

Fool-making situations are presented in the various institutions of comedy. These may be defined as those conditions which render it most likely that a person will act or appear as a fool. The profession of the clown embodies the perfected art of making a fool of one's self or others for public entertainment. To become a fool, one's appearance or conduct must be distorted from expectation in the direction of types such as those described above. Among the important fool-making situations may be itemized the following: (1) involuntary or deliberate distortion of appearance or dress from group norms, e.g., by a mustache or monocle; (2) antic or indecorous behavior in situations requiring proficiency and decorum, e.g., horseplay or badly timed joke by a political candidate. Socrates was made a fool in Aristophanes' play, "The Clouds," by being lowered in a basket. The fool is also made by (3) absurd failures revealing weakness or frustration; (4) defeats by lesser rivals, e.g., being "shown up" in public debate; (5) unflattering comparisons with inferior persons, particularly with fools; (6) situations in which one is forced to make a bluff or to play an unfamiliar role, as, for instance, the youth who is trying to smoke like a man, the nouveau riche and his faux pas in "high society"; (7) lack of timing or insight, which causes one to play an inappropriate role, e.g., the "hero" who rushes on the stage too soon or too late; and (8) being made the butt of a joke which imputes any of the various roles of the fool.

Because fool-making is a collective imputation, it is not necessary, however, that a person actually have the traits or perform the role of a fool. A person is a fool when he is socially defined as a fool. All persons in public positions are exposed to popular humor. Among the social defining processes which assign the role of the fool are (1) jokes and popular humor, (2) name-calling, (3) literary and artistic satire, and (4) propaganda. No one, for instance, is so respected that no jokes or rumors will circulate about him. A ludicrous conception may be built up; the anecdote may become one of the imperishable stories which are part of his reputation. Nicknames are also applied to public personages which help to characterize them and give the public a greater sense of familiarity with them. These epithets are often based upon some outstanding feature of the personality in question; the slightest idiosyncrasy may make him liable to jokes and epithets which assign the role of the fool. Satire may also distort his character through caricature, parody, burlesque, irony, etc. Finally, propaganda may exploit these spontaneous defining processes.

Despite the universality of fool-making processes, it is obvious that all persons who become thus characterized do not remain fools, that fools are selected. What makes a fool role stick? Among the factors responsible for permanent characterization as a fool we may particularly note (1) repeated performances or obvious personal traits which continually suggest the role of the fool; (2) a striking, conclusive, or colorful single exhibition which convinces the public that the person is irremediably a fool; (3) a story or epithet so "good" that it is continually repeated and remembered, making up an imperishable legend; and (4) failure to contradict a fool role by roles or stories of a different category.

ESCAPE FROM THE FOOL ROLE

Instances may be found in which persons popularly defined as fools have escaped from this role by actions or stories which allowed them to be redefined in terms of more favored social types. In general, however, it may be said that the longer a person has been characterized as a fool, the harder it is for him to redeem himself. The strategy of escape is to do something which causes people to take one seriously: aggressive actions which cause one to be defined as a hero or exhibition of "human" traits which arouse sympathy.

Among the major routes of escape from the fool role are the following: (1) Avoidance of the imputation by "taking" a joke and "laughing it off" implies that there has been no injury, that the jibe is ineffectual or inapplicable. (2) A counter-joke or effective repartee "turns the tables" and makes the other a fool; "having the last word" or getting the best of a contest of wits has, in fact, the effect of defining the winner as a clever hero. (3) A similar strategy involves acceptance of the fool role and its use as a "ruse" or "trap" for a clever victory. This is embodied in the sage fool, the rustic wit, or pseudo-fool, who under a pose of simplicity hides unexpected sharpness. By defeating more pretentious opponents, he passes the fool role along. (4) Activity, aggressiveness, or "fight" may transform a fool into a hero, particularly when he picks a larger opponent or identifies himself with a social cause. By choice of a larger opponent there is a double chance of heroic status, since victory will make the person a "giant-killer," whereas defeat is no disgrace but may, on the contrary, cast him as a victim or martyr. (5) We must note also that the social pattern of the "Cinderella" operates as a powerful expectancy in American life, causing people to look hopefully at the "dark horse" or "underdog" for signs of a sudden rise to success. The person who is derided, clumsy, stupid, or made a fool, is a typical starting-point of the Cinderella theme. Any revelation of potentiality or unexpected merit may start this pattern of expectancy into operation. (6) Finally, by suffering or showing "human" traits which arouse sympathy, a person can escape from the fool role. Excessive persecution, e.g., "carrying a joke too far," tends to make a martyr out of the fool. Undue cruelty on the part of opponents, particularly if it is at the same time revealed that he has been injured, that he is human, has feelings, etc., will serve to evoke identification and shatter the definition of him as subhuman. Depiction of human traits by anecdotes of acts of kindness, showing his family life, etc., will perform the same function. If persecution occurs under conditions in which the fool can be identified with a popular cause, so that his sufferings are seen as sacrifices, conversion to the very powerful role of the martyr is possible.

STATUS AND FUNCTION OF THE FOOL

Whether professionalized as clown and jester or found in the butt of popular humor and village idiot, the position of the fool is distinctive. The various statuses of the fool include the household fool or court jester, the folk fool played by peasants, the folklore fool, the comic or dramatic fool, the professional clown or buffoon, and the village idiot. When established as part of social structure, the status of the fool has four characteristics. It is low, ridiculed, tolerated, and licensed. When not established as a formal status, it still persists as a social type or folklore conception in popular humor, particularly as comic butt and antic player of tricks. The status of the fool presents a paradox in that it is both depreciated and valued: It is at the same time despised and tolerated, ridiculed and enjoyed, degraded and privileged. Regarding the low status of the fool, we may note that he is at the nadir of the value system of the group. He is most lacking in honor and the recipient of all indignities. The fool might be defined functionally as a ridiculed status. Being made a fool is a type of disgrace. Ascription of the fool role to any status is a descent. The fool is lacking in rights and responsibilities; nothing serious is demanded of him; the bauble of the fool symbolizes his incompetence, and nobody wants to follow him. His sole privilege is his "license." Despite his low status, however, the role of the fool is valued and appreciated. He enjoys a certain importance and popularity; he may have fame. His pranks and jokes are to his reputation what exploits are to the hero. He is, therefore, not a "nobody." He is appreciated through collective representations of his role, e.g., drama, fame, and folklore. The fact that the role is thus institutionalized in comedy and perpetuated in folklore suggests that the fool has important social functions.

These social functions are to be found principally in certain contributions which the fool makes to group organization and discipline. Some of these may be noted: The fool upsets decorum by antics and eases routine by comic relief. He also acts as a cathartic symbol for aggressions in the form of wit. He takes liberties with rank; and as butt or scapegoat receives indignities which in real life would be mortal insult or conflict-creating. But chiefly the social type of the fool functions as a device of status reduction and social control. Reduction of persons through the fool role is a continuous collective process of status adjustment. Fool ascription acts as a purging device, eliminating upstarts, pretenders, and incompetents from positions of influence. The fool also enforces propriety in conduct and thus acts as a mechanism of social control. Everybody avoids the role of the fool. Fear of ridicule may be as strong as fear of punishment or death. Social satire may be an effective control on political figures otherwise difficult to criticize. Group discipline is thus enhanced by the operation of ridicule as a sanction—as Bergson pointed out in his essay on laughter (1911)— the fool symbol functioning for propriety in a manner similar to that of the villain in the area of mores. Finally, the type of the fool functions in education, providing a negative example in literature and folklore, e.g., as an object-lesson for children in stories of Simple Simon, Humpty-Dumpty, etc. Thus the fool defines certain varieties of untrustworthy conduct. It operates as an avoidance symbol, discrediting leaders, movements, or individuals which show weaknesses in terms of group norms.

❧❧❧❧

CHAPTER IV

SOCIAL ORGANIZATION: INTERPERSONAL RELATIONS AND UNIFORMITIES OF BEHAVIOR

23. Group Description *

ONE OF THE BASIC CONCEPTS in sociology is that of the group. The elements involved in a comprehensive description of any single type of group are set forth in this cogent article by Dwight Sanderson. After setting up the characteristics that distinguish various groups, he singles out a Boy Scout troop as a simple type of voluntary group to which he applies his analysis of group structure. The student could well profit from applying this extensive and thorough outline in the analysis of some types of groups with which he is familiar.

AN ADEQUATE DESCRIPTION of a group seems to involve five major sets of characters. (1) Identity—what limits it or sets it apart from other groups; (2) Composition—the individuals composing the group; (3) Inter-group relations whether the group is independent or is controlled from without; (4) Intra-group relations—forms of interaction between members; and (5) Structure and Mechanism—the established procedures and division of labor for performing specific functions. These characteristics are presented in more detail in the following outline for

* Dwight Sanderson, Social Forces, 16, No. 3 (March, 1938), 309-319. Reprinted by permission of the publisher.
The author (1878-1944) was an entomologist and sociologist. Was a specialist in rural community organization and economic entomology. Among his books are *Insects Injurious to Staple Crops, The Farmer and His Community, Leadership for Rural Life, Rural Sociology* and *Rural Social Organization.*

the description of groups, the items of which will then be briefly explained.

OUTLINE FOR THE DESCRIPTION OF GROUPS

I. *Identity*
    1. Group limits
        a. Exclusive; as by age, locality, sex, social status.
        b. Restricted; as when members must subscribe to certain conditions.
        c. Inclusive; open to all.
    2. Entrance and exit; voluntary, involuntary, by election.
    3. Identification of members; how recognized as by name, garb or insignia.

II. *Composition*
    1. Size or number of elements, i.e. persons or units; kinds of elements.
    2. Homogeneity or diversity of membership; degree of common membership in other groups; social distance.
    3. Stratification or uniformation; classes, social distinction.
    4. Permanent or shifting membership; stability or instability.

III. *Inter-group Relationships*
    1. Independent and autonomous.
    2. Federated, semi-autonomous.
    3. Chartered—controlled.
    4. Degree of dominance.

IV. *Intra-group Relationships*
    1. Forms of interaction between members.
        a. Personal or impersonal, representative, fiduciary.
        b. Contacts—frequency and character of.
        c. Participation—forms and degree of.
        d. Quality or type of participation—competitive, cooperative, domestic, fraternal, etc.
        e. Solidarity—degree of awareness.
        f. Group control of behavior of members—degree of primary loyalty.
        g. Group folkways and mores.
        h. Language peculiarities.
        i. Place of role of certain individuals.
    2. Spatial Relationships
        a. Area covered.
        b. Density or dispersity of group.
        c. Place of meeting.
    3. Temporal Relationships.
        a. Temporary, continuous or seasonal group.
        b. History and traditions.

V *Structure and Mechanism*
1. Leader, type and origin (how selected and if from group).
2. Sub-groups, committees.
3. Stated aim and purpose, with or without; unity or diversity, broad or specialized.
4. Code of behavior for members, definite or lacking.
5. Means of consensus; meetings, discussions, journal, parliamentary procedure, etc.
6. Means of developing and maintaining morale.
7. Extent of institutionalization—ritual, ceremonial, insignia, custom, initiation.
8. Mechanisms for group maintenance or preservation.
   a. Through history and traditions—records, histories.
   b. Through means for homogeneity—party whip, tithing man, committees to secure acquaintance and participation.
   c. For preventing aggression—price agreements, strikes, lock-outs, funds, alliances.
   d. For preventing crises—vice-president, constitutions, parliamentary procedure, reserve funds.
   e. For securing adaptation, or revision of organization—inventory, surveys, conventions, special committees.
   f. For secrecy or privacy—oath, password, grip, etc.
9. Physical basis or essential physical equipment—farm family, employees association.

The significance of these categories for the description of groups will be more apparent with a brief explanation of each.

I. IDENTITY

What is it that delimits a group, that gives it a sort of boundary, or sets it off from those who do not belong?

1. *Groups may or may not have prescribed limitations to membership.* Thus some are (a) *exclusive*, such as fraternities, social clubs, organizations of stockholders; others are (b) *restricted*, that is open to all who will conform to certain conditions, as subscribing to a creed to enter a church, or being a college alumna to join the Association of University Women; while some (c) are *inclusive*, or open to all, as a political party, parent-teacher associations, most civic organizations.

2. *Entrance and exit.* One enters a club voluntarily, but he is a member of a family or of a community involuntarily. To some groups he must be elected, while others may be joined without the knowledge of the members.

3. *Identification of members.* A member of a family is recognized

by his name; a member of a religious order, the army, or a police department, by his garb; and members of many fraternal orders and fraternities are known by their insignia, pins, keys, or fobs.

II. COMPOSITION

1. *Size and elements.* The number of persons in a group. Some are limited, such as families, fraternities, card clubs, while others desire as large a membership as possible. Some groups are composed of individual persons, while others are composed of individuals who are representatives of their groups.

2. *Homogeneity.* Some groups are confined to one sex, age, or nationality, while others include all types of people. A social club will probably have little social distance between its members, but social distance between the membership may be a limiting factor of a parent-teacher association.

3. *Stratification.* Certain groups very definitely recognize differences of social strata, as in the army between privates and officers, or between freshmen and seniors in a college. Others seek to make stratification impossible, as in a veteran's organization, or a political club.

4. *Permanency.* Some groups, such as the church, have a relatively stable membership; some groups are specially for a certain age or period, as Boy Scouts and the college class; while in some loosely organized groups the membership is short-lived.

III. INTER-GROUP RELATIONSHIPS

A social club is an entirely independent antonomous group. Groups which become federated with others lose some of their independence through the effect of the opinion of the larger group, even though they profess their autonomy. Groups which receive their charters from a higher authority, such as fraternities and fraternal orders, certain churches, and trade unions, thereby limit the form and behavior of the local group to certain prescribed standards.

IV. INTRA-GROUP RELATIONSHIPS

1. *The forms of interaction between members.* (a) The nature of the relationship may be personal as in a family or social club, or impersonal as in a business corporation; it may be representative, as in a legislative body or in many councils or federations; or it may be fiduciary as in the board of directors of a building and loan association or the trustees of a church.

(b) Contacts of members of a group range from the hourly association of members of the family, to weekly or monthly meetings of many groups, and annual sessions of national organizations. The nature of these contacts ranges from those which involve all members of the group, as in the family, to those which include only a limited portion of the membership.

(c) Participation in the group varies from that which is universal and intimate, as in a family, fraternity, religious order, or military company in war, to the type of passive participation involved in paying annual dues and having practically no active part in the work of the group, as is common in so-called welfare organizations.

(d) The quality of participation is equally varied, from the domestic attitudes of the family, to the competitive attitudes of a bridge club. The neighborhood is characterized by neighborliness, the fraternity by brotherhood, the cooperative association by cooperation, and so on.

(e) The solidarity of groups, or the degree of awareness which each member has of the group and his loyalty to it, may be almost nil, as in a national learned society, or at a maximum as in a gang or a family feud.

(f) Some groups have almost absolute control of the behavior of their members, as in a religious order or in the army; some control their behavior only on matters affecting the special interests of the group, as in a cooperative marketing association; while some have practically no control over behavior outside of the meetings of the group, as would be the case with many special interest groups, such as a philatelic club, or a social club.

(g) Many groups have folkways or mores peculiar to them. Members of the Grange and some fraternal orders call each other "brother" or "sister"; some churches seat the women on one side and the men on the other; every family has its own folkways and mores; freshmen in college must wear caps; games of chance are prohibited in some churches and exploited by others.

(h) Certain groups have language peculiarities, most obvious in groups of foreign nationality, but also in evidence in the "thee" and "thou" of the Quakers.

(i) The roles of individuals characterize or are peculiar to certain groups, notably in the formation of a football team, in an orchestra, a band or a quartette, and in the husband and wife relation in the family.

2. *Most groups have definite spatial relationships.* (a) The area covered by the group may be as small as a neighborhood, or as large as a state or nation. (b) Density and dispersity will vary according to the area covered. (c) Many groups own buildings which are the homes of such groups as churches, lodges, fraternities, etc.

3. *Temporal relationships.* Some groups are but temporary and plan to dissolve upon the accomplishment of certain purposes, such as a campaign committee. Others are of relatively short duration, as the college class. Some groups are seasonal, as baseball and football and skiing clubs. Most groups are presumably continuous, although the mortality is high and many become quiescent and then revive. Whether the group has a long and well preserved history and established traditions, is a considerable factor in determining the behavior of the present group.

V. STRUCTURE AND MECHANISM

Every group has certain established means of carrying on its life by the assignment of a division of labor to its members and by certain accepted means of procedure, which form its structure and involve definite mechanisms. One of the most common of these group mechanisms is the leader.

(a) Does a group have a recognized leader, is he employed or voluntary, is he elected or does he obtain his position by his own efforts?— these are the questions which reveal the leadership characteristics of different sorts of groups.

(b) Some groups have recognized subgroups. Thus a Scout group is composed of patrols, and a Sunday school of classes; churches have various auxiliary groups; and the work of many organizations is largely handled by committees.

(c) Some groups have stated aims or purposes which dominate their existence, as a reform group or political party. Other groups entirely lack any avowed aim. Parent-teacher associations have rather definite aims, but largely confined to matters of education, whereas the aims of the Grange are very broad and diverse.

(d) If a group has a definite code of behavior for its members, it is a mechanism for group control. The Discipline of the Methodist Episcopal church is such a code, as is that of a religious order, or the regulations of the army.

(e) Groups which do not have frequent contacts must have means of arriving at consensus of opinion so that they may be able to act collectively. For this purpose meetings are held, at which discussions take place; a record is kept of the procedure so that the actions may be consistent and cumulative; parliamentary procedure is used to ensure fairness in discussion and voting. These are but mechanisms for group procedure.

(f) Means of developing and maintaining morale. Journals or group publications; letters to members; person in charge of newspaper publicity; banquets; reunions; special events.

(g) Old groups which have become highly institutionalized often develop a very elaborate system of ritual and ceremonial, with the use of insignia and symbols, as in certain churches, in Masonic orders, in European universities. The degree to which a group is dominated by such usages or by custom or tradition, as over against an entire informality of procedure, is a difference in group structure.

(h) Certain mechanisms of groups are chiefly for the maintenance or preservation of the life of the group, and are sufficiently indicated under the subheads in the outline above. Certain of these mechanisms are characteristic of some groups and are entirely lacking in others.

(i) Physical basis or essential physical equipment. In the case of certain groups the physical conditions associated with them are essential for understanding them. Thus the farm family cannot be adequately described except as associated with its work on the farm, and a factory group of employees has its existence because of their relation in and to the factory. Likewise the physical equipment of certain groups is essential for their existence and they cannot be conceived without it, as yachts for a yacht club or a golf course for a golf club. Such essential physical equipment would seem to be a part of the group structure.

Not all of the points in the outline will apply to any given group, and only those points which are characteristic of the group should be used in its description. It should be noted that we are considering the description of kinds of groups generically rather than of individual groups. We are concerned with the characteristics of a Grange, any Grange, which distinguish it from a Masonic lodge or a farm bureau. It is true that the same scheme may be used for the description of an individual group and that without the description of many individual groups it will be impossible to draw up a valid generic description of the kind of group.

The method of group description suggested will be better understood by the consideration of a concrete example in which a simple type of voluntary group is briefly described by use of the categories in the outline.

DESCRIPTION OF THE BOY SCOUT TROOP

A scout troop is exclusively for males 12 years of age and over. Entrance and exit are voluntary, although sometimes entrance is by election. Members may be identified by their uniforms and badges when they are on scout duty. The troop is limited to 32 scouts, composing four patrols, a scoutmaster (21 years or more), and one to four assistant scoutmasters. Homogeneity is rather high in the membership of a successful troop and there is no stratification except that arising from the different classes of scouts according to their attainments. The troop is chartered by the national organization, but otherwise is practically autonomous. Most troops belong to a local council the area of whose jurisdiction varies; it may include a city, a county or two or three counties. Troops compete with each other at council meets. Membership shifts from year to year as boys drop out at 15 or 16.

Relations within the group are personal and have to do with general interests of a more or less recreational nature. Contacts occur at weekly meetings, at sporadic hikes, lasting either for an afternoon or for a weekend, and at summer camps lasting from one to two weeks. Participation is required to the extent of paying national and local dues and attending meetings. Attendance at hikes and camp is optional. Much of the participation consists of working for merit badges. Solidarity is quite pronounced in successful troops. The quality of participation inculcated is that embodied in the scout laws. Competition exists between patrols, but cooperation occurs within the patrol and within the troop as a whole at inter-troop council meets. The troop exercises no specific control over the behavior of members outside of its meetings, but it exercises considerable influence in attempting to maintain high standards of conduct. The area covered by a troop is usually no greater than that within which members can easily walk or ride on a bicycle to the meeting place. Troops have no spatial jurisdiction; there may be more than one in the same territory. Meetings are usually held in a room at a church, school, or hall, furnished by the sponsoring organization. Most troops last for a number of years, but little is made of their history or tradition.

A troop committee, appointed by the sponsoring organization, finds and appoints the scoutmaster, who is an unpaid leader. Under the scoutmaster are from one to four assistant scoutmasters, and often an older member of the troop is appointed or elected senior patrol leader. Each of the four patrols has a patrol leader and assistant patrol leader. These get their rank by seniority, election, or appointment, as the scoutmaster may decide. The scout oath and twelve scout laws form a code of behavior. Consensus is obtained by meetings and informal discussion. Members are admitted by a formal initiation; the weekly meeting has some form of opening ceremony and the occasions of awarding merit ranks have a definite ritual and insignia.

This is but an outline description and would require considerable elaboration to give one a correct idea of the Boy Scout troop, but it illustrates the manner in which group characteristics may be described.

The above outline attempts a scheme for the description of group structure. Such a description would enable us to be certain of the identity of a group type and to know its gross anatomy. It does not, however, describe the life of the group. Just as the zoologist must describe not only the structure of an animal, but also its physiology and habits, so the sociologist must describe the characteristic behavior of the group. Two types of behavior characteristic of any type of group may be distinguished: that which occurs within the group, as the worship of a church, the sociability of a card club, or community events in a community; and that which involves the behavior of the group towards other groups, individuals, or objects in its environment, such as the opposition of political parties, the competition of football teams, or the sponsoring of scout troops or welfare organizations by churches. Obviously the behavior of individual groups will vary widely, but whatever behavior patterns are characteristic of each type of group should be adequately described if we are to understand its life; for function is as important as structure. The complete description of a group must include both its structure and its functions—its functions for its own members and its functions in society. For groups performing similar general functions may have widely different structures. Thus a recreation group or a scout troop may be organized democratically or it may be "run" by an adult leader. Religion may be organized with the simplicity of the Quaker meeting with no paid leader or with the complexity of the Catholic church in which the local church revolves around the priest who receives his prerogatives from the episcopal hierarchy. The functions of the groups, in that they are the means of religious worship, are similar, but the structure is radically different. On the other hand structure may be similar with very different functions. All sorts of clubs have a very similar structure, at least in their form of organization and superficial aspects, but their functions in terms of interests satisfied range from philately to astronomy, and from athletics to Browning. Or as Hoxie has pointed out in his functional analysis of trade unions, those with seemingly similar structure may be ordinary "business" unions or they may be "predatory" unions. The discovery of the categories which will encompass the various characteristic forms of group behavior and their logical arrangement, is a task which must be undertaken before we can have a complete outline for group description.

Finally, it may be questioned as to just what is the practical use of such descriptions of types of groups, were they ideally completed. The most important results undoubtedly cannot be foreseen any more than can those of careful description in any other field of science. Does the chemist ask what use will be made of the discovery of a new element? One very tangible result, which we have already found from the descriptions of groups so far attempted, is that such an exact description reveals the paucity of our knowledge of groups and opens up many problems and lines of research which are essential before we can adequately describe any given group. Another result, already indicated, is that we shall cease to obscure our understanding by including different kinds of groups under one common sense name. As in other sciences, the purpose of description and classification is not mere taxonomy, but to bring out differences of structure associated with differences of behavior which will enable us to better understand the behavior and to be able to predict what it will be under given conditions.

❧❧❧

24. The Social "World" of the Transients' Camp *

THE TALENTED WRITER OF FICTION sometimes presents social reality in a clear and vivid fashion, and more palatably than the prosaic social scientist. The Grapes of Wrath, Steinbeck's classic novel of the migrant farm family, "tractored out" of Oklahoma and hopeful of a better life in California, contains many such insights into social reality. The selection from that book given here shows how quickly human relationships develop regularities, become "organized," even in so transitory a situation as the overnight camp of the westward-moving migrant farm families.

THE CARS OF THE MIGRANT PEOPLE crawled out of the side roads onto the great cross-country highway, and they took the migrant way to the West. In the daylight they scuttled like bugs to the westward; and as the dark caught them, they clustered like bugs near to shelter and to water. And because they were lonely and perplexed, because they had all come from a place of sadness and worry and defeat, and because they were all going to a new mysterious place, they huddled together; they talked together; they shared their lives, their food, and the things they hoped for in the new country. Thus it might be that one

* John Steinbeck, The Grapes of Wrath, pp. 264-269. Copyright 1939 by John Steinbeck. Reprinted by permission of The Viking Press, Inc., New York.

The author (b. 1902) is an American novelist. Author, Tortilla Flat, Of Mice and Men, The Moon is Down, Russian Journal. Awarded Pulitzer Prize, 1940.

family camped near a spring, and another camped for the spring and for company, and a third because two families had pioneered the place and found it good. And when the sun went down, perhaps twenty families and twenty cars were there.

In the evening a strange thing happened: the twenty families became one family, the children were the children of all. The loss of home became one loss, and the golden time in the West was one dream. And it might be that a sick child threw despair into the hearts of twenty families, of a hundred people; that a birth there in a tent kept a hundred people quiet and awestruck through the night and filled a hundred people with the birth-joy in the morning. A family which the night before had been lost and fearful might search its goods to find a present for a new baby. In the evening, sitting about the fires, the twenty were one. They grew to be units of the camps, units of the evenings and the nights. A guitar unwrapped from a blanket and tuned—and the songs, which were all of the people, were sung in the nights. Men sang the words, and women hummed the tunes.

Every night a world created, complete with furniture—friends made and enemies established; a world complete with braggarts and with cowards, with quiet men, with humble men, with kindly men. Every night relationships that make a world, established; and every morning the world torn down like a circus.

At first the families were timid in the building and tumbling worlds, but gradually the technique of building worlds became their technique. Then leaders emerged, then laws were made, then codes came into being. And as the worlds moved westward they were more complete and better furnished, for their builders were more experienced in building them.

The families learned what rights must be observed—the right of privacy in the tent; the right to keep the past black hidden in the heart; the right to talk and to listen; the right to refuse help or to accept, to offer help or to decline it; the right of son to court and daughter to be courted; the right of the hungry to be fed; the rights of the pregnant and the sick to transcend all other rights.

And the families learned, although no one told them, what rights are monstrous and must be destroyed: the right to intrude upon privacy, the right to be noisy while the camp slept, the right of seduction or rape, the right of adultery and theft and murder. These rights were crushed, because the little worlds could not exist for even a night with such rights alive.

And as the worlds moved westward, rules became laws, although no one told the families. It is unlawful to foul near the camp; it is unlawful in any way to foul the drinking water; it is unlawful to eat good rich food near one who is hungry, unless he is asked to share.

And with the laws, the punishments—and there were only two—a quick and murderous fight or ostracism; and ostracism was the worst. For if one broke the laws his name and face went with him, and he had no place in any world, no matter where created.

In the worlds, social conduct became fixed and rigid, so that a man must say "Good morning" when asked for it, so that a man might have a willing girl if he stayed with her, if he fathered her children and protected them. But a man might not have one girl one night and another the next, for this would endanger the worlds.

The families moved westward, and the technique of building the worlds improved so that the people could be safe in their worlds; and the form was so fixed that a family acting in the rules knew it was safe in the rules.

There grew up government in the worlds, with leaders, with elders. A man who was wise found that his wisdom was needed in every camp; a man who was a fool could not change his folly with his world. And a kind of insurance developed in these nights. A man with food fed a hungry man, and thus insured himself against hunger. And when a baby died a pile of silver coins grew at the door flap, for a baby must be well buried, since it has had nothing else of life. An old man may be left in a potter's field, but not a baby.

A certain physical pattern is needed for the building of a world— water, a river bank, a stream, a spring, or even a faucet unguarded. And there is needed enough flat land to pitch the tents, a little brush or wood to build the fires. If there is a garbage dump not too far off, all the better; for there can be found equipment—stove tops, a curved fender to shelter the fire, and cans to cook in and to eat from.

And the worlds were built in the evening. The people, moving in from the highways, made them with their tents and their hearts and their brains.

In the morning the tents came down, the canvas was folded, the tent poles tied along the running board, the beds put in place on the cars, the pots in their places. And as the families moved westward, the technique of building up a home in the evening and tearing it down with the morning light became fixed; so that the folded tent was packed in one place, the cooking pots counted in their box. And as the cars moved westward, each member of the family grew into his proper place, grew into his duties; so that each member, old and young, had his place in the car; so that in the weary, hot evenings, when the cars pulled into the camping places, each member had his duty and went to it without instruction: children to gather wood, to carry water; men to pitch the tents and bring down the beds; women to cook the supper and to watch while the family fed. And this was done without command. The families, which had been units of which the boundaries were a house at night, a farm by day, changed their boundaries. In the long hot light, they were silent in the cars moving slowly westward; but at night they integrated with any group they found.

Thus they changed their social life—changed as in the whole universe only man can change. They were not farm men any more, but migrant men. And the thought, the planning, the long staring silence that had gone out to the fields, went now to the roads, to the distance, to the West. That man whose mind had been bound with acres lived with narrow concrete miles. And his thought and his worry were not any more with rainfall, with wind and dust, with the thrust of the crops. Eyes watched the tires, ears listened to the clattering motors, and minds struggled with oil, with gasoline, with the thinning rubber between air and road. Then a broken gear was tragedy. Then water in the evening was the yearning, and food over the fire. Then health to go on was the need and strength to go on, and spirit to go on. The wills thrust westward ahead of them, and fears that had once apprehended drought or flood now lingered with anything that might stop the westward crawling.

The camps became fixed—each a short day's journey from the last.

And on the road the panic overcame some of the families, so that they drove night and day, stopped to sleep in the cars, and drove on to the West, flying from the road, flying from movement. And these lusted so greatly to be settled that they set their faces into the West and drove toward it, forcing the clashing engines over the roads.

But most of the families changed and grew quickly into the new life. And when the sun went down——

Time to look out for a place to stop.

And—there's some tents ahead.

The car pulled off the road and stopped, and because others were there first, certain courtesies were necessary. And the man, the leader of the family, leaned from the car.

Can we pull up here an' sleep?

Why, sure, be proud to have you. What State you from?

Come all the way from Arkansas.

They's Arkansas people down that fourth tent.

That so?

And the great question, How's the water?

Well, she don't taste so good, but they's plenty.

Well, thank ya.

No thanks to me.

But the courtesies had to be. The car lumbered over the ground to the end tent, and stopped. Then down from the car the weary people climbed, and stretched stiff bodies. Then the new tent sprang up; the children went for water and the older boys cut brush or wood. The fires started and supper was put on to boil or to fry. Early comers moved over, and States were exchanged, and friends and sometimes relatives discovered.

Oklahoma, huh? What county?

Cherokee.

Why, I got folks there. Know the Allens? They's Allens all over Cherokee. Know the Willises?

Why, sure.

And a new unit was formed. The dusk came, but before the dark was down the new family was of the camp. A word had been passed with every family. They were known people—good people.

ᴥᴥᴥᴥ

25. *Primary Groups* *

Professor Cooley, the author of this selection, is recognized as a pioneer in the field of social psychology. One of his very fruitful contributions to sociology is the concept of primary groups as the "nursery of human nature." Here he explains the universality of primary groups and contrasts their characteristics with what we now designate as secondary groups. He carefully defines "human nature," which he declares to be fundamentally the same the world over. Although more recent psychological discoveries have revealed certain errors in his analysis, such as his statement in this selection about differences in racial capacities, in most essentials his thinking is sound and illuminating. Since 1909, when the book in which this selection appears was published, much progress has been made in

* Charles Horton Cooley. Reprinted from *Social Organization*, pp. 23-31; copyright 1909 by Charles Scribner's Sons, 1937 by Elsie Jones Cooley; used by permission of the publishers.

The author (1864-1929), an American social philosopher, was Professor of Sociology, University of Michigan, at the time of his death. Made contributions of great range and depth to the field of sociology. His important works include developing the scientific research methods of both psychology and sociology; but many of Cooley's ideas, of which the primary group concept is one, have a timeless quality.

BY PRIMARY GROUPS I mean those characterized by intimate face-to-face association and coöperation. They are primary in several senses, but chiefly in that they are fundamental in forming the social nature and ideals of the individual. The result of intimate association, psychologically, is a certain fusion of individualities in a common whole, so that one's very self, for many purposes at least, is the common life and purpose of the group. Perhaps the simplest way of describing this wholeness is by saying that it is a "we"; it involves the sort of sympathy and mutual identification for which "we" is the natural expression. One lives in the feeling of the whole and finds the chief aims of his will in that feeling.

It is not to be supposed that the unity of the primary group is one of mere harmony and love. It is always a differentiated and usually a competitive unity, admitting of self-assertion and various appropriative passions; but these passions are socialized by sympathy, and come, or tend to come, under the discipline of a common spirit. The individual will be ambitious, but the chief object of his ambition will be some desired place in the thought of the others, and he will feel allegiance to common standards of service and fair play. So the boy will dispute with his fellows a place on the team, but above such disputes will place the common glory of his class and school.

The most important spheres of this intimate association and coöperation—though by no means the only ones—are the family, the play-group of children, and the neighborhood or community group of elders. These are practically universal, belonging to all times and all stages of development; and are accordingly a chief basis of what is universal in human nature and human ideals. The best comparative studies of the family, such as those of Westermarck or Howard, show it to us as not only a universal institution, but as more alike the world over than the exaggeration of exceptional customs by an earlier school had led us to suppose. Nor can any one doubt the general prevalence of play-groups among children or of informal assemblies of various kinds among their elders. Such association is clearly the nursery of human nature in the world about us, and there is no apparent reason to suppose that the case has anywhere or at any time been essentially different.

Personal Competition, Human Nature and the Social Order, Social Organization, Social Process, Life and the Student, Sociological Theory and Social Research.

As regards play, I might, were it not a matter of common observation, multiply illustrations of the universality and spontaneity of the group discussion and coöperation to which it gives rise. The general fact is that children, especially boys after about their twelfth year, live in fellowships in which their sympathy, ambition and honor are engaged even more, often, than they are in the family. Most of us can recall examples of the endurance by boys of injustice and even cruelty, rather than appeal from their fellows to parents or teachers—as, for instance, in the hazing so prevalent at schools, and so difficult, for this very reason, to repress. And how elaborate the discussion, how cogent the public opinion, how hot the ambitions in these fellowships.

Nor is this facility of juvenile association, as is sometimes supposed, a trait peculiar to English and American boys; since experience among our immigrant population seems to show that the offspring of the more restrictive civilizations of the continent of Europe form self-governing play-groups with almost equal readiness. Thus Miss Jane Addams, after pointing out that the "gang" is almost universal, speaks of the interminable discussion which every detail of the gang's activity receives, remarking that "in these social folk-motes, so to speak, the young citizen learns to act upon his own determination."

Of the neighborhood group it may be said, in general, that from the time men formed permanent settlements upon the land, down, at least, to the rise of modern industrial cities, it has played a main part in the primary, heart-to-heart life of the people. Among our Teutonic forefathers the village community was apparently the chief sphere of sympathy and mutual aid for the commons all through the "dark" and middle ages, and for many purposes it remains so in rural districts at the present day. In some countries we still find it with all its ancient vitality, notably in Russia, where the mir, or self-governing village group, is the main theatre of life, along with the family, for perhaps fifty millions of peasants.

In our own life the intimacy of the neighborhood has been broken up by the growth of an intricate mesh of wider contacts which leaves us strangers to people who live in the same house. And even in the country the same principle is at work, though less obviously, diminishing our economic and spiritual community with our neighbors. How far this change is a healthy development, and how far a disease, is perhaps still uncertain.

Besides these almost universal kinds of primary association, there are many others whose form depends upon the particular state of civilization; the only essential thing, as I have said, being a certain intimacy and fusion of personalities. In our own society, being little bound by place, people easily form clubs, fraternal societies and the like, based on congeniality, which may give rise to real intimacy. Many such relations are formed at school and college, and among men and women brought together in the first instance by their occupations—as workmen in the same trade, or the like. Where there is a little common interest and activity, kindness grows like weeds by the roadside.

But the fact that the family and neighborhood groups are ascendant in the open and plastic time of childhood makes them even now incomparably more influential than all the rest.

Primary groups are primary in the sense that they give the individual his earliest and completest experience of social unity, and also in the sense that they do not change in the same degree as more elaborate relations, but form a comparatively permanent source out of which the latter are ever springing. Of course they are not independent of the larger society, but to some extent reflect its spirit; as the German family and the German school bear somewhat distinctly the print of German militarism. But this, after all, is like the tide setting back into creeks, and does not commonly go very far. Among the German, and still more among the Russian, peasantry are found habits of free coöperation and discussion almost uninfluenced by the character of the state; and it is a familiar and well-supported view that the village commune, self-governing as regards local affairs and habituated to discussion, is a very widespread institution in settled communities, and the continuator of a similar autonomy previously existing in the clan. "It is man who makes monarchies and establishes republics, but the commune seems to come directly from the hand of God."

In our own cities the crowded tenements and the general economic and social confusion have sorely wounded the family and the neighborhood, but it is remarkable, in view of these conditions, what vitality they show; and there is nothing upon which the conscience of the time is more determined than upon restoring them to health.

These groups, then, are springs of life, not only for the individual but for social institutions. They are only in part moulded by special traditions, and, in larger degree, express a universal nature. The religion or government of other civilizations may seem alien to us, but the children or the family group wear the common life, and with them we can always make ourselves at home.

By human nature, I suppose, we may understand those sentiments and impulses that are human in being superior to those of lower animals, and also in the sense that they belong to mankind at large, and not to any particular race or time. It means, particularly, sympathy and the innumerable sentiments into which sympathy enters, such as love, resentment, ambition, vanity, hero-worship, and the feeling of social right and wrong.

Human nature in this sense is justly regarded as a comparatively permanent element in society. Always and everywhere men seek honor and dread ridicule, defer to public opinion, cherish their goods and their children, and admire courage, generosity, and success. It is always safe to assume that people are and have been human.

It is true, no doubt, that there are differences of race capacity, so great that a large part of mankind are possibly incapable of any high kind of social organization. But these differences, like those among individuals of the same race, are subtle, depending upon some obscure intellectual deficiency, some want of vigor, or slackness of moral fibre, and do not involve unlikeness in the generic impulses of human nature. In these all races are very much alike. The more insight one gets into the life of savages, even those that are reckoned the lowest, the more human, the more like ourselves, they appear. Take for instance the natives of Central Australia, as described by Spencer and Gillen, tribes having no definite government or worship and scarcely able to count to five. They are generous to one another, emulous of virtue as they understand it, kind to their children and to the aged, and by no means harsh to women. Their faces as shown in the photographs are wholly human and many of them attractive.

And when we come to a comparison between different stages in the development of the same race, between ourselves, for instance, and the Teutonic tribes of the time of Cæsar, the difference is neither in human nature nor in capacity, but in organization, in the range and complexity of relations, in the diverse expression of powers and passions essentially much the same.

There is no better proof of this generic likeness of human nature than in the ease and joy with which the modern man makes himself at home in literature depicting the most remote and varied phases of life—in Homer, in the Nibelung tales, in the Hebrew Scriptures, in the legends of the American Indians, in stories of frontier life, of soldiers and sailors, of criminals and tramps, and so on. The more penetratingly any phase of human life is studied the more an essential likeness to ourselves is revealed.

To return to primary groups: the view here maintained is that human nature is not something existing separately in the individual, but a group-nature or primary phase of society, a relatively simple and general condition of the social mind. It is something more, on the one hand, than the mere instinct that is born in us—though that enters into it—and something less, on the other, than the more elaborate development of ideas and sentiments that makes up institutions. It is the nature which is developed and expressed in those simple, face-to-face groups that are somewhat alike in all societies; groups of the family, the playground, and the neighborhood. In the essential similarity of these is to be found the basis, in experience, for similar ideas and sentiments in the human mind. In these, everywhere, human nature comes into existence. Man does not have it at birth; he cannot acquire it except through fellowship, and it decays in isolation.

If this view does not recommend itself to common-sense I do not know that elaboration will be of much avail. It simply means the application at this point of the idea that society and individuals are inseparable phases of a common whole, so that wherever we find an individual fact we may look for a social fact to go with it. If there is a universal nature in persons there must be something universal in association to correspond to it.

What else can human nature be than a trait of primary groups? Surely not an attribute of the separate individual—supposing there were any such thing—since its typical characteristics, such as affection, ambition, vanity, and resentment, are inconceivable apart from society. If it belongs, then, to man in association, what kind or degree of association is required to develop it? Evidently nothing elaborate, because elaborate phases of society are transient and diverse, while human nature is comparatively stable and universal. In short the family and neighborhood life is essential to its genesis and nothing more is.

Here as everywhere in the study of society we must learn to see mankind in psychical wholes, rather than in artificial separation. We must see and feel the communal life of family and local groups as immediate facts, not as combinations of something else. And perhaps we shall do this best by recalling our own experience and extending it through sympathetic observation. What, in our life, is the family and the fellowship; what do we know of the we-feeling? Thought of this kind may help us to get a concrete perception of that primary group-nature of which everything social is the outgrowth.

❧❧❧

26. The Primary Group and the Definition of the Situation *

Cooley's original concept of the "primary group" was presented in the previous selection (25). An equally significant concept in American sociology is the "definition of the situation." In this selection W. I. Thomas presents his original formulation of this concept and discusses it in relation to the "primary group." Both concepts concern the relationship between the person and the group, but the "definition of the situation" points out the significance of the person's image of the social situation in which he behaves. Although its original meaning has been refined in the light of more recent knowledge, the "definition of the situation" remains an essential concept in sociological analysis.

. . . The great common desire of a human society is . . . to remain solidary, and it accomplishes this by the formation of a code of behavior. In a society, the same act is good or bad, organizing or disorganizing, according to its meaning for the welfare of the whole group. Thus, the desire for mastery may express itself in furious and sadistic rage and murder and pillage, and is immoral, disorganizing and criminal when directed against the members of one's own society, but becomes courage, patriotism, heroism and virtue when turned against outsiders, in the protection of women and children, of the state.

The code therefore represents the judgment of society on the activities of its members, it dictates the limits within which the desires may find expression, and it is developed by a method which we may call "the definition of the situation." This defining of the situation is begun by the parents in the form of ordering and forbidding and information, is continued in the community by means of gossip, with its praise and blame, and is formally represented by the school, the law, the church. Of course morality and immorality, organization and disorganization are relative terms; what would be considered disorganization in one society would not be considered so in another—it is perfectly good organization to kill your parents in Africa because they wish to reach the

* W. I. Thomas in *Social Behavior and Personality*, ed. by Edmund H. Volkart (New York: Social Science Research Council, 1951), pp. 226-231. Reprinted by permission of the publisher.
The author (1863-1947) was an American sociologist. Known especially for his work with F. Znaniecki, *The Polish Peasant in Europe and America* (5 vols.). Other important books are *Source Book for Social Origins*, *Sex and Society*, *The Child in America* (with D. S. Thomas).

next world while still young enough to enjoy it—and so the code will
differ widely in different communal, national and racial groups, but will
usually define truthfulness, honesty, obedience, cleanliness, unselfishness, kindliness, industry, economy, politeness, courage, chastity, the
ten commandments, the golden rule, "women and children first," respect to the aged, etc., in terms of positive appreciation.

Moreover, when the code has been defined, no matter what its content, its violation provokes an emotional protest from society designed
to be painfully felt by the offender, and it is so felt, owing to the dependence of the member on society for safety and recognition.   The
epithets, "coward," "traitor," "thief," "bastard," "heretic," "scab," etc.,
are brief definitions designed to be felt as painful.   And the effect of
these definitions is deeper than we suspect.   Many of our profound dis-
gusts, for example, those connected with cannibalism and incest, are so
developed—that is, they are highly emotionalized institutional products.
And all codified acts, even those of no intrinsic importance, become
eventually saturated with emotion.   It is a matter of no intrinsic importance whether you carry food to the mouth with the knife or the
fork, but the situation has been defined in favor of the fork, with grave
emotional and social consequences—disgust and social ostracism.   In
short, any definition, however arbitrary, that is embodied in the habits
of the people is regarded as right.   It was, for instance, a custom to
burn women in India on the death of their husbands, and to strangle
them in the Fiji Islands, and any widow would demand this privilege
although she did not wish it.   The contrary behavior would mean
social death. . . .

And we are not to regard these examples as merely curious or dis-
gusting—slavery, duelling, burning of witches are examples of practices
coming within the definition of moral acts in our own past—but as
evidence of the power which the communal definitions have to control
behavior.   Our immigration problem and our criminal problem are not
mainly questions of inherent mental and moral worth, but questions of
the attitudes and norms of behavior established by definitions of the
situation.

We are in the habit of calling "primary groups" those societies which
through kinship, isolation, voluntary adhesion to certain systems of
definitions secure an emotional unanimity among their members.   By
virtue of their unanimity the mob and the jury are also momentary
primary groups.

Clear examples of the primary group are the South Slavonian *zadruga*
and the Russian *mir*.   When there arises in these communities the
necessity of defining a new situation, it is not even sufficient to reach

a unanimous decision; each member must voice his opinion and agreement, make it explicit. Cases are recorded where in a conflict between the traditional communal definition (say of poverty) and that of the great state, a member has appeared before the communal assembly, sustained by the confidence in a new and authoritative definition, only to wither and collapse before the white scorn of a solidary group. If a member is stubborn his family members and close friends weep, embrace, implore—beg him not to disgrace them and his community by showing the neighbors that they cannot agree. It has been remarked by students of the mir that boys six or eight years of age speak and act like grown men. They repeat the standard definitions of "our community," "our people." . . .

The Polish peasant uses a word, okolica, "the neighborhood round about," "as far as the report of a man reaches," and this may be taken as the natural external limit of the size of the primary group—as far as the report of a member reaches—so long as men have only primary means of communication. But with militancy, conquest and the formation of the great state we have a systematic attempt to preserve in the whole population the solidarity of feeling characterizing the primary group. The great state cannot preserve this solidarity in all respects— there is the formation of series of primary groups within the state—but it develops authoritative definitions of "patriotism," "treason," etc., and the appropriate emotional attitudes in this respect, so that in time of crisis, of war, where there is a fight of the whole nation against death, we witness, as at this moment, the temporary reconstitution of the attitudes of the primary group.

Similarly, in the great religious systems such as Christianity and Mohammedanism, we have a systematic attempt to make the whole world a primary group, to win men away from the merely communal, human and worldly definitions (or to reaffirm these) by a system of definitions having a higher value through their divine derivation. God is the best definer of situations because He possesses more knowledge and more prestige than any man or any set of men and His definitions tend to have finality, absoluteness and arbitrariness and to convey the maximum of prepossession. . . .

But I do not wish to leave the impression that definitions are dependent for their validity on their authoritative source. All usual and habitual practices are emotionalized, become behavior norms, and tend to resist change. The iron plow-share, invented late in the 18th century, was strongly condemned on the ground that it was an insult to God, therefore poisoned the ground and caused the weeds to grow; and until recently the old farmer laughed at the soil-analysis of the city chemist. The man who first built a water-driven saw-mill in England was mobbed; the English war department informed the inventor of the first practical telegraphic device that it had no use for that contrivance; in the last generation there was a persistent opposition to the introduction of stoves and organs into churches, and if we omit recent years, and in recent years only the scientific and practical fields, it would be difficult to find a single innovation that has not encountered opposition and ridicule. . . .

. . . The main purpose of what I have said up to this point was to show that "human behavior norms" are not only very arbitrary, but, precisely because behavior norms, so highly emotionalized that they claim to be absolutely right and final and subject to no change and no investigation. . . . [But] the norms do change, in spite of the emotional prepossessions; traditions and customs, morality, religion, and education undergo an increasingly rapid evolution, and it is evident that a system proceeding on the assumption that a certain norm is valid finds itself absolutely helpless when it suddenly realizes that the norm has lost all social significance and some other norm has appeared in its place.

But why, we may ask, if a society is orderly and doing very well, is it desirable to disturb the existing norms at all? "Little man, why so hot!" And this question reduces itself ultimately to a basis of idealism. It becomes a question of happiness, of the degree of fulfillment of wishes within the society, and on the other hand of levels of efficiency as between societies in the ultimate struggle against death—as in the present war. . . .

Professor Watson emphasized the meaning of higher levels of efficiency, and higher levels of social efficiency are reached through the individualization of function represented best by the scientific specialization of our time. Individualization is a relative term—the individual always remains incorporated in some world of ideas—but practically the creative man secures sufficient individualization to do his work, retains enough recognition to keep him sane, by escaping from the censure of one group into the appreciation of another group. And this escape seems to go on at a rate corresponding with the increased facility of communication. The world has become greatly diversified, containing not only races and nationalities with differing norms and cultural systems, but various worlds of ideas represented by various scientific, religious, artistic circles; and by the fact of reading alone the individual can associate himself with those persons or circles pre-adapted to his ideas, and form with them a solidary group.

Now, the superior level of culture reached by the western world is due to a tendency to disturb norms—introduced first into the material world by the physicists and gradually extending itself in connection with the theory of evolution to the biological world, and just now beginning to touch the human world. And this tendency to disturb norms becomes an end in itself in the form of scientific pursuits whose aim is the redefinition of all possible situations and the establishment eventually of the most general and universal norms, namely scientific laws. And the success of this method from the standpoint of efficiency is shown in the wonderful advance in material technique resulting from research for law in the fields of physics and chemistry, exemplified, for example, in mechanical inventions and modern medicine.[1]

❦❦❦

27. The Application of Fundamental Concepts in Rural Community Studies[*]

LIKE MANY of our everyday "English" words, some concepts used in sociology come to us unchanged from a foreign language. Two of these concepts, highly important in a consideration of inter-personal relations, are the German terms *Gemeinschaft* and *Gesell-schaft*. First systematically developed by Ferdinand Tönnies, these concepts are here capably described and illustrated by Rudolf Heberle in a discussion of the concept *rural community*. He sets forth the importance of considering the ideas and values held in common (the "natural will" basic to *Gemeinschaft*) as well as the contractual and trade elements (the "rational will" characterizing *Gesellschaft*), when one attempts to delineate the geographical area of a community within which association takes place.

THE PROBLEM IN RURAL COMMUNITY STUDIES

THE SOCIOLOGIST, in trying to determine the structure of a rural community, is faced with two problems.

---

[1] The last four paragraphs have been rearranged.

[*] Rudolf Heberle, *Rural Sociology*, 6, No. 3 (September, 1941), 203-215. Reprinted by permission of the publisher and the author.

The author (b. 1896) is Professor of Sociology, Louisiana State University. Born in Lubeck, Germany. Came to the United States in 1938; naturalized, 1944. Since 1940, collaborator, United States Department of Agriculture. Was Labor Market Analyst, War Manpower Commission, 1945. Has written various books in German and contributed numerous articles to professional periodicals. Author, *From Democracy to Nazism*, *The Labor Force in Louisiana*, *Social Movements*.

First, he has to find criteria by which to demarcate in space, so as to be plotted on a map, those groupings of households which are making use of the same service institutions, or which might be considered as units for which new service institutions like schools or community centers should be set up.

Second, it would be important to inquire into the socio-psychological quality of these spatial groupings. The attitudes of the farmers to one another, or to the townspeople; the attitude of both categories to the community as a whole may vary greatly. The entire population may be united by a strong sense of solidarity or they may be rather indifferent towards each other except for the pursuing of certain interests, and there may be more or less formal organization or spontaneous cooperation for such purposes.

The first problem arises from the absence of farm villages and from the fact that in our scattered rural settlements the boundaries of administrative or "civil" divisions almost never correspond to the demarcations of school-church-trade areas and other "service areas."

The significance of this situation may be made clear by contrast with the social structure of rural areas in Europe, where each village forms a municipality at the same time constituting a real socio-economic unit, so that no problem of locating the rural community arises. The sociologists, since Galpin, have developed techniques to delineate groupings of households which can be considered as constituting real rural communities. The service area technique certainly furnishes a valuable result by delineation of those population aggregates which are interrelated by like, common or complementary interests.

But there is a more profound kind of social unity than that which originates from interest—the kind of unity which is present in any normal family group, in a neighborhood where families have been living together and have been friends and helpers in good and hard times for many generations, the kind of unity which exists between people who know that they share the same religious ideas and ethical values. This kind of social unity is denoted by the term "community" in a strict sense, as distinguished from society, or, to use the original terms in order to avoid confusion, by the distinction between Gemeinschaft and Gesellschaft. To assume that this kind of social unity can exist on the mere basis of interests would be fallacious.

While the delineation of service areas may be sufficient for certain purposes, the profounder inquiry into the quality of the socio-psychic structure of any rural aggregation is of importance for a better understanding of rural communities and has some practical significance even for purposes of rural organization.

THE CONCEPTS, GEMEINSCHAFT AND GESELLSCHAFT

Gemeinschaft and Gesellschaft are concepts of pure or constructed types of social entities or social groups. All "social" entities, whether consisting of few or many individuals, whether organized or not, consist in distinction from biological or psychic groups in willed relations. Their existence lies in the affirmation of the entity as such and of the resulting mutual obligations of one will subject to the others. These willed relations can be meant by the individuals as means for the achievement of certain ends, like a contract between buyer and seller, like an agreement between two antagonistic political candidates to support each other against a third competitor, or they can be meant as the self-understood consequences of already existing bonds. In this case they may be without any defined purpose.

Of such kind is the relation between mother and child which, as a social relation, consists in the mutual affirmation of duties and claims resulting as socially sanctioned functions from the biological and psychic relation. Of this type is also the relation between good neighbors of long standing or between sincere and intimate friends.

Social interaction in any social entity is regulated by a set of rules of conduct which are accepted as valid by the members of the group. In Gesellschaft, these rules are established by agreement for certain purposes; they consist of a rationally devised system of conventions, enacted laws and doctrines. In Gemeinschaft, they are an outgrowth of liking, habit and beliefs, formulated in customs, traditional law and traditional morality (sanctioned by religion). In the sense that habit is called man's second nature, these rules in Gemeinschaft seem to form part of the "nature" of the individuals.

Since these codes can be regarded as expressions of the group will (what the members of the group are willing to respect as valid in group matters), Gemeinschaft may be said to be a creation of "natural group will," Gesellschaft an artifact of "rational group will." Or, Gemeinschaft may be thought of as a creation of genuine concord, Gesellschaft as result of agreement. The same functionally defined relation will assume quite different characteristics in Gemeinschaft and in Gesellschaft. A tenancy relation, for instance, will be different in its meaning and implications if the landlord and tenant are closely related kinsfolk than if they are strangers. In the first case, the tenure relation will serve to transfer the use of the farm from father to son, securing subsistence for the retired farmer. In the second case, it will serve to appropriate rent to the landlord, profit to the renter, or wages as the case may be to a share "tenant."

Gesellschaft is the concept of a social entity formed by essentially independent individuals by agreement to achieve certain ends, whether or not these represent like or common interests or mutually complementary interests. The pattern is always that of barter or of alliance. Gemeinschaft is the concept of a social entity already existing before any definite interaction and cooperation arises; it may have its base in biological relations, in the mere fact of living together, or in the most spiritual and therefore human form, in the sharing of ideals and convictions.

The model of Gesellschaft is the society of the market economy, as Adam Ferguson says:

It is here (in a commercial society) indeed, if ever, that man is sometimes found a detached and solitary being: he has found an object which sets him in competition with his fellow-creatures, and he deals with them as he does with his cattle and his soil, for the sake of the profits they bring. . . .

The model and origin of Gemeinschaft is the household group (the Greek *oikos*, the Germanic large family, the old style Chinese family of today) in which all specific social relations are but unfoldings of the basic union of blood, place and mind (spirit).

However, as "constructed" type concepts Gemeinschaft and Gesellschaft can not be used simply to classify empirical social groups as either Gemeinschaften (communities) or Gesellschaften (societies). Any such designation can only mean an approximation of the empirical phenomenon to the concept, in a similar way as one describes a soccer ball as a globe although knowing that it is not really a globe in the mathematical sense. It is with such reservations that the village community of olden times, an aggregate of several large families, is the prototype of a Gemeinschaft in space.

The following structural elements are considered as the essentials of a village Gemeinschaft: (1) Kinship; (2) Neighborhood; (3) Unity of mind and spirit.

Gemeinschaft is not constituted by objective structural elements as such but by the awareness of their existence and by the recognition of mutual rights and duties arising from them. There would be no Gemeinschaft between, let us say, two cousins living in the same village unless they were aware of their kinship and willing to acknowledge the customary and moral obligations arising from such relation. In the perfect case, the entire village is originally one clan or one large family, the individual houses of families thus being mere descendants from the original unit. The Old World villages were largely settled by families closely interrelated by descent from common ancestors and by intermarriage. There are even today villages to be found in Europe where almost everybody is kin by descent or by intermarriage. Such kinship interrelation, while by no means a safeguard against conflict and bitter enmity among the villagers, naturally has a deep effect on all social relations within the group. These can scarcely develop in a purely contractual, utilitarian and rationalistic way; rather will they grow naturally out of such kinship relations, and even business transactions will be influenced by the fact that the partners are kinsfolk.

Neighborhood means more than spatial relation. Mere living together does not constitute Gemeinschaft. On the contrary, spatial proximity is often a source of bitter conflict, for out of it arises dissent over individual rights to land, cattle and other property, unless obligations to solidaristic interaction are recognized as the social consequences of proximity, unless spatial neighborhood becomes neighborliness in attitudes and actions.

Such sense of solidarity will develop out of the usage of the land, which, because of the kinship ties between the villagers, is originally considered as common property, or, at a later stage, as property of the families. Even after individual property has become recognized on certain cultivated lands, its use will still be regulated by the whole community. The very system of crop rotation with three fields which prevailed in the Old World until fairly recent times made this necessary.

Common usage of forest and range still exists in some regions of Europe, or at least residues of such institutions are still discernible in many customs. Springs, wells and streams may be used as community property. The herders of cattle or sheep, as well as the boys or girls to whom are trusted the village's geese and goats, hold a position best described as an "office" controlled and salaried by the community. In many cases, even in Central Europe, there is still to be found a bakery operated for the benefit of all villagers who may send their loaves to the community oven. In small towns are still found the empty shells of former "well-communities" and similar institutions. These are not rationally thought out creations of "community organization" but rather the outcrop of kinship and the spirit of brotherhood resulting from it. This neighborliness pervades all social relations and prevents even trade and barter between the farmer-villagers from becoming entirely contractual and calculative.

Mutual aid is given without thought of accurately calculated compensation. It is the duty of the neighbors to give help in cases of sickness, to attend the funeral of a neighbor, and the folkways require that the neighbors be invited at marriages and baptisms.

These neighborhood obligations and rights cling to the farmstead rather than to the persons who are living on it; they are independent from personal likes or dislikes. In the case of funerals, the roles of pallbearers, etc. are assigned by custom to the people from certain farmsteads. In cases of emergency the villagers will help spontaneously as a natural duty toward their neighbors and kinsfolk. Sometimes, as in the case of insurance against fire hazards the forms of special-purpose associations may be resorted to. But such organizations are not business concerns bent on profit but rather cooperatives with the purpose of making mutual aid more efficient and secure. If in such a community the wealthier farmers hire the poor cottagers as day laborers, this relation will be considered rather in terms of neighborly help, compensated in kind or in money to be sure, but not exactly as an employment for wages. Hired help which live in the farmer's house are treated as part of the family and the farmer and his wife will assume parental obligations for the physical and moral well-being of their servants.

Finally, there is, in the genuine village community, one accepted religion, one code of custom and morality, one dialect, and a common store of material culture traits such as house-types, dress and patterns in furniture, tools and belongings. In other words, the principal values and norms are uniform; there is, in fundamental aspects of the common life, a community of mind and spirit.

In this social structure, each sex, each age, each social rank has its custom-determined functions, rights and duties. Within these limits there is a great deal of freedom, for the individual will be judged not according to appearances but according to his well-known intrinsic qualities. The strong sentiment of solidarity which permeates all spheres of social life works as a brake on pursuance of self-interest and makes on the other hand formal devices of social control largely dispensable.

Far from being a "mechanical" arrangement of will-less individuals, the genuine community is a living union of persons who are directed in their social actions by a strong sense of union, of one-ness one might say, which obliges each member to comply voluntarily with the accepted norms of conduct, to respect the established institutions.

Tonnies' apparently dichotomic concepts however do not denote empirically exclusive alternatives. The very idea of natural will forbids this. No man acts entirely rationally, no Gesellschaft can exist empirically without a foundation in some sort of Gemeinschaft. This is an essential element in the theory. It justified the search for Gemeinschaft elements even in relatively pure Gesellschaft groupings by empirical inquiry.

· · · · · ·

SOME INDICATORS OF GEMEINSCHAFT AND GESELLSCHAFT
IN RURAL SETTLEMENTS

In applying these concepts to empirical community studies one should be aware that they include an entire system of theoretical sociology, comprising a theory of structure, of values and norms, and of social change.

Perceived through the medium of this theory, many apparently insignificant or incoherent traits in rural settlements acquire a very specific meaning as indicators of the prevailing sociological structure. Kinship as a favorable disposition to Gemeinschaft assumes foremost significance. The frequency of consanguinity and intermarriage has been given due consideration in many empirical studies. The inquiry should not stop on the quantitative level but penetrate into the qualitative aspects. Where kinship is numerically significant one may also expect to find other Gemeinschaft traits. It seems, for instance, likely that the need for formal intentional association will be lessened under such conditions. Such associations as there exist will probably vary in degree of integration with the intensity of kinship.

If farmers have the choice between several trade centers or between several merchants in one town, kinship and nationality relations may determine their preference rather than pure economic considerations. This seems to be tacitly assumed by some authors but it should be investigated in each concrete case. For, considering the present trend towards dissolution of definite service areas, such assumption does not seem generally justified. The individual farmer, who, in the earlier period, traded as a matter of course in the nearest village or town where all his neighbors traded now has a free choice between several trade centers in easy reach by automobile. His trade and other service relations may therefore be more determined by rational calculation than formerly. In addition, assimilation of the second and third generation in non-Anglo-Saxon communities tends to reduce the importance of nationality as a determinant of other social relations. In new settlements existence of kinship relations between settlers will greatly facilitate social integration on a Gemeinschaft level.

The importance of the ecological pattern has been recognized sufficiently in recent studies. As a principle, it may be said that, other things being equal, close proximity of farmsteads will help to intensify spontaneous primary contacts and relations and thereby tend to integrate neighborhoods into true Gemeinschaft groups.

Common use of land wherever it occurs in the New World can be taken as a safe indicator of Gemeinschaft in other respects. Irrigation and flood protection, if entirely or partly trusted to the local people, is likely to generate a sense of common responsibility, habits of co-operation and an attitude of solidarity, and thereby to foster concord in many other affairs of the group. The degree to which farming as-sumes the traits of capitalistic enterprise has a certain effect on the structure of social relations within the community. The attitude to-wards the farm itself will be different if the farm is regarded merely as one possible investment among others, than if it is regarded primarily as the homestead of a family for many generations past and future. This again will influence the attitude towards neighbors and the nature of social relations with them. Finally, the attitude towards the settle-ment as a whole will be different: only the farmer who is primarily intent on making the farm a home for him and his descendants will feel really "at home." While it has been widely recognized that differences in soil conservation result from such differences in farming attitudes, it is of equal importance to observe the effects on civic spirit and par-ticipation in community affairs.

Longstanding attachment of families to their farms will strengthen Gemeinschaft between neighbors. Neighborliness will then be a fruit of memory extending to past generations and not merely a recognition of present mutuality of interests. Mobility on the other hand will prevent the development of this deeper sense of solidarity. The highly mobile tenants, the migratory harvest hand, clerical employees in the trade center and other highly mobile elements will therefore, in a sedentary community, remain socially on the fringe of the group.

Gemeinschaft of habitat finds its most perfect and effective expression in mutual aid among neighbors, given without thought of compensa-tion in goods or services of exactly equal value. The story of the farmers in one Frisian-American settlement who rejected a county agent's advice to keep records of their mutual aid services so that at the end of the year the balances could be paid reveals a true Gemeinschaft attitude. Tearing up the already written checks, they said, "We are neighbors, and not in business with each other." Similar attitudes may here and there be found in relations even between farmers and the town people. Such traits deserve observation and meaningful interpretation, since often they can reveal more than could be ascertained through direct inquiry into attitudes.

Where the cultural background of the population is very homogene-ous, Gemeinschaft is more likely to be found than where culture is as heterogeneous as in so many rural communities of the New World. If, therefore, certain observations, e.g., a strong adherence to a traditional house type indicates cultural homogeneity, the presumption would be that other traits of Gemeinschaft could also be found. The opposite will be the case where cultural differentiations coincide with socio-economic stratification. Where agricultural labor is supplied from another racial or ethnic group rather than that to which the landlords belong, the usual denial by the landowner class of equal human dignity to the laborers makes true Gemeinschaft impossible. Only exceptionally, can paternalistic relations modify such situations in the direction of Gemeinschaft.

Where, on the other hand, farm laborers or hired help come from the same class as the farmers, where they share meals and recreation with the farmer's family, where they belong to the same church and attend it together, there it will be safe to assume real Gemeinschaft in these relations. Even seasonal laborers and migratory laborers from far away sometimes return year by year to the same farmers and will be treated somewhat like old friends. Thus, the patterns of conduct customary in labor relations become indicators of more or less Gemeinschaft or Gesellschaft in the structure of the community.

In a true Gemeinschaft, friendly relations with outsiders will never be of purely contractual nature. Where the stranger is treated as if he were a personal friend, one may be sure to find other traits indicative of Gemeinschaft. The essential point is that such treatment should be accorded not merely as an expression of personal liking but as demanded by the folkways.

Personal sympathy however enters as an important element into many intra-community groupings. In many of these groups membership composition will depend largely on personal friendship, kinship and neighborhood relations. One joins a certain group not primarily because one thinks its purpose important but because one wants to please some friend or neighbor who is active in this organization. The more Gemeinschaft, the more likely is such conduct.

This is not an exhaustive treatment of symptomatic traits. Those which have been discussed here as separate have to be seen and interpreted as interdependent and in the whole context of conduct patterns and institutions found in a concrete rural settlement or service center area. Otherwise, bad fallacies can be committed. Caution is advisable especially in the interpretation of economic and technological traits. While the concept of Gemeinschaft visualizes a self-sufficient village, commercialization of agriculture is not always incompatible with Gemeinschaft. If certain products are raised for the market the intra-group relations can still be of a predominantly Gemeinschaft type. Many of the settlements of sectarians, especially those practicing ascetic simplicity in daily life, like the Amish, combine prosperity through production of marketable crops with a very strong Gemeinschaft spirit which is not even limited to the narrow local community.

‎⁕‎

28. Groups and Civilization *

THE PRECEDING READINGS in this chapter emphasize the role of primary and secondary groups in the socialization process and in community life. In this reading Homans examines an even wider horizon: the relation of the small human group to a whole civilization. He maintains that the problems of interpersonal relations are always dealt with successfully at the level of small, informal groups. The basic question facing us all, he says, is this: How can these relationships be equally well handled at the level of large, complex, centralized societies, such as our own, and finally of world civilization itself? The reader will find it profitable to examine Homans' entire recent work, *The Human Group*, represented here by a section from the richly suggestive final chapter.

THE GROUP AND SOCIAL COHESION

AT THE LEVEL of the tribe, the village, the small group, at the level, that is, of a social unit (no matter what name we call it by) each of whose members can have some firsthand knowledge of each of the others, human society, for many millenia longer than written history, has been able to cohere. To be sure, the cohesion has been achieved at a price. Intelligent men have always found small-town life dull, and the internal solidarity of the group has implied a distrust and hatred of outsiders. But society has at least been able to cohere. This is not to deny that groups have succumbed to the severity of the environment and the violence of enemies, but they have had at the same time few problems of internal social organization. They have even tended, as we have seen, to produce a surplus of the goods that make organization successful: morale, leadership, and co-operation between increasingly large numbers of people.

* George C. Homans, *The Human Group* (New York: Harcourt, Brace and Co., 1950), pp. 454-468. Reprinted by permission of the publisher and the author.
    The author (b. 1910) is Associate Professor of Sociology, Harvard University. His fields of interest include industrial relations and sociological theory. Among his writings are *An Introduction to Pareto* and *English Villagers of the Thirteenth Century*.

THE BIRTH OF CIVILIZATION

Throughout human history, groups have used this surplus in the attempt to grow. For most of them, the environment, physical and social, has put an end to the process before it went very far. A few have been more successful. Given an environment neither too severe nor too luxurious, groups have grown and multiplied, and social units larger than the group have begun to appear. The challenge of the environment, to use Toynbee's phrase, posed an internal challenge: If large-scale co-operation could be achieved, it would pay for itself in an increased control over a bountiful nature. In the beginning, the challenge was met most successfully in broad river valleys. There the surplus of co-operativeness, applied to clearing, draining, damming, and irrigating, brought enormous returns and encouraged further co-operation. Finally, one of the groups, much like the others but possessing some of their qualities in a higher degree, consolidated the gains, and a civilization was born. Again and again this has happened. Now a little Chinese principality at the Great Bend of the Yellow River acts as the catalyst, now a city-state in central Italy, and now a tribe, called the Franks, settled on the south shore of the English Channel. The tribes have multiplied; one, more tribal than the rest, has brought the others together.

In our view, and here we are following Toynbee again, ancient Egypt and Mesopotamia were civilizations. So were classical India and China; so was the Greco-Roman civilization, and so is our own Western civilization that grew out of medieval Christendom. These societies on the grand scale have had many characteristics in common. At its height, each has been inventive: it has devised and used a more powerful technology than any at the command of the tribes coming before and after it. Each has been coterminous geographically with a communications network. In fact the existence of such a network has been the necessary precondition allowing one tribe to unite the others. Thus the Mediterranean Sea, with its satellite roads, made possible the Roman Empire. Since the organization of a tribe is incapable of controlling an empire, each civilization has also developed new formal organizations, in law, government, warfare, and religion, linking the tribes to the new center. And almost every one of the civilizations has worked out and adopted a single body of values and beliefs, shared in some degree by all the citizens. Such until recently was Christianity for the Western world.

DECLINE AND FALL

The appalling fact is that, after flourishing for a span of time, every civilization but one has collapsed. The ruling class, if there was one, has lost its capacity to lead; the formal organizations that articulated the whole have fallen to pieces; the faith has no longer commanded the allegiance of the citizens; much of the technology has even been forgotten for lack of the large-scale co-operation that could put it in effect; and after a last and inevitably futile effort to hold society together by force, the civilization has slowly sunk back to a Dark Age, a situation, much like the one from which it started out on its upward path, in which the mutual hostility of small groups is the condition of the internal cohesion of each one. At the end of the cycle the names of the tribes are different from what they were in the beginning—the Saxons are not the Sabines—but tribal behavior is much the same. Society can fall this far, but apparently no farther, and having fallen this far, it may start all over again. In some parts of the world, the cycle of civilization and decay has been repeated at least twice. One can read the dismal story, eloquently told, in the historians of civilization from Gibbon to Toynbee. The one civilization that has not entirely gone to pieces is our own Western civilization, and we are desperately anxious about it. Can it get out of the rut into which the others have fallen?

To account for the decay, the historians have developed many explanations, each more adequate than the last, but the sociologists may still be able to contribute something. Our own theory, in its main lines, would run as follows. At the level of the tribe or group, society has always found itself able to cohere. We infer, therefore, that a civilization, if it is in turn to maintain itself, must preserve at least a few of the characteristics of the group, though necessarily on a much expanded scale. Civilizations have failed in failing to solve this problem. In fact the very process by which civilization emerges has, up to now, made failure inevitable. But let us look more closely.

THE DISSOLUTION OF THE GROUP

The development of civilization has meant technical change, economic expansion, and warfare, usually all three. All have the effect of breaking up old social units without putting anything in their place. One characteristic result was the great cities of the Roman Empire, especially those of the Near East, filled with traders, artisans, and slaves, uprooted from their former homes, whether in Egypt, Canaan, Greece, Gaul, or Spain, and huddled into slums with other people of many different traditions. Another such result is our own great cities, like Detroit and Los Angeles, where, save for some difference in physical surroundings, the same conditions hold. Our study of Hilltown is typical of the reverse of the coin: the decaying society from which the uprooted come. In the old society, man was linked to man; in the new agglomeration—it cannot be called a society—he is alone. He has not had time to be anything else.

Now all the evidence of psychiatry, and it has not been our purpose to include it here, shows that membership in a group sustains a man, enables him to maintain his equilibrium under the ordinary shocks of life, and helps him to bring up children who will in turn be happy and resilient. If his group is shattered around him, if he leaves a group in which he was a valued member, and if, above all, he finds no new group to which he can relate himself, he will, under stress, develop disorders of thought, feeling, and behavior. His thinking will be obsessive, elaborated without sufficient reference to reality; he will be anxious or angry, destructive to himself or to others; his behavior will be compulsive, not controlled; and, if the process of education that makes a man easily able to relate himself to others is itself social, he will, as a lonely man, bring up children who have a lowered social capacity. The cycle is vicious; loss of group membership in one generation may make men less capable of group membership in the next. The civilization that, by its very process of growth, shatters small group life will leave men and women lonely and unhappy.

No harm would be done if new groups appeared to take the place of the old ones, new groups with some of the characteristics of the old. And we know that in fact such groups are always forming. The seed of society is always fertile. Yet it may be that at times the new growth does not keep pace with the rot, and that there is a net increase in the number of isolated individuals, superficially attached to the bare skeleton of formal organization but lacking the old feeling of belongingness. Each of the sociologists—Durkheim, LeBon, Figgis, Brooks Adams—who began, just before World War I, to point out the signs of decay in our society, used the same metaphor. They said that society was becoming a dust heap of individuals without links to one another.

THE NEW GROUPS

The process cannot go on unchecked indefinitely. Society does not dissolve without a struggle, but produces antibodies to check the rot. The reaction often takes a religious form. Among the uprooted of the big cities—Antioch, Alexandria, Ephesus, Rome, Detroit, Los Angeles—

all sorts of religions spring up. They are seldom the religions of the tribes from which the uprooted come, and never the religion of the civilization itself. If men have not found a society satisfying, they will not find its beliefs satisfying either. Whatever spiritual unity the civilization may once have had is broken. The new religions are highly emotional: they cater to the exaggerated emotionality of the isolate. Their elaborate theology is a tribute to his obsessions. But they have something more important to offer than a release for the emotions and a subject for metaphysics. Each new religion is also a new society. Each is made up of cells or congregations, which offer to the isolate some of the feeling of full belongingness that he has lost. This was true of early Christianity, as the Acts of the Apostles and the Epistles of St. Paul bear witness. It was probably true of the mystery cults of the Roman Empire. Who shall say it is not true of the sects that fester in the social wilderness of our own cities, from Jehovah's Witnesses to Communism? Not all the cults survive. In the Roman Empire, Christianity was the only one that survived in strength, and some hope for mankind lies in the fact that Christianity set high ethical standards and addressed itself to man's spiritual, not just his physical, needs. If our civilization goes the way of the others, it may, like the Europe of the Dark Ages, be stimulated to recovery by some new synthesis of moral norms. But whatever the influence of its doctrines may have been, Christianity at least spread its network of new and tough groups, which finally set a term to the decay of the Empire, and, together with the Germanic tribes, formed the matrix out of which a new society could be carved.

In the end, the new groups provided a basis for the reconstruction of civilization, but we must notice that in the beginning they were irreconcilably hostile to the reigning order. Rome was the whore of Babylon, whose destruction St. John confidently predicted. A frustrated person, we are often told, turns to aggression. One is not loyal to a society in which one has been lonely and anxious. The decay of civilization would be much less rapid than history shows it to be if the new groups that absorb the isolated individuals did not have opposition to existing society as their very principle of organization and did not therefore, in the beginning, accelerate the decay.

In the history of Western civilization, the successor of the classical, the problem can be stated in much the same way. Erich Fromm, in his *Escape from Freedom*, says that in the last four hundred years men have been gradually set free from the restraints of traditional society. But in losing these restraints, they have also lost the sense of belonging to a group whose members co-operate in securing the deepest interests of each.   If freedom is to mean no more than emotional isolation, it will not survive.   Men will do any mad thing, even merge in a mass under the sword of a tyrant, to escape from a freedom of this kind.   Every religion, every revolutionary movement claims it will restore the brotherhood of man, and sometimes has really done so in the form of the congregation or cell.   Brotherhood, of the kind they get in a small and successful group, men must have.   But at the level of civilization, the search for the lost brotherhood of man, by creating antagonisms that can only be resolved by force, may end in the worst of tyrannies.   Our best instincts hurt us most.   Although society, like the human body, has immense restorative powers, they are blind.   Left to itself, a broken leg may knit again, but it will certainly knit crooked, and in the same way the forces of equilibrium in society will restore some kind of integration, though the new level may well be lower than the last.   To achieve an advancing adaptation, the maintenance of a civilization rather than a relapse before a new start, intelligence must direct the restorative powers.

GROUP CONFLICT

The problem of emotional isolation, or psychosocial isolation as the social scientists call it, is not the only one that civilization raises, and it may not be the most important.   We have already seen that this problem is inextricably intermixed with the problem of group conflict. As civilization advances, a process often takes place on a large scale that much resembles what took place on a small scale in the Electrical Equipment Company.   An advancing civilization means, among other things, that the technical and economic adaptation of society to its environment changes.   Since the internal system is continuous with the external, this change disturbs the relations between groups within society and exacerbates their mutual antagonisms.   The antagonisms find expression in ideological differences, and civil war may break out. Something very much like this occurred in the sixteenth century, in the last great crisis of Western civilization before the present one. With economic expansion and organizational changes in industry and agriculture, the middle class rose rapidly in importance.   The members of this class were apt to be isolates; they also came, as a group, into conflict with the other classes in society.   The former balance between the classes was destroyed, and antagonisms once kept under control awoke.   In the ideological controversies, which were then religious and political as they are now economic and political, the middle class took one side; the upper and lower classes together took the other.   The issues were not considered on their merits; they became the mere flags of parties whose real energy was drawn from class antagonisms. The result was the civil wars in France and England, and the Thirty Years' War in Germany. Civilization escaped wreck, but only just escaped. England suffered least and even gained by the conflict, which was less severe there than elsewhere; France survived at the price of adopting absolute monarchy, and the development of Germany was so retarded that she has suffered from a national feeling of inferiority ever since. Perhaps we are going through a similar conflict today, but our capacities for wrecking are much greater.

CIRCULATION, COMMUNICATION, AND CONTROL

Other problems raised by an advancing civilization, and closely related both to emotional isolation and to group conflict, are the problems of circulation, communication, and control. Let us take them up in this order. By *circulation* we shall mean the process by which able persons are brought to positions of responsibility in a society. In the small group, the choice of a leader is an obvious and natural thing. The leader is the man who most fully lives up to the ideals of the group. He expresses the aspirations of the group, and it is this, more than anything else, that allows him to carry the group with him. In a civilization at its best, the leaders are of the same kind. Scipio Africanus, William of Orange, Elizabeth, and Washington not only possessed great intellectual capacity but were also felt by their followers to represent the best in society. Their strength lay in this double fact. Yet as civilization advances, as the channels of advancement become more complex, and as conflict widens, the choice of leaders who have the twofold qualification for their job becomes more difficult. Able men may be available, but their skill lies in making money, in intrigue, in using force, or in exploiting the increasing antagonisms between groups. A split grows up between leaders and led, until the latter are no longer led but driven or bribed.

The problem of *communication* is close to that of circulation. We have seen that, in the small group, communication flows naturally toward the leader, and that he cannot do his job unless he is well informed in this way. Now civilization, which is, in one of its aspects, centralization, implies a lengthening of the channels of communication between followers and top leaders in the great formal organizations that articulate the whole. Even in the small group, the seeds of breakdown are latent in the emotional relation between leader and follower, and with every lengthening of the channels of communication, the difficulties increase. The subordinate, dependent on his superior for advancement, may tell the latter only what he wants to hear and only so much as will protect the subordinate's position. It is not enough that good communication should exist between most neighboring positions in the communication lines. If only one link is weak, the flow of information from bottom to top will be impaired. The separate channels of communication from bottom to top may multiply, as the rise of staff departments in every large organization shows, and yet this very multiplication may impede communication. Each channel transmits only part of the story; no one is responsible for paying attention to the whole. And every new channel may increase the insecurity of men located on the other channel, for it by-passes these men and transmits information that, in the hands of a leader inadequately skilled, may bring criticism back down upon them. Finally, adequate communication depends to a great degree on the leader's awareness of the items that ought to be communicated. He hears what he wants to hear, and he wants to hear only what he has been trained to hear. In American industry, for instance, communication is excellent on questions of sales and engineering, but tends to be poor on questions of internal social organization. This kind of information may be inherently hard to communicate, but it is also true that the American administrator is not taught to think it important.

For the ordinary follower in an organization, communication is not a matter of transmitting abstract understanding of a situation. It is a matter of transmitting to the leader an awareness of those problems on which, in the follower's view, action needs to be taken, and of the fact that the follower feels as he does. If action is not then taken by the leader, communication, for the follower, has failed. In the big organizations of modern society, communication in this sense is all too liable to failure. Trade and industrial unions may arise in an unconscious attempt to repair some of the damage, but they are big organizations too, and may fall into the old difficulties. We are in danger of producing a body of men wholly lacking confidence in leadership and organization of any kind whatever. Such a group would much resemble the "internal proletariat," demoralized, without opportunity for spontaneous group action of its own, and sullenly resistant toward its leaders, so characteristic of the later Roman Empire. For the problem is not just that of communication from follower to leader. The leader must also explain, in such a way that the followers will accept it, the plan of action that the society needs to adopt. If communication fails in one direction, it will fail in the other.

We have seen that in the small group, *control* over persons that threaten to depart from the norms of the group is often exceedingly effective but is not imposed from without. Instead it is implicit in the system of relations in the group. We have also seen that the leader, in close communication with his followers, does not ask them to take action that will not receive their spontaneous obedience. As civilization develops, as groups dissolve, as society divides into warring groups, and as the difficulties of communication between leader and follower increase, this spontaneous control tends to dissolve in favor of a control imposed by force and by the central power. Of course it is true that a certain amount of force must always be used in controlling society. What we are talking about now is a civilization that has reached the stage at which, in the view of its leaders, it can be held together only by force. Their diagnosis may be correct, if the dissolution of groups and the increase of conflict have gone far enough. But as for force as a long-run remedy, the evidence of history is that this stage marks the beginning of the downward path of civilization. Forced co-operation only hastens the decay that would have taken place in any event. In the words of Durkheim, "A society made up of a boundless dust-heap of unrelated individuals, whom an overdeveloped state tries to hem and hold in, is a true sociological monstrosity." And yet all dictators, from Napoleon onward, have tried to create something like this monstrosity. Just as Napoleon broke up the ancient provinces of France and divided them into departments, fearing that the provinces with their local loyalties and traditions of self-government would provide centers of resistance to his regime, so all dictators since his time have tried to break up or bring under central domination all social units independent of the state. Rousseau provided them with a rationale for their actions. He argued that the individual should be set free from the trammels of society, but when he faced the question how this should be done, he went on to say that "every citizen should be wholly independent of all the others and excessively dependent on the state . . . , for only the force of the state makes the liberty of its members." In short, man must be compelled to be free.

Let us repeat: all of these problems—psychosocial isolation, conflict, circulation, communication, and control—are handled more or less well at the level of the group. Therefore human society never dissolves beyond this level. What is true of the group must also be true of the civilization if the latter is to maintain itself. Civilization fails when it cannot solve these problems on its own vast scale, and when it even prevents its constituent groups from solving them.

DEMOCRACY

Our own civilization has not wholly failed. It has made some institutional inventions that have turned out, in certain times and circumstances, to be valuable in solving the problems of the group at the level of the civilization. One complex of such inventions is democracy. We do not use the word here in its literal sense of "rule of the people." That gets us into the question of the location of sovereignty in a nation. Sovereignty, which is another word for authority, does not lie in any one element or organ of a nation but in the social system as a whole. Nor do we use it in the sense of "democratic way of life." That, as we have said, gives aid and comfort to the dictators by letting them say that they are as "democratic" as anyone else. So loose is the meaning of democracy in this sense that no one can prove they are not. We use the word here to mean the complex of governmental and legal institutions common to such nations as the United Kingdom and the United States: representative and parliamentary government, universal suffrage, the secret ballot, the habeas corpus, trial by jury, and the various freedoms named in the Bill of Rights.

Note how all these devices are addressed to the problem of maintaining, at the level of a nation if not of a civilization, the values of the small group. The election of executive officers and representatives aims at maintaining for the nation the method of choosing leaders that is characteristic of the small group. Together with the freedoms of speech and press, it also aims at effective communication between the led and the leaders. Trial by jury and the various freedoms are so many admissions that the spontaneous self-control of a society may be much more effective than any imposed control. Finally, representative government is an effort to establish that kind of relationship between leaders and followers on which a spontaneous obedience, rather than a forced one, can be based. A further pursuit of this main idea might lead to many important insights.

But democratic institutions do not exist in a vacuum; they exist in a society, and they cannot live long unless the society is of a certain kind. This is a field in which political science, in co-operation with sociology, must do much more work than it has so far. Democracy cannot be successful unless the nation is well educated and enjoys a standard of living so high that men do not have to worry about sheer survival. Just how high the standard of education and the standard of living need to be we cannot say, but we recognize that at least some minimum level must be achieved. How few countries in which we Americans blithely ask that democratic government be established meet these conditions! How unrealistic we are, and what frustration our unrealism leads us to!

These are only the minimum conditions. There are others. If

democratic institutions do something to create the conditions in which they can survive, they do not do everything. Democracy cannot solve the problem of psychosocial isolation, and it cannot help greatly to solve the problem of conflict. No one believes that, even in the most flourishing circumstances, conflict disappears in a society. Conflict is built deeply into any social order, which would be uninteresting without it. As usual, the question is: How much conflict and in what areas? If social conflict does not go too deep, representative government provides a method for deciding the issues, with much salutary release of emotion. We are all ready to accept a large amount of verbal violence in our politics. Our tolerance for it is high, and we admire a man that gives and takes hard knocks. But if conflict goes deep enough, as the United States once learned, and as the communist propagandists know well, democratic methods do not lead to the peaceful resolution of conflict but to civil war. For democracy to survive, the members of society must enjoy some area of consensus, supported by the informal contacts of daily life, by formal communication networks, and by common ideals. We know little of the nature of this consensus, but we are aware that in some countries of Europe, which were formerly, or now are, democracies in the technical sense, this consensus never existed. Moreover, as we have seen, some characteristics of a developing civilization tend to put the consensus in danger.

Democracy does something to solve the problems of circulation, communication, and control, but its machinery is not applied, and probably cannot be applied, in vast areas of our national life. No one has seriously suggested that production schedules in a factory should be determined by popular vote or even that the factory manager should be elected. And yet in these vast areas the tensions of modern civilization are being generated. We can resolve them not by blindly applying existing democratic methods but by addressing ourselves to the problem to which democracy itself was addressed: How can the values of the small group be maintained on the scale of the civilization?

THE SOLUTIONS OF THE PROBLEM

We have seen some of the problems that an advancing civilization makes for itself. Apparently its rise creates the conditions that lead to its fall. How shall we escape from this dreary cycle? The usual conservative has nothing more to offer than the advice: "Stop change. Any change will be for the worse." But from beginning to end civilization means change. Stop change and, we infer, civilization also stops. And while the conservative is giving his advice, the business firms he admires are making his words idle by stimulating enormous social change. The real problem is this: How can a social order change without either dissolution into a dust heap or cleavage into hostile camps? How can we, to use Elton Mayo's phrase, create an "adaptive society"? Another kind of conservative—he is usually called an "old-fashioned liberal"—growls about "the curse of bigness" and argues that social groups of all kinds should be more independent of state control. He has some idea of the nature of the problem, but his solution is mistaken. Civilization means centralization. It means that men and women will be related to one another in increasingly large organizations, and that these organizations will be brought more and more under the influence of the central directing body of the society, the government. Whether or not modern society requires large-scale organization if it is to maintain its complex adaptation to the natural environment, the fact certainly is that the process of centralization is still going on both in business and in government. If government did not centralize, business would; neither one is in a position to blame the other. The real problem is not how to keep social groups wholly independent and autonomous but how to organize their relation to central control in such a way that they can maintain their own life while contributing to the life of organized society. In the social organism, how can we keep the center strong without destroying the life of the periphery? How can we centralize without stagnating?

As for the modern liberal, not the old-fashioned one, all he has to offer to solve the problems of large-scale organization is more of the same. For big private business he would substitute bigger government business. He rushes into the leviathan state without having the faintest notion how to deal with some of its important human problems. He assumes our present methods are adequate. Take, for instance, the problem of restriction of output, which is a typical problem of the relation between the central direction of an organization and the small working groups of which the organization is made up. The liberal may not know about restriction in American industry, but if he does, he will say that it is specifically a result of business organization and not of modern big organization in general, including the kind he advocates, and that restriction will wither away when the government becomes socialist and the labor leaders are in power. But the difficulties are stubborn and their roots run deeper than we thought. Society is made up, among other elements, of countless small groups of the kind we have described in this book. If advancing civilization, which means an increasingly centralized control, does not destroy them altogether, which hardly seems likely, it will have to deal with them, and yet, as we have seen, advancing civilization tends to weaken the kind of relation between leader and follower in which the leader can carry the group wholeheartedly with him and the follower can accept leadership without fear that his views will be disregarded. Suppose we organize the welfare state and still find thousands of small groups sullenly resisting the advice of their official leaders? That the problem is not academic, the industrial experience of Socialist government shows. If social control is increasingly centralized, the reason must be that such control is necessary, but a central control that cannot be exercised would seem to mean stagnation and not progress. Shall we then use force to bring the recalcitrant into line? History seems to show that this does not solve the problem but rather starts civilization on its downward path. The decline of the Roman Empire began with its birth—the dictatorship of Augustus. This is not an argument against the welfare state; it is a plea that we study more carefully than we have so far the conditions that must be realized if the centralized state is not to stagnate. Let us put our case for the last time: At the level of the small group, society has always been able to cohere. We infer, therefore, that if civilization is to stand, it must maintain, in the relation between the groups that make up society and the central direction of society, some of the features of the small group itself. If we do not solve this problem, the effort to achieve our most high-minded purposes may lead us not to Utopia but to Byzantium. The problem will not be easily solved, but one step we can take in the beginning is to learn the characteristics of the human group.

❧❦❧❦❧

29. Interpersonal Relations in a Bureaucracy *

To THE UNINITIATED a bureaucracy, with its many rules of operation and its highly organized and formalized structure, might seem little subject to personal influences. Actually this impersonality seldom exists, as Ralph H. Turner's article here shows. The bureaucrat's personal relations with his superiors, subordinates, and equals in the hierarchy constantly affect the operation of bureaucracy. Although

* Ralph H. Turner, *American Sociological Review*, 12, No. 3 (June, 1947), 342-348. Reprinted by permission of the publisher and the author.
    The author (b. 1919) is Assistant Professor of Sociology, University of California at Los Angeles. Author, "The Relative Position of the Negro Male in the Labor

Turner has described this process in terms of the Navy disbursing officer, every bureaucratic structure produces strikingly similar conditions sociologically.

EVERY ADMINISTRATIVE STRUCTURE exists in order to achieve certain goals, which goals normally originate outside the structure and are imposed on it from the top. A bureaucratic administrative system is supposed to function as a nearly impersonal machine, individual discretion entering only when alternate procedures are compatible with the system. The ordinary official is expected to apply procedures with blind precision, irrespective of the degree to which they achieve or subvert the general goals.

Needless to say, actual administration often fails to adhere closely to the goals of the organization. Reasons for the divergence may be inadequacies of the procedural pattern and conflicting procedures, conflicting goals within the organization, inadequacies of the bureaucrats themselves, and, most important, the position of each functionary as not only a square on the organization chart but also as a focus of pressures applied by a number of informal structures not envisaged in the formal pattern.

The purpose of this paper is to describe a few of the sociologically relevant influences which bear on a certain type of bureaucratic official, namely, the Navy disbursing officer. Bureaucracy is conceived as defined by Max Weber. Though certain types of influence are more clearly displayed in the position of the disbursing officer, most of what is said will also apply to any Supply Corps officer and, to a lesser degree, to all naval officers. The findings are the result of participant observation by the writer, both as a disbursing officer during the war and as an observer of other officers in a similar position.

From the standpoint of the present analysis there are three characteristics which distinguish the disbursing officer in degree from the remainder of the naval organization. First, disbursing officers handle matters of immediate personal importance to their clients. Navigation, gunnery, etc., may be more vital to the lives of the men, but their problems are vague to those not directly concerned. An error in a pay account or a delay in pay day is more quickly recognized and more loudly protested by the rank and file than deficiencies in most other departments aboard ship. Consequently the disbursing officer and his

Force of Large American Cities," *American Sociological Review*, August, 1951. Other writings on personal values and social structures.

staff are under constant bombardment for favors and incessant criticism for their mistakes—real or imagined—or failures to grant favors.

Second, the disbursing officer is a bureaucrat serving a larger bureaucracy of which he is an integral part. Robert Merton has noted the important fact that a government servant is usually superordinate to his clients, not in any formal sense, but because the client has no direct authority over him and no effective access to anyone of superior authority. Superordination and subordination are clearly defined in the Navy by the label which each man carries on his uniform. Though most of the disbursing officer's clients are enlisted men and hence subordinate, a good many will be officers of senior rank who are thereby empowered to reward or punish him in various ways. Thus in adhering to the formal patterns relating to disbursing the officer must often act counter to the larger formal pattern by defying a senior officer.

Finally, the disbursing officer, unlike most other bureaucrats, is personally accountable and financially liable for any deviation from regulations in the expenditure of government funds in spite of any contrary order from a superior officer.

Three characteristics of the social structure in which the disbursing officer finds himself which make it difficult for him to behave as the ideal bureaucrat will be discussed. First is the frequent conflict between regulations (as interpreted by the disbursing officer) and orders from superiors, both of which are supposed to be obeyed. Second is the subordination of the disbursing officer through rank to many of his clients. Third is the network of informal structures, which exert particular pressure on the disbursing officer because of the crucial services which he dispenses. The facilitating conditions for the operation of these influences include the following: the disbursing officer's incomplete command of voluminous and rapidly changing regulations; the ambiguousness or incompleteness of regulations with respect to many situations; acceptance of properly signed vouchers as proof of fact by the General Accounting Office in auditing disbursing accounts, so that certain documents can be falsified with impunity; those personality traits of the officer which resist strictly impersonal behavior.

Within the formal structure the distinctive problem of the disbursing officer is that of reconciling orders from superiors with regulations when they seem to conflict. Orders may be issued by senior officers in the supply department (of which disbursing is a part) or by the commanding and executive officers of the activity. Conflicts with superior officers in the supply department are usually reconciled fairly smoothly because the supply officer understands the problem of disbursing accountability, often from earlier experience as a disbursing officer, and because of fairly close relationships between them. Conflicts stemming from orders by the commanding and executive officers, who have little knowledge of and little patience with disbursing regulations, and who are generally not accustomed to being asked by a subordinate to discuss the advisability of an order they have issued, present a ticklish problem. If the order seems to be at all important to the officer in question, the senior supply officer can usually be expected to add his pressure, through threats and suggested devices for "getting around" the law. The subsequent careers of disbursing and supply officers can be materially affected by notations which the commanding officer may enter in "fitness reports" submitted periodically to the Bureau of Naval Personnel.

The conflict between regulations (as interpreted) and orders from superiors is not limited to the disbursing function or even to military organizations. The conflict is incipient in every bureaucratic structure because the rational type of authority, as Weber has indicated, involves recognition both of rules and the right of officials to issue orders. Though the hierarchy of officials exists only to administer the rules, which in turn express the purposes of the organization, it is patent that official behavior and commands may often counter the rules. In the small informal organization of a business hiring only a handful of employees, rules may be largely unformulated and procedures passed verbally down the hierarchy as required, thereby eliminating the conflict by making orders supreme. Or the opposite extreme in which authority is expressed solely through a code of rules, each functionary being left to apply the rules without supervision, might be imagined but hardly realized in an actual situation. Because of the inadequacy of either rules or hierarchical authority alone to serve the purposes of bureaucratic administration, both must be present. Thus the ideal type, bureaucracy, is itself a compromise between two ideal extremes, utilizing and compromising two channels of authority which may be in conflict.

Bureaucracies differ, however, in the degree to which they emphasize chain of command or rules. Business organizations tend to vest greater authority in the chain of command, minimizing numbers of rules and winking at violations if the official achieves results. "Cutting through red tape," is the popular phrase for de-emphasizing rules. Government bureaucracies stress rules more strongly because of their different aims and because of fear of abuse of authority by officials, and through civil service regulations functionaries are given more authority to defy superiors in the application and interpretation of rules. Many a former business executive serving as a naval officer in charge of civilian employees in navy yards has been startled to find his orders called into question by subordinates, and to find himself powerless to enforce his orders. As businesses get larger the emphasis on rules to insure uniform practice reduces the contrast with government bureaucracy. Custodians of funds in business or government are more tightly bound by rules and less subject to arbitrary orders from superiors.

In the Navy, and probably in other bureaucratic structures, the intensity of the conflict varies with different levels in the hierarchy. For .the lower ranks of enlisted men the conflict hardly exists because they are explicitly denied the right to make decisions on their own. At the higher levels the official is confronted with fewer and broader orders so that in the top ranks the conflict arises less frequently. Thus the conflict between orders and regulations is most acute at the intermediate levels, from ensign to lieutenant in particular.

In business and in most naval positions, this conflict is resolved in favor of the order, the functionary not being held responsible for violating a rule in compliance with an order from a superior official. As indicated previously, the personal accountability of the disbursing officer denies this way out. Consequently, the Navy, recognizing the possibility of conflict, has provided two procedures for its resolution. The disbursing officer is to point out the apparent discrepancy to the superior and, if no understanding is reached, an inquiry may be sent to the Bureau of Supplies and Accounts. Or, the matter may be referred to the commanding officer who may order the disbursing officer to make the expenditure "under protest," the commanding officer thereby assuming full financial liability. The former procedure was used often during the war for minor issues, but senior officers are often unwilling to wait several months for answers and a disbursing officer who frequently resorts to this tactic is soon in poor standing. A disbursing officer considering the second method invariably pictures himself being transferred to "amphibs" and suffering various awful fates at the hands of a wrathful commanding officer, so the method is seldom employed. However, the occasional disbursing officer who has courage enough to threaten its use usually finds the commanding officer unwilling to assume the personal risk involved in defying him.

The very training given the disbursing officer in the supply corps school teaches him that the above methods are not approved ways of handling such difficulties. The young officer is taught that he must be a "Can do paymaster," in contradistinction to the type of officer who is always ready to cite the paragraph in the Manual which prevents any particular action being taken. The "Can do" officer can almost always find a way to do anything he is ordered to do. This emphasis, of course, partly reflects a general de-emphasis of rules fostered by the war. But it further reinforces the tendency for the disbursing officer to find "informal" ways of dealing with matters and to deviate from the ideal pattern of a bureaucrat.

The second obstacle to impersonal functioning by the disbursing officer is the system of rank. As indicated by Weber, military officers are marked off by class distinction. And Talcott Parsons has observed that, "there is no legitimate order without a charismatic element." It is the union of class distinctions with a strong element of "charisma of office" which gives the rank structure its peculiar and powerful nature. Senior officers are expected to be treated with deference irrespective of their actions. Because of "class" levels, senior officers are usually able to punish or reward a lesser officer indirectly. However, through their charisma officers are generally held in far greater awe than their actual powers or inclinations warrant, and a lesser officer is often afraid even to suggest to a superior that his request is not in keeping with regulations. One of the problems of military organization lies in the rather wide-spread fear of superiors which creates extra labor and ill-feeling on the part of men who feel that they must find some way to conform to an erroneous or careless order. Rank has been too widely discussed to need further elaboration here except to note that the disbursing officer, who is at once both a functionary with specified duties and a position in a system of levels, sometimes finds that he cannot act without violating one of these roles.

A third obstacle to bureaucratic impartiality is the system of informal social groupings. Philip Selznick's three characteristics of the informal structure as found in business and labor union bureaucracies, namely, spontaneity, network of personal relations, and orientation toward control, apply equally to naval situations.

These informal structures are of three sorts. Relatively enduring *friendship patterns* weigh heavily where the disbursing officer belongs to the same primary associations as do many of his clients. Particularly aboard ship where a relatively small number of officers live, eat and play poker together in a small space is this true. "Say, 'Pay,' I sure could use about twenty dollars before payday," or, "Isn't there some way I can get flight pay this month?" is the sort of appeal which comes constantly from friends. As a human being the disbursing officer wants to help his friends, and the penalty for brusque disposal of such requests is social ostracism.

A second type of *simulated friendship* or, in Navy jargon, "earbang-ing" relationships includes less enduring and more uncertain influences. Nevertheless, these are in many cases sufficiently persistent and organized relations among persons to justify the term "structure." They take a multitude of well-known forms: an officer treats one of lesser rank as an equal, he compliments the disbursing officer on the good reputation of his office, he jokes and attempts to appear as an old friend. The aim is always, first, to be defined as a person rather than an applicant in the disbursing officer's eyes, and second, to be defined favorably.

The third and most extensive sort of informal structure is that which may be called an *exchange system*. The officer who assigns staterooms aboard ship finds it easy to get extra food from the galley. The ship's photographer who makes some personal pictures of the supply officer gets first choice when the next shipment of fountain pens reaches "ship's store." Such exchanges are not usually verbalized as such among officers, but the officer who does another a favor has no doubt that there will be a return. However, there also exist extensive and well-verbalized systems for distribution of favors and certain types of supplies, especially at shore stations. The exchange structures extend so far that it is often difficult for a man to secure those services and equipment which are essential to his job unless he can promise some return. Aboard a large ship one attempt was made in the ship's store to sell the limited stock of watches and cigarette lighters on the basis of impartial drawings. Complaints were so many and vigorous from persons who claimed they had been promised a watch or were owed one that thereafter the "spoils" system was used, with much less complaint. Even some enlisted men in key positions, such as the mail clerk and carpenter's mates, are able to exercise influence over officers because of the services at their disposal. Needless to remark, any resort to strictly formal procedure impairs the disbursing officer's potentially exceptionally good position in the system of mutual benefits. Denunciations of these exchange structures are periodically issued by some commands, but such pronouncements are read by only a few and are seldom implemented by more than one or two courts-martial for petty thievery. Furthermore, commanding officers are frequently among the beneficiaries of such systems.

To the participants these exchange systems are widely different from bribery. Bribery is impersonal and is recognized as contrary to law and morals. Favor exchange systems are eminently personal. As long as the system functions smoothly it is just one man doing a favor for a "buddy," and only when a return favor is not forthcoming will the idea of exchange be stressed. And secondly, the exchange system incorporates its own code of behavior. The individual who puts legal technicality ahead of reciprocity is reprehensible, is spoken of with almost moral indignation. The system is not "wrong" or "crooked"; it is a moral system of its own and anyone who puts legality first is a hypocrite. However, there is an ambivalence of attitude toward the system. The official who follows it deliberately and impersonally in order to acquire too great a quantity of goods is disliked, though with a mixture of envy. The system is supposed to operate in leisurely fashion, maintaining the appearance that the goods acquired are secondary to the friendships involved.

The three sorts of systems described operate not only to grant favors to some but to withhold fair consideration from others. Since disbursing officers generally are stereotyped as acting slowly, being tied up in red tape and giving unsatisfactory assistance, prompt careful attention to the business of a client is often defined as a favor. Persons not favorably placed in the informal structures may be deprived of pay because of inadequate attention to their accounts or may suffer undue delay in the handling of their business.

The influence of these systems is felt not only directly by the disbursing officer but also through the enlisted men in his office. Because of their lack of official status, enlisted men develop especially elaborate and powerful informal structures. A new disbursing officer, in the interest of fairness, stopped the dispensing of favors by his enlisted men. A serious morale problem ensued because the disbursing office personnel, no longer able to contribute services, were simply dropped from the status-producing structures, or, as they complained, they had lost their "drag."

Under the combined impact of the informal structures and his formal office, what solutions does the disbursing officer reach? Four types of disbursing officer will be suggested on the basis of their divergent resolutions of the conflicting forces at work. These will be ideal constructs, but have sufficient empirical validity that any disbursing officer should be able to recognize them as applying to other officers he has known and also to tendencies within himself.

The *Regulation* type approximates the true bureaucrat in that he remains impervious to rank, informal structures, and orders of his superiors, but goes further in employing the narrowest possible interpretation of every regulation. For fear of the General Accounting Office his rule is, "When in doubt, don't." He is the stereotyped disbursing officer and the stereotyped bureaucrat. This type is not in a majority during wartime, and consists chiefly of "green" officers who have not yet felt the full pressure of the contrary influences or have not yet learned how easily regulations may be manipulated, and of "mustangs," former enlisted men who have secured commissions.

Opposite is the type who doubts the potency of the General Accounting Office and feels that, "They can't hold me," if money is expended loosely. He will do anything for a friend or superior without debate.

This type is limited to a very few reserve officers who seldom last very long, though many officers have sought escape from the anxieties of their position in the assurance that after the war Congress will pass a "relieving act."

On a different axis, and also fairly infrequent, is the *Sincere* type. He fails to recognize conflicts between regulations and orders from superiors and is unaware of the importance of the informal systems. Apparent conflicts he attributes to his own incomplete understanding of regulations, and rules are seen less as controls than as tools for the execution of orders. He is 100 per cent "sold" on the Navy, is well liked by his superiors and will be assigned positions of favor and responsibility so long as he is a junior officer. His naivete places him in less favor when he reaches higher levels.

The commonest type is the *Realist*. Regulations are seen as illogical concatenations of procedures, restrictions and interpretations, frequently ambiguous, sometimes contradictory, and often, when strictly applied, defeating the purpose for which they were constructed. Rules specify chiefly the papers which must be filed in support of expenditures, and these may be correct without the payment being correct. The most successful career men of the supply corps include many of this type. They assume the regulation facade when the client is not fortunately placed in the informal or rank structure, but know how any payment may be made "legally" if the request comes from an important enough source.

Many conscientious officials join this type when they come to recognize that strict interpretation of rules often works injustice in terms of the rules' obvious intent and that efforts at strict enforcement are frequently nullified because other people know how to prepare papers in "correct form." Such an official begins by helping a client whose claim is payable within the intent of the law but is invalidated by a technicality to give the "right" information to insure payment. Differential treatment of clients on this basis is hard to maintain, so the officer soon finds himself giving such aid without reference to justification, or more frequently, under varying pressures and moods, wavering between a regulation attitude and an opportunistic attitude.

Two general tendencies emerge among disbursing officers as the consequence of orders conflicting with regulations and the pressures of rank and informal structure. One is differential treatment of clientele. Because of the time consumed in extra-routine treatment of persons on the "in," others get summary treatment. The second tendency is for loopholes in regulations to become tools in the hand of the disbursing officer to elevate his own status. Thus he may become more concerned with his own bargaining power than with correct application of rules. In sum, what has been shown is that during this last war powerful influences were at work on the Navy disbursing officer, diverting him from functioning as an ideal-typical bureaucrat. These influences move him, not in the direction of ultra-formalism so frequently observed for bureaucrats in other contexts, but toward personal functioning within systems of power and status in which rules become of secondary importance.

❧❧❧❧

30. The Consequences of Authoritarian and Democratic Leadership *

THE LATE PSYCHOLOGIST Kurt Lewin and his associates did basic research on democratic and authoritarian leadership. They were particularly interested in the impact of such leadership on the social "atmosphere" of experimental groups. The studies upon which this article is based have significance for education and socialization in a society that proposes to be democratic.

IT IS WELL KNOWN that the amount of success a teacher has in the classroom depends not only on her *skill* but to a great extent on the *atmosphere* she creates. This atmosphere is something intangible; it is a property of the social situation as a whole, and might be measured scientifically if approached from this angle. As a beginning, therefore, Lippitt selected a comparison between a democratic and an autocratic atmosphere for his study. The purpose of his experiment was not to duplicate any given autocracy or democracy or to study an "ideal" autocracy or democracy, but to create set-ups which would give insight into the underlying group dynamics. Two groups of boys and girls,

* Kurt Lewin. Reprinted by permission from *Resolving Social Conflicts*, edited by Gertrude W. Lewin, pp. 74-82, Harper & Brothers, New York, 1945.

The author (1890-1947) was a German social psychologist. During the 1940's he founded and directed Research Center for Group Dynamics, Massachusetts Institute of Technology. Taught psychology at Berlin, Stanford, Cornell, and Iowa. Counseller, U. S. Dept. of Agriculture, Washington, D. C., 1942-47. Office of Strategic Services, 1944-45. Chief Consultant, Commission on Community Interrelations, New York. His books include A *Dynamic Theory of Personality* (translated from German by D. K. Adams and K. E. Zener), *Studies in Topological and Vector Psychology* I and II, and *Resolving Social Conflicts*.

ten and eleven years of age, were chosen for a mask-making club from a group of eager volunteers of two different school classes. With the help of the Moreno test both groups were equated as much as possible on such qualities as leadership and interpersonal relations. There were eleven meetings of the groups, the democratic group meeting always two days ahead of the autocratic one. The democratic group chose its activities freely. Whatever they chose the autocratic group was then ordered to do. In this way the activities of the group were equated. On the whole, then, everything was kept constant except the group atmosphere.

The leader in both groups was an adult student. He tried to create the different atmospheres by using the following technique:

Democratic	Authoritarian
1. All policies a matter of group determination, encouraged and drawn out by the leader.	1. All determination of policy by the strongest person (leader).
2. Activity perspective given by an explanation of the general steps of the process during discussion at first meeting (clay mould, plaster of Paris, papier-mâché, etc.). Where technical advice was needed, the leader tried to point out two or three alternative procedures from which choice could be made.	2. Techniques and steps of attaining the goal (completed mask) dictated by the authority, one at a time, so that future direction was always uncertain to a large degree.
3. The members were free to work with whomever they chose and the division of tasks was left up to the group.	3. The authority usually determined autocratically what each member should do and with whom he should work.
4. The leader attempted to be a group member in spirit and in discussion but not to perform much of the actual work. He gave objective praise and criticism.	4. The dominator criticized and praised individual's activities *without giving objective reasons,* and remained aloof from active group participation. He was always impersonal rather than outwardly hostile or friendly (a necessary concession in method).

During the meetings of the two groups, the observers noted the number of incidents and actions per unit of time. It was observed that the autocratic leader put forth about twice as much action towards the members as the democratic leader, namely, 8.4 actions as against 4.5. This difference is even greater if one takes into account only the initiated social approach, namely, 5.2 as against 2.1. Still greater is this difference in relation to ascendant or initiated ascendant behavior: the ascendant actions of the autocratic leader were nearly three times as frequent as those of the democratic leader.

In regard to submissive actions, the proportion was opposite, namely, more frequent by the democratic leader, although in both groups submissive actions of the leader were relatively rare. A similar relation held for the objective, matter-of-fact actions. Here too the democratic leader showed a higher frequency.

On the whole, then, there existed a much greater impact on the members of the group by the leader in autocracy than in democracy, and the approach was much more ascendant and less matter-of-fact.

When we attempt to answer the question "How does the leader compare with the ordinary member in an autocracy and a democracy?" we must refer to an ideal average member who is a statistical representation of what would happen if all activities were distributed equally among the members of the group, including the leader. In Lippitt's experiment the figures showed two facts clearly: first, in both groups the leader was really leading. The autocratic leader showed 118 per cent more initiated ascendant acts than the average ideal member, and the democratic leader 41 per cent more. Both leaders were less submissive than the average member, namely, the autocrat 78 per cent, the democrat 53 per cent. It was interesting to note that both showed also more matter-of-fact action than the average ideal member.

However, the difference between the ordinary member and the leader was much less pronounced in democracy than in autocracy, both in ascendant and submissive action. The democratic leader distinguished himself, also relatively, more by his greater matter-of-factness.

What do these figures indicate about the situation in which the autocratic and democratic group members find themselves? I can only mention a few aspects: In the autocratic group it is the leader who sets the policy. For instance, a child says: "I thought we decided to do the other mask." The leader answers: "No, this is the one I decided last time would be the best one." In dynamical terms such an incident means that the child would have been able to reach his own goal but the leader puts up a barrier against this locomotion. Instead he induces another goal for the child and a force in this direction. We are calling such goals, set up by the power of another person, an induced goal.

A parallel example in the democratic group might be this: A child asks, "How big will we make the mask? Are they out of clay or what?"

The leader answers: "Would you like me to give you a little idea of how people generally make masks?" In other words, the leader in the democratic group, instead of hindering the children in getting to their own goal, bridges over whatever regions of difficulty might exist. For the democratic group, many paths are open; for the autocratic only one, namely, that determined by the leader. In an autocracy the leader determines not only the kind of activity but also who should work with whom. In our experimental democracy all work co-operation was the result of spontaneous sub-grouping of the children. In the autocracy 32 per cent of the work groups were initiated by the leader, as against 0 per cent in the democracy.

On the whole, then, the autocratic atmosphere gives a much greater and more aggressive dominance of the leader, and a narrowing down of the free movement of the members, together with a weakening of their power fields.

What is the effect of this atmosphere on the group life of the children? As measured by the observers the child-to-child relationship was rather different in the two atmospheres. There was about thirty times as much hostile domination in the autocracy as in the democracy, more demands for attention and much more hostile criticism; whereas in the democratic atmosphere co-operation and praise of the other fellow was much more frequent. In the democracy more constructive suggestions were made and a matter-of-fact or submissive behavior of member to member was more frequent.

In interpreting these data, we might say that the "style of living and thinking" initiated by the leader dominated the relations between the children. In the autocracy instead of a co-operative attitude, a hostile and highly personal attitude became prevalent. This was strikingly brought out by the amount of group or "we" feeling as against "I" feeling: Statements which were "we-centered" occurred twice as often in the democracy as in the autocracy, whereas far more statements in the autocracy were "I-centered" than in the democracy.

So far as the relation of the children toward the leader was concerned, the statistical analysis revealed that the children in the autocratic group who were *less submissive* to each other were about *twice* as submissive to their leader, as the children in the democratic group. Initiated approaches to the leader in the democratic group were less frequent than in the autocratic group. In autocracy the action by the member toward the leader had more the character of a *response* to an approach of the leader. The approach to the leader in the autocracy was more submissive, or kept at least on a matter-of-fact basis.

On the whole, then, the style of living in both atmospheres governed the child-child relation as well as the child-leader relation. In the autocratic group the children were less matter-of-fact, less co-operative, and submissive toward their equals, but more submissive to their superior than in the democracy.

Behind this difference of behavior lie a number of factors. The tension is greater in the autocratic atmosphere, and the dynamic structure of both groups is rather different. In an autocratic group there are two clearly distinguished levels of social status: the leader is the only one having higher status, the others being on an equally low level. A strong barrier kept up by the leader prevents any one from increasing his status by acquiring leadership. In a democratic atmosphere the difference in social status is slight and there exists no barrier against acquiring leadership.

This has a rather clear effect on the amount of individuality. In our experiment every individual in the democracy showed a relatively greater individuality, having some field of his own in spite of the greater "we" feeling among them, or perhaps because of it. In the autocratic group on the contrary the children all had a low status without much individuality. The type of sub-grouping showed this difference even more clearly. In the autocracy, there was little "we" feeling and relatively little spontaneous sub-grouping among the children. If the work required the co-operation of four or five members, it was the leader who had to order the members to get together. In the democracy those groups came together spontaneously and they kept together about twice as long as in the autocracy. In the autocracy these larger units disintegrated much faster when left to themselves.

These group structures, in combination with the high tension in the autocracy, led in Lippitt's experiments to a *scapegoat* situation. The children in the autocratic group ganged together not against their leader, but against one of the children and treated him so badly that he ceased coming to the club. This happened to two different children during twelve sessions. Under autocratic rule any increase in status through leadership was blocked and the attempt to dominate was dictated by the style of living. In other words, every child became a potential enemy of every other one and the power fields of the children weakened each other, instead of strengthening each other by co-operation. Through combining in an attack against one individual the members who otherwise could not gain higher status were able to do so by violent suppression of one of their fellows.

One may ask whether these results are not due merely to individual differences. A number of facts rule out this explanation, although of course individual differences always play a role. Of particular interest was the transfer of one of the children from the autocratic to the democratic group, and of another from the democratic to the autocratic one. Before the transfer the difference between the two children was the same as between the two groups they belonged to, namely, the autocratic child was more dominating and less friendly and objective than the democratic one. However, after the transfer the behavior changed so that the previously autocratic child now became the less dominating and more friendly and objective child. In other words, the behavior of the children mirrored very quickly the atmosphere of the group in which they moved.

Later Lippitt and White studied four new clubs with other leaders. They included a third atmosphere, namely that of laissez faire, and exposed the same children successively to a number of atmospheres. On the whole, the results bear out those of Lippitt. They show a striking difference between laissez faire and democracy very much in favor of democracy. They show further two types of reaction in the autocratic groups, one characterized by aggression, the second by apathy.

On the whole, I think there is ample proof that the difference in behavior in autocratic, democratic, and laissez faire situations is not a result of individual differences. There have been few experiences for me as impressive as seeing the expression in children's faces change during the first day of autocracy. The friendly, open, and co-operative group, full of life, became within a short half-hour a rather apathetic-looking gathering without initiative. The change from autocracy to democracy seemed to take somewhat more time than from democracy to autocracy. Autocracy is imposed upon the individual. Democracy he has to learn.

❧❧❧❧❧

31. The Prisoner Community as a Social Group *

IN ANY SOCIETY numerous groups operate under autocratic control— that is, under sets of rigorous rules established and enforced from above without the members having any voice in determining whether the regulations are good and just. Under such conditions the

* Norman S. Hayner and Ellis Ash, *American Sociological Review*, 4 (June, 1939), 362-369. Reprinted by permission of the publisher and the authors.
Norman S. Hayner (b. 1896) is Professor of Sociology, University of Washington (now on leave to serve as a member of the Washington State Board of Prison Terms

appearance of a "community within a community" is not uncommon. Within this autocratic system one or more groups of subordinate members are likely to form—groups that, as N. S. Haynor and Ellis Ash point out, have a distinct set of "mores, attitudes, activities and gradations of status" entirely separate from those established by the official order. An excellent example of this phenomenon is the "prisoner community" described here. If the reader considers this a unique and atypical situation, let him consider objectively the comparable patterns of behavior in any public school. Obviously, much less autocratic control appears in a school than in a prison, but the same "community within a community" does tend to develop.

A CLEAR DISTINCTION should be made between the prison community and the prisoner community. To the casual visitor, the only community at a prison is the one maintained by the administration. Closer acquaintance with any American prison reveals a sub-rosa organization composed entirely of inmates. The major common interest in this prisoner group is release, but there are also, as in a normal community, distinctive mores, attitudes, activities, and gradations of status. It is to the prisoner community that attention is directed in this paper.

Most convicts identify the research man with the administration and are dishonest in dealing with him because they consider him a "screw" (guard). Ordinary statistical or case methods are obviously inadequate to reveal the customs of the prisoner community. The more informal technique of the participant observer seems to be required.

The basic method employed in gathering the data for this study was that of recording at the earliest opportune moment significant social situations in the daily lives of the inmates during a four months' residence at the Washington State Reformatory at Monroe. Frequent short visits over a period of one year supplemented the original observations. Pertinent overt behavior, enlightening casual conversations, and subsequent contact with men released from the institution contributed to the fund of information accumulated. This study is in no sense an exposé of conditions at Monroe. As a matter of fact, the administration is progressive and an objective rating would probably place this institution in a better than average position among the reformatories of the United States. It is the typical characteristics of the prisoner community at Monroe that are being emphasized, rather than what is unique or peculiar.

and Parole). Has written articles on criminology. Author, *Hotel Life*, and *New Patterns in Old Mexico*. Ellis Ash is Director of Public Housing for the City of Baltimore, Maryland.

To secure accurate information, it was necessary for the junior author to be accepted by both inmates and officers. To begin with, both groups were suspicious and both resented the investigator's presence. To obtain the information desired from the prisoners, it was necessary to convince them of his honorable intentions. He had to go through a "proving process" at the hands of the inmate body. This consisted of being placed in situations of their choosing so that they could observe his reactions. He was subjected to cat calls, boos, and hisses; he dodged missiles propelled from unknown and unseen experimenters; he was present during an evident infraction of minor regulations to get his "ratting" (reporting to authorities) response.

After a stay of some two weeks in the institution, the leaders of the inmate body became evident and their acquaintance was definitely cultivated. Acceptance by them meant acceptance by all the inmates. These key men were partially informed of the investigator's purpose in the Reformatory. It was necessary to indicate to the prisoners that, while he was their friend and would perform little services for them not in violation of regulations, still it was impossible to maintain a neutral position in the institution and at the same time flagrantly connive with them. In the beginning, there was no effort to explain the kind of information sought. Interviews were not staged or created artificially. Upon becoming accepted by the inmate body through their leaders, it was possible to mingle with the men without creating an unnatural situation. Many topics were discussed with little restraint. In the prisoner community, as in any other, men enjoy talking shop. Their prejudices for or against particular features of prison life became apparent during the course of these conversations.

Meanwhile, the fact that the field worker had become accepted by the administration was a distinct advantage. The officers as a group did not have leaders whose word was sufficient evidence that a person was acceptable. The confidence of each officer on the staff had to be won individually. By aiding in the organization of a classification clinic, the investigator was able to pay his way with the administration. By offering to relieve various officers on duty in case of emergency, or otherwise, his possible utility was recognized. He was allowed the complete run of the Reformatory at all hours and permission to see anything that went on. Personal bits of information were shared by each officer with him.

Each contact with a man, whether inmate or officer, meant establishing a closer rapport and freer discussion. It was some months, however, before a pattern of community life in the inmate body began to appear.

Although this pattern is not yet entirely clear, some of its outlines are presented here.

In the normal community, contacts are to a considerable extent determined by the type of occupation and the neighborhood of residence. This is also true in a prison. At Monroe, for example, work is divided on the basis of crews, each of which is responsible for specific lines of endeavor. The laundry, power house, tailor shop, office, education, and farm crews are examples. The place of residence, or cell, is usually determined by the crew on which the inmate works. Cells are arranged in two large blocks which are further divided into sides and tiers. In the "old block," the men are under rigid supervision. Immediately after supper, they are locked in their "drum," (cell), for the night. In the "new block" are located most of the trusties, the men with better jobs. Since the work of many trusties requires freedom of movement in both blocks, these selected inmates are allowed to leave their cells in the evening. Each tier in a block becomes a street with its characteristic occupational types. The tierman, who is the middleman between the officers and the inmates for each tier, becomes the runner for his street. If a man settles down in one particular cell for any length of time he tends to develop his closest associations with his neighbors.

The men who have social diseases are segregated on one tier; the "fish" (newcomers) are quarantined on another tier; on still another is the town jail, better known as "deadlock," where incorrigibles are placed. The "hole," or "solitary," is out in the wilderness, so to speak; its occupants are cut off from any communication with their fellow prisoners. In this community, however, prisoners in deadlock or solitary do not lose the respect of the inmate group as a whole; their isolation is physical rather than social.

"Conniving" is a basic process in the interaction between prisoners. It embodies a distinct code of behavior, a set of rules and regulations and a guiding principle for the maintenance of status within the prisoner community. It is responsible for the development of those sub-rosa institutional forms which are an essential part of the community organization. It is a reaction to the dull routine of reformatory life. It is a way of adjusting to the situation, of "making the best of the circumstances." It is not limited to inmate life, but may be identified in any group which operates under coercion.

Each inmate is forced to passive participation in conniving by virtue of his role as a convict. Even though he may wish, as an individual, to adhere rigidly to the rules and regulations of the administration, he must at the same time live up to the "con" (convict) rule—"You must not squeal." This is one of the most important elements in the mores of the prisoner community. A "stool" (spy) for the administration runs constant danger of bodily harm from his fellows if discovered. In most cases, the stool is the scum of the inmate body, the one that possesses no allegiance to the inmate group.

Frequently an inmate will hesitate to engage himself actively in conniving for fear of endangering his opportunities for early parole. This attitude is common to the first-timer from a conventional social background. He soon discovers, however, that he endangers his position more by maintaining this attitude than by relaxing and joining the inmate group. To maintain it means that he becomes an outcast from his fellow cons. The naive first-timer from a normal social environment finds this role much less desirable than that of active participation with other inmates. Under ordinary circumstances, as he becomes "con-wise," he discovers that he desires certain things denied him by the prison administration. In the prison environment, these things assume an importance out of all proportion to their actual value. They are available if he supports the conniving activities. Whole-hearted support will, he finds, mean less danger of discovery and increased benefits.

Variety in the prisoner community, even more than in the outside world, is the "spice of life." It serves to bridge the days on end which would be a constant repetition of formalized responses if each regulation were obeyed to the letter. It is impossible for the officers continually to observe each inmate and many activities contrary to the rules may be enjoyed.

Gambling in the Reformatory is especially popular. It is in violation of regulations; it furnishes a certain spice and thrill; and if one is lucky, he "stands to gain." The excessive interest in this "fighting play" is a commentary on the drab routine of reformatory life. Inmates will gamble on any pretext: the state of the weather many days hence, or the outcome of some local or national situation concerning which there is no scientific evidence on which to base a prediction. Frequently they will bet on whether they can accomplish some other conniving activity and this is an added incentive to the successful completion of that activity. The competitive element is present, the spirit of the game. The medium of exchange for this betting may be any service or commodity capable of transfer from one inmate to another. A cell partner will often pay off a gambling debt by performing the necessary cleaning of the cell for a stipulated period.

Since the loser of a bet in the prisoner community cannot hide, the winner has a distinct advantage. This probably accounts for the fact that there are relatively few inmates who owe large sums to individual prisoners. An inmate might owe small sums to several of his fellows, however, and still maintain his credit. If it becomes apparent that a prisoner is unable to "pay off," the group concerned may take collective action and proceed to rough up the debtor in true pound-of-flesh fashion. In one instance at Monroe, an inmate with a large number of debts endeavored to escape in an effort to avoid group disapproval. He preferred the danger of being shot, of serving time in deadlock, and of being given a longer sentence, to the probable treatment he would receive from the inmate group if he did not pay up. The dramatic nature of the incident was intensified by the fact that the boy had one of the most desirable trusty jobs and was thought of by the administration as an ideal inmate. He decided to leave on the spur of the moment. It was the only release he could think of from the obligations to his fellow inmates. He was captured by the officers within a very short time. The case demonstrates the pressure which an inmate group can exert upon a social deviate.

Let us take another example of conniving. Coffee, or any other beverage with the exception of water, is to be had only in limited quantity at stipulated times. It becomes greatly desired during periods of inactivity, such as "cell time." Once the men are locked in their cells, supervision is relaxed. Unless it becomes obvious that "peace is being disturbed," they are allowed to "go about their business" within the confines of their cells. With due caution, they may smoke "tailor-mades" or roll "skins" (cigarettes), both of which are taboo. Coffee and other delicacies, likewise taboo, are available in the kitchen. An organization must be set up to secure them for distribution. The cost element is always present. In this case, it is the risk involved in bringing the coffee from the kitchen to the consumer rather than the cost of production. Contact must be made with a con who is working on the kitchen crew and has access to the supplies. If this con can procure the coffee, but has no opportunity to smuggle it into the cell block, a middleman is necessary. The one who smuggles it into the block may be unable to hand it over to the consumer. Each participant in the process must have his cut.

Then there is the problem of cooking utensils. Any discarded can will do as a coffee pot. If it is impossible for the cook to obtain this can directly, the proper men must be contacted and paid off. Next, there is the question of a heater. This requires another can or bottle, a wick and fuel. The wick is simple to prepare, but kerosene or some other fuel is precious. Possible sources of supply are the boys working on crews where kerosene is used for cleaning purposes. Again the proper individuals must be approached and paid off. Inmates who are too poor to pay the high price for kerosene use bits of cardboard for fuel. Finally, there is the actual problem of preparation. Some individual in a position to give warning of a screw's approach must be willing to give instant and reliable service. The heater is suspended in the toilet bowl where it is out of sight and where the makings may be easily discarded in case of emergency. Talcum powder is blown into the air at intervals to remove the coffee odor. At last the "jo" (coffee) is ready, together with a skin, and what promised to be a dull evening is transformed into a thrill-packed experience. The successful evasion of a rule is even more satisfying than the finished product. With apologies to Robert W. Service we might conclude: "It isn't the jo that I'm wanting so much as just making the jo."

Occasionally, an extremely successful "brewer" with convenient access to the ingredients will become a wholesaler. He will prepare sufficient amounts of jo to provide for a number of customers and specified quantities will be delivered to the consumers by runners. This may involve a contract for so much coffee over a definite period of time, the brewer assuming all responsibility for delivery.

Although one must pay for services received, barter plays a more important part than in other communities. The man who desires coffee, for instance, may pay for it by providing extra clothes or contacts with the outside. Tobacco is a favorite medium of exchange, but "white" money, i.e., legal currency, is preferred. The men are only allowed to draw two dollars per week from their account and this is in "hickeys" (tokens) rather than in real money. Visitors occasionally succeed in passing money to inmates, but this is dangerous. Generally, it is received through contacts with the farm crew which works at some distance from the Reformatory stockade. The farm crew is an essential feature of the conniving process. This is especially true of the small group that remains overnight on the farm. Men in this group have an opportunity to pick up articles from the side of the road—articles left by motorists during the night. The location of the cache is determined in advance during a visit with a prisoner at the Reformatory. A member of the permanent farm crew may pick up the money and pass it on to a member of the crew that works at the farm only during the day. Each participant must receive some service in return.

The multiplicity of commodities and services available through such means as these requires organization. How is this achieved?

Within the prisoner community there is clear-cut evidence of class divisions. These divisions are based on the relative influence and authority of each class. Since the primary function of the inmate organization is to provide commodities and services denied them by the administration, status is achieved not by "conspicuous consumption" as in the outside world, but by ability as promoters or contact men. Division of labor arises out of unequal opportunities to engage in specific types of conniving. The formal "uppercrust" is popularly known as "politicians' row." This group may or may not include the "right guys," that relatively small select group of natural con-wise leaders. It does include many of the key men in the conniving process.

Politicians' row often takes a hand in gambling activities and sponsors a game on a grandiose scale. A pool may be formed to which many inmates can contribute. The winner makes a substantial sum, but the promoter also profits. Boys who are members of the education crew may easily act as promoters. Since they must make the round of all the tiers each evening to deliver "home study papers" or to give aid on school problems, they are in a position to see every inmate and to find out if he desires to participate in the pool. Payments to winners may be made in a similar fashion.

Entrance to this "community council," i.e., politicians' row, seems to vary with the type of administration. If control is lax and violations of regulations are openly permitted, the hardened racketeers or "ranga-tangs" become the politicians. If, on the other hand, the administration is relatively strong in its control (the present situation at Monroe), politicians' row takes on an entirely different character. The rangatangs, or trouble makers, are under close supervision and do not have an opportunity to work themselves into the key jobs within the institution. This means that they do not have the freedom of movement and association that goes with these jobs. The better-adjusted boys with the best records receive the favored jobs. By virtue of these positions, they become the "town fathers" of the prisoner community and the leading connivers. The importance of membership in politicians' row is, however, largely a matter of tradition. Although members tend to play the role ascribed to them, their actual significance may be more superficial than real. Either a right guy or a rangatang may exploit this situation to advantage. He will endeavor to use willing members of the row as a front for his activities, and will utilize their privileged positions for his individual enhancement.

Another significant fact about the prisoner community is that it is a world of men without women. In a reformatory, the population is primarily composed of young adult males in the virile years of life. The average age of men at the Washington State Reformatory is twenty-two. About four per cent of the 500 inmates (1937) were incarcerated because of their divergent sexual or marital behavior. Sexual starvation is a serious problem in this community. The common trend toward sex topics in male conversations is accentuated. As in other one-sex groups, homosexual behavior is to be expected.

The average warden of a penal institution looks upon sexual perversion as an evil that upsets the routine essential to a well-disciplined group of men. It is antagonistic to the mores of the outside world. It is sometimes regarded as an index to natural criminal tendencies. We find, therefore, that men are committed to penal institutions for sexual perversions, expected to reform in an atmosphere more highly conducive to their practice, and are punished for behavior which is in some cases an integral part of the total personality without being aided in any other way than by being told that it is "wrong."

Normal impulses are many times turned to perversions upon being transplanted to an abnormal situation. In a prison, "smut" stories are told that would cause a "professional" dirty story teller in a college "bull-session" to cry with envy. Faithfulness to one woman is ridiculed. "Get what you can, when you can, from whom you can," is the motto. Men are occasionally "railroaded" into prison to protect the name of some girl who was jointly responsible for the situation. Such an occurrence embitters these men against the entire feminine sex. Status in the prisoner community can be raised by tales of sexual exploits. Many of the young men in a reformatory have never before been confronted with abnormal sex behavior, yet they are suggestible to the point where they may become willing "punks" for a "smoothie" at the game. It is essential to realize that deviations from the conventional sex code within prison walls become acceptable to many merely because they represent an opportunity to defy the forces of law and order. There are also additional incentives in the form of money, candy, and protection. First-timers come in contact with young men no older than themselves who have had a wide variety of sexual experiences. The adventures are told with lurid details; a "proposition" is made; and a convert is won for the cause

"Love for your fellow man" gets a new definition in the prisoner community. Deviations from the conventional sex code are tolerated by the convicts, for perversions are regarded as inevitable. Even if the sex drive is not satisfied in an abnormal manner, the mental conflicts produced in the individual may be more disturbing than the actual consummation of perversions. Not only may the sex attitudes of inmates be distorted by the prison experience, but the lives of sweethearts and wives may be made miserable after the men graduate from this type of "reformation."

It has long been recognized that our reformatories do not actually reform. Contrary to popular belief, however, old timers have no definite educational policy for the youngsters. Inmates learn new and improved techniques in our prisons, to be sure, but this is more or less an incidental feature of the prisoner community. Conversations in the reformatory are primarily with fellow convicts. As in groups in the outside, talk commonly turns to shop. Each type of con describes those varieties of technique with which he is best acquainted. The forger talks of forgery; the embezzler, of stock manipulation; the burglar, of methods for entering homes and stores; the stick-up man, of ways to overcome resistance. Thus many an inmate with a sincere desire to go straight on re-entering society is continually confronted with this kind of conversation. Whether he wishes to or not, he assimilates new crime techniques.

The prisoner community is a social group developed by the outcasts of the larger society. The organization of this community is primarily an economic arrangement devoted to obtaining goods and services denied by the administration. Its entrepreneurs, middlemen, class structure, politicians, and social deviates are comprehensible in terms of the social situation in which the convicts find themselves. The development of conniving, with its code of deception, means that inmates have daily training in traits that make reformation difficult. The prisoner community with its connivings, its perversions, and its exchange of crime techniques re-enforces those behavior tendencies which society wishes to prevent. One cannot expect to break down anti-social habits in an atmosphere that is definitely anti-social.

32. Corner Boys: A Study of Clique Behavior *

INTERPERSONAL RELATIONS and leadership in cliques or informal groups have been the subject of much recent sociological research. William F. Whyte discusses here one of his studies of this type. Through participant observation Whyte was able to analyze the patterns of mutual obligation as well as the leadership structure of a group of "corner boys."

* William Foote Whyte, American Journal of Sociology, 46, No. 5 (March, 1941), 647-664. Reprinted by permission of the University of Chicago Press and the author. The author (b. 1914) is Professor of Industrial Relations, New York State School of Industrial and Labor Relations, Cornell University. Member of executive board, Industrial Relations Research Association. Author, Street Corner Society, Human Relations in Industry, Pattern for Industrial Peace. Editor, Industry and Society.

THIS PAPER presents some of the results of a study of leadership in informal groupings or gangs of corner boys in "Cornerville," a slum area of a large eastern city. The aim of the research was to develop methods whereby the position (rank or status) of the individual in his clique might be empirically determined; to study the bases of group cohesion and of the subordination and superordination of its members; and, finally, to work out means for determining the position of corner gangs in the social structure of the community.

While the explanation of behavior in informal social groupings is generally regarded as a basic problem of sociology, empirical studies of human society, comparable to those now available for animal and bird groupings, are still in the early stages of development. Frederic Thrasher has recognized the phenomenon of informal leadership and has presented some generalizations upon its nature in boys' gangs. F. J. Roethlisberger and W. J. Dickson, in their Western Electric Company studies, have recognized the importance of informal groups of workers in labor relations and have contributed valuable data upon the nature of informal organization in the factory situation. J. L. Moreno has developed a "sociometric" method of charting "social attraction-patterns" which has been applied by him, George Lundberg, Helen Jennings, and others to open a new and promising line of research. W. Lloyd Warner has applied the techniques of social anthropology to the study of groups in modern American society; and, following this approach, Eliot Chapple and Conrad Arensberg have developed a method of studying social behavior by means of detailed observations of interactions.

My research is a product of this period of experimentation, based in part upon the work of Arensberg and Chapple. It differs from Thrasher's gang studies in several respects. He was dealing with young boys, few of them beyond their early teens. While my subjects called themselves corner boys, they were all grown men, most of them in their twenties, and some in their thirties. He studied the gang from the standpoint of juvenile delinquency and crime. While some of the men I observed were engaged in illegal activities, I was not interested in crime as such; instead, I was interested in studying the nature of clique behavior, regardless of whether or not the clique was connected with criminal activity. While Thrasher gathered extensive material upon 1,313 gangs, I made an intensive and detailed study of 5 gangs on the basis of personal observation, intimate acquaintance, and participation in their activities for an extended period of time. Throughout three and a half years of research, I lived in Cornerville, not in a settlement house, but in tenements such as are inhabited by Cornerville people.

The population of the district is almost entirely of Italian extraction. Most of the corner boys belong to the second generation of immigrants. In general, they are men who have had little education beyond grammar school and who are unemployed, irregularly employed, or working steadily for small wages.

Their name arises from the nature of their social life. For them "the corner" is not necessarily at a street intersection. It is any part of the sidewalk which they take for their social headquarters, and it often includes a poolroom, barroom, funeral parlor, barber-shop, or clubroom. Here they may be found almost any afternoon or evening, talking and joking about sex, sports, personal relations, or politics in season. Other social activities either take place "on the corner" or are planned there.

The existence of a hierarchy of personal relations in these cliques is seldom explicitly recognized by the corner boys. Asked if they have a leader or boss, they invariably reply, "No, we're all equal." It is only through the observation of actions that the group structure becomes apparent. My problem was to apply methods which would produce an objective and reasonably exact picture of such structures.

In any group containing more than two people there are subdivisions to be observed. No member is equally friendly with all other members. In order to understand the behavior of the individual member it is necessary to place him not only in his group but also in his particular position in the subgroup.

My most complete study of groupings was made from observations in the rooms of the Cornerville Social and Athletic Club. This was a club of corner boys, which had a membership of about fifty and was divided primarily into two cliques, which had been relatively independent of each other before the formation of the club. There were, of course, subdivisions in each clique.

• • • • • •

As I conceive it, position in the informal group means power to influence the actions of the group. I concentrated my attention upon the origination of action, to observe who proposed an action, to whom he made the proposal, and the steps that followed up to the completion of the action. I was dealing with "pair events" and "set events," to use the terminology of Arensberg and Chapple. A "pair event" is an event between two people. A "set event" is an event in which one person originates action for two or more others at the same time. In working out the relations between men in an informal group, this is an important distinction to bear in mind. I found that observations of pair events did not provide a safe guide for the ranking of the members of the pair. At times A would originate action for B, at other times B would originate action for A.   In some cases there would be a predominance of originations in one direction; but on the whole the data did not support rankings based upon quantitative comparisons of the rates of origination of action in pair events. Qualitatively one could say that when A originated action for B he used a tone of voice and words which in- dicated that he held a superior position.   To take the extreme case, it is not difficult to tell the difference between an order and a request, although both may originate action. It is not safe, however, to rely upon such qualitative differences.   The observer may read into the sit- uation his own impression of the relative positions of the men and thus lose the objective basis for his conclusions.

It is observation of set events which reveals the hierarchical basis of in- formal group organization. As defined by Arensberg and Chapple,

a set is an aggregate of relations such that every individual related in the set is a member either (a) of a class of individuals who only originate action, or (b) of an intermediate class of individuals who at some time originate action and at another time terminate action, or (c) of a class of individuals who only terminate action.

Study of corner-boy groups reveals that the members may, indeed, be divided and ranked upon this basis. Several examples will illustrate.

At the top of the Cornerville S. and A. Club . . . , we have Tony, Carlo, and Dom.   They were the only ones who could originate action for the entire club.   At the bottom were Dodo, Gus, Pop, Babe, Marco, and Bob, who never originated action in a set event involving anyone above their positions. Most of the members fell into the intermediate class. They terminated action on the part of the top men and originated action for the bottom men. Observations of the actions of the men of the intermediate class when neither top nor bottom men were present re- vealed that there were subdivisions or rankings within that class. This does not mean that the intermediate or bottom men never have any ideas as to what the club should do. It means that their ideas must go through the proper channels if they are to go into effect.

In one meeting of the Cornerville S. and A. Club, Dodo proposed that he be allowed to handle the sale of beer in the clubrooms in return for 75 per cent of the profits. Tony spoke in favor of Dodo's suggestion but proposed giving him a somewhat smaller percentage. Dodo agreed. Then Carlo proposed to have Dodo handle the beer in quite a different way, and Tony agreed. Tony made the motion, and it was carried unanimously. In this case Dodo's proposal was carried through, after substantial modifications, upon the actions of Tony and Carlo.

In another meeting Dodo said that he had two motions to make: that the club's funds be deposited in a bank and that no officer be allowed to serve two consecutive terms. Tony was not present at this time. Dom, the president, said that only one motion should be made at a time and that, furthermore, Dodo should not make any motions until there had been opportunity for discussion. Dodo agreed. Dom then commented that it would be foolish to deposit the funds when the club had so little to deposit. Carlo expressed his agreement. The meeting passed on to other things without action upon the first motion and without even a word of discussion on the second one. In the same meeting Chris moved that a member must be in the club for a year before being allowed to hold office. Carlo said that it was a good idea, he seconded the motion, and it carried unanimously.

All my observations indicate that the idea for group action which is carried out must originate with the top man or be accepted by him so that he acts upon the group. A follower may originate action for a leader in a pair event, but he does not originate action for the leader and other followers at the same time—that is, he does not originate action in a set event which includes the leader.

One may also observe that, when the leader originates action for the group, he does not act as if his followers were all of equal rank. Implicitly he takes the structure of the group into account. An example taken from the corner gang known as the "Millers" will illustrate this point. The Millers were a group of twenty corner boys, who were divided into two subgroups. Members of both subgroups frequently acted together; but, when two activities occupied the men at the same time, the division generally fell between the subgroups. Sam was the leader of the Millers. Joe was directly below him in one subgroup. Chichi led the other subgroup. Joe as well as Sam was in a position to originate action for Chichi and his subgroup.

It was customary for the Millers to go bowling every Saturday night. On this particular Saturday night Sam had no money, so he set out to persuade the boys to do something else. They followed his suggestion. Later Sam explained to me how he had been able to change the established social routine of the group. He said:

I had to show the boys that it would be in their own interests to come with me—that each one of them would benefit. But I knew I only had to convince two of the fellows. If they start to do something, the other boys will say to themselves, "If Joe does it—or if Chichi does it—it must be a good thing for us too." I told Joe and Chichi what the idea was, and I got them to come with me. I didn't pay no attention to the others. When Joe and Chichi came, all the other boys came along too.

Another example from the Millers indicates what happens when the leader and the man next to him in rank disagree upon group policy. This is Sam talking again:

One time we had a raffle to raise money to build a camp on Lake ——— [on property lent them by a local business man]. We had collected $54, and Joe and I were holding the money. . . . That week I knew Joe was playing pool, and he lost three or four dollars gambling. When Saturday came, I says to the boys, "Come on, we go out to Lake ———. We're gonna build that camp on the hill. . . ." Right away Joe said, "If yuz are gonna build the camp on the hill, I don't come. I want it on the other side. . . ." All the time I knew he had lost the money, and he was only making up excuses so he wouldn't have to let anybody know. . . . Now the hill was really the place to build that camp. On the other side, the ground was swampy. That would have been a stupid place. . . . But I knew that if I tried to make them go through with it now, the group would split up into two cliques. Some would come with me, and some would go with Joe. . . . So I let the whole thing drop for a while. . . . After, I got Joe alone, and I says to him, "Joe, I know you lost some of that money, but that's all right. You can pay up when you have it and nobody will say nothin'. But Joe, you know we shouldn't have the camp on the other side of the hill because the land is no good there. We should build it on the hill. . . ." So he said, "All right," and we got all the boys together, and we went out to build the camp.

Under ordinary circumstances the leader implicitly recognizes and helps to maintain the position of the man or men immediately below him, and the group functions smoothly. In this respect the informal organization is similar to the formal organization. If the executive in a factory attempts to pass over his immediate subordinates and give orders directly to the men on the assembly line, he creates confusion. The customary channels must be used.

The social structures vary from group to group, but each one may be represented in some form of hierarchy. The members have clearly defined relations of subordination and superordination, and each group has a leader. Since we are concerned with informal organization, the Cornerville S. and A. members must be considered as two groups, with Carlo leading the barber-shop boys, and Dom leading the lunchroom boys.

Observation not only serves to provide a description of the group structure. It also reveals information upon the bases of structure and the factors differentiating between the positions of members. The clique structure arises out of the habitual association of the members over a long period of time. The nuclei of most gangs can be traced back to early boyhood years when living close together provided the first opportunities for social contacts. School years modified the original pattern somewhat, but I know of no corner gangs which arose through classroom or school-playground association. The gangs grew up "on the corner" and have remained there with remarkable persistence. In the course of years some groups have been broken up by the movement of families away from Cornerville, and the remaining members have merged with gangs on near-by corners; but frequently movement out of the district does not take the corner boy away from his corner. On any evening in Cornerville on almost any corner one finds corner boys who have come in from other parts of the city or from suburbs to be with their old friends. The residence of the corner boy may also change within the district, but nearly always he retains his allegiance to his original corner.

The leader of one group spoke to me in this way about corner boys:

Fellows around here don't know what to do except within a radius of about 300 yards. That's the truth, Bill. . . . They come home from work, hang on the corner, go up to eat, back on the corner, up (to) a show, and they come back to hang on the corner. If they're not on the corner, it's likely the boys there will know where you can find them. . . . Most of them stick to one corner. It's only rarely that a fellow will change his corner.

The stable composition of the group over a long period and the lack of social assurance felt by most of the members contribute toward producing a very high rate of social interaction within the group. The structure to be observed is a product of past interactions.

Out of these interactions there arises a system of mutual obligations which is fundamental to group cohesion. If the men are to carry on their activities as a unit, there are many occasions when they must do favors for one another. Frequently, one member must spend money to help another who does not have the money to participate in some of the group activities. This creates an obligation. If the situation is later reversed, the recipient is expected to help the man who gave him aid. The code of the corner boy requires him to help his friends when he can and to refrain from doing anything to harm them. When life in the group runs smoothly, the mutual obligations binding members to one another are not explicitly recognized. A corner boy, asked if he helped a fellow-member because of a sense of obligation, will reply, "No. I didn't have to do it. He's my friend. That's all." It is only when the relationship breaks down that the underlying obligations are brought to light. When two members of the group have a falling-out, their actions form a familiar pattern. One tells a story something like this: "What a heel Blank turned out to be. After all I've done for him, the first time I ask him to do something for me, he won't do it." The other may say: "What does he want from me? I've done plenty for him, but he wants you to do everything." In other words, the actions which were performed explicitly for the sake of friendship are now revealed as being part of a system of mutual obligations.

Not all the corner boys live up to their obligations equally well, and this factor partly accounts for the differentiation in status among the men. The man with a low status may violate his obligations without much change in his position. His fellows know that he has failed to discharge certain obligations in the past, and his position reflects his past performances. On the other hand, the leader is depended upon by all the members to meet his personal obligations. He cannot often fail to do so without causing confusion and losing his position. The relationship of status to the system of mutual obligations is most clearly revealed when we consider the use of money. While all the men are expected to be generous, the flow of money between members can be explained only in terms of the group structure.

The Millers provide an illustration of this point. During the time that I knew them, Sam, the leader, was out of work except for an occasional odd job; yet, whenever he had a little money, he spent it on Joe and Chichi, his closest friends, who were next to him in the structure of the group. When Joe or Chichi had money, which was less frequent, they reciprocated. Sam frequently paid for two members who stood close to the bottom of the structure and occasionally for others. The two men who held positions immediately below Joe and Chichi in the subgroups were considered very well off according to Cornerville standards. Sam said that he occasionally borrowed money from them, but never more than fifty cents at a time. Such loans he tried to repay at the earliest possible moment. There were four other members, with positions ranging from intermediate to the bottom, who nearly always had more money than Sam. He did not recall ever having borrowed from them. He said that the only time he had obtained a substantial sum from anyone around his corner was when he borrowed eleven dollars from a friend who was the leader of another corner-boy group.

The system is substantially the same for all the groups on which I have information. The leader spends more money on his followers than they on him. The farther down in the structure one looks, the fewer are the financial relations which tend to obligate the leader to a follower. This does not mean that the leader has more money than others or even that he necessarily spends more—though he must always be a free spender. It means that the financial relations must be explained in social terms. Unconsciously, and in some cases consciously, the leader refrains from putting himself under obligations to those with low status in the group.

Relations of rivalry or outright hostility with other groups are an important factor in promoting in-group solidarity, as has been well recognized in the literature. Present-day corner gangs grew up in an atmosphere of street fighting against gangs of Irish or of fellow-Italians. While actual fights are now infrequent, the spirit of gang loyalty is maintained in part through athletic contests and political rivalries.

As the structures indicate, members have higher rates of interaction with men close to their own positions in their subgroups than with men who rank much higher or much lower or belong to a different subgroup. That is a significant fact for the explanation of group cohesion.

In the case of the Millers, Sam's best friends were Joe and Chichi. As his remarks have indicated, Sam realized that the solidarity of the Millers depended in the first instance upon the existence of friendly and co-operative relations between himself, Joe, and Chichi. A Cornerville friend, who was aware of the nature of my observations, commented in this manner:

On any corner, you would find not only a leader but probably a couple of lieutenants. They could be leaders themselves, but they let the man lead them. You would say, "They let him lead because they like the way he does things." Sure, but he leans upon them for his authority. . . . Many times you find fellows on a corner that stay in the background until some situation comes up, and then they will take over and call the shots. Things like that can change fast sometimes.

Such changes are the result not of an uprising of the bottom men but of a shift in the relations between men at the top of the structure. When a gang breaks into two parts, the explanation is to be found in a conflict between the leader and one who ranked close to him in the structure of the original gang.

The distinctive functions of the top men in promoting social cohesion are readily observable in the field. Frequently, in the absence of their leader the members of a gang are divided into a number of small groups. There is no common activity or general conversation. When the leader appears, the situation changes strikingly. The small units form into one large group. The conversation becomes general, and unified action frequently follows. The leader becomes the focal point in discussion. One observes a follower start to say something, pause when he notices that the leader is not listening, and begin again when he has the leader's attention. When the leader leaves the group, unity gives way to the divisions that existed before his appearance. To a certain extent the lieutenants can perform this unifying function; but their scope is more limited because they are more closely identified with one particular sub-group than is the leader.

The same Cornerville friend summed up the point in this way:

If we leave the followers, they'll go find some other leader. They won't know what they're doing, but that's what they'll do, because by themselves they won't know what to do. They gather around the leader, and it is the leader that keeps them together.

The leader is the man who knows what to do. He is more resource-ful than his followers. Past events have shown that his ideas were right. In this sense "right" simply means satisfactory to the members. He is the most independent in judgment. While his followers are un-decided as to a course of action or upon the character of a newcomer, the leader makes up his mind. When he gives his word to one of "his boys," he keeps it. The followers look to him for advice and encourage-ment, and he receives more of the confidences of the members than any other man. Consequently, he knows more about what is going on in the group than anyone else. Whenever there is a quarrel among the boys, he will hear of it almost as soon as it happens. Each party to the quarrel may appeal to him to work out a solution; and, even when the men do not want to compose their differences, each one will take his side of the story to the leader at the first opportunity. A man's stand-ing depends partly upon the leader's belief that he has been conducting himself as he should.

The leader is respected for his fair-mindedness. Whereas there may be hard feelings among some of the followers, the leader cannot bear a grudge against any man in the group. He has close friends (men who stand next to him in position), and he is indifferent to some of the members; but if he is to retain his reputation for impartiality, he cannot allow personal animus to override his judgment.

The leader need not be the best baseball player, bowler, or fighter, but he must have some skill in whatever pursuits are of particular inter-est to the group. It is natural for him to promote activities in which he excels and to discourage those in which he is not skilful; and, in so far as he is thus able to influence the group, his competent performance is a natural consequence of his position.   At the same time his performance supports his position.

It is significant to note that the leader is better known and more respected outside of his group than is any of his followers.   His social mobility is greater.   One of the most important functions he performs is that of relating his group to other groups in the district.   His reputation outside the group tends to support his standing within the group, and his position in the group supports his reputation among outsiders.

It should not be assumed from this discussion that the corner boys compete with one another for the purpose of gaining leadership.   Leadership is a product of social interaction.   The men who reach the top in informal groups are those who can perform skilfully the actions required by the situation.   Most such skills are performed without long premeditation.

What the leader is has been discussed in terms of what he does.   I doubt whether an analysis in terms of personality traits will add anything to such an explanation of behavior.   One can find a great variety of personality traits among corner-boy leaders, just as one can among business or political leaders.   Some are aggressive in social contacts, and others appear almost retiring.   Some are talkative, and others have little to say.   Few uniformities of this nature are to be found.   On the other hand, there are marked uniformities to be observed in the functions performed by men who hold similar positions in society, and the study of them promises to provide the best clues for the understanding of social behavior.

❦❦❦

33. Grass-Roots Labor Leader *

IN THIS ARTICLE John W. Alexander and Morroe Berger present a case history of leadership.   They describe the development of the leader role in a workers' group and show the continuous nature of the leadership process.   They also demonstrate the way in which the leader about whom they are writing maintained his relationship with the workers on one hand and the union hierarchy on the other.

* Alvin W. Gouldner, Ed.   Reprinted by permission from Studies in Leadership (New York: Harper & Brothers, 1950), pp. 174-186.

John W. Alexander is an Instructor in Sociology, Columbia University.   Morroe Berger is a political analyst, American Jewish Committee, New York City.   Author,

The popular notion that "leaders are born and not made" is not supported by the way in which Tom Coburn became a leader. Certainly his leadership is directly related to his life experience and the social situation in which he lived.

TOM COBURN, a semiskilled worker in the Acme Brass Mill in a New England town of five thousand people, was in the vice-president's office negotiating for a wage increase for the three hundred production workers he represents as head of the Acme local of the International Union of Mine, Mill and Smelter Workers. Tom remarked that prices had gone up so high that a man's weekly pay envelope didn't contain enough to support his family decently any more. The vice-president turned to Tom and said, slowly:

"Well now, Tom, you're not doing so badly. You just paid off the mortgage on the house a couple of months back."

This is how trade unionism sometimes looks at the grass-roots level: collective bargaining takes on a personal tone since management can obtain through local connections information that would be irrelevant in bargaining on the regional or national level. But what of the union leader's relation to his members? How does this situation look at the grass-roots level? What does it mean to be the head of the union local at no salary plus headaches? How does a grass-roots labor leader, working in the plant alongside the men he represents, exercise and maintain his leadership?

To get one set of answers to these questions we studied the career of Tom Coburn at first hand. We found that Tom's story could illuminate still another set of questions because his parent union, the International Union of Mine, Mill and Smelter Workers, is said to be led by Communists and fellow travelers—two years ago locals began to secede on this very issue—and Tom is in full sympathy with this leadership. So we must ask now, how does the small-town local of such an international union reflect the program and policies of the bigwigs at national headquarters? Is the ideology of the leaders transmitted to the working men in small towns that hear but a faint rumble of the leftist storms and squalls in the great urban centers of radicalism such as New York, Chicago, Detroit and San Francisco? What role does the leader of the grass-roots local play as the link between the rank and file and the union hierarchy, especially where the latter is selling ideology along with traditional business unionism?

"Fair Employment Practices Legislation," *Annals of the American Academy of Political and Social Science*, Vol. 275, May, 1951.

Tom is at the point where the pressure applied from above by the ideological aims of the union hierarchy meets the pressure applied from below by the bread-and-butter aims of the Acme Brass Mill workers. We found that Tom tries to get the ideological message down to his rank and file, but that what he can communicate to them is primarily a general feeling of dissatisfaction with events rather than a specific course of political action.   Tom talks radicalism, but his style of life and his goals are traditionally middle-class.   The middle-class motif in this double pattern of belief and behavior actually reinforces rather than weakens his apparent radicalism: it enables him, as we shall see in a moment, to express his radicalism freely and without regard to the organizational discipline of the Communist party, the leadership of the Mine, Mill and Smelter Workers, or the Progressive party, on whose ticket Tom ran for Congress last fall.

CAREER PATTERN

Tom, now forty-five years old, was born in a rural New England community.   His forebears came from Sheffield, England, where they were cutters and grinders of knives.   Tom's father, following the knife shops around New England, never managed to raise himself and his family of eight children out of the poverty into which all of them had been born. At the age of forty Tom's father died of illness brought on by the constant inbreathing of metal particles produced in the grinding process, and by the cramped position he had to assume at the workbench.

Even before his father's death Tom had already quit school after completing the sixth grade and had started to work in local shops.   His mother took in washing to help support the eight Coburns now left fatherless.   His aims unfocused, Tom took and left a series of factory jobs that required little or no skill.   Then in 1925, at the age of twenty-two, he started a new career pattern by joining a construction gang building a tunnel under a nearby lake for the water line to a large city in the area.   At first Tom fired the boilers in the engine room; later he ran the engines.

This job impressed Tom a great deal.   In the first place, it was his first sustained contact with Negroes, who lived in a Jim Crow camp on the construction site.   With no set attitude toward Negroes as yet, Tom was able to find them interesting friends and "real sports." Secondly, his ideas about workers and bosses crystallized.   This was Tom's first experience in a large-scale enterprise where his relationship to the employer was impersonal.   He says that it was on this job that he learned how the bosses "pit worker against worker, black against white."

Finally, he liked the rough camaraderie he found among the workers, and his sense of loyalty to them was sharpened. There were other ways in which this job was decisive for Tom. At twenty-three he married Martha Wilson, a local girl who had just quit her job in a clock factory. Tom bought a farm and a home, hoping eventually to make a living at full-time farming. But the depression of the 1930's shattered his hopes, and Tom had to keep working for other men. His farm failed, he had mortgage payments to meet, and he now had two young sons to support. In 1937 he found it necessary to return to factory work and took a night-shift job at the Acme Brass Mill about ten miles from his home. This is the plant in which he still works and where he is president of the union. On the job he now has, Tom draws twenty-foot unfinished brass rods through a machine that readies them for cutting by finishing them and making them longer and narrower.

RISE TO LEADERSHIP

Tom's rise to leadership, unlike that of many other union heads, was not the result of a long hard inter-union struggle. Tom got his card in 1941, about a year after the local was organized. At this time it suffered from a lack of willing and capable leadership, perhaps because there were no other unions in town to help out, and because many of the workers in the plant were first- and second-generation Poles who weren't confident of their ability to meet with the more socially polished representatives of management.[1] One day a couple of the active union men asked Tom if he would take over the leadership in order to help the union obtain a majority in the imminent NLRB election. They felt that Tom could deal more confidently with the company officials. He was pleasant to talk to, was liked by the men in the plant, and was certainly loyal to "the boys." But Tom wasn't immediately convinced that he ought to accept the offer. He had his house to take care of, and some farm land around it that he was working in his spare time. Besides, he was pretty busy in the plant, too, selling milk to the workers during lunch hours to pick up extra money. Finally, becoming the union head would in a way deeply commit him to factory work, and he didn't like that. His friends won out, though, and Tom became chairman of the organizing committee. When the union won the NLRB election in 1942 the workers made Tom president.

Tom's personality, of course, had much to do with his rise to leader-

---

[1] Though they might not have made good negotiators, the Poles, Tom told us, made pretty good union members. They sent their children to school as a way of raising their status, and the educated sons and daughters would point out the value of unionism to their fathers and older brothers.

ship. He is easy-going, patient, willing to listen, not given to outbursts of temper. Though he is only a little above average in height, everything else about him is big—his hands, his body, his face and head; yet he is good-looking in a rough, hardy way. Tom often says of himself: "I'm an easy son-of-a-bitch to get along with—you know, hiya boy and a slap on the back." Though he is what most people would call a modest man, Tom likes to impress listeners with the delicacy of his position as representative of the workers both to management and the international union. "You know," he is sure to remark when he talks about his union work, "you got to be careful—you got 'em shoving and pressing from all sides and you got to watch your step."

Though he insists that as a leader he merely does what the union members instruct him to do, Tom actually leads by deliberate attempts to bring the men around to his point of view on political as well as local union matters. His technique is to ask apparently innocent questions in a discussion, and to pursue a line directly to the outcome he seeks. In playing this game Tom puts himself on the same intellectual level as the workers; he does not pose as one who is better-informed than they, though he truly is. Tom is essentially a moderate and careful leader, yet he combines this moderation with a verbal toughness and militancy that are appropriate to the frequently profane, bantering manner of the men he works with. Since he has a genuine sympathy for the working class, he is willing to work hard at being a union man. The Acme workers know and appreciate Tom's concern for their welfare. He is so popular with them that there is no opposition to him at all; only once since 1942 has there been a candidate to oppose him for the presidency, and that contestant withdrew before the election.

Acme officials, too, respect Tom's ability. David Peters, the retired superintendent of the plant with whom Tom had much contact, says that he is probably the best man to defend the Acme workers' interests. Peters, a cautious Scotsman who plays his hand close to his chest, told us: "Tom's a good man for the workers—he reads up on the contract and all that." Yet Peters is not uncritical of Tom. When we asked if he though Tom was pretty intelligent, he said, "Yes, I suppose so. But he wasn't deep. He did his thinking afterwards." Tom's ex-boss gave us the impression that he believed Tom has ambitious motives for his union activity. We asked what Peters thought Tom was looking for, and the old man paused, then raised his eyebrows. "Power and money," he said, looking straight at us.[2]

---

[2] Peters himself is an interesting example of the older type of plant supervisor. He is reputed in town to have been the one man who made the Acme plant a paying enterprise by his enormous knowledge of machines. He struck us as somewhat paternalistic toward the workers and resentful toward the present Acme manage-

THE "MIDDLE-CLASS" PROLETARIAN

Born into a working-class family, Tom's aspirations and the outward aspects of his style of life, we have said, are essentially middle-class. Yet, unlike many other union heads whose outlook is much the same, Tom's middle-class thinking is not the result of any rise in income or any change in living patterns owing to his position as a union leader. He still works in the plant, where he earns one dollar and thirty-nine cents an hour. All he gets from the union is twenty-five dollars every three months for expenses. Tom's middle-class qualities, then, developed in him even before he joined the union. They not only remained with him, but now they actually condition the nature of his leadership by reinforcing his strong working-class sympathies and by preparing him for his role as the transmitter of the union hierarchy's ideology to his rank and file. This is the influence of the double pattern which we have already mentioned. Before we can show its precise effects, however, we must analyze its character more closely.

Tom's acute sense of class cleavage, his working-class sympathies and his radicalism are all separate aspects of his verbal and ideological identification with the workers. Although his father was no radical, the "old gent," as Tom calls him, did impart to his son some notion of what it meant to be one of the underprivileged. Tom's feeling of outrage at the circumstances of his father's death has probably been intensified by his growing conscious leftism, but undoubtedly that sharp event, occurring when he was only fourteen, had a terrific impact upon him. Tom often repeats a remark his mother made to him after she had begun to take in washing. "Tom," she said, "some day there's going to be a war between the rich and the poor." Tom's mother, still alive, seems to have had the realism, resentment and grinding anguish of the poor that is not necessarily translated into political radicalism. Tom can recall no militant class-consciousness in his home, no labor or radical literature, only the spiritless talk of the poor. One of the few bits of workers' lore he remembers is a ditty his father taught him:

> Don't ever let them put your old man on the pan.
> He's worked for you and done the best he can,
> So don't ever let them put your old man on the pan.

ment. We caught a hint of Peters' feeling that men like himself were being edged out these days by the professional managerial class. We asked him if he considered Tom smart enough to be a foreman or supervisor. When he answered, "Not in this generation," there was the clear implication that supervisors now come in at the top level, and neither the David Peterses nor the Tom Coburns have the future they once had.

There is no cynicism in Tom's sympathy for the working class. He likes its informality, the taunting friendliness of men doing a physically tough job. His working-class feeling is so strong that he tries to avoid making remarks that he thinks are not appropriate for a class-conscious worker. When we first asked him what were his ambitions for the future, he shrugged his shoulders at the implication that he might aspire to something beyond the ken of a worker. "Who knows what's going to happen?" he remarked. "I guess I'll just stay on in the plant." Yet further questioning revealed that Tom has for at least twenty years been actively planning to farm for a living. "I want to get the hell away from the goddamned whistle," he told us. He vigorously denied the possibility that he might rise in the plant, basing his objection not on the ground that his road to higher income and status might come via the union rather than through the business hierarchy, but upon the ground of loyalty to the men he has worked with. "How would it look," he asked, "if I was to go up and take a management job after being with the workers all these years? Fellows'd be asking, 'Say, Tom, who the hell've you been working for all this time?'" Everything about Tom, except his fellow-travelerism, suggests the class-conscious militant American Wobbly—in fact, the old Western Federation of Miners, out of which the present mine, mill union grew, was the moving spirit in the organization of the I.W.W. in 1905.

RADICALIZATION PROCESS

What is it that makes Tom a radical, an appropriate medium for the transmission of the International's political ideas to the workers in the Acme plant? The sources of his radicalism cannot be readily identified. Tom was not brought up in a radical home, nor did he get radical ideas from his reading or from any identifiable person he knew before joining the union. We think his leftism, evoked by his contacts as union leader with management, the Acme workers, and the union hierarchy, comes from his experiences as a worker and from his personality. Tom had to go to work at menial jobs while still a boy. He saw others going to high school and college and into their fathers' or their uncles' businesses, but he had to scratch around on jobs without a future. At the same time he has always had a strong sense of loyalty to those he associates with, seeks their approbation, and tends to look at situations without romantically interpreting them.

Tom is unable to say when it was that this general feeling for the workers became a special brand of political radicalism. In 1924, for example, he voted for Coolidge, in 1928 for Hoover, and for Roosevelt in the next four elections. The depression years apparently had much to do with Tom's leftward drift. He clearly recalls the months he worked at the water reservoir, talking over "bad times" with other workers around the brush fire on winter days. He remembers the flow of job-seekers past his house—beaten men who had lost confidence in themselves. The depression years pushed Tom into factory work, something he had been able to avoid ever since he could choose between jobs. And he now realized that farming for a living was out of the question. The depression was but one step in his development. The next one came with his acceptance of the leadership of the local union. Already class-conscious, as the president of the Acme local Tom came into frequent contact with higher-echelon union men who talked his language and the language of leftism. It was this contact that translated Tom's general sympathy for the working class into the more conscious political radicalism of the fellow traveler.

Despite this ideology, Tom's way of living and his aims are middle-class. Early in his adulthood he attached importance to home ownership. He bought his present home in 1926 and by 1944 he had paid off the mortgage. Though small, it is an attractive house, with a sizable, well-kept lawn, a flower garden, and comfortable lawn furniture. The house furnishings are respectable but worn—Tom says he won't buy new furniture (or an inside privy, for that matter) until a dollar will get him what he put into earning it. Tom calls his property Shelter Farm; not many places in the area have names. When we first went to call on him we stopped at a crossroads filling station and asked the way to Shelter Farm. The attendant thought for a moment, then answered, "Well, I guess that's what he calls the place—it's a mile down this road."

Even today, despite his leadership of the union, Tom is not fully committed to factory labor. To him the factory has always been a place to work only when he couldn't make a living in other ways. Tom's working-class qualities are not urban qualities; they are rural in character, and this gives them a middle-class rather than a proletarian tone. If Tom is a proletarian at all, he is a *rurban* proletarian: he lives on a farm that he owns and works, and is employed in a large factory as a semiskilled laborer. This combination is made possible by the rapid, private, and cheap means of transportation, the automobile. Tom, then, is neatly balanced between two poles: his status as a factory worker and union leader, and as a farm-owner and prospective full-time farm operator.

On most domestic issues Tom is in agreement with either the Democratic or the Progressive party, but his special combination of opinions on these questions, on American foreign policy and on the

Soviet Union identify him as a fellow traveler. Yet this is an over-simplification. When all the evidence is considered, it is clear that Tom is an unsophisticated radical who has not had enough contact with leftists to be able to distinguish among the various labels. When we told Tom that he talks like a fellow traveler he answered calmly that he is neither a Communist party member nor a supporter, but that he refuses to be a "red-baiter." To label a man a fellow traveler, Tom feels, is to take part in what he calls "the Red smear." Though he does not accept such socialist principles as government ownership of most of industry, agriculture, and other forms of property, Tom consciously avoids criticizing persons as Communists or fellow travelers. He would not like to see political questions in the United States settled in the violent manner of eastern Europe, he said, yet he offered the common C.P. rationalizations of Soviet foreign policy. When pressed for clear answers, however, Tom said things he usually identifies with "the Red smear." For example, he thought long and hard when we asked him if he considers Russia a free and democratic country. "I don't know," he finally said, "but maybe with this school teacher (Oksana Kasenkina) jumping out of the window, maybe it isn't too pleasant in Russia."

On the conscious ideological level, then, Tom talks like a fellow traveler. In two important respects, nevertheless, he deviates from that pattern. In the first place, because he lacks experience in inter-leftist affairs, he doesn't have the Communist's and fellow traveler's intense hatred of the anti-Communist left. Second, in his speculation about a successor to the presidency of the Acme local he doesn't apply the criterion of adherence to the C.P. line or to that of the International's leadership, or the Wallace movement. The worker Tom would like to see as the next head of the Acme local, Steve Konski, is a vigorous man in his thirties, a loyal Catholic of Polish descent who unhesitatingly expresses his distrust of the Soviet Union and American Communists. Tom's intense loyalty in his personal relations, and his deep concern for the Acme union and its members, dictate that in local matters he must make his decisions without regard to, and even in violation of, the ideology he himself accepts.

LOYALTY TO THE LOCAL UNION

We are now in a position to see how the double pattern, Tom's combination of radical politics and middle-class aspirations, conditions the way in which he functions as the link between the three hundred union men at Acme and the leadership of the International Union of Mine,

Mill and Smelter Workers. This double pattern, first of all, reinforces his loyalty to the *local*, since he aims to advance his welfare not through the union hierarchy but through his part-time and eventually his full-time farming. As a consequence, he owes neither his present power nor his future to the leadership above him.[3] Tom sincerely believes in the fellow-traveling politics of the union hierarchy, and is therefore a willing carrier of its message to the Acme workers. But this willingness is simply the result of the coincidence of Tom's politics and the hierarchy's. Because Tom's aspirations lie entirely outside the realm of unionism and the factory, he adheres to the International's politics by ideological choice rather than economic necessity. Hence Tom is not so reliable a transmitter of the top leadership's politics as, say, a local union head who is dependent upon the hierarchy's good will for his own power and for his future in the labor movement, or the local union head whose membership includes a powerful Communist faction. Tom's double pattern, then, reinforces his loyalty to his local rather than to his ideological mentors, and makes him an uncontrollable transmitter of the International's political line. . . .

Although he owes his position in the local to no one at International headquarters, Tom has always stood well with the top leadership. He shares their political faith. He regularly attends the conventions, personally knows and likes many of the International bigwigs, including Reid Robinson, a fellow-traveling ex-president who fell into disfavor because he had tried to borrow money from an employer with whom the union was negotiating a new contract. Several years ago Tom showed his loyalty to the International in concrete fashion by resisting a strong movement to take many New England locals out of the Mine, Mill and Smelter Workers Union and into the CIO Marine and Shipbuilding Workers of America. Backed by CIO national and state heads, George Bartlett, a former district official in the mine, mill union, led a secession drive over the Communist issue that seriously weakened the International's power and prestige. Tom stood by the International, and his stock with the leaders shot up accordingly. He held his predominantly Catholic local in line even though Bartlett had the support of the Church.

Aside from agreeing with the International on specific political issues, Tom agrees with the hierarchy on the general proposition that trade unions must be alert to politics if they are fully to serve the interests of

[3] In the early days of his leadership Tom was considerably dependent upon Jim Gallagher, the International representative assigned to the local. Tom learned leadership techniques through Jim, but is now entirely independent of him. In fact, Tom now patronizes Jim, who, because of his pretentiousness, is often the butt of jokes among the Acme workers.

their members. Tom feels that a union should provide the worker not only with leadership in the old "business union" sense but also in broader matters which, in his view, are equally essential for the security of the workers as a group. Yet it is not this broader conception that keeps the Acme workers loyal both to Tom and the International, but precisely their faith in the leadership's ability to supply the "business" services of unionism, its ability to deal with management in a manner the workers consider satisfactory. Tom, especially, is judged only on this ability to settle the bread-and-butter issues satisfactorily. By their ability to perform this utilitarian function for the workers, Tom and the International leaders are able also to serve them what an Englishman once called the pot of message. The political ideology is presented to the Acme workers because Tom wants it presented to them. We have no doubt that he can effectively close the door of the local to the International's ideological salesmen if he wants to; and we have no doubt that if the message interfered with the attainment of the Acme workers' bread-and-butter aims Tom would not hesitate to exclude it.

THE WALLACE CAMPAIGN

In unions that hold democratic elections it is possible to check the membership's opinion of the leadership's handling of the main business of unionism. It is not so easy, however, to check the membership's reaction to the political program of its leaders. Fortunately the election campaign of 1948 provides such a test in the case of Acme workers and Tom Coburn. Tom was an early supporter of Henry Wallace for president, attended the nominating convention of the Progressive party, and ran for Congress on its ticket. Tom's candidacy was a real test of his ability to get across an ideological message to the membership, a message which the International was also pushing on higher levels. How did he fare? Very poorly.

One hundred and twenty-five Acme workers signed Tom's petitions to get him on the ballot. In our bull sessions with them they told us they were voting for Wallace and for Tom. Though in private conversations some workers said they would vote for Truman, not a single one we talked to said he would vote against Tom. But Tom's total vote in the two towns where most Acme workers live was only 74 out of 5140 votes cast for the office he sought. He couldn't even get the votes of all those who had petitioned to get him on the ballot. In his own town he got only 8 out of more than 400. In the entire Congressional district the Republican won with almost 63,000 votes, the Democrat got over 58,000 and Tom mustered only 1191.

In one respect this showing surprised us. We had expected that Wallace would do poorly, but we expected that Tom would draw many more votes than he did, especially in the towns near the Acme plant. It turned out that Tom could not transmit the ideological message in this case either for himself or for the head of his ticket. Like the pollsters, we were misled by the verbal responses of Tom's union boys. When approached by Tom or a friend of his to sign the petition to get him on the ballot, the Acme workers willingly did so. When we asked them in a group or individually whether they would vote for Tom, they said you're damned right they would. But when they closed the curtain in the voting booth they acted differently. Tom has their loyalty and support in bread-and-butter union business, but he obviously failed to get across his own and the International's politics.

Business unionism is the vessel on which the ideology of the leadership is carried to the rank and file, but the cargo doesn't always get there with the vessel itself. Leadership can communicate a general approach to larger political issues, but its specific program is something else again, as Tom's campaign experience shows. The union hierarchy gets resolutions passed and runs the conventions, but how far do they influence their members on issues that divide the labor movement itself? The evidence in this case study gives one answer: not very deeply. The union looks one way at the top and another way at the grass roots. The International Union of Mine, Mill and Smelter Workers is a Communist-influenced union, but it has an entirely different aspect at the local level where trade unionism is the reality for most workers. Because he has their respect for his ability to face management in their behalf, Tom gets the unanimous support of the Acme workers; but he can't get them to think his way in the political game. He tries to get a political idea to them because he believes in it; this idea happens also to bind the International leadership. It is Tom, not the International, who stands high with the Acme men; hence it is through him that the message must pass. He lets it pass and gets behind it to give it a shove, but it doesn't get as far as he would like. The Acme workers respond to other loyalties in many situations they face, not merely to their loyalty to Tom and the union.

34. Of Time and the Railroader *

WITH THE INCREASING INDUSTRIALIZATION and related division of labor in our society we have come more and more to "live by the clock." The importance of "time" has grown until it reaches into all aspects of our lives and has come to be a limiting force in all forms of social participation. We raise our children according to a time schedule and the clock becomes an essential part of their lives. As adults, the time schedule demands of our jobs reach out to affect much of our day-to-day social interaction. Perhaps in few occupations does time-consciousness affect the total living pattern as much as it does the "railroader." Here W. F. Cottrell discusses the part that time plays in the lives of railroaders. Because the influence here is extreme, the reader can see the phenomenon in sharp focus and consequently can understand more easily how, to a somewhat lesser degree, the same situation applies to most occupations in our society.

THE FOURTH DIMENSION has been a subject for everything from highly abstract and critical thinking to fantastic imagination. It has served to modify fixed points in an established science and to support time-worn religions. Likewise, calculations in which time is taken as an aspect of all other measurements have imposed new restrictions on human behavior.

That the centuries have witnessed a modification in the concept of time, Sorokin has adequately demonstrated. There is no need for us to raise the question as to whether in the long run the present conception of time may be altered, for, in the moment that we are considering, the use of the Newtonian system of mechanics for the creation of our technology binds us to the use of a mechanical conception of time. We may argue long and bitterly about the nature of time, but we know that if we want to catch a train, see a kickoff, or hear a radio program, our frame of reference forces us to consult an accurate clock.

The vast subdivision of labor which characterizes our technology requires coordination in time and space—neither axis alone is adequate. The backbone of industrialism is the railroad. Split-second timing of industrial operations reflects back along the line of transportation and

* W. F. Cottrell, American Sociological Review, 4 (April, 1939), 190-198. Reprinted by permission of the publisher and the author.

The author (b. 1903) is Professor of Sociology, Miami University, Oxford, Ohio. Interested in child welfare activities, effects of technology upon society. Author, The Railroader.

imposes constantly new and closer limits upon those who operate trains.

Time is an important factor in any social pattern. Social interaction requires time coordination, and to the degree that occupation determines time distribution, time limits all forms of social participation. As technology controls time for the railroader, it also determines the tempo and the interval of other social relationships and sets a pattern for the personality.

After consulting Gulliver on the function of his watch, the Lilliputians came to the conclusion that it was his God. Observing the money spent and the care lavished on his watch, a Martian might conclude the same thing of the railroader. All those who have direct responsibility for the actual operations of trains must carry a fine timepiece which will gain or lose not more than forty seconds in two weeks and which must be cleaned and regulated twice a year by a railroad watch inspector. A delay of thirty seconds in leaving a terminal calls for explanation, five minutes' delay means investigation, and a half hour gives apoplexy to every official from the superintendent to the lowest foreman. On single track roads where trains meet at passing tracks, thirty seconds' delay means that one of the trains will be almost a half mile from a passing track when the other reaches it, and that means delay of a second train, with possible misunderstanding and resultant disaster.

Delays at crossovers may mean a reversal in the order in which trains use the intersection, possible increased delay while clearance is secured, and a whole series of new orders to care for trains that otherwise would be met as a matter of course by other trains over which they have the right of way. The timetable is not only a convenience for the fidgeting tourist who uses it to chart his progress and occupy himself; it is a habit-system, or a "subconscious mind," for the railway "organism." Trainmen meet all scheduled trains in accordance with this table and plan to take sidings or make stops with a margin of time great enough to clear automatic signals for superior trains. The timetable makes all these coordinations as automatic as a conditioned reflex as far as the operating brain in the dispatcher's office is concerned. Delays mean that a new situation must be faced; operative intelligence is required for too many things at once and operating efficiency falls. The fatigued brain of the trick dispatcher is much more likely to err when it is called upon to take a load additional to that involved in planning only for extra trains. The technique of railroading itself makes it necessary to operate thousands of tons, moving at extremely high speeds with an accuracy greater than that maintained on many a factory assembly line.

This operating technique, determined by the nature of *things*, if disaster is to be avoided, is intensified by the interest and insurance calculus of capitalist civilization. To the African, time is like air, a free good, and therefore has no exchange value. To the American business man, who uses it as frequently as any other unit in determining price and exchange value, time becomes a cost factor of no little significance. Passenger trains were first to feel the impact of this factor. The plainsman planning to rejoin his fur-trapping "pardner" was content to rejoin him "after snow melts" or "when the grass turns green," or more accurately "in April" or "six moons from now." Wagon trains made planning of trips calculable within a matter of weeks, stage coaches were due on a certain day, but no efficiency expert computed the value of a half-hour's delay for five hundred people, nor calculated the insurance rate on the whole outfit. Nowadays, business executives accustomed to making decisions involving millions after an interview lasting a few hours or even minutes, demand accurate coordination so that these precious minutes may be calculated far in advance, and even salesmen of less importance schedule their day in minutes. Interdependence with schedules of competing roads and other means of transportation led to increased emphasis on *time*, until the five- or ten-second error permitted on passenger trains became a commonplace.

Then luxury goods began to require the same sort of accuracy. Silk trains, valued in millions, speeding from Pacific Coast ports to silk centers the width of a continent away, were heavily insured. The insurance was high and calculated not in days but hours; the road which could promise accurate delivery could save in insurance sums large enough to make special schedules for silk a paying proposition.

· · · · · ·

The complete interdependence of mass production industries is revealed by such events as the strikes of 1937 in which the absence of single items such as an induction coil or brakeshoe brought the whole automobile industry to a halt. The result is, of course, that the penalties imposed for a few hours' delay in delivering any one of hundreds of items may be fantastic.

Time penalties come to figure highly in the minds of business managers; therefore, railroads have made seemingly impossible promises of delivery because they must bid for regular accounts from shippers who, by Interstate Commerce regulation and antirebate laws, are denied the price cutting and special discounts by which other industries secure contracts. These impossibilities are then turned into realities through pressure on the railroader. The traffic department which has secured a "juicy bit" of business gets apoplectic when a delay threatens to lose it; therefore, down the line, from general manager to car inspector, goes out the edict, "Delay this train at peril of your job." Supervisors are bombarded with messages, "Meet this train"; "No explanation for the delay of this train will be accepted"; "From this date, train operates on such and such a schedule, no delay can be permitted." In the meantime, under the same pressure from "efficiency experts," men are fired or laid off, trains increased in length, the number of service-stops cut, and less money is spent on repairs and maintenance. The second hand of his watch becomes a sword of Damocles to the railroader.

The twenty-four-hour day and the three-hundred-and-sixty-five-day year are as necessary to the railroad as to the calendar. There are no holidays. Christmas day in Chicago is two days before Christmas in Los Angeles, if you are moving east, and two days after Christmas if you move west. No break in service at one point would correspond with delivery date at another except where short distances are involved. So the pressure is incessant. For the railroader, split-second timing never ceases; he is always on call. The plant is never shut down. A wreck, a washout, a split switch, a sudden increased demand for power, an engine failure, frozen steam pipes, clogged toilet facilities, failure of air conditioning, a broken train line—any one of a thousand incidents may threaten to cause delay or to inconvenience patrons, so the railroader must be available even though his shift is over and he is supposedly a "free man." He is a slave to the clock; intense time-consciousness marks the railroader in all his social relationships.

This time-emphasis is, of course, an aspect of the lives of all moderns. They catch the timed trains, eat by the clock, quit by the clock and are clocked in their amusement: "The next feature will begin at 8:12": "Twenty-five cents for the first three minutes, five cents for each additional minute"; "The kickoff will be at 2:30"; and so on, ad infinitum.

Coordination in time takes its toll from all of us but probably among few other classes is it so complete and coercive as among railroaders. It becomes a marked irritant in his relationship with other less time-conscious groups. "Dinner at eight" means eight, not eight-ten or eight-twenty; "I'll meet you at seven" means seven, not seven-thirty or the debutante's eight-thirty. The casualness with which people in other walks of life take delays irritates the railroader and in turn his irritation produces counterirritation among his fellows. A railroad worker expects to lay down his tools with the whistle, or a little before. To the railroader, the callousness with which a building contractor, storekeeper, or other employer, exacts an additional five minutes' work is unforgivable.

The "sixteen hour law" under which the Federal Government regulates the working hours of trainmen and enginemen is absolute. If a hapless crew "lets the monkey get them" or, in other words, finds itself on the road at the expiration of sixteen hours from their terminal of departure, they must stop all active operations. When they sense the approach of the limit, the crew takes to a siding, notifies the dispatcher of their situation and waits for a relief crew to be sent to bring them in. Even delays occasioned by landslide, washout, the derailment of another train, or other accident, do not serve as excuse. If the crew has been on duty during the waiting time, they cannot move the train under penalty of heavy fine on the employing road. If an accident holds the train on the main line while the sixteen-hour limit elapses, its crew may not even move the train to clear traffic for others. Protecting it from collision with track "torpedoes" and "fusees" (flares), they must wait until a crew with legal rest arrives to take charge of it.

Eight hours' rest is required out of every twenty-four in which sixteen hours are worked. A crew may not be called to take a train out before that rest has elapsed, but if another crew *is* called and takes their place and it is later shown that the legal rest of the first crew was up before the train departed, a "run around," or pay for the trip, is given the crew so deprived of their proper "turn." Time is certainly the essence of this contract.

The obverse of this occupational dependence on the clock is the almost complete denial of the opportunity to "time-plan" other relationships. Shopmen working on general repairs, or those on a three-shift basis, such as dispatchers, car and engine inspectors, can normally expect to work one shift and be through, but men on the extra-board, or trainmen and enginemen working on a "chain gang," in which crews take their turns on whatever business is handled, car repairers who may be called out to handle repairs or service extra trains, and many others, find that the demands of occupation make all other plans conditional. Like other aspects of railroading, this is more typical of trainmen than it is of workers in the other crafts.

"We can't plan to have Johnny in the Christmas play because his father may be 'in' right then and we want him to be home." "Mary can't promise to come at that time because her father may want his dinner and he likes to have the children at meals." "I can't join the bridge club because I want to be with John when he is home and I might have to miss too many times." "We did want to have Sunday dinner with the Browns but Will is going to be 'out' and we have to have our dinner Saturday night instead." "We'll go to the benefit if John is 'in' and has his rest, but I can't buy a ticket because he may want to sleep." "We don't want to sign up for that series because you never know whether you can go or not." "The boys were so disappointed. They planned to go fishing with their Dad on the Fourth but there was an excursion and he had to take it 'out.'" "I had the nicest Easter outfit and then we couldn't go to church because Henry was 'called' at nine o'clock." These are typical of the irritations which beset the life of the railroader and his family when he is still on unscheduled freight or the extra-board, which usually occurs while his family, if he has one, is young, and when the demarcation which this sort of life serves to make between the railroader and others, and between various railroaders, is most important. Meals may be required at any hour; sometimes two or three series of meals in a day must be prepared depending upon school schedules and those of men on various shifts. Car inspectors, for example, eat their lunch when they can get it. The noon meal may come any time between eleven and three, depending on the arrival of nonscheduled extra trains, or the amount of "running repairs" that have to be done. The rest of the community,— its schools, its churches, lodges, bridge clubs, official meetings of boards of trustees, town councilmen, benefits, socials, theaters (except movies), —also run on a time schedule, but it is not so rigid as that of the railroad, although it is much more definite and therefore will permit more time-planning than is possible for those railroaders who operate trains.

Membership in any organization with regular meetings is difficult to maintain and the socializing effect of such contacts is lost. Forms of recreation that depend upon no collaboration with others must be indulged in. In cities, there are continuous shows, night clubs and restaurants, taxi dancehalls, and other individualized amusements; in rural areas, fishing and hunting, pool parlors, or saloons are offered; in both, the ubiquitous crap-game and other forms of gambling.

Civic participation is rendered difficult. No membership in governing boards is feasible, promised aid in community service may be impossible when the "layover" between runs comes at the other end of the line or a "bump" may put one on another run. Indifference created by occupationally induced mobility is heightened by this time-factor, and the other members of the community resent the refusal of this group, usually the most financially able, to take any responsibility in community affairs.

Family life is greatly affected. If the wife and mother attempts to make her family an integrated part of the community, she must conform to its timing. Meals must be ready for the children so that they can attend school and Sunday School. Promises as to their participation in athletics, school government, and extracurricular activities must be kept. If this be done, it may mean that the husband and father will see the children only rarely. He can expect that at least half the time his rest will come during the time they are sleeping; their whole day is normally taken at school; if his meals cannot be made to coincide with theirs (and frequently, if he is to get any sleep, they cannot), he may not see his children at all, unless they give up all plans of their own.

The wife labors under a double difficulty. In the absence of the father of her children, she has the whole problem of discipline. She cannot even threaten "when your father comes home tonight" for that may be at three o'clock in the morning. She must be prepared to have meals ready whenever he comes in, which means constant preparation for the unexpected; she seldom knows in which particular meal her husband will share. She cannot plan with any degree of certainty her own recreation or community participation. If she joins club, church, guild, or lodge, and takes office, she may incur the displeasure of a husband deprived of what he regards as his right to her time and attention when he is "in." If she does not join, she is likely to be deprived of almost all recreation since she is denied the equivalent of the forms of recreation her husband may have, and if she chooses to go to public dances or any other public place where couples are expected, she is immediately suspected by all the "good" people of the community. Small wonder that family life during this period is frequently so distasteful and disorganized as to rob later years, when a satisfactory "run" has been earned, of most of its satisfactions. Yet the very situations that make family life difficult also serve to increase the significance of the family in the life of the railroader. In many cases, it is the only group in which he functions, and an idealized attitude toward children frequently results, making for a romantic indulgence of their whims.

Other classes of employees in continuous service, particularly telegraphers and "agents" in small stations, with no relief operator, are made even more dependent upon the clock. Interrupted rest periods are a commonplace. Though the station be officially closed, emergencies may make their presence at the "key" necessary, and many of these men have slept for years with a telegraph repeater in the room, paying no attention to its continuous clatter until the call letters of their own station shock them into instant wakefulness. The newer dependence upon the "dispatcher's" telephone with a selector that rings only the operator for whom it is intended has somewhat reduced this tension, but no operator, whether on or off duty, ever gets out of hearing of his "call bell" without a sense of guilt. To wives anxious to escape the confines of a lonely station, this marriage to a telegraph key is frequently an almost unbearable form of polygamy.

"Agents" in small stations work all trains, the clock around, meeting passengers, selling tickets, arranging for the loading and unloading of freight; securing a doctor to treat the train-sick old lady from Dubuque and a nurse to hold the hand of a homeward bound conventionite who has imbibed not wisely but too much; checking on the whoops of a child about to board the train to discover whether he will become liable for permitting a person with contagious disease to cross a state line; ordering a California-bound farmer's wife with preserves packed in straw to substitue paper in order to avoid another penalty; all under the continuous pressure of time, and with the knowledge that error in transmitting or receiving a "train order" may mean disaster and death.

The higher the railroader climbs on the supervisory ladder, the less he is able to plan his own life. The foreman is expected to supervise even those employees who work night shifts, to meet trains when necessary regardless of the hour, and to be in continuous presence during the day when the regular shifts of "dead workers," "rip track" men, section men, janitors, etc., are working. If he reaches the rare-fied atmosphere of the office of "trainmaster," "roadmaster," or "master mechanic," he is expected to maintain an office in regular contact both with superiors and foremen and to be physically present at numerous points scattered over as much as a thousand miles. Getting up in the middle of the night to catch trains, getting meals when he can, and in emergency, neither getting nor expecting sleep, is the lot of the super-visor as well as his underlings. Is it any wonder that these "real rail-roaders" look with envious contempt at the comfortable "plush polish-ers" in the central offices, who live in a world of the eight-hour day, forty-hour week, and who take all legal holidays?

As "time marches on," its rhythm is set, not by organic impulse, but by the clacking of wheels on rail joints, the clatter of a telegraph key, and the distant whistle of a train departing "on time."

❧❧❧❧

35. Fundamental Notions of the Folkways and of the Mores *

THE MANNERS, usages, folkways, mores, and institutions of every society tend to be regarded by the members of that society as the only right and proper ones. Perhaps Sumner's famous book, *Folkways*, published in 1906, has done more than any other to demonstrate the great variety of human behavior patterns thus regarded. As a result, it has induced many people to pause before they say, "My ways—our ways—are the *only* civilized ways of behaving," or perhaps even to refrain from so thinking. The terms *folkways* and *mores*, first given currency as sociological terms in Sumner's book, have been so widely accepted that even pictorial magazines like *Life* and *Look* use them today. Such popular adoption of technical social science terms is very rare.

DEFINITION AND MODE OF ORIGIN OF THE FOLKWAYS

IF WE PUT TOGETHER all that we have learned from anthropology and ethnography about primitive men and primitive society, we perceive that the first task of life is to live. Men begin with acts, not with thoughts. Every moment brings necessities which must be satisfied at once. Need was the first experience, and it was followed at once by a blundering effort to satisfy it. It is generally taken for granted that men inherited some guiding instincts from their beast ancestry, and it may be true, although it has never been proved. If there were such inheritances, they controlled and aided the first efforts to satisfy needs. Analogy makes it easy to assume that the ways of beasts had produced channels of habit and predisposition along which dexterities and other psychophysical activities would run easily. Experiments with newborn animals show that in the absence of any experience of the relation of means to ends, efforts to satisfy needs are clumsy and blundering. The method is that of trial and failure, which produces repeated pain, loss, and disappointments. Nevertheless, it is a method of rude

---

* William Graham Sumner, *Folkways* (Ginn and Company, 1940, Centennial Edition), sections 1-3, 28-29, 31-32, 34-35, 66-68. Reprinted by permission of the publisher.

The author (1840-1910) was an economist, sociologist, rector. One of first Big Four American sociologists with Ward, Giddings, and Small. Became Professor of Political and Social Science at Yale in 1872. Studied in Universities of Göttingen and Oxford. Among his books are *A History of American Currency*, *What Social Classes Owe to Each Other*, *Earth Hunger and Other Essays*, *The Science of Society* (with A. G. Keller).

experiment and selection. The earliest efforts of men were of this kind. Need was the impelling force. Pleasure and pain, on the one side and the other, were the rude constraints which defined the line on which efforts must proceed. The ability to distinguish between pleasure and pain is the only psychical power which is to be assumed. Thus ways of doing things were selected, which were expedient. They answered the purpose better than other ways, or with less toil and pain. Along the course on which efforts were compelled to go, habit, routine, and skill were developed. The struggle to maintain existence was carried on, not individually, but in groups. Each profited by the other's experience; hence there was concurrence towards that which proved to be most expedient. All at last adopted the same way for the same purpose; hence the ways turned into customs and became mass phenomena. Instincts were developed in connection with them. In this way folkways arise. The young learn them by tradition, imitation, and authority. The folkways, at a time, provide for all the needs of life then and there. They are uniform, universal in the group, imperative, and invariable. As time goes on, the folkways become more and more arbitrary, positive, and imperative. If asked why they act in a certain way in certain cases, primitive people always answer that it is because they and their ancestors always have done so. A sanction also arises from ghost fear. The ghosts of ancestors would be angry if the living should change the ancient folkways.

THE FOLKWAYS ARE A SOCIETAL FORCE

The operation by which folkways are produced consists in the frequent repetition of petty acts, often by great numbers acting in concert or, at least, acting in the same way when face to face with the same need. The immediate motive is interest. It produces habit in the individual and custom in the group. It is, therefore, in the highest degree original and primitive. By habit and custom it exerts a strain on every individual within its range; therefore it rises to a societal force to which great classes of societal phenomena are due. Its earliest stages, its course, and laws may be studied; also its influence on individuals and their reaction on it. It is our present purpose so to study it. We have to recognize it as one of the chief forces by which a society is made to be what it is. Out of the unconscious experiment which every repetition of the ways includes, there issues pleasure or pain, and then, so far as the men are capable of reflection, convictions that the ways are conducive to societal welfare. These two experiences are not the same. The most uncivilized men, both in the food quest and in war, do things which are painful, but which have been found to be expedient. Perhaps these cases teach the sense of social welfare better than those which are pleasurable and favorable to welfare. The former cases call for some intelligent reflection on experience. When this conviction as to the relation to welfare is added to the folkways they are converted into mores, and, by virtue of the philosophical and ethical element added to them, they win utility and importance and become the source of the science and the art of living.

FOLKWAYS ARE MADE UNCONSCIOUSLY

It is of the first importance to notice that, from the first acts by which men try to satisfy needs, each act stands by itself, and looks no further than the immediate satisfaction. From recurrent needs arise habits for the individual and customs for the group, but these results are consequences which were never conscious, and never foreseen or intended. They are not noticed until they have long existed, and it is still longer before they are appreciated. Another long time must pass, and a higher stage of mental development must be reached, before they can be used as a basis from which to deduce rules for meeting, in the future, problems whose pressure can be foreseen. The folkways, therefore, are not creations of human purpose and wit. They are like products of natural forces which men unconsciously set in operation, or they are like the instinctive ways of animals, which are developed out of experience, which reach a final form of maximum adaptation to an interest, which are handed down by tradition and admit of no exception or variation, yet change to meet new conditions, still within the same limited methods, and without rational reflection or purpose. From this it results that all the life of human beings, in all ages and stages of culture, is primarily controlled by a vast mass of folkways handed down from the earliest existence of the race, having the nature of the ways of other animals, only the topmost layers of which are subject to change and control, and have been somewhat modified by human philosophy, ethics, and religion, or by other acts of intelligent reflection. We are told of savages that "It is difficult to exhaust the customs and small ceremonial usages of a savage people. Custom regulates the whole of a man's actions, — his bathing, washing, cutting his hair, eating, drinking, and fasting. From his cradle to his grave he is the slave of ancient usage. In his life there is nothing free, nothing original, nothing spontaneous, no progress towards a higher and better life, and no attempt to improve his condition, mentally, morally, or spiritually." All men act in this way with only a little wider margin of voluntary variation.

•   •   •   •   •   •   •

FOLKWAYS DUE TO FALSE INFERENCE

Folkways have been formed by accident, that is, by irrational and incongruous action, based on pseudo-knowledge. In Molembo a pestilence broke out soon after a Portuguese had died there. After that the natives took all possible measures not to allow any white man to die in their country. On the Nicobar islands some natives who had just begun to make pottery died. The art was given up and never again attempted. White men gave to one Bushman in a kraal a stick ornamented with buttons as a symbol of authority. The recipient died leaving the stick to his son. The son soon died. Then the Bushmen brought back the stick lest all should die. Until recently no building of incombustible materials could be built in any big town of the central province of Madagascar, on account of some ancient prejudice. A party of Eskimos met with no game. One of them returned to their sledges and got the ham of a dog to eat. As he returned with the ham bone in his hand he met and killed a seal. Ever afterwards he carried a ham bone in his hand when hunting. The Belenda women (peninsula of Malacca) stay as near to the house as possible during the period. Many keep the door closed. They know no reason for this custom. "It must be due to some now forgotten superstition." Soon after the Yakuts saw a camel for the first time smallpox broke out amongst them. They thought the camel to be the agent of the disease. A woman amongst the same people contracted an endogamous marriage. She soon afterwards became blind. This was thought to be on account of the violation of ancient customs. A very great number of such cases could be collected. In fact they represent the current mode of reasoning of nature people. It is their custom to reason that, if one thing follows another, it is due to it. A great number of customs are traceable to the notion of the evil eye, many more to ritual notions of uncleanness. No scientific investigation could discover the origin of the folkways mentioned, if the origin had not chanced to become known to civilized men. We must believe that the known cases illustrate the irrational and incongruous origin of many folkways. In civilized history also we know that customs have owed their origin to "historical accident," — the vanity of a princess, the deformity of a king, the whim of a democracy, the love intrigue of a statesman or prelate. By the institutions of another age it may be provided that no one of these things can affect decisions, acts, or interests, but then the power to decide the ways may have passed to clubs, trades unions, trusts, commercial rivals, wire-pullers, politicians, and political fanatics. In these cases also the causes and origins may escape investigation.

HARMFUL FOLKWAYS

There are folkways which are positively harmful. Very often these are just the ones for which a definite reason can be given. The destruction of a man's goods at his death is a direct deduction from other-worldliness; the dead man is supposed to want in the other world just what he wanted here. The destruction of a man's goods at his death was a great waste of capital, and it must have had a disastrous effect on the interests of the living, and must have very seriously hindered the development of civilization. With this custom we must class all the expenditure of labor and capital on graves, temples, pyramids, rites, sacrifices, and support of priests, so far as these were supposed to benefit the dead. The faith in goblinism produced other-worldly interests which overruled ordinary worldly interests. Foods have often been forbidden which were plentiful, the prohibition of which injuriously lessened the food supply. There is a tribe of Bushmen who will eat no goat's flesh, although goats are the most numerous domestic animals in the district. Where totemism exists it is regularly accompanied by a taboo on eating the totem animal. Whatever may be the real principle in totemism, it overrules the interest in an abundant food supply. "The origin of the sacred regard paid to the cow must be sought in the primitive nomadic life of the Indo-European race," because it is common to Iranians and Indians of Hindostan. The Libyans ate oxen but not cows. The same was true of the Phœnicians and Egyptians. In some cases the sense of a food taboo is not to be learned. It may have been entirely capricious. Mohammed would not eat lizards, because he thought them the offspring of a metamorphosed clan of Israelites. On the other hand, the protective taboo which forbade killing crocodiles, pythons, cobras, and other animals enemies of man was harmful to his interests, whatever the motive. "It seems to be a fixed article of belief throughout southern India, that all who have willfully or accidentally killed a snake, especially a cobra, will certainly be punished, either in this life or the next, in one of three ways: either by childlessness, or by leprosy, or by ophthalmia." Where this faith exists man has a greater interest to spare a cobra than to kill it. India furnishes a great number of cases of harmful mores. "In India every tendency of humanity seems intensified and exaggerated. No country in the world is so conservative in its traditions, yet no country has undergone so many religious changes and vicissitudes." "Every year thousands perish of disease that might recover if they would take proper nourishment, and drink the medicine that science prescribes, but which they imagine that their religion forbids them to touch." "Men who can scarcely count beyond twenty, and know not the letters of the alphabet, would rather die than eat food which had been prepared by men of lower caste, unless it had been sanctified by being offered to an idol; and would kill their daughters rather than endure the disgrace of having unmarried girls at home beyond twelve or thirteen years of age." In the last case the rule of obligation and duty is set by the mores. The interest comes under vanity. The sanction of the caste rules is in a boycott by all members of the caste. The rules are often very harmful. "The authority of caste rests partly on written laws, partly on legendary fables or narratives, partly on the injunctions of instructors and priests, partly on custom and usage, and partly on the caprice and convenience of its votaries." The harm of caste rules is so great that of late they have been broken in some cases, especially in regard to travel over sea, which is a great advantage to Hindoos. The Hindoo folkways in regard to widows and child marriages must also be recognized as socially harmful.

* * * * * *

THE FOLKWAYS ARE "RIGHT"

The folkways are the "right" ways to satisfy all interests, because they are traditional, and exist in fact. They extend over the whole of life. There is a right way to catch game, to win a wife, to make one's self appear, to cure disease, to honor ghosts, to treat comrades or strangers, to behave when a child is born, on the warpath, in council, and so on in all cases which can arise. The ways are defined on the negative side, that is, by taboos. The "right" way is the way which the ancestors used and which has been handed down. The tradition is its own warrant. It is not held subject to verification by experience. The notion of right is in the folkways. It is not outside of them, of independent origin, and brought to them to test them. In the folkways, whatever is, is right. This is because they are traditional, and therefore contain in themselves the authority of the ancestral ghosts. When we come to the folkways we are at the end of our analysis. The notion of right and ought is the same in regard to all the folkways, but the degree of it varies with the importance of the interest at stake. The obligation of conformable and coöperative action is far greater under ghost fear and war than in other matters, and the social sanctions are severer, because group interests are supposed to be at stake. Some usages contain only a slight element of right and ought. It may well be believed that notions of right and duty, and of social welfare, were first developed in connection with ghost fear and other-worldliness, and therefore that, in that field also, folkways were first raised to mores. "Rights" are the rules of mutual give and take in the competition of life which are imposed on comrades in the in-group, in order that the peace may prevail there which is essential to the group strength. Therefore rights can never be "natural" or "God-given," or absolute in any sense. The morality of a group at a time is the sum of the taboos and prescriptions in the folkways by which right conduct is defined. Therefore morals can never be intuitive. They are historical, institutional, and empirical.

World philosophy, life policy, right, rights, and morality are all products of the folkways. They are reflections on, and generalizations from, the experience of pleasure and pain which is won in efforts to carry on the struggle for existence under actual life conditions. The generalizations are very crude and vague in their germinal forms. They are all embodied in folklore, and all our philosophy and science have been developed out of them.

THE FOLKWAYS ARE "TRUE"

The folkways are necessarily "true" with respect to some world philosophy. Pain forced men to think. The ills of life imposed reflection and taught forethought. Mental processes were irksome and were not undertaken until painful experience made them unavoidable. With great unanimity all over the globe primitive men followed the same line of thought. The dead were believed to live on as ghosts in another world just like this one. The ghosts had just the same needs, tastes, passions, etc., as the living men had had. These transcendental notions were the beginning of the mental outfit of mankind. They are articles of faith, not rational convictions. The living had duties to the ghosts, and the ghosts had rights; they also had power to enforce their rights. It behooved the living therefore to learn how to deal with ghosts. Here we have a complete world philosophy and a life policy deduced from it. When pain, loss, and ill were experienced and the question was provoked, Who did this to us? the world philosophy furnished the answer. When the painful experience forced the question, Why are the ghosts angry and what must we do to appease them? the "right" answer was the one which fitted into the philosophy of ghost fear. All acts were therefore constrained and trained into the forms of the world philosophy by ghost fear, ancestral authority, taboos, and habit. The habits and customs created a practical philosophy of welfare, and they confirmed and developed the religious theories of goblinism.

•   •   •   •   •   •

DEFINITION OF THE MORES

When the elements of truth and right are developed into doctrines of welfare, the folkways are raised to another plane. They then become capable of producing inferences, developing into new forms, and extending their constructive influence over men and society. Then we call them the mores. The mores are the folkways, including the philosophical and ethical generalizations as to societal welfare which are suggested by them, and inherent in them, as they grow.

TABOOS

The mores necessarily consist, in a large part, of taboos, which indicate the things which must not be done. In part these are dictated by mystic dread of ghosts who might be offended by certain acts, but they also include such acts as have been found by experience to produce unwelcome results, especially in the food quest, in war, in health, or in increase or decrease of population. These taboos always contain a greater element of philosophy than the positive rules, because the taboos contain reference to a reason, as, for instance, that the act would displease the ghosts. The primitive taboos correspond to the fact that the life of man is environed by perils. His food quest must be limited by shunning poisonous plants. His appetite must be restrained from excess. His physical strength and health must be guarded from dangers. The taboos carry on the accumulated wisdom of generations, which has almost always been purchased by pain, loss, disease, and death. Other taboos contain inhibitions of what will be injurious to the group. The laws about the sexes, about property, about war, and about ghosts, have this character. They always include some social philosophy. They are both mystic and utilitarian, or compounded of the two.

Taboos may be divided into two classes, (1) protective and (2) destructive. Some of them aim to protect and secure, while others aim to repress or exterminate. Women are subject to some taboos which are directed against them as sources of possible harm or danger to men, and they are subject to other taboos which put them outside of the duties or risks of men. On account of this difference in taboos, taboos act selectively, and thus affect the course of civilization. They contain judgments as to societal welfare.

•   •   •   •   •   •

MORE EXACT DEFINITION OF THE MORES

We may now formulate a more complete definition of the mores. They are the ways of doing things which are current in a society to satisfy human needs and desires, together with the faiths, notions, codes, and standards of well living which inhere in those ways, having a genetic connection with them. By virtue of the latter element the mores are traits in the specific character (ethos) of a society or a period. They pervade and control the ways of thinking in all the exigencies of life, returning from the world of abstractions to the world of action, to give guidance and to win revivification. "The mores [*Sitten*] are, before any beginning of reflection, the regulators of the political, social, and religious behavior of the individual. Conscious reflection is the worst enemy of the mores, because mores begin unconsciously and pursue unconscious purposes, which are recognized by reflection often only after long and circuitous processes, and because their expediency often depends on the assumption that they will have general acceptance and currency, uninterfered with by reflection." "The mores are usage in any group, in so far as it, on the one hand, is not the expression or fulfillment of an absolute natural necessity [e.g. eating or sleeping], and, on the other hand, is independent of the arbitrary will of the individual, and is generally accepted as good and proper, appropriate and worthy."

RITUAL

The process by which mores are developed and established is ritual. Ritual is so foreign to our mores that we do not recognize its power. In primitive society it is the prevailing method of activity, and primitive religion is entirely a matter of ritual. Ritual is the perfect form of drill and of the regulated habit which comes from drill. Acts which are ordained by authority and are repeated mechanically without intelligence run into ritual. If infants and children are subjected to ritual they never escape from its effects through life. Galton says that he was, in early youth, in contact with the Mohammedan ritual idea that the left hand is less worthy than the right, and that he never overcame it. We see the effect of ritual in breeding, courtesy, politeness, and all forms of prescribed behavior. Etiquette is social ritual. Ritual is not easy compliance with usage; it is strict compliance with detailed and punctilious rule. It admits of no exception or deviation. The stricter the discipline, the greater the power of ritual over action and character. In the training of animals and the education of children it is the perfection, inevitableness, invariableness, and relentlessness of routine which tells. They should never experience any exception or irregularity. Ritual is connected with words, gestures, symbols, and signs. Associations result, and, upon a repetition of the signal, the act is repeated, whether the will assents or not. Association and habit account for the phenomena. Ritual gains further strength when it is rhythmical, and is connected with music, verse, or other rhythmical arts. Acts are ritually repeated at the recurrence of the rhythmical points. The alternation of night and day produces rhythms of waking and sleeping, of labor and rest, for great numbers at the same time, in their struggle for existence. The seasons also produce rhythms in work. Ritual may embody an idea of utility, expediency, or welfare, but it always tends to become perfunctory, and the idea is only subconscious. There is ritual in primitive therapeutics, and it was not eliminated until very recent times. The patient was directed, not only to apply remedies, but also to perform rites. The rites introduced mystic elements. This illustrates the connection of ritual with notions of magical effects produced by rites. All ritual is ceremonious and solemn. It tends to become sacred, or to make sacred the subject-matter with which it is connected. Therefore, in primitive society, it is by ritual that sentiments of awe, deference to authority, submission to tradition, and disciplinary coöperation are inculcated. Ritual operates a constant suggestion, and the suggestion is at once put in operation in acts. Ritual, therefore, suggests sentiments, but it never inculcates doctrines. Ritual is strongest when it is most perfunctory and excites no thought. By familiarity with ritual any doctrinal reference which it once had is lost by familiarity, but the habits persist. Primitive religion is ritualistic, not because religion makes ritual, but because ritual makes religion. Ritual is something to be done, not something to be thought or felt. Men can always perform the prescribed act, although they cannot always think or feel prescribed thoughts or emotions. The acts may bring up again, by association, states of the mind and sentiments which have been connected with them, especially in childhood, when the fantasy was easily affected by rites, music, singing, dramas, etc. No creed, no moral code, and no scientific demonstration can ever win the same hold upon men and women as habits of action, with associated sentiments and states of mind, drilled in from childhood. Mohammedanism shows the power of ritual. Any occupation is interrupted for the prayers and prescribed genuflections. The Brahmins also observe an elaborate daily ritual. They devote to it two hours in the morning, two in the evening, and one at midday. Monks and nuns have won the extreme satisfaction of religious sentiment from the unbroken habit of repeated ritual, with undisturbed opportunity to develop the emotional effects of it.

THE RITUAL OF THE MORES

The mores are social ritual in which we all participate unconsciously. The current habits as to hours of labor, meal hours, family life, the social intercourse of the sexes, propriety, amusements, travel, holidays, education, the use of periodicals and libraries, and innumerable other details of life fall under this ritual. Each does as everybody does. For the great mass of mankind as to all things, and for all of us for a great many things, the rule to do as all do suffices. We are led by suggestion and association to believe that there must be wisdom and utility in what all do. The great mass of the folkways give us discipline and the support of routine and habit. If we had to form judgments as to all these cases before we could act in them, and were forced always to act rationally, the burden would be unendurable. Beneficent use and wont save us this trouble.

❦❦❦

36. Ossification *

WE TEND TO THINK of our society as one in which change is rapid and new ideas are quickly accepted. When we read of extreme resistance to change among primitive societies, the contrast with our own culture is so marked that we forget that sometimes we too resist change. Edward A. Ross jars our complacency. He points up the fact that we tend to change some of our traditions and habits very slowly. For example, we do not like changes that affect our religion and politics, or even our customs of everyday living. Ross explains how and why our social institutions and customs gradually lose adaptability and become "ossified." He gives several concrete examples of the process. In two of the cases he mentions we have shaken off the bonds of the past since the article was published in 1920.

* Edward A. Ross, The American Journal of Sociology, 25, No. 5 (March, 1920), 529-538. Reprinted by permission of the University of Chicago Press.
The author (1866-1951) was Head of the Department of Sociology, University of Wisconsin, 1929-37. Specialized in philosophy and economics at University of Berlin and Johns Hopkins, but sociology held a fascination for him. A dynamic pioneer of wide influence. Prolific writer who could write teachable texts. Among his books are Social Control, The Foundations of Sociology, Russian Soviet Republic, Social Revolution in Mexico, Standing Room Only?, New Age Sociology, Social Psychology.

IN HILLY NEW ENGLAND the settlers discovered that the best way to build a barn is to set the foundation in a hillside, keep the animals in the basement and drive the hay wagons from the uphill side into the second floor on a level. When their descendants migrated to the flat prairies of Illinois, they continued to build barns in the only way they knew. Having no hillsides they built the barn first, built a plank hillside running up into the barn and then got stalled trying to haul loads of hay up this hill!

In olden days the American common schools remained closed during the growing season in order that the farmers might have the help of their children. Thus originated the long summer vacation and as the cities established their school systems they adopted it without question. There are many ways in which school buildings and grounds may be used during the summer to keep children happy and usefully occupied. But no. Although half of us are urban, every June we close the schools of our cities and turn millions of children into the street—to hoe corn and "bug" potatoes!

In an early day in the level West the practice struck root of laying out roads on the section lines. Later the gridiron plan was adhered to even in rough country where it would be more economical to lay out the roads according to the contour, so that they would follow the water courses or the water partings. Today millions of loads are needlessly hauled over hill after hill on their way to market and thousands of hillside roads are washed away every season because men blindly follow precedent.

In general, after a social practice or institution has existed for a generation or two, it is off its original basis of sound reason and will be retained even in a situation so changed that it has no justification whatever. The first users scanning with a cold and critical eye will modify or abandon it if it does not suit their purpose. But after it has been taken over and worked by a later generation which has feelings about it, it loses its plasticity, turns to bone as it were. The process, then, by which social institutions and arrangements lose adaptability and harden into rigid forms may be called *ossification*.

The causes of this tendency are various:

Most of us are mentally lazy. We are loath to put our minds to a stretch, to concentrate our powers upon an intricate matter. Little problems involving only a few factors may challenge and stimulate us like the situations in a game of chess, but we shun complex problems which call for sustained thinking. Hence, we shrink from recognizing a changed situation, from rethinking our task. Indolently we roll along in the rut of habit and precedent until a stone in the rut or an obstacle in the road twists us out of it. Absorbed in their daily round few pause to ask themselves: "Is this thing of any use?" "Am I doing any real good?" The ability to see one's activity in a true perspective is a rare gift, is, in fact *genius*.

There has been for a generation such a furore about social progress that one might suppose it to be an object of universal thought and desire. In truth only a very few care enough for social progress to embrace it in their plans or to make sacrifices for it. They are glad to have it if they can have it at somebody else's expense. The true attitude of these shouters for progress is revealed when one proposes a concrete change affecting their religion, politics, or customs. From their shocked resistance one will perceive that all the time they have been conservatives without realizing it.

Even the strong minds, the highly educated men, tend to abide in their earlier judgments and to retain the emotional attitudes of their youth. If, then, the control of affairs is in the hands of the old, the effete thing will longer escape notice and be longer tolerated than if young men are at the helm. If education falls out of step with life, if knowledge grows beyond the creeds, if laws fail to keep up with the development of social relations, the unprejudiced young will realize it first and will demand changes which the old see no reason for.

At my suggestion Dr. E. B. Gowin, now professor in New York University, reviewed modern history in order to compare epochs of reform and epochs of quiet with respect to the age of their leaders. He found that in ten historical periods of reform or revolution the average age of the dozen leading men in each varied from thirty-two to forty-six years. On the other hand, the average age of their chief opponents or of the leaders in quiet periods varied from fifty-four to sixty-six years. In general, the champions of change have been from fifteen to twenty years younger than the champions of opposition to change.

The long-established becomes an ark of the covenant which we fear to lay hand on lest we meet the fate of Uzzah. Perhaps our forefathers fought and bled for it. It has inspired heroic deeds, noble poetry, and eloquence. We cannot imagine that a thing so cherished has become a stumbling-block or a nuisance. In the face of the imperative need of church union the faithful cling to their denominational peculiarities because of the sacrifices these doctrines once cost. The monastic ideal, the Monroe Doctrine, the policy of avoiding "entangling alliances," uniformity of taxation, the "open door," the "independence of the judiciary," laissez faire, inspire passionate devotion long after their value has become doubtful. The American Constitution has gathered such prestige that scholars who demonstrate the part selfish interests took in its shaping are vilified. Owing to the bloody struggles which have raged about it the Bible has come to be for many a kind of fetish. Its texts are relied on to resolve every doubt life presents and the "higher critics" who call in question the traditional date, authorship, or meaning of the Scriptures bring a tempest upon their heads.

The assumption that what once worked well will continue to work well implies a static notion of society. People generally imagine that society keeps to its track until some large sensible force—a war, a revolution, a law, a religious movement, or a great invention—gives it a new direction. The fact is society can never be stable while its base shifts and its base may be shifted by the cumulative effect of numerous small imperceptible changes—new methods of tillage, a gain of manufacturing on agriculture, cheaper carriage, the opening of new channels of trade, immigration, population growth, the unequal growth of sections and classes, the disappearance of the frontier, the rush to the cities, the access of women to industry, etc. Silently these lowly unnoticed processes make society into something else than we imagine it to be, so that some of the wisdom of the past turns to folly and perhaps some of its folly becomes wisdom. Hence, each generation ought to review all the institutions they inherit and consider of each whether it is still at its peak of fitness. But they will never do this until they recognize the dynamic character of society.

Private interests become dependent on an institution and therefore resist proposals to abandon or alter it. The teachers of Latin and Greek protest against reforming in a modern spirit the traditional courses of study for youth. For thirty years religious leaders have urged that economics and sociology be a part of the training for the Christian ministry. With rare exceptions, however, the theological seminaries have done nothing owing to the vested interest of the professors of the traditional subjects. As a result the clergy are steadily losing influence because of their ignorance of the burning moral issues of the time.

Guild self-interest is, then, an obstacle to adaptive change. Certain persons have specialized in good faith and lo, they are in danger of losing their occupation. It is indeed hard. One cannot well expect them to capitulate to anything less than a mathematical demonstration of their superfluousness and this is impossible outside the field of material production. They are like players who protest against the nature of the game being changed while they are playing it.

In the field of law, ossification is an outcome of the common-law doctrine that precedents are binding. This maxim of *stare in decisis* in turn reflects the popular demand that the law be clear and certain. How can we know what is lawful and what is unlawful for us to do unless we are sure that the judge who reviews our conduct will follow past decisions? Who wants to play a risky game unless the rules appear to be settled? The logic is so irresistible that even equity, "the judicial modification or supplementing of existing rules of law by reference to current morality," accepted the doctrine that precedents bind. As a result it presently lost its discretionary character and became merely a competing system of law. Says Dean Pound, "Well might Falstaff say to an Elizabethan audience, 'there's no equity stirring' when precedents were beginning to be cited in the Court of Chancery." Thus, in meeting the demand that the law be certain, justice has ceased to be either flexible or progressive.

The dominant social class may preserve the outworn because it is to its interest to do so. In America the commercial class has long played upon a popular suspicion and jealousy of government inherited from the eighteenth century when government was an alien arbitrary agency over which the commonalty had no effective control. Now that government has become responsive to the popular will such distrust is unwarranted. Yet the business interests which fear state interference or regulation fan continually these dying embers.

As departments of government multiply to keep pace with the complexity of modern life, the practice of electing all public officials becomes pernicious. The "long ballot" betrays democracy by giving the real selection of such officials into the hands of party "machines" and "bosses." It would have disappeared long ago but for the fight put up on its behalf by the politicians.

The long retention of the "fellow-servant" defense in suits for indemnity brought by injured employees exemplifies the power of the employing class over courts and legislatures. Its injustice had been conceded by all a generation before it was discarded.

The persistence of the county form of local government in the South after the victory of democratic principles there can be accounted for only by the self-interest of a dominant class. A century ago Thomas Jefferson recognized in the New England township system of government the very foundation-stone of democracy. In 1816 he wrote, "The article nearest my heart is the subdivision of the counties into wards (townships)." He realized that if the county was to be the smallest unit of government a few aristocrats or a few bosses would control. It was, indeed, the wealthy class which brought his efforts to naught and prevented the establishment of the township system in the South.

While the dominant class thus causes society to appear at times more stupid than it actually is, there are matters in which it lends society a deceptive air of ready adaptiveness. When this class puts its weight behind a logical change, reform may be effected with startling suddenness. Good roads, the gold standard, banking reform, the acquisition of dependencies, could never have crashed so irresistibly through the dense underbrush of American prejudices but for the driving power of the business interests.

Of the chief elements in society the intellectuals have the least horror of change and the keenest appreciation of the need of it. The commercial class comprises many limber-minded adaptable men who, although they may not see deeply into society, are clear-sighted within their range of vision. These are hospitable enough to needed changes which do not appear contrary to their interests. On account of their lack of education the wage-earning class are often slaves to tradition. Their material interests, however, are not bound up with the inherited order and, once their minds are set free, they stand for radicalism, i.e., the rational and thoroughgoing adaptation of institutions to the needs of society. Owing to their dealing with nature rather than man, the tillers of the soil are limited in their mental contacts. They respond to the influence of their forefathers rather than of their contemporaries and stand for the inherited order save when the need of reform is sharply brought home to them by their own painful experiences. Here is one reason why farmers and working men, although they constitute the two wings of the great producing class and have common interests over against the class which lives from the ownership of property, do not co-operate for long politically.

Of all the economic classes the propertied is least sympathetic with the rational transformation of time-hallowed institutions. Its entire economic position rests upon inheritance and vested rights. Since it shares in current production in virtue not of present exertion but of title from the past, it cannot afford to allow the past to be discredited. Its attitude toward effete institutions is expressed in the maxim, "Let sleeping dogs lie." Since most reforms are detrimental to property in one form or another, the propertied become excessively timorous and develop an instinctive horror of all radical ideas. They grant you there are rotten spots in the building reared by our ancestors, but, they insist, once you begin to tamper and alter, you release new strains and some fine day you will bring the whole structure tumbling upon your head. The domination of the farmers or the propertied therefore makes society like a stiff-jointed rheumatic while the shifting of power from these classes in the direction of the intellectuals, the business men, or the proletariat is apt to make society more supple and adaptable.

CHAPTER V

SOCIAL ORGANIZATION: COLLECTIVE BEHAVIOR

---

37. Lynchers Don't Like Lead *

JOE JORDAN has here described in a vivid manner an extremely violent type of collective behavior—the mob—and shows how it was handled. In sharp contrast with "The Men From Mars" (38, by Houseman) in which mass panic was quickly halted by prompt dissemination of the actual facts, the situation in this case was one in which the facts could not get an audience. Appeals to reason proved useless. It has been said that "a mob acts as one man but as no one man would act alone." All inhibitions are cast off, while the sense of power is greatly enhanced. Violence, irresponsibility, and destructiveness distinguish this type of collective behavior. Sometimes, under powerful personal appeal, reason does prevail over the mob. But at other times, as on this occasion described by Jordan, a display of physical force becomes necessary to reestablish order.

TWENTY-SIX YEARS AGO, on February 9, 1920, a mob at Lexington, Kentucky, bent upon lynching a Negro who was on trial for murdering a white child, charged the Fayette County courthouse. The members of the mob, all white men, were fired upon and repulsed by white soldiers and white civil officers. Six men were killed and fifty or more were wounded. Of the hundreds of newspapers throughout the United States which hastened to praise Fayette County officials for their some-

* Joe Jordan, The Atlantic Monthly, 177, No. 2 (February, 1946), 103-108. Reprinted by permission of the publisher and the author.
The author is City Editor of Lexington Herald-Leader, Lexington, Kentucky. The Atlantic Monthly refers to him as a "Kentuckian from 'way back."

what astonishing stand against mob violence, many pointed out, as did the *Brooklyn Eagle* in a typical comment, that the Lexington incident marked "the first time south of Mason and Dixon's Line that any mob of this sort had actually met the volley fire of soldiers."

At the time, a number of the writers of editorials indicated a cautious belief and hope that the "Second Battle of Lexington" might mark a turning point in the method of dealing with mobs. It now appears that they were right. In 1919, mobs had lynched eighty-three persons in the United States. That figure has not been approached since the Lexington mob was dealt with so vigorously. In 1944, there were only two lynchings in the entire country. To avoid the danger of selecting by chance two unusual years, it is safer to consider five-year averages. In the five years preceding 1920, mobs had lynched an average of sixty-one victims a year; in the five years preceding 1945, lynchings averaged fewer than four a year.

A decisive encounter between determined officers and a determined mob was bound to occur sometime. It occurred at Lexington, that February day in 1920, because the mob picked the wrong town for a lynching party. Fayette County had not seen a lynching in fifty years. It didn't see one then, and it hasn't seen one since. Thousands of outsiders flocked to Lexington on the day of the trial, and some Alabamians who arrived the day before, disclosed to reporters that they had made the long trip to have a part in the expected lynching. They misjudged the temper and underestimated the courage of the county officials, who had issued plain warnings that anyone attempting to take the prisoner from them would be killed.

Will Lockett, the Negro who was to be tried, had killed a ten-year-old white girl at South Elkhorn, in the southern section of Fayette County. It was a revolting crime. The child had been seized when she was walking to a country school less than 400 yards from her home. She had been dragged into a cornfield and there her skull had been crushed by repeated savage blows with a large rock. Her body, half hidden under a fodder shock, had been found after she failed to appear at school.

Lockett, a World War I veteran who still was wearing his Army uniform, had left a country store in the neighborhood shortly before the crime was committed, and was suspected immediately. He was found six hours later, six miles away. A doctor and two other civilians who captured him took him to Lexington hurriedly, for they feared a mob would form and they wanted to get him into the hands of the law.

At Lexington police headquarters, Lockett confessed promptly. He was removed to the county jail, but almost at once the officers decided it would be safer to take him to the state penitentiary at Frankfort. When he was led out of the jail, a crowd already was beginning to form in the street, but it was not large enough to menace the officers who had him in charge, and within an hour he was behind the walls of the Frankfort prison.

As news of the crime spread, the crowd in front of the jail increased, and by dark it numbered several hundred. Its members refused to accept the jailer's statement that Lockett had been taken to Frankfort. There is a traditional procedure in such cases, and it was followed. The jailer consented to admit a committee to search the jail and inspect the prisoners. The committee, which included a farmer by whom Lockett had been employed, looked into the faces of all the frightened Negroes in the jail and went out to assure the crowd that Lockett was not there.

Of course, there have been many similar cases in which the wrong man has been identified and dragged out, but the Negroes in the Lexington jail were lucky that night. The mob then went to police headquarters, where a similar search was permitted. Convinced that Lockett had been taken to Frankfort, the mob's leaders attempted to charter interurban electric cars for the trip to the state capital, but traction-company officials refused to accommodate them, and approximately three hundred men set out in automobiles.

The late Edwin P. Morrow, then Governor of Kentucky, was informed by telephone that the mob was on its way to Frankfort. He acted with characteristic vigor. One hundred special deputies, armed with shotguns and rifles, were sent to the penitentiary to reinforce the regular guards there. Governor Morrow took charge at the prison gate.

Meanwhile Sheriff Bain Moore of Franklin County had taken a force of men to the outskirts of Frankfort, on the Lexington Pike. He stopped the first cars in the caravan from Lexington, had them turned crosswise of the road to establish a blockade, and warned the mob members that they would meet certain death if they attempted to remove the prisoner from the penitentiary. Most of the men turned back. A few who got past the sheriff's barricade were arrested on Governor Morrow's order when they appeared at the prison gate.

The crime was committed and Lockett was arrested on Wednesday, February 4. A Fayette County grand jury indicted Lockett the next day on a murder charge, and his trial was set for the following Monday, only five days after the slaying.

Everybody realized that a serious situation could develop when Lockett was returned to Lexington for the trial. Circuit Judge Charles Kerr and County Judge Frank A. Bullock—in Kentucky the county judge is the administrative head of the county government—conferred with other county officials, with Mayor Thomas C. Bradley of Lexington, and with Governor Morrow. It was decided that there would be no running away from the issue by postponing the trial to a secret date or ordering a change of venue. Governor Morrow promised a company of state troops from Campbell County, in northern Kentucky.

It was admitted that the public did not have so much respect for "Home Guards" as for Regular Army soldiers, and the officials looked longingly toward Camp Taylor, less than a hundred miles away, where the crack First Division Regulars, veterans of World War I, were stationed. The Governor could not obtain Federal troops, however, without certifying that a state of lawlessness existed with which the state authority was unable to cope.

In the interval between Lockett's arrest and his trial, the Lexington newspapers pleaded for peace and order. Negro organizations adopted resolutions "condemning the horrible outrage" and demanding that the guilty member of their race "be punished promptly and adequately." A group of South Elkhorn residents met Saturday afternoon at the courthouse and issued an appeal by T. L. Hardman, brother of the slain girl, which was carried in both Lexington newspapers Sunday morning.

"As a brother of Geneva Hardman, who was murdered by Will Lockett, and as a representative of her family," he said, "I request all of our friends and all those who sympathize with us not to indulge in any violence or create any disturbance when he is brought here for trial. The authorities have acted promptly, the man is under arrest, he has been indicted promptly, and his trial fixed for Monday. I feel sure that a prompt and speedy trial will take place and that any jury impaneled will find him guilty and punish him adequately for the horrible crime he has committed. . . . I would hate to see the life of any other person endangered as the result of violence by reason of conflict over a brute like this, and I therefore urge all citizens, for the good name of the county and in the interest of law and order, to do nothing to interfere with the orderly processes of the law."

In an editorial headed, "Let the Law Take Its Course," the Lexington Leader commented: "If this bereaved brother can assume such an attitude at this time, certainly those who sympathize so deeply with him can afford to await calmly the verdict of the jury. . . . The people of Fayette County can afford to let the law take its course in this case. They cannot afford to incur the just criticism of the people of the nation which would follow a resort to mob rule." The Lexington Herald advanced similar arguments. Sunday morning the congregation of the South Elkhorn Christian Church, composed entirely of neighbors of the murdered child, adopted a resolution calling for orderly administration of the law. Every effort was being made to prepare the public for the crisis expected on Monday.

These appeals appeared to have had the desired effect in Fayette County itself. In a news story the day before the trial, the *Herald* reported: "Indignation on the part of the citizens last night turned into determination that the law should take its course." The *Leader* found that "the mob spirit, which was prevalent immediately after the atrocity was committed, has died down and has been replaced by a willingness to let the law take its course." The *Leader* added, however, that there had been "reports that other counties would send delegations here to 'get' Lockett."

Both newspapers repeatedly assured the public that there could be but one outcome of the trial—speedy conviction and a death sentence. Said a *Leader* news story: "It is anticipated that if Lockett is sentenced to be electrocuted, as it is generally believed he will be, the same military protection will be given him while he is on his way to the penitentiary where the electrocution will take place. . . . It is thought the trial will be a speedy one. After the jury is chosen, the actual trial ought to be over in a very short time." Thus it was hoped to make clear to the public that the issue was not whether Lockett would be punished, but whether the punishment would be carried out lawfully or by a mob.

Adjutant General J. M. Deweese, who was to be in charge of the state troops, issued a brief, forceful warning: "The responsibility for any bloodshed at this trial will rest on those who disregard their duty as citizens and attempt to take the law out of the hands of the constituted authorities." Fayette County Sheriff J. Waller Rodes, who had hurried home from a business trip to Texas to take charge of the county's defense measures, said, "Under no circumstances will the prisoner be taken away from the guards."

At one o'clock Monday morning, the day of the trial, police began stretching steel cables in the empty streets, to keep spectators at a distance from the courthouse. The lines were no more than boundary markers, since it would be easy enough to slip through them. At 3.45 A.M., a special train arrived from Frankfort, bringing Sheriff Rodes, General Deweese, the prisoner, and the state troops. The train stopped before it reached Union Station, and the soldiers marched two blocks with their prisoner and entered the courthouse without incident.

By seven o'clock, a crowd had begun to form on Main Street, in front of the courthouse. It grew rapidly. The trial had been set for nine o'clock. When that hour approached, there were immense crowds on the Main Street and Short Street sides of the building, but officers kept everyone outside the cables except officials, prospective jurors, newsmen, and just enough spectators to fill the courtroom.

The approach to the main entrance of the courthouse is by broad flights of stone steps which lead to the second floor. All ground-floor entrances had been barred. The first flight of front steps ends at a level landing which runs off to the right and left to connect with walks from Upper Street and Cheapside, at an elevation higher than the Main Street sidewalk and the front lawn. Soldiers were stationed behind the stone parapet around the front of this landing. A machine gun had been set up on the landing. At the top of the highest flight of steps. just inside the wide front doors, were more soldiers with rifles and deputies with shotguns. Soldiers also had been stationed in various offices in the building, at open windows commanding the steps.

The defense setup appeared to be adequate. Men attempting to reach the front doors would have to get through the cable barrier (which would not be difficult, but would separate them from the crowd), then cross a bare, level space approaching the steps, and mount the steps in the face of fire from the protected soldiers, who had been posted in positions that would enable them to sweep the steps with rifle and machine-gun fire. That it would be the height of folly to attempt to storm such a position, any man of judgment could see—but mobs are not made up of men of judgment.

The crowd that surrounded the courthouse square was estimated by some observers to number 8000 to 10,000. Such guesses usually are high. A conservative estimate would be 5000 to 6000. Of these, comparatively few were there with any serious idea of attempting to take the prisoner out of the courthouse. Most of them had come out of curiosity, half hoping, perhaps, that they would see fighting. University of Kentucky students (I was one of them) had left the campus in droves, flocking to the downtown district to share in the excitement, in spite of repeated warnings for all peaceful citizens to stay out of the danger zone. The authorities had pointed out that spectators would be in as much danger as participants if a battle developed. Many lookers-on were in a nervously jovial mood, exchanging jokes about how fast they would run if shooting started.

Presently people began to point out a man with a coil of rope over his left shoulder. He pushed his way forward to the cable, at a point directly in front of the steps. In addition to the ones who appeared to be in his party, other grim-faced men began sifting through the crowd and gathering around him. The merely curious spectators who happened to be in that vicinity dropped back and were replaced by additional angry, cursing men who "meant business."

Thus the nucleus of the mob was formed. It appeared to be unplanned, this concentration. Naturally, the ones who actually considered rushing the courthouse would gather at the spot from which the charge would have to start, and as they got together and bolstered one another's courage, perhaps no one of them wanted to appear cowardly before his fellows and so they all persuaded themselves that the thing could be done, that the civil officers and soldiers would not dare shoot white men to protect a Negro murderer.

The courthouse clock struck nine times. Everybody realized that if anything was to be done, it would have to be done soon. The threats and cursing became louder up near the barrier, while those in the background ceased their joking, suddenly aware that the situation might turn dangerous after all.

Inside the courthouse, as we were to learn later from the newspapers, the trial started promptly. Judge Kerr was on the bench. Every seat in the courtroom was filled, but no one was allowed to stand in the spectators' section, behind the rail. In front of the rail, in the space reserved for jurors, attorneys, and court officials, a few men were standing, among them County Judge Bullock. Lockett sat at the defense table, surrounded by four deputies. The bailiff rapped for order, pounding his gavel on a desk across which he had laid an automatic shotgun.

As had been predicted, the trial proceeded with a minimum of delay. A jury was selected quickly. The only question asked each prospective juror was whether he had any conscientious scruples against the death penalty. The court had appointed two leading members of the bar as defense counsel, George R. Hunt and Colonel Samuel M. Wilson. Mr. Hunt filed a demurrer to the indictment, explaining that he was doing it "as a matter of form," but that the indictment appeared to be properly drawn.

Asked whether he wished to plead guilty or not guilty, Lockett mumbled a reply inaudible to the spectators. "Defendant pleads guilty, your Honor," the clerk announced.

Only one witness testified, a man who established the fact of the child's death and told of finding her with a heavy stone on her face. The defendant did not take the stand. Colonel Wilson read Lockett's honorable discharge from the Army, which stated that his character was "very good," and then read a statement in which the defendant asked for a life sentence. "I know I do not deserve mercy," it said, "but I am sorry I committed the crime and I would give anything if the little girl could be brought back to life."

Colonel John R. Allen, Commonwealth's Attorney, made a brief prosecution argument to the jury. "In all the history of crime in the United States," he said, "there has been none to equal this in cruelty. In the name of the law, and of the little girl who was murdered, I ask you to act quickly, and suggest that you return a verdict without leaving the jury box."

While this was taking place in the courtroom, the crowd in the street became more restive. A deputy sheriff engaged in a brief fist fight with a man who had crawled under the cable barrier, and the man was dragged away by two policemen. A newsreel cameraman had been admitted to a cleared space on the lawn and had set up his camera near the equestrian statue of Confederate General John Hunt Morgan. He had taken pictures of the soldiers and the crowd, but apparently he wanted something showing action or emotion. "Shake your fists and yell!" he called out to the nearest spectators. They obligingly did so.

The people who shook their fists and yelled to please the cameraman were just outside the cable barrier, but they were a hundred feet or so east of the nucleus of the real mob. Their action, however, was like a spark in the highly charged atmosphere. It was answered by a roar from the mob—a savage, bestial roar. I was not to hear anything like it again until the radio carried to America the roars with which a Nazi mob responded to an impassioned harangue by Hitler on the eve of Munich.

Men in the forefront of the mob hoisted the cables and went under them quickly, as if the shouts had been a signal. The man with the rope was among the leaders.

General Deweese had taken a stand in an open space at the approach to the first flight of steps. His men had orders not to shoot unless he fired his revolver twice into the air. As the leaders of the charge approached the General, he backed about twenty steps, pistol in hand. When they reached him, he grappled with two of them, and struck one over the head with the pistol. The others surged around him and in a moment had mounted the first flight of steps and reached the landing. They bowled over a machine gunner and kicked his gun aside.

Deweese fired the two signal shots, and a withering volley was discharged. Men piled up on the steps, some wounded, others dropping to escape the bullets. A dozen or more who had passed the landing before the firing began rushed on up the remaining steps to the front doors, but turned back and ran when the soldiers and deputies who had been stationed inside the doors surged out with rifles and shotguns pointed at them.

The one burst of firing, which lasted only a few seconds, had halted the mob, and the soldiers held their fire. Some witnesses estimated that as many as fifty shots had been fired by members of the mob at the defenders of the courthouse; others denied it. That there was some firing from the mob was certain, for three policemen and one soldier were wounded, and today there are still chipped places where bullets struck the stone front of the courthouse.

All the merely curious spectators—except the ones who had been hit —broke and ran as soon as the firing started. The action-seeking cameraman, lugging his camera, tripod and all, sped past many of them before they reached Limestone Street, a block east. (For some strange reason, almost everyone ran east, even those who had been standing west of the steps.) The number of spectators hit never was determined accurately. Some of the soldiers said later that they had fired over the heads of the mob leaders who were mounting the steps. Their bullets went into the crowd or shattered store windows across the street. At least one man was fatally injured, who had been standing backed up against a store front on the opposite side of Main Street. A woman clerk inside a store was struck in the ankle by a bullet.

Of those who had fallen on the steps, the uninjured and slightly injured crawled away, and the others were carried away. One man was taken to a doctor's office near-by and died there within a few minutes. Four others died at hospitals before midnight. The sixth victim died several days later.

Twenty-one wounded persons were treated at hospitals. The newspapers said "scores" were treated at drugstores for less serious injuries, such as being peppered by nearly spent buckshot or being knocked down and trampled. Fearing prosecution, several members of the mob who were shot were reported to have been taken home by friends. Avoiding hospitals, they were treated by their physicians, and no reports were made. That as many as fifty were wounded appears to be a conservative estimate.

In the courtroom, Colonel Allen was making the closing statement to the jury when the crowd's roar was heard, followed by firing. "It's started!" several spectators shouted, leaping to their feet. Deputies pointed pistols and commanded them to sit down. The trial proceeded.

The jurors quickly reached the expected verdict—death. Lockett was called around and Judge Kerr stood to pronounce sentence. At that moment an excited man ran into the courtroom and shouted, "Judge, you better let 'em have the nigger! They're going to tear the courthouse down if you don't!"

Again the deputies pointed their pistols and Colonel Allen—not an honorary but a military colonel, to whom it would be no new experience to be under fire—calmly counseled the crowd in the courtroom to remain seated. Judge Kerr as calmly proceeded with the sentencing, specifying that Lockett should die March 11 in the electric chair at Eddyville Penitentiary and concluding, "May the God of All Mercy have mercy on your soul."

Down in the street, as soon as the first shock was over and the mob members grasped the unbelievable fact that the officers and soldiers actually had fired upon them, had wounded many, and probably had killed a number of them, a cry for vengeance went up. Now they wanted not the prisoner alone, but the men who had stood up against them. Crowds broke for the pawnshops, seeking weapons. Several farsighted pawnbrokers had had their places locked all day, the doors barred and the windows shuttered.

Two shops were open. Joe Rosenberg later reported to police that "forty or fifty" pistols had been taken from his shop; Harry Skuller said he had been robbed of "fifty or sixty" weapons. Boxes of cartridges were picked up along with the pistols. (Later, the two pawnbrokers wasted money on newspaper advertisements appealing for the return of their property. Not a single one of the "borrowed" weapons ever was recovered.)

The shooting had cleared out all the idlers, and the surly crowd that milled around in front of the courthouse was now composed exclusively of those who "meant business." As the news spread, more and more armed men arrived and the situation, to all appearances, was worse than it had been before the shooting. There were reports that dynamite had been sent for, that the courthouse would be blown up, that a special train loaded with mountaineers from eastern Kentucky was on the way to Lexington.

Unknown to the mob was the fact that Governor Morrow had decided he now could certify truthfully to Federal authorities that there existed a state of lawlessness with which the state authority was unable to cope. The First Division Regulars had entrained at Camp Taylor and were on their way to Lexington.

The shooting had begun at 9:28 A.M. Then came the raids on pawnshops and the arrival of reinforcements for the mob. During the succeeding hours, one of the *Leader's* numerous extra editions related, "The courthouse was besieged by increasing numbers of armed men, who displayed an increasingly threatening attitude." By General Deweese's order, Judge Kerr, Judge Bullock, and other county officials remained inside the building, for by that time they were as much the objects of the mob's wrath as the prisoner himself. Lockett sat in a prisoners' lockup adjacent to the courtroom, handcuffed, with his head bowed. He had taken little apparent interest in the trial, and barely had raised his head when he heard the firing outside the building.

As the day wore on, tension increased minute by minute and the besieging force steadily grew larger, but the leaders of the mob bided their time. There were reports that they were waiting for dynamite, that they were waiting for reinforcements, that they were waiting for darkness so they could shoot out the street lights and overwhelm the defenders of the building. The strain was beginning to tell on the "Home Guards," many of whom were teen-age boys whose previous military experience had been confined to drilling one night a week in a National Guard armory. They looked frightened.

Finally, at 3.20 P.M., the special train from Camp Taylor steamed through the yards and stopped at Mill and Water Streets, only two blocks from the courthouse, but out of sight of the mob. Out of the coaches poured streams of battle-hardened veterans, who quickly fell in and marched north on Mill Street with bayonets fixed. Leading them was a color guard bearing the United States flag, a banner which in the sixties often had been carried into Lexington to the accompaniment of despairing groans from the town's leading citizens.

Lexington during the War Between the States had been a Confederate stronghold in a border state. It had been captured and recaptured, and had lived alternately under the United States and Confederate States flags. Now it was being occupied again, but there were no groans that day from the leading citizens as the Regulars executed a smart turn into Main Street and bore down upon the mob, with the Stars and Stripes at the head of the column. Indeed, one of the beleaguered county officials peering out of the courthouse windows—a man who, like most of us Kentuckians, had been taught from childhood to take pride in being an Unreconstructed Rebel—laughingly admitted later that he had been somewhat astonished to hear himself shouting, "That's the prettiest flag I ever saw!"

The soldiers moved steadily east on Main Street and swept the mob before them. No shots were fired from either side. Here and there an occasional inflamed individual attempted to put up an argument and was cracked over the head with a rifle butt; now and then a sullen straggler was hurried along by a light prick with a bayonet point. But for the most part the men who had been so bloodthirsty instantly lost interest in fighting and took to their heels. Magically, within five minutes, all streets approaching the courthouse had been cleared. Khaki-clad sharpshooters looked over the eaves of all structures in sight of the county building.

Never did a city submit more happily to invading forces than Lexington surrendered that day to the United States troops. Martial law was declared, and the citizens marveled at the efficiency with which the soldiers took charge. Twelve patrols were organized and assigned head-quarters. As darkness approached, soldiers began patrolling Negro districts, the tobacco-warehouse district,—which had been threatened because the sheriff and several other county office-holders were interested financially in the warehouses,—and the Union Station, to guard against the expected arrival of the mountaineers, which never came to pass.

Another place that needed guarding was the ROTC Armory at the University of Kentucky, which contained hundreds of rifles and thou-sands of rounds of ammunition. Twice during the day, members of the mob had made unsuccessful attempts to enter it. Directly across Limestone Street from the campus was a fire-department station, which an Army captain selected as convenient headquarters for his patrol. To his request that the station be kept open all night, a surly fire-depart-ment captain replied that he intended to lock up the lower floor and retire with his men to the dormitory above. The fireman was arrested and hustled off to jail. The military was in charge, and before long that fact was impressed upon all citizens, whether or not they sympathized with the mob.

The next day Brigadier General Francis C. Marshall, commanding the U. S. troops, summarized Monday's events in a terse statement: "This community has set a fine example against Bolshevism and lawless-ness and has killed several of its own citizens in upholding law and order."

"Folly's Harvest of Sorrow" was the heading over a *Leader* editorial the day after the riot. It said in part: "The folly of a few men, mad-dened for the moment by a spirit of revenge, seeking the life of a miser-able creature at the very instant condemned to die for his crime, compelled the servants of the law to fire upon a mob in Lexington Monday morning. The majesty of the law was upheld, but at frightful cost."

The *Herald* expressed sympathy for the families of the victims, but added that "there is pride that the law was protected, that the officers of the law observed their solemn oath both to execute and to defend the law." It said the affair proved two facts: that the guilty would be punished surely and swiftly, and that "he who attempts to violate the law goes to meet death."

Jere Reagan, Chief of Police, commented: "There can be no question as to the absolute necessity of firing. Those who forced their way through the lines meant business. I am sorry innocent persons have been killed, but enough warning had been given."

Further evidence that General Marshall was the law in Fayette County was given Thursday, when he directed Judge Kerr to summon a special grand jury to investigate the law violations that had occurred Monday, and to indict the guilty persons. The jury commissioners selected what was recognized immediately as a "hand-picked" grand jury, composed of citizens who would not hesitate to indict the mob members. A week later, this jury was discharged, since it appeared that any indictments the body voted probably would be thrown out of court because the names of the jurors had not been drawn by chance from the jury wheel in the usual manner.

A new jury was drawn from the wheel. It heard witnesses and reported that the members of the mob were "mostly from other counties than Fayette, who were there for the avowed purpose of rescuing the prisoner from the authorities." It called the bloody riot "an unfortunate affair," and concluded that it would be unwise to return indictments, since the subsequent trials "would only tend to aggravate an already tense situation."

"Here we find a new principle injected into the processes of the law," the *Leader* declared in a bitter editorial. "Officers of the law, instead of seeking to punish the guilty and acquit the innocent, must first determine whether the trials of men presumably guilty of serious crimes and misdemeanors would disturb the public mind and 'tend to aggravate bitter feelings in the state.'" There the matter rested.

Lockett had been taken out of Lexington Tuesday night, under the protection of 400 soldiers. No attempt was made to sneak the prisoner out of town. The soldiers openly marched through the streets with him to the Union Station. Thirty-two officers and 472 soldiers remained in Lexington to maintain order. This force was reduced gradually until, on February 22, thirteen days after the riot, General Marshall proclaimed an end to martial rule, "law and order having been restored."

Lockett died in the electric chair at Eddyville Penitentiary on March 11, in the presence of nineteen Fayette County witnesses, including two brothers of his victim. Three days before the execution, he confessed the slaying of four women, one in Indiana, one in Illinois, and two in Kentucky, all by choking. Thus the child he killed in Fayette County had been his fifth victim.

The Kentucky General Assembly, which was in session at Frankfort when the Lexington riot occurred, enacted a law changing the penalty for rape from death in the electric chair to public hanging in the county in which the crime had been committed. Presumably the theory was that the mob lust for vengeance would be appeased by a convenient outdoor hanging which all could witness. A number of revolting exhibitions were staged under this law. The type of persons attracted to such events enjoyed themselves so thoroughly and behaved so atrociously that the law was repealed. Any effort to appease the mob spirit probably was unnnecessary, anyway; the Second Battle of Lexington appeared to have dampened Kentuckians' ardor for lynching parties.

❦❦❦❦❦

38. The Men from Mars *

COLLECTIVE BEHAVIOR depends upon some form of communication. Any expansion in the means of communication, such as radio or television, increases the areas for possible stimulation, direction, and control of behavior. In this entertaining and significant article John Houseman gives a graphic account of a startling and rather disquieting episode precipitated by a radio program designed only for entertainment. To ensure the full dramatic effect in its presentation realism was necessary. So skillful was the technique used that thousands believed an actual invasion from Mars was taking place. The panic, the irrational behavior of many people who chanced to tune in, present an interesting example of the propaganda potentials of radio and television. Houseman rejects the idea that the incident can be dismissed as an example of the "incredible stupidity and gullibility of the American public." Instead, he indicates many other important factors that need to be considered in any explanation of the effects stimulated by the broadcast.

RADIO WAR TERRORIZES U.S.—N. Y. *Daily News,* October 31, 1938.

Everybody was excited I felt as if I was going crazy and kept on saying what can we do what difference does it make whether we die sooner or later? We were holding each other. Everything seemed unimportant in the face of death. I was afraid to die, just kept on listening.
—A *listener*

* John Houseman, *Harper's Magazine,* 197, No. 1183 (December, 1948), 74-82. Reprinted by permission of the author.
    The author is with Metro-Goldwyn-Mayer Pictures. Lecturer in English, Barnard College. Theater, radio director. Co-founder of Mercury Theater, New York, in the 1930's. Supervised Voice of America programs during World War II for the Radio Program Bureau, O.W.I.

Nothing about the broadcast was in the least credible.—Dorothy Thompson

The show came off. There is no doubt about that. It set out to dramatize, in terms of popular apprehension, an attempted invasion of our world by hostile forces from the planet Mars. It succeeded. Of the several million American citizens who, on the evening of October 30, 1938, milled about the streets, clung sobbing to one another or drove wildly in all directions to avoid asphyxiation and flaming death, approximately one-half were in terror of Martians—not of Germans, Japanese, or unknown enemies—but, specifically, of Martians. Later, when the excitement was over and the shadow of the gallows had lifted, some of us were inclined to take credit for more deliberate and premeditated villainy than we deserved. The truth is that at the time, nobody was more surprised than we were. In fact, one of the most remarkable things about the broadcast was the quite haphazard nature of its birth.

In October 1938, the Mercury Theater, of which Orson Welles and I were the founding partners, had been in existence for less than a year. Our first Broadway season had been shatteringly successful—"Julius Caesar," "The Cradle Will Rock," "Shoemaker's Holiday," and "Heartbreak House" in the order of their appearance. In April, Orson, in a straggly white beard, made the cover of *Time* Magazine. In June, the Columbia Broadcasting System offered him a radio show—"The Mercury Theater on the Air," a series of classic dramatizations in the first person singular with Orson as master of ceremonies, star, narrator, writer, director, and producer. He accepted. So, now, in addition to an empty theater, a movie in progress, two plays in rehearsal, and all seven of the chronicle plays of William Shakespeare in preparation, we had a radio show.

We opened on July 11. Among our first thirteen shows were "Treasure Island," "39 Steps," "Abraham Lincoln," "Three Short Stories" (by Saki, Sherwood Anderson, and Carl Ewald), "Jane Eyre," "Julius Caesar" (with running commentary by Kaltenborn out of Plutarch), and "The Man Who Was Thursday." Our second series, in the fall, began with Booth Tarkington's "Seventeen," "Around the World in Eighty Days," and "Oliver Twist." Our fifth show was to be "Life with Father." Our fourth was "The War of the Worlds."

No one, as I remember, was very enthusiastic about it. But it seemed good programming, between the terrors of Dickens' London slums, and the charm of Clarence Day's New York in the nineties, to throw in something of a contrasting and pseudo-scientific nature. We thought of Shiel's *Purple Cloud*, Conan Doyle's *Lost World*, and several others before we settled on H. G. Wells' twenty-year-old novel, which neither of us, as it turned out later, remembered at all clearly. It is just possible that neither of us had ever read it.

II

Those were our golden days of unsponsored radio. We had no advertising agency to harass us, no client to cut our withers. Partly because we were perpetually overworked and partly because that was the way we did things at the Mercury, we never seemed to get more than a single jump ahead of ourselves. Shows were created week after week under conditions of soul- and health-destroying pressure. On the whole they were good shows. And we *did* develop a system—of sorts.

It worked as follows: I was editor of the series. With Welles, I chose the shows and then laid them out. The writing, most of it, was done by Howard Koch—earnest, spindly, six-foot-two—a Westchester lawyer turned playwright. To write the first draft of an hour's radio script took him about five days, working about fifteen hours a day. Our associate producer was Paul Stewart, a Broadway actor turned director. His function was to put the broadcast through its first paces and preliminary rehearsals. Every Thursday, musicless and with rudimentary sound effects, a wax record of the show was cut. From this record, played back later that night, Orson would give us his reactions and revisions. In the next thirty-six hours the script would be reshaped and rewritten, sometimes drastically. Saturday afternoon there was another rehearsal, with sound—with or without Welles. It was not until the last day that Orson really took over.

Sundays, at eight, we went on the air. Beginning in the early afternoon—when Bernard Herrmann arrived with his orchestra of twenty-seven high-grade symphony players—two simultaneous dramas were regularly unfolded in the stale, tense air of Studio Number One: the minor drama of the current show and the major drama of Orson's gargantuan struggle to get it on. Sweating, howling, disheveled, and single-handed he wrestled with Chaos and Time—always conveying an effect of being alone, traduced by his collaborators, surrounded by treachery, ignorance, sloth, indifference, incompetence and—more often than not—downright sabotage! Every Sunday it was touch and go. As the hands of the clock moved relentlessly toward air time the crisis grew more extreme, the peril more desperate. Often violence broke out. Scripts flew through the air, doors were slammed, batons smashed.

Scheduled for six—but usually nearer seven—there was a dress rehearsal, a thing of wild improvisations and irrevocable disaster. (One show was found to be twenty-one minutes overlength, another fourteen and one-half minutes short.)

After that, with only a few minutes to go, there was a final frenzy of correction and reparation, of utter confusion and absolute horror, aggravated by the gobbling of sandwiches and the bolting of oversized milk-shakes. By now it was less than a minute to air time. . . .

At that instant, quite regularly week after week—with not one second to spare . . . the titanic buffoonery stopped. Suddenly out of chaos, the show emerged—delicately poised, meticulously executed, precise as clockwork, and smooth as satin. And above us all, like a rainbow over storm clouds, stood Orson on his podium, sonorous and heroic, a leader of men surrounded by his band of loyal followers; a giant in action, serene and radiant with the joy of a hard battle bravely fought—a great victory snatched from the jaws of disaster.

In later years, when the Men from Mars had passed into history, there was some bickering among members of the Mercury as to who, exactly, had contributed precisely what, to that particular evening's entertainment. The truth is that a number of us made a number of essential and incalculable contributions to the broadcast. (Who can accurately assess, for instance, the part played by Johnny Dietz's perfect engineering, in keeping unbroken the shifting illusion of imperfect reality? How much did the original old H. G. Wells, who noisily repudiated us, have to do with it? Or the second assistant sound man? Or individual actors? Or Dr. Goebbels? Or Charlie McCarthy?) Orson Wells had virtually nothing to do with the writing of the script and less than usual to do with its preliminary rehearsals. Yet first and last it was his creation. If there had been a lynching that night, it is Welles the outraged populace would have strung up—and rightly so. Orson was the Mercury. "The War of the Worlds," like everything we did, was his show.

Actually, it was a narrow squeak. Those Men from Mars barely escaped being stillborn. Tuesday afternoon—five days before the show —Howard Koch telephoned. He was in deep distress. After three days of slaving on H. G. Wells' scientific fantasy he was ready to give up. Under no circumstances, he declared, could it be made interesting or in any way credible to modern American ears. Koch was not given to habitual alarmism. To confirm his fears, Annie, our secretary, came to the phone. She was an acid and emphatic girl from Smith College with fine blond hair, who smelled of fading spring flowers. "You can't do it!" she whined. "Those old Martians are just a lot of nonsense. It's all too silly! We're going to make fools of ourselves! Absolute fools!"

For some reason which I do not clearly remember our only possible alternative for that week was a dreary one—"Lorna Doone." I tried to reach Welles. He was at the theater and wouldn't come to the phone.

The reason he wouldn't come to the phone was that he was in his thirty-sixth successive hour of dress-rehearsing "Danton's Death," a beautiful, fragmentary play by Georg Buechner out of which Max Reinhardt, in an augmented form, had made a successful mass-spectacle in the twenties. Not to be outdone, Orson had glued seventeen hundred masks on to the back wall of the Mercury Theater, and ripped out the entire stage. Day after day actors fell headlong into the rat-ridden basement, leaped on and off erratically moving elevators, and chanted the "Carmagnole" in chorus under the supervision of Marc Blitzstein.

Unable to reach Welles, I called Koch back. I was severe. I taxed him with defeatism. I gave him false comfort. I promised to come up and help. When I finally got there—around two the next morning—things were better. He was beginning to have fun laying waste the State of New Jersey. Annie had stopped grinding her teeth. We worked all night and through the next day. Wednesday at sunset the script was finished.

Thursday, as usual, Paul Stewart rehearsed the show, then made a record. We listened to it rather gloomily, long after midnight in Orson's room at the St. Regis, sitting on the floor because all the chairs were covered with coils of unrolled and unedited film. We agreed it was a dull show. We all felt its only chance of coming off lay in emphasizing its newscast style—its simultaneous, eyewitness quality.

All night we sat up, spicing the script with circumstantial allusions and authentic detail. Friday afternoon it went over to CBS to be passed by the network censor. Certain name alterations were requested. Under protest and with a deep sense of grievance we changed the Hotel Biltmore to a non-existent Park Plaza, Trans-America to Intercontinent, the Columbia Broadcasting Building to Broadcasting Building. Then the script went over to mimeograph and we went to bed. We had done our best and, after all, a show is just a show. . . .

Saturday afternoon Paul Stewart rehearsed with sound effects but without Welles. He worked for a long time on the crowd scenes, the roar of cannon echoing in the Watchung Hills and the sound of New York Harbor as the ships with the last remaining survivors put out to sea.

Around six we left the studio. Orson, phoning from the theater a few minutes later to find out how things were going, was told by one of the CBS sound men, who had stayed behind to pack up his equipment, that it was not one of our better shows. Confidentially, the man opined, it just didn't come off. Twenty-seven hours later, quite a few of his employers would have found themselves a good deal happier if he had turned out to be right.

III

On Sunday, October 30, at 8:00 P. M., E.S.T., in a studio littered with coffee cartons and sandwich paper, Orson swallowed a second container of pineapple juice, put on his earphones, raised his long white fingers and threw the cue for the Mercury theme—the Tchaikovsky Piano Concerto in B Flat Minor # 1. After the music dipped, there were routine introductions—then the announcement that a dramatization of H. G. Wells' famous novel, *The War of the Worlds*, was about to be performed. Around 8:01 Orson began to speak, as follows:

WELLES

We know now that in the early years of the twentieth century this world was being watched closely by intelligences greater than man's and yet as mortal as his own. We know now that as human beings busied themselves about their various concerns they were scrutinized and studied, perhaps almost as narrowly as a man with a microscope might scrutinize the transient creatures that swarm and multiply in a drop of water. With infinite complacence people went to and fro over the earth about their little affairs, serene in the assurance of their dominion over this small spinning fragment of solar driftwood which by chance or design man has inherited out of the dark mystery of Time and Space. Yet across an immense ethereal gulf minds that are to our minds as ours are to the beasts in the jungle, intellects vast, cool, and unsympathetic regarded this earth with envious eyes and slowly and surely drew their plans against us. In the thirty-ninth year of the twentieth century came the great disillusionment.

It was near the end of October. Business was better. The war scare was over. More men were back at work. Sales were picking up. On this particular evening, October 30, the Crossley service estimated that thirty-two million people were listening in on their radios. . . .

Neatly, without perceptible transition, he was followed on the air by an anonymous announcer caught in a routine bulletin:

ANNOUNCER

. . . for the next twenty-four hours not much change in temperature. A slight atmospheric disturbance of undetermined origin is reported over Nova Scotia, causing a low pressure area to move down rather rapidly over the northeastern states, bringing a forecast of rain, accompanied by winds of light gale force. Maximum temperature 66; minimum 48. This weather report comes to you from the Government Weather Bureau. . . . We now take you to the Meridian Room in the Hotel Park Plaza in downtown New York, where you will be entertained by the music of Ramon Raquello and his orchestra.

At which cue, Bernard Herrmann led the massed men of the CBS house orchestra in a thunderous rendition of "La Cumparsita." The entire hoax might well have exploded there and then—but for the fact that hardly anyone was listening. They were being entertained by Charlie McCarthy—then at the height of his success.

The Crossley census, taken about a week before the broadcast, had given us 3.6 per cent of the listening audience to Edgar Bergen's 34.7 per cent. What the Crossley Institute (that hireling of the advertising agencies) deliberately ignored, was the healthy American habit of dial-twisting. On that particular evening, Edgar Bergen in the person of Charlie McCarthy temporarily left the air about 8:12 P. M., E.S.T., yielding place to a new and not very popular singer. At that point, and during the following minutes, a large number of listeners started twisting their dials in search of other entertainment. Many of them turned to us—and when they did, they stayed put! For by this time the mysterious meteorite had fallen at Grovers Mill in New Jersey, the Martians had begun to show their foul leathery heads above the ground, and the New Jersey State Police were racing to the spot. Within a few minutes people all over the United States were praying, crying, fleeing frantically to escape death from the Martians. Some remembered to rescue loved ones, others telephoned farewells or warnings, hurried to inform neighbors, sought information from newspapers or radio stations, summoned ambulances and police cars.

The reaction was strongest at points nearest the tragedy—in Newark, New Jersey, in a single block, more than twenty families rushed out of their houses with wet handkerchiefs and towels over their faces. Some began moving household furniture. Police switchboards were flooded with calls inquiring, "Shall I close my windows?" "Have the police any extra gas masks?" Police found one family waiting in the yard with wet cloths on faces contorted with hysteria. As one woman reported later:

I was terribly frightened. I wanted to pack and take my child in my arms, gather up my friends and get in the car and just go north as far as we could. But what I did was just sit by one window, praying, listening, and scared stiff, and my husband by the other sniffling and looking out to see if people were running. . . .

In New York hundreds of people on Riverside Drive left their homes ready for flight. Bus terminals were crowded. A woman calling up the Dixie Bus Terminal for information said impatiently, "Hurry please, the world is coming to an end and I have a lot to do."

In the parlor churches of Harlem evening service became "end of the world" prayer meetings. Many turned to God in that moment:

I held a crucifix in my hand and prayed while looking out of my open window for falling meteors. . . . When the monsters were wading across the Hudson River and coming into New York, I wanted to run up on my roof to see what they looked like, but I couldn't leave my radio while it was telling me of their whereabouts.

Aunt Grace began to pray with Uncle Henry. Lily got sick to her stomach. I don't know what I did exactly but I know I prayed harder and more earnestly than ever before. Just as soon as we were convinced that this thing was real, how petty all things on this earth seemed; how soon we put our trust in God!

The panic moved upstate. One man called up the Mt. Vernon Police Headquarters to find out "where the forty policemen were killed." Another took time out to philosophize:

I thought the whole human race was going to be wiped out—that seemed more important than the fact that we were going to die. It seemed awful that everything that had been worked on for years was going to be lost forever.

In Rhode Island weeping and hysterical women swamped the switch-board of the Providence *Journal* for details of the massacre, and officials of the electric light company received a score of calls urging them to turn off all lights so that the city would be safe from the enemy. The Boston *Globe* received a call from one woman "who could see the fire." A man in Pittsburgh hurried home in the midst of the broadcast and found his wife in the bathroom, a bottle of poison in her hand, screaming, "I'd rather die this way than that." In Minneapolis a woman ran into church screaming, "New York destroyed this is the end of the world. You might as well go home to die I just heard it on the radio."

The Kansas City Bureau of the AP received inquiries about the "meteors" from Los Angeles; Salt Lake City; Beaumont, Texas; and St. Joseph, Missouri. In San Francisco the general impression of listeners seemed to be that an overwhelming force had invaded the United States from the air—was in process of destroying New York and threatening to move westward. "My God," roared an inquirer into a telephone, "where can I volunteer my services, we've got to stop this awful thing!"

As far south as Birmingham, Alabama, people gathered in churches and prayed. On the campus of a Southeastern college——

The girls in the sorority houses and dormitories huddled around their radios trembling and weeping in each other's arms. They separated themselves from their friends only to take their turn at the telephones to make long distance calls to their parents, saying goodbye for what they thought might be the last time. . . .

There are hundreds of such bits of testimony, gathered from coast to coast.

IV

At least one book* and quite a pile of sociological literature has appeared on the subject of "The Invasion from Mars." Many theories have been put forward to explain the "tidal wave" of panic that swept the nation. I know of two factors that largely contributed to the broadcast's extraordinarily violent effect. First, its historical timing. It came within thirty-five days of the Munich crisis. For weeks, the American people had been hanging on their radios, getting most of their news no longer from the press, but over the air. A new technique of "on-the-spot" reporting had been developed and eagerly accepted by an anxious and news-hungry world. The Mercury Theater on the Air by faithfully copying every detail of the new technique—including its imperfections—found an already enervated audience ready to accept its wildest fantasies. The second factor was the show's sheer technical brilliance. To this day it is impossible to sit in a room and hear the scratched, worn, off-the-air recording of the broadcast, without feeling in the back of your neck some slight draft left over from that great wind of terror that swept the nation. Even with the element of credibility totally removed it remains a surprisingly frightening show.

Radio drama was taken seriously in the thirties—before the Quiz and the Giveaway became the lords of the air. In the work of such directors as Reis, Corwin, Fickett, Welles, Robson, Spier, and Oboler there was an eager, excited drive to get the most out of this new, all too rapidly freezing medium. But what happened that Sunday, up on the twentieth floor of the CBS building was something quite special. Beginning around two, when the show started to take shape under Orson's hands, a strange fever seemed to invade the studio—part childish mischief, part professional zeal.

First to feel it were the actors. I remember Frank Readick (who played the part of Carl Phillips, the network's special reporter) going down to the record library and digging up the Morrison recording of

* *The Invasion from Mars* by Hadley Cantril, Princeton University Press, from which many of the above quotations were taken.

the explosion of the Hindenburg at Lakehurst. This is a classic reportage—one of those wonderful, unpredictable accidents of eyewitness description. The broadcaster is casually describing a routine landing of the giant gasbag. Suddenly he sees something. A flash of flame! An instant later the whole thing explodes. It takes him time—a full second—to react at all. Then seconds more of sputtering ejaculations before he can make the adjustment between brain and tongue. He starts to describe the terrible things he sees—the writhing human figures twisting and squirming as they fall from the white burning wreckage. He stops, fumbles, vomits, then quickly continues. Readick played the record to himself, over and over. Then, recreating the emotion in his own terms, he described the Martian meteorite as he saw it lying inert and harmless in a field at Grovers Mill, lit up by the headlights of a hundred cars—the coppery cylinder suddenly opening, revealing the leathery tentacles and the terrible pale-eyed faces of the Martians within. As they begin to emerge he freezes, unable to translate his vision into words; he fumbles, retches—and then after a second continues.

A few moments later Carl Phillips lay dead, tumbling over the microphone in his fall—one of the first victims of the Martian Ray. There followed a moment of absolute silence—an eternity of waiting. Then, without warning, the network's emergency fill-in was heard—somewhere in a quiet studio, a piano, close on mike, playing "Clair de Lune," soft and sweet as honey, for many seconds, while the fate of the universe hung in the balance. Finally it was interrupted by the manly reassuring voice of Brigadier General Montgomery Smith, Commander of the New Jersey State Militia, speaking from Trenton, and placing "the counties of Mercer and Middlesex as far west as Princeton and east to Jamesburg" under Martial Law! Tension—release—then renewed tension. For soon after that came an eyewitness account of the fatal battle of the Watchung Hills; and then, once again, that lone piano was heard—now a symbol of terror, shattering the dead air with its ominous tinkle. As it played, on and on, its effect became increasingly sinister—a thin band of suspense stretched almost beyond endurance.

That piano was the neatest trick of the show—a fine specimen of the theatrical "retard," boldly conceived and exploited to the full. It was one of the many devices with which Welles succeeded in compelling, not merely the attention, but also the belief of his invisible audience. "The War of the Worlds" was a magic act, one of the world's greatest, and Orson was just the man to bring it off.

For Welles is at heart a magician whose particular talent lies not so much in his creative imagination (which is considerable) as in his proven ability to stretch the familiar elements of theatrical effect far

beyond their normal point of tension. For this reason his productions
require more elaborate preparation and more perfect execution than
most. At that—like all complicated magic tricks—they remain, till the
last moment, in a state of precarious balance. When they come off,
they give—by virtue of their unusually high intensity—an impression
of great brilliance and power; when they fail—when something in their
balance goes wrong or the original structure proves to have been unsound—they provoke, among their audience, a particularly violent
reaction of unease and revulsion. Welles' flops are louder than other
men's. The Mars broadcast was one of his unqualified successes.

Among the columnists and public figures who discussed the affair
during the next few days (some praising us for the public service we
had rendered, some condemning us as sinister scoundrels) the most
general reaction was one of amazement at the "incredible stupidity"
and "gullibility" of the American public, who had accepted as real,
in this single broadcast, incidents which in actual fact would have
taken days or even weeks to occur. "Nothing about the broadcast,"
wrote Dorothy Thompson with her usual aplomb, "was in the least
credible." She was wrong. The first few minutes of our broadcast
were, in point of fact, strictly realistic in time and perfectly credible,
though somewhat boring, in content. Herein lay the great tensile
strength of the show; it was the structural device that made the whole
illusion possible. And it could have been carried off in no other
medium than radio.

Our actual broadcasting time, from the first mention of the meteor-
ites to the fall of New York City, was less than forty minutes. During
that time men traveled long distances, large bodies of troops were
mobilized, cabinet meetings were held, savage battles fought on land
and in the air. And millions of people accepted it—emotionally if not
logically.

There is nothing so very strange about that. Most of us do the same
thing, to some degree, most days of our lives—every time we look at a
movie or listen to a broadcast. Not even the realistic theater observes
the literal unities; motion pictures and, particularly, radio (where neither
place nor time exists save in the imagination of the listener) have no
difficulty in getting their audiences to accept the telescoped reality of
dramatic time. Our special hazard lay in the fact that we purported to
be, not a play, but reality. In order to take advantage of the accepted
convention, we had to slide swiftly and imperceptibly out of the "real"
time of a news report into the "dramatic" time of a fictional broadcast.
Once that was achieved—without losing the audience's attention or
arousing their skepticism, if they could be sufficiently absorbed and be-

witched not to notice the transition—then, we felt, there was no extreme of fantasy through which they would not follow us. We were keenly aware of our problem; we found what we believed was the key to its solution. And if, that night, the American public proved "gullible," it was because enormous pains and a great deal of thought had been spent to make it so.

In the script, "The War of the Worlds" started extremely slowly— dull meteorological and astronomical bulletins alternating with musical interludes. These were followed by a colorless scientific interview and still another stretch of dance music. These first few minutes of routine broadcasting "within the existing standards of judgment of the listener" were intended to lull (or maybe bore) the audience into a false security and to furnish a solid base of realistic time from which to accelerate later. Orson, in making over the show, extended this slow movement far beyond our original conception. "La Cumparsita," rendered by "Ramon Raquello, from the Meridian Room of the Hotel Park Plaza in downtown New York," had been thought of as running only a few seconds; "Bobby Millette playing 'Stardust' from the Hotel Martinet in Brooklyn," even less. At rehearsal Orson stretched both these numbers to what seemed to us, in the control room, an almost unbearable length. We objected. The interview in the Princeton Observatory—the clock-work ticking monotonously overhead, the woolly-minded professor mumbling vague replies to the reporters' uninformed questions—this, too, he dragged out to a point of tedium. Over our protests, lines were restored that had been cut at earlier rehearsals. We cried there would not be a listener left. Welles stretched them out even longer.

He was right. His sense of tempo, that night, was infallible. When the flashed news of the cylinder's landing finally came—almost fifteen minutes after the beginning of a fairly dull show—he was able suddenly to spiral his action to a speed as wild and reckless as its base was solid. The appearance of the Martians; their first treacherous act; the death of Carl Phillips; the arrival of the militia; the battle of the Watchung Hills; the destruction of New Jersey—all these were telescoped into a space of twelve minutes without overstretching the listeners' emotional credulity. The broadcast, by then, had its own reality, the reality of emotionally felt time and space.

V

At the height of the crisis, around 8:31, the Secretary of the Interior came on the air with an exhortation to the American people. His words, as you read them now, ten years later, have a Voltairean ring.

(They were admirably spoken—in a voice just faintly reminiscent of the President's—by a young man named Kenneth Delmar, who has since grown rich and famous as Senator Claghorn.)

The Secretary

Citizens of the nation: I shall not try to conceal the gravity of the situation that confronts the country, nor the concern of your Government in protecting the lives and property of its people. However, I wish to impress upon you— private citizens and public officials, all of you—the urgent need of calm and resourceful action. Fortunately, this formidable enemy is still confined to a comparatively small area, and we may place our faith in the military forces to keep them there. In the meantime placing our trust in God, we must continue the performance of our duties, each and every one of us, so that we may confront this destructive adversary with a nation united, courageous, and consecrated to the preservation of human supremacy on this earth. I thank you.

Toward the end of this speech (circa 8:32 E.S.T.,), Davidson Taylor, supervisor of the broadcast for the Columbia Broadcasting System, received a phone call in the control room, creased his lips, and hurriedly left the studio. By the time he returned, a few moments later—pale as death—clouds of heavy smoke were rising from Newark, New Jersey, and the Martians, tall as skyscrapers, were astride the Pulaski Highway preparatory to wading the Hudson River. To us in the studio the show seemed to be progressing splendidly—how splendidly Davidson Taylor had just learned outside. For several minutes now, a kind of madness had seemed to be sweeping the continent—somehow connected with our show. The CBS switchboards had been swamped into uselessness but from outside sources vague rumors were coming in of deaths and suicides and panic injuries.

Taylor had requests to interrupt the show immediately with an explanatory station-announcement. By now the Martians were across the Hudson and gas was blanketing the city. The end was near. We were less than a minute from the Station Break. The organ was allowed to swirl out under the slackening fingers of its failing organist and Ray Collins, superb as the "last announcer," choked heroically to death on the roof of Broadcasting Building. The boats were all whistling for a while as the last of the refugees perished in New York Harbor. Finally, as they died away, an amateur shortwave operator was heard from heaven knows where, weakly reaching out for human companionship across the empty world:

2X2L Calling CQ

2X2L Calling CQ
2X2L Calling CQ
Isn't there anyone on the air?
Isn't there anyone?

Five seconds of absolute silence. Then, shattering the reality of World's End—the Announcer's voice was heard, suave and bright:

ANNOUNCER

You are listening to the CBS presentation of Orson Welles and the Mercury Theater on the Air in an original dramatization of *The War of the Worlds,* by H. G. Wells. The performance will continue after a brief intermission.

The second part of the show was extremely well written and most sensitively played—but nobody heard it. It recounted the adventures of a lone survivor, with interesting observations on the nature of human society; it described the eventual death of the Martian Invaders, slain— "after all man's defenses had failed by the humblest thing that God in his wisdom had put upon this earth"—by bacteriological action; it told of the rebuilding of a brave new world. After a stirring musical finale, Welles, in his own person, delivered a charming informal little speech about Halloween, which it happened to be.

I remember, during the playing of the final theme, the phone starting to ring in the control room and a shrill voice through the receiver announcing itself as belonging to the mayor of some Midwestern city, one of the big ones. He is screaming for Welles. Choking with fury, he reports mobs in the streets of his city, women and children huddled in the churches, violence and looting. If, as he now learns, the whole thing is nothing but a crummy joke—then he, personally, is coming up to New York to punch the author of it on the nose! Orson hangs up quickly. For we are off the air now and the studio door bursts open. The following hours are a nightmare. The building is suddenly full of people and dark blue uniforms. We are hurried out of the studio, downstairs, into a back office. Here we sit incommunicado while network employees are busily collecting, destroying, or locking up all scripts and records of the broadcast. Then the press is let loose upon us, ravening for horror. How many deaths have we heard of? (Implying they know of thousands.) What do we know of the fatal stampede in a Jersey hall? (Implying it is one of many.) What traffic deaths? (The ditches must be choked with corpses.) The suicides? (Haven't you heard about the one on Riverside Drive?) It is all quite vague in my memory and quite terrible.

Hours later, instead of arresting us, they let us out a back way. We scurry down to the theater like hunted animals to their hole. It is surprising to see life going on as usual in the midnight streets, cars stopping for traffic, people walking. At the Mercury the company is still stoically rehearsing—falling downstairs and singing the "Carmagnole." Welles goes up on stage, where photographers, lying in wait, catch him with his eyes raised up to heaven, his arms outstretched in an attitude of crucifixion. Thus he appeared in a tabloid that morning over the caption, "I Didn't Know What I Was Doing!" The *New York Times* quoted him as saying, "I don't think we will choose anything like this again."

We were on the front page for two days. Having had to bow to radio as a news source during the Munich crisis, the press was now only too eager to expose the perilous irresponsibilities of the new medium. Orson was their whipping boy. They quizzed and badgered him. Condemnatory editorials were delivered by our press-clipping bureau in bushel baskets. There was talk, for a while, of criminal action.

Then gradually, after about two weeks, the excitement subsided. By then it had been discovered that the casualties were not as numerous or as serious as had at first been supposed. One young woman had fallen and broken her arm running downstairs. Later the Federal Communications Commission held some hearings and passed some regulations. The Columbia Broadcasting System made a public apology. With that the official aspects of the incident were closed.

As to the Mercury—our new play, "Danton's Death," finally opened after five postponements. Not even our fantastic publicity was able to offset its generally unfavorable notices. On the other hand, that same week the Mercury Theater on the Air was signed up by Campbell Soups at a most lavish figure.

Of the suits that were brought against us—amounting to over three quarters of a million dollars for damages, injuries, miscarriages, and distresses of various kinds—none was substantiated or legally proved. We did settle one claim however, against the advice of our lawyers. It was the particularly affecting case of a man in Massachusetts, who wrote: "I thought the best thing to do was to go away. So I took three dollars twenty-five cents out of my savings and bought a ticket. After I had gone sixty miles I knew it was a play. Now I don't have money left for the shoes I was saving up for. Will you please have someone send me a pair of black shoes size 9B!"

We did.

39. Camp Meeting *

THIS SELECTION presents a type of collective behavior—the audience
—far different from those described in the two preceding selections
(37 and 38). Written by the essayist E. B. White, long associated
with *The New Yorker*, it presents the keen observations on audience
behavior of which the skilled reporter is capable. Although not the
work of a professional social scientist, the description offers many
interesting illustrations of the interaction between speaker and
audience and among the members of an audience.

OVER IN THE NEXT COUNTY the Methodists have a camp ground, in a
clump of woods near East Machias. They were in session there for about
a week, and I went over on Saturday for the *pièce de résistance*—Dr.
Francis E. Townsend (himself) of California. I had long wanted to
see the author of America's favorite plan, and there he was, plain as day,
right under the GOD IS LOVE sign.

It was a peaceful spot, though it gave one a sultry, hemmed-in feeling,
as hardwood dingles often do. There was a ticket booth, where I paid
my quarter; and beyond was a lane opening out into the *al fresco* temple
where about six hundred people were gathered to hear the good news.
They were Methodist farmers and small-town merchants and their
Methodist wives and children and dogs, Townsendites from Townsend
Club Number One of East Machias, pilgrims from all over the State,
honest, hopeful folks, their faces grooved with the extra lines that come
from leading godly, toilsome lives. The men sat stiffly in the dark-blue
suits that had carried them through weddings, funerals, and Fair days.
In a big circle surrounding the temple were the cottages (seventy or
eighty of them), little two-storey frame shacks, set ten or a dozen feet
apart, each with its front porch, its stuffy upstairs bedroom, and its
smell from the kitchen. Beyond, in a nobler circle, were the back-
houses, at the end of the tiny trails. The whole place, even with
hymns rising through the leafy boughs, had the faintly disreputable air
which pervades any woodland rendezvous where the buildings stand

* E. B. White, *One Man's Meat* (New York: Harper & Brothers, 1939), pp.
188-194. Copyright 1939 by E. B. White. Reproduced by permission of the
author and the publisher.
    The author (b. 1899) is an editorial writer and contributor to the *New Yorker*,
for which he wrote "Talk of the Town" columns for eleven years. From 1938-43
conducted the department "One Man's Meat" in *Harper's Magazine*. His style has
been called indescribable, highly individual, "a kind of precocious offhand humming."
Author, *The Lady is Cold* (poems), *Is Sex Necessary?* (with James Thurber), *A
Subtreasury of American Humor* (with Katherine S. White), *Here is New York*.

unoccupied for most of the year, attracting woodpeckers, sneak thieves, and lovers in season.

On the dais, behind some field flowers, sat the Doctor, patiently awaiting his time—a skinny, bespectacled little savior, with a big jaw, like the Tin Woodman. He had arrived by plane the night before at the Bangor airport a hundred miles away, and had driven over that morning for the meeting. As I sat down a voice was lifted in prayer, heads were bowed. The voice came from a loudspeaker suspended from the branch of an elm, and the speaker was talking pointedly of milk and honey. When he quit, Dr. Townsend's henchman, a baldish fellow with a businesslike manner, took the stand and introduced the man who needed no introduction, Dr. Francis E. Townsend, of California, the world's greatest humanitarian. We all rose and clapped. Children danced on the outskirts, dogs barked, and faces appeared in the windows of some of the nearest cottages. The Doctor held out his hands for silence. He stood quietly, looking round over the assemblage. And then, to the old folks with their troubled, expectant faces, he said, simply:

"I like you people very much."

It was like a handclasp, a friendly arm placed round the shoulder. Instantly his listeners warmed, and smiled, and wriggled with sudden newfound comfort.

"I have come nearly four thousand miles to see you," continued the Doctor. "You look like good Methodists, and I like that. I was raised in a Methodist family, so I know what it means."

He spoke calmly, without any platform tricks, and he sounded as though this was the first time he had ever expounded Townsendism. In words of one syllable he unfolded the plan which he had conceived, the plan which he knew would work, the plan which he promised to see enacted into law, so that all people might enjoy equally the good things of this life.

"The retirement of the elders is a matter of concern to the entire population." Grizzly heads nodded assent. Old eyes shone with new light.

"In a nation possessed of our natural resources, with great masses of gold and money at our command, it is unthinkable that conditions such as exist today should be tolerated. There is something radically wrong with any political philosophy which permits this to exist. Now, then, how did it come about?"

Dr. Townsend explained how it had come about. Flies buzzed in the clearing. The sun pierced the branches overhead, struck down on the folding music stands of the musicians, gleamed on the bare thighs of young girls in shorts, strolling with their fellows outside the pale of economics. The world, on this hot Saturday afternoon, seemed very old and sad, very much in need of something. Maybe this Plan was it. I never heard a milder-mannered economist, nor one more fully convinced of the right and wisdom of his proposal. I looked at the audience, at the faces. They were the faces of men and women reared on trouble, and now they wanted a few years of comfort on earth, and then to be received into the lap of the Lord. I think Dr. Townsend wanted this for them: I'm sure I did.

"Business is stymied," murmured the Doctor. "Almost half the population is in dire want. Sixty millions of people cannot buy the products of industry." The Doctor's statistics were staggering and loose-jointed, but his tone was quietly authoritative. There could be small room for doubt.

He spoke disparagingly of the New Deal, and knocked all the alphabetical schemes for employing idle men. "Do you want to be taxed for these useless and futile activities?"

His audience shook their heads.

And all the while he spoke, the plan itself was unfolding—simply, logically. A child could have understood it. Levy a two per cent tax on the gross business of the country and divide the revenue among persons over sixty years of age, with the one stipulation that they spend the money ($200 a month) within a certain number of days.

"And mind you," said the Doctor, with a good-natured grin, "we don't care a rap what you spend it for!"

The old folks clapped their hands and winked at one another. They were already buying pretty things, these Methodists, were already paying off old cankerous debts.

"We want you to have new homes, new furniture, new shoes and clothes. We want you to travel and go places. You old folks have earned the right to loaf, and you're going to do it luxuriously in the near future. The effect on business, when all this money is put into circulation, will be tremendous. Just let us have two billion dollars to distribute this month, and see what happens!"

The sound of the huge sum titivated the group; two billion dollars flashed across the clearing like a comet, trailing a wispy tail of excitement, longing, hope.

"It may even be three," said the Doctor, thoughtfully, as though the possibility had just occurred to him. "America has the facilities, all we need is the sense to use them."

He said he was reminded of a story in the old McGuffey's Reader. The one about the ship flying a distress signal, and another ship came to

its assistance. "Get us water!" shouted the captain. "We are perish-
ing of thirst."

"Dip up and drink, you fools!" answered the captain of the other ship.
"You're in the mouth of the Amazon River."

"Friends," said the good Doctor, "we are in the mouth of the Amazon
River of Abundance. But we haven't the sense to dip up and drink."

It was a nice story, and went well.

Suddenly the Doctor switched from words of promise to words of
threat. Lightly, with bony fingers, he strummed the strings of terror.
If we're going to save this democracy of ours (he said), we shall have to
begin soon. You've read about strikes in the great industrial centers;
in a very brief time you will read of riots. And when rioting starts, it
will be an easy matter for someone to seize the armed forces of the
country and put them to his own use. This has happened in Europe.
It can happen here.

The glade darkened ominously. Trees trembled in all their limbs.
The ground, hard-packed under the Methodist heel, swam in the vile
twilight of Fascist doom. Still the little Doctor's voice droned on—
calm, full of humility, devoid of theatrics. Just the simple facts, simply
told.

And then the vexatious question of money to carry on with. The
audience shifted, got a new grip on their seats with their behinds. The
ancient ceremony of plate-passing was a familiar and holy rite that had
to be gone through with. The Doctor carefully disclaimed any personal ambitions, financial or political. "I don't want a fortune," he
said, confidentially. "I mean that. I don't seek wealth. For one thing,
it might ruin my fine son. But it does take money to educate people
to a new idea. Give us a penny a day and we'll educate the next Congress."

A joke of two, to restore amiability; another poke at Uncle Sam;
another mention of the need for funds to carry on with; and the speech
was over.

It had been an impressive performance. Most speeches lack the
sincerity the Doctor had given his; not many speeches are so simply
made and pleasantly composed. It had been more like a conversation
with an old friend. I had listened, sitting there near the musicians,
with all the sympathy that within me lay, and (I trust) with an open
mind. Even a middle-aged hack has his moments of wanting to see the
world get along. After all, this was no time for cynicism; most of what
Dr. Townsend had said, God knows, was true enough. If anybody
could devise a system for distributing wealth more evenly, more power to
him. One man's guess was as good as another's. Well, pretty nearly

as good. I pocketed the few scribbled notes I had made and gave my-self over to a mood of summer afternoon despondency and world decay.

The chairman rose and announced that the meeting would be thrown open to questions, but that the time was short, so please speak right up. It was at this point that Dr. Francis E. Townsend (of California) began quietly to come apart, like an inexpensive toy. The questions came slowly, and they were neither very numerous nor very penetrating. Nor was there any heckling spirit in the audience: people were with him, not against him. But in the face of inquiry, the Doctor's whole manner changed. He had apparently been through this sort of thing before and was as wary as a squirrel. It spoiled his afternoon to be asked anything. Details of Townsendism were irksome in the extreme—he wanted to keep the Plan simple and beautiful, like young love before sex has reared its head. And now he was going to have to answer a lot of nasty old questions.

"How much would it cost to administer?" inquired a thrifty grand-mother, rising to her feet.

The Doctor frowned. "Why, er," he said. (This was the first "er" of the afternoon.) "Why, not a great deal. There's nothing about it, that is, there's no reason why it needs to cost much." He then ex-plained that it was just a matter of the Secretary of the Treasury making out forty-eight checks each month, one to each State. Surely that wouldn't take much of the Secretary's time. Then these big checks would be broken up by the individual State adminstrators, who would pay out the money to the people over sixty years of age who qualified. "We're not going to have any administrative problems to speak of, at all," said the Doctor, swallowing his spit. The little grandmother nodded and sat down.

"Can a person get the pension if they hold property?" inquired an old fellow who had suddenly remembered his home, and his field of potatoes.

"Yes, certainly," replied the Doctor, shifting from one foot to the other. "But we do have a stipulation; I mean, in our plan we are going to say that the money shall not go to anybody who has a gainful pur-suit." An uneasy look crossed the farmer's face: very likely he was wondering whether his field of potatoes was gainful. Maybe his potato bugs would stand him in good stead at last. Things already didn't look so simple.

"How much bookkeeping would it mean for a business man?" asked a weary capitalist.

"Bookkeeping?" repeated the Doctor vaguely. "Oh, I don't think there will be any trouble about bookkeeping. It is so simple. Every business man just states what his gross is for the thirty-day period, and two per cent of it goes to pay the old people. In the Hawaiian Islands they already have a plan much like mine in operation. It works beautifully, and I was amazed, when I was there, at how few people it took to administer it. No, there'll be no difficulty about bookkeeping."

"How will the Townsend Plan affect foreign trade?" asked an elderly thinker on Large Affairs.

Doctor Townsend gave him a queer look—not exactly hateful, but the kind of look a parent sometimes gives a child on an off day.

"Foreign trade?" he replied, somewhat weakly. "Foreign trade? Why should we concern ourselves with foreign trade?" He stopped. But then he thought maybe he had given short measure on that one, so he told a story of a corn-flakes factory, and all the corn came from some foreign country. What kind of way was that—buying corn from foreigners?

Next question: "Would a person receiving the pension be allowed to use it to pay off a mortgage?"

Answer: "Yes. Pay your debts. Let's set our government a good example!" (Applause.)

And now a gentleman down front—an apple-cheeked old customer with a twinkle: "Doctor, would buying a drink count as spending your money?"

"A drink?" echoed the Doctor. Then he put on a hearty manner. "Why, if anybody came to me and wanted to drink himself into an early grave with money from the fund, I'd say, 'Go to it, old boy!'" There was a crackle of laughter, but the Doctor knew he was on slippery footing. "Don't misunderstand me," he put in. "Let's not put too many restrictions on morality. The way to bring about temperance in this world is to bring up our young sons and daughters decently, and teach them the evils of abuse. (Applause.) And now, friends, I must go. It has been a most happy afternoon."

The meeting broke up. Townsendites rose and started down the aisles to shake hands reverently with their chief. The chairman announced a take of eighty dollars and three cents. Life began to settle into its stride again. Pilgrims filed out of the pews and subsided in rocking chairs on the porches of the little houses. Red and white paper streamers, festooning the trees, trembled in the fitful air; and soft drinks began to flow at the booth beyond the Inner Circle. The Doctor, waylaid by a group of amateur photographers, posed in front of an American flag, and then departed in a Dodge sedan for the airport—a cloud-draped Messiah, his dream packed away in a brief case for the next performance. On the porch of a cottage called "Nest o'Rest" three old ladies rocked and rocked and rocked. And from a score of rusty stovepipes in the woods rose the first thick coils of smoke from the kitchen fires, where America's housewives, never quite giving up, were laboriously preparing one more meal in the long, long procession. The vision of milk and honey, it comes and goes. But the odor of cooking goes on forever.

✎✎✎✎✎✎

40. The Nature of Personal Influence *

COLLECTIVE BEHAVIOR, like any other form of social behavior, operates within a framework of communication. Sometimes this framework is an indirect one involving the use of mass media, but very often it is a system of face-to-face relationships. In this selection P. F. Lazarsfeld and his associates systematically examine the nature of these face-to-face interpersonal relations in one area of social influence. Their analysis is built around the role of personal influence in determining the actual vote in a presidential election. Although this is a study of "decision making" in politics, the principles described have broad general application to many kinds of collective behavior involving personal relationships.

THE POLITICAL HOMOGENEITY of social groups is promoted by personal relationships among the same kinds of people. But for a detailed and systematic study of the influence of such relationships—the political role of personal influence—a systematic inventory would be needed of the various personal contacts and political discussions that people had over a sample number of days. . . . Such complete data are not available in the present study, but enough information has been collected to indicate the importance of personal relationships so far as their direct politi-

* Paul F. Lazarsfeld, Bernard Berelson, and Hazel Gaudet, The People's Choice: How the Voter Makes Up His Mind in a Presidential Campaign (New York: Columbia University Press, 1948), pp. 150-158. Reprinted by permission of the publisher and the senior author.

A short biographical note on Paul F. Lazarsfeld will be found with selection 6, p. 33. Bernard Berelson (b. 1912) is Chairman, Committee on Communication, University of Chicago. Since 1946, Professor of Library Science, Social Sciences. Dean, Graduate Library School, Chicago, 1947-51. Senior staff officer, Ford Foundation, since 1951. President, American Association of Public Opinion Research, 1951-52. His books include The Library Public, Reader in Communication and Public Opinion (with Morris Janowitz), Content Analysis. Editor, Education for Librarianship. Hazel Gaudet is with the Bureau of Applied Social Research, Columbia University.

cal influence is concerned. Our findings and impressions will be summarized without much formal statistical data. The significance of this area of political behavior was highlighted by the study but further investigation is necessary to establish it more firmly.

In comparison with the formal media of communication, personal relationships are potentially more influential for two reasons: their coverage is greater and they have certain psychological advantages over the formal media.

PERSONAL CONTACTS REACH THE UNDECIDED

Whenever the respondents were asked to report on their recent exposure to campaign communications of all kinds, political discussions were mentioned more frequently than exposure to radio or print. On any average day, at least 10% more people participated in discussions about the election—either actively or passively—than listened to a major speech or read about campaign items in a newspaper. And this coverage "bonus" came from just those people who had not yet made a final decision as to how they would vote. Political conversations, then, were more likely to reach those people who were still open to influence.

For example, people who made up their minds later in the campaign were more likely to mention personal influences in explaining how they formed their final vote decision. Similarly, we found that the less interested people relied more on conversations and less on the formal media as sources of information. Three-fourths of the respondents who at one time had not expected to vote but were then finally "dragged in" mentioned personal influence. After the election, the voters were given a check list of "sources from which they got most of the information or impressions that caused them to form their judgment on how to vote." Those who had made some change during the campaign mentioned friends or members of their family relatively more frequently than did the respondents who kept a constant vote intention all through the campaign.

THE TWO-STEP FLOW OF COMMUNICATIONS

A special role in the network of personal relationships is played by the "opinion leaders." . . . We noted that they engaged in political discussion much more than the rest of the respondents. But they reported that the formal media were more effective as sources of influence than personal relationships. This suggests that ideas often flow *from* radio and print to the opinion leaders and *from* them to the less active sections of the population.

Occasionally, the more articulate people even pass on an article or point out the importance of a radio speech. Repeatedly, changers referred to reading or listening done under some personal influence. Take the case of a retired school teacher who decided for the Republicans: "The country is ripe for a change . . . Willkie is a religious man. A friend read and highly recommended Dr. Poling's article in the October issue of the Christian Herald called 'The Religion of Wendell Willkie.' "

So much for the "coverage of personal contacts." The person-to-person influence reaches the ones who are more susceptible to change, and serves as a bridge over which formal media of communications extend their influence. But in addition, personal relationships have certain psychological advantages which make them especially effective in the exercise of the "molecular pressures" finally leading to the political homogeneity of social groups. We turn now to a discussion of five such characteristics.

NON-PURPOSIVENESS OF PERSONAL CONTACTS

The weight of personal contacts upon opinion lies, paradoxically, in their greater casualness and non-purposiveness in political matters. If we read or tune in a speech, we usually do so purposefully, and in doing so we have a definite mental set which tinges our receptiveness. Such purposive behavior is part of the broad area of our political experiences, to which we bring our convictions with a desire to test them and strengthen them by what is said. This mental set is armor against influence. The extent to which people, and particularly those with strong partisan views, listen to speakers and read articles with which they agree in advance is evidence on this point.

On the other hand, people we meet for reasons other than political discussion are more likely to catch us unprepared, so to speak, if they make politics the topic. One can avoid newspaper stories and radio speeches simply by making a slight effort, but as the campaign mounts and discussion intensifies, it is hard to avoid some talk of politics. Personal influence is more pervasive and less self-selective than the formal media. In short, politics gets through, especially to the indifferent, much more easily through personal contacts than in any other way, simply because it comes up unexpectedly as a sideline or marginal topic in a casual conversation. For example, there was the restaurant waitress who decided that Willkie would make a poor president after first thinking he would be good. Said she: "I had done a little newspaper reading against Willkie, but the real reason I changed my mind was from hearsay. So many people don't like Willkie. Many customers in the restaurant said Willkie would be no good." Notice that she was in a position to overhear bits of conversation that were not intended for her. There are many such instances. Talk that is "forbidden fruit" is particularly effective because one need not be suspicious as to the persuasive intentions of the speakers; as a result one's defenses are down. Furthermore, one may feel that he is getting the viewpoint of "people generally," that he is learning how "different people" think about the election.

Such passive participation in conversation is paralleled in the case of the formal media by accidental exposure, e.g., when a political speech is heard because it follows a favorite program. In both conversation and the formal media, such chance communication is particularly effective. And the testimony to such influence is much more frequent in the case of personal contacts. The respondents mentioned it time and again: "I've heard fellows talk at the plant . . . I hear men talk at the shop . . . My husband heard that talked about at work. . . ."

FLEXIBILITY WHEN COUNTERING RESISTANCE

But suppose we do meet people who want to influence us and suppose they arouse our resistance. Then personal contact still has one great advantage compared with other media: the face-to-face contact can counter and dislodge such resistance, for it is much more flexible. The clever campaign worker, professional or amateur, can make use of a large number of cues to achieve his end. He can choose the occasion at which to speak to the other fellow. He can adapt his story to what he presumes to be the other's interest and his ability to understand. If he notices the other is bored, he can change the subject. If he sees that he has aroused resistance, he can retreat, giving the other the satisfaction of a victory, and come back to his point later. If in the course of the discussion he discovers some pet convictions, he can try to tie up his argument with them. He can spot the moments when the other is yielding, and so time his best punches.

Neither radio nor the printed page can do anything of the kind. They must aim their propaganda shots at the whole target instead of just at the center, which represents any particular individual. In propaganda as much as in other things, one man's meat is another man's poison. This may lead to boomerang effects, when arguments aimed at "average" audiences with "average" reactions fail with Mr. X. The formal media produced several boomerangs upon people who resented what they read or heard and moved in the opposite direction from that intended. But among 58 respondents who mentioned personal contacts as concretely influential, there was only one boomerang. The flexibility of the face-to-face situation undoubtedly accounted for their absence.

REWARDS OF COMPLIANCE

When someone yields to a personal influence in making a vote decision, the reward is immediate and personal. This is not the case in yielding to an argument via print or radio. If a pamphlet argues that voting for the opposite party would be un-American or will jeopardize the future, its warning may sound too remote or improbable. But if a neighbor says the same things, he can "punish" one immediately for being unimpressed or unyielding: he can look angry or sad, he can leave the room and make his fellow feel isolated. The pamphlet can only intimate or describe future deprivations; the living person can create them at once.

Of course all this makes personal contacts a powerful influence only for people who do not like to be out of line. There are certainly some people who gain pleasure from being nonconformists, but under normal circumstances they are probably very much in the minority. Whenever propaganda by another person is experienced as an expression of the prevailing group tendencies, it has greater chances of being successful than the formal media because of social rewards. For example, here is a woman who was for Roosevelt until the middle of the campaign: "I have always been a Democrat and I think Roosevelt has been all right. But my family are all for Willkie. They think he would make the best president and they have been putting the pressure on me." She finally voted for Willkie. This aspect of personal contact was especially important for women.

The rewards of compliance to other people are learned in early childhood. The easiest way for most children to avoid discomfort is to do what others tell them to do. Someone who holds no strong opinions on politics and hence makes up his mind late in the campaign may very well be susceptible to personal influences because he has learned as a child to take them as useful guides in unknown territory. The young man who was going to vote for Roosevelt because "my grandfather will skin me if I don't" is a case in point.

TRUST IN AN INTIMATE SOURCE

More people put reliance upon their personal contacts to help them pick out the arguments which are relevant for their own good in political affairs than they do in the more remote and impersonal newspaper and radio. The doubtful voter may feel that the evaluations he reads or hears in a broadcast are plausible, for the expert writer can probably spell out the consequences of voting more clearly than the average citizen. But the voter still wonders whether these are the issues which are really going to affect *his own* future welfare. Perhaps these sources see the problem from a viewpoint entirely different from his own. But he can trust the judgment and evaluation of the respected people among his associates. Most of them are people with the same status and interests as himself. Their attitudes are more relevant for him than the judgments of an unknown editorial writer. In a formal communication the content can be at its best; but in a face-to-face contact the transference is most readily achieved. For example, here is the case of a young laborer who professed little or no interest in the campaign and who did not even expect to vote until late October: "I've been discussing the election with *the fellows at the shop* and I believe I'll vote, but I haven't decided yet who for." His constant exposure to the views of his fellow-workers not only brought him to the ballot booth but also brought out his final Democratic vote in line with his colleagues.

A middle-aged woman who showed great interest in the campaign was undecided until late October and then voted for Willkie: "*I was talking politics just this morning with a friend, a businessman.* He says business will improve if Willkie is elected and that Willkie promises to keep us out of the war. FDR is getting too much power. He shouldn't have a third term." Her friend had apparently run out for her what amounted to a small catalogue of Republican arguments and he was impressive enough to clinch her vote, which had been in the balance throughout the campaign. Her trust in his judgment settled her mind.

Trust in another person's point of view may be due to his prestige as well as to the plausibility of what he has to say or its relevancy to one's interests. It is obvious that in all influences prestige plays a considerable role. The degree of conformity is greater the higher the prestige of the person in our group who seeks to influence us. The plausibility of the consequences he presents will seem greater if he is important. (Of course, the formal media are also important in this respect.) The heightening of trust through the prestige of certain personal contacts was clear in the case of the driver of a bread truck who changed to Willkie because the prominent president of a business firm had done him the honor of persuading him in that direction. Then, too, there is the case of a middle-aged housewife with little education who was for Willkie from May through September, became undecided in October, and finally voted for Roosevelt. She left Willkie because of the statements of people whom she considered authorities: "I talked with a college student from Case, in Cleveland, and students are for Roosevelt because he has helped recreation. I talked, too, with a man from Chicago who is very interested in politics, and he doesn't seem to think that Willkie is a big enough man to handle international affairs."

PERSUASION WITHOUT CONVICTION

Finally, personal contacts can get a voter to the polls without affecting at all his comprehension of the issues of the election—something the formal media can rarely do. The newspaper or magazine or radio must first be effective in changing attitudes related to the action. There were several clear cases of votes cast not on the issues or even the personalities of the candidates. In fact, they were not really cast for the candidates at all. They were cast, so to speak, for the voters' friends.

"I was taken to the polls by a worker who insisted that I go."

"The lady where I work wanted me to vote. She took me to the polls and they all voted Republican so I did too."

In short, personal influence, with all its overtones of personal affection and loyalty, can bring to the polls votes that would otherwise not be cast or would be cast for the opposing party just as readily if some other friend had insisted. They differ from the formal media by persuading uninterested people to vote in a certain way without giving them a substantive reason for their vote. Fully 25% of those who mentioned a personal contact in connection with change of mind failed to give a real issue of the campaign as a reason for the change, but only 5% of those who mentioned the formal media omitted such a reason. When personal influence is paramount in this way, the voter is voting mainly for the personal friend, not the candidate.

PRACTICAL IMPLICATIONS

In a way the outcome of the election in Erie County is the best evidence for the success of face-to-face contacts. It so happened that for some time the Republican machine in that area worked much more vigorously than its Democratic opponent. When asked whether they knew people who had good ideas about politics, our respondents mentioned considerably more Republican than Democratic local politicians. A few people who did not expect to vote but finally went to the polls mentioned Republican canvassers as the main influence, but we could not trace a similar success for the Democratic machine.

However, one should not identify the personal contacts discussed in this chapter with the efforts of the *professional* political machines. These personal contacts are what one might call *amateur machines* which spring up during elections—individuals who become quite enthusiastic or special groups that try to activate people within their reach. One might almost say that the most successful form of propaganda— especially last-minute propaganda—is to "surround" the people whose vote decision is still dubious so that the only path left to them is the way to the polling booth.   We do not know how the budget of the political parties is distributed among different channels of propaganda but we suspect that the largest part of any propaganda budget is spent on pamphlets, radio time, etc.   But our findings suggest the task of finding the best ratio between money spent on formal media and money spent on organizing the face-to-face influences, the local "molecular pressures" which vitalize the formal media by more personal interpretation and the full richness of personal relationships into the promotion of the causes which are decided upon in the course of an election.

In the last analysis, more than anything else people can move other people.   From an ethical point of view this is a hopeful aspect in the serious social problem of propaganda.   The side which has the more enthusiastic supporters and which can mobilize grass-root support in an expert way has great chances of success.

⋙⋘⋙⋘

CHAPTER VI

SOCIAL ORGANIZATION:
STRATIFICATION AND MOBILITY

41. What Social Class Is in America *

THE CONCEPT OF SOCIAL CLASS is now widely used in popular as well as technical sociological literature. In recent years many studies have been made of social class in American society, but the concept has not been used in the same way by all investigators. W. Lloyd Warner and his associates, the authors of this article, have probably done more extensive work in this field than any other group. Here they describe what they mean by social class in our society.

THE AMERICAN DREAM AND SOCIAL CLASS

IN THE BRIGHT GLOW and warm presence of the American Dream all men are born free and equal. Everyone in the American Dream has the right, and often the duty, to try to succeed and to do his best to reach the top. Its two fundamental themes and propositions, that all of us are equal and that each of us has the right to the chance of reaching the

* W. Lloyd Warner, Marchia Meeker, and Kenneth Eells, Social Class in America: A Manual of Procedure for the Measurement of Social Status (Chicago: Science Research Associates, 1949), pp. 3-32. Reprinted by permission of the publisher and the senior author.

W. Lloyd Warner (b. 1898) is Professor of Anthropology and Sociology, University of Chicago. Noted for his numerous research projects in the South, in the Chicago Negro community, among six Indian tribes, in a Middle Western community, in Chicago industrial plants. Co-author of a number of books, including Color and Human Nature, Social Life of a Modern Community, Social System of a Modern Factory, Democracy in Jonesville. Marchia Meeker (b. 1916) is former Research Assistant, Committee on Human Development, University of Chicago, now at Illinois Institute of Technology. Kenneth Eells (b. 1913) is Associate Professor of Psychology, San Diego State College, San Diego, California. Former Research Associate, Department of Education, University of Chicago. Author (with others) of Intelligence and Cultural Differences.

top, are mutually contradictory, for if all men are equal there can be no top level to aim for, no bottom one to get away from; there can be no superior or inferior positions, but only one common level into which all Americans are born and in which all of them will spend their lives. We all know such perfect equality of position and opportunity does not exist. All Americans are not born into families of equal position: some are born into a rich man's aristocracy on the Gold Coast; some into the solid comfort of Suburbia's middle classes; and others into a mean existence among the slum families living on the wrong side of the tracks. It is common knowledge that the sons and daughters of the Gold Coasts, the Main Lines, and Park Avenues of America are more likely to receive recognition for their efforts than the children of the slums. The distance these fortunate young people travel to achieve success is shorter, and the route up easier, than the long hard pull necessary for the ambitious children of the less fortunate middle class. Though everyone has the common right to succeed, it is not an equal "right"; though there is equality of rank for some of us, there is not equality of rank for all of us.

When some men learn that *all* the American Dream does not fit *all* that is true about the realities of our life, they denounce the Dream and deny the truth of *any* of it. Fortunately, most of us are wiser and better adjusted to social reality; we recognize that, though it is called a Dream and though some of it is false, by virtue of our firm belief in it we have made some of it true. Despite the presence of social hierarchies which place people at higher and lower levels in American communities, the principles of democracy do operate; the Christian dogma that all men are equal in the sight of God because He is our Father and we are His spiritual children, buttressed by the democratic faith in the equality of men and the insistence on their equal rights as citizens, is a powerful influence in the daily life of America.

From grade school on, we have learned to cite chapter and verse proving from the lives of many of the great men of American history that we can start at the bottom and climb to the highest peaks of achievement when we have a few brains and a will to do. Our mass magazines and newspapers print and reprint the legendary story of rags to riches and tell over and over again the Ellis-Island-to-Park-Avenue saga in the actual lives of contemporary successful immigrant men and women. From mere repetition, it might be thought the public would tire of the theme; the names are all that vary and the stories, like those of children, remain the same. But we never do tire of this theme, for it says what we need to know and what we want to hear.

Among people around us, we sometimes recognize men who have got ahead, who have been successfully upward-mobile, and who have reached levels of achievement beyond even the dreams of most men. Many Americans by their own success have learned that, for them, enough of the Dream is true to make all of it real. The examples from history, from the world around us, and from our own experience provide convincing evidence that, although full equality is absent, opportunity for advancement is present sufficiently to permit the rise of a few from the bottom and a still larger number from the middle to the higher economic and social levels. Although we know the statement that everyone is equal but that some men are higher than others is contradictory, and although some of us smile or become angry when we hear that "all of us are equal but some are more equal than others," we still accept both parts of this proposition either by understressing one part of the proposition or by letting all of it go as a paradox we feel to be true.

Our society does an excellent job in giving us an explicit knowledge of, and good argument for, the equalitarian aspects of our life. We have much scholarly knowledge about the workings of democracy, but we have little scientific knowledge about the powerful presence of social status and how it works for good and evil in the lives of all of us. Yet to live successfully and adaptively in America, every one of us must adjust his life to each of these contradictions, not just one of them, and we must make the most of each. Our knowledge of the democratic aspects of America is learned directly as part of our social heritage, but our understanding of the principle of social status tends to be implicit and to be learned obliquely and through hard and sometimes bitter experience. The lives of many are destroyed because they do not understand the workings of social class.

It is the hope of the authors that this book will provide a corrective instrument which will permit men and women better to evaluate their social situations and thereby better adapt themselves to social reality and fit their dreams and aspirations to what is possible.

Our great state papers, the orations of great men, and the principles and pronouncements of politicians and statesmen tell us of the equality of all men. Each school boy learns and relearns it; but most of us are dependent upon experience and indirect statement to learn about "the wrong side of the tracks," "the Gold Coast and the slums," and "the top and bottom of the social heap." We are proud of those facts of American life that fit the pattern we are taught, but somehow we are often ashamed of those equally important social facts which demonstrate the presence of social class. Consequently, we tend to deny them or, worse, denounce them and by so doing deny their existence and magically make them disappear from consciousness. We use such expressions as "the Century of the Common Man" to insist on our democratic faith; but we know that, ordinarily, for Common Men to exist as a class, un-Common superior and inferior men must also exist. We know that every town or city in the country has its "Country Club set" and that this group usually lives on its Gold Coast, its Main Line, North Shore, or Nob Hill, and is the top of the community's social heap. Most of us know from novels such as those of Sinclair Lewis of the Main Streets than run through all our towns and cities, populated by Babbitts or, more explicitly stated, by "the substantial upper-middle class"; and by now, thanks to another group of novelists such as Erskine Caldwell, we know there is a low road, a Tobacco Road, that runs not only by the ramshackle houses of the poor whites of the South, but by the tarpaper shanties of the slums and river bottoms or Goat Hills of every town and city in the United States.

The "superior people" of Marquand's New England, "the North Shore crowd," divided into a top level of "old families" with a set of values and a way of life rated above those of the "new families," are matched by Philadelphia's "Main Line" families in Christopher Morley's *Kitty Foyle* and by similar groups in many other novels which report on the dominance of "the upper classes" in all regions of the United States. Reading them, together with similar novels reporting on Suburbia and Main Street for the middle classes and those on the Tobacco Roads and the city slums for the lower levels, gives one the understanding that throughout the towns and cities of America the inhabitants are divided into status levels which are ways of life with definite characteristics and values. Talking to and observing the people of these communities demonstrate that they, too, know how real these status levels are, and they prove it by agreeing among themselves about the levels and who belongs to them in their particular city.

Although well aware of social class, social scientists have been more concerned with their theories and with quarreling among themselves about what social class is than with studying its realities in the daily lives of the people. Until recently, they have lagged behind the novelists in investigating what our classes are, how they operate in our social life, and what effect they have on our individual lives.

But recent scientific studies of social class in the several regions of the United States demonstrate that it is a major determinant of individual decisions and social actions; that every major area of American life is directly and indirectly influenced by our class order; and that the major decisions of most individuals are partly controlled by it. To act intelligently and know consciously how this basic factor in American life affects us and our society, it is essential and necessary that we have an explicit understanding of what our class order is, how it works, and what it does to the lives and personalities who live in it. Our most democratic institutions, including our schools, churches, business organizations, government, and even our family life, are molded by its all-pervading and exceedingly subtle but powerful influence.

．　．　．　．　．　．

THE STRUCTURAL IMPERATIVE—WHY WE HAVE A CLASS SYSTEM

The recognition of social class and other status hierarchies in this country comes as no surprise to students of society. Research on the social life of the tribes and civilizations of the world clearly demonstrates that some form of rank is always present and a necessity for our kind of society.

Just as students of comparative biology have demonstrated that the physical structure of the higher animals must have certain organs to survive, so students of social anthropology have shown that the social structures of the "higher," the more complex, societies must have rank orders to perform certain functions necessary for group survival.

When societies are complex and service large populations, they always possess some kind of status system which, by its own values, places people in higher or lower positions. Only the very simple hunting and gathering tribes, with very small populations and very simple social problems, are without systems of rank; but when a society is complex, when there are large numbers of individuals in it pursuing diverse and complex activities and functioning in a multiplicity of ways, individual positions and behaviors are evaluated and ranked. This happens primarily because, to maintain itself, the society must co-ordinate the efforts of all its members into common enterprises necessary for the preservation of the group, and it must solidify and integrate all these enterprises into a working whole. In other words, as the division of labor increases and the social units become more numerous and diverse, the need for co-ordination and integration also increases and, when satisfied, enables the larger group to survive and develop.

Those who occupy co-ordinating positions acquire power and prestige. They do so because their actions partly control the behavior of the individuals who look to them for direction. Within this simple control there is simple power. Those who exercise such power either acquire prestige directly from it or have gained prestige from other sources sufficiently to be raised to a co-ordinating position. For example, among many primitive peoples a simple fishing expedition may be organized so that the men who fish and handle each boat are under the direction of one leader. The efforts of each boat are directed by the leader and, in turn, each boat is integrated into the total enterprise by its leader's taking orders from his superior. The same situation prevails in a modern factory. Small plants with a small working force and simple problems possess a limited hierarchy, perhaps no more than an owner who bosses all the workers. But a large industrial enterprise, with complex activities and problems, like General Motors, needs an elaborate hierarchy of supervision. The position in a great industrial empire which integrates and co-ordinates all the positions beneath it throughout all the supervising levels down to the workers has great power and prestige. The same holds true for political, religious, educational, and other social institutions; the more complex the group and the more diverse the functions and activities, the more elaborate its status system is likely to be. We will amplify this point later.

The studies of other societies have demonstrated one other basic point: the more complex the technological and economic structure, the more complex the social structure; so that some argue (the Marxians and many classical economists) that technological advancement is the cause of social complexity and all class and status systems. It cannot be denied that economic and technological factors are important in the determination of class and status orders. We must not lose sight of the fact, however, that the social system, with its beliefs, values, and rules, which governs human behavior may well determine what kind of technology and what kind of economic institutions will survive or thrive in any given tribe or nation. In any case, social complexity is necessary for economic advancement. Furthermore, social complexity is a basic factor determining the presence or absence of class.

The Marxians have argued that the economic changes our society is undergoing always result in a class war in which "the proletariat" will be triumphant and out of which a "classless society" will result. The authors do not agree with them for several reasons. The principal reasons are: (1) the presence of a class order does not necessarily mean class conflict—the relations of the classes can be and often are amiable and peaceful; (2) classless societies (without differential status systems) are impossible where there is complexity for the reasons previously given. Russia's communistic system, supposedly designed to produce a pure equalitarian society, necessarily has citizens who are ranked above and below each other. Generals, there, outrank privates; commissars, the rank and file; and members of the Politburo, the ordinary comrade. Occupants of these higher ranks in Russia tend to associate together; those of the lower ranks form their own groups. Their children are trained according to the rank of their parents. This means that the younger generation learns these status differences, thereby strengthening status differences between levels and fostering the further development of social class in Communistic Russia.

All this has occurred despite the fact the Russians have removed the means of production from private hands and placed them under the control of the State ("the people"). The economic factor which by Marxian doctrine produced social classes is largely absent; yet social hierarchies and social classes are present for the reason that Russia is a complex society and needs them to survive.

These status trends in Russia will undoubtedly continue, for her population is vast, her peoples diverse, her problems immensely complex; and elaborate systems of co-ordination and control are necessary for such a nation to maintain itself. The Communist ideals of economic and political equality cannot produce perfect equality within the complexities of Russian life.

But let us return to the United States. We, too, have a complex, highly diverse society. We, too, possess an elaborate division of labor and a ramified technology. And we, too, possess a variety of rank orders built on the need of maintaining unity and cohesion in making our common enterprises successful. Men occupying high and low positions possess families. Their families and their activities are identified with their social position. Families of the same position tend to associate together. They do this informally or through cliques, associations, or other institutions. This social matrix provides the structure of our class system. Children are always born to their families' position. Through life they may increase or decrease their status. The family thereby strengthens and helps maintain our class order. Social status in America is somewhat like man's alimentary canal; he may not like the way it works and he may want to forget that certain parts of it are part of him, but he knows it is necessary for his very existence. So a status system, often an object of our disapproval, is present and necessary in our complex social world.

If we cannot eliminate the system of status, we can and must work to keep it as democratic and equalitarian as possible. To be successful we must see to it that each American is given his chance to move in the social scale. This ideal of equality of opportunity is essential for our democracy. To do this intelligently, we must know what our class order is and what can be done to make it conform most closely to the needs of the American people.

The remainder of this chapter will briefly summarize what we now know about our social classes and how they are organized and function in the towns and cities of the several regions of the United States. We will start with the New England Yankees and then go on to the Middle and Far West and end up with the South before we take up the question of the common features of American class and what it is as a status system.

CLASS AMONG THE NEW ENGLAND YANKEES

Studies of communities in New England clearly demonstrate the presence of a well-defined social-class system. At the top is an aristocracy of birth and wealth. This is the so-called "old family" class. The people of Yankee City say the families who belong to it have been in the community for a long time—for at least three generations and preferably many generations more than three. "Old family" means not only old to the community but old to the class. Present members of the class were born into it; the families into which they were born can trace their lineage through many generations participating in a way of life characteristic of the upper class back to a generation marking the lowly beginnings out of which their family came. Although the men of this level are occupied gainfully, usually as large merchants, financiers, or in the higher professions, the wealth of the family, inherited from the husband's or the wife's side, and often from both, has been in the family for a long time. Ideally, it should stem from the sea trade when Yankee City's merchants and sea captains made large fortunes, built great Georgian houses on elm-lined Hill Street, and filled their houses and gardens with the proper symbols of their high position. They became the 400, the Brahmins, the Hill Streeters to whom others looked up; and they, well-mannered or not, looked down on the rest. They counted themselves, and were so counted, equals of similar levels in Salem, Boston, Providence, and other New England cities. Their sons and daughters married into the old families from these towns and at times, when family fortune was low or love was great, they married wealthy sons and daughters from the newly rich who occupied the class level below them. This was a happy event for the fathers and mothers of such fortunate young people in the lower half of the upper class, an event well publicized and sometimes not too discreetly bragged about by the parents of the lower-upper-class children, an occasion to be explained by the mothers from the old families in terms of the spiritual demands of romantic love and by their friends as "a good deal and a fair exchange all the way around for everyone concerned."

The new families, the lower level of the upper class, came up through

the new industries—shoes, textiles, silverware—and finance. Their
fathers were some of the men who established New England's trading
and financial dominance throughout America. When New York's
Wall Street rose to power, many of them transferred their activities to
this new center of dominance. Except that they aspire to old-family
status, if not for themselves then for their children, these men and their
families have a design for living similar to the old-family group. But
they are consciously aware that their money is too new and too recently
earned to have the sacrosanct quality of wealth inherited from a long
line of ancestors. They know, as do those about them, that, while a
certain amount of wealth is necessary, birth and old family are what
really matter. Each of them can cite critical cases to prove that particular individuals have no money at all, yet belong to the top class
because they have the right lineage and right name. While they
recognize the worth and importance of birth, they feel that somehow
their family's achievements should be better rewarded than by a mere
second place in relation to those who need do little more than be born
and stay alive.

The presence of an old-family class in a community forces the newly
rich to wait their turn if they aspire to "higher things." Meanwhile,
they must learn how to act, fill their lives with good deeds, spend their
money on approved philanthropy, and reduce their arrogance to manageable proportions.

The families of the upper and lower strata of the upper classes are
organized into social cliques and exclusive clubs. The men gather
fortnightly in dining clubs where they discuss matters that concern
them. The women belong to small clubs or to the Garden Club and
give their interest to subjects which symbolize their high status and
evoke those sentiments necessary in each individual if the class is to
maintain itself. Both sexes join philanthropic organizations whose
good deeds are an asset to the community and an expression of the
dominance and importance of the top class to those socially beneath
them. They are the members of the Episcopalian and Unitarian and,
occasionally, the Congregational and Presbyterian churches.

Below them are the members of the solid, highly respectable upper-
middle class, the people who get things done and provide the active
front in civic affairs for the classes above them. They aspire to the
classes above and hope their good deeds, civic activities, and high moral
principles will somehow be recognized far beyond the usual pat on the
back and that they will be invited by those above them into the in-
timacies of upper-class cliques and exclusive clubs. Such recognition
might increase their status and would be likely to make them members

of the lower-upper group. The fact that this rarely happens seldom stops members of this level, once activated, from continuing to try. The men tend to be owners of stores and belong to the large proprietor and professional levels. Their incomes average less than those of the lower-upper class, this latter group having a larger income than any other group, including the old-family level.

These three strata, the two upper classes and the upper-middle, constitute the levels above the Common Man. There is a considerable distance socially between them and the mass of the people immediately below them. They comprise three of the six classes present in the community. Although in number of levels they constitute half the community, in population they have no more than a sixth, and sometimes less, of the Common Man's population. The three levels combined include approximately 13 per cent of the total population.

The lower-middle class, the top of the Common Man level, is composed of clerks and other white-collar workers, small tradesmen, and a fraction of skilled workers. Their small houses fill "the side streets" down from Hill Street, where the upper classes and some of the upper-middle live, and are noticeably absent from the better suburbs where the upper-middle concentrate. "Side Streeter" is a term often used by those above them to imply an inferior way of life and an inconsequential status. They have accumulated little property but are frequently home owners. Some of the more successful members of ethnic groups, such as the Italians, Irish, French-Canadians, have reached this level. Only a few members of these cultural minorities have gone beyond it; none of them has reached the old-family level.

The old-family class (upper-upper) is smaller in size than the new-family class (lower-upper) below them. It has 1.4 per cent, while the lower-upper class has 1.6 per cent, of the total population. Ten per cent of the population belongs to the upper-middle class, and 28 per cent to the lower-middle level. The upper-lower is the most populous class, with 34 per cent, and the lower-lower has 25 per cent of all the people in the town.

The prospects of the upper-middle-class children for higher education are not as good as those of the classes above. One hundred per cent of the children of the two upper classes take courses in the local high school that prepare them for college, and 88 per cent of the upper-middle do; but only 44 per cent of the lower-middle take these courses, 28 per cent of the upper-lower, and 26 per cent of the lower-lower. These percentages provide a good index of the position of the lower-middle class, ranking it well below the three upper classes, but placing it well above the upper-lower and the lower-lower.

The upper-lower class, least differentiated from the adjacent levels and hardest to distinguish in the hierarchy, but clearly present, is composed of the "poor but honest workers" who more often than not are only semi-skilled or unskilled. Their relative place in the hierarchy of class is well portrayed by comparing them with the classes superior to them and with the lower-lower class beneath them in the category of how they spend their money.

A glance at the ranking of the proportion of the incomes of each class spent on ten items (including such things as rent and shelter, food, clothing, and education, among others) shows, for example, that this class ranks second for the percentage of the money spent on food, the lower-lower class being first and the rank order of the other classes following lower-middle according to their place in the social hierarchy. The money spent on rent and shelter by upper-lower class is also second to the lower-lower's first, the other classes' rank order and position in the hierarchy being in exact correspondence. To give a bird's-eye view of the way this class spends its money, the rank of the upper-lower, for the percentage of its budget spent on a number of common and important items, has been placed in parentheses after every item in the list which follows: food (2), rent (2), clothing (4), automobiles (5), taxes (5), medical aid (5), education (4), and amusements (4-5). For the major items of expenditure the amount of money spent by this class out of its budget corresponds fairly closely with its place in the class hierarchy, second to the first of the lower-lower class for the major necessities of food and shelter, and ordinarily, but not always, fourth or fifth to the classes above for the items that give an opportunity for cutting down the amounts spent on them. Their feelings about doing the right thing, of being respectable and rearing their children to do better than they have, coupled with the limitations of their income, are well reflected in how they select and reject what can be purchased on the American market.

The lower-lower class, referred to as "Riverbrookers" or the "lowdown Yankees who live in the clam flats," have a "bad reputation" among those who are socially above them. This evaluation includes beliefs that they are lazy, shiftless, and won't work, all opposites of the good middle-class virtues belonging to the essence of the Protestant ethic. They are thought to be improvident and unwilling or unable to save their money for a rainy day and, therefore, often dependent on the philanthropy of the private or public agency and on poor relief. They are sometimes said to "live like animals" because it is believed that their sexual mores are not too exacting and that pre-marital intercourse, post-marital infidelity, and high rates of illegitimacy, sometimes too publicly mixed with incest, characterize their personal and family lives. It is certain that they deserve only part of this reputation. Research shows many of them guilty of no more than being poor and lacking in the desire to get ahead, this latter trait being common among those above them. For these reasons and others, this class is ranked in Yankee City below the level of the Common Man (lower-middle and upper-lower). For most of the indexes of status it ranks sixth and last.

CLASS IN THE DEMOCRATIC MIDDLE WEST AND FAR WEST

Cities large and small in the states west of the Alleghenies sometimes have class systems which do not possess an old-family (upper-upper) class. The period of settlement has not always been sufficient for an old-family level, based on the security of birth and inherited wealth, to entrench itself. Ordinarily, it takes several generations for an old-family class to gain and hold the prestige and power necessary to impress the rest of the community sufficiently with the marks of its "breeding" to be able to confer top status on those born into it. The family, its name, and its lineage must have had time to become identified in the public mind as being above ordinary mortals.

While such identification is necessary for the emergence of an old-family (upper-upper) class and for its establishment, it is also necessary for the community to be large enough for the principles of exclusion to operate. For example, those in the old-family group must be sufficiently numerous for all the varieties of social participation to be possible without the use of new-family members; the family names must be old enough to be easily identified; and above all there should always be present young people of marriageable age to become mates of others of their own class and a sufficient number of children to allow mothers to select playmates and companions of their own class for their children.

When a community in the more recently settled regions of the United States is sufficiently large, when it has grown slowly and at an average rate, the chances are higher that it has an old-family class. If it lacks any one of these factors, including size, social and economic complexity, and steady and normal growth, the old-family class is not likely to develop.

One of the best tests of the presence of an old-family level is to determine whether members of the new-family category admit, perhaps grudgingly and enviously and with hostile derogatory remarks, that the old-family level looks down on them and that it is considered a mark of advancement and prestige by those in the new-family group to move into it and be invited to the homes and social affairs of the old families. When a member of the new-family class says, "We've only been here two generations, but we still aren't old-family," and when he or she goes on to say that "they (old family) consider themselves better than people like us and the poor dopes around here let them get away with it," such evidence indicates that an old-family group is present and able to enforce recognition of its superior position upon its most aggressive and hostile competitors, the members of the lower-upper, or new-family, class.

When the old-family group is present and its position is not recognized as superordinate to the new families, the two tend to be co-ordinate and view each other as equals. The old-family people adroitly let it be known that their riches are not material possessions alone but are old-family lineage; the new families display their wealth, accent their power, and prepare their children for the development of a future lineage by giving them the proper training at home and later sending them to the "right" schools and marrying them into the "right" families.

Such communities usually have a five-class pyramid, including an upper class, two middle, and two lower classes.

Jonesville, located in the Middle West, approximately a hundred years old, is an example of a typical five-class community. The farmers around Jonesville use it as their market, and it is the seat of government for Abraham County. Its population of over 6,000 people is supported by servicing the needs of the farmers and by one large and a few small factories.

At the top of the status structure is an upper class commonly referred to as "the 400." It is composed of old-family and new-family segments. Neither can successfully claim superiority to the other. Below this level is an upper-middle class which functions like the same level in Yankee City and is composed of the same kind of people, the only difference being the recognition that the distance to the top is shorter for them and the time necessary to get there much less. The Common Man level, composed of lower-middle- and upper-lower-class people, and the lower-lower level are replicas of the same classes in Yankee City. The only difference is that the Jonesville ethnics in these classes are Norwegian Lutherans and Catholic Poles, the Catholic Irish and Germans having been absorbed for the most part in the larger population; whereas in Yankee City the ethnic population is far more heterogeneous, and the Catholic Irish are less assimilated largely because of more opposition to them, and because the church has more control over their private lives.

• • • • • •

The communities of the mountain states and Pacific Coast are new, and many of them have changed their economic form from mining to other enterprises; consequently, their class orders are similar to those found in the Middle West. The older and larger far western communities which have had a continuing, solid growth of population which has not destroyed the original group are likely to have the old-family level at the top with the other classes present; the newer and smaller communities and those disturbed by the destruction of their original status structure by large population gains are less likely to have an old-family class reigning above all others. San Francisco is a clear example of the old-family type; Los Angeles, of the more amorphous, less well-organized class structure.

CLASS IN THE DEEP SOUTH

Studies in the Deep South demonstrate that, in the older regions where social changes until recently have been less rapid and less disturbing to the status order, most of the towns above a few thousand population have a six-class system in which an old-family elite is socially dominant.

For example, in a study of a Mississippi community, a market town for a cotton-growing region around it, Davis and the Gardners found a six-class system. Perhaps the southern status order is best described by Chart I on page 330 which gives the names used by the people of the community for each class and succinctly tells how the members of each class regard themselves and the rest of the class order.

The people of the two upper classes make a clear distinction between an old aristocracy and an aristocracy which is not old. There is no doubt that the first is above the other; the upper-middle class views the two upper ones much as the upper classes do themselves but groups them in one level with two divisions, the older level above the other; the lower-middle class separates them but considers them co-ordinate; the bottom two classes, at a greater social distance than the others, group all the levels above the Common Man as "society" and one class. An examination of the terms used by the several classes for the other classes shows that similar principles are operating.

The status system of most communities in the South is further complicated by a color-caste system which orders and systematically controls the relations of those categorized as Negroes and whites.

Although color-caste in America is a separate problem, . . . it is necessary that we describe it briefly to be sure a clear distinction is made between it and social class. Color-caste is a system of values and

CHART I

THE SOCIAL PERSPECTIVES OF THE SOCIAL CLASSES[1]

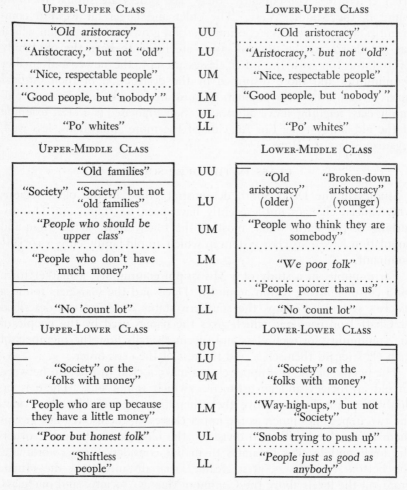

UPPER-UPPER CLASS   LOWER-UPPER CLASS

"Old aristocracy"	UU	"Old aristocracy"
"Aristocracy," but not "old"	LU	"Aristocracy," but not "old"
"Nice, respectable people"	UM	"Nice, respectable people"
"Good people, but 'nobody' "	LM	"Good people, but 'nobody' "
	UL	
"Po' whites"	LL	"Po' whites"

UPPER-MIDDLE CLASS   LOWER-MIDDLE CLASS

"Old families"	UU	"Old "Broken-down
"Society" "Society" but not "old families"	LU	aristocracy" aristocracy" (older) (younger)
"People who should be upper class"	UM	"People who think they are somebody"
"People who don't have much money"	LM	"We poor folk"
	UL	"People poorer than us"
"No 'count lot"	LL	"No 'count lot"

UPPER-LOWER CLASS   LOWER-LOWER CLASS

	UU	
	LU	
"Society" or the "folks with money"	UM	"Society" or the "folks with money"
"People who are up because they have a little money"	LM	"Way-high-ups," but not "Society"
"Poor but honest folk"	UL	"Snobs trying to push up"
"Shiftless people"	LL	"People just as good as anybody"

[1] Allison Davis, Burleigh B. Gardner, and Mary R. Gardner, *Deep South* (Chicago: University of Chicago Press, 1941), p. 65.

behavior which places all people who are thought to be white in a superior position and those who are thought of as black in an inferior status.

Characteristics of American Negroes vary from very dark hair and skin and Negroid features to blond hair, fair skin, and Caucasian features, yet all of them are placed in the "racial" category of Negro.

The skin and physical features of American Caucasians vary from Nordic blond types to the dark, swarthy skin and Negroid features of some eastern Mediterranean stocks, yet all are classed as socially white, despite the fact that a sizable proportion of Negroes are "whiter" in appearance than a goodly proportion of whites. The members of the two groups are severely punished by the formal and informal rules of our society if they intermarry, and when they break this rule of "caste endogamy," their children suffer the penalties of our caste-like system by being placed in the lower color caste. Furthermore, unlike class, the rules of this system forbid the members of the lower caste from climbing out of it. Their status and that of their children are fixed forever. This is true no matter how much money they have, how great the prestige and power they may accumulate, or how well they have acquired correct manners and proper behavior. There can be no social mobility out of the lower caste into the higher one. (There may, of course, be class mobility within the Negro or white caste.) The rigor of caste rules varies from region to region in the United States.

The Mexicans, Spanish Americans, and Orientals occupy a somewhat different status from that of the Negro, but many of the characteristics of their social place in America are similar.

• • • • • •

THE GENERALITIES OF AMERICAN CLASS

It is now time to ask what are the basic characteristics of social status common to the communities of all regions in the United States and, once we have answered this question, to inquire what the variations are among the several systems. Economic factors are significant and important in determining the class position of any family or person, influencing the kind of behavior we find in any class, and contributing their share to the present form of our status system. But, while significant and necessary, the economic factors are not sufficient to predict where a particular family or individual will be or to explain completely the phenomena of social class. Something more than a large income is necessary for high social position. Money must be translated into socially approved behavior and possessions, and they in turn must be translated into intimate participation with, and acceptance by, members of a superior class.

• • • • • •

To belong to a particular level in the social-class system of America means that a family or individual has gained acceptance as an equal by those who belong in the class. The behavior in this class and the participation of those in it must be rated by the rest of the community as being at a particular place in the social scale.

Although our democratic heritage makes us disapprove, our class order helps control a number of important functions. It unequally divides the highly and lowly valued things of our society among the several classes according to their rank. Our marriage rules conform to the rules of class, for the majority of marriages are between people of the same class. No class system, however, is so rigid that it completely prohibits marriages above and below one's own class. Furthermore, an open class system such as ours permits a person during his lifetime to move up or down from the level into which he was born. Vertical social mobility for individuals or families is characteristic of all class systems. The principal forms of mobility in this country are through the use of money, education, occupation, talent, skill, philanthropy, sex, and marriage. Although economic mobility is still important, it seems likely now that more people move to higher positions by education than by any other route. We have indicated before this that the mere possession of money is insufficient for gaining and keeping a higher social position. This is equally true of all other forms of mobility. In every case there must be social acceptance.

Class varies from community to community. The new city is less likely than an old one to have a well-organized class order; this is also true for cities whose growth has been rapid as compared with those which have not been disturbed by huge increases in population from other regions or countries or by the rapid displacement of old industries by new ones. The mill town's status hierarchy is more likely to follow the occupational hierarchy of the mill than the levels of evaluated participation found in market towns or those with diversified industries. Suburbs of large metropolises tend to respond to selective factors which reduce the number of classes to one or a very few. They do not represent or express all the cultural factors which make up the social pattern of an ordinary city.

Yet systematic studies from coast to coast, in cities large and small and of many economic types, indicate that, despite the variations and diversity, class levels do exist and that they conform to a particular pattern of organization.

HOW CLASS OPERATES IN OUR DAILY LIVES

Because social class permeates all parts of our existence, it is impossible to do more than indicate how it enters consciously or unconsciously into the success and failure of business, professional, and other occupations or to show how knowledge of its effects is necessary for increasing the predictive qualities of much of the research done by psychologists and social scientists. Class is vitally significant in marriage and training children as well as in most social activities of a community. Status plays a decisive role in the formation of personality at the various stages of development, for if young people are to learn to live adaptively as mature people in our society they must be trained by the informal controls of our society to fit into their places.

Education is now competing with economic mobility as the principal route to success. Today fewer men rise from the bottom to the top places in industry and business than did a generation ago. More and more, the sons of executives are replacing their fathers in such positions, leaving fewer positions into which the sons of those farther down can climb from the ranks. Captains of industry educate their sons to take their places or to occupy similar places in other industries. Also, more and more top jobs in industry are being filled by men coming from the technical and engineering schools or from the universities. The route up for them is no longer through a hierarchy of increasing skill to management and ownership as it was two generations ago. The prudent mobile man today must prepare himself by education if he wishes to fill an important job and provide his family with the money and prestige necessary to get "the better things of life."

Social-class research demonstrates that our educational system performs the dual task of aiding social mobility and, at the same time, working effectively to hinder it. This ceases to be a paradox when all the facts are examined. In the lower grades, our public schools are filled by children from all walks of life. Since education is free in the public schools, since everyone has a right to it and our laws try to keep children in school, and since it is common knowledge that "if you want to get ahead you must get an education," it would be assumed that children at, and below, the Common Man level would stay in school and equip themselves for mobility. Such is not the case. The social and educational systems work to eliminate the majority of them and permit only a few to get through. It has been estimated that, whereas 80 per cent of the upper- and upper-middle-class children actually go to college, only 20 per cent of the lower-middle and five per cent of the lower-class children get there. The evidence indicates that most, if not all, of the children of the top classes complete their preparation and go on to college, whereas those from the lower classes start dropping out in the grade schools and continue to do so in increasing numbers in high school. Only a very few of them go on to college. The educational conveyor belt drops lower-class children at the beginning and bottom of the educational route and carries those from the higher classes a longer distance, nearly all the upper-class children going to the end of the line.

If the teachers and school administrators in grade and high schools know the class positions of the children who enter their schools they can predict who will and who will not get to college. Furthermore, with such knowledge the educator can act to change a negative prediction to a positive one for the bright, ambitious lower- and lower-middle-class children, whose chances for higher education are now very slight.

The reason for the high mortality rate among the lower-class children becomes apparent when one examines the relation of the teachers and the other children to them. We now know that the intelligence of lower-class children is not responsible for their failures in school for often their I. Q.'s are equal to those of children higher up. Although inferior intelligence has been the most frequent and plausible explanation, I.Q. tests equated to social class demonstrate that differential intelligence is not the answer.

Teachers, it must be said, although one of the most democratically minded groups in America, tend to favor the children of the classes above the Common Man and to show less interest in those below that level. Studies in the Deep South, New England, and the Middle West indicate that they rate the school work of children from the higher classes in accordance with their family's social position and conversely give low ratings to the work of the lower-class children.

· · · · · ·

The democratically minded educator asks how this can be. The answer is that most of it is done through ignorance of social class and how it operates in our lives. To be more specific, part of the general answer lies within the teacher as a product of our class system. The teacher conscientiously applies his own best values to his rating of the child. The middle-class teacher, and over three-fourths of teachers are middle-class, applies middle-class values. For him, upper- and upper-middle-class children possess traits that rank high and are positive; lower-class children have characteristics that are negative and are ranked low.

Perhaps the most powerful influence of social class on the educational careers of our children, and certainly one of the most decisive and crucial situations in settling the ultimate class position of children from the Common Man and lower-class levels, is the influence of other children on the child's desire to stay in school. If the world of the child is pleasant, rewarding, and increases his self-esteem, he is likely to want to stay and do well. If it is punishing and decreases his self-respect, he is likely to do poorly and want to quit.

In a study of children's ratings of other children in a middle western community, Neugarten found that the children of the upper and upper-middle classes were rated high by all other children for such traits as good looks, liking for school, leadership, friendship, and many other favorable personal traits; lower-class children were ranked low or, more often than not, were given a negative rating and were said to be bad looking, dirty, and "people you would not want for friends." When it is remembered that these children were only in the fifth and sixth grades and that each child in these grades was supposedly rated by all other children with no reference to status, we can see how quickly class values influence behavior and have their decisive effect in molding the personalities and influencing the life careers of Americans from their earliest years. School for the children of the populous lower classes is not the satisfactory place it is for the middle and upper classes. Given children of equal intellect, ability, and interest, it can be predicted by the use of class analysis that a large percentage of those from the lower classes will be out of school before the sophomore year in high school and that none of the upper-class children, except those physically or mentally handicapped, will quit school.

If our society is to use more effectively the brains and native talent of this great army of young people, it must learn how to train them. To do this, it must keep them in school long enough to equip them with the skills and disciplines necessary for them to function satisfactorily in our economic and social world. Children, as well as teachers and school administrators, must have a conscious and explicit understanding of social class and a simple and easy way to use such knowledge in solving problems. Personality and I.Q. tests are important instruments to guide the teacher, but unless they are supplemented with instruments to measure and count the effects of social class they are insufficient. . . .

Studies of the relations of workers and managers in business and industry demonstrate how class continues to operate selectively when the young people leave school. Management is bringing college-trained men into the lower ranks of supervisors and promoting fewer from the ranks because it finds that the workers, while good men technically, do not have the necessary knowledge about handling men and relating themselves effectively to the higher reaches of management. Their education is often insufficient to make them good prospects for continuing advancement. The hiring of formally educated men effectively puts a ceiling over the legitimate aspirations of workers expecting to rise in the ranks. The blocking of the worker's mobility and the encouragement of college-trained men is the ultimate payoff of what began in the grade schools. Mobility for workers is becoming more difficult; this means for the United States generally that the American Dream is becoming less real.

Studies of the personalities of workers and managers now being made demonstrate that the effects of social-class and mobility drives are clearly discernible and demonstrably a part of the personality of individuals.

In another area, studies of magazine subscriptions show that the class factor is of real importance in the selection of magazines. Readers from different class levels prefer various magazines on the basis of the different symbolic appeal of the stories and pictures. The Yankee City research showed that class entered not only into the purchase of magazines but into newspaper reading. Later research indicates it has a decided effect on radio listening.

A casual examination of the advertising displayed in various magazines demonstrates that advertising agencies and their clients often waste their money because they are ignorant of the operation of class values in their business. This is not surprising since so many status factors have to be considered. The class distribution of readers of the periodicals published in America varies enormously. The readers of certain magazines are confined to the narrow limits of the classes above the Common Man, others to the lower classes, still others to the Common Man level, but there are some who are not confined to any one segment, being well distributed throughout all class levels. The editors of the magazines last designated, intuitively, by trial and error, or some better means, have chosen reading matter which appeals to all levels. The others, not knowing how to extend their readership or appealing deliberately to a narrow range, have a status-limited range of readers.

The readers to whom the advertiser is appealing may or may not be the potential purchasers of his product. The product may be of such a nature that it appeals to only a narrow segment of the total society; to advertise in those media which have readers largely from other strata or to pay for advertising in journals which appeal to every level is a waste of money.

Although advertising agencies often spend their money foolishly when judged by class criteria, the fault is not always theirs, for frequently the manufacturer or retailer does not know how his product appeals to the different classes. Sometimes the product will appeal to but one level, but often a product might appeal to, and be used by, all class levels, were the producer aware of how his product is valued at different social levels. It is certain that the use and meaning of most objects sold on the American market shift from class to class.

The soap opera is a product of contemporary radio. The average upper-middle-class radio listener has little interest in soap operas; in fact, most of this group are actively hostile to these curious little dramas that fill the daytime air waves. Yet, millions and millions of American women listen daily to their favorite soap operas, and advertisers of certain commodities have found them invaluable in selling their products.

Research has shown that the soap opera appeals particularly to the level of the Common Man. The problems raised in these folk dramas, their characters, plot, and values have a strong positive appeal to women of this class level, whereas they have little appeal to women above the Common Man level.

Other researches demonstrate that furniture, including drapes, floor coverings, chairs and other seating facilities, is class-typed.

Another phenomenon of class, social mobility, is enormously important in the daily lives of Americans and, to a very great degree, determines how they will act on the job or at home. Recent studies of executives in large business enterprises clearly demonstrate that the success or failure of all of them is partly determined by the presence or absence of a "mobility drive." Our research shows that when a family loses its desire to achieve and advance itself, this very often is reflected in the executive's "slowing down" or being unwilling to make the effort necessary for success as a manager. On the other hand, some men are too aggressively mobile and stir up trouble by their overly ambitious desires and their ruthless competition.

Tests combining knowledge of social class and personality demonstrate the necessity of knowing not only what the man's status level is, what it has been, and what he wants it to be, but how the class values and beliefs of his early training have become integral parts of his personality, and ever-present guides for what he thinks, what he feels, and how he acts. Those concerned with selecting executives need a personality inventory and a man's I.Q. to predict how a man will function in a given job; but they also need to find out what his experiences in our status order have done to his individuality and character structure.

Every aspect of American thought and action is powerfully influenced by social class; to think realistically and act effectively, we must know and understand our status system.

◆◆◆◆◆

42. The Conception of the Middle Class *

IN THIS SELECTION G. D. H. Cole, in contrast to Warner and his associates in the preceding article (41), focuses his primary attention not upon all the social classes but upon the "middle classes" of Western society. By defining more clearly the upper class, and carefully distinguishing the bourgeoisie of early capitalist society from our present middle classes, he lays the groundwork for a better understanding of a problem that at present is primarily one of definition. He also considers at some length the relevance of the Marxian doctrine to the present and future situation of the middle classes.

THE VERY TERM "middle classes" implies the notion of a society divided into classes, and at least suggests a main division into three—upper, middle, and lower. How far does such a division into three main classes correspond to reality either in the present-day societies of Western Europe or America, or in these societies at the successive stages of their development? How far does it correspond to reality in other societies, either of the present or of the past? For any society, at any time, the fit is evidently loose; but it is also evidently very much better for some societies at certain stages of their development than for others or for the same societies at other stages. It fits best, on the whole, either a free City at the height of medieval development, or a highly industrialized country at a middle stage of capitalist development, such as Great Britain had reached during the second half of the nineteenth century, or, in a quite different way, a rural structure based on a mingling of landlordism with large- and small-scale farming. It fits much less well either most forms of relatively primitive society, or the types of society in which feudalism and industrial capitalism are intricately

---

* G. D. H. Cole, British Journal of Sociology, I, No. 4 (December 1950), 275-290. London: Routledge & Kegan Paul Ltd. Reprinted by permission of the publisher and the author.

The author (b. 1899) is a British economist, writer, sociologist. Reader in Economics, Oxford University and Fellow, University College, 1925-44, and Honorable Fellow since 1945; Fellow, Nuffield College; Fellow, All Souls College; member Fabian Society. Associated with extensive research projects in economic and social problems for Amalgamated Society of Engineers, trade unions, British Labour Party. Since 1912, connected with Workers Educational Association. Author, Europe, Russia, and the Future; The Meaning of Marxism; World in Transition (U.S.A. only); The Common People, 1746-1946 (with Raymond Postgate); Socialist Economics; Essays in Social Theory.

intermingled, or, I should say, the highly diversified social structures which have been characteristic of West European and American societies in their most recent phases of change.

It seems most convenient to begin by considering, not what is to be called "middle class," but the part of society that is regarded as meriting to be called "upper class." Where there exists a recognized aristocracy, labelled by its possession of land or of mercantile wealth and of privileges attached to such possession, by way either of titles or of offices or of status in gild or municipal bodies, the main body of the upper class can be easily identified, though there may be much dispute about its exact limits. In the familiar case of aristocracies based on landed property, there are usually a small number of great families, extending outwards through the households of younger sons and the marriages of daughters outside the inner circle, so that the feeling of kinship to the great extends far beyond the reality of greatness. Side by side with these great houses are the families of lesser landowners—Anglice, squires; and these in turn throw off shoots of aristocratic sentiment, and sometimes intermarry with the less eligible members of the great families. There may be considerable rivalries and wide differences of culture between the members of these landholding classes; but, whenever they are faced with the rise of claims to social status and privilege resting not on land but on commercial or industrial wealth they tend to be thrown together on the basis of a common claim to be regarded as "gentlefolk," and to develop a common standard of manners and, up to a point, education, in the hope of marking themselves off from their plebeian rivals. Where, mainly for money's sake, they intermarry with the new rich, they feel a sense of degradation which can be removed only by the assimilation of the new recruits to the family to its standards and outlook on life. Of course, some aristocracies are much more closed than others—some, in theory at any rate, altogether closed. Where access is more open. we have the familiar spectacle of the upstart merchant buying land, setting up as a country gentleman, and perhaps in due course preparing the way for the family to achieve ennoblement.

Merchant aristocracies, which are a product of great trading centres, are usually much less closed than aristocracies based on land. They can, indeed, especially in City-States, close their ranks to a considerable extent and establish great hereditary merchant dynasties almost as exclusive as the landed nobility can achieve. This possibility, however, is greatly restricted by the development of national, as against town or city, economies; for even though the United States has its Morgans, Rockefellers and Vanderbilts, and France its deux cent familles, neither of these can properly be described as constituting an "upper class" to the exclusion of everyone else. They are groups, rather than classes— at most, sub-sections of a wider top layer of society.

In unified national societies, a merchant aristocracy cannot constitute a closed order. It has, indeed, on the national plane, to do battle with the strongly entrenched landed aristocracy in order to establish its claim to rank at all, as a group, with the upper class. It infiltrates into this class by individual promotion, and does not, save under very exceptional conditions, join it as a group. Up to what we call the "Industrial Revolution," the numbers of capitalists knocking at the doors of aristocracy were always manageably small: the rise of industrial capitalism based on coal and steam with the accompanying techniques of large-scale production created for the first time a large body of wealthy men, with gradation upon gradation of lesser riches below them, who could vie in pride of possession with the landed and merchant classes, and indeed outvie all but the greatest of the older aristocracy, but were neither assimilable in manners to the existing upper class nor desirous of joining it. These new men emerged distinctively as a middle class, conscious of their difference both from the gentry and from the main mass of the people below their economic level. Whereas the existing aristocracy depended for its upper-classness only in part on wealth or economic position, and quite largely on heredity and family connections, the rising class of industrialists was differentiated at the outset almost exclusively by its economic position as the driving and directing force in the new forms of business enterprise. Individuals here and there might set out to climb out of this class into the aristocracy; but in the main the new men wished, not to become aristocrats, but to achieve political as well as economic influence for their own collective values. They fought against aristocratic privilege, as well as against claims from the mass of the people which seemed to threaten the processes of wealth-accumulation by which they had risen to economic authority. The industrial capitalists thus came to form, on a national scale, a conscious middle class, or at any rate the economic nucleus of such a class. Some of them wished to overthrow the classes above them, and to take their place. Most, at the stage I am here describing, wished only to be assured that the State would order society in conformity with their interests, and were too occupied with their own affairs to wish to take the exercise of political authority directly into their own hands. They were content for the aristocrats who sided with them to do most of the governing and to continue to regard themselves as the upper class, provided that the government did not govern too much, and protected their property against levellers from below as well as against extortions in the interest of the old aristocratic class.

This advancing middle-class group speedily produced its effects on other parts of the social structure. With its expanding consuming power and rising standards of living it transformed the market for consumers' goods and services. It needed many more superior shopkeepers and master craftsmen to minister to its needs, and brought into being a host of shops which set out to do a predominantly middle-class trade. At the same time, it required more attorneys and solicitors, more medical men a cut above the ordinary country surgeon or apothecary, more ministers of religion, especially in Great Britain of nonconformist persuasions, and presently more schoolmasters and schoolmistresses capable of giving its children a sound, middle-class education. The professions and the superior tradesmen, hitherto mainly dependent on upper-class custom, came to provide more and more for middle-class needs, and became therewith themselves more and more "middle-class." The professional elements in the population became a much larger fraction of the whole, and at the same time much more mixed in social origin and outlook. Apothecaries, attorneys, and the top layers of the teaching profession turned into a sort of middle-class gentlemen, and came much nearer in social status to barristers, clergymen, and army officers—the old trilogy of gentlemanly professions. But the new professions—civil engineers, railway technicians, and dissenting ministers—remained much less gentlemanly in social estimation, and much more akin to the various grades of essentially middle-class industrial employers.

Then two further things happened. In England, at any rate, the public schools, greatly increased in numbers, brought about a steadily increasing assimilation of outlook and manners between the children of the lesser members of the older aristocracy and those of a large section of the new middle class; and over the same period the spread of the joint stock system, which greatly fostered large-scale enterprise, brought into existence a new large class of salaried managers and administrators, not only in mining and manufacture, but also in banking, insurance and commerce. The educational process speedily made it impossible to tell at sight or by speech who was a "gentleman" according to the traditional aristocratic reckoning, and who was not. The rise of the salaried element in business, partly replacing small independent master-craftsmen and employers but mainly an additional growth, reinforced the larger capitalists with a considerable group whose prospects, equally with their own, were bound up with the success and expansion of large-scale industrial enterprise. Moreover, the joint stock system immensely multiplied the number of small investors who, playing no active part in the businesses to which their money was made over, lived partly on earnings and partly on the income from their invested savings. Almost the entire professional class became an investing class as well, and thus acquired a stake especially in the larger-scale forms of capitalist enterprise.

These later developments were still at an early stage when Marx formulated, in the 1840s, his theory of the historical evolution of the class-struggle. In *The Communist Manifesto*, as well as elsewhere, Marx insisted that, whereas class-struggles had existed in all historical ages, the essential characteristic of capitalism was to reduce to two only the classes between which the struggle for power would be finally fought out, with the propertyless proletariat, or working class, as the destined victor. At a time when, in the more advanced countries, the middle elements in society were in fact increasing more than ever before in both numbers and influence, Marx represented these elements as in process of being relentlessly crushed out by the advance of capitalism, which on the one hand flung more and more of the master-craftsmen and small employers down into the proletariat and on the other "concentrated" capital into fewer and fewer hands with the rise of great combines, and subordinated to itself what was left of the old aristocratic classes, whose hordes of feudal retainers it transformed into a new host of obedient business subordinates, factory slaves, and obsequious ministers to its material and spiritual wants. Marx, thinking despite his labours among British blue-books largely in German terms whenever his mind turned to the main body of the middle classes, regarded the *petite bourgeoisie* as a class in process of extinction because he thought of it as dependent on obsolescent techniques of small-scale production. As for the rapidly growing new groups of managers, supervisors, technicians, and professional workers, far from regarding these as a new and important factor in the class-struggle, he dismissed them as mere servants of the *grande bourgeoisie*, who could play no independent role in social evolution but could only serve as the commissioned and non-commissioned officers of the army of large-scale capitalism, and could be relied on not to mutiny because it was to their own, as well as to their masters', interest to hold the proletariat—which Marx envisaged as the great majority of the people—firmly at bay.

In Marx's view, then, there were, from the standpoint of the future, only two historically significant classes—capitalists, or *bourgeoisie*, and proletariat. The leading section of the *bourgeoisie*, originally the leaders of the middle classes against the aristocracy, had developed in the advanced capitalist countries into the true upper class, absorbing into itself such elements of the old upper classes as it did not push arrogantly aside, and flinging down into the proletariat its erstwhile allies—the *petite bourgeoisie*—who had failed to make themselves masters of the higher capitalistic techniques. Of course, Marx did not say that this process was anywhere complete: he announced it only as an historical tendency of economic development. He did, however, think that what was left of the "middle classes"—middle, that is, between the higher *bourgeoisie* and the working class—was made up of heterogeneous elements incapable of following an independent policy. Some of them he regarded as standing for obsolete methods: others as mere camp-followers of the advancing capitalist class. He took no account of the effect of the joint stock system in diffusing throughout the middle groups a share in the ownership, as distinct from the control, of large-scale industry; and, far from giving any countenance to technocratic notions or to the allied notion of the so-called "managerial revolution," he stressed the increasing dominance of financial over industrial capitalism, and anticipated a growing concentration of capitalist power in the hands of a small class of financial manipulators concerned with the processes of production only as means to money-making on the grand scale.

This Marxian theory in effect involved a splitting of the middle class, at the point of its decisive victory over the old upper class, into contending factions representing the one a progressive and the other a reactionary relation to the powers of production. But the progressiveness of the *grande bourgeoisie* was, in Marx's view, confined within the limits consistent with the continued capitalist exploitation of the rest of the people, and was destined to turn into reaction when its imperative need for continued expansion came up against the obstacle of the limited consuming power which it allowed to its victims. This was to be the "final contradiction of capitalism," which would lead to its overthrow by the revolutionary proletariat, condemned to "increasing misery" in the midst of potential plenty. Firm in his conviction that political power could only reflect and not generate economic power, Marx had no idea that popular education and the extension of the franchise could lead, without social revolution, in the direction of positive reforms that would so far limit capitalist exploitation as to bring about a significant re-distribution of income between rich and poor, and to compel all parties aiming at political authority by constitutional means to bid one against another by offering instalments of welfare and gradually transforming the "police State" with which he was familiar into the "welfare State" which is to-day at various stages of development not only in Western Europe and the British Dominions, but also in the intensely capitalistic United States. Nor did he anticipate that this growth of political democracy could both prevent the development of a revolutionary will among the general mass of the proletariat and establish that partial alliance between the manual workers and the lower-middle class elements attached to large-scale capitalism which has been a marked feature of the evolution of Social Democracy.

It is, of course, possible to argue that Marx, whatever his errors and over-simplifications of secondary issues, was nevertheless fundamentally right in his verdict concerning the importance of the middle classes as a creative social force, when once the grande bourgeoisie had ceased to be their ally and had become itself the leading element in the upper class. That is a matter which falls outside the scope of this paper to discuss. I am here concerned with Marxism solely from the standpoint of its influence on the conception of the "middle class." Wherever Marxism won acceptance, the middle class ceased to be looked upon as a coherent or creative social group, and came to be thought of as merely a nuisance getting in the way of the real historic conflict between the developed grande bourgeoisie and the proletariat— a decaying class to liquidate which, or any of its elements, was simply doing the work of history.

This notion of the middle classes seemed, in Great Britain, to be confirmed by the eclipse of the once great Liberal Party. If the signs were much less clear in France and Germany, the differences were usually put down to the less advanced stage reached by French capitalism and to the continued power in Germany of the old, feudal aristocratic classes, which still largely dominated the State. Before President Roosevelt's New Deal, the social situation in the United States appeared to lend itself fairly well to interpretation, of which the superficiality was not easily to be seen, in terms of a developing conflict between big business and the Trade Unions, with the rest of the people as little more than spectators. To-day, however, these readings of current history look much less plausible than they did before 1939, or even before 1945. In Western Europe, except in Great Britain and Scandinavia, the conflict between Communism and Social Democracy, by splitting the working class, has handed political power back to predominantly middle-class groups whose antagonism to Socialism ranges them with the grande bourgeoisie, but does not make them by any means entirely its servants. It may be said that this régime could not have been established, and could not survive, but for the powerful support given to it by the United States. That is probably true; but it does not alter the fact that, whatever the reasons, middle-class influence has been waxing and not waning in Western Europe, and has certainly not been extinguished in the United States, despite the very advanced stage of American capitalist development.

No doubt, the Marxian picture can be so re-drawn as to show us the world of to-day as dominated by two great powers, standing respectively for proletarian revolution and for imperialist capitalism, with all other countries in process of being reduced rapidly to the status of helpless satellites of the one or the other. That is how Communists do regard the world, looking upon the "capitalist democracies" of the West as essentially "middle-class" countries in process of being ground to powder between the two great contestants for world power. They may be right or wrong about this: I am not attempting to judge. If, however, it is the fate of Western Europe to be thus counted out as a force in history, this will not be because the internal evolution of the Western democracies has followed the Marxist pattern, but because they are too weak to stand up to external forces which have developed in different ways. Nor am I at all prepared to accept that interpretation of current history which treats the Soviet Union as the unquestionable exemplar of the workers' emancipation or the United States as the no less unquestionable embodiment of capitalist imperialism on the point of falling finally a victim to the "contradictions of capitalism." I cannot see either of them as the fulfilment of Marx's prophecies, according to which Russia was quite the wrong country to be the pioneer of Socialist revolution, and America the very country in which the middle classes ought by now to have been thoroughly snuffed out.

But, observe, Marx spoke usually not of the "middle classes," but of the bourgeoisie, great or small. And this difference of terminology has an important bearing on the entire question which this paper sets out to discuss.

The phrase "middle class" is often used as if it were simply the equivalent of the French bourgeois or of the German and other equivalents of that essentially urban designation. But in truth "middle class" and bourgeois are not only different words, but stand for essentially different ideas. Bourgeois, to any historically-minded person, calls up at once the image of a body of citizens asserting their collective, as well as their individual, independence of a social system dominated by feudal power based on landholding and on the services attached to it; whereas the words "middle class" call up the quite different image of a body of persons who are placed between two other bodies—or perhaps more than two—in some sort of stratified social order. The bourgeois is by his very name a claimant, not for himself alone but for a group with which he identifies his claim, to social power and recognition. He is one who claims, in common with the rest of his group, to be allowed to manage his affairs as suits best the way of life for which his group stands, instead of being subjected to a rule laid down for him by superiors whose values and needs differ fundamentally from those of which he has become conscious as a city-dweller, engaged in the traffic of trade and craftsmanship and seeking ever larger opportunities for the development of the mercantile and mechanic arts.

The "middle class" conception is quite different from this. The *bourgeois*, as such, is not in the middle of anything—at any rate not consciously so. Looking back, we may be able to picture him, if we choose, as standing somehow between an aristocracy based on land and privilege and an unprivileged mass which included the great majority of the people. But this is not, historically, a legitimate way of looking at the *bourgeois* as he emerges into the light of the medieval record. It is altogether wrong either to lump together the main body of the urban workers and the peasants in the countryside as an unprivileged "lower class" or to count the whole body of urban craftsmen as belonging to the *bourgeoisie* equally with the upper strata of gild masters and merchants, and as constituting, with these elements, a coherent "middle class." It is illegitimate to do either of these things because the very term "middle class" implies being in the middle of some unitary structure that can be at least loosely defined. But the *bourgeoisie*, in its earlier phases of development, was not in the middle of anything that can be defined as a unitary structure. It came to be in the middle only later on, when, largely as the outcome of similar struggles in which it had played an ever-increasing part, cities ceased to be mainly enclaves in predominantly rural societies dominated by feudal institutions and came instead to be the predominant elements in societies in which industry, commerce, and the use of money and credit had become the main formative influences. Then, indeed, especially in capital cities and great centres of long-distance trade and exchange, the *bourgeoisie* came to be a middle class standing between the governing class—the aristocracy—on the one hand and the main body of citizens on the other; but this middle status still related mainly to their position in the towns. A revolution in the land system, bringing with it new forms of capitalist agriculture, was needed to create even a partly analogous situation in the rural areas, and to bring into existence a class of capitalist farmers who shared in some degree (though by no means completely) the culture and outlook of the urban *bourgeoisie*. But even where this rural revolution occurred, it did not necessarily carry with it an assimilation of urban and rural workers into a composite "lower class." Such assimilation occurred to the greatest extent only where what is called the "domestic system" spread industrial production widely over the countryside, creating a large body of non-urban industrial workers actually or virtually in the employment of capitalist merchant-entrepreneurs. The more such a situation came about, the more the social differences between city and country became blurred, and whole areas came to be integrated into unitary economic and political systems. This, however, occurred only in exceptional cases, and never completely. Over a large part of Europe, though there was developed an urban *bourgeoisie*, there never did come into existence anything that can properly be called a "middle class," at any rate not on a scale great enough to set its mark on the general course of social and political development. Where the *bourgeoisie* did not spread into the countryside, but remained as an urban *enclave* in a feudal society either developing towards a peasant economy or still dominated by great landed estates worked with serf, or quasi-serf, labour, there was no room for the evolution of a "middle class" on a national scale, and none accordingly for the permeation of the whole society by the characteristically "liberal" values which are associated chiefly with *bourgeois* development. This was the more so because in such societies the professional and intellectual classes developed largely as servants of the State, and thus became bureaucrats rather than "liberals."

This, of course, did not prevent individual members of the *bourgeoisie* in countries in which the town-dwellers remained essentially isolated from the countryside from regarding themselves as members of a "middle class." But, where they did so, they were still the victims of their isolation. They could not, like the *bourgeois* of the advancing capitalist countries, establish a pattern of life and then proceed to impress it upon the entire societies in which they lived: they could for the most part only copy the patterns and values that were being established by their compeers in the more capitalistic countries and pride themselves, on the strength of this, on being the pioneers of civilization *in partibus infidelium*; and the more they copied, and took pride in copying, the greater their isolation became. That is why "liberalism" could never strike real roots over a large part of Europe: that is why there are no foundations to-day over a large part of Europe for political or economic systems which comply with the requirements of "democracy," as democracy is understood in the Western countries that have experienced capitalistic unification. That, in effect, is why there is an "iron curtain" in Europe, and why "democracy" means so different things to Stalin and to Attlee or Churchill or Truman—for, however widely these three may differ in the meanings they attach to the word, they agree in meaning by it something that neither Stalin nor Tito can possibly either mean or even understand.

I think I have said enough in this paper to show that the concept of the middle class is exceedingly elusive, by whatever route one approaches it. Clearly, membership of the middle class, or classes, is not simply a matter of income, either absolutely or of relative income within a particular social structure. Nor is it exclusively a matter of the nature and source of the income received, or of profession or calling. Nor again is it exclusively a matter of education, or of manners; for no definition based on these will avail to mark off one part of the middle classes from the upper class or another from the working class. Nor will it serve to treat the family as a unit; for it is nowadays very common for one child from a working-class household to enter a profession, while another becomes a manual worker, and yet another marries a local shopkeeper, after a spell of either factory or clerical employment. In modern fluid societies, the family ceases in more and more instances to be a unit assignable to a single class. This, of course, is not new, for priesthoods have usually been recruited from a wide variety of social groups; but it is commoner now than ever before, except in pioneering societies such as the United States and the British Dominions, not only for the family to be made up of varying class elements, but also for individuals to shift from class to class on their way through life. This does not mean that classes lose reality; but it does mean that their boundaries become more and more difficult to draw.

•   •   •   •   •   •

What future lies before this ill-defined, heterogeneous "middle class" that can be labelled as a class only because the groups that make it up can be identified neither with the aristocracy and grande bourgeoisie nor with the wage-earners?   Certainly, except in the countries which have passed under Communist domination, it shows no sign of disappearing. It is not, as Marx prophesied, being driven down into the proletariat by the development of capitalism: on the contrary, advancing capitalism has shown itself exceedingly favourable to its multiplication, and declining capitalism, where we have examples of it, seems to drive the middle groups towards Fascism rather than towards an acceptance of the status of proletarians. The evidence for this may be discounted on the ground that it is drawn from countries in which there had been no real decline of capitalism but only an undermining of the middle classes by war and inflation, and that Fascism is to be regarded as a product of these forces rather than of any internal evolution of capitalism itself. The Communist will answer that war and inflation are themselves portents of capitalist contradictions, and that wars have merely hastened and accentuated the tendencies inherent in the capitalist system.   The fact remains that neither in Great Britain nor in the United States has anything that can properly be called Fascism as yet assumed dangerous proportions, or the position of the middle classes been fundamentally undermined.

There is, no doubt, an important difference in this respect between Great Britain and the United States, in that capitalism itself has been seriously challenged in the one country, but not in the other. In America, capitalism, though it has been forced to make substantial concessions to the claims of Labour and to the "Welfare State," is still an advancing system, carrying along with it a prosperous middle income group into which more and more of the superior wage-earners have been able to climb. In Great Britain, on the other hand, capitalism, under pressure from the poorer sections of the population, has been forced to give ground by submitting to levels of taxation that have considerably reduced inequalities of spendable income, though not of capital ownership. But, as against this narrowing of the gulf between the extremes, the process of increasing the size of the middle groups has gone on uninterrupted, and the salary differentials characteristic of big business have been carried over into the administrative structure of the newly nationalised industries. Certainly the development of the Welfare State in Great Britain has not, in raising the living standards of the worst-off, thrown down the professional and managerial groups into the ranks of the proletariat or ground down shopkeepers and farmers into the mass of the unprivileged. On the contrary, it has made large concessions to the claims of doctors, shopkeepers, farmers and small business men, giving them both bigger incomes and greater security than they have ever before enjoyed. It is true that some groups usually ranked as "middle-class" have fared relatively ill—for example, Civil Servants, teachers, and local government officers, as well as small rentiers dependent on fixed money incomes. But there has been no sign of an impending écrasement of the middle class as a whole: rather, a growth of some of its groups compensating for a decline of others, and resulting in a change in its composition and social stratification.

Nor has the supersession of capitalism by proletarian revolution crushed out the middle groups, even in the Soviet Union. One is not allowed to speak of "classes" as existing, save as survivals, in Communist-dominated society; but no one denies the persistence of large differences of income and social prestige, or the existence of a marked tendency towards increasing differentiation, in the Stalinist epoch of Soviet development.

Some writers have gone so far as to claim that these tendencies are signs of the inevitable advent of what James Burnham has dubbed a "managerial revolution" and proclaimed as a necessary product of the evolution of the "powers of production," irrespective of differences of political regime. For my part, I find such notions confusing and grossly over-simplified. If all that is meant is that the development of modern techniques of mass-production and large-scale administration necessarily requires the existence of a large body of highly trained scientists, tech-nicians, administrators and managers, who are bound to claim, for a long time to come, superior rewards and a superior status in society by virtue of their natural or acquired qualities of usefulness, there is nothing to argue about; for no one in his senses is likely to dispute the fact. If, however, it is argued that these occupants of superior positions are bound to become the real masters of society, however it may be nominally governed in its political affairs, I not merely dissent, but see no basis for the contention that does not rest on a sheer confusion of terms. James Burnham, in his much publicised book, *The Managerial Revolution*, supported his argument by shifting at caprice from one definition of his terms to another, treating as "the managers" now the great capitalist entrepreneurs and now the large body of technicians and managerial employees, just as happened to suit his case. Moreover, he resorted to a facile identification of this ill-defined "class" in capitalist countries with the privileged "managers" under the Soviet system, though such evidence as there is goes to show rather separateness than unity between the privileged income groups in the Soviet economic system and the governing party *élite*.

Indeed, I can come no nearer to a conclusion about the future of the "middle classes" than to say that a study of the recent evolution in both capitalist and Soviet countries goes to show, mainly, two things—first, that the road to economic equality, even if open, is much longer and more difficult than many Socialists used to suppose, and that the mere supersession of capitalism by a sort of Socialism by no means wipes out differences of income or of social status, though it does, as Marx long ago said it would, largely substitute income differences based on personal service and capacity for differences based on ownership of property or of inherited economic claims. Secondly, that, as economic differences come to be more closely related to personal capacities and educational advantages, and as education and training come to be more and more state-provided services open to wider sections of the population, social and economic superiority come, in capitalist as well as in socialist countries, to be more individual, and much less family, matters and thus lose a substantial part of their old, undemocratic character. For, after all, the conception of class is, historically, related very intimately to that of family status, not only for landed aristocracies but also for the social groups which base their claims on commerce or industry, or on monopoly, or near-monopoly, of the "gentlemanly" professions. Where the family loses its class character under the influence either of abundant economic opportunity or of an open educational system resting on public provision at the higher as well as at the lower levels, "middle class" tends to become a merely descriptive adjective, designating those in the middle, rather than a term defining a distinctive section of the population. A "middle class" may still be held to exist under such conditions —that is really a matter of words—but a *bourgeoisie*, in the sense historically attaching to the term, cannot.

⋆⋆⋆⋆⋆

43. Portrait of a Striver *

HERE in the colorful prose of J. P. Marquand, one of America's most skilled present-day fiction writers, is a picture of an upward striving young man. The interpersonal relations and the private feelings of an upwardly mobile middle-class man are sharply portrayed—the tensions, the insecurities, the need for watching every step, and the satisfactions. Vividly illustrated is the importance, if one is to achieve social-financial success in this type of setting, of skills in many areas other than that of accurate and rapid performance on one's assigned work.

SHORTLY BEFORE THE OUTBREAK of the European war, Charles had begun taking the eight-thirty. This was a privilege that had raised him above the ruck of younger men and of shopworn older ones who had to take the eight-two. It indicated to everyone that his business life had finally permitted him a certain margin of leisure. It meant that he was no longer one of the salaried class who had to be at his desk at nine.

The eight-thirty train was designed for the executive aristocracy, and once Mr. Guthrie Mayhew, not one of the Mayhews who lived on South Street, not George Mayhew, but Guthrie Mayhew, who was president of the Hawthorn Hill Club and also president of Mayhew Brothers at 86 Broadway, had even spoken of getting an eight-thirty

* John P. Marquand. From *Point of No Return*, by permission of Little, Brown & Company. Copyright 1947, 1948, 1949, by John P. Marquand.

The author (b. 1893) is an American novelist, author of detective fiction, short-story writer. Served as Special Consultant to U.S. Secretary of War, 1944-45. His books include *Thank You, Mr. Moto*; *The Late George Apley* (awarded Pulitzer Prize, 1938); *So Little Time*; *Melville Goodwin, USA*. Member, editorial board, Book-of-the-Month Club, Inc.

crowd together who would agree to occupy one of those club cars with wicker chairs and card tables and a porter, to be attached to the eight-thirty in the morning and again to the five-thirty in the afternoon.

．　　．　　．　　．　　．　　．

Charles remembered Mr. Mayhew's idea vividly, if only because it had come up at the same time that Mr. Burton had suggested that Charles call him Tony.

Charles could still recall the glow he had felt on this occasion and the sudden moment of elation. Mr. Burton had been shy about it in a very nice way, as an older man is sometimes shy. Charles remembered that Mr. Burton had fidgeted with his onyx pen stand and that first Mr. Burton had called him "feller." It had all happened one evening when they had stayed late talking over the Catlin estate, which was one of the largest accounts in the trust department.

．　　．　　．　　．　　．　　．

"Now you may remember," Mr. Burton had said, "that Mrs. Burton and I took a little trip in 1933. You hadn't been with us long then, but I don't believe that you or anyone else will forget how tense things were in 1933, and now and then I found I was getting a little taut, so when things eased up I decided to go away somewhere to get a sense of perspective. That was when Mrs. Burton and I went to Bagdad. You ought to go there sometime."

．　　．　　．　　．　　．　　．

The first morning he and Mrs. Burton had gone to the museum to see the treasure from Ur, parts of which looked like something in a case at Cartier's. You got a lot out of travel if you kept your eyes open. There had been a man in the museum, a queer sort of British archaeologist, who showed him some mud bricks that were actually parts of an account book. When you got used to them, you could see how they balanced their figures; and on one brick, believe it or not, there was even an error in addition, preserved there through the centuries. This had meant a great deal to Mr. Burton.

That clerical error in mud had given him an idea for one of the best speeches he had ever written, his speech before the American Bankers' Association in 1936 at the Waldorf-Astoria. Mr. Burton had opened a drawer and had pulled out a deckle-edged pamphlet.

"Take it home and read it if you have the time," he said, "I dashed it off rather hurriedly but it has a few ideas. It starts with that mistake in addition."

The pamphlet was entitled *The Ancient Art of Banking, by Anthony Burton, President, the Stuyvesant Bank, Delivered before the American Bankers' Association, May 1936.*

"Why, thanks very much, sir," Charles had said, "I certainly will read it." It was not the time to say that he had read the speech already or that for years he had made a point of reading all Mr. Burton's speeches.

"Look here, feller," Mr. Burton said, and he had blushed when he said "feller," "why not cut out this sir business? Why not just call me Tony?"

That was in 1941 but Charles still remembered his great joy and relief, with the relief uppermost, and that he could hardly wait to hear what Nancy would say.

"You know, Charles," Mr. Burton had continued, "Guthrie Mayhew and I have quite an idea. We're going to get hold of Tommy Mapes on the New Haven and see if he can't get us a special car on the eight-thirty. How about getting aboard? My idea is to call it the Cracker-barrel."

"Why, thanks," Charles had said. "I'd like to very much, Tony."

He had worked late that night and he could not remember what train he had taken home, but Nancy had been asleep when he got there.

"Nance," he said, "wake up. I've got something to tell you. Burton's asked me to call him Tony." And Nancy had sat bolt upright in her twin bed.

"Start at the beginning," Nancy had said. "Exactly how did it happen, and don't leave out anything."

They must have talked for a long while, there in the middle of the night. Nancy had known what it meant because she had worked downtown herself.

"Now wait," she had said. "Let's not get too excited. Who else calls him Tony?"

"I don't think anyone else does," Charles had told her, "except the officers, and old Jake when he speaks of him."

"Who's old Jake?" Nancy asked.

It surprised him that Nancy did not know, for she usually kept everything straight, but when he told her that old Jake was a day watchman in the vault who had been there when Mr. Burton had first started at the bank, Nancy had remembered.

"Darling, we ought to have a drink of something, shouldn't we?" she said, but it was pretty late for a drink. "Darling, I knew it would happen sometime. I'm pretty proud of you, Charley."

It was only a week later that they found out that Mr. Burton had also asked Roger Blakesley to call him Tony and they never could find out whom Mr. Burton had asked first.

•   •   •   •   •   •

Though you seldom talked of salaries at the Stuyvesant, your social status was obvious from the position of your desk. Charles occupied one of the two flat mahogany desks that stood in a sort of no man's land between the roll-top desks of the officers and the smaller flat-tops of lesser executives and secretaries crowding the floor of the bank outside the cages. A green rug extended from the officers' desks, forming a neat and restricted zone that just included Charles's desk and the one beside it which was occupied by Roger Blakesley. Charles could see both their names, Mr. Blakesley and Mr. Gray, in silver letters, and he was pleased to see that he had got there first from the eight-thirty, a minute or two ahead of Roger and Mr. Burton and ahead of everyone else near the windows.

Mr. Burton's desk, which had the best light, was opened already and so was that of Mr. Stephen Merry, the oldest vice-president, and so were all the others except one. This was the desk of Arthur Slade, the youngest vice-president of the Stuyvesant, who had died in a plane accident when returning from the West Coast six months before. The closed desk still gave Charles a curious feeling of incompleteness and a mixed sense of personal gain and loss because he had been more friendly with Arthur Slade than with anyone else in the Stuyvesant—but then you had to die sometime. Once Arthur Slade had sat at Charles's own place but that was before Mr. Walter Harry, who had been president when Charles had first come to the bank, had died of an embolism and everyone had moved like players on bases—Burton to Harry, Merry to Burton, Slade to the vacant roll-top—and so on down to Charles himself. The Stuyvesant was decorously accustomed to accident and death and now it was moving time again and it was so plain where one of two persons might be moving next that it was embarrassing. Any observing depositor and certainly everyone employed in the bank, right up to the third floor, must have known that either Mr. Blakesley or Mr. Gray would move to Arthur Slade's desk by the window. Undoubtedly they were making side bets out in back as Charles used to himself when he had first come there from Boston. Undoubtedly the clerks and the secretaries and the watchmen had started some sort of pool.

•   •   •   •   •   •

Tony Burton looked very fit, in spite of his white hair and his roll-top desk which both conspired to place him in another generation. For years Charles had accepted him as a model willingly, even though he realized that everyone else above a certain salary rating also used Tony Burton as a perfect sartorial example, and he was pretty sure that Tony himself was conscious of it. Charles never rebelled against this convention because Tony had everything one should expect to find in a president of a first-rate bank. It was amusing but not ridiculous to observe that all the minor executives in the Stuyvesant, as well as the more ambitious clerks, wore conservative double-breasted suits like Tony Burton's at the same time allowing undue rigidity to break out into pin stripes and herringbones, just like Tony Burton's. They all visited the barber once a week. They all had taken up golf, whether they liked it or not, and most of them wore the same square type of wrist watch and the same stainless steel strap. They had adopted Tony Burton's posture and his brisk, quick step and even the gently vibrant inflection of his voice. In fact once at one of those annual dinners for officers and junior executives when everyone said a few words and got off a few local jokes about the bank, Charles had brought the matter up when he had been called upon to speak. Speaking was always an unpleasant ordeal with which he had finally learned to cope successfully largely from imitating Tony. He remembered standing up and waiting for silence, just as Tony waited, with the same faint smile and the same deliberate gaze.

"I should like to drink a toast," he had said, "not to our president but to everyone who tries to look like him. When I walk, I always walk like Tony, because Tony knows just how to walk; and when I talk, I always talk like Tony, because Tony knows just how to talk; and when I dress, I always dress like Tony, in a double-breasted suit. But no matter how I try, I cannot be like Tony. I can never make myself sufficiently astute."

It was the one time in the year, at that annual dinner, when you could let yourself go, within certain limits, and Tony Burton had loved it. He had stood up and waited for the laughter to die down and then he had spoken easily, with just the right pause and cadence. He had said that there were always little surprises at these dinners. He had never realized, for instance, that there could be a poet in the trust department, but poetry had its place. Poetry could teach lessons that transcended pedestrian prose.

"And I'm not too old to learn," Tony Burton had said, "and I'm humbly glad to learn. Sometimes on a starlit night I've wondered what my function was in the Stuyvesant. I'm very glad to know it is that of a clothing dummy. It's a patriotic duty. It's what they want us to be, in Washington."

That was back in 1941, but Tony Burton still had the same spring to his step, the same unlined, almost youthful face, and the same florid complexion; and he had the same three pictures on his desk, the first of Mrs. Burton in their garden, the second of their three girls standing in profile, like a flight of stairs, and the third of his sixty-foot schooner, the Wanderlust (the boat you were invited on once every summer), with Tony Burton in his yachting cap standing at the wheel. Time had marched on. All of the girls had come out and all were married, and the Wanderlust had been returned by the navy in deplorable condition, but Tony Burton had no superficial scars.

No matter how well Charles might know him, in that half-intimate, half-formal business relationship, he still had a slight feeling of diffidence and constraint. It was the same feeling that one had toward generals in wartime or perhaps toward anyone with power over one. There was always a vestige of a subservient desire to please and to be careful. You had to know how far to go, how long to laugh, and how to measure every speech.

·　·　·　·　·　·

Sycamore Park had been developed in 1938 on the forty-acre grounds of an old estate and the subdivision had been excellently managed by the local real estate firm of Merton and Pease. As Mr. Merton had said, it was a natural, and he had never understood why someone had not dreamed it up long ago—not too far from the shopping center and the trains, and yet in the neighborhood of other larger places. Every place had its own acre, and no house was to be constructed for a cost of less than thirty thousand dollars. It would have been wiser, perhaps, never to have gone there but to have bought a smaller place.

It would have been wiser, easier, and much safer. He had not at that time been moved up in the trust department and in 1939 all he had was twenty thousand dollars in savings, part of which was in paid-up life insurance. He could never analyze all the urges that made him lay everything on the line in order to live on a scale he could not immediately afford, discounting the possibilities of illness or accident and relying on possibilities of promotion. He only remembered having had an irrational idea that time was of the essence, that he would always stay on a certain business level if he did not take some sort of action, and Nancy too, had shared that feeling.

·　·　·　·　·　·

Not since he had left Clyde had Charles ever felt as identified with any community as he had since he had been asked to join the Oak Knoll Country Club. They were in a brave new world involving all sorts of things, of which he had scarcely dreamed after they had moved to Sycamore Park. This cleavage between past and present, Charles realized, was a part of a chain reaction that started, of course, with one of those shake-ups in the bank. Charles had known that he had been doing well. He had known for a year or so, from the way Mr. Merry and Mr. Burton and particularly Mr. Slade had been giving him little jobs to do, that something was moving him out of the crowd of nonentities around him. He was aware also that Walter Gibbs in the trust department was growing restless. There had been a premonition of impending change, just like the present tension. One day Walter Gibbs had asked him out to lunch and had told him, confidentially, that he was going to move to the Bankers' Trust and that he was recommending Charles for his place. Charles was not surprised, because he had been a good assistant to Walter Gibbs, and he was glad to remember that he had been loyal to his chief, ever since the old days in the statistical department.

"Charley," Walter Gibbs had said, "a lot of people around here have been out to knife me. You could have and you never did, and I appreciate it, Charley."

He had known, of course, for some time that Walter Gibbs was not infallible, that he was fumbling more and more over his decisions and depending more and more on Charles's support, but Walter had taught him a lot.

"Slade keeps butting in," Walter had said, and then he went on to tell the old story which Charles had often heard of conflicting personalities and suspicions. Walter had felt that frankly he was more eligible for a vice-presidency than Slade, and the truth was he had never been the same after Arthur Slade had been selected. "If they don't like you enough to move you up," Walter had said, "it's time to get out, Charley."

God only knew where Walter Gibbs was now. He was gone like others with whom you worked closely once and from whom you were separated. Walter Gibbs was gone with his little jokes and his bifocal glasses and the stooping shoulders that had given him a deceptively sloppy appearance. He was gone with his personality that would never have permitted him to be a vice-president of anything.

Charles was ready, not surprised, when Tony Burton, though of course he did not call him Tony then, had called him downstairs and had asked him if he knew what was coming, that he had been with them for quite a while and that they had all had an eye on him ever since he had done that analysis on chain stores. Even if you were prepared for such a change there was still an unforgettable afterglow, and an illuminating sense of unrealized potentiality. It was a time to be more careful than ever, to measure the new balance of power, and not to antagonize the crowd that you were leaving. One day, it seemed to Charles, though of course it was not one day, he was living in a two-family house in Larchmont that smelled of cauliflower in the evenings, stumbling over the children's roller-skates and tricycles, taking the eight-three in the morning, keeping the budget on a salary of six thousand a year. Then in a day, though of course it was not a day, they were building at Sycamore Park. The children were going to the Country Day School. They were seeing their old friends, but not so often. Instead they were spending Sundays with Arthur Slade. There was a maid to do the work. He was earning eleven thousand instead of six, and he was an executive with a future. New people were coming to call; all sorts of men he had hardly known were calling him Charley. It was a great crowd in Sycamore Park and he was asked to join the Oak Knoll Country Club. They were a great crowd in Sycamore Park.

It would have made quite a story—if it could have been written down —how all those families had come to Sycamore Park. They had all risen from a ferment of unidentifiable individuals whom you might see in any office. They had all once been clerks or salesmen or assistants, digits of what was known as the white-collar class. They had come from different parts of the country and yet they all had the same intellectual reactions because they had all been through much the same sorts of adventures on their way to Sycamore Park. They all bore the same calluses from the competitive struggle, and it was still too early for most of them to look back on that struggle with complacency. They were all in the position of being insecurely poised in Sycamore Park—high enough above the average to have gained the envy of those below them, and yet not high enough so that those above them might not easily push them down. It was still necessary to balance and sometimes even to push a little in Sycamore Park, and there was always the possibility that something might go wrong—for example, in the recession that everyone was saying was due to crop up in the next six or eight months. It was consoling to think that they were no longer in the group that would catch it first, or they would not have been at Sycamore Park—but then they were not so far above it. They were not quite indispensable. Their own turn might come if the recession were too deep. Then no more Sycamore Park, and no more dreams of leaving it for something bigger—only memories of having been there once. It was something to think about as you went over your checkbook on clear, cold winter nights, but it was nothing ever to discuss. It was never wise or lucky to envisage failure. It was better to turn on the phonograph—and someday you would get one that would change the records automatically. It was better to get out the ice cubes and have some friends in and to talk broad-mindedly about the misfortunes of others. It was better to go to the club on Tuesday evenings and to talk about something else—and that was where Charles Gray was going.

❧❦❧❦❧

44. India's Submerged Majority: The Unknown Villagers *

THIS DESCRIPTION OF LIFE in the Indian village of Fatepur well illustrates a true caste system, with its extreme social stratification, and the power of ancient folkways, mores, and tradition in a static society. The life of these people, isolated from contacts with the outside world by poverty, ignorance, and suspicion, though carried on less than a mile from the city of Lucknow, is difficult for an American to understand. Because the chief fears, like the wants of all persons, are culturally patterned, those things that these villagers dread are particularly significant. How will the Indian government break through these trepidations, this ignorance and suspicion, to bring a fuller life to its millions?

THE FIRST FEW VILLAGES in India I ever saw close up looked to me like excavated ruins. They were small agglomerations of uneven and crumbling mud walls. There was no living creature anywhere in sight, and no spot of any color but the dun of north India's soil.

Most Indian government workers and foreign missionaries who have tried to work in or even enter Indian villages on a friendly basis have the same story to tell: During the first day or week, or perhaps even the first year, they meet few villagers. If they do meet them, the villagers behave

---

* Jean Lyon, *The Reporter*, 4, No. 5 (March 6, 1951), 21-24. Reprinted by permission of the publisher and the author.
   The author (b. 1902) is an American newspaper woman. Born in China, she came to the United States in 1908, and was educated at Wellesley. Has had varied career as a feature writer, cartoonist, columnist, editor, correspondent, and is at present living in India. Author, *Manners of the Moment*. Frequent contributor to such periodicals as *The Nation, The Reporter, United Nations World*.

as though the intruder were an invisible man. They seem neither to see nor hear him. If he is an official whose questions the villagers must answer, they delight in confusing and misleading him.

The village of Fatepur, less than a mile outside the city of Lucknow in northeast India, seemed no exception to a young college-trained Indian social worker employed by Indian Village Services, a Presbyterian-sponsored organization, when she walked into it eight months ago. Eventually one villager offered her a drink of water and said: "Good morning." Now everyone in the village calls her Bahanji, which means "sister," and she is welcomed in every home from that of the highest-caste Brahman to that of the lowest untouchable. Her friends, no matter who they are, are accepted along with her. That is how I finally was able to enter a village, and to learn at first hand that people live, marry, bear children, and die there.

I was escorted to Fatepur by one of Bahanji's villagers. First we walked down a main road, then along a railroad track, then along a bullock-cart road through a mango grove, and finally on a footpath atop a narrow mudbank that marked the division between guava orchards. An old man, wrapped from head to foot in dusty white cotton, who sat under a pipal tree between the guava groves, did not even glance at us as we stepped around him. He was watching for marauding monkeys, which can't be killed because they are sacred, but which must still be kept from eating the guava crop.

As we rounded the corner of the windowless mud walls of what I later discovered was the untouchables' quarter on the rim of the village, we came to an open space in the center of which was a well. Several men were sitting on their haunches on the flat brick top of the well. Bahanji was standing nearby waiting for us. The men seemed to be carrying on a desultory conversation with her.

"They are talking about the weather," she said. "The clouds look as though we are going to have the first rain of the winter season today. That will be good for their potato crop."

Moving away from the group of men, we walked up a narrow lane between the houses. The lane was muddy, for it was both a path and a village sewer, and we had to pick our way. We came soon to a knot of women squatting on the hard-packed mud floor of a porch, at one end of which was a small clay cookstove. This was a combination kitchen and living room. It had no furniture. The women squatted to cook, to gossip, and to feed their babies.

"Bahanji!" they called. "What do you think the village council will do about Lakshmi?"

Lakshmi, I learned, was a fifteen-year-old girl of the Lodh caste.

Somewhere in the fields, or when she was helping to chase off the monkeys and the sacred bulls from the guava grove, Lakshmi had met a boy from a neighboring village, who was of the Pasi caste. Now Lakshmi wanted to marry the Pasi boy, which was a serious breach of caste laws. The Pasis, like the Lodhs, I was told, were farmers. But the Lodhs were a much higher caste. The Pasis weren't exactly untouchable, but they were very close to it. Not even Bahanji could tell me why. It was one of the many facts that I learned to accept without question, for that was the way the people in Fatepur accepted them.

This was the most urgent matter before the village council, or panchayat (which means "council of five"), and the men had said that the panchayat would surely have a meeting that night if it didn't rain. The women said that of course the panchayat would rule that Lakshmi could not marry the Pasi, but would agree to find her a suitable husband. It would be something of a task, for delegates would have to take time from their fields to visit other villages to find out about the eligible boys. No Fatepur girl ever married within her own village.

Furthermore, said a woman who was feeding her baby under her sari, the panchayat would have to work fast, for Lakshmi was getting old. The woman herself had been married when she was six, and brought to Fatepur to her husband's home when she was eleven. Most girls should be married by the time they were thirteen or fourteen anyhow, she said. Otherwise they would get out of hand.

Another thing the women wanted to discuss with Bahanji was the disappearance of Bahla's wife. It had happened three weeks before, but it was still news in Fatepur. She had gone off one day, while Bahla was in his potato field, and had taken all the family jewelry and money with her. Of course no one knew how much that was. She had never worn as many silver arm and ankle bracelets and toe rings as some of the women did, but that didn't mean that she hadn't had them buried under the mud floor of the house somewhere. And though Bahla's walls had not been washed with cow-dung paint for some time and were beginning to crumble, that indicated nothing about his savings. A wise man didn't advertise what he had. Bahla had simply said that his wife had taken everything.

She was a hard-working woman, they said, always feeding the cattle or working in the fields. She always obeyed her husband and bowed her head submissively when she did his bidding. That was as it should be. But Bahla was hot-tempered. He had beaten her. After their only two children had died last year, when the smallpox took eighty-two of the children in Fatepur's 167 households, he had beaten her more than usual.

No one questioned where she had gone. Where else could a woman go but to her own village, to her parents' house? They only hoped the parents would let her stay until Bahla promised to reform.

These were the subjects the women talked about as we squatted on our heels, brushing off the swarms of flies that settled on us like locusts on a grainfield. In courtyard after courtyard, the women worked as we talked. Some chopped up dried chili peppers. Some swept their porches and courtyards with long bundles of sticks tied together. Some polished to a high sheen the brass plates and bowls from which their families ate, using as a cleanser dry dirt they scraped up with their hands from the courtyard.

There was sickness to talk about, too. Children lay apathetic and wasted, letting the flies settle on their eyelids and lips and noses without even a whimper, and no one knew what to do about them except to propitiate the gods. Bahanji's notes to the clinic in Lucknow might or might not be heeded.

Then there was the woman who had died from the cobra bite. That was a strange thing. It had been a religious festival day, and the members of the dead woman's family had been worshiping a cobra that had been living in their house. After the prayers, the woman had gone into the dark room where the cobra was, to pick up a basket of dry sticks she had left in there, and had touched the cobra instead. But she wouldn't tell anyone what had happened for fear she would anger the god and his wrath would strike her husband and children. Four hours later she had died. The others all knew it had been the snake. But they admired her loyalty, even though they might have applied a home-made remedy for snake bite if she had told them.

As we went into one home after another, Bahanji was able to build up for me something of a picture of the organization of the community.

At the edge of the village were the houses of its one washerman, its one midwife, several cobblers and tanners, and a number of masons (of the cobbler caste) who worked as day laborers on the roads and in the nearby city. These were the untouchables—twenty households of them. For generations their families had been washermen, cobblers, midwives. But even though they were all untouchables, cobblers' daughters married only the sons of cobblers in other villages—never those of washermen. It had always been this way. It was still this way.

These twenty families had their own well. If they drew water from another well in the village, they polluted it for the caste Hindus. Yet one of them washed the clothes for villagers of the higher castes, one of them made their shoes, and one of them delivered their children.

Bahanji tried to explain to me about the midwife. Childbirth is considered a very unclean process, she said. The mother is put as far away as possible from the others in her family, on rags and torn quilts that can be thrown away afterward. Often she is not even warm enough. For the first six days after the baby is born, mother and child must lie in the old rags, with meager food and little attention.

"But don't women who have been through this themselves sometimes protest—or at least slip some comforts to the mother secretly?" I asked.

"Not usually," said Bahanji. "Usually they say, 'I lived through it, and so did my child. You will live through it too.'"

"And if one or the other or both don't live through it?"

"It is fate."

The five Brahman families live on the highest knoll in the village. They are the village's aristocracy. When we visited one family the father was sitting cross-legged on his front porch chopping up fodder for the cattle. He wore a pair of spectacles on his nose—the first spectacles I had seen in Fatepur.

He could read, Bahanji told me, and was the only man in the village who subscribed to a newspaper. Every Brahman father passed the Brahman legacy of literacy on to his sons, and very often to his daughters as well, for theirs was the family that performed the village's religious ceremonies, read to the villagers from the Vedic scriptures, acted as the village priests, and were the village sages. If villagers wanted to know something of what was happening in the outside world, what the new government in New Delhi might be doing for them, or what the landlord-abolition bill meant, they could ask the Brahman families and get some sort of an answer.

A large number of village children had gathered at our heels, and each wanted to guide us to his own house. As we were leaving the Brahman knoll a Brahman woman shouted angrily after us from her doorway. A child near me stopped as though she were in a nightmare and couldn't move. She began to tremble. Bahanji calmed her.

"This is the cobbler's child," she explained to me. "The Brahman lady is very angry because the cobbler's child has polluted her house."

These were the highest and the lowest. Between them were all the other families in Fatepur—in some six or seven caste layers, each with stringent social rules, each with inherited economic tasks, an inherited reward.

Only three things in Fatepur seemed to have changed since India became independent.

One was the way the untouchables were paid. These twenty families were the first to think of an independent India as having anything to do with them. "That," said Bahanji, "was because Gandhi and the Congress Party talked so much about the rights of the untouchables."

Fatepur's twenty untouchable families held a meeting shortly after the new government was formed in New Delhi. They decided that they would no longer work, as they traditionally had, at everyone's beck and call with payment coming only twice a year at harvest time, and then in amounts that were proportionate only to their low status in the village and not to the amount of work they did. They would from now on demand payment in cash or in grain for each job. The washerman would be paid per wash, the cobbler for each pair of sandals he made, the midwife for every baby she delivered. To enforce their decision they would all stick together, and any one of them who broke the common rule would be ostracized.

They also decided one other thing. They would no longer bury the village's dead cattle.

Since not a single household in the village had the equipment for washing its own clothes, and since none knew how to make shoes and none could or would contaminate himself to the extent of delivering babies, the rest of the villagers had to accept the untouchables' decision. Moreover, each farmer started burying his own dead cattle.

But the untouchables have gone on living in the same quarters, doing the same "unclean" work, using their own separate well (they are lucky in Fatepur to have a well and not to have to beg for their water each day of their lives), and their children are less welcome around a Brahman home than termites.

A second thing that happened was that the village's three landlords either sold their lands to those villagers with enough money to buy or turned them over to the government. This happened sooner in Fatepur than in most places, because one landlord was a Moslem and went to Pakistan, and the others were in financial difficulties. But in other places something of this sort is due to happen by law eventually—if the various provincial governments can ever get their laws formulated.

Some of the younger villagers think this is a good thing. The landlord, they say, used to order them to work for him without pay, though he punished them with fines if they refused. He often collected several times over, and he always charged each farmer five rupees (about one American dollar) per acre each harvest for the use of the community well for irrigation.

But some of the older villagers are not so sure that the end of the old landlords means the end of their troubles. As yet, they say, they've seen no government official or tax collector who is any different from the landlords' men. In fact he is usually the very same person, with the very same remarks to make and the very same threats. Furthermore, this new government has thought of some new ways to get money from the villagers. For example, there was the man who collected money for a co-operative seed store but couldn't tell them where the seed store was to be or when it was to be built. "I only know that I'm supposed to collect," he had said.

"There are always hawks hovering over us," the older villagers say.

The third change is in the village council, or panchayat. It used to be made up of the five most respected elders of the village. It was never recognized as official under the British, but in Fatepur it held court on family squabbles, marriage questions, and property disputes. What it decided was the law the villagers obeyed. Now the panchayat has become official, its decisions legal; it is supposed to have on it one untouchable, and it is elected by all the men and women in the village.

At least that is what some officials of the new government who visited Fatepur told the villagers, and so they dutifully elected a new panchayat. The elders refused to run on any such new-fangled ticket, and younger men were elected.

But it all works out without any trouble, the thirty-one-year-old who is the new panchayat's youngest member explained. On most important decisions, the new panchayat calls in the five old men who served the village before. When they have made the decision, the new panchayat announces it to the villagers, saying, "This is what the elders have decided."

"That is the best way," the young man said, "because the elders have always decided for us."

Is Fatepur typical of the seven hundred thousand villages that contain eighty-five per cent of India's people?

Who knows? A few persistent souls like Bahanji, and some of the idealists among the government workers, have broken through the walls of suspicion and isolation behind which the villager has hidden for centuries, like a field mouse frightened of all the animals about him including the other field mice. A few facts about India's villages have been gathered. A few services have been offered both by representatives of the government and of humanitarian agencies.

But the villager still hides. The founders of the India Village Services, Dr. and Mrs. William Wiser, have translated the villagers' feelings this way in a book called Behind Mud Walls:

Our forefathers hid themselves from a covetous world behind mud walls. We do the same. . . . We do not trust the outside world and we are suspicious of each other. Our lives are oppressed by many fears. We fear the rent collector, we fear the police watchman, we fear everyone who looks as though he might claim some authority over us, we fear our creditors, we fear our patrons, we fear too much rain, we fear locusts, we fear thieves, we fear the evil spirits which threaten our children and our animals, and we fear the strength of our neighbors. . . . You and others have told us that with newer methods, we would be spared much labour. Perhaps, but we do not fear work. . . . These new ideas of more results from less labour are untried, and confusing. And how do we know but what they will leave some of us without employment? . . . There is no one outside of our own group whom we dare trust. Everyone who comes to us or to whom we go, thinks of what he can get from us. . . . We have learned bitter lessons, we and our fathers. . . . We feel safe behind the barriers of our mud walls.

᳍ᩁᩁᩁᩁᩁ

45. The White Man's Theory of Color Caste and Rank Order of Discriminations *

AMERICANS tend to pride themselves on those institutions of American culture that permit social and economic "climbing" by able and energetic persons. Taken all together, such institutions are known as an "open-class" system: one in which persons may move freely up, or down, within the socio-economic hierarchy. At the other extreme is a "closed-class," or "caste," system. The essence of the caste system is that a person's status is completely determined by biological inheritance, and that he is prevented from crossing caste lines through marriage. Myrdal, in his famous recent study of the Negro in America, clearly shows that caste is, despite popular belief to the contrary, characteristic of our culture. In this excerpt from his scholarly work Myrdal places the basic caste principle of antiamalgamation first in his "rank order of discriminations" by white people against Negroes in our culture. He also points out that the Negro, while recognizing similar degrees in severity of race discrimination, actually places intermarriage last in his rank order of the things he desires in Negro-white relations. The discrepancy, says Myrdal, between the Negro's actual lower-caste status and his

* Gunnar Myrdal, An American Dilemma (New York: Harper & Brothers, 1944), pp. 57-67. Copyright 1944 by Harper & Brothers. Reprinted by permission of the publisher and the author.
   The author (b. 1898) is a Swedish social economist; government adviser on social, financial, economic questions; industrial and business analyst; authority on United States Negroes; Sweden's most informed man on American affairs; population expert; economic planner for the United Nations. Writes books on monetary and economic

theoretic status, as an equal (defined in terms of traditional American democratic ideals) is what makes up "an American dilemma."

THE WHITE MAN'S THEORY OF THE COLOR CASTE

EVERY WIDENING of the writer's experience of white Americans has only driven home to him more strongly that the opinion that the Negro is unassimilable, or, rather, that his amalgamation into the American nation is undesirable, is held more commonly, absolutely, and intensely than would be assumed from a general knowledge of American thoughtways. Except for a handful of rational intellectual liberals—who also, in many cases, add to their acceptance in principle of amalgamation an admission that they personally feel an irrational emotional inhibition against it—it is a rare case to meet a white American who will confess that, if it were not for public opinion and social sanctions not removable by private choice, he would have no strong objection to intermarriage.

The intensity of the attitude seems to be markedly stronger in the South than in the North. Its strength seems generally to be inversely related to the economic and social status of the informant and his educational level. It is usually strong even in most of the non-colored minority groups, if they are above the lowest plane of indifference. To the poor and socially insecure, but struggling, white individual, a fixed opinion on this point seems an important matter of prestige and distinction.

But even a liberal-minded Northerner of cosmopolitan culture and with a minimum of conventional blinds will, in nine cases out of ten, express a definite feeling against amalgamation. He will not be willing usually to hinder intermarriage by law. Individual liberty is to him a higher principle and, what is more important, he actually invokes it. But he will regret the exceptional cases that occur. He may sometimes hold a philosophical view that in centuries to come amalgamation is bound to happen and might become the solution. But he will be inclined to look on it as an inevitable deterioration.[1]

---

theory, social reform, housing, public finance. Author, *Monetary Equilibrium*; *Population, A Problem for Democracy*.

[1] The response is likely to be anything but pleasant if one jestingly argues that possibly a small fraction of Negro blood in the American people, if it were blended well with all the other good stuff brought over to the new continent, might create a race of unsurpassed excellence: a people with just a little sunburn without extra trouble and even through the winter; with some curl in the hair without the cost of a permanent wave; with, perhaps, a little more emotional warmth in their souls; and a little more religion, music, laughter, and carefreeness in their lives. Amal-

This attitude of refusing to consider amalgamation—felt and expressed in the entire country—constitutes the center in the complex of attitudes which can be described as the "common denominator" in the problem. It defines the Negro group in contradistinction to all the non-colored minority groups in America and all other lower class groups. The boundary between Negro and white is not simply a class line which can be successfully crossed by education, integration into the national culture, and individual economic advancement. The boundary is fixed. It is not a temporary expediency during an apprenticeship in the national culture. It is a bar erected with the intention of permanency. It is directed against the whole group. Actually, however, "passing" as a white person is possible when a Negro is white enough to conceal his Negro heritage. But the difference between "passing" and ordinary social climbing reveals the distinction between a class line, in the ordinary sense, and a caste line.

This brings us to the point where we shall attempt to sketch, only in an abstract and preliminary form, the social mechanism by which the anti-amalgamation maxim determines race relations. This mechanism is perceived by nearly everybody in America, but most clearly in the South. Almost unanimously white Americans have communicated to the author the following logic of the caste situation which we shall call the "white man's theory of color caste."

(1) The concern for "race purity" is basic in the whole issue; the primary and essential command is to prevent amalgamation; the whites are determined to utilize every means to this end.

(2) Rejection of "social equality" is to be understood as a precaution to hinder miscegenation and particularly intermarriage.

(3) The danger of miscegenation is so tremendous that the segregation and discrimination inherent in the refusal of "social equality" must be extended to nearly all spheres of life. There must be segregation and discrimination in recreation, in religious service, in education, before the law, in politics, in housing, in stores and in breadwinning.

This popular theory of the American caste mechanism is, of course, open to criticism. It can be criticized from a valuational point of view by maintaining that hindering miscegenation is not a worthwhile end,

---

gamation is, to the ordinary American, not a proper subject for jokes at all, unless it can be pulled down to the level of dirty stories, where, however, it enjoys a favored place. Referred to society as a whole and viewed as a principle, the anti-amalgamation maxim is held holy; it is a consecrated taboo. The maxim might, indeed, be a remnant of something really in the "mores." It is kept unproblematic, which is certainly not the case with all the rest of etiquette and segregation and discrimination patterns, for which this quality is sometimes erroneously claimed.

or that as an end it is not sufficiently worthwhile to counterbalance the sufferings inflicted upon the suppressed caste and the general depression of productive efficiency, standards of living and human culture in the American society at large—costs appreciated by all parties concerned. This criticism does not, however, endanger the theory which assumes that white people actually are following another valuation of means and ends and are prepared to pay the costs for attaining the ends.   A second criticism would point out that, assuming the desirability of the end, this end could be reached without the complicated and, in all respects, socially expensive caste apparatus now employed.   This criticism, however adequate though it be on the practical or political plane of discussion, does not disprove that people believe otherwise, and that the popular theory is a true representation of their beliefs and actions.

To undermine the popular theory of the caste mechanism, as based on the anti-amalgamation maxim, it would, of course, be necessary to prove that people really are influenced by other motives than the ones pronounced.   Much material has, as we shall find, been brought together indicating that, among other things, competitive economic interests, which do not figure at all in the popular rationalization referred to, play a decisive role.   The announced concern about racial purity is, when this economic motive is taken into account, no longer awarded the exclusive role as the *basic* cause in the psychology of the race problem.

Though the popular theory of color caste turns out to be a rationalization, this does not destroy it.   For among the forces in the minds of the white people are certainly not only economic interests (if these were the only ones, the popular theory would be utterly demolished), but also sexual urges, inhibitions, and jealousies, and social fears and cravings for prestige and security.   When they come under the scrutiny of scientific research, both the sexual and the social complexes take on unexpected designs.   We shall then also get a clue to understanding the remarkable tendency of this presumably biological doctrine, that it refers only to legal marriage and to relations between Negro men and white women, but not to extra-marital sex relations between white men and Negro women.

However these sexual and social complexes might turn out when analyzed, they will reveal the psychological nature of the anti-amalgamation doctrine and show its "meaning."   They will also explain the compressed emotion attached to the Negro problem.   It is inherent in our type of modern Western civilization that sex and social status are for most individuals the danger points, the directions whence he fears the sinister onslaughts on his personal security.   These two factors are more likely than anything else to push a life problem deep down into the subconscious and load it with emotions. There is some probability that in America both complexes are particularly laden with emotions. The American puritan tradition gives everything connected with sex a higher emotional charge. The roads for social climbing have been kept more open in America than perhaps anywhere else in the world, but in this upward struggle the competition for social status has also become more absorbing. In a manner and to a degree most uncomfortable for the Negro people in America, both the sexual and the social complexes have become related to the Negro problem.

These complexes are most of the time kept concealed. In occasional groups of persons and situations they break into the open. Even when not consciously perceived or expressed, they ordinarily determine interracial behavior on the white side.

THE "RANK ORDER OF DISCRIMINATIONS"

The anti-amalgamation doctrine represents a strategic constellation of forces in race relations. Their charting will allow us a first general overview of the discrimination patterns and will have the advantage that white Americans themselves will recognize their own paths on the map we draw. When white Southerners are asked to rank, in order of importance, various types of discrimination,[2] they consistently present a list in which these types of discrimination are ranked according to the degree of closeness of their relation to the anti-amalgamation doctrine. This rank order—which will be referred to as "*the white man's rank order of discriminations*"—will serve as an organizing principle in this book. It appears, actually, only as an elaboration of the popular theory of color caste sketched above. Like that theory, it is most clearly and distinctly perceived in the South; in the North ideas are more vague but, on the whole, not greatly divergent. Neither the popular theory of caste nor the rank order of discriminations has been noted much in scientific literature on the Negro problem.

The rank order held nearly unanimously is the following:

Rank 1. Highest in this order stands the bar against intermarriage and sexual intercourse involving white women.

Rank 2. Next come the several etiquettes and discriminations, which specifically concern behavior in personal relations. (These are

[2] In this introductory sketch the distinction between "segregation" and "discrimination" is entirely disregarded. This distinction, signified by the popular theory and legal construct "separate but equal," is mainly to be regarded as an equalitarian rationalization on the part of the white Americans, indicating the fundamental conflict of valuations involved in the matter. "Segregation" means only separation and does not, in principle, imply "discrimination." In practice it almost always does.

the barriers against dancing, bathing, eating, drinking together, and social intercourse generally; peculiar rules as to handshaking, hat lifting, use of titles, house entrance to be used, social forms when meeting on streets and in work, and so forth. These patterns are sometimes referred to as the denial of "social equality" in the narrow meaning of the term.)

Rank 3. Thereafter follow the segregation and discriminations in use of public facilities such as schools, churches and means of conveyance.

Rank 4. Next comes political disfranchisement.

Rank 5. Thereafter come discriminations in law courts, by the police, and by other public servants.

Rank 6. Finally come the discriminations in securing land, credit, jobs, or other means of earning a living, and discriminations in public relief and other social welfare activities.

It is unfortunate that this cornerstone in our edifice of basic hypotheses, like many of our other generalizations, has to be constructed upon the author's observations. It is desirable that scientifically controlled, quantitative knowledge be substituted for impressionistic judgments as soon as possible. It should be noted that the rank order is very apparently determined by the factors of sex and social status, so that the closer the association of a type of interracial behavior is to sexual and social intercourse on an equalitarian basis, the higher it ranks among the forbidden things.

Next in importance to the fact of the white man's rank order of discriminations is the fact that *the Negro's own rank order is just about parallel, but inverse, to that of the white man.* The Negro resists least the discrimination on the ranks placed highest in the white man's evaluation and resents most any discrimination on the lowest level. This is in accord with the Negro's immediate interests. Negroes are in desperate need of jobs and bread, even more so than of justice in the courts, and of the vote. These latter needs are, in their turn, more urgent even than better schools and playgrounds, or, rather, they are primary means of reaching equality in the use of community facilities. Such facilities are, in turn, more important than civil courtesies. The marriage matter, finally, is of rather distant and doubtful interest.

Such reflections are obvious; and most Negroes have them in their minds. It is another matter, however, whether the white man is prepared to stick honestly to the rank order which he is so explicit and emphatic in announcing. The question is whether he is really prepared to give the Negro a good job, or even the vote, rather than to allow him entrance to his front door or to ride beside him in the street car.

Upon the assumption that this question is given an affirmative answer, that the white man is actually prepared to carry out in practice the implications of his theories, this inverse relationship between the Negro's and the white man's rank orders becomes of strategical importance in the practical and political sphere of the Negro problem. Although not formulated in this way, such a relationship, or such a minimum moral demand on the ordinary white man, has always been the basis of all attempts to compromise and come to a better understanding between leaders of the two groups. It has been the basis for all interracial policy and also for most of the practical work actually carried out by Negro betterment organizations. Followed to its logical end, it should fundamentally change the race situation in America.

It has thus always been a primary requirement upon every Negro leader—who aspires to get any hearing at all from the white majority group, and who does not want to appear dangerously radical to the Negro group and at the same time hurt the "race pride" it has built up as a defense—that he shall explicitly condone the anti-amalgamation maxim, which is the keystone in the white man's structure of race prejudice, and forbear to express any desire on the part of the Negro people to aspire to intermarriage with the whites. The request for intermarriage is easy for the Negro leader to give up. Intermarriage cannot possibly be a practical object of Negro public policy. Independent of the Negroes' wishes, the opportunity for intermarriage is not favorable as long as the great majority of the white population dislikes the very idea. As a defense reaction a strong attitude against intermarriage has developed in the Negro people itself. And the Negro people have no interest in defending the exploitative illicit relations between white men and Negro women. This race mingling is, on the contrary, commonly felt among Negroes to be disgraceful. And it often arouses the jealousy of Negro men.

The required soothing gesture toward the anti-amalgamation doctrine is, therefore, readily delivered. It is iterated at every convenient opportunity and belongs to the established routine of Negro leadership. For example, Robert R. Moton writes:

As for amalgamation, very few expect it; still fewer want it; no one advocates it; and only a constantly diminishing minority practise it, and that surreptitiously. It is generally accepted on both sides of the colour line that it is best for the two races to remain ethnologically distinct.

There seems thus to be unanimity among Negro leaders on the point deemed crucial by white Americans. If we attend carefully, we shall, however, detect some important differences in formulation. The Negro spokesman will never, to begin with, accept the common white premise of racial inferiority of the Negro stock. To quote Moton again:

. . . even in the matter of the mingling of racial strains, however undesirable it might seem to be from a social point of view, he [the Negro] would never admit that his blood carries any taint of physiological, mental, or spiritual inferiority.

A doctrine of equal natural endowments—a doctrine contrary to the white man's assumption of Negro inferiority, which is at the basis of the anti-amalgamation theory—has been consistently upheld. If a Negro leader publicly even hinted at the possibility of inherent racial inferiority, he would immediately lose his following. The entire Negro press watches the Negro leaders on this point.

Even Booker T. Washington, the supreme diplomat of the Negro people through a generation filled with severe trials, who was able by studied unobtrusiveness to wring so many favors from the white majority, never dared to allude to such a possibility, though he sometimes criticized most severely his own people for lack of thrift, skill, perseverance and general culture.   In fact, there is no reason to think that he did not firmly believe in the fundamental equality of inherent capacities. Privately, local Negro leaders might find it advisable to admit Negro inferiority and, particularly earlier, many individual Negroes might have shared the white man's view.   But it will not be expressed by national leaders and, in fact, never when they are under public scrutiny.   An emphatic assertion of equal endowments is article number one in the growing Negro "race pride."

Another deviation of the Negro faith in the anti-amalgamation doctrine is the stress that they, for natural reasons, lay on condemning exploitative illicit amalgamation.   They turn the tables and accuse white men of debasing Negro womanhood, and the entire white culture for not rising up against this practice as their expressed antagonism against miscegenation should demand.   Here they have a strong point, and they know how to press it.

A third qualification in the Negro's acceptance of the anti-amalgamation doctrine, expressed not only by the more "radical" and outspoken Negro leaders, is the assertion that intermarriage should not be barred by law.   The respect for individual liberty is invoked as an argument. But, in addition, it is pointed out that this barrier, by releasing the white man from the consequences of intimacy with a Negro woman, actually has the effect of inducing such intimacy and thus tends to increase miscegenation.   Moton makes this point:

The Negro woman suffers not only from the handicap of economic and social discriminations imposed upon the race as a whole, but is in addition the victim of unfavourable legislation incorporated in the marriage laws of twenty-nine states, which forbid the intermarriage of black and white. The disadvantage of these statutes lies, not as is generally represented, in the legal obstacle they present to social equality, but rather in the fact that such laws specifically deny to the Negro woman and her offspring that safeguard from abuse and exploitation with which the women of the white race are abundantly surrounded. On the other side, the effect of such legislation leaves the white man, who is so inclined, free of any responsibility attending his amatory excursions across the colour line and leaves the coloured woman without redress for any of the consequences of her defencelessness; whereas white women have every protection, from fine and imprisonment under the law to enforced marriage and lynching outside the law.

But even with all these qualifications, the anti-amalgamation doctrine, the necessity of assenting to which is understood by nearly everybody, obviously encounters some difficulties in the minds of intellectual Negroes. They can hardly be expected to accept it as a just rule of conduct. They tend to accept it merely as a temporary expedient necessitated by human weakness. Kelly Miller thus wrote:

. . . you would hardly expect the Negro, in derogation of his common human qualities, to proclaim that he is so diverse from God's other human creatures as to make the blending of the races contrary to the law of nature. The Negro refuses to become excited or share in your frenzy on this subject. The amalgamation of the races is an ultimate possibility, though not an immediate probability. But what have you and I to do with ultimate questions, anyway?

And a few years later, he said:

It must be taken for granted in the final outcome of things that the colour line will be wholly obliterated. While blood may be thicker than water, it does not possess the spissitude or inherency of everlasting principle. The brotherhood of man is more fundamental than the fellowship of race. A physical and spiritual identity of all peoples occupying common territory is a logical necessity of thought. The clear seeing mind refuses to yield or give its assent to any other ultimate conclusion. This consummation, however, is far too removed from the sphere of present probability to have decisive influence upon practical procedure.

This problem is, of course, tied up with the freedom of the individual. "Theoretically Negroes would all subscribe to the right of freedom of choice in marriage even between the two races," wrote Moton. And Du Bois formulates it in stronger terms:

. . . a woman may say, I do not want to marry this black man, or this red man, or this white man. . . . But the impudent and vicious demand that all colored folk shall write themselves down as brutes by a general assertion of their unfitness to marry other decent folk is a nightmare.

Negroes have always pointed out that the white man must not be very certain of his woman's lack of interest when he rises to such frenzy on behalf of the danger to her and feels compelled to build up such formidable fences to prevent her from marrying a Negro.

With these reservations both Negro leadership and the Negro masses acquiesce in the white anti-amalgamation doctrine. This attitude is noted with satisfaction in the white camp. The writer has observed, however, that the average white man, particularly in the South, does not feel quite convinced of the Negro's acquiescence. In several conversations, the same white person, in the same breath, has assured me, on the one hand, that the Negroes are perfectly satisfied in their position and would not like to be treated as equals, and on the other hand, that the only thing these Negroes long for is to be like white people and to marry their daughters.

Whereas the Negro spokesman finds it possible to assent to the first rank of discrimination, namely, that involving miscegenation, it is more difficult for him to give his approval to the second rank of discrimination, namely, that involving "etiquette" and consisting in the white man's refusal to extend the ordinary courtesies to Negroes in daily life and his expectation of receiving certain symbolic signs of submissiveness from the Negro. The Negro leader could not do so without serious risk of censorship by his own people and rebuke by the Negro press. In all articulate groups of Negroes there is a demand to have white men call them by their titles of Mr., Mrs., and Miss; to have white men take off their hats on entering a Negro's house; to be able to enter a white man's house through the front door rather than the back door, and so on. But on the whole, and in spite of the rule that they stand up for "social equality" in this sense, most Negroes in the South obey the white man's rules.

Booker T. Washington went a long way, it is true, in his Atlanta speech in 1895 where he explained that: "In all things that are purely social we [the two races] can be as separate as the fingers, yet one as the hand in all things essential to mutual progress." He there seemed to condone not only these rules of "etiquette" but also the denial of "social equality" in a broader sense, including some of the further categories in the white man's rank order of discrimination. He himself was always most eager to observe the rules. But Washington was bitterly rebuked for this capitulation, particularly by Negroes in the North. And a long time has passed since then; the whole spirit in the Negro world has changed considerably in three decades.

The modern Negro leader will try to solve this dilemma by iterating that no Negroes want to intrude upon white people's private lives. But this is not what Southern white opinion asks for. It is not satisfied with the natural rules of polite conduct that no individual, of whatever race, shall push his presence on a society where he is not wanted. It asks for a general order according to which *all* Negroes are placed under *all* white people and excluded from not only the white man's society but also from the ordinary symbols of respect. No Negro shall ever aspire to them, and no white shall be allowed to offer them.

Thus, on this second rank of discrimination there is a wide gap between the ideologies of the two groups. As we then continue downward in our rank order and arrive at the ordinary Jim Crow practices, the segregation in schools, the disfranchisement, and the discrimination in employment, we find, on the one hand, that increasingly larger groups of white people are prepared to take a stand against these discriminations. Many a liberal white professor in the South who, for his own welfare, would not dare to entertain a Negro in his home and perhaps not even speak to him in a friendly manner on the street, will be found prepared publicly to condemn disfranchisement, lynching, and the forcing of the Negro out of employment. Also, on the other hand, Negro spokesmen are becoming increasingly firm in their opposition to discrimination on these lower levels. It is principally on these lower levels of the white man's rank order of discrimination that the race struggle goes on. The struggle will widen to embrace all the thousand problems of education, politics, economic standards, and so forth, and the frontier will shift from day to day according to varying events.

Even a superficial view of discrimination in America will reveal to the observer: first, that there are great differences, not only between larger regions, but between neighboring communities; and, second, that even in the same community, changes occur from one time to another. There is also, contrary to the rule that all Negroes are to be treated alike, a certain amount of discretion depending upon the class and social status of the Negro in question. A white person, especially if he has high status in the community, is, furthermore, supposed to be free, within limits, to overstep the rules. The rules are primarily to govern the Negro's behavior.

Some of these differences and changes can be explained. But the need for their interpretation is perhaps less than has sometimes been assumed. The variations in discrimination between local communities or from one time to another are often not of primary consequence. All of these thousand and one precepts, etiquettes, taboos, and disabilities inflicted upon the Negro have a common purpose: to express the subordinate status of the Negro people and the exalted position of the whites. They have their meaning and chief function as symbols. As symbols they are, however, interchangeable to an extent: one can serve in place of another without causing material difference in the essential social relations in the community.

The differences in patterns of discrimination between the larger regions of the country and the temporal changes of patterns within one region, which reveal a definite trend, have, on the contrary, more material import. These differences and changes imply, in fact, a considerable margin of variation within the very notion of American caste, which is not true of all the other minor differences between the changes in localities within a single region—hence the reason for a clear distinction. For exemplification it may suffice here to refer only to the differentials in space. As one moves from the Deep South through the Upper South and the Border states to the North, the manifestations of discrimination decrease in extent and intensity; at the same time the rules become more uncertain and capricious. The "color line" becomes a broad ribbon of arbitrariness. The old New England states stand, on the whole, as the antipode to the Deep South. This generalization requires important qualifications, and the relations are in process of change.

The decreasing discrimination as we go from South to North in the United States is apparently related to a weaker basic prejudice. In the North the Negroes have fair justice and are not disfranchised; they are not Jim-Crowed in public means of conveyance; educational institutions are less segregated. The interesting thing is that the decrease of discrimination does not regularly follow the white man's rank order. Thus intermarriage, placed on the top of the rank order, is legally permitted in all but one of the Northern states east of the Mississippi. The racial etiquette, being the most conspicuous element in the second rank, is, practically speaking, absent from the North. On the other hand, employment discriminations, placed at the bottom of the rank order, at times are equally severe, or more so, in some Northern communities than in the South, even if it is true that Negroes have been able to press themselves into many more new avenues of employment during the last generation in the North than in the South.

There is plenty of discrimination in the North. But it is—or rather its rationalization is—kept hidden. We can, in the North, witness the legislators' obedience to the American Creed when they solemnly pass laws and regulations to condemn and punish such acts of discrimination which, as a matter of routine, are committed daily by the great majority of the white citizens and by the legislators themselves. In the North, as indeed often in the South, public speakers frequently pronounce principles of human and civic equality. We see here revealed in relief the Negro problem as an American Dilemma.

❧❧❧❧❧❧

46. Crossing the Color-Line *

IF THE READER has ever observed the members of a large audience of Negroes, he has doubtless noted the wide range of shades of skin color. Probably he reflected on how this racial blending came about —in spite of the widespread taboo on interracial marriages in our society. If he noted that some of the "Negroes" present were of fairer complexion than many "white" persons, he may also have speculated on what is known as "passing": crossing the color-line. Richard Wright, famous Negro writer, describes the book from which this selection is taken as "this definitive study of Negro urbanization." One phase of urbanization for the Negro is that very special type of social mobility—"passing." Here is a fascinating treatment of "passing" by two Negro social scientists.

A ROSE BY ANY OTHER NAME

"PASSING" IS ONE OF THE MOST PREVALENT PRACTICES that has arisen out of the American pattern of race relations. It grows from the fact that one known drop of "colored" blood is sufficient to make an otherwise completely white person a Negro. As there are thousands of Negroes

* St. Clair Drake and Horace R. Cayton, Black Metropolis (Harcourt, Brace and Company, Inc., 1945), pp. 159-173. Reprinted by permission of the publisher and the senior author.

St. Clair Drake (b. 1911) is Associate Professor of Sociology and Anthropology, Roosevelt College, Chicago. Black Metropolis was selected as race relations book of the year, 1946, Schomburg Collection, N. Y. City Public Library. Received the Anisfeld-Wolf Award in 1945 for its contributions to race relations. Horace R. Cayton (b. 1903) is a writer, lecturer, sociologist. Formerly Director of Chicago's Parkway Community House. Worked as Special Assistant to Secretary of Interior, Washington, D.C., 1934-35. Author, Black Workers and the New Unions (with George S. Mitchell) and We Have Tomorrow.

whom neither colored nor white people can distinguish from full-blooded whites, it is understandable that in the anonymity of the city many Negroes "pass for white" daily, both intentionally and unintentionally. But, should white people become aware of their remote colored ancestors they would, in all probability, treat them as Negroes.[1]

There are few figures on the amount of passing which takes place in the United States. Estimates of the number of people who permanently leave the Negro group and are assimilated into white society each year vary from 25,000 to 300,000. These are only estimates, and no conclusive body of statistical data is or ever could be available, especially on those who pass only temporarily or occasionally. There is not, however, a single Negro family known to the authors that has not been aware of instances, sometimes of scores of instances, in which friends, acquaintances, or relatives have crossed the color-line and become white —"gone over to the other side," as Negroes phrase it.

There are various degrees of passing, accompanied by different degrees of estrangement from the Negro group and emotional identification with the white community. Thousands of Negroes pass unintentionally daily. In a large city such as Midwest Metropolis, light-skinned Negroes who go into restaurants, who seek choice seats at a theater, or who are hired in certain jobs are mistaken for white without their being aware of it. A very light woman recently went to an exclusive photographer to have her picture taken. She returned at a later date with her daughter, who was obviously a Negro. The photographer refused to take the daughter's picture and told the mother that he did not care for colored patronage. Only then did she realize that she had been unconsciously passing for white.

Often, when caught in a situation in which he or she is taken for white, a Negro will carry through the bluff even when challenged, in order to avoid embarrassment. A young lady who did not approve of passing related the following incident:

"Speaking of passing—a strange thing happened to me this summer. When I went down to visit my father in Kentucky, I had to change trains at a station on the other side of the Mason-Dixon line. The porter took my bags and escorted me to the coach. I wasn't paying any attention to him. I just took it for granted that he was taking me to the correct coach. When I stepped into the coach, I immediately knew

---

[1] The authors have interviews which suggest that some white people in the North are willing to overlook a small infusion of Negro blood provided the person who is passing has no social ties with Negroes. Several persons when questioned on this matter said that they knew of white people who were suspected of having Negro blood and that it was a joking matter. In one case everybody, including the suspect, saved face by saying it was perhaps Indian blood.

that he had made a mistake. All of these white people were seated and there I was! I said, 'Listen, porter—'and that's all the further I got. He said, 'That's all right, miss, the conductor will call your stop.' He passed my bags overhead and tipped his hat and walked away. So I sat down and was so ill at ease.

"I noticed several of the white people glancing at me and then after the second look, they looked off. I had had my hair freshly done, and when it is fresh it looks dark brown and wavy, and I did look decent because I was wearing my best. I took a magazine and began reading. After a bit, the conductor came up and after removing his hat and apologetically clearing his throat said, 'I know this is highly irregular, miss, but—uh—pardon me—may I ask you what nationality you are? Uh—are you Jewish?' I could have kissed the conductor for giving me that lead, because as soon as he started talking, I knew what he was going to say. I knew that if I said I was a Negro and tried to explain that I wasn't trying to pass, he wouldn't believe it. Also, to have to go back into the Negro coach with the conductor leading the way would be quite embarrassing to me. The Negroes would think I was trying to pass and got caught. So I decided to play up the situation. 'After all,' I said, 'this is highly ridiculous. Yes, I am a Jewess, and I consider this a grand insult.' I wore my haughtiest expression, and I was scared to death. By this time several of the white people had turned around and were listening to us.

"The conductor flushed and was very much embarrassed. I just know how he must have felt. He apologized again and then walked away. I was scared. I didn't enjoy the ride at all, and but for the company of a little eight-year-old white child, I talked to no one. It was lucky for me that I hadn't told Father I was coming. Suppose he had been at the station to meet me—then I would have been in a mess. I told Daddy about it and he just laughed. He thought it was a joke! And that's why I couldn't be bothered with trying to pass. I'd rather be colored and not be bothered. That's why I hate the South."

As the above incident suggests, passing in the South can often lead to serious trouble—it violates both custom and law. There are numerous stories about the dashing young man who comes to a southern town, cuts quite a figure, perhaps becomes engaged to a socially prominent local girl, and then suddenly and mysteriously disappears, never to be spoken of again. It is discovered by accident in such instances, so the tales go, that the man, though he appeared to be white, had Negro blood. In the North, however, where the population is not so sensitized, and in the crowded and impersonal atmosphere of the big cities, little thought is given to the possibility that someone might be passing, and no punitive action is taken by the society even when a person who is passing is discovered. In Midwest Metropolis, many Negroes pass merely for convenience. A light-complexioned girl remarked to one of the authors, "Whenever I am downtown alone I always go to one of the better restaurants. They think I am white, I guess; I never ask them. I wouldn't think of going with my husband, who is dark, for they might refuse us and we would be humiliated. Of course I never speak about this to him, as he is so sensitive about his color." It is common practice for very light women to patronize white beauty parlors where, according to them, they can get better service cheaper and without waiting. Often, too, a light person will purchase theater tickets for darker persons so that the latter will not be Jim-Crowed with other Negroes in the theater, or refused seats on the main floor.

From the initial state of passing unintentionally or passing for convenience, there often develops, in more adventurous persons, a practice of passing for fun. This behavior, too, can be engaged in without any feeling of guilt or disloyalty to the race; it is looked upon as having fun at the white folks' expense. Couples, and sometimes parties, will go to white cabarets and exclusive dancing places just to see what they are like and to get a thrill. Even in these cases, however, the persons involved are rather careful about relating these escapades to their friends for fear of censure from the darker persons. "I wouldn't tell everyone this, but you get around and would understand," said a light-complexioned girl. "The other night I was out with Harry—you know he can pass for white—and after we had seen a show in the Loop he said, 'Let's go over to the Pump Room.' We did and had a glorious time and it wasn't any more expensive than the Rhumboogie. No, I wasn't in the least nervous. How could they tell we were colored? There were no colored waiters who might have recognized us. After this I am going to places like that any time I am out with him." Light-complexioned people who go out with white persons of the opposite sex frequently prefer to go to white places, for there is less fear of detection on the part of the Negro community, which in the case of a woman is a matter of some concern.

A fourth type of passing arises out of economic necessity or advantage. Negro girls have had difficulty in obtaining employment in white-collar jobs. Positions as stenographers, telephone operators, receptionists, and clerks are usually closed to anyone who is known to be colored. As there are many Negro girls of superior ability and training who wish such jobs, it is not unusual for some of them to pass, if they can, in order to obtain such work. There is no way of knowing how frequently such passing occurs, but there are few upper- or middle-class

Negroes who do not claim knowledge of persons who have passed for economic reasons. Men in this category usually pass to obtain technical positions, and there are verifiable instances where eminent positions as scientists, physicians, and public administrators are held by these "white Negroes."

Usually the individual returns to the Negro community for all of his social contacts and uses his light skin color simply as a method of circumventing economic discrimination. Friendships with whites are generally avoided, as they would lead to complications. One girl reported:

"My mother is very fair and passes for white on most of the jobs she has had, but she doesn't like to do it. It always brings about so much trouble. She makes friends and soon they want her to come to. see them and they want to come to see her. One friend that she had had for over a year used to invite Mother to her apartment. This woman knew Mother had two children, and she would say, 'You'll just have to bring those children over so I can see them.' We would have fun talking about it. Well, she finally had to quit; the girl was becoming too chummy."

The final stage of passing—crossing over completely to the other side of the color-line—involves passing in order to associate socially with white people. For a Negro to pass socially means sociological death and rebirth. It is extremely difficult, as one loses in the process his educational standing (if he has gone to a Negro school), intimate friends, family, and work references. People well established in the Negro world and older people seldom pass socially and completely. There is too much to lose and too little to be gained.

WHO CAN PASS?

Scholars have speculated about the amount of Negro blood which a person must have to pass. One concludes that persons with an eighth or less of Negro blood are frequently able to pass as white in a society that is not highly discriminating. Another believes that individuals with one-sixteenth colored ancestry are always able to pass as white. In Midwest Metropolis, a person with still a greater amount of Negro blood can no doubt pass. In other parts of the country, where there are many Mexicans, Puerto Ricans, and South Americans, it is even more difficult to detect persons with considerable Negro blood.

Passing is dependent on many factors other than skin color. Many fairly dark persons with sharp features are taken for Indians, East Indians, Egyptians, or members of other dark groups. The texture of the hair in many borderline cases plays an important role. But no single factor is so important as the general configuration of skin coloring, texture of hair, and facial characteristics in determining whether a person may be "taken for white." Because of the large admixture of Indian blood among Negroes, many have a Mongolian cast to their features. These individuals, if they have straight hair, can pass for non-Negro, even if quite dark. Then there are many subtle characteristics such as dress, general deportment, mannerisms, and degree of self-assurance which all play their parts.

Quite apart from all these factors and from any objective analysis of the individual's physical make-up is the factor of the social situation. In instances where Negroes are out of the conventional role, whites who have stereotyped notions of what Negroes should do, where they might be found, and how they should act are led to mistake obvious Negroes for white or other racial stock. A young Negro student entered a cab at the railroad station and asked to be taken to the University of Chicago. Although he was brown-skinned and had woolly hair, the cab driver asked if he was not Argentinian. A prominent Negro went to an exclusive night club with a white party, and even though he was introduced to the manager as a Negro, the manager refused to believe his eyes or the statement of the white members of the party. This sort of mistake is also sometimes made by Negroes. At a high school where all the students were colored, but it was the custom to have a white speaker for the commencement exercises, a light brown-skinned Negro addressed the audience and was thought by the majority of the student body to be white. Americans, white and black, see with their emotions as well as with their eyes, and actualities are colored by stereotyped expectations.

On the other hand, any white person—including the lightest blond can, if he wishes, pass for colored. Dr. Robert Park, the eminent sociologist, on two occasions passed for a Negro in order to obtain a room in a Negro hotel. A white girl who worked at a social agency in the Black Belt found out to her amazement, after working with Negro people for a year, that almost all of them not only thought she was a Negro, but refused to believe that she wasn't joking when she said she was white. Some white persons married to Negroes habitually pass for Negro in order to gain some advantage or to avoid embarrassment. The white wife of a Negro railroad waiter related the following incident:

"I have an annual pass with the railroad company my husband is with. I used it a couple of times. Yes, I was questioned when I used the pass and I said that although you might not think so, I have colored blood. I was telling the truth because I have red blood in my veins, and that's colored. The man who questioned me was a southerner and I told him that if he doubted my identity he could wire my husband at my expense."

Many persons, especially white southerners and Negroes, believe that they are so sensitized to Negro racial characteristics that they can detect persons who are attempting to pass for either white or Negro. The following incident illustrates a belief in this special ability. Speaking of her mother, who was passing for white for economic reasons, an informant said:

"She used to hold a nice position at a hotel here. One day a man called her name and said, 'You remind me of a little colored girl.' She thought the most suitable answer was, 'You remind me of a little colored boy.' He said, 'Maybe I am.' It turned out that he was colored and lived on the South Side. It is kind of funny how colored people know one another almost ten times out of ten."

The authors found, however, that among the staff of the Cayton-Warner research, one dark-complexioned white girl was constantly mistaken for colored and one very light Negro girl was identified by most visitors, both white and Negro, as not being colored. Mixed parties have been held in the Negro community where white girls have passed for Negro and Negro girls for white, to the utter confusion of all of the guests. Although persons particularly sensitized to racial differences may be a bit more astute in identifying racial characteristics, a point is reached where it is impossible with even the most refined anthropological measurements to distinguish Negroes from whites. The racial identification of such marginal persons is sociological rather than biological; and what really determines their "race" is how much the public knows about their ancestry.

PASSING AS A PROCESS

Few people, regardless of how light they may be, grow up as Negroes and then suddenly make an intellectual decision to pass for white. Those who pass over the color-line do so step by step until the emotional ties which bind them to Negroes are severed, on the one hand, and new relationships with members of the white community achieved, on the other hand. The first step, as has been indicated, is usually unintentional passing, where a Negro with a light skin suddenly realizes that in going about the city, outside of the Negro community, he is taken for white. Later the individual becomes more adventurous and begins to pass for some minor convenience, such as obtaining a Pullman when traveling in the South. The individual then may find a subtle pleasure in fooling white people and going places where he knows he would not be welcomed as a Negro. Still later he may seek employment in the white community with every intention of keeping all social relations among Negroes. But as intimate friendships are established with white fellow-workers, in many cases the individual is gradually drawn farther and farther away from his emotional attachment to members of the black community. For such an individual the final break comes when the irritations of trying to remain colored and the attractiveness of the white world outweigh his trepidation.

For one who is not firmly anchored in the Negro community emotionally, there is much temptation to take such a step. At first he finds that the color-line in Midwest Metropolis seems to disappear for him. There is no close scrutiny by his new-found white working companions and friends. There is no fear of any more reprisal than being fired from a job or losing some new acquaintances. Then more and more difficulties begin to arise. He begins to dread meeting old Negro friends while out with the new white ones. There are cases where daughters have refused to speak to their mothers on the street and sons have looked the other way, when accompanied by whites, upon encountering their Negro fathers. As the new job and the new friends become of more emotional importance, the individual has a constant, haunting fear of being discovered. There is the possibility that an old Negro enemy may turn him in, or that some white person may accidentally discover him and work vengeance on him.

Then there arises a moral crisis. On the one hand, it is hard to continue to live in two worlds; but on the other hand, there is a sense of guilt over being unfaithful to the Negro world with which he and his family have been identified. Then it is that many an individual either announces to a startled office manager, foreman, or fiancée that he is a Negro and would prefer to be known as such, or commits sociological suicide, to be reborn on the white side of the color-line.

An individual who makes the latter choice is not operating in a vacuum. There is the constant and disturbing pressure of the Negro community which both pushes and pulls him. Many very light men, especially, feel uncomfortable in the Negro community. They are very conspicuous when out with Negro groups except when all are as light as they. This is the push which exerts itself on them from birth. They are always suspect—the community feels that in most cases they are only looking for a chance to escape the confines of color. Passing episodes are carefully concealed from most of their Negro friends, for the community would in most cases censure them; and even when they pass solely for economic reasons, only a partial and begrudging sanction is given them. Finally, the condemnation of the Negro group itself operates in the same way as the attractiveness of moving freely in white society, to allow them to make a moral decision to cross over the line. Although there is far from unanimity on the subject, many Negroes would agree with a young woman who said:

"Well, I don't see anything wrong with it, if the person can get something out of it. But personally, I don't like it. I think if for commercial reasons it is done as Mary Malone is doing [she named a well-known Negro girl who passes for white on the stage], that's not so bad; but I wouldn't want to deny my race otherwise. And then I would associate with colored people after I was finished work. What I mean is that I would pass only for business purposes and not because I didn't want to be colored."

There is a widespread belief in the community that Negroes protect other Negroes who are passing. One white woman married to a Negro stated:

"Some people would try to prevent a person from holding a job if they knew he wasn't entitled to it because of color. My husband knows a man who is colored and who is working as a white man, but my husband never recognizes him. There is a sort of code of honor among colored people not to reveal the identity of a person who is working as white."

Although there are occasional instances of Negroes exposing others who are passing, in general there is great tolerance on the part of Negroes if they know they are not being slighted or are being slighted for economic reasons only. The difference in attitude of two colored girls who worked in a downtown department store illustrates this point:

"Mary and I got a job working at Field's one Christmas. Mary had had much more practice at passing than I. But she was scared to death that someone—some colored person—would see her and recognize her. They put her in the costume jewelry section right on the first floor. Negroes would come in and she would try to avoid them and turn her back. Then they made a point of trying to speak to her. Finally she became a nervous wreck and had to quit. They put me in the handkerchief section on State Street, and people were coming in all the time that I knew; but I always spoke to them and would wait on them if they came to my counter. So I got along all right. Lots of people who sensed that I was going to speak to them would just nod and move away quickly. They weren't resentful. I really needed the money; but it wasn't a life-and-death matter, so I couldn't think of not speaking to someone that I knew."

The practice of passing for economic reasons is so frequent and the Negro's economic position is so desperate that some years ago the

Chicago *Defender* gave partial sanction to this behavior in an editorial mainly slanted toward poking fun at the attitude of whites:

In our big department stores in the Loop can be found many sons and daughters who come back "home" at the close of the day, and by the same token would come back home to stay if their identity was found out. They are not as fair as lilies but the fact that most of the stores are "manned" by Jewish girls whose complexion and hair is swarthy helps the situation out materially. It is a shame and a disgrace that we must be forced in order to make a livelihood, to live this life each day, but there is not another way. We pour thousands of dollars, hard earned, into the coffers of the storekeepers and yet we are denied recognition or a chance to earn some of it back except we apply for some menial position like running an elevator or janitorship, and in many places we are even denied this class of employment. That our men and women are superior in every way to the average wage-earner found in these stores is without question, but worth doesn't count when prejudice creeps in, so we must fight fire with fire, and those that are able to "get by" peace be with them and it is our duty not to hinder them in any way. Last Monday was the Jewish New Year and all of that faith were given a holiday—without pay—by the store managers. This, of course, made a number of our young ladies who were Jewish pro tem take two days off. "There are tricks to all trades," said one of them laughingly, "and we had it to do to allay suspicion." So even with the serious side of it there comes something in the lighter vein. But it does seem with a concerted effort this situation could in a measure be changed for the better, patronize the store that offers the most to you and yours and you will be aiding materially in the movement.

A ROSE IS A ROSE IS A ROSE

Although thousands of Negroes are lost to the Negro race each year by passing, scores of thousands have passed for a while only to return to the —for them—warmer and more comfortable milieu of the Negro community.

A prominent colored physician reported that for some years after he left college he passed for white in practicing medicine. He could never feel quite comfortable and was particularly concerned about his relationships with his family. After having established a successful practice, he suddenly decided to return to the Negro group and there achieved a position of prominence which he could never have attained in the larger society. Another well-known Negro businessman for a number of years lived on the North Shore, but he too returned to the Black Belt and, with the capital he had accumulated and the insight into white business practices he had obtained, was able to establish one of the most successful enterprises in the community.

In both of these instances, as in many others, passing was profitable at one period of the individual's life, when he had no money and little experience, but it was equally profitable later on to return to the Negro community. Usually the fact that he has passed is a guarded secret, for it would indicate that at one time he had severed his emotional identification with the community and he would be suspected of demonstrating a similar disloyalty again. Men pass for noneconomic reasons more frequently than women; it is also more common for men to return to the Negro group. Once a light girl has passed, she would be considered disloyal—sullied, and not to be trusted—and would not be able to make such an advantageous marriage were she to return to the Negro group. While it is common knowledge that thousands of Negroes pass, cases of those who return are relatively infrequent. In the lives of many prominent Negroes, however, are gaps which can be explained only in terms of a temporary passing over the color-line.

Passing has been described as a process where one gradually relinquishes his social relationships and emotional identification with the Negro community. It should not be thought, however, that every person who passes completely goes through each step of this process; it is merely the pattern generally followed. Many people are never successful in breaking their ties completely with either group, and severe maladjustment often results.

Passing is one way of crossing the color-line. It does not challenge the mores of the society, for it is surreptitious. It does, however, bring with it miscegenation, introducing a constant stream of Negro blood into the white population. In fact, as Louis Wirth and Herbert Goldhamer state, "One southern state legislator, in speaking against an especially severe bill restricting Negro-white intermarriage, is reported as saying that if the definition of Negro incorporated in the bill were accepted there would not be enough white people in the state to pass it."

Midwest Metropolis is not aware of the volume of passing nor disturbed enough about it to take punitive action. Nevertheless anyone discovered is usually considered a Negro. If such an individual has attained a position of great importance, however, the episode is often hushed up. Negroes claim to be aware of many cases of this kind, and numerous stories on the subject circulate throughout the community.[2]

---

[2] Such stories are hard to verify. Occasionally, however, an incident becomes a matter of public record. Just before the First World War, for instance, a wealthy Chicago publisher, always considered white, was found to be a "Negro" when his darker relatives showed up at his funeral. A similar case appeared in the neighboring state of Indiana in 1940 when a leading businessman and philanthropist was revealed as colored at his funeral.

It is even widely believed that there has been at least one "Negro" president of the United States.

A TWO-WAY PASSAGE

In Chicago people do occasionally cross the color-line. And when they do, they may encounter difficulties. But hundreds of Negroes have lived and are living as white, and a small group of whites have become sociological Negroes. It can and does happen here—but not with the frequency which would warrant the irrational fear of "amalgamation" held by many white people.

What does this race crossing mean? More Negro blood than most suspect finds its way into the white population—not enough, however, to change the physical characteristics of that group at all. Passing is of much more serious import to Negroes. Yearly a number of "white Negroes" pass over the line. This perhaps robs the Negro group of possible leaders and well-trained persons who could add immeasurably to the welfare of the group. But it should be noted that a relatively small proportion of those who can pass really do cross over completely, and there are some who have passed completely but who "return to their race" with capital and experience which allows them to become leaders. It's a two-way passage in many instances.

Intermarriage, on the other hand, operates to introduce more white blood into the Negro group, modifying to an extent that physical type. The study of the "American Negro" is not merely the study of Negroes so designated because they are culturally distinct from the Negroes of Africa, but is also the study of the formation of a relatively distinct physical type. Intermarriage (though nonlegal miscegenation is much more important in this connection) is one of the means by which this new type—the brown American—has come into existence.

THE "BLACK BABY" BUGABOO

Mixed couples usually express a desire for either light brown-skinned children or children who can pass for white. People who oppose passing often cite the "danger" of a "black baby"—a "throwback"—sometime cropping up should the Negro who has passed, or his descendants, marry a white person. Negroes who are passing occasionally hesitate to get married or to have children for fear that "Negro blood will out." This emphasis upon the "black baby" arriving to embarrass its parents has a dual significance. On one hand it reflects the general attitude of the dominant white American culture toward "typical" Negro physical traits—the definition of black skin, thick lips, and kinky hair as "ugly." On the other hand, it expresses a desire that children shall not look so different from the parents as to excite embarrassing stares or malicious gossip.[3]

The "black baby" bugaboo is often cited as the primary objection to passing. Edward M. East, the geneticist, has discussed the probable origin of such black babies as do appear in the following passage:

"A favorite short-story plot with which melodramatic artists seek to harrow the feelings of their readers is one where the distinguished scion of an aristocratic family marries the beautiful girl with telltale shadows on the half-moons of her nails, and in due time is presented with a coal-black son. It is a good framework, and carries a thrill. One waits shiveringly, even breathlessly, for the first squeal of the dingy infant. There is only this slight imperfection—or is it an advantage?—it could not possibly happen on the stage as set by the author. The most casual examination of the genetic formulae given above demonstrates its absurdity. If there ever was a basis for the plot in real life, the explanation lies in a fracture of the seventh commandment, or in a tinge of negro [sic] blood in the aristocrat as dark as that in his wife."

The genetic formulae referred to by East, and generally accepted by geneticists and anthropologists, support the following conclusions:[4]

1. In the case of two persons both theoretically white but having, whether they know it or not, some Negro blood, an accentuation of some Negro characteristics may occur in their offspring, but in all probability the offspring of such unions will be able to pass for white.

2. It is impossible for the offspring of a recognizable Negro and a pure white person to be any darker than the Negro partner, and in all probability it will be lighter.

[3] Esthetic standards vary from culture to culture. Many Central African groups think that thin lips, white skin and straight hair are ugly. And among white people there are many who can recognize "black" beauty or "yellow" beauty as well as white. There are people, too, who in choosing a mate do not put such standards in the primary place. Students of Latin American countries have frequently called attention to the fact that the marriage of whites to very Negroid types is not unusual, and that the white partners feel no shame in such cases. Yet, often, very devoted couples of this type want children who are blends and consider a dark child unfortunate.

[4] In detailing these conclusions we have used the expression "Negro blood" instead of the more precise formulation in terms of genes that govern characteristics such as skin-color, hair form, shape of nose, etc. Obviously, however, blood has nothing to do with heredity, but it is probable that the colloquial use of the term "Negro blood" will remain long after the general public is aware that it really refers to "genes for Negro traits."

3. The offspring of two mixed-bloods (e.g., mulattoes or quadroons) may be darker than either, but in all probability would not be black.

Even a widespread knowledge of these facts will not dispel the "black baby" bugaboo, for what white person can be sure that he has no Negro blood, or what Negro who is passing that he will not marry a "white" person who has a few drops from way back? The chances of such marriages producing a "black baby" are extremely remote—but it could happen. "In all probability" is not a very reassuring phrase. So long as "blackness" of skin is considered a misfortune, the bugaboo will remain. Even if the habit of stigmatizing people because of their skin-color were to disappear, a "black baby" would still be considered a misfortune until everyone knew that an occasional dark child born to lighter parents did not constitute *prima facie* evidence of interracial adultery.

CHAPTER VII

SOCIAL ORGANIZATION: INSTITUTIONS AND INSTITUTIONALIZED BEHAVIOR

47. *Manifest and Latent Functions* *

A SOCIOLOGICAL ANALYSIS of political machines is the method used by Robert Merton to demonstrate the concepts of manifest and latent functions. In this selection new insight is given to the meaning and probable results of gambling and crime investigations, and of "drives to clean up" city or state politics. Merton throws new light on the latent services performed by the political machine for "illegitimate" as well as "legitimate" business. The phenomena described here seem to be pretty well grounded in the institutions of American culture. In confirmation of this assertion, compare Merton's recent analysis with Lincoln Steffens' book, *The Shame of the Cities*, first published as a series of newspaper articles nearly fifty years ago.

SOME FUNCTIONS OF THE POLITICAL MACHINE

WITHOUT PRESUMING TO ENTER into the variations of detail marking different political machines—a Tweed, Vare, Crump, Flynn, Hague are by no means identical types of bosses—we can briefly examine the func-

* Robert K. Merton. Reprinted from *Social Theory and Social Structure*, pp. 71-81, by permission of The Free Press, Glencoe, Illinois. Copyright 1949.

The author (b. 1910) is Professor of Sociology, Columbia University. Associate Director, Bureau of Applied Social Research. Advisory editor, sociology: Harcourt, Brace & Co., *Journal of Legal and Political Sociology*, and *Journal of Human Relations*. Author, *Science, Technology and Society in 17th Century England* and *Mass Persuasion*. Co-editor (with Paul F. Lazarsfeld), *Continuities in Social Research: the Scope and Method of "The American Soldier."*

tions more or less common to the political machine, as a generic type of social organization. We neither attempt to itemize all the diverse functions of the political machine nor imply that all these functions are similarly fulfilled by each and every machine.

The key structural function of the Boss is to organize, centralize and maintain in good working condition "the scattered fragments of power" which are at present dispersed through our political organization. By this centralized organization of political power, the boss and his apparatus can satisfy the needs of diverse subgroups in the larger community which are not adequately satisfied by legally devised and culturally approved social structures.

To understand the role of bossism and the machine, therefore, we must look at two types of sociological variables: (1) the *structural context* which makes it difficult, if not impossible, for morally approved structures to fulfill essential social functions, thus leaving the door open for political machines (or their structural equivalents) to fulfill these functions and (2) the subgroups whose distinctive needs are left unsatisfied, except for the latent functions which the machine in fact fulfills.

STRUCTURAL CONTEXT

The constitutional framework of American political organization specifically precludes the legal possibility of highly centralized power and, it has been noted, thus "discourages the growth of effective and responsible leadership. The framers of the Constitution, as Woodrow Wilson observed, set up the check and balance system 'to keep government at a sort of mechanical equipoise by means of a standing amicable contest among its several organic parts.' They distrusted power as dangerous to liberty: and therefore they spread it thin and erected barriers against its concentration." This dispersion of power is found not only at the national level but in local areas as well. "As a consequence," Sait goes on to observe, "when *the people or particular groups* among them demanded positive action, no one had adequate authority to act. The machine provided an antidote."

The constitutional dispersion of power not only makes for difficulty of effective decision and action but when action does occur it is defined and hemmed in by legalistic considerations. In consequence, there develops "a much more human system of partisan government, whose chief object soon became the circumvention of government by law. . . . The lawlessness of the extra-official democracy was merely the counterpoise of the legalism of the official democracy. The lawyer having been permitted to subordinate democracy to the Law, the Boss had to be called in to extricate the victim, which he did after a fashion and for a consideration."

Officially, political power is dispersed. Various well-known expedients were devised for this manifest objective. Not only was there the familiar separation of powers among the several branches of the government but, in some measure, tenure in each office was limited, rotation in office approved. And the scope of power inherent in each office was severely circumscribed. Yet, observes Sait in rigorously functional terms, "Leadership is necessary; and since it does not develop readily within the constitutional framework, the Boss provides it in a crude and irresponsible form from the outside."

Put in more generalized terms, *the functional deficiencies of the official structure generate an alternative (unofficial) structure to fulfill existing needs somewhat more effectively.* Whatever its specific historical origins, the political machine persists as an apparatus for satisfying otherwise unfulfilled needs of diverse groups in the population. By turning to a few of these subgroups and their characteristic needs, we shall be led at once to a range of latent functions of the political machine.

FUNCTIONS OF THE POLITICAL MACHINE FOR DIVERSE SUBGROUPS

It is well known that one source of strength of the political machine derives from its roots in the local community and the neighborhood. The political machine does not regard the electorate as a vague, undifferentiated mass of voters. With a keen sociological intuition, the machine recognizes that the voter is primarily a man living in a specific neighborhood, with specific personal problems and personal wants. Public issues are abstract and remote; private problems are extremely concrete and immediate. It is not through the generalized appeal to large public concerns that the machine operates, but through the direct, quasi-feudal relationships between local representatives of the machine and voters in their neighborhood. Elections are won in the precinct.

The machine welds its link with ordinary men and women by elaborate networks of personal relations. Politics is transformed into personal ties. The precinct captain "must be a friend to every man, assuming, if he does not feel, sympathy with the unfortunate, and utilizing in his good works the resources which the boss puts at his disposal." The precinct captain is forever a friend in need. In our prevailingly impersonal society, the machine, through its local agents, fulfills the important social *function of humanizing and personalizing all manner of assistance* to those in need. Food-baskets and jobs, legal and extra-legal advice, setting to rights minor scrapes with the law, helping the bright poor boy to a political scholarship in a local college, looking after the bereaved—the whole range of crises when a feller needs a friend, and, above all, a friend who knows the score and who can do something about it—all these find the ever-helpful precinct captain available in the pinch.

To assess this function of the political machine adequately, it is important to note not only the fact that aid *is* provided but *the manner in which it is provided.* After all, other agencies do exist for dispensing such assistance. Welfare agencies, settlement houses, legal aid clinics, medical aid in free hospitals, public relief departments, immigration authorities—these and a multitude of other organizations are available to provide the most varied types of assistance. But in contrast to the professional techniques of the welfare worker which may typically represent in the mind of the recipient the cold, bureaucratic dispensation of limited aid following upon detailed investigation of *legal* claims to aid of the "client," are the unprofessional techniques of the precinct captain who asks no questions, exacts no compliance with legal rules of eligibility and does not "snoop" into private affairs.

For many, the loss of "self-respect" is too high a price for legalized assistance. In contrast to the gulf between the settlement house workers who so often come from a different social class, educational background and ethnic group, the precinct worker is "just one of us," who understands what it's all about. The condescending lady bountiful can hardly compete with the understanding friend in need. In *this struggle between alternative structures for fulfilling the nominally same function* of providing aid and support to those who need it, it is clearly the machine politician who is better integrated with the groups which he serves than the impersonal, professionalized, socially distant and legally constrained welfare worker. And since the politician can at times influence and manipulate the official organizations for the dispensation of assistance, whereas the welfare worker has practically no influence on the political machine, this only adds to his greater effectiveness. More colloquially and also, perhaps, more incisively, it was the Boston ward-leader, Martin Lomasny, who described this essential function to the curious Lincoln Steffens: "I think," said Lomasny, "that there's got to be in every ward somebody that any bloke can come to—no matter what he's done—and get help. *Help, you understand; none of your law and justice, but help.*"

The "deprived classes," then, constitute one subgroup for whom the political machine clearly satisfies wants not adequately satisfied in the same fashion by the legitimate social structure.

For a second subgroup, that of business (primarily "big" business but also "small") the political boss serves the function of providing those political privileges which entail immediate economic gains. Business corporations, among which the public utilities (railroads, local transportation companies, communications corporations, electric light) are simply the most conspicuous in this regard, seek special political dispensations which will enable them to stabilize their situation and to near their objective of maximizing profits. Interestingly enough, corporations often want to avoid a chaos of uncontrolled competition. They want the greater security of an economic czar who controls, regulates and organizes competition, providing this czar is not a public official with his decisions subject to public scrutiny and public control. (The latter would be "government control," and hence taboo.) The political boss fulfills these requirements admirably.

Examined for a moment apart from any "moral" considerations, the political apparatus of the Boss is effectively designed to perform these functions with a minimum of inefficiency. Holding the strings of diverse governmental divisions, bureaus and agencies in his competent hands, the Boss rationalizes the relations between public and private business. He serves as the business community's ambassador in the otherwise alien (and sometimes unfriendly) realm of government. And, in strict business-like terms, he is well-paid for his economic services to his respectable business clients. In an article entitled, "An Apology to Graft," Steffens suggested that "Our economic system, which held up riches, power and acclaim as prizes to men bold enough and able enough to buy corruptly timber, mines, oil fields and franchises and 'get away with it,' was at fault." And, in a conference with a hundred or so of Los Angeles business leaders, he described a fact well known to all of them: the Boss and his machine were an *integral part* of the organization of the economy. "You cannot build or operate a railroad, or a street railway, gas, water, or power company, develop and operate a mine, or get forests and cut timber on a large scale, or run any privileged business, without corrupting or joining in the corruption of the government. You tell me privately that you must, and here I am telling you semi-publicly that you must. And that is so all over the country. And that means that we have an organization of society in which, *for some reason*, you and your kind, the ablest, most intelligent, most imaginative, daring, and resourceful leaders of society, are and must be against society and its laws and its all-around growth."

Since the demand for the services of special privileges are built into the structure of the society, the Boss fulfills diverse functions for this second subgroup of business-seeking-privilege. These "needs" of business, as presently constituted, are not adequately provided for by "conventional" and "culturally approved" social structures; consequently, the extra-legal but more-or-less efficient organization of the political machine comes to provide these services. To adopt an *exclusively* moral attitude toward the "corrupt political machine" is to lose sight of the very structural conditions which generate the "evil" that is so bitterly attacked. To adopt a functional outlook on the political machine is not to provide an apologia, but a more solid base for modifying or eliminating the machine, *providing* specific structural arrangements are introduced either for eliminating these effective demands of the business community or, if that is the objective, of satisfying these demands through alternative means.

A third set of distinctive functions fulfilled by the political machine for a special subgroup is that of providing alternative channels of social mobility for those otherwise excluded from the more conventional avenues for personal "advancement." Both the sources of this special "need" (for social mobility) and the respect in which the political machine comes to help satisfy this need can be understood by examining the structure of the larger culture and society. As is well known, the American culture lays enormous emphasis on money and power as a "success" goal legitimate for all members of the society. By no means alone in our inventory of cultural goals, it still remains among the most heavily endowed with positive affect and value. However, certain subgroups and certain ecological areas are notable for the relative absence of opportunity for achieving these (monetary and power) types of success. They constitute, in short, sub-populations where "the cultural emphasis upon pecuniary success has been absorbed, but where there is *little access to conventional and legitimate* means for attaining such success. The conventional occupational opportunities of persons in (such areas) are almost completely limited to manual labor. Given our cultural stigmatization of manual labor, and its correlate, the prestige of white-collar work," it is clear that the result is a tendency to achieve these culturally approved objectives *through whatever means are possible*. These people are on the one hand, "asked to orient their conduct toward the prospect of accumulating wealth [and power] and, on the other, they are largely denied effective opportunities to do so institutionally."

It is within this context of social structure that the political machine fulfills the basic function of providing avenues of social mobility for the otherwise disadvantaged. Within this context, even the corrupt political machine and the racket "represent the triumph of amoral intelligence over morally prescribed 'failure' when the channels of vertical mobility are closed or narrowed *in a society which places a high premium on economic affluence, [power] and social ascent for all its members.*" As one sociologist has noted on the basis of several years of close observation in a "slum area":

> The sociologist who dismisses racket and political organizations as deviations from desirable standards thereby neglects some of the major elements of slum life. . . . *He does not discover the functions they perform for the members* [of the groupings in the slum]. The Irish and later immigrant peoples have had the greatest difficulty in finding places for themselves in our urban social and economic structure. Does anyone believe that the immigrants and their children could have achieved their present degree of social mobility without gaining control of the political organization of some of our largest cities? The same is true of the racket organization. *Politics and the rackets have furnished an important means of social mobility for individuals, who, because of ethnic background and low class position,* are blocked from advancement in the "respectable" channels.

This, then represents a third type of function performed for a distinctive subgroup. This function, it may be noted in passing, is fulfilled by the *sheer* existence and operation of the political machine, for it is in the machine itself that these individuals and sub-groups find their culturally induced needs more or less satisfied. It refers to the services which the political apparatus provides for its own personnel. But seen in the wider social context we have set forth, it no longer appears as *merely* a means of self-aggrandizement for profit-hungry and power-hungry *individuals*, but as an organized provision for *subgroups* otherwise excluded or restricted from the race for "getting ahead."

Just as the political machine performs services for "legitimate" business, so it operates to perform not dissimilar services for "illegitimate" business: vice, crime and rackets. Once again, the basic sociological role of the machine in this respect can be more fully appreciated only if one temporarily abandons attitudes of moral indignation, to examine with all moral innocence the actual workings of the organization. In this light, it at once appears that the subgroup of the professional criminal, racketeer, gambler, has basic similarities of organization, demands and operation to the subgroup of the industrialist, man of business, speculator. If there is a Lumber King or an Oil King, there is also a Vice King or a Racket King. If expansive legitimate business organizes administrative and financial syndicates to "rationalize" and to "integrate" diverse areas of production and business enterprise, so expansive rackets and crime organize syndicates to bring order to the otherwise chaotic areas of production of illicit goods and services. If legitimate business regards the proliferation of small business enterprises as wasteful and inefficient, substituting, for example, the giant chain stores for the hundreds of corner groceries, so illegitimate business adopts the same businesslike attitude, and syndicates crime and vice.

Finally, and in many respects, most important, is the basic similarity, if not near-identity, of the economic role of "legitimate" business and "illegitimate" business. *Both are in some degree concerned with the provision of goods and services for which there is an economic demand.* Morals aside, they are both business, industrial and professional enterprises, dispensing goods and services which some people want, for which there is a market in which goods and services are transformed into commodities. And, in a prevalently market society, we should expect appropriate enterprises to arise whenever there is a market demand for given goods or services.

As is well known, vice, crime and the rackets are "big business." Consider only that there have been estimated to be about 500,000 professional prostitutes in the United States, and compare this with the approximately 200,000 physicians and 200,000 nurses. It is difficult to estimate which have the larger clientele: the professional men and women of medicine or the professional men and women of vice. It is, of course, difficult to estimate the economic assets, income, profits and dividends of illicit gambling in this country and to compare it with the economic assets, income, profits and dividends of, say, the shoe industry, but it is altogether possible that the two industries are about on a par. No precise figures exist on the annual expenditures on illicit narcotics, and it is probable that these are less than the expenditures on candy, but it is also probable that they are larger than the expenditure on books.

It takes but a moment's thought to recognize that, *in strictly economic terms*, there is no relevant difference between the provision of licit and illicit goods and services. The liquor traffic illustrates this perfectly. It would be peculiar to argue that prior to 1920 (when the 18th amendment became effective), the provision of liquor constituted an economic service, that from 1920 to 1933, its production and sale no longer constituted an economic service dispensed in a market, and that from 1934 to the present, it once again took on a serviceable aspect. Or, it would be *economically* (not morally) absurd to suggest that the sale of bootlegged liquor in the dry state of Kansas is less a response to a market demand than the sale of publicly manufactured liquor in the neighboring wet state of Missouri. Examples of this sort can of course be multiplied many times over. Can it be held that in European countries, with registered and legalized prostitution, the prostitute contributes an economic service, whereas in this country, lacking legal sanction, the prostitute provides no such service? Or that the professional abortionist is in the economic market where he has approved legal status and that he is out of the economic market where he is legally taboo? Or that gambling satisfies a specific demand for entertainment in Nevada, where it is one of the largest business enterprises of the largest city in the state, but that it differs essentially in this respect from movie houses in the neighboring state of California?

The failure to recognize that these businesses are only *morally* and not *economically* distinguishable from "legitimate" businesses has led to badly scrambled analysis. Once the economic identity of the two is recognized, we may anticipate that if the political machine performs functions for "legitimate big business" it will be all the more likely to perform not dissimilar functions for "illegitimate big business." And, of course, such is often the case.

The distinctive function of the political machine for their criminal, vice and racket clientele is to enable them to operate in satisfying the economic demands of a large market without due interference from the government. Just as big business may contribute funds to the political party war-chest to ensure a minimum of governmental interference, so with big rackets and big crime. In both instances, the political machine can, in varying degrees, provide "protection." In both instances, many features of the structural context are identical: (1) market demands for goods and services; (2) the operators' concern with maximizing gains from their enterprises; (3) the need for partial control of government which might otherwise interfere with these activities of businessmen; (4) the need for an efficient, powerful and centralized agency to provide an effective liaison of "business" with government.

Without assuming that the foregoing pages exhaust either the range of functions or the range of subgroups served by the political machine, we can at least see that *it presently fulfills some functions for these diverse subgroups which are not adequately fulfilled by culturally approved or more conventional structures.*

Several additional implications of the functional analysis of the political machine can be mentioned here only in passing, although they obviously require to be developed at length. First, the foregoing analysis has direct implications for *social engineering*. It helps explain why the periodic efforts at "political reform," "turning the rascals out" and "cleaning political house" are typically short-lived and ineffectual. It exemplifies a basic theorem: *any attempt to eliminate an existing social structure without providing adequate alternative structures for fulfilling the functions previously fulfilled by the abolished organization is doomed to failure.* (Needless to say, this theorem has much wider bearing than the one instance of the political machine.) When "political reform" confines itself to the manifest task of "turning the rascals out," it is engaging in little more than sociological magic. The reform may for a time bring new figures into the political limelight; it may serve the casual social function of re-assuring the electorate that the moral virtues remain intact and will ultimately triumph; it may actually effect a turnover in the personnel of the political machine; it may even, for a time, so curb the activities of the machine as to leave unsatisfied the many needs it has previously fulfilled. But, inevitably, unless the reform also involves a "re-forming" of the social and political structure such that the existing needs are satisfied by alternative structures or unless it involves a change which eliminates these needs altogether, the political machine will return to its integral place in the social scheme of things. *To seek social change, without due recognition of the manifest and latent functions performed by the social organization undergoing change, is to indulge in social ritual rather than social engineering.* The concepts of manifest and latent functions, (or their equivalents) are indispensable elements in the theoretic repertoire of the social engineer. In this crucial sense, these concepts are not "merely" theoretical (in the abusive sense of the term), but are eminently practical. In the deliberate enactment of social change, they can be ignored only at the price of considerably heightening the risk of failure.

A second implication of our analysis of the political machine also has a bearing upon areas wider than the one we have considered. The "paradox" has often been noted that the supporters of the political machine include both the "respectable" business class elements who are, of course, opposed to the criminal or racketeer and the distinctly "unrespectable" elements of the underworld. And, at first appearance, this is cited as an instance of very strange bedfellows. The learned judge is not infrequently called upon to sentence the very racketeer beside whom he sat the night before at an informal dinner of the political bigwigs. The district attorney jostles the exonerated convict on his way to the back room where the Boss has called a meeting. The big business man may complain almost as bitterly as the big racketeer about the "extortionate" contributions to the party fund demanded by the Boss. Social opposites meet—in the smoke-filled room of the successful politician.

In the light of a functional analysis all this of course no longer seems paradoxical. Since the machine serves both the businessman and the criminal man, the two seemingly antipodal groups intersect. This points to a more general theorem: *the social functions of an organization* help determine the structure (including the recruitment of personnel involved in the structure), just as the structure helps determine the effectiveness with which the functions are fulfilled. In terms of social status, the business group and the criminal group are indeed poles apart. But status does not fully determine behavior and the inter-relations between groups. Functions modify these relations. Given their distinctive needs, the several subgroups in the large society are "integrated," whatever their personal desires or intentions, by the centralizing structure which serves these several needs. In a phrase with many implications which require further study, structure affects function and function affects structure.

❧❧❧❧

48. Bureaucracy *

CONTEMPORARY American and other Western societies are characterized by highly bureaucratic organization. This structure is true of business and private social institutions as well as governmental agencies. Here Max Weber has systematically analyzed the nature of bureaucratic organization. Although this analysis was written three decades or more ago and is based largely upon German and other European data, there has appeared no statement that is more thorough or significant sociologically.

CHARACTERISTICS OF BUREAUCRACY

MODERN OFFICIALDOM functions in the following specific manner:

I. There is the principle of fixed and official jurisdictional areas, which are generally ordered by rules, that is, by laws or administrative regulations.

* Reprinted from Max Weber: Essays in Sociology, edited and translated by H. H. Gerth and C. Wright Mills, pp. 196-244. Copyright 1946 by Oxford University Press, Inc., New York.

Max Weber (1864-1920) was a German sociologist and political economist. Held chair of political economy at Freiburg. Weber's sociology is based upon his extensive knowledge in economic, political, social, legal, military, and religious fields. Especially well known for his typological studies of charismatic authority, feudalism, and bureaucracy. A pioneer in sociology of religion. Among his translated works are General Economic History, The Protestant Ethic and the Spirit of Capitalism, On the Methodology of the Social Sciences, and The Theory of Economic and Social Organization.

1. The regular activities required for the purposes of the bureau-cratically governed structure are distributed in a fixed way as official duties.

2. The authority to give the commands required for the discharge of these duties is distributed in a stable way and is strictly delimited by rules concerning the coercive means, physical, sacerdotal, or otherwise, which may be placed at the disposal of officials.

3. Methodical provision is made for the regular and continuous fulfilment of these duties and for the execution of the corresponding rights; only persons who have the generally regulated qualifications to serve are employed.

In public and lawful government these three elements constitute "bureaucratic authority." In private economic domination, they constitute bureaucratic "management." Bureaucracy, thus understood, is fully developed in political and ecclesiastical communities only in the modern state, and, in the private economy, only in the most advanced institutions of capitalism. Permanent and public office authority, with fixed jurisdiction, is not the historical rule but rather the exception. This is so even in large political structures such as those of the ancient Orient, the Germanic and Mongolian empires of conquest, or of many feudal structures of state. In all these cases, the ruler executes the most important measures through personal trustees, table-companions, or court-servants. Their commissions and authority are not precisely delimited and are temporarily called into being for each case.

II. The principles of office hierarchy and of levels of graded authority mean a firmly ordered system of super- and subordination in which there is a supervision of the lower offices by the higher ones. Such a system offers the governed the possibility of appealing the decision of a lower office to its higher authority, in a definitely regulated manner. With the full development of the bureaucratic type, the office hierarchy is monocratically organized. The principle of hierarchical office authority is found in all bureaucratic structures: in state and ecclesiastical structures as well as in large party organizations and private enterprises. It does not matter for the character of bureaucracy whether its authority is called "private" or "public."

When the principle of jurisdictional "competency" is fully carried through, hierarchical subordination—at least in public office—does not mean that the "higher" authority is simply authorized to take over the business of the "lower." Indeed, the opposite is the rule. Once established and having fulfilled its task, an office tends to continue in existence and be held by another incumbent.

III. The management of the modern office is based upon written documents ("the files"), which are preserved in their original or draught form. There is, therefore, a staff of subaltern officials and scribes of all sorts. The body of officials actively engaged in a "public" office, along with the respective apparatus of material implements and the files, make up a "bureau." In private enterprise, "the bureau" is often called "the office."

In principle, the modern organization of the civil service separates the bureau from the private domicile of the official, and, in general, bureaucracy segregates official activity as something distinct from the sphere of private life. Public monies and equipment are divorced from the private property of the official. This condition is everywhere the product of a long development. Nowadays, it is found in public as well as in private enterprises; in the latter, the principle extends even to the leading entrepreneur. In principle, the executive office is separated from the household, business from private correspondence, and business assets from private fortunes. The more consistently the modern type of business management has been carried through the more are these separations the case. The beginnings of this process are to be found as early as the Middle Ages.

It is the peculiarity of the modern entrepreneur that he conducts himself as the "first official" of his enterprise, in the very same way in which the ruler of a specifically modern bureaucratic state spoke of himself as "the first servant" of the state. The idea that the bureau activities of the state are intrinsically different in character from the management of private economic offices is a continental European notion and, by way of contrast, is totally foreign to the American way.

IV. Office management, at least all specialized office management—and such management is distinctly modern—usually presupposes thorough and expert training. This increasingly holds for the modern executive and employee of private enterprises, in the same manner as it holds for the state official.

V. When the office is fully developed, official activity demands the full working capacity of the official, irrespective of the fact that his obligatory time in the bureau may be firmly delimited. In the normal case, this is only the product of a long development, in the public as well as in the private office. Formerly, in all cases, the normal state of affairs was reversed: official business was discharged as a secondary activity.

VI. The management of the office follows general rules, which are more or less stable, more or less exhaustive, and which can be learned.

Knowledge of these rules represents a special technical learning which the officials possess. It involves jurisprudence, or administrative or business management.

The reduction of modern office management to rules is deeply embedded in its very nature. The theory of modern public administration, for instance, assumes that the authority to order certain matters by decree—which has been legally granted to public authorities—does not entitle the bureau to regulate the matter by commands given for each case, but only to regulate the matter abstractly. This stands in extreme contrast to the regulation of all relationships through individual privileges and bestowals of favor, which is absolutely dominant in patrimonialism, at least in so far as such relationships are not fixed by sacred tradition.

THE POSITION OF THE OFFICIAL

All this results in the following for the internal and external position of the official:

I. Office holding is a "vocation." This is shown, first, in the requirement of a firmly prescribed course of training, which demands the entire capacity for work for a long period of time, and in the generally prescribed and special examinations which are prerequisites of employment. Furthermore, the position of the official is in the nature of a duty. This determines the internal structure of his relations, in the following manner: Legally and actually, office holding is not considered a source to be exploited for rents or emoluments, as was normally the case during the Middle Ages and frequently up to the threshold of recent times. Nor is office holding considered a usual exchange of services for equivalents, as is the case with free labor contracts. Entrance into an office, including one in the private economy, is considered an acceptance of a specific obligation of faithful management in return for a secure existence. It is decisive for the specific nature of modern loyalty to an office that, in the pure type, it does not establish a relationship to a person, like the vassal's or disciple's faith in feudal or in patrimonial relations of authority. Modern loyalty is devoted to impersonal and functional purposes. Behind the functional purposes, of course, "ideas of culture-values" usually stand. These are ersatz for the earthly or supra-mundane personal master: ideas such as "state," "church," "community," "party," or "enterprise" are thought of as being realized in a community; they provide an ideological halo for the master.

The political official—at least in the fully developed modern state—is not considered the personal servant of a ruler. Today, the bishop, the priest, and the preacher are in fact no longer, as in early Christian times, holders of purely personal charisma. The supra-mundane and sacred values which they offer are given to everybody who seems to be worthy of them and who asks for them. In former times, such leaders acted upon the personal command of their master; in principle, they were responsible only to him. Nowadays, in spite of the partial survival of the old theory, such religious leaders are officials in the service of a functional purpose, which in the present-day "church" has become routinized and, in turn, ideologically hallowed.

II. The personal position of the official is patterned in the following way:

1. Whether he is in a private office or a public bureau, the modern official always strives and usually enjoys a distinct *social esteem* as compared with the governed. His social position is guaranteed by the prescriptive rules of rank order and, for the political official, by special definitions of the criminal code against "insults of officials" and "contempt" of state and church authorities.

The actual social position of the official is normally highest where, as in old civilized countries, the following conditions prevail: a strong demand for administration by trained experts; a strong and stable social differentiation, where the official predominantly derives from socially and economically privileged strata because of the social distribution of power; or where the costliness of the required training and status conventions are binding upon him. The possession of educational certificates—to be discussed elsewhere—are usually linked with qualification for office. Naturally, such certificates or patents enhance the "status element" in the social position of the official. For the rest this status factor in individual cases is explicitly and impassively acknowledged; for example, in the prescription that the acceptance or rejection of an aspirant to an official career depends upon the consent ("election") of the members of the official body. This is the case in the German army with the officer corps. Similar phenomena, which promote this guild-like closure of officialdom, are typically found in patrimonial and, particularly, in prebendal officialdoms of the past. The desire to resurrect such phenomena in changed forms is by no means infrequent among modern bureaucrats. For instance, they have played a role among the demands of the quite proletarian and expert officials (the tretyj element) during the Russian revolution.

Usually the social esteem of the officials as such is especially low where the demand for expert administration and the dominance of status conventions are weak. This is especially the case in the United States; it is often the case in new settlements by virtue of their wide fields for profit-making and the great instability of their social stratification.

2. The pure type of bureaucratic official is *appointed* by a superior authority. An official elected by the governed is not a purely bureaucratic figure. Of course, the formal existence of an election does not by itself mean that no appointment hides behind the election—in the state, especially, appointment by party chiefs. Whether or not this is the case does not depend upon legal statutes but upon the way in which the party mechanism functions. Once firmly organized, the parties can turn a formally free election into the mere acclamation of a candidate designated by the party chief. As a rule, however, a formally free election is turned into a fight, conducted according to definite rules, for votes in favor of one of two designated candidates.

In all circumstances, the designation of officials by means of an election among the governed modifies the strictness of hierarchical subordination. In principle, an official who is so elected has an autonomous position opposite the superordinate official. The elected official does not derive his position "from above" but "from below," or at least not from a superior authority of the official hierarchy but from powerful party men ("bosses"), who also determine his further career. The career of the elected official is not, or at least not primarily, dependent upon his chief in the administration. The official who is not elected but appointed by a chief normally functions more exactly, from a technical point of view, because, all other circumstances being equal, it is more likely that purely functional points of consideration and qualities will determine his selection and career. As laymen, the governed can become acquainted with the extent to which a candidate is expertly qualified for office only in terms of experience, and hence only after his service. Moreover, in every sort of selection of officials by election, parties quite naturally give decisive weight not to expert considerations but to the services a follower renders to the party boss. This holds for all kinds of procurement of officials by elections, for the designation of formally free, elected officials by party bosses when they determine the slate of candidates, or the free appointment by a chief who has himself been elected. The contrast, however, is relative: substantially similar conditions hold where legitimate monarchs and their subordinates appoint officials, except that the influence of the followings are then less controllable.

Where the demand for administration by trained experts is considerable, and the party followings have to recognize an intellectually developed, educated, and freely moving "public opinion," the use of unqualified officials falls back upon the party in power at the next election. Naturally, this is more likely to happen when the officials are appointed by the chief. The demand for a trained administration now exists in the United States, but in the large cities, where immigrant votes are "corraled," there is, of course, no educated public opinion. Therefore, popular elections of the administrative chief and also of his subordinate officials usually endanger the expert qualification of the official as well as the precise functioning of the bureaucratic mechanism. It also weakens the dependence of the officials upon the hierarchy. This holds at least for the large administrative bodies that are difficult to supervise. The superior qualification and integrity of federal judges, appointed by the President, as over against elected judges in the United States is well known, although both types of officials have been selected primarily in terms of party considerations. The great changes in American metropolitan administrations demanded by reformers have proceeded essentially from elected mayors working with an apparatus of officials who were appointed by them. These reforms have thus come about in a "Caesarist" fashion. Viewed technically, as an organized form of authority, the efficiency of "Caesarism," which often grows out of democracy, rests in general upon the position of the "Caesar" as a free trustee of the masses (of the army or of the citizenry), who is unfettered by tradition. The "Caesar" is thus the unrestrained master of a body of highly qualified military officers and officials whom he selects freely and personally without regard to tradition or to any other considerations. This "rule of the personal genius," however, stands in contradiction to the formally "democratic" principle of a universally elected officialdom.

3. Normally, the position of the official is held for life, at least in public bureaucracies; and this is increasingly the case for all similar structures. As a factual rule, *tenure for life* is presupposed, even where the giving of notice or periodic reappointment occurs. In contrast to the worker in a private enterprise, the official normally holds tenure. Legal or actual life-tenure, however, is not recognized as the official's right to the possession of office, as was the case with many structures of authority in the past. Where legal guarantees against arbitrary dismissal or transfer are developed, they merely serve to guarantee a strictly objective discharge of specific office duties free from all personal considerations. In Germany, this is the case for all juridical and, increasingly, for all administrative officials.

Within the bureaucracy, therefore, the measure of "independence," legally guaranteed by tenure, is not always a source of increased status for the official whose position is thus secured. Indeed, often the reverse holds, especially in old cultures and communities that are highly differentiated. In such communities, the stricter the subordination under the arbitrary rule of the master, the more it guarantees the maintenance of the conventional seigneurial style of living for the official. Because of the very absence of these legal guarantees of tenure, the conventional esteem for the official may rise in the same way as, during the Middle Ages, the esteem of the nobility of office rose at the expense of esteem for the freemen, and as the king's judge surpassed that of the people's judge. In Germany, the military officer or the administrative official can be removed from office at any time, or at least far more readily than the "independent judge," who never pays with loss of his office for even the grossest offense against the "code of honor" or against social conventions of the salon. For this very reason, if other things are equal, in the eyes of the master stratum the judge is considered less qualified for social intercourse than are officers and administrative officials, whose greater dependence on the master is a greater guarantee of their conformity with status conventions. Of course, the average official strives for a civil-service law, which would materially secure his old age and provide increased guarantees against his arbitrary removal from office. This striving, however, has its limits. A very strong development of the "right to the office" naturally makes it more difficult to staff them with regard to technical efficiency, for such a development decreases the career-opportunities of ambitious candidates for office. This makes for the fact that officials, on the whole, do not feel their dependency upon those at the top. This lack of a feeling of dependency, however, rests primarily upon the inclination to depend upon one's equals rather than upon the socially inferior and governed strata. The present conservative movement among the Badenia clergy, occasioned by the anxiety of a presumably threatening separation of church and state, has been expressly determined by the desire not to be turned "from a master into a servant of the parish."

4. The official receives the regular pecuniary compensation of a normally fixed salary and the old age security provided by a pension. The salary is not measured like a wage in terms of work done, but according to "status," that is, according to the kind of function (the "rank") and, in addition, possibly, according to the length of service. The relatively great security of the official's income, as well as the rewards of social esteem, make the office a sought-after position, especially in countries which no longer provide opportunities for colonial profits. In such countries, this situation permits relatively low salaries for officials.

5. The official is set for a "career" within the hierarchical order of the public service. He moves from the lower, less important, and

lower paid to the higher positions. The average official naturally desires
a mechanical fixing of the conditions of promotion: if not of the offices,
at least of the salary levels. He wants these conditions fixed in terms
of "seniority," or possibly according to grades achieved in a developed
system of expert examinations. Here and there, such examinations
actually form a character *indelebilis* of the official and have lifelong
effects on his career. To this is joined the desire to qualify the right to
office and the increasing tendency toward status group closure and
economic security. All of this makes for a tendency to consider the
offices as "prebends" of those who are qualified by educational certificates. The necessity of taking general personal and intellectual qualifications into consideration, irrespective of the often subaltern character
of the educational certificate, has led to a condition in which the highest
political offices, especially the positions of "ministers," are principally
filled without reference to such certificates.

•   •   •   •   •   •

TECHNICAL ADVANTAGES OF BUREAUCRATIC ORGANIZATION

The decisive reason for the advance of bureaucratic organization has
always been its purely technical superiority over any other form of organization. The fully developed bureaucratic mechanism compares
with other organizations exactly as does the machine with the non-
mechanical modes of production.

Precision, speed, unambiguity, knowledge of the files, continuity, discretion, unity, strict subordination, reduction of friction and of material
and personal costs—these are raised to the optimum point in the strictly
bureaucratic administration, and especially in its monocratic form. As
compared with all collegiate, honorific, and avocational forms of administration, trained bureaucracy is superior on all these points. And
as far as complicated tasks are concerned, paid bureaucratic work is not
only more precise but, in the last analysis, it is often cheaper than even
formally unremunerated honorific service.

Honorific arrangements make administrative work an avocation and,
for this reason alone, honorific service normally functions more slowly;
being less bound to schemata and being more formless. Hence it is
less precise and less unified than bureaucratic work because it is less
dependent upon superiors and because the establishment and exploitation of the apparatus of subordinate officials and filing services are almost
unavoidably less economical. Honorific service is less continuous than
bureaucratic and frequently quite expensive. This is especially the

case if one thinks not only of the money costs to the public treasury—costs which bureaucratic administration, in comparison with administration by notables, usually substantially increases—but also of the frequent economic losses of the governed caused by delays and lack of precision. The possibility of administration by notables normally and permanently exists only where official management can be satisfactorily discharged as an avocation. With the qualitative increase of tasks the administration has to face, administration by notables reaches its limits—today, even in England. Work organized by collegiate bodies causes friction and delay and requires compromises between colliding interests and views. The administration, therefore, runs less precisely and is more independent of superiors; hence, it is less unified and slower. All advances of the Prussian administrative organization have been and will in the future be advances of the bureaucratic, and especially of the monocratic, principle.

Today, it is primarily the capitalist market economy which demands that the official business of the administration be discharged precisely, unambiguously, continuously, and with as much speed as possible. Normally, the very large, modern capitalist enterprises are themselves unequalled models of strict bureaucratic organization. Business management throughout rests on increasing precision, steadiness, and, above all, the speed of operations. This, in turn, is determined by the peculiar nature of the modern means of communication, including, among other things, the news service of the press. The extraordinary increase in the speed by which public announcements, as well as economic and political facts, are transmitted exerts a steady and sharp pressure in the direction of speeding up the tempo of administrative reaction towards various situations. The optimum of such reaction time is normally attained only by a strictly bureaucratic organization.[1]

Bureaucratization offers above all the optimum possibility for carrying through the principle of specializing administrative functions according to purely objective considerations. Individual performances are allocated to functionaries who have specialized training and who by constant practice learn more and more. The "objective" discharge of business primarily means a discharge of business according to *calculable rules* and "without regard for persons."

"Without regard for persons" is also the watchword of the "market" and, in general, of all pursuits of naked economic interests. A consistent execution of bureaucratic domination means the leveling of status "honor." Hence, if the principle of the free-market is not at the same

---

[1] Here we cannot discuss in detail how the bureaucratic apparatus may, and actually does, produce definite obstacles to the discharge of business in a manner suitable for the single case.

time restricted, it means the universal domination of the "class situation." That this consequence of bureaucratic domination has not set in everywhere, parallel to the extent of bureaucratization, is due to the differences among possible principles by which polities may meet their demands.

The second element mentioned, "calculable rules," also is of paramount importance for modern bureaucracy. The peculiarity of modern culture, and specifically of its technical and economic basis, demands this very "calculability" of results. When fully developed, bureaucracy also stands, in a specific sense, under the principle of *sine ira ac studio*. Its specific nature, which is welcomed by capitalism, develops the more perfectly the more the bureaucracy is "dehumanized," the more completely it succeeds in eliminating from official business love, hatred, and all purely personal, irrational, and emotional elements which escape calculation. This is the specific nature of bureaucracy and it is appraised as its special virtue.

The more complicated and specialized modern culture becomes, the more its external supporting apparatus demands the personally detached and strictly "objective" expert, in lieu of the master of older social structures, who was moved by personal sympathy and favor, by grace and gratitude. Bureaucracy offers the attitudes demanded by the external apparatus of modern culture in the most favorable combination.

❧❧❧❧

49. *Natural versus Artificial Aristocracy* *

THE STRUCTURE AND EVOLUTION of institutions in any society are shaped by the "ideas" and "ideals" of its leaders. Here an early leader and a great architect of our basic institutions, Thomas Jefferson, presents one of his fundamental ideas: good government requires that public office be filled from the ranks of the natural aristocracy by free election of the citizens.

FOR I AGREE . . . that there is a natural aristocracy among men. The grounds of this are virtue and talents. Formerly, bodily powers gave

---

* Saul K. Padover, ed., *Thomas Jefferson on Democracy* (New York: Appleton-Century-Crofts, 1939), Chapter V. Reprinted by permission of the publisher and the editor.

Thomas Jefferson (1743-1826) was an American statesman and third President of the United States. A champion of democratic ideals. Wrote final draft of Declaration of Independence and was one of the signers.

place among the aristoi. But since the invention of gunpowder has armed the weak as well as the strong with missile death, bodily strength, like beauty, good humor, politeness and other accomplishments, has become but an auxiliary ground of distinction. There is also an artificial aristocracy, founded on wealth and birth, without either virtue or talents; for with these it would belong to the first class. The natural aristocracy I consider as the most precious gift of nature, for the instruction, the trusts, and government of society. . . .

May we not even say, that that form of government is best, which provides the most effectually for a pure selection of these natural aristoi into the offices of government? The artificial aristocracy is a mis' chievous ingredient in government, and provision should be made to prevent its ascendancy. . . . I think the best remedy is exactly that pro- vided by all our constitutions, to leave to the citizens the free election and separation of the aristoi from the pseudo-aristoi, of the wheat from the chaff. In general they will elect the really good and wise. In some instances, wealth may corrupt, and birth blind them; but not in suf- ficient degree to endanger the society. . . .

At the first session of our legislature after the Declaration of Inde- pendence, we passed a law abolishing entails. And this was followed by one abolishing the privilege of primogeniture, and dividing the lands of intestates equally among all their children. . . . These laws, drawn by myself, laid the ax to the foot of pseudo-aristocracy. And had another which I prepared been adopted by the legislature, our work would have been complete. It was a bill for the more general diffusion of learning. This proposed to divide every county into wards of five or six miles square . . . ; to establish in each ward a free school for read- ing, writing and common arithmetic; to provide for the annual selection of the best subjects from these schools, who might receive, at the public expense, a higher degree of education at a district school; and from these district schools to select a certain number of the most promising subjects, to be completed at an University, where all the useful sciences should be taught. Worth and genius would thus have been sought out from every condition of life, and completely prepared by education for defeating the competition of wealth and birth for public trusts. . . . Although this law has not yet been acted on . . . , I have great hope that some patriotic spirit will, at a favorable moment, call it up, and make it the keystone of the arch of our government.

With respect to aristocracy, we should further consider, that before the establishment of the American States, nothing was known to history but the man of the old world, crowded within limits either small or overcharged, and steeped in the vices which that situation generates.

A government adapted to such men would be one thing; but a very different one, that for the man of these States. Here every one may have land to labor for himself, if he chooses; or, preferring the exercise of any other industry, may exact for it such compensation as not only to afford a comfortable subsistence, but wherewith to provide for a cessation from labor in old age. Every one, by his property or by his satisfactory situation, is interested in the support of law and order. And such men may safely and advantageously reserve to themselves a wholesome control over their public affairs, and a degree of freedom which, in the hands of the canaille of the cities of Europe, would be instantly perverted to the demolition and destruction of everything public and private.

꧁꧂

50. The Beginning of Religion *

THIS ARTICLE, taken from the first chapter of Clifford Kirkpatrick's *Religion in Human Affairs*, stresses the all-pervading part that religious institutions and beliefs play in the life of mankind. Illustrations of the innumerable forms they have taken are used to emphasize the universality as well as the diversity of "phenomena almost as old as man himself which have loomed large in human experience even down to the present day." Kirkpatrick also makes clear that ethnocentric attitudes often prove serious obstacles to our understanding of the nature and functions of religious institutions.

THE BEGINNING of religion is unknown. From the very dawn of human history man is found bending his knee in supplication to unknown powers, practicing dark rites to achieve his ends, and creating a rich and varied mass of myths, superstitions, and beliefs concerning gods

* Clifford Kirkpatrick. Reprinted by permission from *Religion in Human Affairs*, pp. 1-11, published by John Wiley & Sons, Inc., 1929.
The author (b. 1898) is Professor and Chairman, Department of Sociology, Indiana University. Team research director, U. S. Strategic Bombing Survey, Germany, 1945. Received D. S. Cross, 1918. Chairman, Research Committee on Marriage and the Family, National Council on Family Relations. Author, *Capital Punishment, Intelligence and Immigration, Nazi Germany—Its Women and Family Life, What Science Says about Happiness in Marriage, Report of Research into Attitudes and Habits of Radio Listeners*. Has written articles for numerous periodicals. Contributed ten chapters to *Man and His World*.

and devils, spirits, fays, and god-like heroes. Countless gods have been cast down and have faded from the mind of man; thousands of ceremonies have sunk into oblivion, or linger on stripped of their meaning and original emotional appeal. Invariably, however, new manifestations of man's religious nature have sprung up to take their place.

Many centuries before the birth of Christ clear evidence of a highly developed religion is to be found in Egypt. Since that time an ever-changing panorama of cults and creeds, beliefs and practices has been unrolled. The picture is often blurred. A lack of data makes analysis most difficult. There is a strange fusion of religious beliefs and rites, and when the historical record is complete it frequently discloses only the dry bones of what was once a warm and living human experience. Furthermore, from the Eskimo to the Patagonian, from the Veddah of Ceylon to the Bushman of Africa, one finds the earth covered with countless groups, large and small, each with some means, more or less peculiar to itself, of approaching the supernatural. How is it possible to find uniformity in such diversity, or order in such confusion?

Who can say that the religious experience of an American of the twentieth century corresponds to that of the Australian aborigine or the Hindu mystic, or that any one religion typifies the religious experience of the entire human race? One cannot know the stature of Englishmen from the measurements of two or three Britons. Neither is it possible to draw general conclusions concerning religious experience from a small number of localities or from limited periods of time.

What is religion and what are the criteria of the religious? These are questions that will offer difficulty and perhaps can receive no complete answer. Religion merges with magic and with mythology. It is bound up with social and political organization. It joins hands at times with art and literature. It enters into economic life, as among the Todas where religion centers upon the production and use of milk, and the dairyman is the priest. Ethical and religious concepts are frequently found in close alliance, as in Confucianism. In fact, it is a question whether Confucianism in its original form should not be regarded as a system of ethics rather than as a religion.

Often religions show a strange blend in regard to motive and ritual. As Carpenter points out,

Among the Indians of North America speculation is sometimes highly elaborated in mythological tradition; and out of the fusion of nationalities in Mexico rose a developed polytheism in which lofty religious sentiment seems strangely blended with a hideous and sanguinary ritual. Peru, no less, presented to the Spanish conquerors bewildering and incongruous aspects. In these two cultures native American civilization reached its highest forms. In Mexico the apparatus of religion was minutely organized. There were immense temples, which required large numbers of priests and servitors. The capital alone is said to have contained 2,000 sacred buildings, and the great temple had a staff of 5,000 priests. There were religious orders and temple-schools; rites of baptism and circumcision; feasts and sacrifices and sacraments, in which the monkish chroniclers found strange parallels to their own practice.

Religion may thus be infinitely complex and may enter into every phase of human experience and resist any attempt to isolate it and place it on the operating table for dissection and examination.

Even when the external forms are accurately described, how is the observer to project himself into the minds of the worshipers and share their subtle emotional experiences?

Twice a year was the great Mexican deity Huitzilopochtli presented in the form of dough images to his worshipers, and with elaborate ceremonies was consumed. Tezxatlipoca, in like manner, chief god of the Aztecs, represented by a handsome and noble captive wearing the divine emblems, was slain on the great altar; the body of the victim was respectfully carried down into the court below, divided into small pieces, and distributed among the priests and nobles as blessed food.

How difficult it is to fathom the mental processes of the participants in this ceremony; the anticipated results, the emotions of awe and reverence, the degree of belief in the efficacy of the rite!

Another difficulty is suggested by the above example. Suppose that one of the priests were asked to explain the meaning of the ceremony, have we any assurance that his interpretation would fairly represent the beliefs and feelings of the mass of the people? One should be on guard against assuming religious homogeneity even within the same group. Would a curious observer from Mars obtain the same interpretation of the Christian religion from a theologian and an ignorant laborer?

· · · · · ·

It may be helpful to show more definitely the effects of bias acquired in a particular cultural atmosphere. Not long ago the students of religion made their initial classification of religion on the basis of truth or falsity, thus introducing bias into the analysis at the very beginning. "Dr. Johnson could sententiously declare that 'there are two objects of curiosity: the Christian world and the Mohammedan world—all the rest may be considered as barbarous.'"

Even the very definition of a problem and the use of descriptive terms reflect the bias of a particular culture. Says Parson Thwackum in *Tom Jones*, "When I mention religion, I mean the Christian religion; and not only the Christian religion but the Protestant religion;.and not only the Protestant religion, but the Church of England." Perhaps, after all, such an explicit statement is not objectionable, for it is conceivable that more subtle identification of religion with personal concepts and standards may be fraught with greater danger of error.

• • • • • •

In view of the difficulties outlined a word should be said concerning the aim of this study of religion. Its purpose is to explain something of the origin, nature, and significance in social life of man's religious attitude. No attempt will be made to pass judgment on the ultimate truth or falsity of religious beliefs, for that is the field of theology and philosophy. We are interested solely in observable facts and their relationships, and merely seek to understand rather than to praise or blame religious beliefs and customs. The chemist accepts his elements without terming them good or bad, and without trying to wish others into existence. We shall try to follow this example in our own field of discussion.

It is legitimate, however, to speculate as to the stage in the evolution of man in which the first dim consciousness of the supernatural came into existence. Do animals have religion? The question is interesting, although to attempt a complete answer would anticipate our later discussion of the exact meaning of religion and magic. Some writers have attempted to demonstrate the beginnings of religion in the higher animals. Such a demonstration is facilitated if the famous view of Hobbes be accepted that the essence of all religion is fear. It is alleged that the strange, the mysterious, and the fearful excite in higher animals what is equivalent to the religious thrill of humans. An oft-cited experiment of Romanes consisted in attaching a fine thread to a bone and thus terrifying a dog by producing movements without any visible cause. Spencer mentions the emotion of a dog in the presence of an umbrella mysteriously moved by the wind. Such anecdotes have little significance since the exact conditions and the past experiences of the dogs are unknown. The situation may have had something in common with a past situation involving pain or injury. It is a question also whether a deity exists for the devoted dog in the master who dispenses praise and blame, rewards and punishments. This claim is a more or less futile attempt to interpret canine behavior in human terms.

Frazer, in arguing for the early development of magic prior to the appearance of religion through the mistaken association of ideas, a theory which we shall examine later, says:

The very beasts associate the ideas of things that are like each other or that have been found together in their experience; and they could hardly survive for a day if they ceased to do so. But who attributes to the animals a belief that the phenomena of nature are worked by a multitude of invisible animals or by one enormous and prodigiously strong animal behind the scenes? It is probably no injustice to the brutes to assume that the honour of devising a theory of this latter sort must be reserved for human reason.

Even if mistaken associations of ideas were the whole story of magic it is stretching a point to attribute either worship or sorcery to animals. True, they do form associations or conditioned responses so as to react to some element of a past situation or according to a new *gestalt*, yet no dog shuns the flesh of a rabbit for fear of acquiring the timidity of that animal nor does a cat scratch an image of a dog with the belief that the canine himself will suffer accordingly. While the dog may fawn upon the human he does not pray to a mental image of his master. Animals do not often react to things not present nor do they apparently have conscious anticipation as a rule of the future results of present acts.

What then is the mental basis of the supernaturalism which is essentially peculiar to man? Three things may be mentioned: (1) imagination, (2) complex emotional development, and (3) language, as made possible by highly developed association areas in the human brain. Imagination is the power of the human organism to store up impressions, to condense them into images or symbols and to recombine them and project them into the future. Man makes his gods by means of his imagination just as he does his scientific systems although he is less inclined in the former case to check up his conceptions with the aid of observation. Again the emotional life of humans is more complicated than that of animals. Awe, love, reverence, wonder and other more or less complex emotional states are possible to him and may be associated with ideas or sub-vocal responses corresponding to things not present to the senses. Such systems of ideas and emotions may be called complexes, sentiments or attitudes and constitute the very core of religious life. Finally, it should be noted that the human power of speech makes possible the transmission of religious beliefs and practices from one generation to another.

The conclusion then must be that magico-religious behavior is not found at the sub-human level but there is reason to think that when man acquired his essentially human traits religion soon appeared. It is something of a paradox that the common-sense behavior of animals degenerates in man, at least for a time, into fantastic magic and gross superstition. The animal fears its natural enemy but being blessed with no imagination does not people the world with evil spirits, demons, hobgoblins, witches and wrathful gods nor does it devise the eight Hells of Japanese Buddhism with their excruciating and eternal tortures for hapless souls.

It has already been ventured that man did not have to rise far from the brute level before his religious life began. The best evidence of this is furnished by anthropology and archeology. Let us take a hasty glance at what these sciences have to show us concerning the antiquity of religion. Unfortunately religious practices are not preserved to us as are stone tools, yet Kroeber writes:

As far back as the Mousterian, thirty thousand years ago, certain practices were being observed by the Neanderthal race of western Europe which modern savages observe in obedience to the dictates of their religion. When these people of the Mousterian laid away their dead, they put some of their belongings with them. When existing nations do this, it is invariably in connection with a belief in the continued existence of the soul after death. We may reasonably conclude therefore that even in this long-distant period human beings had arrived at a crude recognition of the difference between flesh and spirit; in short, religion had come into being.

Somewhat later the Cro-Magnon people folded and painted the bodies of their dead, and buried flint implements and food in their graves.

Ancient skulls have been found pierced presumably to permit the egress of evil spirits believed to cause headaches, if we can judge the purpose of contemporary practices of some primitive people. Another line of evidence is found in the cave paintings dating back some twenty thousand years. Whitnall says that, "Practically all the finest paintings are of animals that were used for food." Furthermore these paintings are found in the most distant and secluded portions of the caves and in this respect at least justify the term "Prehistoric Sanctuary" applied by Marret to one of these caves at Niaux. Recently an underwater swim through a subterranean stream by an adventurous archeologist revealed in a cavern at Montespan the clay image of a bear apparently pierced with spear thrusts. Many of the animals painted on the walls of the French caves are found to be wounded in vital spots.

These latter facts take on significance when it is recalled that many peoples the world over have magic rites in which a desired act or achievement is imitated in the hope and doubtless belief that a mysterious connection between the symbol and the reality will give them the effect desired. Living races pierce images of animals they wish to kill, sprinkle water to produce rain and perform other magical rites. Certainly the hypothesis that magico-religious beliefs and practices entered into the life of man at least twenty thousand years ago is in accord with these facts.

Again, the universality of some sort of religion among the peoples of the entire earth suggests great antiquity for religion. If magic and religion were developed but once in the history of the human race as some anthropologists are inclined to believe, then it must have taken a long time for them to diffuse over the world. On the other hand, if magico-religious practices originated several times and in different places it still would probably mean a venerable age for this social invention. If such an invention were difficult to hit upon it would have taken a long period of time for all peoples to make the discovery, while if it were a natural and inevitable product of the human mind it would have come into being in the dim mists of antiquity when mind first reached the human level, perhaps before the original dispersion of the human species. In studying religion, we are consequently dealing with phenomena almost as old as man himself which have loomed large in human experience even down to the present day.

❦❦❦❦❦

51. Trends in Religious Thought That Affect Social Outlook *

ONE FUNDAMENTAL PROBLEM that confronts the social scientist is the interaction between beliefs, attitudes, and social behavior. Two quotations, one from the *Bible* and one from a famous American thinker, indicate the wide range of possible interpretations. "As a man thinketh in his heart, so is he"; and "As he [a man] acts so he feels and thinks." Professor Tillich deals with one important facet of this complicated problem. As a great philoso-

* Paul J. Tillich. Reprinted by permission from *Religion and World Order* edited by F. Ernest Johnson, pp. 17-28, Institute for Religious Studies, New York. 1944.
The author (b. 1886) is Professor of Philosophy and Theology, Union Theological Seminary, New York. Born in Prussia. Early career in teaching at Berlin, Marburg, Dresden, Leipzig, Frankfurt am Main. Tailor Lecturer, Yale, 1935. Terry

pher and theologian, he interprets for us some of the meanings that
religious thought has given about the nature of man and his universe.
He shows how and why these meanings have a direct affect upon our
social attitudes and therefore on our social relationships.

RELIGIOUS THOUGHT is able to affect social outlook, because religion is
our relation to what concerns us ultimately. Religion at its center is
ultimate, unconditional, inescapable concern. Therefore, religion is
the expression of the meaning of our life as a whole. It is related to
every realm of human existence. Religion is not a province beside other
provinces of the human mind. It is never "beside" not even in the
sense of "above." It is the ultimate concern in all preliminary concerns,
the center of all theoretical and practical activities, the inexhaustible
meaning in everything that has meaning. Religious thought can influence social outlook, because religious thought deals with the ultimate
meaning of man's social existence as much as it deals with the ultimate
meaning of man's scientific, moral, political, aesthetic existence. It
cannot be separated from any of them, because religious thought deals
with existence as such. Only as this basic and inclusive concept of
religion is recognized, can the relation of religion to the social realm
be described adequately.

But after the first and affirmative answer to the question has been
stated, a second and restrictive answer must follow. Religion has not
only the fundamental and universal meaning just mentioned, but it also
has a derived and particular meaning, namely, a system of symbols, actions and emotions in which the meaning of our existence is expressed.
Religion in this secondary sense, for instance, an organized church, is a
separate realm and cannot claim authority over the special structures
of the other realms. Therefore religion as a special sphere of human
existence—although based on the ultimate meaning of all human existence—should not try to interfere with the other spheres. It should
not try to exercise scientific or artistic or economic or political authority.
If it does so the other spheres revolt against it, as they did at the end
of the Middle Ages, and thus religion is deprived of its central and all
embracing significance. Church interference is not the answer to the
question of the relation between religion and the social order.

A third answer must be found, uniting the universal affirmative
character of the first one with the restrictive character of the second
one. Religious thought can influence social outlook by showing the
ultimate meaning of human existence and the presupposition of its

Lecturer, 1950. Among his books are *The Religious Situation, The Interpretation of
History, The Protestant Era, The Shaking of Foundations,* and *Systematic Theology.*

realization in human nature and destiny. It is much too narrow to restrict the import of religion to the ethical implications of social life. They themselves are based on an interpretation of man and his world. Without such an interpretation social as well as ethical demands and purposes are without a ground and norm. Without a basic understanding of human finiteness and tragedy, of historical time and the nature of the historical process, of the interdependence of personality and community, of the relation between nature and history, between body and mind, between reason and the irrational—without these no social program has a lasting significance.

The basic definition of religion as ultimate concern implies that religious thought cannot be separated from philosophy. All methodical thought has philosophical presuppositions and philosophy, if it is more than an academic matter, must ask for the meaning of being in general and of human existence in particular. It does so upon assumptions and by means which differ from the ways of religious thought. But it cannot avoid the question of the ultimate. In this sense genuine philosophy has a religious character, not by intention but by implication, and cannot be separated from other forms of religious thought.

It seems to me most adequate to distinguish the different types of religious thought which affect social outlook by their different interpretations of the nature of man. The nature of man can be understood first in terms of his essential, created character—mythologically speaking, of his original goodness. The nature of man can be understood secondly in terms of his existential, self-determined character—mythologically speaking, of his distortion by the fall. Only in man is this dual consideration possible, because only man has the freedom which enables him to contradict his own essential goodness. Human freedom necessitates the distinction between man's essential and existential nature. The nature of man can be understood, thirdly, in terms of a permanent conflict between his essential and his existential nature—mythologically speaking, of the process of his salvation. From this threefold interpretation of human nature follow three possibilities of religious thought affecting the social outlook:

1) A type of religious thought which emphasizes man's essential nature and neglects the existential distortion of it;

2) A type of religious thought which emphasizes man's existential situation and neglects his essential goodness;

3) A type of religious thought which emphasizes the tension between man's essential goodness and his existential distortion.

Each of these types of religious thought has special consequences for the social outlook.

I

If man's essential nature is emphasized over against man's existential distortion, mankind is considered to be a part of nature, developing like nature from potentiality to actuality. On this view history is the actualization of human potentialities. Many things are not yet actualized but they will be in the progress of history. The "not yet," the shortcomings in the historical self-realization of human nature, are natural and will be progressively eliminated. In a process of emergent evolution man will reach the stage in which his essential possibilities are realized. There is a providential harmony between the free will of man (which could disturb the course of natural evolution) and the development of the whole. In the long run man will actualize all his potentialities under the guidance of God Who is interpreted as the moral world order, or the progressive synthesis of the elements of being and value, or the creative ideal of goodness. Although the individual man is free to oppose the general progress and to frustrate possibilities of a creative synthesis in himself and in others, the progressive development as a whole is guaranteed. All human potentialities will be actualized in the process of history. Divine Providence—philosophically speaking, the preestablished harmony between the individual and the whole— is the guarantee of the progressive synthesis.

Man, for this type of theological thought, is essentially intact. Reason, his determining and distinguishing quality, is not distorted, at least not in principle. There is, of course, a gap between man's high bodily and low spiritual perfection; there were and there still are infantile stages in man's development; persistent difficulties attend man's effort to adapt himself mentally and socially to the structure of our world. But this handicap is not insurmountable. In many respects it already has been overcome and it certainly will be entirely overcome in a not indefinitely remote future. The history of mankind is a long educational process in which man's rational possibilities will become increasingly realized. The history of religion is a process of cumulative experience in which ever higher truths and values are realized. God is the driving power toward the victory of reason over pure nature within man and outside of him. Christ is an outstanding, perhaps the outstanding agency of Divine Providence.

This is the theological attitude of bourgeois humanism, since the Renaissance discovered the greatness of man's essential nature and Erasmus defended human freedom against Luther's doctrine of human bondage. This is the theology of the leaders of Deism and Enlightenment, of the German classical philosophers and poets, including Schleiermacher and Hegel. This is the doctrine of Ritschl, of the theology of the Social Gospel, of moralistic theism and so-called theological humanism. In spite of the differences between these theologians and philsophers of religion, they all represent an interpretation of essential life which is based on the belief in the integrity of man's rational nature.

The social outlook which follows from this type of theology is strongly interrelated with the development of modern bourgeois society, of which it is the ideological self-interpretation. Bourgeois society has developed in three main stages in which the bourgeoisie is seen as successfully attacking, controlling and defending. The social outlook was different in each of these stages and so was the attitude toward religion and Christianity. The fighting bourgeoisie had a strong feeling for its historical vocation. The period of reason, the final aim of history has begun. Man has become in principle what he essentially is—mature in his reason. The infantile and adolescent stages of the long "pre-history" of mankind are past. Real history, namely the development of man on the basis of mature rationality has begun with the rise of an enlightened bourgeoisie. Religious symbols which do not fit into this new self-interpretation of man are superstitious remnants of the youth of mankind. They must be dismissed or transformed. The age of autonomy and rational self-determination is at hand. Liberal politics, democratic procedures and progressive education have become possible. Their application will bring to perfection what in principle is given: Man's rational maturity.

In the period of the victorious bourgeoisie the social outlook became less revolutionary and more evolutionary. The belief in reason became less enthusiastic and more sober, more scientific and finally more technical. The fighting reason was replaced by the calculating reason. Progress was slowed down by a large amount of political and social conservatism. The ruling bourgeoisie is afraid of the revolutionary impetus of its fighting period. It can accept more of the traditional religious symbols, using them as a helpful ideology for the masses which are not supposed to know that the enlightened leaders themselves do not believe any more in traditional religion. But this does not prevent the theologians of this period from demanding and hoping for an increase in enlightenment, liberalism, democracy, peace and universal justice. The pursuit of individual interest will not seriously hamper the growing world community; on the contrary, it will be the way to foster it. Pacifism and the Social Gospel are the most important movements representing the social outlook of this period.

When it became apparent that the contradictions within the assumed system of harmonic development were so profound that they practically disrupted the harmony, the third stage of bourgeois society started, the stage of defense and decay. The basic presupposition, man's essential integrity, was still maintained. But the belief that the period of rational maturity already has been reached was given up. A new start, after a revolutionary transformation, is held to be necessary. The substantial advance in theory is frustrated by the slight advance in practice—in social practice, as Marxism emphasized; in personal practice, as the doctrine of man since Nietzsche and Freud has shown. The utopian forms of early Religious Socialism made the same point, identifying the proletarian revolution with the coming of the Kingdom of God. Although these ideas did not transcend the bourgeois frame of thought, especially the interpretation of man's nature by Renaissance and Enlightenment, they prepared the breaking of that frame by making manifest the contradictions within it.

II

The second type of theology, opposing the first, denies that there is any approach to man's essential nature, either because it does not exist or because it has been lost completely. The former possibility is represented by pessimistic naturalism, the latter by pessimistic supranaturalism. Both forms of this theology have made their appearance in great strength in connection with the disintegration of bourgeois society in its third stage. And both forms had a tremendous influence on social outlook.

Naturalistic pessimism developed very early as the inescapable shadow of rationalism. Again and again the leaders of Enlightenment and the profounder spirits of the nineteenth century questioned the optimistic presupposition that there is a harmony between nature and reason, that rational progress is rooted in the nature of things, be it called Divine Providence or pre-established harmony. If we look into the depths of human nature we discover irrational and even antirational forces such as will to power, cupidity, will to death, destructiveness, anxiety and despair. If we look into the depths of man's social existence we discover a cruel fight for survival in the masses and a brutal conquest and maintenance of power in the ruling classes. We discover an unimaginable amount of individual and social suffering and we are inclined to replace the progressivist by a tragic interpretation of human life. This naturalistic pessimism expresses itself in half-theological philosophies or a purely individualistic, will-to-power philosophy. It is the attitude which supports the present attack on the traditional religions and their systems of value. For the quasi-theology of naturalistic pessimism man is neither intact nor distorted. He is as he is, no essential perfection can be posited over against his real existence.

The social outlook following from this type of naturalistic theology is determined by the unrestricted acceptance of the power principle. Instead of Divine Providence which guarantees social progress, different and changing powers, aristocracies, nations, races, cultures, classes, control the incalculable course of history. Liberal and democratic ideas are weapons in the hands of the rulers as long as they can use them and will be discarded in favor of authoritarian systems as soon as they become weapons in the hands of the ruled masses. No rational structure of society is possible, reason can only be used as technical reason in the hands of the powerful groups in order to subject nature and society to their purposes. These are the social consequences of a doctrine of man which denies man's essential goodness.

They are very similar to the social outlook of the supranaturalistic form of theological pessimism which largely agrees with the naturalistic form with respect to man's actual situation, i.e., his existential nature. The same tragic contradictions in human existence to which pessimistic naturalism refers are emphasized in this type of theological thinking. Such concepts as anxiety, despair and melancholy are emphasized most forcefully by people like Kierkegaard and his contemporary followers. They all agree in a tragic, non-progressivist interpretation of history. The story of the "Tower of Babel" is used as the symbol of the tragic impossibility that mankind ever will reach political and cultural unity. On all these points both forms of pessimism agree. The main difference is that the supranaturalistic form affirms the loss of man's essential nature, its paradoxical restitution in the Christian event and its fragmentary visibility in the message of the Christian Church. But this does not refer to the social and cultural life outside the Church. No approach to essential manhood is possible through reason. Therefore no rational system of life can be expected. In spite of the revealed integrity of man's nature in Jesus as the Christ, no historical integrity or progress toward integrity can be imagined. The fulfilment is transcendent only. The Kingdom of God has nothing to do with history. History is left to man in his existential distortion and to the demonic powers controlling him.

The social outlook of this theology is not very different from that of pessimistic naturalism. The principle of power is interpreted as a consequence of human sin and is justified as a means of suppressing sin. Rational criteria to be applied against an existing state do not exist. The irrational power of the government must be acknowledged, even if it is destructive. Revolution is prohibited and in vain, because man's existential nature cannot be changed. So pessimistic supranaturalism betrays a very conservative character; it has no belief in social progress at all. It is interesting to note that Luther's pessimistic supranaturalism very early was compared to Machiavelli's pessimistic naturalism. Political absolutism could use the one as well as the other. Today Karl Barth's pessimistic supranaturalism has helped to destroy the Religious-Socialist attempts in pre-Hitler Germany to stop Nazism by creating a better social order on the basis of Christian principles. And even when Barth became a fanatical anti-Nazi he showed in his letter to the British Christians that it was not the common fight of people of all religions and creeds against the National-Socialist distortion of humanity that interested him, but the defense of the Church as the finger pointing only to heaven and not to earth. He challenges the British Christians to interpret the war in terms of secular humanism and not of religious transcendence. He, like all pessimistic supranaturalists, is not interested in history as such nor in a social transformation for the sake of humanity.

III

The third type of theology attempts a dialectical union of the first and the second type. It presupposes, on the one hand, the essential goodness of human nature; but it denies that human existence is a natural process in which his essential nature is gradually actualized. It presupposes, on the other hand, the existential distortion of human nature; but it denies that human existence is a natural process without the critical and promising presence of essential goodness. Man's essential nature is neither a mere ideology nor a merely transcendent possibility, but it is actual in history. It is not lacking or completely destroyed, but it is fragmentarily and ambiguously visible. Human history is neither a mere progress nor a mere tragedy, but it is a fight between the forces of perfection and those of distortion. The belief in Providence means that in this struggle the negative forces cannot ultimately prevail; but it does not guarantee any kind of harmonious progress. It gives the certainty that the victory over man's existential distortion is won from the point of view of eternity; but it does not give the certainty that there is or will be a victory at any point of history.

There are three main forms of this type, the social outlook of which is important for our present situation—Catholicism, Ecumenical Protestantism, and Dialectical Religious Socialism.

Roman Catholic theology emphasizes the large amount of essential goodness and rationality remaining in mankind after the fall of the first man. Although man's freedom and natural perfection are corrupted, they are not thoroughly distorted. Only the original supranatural gift of community with God is lost. But this was an addition to his essential goodness. Its loss means a weakening, but not an extinction of the divine image in man. Consequently man is able to prepare himself for the reception of grace. And grace, when received, is able to restore the integrity of human nature and reason in a process of progressive sanctification.

The social consequences of the Catholic doctrine of man are as dialectical as the picture of man itself is. On the basis of man's corrupted nature Catholicism acknowledges the principle of power and supports the earthly authorities. In this respect it often approximates the attitude of pessimistic supranaturalism. On the basis of man's preserved rationality Catholicism can accept liberal and democratic forms of life. In this respect it often approximates the theology of optimistic rationality. A balance between the two trends is permanently achieved by the Church and its authoritarian hierarchy on the basis of the restitution of the divine grace which was lost in the fall. Therefore the Church is the central factor in every social outlook of Roman Catholicism. The Church can favor power politics in a special situation and it can favor liberal politics in another situation. The criterion is always the ethical doctrines and political influence of the Church. This excludes Fascist totalitarianism as well as humanistic liberalism. A system in which the Church is not the central factor can be tolerated in terms of compromise but it cannot be accepted as true. There can be no doubt that the present world situation and the breakdown of autonomous Liberalism as well as of totalitarian Fascism offers an unexpected opportunity to the social outlook of Catholic theology.

The second form in which a dialectical union of the first and the second type of present theology is achieved is the theology of Ecumenical Protestantism. An ecumenical theology as a special theological method does not exist; but there are trends visible in all ecumenical thinking that justify the conception of an ecumenical theology. The ecumenical movement is a result of the fact that since the beginning of our century "world" in the historical sense has been established. World traffic and world economy were its presuppositions. World wars are its first actualization. A world union of the churches is its ideal projection. The unity of the Church as the "Assembly of God" or as the "Body of Christ" has always been emphasized—as much as the essential unity of mankind. But today "world" also means the historical-empirical unity of all nations in their interdependence. And "Church" should also mean the historical-empirical unity of all churches in their collaboration.

The ecumenical movement was started in the Anglo-Saxon countries under the strong influence of their missionary activities. It has slowly grasped the Continental churches, where the Continental Lutherans were most reluctant. The collaboration of the Greek Orthodox churches has slightly balanced American denominationalism, but the theological trends which have appeared up to now are essentially Protestant in origin and nature. They show two poles corresponding to the two main theological types we have distinguished. The one pole is represented by American progressivist optimism, the other by Continental tragic pessimism. The Anglican church mediates somewhat between the two poles, providing leadership which appreciates the dynamic impulses coming from the progressivist mood of America as much as the restraining reflections coming from the tragic mood of Europe.

The social outlook of Ecumenical Protestantism has found a very profound, radical and inclusive expression in the statements of the Oxford Conference, some of which show the spirit of a theological vanguard. But on the whole the social outlook of the ecumenical movement does not transcend very far the ideals of Anglo-Saxon democracy in the direction of a strongly social interpretation. The function of the churches according to these programs is not that of the Catholic Church, to balance authoritatively the different social forces. The ecumenical churches are supposed to influence indirectly, by teaching, example, spiritual power, temporal movements and authorities. They expect that the present world situation, especially the reaction against Fascist authoritarianism, will favor the non-Catholic churches at least as much as Roman Catholicism—if they are able to understand the general trend toward a new collectivism.

This condition of the effectiveness of the social outlook of ecumenical theology points to the remaining form of our third type of theology: Dialectical Religious Socialism. It is distinguished from the different utopian forms of Socialism generally and non-dialectical Religious Socialism in particular by accepting the pessimistic view of human existence emphasized by the second type of theology. But it is distinguished from the tragic interpretation of history by its revolutionary activism, and the element of progressivist feeling implied in every revolutionary action.

Religious Socialism in its dialectical form has largely accepted the Marxian analysis of bourgeois capitalism, while rejecting many philosophical doctrines of Marx and his followers. Main emphasis is laid on Marx's description of the dehumanization and alienation of man in the later stages of bourgeois society. This description is confirmed by an analysis of the present situation in all realms of human existence. Dialectical Religious Socialism has developed a theology the social outlook of which is not an accidental consequence but an essential element. Human existence is interpreted with reference to the concrete social existence of our period. Historical concreteness and universal validity are united. On this basis a religious interpretation of history is given, which tries to avoid utopianism as well as historical indifference. It believes in the *Kairos*, the right moment of time, in which eternity breaks into history and demands a decisive step, without assuming that this step will lead into an immanent or transcendent stage of perfection. The doctrine of the *Kairos* unites in a special way theological optimism and pessimism and overcomes the alternative.

Dialectical Religious Socialism is not represented by a powerful group or a mass movement. It is the attitude of small groups all over the world. Neither the churches nor labor movements nor political parties are the representatives of Religious Socialism. But there are individuals everywhere who understand the signs of our time and who have a social outlook on the basis of a more developed theology. It is my conviction, that neither the Catholic Church nor Ecumenical Protestantism but the spirit of these small groups will determine the future of mankind.

⋘⋘⋙⋙

52. Religion and Hard Times: A Study of the Holy Rollers *

MAJOR INSTITUTIONS of a society are often interrelated. The complexity of these interrelationships clearly manifests itself in our religious and economic institutions. Not only do economic conditions affect religious forms and experiences but even in "normal" times the various classes of a society often express fundamental religious beliefs quite differently from each other. This variety of expression holds especially true for Christian Protestantism. Anton Boisen's study of the Holy Rollers reveals that their membership is largely recruited from an economically and socially underprivileged

---

* Anton T. Boisen, *Social Action*, 5, No. 3 (March 15, 1939), 8-35. Reprinted by permission of the Council for Social Action and the author.

The author (b. 1876) is Chaplain Emeritus, Elgin State Hospital, Elgin, Illinois. Research associate and lecturer, Chicago Theological Seminary, 1925-42. Made social and religious surveys for several years. Has had articles in *American Journal of Psychiatry*, *American Journal of Sociology*, and *Journal of Pastoral Care*. Author, *Exploration of the Inner World* (manuscript read by A. R. Radcliffe-Brown) and *Problems in Religion and Life, A Manual for Pastors*.

class. These people seem to find compensation for their social ills in an austere yet colorful religious fervor. Through the author's study and analysis of his observations among this sect the social and psychological significance of religious expression takes on added meaning.

THE PERIOD since the depression began has been marked by the growth of eccentric forms of religion. One of these, the "Holy Rollers," is the subject of this study. This term is applied popularly to a number of sects which cultivate an extreme form of mystical religion. They belong to the "Holiness" group, holding in common the doctrine that in addition to the experience of "conversion" the true Christian must have also the experience of "sanctification." As distinct from other Holiness sects, the Holy Rollers require also the experience of being "baptized by the Holy Spirit." Evidence of this baptism of the Spirit they find in the phenomenon of "speaking with tongues" as described in the account of the Day of Pentecost which is given in the second chapter of the Book of Acts. Along with this go other abnormal manifestations such as dancing, jumping, jerking, thrusting up the hands, falling on the floor and even passing into states of unconsciousness.

• • • • • •

HOW THEY GET STARTED

Back of this growth [in membership] is vigorous missionary activity, directed often by a strongly centralized organization. The leaders are generally men of limited education but earnest and of considerable ability. Some of them derive their support from the organization, but many of them, particularly the local leaders, earn their own living.

While the organization of these sects is patterned after that of the Methodist Church, with much authority vested in the leaders, the Pentecostal sects are essentially laymen's movements. They believe with George Fox that to be bred at Yale or at Chicago is not sufficient to qualify a man to be a minister of Christ and their leaders are drawn from the ranks of the laymen. Throughout it is the zeal of the laymen which carries the burden of the work. Most of them tithe conscientiously and they make genuine sacrifices. At the national conventions of the Church of God in Chattanooga and in Cleveland, Tennessee, fully six thousand delegates were present, out of a total membership of perhaps eighty thousand. They had come from all parts of the country at great expense of time and money. They show the same unreserved devotion in their missionary activities.

• • • • • •

WHERE THEY GET THEIR MEMBERS

Visits to three state and national conventions and attendance at many local gatherings have left an impression of the relative youthfulness of the membership. There were many young people present and only a relatively small number who were not on the sunny side of forty. There remains also an impression that among them were many fine types—attractive women and men of rugged physique, clear-cut features and pleasant expression. It was easy to see that they belonged to the underprivileged classes, town or city workers, most of them employed in shop or factory or W.P.A. One judged that most of them had been raised in the country and were the product of America's country schools and churches.

WHAT THEY PREACH

Although arising among the underprivileged and rooted in the social and economic injustices of our present-day civilization, the Pentecostal sects concern themselves not at all with the problems of social betterment. They are not seeking to save the world but to save individuals out of a world which is getting worse and worse. They believe that the second coming of the Lord is near at hand and their preaching dwells upon the signs of the times. In any case salvation for them has to do chiefly with the life to come. Thus in the convention of the Church of God in Chattanooga, nine of the eleven hymns used in their evening service had an otherworldly theme. Among them were the following first lines: "That home of the soul over there," "When we cross the great divide," "Somebody's going to be left behind." At one point a little girl of seven sang, "I'll never feel at home in this world any more." An examination of their hymn book showed 75 of their 170 hymns related to the future life.

Doctrinally these groups are rigidly fundamentalistic. The Bible is for them the literally inspired Word of God. Jesus is God, born of a virgin, who died for our sins in order to free us from the wrath to come. Man himself is totally depraved. There is no health in him and no hope of salvation except through conversion and regeneration.

Occasionally one will hear derogatory remarks regarding education and educated people. Aside from this there is little tendency toward belittling others.

●　　●　　●　　●　　●　　●

It is important to recognize that the principle of holiness, which is common to all these groups, is primarily a matter of religious experience. These people are commonly austere in their piety. They forbid dancing, card-playing, theatre-going and the like, but they are not interested in holiness for its own sake. They are interested rather in that sense of fellowship of the soul with its Maker to which we give the name of mysticism. Their austerity, their requirement of perfection, is either just a means toward obtaining and keeping that experience or else an expression of their faith in the potency of the experience. The doctrine of the second blessing is thus an expression of their discovery that the religious life is a matter of spirit or attitude rather than of formal correctness; also of the further discovery that there must be a place in the normal religious life for more than one crisis experience.

In the groups with which we are chiefly concerned, those to whom the name "Holy Roller" more properly applies, this emphasis on regeneration is further complicated by another doctrine. In addition to the conversion experience, in addition even to sanctification, there must be the experience of baptism by the Holy Spirit. Evidence of the Spirit's presence they find in the phenomenon of "speaking with tongues." Those who are baptized by the Spirit must "speak with tongues" once at least. They value also other abnormal manifestations such as dancing, jerking, thrusting up their hands, falling on the floor. Even passing into an unconscious state may be interpreted as evidence of possession by the Holy Spirit and have value in their eyes. Let us look at them through the eyes of one of their converts.

A CONVERT'S STORY

The man in question was a middle-aged man of no little ability and fair education who held a responsible job and served as deacon and Sunday school superintendent in a fairly strong Congregational Church. Dropping in one evening at a Negro Pentecostal mission this man, Mr. T., became deeply impressed. He continued to attend and finally felt himself the experience of being "baptized by the Spirit." He valued this experience so highly that he wrote a lengthy description of it and published it at his own expense. A member of this mission gave me a copy. Here are some extracts from his account:

They came forward at once, some twenty of them, (in response to the altar call) and knelt about the altar, and then began the strangest prayer I have ever experienced. Some one began singing, "Savior lead me lest I stray"; others joined in and the song seemed finally to dissolve in a prayer of many voices, mingled with groans, moans, shouts and cryings, and the fantastic musical wail so peculiar to the colored race. This prayer lasted about twenty minutes. It was brought to a close by an ardent prayer from the black man on the platform. When they arose their faces were beaming with joy. Some one then started singing, "Who shall abide in thy tabernacle? He that walketh uprightly and speaketh the truth in his heart." It was begun by a voice a bit out of tune, but taken up by the others it soon improved in form and tone, and with the staccato of clapping hands and the even tinkling of tambourines it became rhythmically irresistible. Again and again they sang it with swaying bodies and beating feet, gaining in power amid the shouts of glory. Suddenly a woman on my right shouted, "Praise him! Praise him!" Jumping up she began to dance, seemingly without thought as to any one's opinion as to the propriety of the act. I was convinced that she was in the grip of some outside power, for she was of such ample proportions physically as to preclude such exhibition under normal conditions. One after another joined her until a dozen were on the floor singing and dancing until the place rocked with their joy.

Then came the testimonies, and there was no waiting. The first to speak was a young colored woman, who said, "I want to praise God for his wonderful way with me. I used to be in the world and loved to dance and play cards and go to the theatre and such like, but praise God, He has changed my life—Glory to Jesus. He has saved my soul from hell through the blood of the cross, and not only that, but He healed my body. I followed the world and its pleasures so hard that I was taken sick. The doctors said one of my lungs was gone and my case was hopeless. I became a mere skeleton, but—Glory to God—I took my case to Jesus and He healed me. Hallelujah, Praise Him—He surely can put flesh on the bones." And she surely looked it.

Well, one by one they testified to the knowledge of a walk with God. From the first I felt wonderfully at home in that humble room. The voices seemed to ring true. Men clearly of little education (as the term goes) preached sermons that were marvels of pointed truth and convincing power, and sinners came forward during the preaching and knelt at the platform, calling upon God.

On one occasion an ignorant colored woman (as the world counts wisdom) addressed the meeting and under the power of the Holy Ghost she broke forth with the marvel of an unknown tongue—a tongue that the intelligent hearer could easily perceive was classic. Although I could not understand the utterance I detected at once its Latin origin. When this demonstration ceased, the sister said, "Now you all know that wasn't me. I can't speak my own language right, much less a foreign one. That wasn't me. That was the Holy Ghost." The leader then called for an interpreter. A sister rose and said, "I am not an interpreter but I can speak the Spanish language and the sister spoke in that tongue. I did not get it all, but the last phrase was 'glory to the precious name of Jesus.' "

After months of faithful attendance at the little mission, Mr. T. finally responded to the altar call. Two evenings later we find him back again in the mission, going through a terrific struggle. He describes it as follows:

Praise God's great name forever. The prayers of the righteous prevailed that night; for the struggle ceased and Satan was defeated.

I remember that I lay face downward on the floor, my left hand beneath me. I have the habit of drumming with my right hand during family prayers on the chair seat. I began to do it then, moderately at the beginning, then faster and faster until the beats became unthinkably rapid. Then the movement of my hand changed. I struck my forehead with my open palm—slowly at first but increasing in force and rapidity until it seemed that my head would be beaten in. Just at the point where seemingly I was killing myself a strange thing occurred: I lost consciousness. How long I remained in that condition I do not know, but this I do know, that in that interval the power of God possessed me entire; for upon regaining my understanding and feeling, I was flat on my back—my legs straight and my arms at 90 degrees with my body, even as Jesus was on the cross—for had I been nailed to that blessed floor, I could have been no more powerless to move.

My eyes were still closed but a light was blinding them even through closed lids and through the white radiance there shot and leaped tongues of yellow fire apparently just above my head. After a little while the flames died away and I was permitted to open my eyes. I imagined myself in another world, but as my vision returned, I saw the old rusty stove pipe and knew that I was in the House of Prayer. I saw that I was surrounded by shining black faces, lighted up, as it were by the glory of God.

Then I said, "So this is it—well, praise God—Holy, holy, holy, Lord God Almighty." Then I began to have intervals of liberty—for waves of glory swept over me and when they came I praised God with a loud voice and in the spirit I clapped my hands and rejoiced. I should judge that I was under the spell of that holy joy for, say, twenty minutes.

For the first time in my life I knew the inexpressible rapture of being entirely controlled by the power of God and it was wonderful past describing.

After a long and glorious season of uncontrollable praise, there came a gradual subsiding and a blessed quietness and in that holy calm I gave honor to the new power, the Holy One, in words that I formed not and which I shall never forget—"Wonderful, wonderful, wonderful, wonderful the Holy Ghost, the Holy Ghost, the Holy Ghost, the Holy Ghost; praise Him, praise Him, praise Him, praise Him; glory, glory, glory to God!"

After several minutes of this wonderful manifestation of God's great power, the speaking ceased and there reigned a heavenly peace—such peace as I had never known.

At that time, as if to superprove the experience and have it fit exactly into the Acts account, a remarkable thing occurred.

Still in a fixed position on the floor, still controlled by the blessed Spirit and powerless to move, I heard the door open and, bending my head, I saw two policemen enter. One of them, a sergeant, said, "What's going on here? It's quarter past two and you're disturbing the peace." Brother R. replied, "This is a Christian meeting." "Christian!" said the officer, "I'm a Christian, but I never saw anything like this."

You remember how some of the people explained the strange demonstration that followed the descent of the Holy Ghost in the Acts account. They said, "They are filled with new wine." Listen to the record two thousand years after Pentecost:

The sergeant turned to me and said to Brother R., "What's the matter with this man?" Brother R. answered with quiet impressiveness, "He is filled with the Holy Ghost." "Filled with jakey," was the sergeant's quick reply!!! Hallelujah, Glory to God! How I laughed and how the saints laughed when we heard that. A. D. 33, the ignorant ascribe the demonstration to new wine. A. D. 1921, the ignorant claim it is "jakey" (drink based on the alcoholic contents of Jamaica Ginger). Praise God, the power is just the same to-day. He brings the experience down to date with a current term. Well, glory to God! there were no arrests that night. The policemen could not stand the power and very shortly they went out into the night.

This account is given in detail because it reveals so clearly the nature of the experiences on which these sects place such high value and the assumptions which underlie the experience. Mr. T. was convinced that the fat woman who danced was in the grip of an *outside power*, that the woman who spoke in tongues was actually speaking correctly in a language which she did not know, and that he himself had had the experience of being entirely controlled by the power of God, because he was doing things he could not otherwise explain. We are struck most of all by the emotional effect which this experience has upon him as well as the emotional condition out of which it arises.

It is worth noting that whereas the conventional Negro churches of the city were chiefly concerned with the problem of white superiority and were endeavoring to solve the problem by imitating the whites, these little missions were so firmly convinced that they had found the greatest of all blessings that they were sorry for those who did not have it. And other white persons besides Mr. T. joined their circle. Rather generally in these radical sects there is a tendency to disregard the lines of color and race. They feel that they have found a new basis of fellowship and they receive with open arms all who share in their experience.

Although this happened to be a group of Negroes, Mr. T.'s description would fit quite well many of the white Pentecostal meetings which I have witnessed. There is action from beginning to end and it is in

large part a musical service. The Negroes have perhaps a better sense
of harmony and rhythm than the whites, but this statement applies to
them all. Even when the preacher is holding forth, there is often an
accompaniment of "Amens" and "Yes, Lords" uttered in the singing
voice. The general prayer is said by all, each person praying after his
own fashion. Sometimes the effect is that of a discordant Babel, but
sometimes the voices blend and harmonize. The testimonies, which
constitute an important part of the service, are interspersed with spontaneous singing. Throughout there is much singing and when these
people sing, they sing not only with their voices, but with their hands
and their feet and their bodies. The general effect of the singing, when
it is done well, is to give the individual a sense of being caught up and
fused with the group. The fact that Mr. T. was a musically sensitive
person may help to explain what happened to him.

WHY THEY ARE GROWING

DIFFERENCES OF CULTURE AND TASTE

The explanation of the growth of these new sects may be sought first
of all in considerations of culture and of taste. They have been recruited from those who, rightly or wrongly, have felt that they were not
welcomed in the older churches. In any case they have not felt at home
in the atmosphere of the dignified service and have found the informality
and spontaneity of the small believers' groups much more to their liking.
And just as these people prefer "St. Louis Blues" to a Beethoven sonata
or the *Chicago American* to the *New Republic*, so also they prefer
"When the Roll is Called up Yonder" to "Our God, Our Help in
Ages Past." They therefore gravitate toward the culturally like-minded.
Many who formerly would have found their home among the Methodists or the Disciples now forgather with the Pentecostals.

•   •   •   •   •   •

WHAT RELIGION MEANS TO THEM

Most important of all is the sense of reality which pervades the
religion of these newer groups. They share the conviction that they
have found God. They feel themselves able to bear witness to his
presence in their own lives. They share the belief that He talks to them
just as He talked to the old Hebrew prophets. Evidence for this they
find in the sense of release from the burden of guilt. They find it also

in certain unusual experiences. Like Mr. T. they find themselves doing things they can't account for, uttering words that do not seem to come from themselves or even passing into states of unconsciousness. These experiences they interpret as due to possession by a power beyond themselves. We may question the correctness of their interpretation, but that does not alter the fact that it has for them tremendous emoional value and that the results are often definitely constructive. To many of them it gives power to re-organize their lives and kindles in them a faith that is contagious.

LESSONS FROM HISTORY

•   •   •   •   •   •

The history of the Christian Church, as Richard Niebuhr has pointed out, furnishes many instances in which . . . [the following] process has been repeated. Little groups of like-minded persons, nearly always of the struggling underprivileged classes, have come together on the basis of some new vision, some vivid sense of the presence of the divine. Others have been drawn into the fold on the basis of a shared experience. Then gradually the voluntary society becomes a church. The original believers are replaced by their children and institutionalization follows. The sacraments become means of grace rather than symbols of confession. The creeds become standards of doctrine rather than confessions of faith. Even religious experience itself tends to become standardized in the form of patterns of behavior which have to be induced by all sorts of meretricious devices. But in general the process is one of leveling. The great prophetic, forward movements are leveled down and conventionalized. The eccentric and regressive manifestations are leveled up and become respectable.

•   •   •   •   •   •

LINKING RELIGION AND SOCIAL ACTION

The otherworldly emphasis among the Pentecostals calls attention to a common tendency to divorce religion and social action. Those who go in for radical mysticism tend to withdraw from the world and its problems. Those who devote themselves to social action often withdraw from organized religion. It may not be an unwholesome thing for those who are caught in the meshes of a bad political and economic system to turn their attention away from evils they can do nothing about to those for which they are personally responsible. Certainly leaders of reform movements have abundant reason to know that there are multitudes of unstable individuals who seek in attempts to reform the system an escape from the need of reforming themselves. But always it is a misfortune when religious zeal stops short of its practical task of bringing the kingdom of heaven down to earth. It seems equally unfortunate when those who are in a position to work for social betterment lose touch with the church. Organized religion moves slowly, but a forward movement is certainly in a much stronger position when it is linked with the great loyalties to which the masses of well-meaning people are already committed.

◄◄◄◄◄►►►►►

53. Religious Liberty v. Police Power: Jehovah's Witnesses *

WHEN OUR CONSTITUTION was drawn up, the memories of religious wars, political persecutions, and discriminations against various religious minorities were still fresh, so definite provisions were incorporated to safeguard religious freedom. It was and is rightly felt that religious freedom is an important touchstone to determine the status of civil liberty in a community, for religious belief and practice are deeply personal matters. But the religious fanatic can be a threat to the community peace, and religious sects sometimes deviate disturbingly from accepted community behavior norms. In such cases the police power of the state is apt to be invoked by those who resent these disturbing forces. The Courts must then decide the issue. This reading illustrates vividly the conflicting roles of church and state as institutions of social control. The conflict situations precipitated by the Jehovah's Witnesses have been before the Supreme Court many times in recent years. These have involved interpretations and decisions of far greater import than may have appeared to inhere in the immediate cases under consideration.

* Hollis W. Barber, The American Political Science Review, 41, No. 2 (April, 1947), 226-247. Reprinted by permission of the publisher and the author.

The author (b. 1910) is in the Chicago Undergraduate Division, University of Illinois. Lecturer, University College, Northwestern, and Chicago. His particular fields are international relations, American foreign policy, and constitutional law of the United States.

IT IS STRESSING THE OBVIOUS to observe that the state must often resolve conflicts between certain of its constitutional powers and certain equally constitutional private rights. Such is the age-old controversy of liberty versus authority, familiar to every social scientist. Such is the contemporary controversy between "Bible-dizzy but patently sincere" zealots of the Watch Tower Bible and Tract Society, more widely known as Jehovah's Witnesses, on the one hand, and the police power on the other. There is nothing novel about a quarrel between religion and the police power, as witness the Mormons; but a new twist is now given by the personalities of Jehovah's Witnesses and their unique ways of practicing their faith.

Much of their attitude is reflected in their slogans, "Religion is a Racket," "Religion is a Snare," and "Millions Now Living Will Never Die." With a fine neutrality, they consign to the leaping flames all existing religious beliefs other than their own, although they are especially antagonistic to Roman Catholicism. Followers of "Pastor" Charles Taze Russell and "Judge" Joseph Frederick Rutherford, they are serene in their belief that the second coming of Christ is due momentarily, that there is no time to build churches, and that the "witness work" must be carried on by the direct method of calling on people in their homes, distributing pamphlets and playing records on portable phonographs describing their publications and beliefs for the edification of whomsoever will listen. Soon He will return and all but members of the Society will be swept away; thus "millions now living will never die." This assurance of immortality beginning in the immediate future constitutes a powerful drive toward fanatical proselyting, and in order to speed the good work every Witness is an ordained minister whose duty it is to spread the Word. Although not universal, it is often true that the Witness assumes an exceedingly aggressive, intolerant, and even boorish attitude toward a prospective convert, apparently assuming that, since he is himself the repository of all religious wisdom, the other must be a dolt if he does not immediately see the light. A variation of the phonograph technique is for the Witness to offer to leave books and pamphlets and to request a "contribution," which may or may not be in proportion to the cost of the printed matter. The Witnesses are very clear on this point—their "literature" is not sold; it is given freely, as is the reciprocal contribution in the amount set by the donor's conscience. This point has an obvious bearing on the commercial (as contrasted with the religious) nature of these transactions—a matter of importance when the Witnesses disobey a city official's demand that they take out permits before peddling or soliciting as is required of other itinerant salesmen of books or merchandise.

The Witnesses' numerous conflicts with the law may be traced in major part to their literal interpretation of Exodus 20:3-5: "Thou shalt have no other Gods before me. Thou shalt not make unto thee any graven image, or any likeness of anything that is in Heaven above, or . . . in the earth, . . . or in the water under the earth. Thou shalt not bow down thyself to them, nor serve them: for I the Lord thy God am a jealous God. . . ." Any kow-towing to governmental licensing regulations, or signs of obeisance such as saluting the flag, come under the prohibition against bowing down to graven images. Thus it is that when one of the faithful refuses to procure a municipally-required permit to distribute handbills, to hold a parade, or to solicit charitable contributions, he maintains that he was "sent by Jehovah to do His work," and that to have applied for a permit would have been "an act of disobedience to His commandment." Similar ideas account for the refusal to salute the flag. The Witnesses persistently maintain that flag-salute and permit-ordinances are contrary to the religious freedom guaranteed specifically in the First Amendment and by construction in the Fourteenth.

●   ●   ●   ●   ●   ●

So far as concerns the law as it now stands, it is clear that it is unconstitutional for a state or city to require students in its schools to give a specified salute and pledge of allegiance to the national flag and government if the students have religious scruples against those acts.

And a city may not levy a tax as a condition precedent to the granting of a permit to canvass or solicit in a religious cause, or to sell or donate religious publications. There are many who, with an eye on the aggressive and at times anti-social attitudes and tactics of Jehovah's Witnesses, will consider that the Court in its most recent decisions has gone too far and leaned over backward in its solicitude for the tender religious sensitivities and constitutional rights of a group which customarily shows little concern for the correlative rights of others. It hardly seems unfair to suggest that the Witnesses, who demand so much tolerance and coöperation from the public, might practice a little tolerance and coöperation themselves. It is here submitted that the Witnesses, at least since 1943, have had no just cause for complaint against the treatment they have received at the hands of the judicial branch of the federal government, and that the position taken by Justice Jackson in his dissents in Douglas v. Jeannette and Prince v. Massachusetts merits extremely careful study as quite possibly the right one. It is not impossible that the Court, in an altogether laudable desire to protect the constitutional rights of a minority—an attitude which liberal democrats will criticize only with great reluctance—may actually have leaned too far in the direction of protecting the religious fanatic who maintains that the one way in which he can worship the deity of his choice is by spreading his prayer rug in the middle of a busy street intersection, and who therefore demands that all traffic be routed around him. In actual fact, the Witnesses are not large enough a sect to cause any great disturbance one way or the other. But the principle is of basic importance, far outweighing the significance of the people who evoke its application.

•   •   •   •   •   •

No one who has dabbled in the great American game of predicting Supreme Court actions can be regarded as ready for promotion to sophomore standing unless he shows appreciation of the great number of variables involved and the consequent likelihood of error on his part. He who would state categorically that the Witnesses will win their next several cases demonstrates the superficiality of his study of constitutional history, even though the sect has recently found a very sympathetic hearing in the marble temple on Capitol Hill. The Court's personnel has already changed since the last decision covered in this article, and it would be foolhardy to attempt a forecast of future changes of legal thinking and social philosophy. But study of a sequence of cases need not culminate in crystal-gazing. It may prove something far more important than the Court's application of certain laws to certain facts: it may show again the Court's devotion to the protection of minority rights, even those of an often bigoted and unpopular minority. Even if all agreed, which they obviously will not, that the tribunal may recently have been a bit too solicitous about Witness rights, there are few who would not prefer that situation to the alternative of seeing a majority disregard them completely. We may begrudge an extra trip to the front door to receive a Witness handbill, but the effort is small enough price to pay for the assurance of living in a community where diversity of thought is still tolerated. However imperfectly we may in the past have practiced it, we still pay homage to the American tradition of religious freedom.

ઐ·ઐ·ઐ

54. The Division of Labor in Society *

ONE of the recurring basic criticisms of modern society is that the
"whole man"—the personality—has been weakened because of
specialization, or "division of labor." Said one philosopher, "It is
a sad commentary that we have come to the state where we never
do anything more than make the eighteenth part of a pin." Said
another, "In so far as the principle of the division of labor receives
a more complete application, the art progresses, the artisan retro-
gresses." Many, comparing the life of the modern workman with
the "free, bold life of the 'noble' savage," have found the second
much more favorable than the first. Adoption of such a philosophy, carried to its logical conclusion, would lead to tremendous
changes in all of social life. This idea, perhaps most popular in the
19th century, still flourishes today. Consequently, in vocational
planning, we may be given contradictory advice: Specialize. Do not
specialize. The result of specialization, in the thinking of Rousseau
and others, is the "splintering" of personalities and societies. Emile
Durkheim, however, in this conclusion to his The Division of Labor
in Society argues that specialization is the chief source of social
solidarity and is becoming the foundation of our present moral order.

I

IF THERE IS ONE RULE of conduct which is incontestable, it is that which
orders us to realize in ourselves the essential traits of the collective type.
Among lower peoples, this reaches its greatest rigor. There, one's first
duty is to resemble everybody else, not to have anything personal about
one's beliefs or actions. In more advanced societies, required likenesses
are less numerous; the absence of some likenesses, however, is still a sign
of moral failure. Of course, crime falls into fewer different categories;
but today, as heretofore, if a criminal is the object of reprobation, it is
because he is unlike us. Likewise, in lesser degree, acts simply immoral
and prohibited as such are those which evince dissemblances less profound but nevertheless considered serious. Is this not the case with

* Emile Durkheim. Reprinted from The Division of Labor in Society, pp. 396-
409, by permission of The Free Press, Glencoe, Illinois. Copyright 1947.
   The author (1858-1917) was a French sociologist and philosopher. Taught at
University of Bordeaux and at the Sorbonne. Successor to Auguste Comte. Par-
ticular interest: moral sociology; central theory: collective representation. Besides
doctoral dissertation from which this selection is taken, Durkheim's main works are
The Rules of Sociological Method, The Elementary Forms of the Religious Life, and
Suicide, A Study in Sociology.

the rule which common morality expresses when it orders a man to be a man in every sense of the word, which is to say, to have all the ideas and sentiments which go to make up a human conscience? No doubt, if this formula is taken literally, the man prescribed would be man in general and not one of some particular social species. But, in reality, this human conscience that we must integrally realize is nothing else than the collective conscience of the group of which we are a part. For what can it be composed of, if not the ideas and sentiments to which we are most attached? Where can we find the traits of our model, if not within us and around us? If we believe that this collective ideal is that of all humanity, that is because it has become so abstract and general that it appears fitting for all men indiscriminately. But, really, every people makes for itself some particular conception of this type which pertains to its personal temperament. Each represents it in its own image. Even the moralist who thinks he can, through thought, overcome the influence of transient ideas, cannot do so, for he is impregnated with them, and no matter what he does, he finds these precepts in the body of his deductions. That is why each nation has its own school of moral philosophy conforming to its character.

On the other hand, we have shown that this rule had as its function the prevention of all agitation of the common conscience, and, consequently, of social solidarity, and that it could accomplish this role only by having a moral character. It is impossible for offenses against the most fundamental collective sentiments to be tolerated without the disintegration of society, and it is necessary to combat them with the aid of the particularly energetic reaction which attaches to moral rules.

But the contrary rule, which orders us to specialize, has exactly the same function. It also is necessary for the cohesion of societies, at least at a certain period in their evolution. Of course, its solidarity is different from the preceding, but though it is different, it is no less indispensable. Higher societies can maintain themselves in equilibrium only if labor is divided; the attraction of like for like less and less suffices to produce this result. If, then, the moral character of the first of these rules is necessary to the playing of its role, it is no less necessary to the second. They both correspond to the same social need, but satisfy the need differently, because the conditions of existence in the societies themselves differ. Consequently, without speculating concerning the first principle of ethics, we can induce the moral value of one from the moral value of the other. If, from certain points of view, there is a real antagonism between them, that is not because they serve different ends. On the contrary, it is because they lead to the same end, but through opposed means. Accordingly, there is no necessity for choosing between them once for all nor of condemning one in the name of the other. What is necessary is to give each, at each moment in history, the place that is fitting to it.

Perhaps we can even generalize further in this matter.

The requirements of our subject have obliged us to classify moral rules and to review the principal types. We are thus in a better position than we were in the beginning to see, or at least to conjecture, not only upon the external sign, but also upon the internal character which is common to all of them and which can serve to define them. We have put them into two groups: rules with repressive sanctions, which may be diffuse or organized, and rules with restitutive sanctions. We have seen that the first of these express the conditions of the solidarity, *sui generis*, which comes from resemblances, and to which we have given the name mechanical; the second, the conditions of negative solidarity and organic solidarity. We can thus say that, in general, the character-istic of moral rules is that they enunciate the fundamental conditions of social solidarity. Law and morality are the totality of ties which bind each of us to society, which make a unitary, coherent aggregate of the mass of individuals. Everything which is a source of solidarity is moral, everything which forces man to take account of other men is moral, everything which forces him to regulate his conduct through something other than the striving of his ego is moral, and morality is as solid as these ties are numerous and strong. We can see how inexact it is to define it, as is often done, through liberty. It rather consists in a state of dependence. Far from serving to emancipate the individual, or disengaging him from the environment which surrounds him, it has, on the contrary, the function of making him an integral part of a whole, and, consequently, of depriving him of some liberty of movement. We sometimes, it is true, come across people not without nobility who find the idea of such dependence intolerable. But that is because they do not perceive the source from which their own morality flows, since these sources are very deep. Conscience is a bad judge of what goes on in the depths of a person, because it does not penetrate to them.

Society is not, then, as has often been thought, a stranger to the moral world, or something which has only secondary repercussions upon it. It is, on the contrary, the necessary condition of its existence. It is not a simple juxtaposition of individuals who bring an intrinsic morality with them, but rather man is a moral being only because he lives in society, since morality consists in being solidary with a group and vary-ing with this solidarity. Let all social life disappear, and moral life will disappear with it, since it would no longer have any objective. The state of nature of the philosophers of the eighteenth century, if not immoral, is, at least, amoral. Rousseau himself recognized this. Through this, however, we do not come upon the formula which expresses morality as a function of social interest. To be sure, society cannot exist if its parts are not solidary, but solidarity is only one of its conditions of existence. There are many others which are no less necessary and which are not moral. Moreover, it can happen that, in the system of ties which make up morality, there are some which are not useful in themselves or which have power without any relation to their degree of utility. The idea of utility does not enter as an essential element in our definition.

As for what is called individual morality, if we understand by that a totality of duties of which the individual would, at the same time, be subject and object, and which would link him only to himself, and which would, consequently, exist even if he were solitary,—that is an abstract conception which has no relation to reality. Morality, in all its forms, is never met with except in society. It never varies except in relation to social conditions. To ask what it would be if societies did not exist is thus to depart from facts and enter the domain of gratuitous hypotheses and unverifiable flights of the imagination. The duties of the individual towards himself are, in reality, duties towards society. They correspond to certain collective sentiments which he cannot offend, whether the offended and the offender are one and the same person, or whether they are distinct. Today, for example, there is in all healthy consciences a very lively sense of respect for human dignity, to which we are supposed to conform as much in our relations with ourselves as in our relations with others, and this constitutes the essential quality of what is called individual morality. Every act which contravenes this is censured, even when the agent and the sufferer are the same person. That is why, according to the Kantian formula, we ought to respect human personality wherever we find it, which is to say, in ourselves as in those like us. The sentiment of which it is the object is not less offended in one case than in the other.

But not only does the division of labor present the character by which we have defined morality; it more and more tends to become the essential condition of social solidarity. As we advance in the evolutionary scale, the ties which bind the individual to his family, to his native soil, to traditions which the past has given to him, to collective group usages, become loose. More mobile, he changes his environment more easily, leaves his people to go elsewhere to live a more autonomous existence, to a greater extent forms his own ideas and sentiments. Of course, the whole common conscience does not, on this account, pass out of existence. At least there will always remain this cult of per-.

sonality, of individual dignity of which we have just been speaking, and which, today, is the rallying-point of so many people. But how little a thing it is when one contemplates the ever increasing extent of social life, and, consequently, of individual consciences! For, as they become more voluminous, as intelligence becomes richer, activity more varied, in order for morality to remain constant, that is to say, in order for the individual to remain attached to the group with a force equal to that of yesterday, the ties which bind him to it must become stronger and more numerous. If, then, he formed no others than those which come from resemblances, the effacement of the segmental type would be accompanied by a systematic debasement of morality. Man would no longer be sufficiently obligated; he would no longer feel about and above him this salutary pressure of society which moderates his egoism and makes him a moral being. This is what gives moral value to the division of labor. Through it, the individual becomes cognizant of his dependence upon society; from it come the forces which keep him in check and restrain him. In short, since the division of labor becomes the chief source of social solidarity, it becomes, at the same time, the foundation of the moral order.

We can then say that, in higher societies, our duty is not to spread our activity over a large surface, but to concentrate and specialize it. We must contract our horizon, choose a definite task and immerse ourselves in it completely, instead of trying to make ourselves a sort of creative masterpiece, quite complete, which contains its worth in itself and not in the services that it renders. Finally, this specialization ought to be pushed as far as the elevation of the social type, without assigning any other limit to it. No doubt, we ought so to work as to realize in ourselves the collective type as it exists. There are common sentiments, common ideas, without which, as has been said, one is not a man. The rule which orders us to specialize remains limited by the contrary rule. Our conclusion is not that it is good to press specialization as far as possible, but as far as necessary. As for the part that is to be played by these two opposing necessities, that is determined by experience and cannot be calculated *a priori*. It is enough for us to have shown that the second is not of a different nature from the first, but that it also is moral, and that, moreover, this duty becomes ever more important and pressing, because the general qualities which are in question suffice less and less to socialize the individual.

It is not without reason that public sentiment reproves an ever more pronounced tendency on the part of dilettantes and even others to be taken up with an exclusively general culture and refuse to take any part in occupational organization. That is because they are not sufficiently

attached to society, or, if one wishes, society is not sufficiently attached
to them, and they escape it. Precisely because they feel its effect
neither with vivacity nor with the continuity that is necessary, they have
no cognizance of all the obligations their positions as social beings demand of them. The general ideal to which they are attached being,
for the reasons we have spoken of, formal and shifting, it cannot take
them out of themselves. We do not cling to very much when we
have no very determined objective, and, consequently, we cannot very
well elevate ourselves beyond a more or less refined egotism. On the
contrary, he who gives himself over to a definite task is, at every moment,
struck by the sentiment of common solidarity in the thousand duties
of occupational morality.

                                   II

   But does not the division of labor by making each of us an incomplete
being bring on a diminution of individual personality? That is a re-
proach which has often been levelled at it.
   Let us first of all remark that it is difficult to see why it would be
more in keeping with the logic of human nature to develop superficially
rather than profoundly. Why would a more extensive activity, but
more dispersed, be superior to a more concentrated, but circumscribed.
activity? Why would there be more dignity in being complete and
mediocre, rather than in living a more specialized, but more intense
life, particularly if it is thus possible for us to find what we have lost
in this specialization, through our association with other beings who
have what we lack and who complete us? We take off from the principle that man ought to realize his nature as man, to accomplish his
ὅικεῖον ἔργον, as Aristotle said. But this nature does not remain constant
throughout history; it is modified with societies. Among lower peoples,
the proper duty of man is to resemble his companions, to realize in
himself all the traits of the collective type which are then confounded,
much more than today, with the human type. But, in more advanced
societies, his nature is, in large part, to be an organ of society, and his
proper duty, consequently, is to play his role as an organ.
   Moreover, far from being trammelled by the progress of specialization,
individual personality develops with the division of labor.
   To be a person is to be an autonomous source of action. Man
acquires this quality only in so far as there is something in him which
is his alone and which individualizes him, as he is something more than
a simple incarnation of the generic type of his race and his group. It
will be said that he is endowed with free will and that is enough to

establish his personality. But although there may be some of this liberty in him, an object of so many discussions, it is not this metaphysical, impersonal, invariable attribute which can serve as the unique basis for concrete personality, which is empirical and variable with individuals. That could not be constituted by the wholly abstract power of choice between two opposites, but it is still necessary for this faculty to be exercised towards ends and aims which are proper to the agent. In other words, the very materials of conscience must have a personal character. But we have seen that this result is progressively produced as the division of labor progresses. The effacement of the segmental type, at the same time that it necessitates a very great specialization, partially lifts the individual conscience from the organic environment which supports it, as from the social environment which envelops it, and, accordingly because of this double emancipation, the individual becomes more of an independent factor in his own conduct. The division of labor itself contributes to this enfranchisement, for individual natures, while specializing, become more complex, and by that are in part freed from collective action and hereditary influences which can only enforce themselves upon simple, general things.

It is, accordingly, a real illusion which makes us believe that personality was so much more complete when the division of labor had penetrated less. No doubt, in looking from without at the diversity of occupations which the individual then embraces, it may seem that he is developing in a very free and complete manner. But, in reality, this activity which he manifests is not really his. It is society, it is the race acting in and through him; he is only the intermediary through which they realize themselves. His liberty is only apparent and his personality borrowed. Because the life of these societies is, in certain respects, less regular, we imagine that original talents have more opportunity for free play, that it is easier for each one to pursue his own tastes, that a very large place is left to free fantasy. But this is to forget that personal sentiments are then very rare. If the motives which govern conduct do not appear as periodically as they do today, they do not leave off being collective, and, consequently, impersonal, and it is the same with the actions that they inspire. Moreover, we have shown above how activity becomes richer and more intense as it becomes more specialized.

Thus, the progress of individual personality and that of the division of labor depend upon one and the same cause. It is thus impossible to desire one without desiring the other. But no one today contests the obligatory character of the rule which orders us to be more and more of a person.

One last consideration will make us see to what extent the division of labor is linked with our whole moral life.

Men have long dreamt of finally realizing in fact the ideal of human fraternity. People pray for a state where war will no longer be the law of international relations, where relations between societies will be pacifically regulated, as those between individuals already are, where all men will collaborate in the same work and live the same life. Although these aspirations are in part neutralized by those which have as their object the particular society of which we are a part, they have not left off being active and are even gaining in force. But they can be satisfied only if all men form one society, subject to the same laws. For, just as private conflicts can be regulated only by the action of the society in which the individuals live, so intersocial conflicts can be regulated only by a society which comprises in its scope all others. The only power which can serve to moderate individual egotism is the power of the group; the only power which can serve to moderate the egotism of groups is that of some other group which embraces them.

Truly, when the problem has been posed in these terms, we must recognize that this ideal is not on the verge of being integrally realized, for there are too many intellectual and moral diversities between different social types existing together on the earth to admit of fraternalization in the same society. But what is possible is that societies of the same type may come together, and it is, indeed, in this direction that evolution appears to move. We have already seen that among European peoples there is a tendency to form, by spontaneous movement, a European society which has, at present, some idea of itself and the beginning of organization. If the formation of a single human society is forever impossible, a fact which has not been proved, at least the formation of continually larger societies brings us vaguely near the goal. These facts, moreover, in no wise contradict the definition of morality that we have given, for if we cling to humanity and if we ought to cling to it, it is because it is a society which is in process of realizing itself in this way, and with which we are solidary.

But we know that greater societies cannot be formed except through the development of the division of labor, for not only could they not maintain themselves in equilibrium without a greater specialization of functions, but even the increase in the number of those competing would suffice to produce this result mechanically; and that, so much the more, since the growth of volume is generally accompanied by a growth in density. We can then formulate the following proposition: the ideal of human fraternity can be realized only in proportion to the progress of the division of labor. We must choose: either to renounce our dream, if we refuse further to circumscribe our activity, or else to push forward its accomplishment under the condition we have just set forth.

III

But if the division of labor produces solidarity, it is not only because it makes each individual an exchangist, as the economists say; it is because it creates among men an entire system of rights and duties which link them together in a durable way. Just as social similitudes give rise to a law and a morality which protect them, so the division of labor gives rise to rules which assure pacific and regular concourse of divided functions. If economists have believed that it would bring forth an abiding solidarity, in some manner of its own making, and if, accordingly, they have held that human societies could and would resolve themselves into purely economic associations, that is because they believed that it affected only individual, temporary interests. Consequently, to estimate the interests in conflict and the way in which they ought to equilibrate, that is to say, to determine the conditions under which exchange ought to take place, is solely a matter of individual competence; and, since these interests are in a perpetual state of becoming, there is no place for any permanent regulation. But such a conception is, in all ways, inadequate for the facts. The division of labor does not present individuals to one another, but social functions. And society is interested in the play of the latter; in so far as they regularly concur, or do not concur, it will be healthy or ill. Its existence thus depends upon them, and the more they are divided the greater its dependence. That is why it cannot leave them in a state of indetermination. In addition to this, they are determined by themselves. Thus are formed those rules whose number grows as labor is divided, and whose absence makes organic solidarity either impossible or imperfect.

But it is not enough that there be rules; they must be just, and for that it is necessary for the external conditions of competition to be equal. If, moreover, we remember that the collective conscience is becoming more and more a cult of the individual, we shall see that what characterizes the morality of organized societies, compared to that of segmental societies, is that there is something more human, therefore more rational, about them. It does not direct our activities to ends which do not immediately concern us; it does not make us servants of ideal powers of a nature other than our own, which follow their directions without occupying themselves with the interests of men. It only asks that we be thoughtful of our fellows and that we be just, that we fulfill our duty, that we work at the function we can best execute, and receive the just reward for our services. The rules which constitute it do not have a constraining force which snuffs out free thought; but, because they are rather made for us and, in a certain sense, by us, we are free. We wish to understand them; we do not fear to change them. We must, however, guard against finding such an ideal inadequate on the pretext that it is too earthly and too much to our liking. An ideal is not more elevated because more transcendent, but because it leads us to vaster perspectives. What is important is not that it tower high above us, until it becomes a stranger to our lives, but that it open to our activity a large enough field. This is far from being on the verge of realization. We know only too well what a laborious work it is to erect this society where each individual will have the place he merits, will be rewarded as he deserves, where everybody, accordingly, will spontaneously work for the good of all and of each. Indeed, a moral code is not above another because it commands in a drier and more authoritarian manner, or because it is more sheltered from reflection. Of course, it must attach us to something besides ourselves but it is not necessary for it to chain us to it with impregnable bonds.

It has been said with justice that morality—and by that must be understood, not only moral doctrines, but customs—is going through a real crisis. What precedes can help us to understand the nature and causes of this sick condition. Profound changes have been produced in the structure of our societies in a very short time; they have been freed from the segmental type with a rapidity and in proportions such as have never before been seen in history. Accordingly, the morality which corresponds to this social type has regressed, but without another developing quickly enough to fill the ground that the first left vacant in our consciences. Our faith has been troubled; tradition has lost its sway; individual judgment has been freed from collective judgment. But, on the other hand, the functions which have been disrupted in the course of the upheaval have not had the time to adjust themselves to one another; the new life which has emerged so suddenly has not been able to be completely organized, and above all, it has not been organized in a way to satisfy the need for justice which has grown more ardent in our hearts. If this be so, the remedy for the evil is not to seek to resuscitate traditions and practices which, no longer responding to present conditions of society, can only live an artificial, false existence. What we must do to relieve this anomy is to discover the means for making the organs which are still wasting themselves in discordant movements harmoniously concur by introducing into their relations more justice by more and more extenuating the external inequalities which are the source of the evil. Our illness is not, then, as has often been believed, of an intellectual sort; it has more profound causes. We shall not suffer because we no longer know on what theoretical notion to base the morality we have been practicing, but because, in certain of its parts, this morality is irremediably shattered, and that which is necessary to us is only in process of formation. Our anxiety does not arise because the criticism of scholars has broken down the traditional explanation we use to give to our duties; consequently, it is not a new philosophical system which will relieve the situation. Because certain of our duties are no longer founded in the reality of things, a breakdown has resulted which will be repaired only in so far as a new discipline is established and consolidated. In short, our first duty is to make a moral code for ourselves. Such a work cannot be improvised in the silence of the study; it can arise only through itself, little by little, under the pressure of internal causes which make it necessary. But the service that thought can and must render is in fixing the goal that we must attain. That is what we have tried to do.

✥✥✥✥✥

55. Business and Ethics *

THE ECONOMIST WILLIAM ORTON attacks here the subject of morals and the economic order from a totally different perspective than that in the preceding selection by Emile Durkheim (54). Discussing the present state of ethics in business institutions, the author contends that the essential foundation of economic policies is, or should be, moral. He also maintains that the determination of economic morals should devolve upon all of society, not upon just a few people. In elaborating his point of view, he illustrates the interrelated character of some of our basic institutions.

* William A. Orton. Reprinted from the October, 1948, issue of Fortune, pp. 118-124, by Special Permission of the Editors; Copyright 1948 Time, Inc.

The author (b. 1889) is Professor of Economics, Smith College. Born in Bromley, England. With War Office intelligence staff, London, 1917-19. Staff officer, industrial relations department, British Ministry of Labour, 1919-22. Came to United States in 1922. Author, Labor in Transition, Prelude to Economics, America in Search of Culture, The Liberal Tradition, The Economic Role of the State. His articles have appeared in Atlantic Monthly, American Mercury, New Republic, and many other periodicals.

WHEN BUSINESS AND ETHICS are discussed as separate spheres or categories of conduct, economists as well as manufacturers are apt to take the cue and insist that "business is business." American businessmen are remarkably tolerant of sermons from all sorts of sources, and, like old-style British labor leaders, they preach some pretty good ones themselves— but not at directors' meetings. There, they feel, is a different universe of discourse: a very complex universe that has to be dealt with on its own terms at the risk of total failure, a universe that is not amenable to sermons. Lord Josiah Stamp, whose death in the blitz was a major disaster for the Germans as well as the English, took an active interest in the relation of ethics to business. Good Christian that he was, he gave to it some of his best work and keenest thought. But he had very little use for sermons. Just as you live in a physical world, he would say, and have to reckon with its imperatives, so you live in an economic world and must pay attention to its laws. If you do not, so much the worse not merely for you but for the bit of practical good you might have accomplished. If or when (in 1926 he said "when") the general quality of human conduct is spiritually elevated over a wide enough area, then business motives may be sufficiently modified to alter the economic postulates. But in the meantime "what is economically sensible and feasible becomes an integral part of what is ethical, and is not rival or antithetic to something which we have independently determined as ethical."

That did not mean, of course, that anything business finds expedient or profitable to do in the short run has an intrinsic ethical sanction. It did mean, emphatically, that the efficient conduct of the world's work is a sounder basis for an ethical system than any amount of talk; for it is common work, rather than talk, that extends and deepens the areas of dynamic community. Once in a while the fact strikes home on the wings of danger. Try coping with a scrub fire, or beaching an injured boat in a cross wind, and you will soon find out who is the good neighbor; and you will not forget. But does it take an emergency to remind us that the impulse to cooperate is as authentic a part of human nature as the impulse to beggar-my-neighbor or blow him into kindom come? Apparently it does. Why else do we hear so much of Darwin and so little of Kropotkin? Thus when one asserts—as I do assert—that the everyday business of life is a sphere not only of economic but of moral significance, the statement seems paradoxical and needs supporting.

WHERE DOES ETHICS STOP?

Surely it is from the natural and necessary relationships of social life that any and every ethical system arises. If it were not for those relationships there would be no moral philosophy; for the moral philosopher (unlike some modern economists) cannot philosophize in a vacuum. What gets him going and makes him useful is the fact that these relationships give rise to problems; problems of will and purpose, not merely of arithmetic. If they did not, they would not be human relationships at all, perhaps not even simian. Family life, for example, is no doubt more difficult for men than for monkeys, and we sometimes fail to pass its tests; nonetheless—indeed for that very reason—it is the finest school in the world. Are we then to suppose that moral and ethical problems suddenly cease to exist outside the sphere of immediate blood relationships? If so, where? The answer, of course, is nowhere. From the crew of a dragger to the setup of a mammoth corporation, the entire work field is a living web of human beings. Their relations to each other are often mediated through forms of association that do not rest on kinship; and in some cases they are so vast and so complex that we cannot concretely envisage them all at once. But to assert, on the basis of that limitation, that the relationships themselves have ceased to be human is such preposterous nonsense that we may well ask how intelligent people ever came to believe it.

As a matter of fact, few of them really believe it; but lots of them think they ought to pretend to. Many a corporation director is more interested in his concern as a working community than as a money-making machine; but he is usually shy to admit it—partly because he thinks the stockholders or the bankers would kick, partly because he is genuinely afraid of being "unbusinesslike." In the external relations of a business, "good will" is as frequently a moral fact as it is a financial fiction. The same is true of the internal relations. The average union leader (or "business agent") is much less indifferent to the success of the concern than outsiders are led to suppose. Collective bargaining is not a vehicle of economic warfare but a normal and necessary part of business dynamics. That it is so frequently depicted in the former aspect is largely due to the fact that much recent legislation has been based on the false assumption. Listening to many of our neo-liberals, you might well picture the American economic scene as a chaotic free-for-all, with its amazing productivity a lucky and inexplicable accident!

A British investigator of unemployment relief toured the U.S. in 1932 to see what was happening. At the end of his trip he said this: "I doubt if there is any country in the world that could have taken the licking this country is taking, and not gone red. Everywhere the men are saying, Sure, it's tough on us, but it's tough on the boss, too. I find no perceptible increase in revolutionary sentiment." The facts bore him out; and the full story has not even yet been told: the way, for instance, well-to-do wives, and their children who had to quit college, stood up to the beating. Was there no moral significance in that? Times have changed since then, you say. Yes, in certain respects they have. But it may still be held, without overoptimism, that the moral solidarity of American economic life is a lot stronger than most intellectuals suppose: so strong that a far richer and more interesting social order can be developed from it.

Ethics is a practical subject. If businessmen (including business agents) are to be bothered with it, they have a right to expect practical results. We shall not get any if the whole matter is left up in the fine air of sermons and sentiments. A technique of approach is needed. There was a time, not so long ago, when the systematic study of ethics and jurisprudence occupied a prominent place in colleges and law schools; but the law schools became vocational institutions cramming cases, and the late-nineteenth-century economists disposed of ethics by proving to their own satisfaction that we don't need any—the preface to J. B. Clark's *Distribution of Wealth* is the classic example. Now that we find we do—that after all there is a case and a need for the moral evaluation of social policies and institutions—we find ourselves very poorly equipped for the job, short of both tools and technique. To indicate certain lines of approach is as much as an introductory essay can attempt; and even that must be regarded rather as a call for co-operation than as an effort to lay down the law.

ETHICS TAKES THINKING

Since ethics pertains to the sphere of natural rather than supernatural community, its proper instrument is intelligence, which implies the ability not only to think clearly but to think objectively. It takes a man-sized effort to think about things as you actually find them in experience, rather than as some theorist or idealist or propagandist tells you they are. Not that these people are necessarily wrong, but that whatever they say has no genuine value until and unless it passes the test of concrete experience. That is a rigorous test in a land as ridden with slogans and stereotypes as this is. The U.S. has one of the oldest and toughest constitutions in the world, coupled with a productive efficiency that is without equal; but its dominant ideas and concepts are still European importations, some of them so stale that they stink. Particularly is this true of the class theory of society: a piece of pure abstraction that becomes positively funny when you try to apply it to the realities of American life. Ask our neighborhood group—the grocer, the carpenter, the electrician, the schoolteacher, and me—which of us belongs to the proletariat; or better still, ask our wives. The proletariat is a myth: a very powerful and pernicious one. That does not mean that it is a falsehood. It is a fact that a large number of working people (hand and brain) own scarcely anything in the way of capital goods and depend on others for the opportunity of employment. The falsehood consists in making out of that fact a controlling concept of society: in imputing to us people, on that sole ground, a solidarity of interest and sentiment that does not naturally arise from it. And the mischief is that when practical policies are based on such an abstraction, they will prove so far out of touch with human reality as to be neither successful nor safe. Only brute force can render them even temporarily effective.

·   ·   ·   ·   ·   ·

WHAT TO THINK ABOUT

So far our argument has been that economic life has a moral as well as a material significance; that in America, despite certain appearances, it is still pretty healthy; and that to get the best out of it our first prerequisite is clearer thinking, and more of it.

But what kind of thinking, then? In this field of business and ethics, we are not thinking for thinking's sake. Good thinking is certainly one of the seven virtues, but we have to remember in which set it belongs; for you cannot run an economic system on faith, hope, and charity, and it would not be virtuous to try. What we are after is that almost forgotten quality called sagacity, which sums up the effects of prudence, temperance, fortitude, and justice. This sounds very abstract; but it is an odd fact that people instinctively recognize sagacity when (rarely) they meet it. It goes so far beyond mere cleverness or expertise. Sir Francis Bacon remarked, toward the end of his life— when he had bitter reason to know what he was talking about—"there is a great difference between a cunning man and a wise man, not only in point of honesty but in point of ability . . . for nothing doth more hurt in a State than that cunning men pass for wise."

The purposes of good thinking in the field of social policy are two: first, to distinguish the elements in the situation that are given and not immediately alterable from those as to which we have some freedom of choice; and second, to discover the grounds and the probable effects of the choices that are open to us. For example, in a free society the elasticities of demand and supply and the results of free technology fall mainly in the former category: we have to adjust our decisions to them, rather than theirs to us. There is no hard-and-fast line; but not even Mr. Stalin can control the weather or the women, though it would appear that he can control practically everything else.

On examination we shall find that the area of the "given"—the inexorable laws and so forth—is much smaller than is generally supposed, and the area of possible choice much larger. And precisely that is our problem. Despite Sir Stafford Cripps, Mr. Wallace, and their encompassing crowds of experts, we are not wholly responsible for bumper crops of wheat, cotton, or potatoes; but we are responsible for what we do with them, and that responsibility is so onerous that we are tempted to wish it away somewhere. Yet we know, or should know by this time, that to narrow down or duck out of the area of conscious responsible choice is the surest way to corrode the morale of any modern society. One of the most tragic facts about totalitarianism is that, in proportion as the responsibility for vital decisions is taken away from the people, the amount of corruption and nepotism steadily increases. That fact can never be fully documented or proved by statistics; but it holds true even of Germany from 1930 to today. Conscious choice coupled with responsibility is the basis of all moral development. It is the school to which history consigns us; and it is a tough one. But we must not imagine that we can get the same education more cheaply elsewhere.

Must we then conclude that it is better to have unsound decisions resting on the broadest possible consensus than sounder ones resting on a narrower basis? For an economist to say that is about as easy as having a tooth pulled—not because he knows more of the right answers, but because he knows more of the penalties that are meted out to wrong ones. Yet it must be said if we are pushed into the field of general principles; and it can be said without too much misgiving provided we recognize what Lord Stamp really meant, in the statement above quoted, by "economically sensible and feasible."

MUSIC AND POTATOES

What did Stamp really mean? He was not defending laissez faire as such; neither, in final analysis, are Hayek, von Mises, and their adherents—though they have exposed themselves to considerable misinterpretation. To enthrone the "consumer as king" is to give him a grand opportunity to make a fool of himself, which he periodically does. I am by no means sure that a society consisting primarily of "consumers" would rate very high in any hierarchy, even that of the animal kingdom. No, the case for democratic freedom does not rest on the fact of our all having common appetites. It rests on the fact that the basis of all "sensible and feasible" economic policies is *moral rather than economic*. There is abundant proof in the history of British social reform down to 1945: the driving power came from a moral consensus of all sorts of people, not from an intellectual consensus of the doctrinaires—many of whom were overridden. The same, on the whole, has been true of America: one hopes it always will be true.

We do not have to dig back into history to establish the thesis. Consider again, for a moment, those bumper crops. Last year the newspapers published a picture of government-owned potatoes being destroyed in bulk by spraying kerosene over them. Everywhere that picture went—from Bangor to Leipzig, and farther—it evoked a shock of horror hardly less than the pictures of Hiroshima. It indicated something, as Henry Beston would say, "outside life." It suggested that somewhere, sometime, in this world or the next, there is a rod in pickle for people—whoever they are, and whatever their theory—who make that sort of response to nature's bounty. The same reaction was aroused by the wholesale destruction of citrus fruit in California. I say (I speak as a fool) that it was a good reaction; and I would rather die as a fool protesting than live as an "expert" proving that it was sensible and feasible. Or consider again, for a moment, our local community—the grocer, the carpenter, the electrician, the schoolteacher, and me. Our interests and our politics vary; but when George Szell brings his magnificent orchestra to town, we know that it is wrong that the schoolteacher cannot afford to buy a ticket. It is so god-damned wrong that you could not interest us in any theory proving that it is right or inevitable. This is not a thesis about schoolteachers' salaries; it is an illustration of the way in which economic policies that really work are arrived at. The basis is moral; and once that basis is denied, or deserted, it makes no difference what economic or political theory you excuse yourself by: the human values go down the drain anyway.

GRAB GROUPS AND THE "COMMON GOOD"

That is why so many of us view-with-alarm the temptation to slough off final economic responsibilities to—well, to anybody except plain you and me. It is not that we distrust the experts. They know their job, know it only too well. But if, as is here contended, the ultimate ground of all economic decisions is moral, then we cannot afford to give our collective conscience into anybody else's keeping. And precisely that is what we are now tempted to do.

It is worth recalling that the older economics of America rested on a strong base of Protestant individualistic religion, in theory as well as practice. In the hands of great teachers, like Francis Wayland of Brown University, it inspired young men to find spiritual as well as material satisfaction in the hard tasks of economic life; and they were not all bosses. It is frightfully cheap to sneer at all that. Granted that the ethical system was not adequate to the needs of an associative society, granted it was exploited by ruthless and greedy men—we are still far from justifying any theory that absolves us all, employers or employees, from personal moral responsibility. That is what the present generation is being offered. Because of the difficulties we have got ourselves into, we are tempted to leave not only the discussion of means but the determination and evaluation of ends to others: and in so far as we do that, our society disintegrates into a welter of mere grab groups, with the nation itself acting as one of them.

The modern tendency is to invoke general phrases, such as the "common good" or the "public welfare" or the "interest and security of the United States," then leave somebody else to define and apply them while we go about our business, and over the cocktails complain of bureaucracy. The U.S., for example, has accumulated an amazing collection of laws about fairness—fair labor standards, fair employment practices, fair return, fair valuation, fair trade (which means private price fixing), fair competition (which damns it); but if you seek from a study of these laws to ascertain the basic meaning of the word "fair," you are in for a course in applied jurisprudence that will reduce you to the mental condition of Pontius Pilate. The same result can be more swiftly achieved by a review of the conflicting criteria of public welfare that have been actually applied, this past thirty years, to either the mining or the railroad industry. The latter case gives a particularly striking demonstration of the fact that you cannot fix fairness by formula. After more than twenty years of trying, both the courts and the Congress were compelled to fall back on another batch of purely ethical terms such as honest, reasonable, just, prudent, and so forth. It is the interpretation of these terms that should and can be kept on the broadest possible basis; and it is both the duty and the ultimate interest of business—all sections of it—to see that we the people, striving yesterday, today, and forever to form a more perfect union, have the materials for intelligent moral judgment fully and frankly available to us.

$$\text{≈}\text{ई}\text{≈}\text{ई}\text{ई}\text{≈}\text{ई}\text{≈}$$

56. *Veblen* *

SOME OF VEBLEN'S COLORFUL PHRASES are probably much more widely known than his name. Here the reader has an opportunity to become more completely acquainted both with the man and with the broad range of his ideas. Staff writers from *Fortune*, after systematically examining the writings of Veblen and of those who have written about him, present in a popular vein his theories about business as a social institution.

THORSTEIN VEBLEN, the Wisconsin-born social philosopher who died obscurely in California in 1929, did what every thinking man would like to do if he had the time, the tenacity, and the mental endowment. Hungry for knowledge and understanding, but absorbed in the problems of their own lives and generations, most men never acquire more than scattered fragments of mankind's immense and constantly growing store of learning. Even the scholars for the most part are forced to live out their lives in the valleys, tending some single one of the narrow gardens into which academic specialists have marked off man's study of himself and his world. Veblen was the one man in a million—or in a thousand million—with courage and capacity to do more. Taking all knowledge for his province, he climbed a mountaintop and surveyed the whole life of mankind.

Because, in his sweeping view, men's beliefs and conduct are shaped primarily by the ways in which they earn a living and acquire wealth, Veblen is often classified as an economist. But his powerful, searching, original mind ranged far beyond the conventional limits of economics. He investigated art and religion and education, fashions and social customs, government and war and peace. He delved deep in history, literature, anthropology, psychology, biology, technology, the physical sciences. He has been called "the last man who knew everything."

But he was no scholarly magpie. Discovering new relationships of cause and effect, he wove everything he learned into a critical, coherent account of the development of Western civilization. His purpose was to understand the society he lived in, to explain the goals men strive for and the reasons for their striving, and to point out the goals they might attain.

What he saw and reported from his lonely peak was disturbing and

* Reprinted from the December, 1947, issue of *Fortune*, pp. 133-202, by Special Permission of the Editors; Copyright 1947 Time, Inc.

unwelcome to his contemporaries.   Most of them simply ignored it, and
tried to ignore him.   Most people still do.   To Americans in general, he
is only a name, vaguely identified as a Gilded Age satirist of business and
the rich, a radical and an eccentric whose reputation for polysyllabic
profundity frightens most readers away from even his famous first book,
The Theory of the Leisure Class. : . .

Yet Veblen has already won the philosopher's reward defined by the
late Justice Holmes: "men who never heard of him" are "moving to
the measure of his thought."   Every American who is skeptical of business glories, suspicious of great enrichment, contemptuous of social
climbing and wealthy ostentation, dubious of the merits of keeping up
with the Joneses, probably owes something to Thorstein Veblen's intellectual adventuring.   More than any other single thinker except
Karl Marx, he inspired and shaped the modern intellectual attack on·
business and the values of a business-dominated civilization.

That attack, currently still at a relative war-prosperity ebb after its
latest depression flood, stems from many intellectual springs.   Even
before the New Deal, the streams of pre-Marxian socialism, Populism,
Progressivism, Marxism, and Brandeisian antagonism to bigness and
monopoly were so intermingled that it was difficult to determine each
one's precise influence.   But it seems clear that Thorstein Veblen's
attitude and vocabulary were major contributions to the common cause.

Veblen, though a blaster of economic complacency, was not first in
the field.   Marx and his predecessors, who strongly influenced Veblen
but never converted him to full acceptance of any socialist system, had
touched off their charges long before *The Theory of the Leisure Class*
appeared.   But conventional U.S. economists at the turn of the century
still regarded business-as-usual with uncritical calm.   Accepting the prevailing attitudes and practices of businessmen as the working out of
immutable natural laws, they held that all goods and services (except
frankly criminal ones) are socially valuable simply because they are
in demand.   Almost their sole concerns were to describe the workings of
the system, and to figure out the precise balance of painful acquisition
and pleasurable consumption that gave each article or service its market
value.

Like Marx, Veblen declared that economics must be an evolutionary
science.   Following the trail blazed by Darwin and Huxley and Sumner, he insisted that economists, too, should study the origins of institutions; they should examine the social as well as the market value not only
of goods and services but also of business practices.   They should, for
example, not stop with asking how a stock exchange or a holding company works, but should go on to ask what human needs and notions

shaped its birth and development, and whether it is still in fact necessary or useful to the common welfare.

That such an approach to economic problems is now a matter of course is in no small measure a result of the fact that Thorstein Veblen spent his life asking and answering just such questions. ". . . As for the professional economists of the present generation and the fundamental aspirations of current economics," wrote Horace M. Kallen in his obituary of Veblen in *The Forward*, "they owe to Veblen more than to any single mind of his own time." Economist Paul T. Homan wrote shortly before Veblen's death: "It falls little beyond the truth to say that almost all the new leads in economic thinking which have been fruitfully followed during the past twenty years are in some degree directly traceable to him."

But Veblen's questions and answers, brilliant and stimulating as they are, have probably had less popular influence than the manner of his asking and his answering. Marx had already put much the same questions, and returned answers very different in kind but basically similar in substance. But Marx's attack was ferocious, and his conclusions openly revolutionary. The verbal blunderbuss of an avowed enemy and would-be destroyer of the capitalist system could—until his disciples seized control of the world's largest country—be safely ignored by capitalist professors and businessmen.

Veblen's approach, on the other hand, was one of aloof and urbane irony. Some vitriol crept into his later books, but in his earlier writing, and especially in *The Theory of the Leisure Class*, he seems to be examining the rich and powerful of the earth, and their envious imitators, with the detachment of a worldly zoologist explaining the antics of a cageful of monkeys. The revolutionary implications are there, but they are masked in a wondrously involved and thoroughly delightful style, deadpan, sesquipedalian, mock-pedantic, and sometimes uproariously funny, that has won Veblen some acclaim as a literary craftsman. With it he made "leisure-class" credos and conduct seem not only antisocial but more than slightly ridiculous.

The professors might try to ignore him, or dismiss him with curt contempt, but neither they nor the world at large could long ignore the insidious sting of such great phrases as "conspicuous leisure," "conspicuous consumption," "conspicuous waste," "invidious distinction," "the kept classes." It was these phrases and this attitude that captured the imaginations of youthful intellectuals rebelling against the materialism of American life at the century's turn. Gleefully they hurled Veblen's barbs at the rich and mighty and pretentious through Teddy Roosevelt's Square Deal and Woodrow Wilson's New Freedom. By the 1920's a knowledge of Veblen had become standard intellectual equipment for U.S. social rebels. The Veblen influence shone clear and strong in the writings of such critics as Stuart Chase, Lewis Mumford, Max Lerner, John Chamberlain, and Sinclair Lewis, such future New Dealers as Henry Wallace, Isador Lubin, Rex Tugwell, and Adolph Berle.

Writers of the *Nation—New Republic* school might be inspired by Marx's militant program, but Veblen was the man to quote. Whether they aimed at revolution or reform, the intellectuals knew that, in that era of prosperity, sophisticated skepticism and urbane ridicule were far more effective weapons than savage denunciation. Through journalists and fiction writers, the Veblen attitude spread in ever widening circles. Then, with the coming of depression, it burst its intellectual bounds entirely and suspicion of big business became a national fashion.

While the Battle of Business raged in the thirties, it was impossible for any business partisan to read Veblen with judicious calm. During the present lull, it may be profitable to investigate the man and the philosophy that produced the satire.

ODD MAN

Even his admirers, calling the man "strange," "aloof," "remote," "complex," have never pretended to understand Veblen fully. But his bias, at least, seems readily explained by the facts of his unhappy life. The definitive biography, a distinguished work of intellectual history, is *Thorstein Veblen and His America*, by Joseph Dorfman. It makes plain that he was always an alien spirit in the U.S., never at home in it, never at ease.

Born on a raw Wisconsin farm in 1857 and reared on another in Minnesota, Veblen was one of nine children of poor Norwegian immigrants. From the first he was set apart from the native community. The frontier "Norskie" settlers of his youth dwelt in clannish isolation, preserving their language and customs, distrusting their Yankee' neighbors and in turn despised by them.

Veblen's sharp, curious mind made him an alien, too, among his parents' stolid countrymen. Even to them he was an "odd" youth—irreverent, jeering, sarcastic, unpopular. But he was enough a part of the midwestern community to share deeply in the 'late-nineteenth-century agrarian unrest that, mixed with the yeast of pre-Marxian socialism brought by the immigrants of 1848, produced the Populist revolt and the continuing radicalism of Wisconsin and Minnesota. Veblen's temperament made him uncommonly receptive to the bitter resentment of the railroads, and the deep suspicion of what he was to call the "massive vested interests that move obscurely in the background" in Wall Street, which dominated that time and place.

Poverty and lack of English helped bar him from a normal social life at Carleton College. Lonely, shy, and debt-ridden, but still as contentious and acid-tongued as ever, he went on to Johns Hopkins and Yale for a Ph.D., hoping to become a teacher of philosophy. His rustic manners and skeptical beliefs, plus the fact that divinity students were then preferred as philosophy professors, closed academic doors to him. Pleading ill health, he went back to Minnesota in defeat, to live off his family (and later his wife's family) for seven miserable years.

In 1891, aged thirty-four, he determined to make a fresh start and went off to Cornell to study the social sciences. Wearing a coonskin cap and corduroy trousers, with long hair, weak drawl, anemic looks, and shambling gait, he was still a bizarre figure in the campus world. But the years of "reading and loafing" had not been so idle as they seemed to his long-suffering kinsmen. Ranging from Icelandic mythology to Cretan history and beyond, he had stored up an impressive knowledge of man's habits and beliefs from earliest times, and thought deeply and originally about them. The quality of his mind and the sweep of his learning at last won him recognition and a $520-a-year academic foothold at the new University of Chicago.

Veblen became a brilliant teacher, but never a popular one. To a few receptive students he gave the incomparable exhilaration that comes of glimpsing a new pattern in the swirling complexities of human life. But he was irked by classroom routine and impatient of dullness and ignorance; he mumbled through most of his lectures. Equally irked by the proprieties, he was the kind of defiant campus eccentric who keeps tongues clacking happily in faculty clubs and parlors. All his life he had trouble getting and holding a job. Embroilment with two wives and a succession of mistresses ("But what is one to do if the woman moves in on you?" he asked) forced him to move on from Chicago to Stanford to Missouri, and finally to the metropolitan haven of New York City, where in the years of World War I and after he helped edit The Dial and lectured at the New School for Social Research. Everywhere he left behind him legends of his unconventional ménages, his ill-fitting clothes and monogrammed cigarettes, his unmade beds and primitive dishwashing machine (barrel plus garden hose).

Veblen never earned more than $2,400 a year by his teaching, and the royalties from his books added only $500 a year at their peak. When the New School fell into financial straits, he was able to stay on only because a former student anonymously paid his salary. Finally, in 1926, he went back to his mountain cabin in California, "a deserted and lonely man," as Lewis Mumford recalls, "feeble, ill, pale, wistful, demonic, proud." He died less than three months before the Great Crash came to fulfill his prophecies of capitalistic disaster.

IS HUMAN NATURE NATURAL?

Veblen's writings revolve around his contrast between the predatory and the productive traits and activities of mankind. Developing this theme, he insisted on a sharp distinction between "business" and "industry." Industry, he said, is the productive process of making goods; business is the predatory process of making profits.

Veblen hailed technologists and engineers, devoted to efficient production, as the real industrialists. Businessmen—in which category he lumped absentee owners, major executives, financiers, salesmen, advertising men, stockbrokers, promoters, and all others not directly concerned with production and essential distribution—he called "parasites" and worse than useless. Intent on "getting something for nothing," they impede the flow of goods by killing off competitors and "sabotaging" the industry they control through a "conscious withdrawal of efficiency" to keep goods scarce and prices high.

The Veblen critique of business would be indisputably true—if it were applied to a world wholly composed of unselfish, non-competitive, cooperative human beings with plenty of everything for everybody. Confronted with the simple facts of existing human nature and material production, his whole argument seems to collapse. But it is precisely at this point that Veblen really begins to argue.

Human nature, he declares, is not foreordained and unchangeable. Seen in the perspective of man's whole life on the planet, what we regard as fixed characteristics of human nature are simply traits that men have developed in the process of adapting themselves to their environment. Since environment constantly changes as men evolve new ways of providing themselves with life's necessities and luxuries, it might be expected that human nature would change with it.

The flowering of the machine process in the Industrial Revolution, for example, has made it possible for the first time in history to produce enough goods so that every human being can have all the material things he needs for a comfortable, healthful life. Hence there is no longer any material reason why men should not stop their quarelling and settle down to peaceable production and sharing of that possible abundance.

But, said Veblen, the adaptation of human nature to this new environment has been and is still being grievously impeded by the "leisure class"—the rich and powerful of the earth. Over the centuries they have developed and still vigorously defend a massive fabric of codes and institutions. These are designed, consciously or unconsciously, to perpetuate the selfishness, pride, greed, competitiveness, ruthlessness, clannishness, and other traits that human beings developed when there was not enough to go around, when men did not know how to produce enough for everybody and the strong took from the weak. Only men's loyalty to these outworn codes and institutions keeps them from entering at last into a world of peace and abundance.

This is the thesis that emerges when one has penetrated the thickets of Veblen's prose; this is the vision of past and future he saw from his lonely mountaintop. To those who understand it, his satirical bitterness becomes in turn understandable. It is the bitterness of the prophet against a world that refused to listen to him, and failed to understand him; against codes of social standing, business success, luxurious living, dress, etiquette, sport, patriotism, and institutions of business, government, education, religion, and all others that, in their existing forms and inspirations, he saw as stumbling blocks on the road to a new life for mankind. This is why, beginning in *The Theory of the Leisure Class*, he devoted all of his immense learning and penetrating imagination to "destructive" explanations of how and why these codes and institutions have developed.

THE BIRTH OF PRIDE

Far back in the beginnings of time, he wrote, before the dawn of history, primitive men actually did live together in sluggish good will. They were peaceful, indolent, non-competitive, mutually helpful. There was no urgent reason why they should not be; their needs and tastes were few and simple. A man might keep a club or trinket or piece of clothing for his personal use, but that was the extent of individual ownership. Everything else belonged to the group and was shared in common.

Then, as humans multiplied and ranging hunters clashed with members of strange groups, the predatory era dawned. Fighting men began capturing and bringing home enemy women. At first the captives were simply trophies of victory, and their capture brought glory not to the captor but to his group.

But, as the centuries passed, the beginning of handicraft and agriculture brought more and more work into human life. Women, the weaker sex, had always done whatever drudgery was involved in preparing primitive food and clothing, so it was only natural that the captives should be put to use at these new tasks. The trophies acquired productive value.

There was some point, now, in the captor's wanting to keep them for himself. The institution of marriage began to take shape, as households with a male head were established. Since strength and wiliness were required to capture women from enemy men, the possession of a number of them came to be a mark of their captor's prowess. He enjoyed not only their personal service and the products of their work, but also the esteem and envy of his fellows.

This, says Veblen, was probably the origin of individual ownership "as a conventional right or equitable claim." With it, because all useful work except hunting was assigned to women and other inferiors (later including captive men as well as women), came the beginning of men's feeling that productive work is inherently shameful, a thing with which no superior man will soil his fingers or his dignity. Thus began what Veblen calls "conspicuous leisure," i.e., leisure enjoyed not for its own sake but as a visible mark of the idler's superiority. And thus arose an "invidious distinction"* between the leisure class and persons forced to work for a living.

With the establishment of this difference between persons, the "regime of status" was born. Social emulation—the desire to equal or excel another in social standing—entered the world as a major motive in human conduct.

But man, says Veblen, is by nature an agent. He is impelled by a sense of purpose and so "possessed of a taste for effective work, and a distaste for futile effort . . . a sense of the merit of serviceability or efficiency and of the demerit of futility, waste, or incapacity." This "instinct of workmanship," developed in the peaceful ages before the predatory era began, is forever at war with man's acquired sense of the dignity of leisure. He cannot rest content with mere idleness.

The leisure class hence needed something to do, some occupation with a sense of purpose and accomplishment about it that offered rewards for efficient performance, yet carried no slavish stain of productive industry. Hunting and warfare were naturals for the purpose. While it remained primarily a source of food, hunting of course dangerously resembled useful industry. But, Veblen hastens to point out, it was not really industry; like war, it was exploit, seizure by force. Other occupations found to meet the leisure-class requirements of purposeful, nonproductive employment were government, priestly service, sports.

Because these were the activities of superior men, they came to be regarded as "honorable"—a concept that in primitive societies "seems to

---

* *Invidious,* adj. 1. *Tending to excite odium, ill will, or envy; likely to give offense; esp., unjustly and irritatingly discriminating; as, invidious distinctions...* 2. *Worthy of envy; enviable; as, an invidious income*—Webster.

connote nothing else than assertion of superior force." For thousands of years, while productive labor remained the despised (and therefore irksome) province of women and slaves, efficiency in these leisure-class pursuits filled the performer with pride and the beholders with admiration and envy. Human beings naturally grew to admire also the "manly virtues" required for success in these pursuits: ferocity, ruthlessness, selfishness, clannishness, shrewdness, trickery.

Hand in hand with conspicuous leisure and the regime of status came "conspicuous consumption"—the accumulation and consumption of goods not solely for their utility but in part, or wholly, to impress the neighbors. Here simple expensiveness is the touchstone. But as chiefs and kings and nobles vied with each other to display more and better-trained and richer-liveried servants, greater houses and castles, more resplendent clothes and jewels, rarer and more abundant food, conspicuous leisure and consumption combined to produce "conspicuous waste" as a ruling canon of leisure-class life.

Veblen defined economic waste as any expenditure of time or effort or material that does not contribute to "the physical comfort and fullness of life" of the community or mankind. The resulting article or activity may, he concedes, give the individual genuine pleasure, and so not be wasteful in the conventional sense. But the pleasure, he argues, derives less from the thing itself than from the prestige attached to it. According to the code of conspicuous waste, the more wasteful any visible activity or service or article is, the more it redounds to the prestige of the consumer, as a display not only of his wealth but also of his contempt for productive effort. Thus fox hunting bestows more social prestige than deer hunting (the deer can be eaten), a butler or footman more than a cook, handmade shoes or lace more than machine-made.

These are the notions whose history Veblen examines in *The Theory of the Leisure Class*. He is far less concerned with conscious "social climbing" or with the rich themselves than with the way their standards have burrowed into the human subconscious and shaped conventional ideas of what is right and good and beautiful.

WOMEN AND SERVANTS

For a long time after captive women began to be put to use, the wife (or chief wife) of the leisure-class household remained little more than its chief servant. But as the honorific value of conspicuous leisure rose, it began to seem more and more essential to the prestige of the head of the house that his wife should not demean him by stooping to any form of useful labor.

This feeling grew even more widespread when the social value of male

conspicuous leisure—or rather the social disgrace of male industry—
began to diminish. Two historic developments made it socially permissible for a gentleman to go to work (though still not to actual production). The spread of law was one; it grew increasingly difficult and
dangerous for predatory men simply to grab what they wanted. And
the Industrial Revolution, changing the world's economy, made it possible for forceful men of the lower classes to rise to wealth by methods
other than armed conquest. The older aristocracy, whose ancestors had
secured their wealth by the "honorable" means of armed force, might
continue indefinitely to look down on people "in trade," but the power
of wealth could not be denied.

The self-made man, however, continued to respect the older aristocracy's codes. He made his obeisance to that of conspicuous leisure increasingly at second hand, through his wife and daughters and servants.
Among both old and new rich, the woman's conspicuous leisure remained a very different thing from that of the man. Like the leisure of
the superfluous servant, it was designed to enhance not her own prestige
but that of her master. It was, in Veblen's phrase, "vicarious leisure."
Her costume, like that of the liveried butler or footman, was designed
to display her master's wealth and contempt for industry not only by
its obvious costliness but also by its obvious evidence that the wearer
could engage in no productive activity while so clothed. Hence the
corset, the long skirt, the bustle, the hoop skirt, the high heel, the
towering coiffure of the eighteenth century. Hence also the artificially
deformed feet of the Chinese—and the New Look. That these things
are uncomfortable is of no more moment than the fact that a woman
may be bored by her enforced idleness. The possessor of vicarious
leisure is not intended to enjoy it.

BEAUTY AND FASHION

How does it happen that such obviously grotesque devices as the
corset, the bustle, the high heel can in themselves, or in their effect,
actually seem beautiful?

The "underlying norms of taste," says Veblen, were probably formed
before men began trying to outdo each other in displays of wealth.
According to these norms, "the requirements of beauty, simply, are
for the most part best satisfied by inexpensive contrivances and structures
which in a straightforward manner suggest both the office which they
are to perform and the method of serving their end."

But the standards of pecuniary display have all but obliterated this
"untutored" sense of beauty. Consciously or unconsciously, we admire
and buy things according to their expensiveness and waste. This ac-

counts for the vogue of dresses, houses, furniture, automobiles, etc., that are large, intricate, and ornate, obviously involving waste of labor and materials.

These things, however, are offensive to underlying tastes, to the "instinct of workmanship" that admires efficiency and dislikes futility. Hence changing fashions. "The process of developing an aesthetic nausea takes more or less time," but eventually one set of grotesqueries is swept away in favor of a new and different set.

But temporary admiration of fashionable things is not usually hypocritical. "A fancy bonnet of this year's model unquestionably appeals to our sensibilities today much more forcibly than an equally fancy bonnet of the model of last year; although when viewed in the perspective of a quarter of a century, it would, I apprehend, be a matter of the utmost difficulty to award the palm for intrinsic beauty to the one rather than to the other of these structures. So, again, it may be remarked that, considered simply in their physical juxtaposition with the human form, the high gloss of a gentleman's hat or of a patent-leather shoe has no more of intrinsic beauty than a similarly high gloss on a threadbare sleeve; and yet there is no question but that all well-bred people (in the Occidental civilized communities) instinctively and unaffectedly cleave to the one as a phenomenon of great beauty, and eschew the other as offensive to every sense to which it can appeal. It is extremely doubtful if anyone could be induced to wear such a contrivance as the high hat of civilized society, except for some urgent reason based on other than aesthetic grounds."

KEEPING UP WITH THE JONESES

So Veblen goes on through the range of human institutions, everywhere finding evidences of the way human adaptation to the new industrial environment is slowed by conspicuous leisure, conspicuous consumption, conspicuous waste. College sports, he asserts for example, glorify and perpetuate the "archaic virtues" of ferocity, trickery, and clannishness. In so doing, sports may be extremely helpful to the individual preparing for life in a predatory world. But as for their pretended benefit to general student health, he drily notes: "It has been said, not inaptly, that the relation of football to physical culture is much the same as that of the bullfight to agriculture."

Religious observances, he further declares, perpetuate the regime of status even in spiritual matters. Men act as if their God were a worldly prince. They seek to glorify Him by building conspicuously wasteful churches like castles: large, costly, richly decorated. They pay Him the servitor's tribute of vicarious leisure by refraining from work on Sunday, going to church in clothes unsuited for work, sitting in uncomfortable pews.

Veblen sums up the ruling motive of modern life as "pecuniary emulation." Men work primarily, he says, to earn a living. But the things a family really needs for comfortable, healthful living can normally be bought with a relatively small income. Beyond that, most men try to earn more money and accumulate more goods primarily to prove their prowess. In a pecuniary civilization like that of the U.S., the success of all but a few such men as scientists, poets, and college presidents is measured in terms of money. Unless a man is so notoriously rich that he can afford to dress in shabby comfort and have bad manners, he normally feels that he must provide continuous evidence that he is at least as successful as, and preferably a little more successful than, most of the people in his community or social class. He can normally do this only by visibly maintaining or excelling their standards of leisure, consumption, and waste in house, furnishings, grounds, dress, automobile, manners, entertainment, sports, clubs, schools. Americans call it "keeping up with the Joneses," "having what other people have," "giving our children the advantages the other children have," or, when purchasing power dwindles, just "keeping up appearances."

Any failure to maintain these standards brings instant social opprobrium. If a man does not spend sufficient money on these things, the obvious conclusion is that he lacks the money, and is therefore less successful than his neighbors. For the ordinary man, this is more than a matter of winning or keeping his community's respect and envy. Just as he feeds his pride by getting and spending, so he loses his self-respect if he is a failure in the eyes of his community and family.

In this race there is no rest. The anxiety about "security," which the ordinary man suffers, is less a fear of losing the means of his family's subsistence (now guaranteed in the U.S.) than of being forced to a drastic lowering of its standard of living. No man can ever be guaranteed against that.

Says Veblen with worldly wisdom: "It is much more difficult to recede from a scale of expenditure once adopted than it is to extend the accustomed scale in response to an accession of wealth. Many items of customary expenditure prove on analysis to be almost purely wasteful, and they are therefore honorific only, but after they have once been incorporated into the scale of decent consumption, and so have become an integral part of one's scheme of life, it is quite as hard to give up these as it is to give up many items that conduce directly to one's physical comfort, or even that may be necessary to life and health . . .

"But as fast as a person makes new acquisitions, and becomes accustomed to the resulting new standard of wealth, the new standard forthwith ceases to afford appreciably greater satisfaction than the earlier standard did . . . The end sought by accumulation is to rank high in comparison with the rest of the community in point of pecuniary strength. So long as the comparison is distinctly unfavorable to himself, the normal, average individual will live in chronic dissatisfaction with his present lot; and when he has reached what may be called the normal pecuniary standard of the community, this chronic dissatisfaction will give place to restless straining to place a wider and ever-widening pecuniary interval between himself and this average standard . . .

"In the nature of the case, the desire for wealth can scarcely be satiated in any individual instance, and evidently a satiation of the average or general desire for wealth is out of the question. However widely, or equally, or 'fairly,' it may be distributed, no general increase of the community's wealth can make an approach to satiating this need, the ground of which is the desire of everyone to excel everyone else in the accumulation of goods."

EMANCIPATOR OF THE MIND

Reminiscent as it is of Christ's admonitions that happiness cannot be found by laying up "treasures upon earth," The Theory of the Leisure Class suggests a plausible explanation of Thoreau's made-in-America observation: "The mass of men lead lives of quiet desperation." Even after discounting Veblen's satirical exaggerations, many a reader of this American classic has probably resolved to sweep pecuniary pride out of his own heart and life.

Veblen himself had no hope that the world can ever be righted by such individual changes of heart. His later books are increasingly permeated by a sense of impending doom. Like Marx, he concluded that the inner contradictions of capitalistic society, including the conflict between production and profit seeking, and the impossibility of satiating "the average or general desire for wealth," must inevitably lead to increasingly severe depressions, wars, revolution, and general collapse.

"What can be done," he asked in The Theory of Business Enterprise (1904), "to save civilized mankind from the vulgarization and disintegration wrought by the machine industry?" Not until The Engineers and the Price System (1921) did he supply an affirmative answer. Parting company with Marx, he denied that the proletariat might bring salvation. Workingmen, he declared, understand the necessities of modern industry no better than businessmen do; the labor unions' "sole and self-seeking interest converges on the full dinner pail." The world can have peace and abundance, Veblen suggested, only if production-minded engineers somehow unite in a "soviet of technicians" and take over the world.

Fortunately for himself, Veblen died too soon to see his fascist-minded proposal flare and fizzle during the early thirties in Howard Scott's Technocracy. Veblen's reputation remains that of a great diagnostician, not a healer, of social ills. But no one who has really explored Veblen's thought—the breadth and subtlety of which are barely suggested in this brief account—is likely to dispute the tribute paid him by a disciple and former student, Columbia University's distinguished economist Wesley C. Mitchell, in a reminiscent speech at the University of Chicago:

"There was the disturbing genius of Thorstein Veblen—that visitor from another world, who dissected the current commonplaces which the student had unconsciously acquired, as if the most familiar of his daily thoughts were curious products wrought in him by outside forces. No other such emancipator of the mind from the subtle tyranny of circumstance has been known in social science, and no other such enlarger of the realm of inquiry."

◆◈◆◈◆◈◆

57. U. S. vs. A & P: Battle of Titans *

TWO BASIC INSTITUTIONAL SYSTEMS in American society are business and government. Both are powerful institutions vested with extensive systems of social control. At numerous points these two areas of power and control have come into conflict. John W. Andrews describes the Great Atlantic and Pacific Tea Company and analyzes its attempt to prevent the Federal government from regulating this corporation's power to eliminate competition. The article illustrates the corporate organization of American economic institutions and the struggle between these corporations and the agencies of government.

* John Williams Andrews, Harper's Magazine, 201, No. 1204 (September, 1950), 64-73. Reprinted by permission of the author.
The author (b. 1898) is a lawyer and writer. Chief, Federal-State Relations Section, U. S. Dept. of Justice, Washington, D. C., 1942-49. Associated with history department, Yale University. Formerly, practicing lawyer in Elihu Root's law firm in New York. Does biological and historical writing. His poems have appeared in a number of magazines including Harper's.

The great atlantic & pacific tea company—the name brings up an image of global enterprise, trade winds and oceans of discovery, the romance of the East. Actually, the enterprise was purely American; two young business men from Maine, expanding, in the middle of the last century, their modest hide-and-leather business into tea, sold at cut-rates in a gaudy little store in Vesey Street, New York. It was not until the nineteen-thirties that it became truly global. It was not until the nineteen-forties that it began seriously to tangle with a companion Titan, the United States government. Today, the continuation of A&P, as America has known it for ninety years, depends on the outcome of a great new anti-trust action, United States versus A&P.

A&P began, back in 1859, as the Great American Tea Company, selling teas for thirty cents that had been selling for a dollar, advertising the elimination of the middleman, and accumulating the anguished squawks of the harried competition. A band played on Saturdays in the store; red, white, and blue globes shone in the windows; and a huge gaslight "T" swayed over the sidewalk. As new stores were opened, they were in the Vesey Street pattern. A Baltimore newspaper of the seventies reported the new Baltimore store as "more resembling the fairy palaces . . . in the Arabian Nights than the business establishments one generally sees in this section." "Tea Clubs" were formed by mail to stimulate the country business, and premiums were given away to the tune of "This is the day / They give babies away / With half-a-pound of tea."

By 1869 the Great Atlantic & Pacific Tea Company had been formed, embodying, it has been suggested, the Founders' ambition to emulate the Union Pacific Railroad in linking the two oceans. By 1880 there were a hundred stores, scattered up and down the Eastern seaboard, and the older founder, George F. Gilman, had retired to a life of splendor in Bridgeport, Connecticut. By the early nineties, George Huntington Hartford, the younger founder, and his sons, George and John, still expanding the chain, had begun the manufacture of A&P products— baking powder made by a chemist behind a screen in Vesey Street. By 1900, there were two hundred stores; by 1912, there were four hundred. A&P wagons—with teas, coffees, and groceries—moved over some five thousand peddlers' routes. By 1916, sales were running close to the forty-five million level.

The true spurt into vastness, however, came just before America's entry into World War I. John Hartford, the younger son, had discovered the magic of "economy stores"—one-man, standardized affairs, operating without deliveries, credit, or premiums, and putting all savings into lower prices. Seven thousand five hundred of these stores were opened in some nine hundred working days; they revolutionized the food merchandising business in America. By the end of 1924, A&P could boast no less than 11,413 stores across America. By June 1926, it had 14,220 stores, sales were close to the half billion mark, earnings before taxes were over $13 million. By 1932, about the time that A&P's competitors, ahead of A&P, were launching into the Super-market, A&P had over 15,000 stores. It was a Titan, vaster than Henry Ford at his peak; vaster than James Cash Penney, Sears Roebuck, and Montgomery Ward together; approximately equal to the entire auto-mobile business of 1932. It was the Great American Food Romance. By 1942, its sales were almost a billion and a half, its profits close to thirty millions.

Today, with sales still climbing and the Atlantic and Pacific truly linked, A&P faces what the management calls the "destruction" of A&P, and the government calls "divestiture in the public interest." If the government is successful, A&P will be split into seven competing retail chains; the manufacturing phases of the business will be divorced from the retail phases and from each other; and the great Atlantic Com-mission Company, the vast A&P purchaser of fresh fruits and vegetables, will be wholly dissolved.

It is a curious case. We have had other divestitures—the Pullman case, which broke up the old empire of the Pullman cars; the Paramount Motion Picture case, in which, after years of trial and error, the courts decreed the separation of the production phase from the exhibition phase; the still undetermined cases against American Telephone & Telegraph and Western Electric, against du Pont, U. S. Rubber, and General Motors, against the Big Four Meat Packers. These cases have made their flurries in professional circles, but the man-and-woman-in-the-street have paid little heed. The A&P case is different. It has reached down into the homes. Husbands and wives discuss it over the break-fast table. You can pick up an argument in any train or street car. Opinion is passionate, personal—even violent.

It is largely on the side of A&P. The Gallup poll of November 20, 1949, showed almost twice as many people for A&P as for the govern-ment. Editorial opinion is even more weighted, if the forty-eight-page reprint of 728 editorials and commentaries, issued by A&P, is an ac-curate reflection. Each of our 150,000,000 people must eat; a wife or husband in each of our 38,000,000 families must buy its daily bread; the A&P case, in its basic issue of consumer prices, involves not only those who buy from A&P, but all who buy. It is not extraordinary that the case should be occupying the attention of such a large proportion of the public. It is not even extraordinary that opinion should be one-sided, considering the fashion in which the story has thus far been presented to the American people.

II

The A&P divestiture action was filed by the United States Department of Justice on September 15, 1949, and, for a day or so, created little or no stir. The Sherman anti-trust laws are part of the folklore of the American people, but the legal and economic implications are, at best, only generally understood; the dry reading matter of an anti-trust action cannot compete with the comics or the morning's murder.

On September 20, 1949, however, the situation began to change. On that day, in some two thousand newspapers across the country—big dailies and little country weeklies—the first of the great A&P advertisements appeared. Under the generalship of Carl Byoir, A&P's public-relations counsel, tall headlines rode across full pages in the finest tradition of expert advertising. "Do You Want Your A&P Put Out of Business?" "Do You Want Higher Prices?" "This would mean higher food prices for you . . . less food on every dinner table. . . . Do they [the American people] want to continue to enjoy low prices and better living? Or do they want to break up A&P and pay higher prices, and have lower living standards? What do you want? . . . If A&P is big, it is because the American people, by their patronage, have made it big."

On Thursday, September 29, 1949 (regular chain-store "ad" day) the second A&P ad appeared—a full page again. "Why Do They Want To Put A&P Out of Business? They say . . . and these are the anti-trust lawyers' own words . . . that we 'have regularly undersold competing retailers.' To this charge we plead guilty: we confess that for the past ninety years we have constantly stepped up the efficiency of our operations in order to give our customers more and more good food for their money." The sub-heads shouted, "Do You Want Higher Prices?" The text painted a picture of America mobilized behind A&P—customers, farmers, suppliers, "our 110,000 employees," the labor leaders. "The entire American system of efficient, low-cost, low-profit distribution which we pioneered will face destruction and the public will suffer."

On October 18, 1949, Attorney-General McGrath, speaking to the Connecticut Bar Association, quickly struck back on behalf of the government. "The successful prosecution of the pending civil suit," he said, "will not increase, but should decrease, grocery prices. . . . The existence of monopoly power and its ruthless use in disregard of the public interest threaten economic freedom, retard efficiency, and curtail progress. Our system of free enterprise cannot survive unless the advantages of competition accrue to all of us."

On the same day, Assistant Attorney-General Bergson, in charge of the Anti-trust Division, spoke in Chicago. "A&P," he said, "has overlooked a very significant fact in its advertisements. The filing of the recent civil suit did not mark the beginning of the Department's anti-trust litigation against A&P. In 1942, the Department instituted a criminal anti-trust case, involving the same conduct that is the subject matter of the civil suit. . . . After six months of careful consideration . . . the Court found A&P guilty. . . . A&P appealed to the Court of Appeals. . . . In February of 1949 that court unanimously held that A&P had been properly convicted. A&P could have asked the Supreme Court of the United States to review this conviction. . . . They chose not to do so. Instead, they paid maximum fines totaling $175,000. . . .

"Suppression of the truth is equivalent to the suggestion of what is false. In a mild way, that sums up A&P's advertising. . . . A typical deception is found in the advertisement which reads, quote: 'They say . . . and these are the anti-trust lawyers' own words . . . that "we have regularly undersold competing retailers," ' end quote. This advertisement asserts that this is the charge against A&P. And to this charge A&P in headline type pleads guilty. . . . These words were deliberately lifted out of context. I'll read you the paragraph of the complaint in which they are found:

Defendants, by coercing and receiving unlawful buying preferences, have become enabled to and *have regularly undersold*, regularly taken patronage away from, and sometimes eliminated *competing retailers*. . . .

"The Court did not convict A&P of being big. . . . A&P was convicted . . . because, and I quote the Court, of the 'predatory application of its mass purchasing power' and the abuse of that power through boycotts, blacklisting, preferential rebates, price wars, and below-cost retailing in strategic areas in order to eliminate local competition. . . . The aim of this case is to restore active and vigorous competition to the food industry."

It was not to be expected that these speeches would reach many ears. A curious story developed at this time, of how certain sections of the press excluded or attenuated coverage of the government's side of the case. Don Hollenbeck treated the matter in some detail in broadcasts over WCBS on October 22 and November 26, and some historian, in years to come, may include a footnote on a possible relationship between newspaper advertising and editorial policy. But even with comprehensive coverage, it would not have been possible for a few inches of a speech by a government official, couched in legal terminology, to make much headway against broadsides which multiplied, week after week, themes designed to dismay and alarm the food-and-price conscious American householder. The scareheads—"Higher Prices," "Less Food," "Less Money in the Pay Envelope" were sandwiched with glowing references to America the Wonderful, American Sportsmanship, and A&P's beneficent mission.

On January 5, 1950, a new theme began to develop—the "They Have Been Wrong Before" theme—"they" being, as usual, the Washington anti-trust lawyers, pictured as engaged in a personal vendetta against A&P. The new ads took up the "Washington Bread Case" and the "North Carolina Potato Case," in each of which A&P was acquitted by directed verdict, and the "Dallas Case," where an indictment against A&P was abandoned by the government in favor of an identical criminal complaint in the Federal District Court at Danville, Illinois. No mention, naturally, was made of the Cease and Desist Order of the Federal Trade Commission in 1938, calling upon A&P to conform to the provisions of the Robinson-Patman Act; nor of the two indictments in 1941, which resulted in fines to A&P; nor of the four civil actions in 1941, in which A&P, with other defendants, consented to decrees prohibiting price-fixing and the coercion of price-cutting grocers.

The "Danville Case" was mentioned, with a promise to tell the public all about it. This promise was fulfilled on May 12, 1950. The superhead ran: "This Time the Anti-trust Lawyers Won a Case Against A&P. . . . They say that this suit [the divestiture suit] is based on the fact that they won a suit against us at Danville, Illinois, in 1946. They did. . . . Immediately thereafter, in a letter explaining his decision, Judge Lindley wrote: 'I Have Not Condemned the A&P System. I Have Not Made a Finding Which Could Be the Basis For a Suit of Dissolution.' So, now we have the anti-trust lawyers saying that their suit to dissolve A&P is based on Judge Lindley's decision; while Judge Lindley himself says his decision could not be the basis for a suit of dissolution."

On the day on which this statement appeared, Judge Lindley gave the *Chicago Daily News* a somewhat different version of his decision.

"I decided," said Judge Lindley, "that they violated the law. I did not attempt to make a finding to be the basis of a suit for dissolution. I was not asked to do this. This was beyond my province in the case before me. Whether the conduct of A&P since my decision has been such as to correct the abuses I found or of such character as to justify a decree of dissolution is a question for the court in which the suit is pending."

Judge Lindley told the *Daily News* that the letter mentioned by A&P was "a casual answer to criticism" following his decision. "He did not remember," said the *News*, "to whom he had written."

III

The Danville case was a remarkable affair, not because of the legal issues involved (there was little or no new law), nor because of the length of the trial (twenty-five weeks), nor the length of the record (some 60,000 pages). It was extraordinary because, for the first time in its eighty-five years of existence, the A&P was revealed in its full stature and inner workings. *Business Week*, when the Dallas indictment was handed up in 1942, remarked: "The Department of Justice did contrive, of legal necessity, to work in a few Winchellisms, which will give the trade a peek through A&P's hitherto blacked-out keyhole." With the Danville trial, the full curtain went up.

A&P was shown to be a completely integrated empire, fourteen corporations piled one on top of the other, pyramiding upward, through two great holding corporations, to the George Huntington Hartford Trust, of which the two brothers, Mr. John and Mr. George Hartford, were the sole trustees. The Trust held 99.97 per cent of the voting stock of the Great Atlantic & Pacific Tea Company of New York; A&P New York held all of the stock of A&P Maryland, which in turn owned outright the three great manufacturing companies—Quaker Maid Company, which made for A&P stores two hundred and more products, from baking powder to vinegar; White House Milk Company, with milk-processing plants in Wisconsin; and Nakat Packing Corporation, America's largest canner of Alaskan salmon and operator of great Alaskan fishing fleets. A&P Maryland owned outright the enormous American Coffee Corporation, buyer of green coffees from Colombia and Brazil; A&P New Jersey, which roasted and packed the coffees and also operated retail stores in twenty-four states; A&P Nevada and A&P Arizona, which operated stores in sixteen additional states; and the super-colossal fruit and vegetable purchaser, Atlantic Commission Company. There was not even a shade of a minority interest anywhere from A&P New York on down.

The retail stores were an empire in themselves, scattered from coast to coast, operating in forty states and the District of Columbia, with A&P Delaware holding A&P rights to do business in the states not yet invaded. Thirty-seven wholesale warehouses supplied the stores, receiving the A&P-manufactured products and the products purchased by the A&P divided into seven great divisions—New England, Atlantic, Eastern, Southern, Central, Central Western, and Middle Western. No division was a separate corporation, but each was fully equipped with a president, vice-presidents, a board of directors, and operating officers. Each division was divided into units, each unit being also an operating segment in itself.

An elaborate system of bookkeeping kept the financial relationships between the parts of the empire in order—bookkeeping "profits" for the companies and for each business phase, goods "sold" from level to level, rebates, discounts, allowances. But the whole was monolithic. "It is all the A&P Tea Company to me," an official testified at Danville, and this concept carried down to the littlest clerk. All of A&P's "real" profits, with the exception of certain profits of Atlantic Commission Company (Acco), were made from the over-the-counter sales to the American housewife.

A&P might spread huge across the United States; it might reveal, in its slightest gesture, the presence of a colossus; its titanic sales (835 million pounds of meat in 1946, 2 million tons of fresh fruit and vegetables, 300 million loaves of bread, 74 million pounds of butter, 100 million dozen eggs, 100 million pounds of poultry, 17,500 tons of cheese, 245 million pounds of coffee, 50 million dozen doughnuts—to mention but a few items) might involve it in activities the world over. But A&P's basic operation was utterly simple, cutting through all its corporate lines. It was just a blown-up grocery store, buying or manufacturing the supplies it sold to the housewife over the counter.

Its basic operating policy was equally simple: to buy at the lowest possible price, and, except where the strategies of empire dictated otherwise, to sell at the lowest possible price. A&P officials referred to this policy as the "two-price level" policy—the lower price (both buying and selling) for A&P and the higher price (both buying and selling) for A&P's competitors. It was excesses in pursuit of this policy that first brought A&P in conflict with laws against restraints of trade.

IV

The A&P's side of the dispute with the government has been so widely heard, and the government's side so little heard, that it seems essential for understanding to set forth the story of the A&P's methods as the courts found them (Judge Lindley in the District Court and Judges

Minton and Kerner and Chief Judge Major in the Circuit Court). According to their version of the story, A&P entered a new phase as early as 1925.

At that time, in the various produce centers of the country, A&P maintained "brokerage" offices, ostensibly independent of A&P and often run under the names of the managers, but actually under the strict control of headquarters in the Graybar Building in New York, where the Hartfords had their offices. These brokerage offices bought merchandise for A&P, exacting, through the weight of A&P's vast purchasing power, large reductions in cost, and receiving also, on top of these discounts, a brokerage commission which went into A&P's coffers as a further reduction in cost—a differential not available to A&P's competitors. (This unequal device, in the early days of the Depression, had been one of the causes for the outcry against chain stores, which resulted in the passage of the Robinson-Patman Act.) "In 1935," said the Circuit Court, "gross revenues from this source amounted to $2,500,000."

After the Robinson-Patman Act had outlawed this device, A&P made the first of its shifts of method. The "brokerage" offices were rechristened "field buying offices" and, as the Circuit Court put it, "buyers, instead of getting credit for alleged brokerage, induced their suppliers to reduce their price further to A&P by the amount of the brokerage fee." This was called "net buying." The "inducement," the Court found, included "blacklisting" of recalcitrant suppliers. An A&P official had written: "Any canner who declines to work on a net basis . . . we feel should then be placed on the Unsatisfactory List." Lists of manufacturers were prepared, with appropriate symbols:

N—Have agreed to a NET basis. (Be sure it's really net when trading.)
G—Have definitely agreed to hold the brokerage for us until our Headquarters officials figure out a practical method for this to be paid legally. . . .
R—Refused either plan and under no circumstances is any business to be given except with the writer's OK.
P—Have been approached but no definite agreement and should be aggressively followed, therefore, until agree to either net or gross . . . no business should be done without the writer's approval.

Blacklisting has, for years, been held by the courts to be an unfair method of competition.

Promptly, A&P ran afoul of the Federal Trade Commission. The A&P attorneys argued mightily for the legality of "net buying"; but a Cease and Desist Order was issued against A&P, requiring it to cease accepting allowances and discounts in lieu of brokerage. A&P appealed to the Third Circuit, which upheld the order, and to the Supreme Court, which refused review.

A&P then made its second shift of method. In a national release to the trade, it announced that it would no longer buy from any supplier who offered to sell to it through a broker or who so sold to others. The new device was called "direct buying," and it did not bother A&P that its action "clearly affected the business of brokers." The District and Circuit Courts both quoted the remark of an A&P official: "The brokers are dying hard." Nor did it bother A&P that their action affected that part of the trade which could not buy direct. But the device boomeranged when the Danville case came to trial.

An A&P official had written in connection with "net" buying: "If net prices are not agreeable to a seller, a quantity discount or advertising contract should be essayed, effective the date brokerage payments stop and payable to Headquarters." The same devices were being used in connection with "direct buying." But such discounts and allowances, under the Robinson-Patman Act, could be paid preferentially only where the seller could make savings in his costs of manufacture or shipment because of the quantities purchased, or where true services were rendered.

The trouble was that A&P's discounts did not seem to bear any direct relationship to the economics inherent in large-scale manufacture for a large buyer. A&P's contracts with suppliers were "rigged," as the Circuit Court put it; they were designed to give a "semblance of compliance with the Robinson-Patman Act"; but the primary consideration with A&P seemed to be "to get the discounts, lawfully, if possible, but to get them at all events."

"Whatever the system used," said the Circuit Court of this pattern of A&P's buying, "or by whatever name designated, A&P always wound up with a buying price advantage. . . . Only A&P was blessed, and the supplier had to make his profit out of his other customers at higher prices, which were passed on to the competition A&P met in the retail field."

The device of advertising allowances effected the same result. Newspaper space advertising allowances "were contracted for, not alone at the cost of the advertising, but at cost plus one hundred per cent to A&P." A&P would also contract with its suppliers for a percentage allowance, agreeing in the vaguest terms that it would display the goods of the supplier in just such a fashion as it would ordinarily be expected to display them. In other words, it would get paid for what the Court refers to as "pretended services," which no supplier would pay for who was not under pressure to do so. It was A&P's policy, "and a usually successful one," to get "a larger allowance of this kind than its competitors. If it did not get the allowance it sought, the threats to take away the business of A&P were used and brought the supplier into line."

These practices, illegal under the Robinson-Patman Act, and outlawed by Congress to give the small fry a chance to compete with the great chains, did not make for the kind of fair competition which must exist if the little fellows are to survive in the jungles of Big Business.

Atlantic Commission Company, wholly-owned buying arm of A&P, engaged in these same practices—and others. In the early days, Acco had exacted the highest possible discounts, piling on top of them a buyer's brokerage, shifting with A&P to net buying, shifting again with A&P to direct buying. "Its practices over the years," said Judge Lindley, "leave a bad odor."

Acco's other activities still further cut away the chances of the smaller concerns. Acco acted as broker-*seller* for the surplus produce of suppliers, collecting brokerage which went into A&P's pocket, selling at prices which made the goods expensive to A&P's competitors, and also getting first choice of the supplier's produce and selling the balance, which "might be and often was an inferior grade." Acco acted as broker-*buyer* for jobbers who sold to A&P's competitors, collecting brokerage which went to A&P, while the higher price was passed on to the competition. Acco used its huge buying power to buy on cash terms, but refused to accept the "risks-in-transit" burden which less favored competitors had to assume. Acco bought on a "sales arrival" basis, forcing the shipper to assume the risks of any price-change. Acco took merchandise on consignment—it could buy for A&P at A&P's large discount, or it could sell and pocket a commission. Each of these devices still further increased the two-price differential in favor of A&P.

Acco sold produce to jobbers in carload lots, with simultaneous agreements to buy back less than carload lots—but at the lower or carload rate—and it gave its less-than-carload-lot business to jobbers who bought through Acco, price and quality being the same.

Acco even exacted *double* brokerage. "Vetter at Louisville," said Judge Lindley, "bought the same merchandise through Macaluso and Acco, although the purchases had been completed through Macaluso. . . . Other dealers paying unearned brokerages to Acco were the Gordon Fruit & Produce of New Haven, and DeCarlo of Buffalo, and the Mercurio Company of Providence. These odorous unjustified transactions cannot be excused in any manner."

Acco "made a determined and persistent effort to establish a close relationship with and influence over growers' co-operatives." Judge Lindley mentions the Northwest Apple Growers, Sowega Products,

Farmers' Co-operative Exchange of North Carolina, and Florida Citrus Exchange, the transaction with the latter coming, as the Court put it, "dangerously near being an agreement in restraint of trade in itself."

Acco promoted the famous Super-Coop, which caused the food trade, in 1940, to cry out, "monopoly!" Super-Coop was designed to "secure a larger and more effective control of the shippers by Acco. . . . Acco was to benefit in the form of a lower expense rate"—the usual A&P purpose—"resulting from the larger volume handled, a greater availability in quantity and selection of supplies for A&P, and an organization readily useful as a propaganda agency to fight A&P's enemies." Super-Coop "was camouflaged to make it appear as though the shippers were the moving force in the organization." John Hartford was doubtful as to Super-Coop's legality, and it was finally dropped by A&P, but not until it had become notorious.

The trouble with Super-Coop was the same old trouble. A&P, "by the use of its intergrated power and control," could buy merchandise at prices it "would not otherwise have obtained, at prices less than those of competitors, with a resulting handicap to competitors."

A&P even turned its manufacturing potential to the same use. When it could not get the discounts or allowances it thought were its due, it would threaten to go "into the manufacturing and processing business itself, since it already possessed a considerable establishment and experience that would enable it to get quickly and successfully into such business if a recalcitrant supplier, processor, or manufacturer did not yield." The prime illustration in the record is the case of the Ralston Purina Company, which raised its discount rate to A&P from 7½ cents a case to 17½ cents a case. The government, at Danville, introduced a letter from Ralston which read in part: "The discounts allowed in this contract are not made in lieu of brokerage, but represent an arbitrary reduction from our list prices which it was necessary to make to hold the flake cereal business of the Great Atlantic & Pacific Tea Company and to secure from them an agreement not to enter into the business of manufacturing flakes for five years."

Counsel for A&P, in their appeal brief, dismissed this letter as "no more than the extravagant words of a supplier trying to defend prices that he knew were too high." On this and kindred evidence, however, the Circuit Court was convinced that this type of threat, designed still further to decrease the chances of the competition, represented a general A&P practice.

According to the findings of the Court, A&P seems not to have left even the smallest stone unturned. It forced suppliers to discontinue store deliveries, because, with its warehouse system, it could reap no advantage and was unwilling for its competitors to do so. It forced suppliers to abandon premiums, not wanting itself to bother with them. On "bag and label allowances" it realized a "substantial difference between the cost to it and what it realized out of the transaction from other suppliers." "Everything," said the Circuit Court, "was grist to the mill that was grinding down prices to A&P to enable it to maintain the two-price level to its advantage."

But it was at the retail level—down at the grass-roots where Mr. and Mrs. America buy their daily bread—that the effects of this policy had their clearest impact. The two-price level, so carefully cultivated at the buying level, could, at the selling level, be translated into an overwhelming power to harry or eliminate competition. "Profit margins are slight," said Judge Lindley. "The difference between profitable operation and loss is fractional. . . . When the net profit is in the neighborhood of 2 per cent, an advantage of 5 per cent in buying in one dealer immediately places him in an overpowering position so far as his competitors are concerned."

A&P's practices had created this advantage. With the funds realized from savings on buying prices—whether by discriminatory preferences, discriminatory allowances, or whatever—the A&P policy makers could manipulate the retail policies of their empire pretty much at will. A&P's retail operating policy, it clearly appears, was to capture volume—25 per cent of the available business, said the government, and Judge Lindley said: "I think it clear that the amount of available business in any given area was the starting point on which A&P's activity in that territory was planned, and that, in many instances, it was A&P's definite program that its supermarket merchandising should eventually enjoy 25 per cent of the available business. . . . To reach this goal, reduction of gross profit rates was continuously made in various places. . . ."

He gave examples of below-cost operations: "Boston," he said, "operated at a loss from 1934 to 1941; Providence from 1934 to 1940. . . . Toledo operated at a loss from 1932 to 1938 inclusive; Indianapolis in all the same years except 1936; Detroit in the years from 1932 to 1937 inclusive; Cincinnati from 1932 to 1937 inclusive. . . . For two years after 1938 the Atlantic Division was operated at a loss, resulting in an increase in volume from $108,000,000 to $151,000,000." In 1941, in the Albany unit, the sales activity resulted "in the astonishing actual retail operation of the entire unit at a net loss of $28,999." And there were many other illustrations in the record; for example, in 1939 the New England Division and Atlantic Division both lost money—$252,665 for the first, $288,752 for the second.

Judge Lindley discussed the government's deduction from the record —that, in 1925-1926, of A&P's thirty-three units, only one had more than 15 per cent of the total available business in its territory, eleven had from 10 to 15 per cent, twelve from 5 to 10 per cent, and nine had less than 5 per cent; whereas in 1941, of A&P's thirty-nine units, eight had from 15 to 20 per cent, eighteen from 10 to 15 per cent, ten 5 to 10 per cent and three less than 5 per cent. He referred to the board of directors' meeting of the Central Division in May 1941, when a program of supermarkets and special development stores was outlined, "aiming at obtaining 20 per cent of the available food business in cities where there was an available volume of $20,000 or more per week." "There were in the Division," he said, "eight cities where A&P had over 50 per cent of the available business, fifteen cities from 40 to 50 per cen, fifty-one from 30 to 40 per cent, fifty-one from 20 to 30 per cent, fifty-five from 10 to 20 per cent, seven with less than 10 per cent."

The Circuit Court drew a sharply outlined picture of the relationship between low-price or below-cost sales and the capture of volume. "If Area X is having a tough experience competitionwise," it said, "or the area looks prospective in which to increase the volume of business, the gross profit percentage in this area is lowered. This lowers the price at which goods may be sold and the volume increases at the expense of somebody. Sometimes the gross-profit rate is fixed so low that the store runs below the cost of operation, even with all the advantage derived by the store in reduction of the cost of its merchandise occasioned by the headquarters' allocation of its predatory profits and accumulations."

The Circuit Court noted the general formula by which A&P operated. "When the gross profit rate is reduced in Area X," it said, "it is an almost irresistible conclusion that A&P had the power to compensate for any possible decline in net profits by raising the gross profit rate and retail prices in Area Y. . . . Thus Area Y, at the desire of the policy makers of A&P, can be brought to aid in the struggle in Area X, which in numerous instances, as the record shows, sustained heavy net losses for periods extending over a substantial number of consecutive years. There must inevitably be a compensation somewhere in the system for a loss somewhere else, as the over-all policy of the company is to earn $7 per share per annum on its stock."

The Circuit Court summed up the entire A&P enterprise—the immense food empire, sprawled across the United States, engaged in processing and manufacturing, wholesaling and retailing, and pressing its advantages at every point. "The inevitable consequence of this whole business pattern," said the Court, "is to create a chain reaction of ever-increasing selling volume and ever-increasing requirements and hence purchasing power for A&P, and for its competitors hardships not produced by competitive forces, and, conceivably, ultimate extinction."

The Court, obviously, had two major elements in mind, though in the long run they would come to one and the same thing. "There is evidence in this record," it said, "of how some local grocers were quickly eliminated under the lethal competition put upon them by A&P when armed with its monopoly power." The evidence in the record, cited by Judge Lindley, included, among others, the plight of one Culwell, of Dallas, Texas, who "testified that . . . A&P conducted every day sales at retail prices below his cost. His sales in 1937 were $73,000, profit, $4,000; his sales in 1938, $65,000, his profit, $3,000; 1939, sales were $62,000, net profit $2,000; 1940, $60,000, net profit $2,000; 1941, $59,000, net profit $1,100. In June 1942, A&P moved its neighboring store fourteen blocks away. Culwell's business jumped from $59,000 in 1941 to $80,000 in 1942, net profit to $3,000. The Court also included the boast of an A&P executive of "past achievement of financial ruin to other competitors," and a letter from an A&P official to the manager of the Richmond warehouse, "I certainly don't think that the Sanitary next door to you at Carey Avenue is a competitor and the hotter we can make our program the quicker this outfit will realize that they have no place in the supermarket business in Richmond."

The second aspect was not less important—affecting, as it does, the ultimate consumer, the housewife. Already, on the facts found, the housewife who did not buy at A&P was paying higher prices in her particular food store, because of the deliberately executed two-price-level buying policy of A&P. But the housewife who purchased "good foods at lower prices" in the A&P itself was also subject to A&P's strategical manipulations. Where volume was being captured through below-cost selling, she might benefit; but in areas supporting the below-cost areas, her prices would be higher—at the whim of A&P.

And, potentially, there might be nothing except A&P's own self-imposed restraint to keep prices down. Already A&P could balance division against division, unit against unit, store against store. Already, because of its size, backed by the practices cited above, it could undersell at will. In plain language, the Court could forsee a time when A&P's low-buying, low-selling, volume-capturing practices would have eliminated competition. Then prices could be raised at will. It seems a correct analysis of the Court's view that A&P already possessed the power to slay or let live, and that this was a situation the Sherman Act had been expressly designed to prevent.

V

So much for the charges against the A&P as the courts have found
the facts. What are we to say about them? That is a difficult question
to answer. In the first place, the housewife—or her husband—who
reads this article should bear one point in mind: It is impossible to
evaluate the activities of the A&P empire from the worm's-eye-view one
gets from trading with one particular A&P market. It requires the
over-all view—that which a court obtains after six months of trial, or
which attorneys get, on either side, after months and years of preparation for trial.

Beyond this, there is the matter of the anti-trust laws themselves.
They are "good laws"—even A&P makes that statement in one of its
ads, though protesting their application to itself. Whatever their
faults of vagueness and occasional ineptitudes, they have contributed
as much to the greatness of America as the businesses, big and small,
that they were designed to control and protect. Not long ago, there
appeared a magazine article entitled, "Competition Is So Vulgar,"
dealing with the accepted system of restraints of trade which has been
Great Britain's way of doing business for generations. Competition,
as we know it, is a comparative rarity in Britain. Prices have long been
set and policed to protect the weakest links in the production and distribution chains. We are paying a lot of money these days for Britain's
inability to compete effectively in world markets, a situation due, at
least in part, to her non-competitive system. And it is interesting to
note that many people in Great Britain, and also in the nations on the
Continent which have promoted the doctrines of nationalization, are
now looking with increasing interest at the American anti-trust laws,
which they once thought were only "window dressing," as a possible
alternative to government control. Whenever these laws are stiffly
enforced in the United States, there is always an outcry; yet even those
who join in it recognize the value of competition to American industry.

One may add that it is unfortunate that the A&P advertising campaign
to date should have been couched in such terms that if divestiture of
A&P should be ordered by the courts, important segments of the American public will doubt the soundness of the judicial process. Not long
ago I received a letter from a woman of profound understanding in
many matters; she wrote: "Whether the A&P combination is legal or
illegal, honest or dishonest, the low A&P prices have been a boon to all
housekeepers, rich and poor alike." Such opinion is very general, but
it misses the point. The Sherman Act does not directly concern itself

with prices, whether high or low. It concerns itself with the full play of competition, on the theory that competition, given full play, will further the American principle of "freedom to compete" and will, in the long run, keep prices down. Even a distinguished judge missed the point. "What does it matter," he asked, "what will happen fifteen years from now?"

The issue is deep and far-reaching. Monopoly and high prices come when competition dies. When competition is dead, it can scarcely be revived, yet control must be exercised—and the only control presently available is governmental control. This is another way of saying that business monopoly leads to governmental monopoly, which is another way of saying socialism.

The question of whether or not the courts will order dissolution of A&P will be long in doubt. The government will argue that "A&P has made it clear that it is incapable of abandoning its predatory activities merely because a court orders it to do so"; hence, that divestiture is necessary. A&P will argue, at a minimum, that it has put its house in order. Whatever may be the decision in the District Court, appeals seem certain—to the Circuit Court, and, thereafter, to the Supreme Court. It will be several years before divestiture, if ordered, becomes an accomplished fact.

In the meantime, it is important that no propaganda campaigns should be permitted to obscure the true issue at the root of the A&P case. Anti-trust experts have a phrase: "Show me the power and I will show you its abuse." Or, as that American oracle, a taxi-driver, remarked to me recently, "What's the use of power if you don't abuse it?" There is no such thing as a permanently benevolent tyranny.

᯽᯽᯽᯽

58. Levels and Standards of Living *

THIS SELECTION, from T. Lynn Smith's sociological study of Brazil, considers in some detail the conditions and factors responsible for the wide variations in living conditions in that large and diverse country. In this study the author makes clear the meaning of the technical term "level of living"—an important socio-economic concept which is the social science equivalent of the layman's term

---

* T. Lynn Smith. Reprinted from *Brazil: People and Institutions*, pp. 345-48, 358-364, 367-72, 375-80, 383, 391, published by Louisiana State University Press, 1946, by permission of the publisher and the author.

"standard of living," the goods and services that persons or families use or consume. He explains the largely unquestioning acceptance of low living levels in terms of the technical concept "standard of living," or what people seriously aspire to. From this analysis the reader will understand at least in part why Brazilian levels and standards of living are comparatively lower than in the U.S.A., and why they vary so widely within Brazil.

IN THE LAST ANALYSIS the level of living of a given people resolves itself into a consideration of three factors: (1) the quantity and quality of the natural resources available for exploitation by man; (2) the output per worker; and (3) the manner of distributing the results of man's efforts among those who share in the productive process. Even the shares the economist attributes to capital, management, and land ultimately find their way to the person or persons performing the managerial function, advancing the capital, or owning the land. The above generalization should not be interpreted as meaning that natural resources by themselves are of any import; for unless man's culture is developed to the stage that society possesses a rich storehouse of knowledge of the ways in which the gifts of nature may be utilized, and unless it contains values and patterns that propel man to labor in order to satisfy felt needs or to engage in activities that are deemed commendable by the society in which he lives, the presence of certain physical substances may be of no significance. The output per worker of course must also take into account the ratio of workers to dependents in the population, or the number of mouths that must be fed by the average person's share of the product. Furthermore, even though a nation may have unlimited natural resources and a sizeable output per worker, the standard of living may remain very low if the rewards to capital or to management are far out of line with the proportion going to labor. This is most pronounced in a slave society, where labor is at the same time capital, and where the share of the products that go to labor depends upon the enlightenment and kindliness of the members of the master class.

In countries like Argentina, the United States, and Brazil, where the pressure of population upon resources is much less than in many other parts of the world, the productivity per worker is largely determined by the extent to which labor is expended in the productive process. Where

The author (b. 1903) is Professor of Sociology, University of Florida. Served as Director, Institute of Brazilian Studies, Vanderbilt University, 1947-49. Senior Agricultural Analyst to embassies of Rio de Janeiro, San Salvador, and Bogota, U. S. Dept. of State, 1942-45. Honorary degree from University of Brazil in 1946 in recognition of Brazil: People and Institutions. Among his works are The Sociology of Rural Life and Population Analysis.

labor is used lavishly, which is to say combined with relatively small in-
puts of capital and management, the output per man is much less than
where each human being makes considerable use of tools, machinery,
and power in the work which he performs. In other words, in the
countries mentioned above, production per worker, and particularly per
capita agricultural production, becomes chiefly a function of the extent
to which the hand of man is strengthened for his struggle with nature.
Where, as in huge expanses of Brazilian territory, man's only aid against
the jungle is the axe and fire, the output per worker may be so small as
to permit only a low level of living. On the other hand, if each worker
has an abundance of land, tools, equipment, and power, capital is not
being husbanded. Under these circumstances the increased production
per person creates a greater product to be divided, and permits a higher
level of living. When this is the case the prevailing level of living comes
to depend largely upon the system of distribution; and the whole axis of
human thinking must shift if unemployment, "overproduction," and
misery are to be avoided.

The quality of the population has much to do with the relative importance of management in the productive process. If each human
being is himself the thinking, deciding, acting agent performing the
managerial functions (as is the case in the "colonial" parts of South
Brazil and on the typical midwestern farm in the United States), this
important factor of production is not relegated to the secondary position
it occupies on many large plantations, fazendas,[1] haciendas, and estan-
cias.[2] Where the worker himself also receives a return for the performance of managerial activities, as well as for his labor, much has been
done to ensure a relatively high general level of living. On the other
hand, in the types of large-scale agricultural operations mentioned above,
the managerial activities of the major domo frequently are merely
nominal, with the result that the managerial function in the productive
process might be said to be carefully husbanded. Under these circumstances both the poor combination of productive factors and the
failure of the mass of the workers to receive a return for managerial
activities dictate a comparatively low level of living.

As was indicated above, where resources are abundant and where the
correct combination of productive factors makes the output per worker
large, the level of living becomes almost entirely a function of the system
of distribution which is employed. However, as was also suggested
above, in the agriculture of the western hemisphere, under present forms
of social and economic organization, the system that makes for the

[1] Large estates.
[2] Large cattle ranches.

greatest production per capita also does much to ensure that the distribution of income among the agricultural population does not have a depressing effect upon the average level of living. (The distribution of incomes between agriculture and other industries is quite another thing.)   In the present stage of technical knowledge and its application to agricultural enterprises, the greatest production per farm worker takes place only in the areas where the worth of the human hand is very great. It comes precisely in those areas in which home training and education are directed to the end that each worker becomes his own manager; where in addition to doing the essential labor on the farm, he also is a capitalist, owning the land as well as the tools, machinery, and livestock. It should be repeated for emphasis that other things being equal, the greatest production per worker (counting all of them) probably comes in the family farm system, under those circumstances in which the farmer has sufficient land to fully occupy himself and the members of his family, and where he also fully magnifies the strength of his arm by the use of tools, equipment, power, and an understanding of the processes of agriculture.   Under such a family farm system, where from birth the child is molded in the direction of becoming a self-reliant person capable of exercising the functions of manager and capitalist, and also equipped with attitudes allowing for the dignity of manual labor, the worth of the average human being is very great—to use a Brazilian word that is too rich in meaning to be restricted to coffee, man has been "valorized."   In a society organized on these lines the level of living may come to be very high.

LEVEL OF LIVING

The general level of living of the masses in Brazil is comparatively low. It also seems fairly certain that this low level is closely associated with a low standard of living, or that the masses of lower-class Brazilians see very little discrepancy between the amount of goods and services which they actually are privileged to consume and that to which they feel rightfully entitled.   This is not to say that all Brazilians have a low level and low standard of life.   On the contrary, in Brazil there are significant elements in both the city and the country that have as high levels and standards of living as will be encountered elsewhere in the western world.   The upper classes of Brazilian society certainly consume as much in the way of material goods and services as their fellows in other countries; since they are less specialized, and perhaps less driven by competition, they are also equipped educationally, emotionally, and temperamentally for the maximum enjoyment of a luxurious mode of living.   Indeed the capacity of people in Brazil's elite classes to appreciate luxurious living is perhaps far beyond that of upper-class members in most other societies. Furthermore, apparently it never occurs to a member of this class to question for one moment his inherent right to the enjoyment of these superior elements of living, so that we may be sure the standard of living is high.

However, because of the concentration of property and wealth, the relative absence of middle-class groups in many regions, the concentration of the population, both rural and urban, in the unskilled labor categories, the lavish use of labor in the production process, the ease with which a vegetative existence can be carried on, and the lack of social, economic, and climatic propulsions to continuous work activities, the classes which constitute the bulk of Brazil's population live in poverty. In diet, housing, clothing, and all the educational and cultural aspects the level of consumption must be classed as very low. Rather general contentment with their lot or at least a resignation to it, the relative absence of class struggle, little evidence of mental anguish and conflict, a rigid adherence to long-established cultural practices, all are indicative of the fact that the standard of living also is low. For example, the aspiration to landownership is probably a rare phenomenon among Brazil's millions of rural workers. On the other hand, hundreds of thousands of Brazilian caboclos,[3] matutos,[4] and sertanejos[5] would feel deprived of their rights if interfered with in building a hut of wattle and daub, pau-a-pique, or thatch, with a thatched roof, on the spot of their choosing. They do have standards.

•   •   •   •   •   •

FACTORS CAUSING VARIATIONS

The study of standards and levels of living in Brazil is still in its infancy. But, although all of the details of the complex of factors that have contributed to the present low level on which the bulk of the Brazilian population is living are not known, still it is possible to indicate in a general way the manner in which some of the more important determinants have worked and continue to operate. Probably the more important factors may be reduced to the three following categories: (1) a very high ratio of dependents to contributors or producers; (2)

---

[3] Any lower-class rural person.

[4] Forest dwellers.

[5] The common man who lives in the sparsely populated semi-arid area of northeastern Brazil.

the very low production per worker; and (3) the lavish use of labor in the production process, which results in labor being entitled to a comparatively small proportion of the product and the necessity of dividing this reduced share among many workers. These will be considered in order.

HIGH RATIO OF DEPENDENTS TO CONTRIBUTORS

There can be no doubt that Brazil's standard of living is adversely affected by the high ratio of dependents to contributors that prevails in the population. In a large measure this is purely demographic, the inevitable result in a country where the birth rate and the death rate are both very high. This can result only in a situation wherein the number of children is exceedingly high in proportion to the persons of working or productive age. This is certain to occur in a country having both a very high birth rate and a high death rate, unless strong immigration is constantly replenishing the people of active working age. . . .

By counting persons under 15 and 70 or over as dependents and those between 15 and 69 as contributors or producers, one may secure a useful yardstick for evaluating the economic significance of differences in age distributions. On this basis, in 1920 there were 80 dependents for every 100 producers in Brazil, while in the United States the comparable figure was only 53. Were data for 1940 available, the differential would undoubtedly be much greater. In any case, these data serve to indicate that the age distribution of the population of Brazil limits very definitely the size of its potential labor force, making the percentage of population that might be utilized as workers very much smaller than in the United States. This is one very important determinant of the prevailing level of living.

SOCIAL STRATIFICATION

Another factor that serves to increase the number of consumers in relation to the proportion of workers is the high degree of social stratification that prevails in the Brazilian population. The aristocratic tradition by no means came to an end with the abdication of the emperor. It is true that many of the members of the distinguished families who are descended from the barons and counts of the 1880's now perform essential economic functions in Brazilian society; but it is also true that the inheritance of wealth and social position have permitted many members of Brazil's elite class to live a life of ostentation while making no substantial contribution to the national wealth and income. The presence of such "drones" also tends to swell the number of dependents to contributors. Furthermore, because of the generous size of the "helpings" which they receive out of the relatively small national income, the presence of these nonproductive elements in the population has a depressing effect upon the general level of living far out of proportion to their numbers.

LOW PRODUCTION PER WORKER

Another series of factors that determines the relatively low level or standard of living prevailing in Brazil includes all the numerous social, economic, and cultural determinants that make for a low productivity per worker.

(1) Concentration of Landownership

Because such a large proportion of Brazil's population is rural and therefore dependent upon agricultural and collecting enterprises for a livelihood it seems logical to begin the enumeration of these by mentioning the concentration of landownership and control. As has been indicated in another place, Brazil is the land of large fazendas, a country in which the great bulk of all the people fall in the category of agricultural laborers. In Brazil, as elsewhere, the status of agricultural labor is perhaps the least desirable one in the entire social scale. Probably it is impossible for any system of large agricultural estates to result in a high standard of living for the workers. Certainly it seems beyond all possibility of dispute that the very unsatisfactory standard of Brazil's working masses is directly due to the concentration of landownership and control that has prevailed from the first settlement of the country until the present time. Even though the slave might flee the fazenda and join with others in a *quilombo* (community of fugitive slaves) he still lacked the knowledge and skills essential for independent existence as a farmer. The miserable lot of the swarms of squatters (*posseiros*) throughout Brazil's vast interior is mute testimony to the validity of this statement.

The reasons for the unfavorable economic and social status of the farm laborer are, in turn, not difficult to discover. Agricultural labor cannot be done in a factory building where the watchful eye of a supervisor can take account of the activities of many workers, nor on huge assembly lines where the failure to perform specified tasks in the manner prescribed and time allowed immediately directs the supervisor's attention to the derelict employee. In most agricultural operations a good combination of labor and management is possible only where the two functions are both performed by the same individual. For the most part this is done only on the family-operated and family-worked farm. Despite the presence of overseers, major domos, and other bosses of one kind and another, the plantation system is almost sure to result in the sparing use of management and the lavish use of labor in the productive process. . . .

As has already been indicated, the agricultural laborer loses in two respects when large-scale agricultural operations dictate that he shall specialize and shall perform only the functions of laborer and not those of manager. Under these circumstances the head of a rural family is entitled to and receives only the share of the product that belongs to labor. Unlike the operator of a small farm, be he owner or renter, such a worker is not entitled to receive any remuneration for the managerial ability in this line which he might possibly develop, his potentialities as a manager go to waste, and in the deadening process of routine work experience demonstrates that they also waste away.

There are also many other reasons for the low production per worker. When, as in Brazil, there is concentration of landownership and control and when the bulk of the rural people are found in the farm labor category, there are few stimuli propelling the individual to attempt to climb up the social ladder. Social pressures urge resignation to or acceptance of one's lot, rather than continued effort to better one's condition. Social ostracism is likely to result from trying to be better than one's fellows, rather than from failing to "keep up with the Joneses." Of such an innovator his Brazilian fellows are likely to say: "He would like to encircle the world with legs that have never encompassed a horse." Since the operation of the agricultural ladder would destroy the Brazilian fazenda system in a single generation, its persistence throughout the centuries of itself is sufficient evidence that the opportunities and propulsions to advance have not been sufficient to make for much climbing on the part of the Brazilian lower classes. The extra effort called forth by such climbing has not contributed to increase the goods and services that are consumed by the Brazilian population.

Probably the most tragic effect of the high degree of landownership and control prevailing in Brazil is the fact that it perpetuates a rural population that is incapable of exercising economic functions other than those of the laborer. In other countries where the estates are built up through the process of dispossessing small owner-operators and consolidating their former holdings into large plantations, as occurred throughout parts of our own Southland, the process has first produced and then perpetuated such a class. Brazil skipped the first of these

stages almost entirely: she obtained the laboring class for her agriculture
by enslaving the Indians and importing Negro slaves from Africa. Both
of these peoples lacked most of the skills involved in the management
of agricultural enterprises, so that the present-day rural Brazilian population could have received very little in management skills from them
had the system of slavery never confined them to the sugar *engenhos*[6]
and cattle fazendas. Nor did they receive as a cultural heritage from
those of their white ancestors who mingled their blood with that of
the darker slaves, any substantial contributions to help overcome the
deficiency. Very few traits of Europe's peasant agriculture were able
to sift through Brazil's coastal sugar plantations into the vast interior
regions. In summary it should be stated that the net effect of the
concentration of landownership and control in Brazil is to lower the
level of living of the population. By relegating the bulk of the people
to the status of farm laborer, the system results in a poor combination
of labor, capital, and management; it gives to most breadwinners only
a share in the product that might go to labor; it fails to use the desire
to better one's self as a propulsion to steady, efficient labor and thrift;
and it produces generation after generation of people who are lacking
in a knowledge of managerial skills and capitalistic (thrifty) attitudes.

(2) *Deficiencies in the Diet*

Poor diet, one of the leading factors in the poor health situation . . . ,
also renders much of the population incapable of sustained work activities. Loss of efficiency and initiative may be induced by a deficient
diet, even though the workers are not reduced to complete disability.

That the Brazilian diet is deficient in essential nutritive elements,
often lacking in quantity, and almost always in quality, seems to have
been established by Brazilian scholars and scientists. . . . Spurred on
by the widespread acceptance of the belief that tropical countries, including Brazil, were backward because of climatic influences and because
of race mixture, a number of Brazil's leading scientists and scholars
have advanced the thesis that in reality the responsible factors are those
of diet and disease, especially malaria and hookworm. Says E. Roquette-
Pinto: "I continue, however, to preach the same sermon as ever: the
evils of race mixture are the evils of hunger and misery." If he, Josué
de Castro and other scholars have not definitely disproved the cases for
climatic determinism and physical deterioration of the ethnic stock
being brought about by interracial crossing, they have at least thrown a
great deal of light upon the dietary problems of Brazil.

[6] Plantations.

One of the best summaries of the situation, and one that makes the necessary allowances for differences between the social classes, is that by Ruy Coutinho. After indicating that hygiene and sanitation, and also the economic situation, along with the diet (and not the lack of Nordic blood) are the basis of the unsatisfactory showing of tropical peoples, he summarizes the dietary situation in Brazil:

If in countries with a high economic and cultural level, such as the United States, England and Canada, there is a large proportion of malnourished people, in countries such as Brazil the proportion must be excessive. In reality, observation reveals how inferior is the nutritional level of the Brazilian. The dietary and hygienic conditions of our poorer classes are miserable, a result of their insufficient wages. They are undernourished— their diet is lacking in quantity and quality.

Their diet is insufficient in calories, with a low percentage of proteins, notably those of class one; deficient in vitamins and mineral salts. These lower classes have as nourishment mandioca flour, dried meat or fish, three poor foods; they are, however, the only ones obtainable with their incomes, although sometimes they are supplemented by beans, already a luxury, and bacon.

The same author also summarizes the dietary position of the middle classes: "Even the Brazilian of the middle class is badly nourished. He uses cereals and sweets in excess, to the exclusion of other dietary elements of greater nutritional value. We do not have the habit of eating salads, and sweets take preference over fruits. . . ."

Finally, according to this authority, not even Brazil's well-to-do classes eat wisely of a well-balanced diet.

In Brazil the wealthy class, although it eats much, does not eat well. Its members do not understand how to nourish themselves. If they do not live on dried meat, dried fish, corn meal or mandioca flour and feijoada [a favorite Brazilian dish which included beans, numerous kinds of meats, rice, and mandioca flour], pungent gravies, fatty dishes, conserved meats and vegetables, fine "foie gras" and "leberwurst." . . . In this way the wealthy use an excess of fats and proteins to the neglect of vitamins and mineral salts. These latter elements are furnished almost exclusively by eggs, milk, and fresh fruits and vegetables—foods which enter in relatively small proportions into the diet of the wealthy, who prefer preserves, sweets, and pastries.

•   •   •   •   •   •

That changes have taken place in the last eighty years, and that the agricultural practices and diet are better now than they were, offers encouragement, for once established, such deficient habits and the paucity of agricultural skills are transmitted from one generation to another, as are other parts of the cultural heritage. Frequently, in these parts of man's social environment years may pass with very little change. This is particularly true in an environment that is overwhelmingly rural, as is Brazil. The result is that the Brazilian population of the present day is much more poorly nourished than is necessitated by the agricultural resources and possibilities of the country; but it can only be better nourished if the *wants* and the *agricultural practices* of the people can both be changed.

(3) Poor Health

Poor health is another factor which greatly reduces the production per Brazilian worker and contributes to the very low levels of living that prevail throughout most rural sections of the country. Although stated in a manner designed to attract attention, there is at least a grain of truth in the assertion often made by Brazil's leading thinkers that large segments of the rural population are more suitable as clinical materials than as workers. . . . Were the health better, undoubtedly productivity per worker would be much higher. On the other hand, since the bulk of the income is required to maintain the present inadequate diet, poor health follows as a result of present levels of living.

• • • • • •

(4) Incentives to Work, Attitudes towards Labor, and Alternative Opportunities

Another factor making for the low productivity per worker, and accordingly for the low levels of living prevailing throughout Brazil, is the general weakness of the propulsions to regular work activities. In the states from São Paulo north, and to a certain extent in the southern region, the Brazilian caboclo, or rural worker, lacks a great many of the propulsions to work that are the heritage of his fellows in many other lands. Most obvious of these are the ones associated with the climate, but probably the most significant are those that life embedded in the social environment the caboclo has inherited.

(a) *The climate.* The extremely mild climate and the rich gifts of nature that may be had merely for the collecting make it possible for many Brazilians in the interior of the country to lead a vegetative existence, to put forth a very minimum of effort. So readily collected or produced are the simple food requirements (except in parts of the northeast), so slight the minimum requirements for clothing, so easily constructed some kind of shelter, so readily furnished in an acceptable manner with a rough table and a few hammocks, that it is possible for life to be maintained in most of Brazil with an output of effort far below that required in more rigorous climes.

•   •   •   •   •   •

(b) *Cultural factors.* But probably climate is not the most significant factor in Brazilian work habits. In many regions the rural Brazilian of the working class has also inherited a social environment that serves as a brake upon the amount of effort expended. The caboclo's house of wattle and daub, or pau-a-pique, or thatch, with its rough tile or thatch roof and dirt floor, humble as it is, comes up to standard. To be housed as well as his fellows a minimum of household equipment is required, frequently little more than a few chairs, a rough table, and some hammocks. To provide a house and furnishings that are socially acceptable in the caboclo's environment does not require the years of sustained effort that it does in the family farm section of São Paulo, Santa Catarina, Paraná, or Rio Grande do Sul.

Probably even more significant than this lack of propulsions from the field of material culture are those that are embedded in non-material culture of the lower-class rural Brazilians. Particularly pernicious is the socially acquired mind set, or system of attitudes, towards manual work that are prevalent in the country. In Brazil almost the entire nation has inherited all of the vicious attitudes towards human toil that are the inevitable aftermath of a system of slavery. To work with the hands is considered degrading, is the indelible mark of inferior social position, is a stigma to be avoided as one would shun the plague. Thus, there is a popular saying in Brazil that *"trabalho é para cachorro e negro"* (manual labor is for the dog and the Negro). The colonist, who may have been a servant in Portugal, upon setting foot in Brazil considered it beneath his dignity, beneath the position of a white man, to labor with his hands. Even the skilled labor of the artisan was thought of as degrading to the white man, i.e., the free man; and labor in farming, which has always been and remains the basis of Brazil's economy, is said to have been considered the most disreputable of all, even more so than working at the tasks connected with mining.

It is well known that a comparable attitude towards manual labor still plagues those parts of the United States which knew the slave system and the extreme social stratification that went with it. In Brazil, however, slavery was almost universally practiced, the use of slavery being prohibited only on the lands given by the empire to the states to be used in establishing colonies of small farmers on the land. In effect this restricted slavery to any considerable extent only in the southern part of the country. Furthermore, in Brazil slavery was not abolished until 1888. Finally, the concentration of land and power, and the resulting social stratification, was even more pronounced than in the southern part of the United States, with the result that the members of the elite class were numerically less important and the laboring classes proportionately more important than in our own country. This quantitative difference also increased the social chasm separating the two layers of society, and at that time Brazil contained almost no small-farming classes, comparable to those of the southern uplands, to fill the gaps between the master and slave classes and to form the nucleus of a middle class. In view of all this, it is not difficult to understand why "the dignity of human labor" should be a concept foreign to the bulk of Brazilian thinking.

The hope of improving his economic position, of climbing the agricultural ladder and becoming the operator of his own farm, is a social propulsion that does much to stimulate agricultural laborers in some countries to regular work activities. Such social climbing is occurring in western São Paulo, and in portions of the other southern states. However, most Brazilian caboclos, matutos, sertanejos, seringueiros, or other rural workers, have no comparable stimulations. Except in restricted areas, particularly in the south, the large estate still reigns supreme throughout Brazil. The prevalence of this, as in our own South, is irrefutable proof that the agricultural ladder is not working. Outside the four southernmost states, such division of land as has occurred has been due either to a limited number of governmentally sponsored colonization projects, or to the equal inheritance of property among the numerous progeny of the *fazendeiros*. The average caboclo probably has never entertained for one moment the thought that some day he might operate a small farm of his own. He is mainly concerned with the kind of treatment received from the owner of the land on which he squats and builds his rude shelter and makes his *roca*, or on whose fazenda he labors as a *colono, agregado,* or *camarada*.

(c) *The rudimentary condition of popular education.* Finally, as indicative of the weakness of the motivations to sustained productive effort on the part of the bulk of the Brazilian laboring class must be mentioned the rudimentary nature of the school system and the resulting widespread illiteracy among the population. In the last analysis, man arises above the level of creature needs only through the acquisition of new wants and the ensuing struggle to obtain the means for satisfying them. If these are not inculcated by the family institution, which itself must possess them before it can hand them down, only the school and other educational institutions, such as the church, can do much to create the new wants and to inculcate the skills which will assist in obtaining the means for their satisfaction. Where two thirds of the population never enter a school, and where only a very small minority of the population ever acquire more education than an elementary knowledge of the three R's, the motivations to work are correspondingly weakened.

* * * * * *

LAVISH USE OF LABOR

All the factors enumerated so far have an important bearing upon productivity per worker. But perhaps the most important of all is the manner in which the essential elements of production—land, labor, capital, and management—are combined in the Brazilian productive process. Analysis, study, and reflection will make it more and more apparent that, to a very great extent, the comparatively low standard of living in Brazil is a function of the extremely lavish use of labor in the productive process. The factors previously analyzed all have an important bearing on existing standards of living, but even with these handicaps the average level of living might be greatly improved if labor were used less lavishly in combination with capital and management.

* * * * * *

The significance of all this lies in the fact that the squandering of labor results in a low productivity per worker. Enough is not produced to permit a high average level of consumption. Widespread poverty and misery must continue to prevail until the human being is "valorized" and labor is used less lavishly in the productive process. In part this can only come if the people's wants, their standard of living, can be increased.[7]

[7] A story told in Maranhão is pregnant with meaning on this point. The caboclo and his family were accustomed to bringing in weekly two sixty-kilo sacks of babassú kernels which they had collected. The price of five cents per kilo gave them a cash income of $6.00 per week. With the increased demands for vegetable oils due to our war effort, dealers raised the purchase price to 10 cents per kilo. Now the caboclo began bringing in only one sack. Expostulated the dealer, "You're crazy! Now the price has gone up and you collect less babassú than you did before!" "No," replied the caboclo. "It's you that's crazy! Now you pay me as much for one sack as you used to for two!"

59. The Responsibility of American Medicine *

SINCE AN INSTITUTION is, by one definition, a complex, integrated, relatively crystallized system of organization and operation to meet some persistent value deemed basic in a society, it is likely to change very slowly. This selection is the first of four (59, 60, 61, and 62) illustrating differing perspectives regarding institutional change, in each case the "target" of possible institutional change being the system of American medical care—the present system versus some system involving national health insurance. On the occasion of his inauguration as president of the American Medical Association in 1950, Dr. Elmer L. Henderson undertook before a nation-wide radio audience to defend the institution as it now operates. His address is presented here in order that the reader may see this defense in its entirety. It should be read with care not only to understand the argument advanced but to make possible a better understanding of the reaction it precipitated in one writer, whose selection (60) immediately follows.

Dr. Irons, Dr. Bauer, Mr. Speaker, Members of the American Medical Association—and Fellow Americans:

In the annals of American medicine, this is an historic occasion. Tonight, the American Medical Association, in its inaugural ceremony, is speaking not just to doctors, but to the American people—on two Nationwide radio networks, reaching into every State and into every corner of the country. There is a vital reason for this new policy. Our affairs are no longer just medical affairs. They have become of compelling concern to all the people. American medicine has become the blazing focal point in a fundamental struggle which may determine whether America remains free, or whether we are to become a Socialist State, under the yoke of a Government bureaucracy, dominated by selfish, cynical men who believe the American people are no longer competent to care for themselves.

* Elmer L. Henderson, M.D., American Medical Association Presidential Inaugural Address, The Journal of the American Medical Association, 143 (July 1, 1950), 783-785. Reprinted by permission of the American Medical Association and the author.
    The author (b. 1885) is a surgeon and medical officer. On staff of Kentucky Baptist Hospital and St. Joseph's Infirmary, Louisville. Special surgical consultant, Air Surgeon's Office, U. S. Army, since 1942. President, World Medical Association, 1950. Member, survey mission to Japan on Social Security, 1948. Leader in medical associations since 1918.

STATE SOCIALISM IS THE ISSUE

In light of the challenge which confronts us, it is with a deep sense of responsibility that I begin my year of stewardship as President of the American Medical Association. American medicine, which has led the world in medical advances, and which has helped to make this the healthiest, strongest Nation on the face of the globe, has been made the first major objective of those ambitious men in Washington who would make the American people walk in lockstep under a rigidly-controlled, Government-dominated economy.

The American medical system has been made a target for the barbs and criticisms of a comparatively small group of little men—little men whose lust for power is far out of proportion to their intellectual capacity, their spiritual understanding, their economic realism or their political honesty. These men of little faith in the American people propose to place all our people—doctors and patients alike—under a shabby, Government-dictated medical system which they call "Compulsory Health Insurance." And this, factually, is Socialized Medicine, regardless of how hard they try to disclaim it.

But it is not just "socialized medicine" which they seek; that is only their first goal. Their real objective is to gain control over all fields of human endeavor. Their real objective is to strip the American people of self-determination and self-Government and make this a Socialist State in the pathetic pattern of the socially and economically-bankrupt Nations of Europe which we, the American people, are seeking to rescue from poverty and oppression.

This we must all recognize: There is only one essential difference between Socialism and Communism. Under State Socialism human liberty and human dignity die a little more slowly, but they die just as surely! Never will our people accept the Socialist program that grasping men in our Government have planned for them, if they once understand that fundamental fact. And tonight, I call upon every doctor in the United States, no matter how heavy the burdens of his practice may be, to dedicate himself, not only to the protection of the people's physical health, but also to the protection of our American way of life, which is the foundation of our economic health and our political freedom.

IT ISN'T MEDICINE WHICH HAS FAILED THIS GENERATION

The moral and spiritual health of a people certainly is of equal importance with their physical well being.

It is not American medicine which has failed to measure up to its obligations. It is not American business nor American agriculture which has failed, nor the fine, loyal working people of America who have failed. It is the administrative arm of our Government in Washington which has failed us in this generation—a Government which is sick with intellectual dishonesty, with avarice, with moral laxity and with reckless excesses! That condition we simply must change, if we are to survive as a strong, free people, and all of us—every one listening to me tonight, regardless of what his way of life may be—shares the responsibility.

THE AMERICAN PRESS TAKES ITS STAND FOR FREEDOM

There are many who recognize this need. Only two days ago, newspaper publishers of the National Editorial Association, which represents 5,200 country newspapers in every section of America, made a pilgrimage to Plymouth Rock to rededicate themselves to the principles and the ideals on which this country was founded—and to consecrate themselves anew to the fundamental freedoms of our America. Tonight, in behalf of American medicine, I want to pay tribute to the American press for its staunch devotion to the welfare of our people. If it were not for leadership of the American press, in defending our fundamental liberties, American medicine, even now, might be socialized—and under the heel of political dictation.

The newspapers of America, with comparatively few exceptions, have taken a strong stand, not only against socialized medicine, but against all forms of State Socialism in this country—and the doctors of America are proud to take their stand beside the fighting editors of America in the battle to save our freedom and the system of individual initiative which maintains it.

THE REAL MIRACLE OF AMERICAN MEDICINE

I am taking office as President of the American Medical Association at the half-way mark of the fabulous 20th Century—and I want to review briefly some of the advances we have made before turning to the goals which lie ahead.

The history of American medicine is a vibrant, continuing story of human progress. Because of that progress, millions of Americans are alive today who otherwise would have died at birth, during infancy, in childhood, in youth or in middle age. The story of never-ending medical progress in this country is not just a story of so-called "miracle drugs" and "miracle discoveries." The real miracle of American medical progress is the miracle of America itself—the motivating power of the American spirit, of free men, unshackled and unfettered, with freedom to think, to create, to cross new frontiers.

Part of the great miracle that is America is our freedom to share, to cooperate, to work together for the common good. That is the spirit which not only has provided the motive power for American medicine, but which has permeated the entire fabric of our American life—inspiring labor and business and industry—science and education, and all our fields of endeavor. It is only the course of wisdom and common sense, therefore, to examine the past, present and future of our medical system —to appraise what has been done, what is being done, and what can be done. For if Government—under the guise of misleading promises of health "security"—finally regiments physicians, dentists, nurses, druggists, scientists, hospitals, medical schools and patients under a totalitarian plan which Washington directs and the people pay for—the spirit of individual initiative not only will be killed in the realm of health. Gradually, it will die in all phases of American life, just as it is dying today in other Nations which first embarked on socialized medicine and then took the final, irrevocable steps down the path of State Socialism.

DRAMATIC HIGHLIGHTS OF AMERICA'S MARCH TOWARD GOOD HEALTH AND LONG LIFE

Let's look at the facts: In America, since the turn of this century, the death rate has been cut almost in half. In 1900, the average life expectancy at birth was only 49 years. Today, new-born babies have a life expectancy of more than 68 years—a gift of 19 years of life! For American mothers and babies, the risks of childbirth have been greatly reduced. Both the maternal and infant mortality rates are the lowest in our history. The death rate for mothers in this country is the lowest reported by any Nation in the world! I wonder whether the politicians who want control over medicine can point to any comparable achievement.

At the turn of the century, pneumonia and influenza, taken together, and tuberculosis were far out ahead as the leading causes of death. Today they have been pushed down to sixth and seventh places, respectively, with death rates less than one-fifth and one-sixth of what they were in 1900. If our would-be overseers in Washington had made similar progress in the art of Government, we might look upon their pretensions in the field of health with less fear of the consequences!

Dread diseases like typhoid fever, diphtheria and smallpox—which 50 years ago took a heavy toll in sickness and death—virtually have been eliminated as National health problems. And all of the infectious diseases have been brought under effective methods of prevention, control and treatment.

The fight against disease and premature death is of significance and dramatic interest to every man, woman and child in our country. It is being waged today with weapons which were largely unknown or undeveloped in 1900—new and revolutionary methods of examination, diagnosis and treatment; new drugs, new anesthetics, new surgical techniques, new vaccines and serums, new facts about nutrition, new kinds of equipment and facilities, new methods of sanitation, public hygiene and medical education.

BETTER MEDICAL SCHOOLS AND MORE DOCTORS

A vital part of the great advance has been the continual expansion and improvement of our hospital system, and the constant raising of standards in our medical schools. Yet only recently, the advocates of a Government-controlled medical system had the amazing effrontery to castigate American medicine because, they asserted, there were more schools of medicine in 1900 than there are today!

The truth is that in 1900, the American landscape was dotted with scores of unaccredited, second- and third-rate medical schools, many of which were actually diploma mills for the production of quack doctors! Is that the condition to which these political medicine men would have us return? Today, as a result of the American Medical Association's fight for higher standards, that dangerously deplorable situation has been eradicated—and we now have 79 Class A medical schools with approximately 25,000 students. And the number of doctors in America is increasing at a more rapid rate than the general population!

The misleading propaganda which has emanated from Washington on this issue is an affront to the American people's intelligence. Typical of this flagrant misrepresentation is the attempt to create a crisis over an alleged "doctor-shortage" in this country. The simple truth is that the ratio of doctors to population is higher in the United States than in any Nation on earth except Israel, where the unfortunate refugee doctors of all Europe are gathered. It is equally true, as we are confident most of the people are aware, that the individual physician today can provide far more medical service than even a decade ago, because of technological improvements.

HOSPITAL FACILITIES VASTLY EXPANDED

Now let's look at a half century of progress in the hospital field. In 1900, there were less than 1,000 approved hospitals, with approximately 400,000 beds. Today there are more than 6,300 registered hospitals, with almost 1,500,000 beds, serving more than 16,000,000 patients a year. And the number of hospitals also is increasing steadily.

VOLUNTARY HEALTH INSURANCE TAKES THE ECONOMIC SHOCK OUT OF ILLNESS

Finally, in the field of medical economics, the past twenty years have given our Nation the new instrument of Voluntary Health Insurance to provide people with prepaid medical care and thereby take the economic shock out of illness. Today, hundreds of excellent Voluntary Health Insurance plans are available. There are non-profit plans sponsored by doctors and hospitals. There are commercial plans offered by insurance companies. There are fraternal group plans, labor-sponsored plans and industry-sponsored plans.

This has been one of the great advances in medicine in our times, because it is increasing the availability of medical care to people in all income groups. Compulsory Health Insurance is not the answer to this problem. The Voluntary way is the American way to cope with the problem—and the people, by their support of the Voluntary systems, are demonstrating that fact. In 1946, there were 40 million Americans enrolled in the Voluntary Health Insurance plans. In 1949, the number had increased to 61 million—and now it is approximately 70 million. Within the next three years, in the opinion of leading medical economists, 90 million persons will be enrolled in the Voluntary prepaid medical plans—and when that number has been reached, the problem will have been largely resolved.

This, then, is a brief, over-all picture of just one chapter of American accomplishment—the stimulating, hopeful march of medical progress in the past half-century.

ASTOUNDING PROGRESS AHEAD, IF FREEDOM OF INITIATIVE IS MAINTAINED

Mindful of that astounding progress, we can look forward to even more amazing medical progress in the next half-century, if the American spirit of freedom, initiative and adventure is kept alive. The doctors believe that solutions to current problems of medical care and service can be reached without recourse to legislation, without compulsory payroll taxes and without political pressure!

In the half-century ahead, I think we can expect that doctors and their scientific allies will achieve victory over cancer. I think we will conquer infantile paralysis, arthritis, rheumatic fever, premature heart disease and high blood pressure. It is reasonable to expect that pneumonia, influenza, tuberculosis, the common cold and other infectious conditions will be reduced to an absolute minimum by new methods of prevention, control and treatment. And certainly the years ahead will bring a wealth of new knowledge concerning the human mind as well as the human body.

We are on the threshold of great progress which will do much to alleviate human suffering and to prolong human life. But if we are to achieve this maximum progress in the future, we must keep alive the American spirit and the American methods which have made possible the progress of the past and present! This is the spirit, and these are the very methods, which Government domination of medical practice would destroy! In behalf of American medicine, I want to express my deep appreciation of the wonderful support the medical profession has received from civic groups all over America in its fight for liberty.

AMERICA RALLIES TO THE CAUSE OF FREEDOM

Today nearly 10,000 National, State and local organizations, with many millions of members, have taken positive action against socialized medicine—and there is a rapidly broadening front against all forms of State Socialism as a result of the fight that American medicine has been making. We are proud to have such outstanding organizations as the American Farm Bureau Federation, the American Legion, the National Grange, the Veterans of Foreign Wars, the General Federation of Women's Clubs, the American Bar Association, the American Council of Christian Churches, and thousands of other groups, standing beside us in this battle for good medicine and sound Americanism!

With the help of God and the American people, the medical profession will continue to minister to the sick, to relieve human suffering —and to uphold the ideals which have made America the hope of freedom-loving people everywhere.

⊷⊰⊷⊰⊱⊷⊱⊷

60. Letter to a Family Doctor *

As POINTED OUT in the headnote to the Henderson speech (59), which immediately precedes, this is one of four selections to be considered as a unit. Here Bernard DeVoto reacts negatively, with much vigor and acid, to that speech. He argues that not only are improvements long overdue in American medicine but that the American Medical Association, instead of obstructing, should itself be midwife to these badly needed institutional changes.

DEAR DOCTOR JAY:

My check for $14.45 accompanies this letter. I have taken two deductions from the $15 for which you billed me. The first one, thirty cents, is the 2 per cent for current payment customary in commercial transactions; business ethics, I gather, now govern our relationship. I will explain the remaining twenty-five cents in a moment.

I fully understand why you have been forced to raise your fee for house calls from $10 to $15, though I am not able to adjust my own professional fees so readily to the rise in living costs. I am still being paid for the Easy Chair just what I was getting in June 1946 when I wrote a piece attacking the anti-vivisectionists for which you and about a thousand other medical men wrote me letters of approval. (Many of them phrased so similarly as to suggest that someone had sent out word to give me a hand.) Still, though my income is not large enough to enable me to pay for my children's education this year without dipping into savings, I realize that it is large enough to put me, statistically, in the topmost 5 per cent of Americans. I am therefore glad to send you the $15, less deductions, as payment for your treatment of my son's cold plus my share of your treatment of others who cannot afford your full fee or perhaps any of it. The 95 per cent of my fellow-countrymen who are less able than I to afford medical treatment thrust themselves on my attention. I will help American medicine take care of them—as long as I can.

* Bernard DeVoto, Harper's Magazine, 202 (January, 1951), 56-60. Reprinted by permission of the author.

The author (b. 1897) is editor of "The Easy Chair," Harper's Magazine. Formerly in editorial capacity with Saturday Review of Literature. Taught at both Northwestern and Harvard Universities. Writer of United States history, fiction, literary criticism; authority on Mark Twain. Known for his non-conformity. His books include The Year of Decision, Mark Twain's America, The World of Fiction. His historical work, Across the Wide Missouri, was awarded the Pulitzer Prize and the Bancroft Prize in 1947.

I do not know how long that will be. This month the hospital to whose staff you belong asked me to contribute to its endowment drive. The last time it did so I sent what was for me a thumping big check, much larger than I could really afford. I would be glad to contribute now, all the more glad because of the magnificent care I received during the three weeks I spent there last April. But this year I cannot afford to give the hospital a dime. One reason, besides taxes and the inflation, is that the cost of those three weeks, the fee of the surgeon who operated on me, and the loss of income while I was convalescing used up all my margin. The chairman of the drive tells me that it is going to fall far short of its goal; many people on whom it could once depend for contributions can no longer afford them. He, you, and I all know how grave a danger this is to the hospital, to your profession, and to the public. Who is going to pay the hospital's deficits and who is going to support its medical research now that we of the middle class no longer can? I understand your trade association, the AMA, to say that though it cannot answer that question it will not permit the government to pay for them.

I thank you for the publicity matter which you inclosed with your statement. I am especially glad to have the copy of Dr. Elmer L. Henderson's inaugural address, "Medical Progress versus Political Medicine." I understand that in sending me this material you were helping in the crusade which Messrs. Whitaker & Baxter outlined for you in "A Simplified Blueprint of the Campaign against Compulsory Health Insurance." You must, they tell you there, "do double duty until this issue is resolved." You must, they say, "help in treating the ills of the body politic." But I must tell you that as part of the body politic I do not think you are qualified either to diagnose or to treat such illnesses, and I know that advertising agencies will make any diagnosis asked for on a fee-for-service basis.

Your proprietary advertising reached me opportunely. I was following the ads which you were running in the Boston newspapers. I found them dishonest, and they further annoyed me by the copywriter's assumption that I am a fool. But they harmonized well with the ads on the opposite page, which were trying to sell me water from a radium spring that is guaranteed to cure everything from impotence to cancer. They set out to rouse the same fears to the same ends. Your radio commercials interested me too. Little dramatic sketches presented you as the old family doctor, with the nobility and self-sacrifice which copywriters now have you wearing like a streetwalker's smile, and assured me that you were guarding my health (without fee, the implication was) and simultaneously protecting me from political enslavement. I observed that as soon as you signed off, another little drama came on. There was a woman who was very, very tired. She was so exhausted and suffered so much from backache that she could not greet her husband with the loving eagerness which alone could save their marriage. It turned out that she needed the dollar economy-size of a cathartic which acts painlessly, and I rejoiced that the advertising agencies were saving freedom, monogamy, and peristalsis in the same half-hour.

You and a tobacco company will relieve throat irritation; you and Seneca Snake Oil will get rid of gallstones. Your advertising has already cost you a very great deal of the prestige which the advertising agency told you would put your campaign over. And it has radically changed the relationship between you and me. Your ads speak of the trust between physician and patient, so noble it says here, so sacred, so certain to be destroyed by what the propaganda calls socialism. But I do not like any kind of solicitation that trades on prestige or on such fears and hopes as illness necessarily involves, and I will not tolerate political solicitation in a relationship of trust. Solicitors who call at my house must use the back door.

My second deduction, the twenty-five cents, signifies that I will not help pay for the $25 assessment you sent to the AMA to run these ads and print these pamphlets. I will not help you finance distortion and demagoguery. In an envelope that has your name and degree on it you tell me by way of Dr. Henderson that "all infectious diseases have been brought under effective methods of prevention, control, and treatment." I am to have no more colds, then, and my friend's daughter need not have died of poliomyelitis last summer. Cure guaranteed, Dr. Henderson's ad says in effect, and it was only through inadvertence that he did not mention the great increase in chronic diseases, especially among the elderly, and that he did not point out how our increased longevity makes more medical service necessary, not less. There is much further disingenuousness in his anthem of self-praise but let us pass over it. I am willing to grant him that on the whole "the history of American medicine is a vibrant, continuing story of human progress." But when you follow him into a political agitation that is at once arrogant, insolent, and dishonest, someone has got to call you.

"It is," the two of you say, "the administrative arm of our Government in Washington which has failed us in this generation—a Government which is sick with intellectual dishonesty, with avarice, with moral laxity, and with reckless excesses." You say that to me when you send me his speech, Doctor. You sound like Mr. Vishinsky, and that eloquent rabble-rouser was surely pleased by your allusion to "the totalitarian plan which Washington directs and the people pay for."

You and Dr. Henderson are to be highlighted in your nobility against the government's viciousness, and I am to rejoice that, all other moral heroisms having been defeated, yours will keep us free. And the conspiracy, though so powerful, is so small. You tell me that the people who do not stand on the AMA's party line are "a comparatively small group of little men—little men whose lust for power is far out of proportion to their intellectual capacity, their spiritual understanding, their economic realism, or their political honesty." Expert hysterical rabble-rousing, Doctor, and you add, "Their real objective is to gain control over all fields of human endeavor. Their real objective is to strip the American people of self-determination and self-government and make them a Socialist State in the pathetic pattern of the socially and economically bankrupt Nations of Europe which we, the American people, are seeking to rescue from poverty and oppression." You go on to say that the issue is "whether we are to become a Socialist State, under the yoke of a Government bureaucracy, dominated by selfish, cynical men who believe the American people are no longer competent to care for themselves." You and Dr. Henderson and his publicity adviser, from your advertising agency I suppose, appear to believe that the American people are no longer competent to think for themselves. But you make me wonder how competent you are.

Much might be said about this delirious rant, which would have landed Dr. Henderson before the Un-American Activities Committee if it had been circulated by a group of excited college boys who had just heard of Marx. One thing is this: you and Dr. Henderson are saying what is not so. Another is this: Dr. Henderson acquires no immunity by wrapping the flag round the vested interest of the AMA's bureaucracy and trustees. Your acquiescence in his claptrap withdraws you from my respect but I take it to be a consequence of the fact that you have not done much thinking about the subject he is misrepresenting. Medicine is your field, not economics, sociology, or government. You come innocent and virginal to social thinking. It is a fair bet that, like thousands of other physicians whose rage Dr. Henderson is whipping up, you have not even read the bills for compulsory payroll deductions for medical insurance which, after all, are what he is talking about. You probably do not know what the bills say, and you had to work so hard on biochemistry at college that you did not learn to detect the propaganda in such phrases as "socialized medicine," "statism," "socialism," and "totalitarianism." With what valorous stupidity you charge head down at those red rags—and all they are concealing is certain bills which would require some people to take out medical insurance. Bills that are an admittedly clumsy attempt to remedy an intolerable situation which your trade association refuses to face realistically and which, it makes clear, must be solved without its help.

You are a busy man, I know. You have not got time to find out for yourself, though every day you see some of the conditions that the bills are trying to alleviate. So you check your intelligence with the AMA, whose refusal to do anything grows more reactionary as conditions grow more alarming. And with your intelligence and your $25 in its pocket, the AMA systematically distorts the facts and misrepresents the conditions to you. You docilely swallow the cure-guaranteed elixir which your propagandists prescribe. And, docile to them but truculent to me, you send me Dr. Henderson's nonsense and forfeit your status.

A friend of mine, a Vermonter, has a useful locution. He does not say, "Joe is a damned fool." Knowing the mixed nature of the human being and the fallibility of human judgment, he says instead, "Joe puts me in mind of a damned fool." What you put me in mind of, Doctor, is a sap.

You had better stop acting like a sap. Our constitutionally elected government, which has to do something about an increasingly alarming social situation that the AMA refuses to deal with at all except on its own long-obsolete terms—do you really think it is what Dr. Henderson says it is? You had better think again, fast and hard. And this pamphlet called "Old Doc Truman's Pink Pills." Have you read it, Doctor? Take the passage that begins on page 27. It equates the Democrats, the party which a majority of our citizens have maintained in power, with Communists, and in doing so it makes some of the most scabrous and feculent statements I have ever seen in print. Its distributors have learned a little caution, but not much, from the public outrage that followed the notorious "Dear Christian Colleague" letter which one of your propaganda organizations sent out. As it describes the plot of various committees and learned foundations to deliver medicine and the United States over to Stalin, it insistently repeats Jewish names. It never quite says right out that the Democrat-Communist plot is a Jewish plot but it is so written as to make many a reader believe that it is. Thus it arrives at a standard technique of totalitarianism: anti-Semitism. Do you accept responsibility for this? You will be held responsible. I got the pamphlet from the office of your State medical society and the girl there said that it was for distribution to patients. You paid the $25 assessment. The noble old family friend has corrupted the relationship of trust with anti-Semitism.

I know that you, personally, do not approve of this, but there it is. Thousands of your colleagues do not, either, and still there it is. Take a tumble to yourself.

And take a tumble to your leaders. Dr. Henderson says that in three more years ninety million people will be enrolled in voluntary health-insurance plans and that "when that number has been reached, the problem will be largely resolved." Even if his wild guess should prove accurate, and even if all those voluntary plans should prove adequate, will the problem be "largely resolved"? Dr. Henderson will be satisfied if the remaining 40 per cent of the population are without insurance—will you be satisfied? And are you sure that the AMA will support the voluntary plans which it is now praising? For years it opposed voluntary health insurance as violently as it now opposes payroll deductions. Twenty-six state medical societies, I make it, have sponsored legislation which limits such plans to those that are controlled wholly by physicians. That is, plans in which neither the public nor the subscriber has effective power. Many medical societies have threatened disciplinary action—up to measures which would make practice impossible—against any of their members who participate in any other kind of plan. Some have been convicted of conspiracy in restraint of trade—which is a crime, Doctor—and others are under indictment for such interference with voluntary prepayment plans. The AMA has fought hard against comprehensive prepayment plans. It has tried to kill those that have succeeded. On the showing so far, is it honest about voluntary insurance or is it throwing dust in my eyes and yours?

Like a lot of physicians, a lot of us laymen are fed to the teeth with the AMA's methods. With its persistently negative approach to everything. With its unvarying misrepresentation of the efforts other countries are making to solve the problem. With its "crusade" and its "battle" and its vilification of the government, the public, and its own members who speak out. With its uniformly misleading attack on "government medicine." Everyone in the military services is under a system of "government medicine"; so is everyone in a veterans' hospital or receiving out-patient treatment from one. The Public Health Service is "government medicine." Several thousand of your colleagues who have had the best training available are practicing "government medicine." Are they venal, inferior, and suppressed?

One of your ads listed "damage to research" among the ills certain to follow "government domination of the people's medical affairs under compulsory health insurance." What about that? The hospital which asked me for a contribution is carrying out fundamentally important researches that are being paid for by the government. They are entirely in the hospital's hands. How have they been damaged? As a member of a committee of the National Research Council, you regularly go to Washington to appraise projects in medical research for which the government is to pay. Your committee is composed exclusively of medical men who are not in the government service. You decide whether a project is valuable and how much ought to be spent on it; the project then passes to representatives of the government just long enough for them to allocate the money for it; it then passes entirely out of their hands and the government has no more to do with it till private medicine has finished the job. . . . Why do you submit to a patent misrepresentation? Why do you try to deceive me?

The advertising, propaganda, and vilification which the AMA conducts is steadily, and now seriously, undermining your professional standing and prestige. The public very much needs both. The traditional system of medical practice has burst its seams; it is now inadequate and outworn. We are going to have something different. No matter what your propagandists say, it is certain to be not a single system but multiple and mixed. And there is no chance whatever that the AMA will get what it demands—no chance that the mixed system will be developed and administered solely by doctors. This is a public matter, a community and national matter. It requires innumerable skills which medical men simply have not got, and it must be under the unremitting scrutiny of representatives of the public with power to act. Medical knowledge is only one of many kinds of knowledge that are required for social action.

But you and your colleagues can shape the future of American medicine if you will accept the responsibility. If you study the problem and act to solve it, not to prevent its being solved. If you turn back the AMA's headlong opposition to every change not approved by the extremely small group of men who enforce its reactionary policy on its whole membership. (Is there no lust for power on the top level of the AMA? And how much of this policy is designed to secure to a very few men the largest possible incomes while the average income of medical men is smaller than it would be if people could afford to pay their doctors' bills?) If you stop acting like a sap, then you can count on shaping the solution. But time passes, the problem grows more desperate all the time, and a solution will be worked out somehow—with, without, or in spite of you. It had better be with your help.

Desperate social problems have to be solved, Doctor; they are solved as needs must, if it comes to that. Even if we accept Dr. Henderson's figures, 40 per cent of the population will have no insurance protection against medical expense. Of his 60 per cent, only a part will have adequate insurance. Ward service in the hospital that is trying to raise funds now costs $10 a day, the cheapest room $18 a day. Last week in the out-patient department I saw a patient getting a prescription filled at a drug window. It called for six capsules of aureomycin a day for ten days. The hospital was selling him the capsules at cost, forty cents apiece, $24. If his job paid him $40 a week, he could not afford them. In that case the hospital would give them to him, but the hospital had to pay $24 for them—and it can no longer get its deficits paid by contribution. Yet aureomycin is cheap compared to certain other remedies which medical research—in part supported by government appropriation—has developed. How could he afford ACTH, or the hospital afford it for him?

There are other considerations too. You know that, in spite of what your advertising says, the only places where American medicine can fully live up to its possibilities are the teaching hospitals. You know that elsewhere it is not doing as well as it wants to and must. You know that there are many areas inadequately provided with doctors, hospitals, and the proper equipment for tests, treatment, and research. You know that some doctors are not well enough trained—with the cost of training climbing before your eyes—and that some hospitals are not good enough—with the cost of making them better steadily mounting.

You know too that thousands of physicians disapprove of the AMA policy, are alarmed by it, and want to substitute for it one which will enable the profession to grapple successfully with all these problems. And you know that the hard facts of a rapidly changing world are forcing thousands of other physicians into activities—contract practice is one of them—which the AMA condemns. You know that many thousands of your colleagues agree with Dr. James Howard Means, who is not a Communist, who I think is not a Democrat either, but who is Chief of Medicine at a great hospital and Professor of Clinical Medicine at a great medical school. "A learned profession has sunk, or been dragged, in its political sphere, to a distressingly low level," Dr. Means wrote, and he went on, "What organized medicine needs . . . is a new and more enlightened leadership."

That puts it up to you, Doctor. For the campaign of what the AMA calls "public education" run by an advertising agency, you had better substitute one of self-education. You had better adopt the scientific attitude and find out what the facts are and what, besides propaganda, can be done about them. You might begin by reminding Dr. Henderson of his oath: "I shall strive constantly to maintain the ethics of the medical profession and to promote the public health and welfare." The public does not consider misrepresentation ethical. The AMA is not promoting public health and welfare by intimidating its members, trying to frighten laymen, lapsing into anti-Semitism, and accusing a

government which has also sworn to promote the public welfare, of
conspiring with Communists to stamp out freedom in the United States.
You can hold your leadership to proper ends, Doctor, or you can
repudiate it.   You have that option.   But if you are to retain the public
respect that has been yours or if you are to do your part in guiding the
future of medicine in the United States, you have no other choice.

✺❦✺❦✺❦✺

61. The Pains of a New Idea*

ONE WAY OF INCREASING UNDERSTANDING of a proposed institutional
change is to compare the process with that which accompanied some
other institutional change in the past.   This is the method used in
the present selection by Shirley Basch, who compares the arguments
formerly used in opposing free public education with those currently
being used in opposing national health insurance.   Obviously the
reader is expected to draw the conclusion that the same happy results
would obtain if the institution of medicine were altered in somewhat
the same way that our educational institutions were changed early in
the 19th century.

AMERICANS A CENTURY AGO were fiercely divided on the question of tax-
supported education for all children.   No punches were pulled.   The
opponents had ten main arguments and in flowing oratory they presented them.

History seems to be running the film over again today.   Americans
once more have two different opinions, this time on national health
insurance.   The fight is on, no punches are pulled, and once more the
oratory is loud and passionate.

The strange thing is that the current arguments are exactly the same
as those of a hundred years ago.   And they are presented in almost
exactly the same words!   Then it was the public's education, today it
is the public's health.   That seems to be the only difference.   The
record speaks for itself.   The quotations in the column to the left, with
one exception, are from the *Philadelphia National Gazette*, 1830, those
at the right from recent writings and speeches.

* Shirley Basch, *Survey Graphic*, 84 (February, 1948), 78-79.   Reprinted by permission of the publisher and the author.
The author is the wife of a physician in the U. S. Public Health Service.

UNIVERSAL EDUCATION	NATIONAL HEALTH INSURANCE

1. ONLY THOSE WHO CAN PAY HAVE A RIGHT TO IT.

"Literature cannot be acquired without leisure, and wealth gives leisure. . . . The 'peasant' must labor during those hours of the day, which his wealthy neighbor can give to the abstract culture of his mind; otherwise the earth would not yield enough for the subsistence of all. Languor, decay, poverty, discontent would soon be visible among all classes."

"This attitude arose, in part from the false promise that it is a function of government or philanthropy to 'give health to the people' whereas in truth, health, like freedom and wealth, cannot be given, but must be earned. . . . The assumption that people have a 'right' to health is as false as the notion that everyone is entitled to freedom from want. Nothing could be more viciously destructive of initiative, effort and progress. Health is a privilege, not a right. . . ."

(Edward J. Stieglitz, M.D. in "A Future for Preventive Medicine." 1945)

2. THE IDEA IS FOREIGN TO OUR COUNTRY.

"Some of the writers about universal public instruction and discipline seem to forget the constitution of modern society and declaim as if our communities could receive institutions . . . like those of Sparta. . . . No government, no statesman, no philanthropist can furnish what is incompatible with the very . . . being of civil society."

"In my view we need look no further for evidence that this legislation embodies proposals which find no roots in the soil of free America. . . . The system here proposed is alien to the deepest instincts of the American people."

(National Physicians Committee in "Compulsion the Key to Collectivism." 1946)

3. IT SHOULD BE LEFT TO PRIVATE ENTERPRISE.

"Education generally, to be effective, must be left to the enterprise and competition of individuals, to the sagacity and liberality of parents, and to the efforts of enlightened associations."

"I believe that the whole business open to private enterprise and free of teaching school should be thrown

"All these activities demonstrate that an effort is being made to change radically the free system of caring for the sick as we have always known it. The broad purpose is nothing less than the shifting of responsibility from its threefold traditional base—the individual, the medical profession, and the local

competition, just like . . . running a shoe factory."
(From Zachery Montgomery in "The School Question." 1866)

community—to the federal government and the states."
(From *The Nation's Business.* 1940)

4. GOVERNMENT MUST NOT CONCERN ITSELF WITH IT.

"It is an old and sound remark that government cannot provide for the necessities of the people; that it is they who maintain the government, and not the latter the people. Education may be among their necessities; but it is one of that description which the State or National councils cannot supply except partially and in a limited degree."

"That the protection of the health of the citizen is a natural function of government is debatable. The best government is that which governs least, and all history persuades us that freedom is smothered by increasing government paternalism."
(L. S. Goin, M.D., California Medical Society, in the Twentieth Annual Debate Manual. 1946)

5. IF PUBLIC FUNDS SUPPORT IT, POLITICAL BUREAUCRACY WILL BE RAMPANT.

"In this country, nothing could prevent [public education] from becoming a political job, if a government concern."

"Shall patients and doctors retain their freedom of judgment in this matter of medical care or shall this freedom be surrendered to a federal bureaucracy?"
(H. H. Shoulders, M.D. in his 1946 presidential address to the American Medical Association)

6. REQUIRING PEOPLE TO PAY FOR ITS SUPPORT IS DANGEROUS.

"Authority—that is, the State—is to force the more eligibly situated citizens to contribute a part . . . of their means for the accommodation of the rest, and this is equivalent to the idea of an actual, compulsory partition of their substance. . . . We have no confidence in any compulsory equalizations."

"Compulsion is the key to Collectivism. If the Wagner-Murray-Dingell proposals were enacted into law they would introduce a compulsory tax to pay for a compulsory service—medical, dental, and nursing care—directly affecting the most vital and most sacred functions of each individual citizen of the United States."
(National Physicians Committee. 1946)

7. IT IS "AGRARIANISM"—OR "SOCIALISM."

"The Scheme of Universal Equal Education at the expense of the

"Such frauds like compulsory health insurance . . . anticipate the

State is virtually Agrarianism. It would be a compulsory application of the means of the richer for the direct use of the poorer classes."

establishment of universal state medical service for everybody. That is socialism as unadulterated as if it came from the sanctified pen of Karl Marx himself." (From *The Nation's Business.* 1940)

8. IT WILL DESTROY INITIATIVE AND AMBITION.

"One of the chief excitements to industry among the working classes is the hope of earning the means of educating their children respectably and liberally; that incentive would be removed, and the scheme of State and equal education be thus a premium for comparative idleness, to be taken out of the pockets of the laborious and conscientious."

"Ambition is destroyed in a large percentage of the population when all the provisions of socialized medicine are put into effect. . . . The proposed bill . . . makes it possible for the government to take directly . . . earnings . . . of conscientious moral workmen . . . and give them to the lazy, shiftless, immoral individuals for sickness which they may have largely brought on themselves by riotous, immoral living."

(Edward H. Ochsner, M.D., Chicago Medical Society in 1946 Senate Committee hearings on a National Health Program)

9. IT WILL LOWER STANDARDS.

"Universal Equal Education is impossible . . . unless the standard of education be greatly lowered and narrowed."

". . . any attempt to introduce compulsory health insurance in the United States . . . would inevitably result in a serious—even criminal—deterioration in the quality of medical care."

(National Physicians Committee. 1946)

10. IT IS BEST TO INSURE IT ONLY FOR THE NEEDY.

"[State and National Governments] may endow public schools only for the indigent. . . . But to create or sustain seminaries for the tuition of all classes . . . is beyond their province and power."

"It is our recommendation that the Federal government consider some plan for aid to the states in taking care of those persons who cannot pay for it."

(Peter D. Ward, M.D., American Hospital Assn. in the Twentieth Annual Debate Manual. 1946)

And after all the smoke of the century-ago battle cleared away, we had the start of a public school system unsurpassed in the world. The dire predictions of its calamitous effect are now a shadowy memory.

≈§≈§§≈§≈

62. Compulsory Medical Care Insurance, 1910-1950 *

IN THIS ARTICLE Odin W. Anderson places the issue of compulsory medical care insurance in historical perspective. While tracing the course of events and developments over the past forty years he gives insight regarding the nature and role of pressure groups in advancing and opposing proposals for social action. Whether national compulsory health insurance is established by law in this country or not, this study helps to show how, out of opposing pressures, consensus develops on some points, crucial issues are re-defined, and cultural change gradually takes place.

THE AGITATION FOR AND AGAINST the adoption of a compulsory system of medical care insurance in the United States began shortly before World War I. It is the purpose of this article to trace the main events and developments of issues during these forty years, dividing the time into three broad periods. The first period, 1910–20, reached the legislative stage in several states, but no bills were passed. Action for compulsory medical care insurance appeared to be ill-prepared and hasty, and subsided abruptly as soon as unexpected opposition mustered its forces effectively. The second period, 1921–33, was a quiet one devoted to study of basic facts and problems only superficially comprehended in the first period. The third period, beginning in 1933, has been characterized by action similar to that of the first period, but on a much broader base of support and opposition, and in a profoundly different social, political, and economic context.

* Odin Anderson, The Annals of the American Academy of Political and Social Science, 273 (January, 1951), 106-113. Reprinted by permission of the publisher and the author.

The author (b. 1914) is a medical sociologist. Associate Professor in charge of the Social Aspects of Medicine, Department of Clinical Preventive Medicine, University of Western Ontario. Research assistant and instructor, Bureau of Public Health Economics, School of Public Health, University of Michigan, 1942-49. Author of monographs and articles for professional journals.

FIRST PERIOD, 1910–20

During the first period the American Association for Labor Legislation (AALL) was the chief group calling attention to the problem of medical care insurance and making concrete suggestions for its solution. The AALL was organized in 1906 by a handful of prominent economists. By 1913 it had over 3,300 members consisting of economists, lawyers, political scientists, historians, and members of other fields concerned with social problems. It passed out of existence in 1942.

It is important to note that the AALL was dedicated to the improvement of various phases of society within the contemporary economic and social structure and ideology. The organization was primarily interested in the effects of industrialization as seen in industrial accidents, occupational diseases, and general working conditions. Workmen's compensation was greatly emphasized and pushed as the prime method of reducing industrial accidents and diseases and protecting the earning power of the workers. In this regard the AALL was very effective, because workmen's compensation laws were enacted in thirty states by 1915. The AALL was thus flushed with a seemingly easy victory and was looking over the social scene for some other problem to attack.

Medical care insurance was selected as the next logical step for action. Workmen's compensation protected the workers against the economic loss of accidents and illness arising out of employment, while medical care insurance was designed to cover workers for illnesses and accidents not related to employment.

In 1912 the AALL established a Committee on Social Insurance, the first of its kind in the United States, which in the next few years carried the main burden of medical care insurance study and activity. Three of the members of the committee were also members of the Social Insurance Committee established by the American Medical Association (AMA) in 1915. They were Alexander Lambert, I. M. Rubinow, and later S. S. Goldwater, all physicians. As will be seen, these cross connections had interesting results.

At the seventh annual meeting of the AALL held in Washington, D. C., in December 1913, Joseph P. Chamberlain delivered the first paper on medical care insurance, recommending a compulsory system for state and Federal consideration.

In 1914 a subcommittee of the Committee on Social Insurance was appointed to draft a bill in preparation for an active campaign in the states and in Congress. By the end of 1915 a model bill was drafted to be introduced in several state legislatures in January 1916. At the same time it was reported that the AMA had appointed a committee to co-operate with the Committee on Social Insurance "in putting the finishing touches on the medical sections of the bill." Also, several other important organizations appointed committees early in 1916 to study the proposal of the AALL. The Secretary of the AALL optimistically wrote in the annual report: "The opportunity now appears good for a big educational campaign for the conservation of health, with fair prospects for legislative commissions to investigate in 1916 and for compulsory health insurance legislation in this country in 1917."

OPPOSITION AROUSED

So far so good for the protagonists, but opposition emerged very rapidly after the AALL had unstrategically exposed itself completely. It was naïvely assumed that a reform which they thought should be deemed good by everyone would triumph on its own merits.

As long as medical care insurance was discussed without relation to specific and concrete actions, the potential opponents apparently were not aware of its implications. However, when ten state commissions were established to study the subject and make recommendations, and bills were introduced in sixteen state legislatures, the proponents were surprised at the opposition's vehemence and gathering strength. Within the AALL itself, Frederick L. Hoffman, statistician for the Prudential Insurance Company of America, resigned from the Committee on Social Insurance in 1916 when it endorsed compulsory medical care insurance. He and I. M. Rubinow became opposing symbols of the controversy. They were inveterate traveling lecturers; both used words effectively, and both had a following.

By 1918 the movement had reached its peak as represented by activities of state commissions in the state legislatures. The most intense activity was found in California and New York. At this point the seemingly favorable attitude of organized medicine turned into vigorous opposition. Simultaneously, pharmaceutical companies, accident and health insurance companies, companies selling industrial insurance, and healing cults proved to be too much for the proponents of compulsory medical care insurance. Furthermore (and this was a dismaying discovery for the AALL), Samuel Gompers, president of the American Federation of Labor, was very outspoken in his denunciation of government-operated social insurance schemes. Numerous state federations of labor supported the AALL proposal, particularly in New York State, but their support came too late and Gompers' prestige was too great.

AMERICAN MEDICAL ASSOCIATION

It appears to be coincidental that the prominent physicians in the American Medical Association were able to have a committee established in 1915 to study the issues of medical care insurance and report to the House of Delegates from time to time. The apparent purpose was not to advocate any compulsory insurance, but, according to I. M. Rubinow who became the executive secretary of the committee, "to bring about friendly understanding between all parties concerned and to protect the legitimate economic interests of the profession."

A few months before Rubinow's statement, the *Journal of the American Medical Association* ran an editorial regarding the model bill of the AALL: "It is hoped that physicians will take advantage of this opportunity [of studying the AALL bill] and that it will be possible to avoid that lack of co-operation between physicians and legislators which, for a time, marred some of the foreign legislation."

By 1920 officials of state medical societies were reacting vehemently against any deliberation on compulsory medical care insurance, particularly in New York, Michigan, Illinois, and California. A powerful group of delegates assembled at the annual session of the AMA in New Orleans in 1920 "to get Lambert" as they put it, who was then president of the association.

At the same session, the House of Delegates established a basic policy which has not been revised to the present day, and expressed it in the following resolution:

The American Medical Association declares its opposition to the institution of any plan embodying the system of compulsory contributory insurance against illness, or any other plan of compulsory insurance which provides for medical service to be rendered contributors or their dependents, provided, controlled, or regulated by any state or Federal government.

The end of the controversy over compulsory medical care insurance was just as abrupt as the foregoing resolution was final.

SECOND PERIOD, 1921–33

After the emphatically worded resolution in 1920, the American Medical Association at several annual meetings considered resolutions concerned with definitions of "state medicine" and similar forms of medical care organized and operated by government.

In 1921 the Sheppard-Towner bill to provide grants-in-aid to states for maternal and child health programs was up for consideration in Congress. The bill aroused bitter controversy at the hearings, and many physicians testified in opposition. Although the bill was not proposing a system of compulsory medical care insurance, physicians regarded it as an entering wedge for encroachment of government in private practice. Nevertheless, the Sheppard-Towner Act was passed in 1922 with active support from citizens' groups. The act was disapproved officially by the House of Delegates at the annual meeting of the AMA in 1922.

Problems regarding the economic and social aspects of medical care were discussed on several occasions in 1925 and 1926 at conferences attended by physicians, members of the public health profession, and economists. These conferences were called to formulate plans for a study of the structure of medical services of the country, especially the economic aspects. As a result of the deliberations of these conferences, the Committee on the Costs of Medical Care (CCMC) was established. Its work was financed by six foundations: Carnegie Corporation, Josiah Macy Jr. Foundation, Milbank Memorial Fund, Julius Rosenwald Fund, Russell Sage Foundation, and Twentieth Century Fund.

The committee consisted of 42 persons—14 private practitioners of medicine, 6 from public health, 8 from institutions interested in medicine, 5 economists, and 9 persons representing the general public.

From 1928 to 1932 the CCMC released twenty-eight reports on the incidence of illness, the cost of medical care, and related aspects of health. The period of study seemed to be one of watchful waiting. The AMA editorialized: "Most physicians and most economists and most social workers are willing to wait until the Committee on the Costs of Medical Care, a group with which the medical profession is co-operating wholeheartedly, has brought into the situation, data on which to base reasonable action for the future."

The effect of the final report dealing with recommendations for action on the basis of findings was immediate. Majority and minority reports split the CCMC and supporters of its objectives into factions. The lead in opposition to the majority report was taken by the AMA and some of the physician members of the CCMC.

The majority of the members of the committee were of the opinion that "medical service, both preventive and therapeutic, should be furnished largely by organized groups of physicians, dentists, nurses, pharmacists, and other associated personnel" and that "the costs of medical care be placed on a group payment basis," through the use of insurance, taxation, or both.

The minority group, while agreeing with the majority report in many matters, objected to the proposal for group practice and the adoption of insurance plans unless sponsored and controlled by organized medicine.

The editorial response of the AMA to the majority report has become a classic, and was presumably directed at the aspects of the report dealing with group practice and areas of government responsibility, and not at voluntary insurance, as such, if sponsored and controlled by organized medicine. The editorial read:

> The alinement is clear—on the one side the forces representing the great foundations, public health officialdom, social theory—even socialism and communism—inciting to revolution; on the other side, the organized medical profession of this country urging an orderly evolution guided by controlled experimentation which will observe the principles that have been found through the centuries to be necessary to the sound practice of medicine.

THIRD PERIOD, BEGINNING 1933

The recommendations of the Committee on the Costs of Medical Care and the reactions to them formed the base of the third period of the compulsory medical care insurance movement. The main issues and factions were brought to the surface as the movement gained momentum and breadth during the following years. It will be recalled that the American Association for Labor Legislation, an organization composed chiefly of professional people, was the group most instrumental in initiating interest in and action for some type of compulsory medical care insurance in the first period; but during the third period, beginning in 1933, which has not yet ended, the Federal Government, through official committees and legislative activity, and later state governments, have been the agencies which spearheaded the reopening of the issue of government-sponsored medical care insurance. What government has done during this period has conditioned the attitudes and actions of other groups which feel that they have a stake in the future of medical care. There has been general agreement that a problem exists, and the depression made it more acute; but there has been profound disagreement as to what should be the solution.

The depression and the deliberations over the nature and scope of the impending social security program provided the framework for discussions and action regarding compulsory medical care insurance. The precedent-setting Federal *Rules and Regulations No.* 7 of 1933 defined policies and procedures under which medical care might be given to those receiving unemployment relief in the states. Representatives of the American Medical Association participated in the formulation of the rules and regulations and gave their sanction. Access to medical care was now recognized by government as a basic minimum right together with food, clothing, and shelter.

COMMITTEE ON ECONOMIC SECURITY

In 1934 the President appointed the Committee on Economic Security to make recommendations for a program "against misfortunes which cannot be wholly eliminated in this man-made world of ours." In addition there were numerous committees established as advisory to the Committee on Economic Security, with a very broad range of representation of fields of interests and organizations. The research duties of the committee were divided into several problem areas; among them, medical care.

Medical care insurance was given short shrift, however, inasmuch as Edwin E. Witte, executive director of the Committee on Economic Security, reported that medical care insurance could not even reach the research stage, not to mention its incorporation in the social security program. He wrote:

When in 1934 the Committee on Economic Security announced that it was studying health insurance, it was at once subjected to misrepresentation and vilification. In the original social security bill there was one line to the effect that the Social Security Board should study the problem and make a report thereon to Congress. That little line was responsible for so many telegrams to the members of Congress that the entire social security program seemed endangered until the Ways and Means Committee unanimously struck it out of the bill.

As a corollary, the AMA was also the object of pressure. Its *Journal* editorialized, on November 24, 1934:

The headquarters office of the American Medical Association has been besieged with telephone calls, telegrams and letters on this subject. . . . Some physicians are apparently opposed to all change and feel that the American Medical Association should officially make itself felt in opposition to the entire program of the government.

FOLLOWING THE SOCIAL SECURITY ACT

The Social Security Act was passed in 1935. Thereafter the Government sponsored a series of activities which either deliberately or coincidently resulted in the introduction of the first compulsory medical care insurance bill in Congress to attract any widespread attention, the so-called Wagner bill of 1939 (S. 1620). The series of activities was as follows:

1. The National Health Survey was made in 1935–36—a large-scale study of the incidence of illness and the underlying social and economic factors.

2. In 1935 the President appointed the Interdepartmental Committee to Coordinate Health and Welfare Activities, entrusted with the task of making sure that the provisions of the Social Security Act were being effectively applied, and suggesting improvements. One of the chief interests of the committee was the problem of medical care.

3. Out of the Interdepartmental Committee was created the Technical Committee on Medical Care in 1937, consisting chiefly of experts from the Federal agencies concerned in whole or in part with health.

4. Early in 1938 the Technical Committee recommended, among other things, that there was a need for a general program of medical care and insurance against loss of wages as a result of illness.

5. Thereupon, the Interdepartmental Committee called the National Health Conference held in Washington, D. C., in July 1938, to discuss the findings and recommendations submitted by the Technical Committee. Invitations were sent to a large representation of people from the medical profession, from agencies working in health, and from labor, industry, agriculture, and other groups of citizens. The purpose of the conference was to clarify issues and stimulate constructive criticisms. No specific recommendations were expected from the conferees.

SUCCESSION OF BILLS

The Wagner bill of 1939 was followed by: the Capper bill in 1941 (S. 489); the Eliot bill in 1942 (H. R. 7354); the Wagner-Murray-Dingell bill in 1943 (S. 1161); a reintroduction of S. 1161 by Representative Dingell, Michigan, early in 1945 (H. R. 395); and in November of the same year, a new Wagner-Murray-Dingell bill (S. 1606). In 1947 there appeared the first counter-proposal to compulsory medical care insurance in the bill (S. 545) sponsored by Senator Taft and others to assist states in providing medical care for the indigent. The opposite type of bill was introduced in the same year by Senators Murray, Wagner, and others (S. 1320).

In May 1948 another health conference, the National Health Assembly, was held in Washington, attended by 800 professional and community leaders. Again all phases of the problem of medical care were examined. The Medical Care Section of the assembly unanimously agreed that the *principle* of contributory insurance should be the basic method of financing medical care for the large majority of the American people, but differed in their views on the method of implementation. Independent of the National Health Assembly, the Federal Security Administrator, Oscar R. Ewing, recommended a compulsory system, and in the report to the President marshaled a great array of data in an attempt to justify his conclusions.

In 1949 bills in Congress on medical care became so numerous that they were difficult to follow, but two bills emerged as the focus of the conflict over compulsory medical care insurance—the administration bill, S. 1679, and the opposition bill, S. 1970. The latter bill proposed a "voluntary" approach by providing for Federal grants to the states to assist co-operating voluntary prepayment plans to make their services generally available to those wishing to utilize them. The difference between the two bills reflects diverse philosophies.

Because of the intense and prominent activities on the Federal level, parallel actions on the state level have been overlooked or discussed as of little importance, except in California. However, since 1935 compulsory medical care insurance bills have been introduced in over a dozen states, and in some of them repeatedly. In California, by law of 1949, compulsory insurance against the cost of hospitalization was introduced for all persons covered by compulsory unemployment insurance.

As stated previously, it appears that government activity was the stimulus for counteractivity on the part of proponents of voluntary health insurance. Today these plans are widespread.

DEVELOPMENT OF ISSUES

To close the discussion of the third period let us trace the development of issues to the present time, so that we can be assisted in delineating current issues. Not until the National Health Conference held in Washington in 1938 did the issue of compulsory medical care insurance become a national issue in the sense that a great variety of groups throughout the country became aware of the problem and acted accordingly.

The shifts in issues since 1933 may be broadly indicated as follows:

1. In 1933 medical care insurance, regardless of type of sponsorship, was an issue.

2. By 1939 insurance as a device to spread the economic risk of illness ceased to be an issue. The hospitals had for several years supported insurance plans pertaining to hospitalization, and the AMA recognized

them and began to direct attention to medical plans along similar lines.

3. Also by 1939 an insurance system covering the Nation regardless of type of sponsorship was an issue.

4. By 1946 both the American Hospital Association and the AMA subscribed to a nation-wide system sponsored and operated by themselves.

5. The remaining basic issue has become a national compulsory medical care insurance system or a national voluntary system. There are important subissues, such as the questions of scope of service, extent of coverage of population, and pace of development.

Basically the AMA is in the forefront of the chief opposition group, and organized labor—the CIO and the AFL—is spearhead for some form of compulsory insurance. It will be recalled that the collapse of the movement for compulsory medical care insurance in the first period was partly due to the lack of effective support from organized labor; but the reverse is true today.

BASES OF AGREEMENT

So much attention is being paid to disagreements between opposing factions that bases of agreement are ignored. The bases of agreement holding all parties and individuals within sparring distance of one another is the consensus that all should have access to medical care irrespective of income. Given this consensus, the next step is the struggle over means. The means is insurance, but there is disagreement as to sponsorship and control.

Another common orientation is that groups on both sides of the question of compulsory medical care insurance have a basic faith in the present political and economic institutions. The individuals and organizations supporting compulsory medical care insurance are not necessarily revolutionary; nor are those opposing such a system necessarily reactionary. As specific objects of a reform movement, physicians are naturally very much affected, and to them it seems a revolutionary step; but in the perspective of a deep-seated and world-wide movement gaining momentum in the United States with the Social Security Act in 1935, compulsory medical care insurance is a rounding out of a broad social program.

The exact form a national medical care insurance program might take would probably depend on the ability of the Blue Cross and Blue Shield plans to modify and deflect an all-out Federal state compulsory medical care insurance system, and on the as yet unclear trends of the burgeoning union health and welfare plans. In other words, the third period of the medical care insurance movement in the United States is by no means over. Events are moving so rapidly that the last part of this article will become out of date in a year.

≈≋≈≋≈≋≈

63. A Perspective on American Education *

"THE FORM OF ANY INSTITUTION is whatever a society chooses to make it." This statement is as true of our educational institutions as of any others. Here the communications expert, Charles Siepmann, describes his position regarding the present role of education and his beliefs as to the function it *should* perform. He sees conflicting demands being placed upon schools: on the one hand they are being asked to acquaint students with their social environment and to train them to live in the present world; on the other they are being asked to teach students to use originality and to promote in them the skills to mold and improve society when they become adults. Siepmann also expresses concern over the consequences he feels "mass education" may have for the quality of training received by students.

FOR THOSE WHO GO FAR WITH IT education is, on one side, a lonely business. For to be eminent in mind or in imagination is, as with all eminence, to stand alone and apart. Education is also awful, for it leads us inexorably beyond the known to the unknowable—so that, like Socrates, we end with the recognition that we know nothing. Consequently, the chief attributes of a truly educated man are humility and a certain suspension of judgment (not to be confused with skepticism) in recognition, always, of "that reserve of truth beyond what the mind reaches but still knows to be behind." This quality of mind is common both to great scientists and to great men of faith.

Education, moreover, requires courage—more and more courage as we

* Charles A. Siepmann. From Radio, Television, and Society, pp. 252-262, copyright 1950 by Oxford University Press, New York. Reprinted by permission of the author and the publisher.

The author (b. 1899) is Chairman, Dept. of Communications, School of Education, New York University. Formerly adviser to the President on the educational and social significance of radio in U. S.; Consultant, O.W.I. 1942. Born in England; with British Broadcasting Corp. in its pioneer days. Member British Government Committee on radio's wartime role before 1939. Specialist in radio propaganda. Author, Radio in War Time, FCC's "Blue Book," and Radio's Second Chance.

attain to its upper reaches. It is by nature and of necessity selective, and no mere spreading of its "facilities" will make it otherwise. From higher education, in its proper sense, most should be warned away, for they will not have the stomach—to say nothing of the mind—for it. Education (in terms, at least, of intellectual attainment) is the one realm in which an "aristocracy" has natural and inalienable rights. Only the fool or the sentimentalist will find this incompatible with democratic principles. "The mind is its own place."

To most of us these are unfamiliar as well as, perhaps, uncomfortable thoughts. For few of us have ventured in education beyond its charted territory or have ever, like Cortez' men when they stared for the first time at the Pacific, "looked at each other with a wild surmise—silent, upon a peak in Darien." To teachers, in particular, such thoughts may prove a stumbling block, making necessary a distinction, often overlooked, between teaching and scholarship. What has been said applies preeminently to scholarship—and to the teacher in so far as he is scholar also. Scholars are trailblazers. Teachers are roadbuilders, "making the rough places smooth" for millions to follow where the few have led. (The distinction, though necessary, is, in a sense, artificial, for the good teacher is part scholar also. There is—or should be—no clear, dividing line.)

Yet it is true of both teaching and scholarship that as we withdraw our gaze from the horizon, we lose direction even in the early, intermediate stages of our road-making. To "make the rough places smooth," to make education easy going is only part—a subordinate part—of teaching. We shall have done disservice to our charges should we conceal from them how long and hazardous is the road on which they have set out. It is a false security that we implant (which life itself will all too soon unmask) that seeks to conceal this fact. The true security, which honest teaching offers, is that which helps us to be, as St. Paul said, "perplexed, but not unto despair." Finite man may not look for more than this of comfort as he explores the infinite.

Education, then, being the progressive enlargement of man's view of himself and of the universe about him, is everybody's business. Somewhat inconsequentially, however, (considering how inherently complex a task it is) everyone regards himself as an authority on the subject. In so far as it bespeaks concern and interest, the attitude is healthy. It is salutary, too, as it recognizes—what is true—that we learn more, in the long run, from life's experiences than from formal education. Anything from which we learn something is, in a broad sense, educational. But "education" and "learning" lose any vestige of meaning when interpreted too broadly. We reach the farcical, for instance, when (as actually happened in radio's early days) a network offered, as evidence of its educational endeavor, a live performance by Amos and Andy before the Federal Radio Commission! If this is education, so is the braying of an ass. Clearly, to keep our discussion of education within manageable bounds we must somehow circumscribe its meaning.

For working purposes let us, then, conceive of education as being distinguished by three characteristics: (1) purpose; (2) design; (3) continuity. Its purpose is, as we have said, that progressive enlargement of a man's understanding of himself and of the universe that is the only basis for reasoned and reasonable action. Its design will be related to the several, sequent stages by which such understanding is attained and to the means by which human faculties, necessary to understanding, can best be trained and developed. Its continuity will be such as to keep the muscles of the mind supple. Continuity is essential to the execution of the design and to preclude the haphazard, intermittent, and disorderly impact of experience. It provides for ordered learning and for the saving of time.

The context of all education is twofold—individual and social. Its business is to make us more and more ourselves, to cultivate in each of us our own distinctive genius, however modest it may be, while showing us how this genius may be reconciled with the needs and claims of the society of which we are a part. Though it is not education's aim to cultivate eccentrics, that society is richest, most flexible, and most humane that best uses and most tolerates eccentricity. Conformity, beyond a point, breeds sterile minds and, therefore, a sterile society. It is this that foredooms authoritarian regimes, which are the first to insist on strict conformity and the last to concede the social advantages of individual difference.

Authoritarianism, however, is only an extreme example of a danger ever-present in all institutionalized education—the insistence, within communities, on a strict observance of convention coupled with a deep-seated fear of new and "therefore," dangerous thoughts. Man "hates to stand alone in his opinion"—and hates even more for others to do so. The position of the teacher is thus paradoxical. His task (at least in a democracy) is to educate for change, to breed a healthy discontent, and to feed in the young the fires of constructive reform. For is there one of us so well-contented with himself or with his lot that he would wish to see his child grow up in his own likeness? The question is, alas, rhetorical, for it would seem that there are not one, but many. We cling to what we have and what we are, and there are still relatively few who, recognizing ideas as dangerous, are prepared to face the danger.

The teacher is thus circumscribed by social conservatism in his efforts to liberate the child from a conformity that in a hundred ways has been at work on him from early infancy, and to defer for as long as possible the corroding influence of custom and habit that masters most of us long before we reach middle age. The teacher's actual power to influence children is, incidentally, much overrated. Forces outside the classroom —preeminently the home and today, perhaps, the mass media of communication—are much stronger and more permanent in their effects. Educators should be the indirect pacemakers of social progress and enlightenment. In practice their influence, like their pay, is modest and, like their social status, respectable and generally speaking uninspiring.

Education is a long process. Indeed, if properly conceived and intelligently pursued, it never ends. Formal education (which alone ends) provides the springboard for what should be a life pursuit. Its task is to make us literate; socially conscious, adaptable, and active; competent, to some degree, in our mastery of useful skills; capable of enjoying leisure fruitfully; and, last but not least, the sum of all these things—masters in some sense of the not so gentle art of living. The aim of all true education is philosophy—a broad, synoptic view of life compounded of character, imaginative insight, and applied experience.

In a democracy universal education is not a luxury but a necessity. A semiliterate electorate, ignorant, indifferent, and inert, constitutes a standing invitation to disaster. We have universal education of a sort, but it is not adequate. But those who complain of its shortcomings tend to overlook its comparative youth (in 1870 the movement was still only getting under way) and the burdens that have been increasingly loaded on it.

In the 70 years between then (1870) and 1940 the population slightly more than tripled. But in 1870 some 80,000 students were enrolled in secondary schools and 60,000 in colleges, whereas by 1940, 7,000,000 were enrolled in the former and 1,500,000 in the latter (while, in addition, more than 1,000,000 were engaged in part-time, vocational and adult education). Thus, while the general population was increasing three times over, the enrollment of high schools was being multiplied about 90 times and that of colleges about 30 times. And the end is not yet. Even now one young person in six fails to reach high school and half of those who enter drop out before the end.

Not only has enrollment increased at a staggering pace but so have the demands upon the teacher to provide instruction in ever-widening and varied fields of knowledge. Modern industry demands more and more technicians, and, in the rush to provide them, there are those who overlook the cultural importance of a liberal education as the necessary ballast for a civilized way of life. It is small wonder, then, that education remains largely unfinished business and that we number, to this day, millions of citizens unfitted, educationally speaking, to pull an oar in the great Ship of State.

Public impatience with education is altogether too easy a way of shifting the burden of responsibility from where it properly belongs—squarely on the shoulders of the public. We could have better education if we wanted it. It is ironical that men who will blithely vote vast sums for better roads and improved garbage disposal will lobby to avoid an increased tax rate to provide better school facilities. In one sense it is always true that "there is never anything wrong with the educational system of a country. What is wrong is the country. The educational system that any country has will be the system that country wants."

There is, however, an aspect of universal education that can be less readily dismissed—namely, the risk taken and the price paid for this brave experiment. It is pure self-deception to assume that, when educational facilities are increased ninetyfold, something is simply "added" to the existing system, that it becomes more all-embracing while retaining its essential characteristics. The fact is that the whole structure of education is rocked to its foundations. Nothing is as it was before—and least of all the institutions of higher learning already operating when universal education was, to all intents and purposes, achieved. The intermediate price paid is (or at least may well be) a general lowering of standards, the dilution of scholarship, and a downward adjustment of the pace of education to that of the more backward student. (Mass education is almost inevitably egalitarian, exceptional students creating a certain problem for the harassed teacher by being out of line in terms of the level of instruction aimed at the total group.) The risk is that, in the process, we lose sight of the true goal and of the quintessential character of education as described at the beginning of this chapter. The necessity to level down becomes elevated to a virtue, while the prospect of leveling up is relegated to an indefinite future and assumes the character of wishful thinking.

Materially, the gains of universal education are reflected in our industrial pre-eminence in the world today. Culturally, they are, perhaps, to be measured by the quality of our mass media of communication, by the chaotic, if transitory, state of our moral code, and by the seemingly increasing contempt for and disregard of high standards of excellence. The fact that the word intellectual is now rarely seen in print without inverted commas or used other than as an opprobrious term is of itself, perhaps, significant. To overlook such possible intermediate consequences of perhaps the bravest and noblest enterprise that any nation ever undertook is to dishonor the idealism and to confound the high hopes that launched it. To reckon with the consequences involves the occasional raising of our eyes from the immediate job in hand to recover true vision and perspective by a fresh glimpse of education's far horizon. It is essentially a matter of perspective, of reconciliation to the fact that universal education will not bear fruit short of, perhaps, two hundred years ahead. Those teachers are not fools who knowingly cast their bread upon the waters, hoping only that it will return to them after many days.

One further consequence of "wholesale" education may be mentioned, which has to do with the demand-supply relation. If there is less respect for education now (because there is less understanding of its true, final purpose), it still has a considerable, if residual, prestige. Even those least acquainted with it pay it lip service. Increased facilities at the primary and secondary levels have fired many to storm the heights of higher education, and, to meet the demand, colleges have sprung up on all sides, many of them peddling degrees for a modest fee, with a reckless and sometimes cynical disregard for academic standards. What was formerly a cherished and hard-won prize has all too frequently become a readily salable commodity. The one-time symbols of true accomplishment—the A.B., M.A., and even the doctoral degrees—have themselves become the objective to be realized, the commodity to be acquired, rather than the accomplishment they should symbolize. Such idolatry is dangerous, bringing the gods themselves into contempt.

Perhaps the greatest of all the risks involved in universal education is this leveling-off of the high peaks of educational attainment to a broad plateau—the elimination, as it were, from the educational landscape of its mountain ranges. Would India be the same without its Everest? Economics apart, is the continuance of such a leveling process actually necessary? It would hardly seem so. And yet so powerful is the influence of a trend that it appears to master and condition our thinking. A good example is the report of the President's Commission on Higher Education. Among its proposals is the doubling of college and university enrollment by 1952. This proposal provoked much enthusiasm and little adverse comment. Yet might it not be true that the best interests of our society would have been better secured by a proposal the exact reverse of this one? Have we not now reached a point at which education in depth, rather than in breadth, should be the order of the day? Is not Dr. Conant nearer the mark in pleading for higher standards at the university coupled with greater opportunities for university education for those now debarred, by economics rather than lack of ability, from attendance? Every form of society—and a democracy above all others—must guard against one liability, while constantly nurturing one priceless asset. The liability is a semiliterate and backward mass; the asset is an intellectual elite. It is not undemocratic to prize the qualities of leadership and intellectual distinction. Though we move forward together, there must be someone in the lead. Move we must, but the *direction* in which we move is all-important. There must be those to point the way.

But to create leaders (perhaps the nation's outstanding need of education) involves leadership. Liberal education, as we have seen, is always subject to the retarding influence of what is rather vaguely called a "social lag." Its subservience, however, to social climate is never more than partial—and is roughly in inverse proportion to its own dynamic. Teachers are vital and significant as they show the will and capacity to affect the environment. Education, indeed, is a constant dialectical process, helping us to see the nature and the cause of current defects in ourselves and our society and to find acceptable ways of removing them.

The main function of primary education is to *acquaint* children with their social environment—the history, tradition, and character of the society and the world of which they are a part. Its concern is with basic skills, with social adjustment and personal security. The function of secondary—and still more of higher—education is to *affect* the environment. Teachers are not, and should not be, social reformers. But they should be the catalytic agents by means of which young minds are influenced to desire and execute reform. To aspire to better things is a logical and desirable part of mental and spiritual growth.

Clearly, then, education is not just an elegant frill or adornment, or merely a matter of cultivated manners or correct deportment. It is the deeper perception that, in a quite literal sense, "manners makyth man"; it is the creation of a cast of mind all-pervasive in its influence on conduct and outlook—and in particular on human relations. For "manners" read social mores, and you have the central concern of all true education.

❦❦❦❦

64. Education in American Culture *

IN THIS SELECTION W. B. Brookover analyzes what Americans expect
of their formal educational institutions. Using data from public
opinion polls the author provides insight into the role of high-
school and college education in American culture.

AMERICANS HAVE COME to look upon education as a distinctive feature of
their society. Numerous social scientists have described it as a dominant cultural trait. This is commonly expressed in terms of a tremendous faith in the goodness of education. To most Americans the
education provided by the schools is a desirable thing. Interference
with the child's opportunity to attend school and to acquire the benefits,
vague as they may be, that accrue from such attendance is universally
frowned upon and a criminal offense in all states if the child is under
14 to 16 years of age. Although we will examine later some of the
more specific outcomes that are expected of participation in the formal
educational experience, it is important to understand the underlying
belief that some of this education is good for nearly every child. This
is often expressed when the question of school attendance for children
of limited abilities is discussed. Americans then not uncommonly
take the position that even though such a child may not learn much
of the standard curriculum to which he is exposed, he benefits by
going to school. Clearly they anticipate some vague benefit to the
individual or society.

In another situation a person who is critical of the particular training
that a school provides in some area would generally reject entirely any
suggestion that it might be better for the child not to attend such a
school at all. In much the same way that he believes some religious
belief is good, so also he believes some education is good. In certain
situations limits to the amount of school attendance are advantageous,
but in almost every case some education is desirable and in most situations more education is better. This type of thinking is illustrated by
the position of the personnel director of a large business whom the
writer chanced to engage in conversation. As soon as he learned that
he was addressing an educator, he launched on what appeared to be

* Wilbur B. Brookover, Sociology of Education, chapter on "Education in American Culture," to be published by the American Book Company. Reprinted by
permission of the author.
    The author (b. 1911) is Associate Professor of Social Science and Sociology, Michi-
gan State College. Special fields of interest: sociology of education and minority
groups in American society.

an oft-repeated diatribe against the type of training that young men were receiving in American high schools and colleges. He explained that his company had instituted a training program whose main function was to counteract the learning that the new employees had acquired in school. It was suggested that perhaps his company would be better served if it employed youth who had not yet had extensive formal educational experience at this level. The personnel man was horrified at this suggestion. "Of course we can only use college graduates in these kinds of jobs." Why was this, if the company had to retrain the men so extensively? For this query he had no answer. The company's employees must have the educational symbol. High school and college education was good although it had little value in the work for which they were employed. This common cliché was investigated in a *Fortune* public opinion poll in which business and professional men were asked, "Do you think the following statement is more true than false, or more false than true: 'A boy or girl fresh out of college is not much use to an employer until he has unlearned a lot of things the professors taught him'?" Slightly over half of the business and professional men thought this was more false than true, while less than one third thought it more true than false. The remainder had no opinion on the subject. Although a sizable proportion accept this idea that a college education has no practical value, the majority of this upper middle class group rejected the belief.

This criticism of the training received in the educational system suggests, and may be related to, the American image of the educator. On the higher educational level particularly, and to some extent on the elementary and secondary levels, the teacher is seen in the image of the impractical visionary who could not meet the competition of the less protected world of affairs. In this image the teacher is the object of many jokes and comments that border on ridicule. So also this is the base of numerous derogatory remarks concerning the "brain trusters" who may be engaged as consultants or officials in government. Highly educated persons and particularly those who have been college professors are frequently suspect in non-academic positions. A man with a Ph.D. reports that he has studiously tried to avoid being identified as "Doctor" because he learned early in his tenure in the offices of a national organization that this title made him the object of unfavorable comment among his colleagues. Elmo Roper in a *Fortune* Survey asked his sample if they thought it more true than false that "Most college professors are not practical enough to run a business successfully." Only a little more than one third of the total sample thought this was true, but over half of the business executives and other professional people agreed with the statement. The image of teachers at the lower levels is less of the visionary and more of the inept person who can't do anything but teach or perhaps some related types of work. This somewhat unfavorable image of teachers generally does not preclude the possibility that they may be consulted for expert knowledge and assistance in all kinds of situations in which they may be expected to have special qualifications. In fact, this common practice no doubt contributes to the relatively high esteem in which the educator is held despite the visionary image.

The image of the educator we have just examined may represent a current manifestation of an earlier and sometimes currently held belief that too much "book learning" is impractical. In colonial and pioneer America, when the labor of the youth was a decided asset, "schooling" beyond that required for the acquisition of some facility in reading, writing, and simple arithmetic was generally considered to be a waste of time; the real education in the essentials of making a living and understanding the world in which they lived was acquired in the "real" work of the household. More advanced education was desirable for the few who entered into the professions of law, medicine, or the ministry, but not for the masses of farmers and artisans. Occasionally similar ideas are expressed even in mid-twentieth-century America. This reaction appears most frequently in isolated communities of the nation, but may be encountered rarely in other segments of the society. In general the contrary is the predominate cultural trait in respect to school attendance. The idea of the education of the masses, cited by Thomas Jefferson as an essential for democratic government, has constantly been extended to more and more people and for increasingly longer periods of time. This change in attitude is demonstrated by the fact that 83 per cent of the parents interviewed in the Fortune Survey wished to have their sons go to college and 69 per cent desired the same thing for their daughters. This evidences the great faith that Americans have in the extended formal education of the masses.

This faith has become so strong and so nearly universal that the extension of provisions for it is one of the most generally acclaimed aspects of the culture. Education is good for children; it is good for war veterans; it is good for adults; it is good for almost anyone. What it is good for is not always clear. In 1944 80 per cent of parents responding to a National Opinion Research Center poll reported that they are satisfied with what their children were getting from their education in school. Thus far social scientists have devoted little attention to an analysis of this faith in the efficacy of education, so its actual character is not clearly understood. But certainly no sociology of education in America will be complete until the exact nature of this faith with its seemingly contraditory patterns and its function in the culture is understood. Moreover, the research on which this study must be based has not yet been done. We shall attempt, however, in the following section, to suggest some of the more specific expectancies that may be found to be involved in this faith.

AMERICAN EXPECTATIONS CONCERNING EDUCATION

If students in America's schools at any level are asked what outcomes they expect from their own attendance or that of many other youth in the numerous institutions for mass education, any response even vaguely related to Jefferson's idea of making democracy feasible almost certainly will be rare. The same result will appear if the parents of the students are asked why they desire education for their children. Yet even though they seldom verbalize it, many people, particularly among the intellectuals, make an abstract association between the belief in mass education and the achievement of a democratic society.

If we were concerned with what is known as the philosophy of education, we might dwell at some length on this aspect of the role of education in American culture. We are, rather, concerned with the more realistic meaning of education as conceived by the masses of people involved in the cultural process. This direction of interest is not to deny that the schools perform a major function in transmitting the ideals and sentiments necessary in the development of democracy. Neither is it intended to suggest that democratic society could function without citizens who possess some measure of the skills that are provided by the schools. We are simply saying that only in a vague way do Americans expect the education that they value so highly to contribute to the development of democracy. Only 14 per cent of the parents interviewed by N.O.R.C. said that training for citizenship was the most important thing they hoped to have their children receive from education.

TRAINING FOR A VOCATION

Throughout democratic society perhaps the most salient expectation from education is preparation for a particular occupation or the acquisition of the skills necessary to earn more money. For several decades the argument most frequently used by educators and others in favor of higher levels of education has been that the greater the education, the greater the earning power of the individual. Associated with this have been constantly increased educational requirements for entrance into numerous occupations. These and other influences have made American people acutely cognizant of the relation between education and vocational success.

Although this awareness holds to some extent for education at the elementary and secondary levels, it is most strikingly seen in the expectation from college education. In the *Fortune* Survey those people who would like to have their son or daughter go to college were asked, "Why would you like to have a son (daughter) of yours go to college? What would you want him (her) to get out of it?" The majority responded with some form of "preparation for a better job, a trade or profession, greater earning power." Despite the more frequent expression of this desire for sons than for daughters, 48 per cent did mention some type of vocational aspirations for their daughters. In the same poll all parents were asked to select from a list of things, the most important to be obtained in college. From this list 57 per cent mentioned "Training for a particular occupation or profession" as important for their sons, and 33 per cent mentioned the same for their daughters. However, 46 per cent named marriage and family-life preparation for daughters. This goal for them is similar to vocational training for boys.

The same desire for vocational training in the lower levels of education is expressed by a substantial proportion of parents. The 26 per cent in the N.O.R.C. poll who listed vocational training as the most important goal ranked next to the number who considered the regular subjects and character education most important. Even though the expectation of training for occupations is more salient when the higher level of education is considered, much of the desire for training in the basic skills of reading and writing clearly is associated with earning a living. This association is indicated by the comment of a street cleaner's wife, who responded to the inquiry concerning the most important thing to be obtained from an education with the comment, "To learn all they can. Now me, I can't read or write, but if I could, I could make some money."

BASIC SKILLS

The polls, as well as many other sources, make it clear that parents generally expect the acquisition of certain skills traditionally taught in the American schools. The fact that only 34 per cent mentioned the "regular subjects" as the most important things to learn does not mean that the others did not expect these to be included; it indicates merely that these people did not give them first priority. Probably everyone expects the school to teach the children reading, writing, some skill in mathematics, some knowledge of history, and other of the traditional school subjects. The controversy that periodically breaks out in American communities over this issue is in reality a question of techniques and procedures for teaching these skills rather than one of whether or not they should be taught. This function of the schools is so clearly established in American culture that everyone takes it for granted, and many do not mention these skills as expected outcomes because their acquisition is synonymous with education itself.

Because the regular-subjects classification is not rigidly defined, some may include such things as geography, foreign languages, government, health, and other subjects common to the curriculum. The patterns of expectancy with regard to any of these are not clearly defined and may vary considerably from community to community. At the secondary and higher educational level these subjects may be fused with the expectation of vocational and related training. In this they are hardly classified as basic skill subjects. At the elementary level, however, the teaching of the so-called basic skills is clearly expected and the teachers dare not deviate far from the cultural norms in this respect.

TRANSMISSION OF ACCEPTED CULTURAL VALUES

Although transmission of the accepted values and behavior norms of the community does not have the highest level of saliency as an expected outcome of education, the school obviously is expected to train youth in these values. The lower degree of saliency of these elements no doubt reflects the fact that the typical American would never think of the possibility that the "right" way to think and act might not be taught. Certainly any teacher who would in any way appear to be teaching something that wasn't "right" as defined by the generally accepted norms would not be considered a "good influence" on the children. The cases of dismissed teachers provide ample evidence that they are expected to teach the values of the culture. Although the category of "character education" used in the N.O.R.C. poll includes a variety of things, such as "good intellectual habits" and "learning to live," a portion of the 34 per cent who said this was the most important thing children should get from their education had in mind the inculcation of cultural values. This conclusion is indicated by such comments as: "Train them to become good men and women. Bring out their best character," and "A sense of high moral values. . . ." and still another, "Develop high ideals and learn to live by them." Probably the one in five parents responding to the Fortune poll who wished their son or daughter to "develop a good moral character" in college had a similar pattern in mind. Although such poll results are not entirely valid evidence of an expectation that the accepted values will be transmitted, they definitely convey the feeling that the schools' products should not go very far afield in their behavior codes. It would require much more carefully conceived research to learn the exact degree to which teachers might deviate from the accepted norms in their teaching about moral codes and values. In the absence of evidence to the contrary, the observations at this point indicate that the moral codes and values of the community are expected to pervade the schools' activities.

SOCIALLY ADJUSTED PERSONS

In recent decades the philosophy of education expressed in the writings of John Dewey and others, and the concepts of modern psychology, sociology, and social psychology, have permeated the American culture to the point that some people now expect the schools to contribute to the social adjustment of youth. At the same time that the school provides numerous other types of training many parents want it also to teach the child how to "get along with other people" and otherwise develop an acceptable personality. In both the polls of what is expected in college and education in general referred to above, approximately one in seven parents mentioned this type of training as the most important. Many others would no doubt include this in the list of things that they would want for their children. When given the opportunity to name three qualities needed as preparation for college entrance, approximately one out of three parents listed this goal.

Some people, however, consider such training in social adjustment outside the function of the schools, something that should be obtained at home or in other situations. These may feel that when the school emphasizes training in social adjustment it does so at the expense of teaching basic skills or vocational skills that to them are more important. Many communities have been the scenes of heated controversies over this issue. As a rule the differences are based on the assumption of some that the school that seeks to develop well-adjusted personalities cannot and does not wish to provide high-level training along other lines. Others maintain that the best training in the basic skills occurs in an atmosphere that also leads to proper adjustment for harmonious social relations. Despite the absence of final and conclusive evidence on which to decide this issue, much evidence from the social sciences supports the latter position.

GREATER OPPORTUNITY FOR SOCIAL MOBILITY

Innumerable American parents have admonished their children to continue in school because "I don't want you to have as hard a time as I have had." In the parlance of the sociologists such comments mean that the parents want the child to achieve a higher social status where life is presumably less arduous than has been their experience. In the formulation of the *Fortune* poll on higher education Roper and his associates used the phrase "A better chance to get ahead in the world" to refer to this desire for upward mobility. In this case 37 per cent of the parents mentioned this goal as one of the three gains they wished their sons to get from college, and 20 per cent stipulated it for their daughters. Significantly, parents who have had only high-school or grade-school education mentioned "A better chance to get ahead in the world" more than twice as frequently for sons and three times as frequently for daughters as did the parents who were college graduates. This result reflects the higher status of the latter parents, who feel that the social position of their children is more secure. From this position the parents were much more likely to desire for their children "A sharper, better trained mind in dealing with all sorts of problems" or "The intelligence and wisdom necessary to live a full life," the need to rise in the social scale having been replaced by the less pressing need to maintain the position that the family holds.

Because the great majority of the children from all status groups attend school through the elementary grades, the interest in social mobility has less application on the lower levels of education. As the child advances through high school and college, the desire for social mobility becomes an increasingly important motivation for the lower-status children and their parents. Among higher-status families the higher levels of education are taken for granted as a minimum essential for maintaining the family position.

Higher levels of education are sometimes opposed by social groups that desire to maintain their integrity and a degree of social isolation. The Amish, for example, recognize that high-school and college education for their children frequently results in movement out of the isolated Amish group. Since this effect is contrary to the policy of cultural isolation, the members of this ethnic group strongly oppose education beyond the elementary grades. There are other groups of this sort in American society. But when viewed in general terms they account for a relatively small segment of the society. Still other groups have ambivalent desires in regard to education. In many rural communities farm people wish to keep the boys and girls on the farm, but at the same time hope to have their children get ahead through education. As a result of this conflict in desires, they provide the opportunity for the youth to go to high school and college but are then disturbed when the educated child does not settle down in the rural community. The decreasing opportunity for farm youth to find employment on the farms does, of course, complicate this situation. One of the goals of agricultural extension educational programs, such as the 4-H clubs, is to keep the youth interested in the farm as a life work; but as participants advance in the agriculture training program, they make contacts with other groups and interests that frequently lead them away from the farm.

In spite of the variations among some subcultural groups the polls indicate that many people in the lower status groups expect higher levels of education to provide an avenue for upward social mobility. When coupled with the belief in an open-class society this expectation becomes a very significant aspect of the American culture.

A CURE-ALL FOR SOCIAL PROBLEMS

The faith that Americans have in mass education often takes the form of looking upon education as a panacea capable of solving all the problems of society. This hope that education will make a better world, with a complementary fear that it cannot do so, was succinctly voiced by a garage mechanic to a newly elected school board member:

"It don't make much difference about me, but I want my kids to have the chance I missed. I wouldn't want to live in a big city, except only so that my boy could get a free college education which he can't get here. But what he learns in high school is good stuff. He can talk about things that I can't hardly understand. I hear they want to cut down on the schools. Don't let them do it. The future for us is in our kids. *Maybe the education they're getting won't straighten out everything in the world, but if they can think clear, that'll be a hell of a big part of the battle for something better than we've had the last few years. . . ."*

Such an expression is more likely to come from the members of lower status groups who feel less satisfied with the world as it is. In their study of Middletown the Lynds noted the value placed upon education by these people in the observation that "if education is oftentimes taken for granted by the business class, it is no exaggeration to say that it evokes the fervor of religion among a large section of the working class." This belief that education will solve all the problems of society is no doubt related to the previous expectation of increased mobility. The latter relates more particularly to the individual youth whereas the former involves the solution of such problems as depression and un-employment, intergroup conflict, crime and delinquency, poverty, and most any other cause of discomfort or unhappiness.

After teaching courses in social problems over a period of several years, the writer has learned that students without hesitation suggest that education is the solution to all the foregoing problems. Among Americans this anticipation is so great that they occasionally become highly critical of the schools when disillusionment occurs concerning the school's ability to solve some problem. Yet disillusionment is inevitable, for education cannot possibly have the anticipated impact on the total social system. McKeel clearly stated the difficulty: "When we become acutely conscious of social and economic problems we begin to think of education as a cure-all. . . . We forget that education is only a segment of our entire culture. . . . Education, . . . to be effective, must be geared to the actual structure before it can turn the wheels of change to advantage." The possibility of realizing this naive assumption that education will serve as a cure-all is remote in the light of the many other forces that operate to create the problems involved. Only through major modifications in the relations between the patterns of formal education and other aspects of the social-cultural milieu can there be hope of its realization.

GOOD ATHLETIC TEAMS, BANDS, AND OTHER ENTERTAINMENT

Nothing arouses dissatisfaction among the patrons in an American high school community more quickly than the failure of the school to produce winning athletic teams or a successful competitive band if the neighboring schools participate in such activities. For several decades the extra-classroom activities, such as competitive team athletics, musical groups (bands, orchestras, and choruses, etc.), and speech and dramatic activities, have been assuming an increasingly important role in sec-ondary and higher educational institutions. They are no longer optional activities that the school staff may provide for the training and enter-tainment of the students if they wish; instead, the patrons expect the school to provide special coaches or directors for such activities and in turn look for these specialists to produce the most successful performers in the school's several sports, dramatics, or musical organizations. On the athletic field particularly, any feeling on the part of the patrons that the teams are not winning as consistently as expected will almost certainly result in a demand for a new coach or some other action to correct the failure. To a somewhat lesser degree the same course is true of the other activities mentioned; in these, however, there is greater variation from one community to another in the nature of the expectations.

Although no adequate analysis of such activities has been made, the demand for winning teams and colorful bands probably is, in part at least, a matter of community pride and ethnocentrism. Since more publicity is given to these activities and they are more available for public display than other aspects of the school's program, they become symbolic of the quality of the school. Students, patrons, and other citizens of the community take pride in the achievements of a successful team or band and use such achievements as the yardstick in comparing their school with others. Of course not all people react in this fashion, but for many the consistent production of winning teams and/or musical groups is sufficient evidence that the staff is providing a good educational program. Others more specifically interested in some other aspect of the school program, however, may be highly critical of the expenditure of energy on such more observable performances.

Although it has been contended that the time spent in the training for and performances of competitive sports, musical contests, and similar activities is at the expense of "more important" educational functions, this neglect need not occur. Schools that consistently present successful contenders to their communities may at the same time provide superior training in all other expected areas. There is no satisfactory evidence on which to base a conclusion concerning the relationship between successful teams, bands, or dramatics and the quality of the less observable educational programs. Some educators would take the position that the former builds up school morale and interest so that improvement is noticed in the entire school program. One experienced school administrator who had worked for many years in schools with losing teams became converted to such a position after a year with successful athletic teams. He had publicly expressed disapproval of the "overemphasis" on athletics, but after serving as the principal of the winning school he commented to the coach, "Although I don't like the emphasis on athletics and don't want anything to do with it directly, I'm convinced that good teams make a better school. The students are more interested and do better work in their studies." This change of heart may have been a rationalization to justify his bowing to the demand for greater emphasis on athletics, but if so, it is so widely accepted that it deserves careful research.

In many small communities the desire that the school provide various public activities may be partially based on the need of the community as a whole for some type of entertainment and recreation. In some localities the school plays, ball games, and operettas and other musical performances provide the main source of public entertainment. In those places failure of the school to present a "Senior Play" or sponsor a basketball team would delete a major element of the community culture. For the adults the educational function of these activities is secondary to their function as community entertainment, but this point of view does not lessen the demand that the school provide them. In fact, it makes the pattern of expectancy even more imperative.

SUMMARY

Americans obviously expect their schools to provide a wide variety of different functions and services. These expectations are not always harmonious or easily met by the same system. Frequently, therefore, an undercurrent of dissatisfaction and criticism of the schools exists: some expect more of one thing, and others expect something else. No school is ever likely to provide the type of program desired by everyone in the community in which it functions. In spite of this inability of any school to satisfy all its patrons we have noted that four out of every five persons interviewed in a nation-wide poll were satisfied with the education being received by their children. Some of these responses only meant that they were relatively satisfied, for 43 per cent of those interviewed suggested some kind of changes. The tremendous range of expectations, a portion of which we have discussed, and the relatively high degree of satisfaction with the way they are being provided reflect the great faith Americans have in formal education. It is almost a magical force that can do anything when the proper incantations are performed.

ᴥᶘᴥᶘᶖᴥᶖᴥ

65. Leisure *

CONTINUING ADVANCES since the beginning of the Industrial Revolution have made it possible for modern man to supply his material needs with less and less expenditure of time. This development has freed an increasingly larger share of time for other activity.

* George A. Lundberg, Mirra Komarovsky, and Mary A. McInerny, Leisure: A Suburban Study. Copyright 1934 by Columbia University Press. Reprinted by permission of the senior author and the publisher.
For brief biographical sketches of George Lundberg and Mirra Komarovsky see

Much of this freed time is often referred to as "leisure," and its increase has stimulated the growth of elaborate institutional structures to fulfill man's needs for satisfying ways in which to occupy his time when he is not at work. This selection by George Lundberg and associates is an exploration of the nature of leisure and a consideration of the features that mark "spare-time" institutions.

"THE MORE MACHINES WE HAVE the easier will be the work, the shorter will be the working day, the lighter and happier will be the lives of all."[1]

This wistful statement comes out of a land which is just beginning to be remade by the machine. To it millions are looking for release from centuries of bondage. In view of what has occurred in countries where mechanization is more complete, what hope may one reasonably entertain for the realization of this dream? True, it is Ilin's main theme that only under a socialized régime will these results be obtained. But even assuming that the full product of the machine goes to the workers themselves, is the fond expectation justified?

It would perhaps be futile to deny that many types of work have been made easier, in a certain sense, by the machine. In some cases the change may consist chiefly of a substitution of nervous for muscular energy. But let us grant that on the whole work has become easier. Let us grant further that the machine has shortened the working day and that it could be much further shortened in an intelligently organized society. When we have made these concessions, we are, unfortunately, still far from having insured the conclusion that then "the lighter and the happier will be the lives of all."

There are, unhappily, many reasons why mere freedom from vigorous physical toil and long hours of labor will not in itself insure men against heavy and unhappy lives. Some of these reasons we shall consider later. A few random illustrations will suffice here. There is the enforced leisure of the physically handicapped—the blind, the deaf, and the convalescent. They are frequently far from happy even when no economic worries are present. There are prisoners whose wretchedness may be increased by lightness of work or lack of work. Millions of unemployed find their leisure more burdensome than their work ever was. Some "retired" people, having abandoned the occupations of a lifetime while they are still in good health, to engage avowedly in the business of enjoying life, find this pursuit the most burdensome and unsatisfying

---

selection 3, page 14, and selection 19, page 133, respectively. Mary A. McInerny was formerly with the Columbia Social Science Council for Research.

[1] M. Ilin, New Russia's Primer (1931), p. 16.

of all. It was perhaps alternatives like these that Mahatma Gandhi had in mind when he said that modern machinery would leave India's millions with "too much leisure." Clearly, something more than a short and easy working day, even with economic security, is needed before we have any assurance that the lives of men will be happier and lighter. It all depends on what we do with the additional leisure and our attitude toward these activities.

Leisure is popularly defined as the time we are free from the more obvious and formal duties which a paid job or other obligatory occupation imposes upon us. It is in this sense that we have used the term. Tentatively, and for practical purposes, we shall accept this definition because it is relatively objective. In so doing, we shall not overlook the important subjective differences which distinguish mere idleness, rest, or loafing, from relaxation, recreation, or a certain mental release or exaltation. In this more limited sense, leisure is primarily an attitude, a state of mind, a process of pleasurable adjustment to one's situation. Leisure in this subjective sense will always depend upon personality, temperament, education, and the activities that have preceded. An activity which is recreation to one person is onerous labor to another. The same activity may be either labor or relaxation to the same person at different times. But by the same reasoning it would be impossible to define work objectively on the basis of overt activity, for it is frequently largely interwoven with recreational elements. Yet for many purposes we find such broad classifications of activity useful.

• • • • • •

The production of the material necessities of life, which has for centuries been the dominant concern of nearly the whole population, including women and children, is today carried on by a relatively small number of people. The "gainfully employed," a class which includes the producers of luxuries (in goods and services) as well as of necessities, today comprise only about two-fifths of our population. In the face of such facts and with even more striking prospects for the future, it is not surprising that Nicholas Murray Butler declares that "guidance in the right use of leisure is vastly more important than what is now known as vocational guidance."

The great increase in the amount of leisure for the masses of men is, however, only one aspect of the new problem. The very changes which caused shorter working hours also disrupted to a large extent traditional leisure pursuits. The technological revolution and the resulting drift to the city resulted in profound physical, institutional, and sociological changes in customary leisure opportunities and activities. For example, spontaneous and informal neighborhood life, which formerly provided a chief use of leisure, has largely disappeared as a result of the tremendous mobility of modern urban society. Neighborhood life depends upon relative stability; it cannot flourish where a substantial part of the population moves every year or two. In the city, furthermore, occupation tends to supplant geographic location as a basis of fellowfeeling and association. Congested living quarters and the disappearance of the yard and other outdoor facilities have further shifted recreation to the school, the club, and the commercial recreation place.

These new conditions under which spare time is spent have also altered profoundly the uses of leisure. Home and neighborhood games and sports are supplanted by billiard "parlors" and public dance halls. Huge stadia offer a vicarious satisfaction for the urges which conditions no longer permit us to fulfill directly. Instead of singing around the piano, we turn on the radio. The innumerable petty activities of barn, pasture, and garden, many of them heavily mixed with recreational elements, are foreign to the apartment dweller. Even the "job" of the ordinary man was formerly often fraught with variety and high adventure and therefore had its own recreational aspects. There is little possibility of dramatic developments or variety in the operation of a punching machine. The former type of work might leave one tired, but not taut; restful sleep was its remedy. The latter type results in a craving for explosive stimulation as a relief. Add to these considerations the exploitative aspects of advertising, salesmanship, and the modern facilities of communication, and we secure some idea of the altered conditions of leisure.

Professor Jacks has summarized the situation of the modern city dweller as follows:

On every side he is surrounded by artful operators who have studied his weak points, often with the aid of psychology, and beset him with the offer of ready-made pleasures to be purchased at a price. . . . Even those of us who are immune from the attractions of the cinema, the race-course and the public-house are not masters of our leisure time, at least to the extent we should like to be. We are largely at the mercy of our neighbors, who have facilities of getting at us unknown to the ancient Greeks or even to our grandfathers. Thanks to the telephone, motor car and such-like inventions, our neighbors have it in their power to turn our leisure into a series of interruptions, and the more leisure they have the more active do they become in destroying ours. Nor are we less active in destroying theirs. We spend a great deal of our leisure in mutual botheration. In whatever conditions you place a man, the use he can make of his own leisure will always be limited by the use that other people are making of theirs.

These are some of the conditions which have made leisure a community problem.

We are confronted, then, with radically altered conditions under which to spend our leisure and a greatly increased amount of leisure to spend. What will people do under these conditions? One student of the problem [Professor Jacks] has stated the question in this way:

Will they take as the model for their leisure the sort of life now most favored by the "idle rich" and get as much of that sort of thing as their means enable them to procure—display, luxurious feeding, sex excitement, gambling, bridge, golf, globe-trotting and the rest? Or will they spend it in the way the idle poor—by whom I mean the unemployed—are now spending the leisure forced on them by the industrial crisis, which consists for the most part, in just stagnating, physically, mentally, and morally? Or will it be a mixture of the two—stagnations relieved by whatever doses of external excitement people may have the cash to purchase?

.   .   .   .   .   .

COMPETITIVE CONSUMPTION AS A LEISURE PURSUIT

"It began to be recognized," says the President's Committee on Recent Economic Changes, "not only that leisure is 'consumable' but that people can not 'consume' leisure without consuming goods and services, and that leisure which results from our increasing man-hour productivity helps to create new needs and broader markets." Here we have very excellently revealed the current preoccupation of economists with the productive aspect of their subject. From this point of view the problem of leisure is a problem of increasing man's consumption of material goods so that business and profits may be bigger and better. This, apparently, is the highest and final object of endeavor. Increased sales bring increased employment and higher wages. Purchasing power is thus increased, which in turn makes possible still bigger business. If as a result of big business, improved methods of production are devised by which a task that used to require four days now requires only two, the chief significance of this development, in current theory, is that in the time saved, the laborer will be able to consume some goods and services for which he has hitherto not had time to develop an appetite. Herein we have the modern version of the fascinating experience of growing more corn to feed more hogs, to make more money, to buy more land, to grow more corn, to feed more hogs, and so on. This exhilarating round, at an ever-increasing tempo, represents, apparently, the highest aspiration of Western civilization.

There is no denying the hypnotic centripetal power with which the increasingly rapid swirl of this circle is capable of holding man. As a method of bridging the gap between birth and death, keeping occupied, it has much to be said for it. It undoubtedly keeps many out of mischief. The people most completely in its sway are not infrequently the pillars of society. Among other things, it prevents philosophic meditation and other morbid reflections which tend to afflict some preachers, professors, artists, and others who won't work according to the formula. Nevertheless, the charmed circle is unpleasantly suggestive of a squirrel cage and its activities suitable rather to the brain of a squirrel than to that of man.

What is the alternative? It is conceivable that under another system of ideals and education men might prefer to utilize at least part of the leisure which the machine has won for them in some form of self-activity which would not greatly affect economic production of profits. We might, for example, hold up what men are rather than what they buy as a standard of worth. On this theory the greatest satisfactions of life, as well as the best balanced personalities, come from the acquisition and exercise of skills and activities of various sorts not necessarily of economic significance. The consumption of blue sky, sunshine, and sylvan solitude, or the amateur dabbling in the fine arts is of this nature. Merely as a method of killing time and consuming energies it may be no more absorbing than the frantic game of keeping up with the Joneses. The justification for this substitute, therefore, must be based on other grounds. We must show that this substitute is in some way more compatible with man's biological nature and that its indulgence contributes more to that balance and integration of personality which is generally recognized as desirable.

The value of leisure-time activities, play, and recreation is usually conceded to lie in the nervous release which they afford from the customary and coercive activities which the social order imposes upon us. To the extent, therefore, that the pursuits of our leisure time tend to become organized under convention patterns determined by competitive consumption they lose their unique and primary value as recreation and so become merely another department of activity devoted to the achievement of prestige or status. Is it true that at present a great many leisure-time activities, dictated as they are by the dominant economic motive of the age, partake of this nature? Says Joad: "If the business man plays golf, it is, as he will tell you, to keep himself fit for business; if he takes a holiday he is submitting to boredom for the same reason." Is it true that an increasing number of people find themselves coerced by such considerations into a meaningless round of "recreational," leisure activities, which they heroically endure but which are devoid of capacity to minister to release of nervous tensions and to the development of personality which constitute the true purposes of recreation? Explosive and orgiastic "parties" are the pathological substitutes for the leisure pursuits which are the normal release of the tensions resulting from the job. Orgies have almost become a social obligation. As one girl put it, "Without cocktails the pleasures of life would be insupportable." While on a visit to Coney Island Maxim Gorky remarked: "What an unhappy people it must be that turns for happiness here." What shall we, in fact, say of a civilization which has so encumbered life that one of every twenty of us is destined actually to be committed to a hospital for mental diseases? How shall we appraise a prosperity which insures that one out of every ten of us will suffer such mental impairment as to make us eligible for psychopathic institutions? It is considerations of this kind which justify us in turning our attention to consumption of the products which might minister to the enrichment of life. One of the chief of these products is leisure.

The indictment of current leisure-time activities, then, rests not upon the mere fact that they are different from what they used to be or that they tend to be increasingly commercial. Nor should our criticism rest upon the a priori generalizations of artists and aesthetes regarding "higher" and "lower" forms of activity. The charge is that leisure or recreation of a certain type is neither leisure nor recreation in any basic biological or psychological sense. Slavish pleasures and mechanical leisure are contradictions in terms. That the shorter working day necessarily means more leisure of a desired or desirable kind is a non sequitur which is almost universal but is palpably false. All it necessarily means is more time for other pursuits, or for simple boredom. Boredom is receiving increasing attention as a factor in mental disease. As Edman has said, "Leisure is an affair of mood and atmosphere rather than simply of the clock. It is not a chronological occurrence but a spiritual state. It is unhurried pleasurable living among one's native enthusiasms."

Accepting the above conclusions as to the nature of leisure, we may now formulate provisionally a summary description or definition of this aspect of life. There appear to be four criteria which distinguish leisure, whether regarded as an activity or as a passive state. In the first place, leisure has, in a relatively high degree, both its original incentive and its fulfillment, in the individual himself rather than in coercions of the social and the economic order. Secondly, leisure must possess the capacity of being relatively permanently interesting. This implies such qualities as variety, and suggests, thirdly, that true leisure should involve activities or states as different as possible from those which are consciously forced upon us by our station in life. Finally, leisure should at least be compatible with, if not conducive to, physical, mental, and social well-being.

✎✐✎✐✎✐

66. A Portrait of the Farm Family in Central New York State *

SINCE THE MAJOR PROCESSES of socialization take place within the family, it is always considered one of the basic social institutions. The structure and function of the family, however, vary greatly, in both space and time, even within our own country. This selection portrays one style of family life, typical of farm families of the northeastern United States in the 30's and shows in what ways it is similar to, in what ways different from, the pioneer patriarchal farm family from which it descended. Although Howard Beers has here described an institutional form that has undoubtedly undergone considerable change since this was written, the present picture would probably still consist largely of a further "modification of old patterns, a partial acceptance of new patterns."

PICTURES OF THE GRANDPARENTS or great-grandparents hang today beside needlework samplers and faded hair flowers in heavy frames on the walls of an occasional farmhouse parlor. Heirlooms now, they typify a cultural period that had also its characteristic patterns of social arrangement. The early designs for living are heirlooms, too, but not yet as completely relegated to the walls of memory as are the paintings and the handwork in those parlor frames. Sometimes, indeed, we have nostalgic urges to recall them entirely from the past to play again the old roles of certain status in the present period of greater social confusion. But cultural systems change and if there were to be any permanence of role and status it would be too often a kind of social rigor mortis. Specific patterns of family life are therefore neither universal nor permanent. Our pictures of the farm family, as of every

* Howard W. Beers, American Sociological Review, 2 (October, 1937), 591-600. Reprinted by permission of the author and the publisher.

The author (b. 1905) is Head, Department of Sociology, University of Kentucky. Associate Economic Analyst, FERA, 1934; principal research supervisor, WPA, Washington, 1936. Has published articles in numerous professional journals.

other social grouping, must be adjusted at intervals to cultural change in each locale and in each social stratum.

A classic picture of the early farm family in New York State has been worded by James Mickel Williams. The figure in his portrait is an English puritan family reaching New York via New England, gradually reshaped by the conditions of pioneering, but with basic patterns enduring throughout the period of subsistence farming and continuing even into the recent periods of commercial agriculture and contemporary metropolitan dominance. The pioneer American family was large, biologically vital, and of strong social texture. It was "the beginning and the end of rural social organization." Family groups were geographically isolated, economically self-sufficient and socially self-contained. Parents were often "the school, the church, in extreme cases the state." Fathers were austerely dominant. Wives were obedient, faithful, subordinate in person and in law. Strict obedience was required of children. Actually the subjection of wife and children to the father exemplified their common submission to natural processes, never completely understood, always uncertain. The common and paramount interest of family members in the outcome of the farm enterprise necessitated agreement on all matters. Farming and living were synonymous. There was need for an executive in each family who could give direction to the process of living. The natural executive was the father, hence our usual judgment that the farm family was patriarchal. There followed from these conditions a strong family pride and exclusiveness, rigid adherence to custom. Self-restraint, thrift and industry were predominant in attitude and in action. There were strong standards of modesty and morality. There was respect for authority, whether parental, religious or legal.

The matrix of rural custom in which these family-forms were set has been only stiffly flexible, yielding slowly to urban encroachment. The very strength of its original position has not only retarded change but it has added to the discomforts of change. Social confusion is in proportion to the rate of change of the mores. Life is well-ordered and relatively easy when standards and rules are fixed, commonly known and commonly unchallenged. The psychological strains and tensions accompanying rapid social change are most acute where there has been greatest reliance on precept and formula. The potentialities for intra-group conflict, therefore, have recently been great in the farm family. City folk were earlier inured to the presence in one family group of widely variant interests and activities than were farm people. Perhaps this is why Burgess found evidence that adolescent-parent relationships are less well adjusted in the rural than in the city home. Alterations of farm family life may be occurring today in a maximum-discomfort stage of cultural change.

The family type described by Williams was at one time common in many parts of the northeastern hay and dairy sections. It was the biological and social ancestor of present day farm families in Central New York State. These families are living today on family-size farms which they own or rent and from which they derive their chief income. In the sample studied, all members are native born. They are in the second and third stages of family development, with husbands averaging 43.5 years in age, two years older than the wives. The parents were married an average of 18 years ago. An average of 3.6 children have been born per family. An average of 2.7 of these children per family are living with their parents at the time of observation. The families have been settled on their present farms an average of 10.8 years. Three-fourths of the wives and four-fifths of the husbands were born on farms. The families are similar, then, with respect to race, general culture, and occupation. They differ among themselves with respect to age, stage of family development, economic status and other factors. There are many interfamily variations like the individual differences among persons. The family patterns in this group are only once or twice removed from those of native white families in town, for they all stem from the early patriarchal type. The country cousin, however, remains biologically more vital than its urban kin. Even though farm birth rates have declined, perhaps more rapidly than city birth rates, the farm family still is formed earlier and is larger. The age of marriage in the United States has been increasing among classes of higher economic status, but it has been declining among farm people, as among other low income classes.

This portrait of contemporary farm families in a particular area will emerge more distinctly if one model sits against the background of descriptive data for all the families studied. Excerpts from a case narrative will help to clarify the outlines of our discussion.

The X family lives eight miles from a village of 2500 people in a rugged south central dairy section of New York State. To reach their home, one drives out through the broad valley and up a winding black-top road through the Gully. Turning right into an uphill lane, one stops between the frame house (straw yellow with white trimmings) and the unpainted barns. A flashlight beam points the way through a dark, rainy night to the back entrance.

This has been their home for 17 years. Mr. X is 43 years old, and his wife is 41. Both were born and reared on nearby farms. He finished common school. She attended the village high school for two years. Neither has had any occupational experience other than farming, and the farm is now their sole source of income.

Four children have been born to the mother, but the first boy died of pneumonia in his second year. The second boy, now eighteen, is a sophomore at college. The next child is a boy of eleven, in seventh grade. The youngest, a daughter of six, is in school for the first time—four born, three living, and two at home.

When married 20 years ago, Mr. and Mrs. X lived for three years with Mr. X's parents, working the homestead on shares. Then they bought their present farm of 96 acres going in debt for the full cost. Their small cash reserve was invested in repairs to buildings.

An average season's work on this farm involves handling 15 acres of hay, 12 of spring grain, five of ensilage corn, seven of buckwheat, three of potatoes, one acre of field beans, two acres of wheat, four of alfalfa, the care of nine milk cows, some young stock and 100 hens. Mr. X is now rated by local leaders as a careful and successful farmer.

The basic differences between early farm and city families were due both to rural isolation and to occupation. Today we find the kind of work that families do is becoming relatively more important than their place of residence. The social length of a physical mile varies from moment to moment. Farmers in central New York State undoubtedly knew of the Hindenburg Zeppelin disaster before the flames were extinguished. Certainly many of them while at breakfast took vicarious part in the coronation of a British King. Furthermore, as the influence of distance declines and the influence of occupation becomes more marked there comes increasingly into the picture a third differentiating factor, namely, that of economic status. Socio-economic differentiation within the rural community is becoming more pronounced. It is less and less possible to portray sharp contrasts between "the rural" and "the urban" family because of greater social heterogeneity within both rural and urban groups. Hitherto rural people in America have belonged largely to the middle classes. Recently, increasing numbers have moved into social positions of lessened status. As this happens it is important to note that "the climbing of the ladder of gentility" [successfully accomplished by Mr. X] "has suddenly become a much more difficult task than has heretofore been the case."

Underlying or accompanying the vital and economic changes of the farm family, there are changes in psychosocial relationships, changes in status and role. One factor basic to the definition of status is the division of labor among family members. Hence, any change in work pattern is significant.

Mr. X is primarily responsible for the outdoor work and the chores. In

summer the oldest boy, home from college, helps regularly with work outdoors. He is chief teamster during the summer, operates the mowing
machine, binder and other implements. Practically no outside help is
hired. The younger boy does some of the mowing, "drives on the horse-
fork" during haying, he does some milking, helps with general chores, helps
with gardening and is entirely responsible for feeding the poultry. He drove
the team and hay-rake last summer. All members but the little girl share
responsibility for the home garden. Mrs. X washes the milk utensils. She
takes sole responsibility for work in the house. The little girl occasionally
helps to wash dishes and to dust. She likes the latter chore in particular.
The younger boy carries wood (they burn no coal) for the stoves. Mrs. X
says that her husband was not "handy with babies," so she had no help in
the care of the younger children. The coming of children altered the
division of labor in this home. Mrs. X helped with the milking and with
general farm chores until the children arrived.

In the farm family of today, specialization is more marked than it
was during an earlier period. Formerly, it was not unusual for girls
to help with the outdoor work and for boys to help in household routines. Today, however, the processes of economic production have
largely left the house for field and barn. Sanderson has raised an interesting question with respect to this change. "It is undoubtedly true
that there is less need for home production . . . but if the wife and the
family are to be relieved of all domestic activities . . . do they secure
the satisfaction and is there a possibility of developing the affection
that would result from a sharing of common activities which make
possible an interchange of personal service, of what the Binkleys call
'domestic interaction'?"

Child labor is traditional on farms and it has been reduced in quantity
more by compulsory school attendance than by any shifts in rural
attitude. This is well evidenced by nation-wide rural negation of the
proposed constitutional amendment regulating the labor of children.
In an earlier time, custom allowed rural fathers the privilege of getting
all the work they could from their sons while the latter were legal
minors. Social maturity was recognized at 21, but not before. This
father-son work relationship is still almost unique to the farm family.
It constitutes a type of vocational training inherent in family farming.
A father-son relationship that is markedly different in at least one
phase from the pioneer pattern, however, is found in the X family.

When the older boy started college he had saved $120 in cash. Most of
this had accumulated as follows: The boy once had wanted a calf. The
father gave him a calf on condition that he raise it carefully and be responsible for its care. When the calf became a cow the father was to get the milk

for the expense of feeding. The cow's first calf was vealed and the boy got the money on condition that he put it in the bank. So every calf to which this cow gave birth was vealed and the boy kept the money. In the end the cow was sold. The same plan is being followed with the eleven-year-old who now has a calf that he is feeding.

Although there is greater division of labor in today's farm home, many activities are still shared, and propinquity still fosters family solidarity. Farm families vary in these customs, but the X family is representative for central New York.

The family members are all home together an average of six evenings per week. When asked what the family usually does in the evening to pass time pleasantly, Mrs. X said, "Well, when the boys are home they like to have Mr. X play checkers with them or something like that. I read a great deal. Mr. X reads as much as he can with his poor eyes. Then we have music, too. Lots of times we get around the organ and sing." The family always gathers at meal time with the exception of luncheon on school days when the children are not at home. But when the family is at home, each waits for the others to assemble before starting to eat. Reading aloud is customary, as it was in both of the parental homes. The Bible is read aloud once each day. As a rule, shopping in town is a family activity. There is family observance of the usual holidays. On Christmas the family goes to the home of Mrs. X. On Thanksgiving they go to the home of Mr. X. On New Year's Day they observe a holiday at home. On Decoration Day they go to the cemetery to decorate the graves of their first-born and their dead kin. Birthdays are always celebrated with at least a cake.

Religion and ritual are less intimately a part of the family pattern today than they were yesterday. In this respect, the X family is closer to pioneer customs than to modern city folkways.

In the extra parlor, a well-thumbed Bible and an accumulation of Sunday School papers cover the surface of a small table. On the wall above hangs the framed marriage certificate. On the opposite wall hangs a placard with the message, "His Mercy Endureth Forever." At one end of the room is an old melodeon on which a well-worn hymn book is open at *Rock of Ages*. There is no other music visible.

Daily Bible readings and strong social dependence upon church activity appear in the case of the X family. Neither they nor their neighbors follow the old custom of "saying grace" at meals. Yet every one of the marriages among these farm families was performed by a minister of religion rather than by a civil officer. Wives in particular declared that they "would not feel married unless a minister had performed the ceremony." The marriage mores of rural life are still intimate with institutional religion, but family activities are affected less directly by religion than they were in an earlier period.

The shared activities, propinquity and group rituals in these families are not ordinarily accompanied by overt demonstrations of affection. Here, as elsewhere, traditions of restraint and habits of emotional control are vestiges of the pioneer attitude. It is likely, however, that practices with respect to shared activity, demonstration of affection or family ritual vary more from family to family now than they would have varied three generations ago in the same area.

Along with propinquity and the patterns of work and leisure, division of executive authority in the home is equally basic to family structure. As Sims has written, "Although the rural family inclines to the patriarchal type, it often manifests noteworthy democratic traits." It might now be argued that the farm family inclines more and more to the democratic type of organization. The old conditions of risk and uncertainty in agriculture have not been entirely supplanted but there is now less mystery about the processes of production. Uncertainties of biology and weather, although replaced by uncertainties of the market, are no longer so insistent that each family group have a patriarchal head.

The present importance of markets, and the consequent emphasis upon intense, specialized production is introducing certain new influences on role and status within the family, giving some impetus to the democratic trend.

On a check list, which Mr. and Mrs. X completed independently, each gives the other credit for helping earn the family income. Each of them reports it to be earned by "father and mother together." Mrs. X is responsible for buying food. Purchasing children's clothing is a shared responsibility. Borrowing money is a matter that rests largely with Mr. X, although both parents discuss any problem of this sort before action is taken. If a problem directly concerns the children, they are called into council. Buying machinery is a matter for Mr. X's decision. He decides what crops to plant, when and where to plant them. If there is any remodeling to be done in the house, a joint decision is made. Contributing to the church is a matter for consensus. Mr. and Mrs. X select together the papers to which they will subscribe. Writing checks is done only by the husband. He buys the insurance, although whether or not it shall be taken is first agreed upon. Training the children is shared; seeing that children study lessons is also shared. Giving the children permission to leave the home or to go away is joint; punishing children is done by both. Both parents give the children spending money. Both of them help in planning the children's education, although Mrs. X said, "Now some of these things, like choosing the children's vocation, neither one of us ever thought that was our place."

There is little evidence here of uncompromising paternal dominance. The husbands in these families rarely take upon themselves the sole responsibility for making decisions, even when problems of business are up for solution. A discussion involving at least the husband and wife precedes the reaching of a decision in seven homes out of eight. In nearly half of the homes, children also are consulted. However, the importance of family discussion varies according to the kind of problem awaiting solution. Questions relating primarily to the farm business are more likely than others to be decided by the husband without consulting the wife. Decisions about the purchase of machinery or what crops to plant are of this type. On the other hand, if the question is whether or not to borrow money, to buy insurance, or to buy a car, there is likely to be a family discussion before any final action is taken. These questions relate directly to family welfare rather than solely to the farm business. If money is borrowed, thrift is forced upon the members of the family. If insurance is purchased, other things will have to be foregone. A new car will be either liked or disliked by each family member, hence each one has an interest in the decision.

The tendency for husbands to be solely responsible for financial decisions is more marked in families on large than on small farm enterprises. There is a suggestion in the evidence that as standards of competitive business efficiency enter farming, the splitting of executive responsibility into home and farm divisions may become more pronounced. The prophets of chemurgy as well as the discoveries of conservative research point to extreme and imminent changes in the practices and skills of agricultural production. The rate and final extent to which country life may be deruralized, of course, cannot even be conjectured, but even now milk-dresses and bathtub-tomatoes are more than pure fantasy.

There are also some new problems of financial administration in the home. In the days of family self-sufficiency, production and consumption were one dual process, begun and finished on one farm unit. Cash was unimportant. Now, however, the medium of exchange has a new significance to each family member. How do families meet the problem of an equitable or satisfactory distribution of cash among the separate members? There is little evidence of any one answer sufficiently extant to be called a folkway, but it is likely that low income or disagreement over distribution of income is a new source of tension in the farm family.

Some phases of the parent-child relationship have been mentioned above. In the X family, we found each child attending school, the oldest boy in college. This illustrates an attitude frequently voiced by mothers who want to educate their children into white-collar strata. We found each child with a definite place in the work pattern, a place of responsibility increasing with age, and allocated to house or field and barn on the basis of sex. We found parents and children playing as well as working together. We found children included occasionally in family councils, we found the boys with property and money of their own, we found ritualistic observance of the children's birthdays. (The manner of giving money to children in the X family is not general in the area studied. Irregular amounts of spending money are more customary in other families.) We found both parents sharing some responsibilities for guidance and control, yet allowing children relative freedom in such matters as choice of vocation. However, we still find that unfailing obedience is expected.

"Mr. X, how do you get the children to do what you ask them to do?"
"Why, we just tell them." Mrs. X added, "We never believed in bribing them or paying them to do things." Mr. X continued, "We always cal'clate that if they are told to do anything they are s'posed to do it."
"What methods of punishment do you use?"
"Oh, the whip and the strap. Often we deny them something they want. But we always make it clear to them just why we are doing it."

The changed status of wife and mother is at once cause and effect of changing family relationships. It has been only recently that a writer of syndicated newspaper features could, with impunity, advise a farm wife to "calmly announce to your husband that unless you can have a maid on your farm next year you will refuse to do any canning, gardening or chicken raising. Plan to cut down your work at least 40 per cent."

But women have been enfranchised. The law now recognizes their property rights. Educational levels have been raised. They participate freely in the organizational life of communities. Their roles with respect to household and farm work have changed. Some of these things have tended to give them a social status both within and out of the home that is more than ever like that of their husbands. The relationship of the mother's position to patterns within the family has been recognized in the foregoing discussion. It is related also to the role of the family in the community, a role that has changed since the days of pioneering. Mrs. X does not operate the family car but 43 per cent of the farm wives in neighboring homes are licensed drivers.

The organized participation of the family centers largely in the church. All members of the family attend church and Sunday School regularly. They have not joined the Grange. Mr. X belongs to the Farm Bureau and Dairymen's League. Mrs. X is a faithful attendant at meetings of the Missionary Society. They have not been to a moving picture since they were married. Mr. X goes to the village or a nearby city about twice a week and Mrs. X not more than once a month. Entertainments take them out not more than once a month. Mrs. X visits with neighbors on the telephone from one to three times a day. Mr. X confesses, however, that he probably does just as much visiting if not more than his wife. He meets neighbors on the road and stops to chat with them or he exchanges work with his neighbors and gossips while he works. Once a year they have friends from the city who come to spend a week or a few days with them. Mr. X has been on the church board; he has been a church steward and has been on the church building committee. Mrs. X teaches Sunday School and is vice-president of the Missionary Society. Mr. X is now collector and school trustee of the school district.

The proportion of husbands who did not participate in any organization (15 per cent) is greater than for wives (12 per cent). Similarly husbands attended an average of only 2.6 organizations while the wives attended an average of 3.2 organizations. This is a reversal of pioneer customs. Commercial recreation is infrequent. The husbands and wives attend moving pictures only about once in two months. Town contacts were twice as frequent for husbands as for wives because of business trips.

The local leadership of their communities comes from these families. Three-fourths of the men and over half of the women had a record of some past or present office in an organization. This changed community role of the farm wife, however, has not yet removed her from the family group enough to threaten the integration of the home, for wives with leadership records were found in those homes in which there are many shared activities. Furthermore, this activity in organizations often helps mothers to cope with current change. "Parent-teacher associations, child study clubs, and similar organizations render an important service in establishing norms of child behavior and strengthening the morale of the associated members in their efforts to maintain them."

Although the strength of the great family as a rural social control has weakened materially we find the kinship group still important. One-fourth of the households studied included some relative whose only home was with the family group.

The X's "go visiting" about once a month and receive visits from others with the same frequency, usually entertaining these guests at dinner. Most of this visiting is with nearby members of the great family. Nearly half of the families typified by Mr. and Mrs. X and their children attend an annual reunion of the paternal great family and the same proportion attend a similar gathering of the mother's great family. When we analyze their habits with respect to visiting we find that one-fourth of these families visit from one to four kin families of the husband and a similar number of kin families of the wife. Only one family in eight reports visiting no homes in which there are relatives of the husband, and one family in three reports visiting in no homes containing relatives of the wife.

In many respects, then, the portrait of today's farm family in Central New York could well hang on the same wall with needlework samplers and framed hair flowers. In other respects, it would not be out of place in a modern mural. It is a modification of old patterns, a partial acceptance of new patterns. It is smaller than the pioneer family, yet it is still among our chief sources of population increase. The rural social organization of the area is no longer familistic, but it is at least "semi-familistic." The roles of parent and child are less fixed in the mores. There is a definite heritage of paternal dominance, but the outlines of the heritage become progressively more dim. Obedience and subjection of children stand forth still as parental goals but with less and less filial recognition. Specialization and education have affected the division of labor, but shared work and shared leisure are still formative of the family pattern. Propinquity continues to foster solidarity, resisting the centrifugal effects of urbanization. There has been definite democratization in the changes of role and status. That is evidenced particularly in the joint executive function of mother and father. The rate at which this change occurs accelerates with the advance of business efficiency and industrialization in agriculture. Both rate and direction of future change in the farm family pattern are, therefore, quite as likely to depend upon larger economic and social influences affecting agriculture as upon the dictation of tradition.

It is significant that the family pattern of these farm folk is so widely valued today. As an accepted design for living, it is a stated or implied goal of those current governmental efforts at agricultural adjustment which propose to make the family farm more general and more secure.

67. Intrafamilial Relationships in a Farm Village of Shantung Province, China *

THE ONE SOCIAL INSTITUTION that has fundamental importance in all societies, regardless of time or place, is the family. But the composition of the family, its typical life cycle, and the roles played by males and females of various ages and relationships—all these differ from society to society. In this selection Martin Yang, a Chinese social scientist, gives us a view of the culturally defined roles and patterns of interpersonal relationships that characterized families in his native village.

THE REAL CORE OF FAMILY LIFE lies in the behavior of the individual members toward one another. Marriage and descent are its foundations and determine its most important interrelationships. Within the family circle the individual develops his personal attitudes, a self-evaluation and interpretation of his place in the larger society, and a sense of the significance of his relations with people outside the family.

Since marriage in an old-fashioned Chinese family is arranged by the parents, and since the two young people do not know each other before the wedding, the problem of adjustment for the newly married couple is a difficult one. They do not have their own home, but live with the husband's family. Although the couple often achieve a genuine affection for each other after a brief period of living together, they must not let their love be apparent and the husband, if he is to be considered a filial son and a good brother, must maintain closer relations with his family than with his wife. A young husband must not mention his wife too often; he must not praise her in family gatherings or to the villagers; if she passes by when he is with other persons, he must not speak to her unless either one or the other has an urgent message. When a husband returns from a trip he must greet his parents and his brothers and his sisters before he greets his wife. Only after several hours have elapsed may he excuse himself and join his wife in their room, and that only on the pretext that he must clean up and change his clothes. Although

* Martin C. Yang. Reprinted from A Chinese Village, pp. 54-67. Copyright 1945 by Columbia University Press. Reprinted by permission of the publisher and the author.

Martin C. Yang (Mou-Ch'un Yang) was born in Taitou, Shantung Province, China. Lived in the village until he entered high school. Dr. Yang made annual visits to his birthplace until recent years. A Chinese Village is built on facts experienced and recorded by one who combined sympathetic insight with scientific detachment.

he may be most anxious to be with his beloved one, and his family (especially his mother and sisters) understand this perfectly, he must nonetheless affect indifference.

A young wife must also keep from showing that she loves her husband. The general attitude is that a decent wife should love her husband, but must not let her love spoil his career or make him neglect his duty to his family. A good wife stays at her work with her mother-in-law or sisters-in-law during the day, and at night she must wait until all the family members have retired before she can go to her room and be with her husband. She should avoid sitting with her husband at social gatherings and should act as if she does not know him. She, too, must avoid referring frequently to him, or when it is necessary for her to do so, she should not use his name nor say "my husband," but instead use the pronoun "he." In speaking to her younger brother-in-law, or younger sister-in-law, she may refer to her husband as "your No. x brother." When her husband returns home from a prolonged trip, she does not greet him. Instead she prepares hot water and a meal for him, according to her mother-in-law's order. However, every member in the family knows that, after his mother, she is the one who is happiest at his return. The younger sister-in-law may tease her and this she will secretly enjoy.

A newly married wife cannot but feel lonesome and strange, because she is really in a strange home with strange people. The sudden separation from her mother, the stern face of her mother-in-law, the pretended dignity of the father-in-law, and above all, her sudden introduction to the continuous housework, all make her feel that she is completely at the mercy of these people. Since she cannot go back to her mother, the only one from whom she can seek protection is her husband. She will generally respond with great warmth and gratitude if she is well received by him. It is true that the husband has been hardened by the heavy work, by the rude country life, and in many cases by his never-joking father. But, on the other hand, he is just a fully grown adolescent who has not been permitted to be alone with any grown-up girl before. Now he has a wife to whom he can express his romantic ideals and reveal his love. For these reasons the young people usually become much attached to one another.

The partners of an unsuccessful marriage are in an unhappy plight. Divorce is out of the question: they must make the best of it. Outwardly they may seem no different from any other couple. They will not quarrel openly; the husband will not beat his wife; she does her work dutifully. However, it is easy to note that the loved wife is active, cheerful, and energetic, while the unhappy wife is listless and slow in her work. Although a newly married couple must put on a show of indifference in the presence of others, a keen observer can soon discern whether the indifference is pretended, as in the case of a happy couple, or real. The indifference of the ill-mated pair continues even in the privacy of their room. The husband goes to bed with a great sigh; the wife can only weep in secret and swallow her tears into her stomach. The husband will not approach her unless driven to do so, and she will be merely permissive. The two live together and have children, but their marriage is a gloomy one.

However, if an initially unhappy marriage survives at all, if the hopelessness and sorrow and burden of work do not break down the unhappy wife, the relationship between the couple improves with time. A woman who survives these hardships without committing suicide or breaking down becomes a heroine in the eyes of her relatives. She has proved that she has patience, far-sightedness, and unusual wisdom and kindness. As the couple grow older and their children reach maturity, their feelings toward each other mellow. Husband and wife can now sit together and talk more freely at family gatherings; they can walk together in public. The husband can joke at the expense of his wife in the presence of other people, even before the father-in-law, and the wife can also offer some humorous counterattack. In referring to each other in conversation, they no longer use the pronouns "he" and "she," but say "child's father" or "child's mother." If the name of their first child, for example, is Lien-pao, then the wife would say to her mother-in-law: "Lien-pao's Daddy said that."

In privacy, romantic love decreases, while the feeling of companionship grows stronger. In their bedroom the wife will tell her husband what has happened in the household during the day and what she thinks about their problems. She will also talk to him about their children. The husband tells her about the crops in the field, the work of his brothers and the hired laborers, and so on. Because of his consciousness of being a man, a filial son, a good brother, and a dignified husband, he is supposed not to listen to, or at least not to believe, his wife's complaints about other household members. In spite of this he frequently accepts her statements, and secretly acts on her suggestions and advice on other matters.

As the husband and wife mature, they come to have their own home and undivided authority over their children. The companionship ripens and is no longer kept secret but becomes the foundation of the newly independent family. The wife now becomes the undisputed head of the home. Arranging the children's marriages falls to her. The husband oversees the farm and deals with all matters pertaining to it, but since there is no clear-cut demarcation between domestic and farm affairs, and since cooperation and mutual advice between husband and wife is well-established in practice, this division occasions no real separation. According to a Confucian idea, the husband and wife relationship in this period is "Husband leads and wife follows." But in practice the wife may play the leading part while the husband follows, depending upon which is the more capable in this matter or that. The wife may become more eager to take on responsibility, but this does not mean that her respect for her husband diminishes, or that she does not acknowledge him as head of the family.

When a couple reaches the age of fifty or sixty, the wife generally becomes the dominant person in the household. She is now the mother-in-law of one, two, or even four daughters-in-law. She is the grandmother of a long line of children and is also the overseer of a large household. The middle-aged sons have almost invariably developed strong attachment to their mother but not to their father. The father's authority in the fields, now that he does not work there, is considerably lessened. He has lost his role in business transactions because he is too old to take the farm products to the market town and deal directly with the dealers. To a certain extent, his importance in relations with the neighbors is diminished, because people find that he is no longer the real authority and that his position as family head is more nominal than real, although he is still respected by all the household. His wife must see to it that he is well fed, well clothed, and well cared for. He preserves also the privilege of venting his anger upon any member of the family, except his daughters-in-law. Nevertheless, he sometimes recognizes his real position, and this may make him envy his wife. He may show this in quarrels which will elicit soothing words and apologies from her, but the real situation will remain unchanged.

After the sons and their families have departed to establish independent homes, relations between the old couple may undergo still another change. The wife now loses all her authority and is on equal terms with the husband. They may have a common feeling of neglect, and a need to look to each other for real sympathy and understanding. They thus reestablish the earlier companionship, except that where it was positive, creative, and had the achievement of a prosperous household as a mutual concern, it is now self-pitying and negative.

The relationship between father and child has none of the warmth and freedom existing between mother and child. The father's attitude is dignified, even remote; his authority is unquestioned and he expects submissiveness from his sons. Although in a farm family some informalities are permitted—as, joking in the presence of one's parents, taking a place of equal importance to that occupied by one's father, not rising when the father approaches—yet the father and son relationship is far from free or intimate. When the son is an infant, the father may on rare occasions play with him or take him out. When the boy is old enough to help in the fields, father and son walk together and work together quite often. But by the time the boy reaches the age of fifteen, the father assumes a more dignified attitude toward him and is frequently severe. The son feels uncomfortable with his father and prefers to work with other men in the fields. When father and son do work together, they have nothing to say, and even at home they speak only when there is business to discuss. At street gatherings or in places of amusement, they mutually avoid each other.

The relationship between mother and son, on the other hand, is comparatively close. Although a boy who reaches the age of ten is dependent entirely upon his father's authority and teaching, this does not interfere with his intimacy with his mother. Because of the lack of female companions and the meager possibilities for recreation, a young man spends much time talking to his mother during his formative years. After supper, when the father is absent and she is busy with the household chores, he talks with her freely of the things which concern him and even tells her if he is perhaps getting interested in his ku-chia piao-mei, the daughter of his father's sister. The mother may also use this opportunity to tell her son that she is arranging for his marriage and ask him if it is all right. He may make detailed inquiries about the girl, or he may insist that his ku-chia piao-mei is the girl he likes best and that his mother should arrange so that he can marry her. At this time the son may also complain of his father's harshness or confide that he would like to learn some trade other than farming, or that he would like to continue study. In her turn, the mother may tell him what she and his father think of him. A son at this time has no one, except his mother, to whom he can tell his thoughts freely, and this provides an unshakable foundation for the long-lasting mother-son relationship.

The affection between mother and son is threatened when the son marries. If the mother is selfish or narrow-minded, as many mothers are, she will become jealous of the young wife. Not a few of the difficulties between mother-in-law and daughter-in-law are unconsciously based on such jealousy. A common saying has it that "A son is lost when he is married." Should the marriage prove unsuccessful, the son may blame his mother because he holds her responsible for the match. A reasonable mother, who is happy to see her son and daughter-in-law getting along well, helps to preserve the original relationship between herself and her son. On the other hand, if he does not prolong his romantic indulgence but is mature enough to appreciate his parents' efforts on behalf of the household, he comes back to his mother the sooner. This does not mean that he deserts his wife, but simply that he resumes the talks with his mother that were interrupted during the early years of his marriage. If the daughter-in-law is reasonable and far-sighted, she does not oppose this intimacy, but rather attempts to strengthen the bond between herself and her mother-in-law and seeks opportunity for family talks, persuading her husband to join them. If these three cooperate, then, the mother-son relationship will resume its former intimacy after ten years or so. When the son and his wife are middle-aged parents, the mother-son relationship comes to include the son's family. In the winter, when the men are not busy in the fields and supper is usually finished earlier, sons, wives, and grandchildren will gather in the old mother's room and the grandmother will play with her youngest grandchildren, while the wives and older grandchildren and the sons talk about what they have seen and heard outside. The father may take part in this gathering if he likes, but he usually keeps himself aloof in order to maintain his patriarchal status. If he attempts to disrupt the free atmosphere, he will be chased out by his old wife.

Legally, the son is the head of the household after his father is dead, and the mother is under his authority. A woman's position is defined in a local saying, "At her parents' home she obeys her father; after marriage, her husband; when he dies, her son." When land or a house is sold, it is done in the name of the first son, the mother only being asked to vouch for it. The deed is worded as follows: "Seller, Wang Chuan-chia, with his mother's permission and through the medium of Chang Yuan-ch'ang and Ch'en Kao-fa, sells a piece of land of five mow [the locality and the four neighboring fields are indicated] to Lee Lien-pang at the negotiated price of fifteen hundred dollars. . . ." These legalized relations are seldom realized by the people in general and do not figure in everyday life. It is only when controversies arise regarding family property or the continuity of family line that the legal aspects are discussed by relatives and neighbors.

When a girl is born, she is cared for by her mother in much the same way a boy is. The father maintains his usual attitude of indifference. When the next baby is born, the three- or four-year-old girl has a place of her own or is temporarily taken care of by her grandmother rather than sharing her father's side of the bed as a boy does. When she is six or older, she gradually starts helping her mother to look after the younger sister or brother. By the time she is thirteen, she begins to learn to sew, cook, spin, and many other things. By fifteen, she is indispensable to her mother. Mother and daughter develop an intimate relation, and the father and daughter become more distant. He may have genuine affection for his daughter, especially if the latter conforms to the prevailing standard of a good girl, but the affection between them must be restrained. His knowledge of his daughter is gleaned indirectly through her mother. Generally, a daughter's marriage is arranged by her mother and only the mother can ask the girl's opinion in the matter. The father is consulted, of course. After the arrangement is made, the mother supervises everything the girl makes for her wedding and also persuades the father to be generous with the dowry. At the wedding both mother and daughter feel sad, which brings them even closer together than they were before. For two or three days before the ceremony, mother and daughter lie awake talking all night. The mother tells her daughter everything she knows about marriage, except the sexual details, and instructs her in the ways in which a bride should behave. Needless to say, the impending separation is difficult for both. When the girl has gone, her mother tries to learn whether or not she has been satisfactorily received by her husband and if she is kindly treated by the senior members of the household. If all goes well, the daughter appears happy when she pays her first visit home and the mother is happy too, but if the situation is not a good one, the daughter will cry at her mother's feet and the mother suffers unspeakably.

If a grown-up girl does not do her work well or does not behave properly, the person held responsible is her mother. In the same way, if a daughter-in-law is not satisfactory to her mother-in-law, the latter says that she has not been disciplined by her mother. This shows how commonly accepted the closeness of mother and daughter is. When a father hears his daughter criticized by the villagers, he does not go to the girl directly, but to her mother, and she is not permitted to say that she knows nothing of it, or is not responsible, but must apologize and then try to find the reason for her daughter's reputation. If it is based on fact, she must correct it. The villagers know that a daughter's personality is a reflection of her mother's and the mother shares in any blame directed at the former.

Relations between mother-in-law and daughter-in-law are sometimes strained, sometimes harmonious, but always less intimate than those of a daughter and her own mother. A daughter-in-law's obligations to her mother-in-law and to her husband are similar, but there are many points of friction inherent in the situation between the two women. The son's transference of affection from his mother to his wife, creates tensions between the women. The wife now takes care of mending and sewing his personal garments; to everybody else these changes seem natural, but to the mother, it is a great blow. She feels that she has been deserted by her son, that she has lost her greatest treasure. For this she cannot blame him, because she loves him so well, yet needing somebody to blame, she naturally turns to his new wife. At first, she may say that her daughter-in-law should not be so appealing to her son as to make him neglect his parents, brothers, and family duties. Later she may come to believe that the young woman purposely defames her to her son, and a bitter resentment may grow up in her mind. Also, as a result perhaps of the traditional expectations or of the loneliness and feeling of insecurity occasioned by the new environment, a daughter-in-law is always ready to feel that she is being ill-treated by her mother-in-law. Thus suspicion and self-pity on both sides create fertile ground for the sowing of conflicts, and minor incidents assume undue importance.

It is commonly said that when a mother-in-law treats her daughter-in-law badly it is because she was herself so treated when she was a young married woman and is now trying to avenge her own past wrongs. Except for the daughter-in-law, there is no person in the household on whom the mother is able or willing to avenge herself.

In many cases, however, the mother-in-law tries to be kind to her daughter-in-law, and the latter responds favorably. There are not a few mothers who are soft-hearted and far-sighted enough to see the importance of cooperation amongst the family members to the well-being of the large household. There are also not a few daughters who have been brought up in homes where broad-mindedness, obedience toward the senior generation, tolerance, filial piety, diligence, frugality, sincerity, and faithfulness have been the objectives in the training of the children. When such a mother and daughter come to live together, they will treat each other with consideration. The mother-in-law appreciates the fact that the girl has been abruptly separated from her parents and brought to an entirely new environment, and that she may be pretty miserable. She also understands that kindness and sympathy will make her loyal to the family and that her loyalty is tremendously important. Therefore, she will try to help her daughter-in-law become accustomed to her new home, and will not want her to work too much, will see that she eats enough and that she gets along well with her husband. She will on occasion look after the young children. If treated this way, the daughter-in-law will try to show her faithfulness to her husband and the whole family. If something untoward happens, the mother-in-law will assume the attitude of a mother in trying to rectify the situation and the daughter-in-law will accept the correction or blame with meekness. In this way the girl transfers her affection to the new family and accepts her position among them without continuing to long for her old home.

Relationship between a woman and her husband's father is very formal. She sees him and speaks to him, but only to a very limited extent. It is considered improper for a father-in-law to enter his son's room after that son is married. This holds true even when the daughter-in-law is not actually in the room. A father may joke with his son's wife only at a family gathering, and the joke must be free from any romantic implication. A young daughter-in-law must respect her father-in-law; she should not burst into laughter in his presence, but merely smile if a joke is told. When she is in her husband's parents' room, she must stand up when her father-in-law enters; she owes him as much deference as her husband does.

It is a breach of etiquette for a father to ask about his daughter-in-law's affairs, except when the latter has committed some wrong.

If he should behave improperly toward her he would be disgraced in the eyes of his own son and of his daughter-in-law's family. Should sexual misconduct be involved, the young members of her family confront him with the reins and feed of a mule, and do everything else they can to insult him. He loses the respect of his own family, of the villagers, and all his relatives and friends. Hereafter, everyone calls him a mule. We do not know definitely why this term is used, but we may hazard a guess. Sexual relations between a man of the older generation and a young person in the same family are considered bestial. So far as the farmers know, only mules mate with animals not of their own kind. Horses are very rare in this area and the local people are unfamiliar with them; and also a horse is rated much higher than a mule, so the condemned man is not worthy of being called a horse. This treatment is accorded a man who has any improper interest in his daughter-in-law, or who does anything to make her think he is sexually inclined toward her.

During boyhood, brothers are playmates and are on more or less equal terms. Fights between them are not frowned upon. Later, the elder brother is expected to be friendly to his younger brother, but there is some restraint in the situation. The younger one is expected to respect the elder. Before they marry, or when only the eldest has married, they continue to get along well with each other. They work together in the field or at home under their father's direction, and though there may be rivalry or even occasional clashes there is also cooperation, mutual help, and mutual confidence. After they have all married, the relationship usually becomes less pleasant. At first, they try to maintain the original friendliness. But gradually their efforts become less and less effective, for they cannot but be influenced by their wives' insinuations and their children's complaints. Quarrels or distrust rise more easily to the surface. If the parents cannot act as arbitrators or mediators, the household is likely to break up. A number of families in the village have held together for a considerable period after the sons were married, and in several cases even after the parents had died. But, for the most part, married sons set up their own households after their children are born.

In the early years of life, a girl is usually dominated by her brother in play or disagreements. This is due partly to the fact of male priority in a Chinese family. The girl's bound feet may be another reason for her "unconditional surrender." When a boy is twelve or fifteen years old, he begins to feel that it is his duty to protect his sister, even if she is older than he. A Chinese girl over twelve years is not allowed to associate with any boy other than her own brother or her father's brothers' sons. Since her desire for male company grows stronger as she gets older, she eagerly accepts her brother's company and protection. Unmarried brother and sister have a free and intimate relationship. He may tell her if he is interested in a certain girl or ask her about feminine psychology. A sister may act as a go-between for her brother and a girl he is interested in. He may confide to her his as yet unrevealed ambitions and he may ask her to speak for him to their mother. A sister, however, would not reveal her heart to her brother, for she is too shy and timid. A brother may admit his own romantic aspirations, but would not like to know that his sister is interested in a certain boy. He would feel shame at the knowledge that she longs for love, for he must feel that she is pure. He resents any boy's advances to her, as, unconsciously, he already hates the young man who will be his sister's husband. Though confidences are not mutual, a girl derives satisfaction from her brother's companionship, and since she is not permitted to know any other boy, his friendship is very dear to her.

After his marriage, the brother's attitude is apt to change to indifference or even hostility. He now has a wife who is closer to him than his sister ever was, and he no longer needs to turn to the latter for feminine sympathy and help. The brother's new wife helps to widen the breach between brother and sister for she is usually jealous and suspicious of their relationship. Also, she may be unpleasant to her young sister-in-law as a means of releasing aggression against the girl's mother, for most brides suffer from their mother-in-law's domination. The brother, at the instigation of his wife, may blame the sister for minor household difficulties, thereby increasing the rift. The mother, if she is still living, protects her daughter from any open acts of hostility on the part of the young couple; this is one reason why a mother fears to die before she can see her daughter safely married. An amicable adjustment of these relationships is usually worked out eventually.

•   •   •   •   •   •

A daughter-in-law is inclined to believe that the trouble which she has with her mother-in-law is the result of her sister-in-law's influence and antagonism to her. On the other hand, the unmarried daughter feels that her brother's wife is her rival, and resents her because she has taken her brother away from her and her mother. It is very rarely that one sees a girl being a true friend of her brother's wife. Under ordinary conditions, the girl maintains an attitude of indifference toward the sister-in-law, and the latter is polite but quite remote. A daughter-in-law, for her mother-in-law's sake, makes concessions to her husband's sister, and she, in her turn, may look after her brother's young children when their mother is busy. She may also voluntarily, or when ordered by her mother, lend a hand when her sister-in-law needs help. On the whole, however, the relationship is not well defined; the village opinion is that it is hardly good. When a mother arranges her daughter's marriage, she always asks how many sisters the prospective husband has. Other things being equal, she probably chooses the man with the fewest sisters.

A brother's wife can have great influence on the behavior of her husband's unmarried sister. According to village opinion, when a sao-tze (a term by which a girl refers to her elder brother's wife) and a hsiao-ku (a term used by a daughter-in-law to refer to her husband's younger sister) do come together either in work or in relaxation, the conversation is very likely to be about personal affairs. The sister usually likes to listen, and she may even unconsciously incite her brother's wife to talk. This is an important source of sexual knowledge and may also furnish temptation to commit some socially condemned act. A girl can also learn from her brother's wife sewing, cooking, embroidering, taking care of a baby, taking care of a husband, dealing with a mother-in-law and sister-in-law, and so on—all very useful to her.

• • • • • •

A woman and her husband's younger brother have a free and easy relationship. But if the brother is very young and the woman is middle-aged, the latter is supposed to play a mother's role to him, especially if the boy's mother is dead. In not a few cases motherless boys have been brought up by the wives of their eldest brothers, and these boys pay high tribute to their sisters-in-law. That the wife of one's eldest brother should be looked upon as one's mother is a proverb well known by the local people.

Between a woman and her husband's elder brother the relation is marked by respect and by a distance that borders on avoidance. Like the father, the elder brother does not enter the bedroom of the younger one after the latter is married, unless it is absolutely necessary. Even then the younger brother's wife must be informed beforehand so that she may leave the room. Only in family gatherings or in the old parents' room, when all the family members are present and talk is free, may an elder brother-in-law joke without embarrassing the wives of the younger brothers. The formality decreases when all the brothers and their wives reach middle age. In a farm home, all the family members must work and eat together, and formalities cannot be strictly observed. Sexual relations between a man and his brother's wife are forbidden, but the taboo is not as strict as it is for the father-in-law. . . .

The relationship between a man and his father's brother is almost the same as that between him and his parents when the large family is still together under one roof. The nephew is required to listen to his father's brother, and if the uncle is not married, he has as much authority over his nephew as the boy's father has. He may punish the boy without interference. After the uncle is married and has his own children, he must refrain from exercising his authority. If his nephew defies him, he should ask the boy's own father or mother to correct him. If he scolds the boy, his scolding should not be as severe as the boy's parents would administer. When a man has his own children, he should be especially nice to his brother's children because his kindness or severity will be reciprocated. Also, kind treatment to nephew or niece is a way of showing good feeling toward one's brother. Another manifestation of filial feeling is punishing one's own children unhesitatingly if they have not been sufficiently respectful to one's brother and his wife. The punishment must be purely disciplinary. Unfair treatment, actual or imaginary, of a brother's children, is a source of much misunderstanding between brothers and of family trouble in general.

The relationship between grandparents and grandchildren is a loving one, expressed with a tenderness similar to that between a mother and her child. The happiness of having a grandchild is the goal of all middle-aged parents, and the greatest pleasure of an old man or woman is to hold a grandchild in his arms.

The adjustments necessary between the members of a large family are delicate ones and it is only when they can be made with a minimum of friction that a large household can hold together. Jealousies and disagreements between certain members will throw the entire organization out of balance, and, if no immediate remedy is found for the situation, the household may break up. It is the most important duty of the head of a household to keep these relationships functioning smoothly. The task would be impossible, even for a family head of great tact and skill, were it not that so many traditions, rituals, and social sanctions operate as controls in the situation.

There are two basic relationships: that between parents and children (with the emphasis, of course, upon the sons), and that between a son and his wife. Theoretically, these two should be complementary. In practice, however, they are antagonistic to one another. It is true that when parents find a wife for their son they hope that the couple will be compatible and are pleased on the wedding day to receive such congratulations as "Harmony in one hundred years"; "A heavenly sanctioned union"; "Sincerity and love between husband and wife." However, the parents are displeased when the young couple are too devoted to each other, for this menaces the relationship between parents and son, especially that between mother and son. We have previously seen how a mother becomes bitter if her son loves his wife or his wife loves him too much. We also pointed out how a father's instruction may be neglected, rejected, or misinterpreted if his son listens too attentively to his wife's words. In case he is not satisfied with his wife, he must, if he wants to be a filial son, not quarrel too much with her lest his parents' consciences be hurt, nor must he complain too much. That is why, as we have seen, a young husband is required to assume an attitude of indifference while his parents or other family members are present, and why such mottos as, "Listening to wife's words and turning one's back to one's bone and flesh relations is not the behavior of a righteous man," are highly praised by all Chinese parents. Marriage is not primarily for the happiness of the husband and wife alone, but also for the parents—to help in their work, to wait upon them, to satisfy their desire for grandchildren while they are living, and to continue their "incense and fire" when they die.

❧❧❧❧❧

68. Roles and Marital Adjustment *

INSTITUTIONS, as the literature of sociology points out, develop to fulfill persistent basic social needs. Sometimes institutional experience is unsatisfying, however, because persons have learned to

* Leonard S. Cottrell, publication of the American Sociological Society, XXVII, No. 2, Papers, May, 1933, University of Chicago Press, 1933. Reprinted by permission of the author and the publisher.
The author (b. 1899) is a social psychologist, Russell Sage Foundation. Chief

play roles unsuited to the institutional situation in which they find themselves. Or their expectations regarding the behavior of others in the institution are unfulfilled. In this selection L. S. Cottrell discusses the importance of an understanding of role-playing and role-expectation in studying the adjustment of husbands and wives to the institutions of marriage and the family.

There are certain points concerning the concept of the rôle which, though recognized by those who developed and refined the concept, need for our purposes added emphasis.

First, in our use of the concept rôle we are prone to think of certain characteristic responses or tendencies to respond which the person makes or tends to make to persons or situations. Frequently we fail to recognize clearly enough what might be called expectations entertained by the subject as to actions or responses which are to come from other persons. The writer recognizes that it is impossible to separate these two things since in reality they are aspects of the same thing. There is no conception of one's rôle, conscious or unconscious, without reference to what action is expected of the situation of which the rôle is a part. It is well, however, to emphasize the expectancy aspect, particularly in using the notion in the study of marriage situations. A number of our cases of marital difficulty seem capable of analysis in terms of the inability of one mate to fit into the expected response pattern called for by the other.

A second point to be called to mind is that in marriage the partners do not play single rôles with respect to one another, although a single rôle may be most characteristic of a given person in his marriage relations. Cases seem to indicate a multiplicity of rôles. For example, a wife may play a much depended upon mother-rôle, a hated sister-rôle, and a loved brother-rôle at different times for her husband. The husband may in turn be for his wife her distantly respected father, her hated younger brother, and her loved older sister. The startling ambivalence frequently displayed by married persons for one another may not be true ambivalence in the strict Freudian sense. It may actually be the result of corresponding attitudes for different rôle patterns derived from early family relations. Thus a husband may call out affectionate as well

sociologist, and director of survey analysis, research branch, information and education, O.C.S., War Dept., 1942-45. FERA and WPA research analyst, 1935. Co-author, *Part Time Farming and Industrial Employment in the Southeast*, *Delinquency Areas*, *Predicting Success or Failure in Marriage* (with E. W. Burgess), *Development in Social Psychology*, *American Opinion on World Affairs in the Atomic Age*. Has written numerous confidential research reports on morale of U. S. troops.

as hostile responses from his wife by playing rôles of members of her family who earlier called out the different responses. Of course it is not at all necessary nor even likely that either husband or wife will be aware that he is playing such rôles.

A third point to be mentioned is that rôles may be stereotyped and unique. The stereotyped rôles, for example, of husband and father, wife and mother, are defined in the folkways and mores of society. But within these definitions by a given culture there are individual patterns or rôles that are determined by the peculiar social experience of the individual. Thus an adult may continue to play an infantile rôle as a result, let us say, of his having been the youngest child in a family that has coddled him a great deal.

A fourth point which needs emphasis is that, frequently, we might say usually, many of the rôles that persons play are unconscious. If all of the rôles a married pair play for one another are not unconscious, the most significant ones are frequently so.

We shall not here attempt an exegesis of the conception of the unconscious. It is sufficient for our purposes to realize that, if we analyze any act or series of actions, we find that there are phases of the act which can be said to be unknown to the actor, and are, moreover, not subject to his unaided conscious scrutiny and reflection. The conscious phase of the act in which the individual has defined for himself or has defined for him his objects and purposes and motives is one phase only. There are preliminary to and concomitant with his acts, goals, motives, etc., of which he is unconscious. Examples might be taken from the cases cited by Mr. H. D. Lasswell in his *Psychopathology and Politics* in which the conscious political activity directed against a present order turns out to be a displacement of drives and hostilities of the child with respect to its parent or sibling. Of these more primary and elementary motives the person is not aware and accepts his own definitions of goals and reasons as the only ones present in the action. Our contention here is that the same kind of unconscious character can be attributed to much of marital activity.

There may be some objection to thinking of rôles as unconscious. We do not hold that all rôles are unconscious. Some seem to be completely unconscious; some only partially so. We are not wedded to a word. If the term "rôle" is to be used only for conscious action patterns and relationships, then we must give another name to these unconscious patterns and relationships that exist in fact.

The narrowed angle of approach represented in this paper, namely, the study of marriage as an adjustment of rôles, may be indicated by laying down certain propositions.

First, marriage adjustment may be regarded as a process in which marriage partners attempt to re-enact certain relational systems or situations which obtained in their own earlier family groups. Or, in other words, marriage partners tend to play the habitual rôles they evolved in their childhood and adolescence.

Second, the kinds of rôles that marriage partners bring to the marriage will determine the nature of their marriage relationship and the degree of adjustment that they will achieve.

Third, that maladjusted marriages may be regarded as results of the failure of marriage situation to provide the system of relationships called for by the rôles which the marriage partners bring to the marriage.

Now the writer is quite aware that these propositions leave out of account a great many important factors—cultural, economic, etc.—and there is no effort to deny that such factors are of importance. Let it be emphatically affirmed that these propositions are laid down in an effort to make a logical delimitation of the problem. However, there is considerable justification for the opinion that the unique rôle patterns are the chief determinants of the success or failure of marriages in which the persons come from similar cultural backgrounds. And it should not be forgotten that the greater number of marriages are contracted by persons of reasonably similar cultural backgrounds.

Let us consider the case of Mr. and Mrs. A. who have been married about a year.

Mr. A. (aged 24) is the youngest of a family of seven. When asked to tell about his childhood, he launches into a rather enthusiastic account of his happy and satisfactory family life. From his story one gathers that his mother was a powerful and aggressive personality, the chief center, drive, and control factor in the family. She ran the father's affairs, planned the children's vocational and social activities, maneuvered the daughters' marriages, and tried to maneuver the sons' marriages. Mr. A. boasts of her iron will. He is proud of her determined look, and tells how her spirit never sagged. He tells how she faced death with the same unshaken will and determination never to admit defeat.

The father is described as a pleasant, reliable, steady, quiet, and meek person who seemed to figure merely as an unimportant though kindly fixture in the household. He worked steadily, turned his earnings over to his wife, never seriously opposed her, and after her death, agreeably allowed his daughters to place him in an old people's home.

The three sisters are described as being very much like the mother, particularly the two older ones. These two have married husbands to whom they play pretty much the same rôle which their mother played toward her husband. The youngest sister, whom we shall call Martha, is two years older than Mr. A. Although not quite so Amazonian as her sisters, she is fairly aggressive, active, and adequate in meeting situations. She has played a decidedly mothering rôle to Mr. A., especially since the death of their mother when Mr. A. was about fifteen years old. He says of Martha in an interview, "We have always been very close together. She has comforted me and consoled me in my troubles. I have confided in her and she has shielded me. She used to advise me and tell me what to do." He used to sleep with his sister, and he tells of his surprise on discovering recently that people thought such an arrangement strange. He says: "Even after I was 16 or 17 if I was blue or worried about my future she would take me to bed with her and comfort me." This occurred more frequently after the mother's death. Soon after his marriage he felt he *had* to leave his wife, to get away and think things out. He went home for a visit. The first few days he was very worried and upset. He couldn't sleep at night and one night fell to weeping. Martha took him to bed with her and consoled him. He says: "I felt a motherly warmth and felt released from my troubles and went to sleep. After that I slept in her room every night and felt much better." Mr. A. denies ever having sexual impulses or ideas about Martha at any time, although they have discussed sex quite freely.

In speaking of all the sisters he says: "I was always proud to go places with my sisters. They were lively and popular and I was proud of them. I could walk around and enjoy myself and they could take care of themselves." (This was said in comparing his sisters with his wife, who depends too much on him, he says, for pleasant times at social gatherings.)

Mr. A. does not feel that there was much conflict in his home. Things seemed to be secure and to run smoothly under the orderly supervision of the mother. He feels that the home life was happy. He says: "There was always something going on at my home. My mother and sisters were always doing interesting things, having people over and having jolly times that I like to remember. They didn't sit around like she does (alluding to his wife) and wait for something to happen. My father is quiet and never participated much in what was going on, but he enjoyed watching and listening to other people. I am like my father. I liked to watch and listen, and, if I felt like it, put in a word or do something. I hate to feel I *have* to talk or take the initiative." (This remark also was made with reference to his wife's irritating dependence upon him.)

Mr. A.'s two brothers are interesting. The older brother, who is also the oldest child, is called the black sheep. His relations with the mother and with the sister next to him were particularly hostile. He rebelled and left home early. The next brother is the middle child. He was the mother's favorite. He was and still is a dependable, quiet, kindly, non-aggressive person. The children say he is the mainstay of the family. Mr. A. describes him as a kind of parent to the younger children.

Mr. A. says that his parents and siblings were always kind to him. "They always took care of me, and my brother told me he would send me to school. My sisters like to have me come to their homes, and they enjoy giving me the comforts of a home. They say, 'You need the comforts of a home'; and I believe they are right, because I often wish I could feel that I had a father and mother and a home I could go back to."

He was punished very little. A typical instance is revealing. His mother and brother scolded him and threatened to punish him for not practicing his music. They told him he should be willing to practice for them if they paid for his lessons. Mr. A.'s comment is interesting: "I remember I was very angry that they should expect anything from me just because they paid for the lessons. I hated to feel obligated." (This represents an attitude characteristic of Mr. A.—that of expecting the environment to minister unto him with no obligation or responsibilities on his part.)

One gets the impression from Mr. A.'s conversation that he was an extremely dependent, much indulged, and coddled child; that he resented any responsibility or expectation or demand from him on the part of the environment; and that he felt insecure in situations where he was thrown on his own initiative. He tended to assume a passive rôle, expecting the environment to furnish aggressive support, backing, and leadership. On several occasions he made what he describes as attempts to win his independence by leaving home. He usually went under the tutelage of a decisive and aggressive boy friend who told him he ought to learn to stand on his own feet. On each occasion when he faced a shortage of jobs or money he felt forced to retreat home. After a few attempts he was ashamed to go home and would retreat to the family of the girl he finally married. He said: "I just can't bear feeling all alone in a strange place with no money and no home I can go to."

Mr. A. met his wife shortly before his mother's death. He says: "I was timid and bashful, but she was pleasant and talked to me and I felt comfortable with her." Soon after Mr. A.'s mother died the girl's family moved to another city. A. wept the night before her departure and said: "First I lose my mother; then I lose you." (The girl had the same first name as Mr. A.'s mother.) He told her he loved her at that time, but felt that he had said more than he meant; and the next day he contrived to arrive at the railroad station too late to see her off. Largely through the girl's efforts, a correspondence was kept up between the two. Later, after some of his unsuccessful forays into the world of affairs, he would seek the shelter of the girl's home. She would be very sympathetic about his trials and tribulations and she readily accepted his alibis for failure and excused him to himself. When she consoled him on his retreats from unsuccessful attempts to make good in the world (which, by the way, he expected to do in short order) he would tell her that she was just like his sister. As he was forced to repeat his returns to the girl's family, he became more and more uncomfortable; for he felt himself more and more obligated to assume responsibilities with respect to the girl. He seemed unable to do without a good deal of sympathetic reassurance; but he became increasingly panicky as it grew more evident that marriage was expected of him.

Before we discuss further the relations between Mr. A. and his wife, it is necessary to describe briefly Mrs. A.'s family. The families of both Mr. and Mrs. A. represent the same cultural and economic levels; if there is any difference, it is slight and in favor of Mr. A.'s family.

Mrs. A. (aged 23) describes her father as a successful merchant until a few years ago, when he developed an interest in gambling and taking extended vacations. He had never saved money but his business kept the family in good circumstances. For some time now, however, he had been very improvident and irresponsible. He has obtained good positions, but has given them up for very trivial reasons. Mrs. A. says she used to admire and respect her father, but since he has allowed the family to come upon evil days she has lost respect for him and feels very resentful toward him. The father accuses the mother of being responsible for the condition of the family. He says: "You should have taken the money from me and not allowed me to gamble." And "You should have made me attend to our business." Mrs. A. feels her father has acted as something of a spoiled child toward his wife.

The mother is described as patient, long suffering, submissive. Mrs. A. feels that she is close to her mother because, as she says, "I am very much like my mother and can understand her." She has always taken sides with her mother in family arguments, which seems to align the father and older brother against the mother and Mrs. A. These arguments turn out to be tongue lashings from the father and older brother, with the mother and daughter passively resisting.

The oldest brother is very harsh toward the mother, but she submits to his dominating and overbearing treatment. She appears to resent it somewhat, but she excuses him. When he flies into rages and leaves home to avoid paying room and board, the mother will feel sorry for him and will cook up cakes and other dainties, which she carries to his abode and lays at his feet. She treats the father in much the same way, patiently accepting his occasional beratings. When some of the children complain of their father's incompetence the mother will make excuses for him. She will say, "Your father has worked hard all his life and now just look at him. It isn't fair."

There are three children in the family, an oldest son, Mrs. A., and her younger brother. Mrs. A. speaks bitterly of the intense hatred she bears her older brother, who appears from her description to be a very domineering, overbearing, egocentric person. But she follows her statements of hostility toward him with the admission that she secretly admires his aggressiveness and capabilities and envies his assertiveness. She has wished all her life that he would love her. When on rare occasions he would be kind to her or give her a birthday gift, she would feel much encouraged and hope for better relations. She would experience great disappointment when he would resume his usual tactics.

The son's hostilities toward his mother and sister seem to date from early childhood. Mrs. A. has fought back somewhat, but she usually cries, feels blue, and suffers inwardly. She still dreams of having bitter fights with him, but in these dreams her rôle is one of defending herself against his attacks. Occasionally she will dream of a more aggressive rôle in which she vehemently commands her brother to get out of the house. She says that one reason she liked Mr. A. was that he seemed to be the opposite of her brother in every way.

Mrs. A. is fond of her younger brother and feels that they were quite close as children, though their relationship is not so close now.

Mrs. A.'s conversation gives one the impression of a person with some hostile drives, who, nevertheless, tends to assume a passive rôle in all situations. She tends to wait for something to happen, for others to make suggestions and to take the initiative. Her lack of decisive self-assertion is a characteristic which drives her husband, so he says, to distraction.

With this all too meager account of the backgrounds of our subjects, let us turn again to their relationship with one another.

Mr. A. became more and more frightened and restless as it became clearer to him that the natural and expected result of his relationship to Mrs. A. was marriage. He made some attempts to extricate himself by protesting to her that they were in no position to marry and by leaving her home. Quoting from an interview with him: "I wanted to be away to be free to work out my problems alone, but I felt myself dragged deeper and deeper." Early attempts to leave and get a job resulted in failure and an inevitable return to the girl, who was always ready with her sympathy and mothering solicitude. Her family was hospitable;

but what worried Mr. A. was that they assumed his frequent returnings for prolonged visits to mean that he was intent on marriage. The father finally became more urgent and tried to encourage the diffident young man by letting him know that what he needed to settle him down was marriage.

These urgings and expectations on the part of the family plus the pleadings of the girl, plus his own inability to do without some sympathetic reassuring, proved too much for him. Finally, he says, he shut his eyes and jumped. We do not have time to give his description of his mental anguish as he walked the streets for two days trying to make up his mind. "Then," he says, "with super-human effort I forced myself to go to the courthouse and say 'I want a marriage licence.'"

After the marriage Mr. A. began to have many fears and forebodings. He was afraid Mrs. A.'s mother or father would die and he would have to help take care of Mrs. A.'s younger brother. He feared that he had wrecked his chances to realize his best self and should get out of the marriage. He began to find Mrs. A. ugly; and this, he said, outraged his aesthetic sensibilities. But the main theme throughout his interviews is: "My wife is a drag on me. She depends too much on me. Instead of feeling myself being pulled forward, I feel like she is pulling me backward. Why can't she be like my sisters? She is weak and casts a gloom over my spirit that I can't shake off. I must go away so I can feel free again and be on my own."

He did break away once to go to his sister for comfort and solace. He said: "While I was there I was happy again unless I thought of my plight. My sister said 'all you need is the comfort of your home' and she was right. While I was with her I felt all right."

The wife complained that she didn't feel secure with her husband. She wished that he could be like other men who seem to know what they want to do and how to go about it, who seem to take charge of things and forge ahead and not appear so helpless. She resented the fact that, although her husband was out of work and she was supporting him, he seemed to take that for granted as his due. Moreover, he showed great irritation toward her if she came home tired and, as he puts it, "sagging and weak looking." He says: "I simply can't stand that sagging, droopy look."

Their sexual adjustment is interesting when seen on this background. Neither knew how to proceed and their first attempts at intercourse were clumsy and unsuccessful. The husband's history shows considerable curiosity during childhood, and avoidance and fear in adolescent encounters. Even after receiving coaching from a physician and becoming somewhat adept in sexual technique, he is still described by his wife as clumsy and diffident in his approaches. He himself reveals a certain resentment and resistance to assuming the rôle of aggressor in relation with his wife. He has to assume a rôle in the sexual situation that runs contrary to his desires.

In both husband and wife there are evidences of strong repressions of sexual drives. These specifically sexual attitudes are undoubtedly a part of the situation, but they may also be thought of as parts of the basic rôle patterns, particularly in the case of the husband.

This represents the barest outline of some of the high spots in the case, but if we could present all of our materials they would hardly do more than amplify the picture which must be evident from even such a scant description.

The central problem in this case is a problem of basic rôles, which are apparently the result of the early family relationships.

The husband is looking for a solicitous, protecting, aggressive, decisive, parent environment which the wife, who expects something of the same sort of environment, cannot supply. She was able to furnish sympathy and to that extent supplied the rôle of mother and sister in the husband's family. But she is not equipped to supply the more positive and aggressive part of the rôles that these people represented in Mr. A.'s personality development.

Neither of them is quite fully aware of what the basis for their trouble is. The husband thinks his marriage is a mistake, that he is not cut out for marriage, that his artistic temperament needs complete freedom to realize itself. The wife thinks the husband is sulky, inconsiderate, selfish, and jealous of her interest in her family. They both think that relief of the financial tension would be a partial solution.

Those who take the psychoanalytic approach would probably classify the man as a homosexual type, and interpret the difficulties on that basis. If we recognize that for the male the category "homosexual" applies to general psycho-sexual traits of passivity rather than to certain specific sexual attitudes merely, then the classification is probably valid. But it should be pointed out that the classification is not fully descriptive of the rôle pattern Mr. A. represents. He is not only passive but has an infantile dependent attitude or rôle which is not necessarily characteristic of the homosexual.

The case might also be interpreted as a result of guilt feelings which arise when Mr. A. engages in sexual activity with a person who stands as a substitute for his sister Martha. Sexual impulses with reference to his sister must have been heavily repressed and, when they are allowed expression on a love object that stands for her, they give rise to strong guilt feelings from which Mr. A. seeks to escape by terminating the marriage. Even here, however, we get into a usage of the notion of rôles. But it is apparent that this specifically sexual explanation leaves out of account too much of Mr. A.'s general pattern of response to all types of situations.

The writer would suggest that, at the present stage of the game, it seems preferable to use concretely descriptive categories of rôle types. It may turn out later that some such set of master categories as those now used in the psychoanalytic field will apply. But their application should be made when empirical evidence justifies such usage.

Turning to a different approach, it should be pointed out that analysis of marital problems in terms of the usual categories of economic, cultural, response, temperamental, health, and other tensions is rather sterile unless such analysis is done with the insight that rôle analysis supplies. Any and all of the usual tensions may and do appear in a given case, but frequently they are meaningless unless seen in reference to the basic problem of rôles.

⇜⥱⇜⥱⇝⥲⇝

CHAPTER VIII

SOCIAL ORGANIZATION: ECOLOGICAL

69. The Role of the Village in American Rural Society *

SOME ELEMENTS OF HUMAN ECOLOGY may be seen more clearly if examined in a relatively simple setting. This description, by T. Lynn Smith, of the American village defines it as an ecological unit —the essential link between rural and urban worlds. In addition to his description of the roles played by the village as a center of trade and commerce and as the nucleus of the emerging rural community, the author analyzes various other functions it performs.

INTRODUCTION

As A CENTER of trade and commerce, the village has long played a vital rôle in American rural society. Contrary to a widespread popular belief, this function of the village continues to wax in importance. At the same time the village is also forging to the front as the social center of rural America, coming into its own as the nucleus of the emerging rural community. As the line of cleavage between the rural and urban worlds, as the point of contact between urban and rural patterns of behavior, and as a residential center for certain more dependent parts of the national population, it also performs other functions of vital importance in our general web of life. Current developments such as the

* T. Lynn Smith, Rural Sociology, 7, No. 1 (March, 1942), 10-21. Reprinted by permission of the author and the publisher.
For a biographical sketch of the author see selection 58, p. 491.

increased mobility of the aged population, the expansion of the social security program, and above all the War, bid fair to increase still further the importance of the American village. The present discussion considers the village as an element in our national structure and indicates a few of the more essential functions that it performs.

Before beginning the analysis of the rôle of the village it is necessary to attempt some clarification of the terminology pertaining to small locality groupings. First it is essential to state precisely what is meant when the term village is used and to differentiate this concept from other closely related ones. This involves several considerations. There are those, such as Professor Sauer of the University of California, who would restrict the designation village to those small population aggregates that are composed for the most part of the homes of farmers. There is much merit to such a position. Undoubtedly throughout most of the world the use of the village pattern of arranging the population on the land has led to a situation in which agriculture is the primary occupation of the majority of persons living in the smaller population aggregates. However, such a standard would practically eliminate the term village from domestic application in the United States where scattered farmsteads is the prevailing mode of settlement. In the United States size must be the principal criterion utilized in the definition of the village.

At the present time, using size as the criterion, the following definition of village is in rather general use: a population center containing between 250 and 2,500 inhabitants, irrespective of the occupations of the residents. The upper limit coincides with present census practice in differentiating between urban and rural populations and sets villages apart from urban aggregates. The appellation town is proposed for centers of population varying in size from 2,500 to 10,000 inhabitants, and city for places with more than 10,000 residents. The lower limit is less satisfactory, but it does meet the principal objective of differentiating the village from the hamlet or the smallest aggregation of homes. It is recognized, however, that it might be better to choose 100 or some other figure as the line of demarcation between the two.

A second consideration of terminology is clarification of the difference between the terms village and community. Where nucleated settlement patterns prevail, the community consists of the village center with its cluster of residences and the lands that are tributary to it. In order to care for their crops the village population must commute regularly to their fields. The boundaries of the locality group are definite, and there is little chance for uncertainty to arise concerning village functions and community boundaries. However, in some cases, too close identification of village and community or commune results in references to villages as being constituted of several separate nuclei or hamlets. Obviously this is a misnomer; such a collection of hamlets is a community or commune rather than a village. On the other hand, in the United States where the village serves largely as a trade and service center and not as a residential center for farmers, it is only one part of the community. In this case the lands tributary to the village center are not so easily identified; there may be some confusion relative to the community attachments of many farm homes; and there remains the additional task of determining the limits of the web of life centering in the village which gives to the nucleus and the tributary farm homes the fundamental characteristics of a community. Throughout most of the United States the village is merely one part of the rural community.

• • • • • •

THE FUNCTIONS OF THE VILLAGE

1. TRADE AS THE PRIMARY FUNCTION OF THE AMERICAN VILLAGE.

Most villages in the United States came into being as trade and service centers for the farm families living on the land in the surrounding territory. Today trade, manufacturing (broadly interpreted to include carpentering, bricklaying, and other skilled trades), communication and transportation, and the professions continue to constitute the *raison d'être* of most of our villages. Of the gainfully-employed male residents of United States villages, only a small portion are engaged in agricultural pursuits. In other words the primary function of the American village is to serve as a trade and service center for the farmers in the surrounding area. This is in sharp contrast with the principal function of Old World and Latin American villages which are primarily residential centers for farm families, the trading function being of secondary importance.

There are of course important differences between the villages of the nation. Many of those that are located on the fringes of cities and towns are primarily residential areas or manufacturing centers. In certain parts of the country, and particularly in the Mormon and Spanish settlements in the Rocky Mountain and southwestern parts of the country, the village pattern of settlement has been used. Just as in Europe, Asia, or Latin America, these villages are composed principally of farm homes. But most American villages are primarily trade and service centers; these should be listed as their most important functions.

2. THE VILLAGE AS THE NUCLEUS OF THE EMERGING RURAL COMMUNITY.

The United States long has suffered for want of a strong, clearly defined, and well integrated rural community. Colonial America was for the most part cut to the neighborhood pattern. With minor exceptions the principal locality groupings were small in size, consisted of persons closely knit together by intimate social bonds, and were areas within which the social interaction was almost exclusively on a face-to-face basis. But despite a high degree of self-sufficiency on the part of each family, it still was necessary to go outside the group for satisfaction of many elemental needs. As settlement edged forward from the Appalachians to the Pacific, federal policies of land distribution and the scattered farmsteads type of settlement played important roles in keeping locality groupings small, i.e., in the neighborhood stage. Until the opening of the twentieth century, closely knit neighborhoods formed the warp and woof of rural society, and for the bulk of the farm population larger areas of association were relatively unimportant. Prior to 1900 it was customary, and to a considerable extent justifiable, to speak of the American farmer as the "man without a community." With the passage of time and especially with the development of improved methods of communication and transportation, neighborhood ties have weakened, the vista of the farm family has broadened, and there is emerging in rural America a locality group that can meet most of the criteria of a real community.

These changes have meant a considerable disorganization of old structural patterns, but out of it all the village is rapidly finding its place as the center of this larger and more complex web of rural living. In addition to the economic institutions and agencies which are primary, the village is becoming of increasing importance in other social spheres. Neighborhood institutions, such as the open-country church or the one-room school, and informal recreational activities, are declining in importance or passing. On the other hand the village church is enrolling increasing proportions of farm members; centralized schools usually are located in the village center; and the movies and other forms of commercialized entertainment in the village are becoming largely dependent upon the farm population. It seems fair to say that the social functions of the village already promise to rival its economic functions.

3. THE VILLAGE AS AMERICA'S "OLD FOLKS' HOME."

Villages also perform some very highly important demographic functions for our national society. In contradistinction to the farms which are the seed bed of national population and the cities which are the consumers of population, the village is the place where a disproportionately large share of the nation's old persons live out the declining years of their lives. As Brunner and Kolb have correctly stated the village is "rural America's old folks' home." The importance of its function as an uncongested, healthful, and inexpensive abode for the aged should not be minimized. If it has played this part during years of peace, war is likely to enhance still further this role of the American village.

Unfortunately for those of us who are interested in rural population, the data pertaining to the demographic characteristics of the village population leave a great deal to be desired. However, enough data are available to establish the fact that the villages contain a disproportionately large share of the old people of the nation. Thus in 1930 the inhabitants of the 3,087 incorporated villages with between 1,000 and 2,500 inhabitants (the only ones for which data are available) contained only 3.9 per cent of the national population. But in these same villages resided 5.6 per cent of all persons aged 65 and over in the United States. On a relative basis, this means that the aged population was 40 per cent more important in the villages than it was in the national population. Furthermore, in almost every state in the union, the village population contained a disproportionately large share of the aged. Exceptions to this rule are to be found only in three recently settled western states (Arizona, Idaho, and Montana) in which many pioneers had not yet reached the most advanced ages. Throughout much of the nation and particularly in the northern and midwestern states, the villages contained old persons in proportions that were half again as high as the percentages in the respective states. It is not overstating the case to assert that the provision of a place of habitation for the aged members of the population is one of the more important functions of the village.

Closely allied to this demographic function is the low sex ratio of the village population and the high proportion of widowed and divorced females who reside in the small incorporated centers of the nation. It is likely that a large proportion of these widowed and divorced females have moved in from the surrounding farms.

4. THE VILLAGE AS THE ARENA OF RURAL-URBAN CONFLICT.

The fact that the social and economic environment of city and country people is vastly different is widely recognized. Also rather well understood is the proposition that these differences in the man-made environment or culture of the two groups have significant influences in molding the personalities of rural and urban people. That these personality differences and the differing folkways, mores, and cultural patterns in which they have their roots lead to a constant and often severe conflict between the urban and rural parts of our society is also rather generally understood. But that the village is the arena in which this conflict occurs has seldom if ever received any detailed analysis. My immediate purpose is to illustrate the nature of this important village function.

It is because the American village serves, not as a residential center for farm families, but as a market, a trade center, and a social center for families living in the surrounding open country territory that it becomes the arena for rural-urban conflict. The stress laid upon this point is not to overlook the important fact that many rural-urban contacts result in an end highly satisfactory to both segments of society. It is merely to emphasize that the village serves as the focal point in which urban values, attitudes, and patterns of living clash head on with those from the country, and that a great deal of conflict is generated by this brusque contact. This clash of interests arises in a great many aspects of life, but it may be illustrated with a few simple examples.

Consider first one of the economic aspects. Long after the city man has become so highly specialized that he is either a laborer, a capitalist, or engaged in managerial activities, the great bulk of the farmers continue to perform all three of these economic functions. For this reason and also because he deals largely with living growing things, lives in a sparsely-populated district, and has few but intimate and enduring social contacts, the farmer has a set of attitudes towards such things as hours of work, wage rates, and prices that is considerably different from those possessed by any one class of city men. As indicated above, village banks, retail outlets, and other business firms are the media of contact between these divergent urban and rural attitudes, values, and patterns of behavior.

Thus we may cite the example of the farmer who takes his car to the village garage for a repair job. Even in the smallest crossroads'center the garage is an institution that brings into the rural area the wage scales and commodity prices of Detroit and other large cities. The farmer is used to differentials: he rarely pays wage rates that are comparable to those of the city. But unless he can do the work himself, he must pay the national wage and price scales in the garage. Nothing outrages the farmer more than this situation, especially in those numerous cases in which the mechanic is the "good-for-nothing" son of a neighbor who has gone off to the village looking for an "easy job."

In the field of educational theory and practice, the village is also the scene of conflict between the traditional rural attitudes and behavior and the innovations introduced by urban trained teachers and curricula designed to meet the needs of city children. Sharp conflicts are engendered in respect to content, teaching methods, discipline, and school organization and administration. Not unusual are the cases in which the farm districts are hotbeds of discontent deeply angered with the "frills" of a school curriculum, completely horrified by the "progressive methods" of instruction, fully disgusted with "lax" school discipline, and thoroughly rebellious about actual or proposed delineation of school administration or attendance areas. Gerrymandering of school districts, which the farmer often thinks is for village advantage, and consolidations are frequently basic in all these disputes. My intention is neither to praise nor to blame either side to the disputes, merely to emphasize that the village is the place in which the clash of systems occurs.

The village is also the place in which the modernistic religious practices and beliefs of the city collide with the traditional religious attitudes and expressions of the countrymen. As has been shown by the excellent studies of Brunner and his associates, the village is increasingly becoming the focal point for rural religious activities. But in the village church the farmer comes into contact with a trained minister who has been exposed to the facts and theories of modern biological and physical science, the current contributions of the social sciences relative to social and cultural change or the social functions of the church, and perhaps to some elements of the higher criticism. The pulpit of the village church serves as the faucet through which these ideas are let loose on the countryside. Probably to the villager, and certainly to the farmer, much of the preaching of contemporary liberal or unorthodox ministers is in fundamental conflict with many traditional beliefs that are deeply imbedded in cultural and emotional foundations. Probably the conflict between "modernism" and "fundamentalism" reaches its acme in the village church.

The foregoing analysis should be sufficient to demonstrate that the village is the principal arena for the clash of rural and urban attitudes and patterns of living. Before leaving this subject, however, it should be indicated that these differences, as all others, must ultimately be resolved. Men cannot fight all the time. Some of the ways in which a *modus vivendi* are obtained are extremely interesting. *Sub rosa* the garage may fail to charge the stipulated prices or wage scales; as attested by *The Reader's Digest* survey, the vigilance of rural mores keeps exploitation at a minimum in village garages; public employees may keep longer working or office hours in the village than in the city; departures from traditional curricula or teaching methods may be less "progressive" than in the larger centers; and the minister's orthodoxy may be carefully examined before he is employed by the village church.

❦❧❦❧

70. Littletown *

THE STORY OF AN AMERICAN VILLAGE

IN THE PRECEDING SELECTION (69) Professor T. Lynn Smith discusses the rural village in broad generalizations. This selection by W. G. Mather, Jr., in contrast, offers a case study of one rural town in New York. After briefly reviewing the history of the community, he proceeds to depict the way of life in the village. Dismal though the picture is, it was typical of the pattern of life in many rural communities at the time this was written (1935). As the concluding paragraphs of the article imply, however, communities have a way of persisting, even though shifts in the organization of American society may distinctly change their character.

THE OTHER DAY a farmer called on Jonas Handman to deliver a basket of apples. He knocked on the kitchen door, waited for a while, then went round to the front door and knocked there. Nobody came. Handman had said that he wanted those apples, so the farmer put the basket down on the porch and went back of the house to the barn. There he found Jonas hanging by his neck, dead.

Jonas had never been known to do any real work about Littletown; while his father was living he never had to. And when his father died he left him the store blocks downtown. Jonas seemed to get along very well on the rents up to a few years ago, and was in the pool room most of the time. There were two stores, one with a hall over it that hasn't been used for years except for a few months some time ago by the Girl Scout troop. Last year Bill and Ed Brown started a garage in the store part of that block, when the grocery which Jed Simmons had run was closed out after his funeral. The other block had been vacant for a few years, except for a rummage sale or bake-sale in it now and then. The garage did not pay much rent, and you can't charge a women's society for sales, so it seemed that things had turned out badly for Jonas. We hadn't realized they were that bad though.

The truth is, we don't miss Jonas Handman very much. He was never, so to speak, a contributing member of our community. But his suicide is the third within the past year.

* William G. Mather, Jr., Harper's Magazine, 170 (January, 1935), 199-208. Reprinted by permission of the author.
The author (b. 1901) is Professor of Rural Sociology, Pennsylvania State College. Interests center in rural sociology, the church, and welfare, in each of which fields he has published.

Littletown is small, as its name implies, with only some fourteen hundred people. And three suicides in one year are altogether too many for that population.

Some of us are beginning to worry about what is going to happen to our town. The past thirty years have seen many changes in the world, and from the point of view of the small-town man they have not all been good in their effect. There seems to be a sinister force at work, threatening the very existence of many small towns.

Take the little hamlet a few miles from us called The Flats. Thirty years or so ago The Flats was a busy little crossroads with two cheese factories, two stores (one with a hall over it), a blacksmith shop, a shingle mill that took its power from the creek, a school, and a church. They had great times with family reunions, square dances, warm-sugar parties, and the like, and it was known as one of the best communities in our neighborhood.

To-day not a single one of those signs of business life remains. There is only the old church, empty and unused, and the school with only a handful of pupils. One out of three of the houses within two miles of the crossroads in every direction is unoccupied and falling to pieces.

No wonder that we in Littletown are becoming nervous. As the advertising posters begin to be pasted on the inside of the show windows of store after store of ours that closes, the ghost of The Flats comes over the hill and haunts us. Twenty years, forty years—and shall we also belong to the Past?

II

Littletown is a cozy village in a hollow of the beautiful, surprisingly abrupt hills of southwestern New York. The Baptist church, a few rods down Spring Street from the main corner, is at an elevation of 1400 feet above sea level, while the tops of the hills round about are 1800 and 1900 feet. The only flat land is found in the valleys, and in only small patches there; in one summer alone three men, tilling the rolling slopes, were hurt by the overturning of tractors. The land has been farmed for a century and a third but is untamed yet!

An ancient glacial lake lay to the north of Littletown long before even the foot of a Seneca Indian had disturbed the deep grass of the pastures of the deer, and the lake left behind, with its shoreline and outlet banks, a level but tortuous passage through the hills to the more gently rolling valley of the Genesee. Along this path wound the old cart road to the cities of the north in the early days of settlement in the 1790's; and when Clinton's Ditch traversed the State from east to

LITTLETOWN 601

west a canal was dug over the same gentle path to connect Rochester, with her port on Lake Ontario, to the Allegheny River.` It was possible in those days to move slowly up the canal, through Littletown and across to Oleander, where one turned down the Allegheny to the Ohio, thence to the Mississippi and the Gulf. The canal is gone now, but the locks still stand, with now and then a crumbling skeleton of a gate between them; and there are men in Littletown who will tell you of unloading salt at the Port of Littletown in those days, and women who remember the Sunday School outings when heavily loaded, bunting-draped barges moved off for a day in some grove along the canal.

The Pennsylvania Railroad bought the canal and used the tow path as a base for its rails; part of the Erie main line follows the same route, and is well traveled; but the Pennsylvania is a branch line, built to serve the little towns along the old artery of travel.` Such is the way of Time that it is running fewer trains each year, the rails are beginning to gather rust, and a concrete highway makes the tires whine as cars speed over the old route of the post road, the canal, and the iron horse.

It was nearly a century and a half ago that a group of men discovered the valley in which Littletown lies. It seemed a good place for a town, this little flat patch with passes through the hills to all four points of the compass, so they took up land rights. One faction wanted the village at the north end of the hollow; the other, at the south, against the hills. Each set up a store and a tavern on its chosen spot; but the liquor must have been better at the latter place, for North Littletown is now just a filling station, a house for tourists and a school.`

The village grew slowly but was regarded as a coming town.` A new post road from Buffalo to Pennsylvania was surveyed about 1870, and Littletown was on one of the two possible routes. The village was astir; two post roads, a canal—what more could one ask to insure prosperity? And then the road went through Oleander, a village of the same size, almost a day's journey (in reality, only sixteen miles) up the swampy valley to the west. Old timers shake their heads and date that city's rise from the changing of the road. "When I was a boy Oleander wasn't as big as we are now," they say, and sigh the sigh of men who have guessed wrong.

But the long grass was still there, and the cows were there, going about the business of the cud unmindful of the fate of village empires down below them. Within ten years after the incident of the road, the milk from more than two thousand cows was being handled in the many cheese factories tucked away in the folds of the hills, and more than three-quarters of a million pounds of rich, mild-flavored cheese were marketed through the Littletown exchange each year. Almost all of the land, even in the remotest hills, was in pasture or grain.

The little cheese factories are just about all closed now, for cheese can be made at lower cost in Wisconsin and Minnesota; but there are a few left, and a chain store and a national meat packer still maintain cheese warehouses in Littletown. The War helped to change the nature of the dairy industry, as it boosted the sale of condensed milk, and several large condensaries were established in and near our village. One of them is still operating, the milk being hauled in by trucks that rumble through when the sleepy storekeepers are sweeping out in the morning.

Milk prices are low now, and the dairymen who have to pay for long hauls of milk are finding it hard to keep going. The old days of milk-prosperity—if they could be called that—do not seem likely to come again; dairying is a serious, corner-cutting, belt-tightening business, and a good many hill pastures are growing up to brush and scrubby timber.

There was another time when Fortune gave her Mona Lisa smile to Littletown, and now and again we get a little publicity in some newspaper because of it.

It seems that away back in the early days a bowlegged man called Seneca Pete used to drive an old gray mule down from Buffalo with two empty kegs strapped on her back. A mile or so from the village is a scummy spring in a swampy hollow, that used to form a thin film of oily substance over its surface. When flint and steel were struck close to its edge, it would burn for a time. The Senecas guarded it as a treasure, dipping their blankets into it and straining out the precious oil that had oozed up from the rock below. It was thought to be good for a snakebite, good for wounds, good for general principles; and Seneca Pete would load up his mule and plod back to Buffalo, there to sell the famous "Seneca Oil" to the doctors. It was the first petroleum discovered in America.

When Drake proved the worth of drilling a shaft for oil Littletown heard the news with joy. When oil ran out of its own accord, without need of a drilled hole, how much more must there not be below the surface, waiting for the bit to free it and send it spouting up into the sun?

A well was drilled close to the edge of the old spring. The top of the casing still stands in the weeds, ragged, rusty, ashamed. But over the hills, only eight miles away, begins the rich oil field from which the world's best crude is pumped. Fortune missed us by that slight a margin.

A few years ago the men whom oil had made rich came to our town and built a monument in tribute to the spring that had led the way.

We are proud of that bowlder with its bronze slab and generally motor our visitors out to see it. But we would rather have a derrick.

In the first decade of the present century, Littletown made its bid as a manufacturing center. A knife factory, a pulley works, a cheese-box factory, and a novelty concern erected buildings and began operations. Perhaps a hundred men were employed, with two dozen others in the two older mills that had been long established for the grinding of feed and flour and the sawing of lumber. An enterprising citizen with little taste put up a whole street of somber houses, all alternately alike, on the edge of town. We had our factories and our slums. We were on the way to becoming a big town.

The knife factory died first and one of the banks took it over. The novelty firm moved on. The pulley works went under two years ago. The box factory merged with the sawmill.

The buildings still stand there, sagging, empty, and the Chamber of Commerce is busy dangling bait before the eyes of small city businesses, hoping to entice them here. A year or so ago some of the younger business men became impatient and from somewhere managed to raise two thousand dollars, which they gave, together with an old barnlike structure, to a man with an idea for an airplane. The plane almost flew, at that.

Commerce, oil, manufacturing—they have all paid us but fleeting visits. They roused our hopes, they made us dream. Yet on the hillsides the sleek cows still graze, the milk trucks roll through town in the early morning, and the only mills that stood the test of time are the feed and flour mills, grinding out food for the cows. Even the sawmill is owned by the same men that own the feed mill. And it makes cheese-boxes. We have not wanted to be rural, but it seems that we cannot help it.

III

Although Littletown is small, it does not lack facilities for trade. There are three chain groceries in town, hated like poison by the proprietors of the locally owned groceries, of which there are also three. The local stores are forever urging us to keep our dollars at home, to support home industries, to remember old friends; but so far only one of them has cleaned up his place of business, painted the front an attractive color, enamelled the shelves, and removed the cat from the warm show window. He gets some of the business that the bright, neat chains get, but the other two have their troubles.

We did have two bakeries, one of them half a grocery also. The bakery has gone bankrupt; the combination hangs on. Bread trucks come in daily from Oleander with fresh rolls and bread and pastry, attractively done up in boxes or transparent paper with no flies inside, and most of our housewives prefer to buy their baked goods that way.

If you wish to buy a pair of shoes in our town, you have many opportunities. When the last census was taken, there were only two thousand eight hundred and forty-four feet in the village, but there are six places in which to buy shoes. There are two men's clothing stores, one pool room, one men's and women's clothing store, and two drygoods stores—all selling shoes. Of course, no one of them has a large assortment of either sizes or styles, but you may find what you want if you are lucky.

There are two meat markets, one run by the man who also manages the moving picture theater. But two of the chain groceries also carry meat, and so one of the markets has put in a line of bread and rolls, cakes, and canned goods. He is new to town and swears that if the competition extends to other stores he will put in dresses and cameras and a soda fountain.

There is the ever-present ice cream parlor, whose owner, in partnership with his brother, also runs an ice cream factory. They make very good ice cream, putting real cream from the local dairies into it; thus it costs more to make than do the frozen puddings turned out by the Buffalo factories, and so their business remains small. The drugstore on the opposite corner from the ice cream parlor carries the Buffalo brand.

There are two drugstores and they both sell drugs in addition to watches, alarm clocks, cameras, radios, candles, wall paper, candy, mirrors, pictures, greeting cards, toys, and what not. And there are two pool rooms, two hardware stores, two electric stores, the proprietor of one of which doubles as funeral director, three restaurants, two gift shops with jewelers' counters, two hotels, four garages.

Yes, we have the facilities for doing business. Two of everything at least, including two banks to handle the inevitable bankruptcies that come more frequently in recent years. If Prosperity ever dared walk down our main street it would be plucked raw before it had gone half a block.

We used to have business too. The farmers' teams crowded the streets, and their children the stores, and everyone was happy. They used to give you a bag of candy when you paid your bill. But business is drifting to Oleander now, with its ten-cent stores and its larger stocks of suits and dresses and furniture, only twenty-five minutes away over a good paved road that we were mighty pleased with when it was first laid down.

Sometimes we look back on the paving of that road and grin crookedly. We were proud as Punch when the job was finished. There were editorials in the paper, photographs of leading citizens, and all that. We came within an inch of having one of these celebrations with a symbolic wedding too. If our storekeepers could have seen how much of their business was going to roll over that road to Oleander, they would have worked for a symbolic funeral instead.

But they didn't see it and went right on doing business as they had done it for years before, when we had to buy from them or go without. But now, if we don't like what they have or the price that they set upon it we can try in Oleander without much trouble. A lot of small-town business men are making that same mistake; they do not seem to realize that the swamps and hills that cut their customers off from the rest of the world are being filled and levelled now, and that their business is in competition with every other store of the same line within forty miles. Even Oleander, now with nearly twenty thousand people, complains that some of its trade is going to Buffalo, seventy miles to the northeast; and Oleander has some large stores.

Of course, it is true that a man in a small town like ours cannot expect to have a large store; but sometimes I wonder if it is necessary to break up what little business we do have among so many men and make it still smaller.

One of the things that keeps business poor is the fact that there just aren't as many people to buy goods as there used to be. Our village declined 11.7 per cent in population between the last two federal censuses. As for the countryside round us, a drive over the dirt roads in any direction will show what is happening there, as house after house stands empty with its shutters banging in the wind. It does no good to call those dirt roads "side" roads; they were main roads when our village was growing and our present number of stores were founded, and the people who traded with us came over them to market.

Modern methods of agriculture have made it possible for one farmer to handle more stock and more land than several farmers could in the former days, and the surplus farmers have moved away. The poorer land is going out of cultivation, as not worth a man's time, and the better land is being tilled more cheaply and better. The population of the old canal and post road days is not needed any more. Men do not go down the meadows four and six abreast, swinging their scythes, at harvest time; one man rides round on a mower. One man sitting on a tractor turns two or three furrows at once. One man milks two cows at once while leaning against a post and watching the machine suck and blow. Farming is a business now, and the sheriff sells out the man who cannot run his farm in a business way.

I cannot sigh over the departure of the old days of hand agriculture. I was raised on a farm. I have had a double-shovel give my ribs a Dutch rub when plowing corn in the old stump field, and I am glad that men can farm now more safely for their bones and their religion. The women in farm homes too do not long for the days when the dining room was full of harvesters and the kitchen full of the fumes of hell. The new ways are better. But that does not alter the fact that they mean fewer feet to be shod, fewer legs to be overalled, fewer freckled, sun-browned misses to wear the new, soft drsses.

IV

The people that live in Littletown are nice. The Legion and the Ku Klux would accept them all. We have very few foreign families— you could count them on one hand—and still fewer colored. There are the usual number of faithful elderly spinsters waiting to join Ma and Dad, who died and left them without the job that had been husband and children to them; the usual number of widows and widowers living alone with their memories in rambling, solitary houses; the usual number of retired farmers sniffing the wind wistfully in the morning; the usual number of children playing in the yards of the smaller houses on the side streets. There are not many young people though; the population takes a running jump over the twenties, and the few that are left keep asking, "What's doing in the city? Are jobs opening up there yet?"

It makes it rather hard on the young folks in high school. They are determined not to be like Mother and Dad, but there are few in between to copy after. So they read the magazines and go to the movies and get their styles of dressing and acting from there. A little too much lipstick, talk rather coarse and loud, clothes just a bit extreme, and a faraway look of cities over the horizon when the school bell has rung for the last time, tell their story.

A year or two ago one of the men from the college of agriculture gave the young folks in our high school a questionnaire about their choice of a vocation. Only 16.5 per cent of them said they were planning to do work similar to their father's, and only 13.8 per cent were intending to stay in town. Their dreams will change of course, and disappointment will also come; but that does not change the present situation much. Our young folks do not like us and see no future for themselves with us.

On Sunday morning the bells in five steeples ring the call to worship, and the doors of five churches open for the crowds of worshippers who will not come. All of our churches have a seating capacity far in excess of their resident membership. Yet we are a fairly religious town; for a census that the churches took one year showed that over half of our population belonged to some church, and the average for the United States is less than that. The proportion is considerably smaller, however, among the country people; relatively few of them come to our churches, and they have none of their own. They say that their clothes are inferior to ours, and that we are not friendly with them. I think that their clothes are on the whole as good as ours, but they are probably right about the lack of cordiality; we have had our eyes fixed on the dream of being a big city for so long that we have forgotten the people who tend the cows that fill the milk trucks that rumble through town.

Our churches are costly affairs. In 1930 we spent, one of the ministers estimated, $17,507 for the four Protestant churches alone. Thirty years before that the records show that the cost of those same churches, with more members, was only $7,089. I do not attribute this rise to extravagance but to the upward tendency of our necessities; thirty years ago we did not feel that a college education was necessary for our ministers; but we do now, for so many of us are college-educated that we abhor scientific blunders in the pulpit. And college men cost us more than illiterate, or semi-so, ministers. The same is true of our pipe organs, our redecorated buildings, our robed choirs. Those things are part of our modern culture.

Our extravagance comes, however, in our insistence that each small church group must have those things for itself. The Methodists, with only ninety-four members, must have those things just as do the Baptists, with two and one-half times as many people over whom to spread the cost. Some people I know have actually declined to join one of our churches, not because they did not feel spiritually ready, but because they knew that they could not stand the financial pressure that is put upon its members. The gospel is far from free in our town.

Some efforts have been made toward inter-church co-operation. Union services are held on summer evenings, and even the smallest building is adequate to hold the combined audiences. The young people of three of the churches began a joint society, but the older folks of one church withdrew their young people after a few weeks, saying that they were having too good a time with the others and feared they might be "weaned away" from their own church. Two of the churches have had a joint men's class for a few years, and the men got along with one another there as well as they did in the lodges or the business men's clubs; but when talk began of union of the two churches at a time when one of them was without a minister some of the women said things that put a stop to it.

It may be after we have had a few more burials in our beautiful green cemetery on the hill that church union will come nearer, and we shall become fellow-Christians as well as fellow-Littletownians—but there are those who will term my hope sinful.

Although we are losing population, our school is becoming more crowded every year. The classrooms are full of seats. It seems that out in the country districts, as the little schools lose students until only a few are left and the cost per pupil becomes high, the schools are closed and those few children are taken in to our school by buses. Also, more young people above the age at which they are legally required to go to school are wanting to continue on through the high school; they feel the need of higher education in this day. We shall have to build a new building for them eventually, and yet we hesitate at the cost and keep putting it off. A large part of our taxpaying towns-men are retired farmers whose income is small and limited, whose children are already educated and gone, but whose influence is great.

We have a beautiful little library, built by funds which a good woman left for the purpose, and the young folks use it very well. Their parents, except for women who do a deal of novel-reading, do not use it much. We are not enthusiastic in the cultivation of our minds but are fairly satisfied to let them be as they are. One of the doctors was fuming the other day that there were eight card clubs in town but not one mother's club.

When evening settles down upon us there are several things that we can do. Generally we sit at home and listen to the radio, which is pleasant in the summer when it can be heard through an open window on the porch. If the night is fair we visit friends; and if there is some-thing extra on at one of the lodges those of us who are not officers, who would go anyway, attend.

We have two lodges, the Odd Fellows and the Masons, the former with a large proportion of farmers in its membership. The leaders of both complain that meetings are poorly attended, not like the good old days. But the rooms are open in the afternoons, and the older men drop in to play checkers and cards and talk. The women have their Rebekahs and Eastern Star and put on bake-sales now and then.

There are, besides the Legion—which is getting a bit fat—and the Grange, a number of other organizations in town. A D.A.R. chapter that was recently formed by some lady who belonged to no other club, I think, and who wanted to join one; a chapter of Daughters of Union Veterans; a Current Topic club that should properly be called Current Gossip; the Shakespeare Club that discusses astronomy and art; any number of card clubs that are the breath of life to the two little gift shops; and in each section of town a "sunshine" club that sends flowers and gifts to the sick. The women spend a great deal of time at these various clubs; for they are, like most small-town women, forever lonesome and inquisitive about one another's affairs.

We have two business men's clubs, whose main occupation is talking about bringing "new business" to town, but none of them includes in its membership farmers, whose milk trucks bring in all the new business that ever does come.

For sport, the younger men have organized a soft-ball league that fights noisy battles in the park at twilight. The barbers have a team, the railroad men, the feed-mill men, and so on; "Lucky Tigers," "Keystones," "Barney Googles" they call them, and get real sport out of the games. Baseball loosens up the muscles that have been fighting rust on the rails or waiting behind the counters for business to come home and be forgiven, and also takes their minds off the complaining women who wait for their men folk to return at sundown and listen respectfully while they retail the gossip of the day.

V

Last year the farmers took a step that disgusted the business men. They organized a co-operative feed store in one of the empty buildings, to handle feed and flour and the like, buy seeds and fertilizer, and ship some produce as well. The business men regard it as very ungrateful of them, especially in the midst of this business depression. If they had only taken some stock in the knife factory or the airplane industry now, the farmers would have been showing real co-operation. But this event proves to them that the farmers do not understand civic needs.

One would think that the young people, even more than the women, would be very busy; for they have any number of organizations for them in the school and the churches and the Scouts and the Hi-Y. Some organization is putting on a sale of some kind, raising money for some purpose, almost all the time. But the truth is, as I have observed, that a few of them belong to nearly everything, with no time even to study, while a great many belong to nothing and do nothing except stand on the street corners and giggle.

There really is not much else for those who are not dashing off to some meeting or other to do. They can go to the movies, which cost money, or they can shoot pool, which also costs money and is not too well thought of, or they can go home. They rarely do that except to work at their lessons. What they fall back upon is the promenade. From the library they drift down one side of the street to the filling station, then cross over and back up the other side, and so on around again. Now and then they pair off and slip away down a side street where the lights are more dim.

One winter a new minister suggested opening up some of the rooms of a church and installing ping-pong tables, checkers, a piano, and the like on Friday and Saturday nights. He didn't get far with that idea. "What for?" was the attitude of his board. "We spend a lot of money on our young folks now, and then when they get through school they go off to the city and we never get it back. And besides it isn't right to use the church property that way."

So the card-tables gossip about the goings-on among the younger generation of this awful day; one of the older ministers fulminates weekly about the drinking and necking proclivities of youth, and the business men complain that the young people do not remain to marry and settle down and breed a trading population for the town. And all the while the more ambitious and worthy of the young folks are whispering impatiently among themselves, "Let's get out of here to where something's doing!"

And that probably is the very spirit that led their ancestors to come to Littletown in the first place.

We used to have, not so long ago, considerable doing in our town. Every fall we had a fair, of which we were justly proud. We had halls for exhibits, a race track, a grandstand. I can remember when I used to swallow a whole bag of popcorn without tasting it, as La Paloma won by a nose from Gelter's Pride or while I watched Zanzibar the snake eater for one dime, ten cents, the decimal part of a dollar. But the fair stopped some years ago for lack of entries, and enthusiasm, and patrons, and money; and last year we arranged to sell the old buildings that remained in order to pay off a debt we owed the printer.

The grove just south of town, a clean place of hard maples lifting round bare trunks above the grass, used to be the scene of camp meetings, chautauquas, and political rallies. Tents were pitched amid the trees, water brought from the spring, horses staked out, and the whole family settled down to enjoy religion or whatever there was, while one of the boys ran the farm between hayings. Jolly, informal, full of fist fights and love-making, of prayer and mud-slinging, summer camp meetings were the balm of sultry days. Brush grows up in the old grove now, and the cows scratch their lean necks against well-nigh obliterated hearts with arrows stuck through and letters, "H.C. and V.T." O Time, how could you?

Here it lies, the little village in the lap of the hills, about it the marks of its former happiness and hope, and before it the shadows seen only by itself and the old men who sit on the bench before the pool room on calm afternoons. They too have lived and dreamed.

And the storekeepers agitate home trade, dangle decaying buildings before decaying industries as an attraction to come to Littletown and die, and at the last do as Jonas Handman did. Just between the main highways of travel, just on the edge of the oil field, not big enough to be a city, not small enough to be a hamlet—wanting things, almost getting things, too alive to die and too dead to grow, what shall become of us?

We have the poor comfort of knowing that our lot is not solitary. There are many villages like ours to-day, facing what we face. We hear talk of the decentralization of industry, of the putting of great factories into small units scattered over many towns, but we know that salvation for us does not lie in the scheme. It may be done, but we know that it will be the villages nearer the great cities than we are that will profit. And the extent of their profit is doubtful; industry began in small towns once and left them; we had factories once, and they are gone; nor have the prodigals shed many tears of penitence as yet. Many villages like us are waiting for either factories or farmers to come back; for over one hundred thousand acres of farm land have been abandoned in our county alone, many times that in the State, and millions in the whole country.

Everywhere that this has occurred there are villages with Jonas Handmans.

Of this, I think we are certain: that the process of shrinking will go on until there are just enough farmers left outside our village to supply the milk that the market demands. And when that point is reached there will also be just enough stores left in Littletown to supply the needs of these farmers. The churches will either die or merge the one with the other until there are just enough churches to accommodate us all, villagers and farmers, in our worship. The little district schools will probably draw together in consolidation until our youth can find in the minimum number of good schools the maximum preparation for life.

These things will not happen easily. They will be accompanied by struggle and pain. But if we can see where we are going, and help one another on the way, we may be able to reduce the Jonas Handmans.

Littletown is not going to die. Littletown is going to start over again, this time with its eyes open, its goal more real. We shall gain a spiritual dividend from the re-organization of our village life, I think; for whatever we do we shall have to do together—and that is good for the soul. One with the countryside, with the old false barrier between village and farm forgotten, with the common interest of storekeeper and dairyman at last known and understood, the renascent Littletown may be a better place than before.

For life still goes on about us. Lovers marry and are given in marriage; children play in the front yards; men sweat in the fields; women peel vegetables in the kitchens; and the cows come home at evening in long patient lines, trailing down from the hill pastures.

And wherever there is life there are the needs of life, that cannot be met by any one man alone.

꧁꧂꧁꧂

71. The Intolerable City: Must It Keep On Growing? *

MANY URBAN AMERICANS have only recently migrated from rural and village communities to the city. Some of these migrants, and their friends who remain in rural areas, condemn the city as an unbearable and evil place to live. Many sociologists also maintain that the urban social environment—particularly that of the metropolis—seriously limits the type of social relations that produce well-adjusted people. Although some question this hypothesis, a description of the conditions that give rise to it are worth consideration. In this article Lewis Mumford presents a dramatic picture of the city and examines the possibility that new developments in transportation, community planning, and decentralization may modify the city's fundamental nature.

THE MOUTHS of our great cities are gigantic hoppers. Into them pour the foods we coax from the earth, the energy we snare from the sun,

* Lewis Mumford, Harper's Magazine, 152 (February, 1926), 283-293. Reprinted by permission of the author.
The author (b. 1895) is an American author; critic. Visiting Professor, University of North Carolina, since 1948 and has taught at other major universities. Writings and personality of Professor Patrick Geddes most important influence on his life. Learned to use the city actively as a powerhouse of educational equipment. His books include Technics and Civilization, Faith for Living, Values for Survival, Green Memories, The Story of Geddes, The Culture of Cities, The Condition of Man.

the metals we disembowel, the men and women we draw from the smaller communities. What comes out of these hoppers? Ordinarily, people think that wealth is increased and life is far more attractive and thrilling; for if this were not so, who would be drawn into New York, Chicago, Los Angeles, Detroit, Philadelphia, and why should any other city boast about its increases in population and attempt to put itself in the same census tables? Surely, this is the best that modern civilization can offer, this New York with its dazzle of pointed towers, this Chicago with its sweep of avenues, this Detroit with its thick pageant of motors?

But let us look at the hopper more closely and see what is actually coming out of it. Census reports, mortality statistics, and income-tax returns do not tell the whole story: there is something beneath all that, the life of the ordinary man and woman. In the long run the things that tip the balance are those that cannot be weighed: they must be seen, felt, handled, endured. Recently, the New York State Housing and Regional Planning Commission confessed that only one-third the population of New York City had an income sufficient to enable the family to live in decent modern quarters. Let us single out Mr. Brown, who is one of this fortunate minority, and follow him through the routine of his day.

As an inhabitant of a vigilant city, Mr. Brown is proud of the low death rate his health department boasts; unfortunately, the statistician keeps no account of the living rate, so we must make a first-hand appraisal. Mr. Brown usually comes home at the end of a day with that tired feeling, and all the quack medicines in the drugstore do not quite relieve him of it. He is proud of the fact that he keeps books or sells insurance on the eighteenth story of a skyscraper; but so much of the ground was used to build those splendid offices that Mr. Brown works most of the day under artificial light; and in spite of the slick system of ventilation, the middle of the afternoon finds him dull.

The journey home undoubtedly calls forth physical effort; unhappily it is not invigorating. The Swedish massage he receives at the hand of the subway guard does not improve his appetite; nor is it helped by the thick fumes of gasoline when he walks out upon the street. Eventually, Mr. Brown sits down at his dinner table and looks out on an airshaft or a court where a dozen other kitchens have been busily preparing a dozen other meals: it never varies. No change in color, no hint of sunset or moonlight, no variation from season to season as the vegetation flourishes or shrivels: only the smells that creep through the windows tell the difference between Thursday and Friday.

Once upon a time Mr. Brown used to stretch his legs and play with the children; the six-room flat was common in Boston and New York; the seven-room house flourished in Philadelphia and Chicago and St. Louis. Now the walls of the rooms have contracted: Mr. Brown pays so much for his four cubicles he is perhaps forced to harbor an ancient aunt or his wife's parents in the same narrow quarters; and, as likely as not, there are no children. When the Browns have put by a little they will have either a baby or a cheap car: it is hard to decide which, for the upkeep is high in both cases; but the car has this advantage—it would enable the whole family to get out into God's own country on Sundays.

This pursuit of God's own country would make the angels themselves weep: it means a ride through endless dusty streets, and along an equally straight and endless concrete road, breathing the dust and exhaust of the car ahead, and furnishing an equal quantum of exhaust and dust to the car behind; a ride with intervals spent at hot-dog stands, and long hours wasted at ferry houses and bridges and main junctions and similar bottlenecks, where the honking of impatient horns reminds Mr. Brown in the spring of the frog ponds he was not quite able to reach. As the main city grows, the country around becomes more suburban and the fields and hills and lakes are more difficult to reach. A generation ago Mr. Brown's father used to catch shad in the Hudson, or he might have spent the Sunday rambling with his youngsters along the bays and inlets of Long Island Sound. To-day a vast load of sewage has driven away the fish; and the expansion of great country estates for the lords of the metropolis has blocked and fenced off the rambler. Nor does New York alone suffer. Buffalo was forced to jump sixteen miles from the city line the other day to recover a paltry thousand feet of lake front for its citizens. By the time open spaces are set aside, however, the population has multiplied so furiously that, on a summer Sunday, the great parks are as congested as the city's streets—so much for solitude and natural beauty!

When dinner is over neither Mr. Brown nor his wife is in condition to listen to great music or to attend the theater. First of all, they are not in financial condition to do this because ground rents are high in the amusement district, and the price of seats has risen steadily to meet the increase in rents. Unless the occasion is important or Mr. Brown is willing to scrimp on the week's lunches, he cannot afford to go. Again, he is in no mental condition to participate in play that demands mental activity or emotional response above the spinal cord; and if this were not enough, the prospect of another hour in the subway kills most of the impinging joys. The seventy theaters that exist in sophisticated New York are, really, only one to a hundred thousand people; there are a score of little towns in continental Europe that are far better provided with drama and music. The fact is that, with all New York's wealth, its cultural facilities are *relatively* limited: they would be insufficient were it not for the fact that only a minority can afford to enjoy them regularly.

But Mr. and Mrs. Brown have their amusements? Oh, yes, they have the movies; that is to say, the same entertainment, served in almost the same form, as it comes in Peoria or Tuscaloosa or Danbury—no more and no less. If they are too tired to "drop around the corner" they have another consolation, the radio: this, too, works no better than it does in the despised, backward villages of the hinterland, and if the Browns happen to be situated in one of the mysterious "dead areas" it does not work nearly so well! In short, Mr. Brown travels through the pulping mill of the subway, endures the tawdry monotony of his flat, divorces himself from the natural enjoyments he can never quite recover on Sunday—for what? For an occasional visit to the museum or the opera? He could have as much if he lived a hundred miles away. His sacrifices are in reality made for a much more mystical purpose: his presence increases the "greatness" of his city. By adding to its population, he raises the capitalizable value of its real estate; and so he increases rents; and so he makes parks and playgrounds and decent homes more difficult to obtain; and so he increases his own difficulties and burdens; and his flat gets smaller, his streets bleaker, and his annual tribute to the deities who build roads and subways and bridges and tunnels becomes more immense.

Mr. Brown grumbles; sometimes he complains; but he is only just beginning to doubt. His newspaper tells him that he is fortunate; and he believes it. He fancies that when another subway is built he will find room in it for his feet—if he leaves the office promptly. I shall deal briefly with this fond hope a little later.

II

What is true of Mr. Brown is true also of the people who live on the East Side, the South Side, the Hump, the Stockyards District, or "the other side of the railroad track." Since, however, they lack Mr. Brown's snobbishness, they have a touch of neighborliness for consolation, and may occasionally manufacture a little special amusement for themselves in wild dances and hearty weddings and funerals full of pomp and dignity and excellent wine. If these groups, through advances in wages, could be raised to the level of Mr. Brown's station, they would not exactly be in Paradise; but suppose Mr. Brown stood at the apex of the pyramid—perhaps that would be Paradise? Perhaps that would justify Mosshunk's trying to become Boomtown, Boomtown's trying to become Zenith, Zenith's trying to become Chicago, Chicago's trying to become New York, and New York's trying to become like Mr. Hugh Ferriss's picture, The Future?

Well, let us consider what Mr. Smith-Robinson, the millionaire widget manufacturer, gets out of the great city, with its increasing population, its multiplying turnover, its skyscrapers, its subways—in short, all the symbols of its dominant religion of material expansion.

Mr. Smith-Robinson lives in a twenty-story apartment house on Park Avenue. It is like Mr. Brown's plain apartment, but it has ascended the ladder of evolution: the blastula has become a gastrula, or to speak more plainly, the four-celled unit has multiplied to sixteen units, six of them being sacred chambers devoted to lustration and baptism. To overcome the bare efficiencies of the building, we shall call in the services of a fashionable architect; he will arrange the scenery to persuade his client that he is a Spanish ambassador, an Italian prince, or a medieval English baron—but woe to the poor client if he take it into his head to draw back the hangings and look out the window. The chances are that he will find himself facing directly a blank honeycomb of windows, exactly like Mr. Brown's exhilarating view—only there are more of them. After all, the company that built the apartment was not in business for its health: they covered every square foot that the building laws and zoning ordinances would permit. Though they may call the few tubs of trees and shrubs at the bottom of the court a Persian garden, it is a feeble attempt to confuse the mind: the virtues of a Park Avenue apartment are those of an honest barracks.

So numerous are the lofty palaces and cloud-capped pinnacles where the "emergent minority" live, that the streets are vastly overtaxed by the traffic of their automobiles. When Mr. Smith-Robinson comes down from the country estate he sooner or later acquires, he finds that it pays to leave the car at the outskirts and take the rapid transit into town. The theaters, the clubs, the teas, the dances, the dinners, the concerts, the opera, and all the other devices for "performing leisure" which Mr. Thorstein Veblen has catalogued have, perhaps, a strong appeal to Mr. Smith-Robinson; but more and more, for all that, he is tempted to adopt the Friday-to-Tuesday week-end in the country. He finds, curiously, that as his income increases, the devices for reducing it become more and more effective. He bequeathes a young fortune to his fellow citizens to buy them a park; his executors are able to get hold of only a small wedge of land. Or he adds a wing to a hospital, and finds that it is overcrowded before the first year is over. As the

avenues become clogged, as crimes increase, as he becomes conscious
of the danger of merely walking abroad on the streets, our fortunate
citizen perhaps grows a little thoughtful; at the least, he reads with
great interest the weekly bulletin of plans for doing away with traffic
congestion by sinking endless millions into ingenious feats of engineering. These plans are to Mr. Smith-Robinson what new subways are
to Mr. Brown; and with the fond hopes that they too embalm I shall
deal shortly.

III

In the meanwhile, neither Mrs. Brown nor Mrs. Smith-Robinson is
an altogether happy woman: the city they live in was at best designed
for adults, and there is no place in it for the coming generation. So
much money is spent in the detection of criminals, in the treatment of
preventable disease, in the building of refuges for the mentally unstable
and, above all, in the labyrinth of sewers and subways, that there is
relatively little left for the more fruitful processes of living and learning.
The schools are driven, by mere weight of numbers, to offer an education which caricatures our democratic technic of living; and no pabulum
that may be added to the curriculum quite makes up for the impoverish-
ment of educational opportunity in the city itself.

As for play, it is almost out of the question; even generous Chicago
cannot keep up with its necessities. The acreage of parks and playgrounds in our metropolitan hives bears no relation at all to the density
of population; for although by crowding people together and piling
story on story we may almost indefinitely multiply the normal density,
Nature does not permit us to pile one lawn upon another, or one tree
upon another; and even if the rooftops were used for playgrounds, too,
there would not be an adequate amount of open spaces. Indeed, as our
cities continue to grow, and become more deeply in need of parks, the
difficulties of holding open the land they do possess become greater:
art galleries, museums, universities, art centers, and similar institutions
run without commercial profit naturally covet land that need not be
bought—and as ground rents rise their demands become more im-
portunate.

So note the paradox. As a city increases in "population and wealth"
it becomes less able to afford the things that make life gracious, interesting, and amusing. The difficulties of carrying on mere physical
existence are so terrific that a major part of a city's money and energy,
which should be spent on making life itself better, is devoted to the
disheartening task of keeping "things" from getting worse. For a

fortunate and able minority the city provides power and riches—much power and much riches. But the chief benefit of a big income is that it enables the possessor to escape from the big city. Hence the estates that are being planted from Chestnut Hill to Santa Barbara; hence the great drift of the middle classes into suburbia. If metropolitan life were the best civilization can now offer, it would be impossible to explain the fact that the suburbs are increasing in size, number, and population. The smaller cities that copy the defects of New York and Chicago, towns that ache for skyscrapers and apartment houses and pray to heaven for a little traffic congestion—even these cities are in the same boat; for many of them are being engulfed by suburbs which take advantage of the city's business facilities and escape the increasing burden of taxes.

IV

Manifestly, the suburb is a public acknowledgment of the fact that congestion and bad housing and blank vistas and lack of recreational opportunity and endless subway rides are not humanly endurable. The suburbanite is merely an intelligent heretic who has discovered that the mass of New York or Chicago or Zenith is a mean environment. Is the suburb, then, a "solution"? Will the metropolis of the future cover a radius of at least fifty miles from the central district; will Boston, New York, Philadelphia be merely high points of congestion in a vast belt of suburbs and industrial districts stretching along the coast? That is the assumption upon which many of our city surveys and regional plans, to say nothing of real estate speculations, are being tacitly made. Let us examine this beautiful prospect.

The suburb is an attempt to recapture the environment which the big city, in its blind and heedless growth, has wiped out within its own borders. With the aid of the suburb, business and living are divided into two compartments, intermittently connected by a strip of railroad. For the sake of clearness, let us isolate the case of Mr. Jones, the typical suburbanite, the perennial theme of the cockney cartoonist. Twenty years ago Mr. Jones built a house in Grassmere. It contained some of the closets, rooms, niches, fixtures, furniture which had been oddly missing in his city apartment, and it was surrounded by a garden which, until the garage began to demand space, and the car itself most of the family's time, was well-cultivated. The streets were embowered with trees, the school was small and surrounded by a playing field; within ten minutes walk was Chestnut Woods, a great place for picnicking.

When Mr. Jones moved to Grassmere it was Eden; almost it was. All

the suburbs along the line were small, the railroad company was obsequious and kept the fares low; and if the journey to the office was a
little tiresome, the newspaper presently increased in size and reduced
the mental distance. The sacrifice of the climax of the third act was
a small price to pay, in fact, nothing at all to set over against the children's gain. As long as Mr. Jones had "business in the city" this was
perhaps the best possible arrangement for the life of his family.

In establishing himself in Grassmere Mr. Jones forgot only one thing:
he forgot that he had not really escaped the city. The very forces
that created the suburb moved out, inexorably, with icy relentlessness,
and began to smear away this idyllic environment, which had the
neighborliness of a small community and the beauty of gardens and
parks and easy access to nature. Inevitably, the suburb grew and,
growing, it became more like the city it had only apparently broken
away from: the market street lengthened into a garish main street,
ungainly offices and lunchrooms sprang up, an apartment house was
built near the railroad tracks. Land values boomed; but taxes, alas!
rose too. Potentially, Mr. Jones was more prosperous; but if he wanted
to keep his house as a permanent home every increase in land values
and taxes had the effect of making him poorer. If he had a little extra
land he was forced to sell it as building lots; that brought neighbors
uncomfortably near. The simple dirt road, which had cost little, was
replaced by asphalt; traffic increased and it was necessary to widen Main
Street: both improvements cost money. The old method of sewage
disposal and the old water mains were no longer adequate for the
doubled population; Grassmere enlarged them—and that cost money.
New streets were opened at the behest of the leading real estate man,
who happened to be Mayor during the boom period; while these streets
waited for new owners and housebuilders, they "ate their head off."

All the costs of sewers, paving, unnecessarily wide residential streets,
street lighting, gas, electricity, and police went up so rapidly that
presently the newcomers could no longer afford a roomy, comfortable
house like that which the Joneses had built: they put up monotonous
semi-detached rows or plumped into apartments. Mr. Henry Wright
has pointed out that the cost of these little accessories has been steadily
mounting during the last century, and now comes to about forty-five
per cent of the total cost of a house. When all the land is covered
with asphalt, when all the streets are designed indiscriminately for
through loads of traffic, when the land itself is sold by the front foot,
the single family house becomes a forbidding luxury, and there is no
choice at all for the greater part of the population but to build multi-
family houses. The "Own-your-own-home movement" does not recog-

nize that the real difficulty under these conditions consists in keeping your own home.

When his suburb became choked with new buildings, Mr. Jones began to wonder if he might not endure an extra hour's travel each day for the sake of quiet, lower tax rates, a tennis court, and a more congenial community.

Unhappy Mr. Jones! If he moves farther into the country' the improvement is only temporary. So long as the office buildings and the lofts crowd higher into the sky, so long as the factories are planted more thickly along the railroad sidings that line the entrance to the great city, so long will the blessings of suburbia be little more than a momentary illusion. The sort of life the suburb aims at is of course only partial: inevitably the suburbanite loses many of the cultural advantages and contacts of a complete city; but even its limited effort to obtain two essential things—a decent home for children and a comely setting for life—is thin and ephemeral in its results. The suburb is not a solution. It is merely a halting place. So long as the big city continues to grow, the suburb cannot remain suburban. Its gardens are doomed, its quiet streets are doomed, the countryside around it is doomed, a doom hangs over every aspect of its life—sooner or later it will be swallowed up and lost in the maw of the great city. Spring Gardens was anciently a suburb of Philadelphia; Cambridgeport, of Boston; Flushing, of New York—and where are the snows of yesteryear?

V

The conditions that we have been examining are those that attend uncontrolled and unregulated urban growth. They are not evils which are inherent in the constitution of cities; but neither are they accidental defects which will be wiped out by a little adroit street-widening or municipal regulation. It is true that during the last forty years a great corps of technicians has arisen, city planners, engineers, transit experts, and municipal administrators who devote themselves to easing the burdens of congestion and repairing the more obvious damages. Unfortunately, however, for the hopes that these excellent minds awaken, none of their remedies permanently remedies anything—and they themselves are the first to confess it! Our technicians usually accept the fact of unregulated and unbounded urban growth as "given." So instead of attempting to remove the causes that create our mangled urban environments, they attempt only to relieve a few of the intolerable effects. They exhaust the devices of mechanical engineering and finance to provide palliatives for expanding cities and expanding populations, and they flinch, most of them, from asking the one question which promises any permanent and effectual answer—how can we provide a stable environment for a stable population?

It is quite fatuous to ask what promise there is of reconstructing New York and Chicago internally, to make them fit for permanent human habitation. Our efforts to combat the evils of congestion never get within miles of that: the most Mr. Brown hopes for is that the next subway will give him more standing room, in New York; or that a series of double-decked streets will give more clearance to his automobile, in Detroit. As urban growth takes place now, Mr. Brown might as well dream of free airplane excursions to the North Pole. Each new transit line opens up new tracts of land, or increases the capacity of the existing areas to bear a heavier load of people. Thus the remedy increases the population in the Central District and at the outskirts; with this increase, land values rise again and, in turn, a still heavier load falls upon the land.

The same principle applies to those marvelous double-decked avenues and underground ways that modern engineering so eagerly threatens us with. As exhibitions in constructive audacity, these schemes are highly admirable; as instruments of business enterprise they are also, perhaps, admirable; in fact, they are altogether delightful for any purpose except for that for which they are intended—namely, the relief of congestion. The reason is plain: the cost of each new bank of streets or each new boring of tunnels must fall back, eventually, upon the land; and in order to meet the taxes and carrying charges of our monster skyscrapers, still greater monsters must be erected. In short, the remedy just adds a little more of the disease. To build streets in anything like the initial ratio to the original density of population would throw an intolerable charge upon the buildings—unless it were possible to increase the height, and so destroy the ratio! None of our current plans for city improvement break out of this vicious circle; for the only way of breaking out is by limiting the increase of population within a single congested area, whereas none of our present improvements would be tolerated, on business principles, if they did not promise just the opposite of this.

Since all this holds for the present metropolis, we might as well put down in the cellar those purely fanciful solutions of our urban problems upon which Mr. Hugh Ferriss exerts his able and masculine draughtsmanship. Physically, there is perhaps no limit to the heightening and extension of New York and Chicago; the real limitations on city development are not physical but social. They lie in the very nature of a humane life, in the fact that the city is not essentially an agglomeration of houses, but an association of human beings. "Men come together in order to live; they remain together in order to live the good life." Only a megalomaniac imagines that life in a two-hundred story building is in any way better or greater than life in a two-story building, or that air pumped into the city from stations leagues away is superior to air breathed directly, without going through an elaborate mechanical apparatus. The capital objection to immuring oneself in the canyons of the existing metropolis, or the far more colossal canyons that exist in the real-estate speculator's imagination, is that the things that make life tolerable are not a single whit furthered by all this mechanical apparatus. And after all, someone must live at the bottom of these eyries that our bold architects project from Cloudcuckooland; and, unless I am greatly mistaken, life below the fortieth story would be as precarious and dull as it is to-day in those parts of the city that are not on show.

So we come back to the problem: How are we to obtain the physical foundations of a good life in our cities?

VI

The problem would be utterly discouraging were it not for two conditions. One is that the growth of modern invention has diminished the necessity for urban concentration. The other is that human beings are still, after all, human; and though they would doubtless stand for even worse conditions if they thought their sacrifices and discomforts could not be helped, they are not likely to stay in the same posture once they find that an avenue of escape is open. Without any great optimism, I think it is now becoming plain that the more intelligent and sensitive part of the population is becoming a little bored by "greatness," and they are beginning to feel towards their skyscrapers the way an Egyptian slave perhaps felt towards the Pyramids. Also, perhaps for the first time, there is the promise of conditions which would favor and encourage a fundamental social and economic change.

All our plans for city improvement have hitherto been based on conditions which existed in the past; the city planner genially assumes that these forces will operate equally in the future. There is this fatality about such plans: they rarely catch up even with the past. Against this school of thought stands another group that has grown up slowly in the last generation: it first centered about Mr. Ebenezer Howard and his garden-city group, and it now has distinguished adherents in every country. These planners believe that we can effectually take care of the past only by preparing for a more desirable future. For them, the congested metropolis is not primarily bad or miserable: it is merely wasteful, inefficient, technologically obsolete. That is to say, it arose out of industrial and commercial conditions which have ceased to operate in full force to-day, and may not operate at all to-morrow.

Let me explain. During the railroad era the favored urban spots were at the terminals of trunk lines: urban growth took place linearly, along the tracks. The result was vast urban agglomerations—it is impossible to call them "cities"—at points where the traffic ended, coalesced, or crossed. Modern motor transportation and modern airplane traffic do not abet this tendency: They favor a more even distribution of population, like that which characterized the wagon and canal period; for the net of motor roads makes it possible to serve any point in a whole area by car or truck, instead of simply those points "on the line." Economically, this works towards regional rather than metropolitan development; towards industrial decentralization rather than toward further congestion.

Now, the first outcome of motor transport has been in the domain of living rather than in industry. All over the land a great body of people, fed up with the life they have been forced to live in the old centers, have taken to wheels: they drive around the country, more or less consciously seeking a better environment. They are no longer content to live where they can work; they want work, rather, where they may have a little opportunity for truly living. They do not make the search, generally, with either imagination or intelligence—for the moment a large number of them think Florida is the paradise of the heart and the end of human aspiration; but at worst, they manage to plant a bungalow in the middle of some deserted field beyond the city's limits —mean and pathetic, perhaps, but a symbol of the desire to recover freedom and a sense of the human scale.

At present this going and coming of motors is as anarchic as the buying and selling of urban lots. Giant power and industry planning are the two positive forces which are capable of turning this loose human desire into socially constructive ends. Giant power, as distinguished from superpower—the mere commercial linkage of generating stations— carries with it the notion of distributing electricity in districts where a balanced day and night load may be carried along the same mains: this requires a community devoted to both domesticity and industry, not a community in which these things are separated, as they are in the big city and its suburbs. Such a development has been engineered through public ownership in Ontario with a deliberate social purpose; but in certain regions it is likewise being fostered and stimulated by the commercial companies. In outlining their policies on power, Governors Smith and Pinchot have emphasized the opportunities Giant Power offers for building up the rural community, and restoring life to the whole countryside; and in the preliminary report of the New York State Housing and Regional Planning Commission the writers showed how a whole belt of the State, now poorly developed and cultivated, might be opened up, through motor transportation and electric power, for the creation of new communities. Mr. Henry Ford's attempt to lower the vast overhead of metropolitan industry and to restore a smaller factory unit to the old mill sites in the open country is a significant industrial departure in the same direction—and it is a departure, too, in this special sense, that it leaves the great and growing city of Detroit behind it.

The benefits of motor transportation and electric power are, I hasten to add, potential; against their free operation is the drag of habit and routine and business enterprise, which keeps industry fettered to the sites where high land values can be maintained and charged back to the consumer, and where vast private fortunes may be built up through the congestion of population. These new tendencies, however, show that the continued growth of the great city is not merely vicious—it is technologically futile. As industrial processes become more refined, as electricity supplants raw coal, as industrial production becomes planned and socially regulated, as the working population achieves even such relative stability as it has now attained for example in the garment trades, as all these things happen, industry has less and less to gain by haphazard overcrowding. Whereas for a century we have lived where industrial and commercial opportunities seemed greatest, we can now reverse the process, and deliberately plant our industries and our communities in regions where the human opportunities for living are best. In the light of this, our ingenious plans for super-cities, with super-congestion, super-subways, super-tenements, and super-skyscrapers are, if I may be allowed a pun, a little superficial.

The alternative to super-congestion is not "back to the farm" or "let things go." The real alternative to unlimited metropolitan growth is limited growth and, along with it, the deliberate planning and building up of new communities. Once we abandon our naïve belief in the quackeries of engineering, we shall perhaps be willing to face the wholesale change that this implies; for it breaks entirely with the notion that congestion is a boon, that city growth beyond a certain limit is desirable, and that we can solve our human and social problems by placing them all on the plane of mechanics.

But how can the growth of cities be controlled? Is the flood of population not as inevitable as a river flood? It is indeed; but river floods are not inevitable. The comparison serves very neatly; and it was well put recently by Mr. Benton Mackaye. There was a time when the cities along the Ohio used to protect themselves from spring floods by raising dykes; presently, a great tide of water would rush down the valley and flow over the dykes; and then more elaborate ones would be built. As long as cities attempted river control by this sort of patchwork they were perpetually defeated. Genuine flood-prevention dates from the time that the flood-engineers planted forests in the hills to retain the moisture and hold back the waters; when they dealt with causes, rather than effects.

Need I point the parallel? Effective community planning cannot go on so long as each new flood of population can break down the dykes. Any effective effort to provide good living conditions within our existing cities rests upon achieving a fairly stable population: this can be accomplished only by building up new communities in the hinterland, which will hold back the flood, or, to make the metaphor more exact, will not merely hold it back but also drain off some of the surplus from existing centers. What we need is a policy of "community afforestation." Our present small towns and villages are unable to retain their young people because so many of them are scrub communities; neither can they, in their present state, attract new industries or foster new homes. If we are to prevent congestion, we must deliberately create communities which will be fully equipped for work, play, study, and "living." Our new communities must be at least as well designed as a Gary school; in other words, they must be, in English usage, complete garden cities.

VII

How would these new communities differ from existing cities? First, in placement; they would be established in relation to the best remaining water and power resources, and in country districts where land values were still low. They would be surrounded by a permanent belt of agricultural land, to provide a continuous local food supply of green vegetables, and to preserve open spaces without taking them altogether out of productive use. Second, provisions for all the institutions necessary for a community of a given size, say ten thousand or fifty thousand, would be made from the beginning. That is, the land needed for schools, churches, libraries, theaters, hospitals, municipal buildings, associations, playgrounds, and parks would be calculated, platted, and reserved; at the same time, the land needed for shops, factories, and offices would be allocated, with due respect to convenient access, to amenity, and—in the factory district—to prevailing winds and outlooks. The residential parts of the city, instead of being intersected by innumerable streets, would be planned for quiet, safety, and beauty; so that while traffic roads would doubtless be much wider than our present roads, the homeways would be much narrower and much more lightly paved. In general, no houses higher than three stories, and no office higher than five, would be permitted; but that would not prevent the erection of a single tall building, or a small group, as high as, say, ten stories if the height served some direct purpose, such as the grouping of municipal departments, or medical services. The high building would not, however, be permitted as a mere rent-barracks—any more than it is to-day in most European cities.

The provision of gardens and playgrounds would likewise be made on the initial plan; and since the population would be definitely limited, their adequacy would be permanently insured. The time now wasted in subway travel would, since the area of the city is limited, be available for sport, rest, education, or entertainment. Land values increase in the business district of such a city; but the increase is kept for communal purposes. Hence, the stimulation of land values becomes no ordinary part of the processes of business or industry. If some potent institution, like an expanding industry or a great center of learning, caused such a city to attract more people than originally provided for, the further extension of the city, once it had filled its sites, would be taken care of by founding another city, similarly restricted in area and population, similarly surrounded by a rural belt. Mr. Waldo Browne, in an excellent discussion of our overgrown universities, has suggested that institutions like Harvard, instead of automatically getting bigger, should "swarm," and create new Harvards in Indiana or California. It is an excellent principle: in precisely this manner growth would take place in the garden city.

I have painted only a partial picture of the new community; but I trust no one will think I have been dealing with an imaginary town. On the contrary, I am just translating into general terms the realities of Letchworth and Welwyn, with a touch now and then of other communities—including an interesting housing development where I happen to live, unique among all the urban dormitories of New York in the fact that, promoted by a limited dividend corporation, it carries with it an adequate amount of garden and playground from the beginning, as part of the normal cost of housing. There is nothing "ideal" in Letchworth or Welwyn or Sunnyside in the sense that the men and women who live there have suddenly become beatified, marvelously intelligent, feverishly public spirited. Let me emphasize, on the contrary, that this sort of community is merely human. What

makes it desirable, against the congested metropolis, is that our New
Yorks and Chicagos are a little less than human—admirably fitted for
the habitation of robots. The planning of a merely human community
is a prodigious advance upon our current metropolitan plans to "decrease
(i.e. further) congestion." It will be time enough when we have
provided humane conditions to conceive of habitations fit for Men
Like Gods. At any rate, garden cities call neither for super-human
powers, nor for a religious conversion—unless the subordination of
speculation and profiteering to the welfare of the community implies,
in fact, a religious conversion.

Once the desire for better living conditions is effectively expressed,
there is nothing in modern industry itself to hinder its being worked
out; for the building of new garden cities calls for no violent departure
from normal American practices. For three hundred years we have
been planting new cities: it would be strange if, at the height of our
mechanical powers, we had suddenly become paralyzed. Every day
new factories are founded, or old ones forced to expand and to move:
outside of highly localized industries, such as those connected specifically
with mines or ports, there is no reason why a fresh start should not be
made in the new centers, instead of adding to the clutter and confusion
of existing ones. Finally, every day new houses are built: it needs only
social foresight, and financial co-ordination to connect the erection of
houses with the spotting of new industries.

Here then is the choice—between growth by the "mechanical extension" of existing urban areas, and growth by the foundation of new
communities, fully equipped for working, learning, and living. In the
growth by mechanical extension we move inertly towards the intolerable
city whose various phases I have described. With a tithe of the constructive power we now spend on palliatives, we might found a hundred
fresh centers in which life would really be enjoyable, in which the full
benefit of modern civilization and culture might be had. It is not easy,
I confess, to translate this alternative into stunning sky-pictures: hurtling
masses of steel would perhaps seem far more attractive on paper, especially for minds that are starved for something to worship, and will worship a skyscraper, provided it be big enough. Nevertheless, the
alternative is genuine; the "way out" it offers is real. Shall we make the
attempt? Perhaps not. The likelihood is that we shall go a little
farther along the road of super-congestion, before our disillusion becomes complete, and our physical state odious. Sooner or later, however, we shall find out that, in Professor Patrick Geddes's tart phrase
metropolitan growth means "more and more of worse and worse."
When the super-city crumbles in our imagination, I do not think any-

thing will keep us from achieving solid human communities, in fact. They existed once. They will exist again; and by promoting them we should make life in our present centers more tolerable.

≈§·≈§§≈§≈

72. Urbanism as a Way of Life *

THE PROCESS OF URBANIZATION has had significant effects on social relations and personality organization in Western societies. Louis Wirth here analyzes urban social systems in terms of size, density, and heterogeneity and examines their impact on personal as well as collective behavior in the city. The general principles developed in this article can profitably be applied to rural or small town communities such as the one described in "Littletown" (70, by Mather). Also, the description of the behavior of "Villagers in Metropolis" (74, by Riemer), which further enriches an understanding of urban society, will be found to complement this article.

A THEORY OF URBANISM

SIZE OF THE POPULATION AGGREGATE

EVER SINCE Aristotle's *Politics,* it has been recognized that increasing the number of inhabitants in a settlement beyond a certain limit will affect the relationships between them and the character of the city. Large numbers involve, as has been pointed out, a greater range of individual variation. Furthermore, the greater the number of individuals participating in a process of interaction, the greater is the *potential* differentiation between them. The personal traits, the occupations, the cultural life, and the ideas of the members of an urban community may,

* Louis Wirth, *American Journal of Sociology,* 44, No. 1 (July, 1938), 10-18, 22-24. Reprinted by permission of the author and the University of Chicago Press.

The author (b. 1897) is Professor of Sociology, University of Chicago. Born in Germany, he came to this country in 1911. Has had distinguished career as director, research fellow, consultant in various capacities. President, American Council on Race Relations. Associate editor, *American Journal of Sociology,* 1926-28 and since 1931. Past president of the International Sociological Association. Co-author, *The City, Our Cities: Their Role in the National Economy.* Author, *The Ghetto, Community Planning for Peace Time Living.*

therefore, be expected to range between more widely separated poles than those of rural inhabitants.

That such variations should give rise to the spatial segregation of individuals according to color, ethnic heritage, economic and social status, tastes and preferences, may readily be inferred. The bonds of kinship, of neighborliness, and the sentiments arising out of living together for generations under a common folk tradition are likely to be absent or, at best, relatively weak in an aggregate the members of which have such diverse origins and backgrounds. Under such circumstances competition and formal control mechanisms furnish the substitutes for the bonds of solidarity that are relied upon to hold a folk society together.

Increase in the number of inhabitants of a community beyond a few hundred is bound to limit the possibility of each member of the community knowing all the others personally. Max Weber, in recognizing the social significance of this fact, pointed out that from a sociological point of view large numbers of inhabitants and density of settlement mean that the personal mutual acquaintanceship between the inhabitants which ordinarily inheres in a neighborhood is lacking. The increase in numbers thus involves a changed character of the social relationships. As Simmel points out:

[If] the unceasing external contact of numbers of persons in the city should be met by the same number of inner reactions as in the small town, in which one knows almost every person he meets and to each of whom he has a positive relationship, one would be completely atomized internally and would fall into an unthinkable mental condition.

The multiplication of persons in a state of interaction under conditions which make their contact as full personalities impossible produces that segmentalization of human relationships which has sometimes been seized upon by students of the mental life of the cities as an explanation for the "schizoid" character of urban personality. This is not to say that the urban inhabitants have fewer acquaintances than rural inhabitants, for the reverse may actually be true; it means rather that in relation to the number of people whom they see and with whom they rub elbows in the course of daily life, they know a smaller proportion, and of these they have less intensive knowledge.

Characteristically, urbanites meet one another in highly segmental roles. They are, to be sure, dependent upon more people for the satisfactions of their life-needs than are rural people and thus are associated with a greater number of organized groups, but they are less dependent upon particular persons, and their dependence upon others is confined to a highly fractionalized aspect of the other's round of activity. This is essentially what is meant by saying that the city is characterized by secondary rather than primary contacts. The contacts of the city may indeed be face to face, but they are nevertheless impersonal, superficial, transitory, and segmental. The reserve, the indifference, and the blasé outlook which urbanites manifest in their relationships may thus be regarded as devices for immunizing themselves against the personal claims and expectations of others.

The superficiality, the anonymity, and the transitory character of urban-social relations make intelligible, also, the sophistication and the rationality generally ascribed to city-dwellers. Our acquaintances tend to stand in a relationship of utility to us in the sense that the role which each one plays in our life is overwhelmingly regarded as a means for the achievement of our own ends. Whereas, therefore, the individual gains, on the one hand, a certain degree of emancipation or freedom from the personal and emotional controls of intimate groups, he loses, on the other hand, the spontaneous self-expression, the morale, and the sense of participation that comes with living in an integrated society. This constitutes essentially the state of *anomie* or the social void to which Durkheim alludes in attempting to account for the various forms of social disorganization in technological society.

The segmental character and utilitarian accent of interpersonal relations in the city find their institutional expression in the proliferation of specialized tasks which we see in their most developed form in the professions. The operations of the pecuniary nexus leads to predatory relationships, which tend to obstruct the efficient functioning of the social order unless checked by professional codes and occupational etiquette. The premium put upon utility and efficiency suggests the adaptability of the corporate device for the organization of enterprises in which individuals can engage only in groups. The advantage that the corporation has over the individual entrepreneur and the partnership in the urban-industrial world derives not only from the possibility it affords of centralizing the resources of thousands of individuals or from the legal privilege of limited liability and perpetual succession, but from the fact that the corporation has no soul.

The specialization of individuals, particularly in their occupations, can proceed only, as Adam Smith pointed out, upon the basis of an enlarged market, which in turn accentuates the division of labor. This enlarged market is only in part supplied by the city's hinterland; in large measure it is found among the large numbers that the city itself contains. The dominance of the city over the surrounding hinterland becomes explicable in terms of the division of labor which urban life occasions and promotes. The extreme degree of interdependence and the unstable equilibrium of urban life are closely associated with the division of labor and the specialization of occupations. This interdependence and instability is increased by the tendency of each city to specialize in those functions in which it has the greatest advantage.

In a community composed of a larger number of individuals than can know one another intimately and can be assembled in one spot, it becomes necessary to communicate through indirect mediums and to articulate individual interests by a process of delegation. Typically in the city, interests are made effective through representation. The individual counts for little, but the voice of the representative is heard with a deference roughly proportional to the numbers for whom he speaks.

While this characterization of urbanism, in so far as it derives from large numbers, does not by any means exhaust the sociological inferences that might be drawn from our knowledge of the relationship of the size of a group to the characteristic behavior of the members, for the sake of brevity the assertions made may serve to exemplify the sort of propositions that might be developed.

DENSITY

As in the case of numbers, so in the case of concentration in limited space, certain consequences of relevance in sociological analysis of the city emerge. Of these only a few can be indicated.

As Darwin pointed out for flora and fauna and as Durkheim noted in the case of human societies, an increase in numbers when area is held constant (i.e., an increase in density) tends to produce differentiation and specialization, since only in this way can the area support increased numbers. Density thus reinforces the effect of numbers in diversifying men and their activities and in increasing the complexity of the social structure.

On the subjective side, as Simmel has suggested, the close physical contact of numerous individuals necessarily produces a shift in the mediums through which we orient ourselves to the urban milieu, especially to our fellow-men. Typically, our physical contacts are close but our social contacts are distant. The urban world puts a premium on visual recognition. We see the uniform which denotes the role of the functionaries and are oblivious to the personal eccentricities that are hidden behind the uniform. We tend to acquire and develop a sensitivity to a world of artifacts and become progressively farther removed from the world of nature

We are exposed to glaring contrasts between splendor and squalor, between riches and poverty, intelligence and ignorance, order and chaos. The competition for space is great, so that each area generally tends to be put to the use which yields the greatest economic return. Place of work tends to become dissociated from place of residence, for the proximity of industrial and commercial establishments makes an area both economically and socially undesirable for residential purposes.

Density, land values, rentals, accessibility, healthfulness, prestige, aesthetic consideration, absence of nuisances such as noise, smoke, and dirt determine the desirability of various areas of the city as places of settlement for different sections of the population. Place and nature of work, income, racial and ethnic characteristics, social status, custom, habit, taste, preference, and prejudice are among the significant factors in accordance with which the urban population is selected and distributed into more or less distinct settlements. Diverse population elements inhabiting a compact settlement thus tend to become segregated from one another in the degree in which their requirements and modes of life are incompatible with one another and in the measure in which they are antagonistic to one another. Similarly, persons of homogeneous status and needs unwittingly drift into, consciously select, or are forced by circumstances into, the same area. The different parts of the city thus acquire specialized functions. The city consequently tends to resemble a mosaic of social worlds in which the transition from one to the other is abrupt. The juxtaposition of divergent personalities and modes of life tends to produce a relativistic perspective and a sense of toleration of differences which may be regarded as prerequisites for rationality and which lead toward the secularization of life.

The close living together and working together of individuals who have no sentimental and emotional ties foster a spirit of competition, aggrandizement, and mutual exploitation. To counteract irresponsibility and potential disorder, formal controls tend to be resorted to. Without rigid adherence to predictable routines a large compact society would scarcely be able to maintain itself. The clock and the traffic signal are symbolic of the basis of our social order in the urban world. Frequent close physical contact, coupled with great social distance, accentuates the reserve of unattached individuals toward one another and, unless compensated for by other opportunities for response, gives rise to loneliness. The necessary frequent movement of great numbers of individuals in a congested habitat gives occasion to friction and irritation. Nervous tensions which derive from such personal frustrations are accentuated by the rapid tempo and the complicated technology under which life in dense areas must be lived.

HETEROGENEITY

The social interaction among such a variety of personality types in the urban milieu tends to break down the rigidity of caste lines and to complicate the class structure, and thus induces a more ramified and differentiated framework of social stratification than is found in more integrated societies. The heightened mobility of the individual, which brings him within the range of stimulation by a great number of diverse individuals and subjects him to fluctuating status in the differentiated social groups that compose the social structure of the city, tends toward the acceptance of instability and insecurity in the world at large as a norm. This fact helps to account, too, for the sophistication and cosmopolitanism of the urbanite. No single group has the undivided allegiance of the individual. The groups with which he is affiliated do not lend themselves readily to a simple hierarchical arrangement. By virtue of his different interests arising out of different aspects of social life, the individual acquires membership in widely divergent groups, each of which functions only with reference to a single segment of his personality. Nor do these groups easily permit of a concentric arrangement so that the narrower ones fall within the circumference of the more inclusive ones, as is more likely to be the case in the rural community or in primitive societies. Rather the groups with which the person typically is affiliated are tangential to each other or intersect in highly variable fashion.

Partly as a result of the physical footlooseness of the population and partly as a result of their social mobility, the turnover in group membership generally is rapid. Place of residence, place and character of employment, income and interests fluctuate, and the task of holding organizations together and maintaining and promoting intimate and lasting acquaintanceship between the members is difficult. This applies strikingly to the local areas within the city into which persons become segregated more by virtue of differences in race, language, income, and social status, than through choice or positive attraction to people like themselves. Overwhelmingly the city-dweller is not a home-owner, and since a transitory habitat does not generate binding traditions and sentiments, only rarely is he truly a neighbor. There is little opportunity for the individual to obtain a conception of the city as a whole or to survey his place in the total scheme. Consequently he finds it difficult to determine what is to his own "best interests" and to decide between the issues and leaders presented to him by the agencies of mass suggestion. Individuals who are thus detached from the organized bodies which integrate society comprise the fluid masses that make collective behavior in the urban community so unpredictable and hence so problematical.

Although the city, through the recruitment of variant types to perform its diverse tasks and the accentuation of their uniqueness through competition and the premium upon eccentricity, novelty, efficient performance, and inventiveness, produces a highly differentiated population, it also exercises a leveling influence. Wherever large numbers of differently constituted individuals congregate, the process of depersonalization also enters. This leveling tendency inheres in part in the economic basis of the city. The development of large cities, at least in the modern age, was largely dependent upon the concentrative force of steam. The rise of the factory made possible mass production for an impersonal market. The fullest exploitation of the possibilities of the division of labor and mass production, however, is possible only with standardization of processes and products. A money economy goes hand in hand with such a system of production. Progressively as cities have developed upon a background of this system of production, the pecuniary nexus which implies the purchasability of services and things has displaced personal relations as the basis of association. Individuality under these circumstances must be replaced by categories. When large numbers have to make common use of facilities and institutions, an arrangement must be made to adjust the facilities and institutions to the needs of the average person rather than to those of particular individuals. The services of the public utilities, of the recreational, educational, and cultural institutions must be adjusted to mass requirements. Similarly, the cultural institutions, such as the schools, the movies, the radio, and the newspapers, by virtue of their mass clientele, must necessarily operate as leveling influences. The political process as it appears in urban life could not be understood without taking account of the mass appeals made through modern propaganda techniques. If the individual would participate at all in the social, political, and economic life of the city, he must subordinate some of his individuality to the demands of the larger community and in that measure immerse himself in mass movements.

THE RELATION BETWEEN A THEORY OF URBANISM
AND SOCIOLOGICAL RESEARCH

• • • • • •

Being reduced to a stage of virtual impotence as an individual, the urbanite is bound to exert himself by joining with others of similar interest into organized groups to obtain his ends. This results in the enormous multiplication of voluntary organizations directed toward as great a variety of objectives as there are human needs and interests. While on the one hand the traditional ties of human association are weakened, urban existence involves a much greater degree of interdependence between man and man and a more complicated, fragile, and volatile form of mutual interrelations over many phases of which the individual as such can exert scarcely any control. Frequently there is only the most tenuous relationship between the economic position or other basic factors that determine the individual's existence in the urban world and the voluntary groups with which he is affiliated. While in a primitive and in a rural society it is generally possible to predict on the basis of a few known factors who will belong to what and who will associate with whom in almost every relationship of life, in the city we can only project the general pattern of group formation and affiliation, and this pattern will display many incongruities and contradictions.

URBAN PERSONALITY AND COLLECTIVE BEHAVIOR

It is largely through the activities of the voluntary groups, be their objectives economic, political, educational, religious, recreational, or cultural, that the urbanite expresses and develops his personality, acquires status, and is able to carry on the round of activities that constitute his life-career. It may easily be inferred, however, that the organizational framework which these highly differentiated functions call into being does not of itself insure the consistency and integrity of the personalities whose interests it enlists. Personal disorganization, mental breakdown, suicide, delinquency, crime, corruption, and disorder might be expected under these circumstances to be more prevalent in the urban than in the rural community. This has been confirmed in so far as comparable indices are available; but the mechanisms underlying these phenomena require further analysis.

Since for most group purposes it is impossible in the city to appeal individually to the large number of discrete and differentiated individuals, and since it is only through the organizations to which men belong that their interests and resources can be enlisted for a collective cause, it may be inferred that social control in the city should typically proceed through formally organized groups. It follows, too, that the masses of men in the city are subject to manipulation by symbols and stereotypes managed by individuals working from afar or operating invisibly behind the scenes through their control of the instruments of communication. Self-government either in the economic, the political, or the cultural realm is under these circumstances reduced to a mere figure of speech or, at best, is subject to the unstable equilibrium of pressure groups. In view of the ineffectiveness of actual kinship ties we create fictional kinship groups. In the face of the disappearance of the territorial unit as a basis of social solidarity we create interest units. Meanwhile the city as a community resolves itself into a series of tenuous segmental relationships superimposed upon a territorial base with a definite center but without a definite periphery and upon a division of labor which far transcends the immediate locality and is world-wide in scope. The larger the number of persons in a state of interaction with one another the lower is the level of communication and the greater is the tendency for communication to proceed on an elementary level, i.e., on the basis of those things which are assumed to be common or to be of interest to all.

It is obviously, therefore, to the emerging trends in the communication system and to the production and distribution technology that has come into existence with modern civilization that we must look for the symptoms which will indicate the probable future development of urbanism as a mode of social life. The direction of the ongoing changes in urbanism will for good or ill transform not only the city but the world. Some of the more basic of these factors and processes and the possibilities of their direction and control invite further detailed study.

73. The Pattern of Movement of Residential Rental Neighborhoods *

PREVIOUS READINGS in this section mainly have treated various types of ecological structures. In this selection Homer Hoyt illustrates the process of urban change through the technique of ecologi-

* Homer Hoyt, The Structure and Growth of Residential Neighborhoods in American Cities (Washington, D. C.: Federal Housing Administration, 1939), pp. 112-122. Reprinted by permission of the author.

The author (b. 1896) is President, Homer Hoyt Associates, Larchmont, New York. Has had varied career as urban land economist, consultant, lecturer, research director,

cal analysis. The important influence of changes in means of
transportation, especially the shift to the automobile, on the rate and
type of movement shown by residential neighborhoods is clearly
illustrated. Since the author has used data from many of the major
cities of this country, the reader may be able to confirm from his
own observations the validity of Hoyt's generalizations and the rep-
resentativeness of his data.

Of the various shifts that take place in the internal structure of a city
as a result of population growth, the movement of the residential rental
neighborhoods most vitally concerns the home owner or the investor in
residential mortgages. . . .

. . . From the high rental areas that are frequently located on the
periphery of one or more sectors of American cities, there is a downward
gradation of rents until one reaches the low rent areas near the business
center. The low rent areas are usually large and may extend from this
center to the periphery on one side of the urban community. The high,
low, and intermediate rental neighborhoods, however, did not always
occupy these locations on the urban site. Their present positions are
the points reached in the course of a movement taking place over a
period of time. It is not a movement of buildings but a shifting and a
change in the character of occupants that produces neighborhood
change. New patterns of rent areas are formed as the city grows and
adds new structures by both vertical and lateral expansion.

•   •   •   •   •   •

*The high rent neighborhoods of a city do not skip about at random in
the process of movement—they follow a definite path in one or more
sectors of the city.*

Apparently there is a tendency for neighborhoods within a city to
shift in accordance with what may be called the sector theory of neighborhood change. The understanding of the framework within which
this principle operates will be facilitated by considering the entire city
as a circle and various neighborhoods as falling into sectors radiating out
from the center of that circle. No city conforms exactly to this ideal
pattern, of course, but the general figure is useful inasmuch as in our

housing economist, real estate analyst, debate coach, university professor, statistician.
With Federal Housing Administration, 1934-40; Urban Land Institute, 1940-41;
Chicago Planning Commission, 1941-43. Author, *One Hundred Years of Land
Values in Chicago* and *The Economic Status of the New York Metropolitan Region
in 1944.*

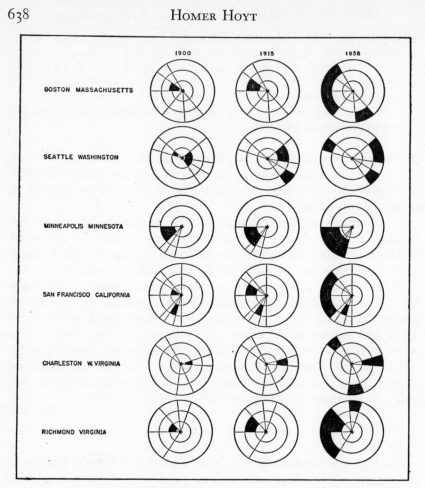

Shifts in location of fashionable residential areas in six American cities, 1900-1936. (The fashionable residential areas are indicated by solid black.) This chart depicts graphically the sector theory of city growth, as formulated by the author of this article. According to this interpretation, residential areas tend to take the form of sectors rather than concentric zones. (Courtesy Federal Housing Administration)

American cities the different types of residential areas tend to grow outward along rather distinct radii, and new growth on the arc of a given sector tends to take on the character of the initial growth in that sector.

• • • • • •

High rent or high grade residential neighborhoods must almost necessarily move outward toward the periphery of the city. The wealthy seldom reverse their steps and move backward into the obsolete houses which they are giving up. On each side of them is usually an intermediate rental area, so they cannot move sideways. As they represent the highest income group, there are no houses above them abandoned by another group. They must build new houses on vacant land. Usually this vacant land lies available just ahead of the line of march of the area because, anticipating the trend of fashionable growth, land promoters have either restricted it to high grade use or speculators have placed a value on the land that is too high for the low rent or intermediate rental group. Hence the natural trend of the high rent area is outward, toward the periphery of the city in the very sector in which the high rent area started. The exception to this outward movement is the development of de luxe apartment areas in old residential areas. This will be treated more fully on a following page.

What determines the point of origin of the highest rental areas of the city and the direction and pattern of their future growth? The answer to this question is of vital importance to all students of urban growth, for the high rent sector is the pole or center of attraction that pulls the other residential areas with it.

In all of the cities studied, the high grade residential area had its point of origin near the retail and office center. This is where the higher income groups work, and is the point that is the farthest removed from the side of the city that has industries or warehouses. In each city, the direction and pattern of its future growth then tends to be governed by some combination of the following considerations:

(1) *High grade residential growth tends to proceed from the given point of origin, along established lines of travel or toward another existing nucleus of buildings or trading centers.*—This principle is illustrated by the movement of the high grade residential neighborhood of Chicago along the main axes of the roads like Cottage Grove Avenue, leading south around the bend of Lake Michigan to the east, of main roads like Madison Street leading westward, and of roads following the lake northward to Milwaukee. In Detroit, Mich., there was a trend of fashionable growth along the radial line of Woodward Avenue, the main thoroughfare to Flint and Pontiac, beginning within the Grand Boulevard Circuit and later extending to Highland Park, Palmer Woods, Ferndale, Royal Oak, and Birmingham.

(2) *The zone of high rent areas tends to progress toward high ground which is free from the risk of floods and to spread along lake, bay, river, and ocean fronts, where such water fronts are not used for industry.*—The movement of high grade residential neighborhoods away from river

bottoms to higher ground or to wooded hills is illustrated by numerous examples. In San Francisco, Calif., the wealthy moved from the lowland along the bay to Knob Hill which was less subject to fogs and smoke. In Washington, D. C., the high grade neighborhoods moved from the mud flats along the Potomac in the southeast quadrant and from the lowland in the southwest quadrant, to the higher land in the northwest section. In Springfield, Mass., the best areas moved from the lowland along the Connecticut River to rising land and to Longmeadow. In Kansas City, Mo., St. Louis, Mo., and Cincinnati, Ohio, there has been a movement of settlement away from the river bottoms to the higher land.

In cities located on relatively flat land near rivers, bays, lakes, or oceans, the high grade residential neighborhood tends to expand in long lines along the water front that is not used for industrial purposes. Thus in Chicago, the lake front on the north side is the front yard of the city and is preempted for high grade residential use for a distance of nearly 30 miles north of the business center. In New York City, a high grade residential area grew northward along the Hudson River on Riverside Drive from 72d Street to Riverdale in the West Bronx. In Miami, Fla., the high rent areas extend along Biscayne Bay to the north and southeast and along the ocean front on Miami Beach. In Detroit, Mich., a high grade development extends along Lake St. Clair at Grosse Pointe. On the New Jersey coast, there is a long string of resorts along the ocean front with the highest paid residential use confined to the strip along the beach. In Charleston, W. Va., one high grade residential area extends along the high bank of the Kanawha River.

Thus, where such lakes, rivers, bays, or ocean fronts exist and offer the attractions of bathing, yachting, cool breezes in summer, and a wide expanse of water with its uninterrupted view, rent areas tend to follow the contour of the water front in long, narrow lines of growth.

(3) *High rent residential districts tend to grow toward the section of the city which has free, open country beyond the edges and away from "dead end" sections which are limited by natural or artificial barriers to expansion.*—The lure of open fields, golf courses, country clubs, and country estates acts as a magnet to pull high grade residential areas to sections that have free, open country beyond their borders and away from areas that run into "dead ends." Thus the high-grade neighborhood of Washington, D. C., grows northwest toward expanding open country and estates. Thus, the expansion of high-grade neighborhoods to the north of Baltimore, Md., to the south of Kansas City, Mo., and to the north of New York City in Westchester County is into areas with a wide expanse of country beyond them.

(4) *The higher priced residential neighborhood tends to grow toward the homes of the leaders of the community.*—In Washington, D. C., the White House; in New York, the homes of the Astors and the Vanderbilts were the magnets that pulled the members of society in their direction. One fashionable home, an outpost on the prairie, standing near Sixteenth Street and Prairie Avenue in Chicago in 1836, gave prestige to the section and caused other leaders of fashion to locate near the same spot.

(5) *Trends of movement of office buildings, banks, and stores, pull the higher priced residential neighborhoods in the same general direction.*— The stores, offices, and banks in the central business district usually move in the direction of the high rent area, but follow rather than lead the movement of the high rent neighborhood. Sometimes, however, when an office building center becomes established at a certain point, it facilitates the growth of a high rent area in sections that are conveniently accessible to it. Thus the office building center in the Grand Central District in New York City has aided the growth of the de luxe apartment area in Park Avenue and also the exclusive suburban towns in Westchester that are served by fast express trains entering the Grand Central Station. The establishment of an office building center at Grand Boulevard and Woodward Avenue in Detroit, Mich., aided the growth of the high grade area to the north and west of it. In Washington, D. C., the northwestward trend of the office buildings, while the result of the pull of the high grade areas to the northwest, also favored the further growth of the northwest area because it made those areas more accessible to offices. Similarly, the trend of office buildings on North Michigan Avenue in Chicago favored the northward growth of the de luxe apartment area.

(6) *High grade residential areas tend to develop along the fastest existing transportation lines.*—The high grade residential areas in Chicago grew along the main plank road, horse car, cable car, and suburban railroad routes. In New York City, the elevated lines and subways paralleled Fifth Avenue. Fast commuters' trains connect New York City with the high grade suburban homes in Montclair, the Oranges, and Maplewood in New Jersey, in Scarsdale, Pelham, and Bronxville in Westchester, and in Forest Hills, Kew Gardens, Flushing, and Hempstead in Long Island. In Detroit, Mich., the high grade areas are located close to main arteries leading directly to the center of the city— Jefferson, Woodward, and Grand River Avenues. In Washington, D. C., the best areas are on the main transportation arteries—Connecticut Avenue, Massachusetts Avenue, and Sixteenth Street leading directly to the White House.

(7) *The growth of high rent neighborhoods continues in the same direction for a long period of time.*—In New York City, the march of the fashionable areas continued up Fifth Avenue from Washington Square to Central Park for over a century. The high grade neighborhoods in Chicago moved south, west, and north from their starting points in or near the present "Loop" to present locations—7 to 20 miles distant—in the course of a century. In the century after the Revolutionary War, the high grade area of Washington, D. C., moved from the Capitol to the Naval Observatory. The high rent areas of Detroit, Mich., moved from points near the present business center to Grosse Pointe, Palmer Woods, and Birmingham, 6 to 10 miles away.

In Miami, Fla., Minneapolis, Minn., Seattle, Wash., Charleston, W. Va., Salt Lake City, Utah, and many other cities, this same continuous outward movement of high rent areas has been maintained for long periods of time. Except under the unusual conditions now to be described, there have been no reversals of this long continued trend.

(8) *De luxe high rent apartment areas tend to be established near the business center in old residential areas.*—One apparent exception to the rule that high rent neighborhoods do not reverse their trend of growth is found in the case of de luxe apartment areas like Streeterville in Chicago and Park Avenue in New York City. This exception is a very special case, however, and applies only to intensive high grade apartment developments in a few metropolitan centers. When the high rent single-family home areas have moved far out on the periphery of the city, some wealthy families desire to live in a colony of luxurious apartments close to the business center. Because of both the intensive use of the land by use of multiple family structures and the high rents charged it pays to wreck existing improvements.

Such apartments can rise even in the midst of a poor area because the tall building itself, rising from humble surroundings like a feudal castle above the mud huts of the villeins, is a barrier against intrusion. Thus, when the railroad tracks were depressed under Park Avenue in New York City and the railroads were electrified, that street, originally lined with shanties, became the fashionable apartment avenue of New York City. In Chicago, the wall of apartments on the sands where Captain Streeter once had his shack is now occupied by the most exclusive social set. In both cases, there was a renaissance of an old neighborhood. It is only where intensive apartment uses occupy the land that such an apparent reversal of trend occurs.

(9) *Real estate promoters may bend the direction of high grade residential growth.*—While it is almost impossible for real estate developers to reverse the natural trend of growth of high grade neighborhoods, even

by the expenditure of large sums of money and great promotional effort, it is possible for them to accelerate a natural trend or to bend a natural trend of growth.

Miami Beach, directly on the Gulf Stream in Florida, was favored by nature as the site for high grade resort homes. When it was a mangrove swamp, separated from the mainland by Biscayne Bay, it was almost inaccessible. Carl Fisher, by building a million dollar causeway and by pumping up 2,800 acres of land out of the bay and erecting thereon golf courses and hotels, made it possible for these natural advantages of Miami Beach to be utilized. Similarly, George Merrick acquired a great tract of land at Coral Gables, Fla., and, by spending millions of dollars in laying out streets, in planting flowering trees, and in establishing restrictions, gave the area a high grade character which it did not otherwise possess. So, likewise, did the developers of Roland Park in Baltimore, Shaker Heights near Cleveland, and the Country Club District of Kansas City take large areas in the line of growth and establish high grade communities by means of building restrictions, architectural control, community planning, and other barriers against invasion.

In all these cases, the high rent area was in the general path of growth; but which area of the many in the favored area became the fashionable center depended upon the promotional skill and the money expended by individual promoters.

As a result of some or all of these forces, high rent neighborhoods thus become established in one sector of the city, and they tend to move out in that sector to the periphery of the city. Even if the sector in which the high rent growth begins does not possess all of the advantages, it is difficult for the high rent neighborhood to change its direction suddenly or to move to a new quarter of the city. For as the high rent neighborhood grows and expands, the low and intermediate areas are likewise growing and expanding, and they are taking up and utilizing land alongside the high rent area as well as in other sectors of the city. When these other areas have acquired a low rent character, it is very difficult to change that character except for intensive apartment use. Hence, while in the beginning of the growth of the city, high rent neighborhoods may have a considerable choice of direction in which to move, that range of choice is narrowed as the city grows and begins to be filled up on one or more sides by low rent structures.

It is possible for high rent neighborhoods to take over sections which are marred by a few shacks. These are swept aside or submerged by the tide of growth. Negro houses have even been bought up and moved away in some southern cities to make way for a high grade development. This possibility exists where the houses are flimsy or scattered, where the land is cheap, where it is held by one owner, or where the residents are under the domination of others. It is extremely difficult otherwise. The cost of acquiring and tearing down substantial buildings and the practical impossibility of acquiring large areas from scattered owners, usually prevent high grade areas from taking over land once it has been fairly well occupied by middle or low grade residential uses.

Now that the radius of the settled area of cities has been greatly extended by the automobile, however, there is little difficulty in securing land for the expansion of high rent areas; for the high rent sector of the city expands with an ever widening arc as one proceeds from the business center.

The next vital question to be considered is how the various types of high rent areas are affected by the process of dynamic growth of the city and how the various types are related to each other in historical sequence.

The first type of high rent development was the axial type with high grade homes in a long avenue or avenues leading directly to the business center. The avenue was a social bourse, communication being maintained by a stream of fashionable carriages, the occupants of which nodded to their acquaintances in other passing carriages or to other friends on the porches of the fine residences along the way. Such avenues were lined with beautiful shade trees and led to a park or parks through a series of connecting boulevards. Examples of this type of development, in the decades from 1870 to 1900, are Prairie and South Michigan Avenues, Washington and Jackson Streets and the Lake Shore Drive in Chicago, Fifth Avenue in New York City, Monument Avenue in Richmond, Va., and Summit Street in St. Paul, Minn. The fashionable area in this type of development expanded in a long string in a radial line from the business center. There was usually an abrupt transition within a short distance on either side of the high grade street.

The axial type of high rent area rapidly became obsolete with the growth of the automobile. When the avenues became automobile speedways, dangerous to children, noisy, and filled with gasoline fumes, they ceased to be attractive as home sites for the well-to-do. No longer restricted to the upper classes, who alone could maintain prancing steeds and glittering broughams, but filled with *hoi polloi* jostling the limousines with their flivvers, the old avenues lost social caste. The rich then desired seclusion—away from the "madding crowd" whizzing by and honking their horns. Mansions were then built in wooded areas, screened by trees. The very height of privacy is now attained by some millionaires whose homes are so protected from the public view by trees that they can be seen from outside only from an airplane.

The well-to-do who occupy most of the houses in the high rent brackets have done likewise in segregated garden communities. The new type of high grade area was thus not in the form of a long axial line but in the form of a rectangular area, turning its back on the outside world, with winding streets, woods, and its own community centers. Such new square or rectangular areas are usually located along the line of the old axial high grade areas. The once proud mansions still serve as a favorable approach to the new secluded spots. As some of the old axial type high rent areas still maintain a waning prestige and may still be classed as high rent areas, the new high rent area takes a fan-shaped or funnel form expanding from a central stem as it reaches the periphery of the city.

The old stringlike development of high rent areas still asserts itself, however, in the cases of expansion of high rent areas along water fronts like Lake Michigan, Miami Beach, and the New Jersey coast. The automobile, however, has made accessible hilly and wooded tracts on which houses are built on the crest of hills along winding roads.

The fashionable suburban town, which had its origin even before the Civil War, has remained a continuous type of high grade area. Old fashionable towns like Evanston, Oak Park, and Lake Forest near Chicago, have maintained their original character and expanded their growth. Other new high grade suburban towns have been established. The de luxe apartment area has been a comparatively recent development, coming after 1900, when the wealthy ceased to desire to maintain elaborate town houses and when the high grade single-family home areas began to be located far from the business center. A group of wealthy people, desiring to live near the business center and to avoid the expense and trouble of maintaining a retinue of servants, sought the convenience of tall elevator apartments.

The high grade areas thus tend to preempt the most desirable residential land by supporting the highest values. Intermediate rental groups tend to occupy the sectors in each city that are adjacent to the high rent area. Those in the intermediate rental group have incomes sufficient to pay for new houses with modern sanitary facilities. Hence, the new growth of these middle-class areas takes place on the periphery of the city near high grade areas or sometimes at points beyond the edge of older middle-class areas.

Occupants of houses in the low rent categories tend to move out in bands from the center of the city mainly by filtering up into houses left behind by the high income groups, or by erecting shacks on the periphery of the city. They live in either second-hand houses in which the percentage needing major repairs is relatively high or in newly constructed shacks on the periphery of the city. These shacks frequently lack modern plumbing facilities and are on unpaved streets. The shack fringe of the city is usually in the extension of a low rent section.

⋙⋘⋙⋘

47. Villagers In Metropolis*

Are city planners following a mistaken lead when attempts are made to revive village structures in the metropolis? Do we need to shift our thinking about the neighborhood so as to emphasize less its characteristic as an "area clearly delineated in space" and emphasize more the fact that it is "a phenomenon anchored in the mind?" These are some of the questions to which the author applies himself. His answers are interesting and challenging.

I. RURAL AND URBAN SOCIAL CONTROL

While village structures vanish more and more from the urban environment, the professional city planner endeavours to keep alive or to revive in the city a social climate characterized by close internal cohesion among neighbours. The paradox ventured in the title of this article presents a goal, a desideratum rather than a fact.

Village structures are determined by a way of life (1) deeply embedded in tradition and (2) controlled by a close-knit welter of informal social relationships among the members of the group. Geographically, the village is characterized by close residential propinquity of those members of the community who—at work and play—are bound to each other by frequent social contacts.

In the large modern city of the United States, all these criteria were realized only in the flourishing immigrant neighbourhoods of the nine-

* Svend Riemer, British Journal of Sociology, II, No. 1 (March, 1951), 31-43. London: Routledge & Kegan Paul Ltd. Reprinted by permission of the author and the publisher.

The author (b. 1905) is Associate Professor of Sociology and Anthropology, University of Wisconsin. His writings have appeared in numerous professional journals. The family, urban sociology, housing, and neighborhood planning form his particular interests.

teenth century. Here, indeed, the village pattern of the old world was frequently transferred to urban residential sections in the new world. These immigrant neighbourhoods, however, were never successful in retaining their populations.

Successive waves of European and other nationality groups moved through the quasi-village environment of the American immigrant neighbourhood. In the process of urbanization, immigrant populations gradually lost themselves in the anonymous environment of other residential sections where they established themselves individually as members of the urban community at large without intermediate in-group loyalties. Since the cessation of large-scale immigration to the United States in 1924, these village-like immigrant communities have gradually evanesced. Some nationality groups moved to secondary settlements of higher status in a more Americanized, i.e., urbanized, environment; others lost control over their members in the younger generation who spread wide and far over the entire city.

Suburban real estate developments have attempted, at times, to provide their customers with an arrangement of construction that promised village comforts lost in the large city. With a village green and possibly a swimming-pool, a community centre or a country club in the middle of the settlement, and a protecting wall surrounding the entire area, these "guaranteed neighbourhoods" found their greatest advantage in the exclusion of others than the residential population from expensive recreational facilities. They promised protection against invasion by lower status groups. They guaranteed permanence of the family residence unendangered by the degrading influence of undesirable association.

Such village construction in the parkland of the dormitory suburb serves only the purpose of segregation without necessarily creating that overlapping and intertwining of economic and social interests in the resident group characteristic for true village structures. As a matter of fact, residential anonymity reaches its highest degree in the suburban settlement of advanced status groups. Neighbouring, in this environment, tends to be limited to the children as the only constant users of joint recreational facilities.

Rapid urban growth, of course, ensnares actual village communities in the orbit of urban extension, either at the periphery of the growing metropolis or in the midst of vast connurbations. Again, true village structures are lost as peasants and farmers turn into commuting city workers, as close economic interdependence fails to coincide with residential propinquity, and as the common interests of the residents are reduced to the private or consumption aspects of their lives.

Thus, while actual village structures are gradually being lost in the urban environment, the efforts of the planner point in the opposite direction. The planner endeavours to revive village structures in the city. He promotes a type of neighbourhood planning which by the arrangement of construction, by landscaping and by the provision of a full scope of services for purposes of everyday living, by visual separation of the area from adjacent territories and its orientation inwards towards the playground—and other recreational facilities offer the physical setting for the development of social relations typical for the village rather than the city. The reason for this anachronism lies in the attempt to stem the tide of social disorganization which—like delinquency, divorce, crime, suicide and vice—is attributed to the anonymity of urban living.

The planned neighbourhood in the city is considered a substitute for those informal means of social control assumed to keep the villager and the small town dweller in line, forcing him—through gossip, ridicule, contempt and ostracism—into the wholesome strait-jacket of provincial conformity. Two questions arise at this juncture:

(1) Whether it is indeed these informal means of social control that keep the small town clean from undesirable symptoms of social disorganization, and

(2) Whether the typical city dweller is susceptible to a transfer of these means of social control to the urban environment.

To both questions, our considered answer is "No."

Small town and village people are made to conform to socially approved behaviour by the inescapability of economic pressures. The overlapping of numerous economic as well as social relationships within a limited geographical area gives to even the most superficial of social contacts economic significance. Any displeasure aroused within the sphere of leisure-time activities might have economic repercussions. The people with whom financial negotiations are entertained are the same with whom the villager rubs elbows in his private life. If the minister's son steals apples, he might find that he did so in the orchard of that member of the congregation who decides about his father's reappointment. If the local grocer becomes negligent in his church attendance, a malicious whispering campaign may cost him a lot of patronage. Informal means of social control—such as gossip and spying upon each other—are certainly at work. But they could remain powerless were it not for the fact that they are backed up by economic pressures in an environment where confinement in space forces all residents either to buy from or sell to each other.

The low level of social disorganization in the non-urban environment does not necessarily reflect upon social controls in the village, the small town and the farm. Delinquents bent upon a criminal career sooner or later vanish from the small town environment and move to the city. They move because of economic pressures exerted upon them and their families. All non-conformists tend to withdraw from an environment in which their deviant behaviour is easily discovered. They move to the city where employment is not dependent upon the private conduct of the individual.

What are the chances for the transfer of these controls to the urban environment? Without proof to the contrary, we must be sceptical about their efficacy in the city. Even in the best-planned urban neighbourhood, economic pressures upon the private conduct of the individual are lacking. Whether informal social contacts by themselves will turn the trick of reducing deviant behaviour has yet to be shown. In the small town, the combination of economic with social contacts keeps the individual in line. This combination is absent from the urban neighbourhood planned for the private spheres of daily living only.

Even in leisure-time activities, the typical city dweller is not at all prone to limit himself to contacts with neighbours dwelling in close propinquity to his own home. Apart from very special situations such as recent arrival to the city with few pre-established personal or institutional contacts, or apart from special local conditions with numerous small children in families thus restricted in their movements, apart from such special situations the city dweller tends to take advantage of his unique privilege to roam far and wide in search of a select group of friends and select recreational facilities to serve his very special needs for entertainment and self-expression.

The "freedom of the city" is the freedom to choose from innumerable potential social contacts. Social contacts are not forced upon the city dweller on the basis of residential propinquity. It is doubtful that the city dweller will ever forgo the privilege of association by choice. Under the circumstances, many planned neighbourhoods will never function as cohesive social units. The generous provision of park- and play-space within the confines of the planned neighbourhood may well be enjoyed as an unusual asset of the individual dwelling unit. Still, the neighbourhood and its facilities may fail to promote that experience of belonging which the planner—following the example of the village and the small town—tries to reproduce in the large city.

II. NEIGHBORING PATTERNS

To assess the city dweller's readiness to avail himself of the facilities provided in the conventional neighbourhood unit plan, we have to know about his propensity to "neighbour" under conditions of planned or unplanned urban environment. Such information is sorely lacking. Most neighbourhood planning has proceeded on the basis of foregone conclusions.

Experimental research about actual neighbourhood experiences has provided the author with two types of pertinent documentation. Family contact patterns were ascertained by way of interview in both Milwaukee and Madison, Wisconsin. In addition, students of the University of Wisconsin were induced to write about their individual neighbourhood experiences with the help of a Problem Guide. The materials so collected cover a wide range of actual neighbourhood experiences in communities of different size and families of different composition. No attempts were made to apply sampling methods that would have provided reliable conclusions. The intent of this research was truly "experimental." It was devised to produce that familiarity with a new field of investigation without which the formulation of pertinent hypotheses is impossible. The resultant conceptualization of the field of neighbourhood study appears on the following pages.

The empirical approach to our problem may concern itself with either

(1) Neighbourhood consciousness, or
(2) Neighbouring behaviour.

At closer scrutiny, neighbourhood consciousness reveals itself as an elusive phenomenon. Residents in a limited residential area of Milwaukee were asked what they considered "their" neighbourhood. Fifty-three out of 197 interviewees responded by pointing to an area of not more than a city block. Another 78 of the interviewees referred to an area of more than seven blocks. Obviously, these two groups did not have the same thing in mind when talking about their neighbourhood. Nearly all answers to this question were introduced with expressions of doubt such as "I don't know," "never thought about it," etc. These people were not only vague about the subject of discussion, but felt actually forced to make a choice between different types of experiences to which the term "neighbourhood" could be applied.

The neighbourhood may be considered as either a geographical or a social unit. As a geographical unit, the neighbourhood is considered a contiguous territory in which close neighbourly relations exist. As a social unit, the neighbourhood refers to social relations which may or may not pre-empt a contiguous city area. Neighbourhood consciousness as a social experience is subject to different interpretations.

WHAT DO YOU CONSIDER "YOUR" NEIGHBOURHOOD?
(*Responses from a residential environment
in the city of Milwaukee*)

One block or under	53
Two to three blocks	12
One square block	14
Three to six blocks	11
Two square blocks	13
Seven to ten blocks	20
Eleven to twenty blocks	21
Over twenty blocks	37
Whole city	2
Area outside neighbourhood	4
No neighbourhood	10

To consider the neighbourhood as a phenomenon anchored in the mind, rather than a phenomenon located in an area clearly delineated in space, a phenomenon resting in prevailing attitudes, customs and preferences, rather than a certain number of square miles of real estate, such shift in our thinking about the neighbourhood presents a departure from the customary approach. Uncritically, the neighbourhood has been discussed as a unit that combines both spatial and social characteristics. For purposes of analysis, we have to separate from each other the social and the spatial aspect of the phenomenon under observation. Only in this manner can we do justice to the practical problem that consists of placing these two aspects in best possible relationship to each other.

From the same urban environment, we receive most contradictory statements about neighbourhood experiences and neighbourhood activities prevailing in the area. The same residential area will be assessed very differently by people living at close distance from each other. More than that: neighbourhood experience is under the influence of individual dynamics. It does not change only from individual to individual but undergoes continuous changes in the individual life history. Neighbouring means something different at elementary-school age, at high-school age, at the age of family formation and in old age.

Furthermore, neighbourhood experiences may be associated by the same individual with different dimensions of social participation. Education and occupation, informal and organized leisure-time activities may lead to different clusters of social contacts which—rightly or wrongly —are referred to by the term "neighbourhood relations." These distinctions will stand out more clearly in our discussion of neighbouring behaviour.

If the existence of neighbourhood relations is to be based on overt behaviour, we must focus on behaviour that establishes social contact. We ask ourselves to what extent these social contacts remain confined to a contiguous city area. To make a "true" neighbourhood, one further condition would have to be satisfied. The neighbour—according to the history of the word—means literally near-dweller. Residential propinquity, therefore, is a necessary prerequisite to neighbourhood formation.

In the early cities of Western Civilization, residential propinquity led unavoidably to social interrelationship. In the farming environment, near-dwellers depended upon each other for help in emergency situations. City living diminished the exchange of mutual help among those living close to each other. In the city, distances were not such as to prohibit help from others than those living nearby in the large population settlement. Near-dwellers in the city were held together in the city by co-operative municipal function. Neighbourhood groups developed social cohesion by assuming collectively the responsibility for urban defence, water supply, fire protection, etc. In the course of the centuries since medieval city foundation, such responsibilities were gradually centralized and placed upon the shoulders of the urban community at large. Deprived of definite service functions, the urban neighbourhood retained only the loose bonds of informal social contacts which previously had flourished as adjuncts to decentralized urban self-government.

Even the informal social relations between neighbours in the city are withering away to-day. Many informal social relations take the city dweller far away from his family residence. The same is certainly true for formal social relations which carry the city dweller to the residential, commercial and industrial sections of town.

It is not necessary to demonstrate that the dormitory suburb is far removed from urban places of employment. It is more interesting to show that even such important functions as shopping and worship have been far removed from the range of what might properly be called a contiguous residential neighbourhood.

The extension of shopping relations beyond the confines of the residential neighbourhood is dependent upon new developments in urban food distribution. It is dependent upon improved storage facilities in the individual family home in the form of sizeable refrigerators or freeze lockers. It is dependent upon the availability of private motor-transportation. It is dependent, finally, upon the concentration of commercial food distribution in the hands of large chain-stores able to offer lower prices than the local grocery store. Weekly rather than daily shopping needs are carried beyond the confines of the individual neighbourhood. We venture to guess, however, that the volume of weekly shopping is continuously being enlarged at the cost of daily shopping. The long-term destiny of the local grocery store is easy to predict.

Worship is not necessarily confined within the residential neighbourhood. Due to prevailing heterogeneities, it takes more people than those living in easy walking distance from each other, to provide sufficient numbers for the operation of a church. Urban residential settlement is not based on denominational segregation. Consequently, church membership must reach out beyond spatial proximity to the individual church building. Those affiliated to a certain religious denomination are too sparsely settled in the urban fabric to draw desired facilities for worship close to all individual family homes.

Similar conditions prevail in other urban activities. If we consider all city contacts of the individual family, the limited importance of "neighbouring" becomes immediately apparent. The activity radius of the individual family extends over the entire city. The family picks and chooses from what the city has in store for it. In the process of choice, proximity to the family residence is obviously not the only principle of selection.

Still, family contacts are not spread at random over the entire urban fabric. They tend to cluster in characteristic patterns. . . .

· · · · · ·

Seen within this broader framework of family contact patterns, the urban "neighbourhood" appears as a special case within the pattern of selective contact clusters. It forms a selective contact cluster, with the added criterion of being contained in close proximity to the family residence. It becomes an empirical question, then, what contact terminals are—and under what conditions—contained close to the urban residence.

Our observations, then, reveal a phenomenon closely related to neighbouring although not identical with it: namely, the phenomenon of contact clusters established either close to the family home or close to any of the more important contact points in the city area. They are not neighbourhoods proper because this term cannot be divorced from the circumstance of "near-dwelling" or from "proximity to residential location." Different walking distance areas, not necessarily close to the family home, gain social significance for the city dweller.

Walking distance areas tend to be of either of the five following types:

(1) Residential.
(2) Occupational.
(3) Educational.
(4) Commercial.
(5) Associational.

They shall be so designated according to the most frequent activity around which other contact points are clustered. In practice, an overlapping of several important activities within one and the same walking distance area will be the rule rather than the exception. The reason for the formation of such contact clusters is found in the ease of communication between one contact point and the others. It is invited also by the initiation of contacts due to chance of physical presence. The dentist close to the place of work and the ice-cream parlour close to the high school are most likely preferred to others in less accessible location. Different recreational facilities in close proximity to each other appeal to the same patronage.

In the course of the individual life cycle, the total contact pattern of the individual city dweller is subject to continuous change. Before the contact pattern reaches out to city areas far remote from the individual residence, and when they shrink again in old age, or as long as they are limited due to new arrival in the city, the "neighbourhood," i.e., the residential walking distance area, gains overwhelming importance by default. The pre-school child may be limited to contacts within the city block. The schoolchild branches out, and at high-school age, friendship and recreation and education pull the young city dweller out over a considerable section of the city. Occupational activities establish new clusters of contacts close to place of work. Shopping activities extend farther for adults and with the availability of private motor-transportation. Friendship established at work will open new contact areas for the individual city dweller in other residential areas than his own. Marriage and movements of friends and relatives and the city dweller himself furthermore extend and complicate the picture. In old age, the pattern is apt to shrink due to decreasing mobility and diminishing interests.

If the primary group is to be discovered as a socializing factor in the city environment, it will not necessarily have to be tied to the residential neighbourhood. Close and intimate contacts are established in those contact areas of the city which gain significance for the individual not only due to number of repetitive contacts and waking hours spent in this environment, but in addition due to the importance of different overlapping social contacts.

III. FROM NEIGHBORHOOD TO CITY PLANNING

Unfortunately, the endeavour to reactivate primary group relations in the large modern city has been tied to the assumption that such primary group relations are worth promoting only in the vicinity of the family home. Our thinking about social relations in the city has been dominated by the spatial dimension. A small town culture trait has thus been superimposed upon the urban environment. In the small town, the coincidence of intense social relations with proximity to the individual residence can be taken for granted. This need not be so in the city. In the city, man has gained the freedom of making social contacts with little regard to geographical distance.

The city offers opportunities to select social contacts from a large number of people and facilities gathered in the urban environment and connected by convenient and rapid means of transportation. These conditions permit the city dweller to pick and choose the social relations he wants to bother with. He does not find, like the small town dweller, the opportunities for personal and institutional contacts limited to the walking-distance area surrounding his living quarters. Social relations are not thrust upon him. He enjoys the freedom of choice.

City planning is needed in view of limitations in the urban transportation system. Transportation may be inconvenient or unduly time-consuming. For these reasons, the arrangement in space of different urban construction has to be carefully planned. Exclusive concentration upon neighbourhood planning, i.e., the planning of the walking-distance area around the individual family home, neglects those manifold opportunities which alone justify the urban way of life, which have led to city formation and which draw the farmer and the small town dweller into cityward migrations. One-sided attention to residential neighbourhood planning runs the danger of ignoring fundamental advantages that led to large population settlements in the first place. It clashes with the attitude of the typical city dweller who wants to roam within the entire urban fabric in search for occupational, educational, recreational and associational opportunities, assisted by an efficient system of transportation that releases him from the fetters of spatial confinement.

We have not yet freed ourselves, however, in thought and action, in scientific observation and planning, from domination by the spatial dimension. Preparatory to planning, urban sociology starts with the observation of "natural areas" in the urban environment and promotes the correction of minor inadequacies. The full scope of city planning invites the analysis not of urban environment as it has grown at random.

It challenges the social scientist and the planner to deal with more elementary data. These data may be found in individual and family contact needs.

Such contact needs may reach out for either informal or formal personal relations. By and large, informal personal relations call for the proximity of certain residential units to each other. Formal personal relations, on the other hand, are tied to and carried out within commercial and public urban construction. For planning purposes, we have therefore to ascertain

(1) The spread of family contact patterns in the city.
(2) The service radius of commercial and public facilities in the city.

The purpose of functional city planning can be no other than to relate to each other family contact needs and the service areas of commercial and public facilities. They have to be related to each other in such a manner as to minimize inconvenient and time-consuming transportation.

In a well-structured urban environment services and people must be related to each other in an economical manner. Optimal conditions can be obtained by the promotion of walking-distance areas which tend to grow out of individual adjustments to the urban environment anyway. In terms of urban construction, such walking-distance areas require the clustering of commercial and public construction. Such groupings of urban construction cannot be called "neighbourhoods" because most of them will be located at longer than walking distance from the majority of family residences which they serve. These walking-distance areas have one thing in common, however, with our concern for urban neighbourhoods. They establish walking-distance areas at some maximum distance from the city residence. Here they are contained in walking distance from each other, albeit not in walking distance from the residences of most city dwellers. The city planner must concern himself with the relative desirability of different possible clusterings of commercial and public facilities in the urban environment.

The service radius of urban facilities is not entirely a matter of choice and desired convenience. If it were so, every city dweller would want to have all services located either next door or—if they entail nuisances— at close distance hidden by a pleasant group of trees. To provide for the satisfaction of such needs is economically impossible. To operate economically, with a profit or at reasonable cost, all urban services demand recruitment areas of different size from which to draw their clientele. The more specialized the type of service, the fewer the people who avail themselves of the service at all, and the less frequently they will make use of the service, the larger the service area will have to be.

To establish walking-distance areas in the city environment, the city planner is charged with the task of combining into a cluster of construction commercial and public facilities dependent upon service areas of equal size. A number of concentric service areas will thus be made to overlap. With increasing specialization of service, ever larger areas will be required to provide sufficient patronage. The deciding factor for the combination of some and not other services is the service radius of these facilities, which also determines the distance at which these service clusters will have to be located from each other to operate efficiently.

While a well-structured urban environment may thus be planned for, an environment that does not leave any service loopholes in the urban fabric and meets the demand for "walking-distance areas" at varying distances from the city residence, the need for informal personal relations is thereby not considered. Informal social relations call for proximity to each other of those residences the occupants of which want to associate frequently, at a minimum of inconvenience and time spent.

The scope of neighbourhood planning becomes apparent if it is realized that either of two conditions must be fulfilled to encourage the city dweller to limit his informal associations to near-dwellers. The city dweller must be either:

(1) Willing to limit the majority of his leisure-time activities to association with those people who live by chance next door or in easy walking distance, i.e., he must be void of personal or activity interests that will draw him to some other location, leaving the planned neighbourhood without social function; or he must be

(2) Willing to congregate within the residential neighbourhood with like-minded and like-interested people, i.e., he and his friends must stand ready to move to put life into well-planned neighbourhood construction.

Such conditions are the exception in the modern city. It is doubtful, therefore, that even a semblance of village life will find acceptance in the modern metropolis.

⋘⋙

75. The Strangest Place In Chicago *

SOMETIMES A DESCRIPTIVE PIECE of writing or a story brings to life
with startling impact ideas that otherwise seem dull and mechanical,
commonplace, or meaningless. In this article John Bartlow Martin performs such a feat. He never uses the social science terms
"invasion," "succession," or "segregation." He does not discuss
rentals, slum areas as such, city planning, or race discrimination in
its varied aspects. He simply describes a building in its physical
aspects, its locale, the life that goes on there, and the differences
between that place some thirty years ago and today. He makes it
live for us. Invasion and succession! That's what happened here!

FROM THE CHICAGO LOOP, where sunlight off the lakefront strikes the
shining towers, State Street runs straight south, wide, busy with streetcars and heavy trucks. Quickly the buildings get shabby—little stores
selling auto parts, a junkyard crammed with rusting wreckage. The city
is harsh: concrete streets, brick building walls, black steel viaducts.
Beyond 22nd Street the faces of the people are black. This is the South
Side Negro section. Here the street is quieter, the sun is hazy and
dirty and pale, the sky is a network of trolley wires. Across an expanse
of new-turned earth stretches a new public housing project, with a
playyard for the children, and at 32nd Street begins the new campus of
the Illinois Institute of Technology, sleek brick-and-glass buildings surrounded by new trees and new grass. And just beyond the Institute
rises a great gray hulk of brick, four stories high, topped by an ungainly
smokestack, ancient and enormous, filling half the block north of 34th
Street between State and Dearborn. It is the Mecca Building.

Let us note its setting. Across State Street are a cleaning shop, a
barber shop, a grocery, the Railroad Men's Social Club, McClain's Hair
Goods, a Bar-B-Q, the office of H. Young the Icer, the Church of
God & Saints of Christ in an old storefront. An old man pulls a
handcart filled with junk across an empty lot. From a deep hole
tunneled under the sidewalk emerges the head of a little Negro boy,

---

* John Bartlow Martin. This is an abbreviated version of "The Strangest Place
in Chicago," which originally appeared in Harper's Magazine, December, 1950.
Reprinted by permission of the author and Harold Ober Associates.

The author (b. 1915) is a journalist. Writer of real-crime articles for Saturday
Evening Post and Harper's. His article "The Blast in Centralia No. 5" was a piece
of masterful reporting. Author, Call It North Country, the Story of Upper Michigan;
Indiana, an Interpretation; Butcher's Dozen and Other Murders.

playing. The sidewalk is cracked and broken. Nearby are rickety wooden tenements.

The Mecca Building is U-shaped. The dirt courtyard is littered with newspapers and tin cans, milk cartons and broken glass. Pigeons roost on a car on blocks. A skinny white dog huddles in a doorway. Iron fire escapes run up the building's face and ladders reach from them to the roof. There are four main entrances, two on Dearborn and two on State Street. At each is a gray stone threshold and over each is carved "The Mecca." The Mecca was constructed as an apartment building in 1891, a splendid palace, a showplace of Chicago. Today it is still an apartment building and a showplace but of a very different sort. It has become one of the most remarkable Negro slum exhibits in the world. Let us pass through the arched doorway of the Mecca; let us see what the Mecca looks like inside, see who the people in it are and how they live, whence they came and why they stay.

Inside, a powerful odor assails the visitor at once, musty, heavy, a smell compounded of urine and stale cooking and of age, not necessarily an unpleasant odor but a close powerful one, which, like that of marijuana, once smelled is never forgotten. The stone slab step is hollowed. The lower part of the walls of the vestibule once was covered with marble but now the marble has been stripped away in ragged patches, revealing naked brick and mortar. It is dark here. Ahead stretches a corridor; it is like a tunnel, it seems endless and it is indeed a block long, running all the way to the Dearborn Street entrance; down its whole length hang only five light bulbs, glowing feebly in the gloom. Tan paint is peeling from the wall, the doors of apartments open into the corridor. This is the base of the U in the U-shaped building.

The arms of the U are identical. They are great halls, each lit by a skylight four stories overhead which, because of the dirt that has accumulated on the glass through years of neglect, admits the kind of unreal light found underseas. This light slants down in great long angling shafts filled with floating dust, shifting as the sun moves across the sky, falling in fitful patches on the floor. Around the walls run three balconies guarded by ornate wrought-iron grillwork, and off these balconies open the doors to the apartments, like tiers of cells in a prison cellblock. The floor in the center of the well is of hardwood, splintered now, and beneath the balconies it is of tile, broken in many places. A janitor with a wheelbarrow is slowly patching the tile with concrete; his shovel makes a rasping, scraping sound. From somewhere in the building comes always the sound of distant human voices—women talking, a baby squalling, children screaming, men muttering, no words distinguishable. Spittle splats flatly on the tile floor, falling from a great height, spat by a man or a woman standing on an upper balcony. All day long people stand at the balconies, leaning on the wrought-iron railings with hands clasped out over them, gazing out at other people facing them across the well in silence, gazing down at the floor far below, spitting, small human figures in a vast place, two or three on each of the four floors, occasionally calling back and forth to one another but most of the time just standing silent. The building is never entirely quiet, not even very late at night, since so many people live here; but it is so vast that it seems quiet, even amid uproar.

In the center on the ground floor is a long narrow bank of mailboxes, tarnished brass, 176 of them. One has thirteen names on it, including seven different family names, indicating that thirteen adults expecting mail occupy that particular apartment. Late in the morning the post-man comes, a man in blue. Three tenants wait respectfully at the side while he distributes the mail. On the balcony above, two men leaning on the railing watch him critically: "He'll never get it all done doing it one at a time," and, "He's a new man." At last he finishes, and tenants emerge from their apartments to get their mail. From a high balcony a toddler throws a chunk of broken tile; it bounces on the floor by the mailboxes. A stooped old woman wearing a black sweater and black shawl, only her hair and her eyeballs white, moves slowly and painfully in the shadows beneath the balcony, keeping close to the wall as long as possible, touching it with bony fingers, and only leaving it when she must to venture across the open floor to the mailbox; gets her mail, then retreats along the wall to the stairs, where a man steps aside, saying kindly, "You come down to see what you got, didn't you?" and she says, in a gasping voice, "I'm going take my good time," then begins to ascend, pulling herself up by the railing, first her right foot up one step, then the left slowly after it, her body bent so low that her face almost touches the next step, stopping at the landing to rest and stare at the peeling walls with watery, half-blind eyes. Near the mailboxes three children are jumping rope, using a doubled rope, two boys swinging the two long strands in sweeping arcs while a girl rocks to and fro at one side to get into the rhythm before jumping in. Children ride battered tricycles across the floor, safe here from the traffic of the streets. On a balcony children are playing store, using a cardboard box. One of them throws a fistful of paper over the railing and it flutters down: policy slips, there must be a policy station here.

The wind blows in off Dearborn Street and a young woman neat in black enters, walking a leashed dog and humming a hymn. Somewhere a child is crying over and over, "Mummy, Mummy." In the long dark corridor a dog is nosing at garbage from an upset garbage can. From somewhere comes a clatter, perhaps of a falling garbage-can lid, and the high mad cackling laughter of an old man. A very young child standing on the third floor balcony urinates through the ornate iron grillwork and the urine falls to the ground floor far below and a woman calls to him, "Don't you do that, you got no right to do that, I'm going to tell your mother." The ice man comes wearing a leather protector on his shoulder and back, carrying a cake of ice that gleams whitely against his black face and hat. A woman calls from the third floor, "Bring fifty pounds to 304½," and he plods to the stairs.

In the shadows against a pillar marked with match-strikes leans a man, his shirt-collar buttoned but without a necktie, his hat-brim slanting low over his scarred face, a cigarette slanting from his mouth; he is just standing there watching. How many people live here? He laughs. "I don't know." Two thousand? "Oh, more than that. There's 176 apartments and some of 'em's got seven rooms and they're all full." A heavy round-faced man in a long white apron holding a ball-peen hammer approaches: "You are visiting some of the historic sites of the city? You found one all right. If it don't fall in on you while you're lookin'." How many people live here? "That," he says, "is a mystery. You'll find them sleeping in bathtubs, sleeping in the kitchen under the sink, anywhere they can sleep." Nobody, in truth, knows how many people inhabit the Mecca Building. The janitor, Jimmy Sanders, estimates 2,300; the Democratic precinct captain, William Patrick Fitzgerald, who has lived here eighteen years, estimates 1,400; the owner doesn't know. All the inhabitants except one woman are Negroes. The Mecca Building contains more people than most Chicago precincts; indeed, it constitutes a precinct in itself, the 27th Precinct of the 2nd Ward.

On the third floor an old woman stands by the railing, a towel wound round her head, a big gold ring on her finger. Watching dispassionately as children run in from school for lunch, their screams ringing piercingly through the building, she says judiciously, "That size runs to roller skates," and then, "When I first came here they used to control the children. White people hadn't been gone so long, 1917 it was. They used to have a policeman here nights, you could hear a needle drop. Now they's shooting here five times a night. Them young men and the young girls is the worst. I'd move out tonight if they'd find me a house. I moved out for a while once but I came back to have company, my daughter lives here and my granddaughter was born here," and she turns and shuffles into her flat.

In the flat, wallpaper hangs from the walls in great sheets. Clean newspapers are spread on the floor. Over the dresser are some artificial flowers, and a transparent plastic wrapper covers the bed. The sideboard, radio, and table are cluttered with family photographs. Mottoes and pictures hang on the walls, a picture of Jesus Christ and a crucifix put out by a liquor store, a plaque, "My Help cometh from the Lord," and also secular shrines: a large frame holding the pictures of Abraham Lincoln and Frederick Douglass flanked by Booker T. Washington, Paul Laurence Dunbar, W. E. B. DuBois, and other race leaders. And a framed faded campaign picture of Franklin D. Roosevelt. She calls Lincoln "Abraham." She was born in Alabama. She is bent and stooped, aged. She says, "I live here all by myself, me and my Lord," and then, as her visitor departs, she touches his arm and says gently, "Do you know anything about that man we call Jesus, do you know him personally, you ought to get in touch with him." Outside her door a teen-age boy is standing at the balcony railing, trying to spit clear across to the other side.

In the long first-floor corridor the janitor passes, Jimmy, a short squat man in a leather cap and jacket, ambling along with a Yankee drill in his hand. "I'm the maintenance man," he says. "I do a little of everything—work a little, fight a little, sleep a little, play a little." Right now he is accompanying the rent collector, a white man, a wiry Scot named John. "I go around with him," Jimmy says, shifting the stub of his dead cigar to the other corner of his mouth, "because the young fellas in the building think he's got money with him." About a year ago the young fellows robbed an insurance collector of $17. The rent collector, John, says, "I lost all my hair fighting with these people," and laughs. Actually, he has little trouble collecting rents, which are cheap. His troubles are of a different sort: he and Jimmy fight a hopeless rearguard action against decay and vandalism. "Last night they shot out the light bulbs," says Jimmy. "And the windows—in the last year I bet I put in over two hundred windows. They break 'em fast as you put 'em in." Who does it? "Outsiders, most of it. And the kids here. The kids get to playin' and throwin' at one another and first thing you know they break the glass. There's nothin' you can do about it. You can't kill one 'cause he broke the glass."

As the rent collector walks along, a woman calls from the third-floor balcony, "Hold your head up, John, John, hold your head up, I want to talk to you," but John plods on, grinning secretly. A sign by the basement stairs reads, "Put All Complaints in Mail Box." Near the State Street entrance another janitor has temporarily left his job of cementing a broken place in the floor and is stooping over at an apartment door, digging with a knife at something in the door. He gets it out: a bullet. "That's a thirty-eight," he says, turning it over in his hand, shiny and twisted. Then, to a woman who has come to the door, "They try to shoot you out last night?" She laughs. "Yeh, try to kill me. Like shootin' rabbits in a swamp down yonder." He says, "They was really shootin' here last night. Some of 'em shootin' for fun, some of 'em fightin'. That's every night around here. Couple of 'em got shot the other night." Any ever killed? "Oh, yes, one got killed summer before last up there in that corner," pointing upward. Why? "I don't know."

Down the stairs comes a man on crutches, his left leg off above the knee, his pants leg pinned up, coming down the steps, the crutch and his good leg visible first, then the man, thin, wearing white pants and a brown coat and hat; he walks diagonally past the mailboxes to the grocery, pausing to adjust his pipe.

High on the fourth west gallery, close up under the skylight, the balcony seems narrow. Two boys wrestle on it, and one falls heavily against the iron railing, which trembles but holds firm. It is four stories down to the ground floor; nobody ever heard of a child falling. An old woman is sweeping the floor. High up here at the north end a dozen young men and women are congregated, well-dressed, two of the men off to one side leaning idle on the railing and peering sullenly down, the others close together, laughing, fooling around with each other, the girls in tight white sweaters, the young men in snapbrim hats and suitcoats over sweaters

•   •   •   •   •   •

When the Mecca Building was constructed it was considered one of the largest and finest apartment buildings in Chicago if not in America. It catered (almost needless to say) to a white clientele. But after 1900 the Negro migration to Chicago forced the black belt to expand, and by 1912 the Mecca Building was the home of the Negro elite—doctors, lawyers, business men.

A woman who lives there still, Mrs. Florence Clayton, arrived in 1916, and she remembers, "There were carpets on the stairs and halls. There were goldfish in the fountain. On the first floor there were lounge chairs and outdoors we had a flower garden and beautiful trees and green grass, you could go out there, oh, it was lovely. The courtyard was all fenced in and there was a lovely walk through the flowers."

The building started to deteriorate during the 1917-18 war. So did the whole neighborhood. Booming war industries pulled thousands of Negroes to Chicago. The luckier ones abandoned the region of 35th and State to the poor and the wicked. The black-and-tans where

Chicago jazz flowered were right here. Jimmy, the janitor, recalls, "There were lots of fights and cuttings. Building was full of prostitutes. I saw a man throw a prostitute over the third floor railing—from the third floor to the first floor. Didn't hurt her much. She only weighed ninety pounds, kind of light. Finally one of the pimps killed the building watchman. Did it over a woman. And she wasn't even living with him." Jimmy pushes his leather cap back off his forehead. "That about ended it, though. They got a new watchman and he was a killer. He was just a little man but he had great big eyes and he'd shoot you with either hand. He had a cemetery of his own before he died. He only killed nine people—between the basement here and that wire fence. The building got kind of decent after that—families, working people."

And then the Depression came along, and the wicked left, and almost none but the poor remained. The Depression was awful in the black belt. About 1932 the bottom fell out. One woman who lived here then recalls, "The building was partly empty. One lady told me she was sitting down on the curb and the police passed and it was cold and they asked her what was the matter and she said she'd been set out and they told her to come on in here and the first flat she'd find, sit down. They carried her to court later but they didn't make her get out, they couldn't; people had no work to do then. It was always warm and nice in here during the Depression."

The Depression accounts for the presence today of the building's only white tenant, a heavy, soft-faced, white-haired woman of sixty-six. "I'd been a housekeeper at a hotel and one of my maids, a colored girl, she was married to a white doctor and they lived here in the Mecca Building. I couldn't find a job, I just got stuck, I couldn't make it, and they took me in." Some of the Mecca inhabitants who moved in while they were on relief are now earning good money in the steel mills or on Pullman cars and one or two earn upward of $5,000 a year, but they are imprisoned here by the scarcity of dwellings for Negroes. A few of the long-time tenants remain by choice, oddly proud of the building. A few earn money by living there—they sublet rooms in their apartments for as much as $12 a week. The janitor Jimmy says, "Every day people come in, many as ten or twelve a day, lookin' for a place, they been walkin' the street, lookin' for some place to go, say, 'Janitor, if you can get me an apartment in here I'll give you $100,' but there ain't none."

There are several women's clubs in the building, such as the Old-Age Pensioners Club and the Twelve Tribes. Fitzgerald, the Democratic precinct captain, has been elected sweetheart of these. Fitzgerald, a

neat, well-dressed, youngish man, has said, "If there's a weddin' I'm
there, if there's a death I'm there, if there's a birth I'm there. I had a
baby born in my car a while back, trying to get the mother to the
hospital." Fitzgerald is a court bailiff by day. The Mecca precinct
has voted Democratic since 1932. Like the other tenants, Fitzgerald
worries about the children. "In summertime the police chase them off
the street. One day I come home and the police had backed up a
wagon ready to take a whole load to the station for standing in front of
the building. I had to put a stop to it. I had three ball clubs last
summer and got uniforms for 'em all."

In a vacant store on the ground floor is the Mecca Center, for children. Nobody knows how many children are being raised in the Mecca
Building but most people guess five hundred, and now at 4:30 P.M. on a
Thursday fifteen of the five hundred are in the Mecca Center. The
Center is a big square bare room, a dais at one side, a great clutter of
dusty newspapers behind a desk, a piano and a windup Victrola against
one wall, a tom-tom and Indian heads in the display window. Two
older boys are playing Ping-pong and at a small table two younger ones
are playing checkers but the rest of the younger ones, probably from
nine to twelve years old, are chasing each other around the room, snap-
ping cap-guns at each other, and soon the checker game stops and all
thirteen of the younger ones are chasing each other, climbing over tables
and chairs, leaping through the air onto each others' backs, screaming
wildly; the Ping-pong players, older, proceed with their game, each with
an arm outstretched to fend off the littler kids, occasionally pausing to
take a cut at a near one's head; a dozen chairs stacked against a wall
collapse as a boy's body crashes into them. A man in a hat is standing
in a corner watching, saying vaguely, "She was supposed to come and
be a musical program but I ain't seen her come in."

On the wall is a program schedule allotting various hours of the week
to such activities as "Teen-Age Club," "Children's Story-Telling Hour,"
"Parents' Club Meeting." Right now, it is "Children's Game Period."
The man watching says sharply, "You—let that Victrola alone," to a
boy climbing onto it in order to leap onto another boy's back. A
woman arrives bustling in. "I teach music and dramatics and folk
dancing. I have about sixty enrolled. From six to eight we have singing and at nine physical culture and clubs." She is taking off her gloves,
as unmindful of the children as they are of her; the children are growing
more serious in their play, the temper has changed, ugliness has crept in,
they battle silently, not laughing or screaming, only panting hard. The
man is making plans to take some of them to the circus.

In one apartment in the building a woman and her husband are raising nine children, raising them in one room. This summer afternoon she is sitting in a chair by the door of the one room, her baby on the bed, evidently asleep but looking dead it is so thin and still, and the mother is saying, "It is hot at night, at night you burn up. My husband and I sleep in the bed. The kids sleep on the cot." The nine kids. They are from nine months to fifteen years in age. The room is eight feet by eleven. In it are one bed, one davenport, one radio, one light bulb, one picture, two straight wood chairs, one wicker table (on which stand a seashell, a jar of deodorant, and a can of face powder), one calendar. Back of the bed is a closet curtained with a rag. One necktie hangs on a nail in the wall. The plaster is broken. Her husband earns $45 a week as a machine operator. They pay $6 a week for this room. They have lived in this room four years.

The mother is twenty-nine years old. When she and her husband first came to Chicago they lived in one room on Wentworth Avenue, then in three rooms on Prairie Avenue until "the lady sold the building," then in five rooms elsewhere on Prairie Avenue again "till the lady sold the building," then in four rooms elsewhere on Prairie "till the man sold the building," then here. They came here on August 6, 1946. "My husband knew the man that had this apartment so he let us have a place in it that same evening. We were out on the street." They can find no other place to live. "I looked so much that I'm just disgusted about it. They say you're a citizen of Chicago and on votin' day they're right up to your door to vote. My husband, he wrote to the Mayor of Chicago and everyone else and I don't see no results," and she rises and fumbles behind a curtain on the window ledge and finds two letters. She is young, quick-moving, pretty; her teeth flash and she wears big gold earrings and she appears about the age of her oldest daughter, fifteen, who now comes in and stands in the doorway looking reproachful. One letter is a long form letter from the Chicago Housing Authority:

"Dear Friend,

". . . The housing projects now in operation have such lengthy waiting lists that no additional applications are being taken at this time. . . ." The other is a personal letter from a Housing Authority official: "Mayor Kennelly has referred to us for reply your letter of March 2, concerning your need for adequate housing. We are very sorry."

"All this stuff's just a racket," says the mother of nine. "They ain't doing nothing about it. Makes me sick." She hitches her chair around to face the wall. "After all, my husband works and makes an honest livin' and he do support his family the best that a workin' man can. His children do get clothes, the onliest kick that they can have is that they don't have no place to live. And that's not his fault." The baby on the bed stirs a little, then lies still again.

Until 1941 the Mecca Building was owned by a New York estate. The janitor Jimmy only once saw a representative of the estate. In 1941 the estate sold the Mecca to its next-door neighbor, the Illinois Institute of Technology. The Institute bought the building for only one purpose: to tear it down. The Institute was expanding its campus in accordance with a neat plan integrated with the neat plans of numerous other agencies for clearing the South Side slums. It wanted to replace the Mecca Building with a laboratory. But its plans ran head-on into an important need of the people who dwelt in the Mecca Building, the need for a place to live.

For nine years it has tried to evict them, taking them to court and warning them the Mecca is a firetrap. Thus far the tenants have managed to generate enough political pressure to stay. Recently, when the Institute again started eviction proceedings, State Senator C. C. Wimbish, a lawyer who has represented the tenants in court, said, "If they try to put these people out, they'll have a race riot down there on State Street and I intend to make it as tense as possible. Any roof is better than no roof."

It is quiet in the building on a summer morning, quiet as a tomb. Spit falls flatly on the ground floor, spat by a silent watcher high on the balcony, and in a dark corner recess on the topmost floor a young girl, pretty, wearing a tight white sweater, strains against a young man leaning on the wall. An old man in blue pajamas, his eyes wild and staring, his body very thin, totters along, clutching at the railing, saying in a high, cracked voice, to a visitor, "Call me a telephone number please, mister, will you call me a telephone number," but a large woman steps from a doorway and shakes her head at the visitor, making circling motions beside her temple, and moves to take the old man's arm, and seeing her he starts, as though to run, then weeps, and she leads him away. A puff of blue smoke hangs in the dead air on the second balcony where a man is leaning on the railing, smoking. A janitor collects garbage in a cart that rumbles on the broken tile like a tumbril. Everything echoes in the halls, voices are hard to comprehend, are confused with distant sounds.

A visitor twists the bell on Mrs. Griffin's apartment and she calls, "Who is it?" then unfastens the chain. Her mother is sitting by the window in the sun, as always. Mrs. Griffin says that when she got the most recent notice to vacate, she went house-hunting: "I found a place to buy at a real estate office way up on the North Side but no other colored people live right there, and I don't want to get bombed on," as indeed many Chicago Negroes have been when they tried to leave the black belt. She goes over beside her mother, who is rocking. "I think this housing situation is terrible, it's all politics, that's all. I'm not mad at the school. It's their property, we know that. I'm mad 'cause all this politics. Put 'em in office and they didn't did nothin'. They build streets and superhighways and recreation—not houses. They should turn that money loose and stop it—people has got to have some place to live. They gonna do *anything* if they don't."

She laughs, but does not sound amused: "They say they gonna place us somewhere. *Place* us! I don't wanta be placed anywhere myself. They might place me in some mudhole somewhere and I never did live in that," and she laughs again. Her mother mutters something. "I don't know what they going to do with us. After all, there's no use in pushing us around from one place to another, that's no way to live." And then, after a pause, "It's all so mean."

Her mother, rocking, has started muttering steadily; she is looking out the window, her head in its white lace cap bobbing gently up and down. What is Mrs. Griffin going to do?

"I don't know. I'll have to have a place for my mother. I couldn't tell you what I'm going to do, to save my neck." Her mother, rocking, begins to mutter louder, but her words are not intelligible, it is just a human voice, muttering, and it is impossible to tell whether in anger or in joy, it is only sound.

⌘⌘⌘⌘⌘

76. A Coming Citadel of Democracy *

MANY LOCAL VARIATIONS in the cultural definitions of required, prohibited, and permitted behavior are recognized as still existent throughout the South. Moreover, certain geographical, cultural, and historical uniformities set it off as a distinctive major region within American society. Nevertheless, as Benjamin E. Mays points out here, recent years have witnessed many changes in the accepted patterns of interracial relations. Although restricted to a discussion

* Benjamin E. Mays, . . . and the Pursuit of Happiness (National Urban League, 1951), pp. 18-19. Reprinted with permission of National Urban League, Inc., 1133 Broadway, New York 10, New York, and the author.

The author (b. 1895) is President, Morehouse College, Atlanta, Georgia. Outstanding leader in education and religion, often chosen delegate to world conferences.

of cultural changes in certain institutions, the selection illustrates the ecological concept of *region*. In selection 90 will be found a compact treatment of regional differences.

ONE WHO COMES to the United States or the South for the first time will not be able to see how the South is changing in the area of human relations. For example, a visitor from South Africa who came to More-house College recently, saw so much segregation in the South and so much discrimination in America that he told me that his three and a half months in the United States had convinced him that the Apartheid movement in South Africa is the best thing for South Africa. I was shocked and amazed at such a declaration.

But as one who was born in the deep South, left it for the first time at twenty to work in the North, and has lived all his life in the South except eight years in college and university in the East and West, I can write with authority about the changing South. When I do this I must make it plain that the South (and the North for that matter) has by no means solved its racial problem. But enough progress has been made for one to be encouraged. There is no need of despair.

The South is definitely changing. There is more regard for the Negro's person than there was two or three decades ago. The Negro is becoming a human being in the South. I remember when it was almost an unpardonable sin for one Negro to call another Negro "Mr.," "Mrs." or "Miss."

My wife and I were social workers in the deep South at one time. Because we called our Negro colleagues "Mrs." and "Miss" and because my wife wrote "Mr.," "Mrs." and "Miss" after her clients' names, we were reported to headquarters and accused of insisting on being "Mr." and "Mrs." We continued our practice of calling Negroes "Mrs." and "Miss" because we believed then and we do now that it is right to respect the person of every individual.

Frankly I do not believe these incidents would happen in the South today; if so it would be in isolated, backward sections and not in cities. Thousands of white people in the South give Negroes their proper titles and few would object to Negroes giving them to members of their own race. Even when "doctor" or "professor" is used to avoid using "Mr." this person would not try to tell Negroes what to call Negroes. "Boy," "Auntie," and "Uncle" are becoming relics of the past. Many southern newspapers do not hesitate to give Negro women their proper titles,

---

Highly successful lecturer in over one hundred colleges in the United States. Author, *The Negro Church* (with J. W. Nicholson) and *Seeking to Be Christian in Race Relations.*

carry pictures of outstanding Negroes and treat Negro news with increasing fairness. This is a tremendous change because it reflects a change of attitude toward the Negro and indicates that his person is being respected.

This change of attitude in the South reflects itself again in the area of public travel. I remember the time when it was almost dangerous [for Negroes] even to request Pullman accommodation in many areas of the South. It was certainly dangerous, at one time, to ride Pullman in the South. In 1923, enroute from Birmingham, Alabama, to St. Louis, Missouri, I was driven from my Pullman by a group of white passengers with guns. For a long time, Negroes got lower 13, which was a berth in the drawing room. Anything to get Negroes out of sight. All that is gone now. The only symbol of segregation on the Pullman today is the practice in some places to put Negro passengers on the end of the Pullman car—lower 1, 2, 11 or 12. Recently the Supreme Court ruled that segregation on the diner was unconstitutional. Many Negroes on through trains traveling from the North to the South ride unsegregated. The amazing thing is nobody is disturbed. In Pullman travel twenty-five years ago, every white passenger going through a car where a Negro was seated turned around and looked daggers at him and the look meant: "You are out of your place." A Negro passenger is not noticed now any more than white passengers. It is perfectly safe for Negroes to ride Pullman today anywhere in the South without embarrassment.

Two decades ago, the white primary was dominant and in most southern states Negroes could not vote. The Supreme Court has abolished the white primary and Negroes are voting all over the South. In many small towns and in some rural areas it is dangerous for Negroes to vote. But it is generally accepted in the South that Negroes are going to vote and are entitled to the ballot. When I was a boy lynching was an accepted institution in the South condoned by leading people. Today, lynching by mobs is rare and loudly condemned.

Perhaps the most significant change is in the area of education. When I was a boy it was dangerous for anyone in my section even to utter the word that a Negro school should be as good as the one for white pupils. Today, it is generally accepted by the white South that Negro schools should be just as good as those for whites. It is yet to be proved that equality can be achieved in education in a segregated system. Nevertheless, the South has come a long way in accepting the fact that it must give to its Negro citizens the same kind and quality of education that it provides for its white citizens. And great efforts are being made all over the South to improve the education given Negroes.

In 1925, few people, if any, would have believed that in 1950 Negroes would be enrolled in the State Universities of Louisiana, Arkansas, Oklahoma, Kentucky, Virginia, Texas, Maryland, and West Virginia. But they are there.

I am aware of the fact that most of these changes are not the result of voluntary acts on the part of the South. But the fact remains that a New South is emerging and it may yet become a citadel of real democracy unsurpassed by any section of the Western World.

⌘⌘⌘⌘⌘

77. Community and Association *

MacIver has in very recent years published three important works elaborating on the nature of the modern state. This selection clearly delineates the early analytical groundwork that was basic to these further elaborations. When the author wrote this, the modern totalitarian state with its dreadful tyrannies had not yet appeared. Yet so powerful is this sociological analysis of the nature of community and its clear-cut differentiations from the State as a refutation of the governmental theories upon which totalitarianism is based, that one finds difficulty in believing it was not written *after* the fact. The confusion of thought that identifies community as such with its instrument, the state, is here exposed, and the monstrous results of such identification are foreseen. Who, today, can question this statement? "The individual should not be summed up in his citizenship, otherwise the claim of citizenship will itself become a tyranny and its essential moral value be lost."

THE GENERAL RELATION OF COMMUNITY AND ASSOCIATION

ONE OF THE GREATEST of the difficulties which at the present day beset the social analyst is the confused nature of his vocabulary. Unlike the students of most other sciences he must accept the terms of everyday life. These terms are lacking in all precision, and if the sociologist

* Robert M. MacIver, *Community, A Sociology Study* (New York: The Macmillan Company, 1928), pp. 22-28. Reprinted by permission of the publisher and the author.

The author (b. 1882) is Lieber Professor of Political Philosophy and Sociology, Columbia University. Special Lecturer, Public Law and Government. Born in Stornoway, Scotland. Author, *Community* (received a Carnegie Award); *Society, Its Structure and Changes; Social Causation; Toward Abiding Peace; The Web of Government; The Ramparts We Guard.*

is to avoid disaster he must not hesitate to refine them to his own purposes. This is the case with the essential terms of our subject-matter, the terms society, community, association, and State. The looseness with which these terms are often used even by professed authorities is remarkable, and the results most unhappy. That must be our excuse if at the outset we insist, in spite of popular usage, on limiting each of these terms to a single and definite meaning.

Society, the most general term of all, I intend to use in a universal or generic sense to include every willed relationship of man to man. If, then, we distinguish community, association, and State from society, it must be by delimiting the former as special kinds or aspects of social fact. The essential distinction here involved, one of the utmost importance, is that between community and association.

By a community I mean any area of common life, village, or town, or district, or country, or even wider area. To deserve the name community, the area must be somehow distinguished from further areas, the common life may have some characteristic of its own such that the frontiers of the area have some meaning. All the laws of the cosmos, physical, biological, and psychological, conspire to bring it about that beings who live together shall resemble one another. Wherever men live together they develop in some kind and degree distinctive common characteristics—manners, traditions, modes of speech, and so on. These are the signs and consequences of an effective common life. It will be seen that a community may be part of a wider community, and that all community is a question of degree. For instance, the English residents in a foreign capital often live in an intimate community of their own, as well as in the wider community of the capital. It is a question of the degree and intensity of the common life. The one extreme is the whole world of men, one great but vague and incoherent common life. The other extreme is the small intense community within which the life of an ordinary individual is lived, a tiny nucleus of common life with a sometimes larger, sometimes smaller, and always varying fringe. Yet even the poorest in social relationships is a member in a chain of social contacts which stretches to the world's end. In the infinite series of social relationships which thus arise, we distinguish the nuclei of intenser common life, cities and nations and tribes, and think of them as *par excellence* communities.

An association is an organization of social beings (or a body of social beings as *organised*) for the pursuit of some common interest or interests. It is a determinate social unity built upon common purpose. Every end which men seek is more easily attained for all when all whom it concerns unite to seek it, when all co-operate in seeking it. Thus you may have an association corresponding to every possible interest of social beings. Community bubbles into associations permanent and transient, and no student of the actual social life of the present can help being struck by the enormous number of associations of every kind, political, economic, religious, educational, scientific, artistic, literary, recreative, philanthropic, professional, which to-day more than ever before enrich communal life.

A community is a focus of social life, the common living of social beings; an association is an organisation of social life, definitely established for the pursuit of one or more common interests. An association is partial, a community is integral. The members of one association may be members of many other and distinct associations. Within a community there may exist not only numerous associations but also antagonistic associations. Men may associate for the least significant or for the most significant of purposes; the association may mean very much or very little to them, it may mean merely the excuse for a monthly dinner-party, or it may be the guardian of their dearest or highest interests—but community is something wider and freer than even the greatest associations; it is the greater common life out of which associations rise, into which associations bring order, but which associations never completely fulfil. If we reflect, we perceive at once that there is a vast difference between the living together of men which makes a village or city or country on the one hand, and the association of men in a church or trade-union—or even, as we shall see, in a State—on the other. Often state-areas do not even coincide with the areas of effective community, as, for instance, when a subject-people, incorporated in an alien State, continues to lead its own manner of life. A distinction of name is essential.

It may be well to show how infinitely associations vary in degree of permanence and significance, and the main reason of these variations, before we consider the relation to community of the most permanent and most comprehensive of all—the State.

Men may mass together without becoming organised. A mere aggregation is not an association. Take the case of a crowd casually collected to watch a fire. The aggregation serves no end, each individual of the crowd could watch the fire quite as well—better in fact—if the others went away. A common interest keeps them together, but it does not bind them to one another, it need bring no individual into social contact with any other. It is a physical and not a social contiguity. No association is dissolved when the fire burns out—or when the policeman moves the crowd away. But suppose the crowd had resolved to fight the fire and had organised themselves to that end. At once the aggregation would have been transformed into an association, its individuals would have fallen into social relations with one another, and the order which is attendant on social purpose would have permeated the whole. As soon as men see that any interest they share is furthered by organisation, they are preparing an association. So here an association would have come into being for an hour—and in an hour would have passed away.

Take next the case of men gathered to celebrate some occasion, say the centenary of some historical event. Here there is a purpose depending on and realised through association. The meeting-together is an essential element of the celebration. Time and place and procedure are predetermined, it is an organised association, not a casual aggregation. But the purpose may be only a trivial thing in the life of each member of the assemblage. It brings him into social contact, but a very transient and partial contact, with the rest. There is a consciousness of common interest realised in association, but it finds only a momentary expression. When the parade is over or the procession has passed, or the bonfire turned to ashes, or the dinner and the speeches are ended, the association dissolves. Because the purpose was transient, the association it created could not endure.

Consider next an association created for the achievement of some specific reform, political or religious, say for the passing of a bill or the formulation of a creed. Here a more permanent purpose animates the association, and works a deeper organisation. Each member of the association has a definite point of contact with every other. It is because each member has a certain individuality that he is a member. If he were different in a certain important way, he would not be a member. And in the association each holds a definite place, determined in part at least by his individuality. (For it is a general law of association that the deeper the purpose at work, the more complex becomes the organisation.) Yet since the purpose is specific and temporary, the association which pursues it pursues its own dissolution. When the bill is enacted or the creed formulated, in the fulfilment of its sustaining purpose the association itself dissolves. When slavery was abolished, the associations for the abolition of slavery were abolished also. Every such association dies of its success. Sometimes an association lives on when its primary purpose belongs to the past, becoming either a venerable relic, like, say, the Honourable Society of Fishmongers, or a social obstruction, like the Grand Army of the Republic.

Let us turn next to an association of a very different type, the association of marriage. The purpose on which this association rests is the deep foundation of all life, and that purpose is fulfilled not in the mere procreation of offspring and their tutelage until they attain the autonomy of manhood or womanhood. The profound purpose of the marriage-association includes the present as well as the future generations, and fulfils the lives of those who enter into it no less than it creates and develops the lives of those who issue from it. It is, therefore, a continuous and—unless perverted—permanent purpose of human life, and the association it creates is likewise continuous and permanent, strongly rooted in the heart of life.

Thus to a permanent purpose there always answers, in the nature of things, a permanent association. This appears still more clearly when we turn to such associations as Church and State. These rest on purposes more lasting than any individuals, and are thus maintained through periods of time infinitely larger than the life-periods of individuals. In so far as they are purposes necessary to the fulfillment of life, they create associations as immortal as life. And as the most enduring purposes are also those which grow and change the most, there is a continuous evolution of the greater associations.

Lastly, associations vary as much in extent as in permanence, and for the same reason. Wherever there is a character common to social beings, a common interest is implicit, an interest, that is, which can be furthered by organisation, by association. The extent of a common interest *should* measure the extent of its correspondent association. The most intimate interest is that which most directly unites just two human beings, as in the association of marriage; but at the other extreme are interests universal as mankind—the interest we call justice, for example—and the history of society is in part a history of the widening of associations (and therefore of community) as men more and more recognise how much they have in common with other men, and more and more understand that every common value is protected and furthered by association. So out of the small circles of primitive society have grown the great and ever-widening associations of the modern world.

We have been speaking of the State as simply one among other associations, but the State has obviously a very peculiar and distinctive place. Other associations are limited to the pursuit of one or at most a few interests, the State seems to have some care for nearly every interest. Other associations cannot on their own initiative enforce their decisions on recalcitrant members, the State can and does. Other associations have their members scattered over a city or district or country, the State includes within its membership, or at least within its control, all the dwellers within determined communal frontiers. It is, therefore, highly important to determine the relation of the State, first to community itself, and next to the other associations within community.

COMMUNITY AND STATE

Because the State, like community, has territorial frontiers and because it exercises control over all, or nearly all, other associations, many writers speak as if community and State were one. This seems to have been the view of Hegel and is certainly the doctrine of the neo-Hegelian writers on the State, as well as of many others to whom that epithet scarcely applies. Here is a representative statement of this doctrine from the late M. Fouillée: "Imagine," he wrote, "a great circle within which are lesser circles combining in a thousand ways to form the most varied figures without overstepping the limits that enclose them; this is an image of the great association of the State and of the particular associations that it embraces." (La Science Sociale Contemporaine, p. 13.)

We shall see later that this doctrine, which makes the State the limit of community and makes all other associations but elements of the State, is contradicted by the whole evolution of the modern State. For the present it will suffice to show that the doctrine, so strangely maintained in the face of history, is contrary to the present fact. Here we are not concerned with what the State ought to be and to include, but with what the State actually is and does include. So regarded, it is quite obvious that the State is neither conterminous nor synonymous with community. Every State has rigid territorial limits, but the modern world, marked off into separate States, is not partitioned into a number of isolated communities. We have already seen that community is a matter of degree, that it is a network of social interrelations, here denser, here thinner, whose ever new-woven filaments join men to men across countries and continents. The State, unlike community, is exclusive and determinate. Where one State ends, another begins; where one begins, another ends. No man can without contradiction owe allegiance to two States, any more than he can serve two masters, but he can enter into the life of as many communities as his sympathies and opportunities will allow.

Quite obviously the metaphor of Fouillée is false. Let us draw our exclusive circles and call them England, France, Germany, and so on. By hypothesis, all associations fall within these circles, and do not intersect them. Well, in which circle shall we place the international economic associations without which none of the great States could to-day exist at all? In which shall we place the numerous international unions, industrial, scientific, religious, and artistic? "Without overstepping the limits that enclose them"—that is the foundation of the neo-Hegelian doctrine of the State, and it is a foundation which is false in fact.

But, it will be answered, every association, international or intranational, is controlled by the State. Intranational associations are controlled by the separate States, international associations by agreement between States. No members of any State can enter into any association whatever unless that State permits it. Thus every other association is subordinate to the State.

We may grant the contention. At a later stage we shall see more clearly whence and why the will of the State has this pre-eminence. At that stage we shall understand more fully the distinction between community and State. Meantime we must insist that there is a false inference if we say that because the State has control over every other association, therefore all other associations are absorbed into the State, are simply parts of the State, or are completely circumscribed by its frontiers. If we hold this view, the process of conflict through which modern States have attained their present democratic forms, and in especial the long agony of strife due to the opposing claims of churches and of States, is without meaning for us.

There is an easy and direct way by which we can discover the limits of the State. The essential feature of the State is political order, the primary instrument of the State is political law. There has been community where no State yet existed, and even to-day we may discover, among certain Eskimo peoples, for instance, primitive forms of communal life still uncoordinated within a State. Where there is no political law, there is no State. Political law is thus the criterion of the State, and in learning the nature and limits of political law we are learning the nature and limits of the State.

Political law is in its proper nature unconditioned, formulated, and mainly negative. These characters reveal the limits of the State.

It is unconditioned. The laws of other associations bind their members, but if you don't like the laws you can leave the association—unless the State forbids. If you disapprove of the laws of your club or business-association or trade-union or church, you can resign. If any such association tries of its own accord to enforce its laws on you, it comes into collision with the powers of the State. It can properly do no more than deny you its special benefits and privileges. So with communal or customary law, properly so-called. If you break the customs, traditions, fashions prevalent in your community, you may expect its disapprobation. It will boycott you, refuse to enter into social relations with you, but unless you break also the law of the State, it cannot otherwise visit upon you its displeasure. But if you break a political law, you do not merely lose privileges. The State will do more than deny its benefits, it will punish. It has behind it the united force of the community, the final sanction attached to no other kind of social law. Nor can you simply resign your membership of the State to escape its law. Even if you go beyond its frontiers its claims may follow you, and within the State, even if you shut yourself up within your walls, you are subject to the laws of the State, to all the conditions it may impose either directly or by delegation of authority.

Why does the State hold this unique position? Why has it behind it the united force of the community? The force of the law is not an ultimate thing, it is always and essentially dependent upon will. The State has this power of compulsion because its members *will* that power, because they subject themselves to its law and unite their force to maintain it. To what end?

No man can wholly cut himself off from social relations while he remains in the world of men. We are forced from all sides, by every instinct and every need, into society, into relations with our fellows. Such relations must be ordered, or life is impossible. Mutual good demands mutual service, mutual forbearance and restraint. Thus wherever society exists there exists a system of obligations and rights. Society incessantly creates these reciprocal relations between every man and all other men. Sometimes they remain unformulated and traditional, as in a primitive community ruled by "unwritten law," but nearly always the most essential of these relationships of right and obligation are set out in clear formulæ, as political laws, and protected by a central authority endowed with communal power. Any body of men so organised that a central institution or government takes over the maintenance and development of the essential system of rights and obligations accepted among them is properly called a State. A State is thus the fundamental association for the maintenance and development of social order, and to this end its central institution is endowed with the united power of the community. It is not meant that the members of a State consciously realise why they give or permit it this final authority—if they did they would never have suffered the endless perversions of government—but only that as their political consciousness emerges, as they ask themselves why they should contribute this might to the State, the answer appears in this form. As the State develops, as its members grow in social wisdom, in the consciousness of their own needs and the possibilities of satisfying them through political order, the power of the

State comes to rest more and more on its service of that end—or else there is distraction, weakness, cleavage, finally perhaps revolution.

Subjection to law is political obligation, which is only the reverse side of political right. Beyond law, beyond government, and beyond force lie the common ends, the common will of community. The end is here as always the revelation of meaning and the justification of existence. If the citizen owes obedience to government it must be in virtue of some social good which in turn determines the respect the government shall show to him. Political right and political obligation, as all right and obligation, are derived from the same source and are meaningless if separated. Already we see that the State and its government are not ultimate social phenomena but rest on what is yet deeper, communal life and will.

The special limits of the State are revealed when we consider the further characteristics of political law.

In the second place, political law is expressed in definite formulæ. A political law defines certain categories of persons as coming within its scope, and prescribes for them as precisely as possible certain forms of conduct. It is obvious, therefore, that it can apply only to general situations and can enforce only *external* fulfilments. Thus the State is at once outside large spheres of human activity. It cannot control motives save indirectly. It can enjoin actions, or rather activities, but not the spirit of their fulfilment. But large classes of action are wholly dependent on the spirit in which they are fulfilled, and many associations exist simply to foster types of ideal or spiritual values. The State *cannot* determine these associations, and it *should not* prescribe any of those actions which derive their only value from the spirit of their performance. The State can compel people to attend church, but it cannot compel them to worship, and therefore the former compulsion is folly. The State cannot create by its *fiat* a church or an artistic or literary association. It can protect and maintain and even organise such associations— to do so may be part of its function—but it cannot, if it is true to its own nature, determine and control them. Further, in its generality and externality it cannot touch (save by way of repression) that spontaneity and initiative of individual life which is the beginning of all social process and the root of all social value. There are times, pre-eminently the time of war, when cumulative force matters for the time being more than spontaneity, and the State inevitably becomes repressive. But this, like nearly all the special phenomena of war, is a throwback to the barbaric order. Certainly this repressiveness, when continued into the time of peace by the momentum of the war-habit, of necessity breeds grave social disturbance and dissension. The State must, therefore, be clearly distinguished from the community which creates it. Community is the common life of beings who are guided essentially from within, actively, spontaneously, and freely (under the conditions prescribed by the laws they make) relating themselves to one another, weaving for themselves the complex web of social unity. But the State works with an instrument which is necessarily formal, prescribing the general external conditions of social life, upholding the main system of those social obligations which may be externally fulfilled. Its instrument resembles, in Aristotle's phrase, no "leaden rule" which can adapt itself to the actual mouldings of the social structure, but an unbending rod which can measure only its general outlines.

Because it can determine only the external forms of conduct, the law of the State must be mainly (though by no means wholly) negative. It must for the most part be content (as the neo-Hegelians themselves are forced to admit, though they do not see the significance of the admission) to "hinder hindrances" to social welfare. It can prevent or punish wrong-doing rather than endorse right-doing. It can create for men the external social conditions necessary for the well-living of their lives. It can enforce these outer obligations without the fulfilment of of which the inner obligations cannot be fulfilled. For this reason the sanction of political law is punishment and not reward. We reward and honour only what the theologian called "works of supererogation," not the minimal fulfilment of external law.

It is needless to say that in thus stating the limits of political activity we are not belittling the immeasurable value of that activity. The point is that the State is not equivalent to community, that the political association does not include and cannot control the whole life of men. The State is seen to be not community but a peculiarly authoritative association within it. The State is determinate, a closed organisation of social life; community is indeterminate, an ever-evolving system spreading beyond and only partially controlled within the definite framework of any State. That framework gives to the portion of community which it encloses a certain unity and definition, but neither cuts it off from a wider community of which it is essentially part nor within that portion substitutes its own external mode of action, its necessity, for the spontaneity that is the mark of all life, social and other. Social life can no longer in practice and should no longer in theory be summed up in political life. The individual should not be summed up in his citizenship, otherwise the claim of citizenship will itself become a tyranny and its essential moral value be lost. "The modern wilderness of interests" is not to be straightened out into the simple road of citizenship. For the main road of citizenship, which we must make straight as possible, though it intersects a thousand paths of social interest, cannot and should not absorb them.

These paths of social interest do not stop at the frontiers of States. The political interest is determinate and has limits, the social has none. Hence for the proper understanding of international relations it is most necessary to distinguish community and State. On the assumption of identity we can have no social unity among the nations until they are absorbed within some world-state. For each State by its very definition is a determinate and self-contained unit. In respect of the sphere of its sovereignty every State is demarcated absolutely from every other. Consequently, if political relationship were identical with social relationship, the members of one State would remain totally alien from the members of every other State. Communities would stand to one another as Spinoza and Hobbes imagined them to stand, isolated as the pre-civil individuals of their imaginations, totally irresponsible until some contract is agreed upon, even then totally irresponsible because there is no possible higher will to make agreement binding. But, of course, it is in international relations that the distinction of State and community is most clearly revealed and that the common interests of universal society most manifestly weave new unities in spite of political separation. A man may perhaps "denationalise" himself (though that is hardly the proper word) by leaving his country, but he cannot "de-socialise" himself without leaving the world of men, or at least of civilised men.

Community, therefore, and not the State, is the "world the spirit has made for itself." "The spirit" does not isolate itself in States, as Hegel's argument assumes. On the contrary, the growth of civilisation means the growth of ever-widening community, the "realisation" of social interest beyond the limits of politically independent groups. Society widens and the sense of community grows. In particular, the privileged classes of the different peoples, the authors of most past wars, become more and more allied by social intercourse, by common commercial and intellectual interests. M. Tarde has pointed out how classes of men whose occupation, even if in a competitive way, brings them into constant association with one another, develop a friendlier spirit towards one another than classes not subject to this socialising influence. The same holds of peoples. It is not civilisation but intercivilisation that develops mutual sympathy between States. The highly socialised Greek cities, because each held to an ideal of autonomy and self-sufficiency, the ideal of "completely independent totality," were not intersocialised, and, accordingly, displayed the intensest hostility to one another. But the aloofness of Greek states is impossible in the modern world, which is pervaded by intersocialising influences of literature and commerce. Common ideas and common trade have formed everywhere social bonds which cut across the line of States, and have made western Europe, looked on as a whole, an effective community. Thus an educated Englishman comes to have more in common with an educated Frenchman than he has, say, with an English agricultural labourer. The alien, shut out from his State, may yet have a closer, social affinity to him than his fellow citizen. And yet the prevalent political philosophy blindly declares that "the State" is "the world the spirit has made for itself," and that "between State and State there can be no consciousness of common good." Because certain dangerously antiquated modern governments retained that philosophy, they have overwhelmed our common civilisation in the consciousness of common evil.

If we turn for a moment from fact to ideal—two things which the neo-Hegelians constantly confuse—we may admit the desirability of a wider political co-ordination of community than at present exists. This is to be achieved not by our going backwards and cutting off the bonds of relationship which make community wider in area than any single State, but by our going forward on the road of federation and making a union of States great enough to comprehend the existing intercommunity. The recognition of likeness of interests, purposes, and needs is increasing and not diminishing in the people of different nations. It is the State that is inadequate, not community that is overstepping its due bounds. The State must always, as we have seen, remain inadequate to comprehend and regulate *all* community. But it is more inadequate than need be, so long as the political relations of States are capricious and uncoordinated. At present civilised States are like masters who maintain splendid order and discipline within their workshops, and thus feel free to go out and racket in the streets.

CHAPTER IX

COMMUNICATION AND SOCIAL
PROCESSES

78. The Business of Communication *

THE LARGER AND MORE COMPLEX a democracy becomes, the greater
is the need for speedy, accurate, and comprehensive institutions of
communication. Probably the average reader is not clearly aware
of the globe-girdling revolution in communications that has recently
taken place—largely within his parents' and his own lifetimes.
This revolution continues today. With great discernment Robert
Leigh, like a skilled physician, diagnoses the difficult situation confronting the public library today. This situation is largely the
product of great expansion in the field of mass media communications. On the basis of his diagnosis Leigh formulates a conception
of the role that the "noncommercial agencies of communication,"
particularly the public library, need to play.

THE COMMUNICATIONS REVOLUTION

NEWSPAPER, MAGAZINE, and book publication in the United States
has always been essentially a private undertaking. Comparatively new,

* Robert D. Leigh, The Public Library in the United States (New York: Columbia University Press, 1950), pp. 26-39, 50-51. Reprinted by permission of
the publisher and the author.

The author (b. 1890) is a research executive; Visiting Professor of Government,
Columbia University. Special adviser and executive officer, Science Committee,
National Resources Planning Board, 1941-42. Director, Commission on Freedom
of the Press, 1944-46. Director, Public Library Inquiry, Social Science Research
Council, 1947-50. Author, Federal Health Administration in the United States,
Group Leadership, Peoples Speaking to Peoples (with Llewellyn White), and In-
equality of Opportunity in Higher Education (with David S. Berkowitz).

however, is the emergence of very large communication units fashioning their products ingeniously to gain and to hold huge mass markets. This development is so recent, so rapid, and so fundamental that it may properly be called a twentieth-century communications revolution. True, it began more than a century ago with the invention of power-driven printing machinery, and has been followed at intervals by improvements in the printing and engraving processes and in rapid transport and communication of messages, which together ushered in the modern metropolitan daily newspaper. But the appearance of mass magazines (with circulations in the millions), book clubs and chain-store book distribution, the phonograph, the radio, and motion pictures is within the memory of persons now in late middle age.

And the more recent advent of television, of photography as a means of reproducing text cheaply and rapidly on paper or film, and of the electronic transmission of texts page-by-page over great distances, reminds us that we are still in the midst of the communications revolution. It may not be exaggerating to say, as some informed people have said, that the transmission of sights, sounds, and words by electrical impulse will prove as powerful and radical an influence on our political and cultural life as was the invention of printing in the sixteenth century.

Changes such as these, occurring gradually, but adding up over a short period to a major transformation, are usually not accompanied immediately by the necessary adaptations of related social habits and institutional machinery. It would be surprising if the public library had made such an adaptation. For the library appeared and assumed its present institutional form in a world of scarce and expensive books, of equally expensive magazines written for a limited clientele, of newspapers with comparatively narrow range of topics and coverage—a world in which there was no radio, phonograph records, or film. That world differs strikingly from that in which we live today, with its almost bewildering abundance and cheapness of print of all kinds, with news, discussions, pictures, music, and drama, even the facsimile of events themselves as they happen, delivered through film or electric impulse in a constant stream to the citizen-consumer in his office, his home, or other place of relaxation.

THE AUDIENCES OF THE MASS MEDIA

Indeed, the two most striking characteristics of modern mass communication are its sheer abundance and its easy accessibility—one might also say, its obtrusiveness. A public library has thousands of books on its shelves. But a person who wants one of them must go to the library for it. If it is available on the occasion when he calls for it, it is lent to him to read for a limited period. Usually he may not telephone in advance to see whether the trip to the library will be worth while. Almost never, unless he is blind, ill, or otherwise disabled, may he order the book delivered to his home as he habitually does when purchasing groceries or a new hat.

The daily newspaper and the magazine, on the other hand, are delivered to his door; radio and television are his to enjoy in his home by simply turning a knob. In some public places he cannot escape them; he is part of a captive audience. Even the books which he buys may come to him with his morning's mail; those of a limited type which are issued in paper covers or of pocket size may be seen and bought in at least 75,000 stores and newsstands. To see a movie he must bestir himself to go a few blocks to the neighborhood or downtown theater. But there are more than eighteen thousand of these theaters, most of them in convenient locations and open throughout the afternoon and evening seven days a week. There are only about half as many public library buildings in the United States. And the smaller ones (constituting a majority of the whole number) are open only for a limited number of hours daily or weekly.

The citizen response to abundance and accessibility of communication is impressive. It is estimated that the average adult in the United States is engaged for a quarter of his waking hours in reading newspapers, magazines, books, listening to the radio, or seeing movies. If this time were to be consolidated into a continuous period it would occupy all the evening from the end of the family dinner until bedtime. It is half the time devoted daily to sleep; more than the time occupied in eating.

The extent of popular addiction to consuming mass communication, however, differs from one medium to another. Our survey of citizen use and our analysis of other surveys indicate that:

1) Practically all adults listen to the radio and read the newspaper (90 to 95 per cent listen to the radio fifteen minutes or more per day; 85 to 90 per cent read one or more newspapers more or less regularly).

2) About two thirds of the adults read some magazine (60 to 70 per cent read one or more magazines more or less regularly).

3) About one half of the adults attend the movies periodically (45 to 50 per cent see a motion picture once every two weeks or more often).

4) About one fourth of our adult population read books as a habit (25 to 30 per cent read one or more books a month, 50 per cent claim to have read at least one book in the last year).

In gross numbers of words, pictures, and sounds received per minute by the average adult in the United States, then, books play a relatively minor role. Some of the reasons for this position of book reading are obvious. Both motion pictures and radio reach beyond the group of people able to read; radio is easily available, also, for those who cannot see. The cost of books per unit is greater than for the other media, except for drug-store editions of paper-bound reprints and mysteries. Even with book clubs and free libraries, systems of book distribution are neither so convenient nor so widespread as those of the other media.

As for television, the newest medium to compete for the leisure time of the American people, there are not yet enough sets in use, nor have the purchasers had the sets long enough, to make comparative figures of any great value. From surveys of the present owners of television receivers, however, we find that adults sit before their television screen on an average of two to three hours a day, children almost as many hours daily. These figures, showing extremely heavy use, must be thought of in terms of the present scarcity. We cannot tell what the quantity and extent of use will be when television sets are no longer a novelty, when they have reached a public far wider than the present group of enthusiasts and have become a regular item of home equipment (an audience of fifty million, with nineteen million family sets is the estimate for 1953).

Heretofore each new mass medium, despite predictions to the contrary, has supplemented rather than replaced existing media. Television gives some indication that it may not follow this course. Surveys of television users report a decline of 30 per cent in reading during the first six months of ownership, 15 per cent a year or more later. They report similarly a drop in movie attendance of 33 per cent in the early period, leveling off gradually to approximately 15 per cent. The decline in radio listening is greatest. Of the television set owners, 75 to 90 per cent say that they listen less to radio, especially during the evening hours when radio has its largest audiences. All these survey figures must be thought of as exploratory and suggestive, rather than definitive. They do indicate, however, that television is likely to take its place as a formidable agency of mass communication with regard to both amount of use and number of users.

When we pass beyond the statistics of average minutes per day of exposure to the various media, some qualifications need to be made. A single radio program of great popularity may have an audience estimated to be thirty million; this number equals the total sales of the fifteen best selling novels for the last five years. Newspaper sales in the United States for five days in 1948 surpassed the total sales of general fiction and nonfiction (trade books) for that year. But these comparisons do not reflect accurately the total exposure to the medium. The day's newspaper goes out with the ash can. A radio program, once heard, is gone with the wind; but the novel *Gone with the Wind* belies its title. It is saved after reading to be lent and read by others; public library copies are used by many readers; it is translated into foreign languages and into the international language of the motion picture. An even longer history of repeated use awaits a book such as Tolstoy's *War and Peace* that becomes a classic in other than the current sense.

Despite these qualifications, however, books remain the most limited of the major agencies of communication so far as numbers in their audiences can be counted. This fact is important to public libraries, because books are the library's principal stock in trade.

THE LIBRARY'S PUBLIC

Public libraries are not the chief distributors of the books that are read by the American people. Defining adults as persons of high school age and beyond, our analyses indicate that about two thirds of the books people read are distributed through commercial channels: 35 to 40 per cent by direct purchase; 18 to 25 per cent as loans from friends or neighbors, who presumably purchased them or received them as gifts; 7 to 9 per cent from commercial rental libraries. Only about one fourth of the books read are from public libraries.

The best estimates from existing data, using the borrowing of one volume or more a month as a basis, are that the public library's clientele for book circulation consists of about 10 per cent of the adult population; about 18 per cent, if we use the reading of one book a year as the basis. These percentages are considerably less than the proportion of all adults in the average community who by signing a registration card indicate that they intend to borrow books from the public library. It may be more than coincidence that the surveys show the ratio of these library registrants to all adults—usually about one out of four—to be the same as the ratio of adult book readers to all adults in the community. Thus, we may assume that nearly all the community's regular book readers take out registration cards at one time or another, constituting the public library's potential users, but that only a minority of them at any one time use the library regularly.

If we look at the 10 per cent of adults who are regular users of the public library, we are obliged to make one further qualification. The members of this group do not use the library with equal regularity. Here public libraries and book reading are in contrast with some of the other communication media. Nearly all newspaper readers, the studies show, devote about the same amount of time to newspaper reading. Also, the use of radio and magazines is comparatively uniform, though less so than for newspapers. Movie attendance is evidently concentrated as compared with newspapers, radio, or magazines. But concentration is greatest with regard to the use of books, including the borrowing of books from public libraries. The available studies reveal that about 10 per cent of the book readers account for about half of all the book reading in the community; and about 10 per cent of the public library's borrowers take out one third of all the books borrowed in a two-week period, only 5 per cent of the borrowers accounting for two fifths of the annual circulation, 20 per cent for three quarters of the books charged out during the year. Clearly, a minority of the 10 per cent of adult library users are real library "fans," constituting a larger percentage of the total users of the library than movie and radio fans represent in their total audiences.

So far we have limited ourselves to the use of books, libraries, and the other agencies of communication by adults. The number of children and young people in school who use the libraries is larger in proportion to their total numbers in the population than the proportion of adult library users to the total number of adults. The best estimates indicate that about one third of the former use the library, compared with one tenth of the adults (use being defined as the borrowing of a book once a month or more often). In most communities library registration of juveniles is also proportionately higher than adult registration, usually averaging nearly 50 per cent of the juveniles in the population compared with the average 25 per cent registration of adults. These figures for juveniles are not based on as reliable or as comprehensive studies as those made of adult library use. And as yet there are no reliable estimates stemming from adequate surveys, of the comparative use by children of books, magazines, radio, newspapers, and movies.

From all the existing data it seems clear that in terms of the total population a small minority of adults and a larger proportion of children, but still a minority, are regular users of public libraries. In no sense does this mean that the library patrons are an inconsequential minority or that public library service is an unimportant segment of the whole machinery of public communication. It means only that in quantitative terms the commercial media reach many more people, even with books.

CELEBRITIES AND PERSONALIZING

The wide coverage of the population attained by the commercial media is not due merely to their abundance and accessibility. It is also the result of careful fashioning of their content and zealous promotion so as to reach the maximum number of consumers. Most mass communication agencies have adopted the usual—probably necessary—techniques of those who make and sell articles for mass markets: standardizing their products, giving them attractive labels, and promoting their sale by extensive and expensive programs of commercial advertising. Indeed, some of the media—radio, newspapers, and magazines—are themselves the instruments for the direct advertising of mass-distributed products as well as for the distribution of ideas, news, and entertainment.

One characteristic of processing for the mass market may be called celebrity-building, or personalizing. We are daily witnesses to this practice in the mass magazines, newspapers, radio, motion pictures, and books, by which attention is centered on stars as authors, actors, or performers rather than upon the content of the subjects dealt with. In some cases the star is created out of obscurity by a careful process of commercial promotion. In other cases a personage well known for activities outside the communication field is used as a ready-made celebrity. A star, once built up by the success of a novel, story, or motion picture, is carefully guided along the path of continued success by variations on the first performance all in the same key. The process of discovering and cultivating celebrities differs somewhat in the various media. But increasingly star-building has become a combined enterprise ranging across the commercial agencies of mass communication. Books are written for and from movies; they are digested in mass magazines; they are distributed by book clubs; authors are guests on radio programs and appear at book fairs, autograph parties, and literary teas fully reported in the newspapers. Star-building is highly competitive; it involves large financial risks. There are frequent flops. Its successes are numerically small, but widely publicized.

The trade-book publishing field, which is of special interest to public libraries, uses this expedient widely. It is apparent in the publisher's choice of volumes promising big sales on which to put his money for promotion. For personalization has a wide appeal. It is a common denominator of interest, reaching out to the marginal, least-interested person, who is the special concern of the medium seeking to saturate the market. The best sellers are of various grades and quality as judged by experts and critics in the fields that the books cover. They usually include each year several publications that eventually join the more permanent contributions to knowledge and literature; they include some that serve a useful current purpose, but have no permanent use; they include a goodly number of what experts judge to be trash. The important point is that the selection of books for zealous promotion to achieve big sales is made not on the basis of their quality but because of their salability—often a different consideration. In the trade-book publishing field only 150 to 200 of the 4,000 books published each year actually hit the jackpot. But because of best-seller emphasis, the books selected for the big markets are those that most people in any year hear about and read.

The concentration on celebrities and best sellers in book and mass magazine publication is important for public libraries, because it affects directly the current demand for their books. Salability is not an acknowledged basis for the selection of books by an institution performing an educational function. As an educational institution the library might justifiably aim to choose each year from the 4,000 titles those volumes judged by experts to be most reliable and informed in their facts and judgments or of real literary merit rather than those designed to be most salable. It might, then, through lists in newspapers, by the use of an available, donated radio hour, and by bookjacket displays, attempt to bring its annual purchases to the attention of the reading public, and thus have the library's selections more widely read. As compared with the booming, insistent voices of commercial advertisers on behalf of the best sellers, however, the library's promotion is likely to seem a scarcely-audible whisper. . . . In this situation present library selection of current books is determined for them to a considerable extent by promotion at the hands of commercial media.

SENSATIONALISM AND DISTORTION

Personalization is only one of the devices used by the commercial media which results from the necessity of fashioning the product to the mass market. Equally common as a means of attracting a maximum of readers and audiences are the dramatization of events by sensationalizing them (especially setting them in the formula of combat between personal adversaries), emphasis on the unusual or the forbidden, such as murder, scandal, and sex, or on the dream worlds of mystery and romance. These emphases in selection of the content for communication in the commercial mass media are made in various ways and to different degrees. But they are elementary rules of choice in newspaper and magazine offices, motion picture and radio studios.

A positive result of fashioning the picture of men and events especially so as to reach multitudes is that significant glimpses of the larger world reach many more people than would be the case without such devices. The negative side of the process is that it tends to distort the picture of reality. Life as it is actually lived has much quiet co-operation as well as combat, much drab but useful activity; there are many significant things as well as people; there are complex and related factors which need to be understood in dealing with life's problems. Murder and other crimes are unusual, not normal happenings, as the dull but useful census figures reveal. Communication of the story of men and events in terms of balance and of complex reality may be quite impossible as a function of the media designed to serve audiences of millions. But without such communication smaller but important audiences often numbered in the thousands are left without material they want and need.

AVOIDANCE OF THE UNPOPULAR AND THE EXPERIMENTAL

A third emphasis in the selection of content by the mass media, resulting from the necessity of reaching and holding the largest possible audiences, is the avoidance of ideas that are unpopular or disturbing to a sizable segment of their clientele. The material selected, consequently, tends to reinforce majority ideas, attitudes, and preferences. In a society as heterogeneous as ours this practice probably serves an important positive role. By dramatizing the tradition and emphasizing the major understandings and concepts which have given our society its special character, the media promote unity and stability. The advantage of this emphasis is seen especially in time of war, when such qualities are most needed. On the other hand, we have indicated that we share the democratic assumption that minority views, including disturbing criticisms, have an important function in a free society. And by their selection of content the mass media tend to underemphasize these sometimes unpalatable but germinal ideas and opinions.

In the field of music and the arts there is a somewhat similar tendency on the part of the agencies of large-scale communication to overemphasize the accepted, to repopularize the popular, to underemphasize or to neglect the less celebrated, the new, the unorthodox, and the experimental. The makers and performers of serious music recordings, the music publishers, and the radio broadcasters, for example, present repeatedly what have been called the "Hundred Best Pieces" (the more famous compositions of Beethoven, Brahms, Mozart, Tschaikowsky, Sibelius, Wagner, and a few others). They seldom present the less-well-known works of these same classicists, the preclassical works on which the classics were built, or serious contemporary compositions not yet tested by many performances.

Again, the emphasis of the mass media has important positive aspects. Through the comparatively new machinery of extensive communication many millions of people have for the first time ready access to music of the highest quality performed with the greatest skill. Negatively, however, the commercial media do not extend their programs over the whole range of serious music, but rather, exploit to the full a limited number of compositions which are already famous. In the field of the arts, as in the field of social comment, a balance between the popular and the not-yet-popular is necessary to maintain artistic vitality and growth. Our present musical, literary, and other classics were once contemporary, unorthodox, and experimental. Only by the testing and criticism attendant upon repeated reading and listening was there gradual selection of those that have survived as classics. Following our assumption, then, society has a double concern with communication of the artist's products: an interest in the full enjoyment of the classical heritage and an interest in keeping open the springs of creation which replenish the main stream of culture. In their understandable concern for the mass market, the agencies of public communication contribute much more adequately to the first interest than to the second.

THE NEWNESS OF NEWS

Superficially in contradiction to the preference of the mass media for long-established, generally approved opinions, prejudices, and tastes is their tendency to stress newness in reporting the day's happenings. Evidently interest in the news of the hour, however unpleasant or disturbing, is very widespread. Often this interest is almost independent of learning what is most significant in the flow of events. The popular desire is ministered to with great zeal and ingenuity by news gatherers and distributors. They have developed the news function into a highly competitive game which yields rich results in furnishing the public with full, uncensored access to a kaleidoscope of current items and activities. On the other hand, they have developed canons of selection which rule out as not newsworthy that which has occurred outside narrow limits of recency.

Indeed, preoccupation with the facts, ideas, and problems of the moment is a characteristic of all the commercial agencies of public communication. It centers their efforts on immediate sale and consumption of the current product with almost no machinery for preserving valuable contemporary items for later use. As a result, the newspaper of day before yesterday, last night's radio program, the magazine of two months ago, last year's popular novel or motion picture are often unobtainable through the regular commercial channels of distribution. Furthermore, neither in city dwellings and bookstores nor on newsstands are there more than the most meager facilities for storing the products of current mass communication for future use.

* * * * * *

THE LIBRARY'S APPROPRIATE SERVICES

Our review of the characteristics of the commercial agencies indicates that they leave undone or slight the performance of communication services which are indispensable for the health of our society. The unperformed tasks would seem to constitute the uniquely appropriate functions for noncommercial agencies of communication, of which the public library is one. They are:

1. To serve as centers for contemporary materials selected from each year's output by the judgment of experts as the most reliable and authoritative, including artistic products of merit as determined by competent critics; and the promotion of the use of such materials by all available means.

2. To serve as centers where materials selected to give adequate and balanced representation to new, critical, often unpopular ideas, and to the preclassical, contemporary, unusual, and experimental in the arts can be brought into full use.

3. To serve as centers for the selection, organization, and promotion of the use of materials which are not new, but of great current relevance because of their enduring quality.

4. To serve as centers of selection, collection, and organization of the whole range of valuable materials in the form of print, picture, record, and film, in such a way as to focus the full resources of record quickly and easily on a particular subject or problem for those seeking such a service.

These four functions are not likely to be performed adequately or at all by the commercial media, characterized as they are by large volume and maximum coverage of the population. It is clear that the functions are not justified by the numbers of people reached so much as by the socially-valuable interests which they serve. They are functions which are made more rather than less necessary by the very flood of materials produced and distributed by commercial means. They seem, moreover, to be functions especially appropriate for performance by the library as a public institution.

79. *Freedom of the Press* *

THE PROBLEM AND THE PRINCIPLES

As POINTED OUT in the headnote to the preceding selection (78, by Robert Leigh), mass communication is essential to the functioning of contemporary society. Of all the agencies of mass communication, the press is, perhaps, the keystone. If it fails to function effectively, the whole fabric of our society is endangered. In the present selection is contained the essence of a searching anaylsis of the role of the press in modern society. Freedom of the press, it is contended, today is in danger. The crucial importance of this principle for democratic society and the problems that currently confront us in this connection are concisely stated.

THE PROBLEM

THE COMMISSION set out to answer the question: Is the freedom of the press in danger? Its answer to that question is: Yes. It concludes that the freedom of the press is in danger for three reasons:

First, the importance of the press to the people has greatly increased with the development of the press as an instrument of mass communication. At the same time the development of the press as an instrument of mass communication has greatly decreased the proportion of the people who can express their opinions and ideas through the press.

Second, the few who are able to use the machinery of the press as an instrument of mass communication have not provided a service adequate to the needs of the society.

Third, those who direct the machinery of the press have engaged from time to time in practices which the society condemns and which, if continued, it will inevitably undertake to regulate or control.

When an instrument of prime importance to all the people is available to a small minority of the people only, and when it is employed by that small minority in such a way as not to supply the people with the service they require, the freedom of the minority in the employment of that instrument is in danger.

This danger, in the case of the freedom of the press, is in part the consequence of the economic structure of the press, in part the consequence of the industrial organization of modern society, and in part the result of the failure of the directors of the press to recognize the

* Commission on Freedom of the Press, A *Free and Responsible Press* (Chicago: University of Chicago Press, 1947), Chapter I. Reprinted by permission of the publisher.

press needs of a modern nation and to estimate and accept the responsibilities which those needs impose upon them.

We do not believe that the danger to the freedom of the press is so great that that freedom will be swept away overnight. In our view the present crisis is simply a stage in the long struggle for free expression. Freedom of expression, of which freedom of the press is a part, has always been in danger. Indeed, the Commission can conceive no state of society in which it will not be in danger. The desire to suppress opinion different from one's own is inveterate and probably ineradicable.

Neither do we believe that the problem is one to which a simple solution can be found. Government ownership, government control, or government action to break up the greater agencies of mass communication might cure the ills of freedom of the press, but only at the risk of killing the freedom in the process. Although, as we shall see later, government has an important part to play in communications, we look principally to the press and the people to remedy the ills which have chiefly concerned us.

But though the crisis is not unprecedented and though the cures may not be dramatic, the problem is nevertheless a problem of peculiar importance to this generation. And not in the United States alone but in England and Japan and Australia and Austria and France and Germany as well; and in Russia and in the Russian pale. The reasons are obvious. The relation of the modern press to modern society is a new and unfamiliar relation.

The modern press itself is a new phenomenon. Its typical unit is the great agency of mass communication. These agencies can facilitate thought and discussion. They can stifle it. They can advance the progress of civilization or they can thwart it. They can debase and vulgarize mankind. They can endanger the peace of the world; they can do so accidentally, in a fit of absence of mind. They can play up or down the news and its significance, foster and feed emotions, create complacent fictions and blind spots, misuse the great words, and uphold empty slogans. Their scope and power are increasing every day as new instruments become available to them. These instruments can spread lies faster and farther than our forefathers dreamed when they enshrined the freedom of the press in the First Amendment to our Constitution.

With the means of self-destruction that are now at their disposal, men must live, if they are to live at all, by self-restraint, moderation, and mutual understanding. They get their picture of one another through the press. The press can be inflammatory, sensational, and irresponsible. If it is, it and its freedom will go down in the universal catastrophe. On the other hand, the press can do its duty by the new world that is struggling to be born. It can help create a world community by giving men everywhere knowledge of the world and of one another, by promoting comprehension and appreciation of the goals of a free society that shall embrace all men.

We have seen in our time a revival of the doctrine that the state is all and that the person is merely an instrument of its purposes. We cannot suppose that the military defeat of totalitarianism in its German and Italian manifestations has put an end to the influence and attractiveness of the doctrine. The necessity of finding some way through the complexities of modern life and of controlling the concentrations of power associated with modern industry will always make it look as though turning over all problems to the government would easily solve them.

This notion is a great potential danger to the freedom of the press. That freedom is the first which totalitarianism strikes down. But steps toward totalitarianism may be taken, perhaps unconsciously, because of conditions within the press itself. A technical society requires concentration of economic power. Since such concentration is a threat to democracy, democracy replies by breaking up some centers of power that are too large and too strong and by controlling, or even owning, others. Modern society requires great agencies of mass communication. They, too, are concentrations of power. But breaking up a vast network of communication is a different thing from breaking up an oil monopoly or a tobacco monopoly. If the people set out to break up a unit of communication on the theory that it is too large and strong, they may destroy a service which they require. Moreover, since action to break up an agency of communication must be taken at the instance of a department of the government, the risk is considerable that the freedom of the press will be imperiled through the application of political pressure by that department.

If modern society requires great agencies of mass communication, if these concentrations become so powerful that they are a threat to democracy, if democracy cannot solve the problem simply by breaking them up—then those agencies must control themselves or be controlled by government. If they are controlled by government, we lose our chief safeguard against totalitarianism—and at the same time take a long step toward it.[1]

---

[1] A third possibility is that government itself may come into the field with an alternative system of communications. The Commission has given little consideration to this possibility, except in international communications. Yet the example of Station WNYC, controlled by New York City, suggests what government may do in domestic communications if it regards private service as inadequate.

THE PRINCIPLES

Freedom of the press is essential to political liberty. Where men cannot freely convey their thoughts to one another, no freedom is secure. Where freedom of expression exists, the beginnings of a free society and a means for every extension of liberty are already present. Free expression is therefore unique among liberties: it promotes and protects all the rest. It is appropriate that freedom of speech and freedom of the press are contained in the first of those constitutional enactments which are the American Bill of Rights.

Civilized society is a working system of ideas. It lives and changes by the consumption of ideas. Therefore it must make sure that as many as possible of the ideas which its members have are available for its examination. It must guarantee freedom of expression, to the end that all adventitious hindrances to the flow of ideas shall be removed. Moreover, a significant innovation in the realm of ideas is likely to arouse resistance. Valuable ideas may be put forth first in forms that are crude, indefensible, or even dangerous. They need the chance to develop through free criticism as well as the chance to survive on the basis of their ultimate worth. Hence the man who publishes ideas requires special protection.

The reason for the hostility which the critic or innovator may expect is not merely that it is easier and more natural to suppress or discourage him than to meet his arguments. Irrational elements are always present in the critic, the innovator, and their audience. The utterance of critical or new ideas is seldom an appeal to pure reason, devoid of emotion, and the response is not necessarily a debate; it is always a function of the intelligence, the prejudice, the emotional biases of the audience. Freedom of the press to appeal to reason may always be construed as freedom of the press to appeal to public passion and igno-rance, vulgarity and cynicism. As freedom of the press is always in danger, so is it always dangerous. The freedom of the press illustrates the commonplace that if we are to live progressively we must live dangerously.

Across the path of the flow of ideas lie the existing centers of social power. The primary protector of freedom of expression against their obstructive influence is government. Government acts by maintaining order and by exercising on behalf of free speech and a free press the elementary sanctions against the expressions of private interest or resentment: sabotage, blackmail, and corruption.

But any power capable of protecting freedom is also capable of endangering it. Every modern government, liberal or otherwise, has a specific position in the field of ideas; its stability is vulnerable to critics in proportion to their ability and persuasiveness. A government resting on popular suffrage is no exception to this rule. It also may be tempted—just because public opinion is a factor in official livelihood —to manage the ideas and images entering public debate.

If the freedom of the press is to achieve reality, government must set limits on its capacity to interfere with, regulate, or suppress the voices of the press or to manipulate the data on which public judgment is formed.

Government must set these limits on itself, not merely because freedom of expression is a reflection of important interests of the community, but also because it is a moral right. It is a moral right because it has an aspect of duty about it.

It is true that the motives for expression are not all dutiful. They are and should be as multiform as human emotion itself, grave and gay, casual and purposeful, artful and idle. But there is a vein of expression which has the added impulsion of duty, and that is the expression of thought. If a man is burdened with an idea, he not only desires to express it; he ought to express it. He owes it to his conscience and the common good. The indispensable function of expressing ideas is one of obligation—to the community and also to something beyond the community—let us say to truth. It is the duty of the scientist to his result and of Socrates to his oracle; it is the duty of every man to his own belief. Because of this duty to what is beyond the state, freedom of speech and freedom of the press are moral rights which the state must not infringe.

The moral right of free expression achieves a legal status because the conscience of the citizen is the source of the continued vitality of the state. Wholly apart from the traditional ground for a free press—that it promotes the "victory of truth over falsehood" in the public arena— we see that public discussion is a necessary condition of a free society and that freedom of expression is a necessary condition of adequate public discussion. Public discussion elicits mental power and breadth; it is essential to the building of a mentally robust public; and, without something of the kind, a self-governing society could not operate. The original source of supply for this process is the duty of the individual thinker to his thought; here is the primary ground of his right.

This does not mean that every citizen has a moral or legal right to own a press or be an editor or have access, as of right, to the audience of any given medium of communication. But it does belong to the intention of the freedom of the press that an idea shall have its chance even if it is not shared by those who own or manage the press. The press is not free if those who operate it behave as though their position conferred on them the privilege of being deaf to ideas which the processes of free speech have brought to public attention.

But the moral right of free public expression is not unconditional. Since the claim of the right is based on the duty of a man to the common good and to his thought, the ground of the claim disappears when this duty is ignored or rejected.   In the absence of accepted moral duties there are no moral rights.   Hence, when the man who claims the moral right of free expression is a liar, a prostitute whose political judgments can be bought, a dishonest inflamer of hatred and suspicion, his claim is unwarranted and groundless.   From the moral point of view, at least, freedom of expression does not include the right to lie as a deliberate instrument of policy.

The right of free public expression does include the right to be in error.   Liberty is experimental.   Debate itself could not exist unless wrong opinions could be rightfully offered by those who suppose them to be right.   But the assumption that the man in error is actually trying for truth is of the essence of his claim for freedom.   What the moral right does not cover is the right to be deliberately or irresponsibly in error.

But a moral right can be forfeited and a legal right retained.   Legal protection cannot vary with the fluctuations of inner moral direction in individual wills; it does not cease whenever a person has abandoned the moral ground of his right.   It is not even desirable that the whole area of the responsible use of freedom should be made legally compulsory, even if it were possible; for in that case free self-control, a necessary ingredient of any free state, would be superseded by mechanism.

Many a lying, venal, and scoundrelly public expression must continue to find shelter under a "freedom of the press" built for widely different purposes, for to impair the legal right even when the moral right is gone may easily be a cure worse than the disease.   Each definition of an abuse invites abuse of the definition.   If the courts had to determine the inner corruptions of personal intention, honest and necessary criticisms would proceed under an added peril.

Though the presumption is against resort to legal action to curb abuses of the press, there are limits to legal toleration.   The already recognized areas of legal correction of misused liberty of expression— libel, misbranding, obscenity, incitement to riot, sedition, in case of clear and present danger—have a common principle; namely, that an utterance or publication invades in a serious, overt, and demonstrable manner personal rights or vital social interests.   As new categories of abuse come within this definition, the extension of legal sanctions is justified. The burden of proof will rest on those who would extend these categories, but the presumption is not intended to render society supine before possible new developments of misuse of the immense powers of the contemporary press.

THE PRINCIPLES IN THE PRESENT SITUATION

The principles we have attempted to state are those general truths which are valid as goals for all civilized societies. It must be observed that freedom of the press is not a fixed and isolated value, the same in every society and in all times. It is a function within a society and must vary with the social context. It will be different in times of general security and in times of crisis; it will be different under varying states of public emotion and belief.

The freedom we have been examining has assumed a type of public mentality which may seem to us standard and universal but which is in many respects a product of our special history—a mentality accustomed to the noise and confusion of clashing opinions and reasonably stable in temper in view of the varying fortunes of ideas. But what a mind does with a fact or an opinion is widely different when it is serene and when it is anxious; when it has confidence in its environment and when it is infected with suspicion or resentment; when it is gullible and when it is well furnished with the means of criticism; when it has hope and when it is in despair.

Further, the citizen is a different man when he has to judge his press alone, and when his judgment is steadied by other social agencies. Free and diverse utterance may result in bewilderment unless he has access—through home, church, school, custom—to interpreting patterns of thought and feeling. There is no such thing as the "objectivity" of the press unless the mind of the reader can identify the objects dealt with.

Whether at any time and place the psychological conditions exist under which a free press has social significance is always a question of fact, not of theory. These mental conditions may be lost. They may also be created. The press itself is always one of the chief agents in destroying or in building the bases of its own significance.

If we now fix our problem in space and time and look at the press in the United States today, we see that the conditions of our society and of the press in our society require new applications of the principles we have stated.

The aim of those who sponsored the First Amendment was to prevent the government from interfering with expression. The authors of our political system saw that the free society they were seeking to establish could not exist without free communication. As Jefferson put it: "The basis of our governments being the opinion of the people, the very first object should be to keep that right; and were it left to me to decide whether we should have a government without newspapers or newspapers without a government, I should not hesitate a moment to prefer the latter. But I should mean that every man should receive those papers and be capable of reading them."

Our ancestors were justified in thinking that if they could prevent the government from interfering with the freedom of the press, that freedom would be effectively exercised. In their day anybody with anything to say had comparatively little difficulty in getting it published. The only serious obstacle to free expression was government censorship. If that could be stopped, the right of every man to do his duty by his thought was secure. The press of those days consisted of hand-printed sheets issuing from little printing shops, regularly as newspapers, or irregularly as broadsides, pamphlets, or books. Presses were cheap; the journeyman printer could become a publisher and editor by borrowing the few dollars he needed to set up his shop and by hiring an assistant or two. With a limited number of people who could read, and with property qualifications for the suffrage—less than 6 per cent of the adult population voted for the conventions held to ratify the Constitution—there was no great discrepancy between the number of those who could read and were active citizens and those who could command the financial resources to engage in publication.

It was not supposed that any one newspaper would represent all, or nearly all, of the conflicting viewpoints regarding public issues. Together they could be expected to do so, and, if they did not, the man whose opinions were not represented could start a publication of his own.

Nor was it supposed that many citizens would subscribe to all the local journals. It was more likely that each would take the one which would reinforce his prejudices. But in each village and town, with its relatively simple social structure and its wealth of neighborly contacts, various opinions might encounter each other in face-to-face meetings; the truth, it was hoped, would be sorted out by competition in the local market place.

Those circumstances which provided variety and interchange of opinion and easy individual access to the market place of ideas have changed so radically as to justify us in saying that this country has gone through a communications revolution.

Literacy, the electorate, and the population have increased to such a point that the political community to be served by the press includes all but a tiny fraction of the millions of the American people. The press has been transformed into an enormous and complicated piece of machinery. As a necessary accompaniment, it has become big business. There is a marked reduction in the number of units of the press relative to the total population. Although in small communities we can still see a newspaper plant and product that resemble their Colonial prototypes, these are no longer the most characteristic or the most influential agencies of communication.

The right of free public expression has therefore lost its earlier reality. Protection against government is now not enough to guarantee that a man who has something to say shall have a chance to say it. The owners and managers of the press determine which persons, which facts, which versions of the facts, and which ideas shall reach the public.

This is one side of the shield—the effect of the communications revolution on the right of the citizen to publish his beliefs. The other side is the effect of the communications revolution on the press as the agency through which the members of a free society receive, as well as exchange, the judgments, opinions, ideas, and information which they need in order to participate in the management of that society. The press has become a vital necessity in the transaction of the public business of a continental area.

In local affairs there is still a chance for face-to-face observation to get in its work. Many private groups, formal and informal, throw an extensive web of alternative communication over the country or over parts of it. But there is obviously less opportunity for direct observation and news by word of mouth in a metropolitan region, in a great nation, or in a world society than there is in a village, a small state, or a single country. For the most part the understanding of the leaders and people of China, Russia, England, and Argentina possessed by the citizens of New Hampshire, Kansas, Oregon, and Alabama will be gained from the agencies of mass communication. Hardly less is the dependence on these agencies of midwest farmers for their understanding of a strike in Detroit or a change in the discount rate by the Federal Reserve Board in Washington.

The complexity of modern industrial society, the critical world situation, and the new menaces to freedom which these imply mean that the time has come for the press to assume a new public responsibility.

Through concentration of ownership the variety of sources of news and opinion is limited. At the same time the insistence of the citizen's need has increased. He is dependent on the quality, proportion, and extent of his news supply, not only for his personal access to the world of event, thought, and feeling, but also for the materials of his duties as a citizen and judge of public affairs. The soundness of his judgment affects the working of the state and even the peace of the world, involving the survival of the state as a free community. Under these circumstances it becomes an imperative question whether the performance of the press can any longer be left to the unregulated initiative of the few who manage it.

The moral and legal right of those who manage it to utter their opinions must remain intact; this right stands for the valid kernel of individualism at the heart of all social life. But the element of duty involved in the right requires a new scrutiny; and the service of news, as distinct from the utterance of opinion, acquires a new importance. The need of the citizen for adequate and uncontaminated mental food is such that he is under a duty to get it. Thus his interest also acquires the stature of a right.

To protect the press is no longer automatically to protect the citizen or the community. The freedom of the press can remain a right of those who publish only if it incorporates into itself the right of the citizen and the public interest.

Freedom of the press means freedom from and freedom for. The press must be free from the menace of external compulsions from whatever source. To demand that it be free from pressures which might warp its utterance would be to demand that society should be empty of contending forces and beliefs. But persisting and distorting pressures—financial, popular, clerical, institutional—must be known and counterbalanced. The press must, if it is to be wholly free, know and overcome any biases incident to its own economic position, its concentration, and its pyramidal organization.

The press must be free for the development of its own conceptions of service and achievement. It must be free for making its contribution to the maintenance and development of a free society.

This implies that the press must also be accountable. It must be accountable to society for meeting the public need and for maintaining the rights of citizens and the almost forgotten rights of speakers who have no press. It must know that its faults and errors have ceased to be private vagaries and have become public dangers. The voice of the press, so far as by a drift toward monopoly it tends to become exclusive in its wisdom and observation, deprives other voices of a hearing and the public of their contribution. Freedom of the press for the coming period can only continue as an accountable freedom. Its moral right will be conditioned on its acceptance of this accountability. Its legal right will stand unaltered as its moral duty is performed.

◆◇◆◇◆◇◆

80. Communication—Problem for the Front Office *

THE TWO PREVIOUS SELECTIONS (78 and 79) have dealt with communication in the "mass" society.   A typical aspect of that society
is the modern business corporation with its extensive bureaucratic
organization.   The official channel of communication in an organization of this type is supposed to be a direct line of authority
characterized by autocratic control.   Such a system of autocratic
control frequently conflicts with the basic democratic values of our
society.   To circumvent this official system, the person within the
bureaucracy frequently uses another informal system of communication channels and interpersonal relations.   To these contradictory
systems of values and communication the *Fortune* writers give their
attention in this skillfully designed and interesting article.

BUSINESSMEN have a new hair shirt.   They are beginning to worry out
loud about an apparent contradiction in the Free Society: how do you
reconcile political democracy with the authoritarian discipline of business?   The question is succinctly put by Pitney-Bowes's Walter
Wheeler Jr.: "We in industry have a problem which must be solved
if business is to survive in its present form . . . a conflict between the
freedom of expression which all citizens enjoy in their private and political life, and the relatively autocratic life which we find in industry."
   It is a root question that has been posed here.   And the fact that it
has been posed most penetratingly by businessmen rather than by
political philosophers is another and very revealing bit of evidence of
the profound transformation taking place in American capitalism.
Success, not failure, raised the question.   For increasingly it is to the
corporation—rather than to the rest of society—that employees look for
their satisfactions, their aspirations, and the meaning they seek for their
lives.
   The result is an entirely new kind of community.   For better or
worse the modern corporation has become not only the most efficient
form for organizing large-scale production and distribution; it has become a community within the community with a true social structure
of its own.   And one with a set of status symbols, codes, and allegiances
as complex as anything ever seen before.
   Management has not been unaware of the fact that it has a community on its hands; through pensions, medical plans, and the like it

   * Reprinted from the May, 1951, issue of *Fortune* by Special Permission of the
Editors; Copyright 1951 Time, Inc.

has been assuming more and more material and economic obligations to its members. But the community also has *social* needs—and business has been slower in facing up to the implications of this. To be sure, business has gone in for "human relations" with a vengeance; it has studied the foreman and the worker on the line, plumbed their inner feelings with "nondirective" interviewing, given them councils to express themselves with, tested their morale so often that questionnaire-filling-out has become almost occupational.

But the executive? He is above the cutoff point. For "human relations," unfortunately, has generally applied only to relations below that rather vague level called "management." Which is, in a sense, going at the problem backward. Efforts at democracy in the shop, it has been made painfully clear, are so much folderol unless they are an extension of a basic top-management attitude. Furthermore, as business is beginning to suspect, perhaps it is management that needs the attention first. It is the executive (and those related to or aspiring to his function) who identifies his life most closely with the corporation. And the higher up in the hierarchy, the more pronounced the identification. It is a complex structure indeed—but a better knowledge of it, this article hopes to demonstrate, is the prerequisite for any successful attack on the problem of democracy and business.

A good many managements have been tackling the problem as one of "communication." There are other ways of approaching the problem—through organization planning or management training, for example, but whatever the angle of attack, the experimenting and self-examination going on have a way of converging on the same points. Do we need entirely new channels of communication? How can the boss find out what is going on down below without short-circuiting the line? And vice versa? In short, is more democracy desirable, and if so, how do you get it without losing control?

Clear answers are few; the research is only now under way, and sometimes it has got tangled up with "human engineering" and other such dubious approaches. But already it is possible to see that an extraordinary amount of mythology has crystallized around the subject of management behavior. The truth that is becoming visible is somewhat surprising.

THE "ROPES"

The moment businessmen take a hard look at the problem they come smack up against one simple but all-important fact: before they can do anything about the social structure, they have to know what it is.

And that does not come easily. People sense the structure, they behave in harmony with it, they curse it, and they praise it. They still know little about it. Anyone who sits down and tries to chart on paper the actual web of his relationships in an organization will find it a fresh—and tough—intellectual experience.

Hitherto, business has ducked the implications of the social structure by speaking of two systems—a "formal system" and an "informal system," the latter being thought of as either a harmless deviation from what ought to be, or aberrations stemming from the cussedness and perversity of human nature. Carefully used, the distinction can be useful, but it is only verbal. The "formal system" doesn't really exist—except on the organization chart; for there is only one system that really counts: the actual operating system—that seemingly intangible phenomenon called "the ropes," "the setup," "the system" (the kind you don't buck), or, simply, "our way of doing things."

It is a bewildering complex of relationships. A man's particular job, of course, is the single greatest element in fixing him in the structure. But this is only one of many influences; he can be affected also by office layout, by nepotism, by car pools, by commuting companions, by lunch groups, by seniority, and by other factors of which he himself may be only dimly aware.[1]

The relationships, moreover, are never static. Even "the grapevine" is without definite form; top executives are often petulant about it, as if there were one master circuit in which, somehow, they are not included. Yet there is no one "grapevine," but a series, running up, down, across, and so constantly adapting to the pressures of the moment that sometime soon people will probably be speaking of ad hoc grapevines.

It is through these social groupings that men find individual expression in the organization. They are not necessarily incompatible with the organization's goal, but in any showdown between the two it is the social needs that are filled first. When "cliques" and "grapevines" become superactive it is a sure sign of maladministration; they can grow only in a vacuum.

In wisely run corporations, of course, the impulse for association works out to the company's benefit. From this some have deduced that if business and personal life can be made to coincide even more, it will be better for all concerned. In one of the most advanced corporations the medical director feels the company should have the right to advise

---

[1] By all odds the best description of this phenomenon is to be found in the account of the aspiring young banker in J. P. Marquand's *Point of No Return*. [Ed. Note: see selection 43]

junior executives on their choice of a wife—this second vow, he feels, should not conflict with the one the junior executive made to the corporation previously. In another corporation the personnel director holds that executive communication would be greatly improved if the executives, instead of being scattered about the suburbs, were to be grouped in one area so as to be as homogeneous as the workers. How valuable this fraternalism is in breaking down barriers is difficult to tell; it will be many years before its effect on the corporation is determined. By which time, possibly, the corporation may have become the modern monastery. But that is another question.

Even the most rigid institutionalizing of friendship, however, is bound to be crossed up somewhat because of the fact of specialization. The growing fragmentation of the corporation into a multitude of divisions and departments has fostered allegiances *within* the business that can be quite as destructive as any outside ones. Indeed, the sub-unit loyalties are often so overdeveloped that there is, in effect, an aggregate of formalized cliques.

This kind of overidentification cuts across as well as up and down. Almost invariably in an organization there is a psychological dividing line somewhere; above it people think in terms of the over-all organization goals; below it people see the day-to-day operating details as the only problems worthy of notice, and can—and often do—effectively sabotage the orders of the "dreamers" up top. If only "they" would leave them alone . . .

Out of these allegiances come the unwritten codes of business—and whatever the manuals may say, it is these codes that really govern behavior. Business has recognized this phenomenon in the shop: how the workers, for example, will ostracize a man who has broken the code by being a "rate-buster." It has been slower, however, to recognize the parallel up top; how, in a more decorous but equally effective way, fellow executives will close in on a man who has flouted one of their codes—and with the boss never the wiser.

Here we glimpse a little recognized aspect of authority. To be exercised, it needs the sanction of codes. As an order goes down it will be reinterpreted in terms of the way people are "accustomed to doing things," and though there may be no conscious effort at sabotage, if there is any serious conflict between the codes and the order, the order gets changed. In one respect, at least, the authoritarianism that management is now starting to worry about is something of a fiction.

One of the qualities that make codes so baffling to management is their extraordinary and irrational longevity. Many may be shrouded in conditions almost forgotten by management. Years ago, to cite one example, a group of engineers started a company. At first it was, in effect, merely a collection of professional associates. But though it grew and has now swelled out to a rounded sales-and-manufacturing outfit, the old codes—that the engineering department is the elite, needs no supervision, etc.—are still in force. Since the present engineers are, in fact, no more important than anybody else, the collision of code and reality has produced tensions that only recently have been diagnosed for what they were. The parallel exists in many another firm; obsolescent or not, the unwritten codes are a long time dying.

So even with the more formal codes. Who is the executive so brave, for example, as to deny that a man given responsibility for a job gets commensurate authority; that he does not have to take orders from people of lower status; that he is responsible to only one superior? Yet a few moments' reflection on the realities of management shows that in practice these codes are largely fictions. Thanks to our elaborate committee systems, "liaison problems," S.O.P., and the staff setups in which the low-ranking executives have to act "in the name of" the boss, these rules are often contravened.

THE EGALITARIANS

This difference between beliefs about the social structure and reality becomes most striking when one is trying to find out about status. The status problem, it would seem, does not exist. "We're sort of unusual here—pretty much of a family, you might say." "We don't give a damn about that sort of thing." "There's no rank in this office—but then, that's typical of the Midwest." "Hell, the janitor can come in and chin with me any time he wants." And so on.

The fact of the matter, of course, is that the American office is a veritable temple of status. Though they may seem almost imperceptible, the symbols are manifested everywhere. Some have a useful purpose—the memo pad "From the desk of . . ."; the routing slip (should the names on the memorandum be listed by seniority, or alphabetically?); who sits with whom in the company dining room. Others are rooted in propriety: who can call whom by nickname, at what level people may smoke. To what grade of washroom is one entitled? Is the office carpeted or does he rate only linoleum? Some are rooted in functions only marginal: the facsimile signature stamp, for example —evidence that a man's importance is such that he must write to a great number of people, even if he doesn't use the facsimile signature in doing it. All these are favorite topics of office humor, of course—but as this fact itself is witness, the symbols *communicate*.

Which is quite as it should be. It is ambiguity of status and not overemphasis that is most provoking—one has only to think of the subtle probing that goes on between two strangers in business to find out just where the other fits in. (It is in this respect that the professors enjoy so great an advantage in gaining access to top brass. "They know we don't make much money," says one professor of industrial relations, "but, by God, they can't place us.")

And there are symbols of equality too. A. P. Giannini used to take inordinate pride in the fact that he worked at a desk in the main room just like everyone else. There is the bonhomie of the office party, the Open Door, and the first-name-calling that marks so many companies. In one well-known concern the president is addressed by his first name by practically every one of his 300 "key men." (Except those nearest him in rank. They call him "Mister.") But while the partitions seem to be coming down, the importance of status has not changed at bit. It can be put down as an axiom, in fact, that the more uniform the trappings of office, the more important the differences between them. Which, in a sense, is a tribute to our national practicality, for thus do we enjoy all the benefits of status symbols while at the same time luxuriating in the warm glow of egalitarianism their modesty gives us.

In addition to status, there is also caste—which is to say, the rank can be sliced along any axis. Ordinarily there is some one department that is considered more aristocratic than the others. It doesn't often get as pronounced as it did at a chemical firm some years back—all employees were required to tip their hats to the chemists of the company—but with few exceptions even those in the lowest level of such departments feel superior to their counterparts elsewhere, no matter how identical their work. In the same fashion, secretaries derive caste from the position of their superiors, and many are the chronic if muted squabbles as to just who has the more important boss.

It is all very well to smile at this sort of thing—but woe be to him who ignores it. The boss of a New York company, a great believer in scientific management, recently brought in some human engineers to tone up the office. Among other things, the human engineers converted the private secretaries of four executives into a steno pool for the same four executives; this way, the human engineers diagramed, there would be a more uniform work load for everyone concerned. The result: interminable coffee hours, frequent war councils in the washroom, general bedlam among the secretaries—not to mention the wounded pride among the executives. Which just goes to show, the boss has since observed, how stupid some people can be.

It is not in the symbols of status nor in codes or allegiances, then,

that the trouble lies. It is in overlooking the tremendous effect they
have on communication. And while it may be a case, as the semanti-
cists like to argue, of confusing the symbol with the reality, the distress
it causes is nonetheless real. And it is more than a question of offend-
ing secretaries. Recently, for example, a large midwestern corporation
almost lost one of its most valuable V.P.'s. In a shift of offices,
inadvertently he was given a metal desk instead of the mahogany
variety common to his bracket. Why? He pondered and fretted, and
began reading hurts, omens, and hidden meanings in every casual conversation. Eventually the matter came out in the open, for the V.P.
could go on no longer; he was on the brink of a complete nervous breakdown.

Silly? Ask the man who's had one.

THE UPWARD LOOK

Disregard for the social structure comes naturally. Who, theoretically, are people most interested in communicating with? Those
beneath them, of course. So goes the folklore of business. Executives
talk of communication as essentially a downward proposition, and yet
they expend most of their energies communicating not downward but
up. They are students of the boss; they spend a large part of each day
reading between his lines, interpreting his gestures, pondering what he
is really up to.

So far so good. The corollary, however, is something else again.
For the trouble is that the average executive spends so much time
analyzing upward that he has little time left to do the same in the other
direction. The boss is a "funny sort," "a hard character to dope out,"
"a very complex guy." Subordinates? They are guys who do work.

Economic Man, thanks to studies of the worker of the last quarter
century, has been exploded. Alas, his blood brother in the front office,
Logical Man, is still around. There is, to be sure, a double standard
on this—people *know* the boss isn't logical—but when they look at those
below, they tend to interpret their behavior in terms of logical cause
and effect—emotion and sentiment being mere aberrations.[2]

The impact of this on communication is profound. For one thing
the boss is led to address himself only to the surface manifestations of
discontent, and to confuse non-logical behavior with illogic—which is
not the same thing. Similarly, because he may forget that his power

---

[2] There are, of course, exceptions: the sales force, research people—and somewhere
in most organizations there usually seems to be an unofficial "V.P. in charge of screw-
balls" or his equivalent.

over his subordinates makes them as preoccupied with him as he is with his own boss, he fails to grasp the tremendous implications his simplest actions can have—how a lifted eyebrow, for example, can set a whole chain of speculations in motion.   He makes a small—and to him innocuous—shift and is amazed, distressed, and disgusted at the wild rumors and gossip that finally bounce back to him about what "they" really meant by the shift.   After all, we're supposed to be grown-up people in this organization.

Furthermore, so quickly does the boss forget how *he* used to feel that he deludes himself about the quality of the information he gets.   It is virtually impossible to find a boss who doesn't want straight dope and difficult to find one who doesn't believe he gets it.   (Out of 100 executives questioned by FORTUNE, less than a third said they thought their subordinates tended to sugar-coat.)   The desire may be sincere—certainly it is true that the boss is often more willing to permit free speech than the subordinate is willing to dare it.   Generally, however, you can postulate that subordinates give the boss bad news only if they would catch hell if they didn't.

And what of the effect of all this on the subordinates?   Thanks to the concept of Logical Man, they must chafe often at the difficulty of getting a "reading" from the boss on their work.   To the boss, naturally, this is an exasperating point of view: no comment is really praise—if your work wasn't up to snuff in this organization you'd hear about it quick enough.

Whatever may be bothering the subordinate, he knows that he is expected to behave "logically"; that he would lose face if he confessed to his boss what was really on his mind.   And so he keeps his troubles to himself, and if he expresses them at all it is only through the medium of "factual" matters likely to have little bearing on the real gripe.   After all, we're grown-up people in this organization.

"Two of the most important and time-consuming pastimes of the human mind," Harvard's Fritz Roethlisberger has noted, "are to rationalize sentiments and to modify sentiments by logic."

Even when people do take a good look at the manifold foibles and pressures of the structure beneath them, they are tempted to shrug it all off as just a case of "the personal factor" at work.   But if it were, there would be little hope for really doing much about better communication.   There are only so many good people to go around and if communication could be explained only in terms of personality, we would seem to be at a dead end.

Fortunately, it is not true.   It is not true because of a fact business is only now beginning to realize: *the way people behave in an organiza-*

tion is influenced as much by its social structure as by their own personalities.

This goes down hard with most people; as with accents, it applies only to others.   Yet few societies exert the selective and molding force of the corporation; however unconscious of it they may be, executives in the same company tend to think, talk, and act alike—and to hire and promote people who similarly "fit in."   And if a "misfit" does manage to stay on it's quite probable that he will either be boxed off as a sort of kept iconoclast, or remold himself to the pattern and take up a hobby.   And be outraged if it is suggested that the structure has influenced his behavior.

Perhaps the most graphic—and significant—demonstration of the structure's force cropped up in the course of a routine morale survey Sears Roebuck made of its retail stores in 1949.   For years the stores had been organized along either of two lines: (1) a relatively centralized pyramidal structure; (2) a "flat" type that put great emphasis on delegation of authority.   Otherwise, they were pretty much alike.   But when the time came to make a breakdown of findings of the survey, Sears' personnel department found that the chart was shaping up in a surprising way.   With few exceptions, the stores whose morale standing placed them at the top of the chart were the "flat" type; the stores at the bottom, the pyramidal type.   Their curiosity aroused, the personnel people went on to make a check of where most of the "promotables" were coming from.   Answer: the "flat" stores.

Significantly, Sears also found that it would be unwise to charge ahead and convert everybody to the "flat" structure.   "The executives that the pyramid had—in effect—selected," says Sears' Jim Worthy, "would have had a rough time functioning well in a looser setup.   To change the structure, you have to change the guys."

Similarly, structure has a lot more to do with determining leaders than the personal factors people usually like to dwell on.   Examine almost any organization and you find that the person in a position of "centrality"—i.e., the spot where the most information channels converge— is the man others regard as a leader.   The executive V.P. is a case in point.   If the other V.P.'s report directly to him rather than to the president, the executive V.P. is likely to be the operating leader—and the president, if he tries to exercise control, is apt to find he's only interfering.   Sometimes this is as it was meant to be; other times it is almost inadvertent.   It is not an unusual organization in which someone, because of a fortuitous position in the communication network, exercises authority out of all proportion to his official position.   Even the province of that most absolute of rulers, the captain of a ship, can be just as subject to this influence.   In World War II carrier warfare, for example, it was found necessary to center the vast flow of incoming data in a Combat Information Center in the bowels of the ship.   The captain, as a result, was often reduced to little more than glorified helmsman—and in one battle a lieutenant commander (and a *reserve*, at that) maneuvered a carrier task force, a rear admiral relaying the orders for him.   Control communication and you control.

* * * * * *

PARTICIPATION—OR ACTIVITY?

In the how-to-keep-a-taut-ship-happy approach, participation takes two general forms.   The first consists of setting up such a heavy downward flow of information that people not involved in something will be made to feel as if they were.   It doesn't work very well.   Where there is no opportunity for interchange—which is to say, no communication—information may be useless.   Indeed, there can be too much of it; all too often it has so little relevance to the employee that it can confuse him more than it enlightens or flatters him.   And confuse the boss, it might be added, into believing participation can come out of the mimeograph.

The second form, not to be confused with the "conference training" whose label it frequently appropriates, consists of a very elaborate series of devices for telling people something and making them feel at the same time that they are thinking it up themselves.   It doesn't work very well either.   A bit of the old oil now and then, of course, can be in order, but in this kind of manipulation the disadvantages outweigh the advantages.   For one thing, since the implicit premise is that logic can convince others how right you were all along, it prevents the user from finding out the true feelings of subordinates.   For another, the device doesn't fool people very long.

All this, it is said, is "participation."   It is not; it is merely *activity*. And the two are by no means the same—particularly when the activity is to avoid participation.

* * * * * *

But much more puzzling than the matter of *how* to participate is that of *who* is to participate.   How many more people are to be brought into the decision-making process?   How much further down the organization do you take policy problems?   And this, inescapably, brings us to the key question of participation. Why? What is it business really wants out of participation, better morale—or more profits?

The question, according to current lore on the subject, is almost heretical. For just as some businessmen evade the choice by phony democracy, more of them deny that the necessity for choice exists at all. Participation is good business. Better human relations means better job performance. Democracy, in short, pays off. So it may. But is this the businessman's real motive? No. He is simply following an old American custom: explaining away his decent instincts in terms of dollars-and-cents benefits.

For the fact is that a great many businessmen are interested in more participation because they think it is right—and not because they think it necessarily means more profits. Most often, it does mean more profits. But the two are not to be equated so easily. Sometimes more participation may produce no gain in measurable efficiency. And while the corporation may benefit in other ways, the problem must be faced for what it is, not one to be resolved on technical grounds. It is a matter of conscience.

"We kid ourselves a lot," says one executive. "We talk about doing all this because it pays off in the annual report. We'd be scared to admit to ourselves anything else. But I think I know why we're doing it—it's because these people here have a right to express themselves. Putting the emphasis on efficiency as the reason is like Stakhanovism, and that's not really what we are doing anyway. I think we'd do better to face up to the fact."

What is the goal of the corporation? Here is the heart of the matter. Is the goal quick profits in a special situation? Expansion? Keeping an already established market? Giving its members the opportunity to develop their potentialities? Until the goal is hammered out, the question of participation and the question of efficiency remain somewhat abstract. And the hammering out—as many a board-room argument indicates—is no mere hairsplitting.

•　　•　　•　　•　　•　　•

There is growing agreement on a major premise: that the social structure of the corporation is the key to its performance—and management doesn't know enough about it. The new approach this calls for goes by many labels—"democratic leadership," "permissive management," and "communication skills." Essentially, however, it resolves itself into training in how to look downward into the organization instead of always up—how, in short, to get the boss to participate.

At the same time, more basic research is badly needed—ironically, for some of our most valuable clues on management behavior we must still go back to a study of workers' behavior in a factory in Hawthorne twenty-odd years ago. The obstacles to research in this field, to be sure, are formidable. Measuring executive behavior is a lot tougher than measuring the behavior of people who are doing something readily measurable; furthermore, what such studies reveal is apt to come closest to piercing the inner core of business mythology. Yet the pilot studies in the field have demonstrated that this kind of research can help clear up a good many problems bothering management.

One that should be cleared up is whether or not business is saddled with a structure that is inherently authoritarian. Many thoughtful businessmen seem to be worried by the question. Which leads us to one final point.

The soul-searching over the "authoritarian structure" can lead to a healthy self-examination. It can also lead to unrealistic expiation. For if the structure is conceived of as necessarily authoritarian, then democracy in industry can only be extracurricular. Hence, the conferences, clinics, and so forth that, one suspects, are occasionally staged more for the fact of their democratic techniques than for their content.

Democracy is a tricky word. It is easy to confuse it with a sort of fatuous egalitarianism in which everybody has an equal say in everything. But democracy was never meant to be that fuzzy and mawkish an ideal. It has always implied leadership, and leadership has always implied some sort of hierarchy; indeed, our own democracy could not function save for the complex of hierarchies that make it up. In business, as in every other kind of organization, democracy lies in the intangibles—the permissiveness of the leader and the assent of those below. And in this matter of assent, as we have seen, the business hierarchy is not so authoritarian as it is sometimes thought.

So we suggest that the word "authoritarian" is a hopelessly misleading way of describing the essential nature of the structure. The structure should be adapted and broadened, certainly; but the best way to reconcile it with the democratic ideal is not through any spurious affectations of democracy, but through the spirit that animates the relationships throughout the organization.

⊸ई⊸ईई⊸ई⊶

81. Gossip in the Small Town *

SAYS E. W. BURGESS, regarding the book by Albert Blumenthal from which this selection is taken, ". . . the main characteristics of small-town life stand out in clear perspective: close acquaintanceship of everyone with everyone else, the dominance of personal relations, and the subjection of the individual to continuous observation and control by the community. These are essentially what are referred to by the phrase 'small-town stuff.' " Of the informal social controls within the village none is more characteristic than the subject of this chapter: gossip.

ONE OF THE FAVORITE THEMES of novels, stage plays, and jokes has long been the petty gossiping in small towns. Even the small-town residents themselves poke some fun at the inevitable and perennial gossiping in their midst, and are continually crying out against it and grumbling about it. For all that is so traditional about the small and isolated community is woven about the far-reaching power of gossip—of communication by word of mouth.

In Mineville, "gossip" is a term much used, especially by women and in description of them. It has two general meanings. Sometimes it includes all local news which is transmitted by word of mouth; and at other times it means only that information involving a fellow-resident which any particular resident would not want told of himself, or which people feel they must whisper stealthily lest they incur the displeasure of someone. Whether or not the resident wishes the word to carry a derogatory stigma is told by the intonation of his voice or by other gestures. In the following discussion it will be used in both senses under the assumption that the context will indicate to what extent a distinction is meant to be made between mere talk, and that sort of talk which anyone thinks should be whispered or not told.

WHO ARE THE GOSSIPERS?

Over the telephone a Mineville woman may quite frankly say, "I thought I would call up and see if you have heard the latest gossip."

---

* Albert Blumenthal, Small-Town Stuff (Chicago: The University of Chicago Press, 1932), pp. 128-143. Reprinted by permission of the publisher and the author.

The author (b. 1902) is Associate Professor of Sociology, University of South Dakota. Small-Town Stuff was issued as a Ph.D. thesis, University of Chicago, under the title, A Sociological Study of a Small Town. Dr. Blumenthal's main fields of interest are community study, theory analysis, and criminology.

But while she is herself in the midst of spreading a scandal she is not unlikely to cast discredit upon another woman by calling her a "terrible old gossip." This illustrates the tendency of the people to make light of their own gossiping and that of their friends and to condemn it in others. For whether or not a person is rated as a gossip in the discrediting sense of the term depends not upon what he actually says but upon the attitude toward him held by the person making the rating.

Violent outbursts of anger and disgust at the "damned gossipers" are characteristic of most Minevillers when some of their own private affairs are aired in public. The part they themselves play in airing the affairs of others they seem to overlook. While it is true that most of them pretend to refrain from circulating information which will be harmful to the other fellow, all townsfolk (excepting infants and very small children) are dispensers of gossip, be it harmful or not. Those persons who might locally be known as non-gossipers are merely persons who are comparatively little interested in collecting whispered information and who, when they secure it, impart it more tactfully and considerately than the people as a whole. But even they have a few strong dislikes which cause them to show little consideration for some people.

In classifying the gossiping proclivities of the people the first criterion to suggest itself is that of sex, because from time immemorial men have jested about woman's tendency toward personal gossip. The explanation is clear. She merely talks of that about which her life is centered. She spends comparatively little time discussing the stock market, sports, politics, and impersonal problems of workaday life such as do the men. Her preoccupation is with local events—particularly those local events which have a strong tinge of the personal such as bridge parties and moral scandals. She frankly admits that when she goes calling she "talks about everybody in town." She touches at great length upon the care of babies, children, and husbands; illnesses, childbirth, cooking, clothing, and other subjects closely related to the home—always illustrating her theory in terms of Mineville personalities. Unlike her husband, she never tires of talking shop, and when she talks shop, persons are generally involved. Also, she can gossip for an hour over the telephone at will while he works with a lone partner in a dark recess far below the surface of the earth. In this way she may act as a gossip collector for him during the day and retail her findings to him when he returns from work. He may tell her what he has heard "at the mine," but this usually is much less than she has to tell him, and less personal.

A usual remark about those in the community who are known as "gossips" is: "Tell Mrs. So-and-So anything as a secret if you want it advertised all over town in a hurry." But Mineville has so many proficient gossipers that to select only those who are reputed to be gossips and to ignore the rest would be to produce an erroneous picture. A few typical examples will serve to bring out this point.

First we may note some factors which cause Mrs. Dunwell to be rated as the community's leading female "gossip." Mrs. Dunwell occupies a position of social prominence which normally places her somewhat in the public eye aside from publicity which she might derive from her gossiping. She is frank and quick to "jump to conclusions"; she spares no one, not even herself, when she decides to give her opinion. This impulsive frankness causes her to reveal passing flurries of envy and jealousy which would remain undisclosed in the case of the ordinary woman. Consequently, she is readily accused of having a tendency to exaggerate and distort, and is feared and disliked by many. But there is no doubt that were she less prominent and less frank to all persons anywhere, she might gossip equally as much without being renowned as a community gossip, in the derogatory sense of the term.

The leading gossips tend to be persons with unusual ability to remember "everything about everybody." One of these is Ed Slade, who is known more as a "talker" than as a "gossip" because he is not a woman. Another was Mrs. Drake, who was not known as a gossip mainly because she was a recluse. Both Mr. Slade and Mrs. Drake were recognized as vocal social historians of the community, as can be seen from the following advice given when certain inside information was sought:

Miss X: You should see Ed Slade. He can tell you anything you want to know.

Mr. X [her father—interrupting]: Yes, see Ed Slade. He knows all about everything in town. I came in 1889 and he was tending bar before he worked for me at that time. He can tell you lots and more too.

Mrs. X: And he will be glad to tell you things. It's odd how some people can remember things. There was Mrs. Drake. Whenever I wanted to know anything I used to go over to her. She seemed to know everything about everybody and everything in town. It's too bad she died. She could have helped you.

She was not a gossip. She never told unless you asked but when you asked she sure knew.

Mr. X: Sid Marshall is quite a talker. He came here after I did but he sure could tell you about everything since he came.

It is interesting that the men are especially prone to speak of the talkative members of their sex as "talkers" while females with the same propensities are classified as "gossips." In reply, the women contend, and perhaps not without justification, that the men are the "worst gossipers." Whatever the truth may be, Mineville has some very talkative males who are much better situated to secure and spread the news than are the women. Among these is Sid Marshall.

"Sid" is the proprietor of a tailor shop in which an almost perpetual talk-fest is in progress throughout the day and often until late at night. Man after man "drops into Sid's place" for a sociable chat and leaves such news as he has in return for a large supply from Sid and others who may have been present. Everything is discussed: from the habitual debtors of Mineville to the debtor nations of the World War; from the scandal of a Mineviller who just passed by the window to that involving presidents and kings. Religion, politics, psychology, economics, milady's styles, fishing trips, smutty stories, the weather, and the merits of one another's chewing tobacco—nothing is barred. But it would be a mistake to conceive of this visiting center as those of small towns are so often caricatured, that is, as made up of men of naïve intelligence who presume great wisdom. Their ideas and attitudes on problems of larger import are not provincialisms, but rather are the same as those had by city people, because of being derived from the same immediate sources: editors of leading periodicals, the radio, and the movies. On the other hand, on local matters the individuals force one another to keep close to facts by the ruthlessness by which they pounce upon him who errs.

There is no better place in Mineville to sense shifts in public opinion than Sid's tailor shop. For news generally is not "out" long before someone brings it to Sid's, whose position is much like that of the editor of a paper in that he tends to hear all sides of questions more rapidly than people in general. From these diverse points of view he tries to arrive at the true statement of a situation. He becomes one of the best-informed men in town on local affairs, and his shop is one of Mineville's best substitutes for a daily newspaper and scandal sheet— a function pleasant to him and in no sense to his discredit, even though he is subjected to criticism by women who imagine that they are the particular objects under discussion in his shop.

. . . . . .

There are, of course, other outstanding agents of gossip and other gossiping centers on Main Street. Not only are there several business men who are very proficient gossips, but most of the business establishments have particular persons who "hang around and talk." In fact, wherever the people assemble informally a gossiping center tends to arise.

Those traditional gossip-dispensing bureaus, the barber shops, where the barber tries to talk about as many interesting things as possible to his customers, have changed somewhat since the war. One of the barbers observes:

Do you remember how there always used to be a gang of men hanging around the barber shops? I try to discourage them from hanging around my place nowadays since women and girls are an important part of my trade. Boy, how the guys used to talk in the old days! I'll bet there were more dirty jokes and more dirty remarks passed in the barber shops than anywhere in town. And how they gossiped! But things have changed. If the fellows do hang around now they have to be careful what they say in the presence of women and girls and so there isn't much to encourage them to loiter in a shop. Besides, women don't like to come into a shop if a lot of men are sitting around. There is plenty of talk now, but the subjects are different—as long as women are in the shop, at least.

Away from Main Street and from home the men do most of their gossiping in the mines and mills. Each group of workers tends to have certain members who stand out for their general talking abilities. Of forty-six men on one shift at the Salmon Mine two of these entertainers are in the limelight. To quote a fellow-workman:

Talk about gossip! On our shift we have Fred Hare and Charlie Ratner in the center of the bunch before we go down the mine and at eating time, and I'll bet there ain't a woman in town who can equal those fellows. They never run out of gossip. You ought to see how they monopolize the conversation. It seems almost impossible that they can possibly know so much. Month after month their supply of gossip holds out.

Even among children there are prominent agents of gossip. They function much as do their elders, and when they are indiscreet they are subjected to the same disrepute. Breta Gaynor (age eleven) is a good example in the grade school. She talks incessantly and keeps widely informed upon the affairs of the school children, and upon those of adults as well. At a tender age Mineville children commence to take a naïve interest in the events of community gossip because they are likely to have had some acquaintance with a large share of persons and things of which they hear adults talk. The more intelligent five-year-old kindergarten children, for instance, have already reached a stage at which they are able to impart surprising bits of information to their teacher.

Influenced by small-town conditions, as are mature residents, Mineville children have leisure time, frankness, curiosity, and close contacts with large numbers at school to facilitate their gossiping. Through the grade school and through the high school waves of gossip of all sorts surge. Indeed, the schools are the largest gossiping centers in town although townsfolk, as a rule, are not aware of the fact.

GOSSIP AND THE FORMATION OF PUBLIC OPINION

Talking of things in general appears to be the favorite indoor and outdoor sport in Mineville. This is due in part to the neighborliness and community of interest among the people, and in part to the deficiency of other leisure-time activities in which there is an element of sociability. An interesting sidelight upon the effect of a community of interest was observed by a candidate for a county office:

I'll tell you something that surprised me. Because I was never much of a mixer, I thought I would have a hard time when I ran for office. I thought I wouldn't be able to find anything to talk about to people I didn't know. It sure surprised me how easy it is to find something to talk about. We have so much in common with one another in this town, and even in the county, that we know a lot about people we've never talked to. For that reason I found that I could predict pretty well what would be an interesting topic of conversation to nearly everyone. I always knew some of their friends, where they worked, something about their children, and so forth. In a jiffy I could bridge the gap between not knowing people and becoming intimate with them. The trouble was not in finding something to talk about but rather that I had to be careful not to talk too much about intimate things for fear someone would start talk going around that the people shouldn't vote for me because I'm just an old gossiper anyhow. And then, I was pretty sure that some of the people were trying to get me to feel intimate with them so that I would confide things in them which they could use against me politically.

With such community of interest, and a general desire to tell the other fellow the latest news, it is not surprising that an exceptionally live bit of news, such as the death of a prominent citizen, attains almost complete circulation in the community in about two hours. Most of the people are likely to have the news in an hour. In a few minutes it reaches all of the business establishments on Main Street. "Too bad about Mr. So-and-So," the merchant characteristically says to his customers one by one. And wherever a group is congregated along the street the death becomes a topic of conversation. Meanwhile, with half of the people in town having telephones and by the age-old practice of "running in" to tell a neighbor, the news soon reaches those who perchance have not visited Main Street or otherwise encountered someone who might tell them. Community expectation of rapidity of circulation is attested by the fact that should such a death occur at nine o'clock in the morning and the information not reach a resident until late in the afternoon, his usual expression is, "I can't understand why I didn't hear that sooner," and others say to him, "Where have you been? Everybody knew that by noon."

For several days such a topic is likely to be focal in the community. The man, his last illness, his family, etc., are discussed and rediscussed. A multitude of diverse bits of information and points of view have been brought into play before the subject drops out of the limelight.

Because as a social unit it is small and isolated, Mineville offers a most interesting laboratory for the study of public opinion. The participant-observer can witness the crystallizing of opinion in detail from its initial gropings to the final product in which more or less uniform attitudes and ideas in respect to a matter are characteristic over the whole community or in large factions. He will be struck with the rapid and varied shifts of opinion from one side of a question to another. He will see occasional cases when opinion becomes so fixed that there is a community-wide tendency for the people to become emotional if they are asked to consider the merits of the minority side of a matter. But he will find that such cases of callousness are usually temporary periods of high resistance, and that in the long run the "truth" is acknowledged by the people as a whole, if an item of gossip is sufficiently alive to keep it before them long enough. The people are so persistently confronted with untruths or partial truths in local rumor that they have a wholesome skepticism regarding it which naturally results in a rigorous, although often unconscious, piecing-together of evidence before a final conclusion is reached.

When news "gets out," one of the first steps of a resident is to trace it, and, as a rule, he is quite keen in tracing the origins and course of gossip because of his insight into the relations of Minevillers to one another. Resolutely he sets about to build his theory as to the channels through which an item of gossip has passed, through certain outstanding gossipers, and through a network of relatives, friends, and others who have frequent and intimate contact with one another. He knows much of the probable motives of these people and of the reliability of what they might say. In questioning the truth of a bit of news, for instance, he will say, "She got it from Mrs. Jacobs and it's a cinch Mrs. Jacobs got it from Mrs. Black and you know what a liar Mrs. Black is."

HOW GOSSIP DESTROYS PRIVACY

We have already indicated how gossip brings together odds and ends of one's private life which he reveals about himself to numerous persons over a long period of time. We have not yet discussed the factor which accounts for the feeding of most of the very intimate personal information into the streams of gossip, that is, betrayed confidences.

Everyone trusts that certain persons in possession of intimate facts of his personal life will not betray him. He would feel most wretched if he actually believed that no one is to be trusted to hold such knowledge in due respect. His father, mother, wife, brother, and several good friends he assumes will shield parts of his life from the public gaze. And while we have no evidence upon which to assert that his faith is not justified for the most part, bit by bit details of his private affairs sift out by way of betrayed confidences. This happens everywhere, but the consequences are especially serious in a small town such as Mineville where people seize with alacrity upon such information and shortly insure its perpetuation by making it a public acquisition. Husbands, for instance, little know what information of their private affairs their wives may have told "in confidence" to women friends who in turn have broadcast it to the community "in confidence." It is by means of just such a network of interlocking confidences that the "whole town" secures the most whispered of information almost as readily as it does ordinary news, despite the strong inhibitions the people have regarding "talking about" others because of being afraid that their words will "get back" to the person "talked about." Fortunately, however, most Minevillers do not seem to realize how well others know them, and so the human longing for someone in whom to confide, to whom to unburden the weight of troubles, still finds extensive expression in the town.

By way of illustration, the following phenomena attending broken confidences may be noted as commonplace in Mineville, as elsewhere:

a) There are irresponsible information purveyors—persons who must tell.

b) While people are on intimate terms they normally confide in and otherwise learn a great deal about one another. When their relations are temporarily or permanently broken, the situation is ripe for the wholesale breaking of confidences.

c) The desire to appear interesting to others often causes indiscretion to the point of violation of confidences.

d) Persons are led into disclosing confidential information in order to prove points in arguments.

e) There are "accidental slips" which are not realized as broken confidences until after they have occurred.

f) Many confidences are broken because as time passes people are likely to forget that they received the information concerned in confidence.

g) Some people care less about privacy than others and so they easily disregard what are to them the excessive requests of others for secrecy. The leading female gossip of the town, as has been indicated, secures her disrepute largely because of telling about others that which she does not care if others tell about her.

SCANDALS

Novelists have painted vivid pictures of small-town life which have captured the popular imagination and have made small-town people appear to be a peculiar species of scandal-hungry creatures. Somehow the lurid exposés featured by city daily papers have been considered to be more worthy of sophisticated people than rural gossip, and there has been a tendency to minimize the fact that city folks do a great deal of gossiping among their more intimate associates.

If Minevillers have a greater interest in scandal than urbanites, it is because of a difference in situation, not in people. It so happens that besides sensational news derived from city dailies, the residents of the town are living under conditions conducive to the ferreting-out, spreading, and perpetuation of an extensive fund of local scandal. And this news is the more interesting because it affects the status of persons with whom they are obliged to have close social relationships. Certainly it would be more interesting if one were to know that the only iceman in town has tendencies to be a paramour than it is to read in a city paper of the same proclivities on the part of some strange iceman one has never seen.

There is a fund of whispered gossip about every resident of a small town. Actually but an infinitesmal part of this is communicated directly to the person concerned, although the people say, "Everything gets back sooner or later in this town." Such news characteristically travels in channels which avoid him. It frequently buzzes among his closest friends and yet escapes him. This is particularly true of scandal.

•   •   •   •   •   •

FEAR OF GOSSIP

In Mineville, individual variation in respect to fear of gossip is very wide. There is to be found the whole gamut of degrees from persons who are excessively fearsome lest their affairs become matter of gossip to those who defy, ignore, or are not well cognizant of the relentlessness with which news travels and the thorough circulation which it attains.

In the main, however, Minevillers wittingly and unwittingly are affected by a strong fear of gossip. Long experience has shown them that information tends to become distorted in passing from person to person, and so, even though the public in question is small enough that the truth is likely to become generally known in time if it is known to a few persons, the people do not wish to have their affairs thrown into the gristmill of conversation and argument through which so much news must pass before it is accurately consumed. This reluctance to be "talked about" does much to inhibit the circulation not only of reprehensible gossip but of permissible news. A warning voice is ever ready to whisper into the resident's ear, "Be careful! It will get all over town," or "What will people say?" And even in formal meetings someone may arise to say, "We'd better watch our step or the whole town will be on our necks before we adjourn."

No resident of Mineville supposes that he is not "talked about." Even obscure townsfolk complain that they live under the spotlight of the public eye and hence must become hardened to the inevitable gossip, if they are to have peace of mind. But withal, there is so much open defiance to gossip as to suggest that many residents do not realize the harm which their acts may bring upon their reputations at present, and even twenty years in the future.

❦❦❦❦

82. Confessions of a Diaper Salesman *

AMERICANS GENERALLY, and business men in particular, have repeatedly pointed out that competition is a basic and characteristic process in our society. We often encourage competition, for example, in recreation, education, and religion, as well as in the world of business. After World War II, during which salesmen were relatively unimportant appendages of business, the *Fortune* editors commemorated the postwar return to competitive selling with this article. Here they present, to use their own introductory remarks, "the somewhat fictionalized account of a well-educated girl who happened into a field of enterprise where high pressure has already

* Reprinted from the March, 1949, issue of *Fortune* by Special Permission of the Editors; Copyright 1949 Time, Inc.

had its collision with ethics." In their competitive struggle, incidentally, the diaper salesmen described here appear to have exploited to the full the techniques of modern communication.

I SHALL START at the beginning. I had to take the job, for at that time
I had very little money. And so one morning, clutching a classified
advertisement in my hand, I walked into the downtown office of the
Compleat Diaper Service, and I must say with not much confidence.
I had the feeling that my education and upbringing were ill suited to
whatever Compleat might want me to do.

It was a small, bare room with a big table on which there were several
telephones. There were two men there. One, a tired-looking man
with gray hair, introduced himself as Mr. Yondel, the sales manager;
the other, a small, wiry chap with a very deep tan, he introduced simply
as Sidney.

I had no sooner started to speak than they beamed at each other.
"Sidney, the accent!" said Mr. Yondel.
"Class!" said Sidney. "With a capital K!" He seemed very amused.
Instantaneously I was hired. Mr. Yondel gave me a short explanation of what the firm did, which seemed simple enough. It was a sort
of laundry (the actual plant was out in the suburbs) with a huge stock
of diapers. For $2.50 per hundred it would rent diapers to mothers.
Twice a week deliverymen, of whom there were forty, would pick up the
soiled diapers and leave fresh ones.

The trick, explained Sidney (who I learned later was the co-owner
and idea man of the business), was not so much to get customers as to
get them *in time*. To try and make the sale after birth, he said, was
uneconomic; there was already lost revenue and, besides, every other
diaper service would be doing the same thing. "Theoretically, we got
nine months to play around with," he said, "and the closer we get back
to when the whole thing starts, the firmer the sale and the less we got to
worry from the competition. Sell the mother while she's in the hospital, O.K. A month, two, three months before that, better. And if
you can figure out a way—" He winked and added something in quite
poor taste.

The enormity of the job became more evident at the next morning's
sales meeting. Besides Sidney and Mr. Yondel there were five others:
two unimpressive-looking men, two matron types, and myself. Sidney
opened the meeting.

"One thought this morning—high pressure." He glared at us men-
acingly. "Everybody's afraid of the word! Been so easy selling last
couple of years everybody's squeamish about doing any work. Namby-

pamby, lazy—L-A-Z-Y. Order takers, that's what we've become. Sure we got a fine service—" (and I must say we really did) "—but now every damn fool's getting into the business. And we got prejudice, ignorance—thousands people never even heard of diaper service. What's the answer? Pressure, brother, *high* pressure, and lemme tell you the guys that don't wise up are going to get left behind, but fast."

"All the time we got to keep punching." He made little jabbing motions with his fist. "The old Compleat motto—we don't care how you get it, but get the Geschäft. Ideas. Angles. Gimmicks. Right after the war, for instance. We couldn't take on any more business— not enough diapers. But did Sidney take it easy? Sidney did not. Sidney hears about a ship being held up out in quarantine—full of war brides and babies are swarming all over the place. So Sidney starts to thinking. Two days later. Every housewife in the city picks up the paper and sees this piece that's terrific with human interest. Helicopter delivers gift of diapers to war-bride ship! *COMPLEAT* diapers! See? Punching, punching all the time! The old Geschäft!"

Sidney sat down and Mr. Yondel took over. He picked up one of the telephones and in a droll fashion slowly began inspecting it. "You people," he said, "seem to have forgotten how to use this thing. It is really a very simple instrument."

"Watch this," Sidney whispered to me, "a real artist, that Yondel."

Mr. Yondel took a typewritten list from his pocket, scanned it, and then began dialing. In a few seconds an answering squawk came from the phone. As it did Mr. Yondel sort of subsided in his chair and his face assumed such an expression of kindliness I could scarcely recognize him.

"Mrs. Kelly? . . ." He settled back farther in his chair. "Mrs. Kelly, 'tis Father O'Rourke . . . Well, our parishes overlap a bit . . . I just wanted to add my word to Father Casey's and say how happy I am that a little one is on the way." In very short order he was speaking of his concern for mother's health and baby's safety, and thus to diaper service. The Father had heard of one that was particularly sanitary. Compleat, he believed the name was. How much did they charge? He didn't really know . . . perhaps the Compleat people themselves might be calling one of these days. . . . Mrs. Kelly was welcome indeed. Mr. Yondel murmured a blessing and quietly put down the phone.

"See what I mean?" said Sidney, enchanted. "We don't care how you get it, but get the Geschäft."

It was on phone work that I was started and I am ashamed to say that I was wonderfully good at it. Sometimes I was a nurse, other times the secretary of some nonprofit institution; if a father answered, I was the representative of the Fortunate Fathers' Club. Frequently I told them just who I was. Whatever I elaborated—and Mr. Yondel gave me carte blanche—I stuck close to certain fundamentals; I told them I was sending them a free subscription to a baby magazine (an excellent magazine jointly sponsored by baby-food companies, layette manufacturers, etc.) and, of course, in addition to trying to sell them, I always asked if any of their friends were expecting also.

Our deliverymen were a big help, for they got many leads from customers and did a bit of canvassing on their own. This was because of a contest Sidney had set up; for each new lead they would get ten points; for each new customer, fifty. When they had piled up a thousand or so points they could choose a prize; with 1,700 points, for instance, they would get an electric toaster; for 4,400 an inner-spring mattress. To make the prizes more compelling Sidney sent the prize catalogues and contest circulars direct to the deliverymen's homes, since he had found that then their wives would make life miserable for them if they didn't get a lot of points. Just another example of getting the Geschäft, he explained.

We were being badgered too. Baby-Pleez, Compleat's greatest antagonist, was expanding very forcefully, and Mr. Yondel kept bearing down on us for more and more names. I called on several maternity shops and tried to arrange an understanding, but it turned out we had more names to give them than they us. Layette departments of big stores weren't much help either, for I found that most women are far too superstitious to buy layettes until after the baby is born. On door-to-door work, however, I hit my stride. Often I would start with only a few names supplied by our deliverymen (and primed by an ecclesiastical call) and then pick up enough for a two or three-day route as I worked from one block of flats to another. Most of the mothers-to-be were glad to see me, and would talk interminably, but sometimes I would come upon someone who had cast aside the word of the church and chosen Baby-Pleez instead of Compleat. Here I would not importune, but use what Mr. Yondel called "the-seed-of-doubt technique." Did mother realize there were *thirteen* different kinds of bacteria that thrived on diapers and that Baby-Pleez's were not Extra-Germ-Proofed, like ours? After all, you never could be sure . . . baby's tender little skin . . . all those germs . . . Surprisingly often, we would get the order if we were patient and called back in a few days.

But labor as we might, Baby-Pleez was becoming a greater threat every day. They had put on a girl who went around making free pencil sketches of their customers' babies. As a reprisal Sidney hired a nurse as a "baby consultant" but soon the word got around that Compleat was offering free nursing service and we had to put a stop to that. Worst of all was the battle of the cans. Even when we had definitely obtained the order, Baby-Pleez's men would leave their metal diaper containers on the customer's doorstep. Other competitors did the same and when the bewildered mother returned home from the hospital she could hardly get to the door for the pile of cans and bundles. Our men were told to use their initiative in such cases. So, apparently, were Baby-Pleez's.

"It's war," Sidney told us one morning, with great zest. And Compleat was fighting back. Mr. Yondel was putting on two extra people for full-time phone work, and Sidney was pepping up the deliverymen by writing personal letters to their wives. "Sort of twitting them, in a nice way," he explained, "about other guys' wives getting more prizes than they did."

Most important, a big hospital drive had been planned. Even though we supplied many hospitals with diaper service, we hadn't had too much luck in getting leads from them; Mr. Yondel had "reached" an interne or nurse in only three hospitals, and the few hospitals that allowed us to solicit patients openly were very small. We would simply have to do better in the "unfriendly" ones. Mr. Yondel assigned me to the biggest. "Only one thing to remember—if they spot you and ask what outfit you're with," he cautioned me, "be sure and protect the good name of the firm. Tell them you're from Baby-Pleez."

It was absurdly easy. I simply walked in during visiting hours, ducked into a lavatory off one of the wards, and changed into a tan smock I had crammed in my handbag. It looked very official and most of the lying-in patients assumed I was approved by the hospital. I tried to get orders from them, but even when I got only their names and addresses that was all right; Sidney would have a deliveryman leave a can of diapers at their homes just the same, for the relatives or father would almost always take it for granted the mother had ordered them and pay up.

Most of the competitors' people didn't dissemble half so well as I; they were far too pushy. Often the wards would become so crowded with nurses' aides and Red Cross workers from Baby-Pleez and the others that the staff would begin to get suspicious. Wisely, I would retire before they were fully alerted and phone the intelligence to Mr. Yondel. Generally he was able to redirect me to a hospital where at the moment the field was wide open.

All in all, the weeks that followed proved to be the most productive I had spent with Compleat, and I was sorry when, for personal reasons, I had to tell Sidney and Mr. Yondel that I was leaving. In a way I hated to go, but it was a good time; the campaign had just reached a triumphant climax. I should mention, though, that actually we didn't beat Baby-Pleez at all. Oddly, they seemed to do as well as we did, but Sidney said he didn't care—between them they had so badgered and needled mothers that everyone was beginning to look on diaper service as an absolute necessity. Sixty-five per cent of the babies being born in the city were now using diaper service, Sidney estimated, and he thought that, if they kept in there punching for the old Geschäft, before long they could get it up to 80 per cent.

This seemed to depress Mr. Yondel. The afternoon I said goodbye he pointed to a new seal of approval some hygiene association had given them. If they kept up at this rate, he said, fingering the telephone, pretty soon they'd be so respectable all the fun would go out of the business. Sidney winked at me over Mr. Yondel's shoulder and said yes, sir, things were going to be strictly ethical from here on in.

As I stood by the elevator watching them for the last time they were chuckling together over something. Then Mr. Yondel picked up the phone. His face was contorted with rage. "Is this the Baby-Pleez Diaper Service?" I could hear him saying, as the elevator doors closed. "This is Dr. Morris at the Memorial Hospital. We're going to the police! There's a woman of yours up in one of our wards, and un- less . . ."

᪉᪉᪉᪉᪉

83. Conflict in a New England College Town *

MANY AMERICAN COLLEGES and universities with fairly large staffs are located in relatively small communities. These staff members often have characteristics and values that differ from those of the townspeople. In such situations the townspeople tend to regard the staff of the institution of higher learning as an out-group, and vice-versa. It is often but a small step further for relationships of hostility to develop between them. From his own experiences Dean Rapport describes one such "town-gown" conflict. Though it has certain unique characteristics, it also has much in common with that

* Victor A. Rapport, Social Forces, 17 (May, 1939), 527-532. Reprinted by permission of the publisher and the author.

The author (b. 1903) is Dean, College of Liberal Arts, Wayne University. For- merly Associate Professor of Sociology, University of Connecticut. United States Army Colonel, 1940-46. Has published numerous articles in professional journals.

found under similar circumstances elsewhere. He concludes that under such conditions conflict is likely to remain a permanent, institutionalized relationship, since the cultures of the two groups are so divergent. The reader can perhaps test, from his own experience, the soundness of this conclusion.

A CONFLICT SITUATION which exists between college and town groups is neither new nor unusual, yet the conflict manifesting itself around Storrs, the seat of Connecticut State College, seems sufficiently individual in certain particulars, typical in others, to warrant description. Deep-seated hates, the products of years, do not prevail since the college itself is young. Antagonisms which have festered with time are absent. Instead, however, is the intensity accompanying new suspicions and dislikes, the force of pioneers who inherit no traditions of struggle but, rather, live the struggle themselves. And the conflict, although new, expresses ancient motivations to conflict, rallying cries of past centuries and foreign places.

An investigation made by the author over a period of two years provides illustrations of certain characteristics of conflict and demonstrates conflict patterns. Some doubt is cast by the facts on the accepted outcomes of conflict, although there is a partial manifestation of several of these effects. The research was by personal interview with a large number of the residents of the Town of Mansfield, (in which Storrs is located), and with members of the college faculty. The results do not adapt themselves to statistical interpretation; they are exclusively opinions expressed in conversation of a purposely casual nature.

Out of the statements, the following characteristics and patterns of conflict became evident: (1) the groups are highly self-conscious with respect to status and welfare; (2) organization both with and without recognized leaders is frequent, although the organizations are transitory; (3) propaganda and false reports are constant; (4) there is distinct confusion between the accepted and assigned reasons for the conflict and what appear to be the real reasons; (5) the unifying and (6) the disorganizing effects of conflict are both apparent. Finally, (7) whether the conflict will be resolved by the operation of accommodation, assimilation, or amalgamation is open to question despite indications of the existence of these processes in the present situation.

Before entering upon a description of the conflict, it would be best to clarify the peculiarities of the New England setting. Connecticut

Co-author, *The Recreational Uses of Land in Connecticut*. His topics of interest include manpower planning in the field of education, criminology, social implications of selective service.

State College is located in Storrs, a village in the Town of Mansfield.

It should be remembered that the New England town is a relatively autonomous political division of the state, somewhat corresponding to the western township. Since county organization and function are relatively insignificant in New England, the town becomes a highly important grouping. Within the town are districts or villages—sometimes cities—which may or may not be separately incorporated, but which still owe a responsibility to the town. Thus, any resident of the Town of Mansfield, be he in Eagleville, Merrow or Gurleyville, is concerned with Storrs and the doings of its people, the college group.

This demarcation of the college group from the remainder of the town is indicative of the self-consciousness with respect to status and welfare. One frequently hears the former referred to as "the college" rather than as a group of individuals. Many of the townspeople make a clear distinction between themselves, who are residents of the town, and the college people who are in the same category as summer residents in a resort town. This is true despite the fact that many of the faculty have been taxpayers and property owners in the town for a score of years. Within the town group, one is "new people," according to one informant, for at least thirty years; the acceptance after that length of time does not appear to hold for those at the college. The college group, on the other hand, generally restricts its social life to colleagues and, in general, is quite ignorant of the town affairs. The self-consciousness with respect to welfare will be discussed later under organization.

Certain individuals, it should be indicated, are excluded from the conflict because of either or both of two reasons: (1) non-participation and (2) exemption. The non-participants are in both groups; these people do not feel antagonistic toward the other group, mix freely, and tend to merge with the exempts, those college people who are stamped as "regular" by the town group, and vice versa. The reasons for inclusion in the exempted group vary considerably with no characteristic pattern. In many instances, the older professors are included, though not all the older professors are exempted nor are all the exempts of the older group at the college. The exempted townspeople are frequently retired or professional men who reside in Mansfield, though not all the exempts are of this category nor is this whole group exempt. Young professors, recently arrived in Connecticut, and old farmers are accepted by the opposite groups—just why, nobody seems to know.

An illustration of the operation of the self-consciousness with respect to status is seen in Mansfield Center, another village of the Town of Mansfield, located about four miles from the college. Many residents of this community have long felt strongly about the college group.

Some years ago a lone professor and his family took up residence in the village. They were not a part of it for several years and were constantly made to feel that they did not "belong." Cracks finally began to appear in the icy reception they met, and in time they found themselves accepted as satisfactory citizens. What they had done to effect this change, they were unaware. They had merely continued about their own business, greeted people pleasantly but without trying to make friends, cultivated their garden, trimmed their lawn, and lived. It is probable that the combination of all these factors was the successful formula to break down the conflict attitudes. More and more of the college families moved into Mansfield Center as Storrs became overcrowded. The village soon heard mutterings about "The college people are taking over all the fine old houses," and "A farmer can't get a place any more with the rents that these college people pay" and "The Center ain't the same with all these new people coming in." As time went by, some of the new people became exempts, others did not.

The organization of the conflicting groups is primarily for political purposes. When the townspeople believe that "the college" is coming to the town meeting (a good old New England custom) for the purpose of promulgating legislation designed to further the ends of the college group, word goes out to the back country that all are needed to fight the measure. On the other hand, the college faction is constantly cautious about being absent lest "the town" force an ordinance prejudicial to the interests of the college. That each is motivated by selfish interests which are not conducive to the greatest welfare of the town is the firm belief of the opposing groups. Leaders are self-constituted or chosen from time to time in these political controversies, but frequently the groups follow concerted action without individuals at their head. A particularly serious issue arose about ten years ago when it was proposed to replace the antiquated grammar school at Storrs with a modern building. The opposition from the town centered around the argument that the existing school had been satisfactory for a great many years and ought to be good enough now, and, further, that "the college" felt that it needed something better for its children than was provided for the remainder of the town. That the children of faculty members represented only about one-third of the school population was overlooked. The building was approved at a town meeting and erected, but the wounds of the conflict have not yet healed. It is chiefly in these political disagreements that the propaganda and false reports are most current. The latter also are frequent in personal gossip principally concerning faculty members.

The confusion between assigned reasons and real reasons is particularly interesting. Among those persons who were interrogated, few had any real justification for disliking the other group, they "just felt that way." In most instances, when pressed for a reason, the informant was forced to pause for reflection before the "reason" was forthcoming.

The "reasons" on both sides are fundamentally the same. The objections of the people of the town to the college group fall under five general headings. The college group (1) takes no interest in the town; (2) is trying to run the town for its own selfish interests; (3) is "too snooty"; (4) represents impractical and incompetent theorists; (5) is composed of non-Connecticut newcomers. The college group felt that the townspeople (1) are trying to run the town for their own selfish interests; (2) are old-fashioned, stubborn Yankee farmers; (3) lack intellectual stimulation; (4) lack broad vision.

An analysis of the assigned reasons for the antagonisms reveals that some are justified while others are merely rationalizations. The political situation, which has been discussed in part previously, has counted heavily in arousing opposition attitudes. The charge has frequently been levelled at the college group that it lived in houses rented from the college (thus not contributing to taxation), traded outside the town, and in general represented no financial gain to town funds. These facts are generally untrue. A large number of the faculty live in non-college houses, almost all have automobiles which are taxable, and even those who live in college houses contribute indirectly to the town in that Mansfield receives a special grant from the State to compensate for the tax-exempt property which the State of Connecticut holds in the town. Regardless of the general untruth of the claim, it still carries great weight in the minds of the townspeople. They resent the "non-contributing" college people coming to town meeting and voting how the town's money shall be spent. A feeling common to many of the townsfolk is that the faculty receives instructions from the administration of the college—or some unnamed group in power—and must vote accordingly.

Some years ago, "the college" was accused of taking no interest in town affairs. When a few members of the faculty interested themselves to the extent of running for office as members of the school board or for other minor offices, the tune changed to one charging an attempt to dominate town affairs. One professor who served for ten years on the school board was complimented implicitly by having a candidate placed in the field for the express purpose of opposing the professor's policies on the board. It was felt that Professor X could not be defeated for office—"the college" would elect him—but the town's leading merchant was elected to fight every proposal which the learned gentleman might make. It is interesting to note that the merchant, who was an "exempt" as far as the college was concerned, found himself agreeing with Professor X, much to the displeasure of the former's constituents.

That the college group is "snooty" is both a justified and a false accusation. While certain of the faculty hold themselves aloof from the non-college group, others are anxious to be felt a part of the town. Their isolation is often more a result of exclusion by the townspeople than a product of their own desire. Herein is manifested a situation common to groups considered "clannish"; they are frequently so because they are not *allowed* to participate. In Mansfield, a number of the residents say that they want nothing to do with the college group, and then charge them with feeling themselves "too good to associate with plain people." An illustration of this occurred when a faculty member went into the village store one day attired in the old clothes in which he had been working in his garden. There he met one of the townspeople who was noted for his dislike of "the college." The two fell into a long conversation about a variety of things, and then the faculty member left. After his departure, the townsman asked "Who is that fellow? He seems mighty pleasant." When told that it was Professor Y, the man felt that he had been imposed on, and continued in his opinion that the college group was "snooty."

The charge that the people at the college are theoretical and impractical is largely derived from the origin of the college as a land-grant and primarily agricultural institution. The proposals of the agricultural faculty for improvement of farming techniques are frequently met with the statement that if those men had to farm like other farmers, they couldn't get along. "As long as they've got the State to pay for all their nonsense, they can try out those damn fool notions." Or, as a variant of that theme, "Anybody could be a successful farmer if he had all the money in the world to buy equipment in the first place." With the introduction and increase of non-agricultural subjects, the attitude of the townspeople was strengthened by the strange fields and the more citified men who were brought in to teach. Now, more than ever, the rift widened.

Not only were the new faculty members urban products, in the large, but they were often from places far distant from Connecticut or even New England. Here the political conflict arose again when it was felt that persons not familiar or sympathetic with local problems were dictating (or attempting to dictate) how town affairs were to be conducted. This is not particularly strange when it is realized that many of the families have been in Mansfield for many generations, and at least five of these families ante-date the Revolution by almost a hundred years. One of the local families is directly descended from a Mayflower pioneer who left the Massachusetts Colony and settled in Mansfield. That "Westerners" (people from Ohio, Illinois, Indiana, Kansas, and Iowa) should tell them how to run *their* town was something to resent. One local resident feels that the cause of the confusion in the United States today is the adoption of all these new-fangled devices, and that all the country needs to restore equilibrium is a return to the old ways of doing things. Automobiles and telephones are foolishness, the local store should resume business on a barter basis with the farmers, and we should drive oxcarts to Norwich, twenty miles away, to do our "trading." Why we have to import strangers to teach weird subjects when there are a lot of Connecticut boys and girls available is a mystery.

The college group, on the other hand, cannot sympathize with the Connecticut tradition of proceeding slowly. Its belief that the towns-people are trying to run the town for their own selfish interests and that they are old-fashioned and stubborn arises from the reluctance of the town to accept in their entirety the proposals for radical change in school and fiscal matters. With all the experts in education and finance it is not surprising that there should exist a desire to operate a sort of laboratory here in Mansfield. The people of the town are not ready to enter whole-heartedly into such proposals. Impatient with this attitude, the college group becomes rapidly critical.

The charges that the local people lack intellectual stimulation and broad vision impress the writer as coming frequently from the fact that the townspeople "don't talk our language." This conflict situation is not limited to gown versus town; it is frequent within the college itself. We of the faculty often become so engrossed in our own fields that we are unwilling or unable to talk with someone else about his work, and his unwillingness becomes to us a sign of his narrowness. The definition of a bore as "a person who always wants to talk when I want to talk" is applicable with slight transformation in this situation.

The real reasons for the conflict are common to all conflict situations. There is a clash of mores, a conflict of interests, which cannot be resolved. The jealousy of success by either group cannot be overcome by rational argument. That there is some justification on both sides is without question, but that much of the dispute is rooted in lack of understanding, in untruths, and an unwillingness to see the opposite side is equally evident.

The unifying effect of conflict is seen in the coming together of disputing groups of the townspeople to oppose the faculty, which, in turn, disagrees about many matters of college policy but which is quite homogeneous in opinions as to town affairs. The disorganization which conflict brings is retarding the normal progress which the town would make were these two factions not present.

Accommodation and assimilation are not totally absent, although whether either process will ever be complete is doubtful. Each side accepts the presence of the other, occasional joint efforts are carried out with the usual pattern being that of the college group joining the town group; rarely does the reverse occur. Such groups as the local Red Cross, the Parent-Teachers Association, and a choral society are effecting certain joint association, but it should be noted that these are primarily groups of women. Less association of the men takes place. As has already been mentioned, exempts of both groups are universally welcome and represent well assimilated individuals. A negligible amount of intermarriage between the groups has occurred.

Discussion of this type of conflict is usually designated as "town versus gown"; the implication is that the town is the aggressor, the college the defender. Long before Simmel, Gumplowicz or Marx, men knew that "it takes two to make a fight." It is the writer's opinion that the gown versus town phase of the conflict has been neglected. The college group, it would appear, is equally responsible for the existence and preservation of the conflict situation.

Finally, the question arises as to whether, as is frequently stated regarding conflict, this situation is true only during a period of change. It may be said that the conflict is occurring while the college is growing, but the writer believes that such divergent groups will not, as has been said, complete the processes of accommodation, assimilation and amalgamation with the eventual eradication of the conflict. Each group is protected from being absorbed by the culture of the other, and, as a result, each will continue with its own culture. Evidence in support of this is seen in towns where colleges have existed for several hundred years and where the town versus gown and the gown versus town conflicts still prevail.

⋖᪣⋖᪣᪣⋗᪣᪣⋗

84. The Battle of Athens, Tennessee *

HUMAN SOCIETIES are often characterized by the struggle for dominance. Those who exercise controls in government, economics, or

---

* Theodore H. White, *Harper's Magazine*, 194 (January, 1947), 54-61. Reprinted by permission of the author.

any other social area are frequently tempted to abuse their power and exploit those over whom they wield authority. Unless checks are provided and constant vigilance is practiced these abuses are likely to occur. The "Battle of Athens," described here by T. H. White, is a story of the abuse of power by a small group of corrupt politicians who were part of a state-wide political machine. It is a story of the conflict, both verbal and physical, that ensued when an intelligent leadership persuaded the citizens they could regain control over their local affairs by use of the ballot.

THE Sweetwater River, a pleasant mountain stream that falls into the basin of the Tennessee, cuts through McMinn County beneath a canopy of high tension wires. The people of McMinn County, like the taut, coppery wires, hum with subdued peaceful activity until they are disturbed; and then, like the wires, they snap in a shower of sparks and violence. It took several killings, ten years of extortion and thuggery, a world war and an official invasion by legal gunmen to bring on the violence of August 1, 1946, and the bloody siege of the Athens jail. But when it was over, democracy was firmly established and authority once again rested with the citizenry.

The people of McMinn County are God-fearing men and women. When the Robert E. Lee highway climbs out of the Shenandoah Valley, which can take its religion or leave it, into east Tennessee on the road to McMinn the highway is sprinkled with signboards telling the godless wayfarers that "Jesus is coming soon" or warning them "Prepare to Meet God." McMinn itself is relatively free of such shrieking witnesses to faith; McMinn's religion is Methodist and Baptist, quiet, bone-deep, and sober. On Saturday afternoon when farmers throng the town, preachers are allowed to call sinners to repentance in the shade of the courthouse at the county seat. But most of McMinn meets God in the serenity of Sunday morning at the red brick or white board house of worship in peace and devotion. The church-goers have made liquor illegal, and Sunday movies are unlawful, too.

Next to religion, politics is the most important thing. But until 1946, religion absorbed so much of the spirit of right-thinking people that politics fell automatically to the bad. First, it was the Republicans. They had McMinn County for years and years. The Republicans would let a Democrat get elected now and then, but the sheriff

---

The author (b. 1915) is a journalist. Correspondent-in-chief, Europe, Overseas News Agency. Formerly editor of *The New Republic*. Author (with Annalee Jacoby), *Thunder Out of China* (Book of the Month Club selection). Arranged and edited *The Stilwell Papers*.

was theirs and they held tight to the county trustee who disbursed funds and issued poll-tax certificates. Then, from 1936, when Paul Cantrell won the election and established an eastern outpost of the Crump machine, it was ten years of Democrats.

Paul Cantrell, state senator from the McMinn area and boss of the county, was a medium-sized, bespectacled man of sallow complexion, a big head, and little neck. Cantrell loved two things: money and power. He had a nervous, fidgety way about him; he rarely looked directly at a man when he talked to him; towards the end, an armed deputy accompanied Cantrell as guard when he strolled through Athens, the county seat. Pat Mansfield, his sheriff, was a tall, handsome man from Georgia. Pat was kind to his family and gave money to his church. He might have been popular but many people resented the sour troop of plug-uglies he had recruited to be his deputy sheriffs. Pat did Cantrell's bidding.

The Cantrell forces were hard, well-connected people. Cantrell was allied with Burch Biggs in neighboring Polk County; the pair were tied tight to the Crump machine, and Crump ran all of Tennessee. They were so close to the Crump machine that George Woods, who represented McMinn in the state legislature, was speaker of the house in the legislature of the State of Tennessee.

The machine bossed the county with a rough hand. The sheriff had sixteen regular deputies and about twenty or thirty other men he would deputize in "emergencies." Three of the deputies had served penitentiary terms. One of them had been convicted of taking a little girl out and violating the age of consent. It wasn't rape, but then it wasn't good, either; and God-fearing people like those who farmed and worked in McMinn didn't like it. When the deputies arrested a man they often slugged him until he was sensible. Nobody talked back much in public because it wasn't safe. The deputies threatened to kill people they didn't like. They were brutal men, ready to beat, blackjack, or bully anyone. One GI who was home on leave during the war was shot and killed by a deputy at a public entertainment house near Athens; a sailor home on leave was killed at the other end of the county.

The gambling joints and bootleggers were all tied to the machine. They paid off the proper people and operated punchboards and slot machines, sold liquor, did as they pleased. As a matter of fact, if someone was in the pen the best way to get him out was to work through the small-time racketeers to get the machine to go easy.

The take from the bootleggers and gamblers wasn't the only source of revenue for the machine. The county was directed by fee-grabbers. A tourist comes riding down the highway; maybe he has a bottle of beer. The deputies arrest him and take him to court. In the court is a little man, called "the informer," who says he is a lawyer. He advises the tourist to plead guilty, pay his fine, and go his way. Sixteen dollars and a nickel. No one will ever know how many people paid their sixteen dollars and a nickel, over and over again, to support the sheriff and his deputies. The sheriff was paid five thousand dollars a year and expenses, but he got seventy-five cents a day for every man in jail that had to be fed. When a drunk was arrested, he was put back on the street next day with a clear head and an empty stomach, but the charge to the county was two days' food at seventy-five cents each. In ten years, county expenses for the sheriff's office had run to over three hundred thousand dollars. McMinn has an audit committee working on the books now.

There was nothing that could be done about it, because you couldn't vote the machine out of office. The machine had taken the county from the Republicans by a famous vote-grab in 1936; some people still tell how the last ballot box from a normally Republican precinct was fixed to show just enough lead to carry the county.

From then on, no matter how people voted, the machine counted the votes. In the key districts when the polls closed the deputies took the ballot boxes to jail, or another safe place, and counted them without any opposition watchers present. Then they would announce the results and always the Cantrell men won. There was nothing that could be done about that either. Appeal to the courts was useless; the Republicans tried that but no suit-at-law was ever won by the opposition.

Things had been that way for a long time when the war came, taking thirty-five hundred boys from McMinn homes and flinging them across the face of the earth. Folks kept writing to their sons about affairs in McMinn County; sometimes the boys would visit on furlough and then write to their friends in camps all around the world. There were four years to think about McMinn County, and Ralph Duggan, who was a lieutenant in the Navy, says he thought a lot more about McMinn County than he did about the Japs. Many were thinking as Ralph did —that if democracy was good enough to put on the Germans and Japs, it was good enough for McMinn County, too. It got to be a saying in Athens: "Wait till the GI boys come home."

By spring of 1946, the GI boys were trickling back to McMinn from France and Germany and Italy and the Pacific. The people of McMinn say there is nothing but what some good doesn't come of it, and what happened afterwards in McMinn came from the war. The boys learned a lot about fighting and more about patriotism in the Army;

when they came home they were ready to do something about democracy in Tennessee.

In February they set to planning. They met secretly because the Cantrell forces had the guns, the blackjacks, and the law; and the deputies could make life hell for anyone they could catch. Once in the summer campaign, they seized one boy, locked him up, took his poll-tax receipt from him, and then, threatening his life, made him sign a statement that no such incident had ever taken place. There were five GI's and one civilian in on the first secret meetings. They decided that in the summer election for sheriff and county officials the GI's would put up a complete slate of their own. Mansfield, Cantrell's sheriff, was going out of office and Cantrell was running for sheriff himself.

The veterans sounded out general feeling and in May they called a mass meeting. To get into the GI meeting you had to show your discharge papers, or your membership card in the American Legion or VFW. The veterans picked a non-partisan slate: three Democrats, two Republicans. Knox Henry, a tall handsome boy who had been hurt in North Africa and ran a filling station, was the man for sheriff. He was Republican, but the county trustee was to be Frank Carmichael, a farmer and a Democrat. Carmichael had been a major in the war and was badly wounded at Saint Lô. The other candidates were GI boys, too, except Charlie Pickel who had been in the first World War and had returned with his wounds to be a carpenter. Jim Buttram, a sturdy, solid chunk of combat infantryman, was to be campaign manager. Jim's family had a grocery store in Athens and Jim was new to politics.

With the slate chosen, the campaign picked up speed. Ralph Duggan, who had come back from the Navy to his law practice, was legal adviser and they pored over the Tennessee Code to see what the laws allowed them. The business men who feared the Cantrell forces contributed money secretly. They were afraid to give openly because the machine could raise the taxes, or arrest them, or generally make life hard. But eight thousand dollars came into the campaign fund and soon loudspeaker trucks were rolling over the hill roads, the *Daily Post-Athenian* was carrying campaign ads, and the local radio station was putting out fifteen minutes of talk a day. Up and down the pockets and roads went GI's calling meetings in evenings at schoolhouses or homes, begging, urging, pleading with everyone to get out and vote. It wasn't hard to pin scandal on the Cantrell forces; McMinn County had lived with the scandal for almost ten years. Nothing had been done about it for two reasons: first, the only alternative was the old

Republicans; and second, it did no good to vote because the Cantrells always counted themselves to victory anyway. So over and over, like the beating of a drum in the darkness, the GI campaign chanted its theme: "Your vote will be counted as cast, your vote will be counted as cast."

"Everybody knew we were trying to do the right thing," said Jim Buttram. "We had twelve public meetings and we knew they were damned good. About three weeks before elections we knew we had won the votes and the hearts of the people of McMinn County. But the hardest thing to do was to build an organization to help us see we got a fair count on election day."

The GI's asked the governor for help; but the governor was elected with Crump backing and was silent. They asked the Attorney General in Washington for help; he did nothing. They made contact with the FBI office in Knoxville; the FBI agent said he couldn't do anything unless Washington told him to, and Washington wasn't telling. The GI's were on their own.

II

Election day dawned sweet and clear over McMinn County. McMinn numbers twelve voting precincts but the decisive vote is cast in two townships, Etowah and Athens. Etowah is some ten miles in the hills from the main highway, but Athens, the county seat, is dead center. Athens sprawls fragrant and green about the old white courthouse; the Robert E. Lee hotel sits on one side, Woolworth's and a movie house on another, stores and offices on the other two sides. One block up from the courthouse lies the red brick county jail. Maple trees and green lawn surround the courthouse; old people sun themselves on the benches, children romp on the grass, blue-denimed farmers stroll casually about buying supplies for home and land.

Election day saw Athens an armed camp. As the voters came to the polls, they found the Cantrell machine in ominous demonstration of force. Almost two hundred armed deputies strutted about, pistols and blackjacks dangling from their belts, badges gleaming. The deputies were strangers. Mansfield claims he asked the governor for National Guardsmen to help him, and the governor authorized him to get deputies where he could. The machine had turned up a sodden gang of plug-uglies, most of them from foreign counties, some from as far as Georgia. Fred Puett, the Chamber of Commerce secretary, said that they looked as though they were drugged; their eyes seemed as cold and arrogant and hard as those of a band of Nazis.

By the Tennessee Code of Law, each polling place must be staffed with watchers from both parties, and the GI's had chosen boys of the best families, with the best war records, to stand as their representatives at each place. As the polls opened in Etowah, one of the GI watchers asked to see the ballot box opened and demonstrated empty as required by law. "Hell, no," said one of the deputies; an argument sputtered, a highway patrolman was summoned and Evans, the GI poll watcher, was hauled off to jail.

At 9:30 trouble flickered in Athens; the machine charged Walter Ellis, a GI watcher, with an unspecified federal offense, took him from his appointed place at the polls and put him in jail, too. At three in the afternoon Tom Gillespie, a colored man, appeared at the eleventh precinct complete with poll-tax receipt. "You can't vote here," said the machine watchers.

"He can too," contradicted the GI spokesman.

"Get him," yelled one of the deputies and someone slugged Gillespie. Gillespie broke for the door and ran down the street. As he ran, a deputy at the door drew his pistol and shot him in the back. Gillespie was taken to the hospital. Fifteen minutes later, Bob Hairell, another GI watcher at the twelfth precinct, was in trouble. The machine wanted to vote a nineteen-year-old girl; Hairell objected. One of the deputies settled the argument by pulling his blackjack and laying Hairell's head open. Hairell was off to the hospital. The *Daily Post-Athenian* sent a reporter to get the story on Hairell. He, too, was slugged and told not to ask questions.

At four, the polls closed. In the eleventh precinct, the two GI watchers, Charles Scott, Jr. and Ed Vestal, were thrust to one side as the machine prepared to count the vote. Through the plate glass door of the polling place, the people could see the two boys penned in their corner of the large room. By this time, Jim Buttram, the campaign manager, had decided that the vote of the eleventh precinct wasn't worth trading off against the lives of two of his men. Twelve armed deputies had cleared the sidewalk in front of the eleventh precinct polling place, but hundreds of people stood on the opposite side. They watched Jim and Mr. Scott, father of Charles Scott, cross the street to speak to Mansfield, the sheriff.

Mansfield was sitting in a red 1946 Dodge. There were six men in the car. Buttram offered to give him the precinct in return for the release of the watchers.

"Are you trying to tell me how to run this election?" asked Mansfield. "You go over and get them yourself if you want them."

"You wouldn't want me to get shot, would you?" said Jim. A deputy sitting beside Mansfield lifted his thirty-eight from his lap and said: "Buttram, I ought to shoot you right now, you're the son-of-a-bitch who started the whole thing."

Mansfield knocked Moses' gun down and told him to shut up, he was doing the talking.

Mr. Scott leaned over and said: "If you won't let my boy out of there and anything happens to him, you'll have to pay for it."

Pat grabbed his gun, snarled, "Let's settle this right now," and started to open the door of the car. Buttram slammed the door on him, and he and Scott hastily made their way back to the cover of the crowd.

A few minutes later Neal Ensminger, the editor of the local paper, strode over to the precinct door to see if he could get a tabulated count. As he asked one of the deputies a question, the two GI's in the polling place broke for safety. With his shoulder down, young Scott burst the door and pounded out, followed in a moment by Vestal. Bleeding, they ran across the street to the crowd as the deputies trained their guns on the boys. By this time women were screaming, children were crying, and the veterans—still unarmed—stood cursing and shouting from the opposing pavement. The deputies held their fire as the two boys slipped among the people.

It was five now, and following their practice the Cantrell forces removed the ballot boxes of the eleventh and twelfth precincts to the security of the jail for counting.

III

The GI's had promised to get the vote counted as cast, and they gathered at their campaign headquarters around the corner to confer. As they stood in the street, two Mansfield deputies approached to break up the group. Otto Kennedy was watching from his tire store as the deputies walked up the street. With Otto was his brother Oley Kennedy, just out of the Navy, and his brother J. P. "Bull" Kennedy, just out of the Army.

"Pat Mansfield said he was going to give us a fair and square election," said Kennedy, "and then we saw those sons-of-bitches from Georgia, walking around with their guns and badges, telling us to kiss their neck. They'd put our boys in jail, they were running all over us. I stepped up to the door. I saw them coming. I just couldn't take it. I said to my brother: 'Bull, let's get them.'"

As the deputies stepped into the crowd, the GI's closed about them. They hit hard and high and low. The guns were taken and distributed among the GI's. Three more deputies, then two more walked into the crowd. All were disarmed and the guns handed out. The deputies were loaded on cars, taken to the woods, stripped of their clothes, and left to walk their way out.

The GI's were still indecisive and the Kennedys became cautious. They had struck the first blow; they were vulnerable. Otto decided to go home, telling the veterans that if they decided to do anything the Kennedys were ready to come back; otherwise they were staying away. Dusk was settling and the vets talked. A city policeman walked by to say that Mansfield was coming with tommy-guns and tear gas. Then something happened.

From dusk to dawn, the story of the siege of Athens dissolves into anonymity. The people had voted the GI ticket, trusting the GI guarantee of a fair count. Five districts which had been fairly tabulated by evening had already given the GI's almost a three-to-one lead. But the ballot boxes of the eleventh and twelfth precincts were being counted in the jail. Tomorrow the Cantrell forces would have victory and no one would be safe. On the one hand, the Common Law says that every citizen has the right to prevent a crime or felony from taking place; on the other hand, to take the jail by storm against the lawfully deputized thugs seemed perilously close to insurrection. A very fine point of law is involved and Crump still runs Tennessee. Therefore, no man knows or tells who played precisely what role in Athens on the night of Thursday, August 1, 1946.

Down the highway from Athens is one of the armories of the National Guard. By eight o'clock rifles and machine guns were held by dozens of the veterans. It was a quiet movement. There was no raving or shouting. They collected at their headquarters and gravely, under cover of darkness, walked the two blocks to the jail where the sheriffs had taken the ballot boxes. Behind the jail is a barbed wire enclosure. Facing it, across the street, is a low hill covered with vines and several houses and buildings. The deputies had made a mistake that the battle-wise GI's recognized immediately: they had concentrated forty or fifty of their number in jail and left no reserves in town. The GI's deployed in the darkness in a semicircle above the jail, on the hill behind the cover of vines, on rooftops. A veteran strode into the street and yelled at the silent jail a demand for the ballot boxes and the release of the GI prisoners.

A voice answered, "Are you the law?"

The GI yelled back, "There isn't any law in McMinn County."

A lone shot went off from within the jail. The man that answered from the hill answered with a tommy-gun.

There were several hundred veterans in the semicircle and hundreds of boys and civilians. Some had rifles, a few had tommy-guns, others had bird guns and hunting pieces. The fusillade rose and fell above the night, echoing into the suburbs and hills. Bullets spattered the Chamber of Commerce and the newspaper office a block away. A block down the road, a man standing on the corner of the courthouse square was nicked in the arm.

The local radio station had sent a reporter with a microphone to cover the action; up and down the county farmers tuned in to the running account. Some of them put their clothes on, got their guns, came to join in the shoot. Boys too young to cock a rifle came down to see the fun and remained to learn how to shoot in the night.

The deputies were safe behind the thick brick wall of the jail, and the bullets of the GI's could do no more than cut out chunks of the wall. As the sporadic shooting dragged on hour after hour, the veterans realized with a sick feeling that night was wearing away and, with daylight, state patrolmen—perhaps even the National Guard—might be called in to reinforce the garrison of deputies. Defeat would mean that McMinn County would never be safe again for any man who had taken part in the night's firing. It was go through with it, or get out of town.

At midnight a detachment went over to the county farm where a case of dynamite was located. During a lull, the veterans yelled that unless the ballot boxes and prisoners were released in twenty minutes they would blast the jail. An hour went by and the jail made no answer. Somebody fitted a cap to a stick of dynamite and tossed it into the street. A second stick followed. On the third throw, two sticks were tied together and thrown across to the sidewalk of the jail. The fourth throw of two sticks landed on the porch of the jail and tore it wide apart. Somebody had learned about demolition in the war; for the last try they decided to prepare a homemade satchel charge of the rest of the case and place it under the jail wall. But before the charge could be placed, the jail was yelling surrender. It was 3:30 in the morning.

"We're dying in here," came a call. "Don't use any more dynamite, we're giving up."

No one was dying. Four of the deputies were pretty badly hurt and required hospitalization; ten of the GI's were wounded in the day's action but the war was over.

The vets ordered the deputies to march into the courtyard with their hands up, leaving their guns behind. As they marched out, the crowd gathered round, yelling, cursing, and booing. Someone in the crowd reached out with a razor and slashed at one of the deputies, laying his throat open. Duggan tried to stop the man; the man explained that the deputy had arrested him before, taken him to jail and kicked in four of his ribs. Duggan tried to reason with him, but he made another razor pass. Then Duggan slugged him into obedience and led the deputy off to the hospital. Behind them a file of deputies, guarded by GI's, paraded through the street to the courthouse and back so that the people might see and taunt their unthroned impotence.

By this time dawn was lighting the county and the radio station, broadcasting the victory, was bringing farmers in from all the hills to see what was happening. The state capital had been alerted and the State Commissioner of Public Safety, Lynn Bomar, called up to locate a GI to negotiate. Ralph Duggan answered the phone and spoke to George Woods at the state capital. Woods, who was Election Commissioner of the county, promised—if given a safe conduct—to return to Athens on Monday and certify the election of the entire GI slate. Duggan announced the victory to the crowd at six in the morning and then went home.

Violence flickered on for several more hours. The GI's had had their fill, but the civilians and boys were carrying on. They smashed in windows of the deputies' automobiles, turned them over, burned cars indiscriminately. It was the GI's now who had to restrain the civilians and protect their prisoners. By ten o'clock, however, the fury had spent itself and the GI's were carefully escorting their prisoners out of town. At three, a giant mass meeting was held in the courthouse, men jamming the assembly hall, overflowing onto the steps and the lawn. The Reverend Bernie Hampton read the twenty-third psalm and asked the body of citizens what their will was. Someone suggested the appointment of a three-man committee to administer the county till things settled down. The three-man committee was elected immediately and from Friday to Monday it conducted the county's affairs on a volunteer basis.

It summoned the county court—the local legislative body—to a meeting on Monday morning. The county court declared vacant the offices held by machine contestants in the elections and declared the GI slate duly elected. Six of the twelve precincts' votes were thrown out entirely, for no fair count had been given there. When the GI's broke into jail they found that some of the tally sheets marked by the machine had been scored fifteen to one for the Cantrell forces. Where the GI's witnessed the count, the margin was three to one GI. Thus it was decided that only in those precincts where both parties had watched should the count be accepted. By Monday afternoon, Knox Henry was sheriff of McMinn County and the law was safe.

IV

McMinn is quiet and peaceful again. The courthouse has been painted for the first time in years, and the big clock has been fixed so that it strikes the hours loud, clear, and free over the entire town. The jail has been repaired but it is curiously empty. Within a month Henry was running McMinn County with eight youthful GI deputies. Saturday night no longer filled the cells with fifty or sixty men waiting to be fined; by the end of the month, Saturday night found only three men in jail. The four city policemen had been fired and replaced by veterans. Pat Mansfield was back in Georgia, working as a fireman on a railway. Paul Cantrell was in Nashville and didn't want to come back.

The gambling joints have been closed down, the bootlegging ring has been smashed, fee-grabbing ended. There are no more slot machines or punchboards. Henry has pledged the new regime that the sheriff will live on his lawful salary.

The GI party, too, has been disbanded, but a Good Government League has succeeded it. The Good Government League has branches in fifteen different communities of the county and is the public whip. The county court still has a majority of old Cantrell men, but they don't come up for election till next summer. Meanwhile the Good Government League suggests various actions to it, and the court pays heed.

The first thing the county court was persuaded to do was to establish an audit committee. The Good Government League wants to see what resources are available for the two most pressing local problems: schools and roads. Schools are pretty bad in McMinn. Pay for teachers is so poor that all the best teachers are leaving. In some places in McMinn, teachers get eighty-five dollars a month for the eight months they work; that averages less than fifteen dollars a week, year-round, as take-home pay. Even a waitress at the hotel makes more than that. Highest pay is at the high school and that comes to only thirty dollars a week for a teacher with a master's degree. The Good Government League wants to divert money from the sheriff's heavy budget to the education budget. When the schools and school buses are fixed, they want to do something about the roads. Maybe after that the League will move on to such long-range plans as a permanent county-manager system and a new structure of government.

The GI's like McMinn and they think they can keep it healthy. There will always be bootlegging unless the church people let the county make liquor legal. But now the government will be master of the bootleggers instead of the bootleggers masters of the government. The GI's say they aren't interested in "issues"; they aren't interested in unions or poll-tax laws or running the country. This was a McMinn matter, strictly a battle to give McMinn fair and square elections and force Boss Crump back to Shelby County.

It is true, of course, that Crump still runs the rest of Tennessee and that Crump helped send back to Washington a man named Kenneth McKellar. And until November 1946, McKellar was president of the Senate of the United States of America, called the greatest deliberative body in the world.

◆◆◆◆◆

85. Altruistic Love *

COOPERATION, in its many and varied forms, is perhaps the most distinctively human of all social processes. The truth of this proposition is not at first glance apparent because in our society, and in our time, vastly greater attention is generally devoted to publicizing conflict rather than cooperation. Sorokin, the foremost sociological philosopher of our time, in these brief excerpts directs our attention to some of the more extreme, even spectacular, forms of individual cooperativeness: the American "good neighbor" and the Christian saint.

IN ITS DECLINING SENSATE PHASE Western culture has become increasingly negativistic. In papers and magazines it devotes the front page to hair-raising murder stories, to sex scandals or perversions, to hypocrisy

* Pitirim A. Sorokin, Altruistic Love: A Study of American "Good Neighbors" and Christian Saints (Boston: The Beacon Press, 1950), pp. 3-5, 81-84, 197-198. Reprinted by permission of the publisher and the author.

The author (b. 1889) is Professor and Chairman, Department of Sociology, Harvard University; Director Research Center in Altruism. Born in Russia. Active in Russian Revolution. Arrested repeatedly, jailed, forbidden to teach, condemned to death by Soviet government in 1917, banished, 1922. Received many academic honors for System of Sociology. Among his other works are Social Mobility, Social and Cultural Dynamics (4 vols.), Crisis of This Age, Russia and the United States, Society, Culture and Personality: Their Structure and Dynamics, and Social Philosophies of an Age of Crisis.

or insanity, hardly ever mentioning any good deed or anything truly positive. It does the same in fiction; in cinemas and plays; in operas and songs; in painting and sculpture; in radio and television. Sex, insanity, and crime constitute roughly from 80 to 90 per cent of the topics in these fields of contemporary Western culture. The situation is no different in other fields. Our sensate culture there also dwells mainly in the region of subsocial sewers; breathes mainly their foul air; and drags down into their turbid muck everything heroic, positive, true, good, and beautiful.

In the sensate social sciences this concentration on the pathological has manifested itself in several ways. One of these is a proliferation of various "debunking" interpretations of man, culture, and values: mechanistic, reflexological, biological, materialistic, organismic, endocrinological, behavioristic, etc. These interpretations have deprived man and his culture and values of everything divine, spiritual, supermaterialistic, or human. They equate man and his culture and values with atoms, electron-protons, reflex mechanisms, reflex organisms, the libido, and so on. Another manifestation of this pathological bent in the social sciences has been their concentration on a study of the negativistic and pathological types of human beings and human actions, and their reluctance to study the positive types of Homo sapiens and human relations.

For decades Western social science has been cultivating, urbi et orbi, an ever-increasing study of crime and criminals; of insanity and the insane; of sex perversion and perverts; of hypocrisy and hypocrites. A vast set of special disciplines has been developed for these purposes: criminology and penology, with their subdivisions and branches; psychiatry, psychoanalysis, and mental hygiene, with still more numerous branches and proliferations.

In contrast to this, Western social science has paid scant attention to positive types of human beings, their positive achievements, their heroic actions, and their positive relationships. The criminal has been "researched" incomparably more thoroughly than the saint or the altruist; the idiot has been studied much more carefully than the genius; perverts and failures have been investigated much more intensely than integrated persons or heroes. In accordance with the total nature of our negativistic culture, our social science has been semi-blind about all positive types and actions and very sharp-eyed about all negative types and relationships. It seems to have enjoyed moving in the muck of social sewers; it has been reluctant to move in the fresh air of high social peaks. It has stressed the pathological and neglected the sound and heroic.

The result is that our social science knows little about positive types of persons, their conduct and relationships. Not having studied these, it lacks also a more adequate knowledge of the negative phenomena: for a knowledge of the positive is necessary in order to have a full knowledge of the negative.

The time has come when this one-sidedness of sensate social science must be corrected. For a fuller knowledge, we must concentrate increasingly on a study of positive values, personalities, relationships, and phenomena. The study of American "good neighbors," together with those of saints, great altruists, and creative geniuses, is one of numerous studies to stress the positive. As we shall see, these studies throw light even on negative phenomena.

．　　．　　．　　．　　．　　．

If criminals are deviants falling below the legally prescribed norms of moral conduct, "good neighbors" are also deviants, but above the level of moral conduct demanded by the official law. As a rule "good neighbors" discharge not only the duties prescribed for and demanded from all, but something extra, above the minimum of social conduct required by official law. This extra something ordinarily does not conflict with the official law, but rather supplements it. In such cases "good neighbors" do not get into trouble with the official law or its enforcers.

In other cases this "superlegality" of altruistic deeds and of their commands does contradict the official law norms. It violates some of these norms—for instance, the refusal of conscientious objectors to be drafted; the refusal of some "good neighbors" to join a witch hunt for officially declared communists or other "subversives." In such cases, "good neighbors" undergo the same conflict with official law that has been the inevitable fate of almost all the great moral innovators and altruists: Buddha, Socrates, Plato, Aristotle, Jesus, the Apostles, Mohammed, Al Hallaj, up to M. Gandhi and Sri Aurobindo. Since the ethical code and altruism of such unselfish persons far transcends the often antiquated, always narrow, fairly low, local, group-selfish moral level of official law, they cannot help colliding with official law and its enforcers. And not only with its enforcers (government, judges, police, etc.), but also with many portions of the population who support the antiquated norms of official law; for whom, therefore, our altruists and "good neighbors" appear as suspicious or revolutionary "subversives," or as persons who through their high moral demands or conduct endanger the vested interests, privileges, and peace of mind of the supporters of the status quo.

This explains why virtually all altruists—even the greatest ones of history—have collided to a certain degree with official law and its agencies, and with many persons and groups. However paradoxical it may seem, the fact is that *all altruistic actions and persons have generated social antagonisms and conflicts*. They have brought not only peace but also war. "The Athenian Committee on un-Athenian Activities" and Socrates; "The Jewish Committee on un-Jewish Activities" and Jesus; some sectarian "Hindu Committee on un-Hindu Activities" and Gandhi; "The American Committee on un-American Activities" and several American "good neighbors"—they and their like are a perennial symbol of this conflict with members of even their own nation or group. Besides the members of their in-group, such altruists and "good neighbors" have invariably collided with many out-groups and their members. This is an eternal tragedy!

Since the bulk of our "good neighbors" are mostly law-abiding citizens, not deviating much from the level of official law; since their activities supplement rather than supplant the conduct demanded by official law, the bulk of our neighbors do not record any particular trouble with official law and its agencies. Only a small part have had collisions with them. And even these collisions have been comparatively mild. A somewhat greater proportion have had some conflicts with various individuals and groups upon whose toes they have somehow stepped. But even these collisions have been tempered and free from violence.

As a rule, the greater the altruism of a person, the sharper and more numerous are likely to be his collisions with official law and its enforcers, and with the persons and groups whose values are "depreciated" and challenged by such altruism. Christ would be likely to get into sharper and greater collisions than any of our ordinary "good neighbors" or Christian ministers and priests today.

Is there a way out of this tragic dilemma? Can there be a pure and lofty altruism, not generating collision and conflict? This problem is beyond the scope of the present study. It is analyzed elsewhere. Tentatively, the answer is that there is such a way, but that it requires, among other conditions, an extension of our "in-group" feelings to all humanity; and this extension must be real, manifested not only in our speech reactions but in our entire behavior. Otherwise such conflicts and collisions are unavoidable. Jesus rightly said that he brought not only peace but the sword. So does any unselfish person or deed!

*   *   *   *   *   *

The activities of the American "good neighbors" supplement the inadequacy, bureaucracy, formalism, coldness, and other shortcomings of the relief activities of institutionalized service agencies. The largest percentage of the good deeds of our "good neighbors" comprise deeds that alleviate boredom, lonesomeness, grief, and various other troubles. Contemporary American life is full of boredom and loneliness for millions, and the official agencies fail to remedy this "vacuum" in our lives. If we consider all the good deeds of all the "good neighbors," their vitalizing, moralizing, beautifying and encouraging effects are likely to be more important than all the official relief of the institutionalized agencies. Real sympathy, a warm heart, unquestioning friendship, and generous love are the free gifts of the "good neighbors."

The social function of the saints, aside from the above rôle of the good neighbors, consists of being a living incarnation of the highest goodness, love, and spirituality of a given society. The saints are creative heroes in the field of moral values and they set a visible example for imitation. In the field of altruistic love the bulk of the saints are masters and creators of "love-energy," which they generate in large quantities of the purest quality. Without these masters of "love-production," society is bound to suffer greatly from a catastrophic scarcity of friendship and harmony among its members, and from an overabundance of deadly hatred and strife. Whatever the form in which these masters of "love-production" appear, be it religious or non-religious, a minimum of such apostles of unselfishness is as necessary for any creative and happy society as is a minimum of experts in the production of vital material goods. The concrete forms of love of these saintly apostles change, but their substance remains perennial and immortal; no society can live a long, happy, and creative life without the heroes of love and spirituality.

❧❧❧

86. Some Sociological Aspects of Consumers' Cooperation *

AMONG THE SOCIAL PROCESSES that characterize American economic behavior, competition may seem most typical; cooperation, however,

* Leonard C. Kercher, Rural Sociology, 6, No. 4 (December, 1941), 311-322. Reprinted by permission of the author and the publisher.
The author (b. 1901) is a sociologist. Chairman, Division of Social Science,

is also very important. This selection by Professor Leonard W. Kercher deals with the Finnish consumers' cooperative movement in the Great Lakes region. It presents some of the distinctively sociological factors that conditioned the launching and operation of these consumer cooperatives. These factors include several major areas: "cultural heritage and change, social aspects of personality, group organization and interaction, community structure, and institutional organization and functioning." Thus the article serves to illustrate *cooperation* as an institutionalized process and also to show how various factors influenced the origin and development of a specific *social movement*.

AROUND THIRTY-FIVE YEARS AGO Finnish immigrants in the Upper Lake region of the North Central states initiated a cooperative movement that has become the strongest and most unified distinctly Rochdale consumers' movement in this country. It is today a mixed rural-urban development of about 110 local distributive societies scattered mainly over northeastern Minnesota, northern Wisconsin and Upper Michigan. It has around 40,000 individual members, about 75 per cent of whom are engaged in farming. The local societies are organized into district and regional federations, the most important of which is the Central Cooperative Wholesale, a regional business and general purpose organization located at Superior, Wisconsin. A study of this Finnish-initiated consumers' cooperative movement brought into relief certain factors that appear to have special significance in the successful initiation, development and operation of cooperative enterprise. The more important of these factors that are more distinctly sociological in character are briefly reviewed in this article.

•   •   •   •   •   •

By inclination and experience immigrant Finns were mainly peasant farm workers who came to the New World in the hope of settling on small farms of their own. But generally they were poor and had to turn to whatever work there was at hand to earn the necessary funds. In the three major economic exploitations of the region they, therefore, usually played the role of common laborers; either miners or lumberjacks first, and then later, farmers. For their work in the mines

---

Western Michigan State College. Selection above is based on doctoral dissertation, "The Finnish Dominated Consumers' Cooperative Movement in the North Central States." This material is included in *Consumers' Cooperatives* (co-author, Vant W. Kebker). Other books of which he was a co-author are *Sociological Foundations of Education* and *Twentieth Century America: Trends in Civilization*.

and logging camps they received very moderate and uncertain wages. The low and variable incomes, as well as unfavorable working conditions, were sources of much unrest among these Finnish workers and were among the principal reasons why they took a leading part in the major labor strikes in the area.

In line with their original aspirations many Finns as soon as possible developed part-time farming activities. But, before they had accumulated adequate resources large numbers of them were forced to turn to full-time farming for a livelihood after being permanently displaced from mining or lumbering occupations. As pioneer farmers they struggled ceaselessly against unfavorable conditions of climate and soil on the one hand, and against exploitative conditions in the local markets on the other. High monopolistic prices charged by local merchants is one of the most frequently repeated reasons given by the members for starting their local consumers' cooperative.

In addition to economic handicaps these early Finns also experienced insecurity with respect to group and individual status and achievement. They unwillingly occupied the most menial of positions in the economy and found advancement extremely difficult. The language barrier, as well as other cultural or occupational differences, served to discourage genuine social relations with other groups in the community. Individual Finns found it next to impossible to achieve in relation to the whole community one of the deepest needs of personality—a sense of belonging. From the beginning they were thrown back upon their own nationality group in order to realize individual and collective goals. They have consequently evidenced a marked tendency to be clannish and to keep intact their social and cultural heritage in the New World. This social isolation and strong primary group unity made more possible the group-wise attainment of desired goals.

Virtually all of the Finnish immigrants who initiated the cooperative movement under study, came to the Upper Lake region between 1900 and 1910 as young men who had little if any direct experience with cooperation in their native country. They brought with them, however, a workingman's culture including a liberal social philosophy which had been molded by a half century of struggle on the part of Finnish-speaking lower classes to attain national unity and economic security. Various interrelated associations and institutions of this cultural heritage were transplanted and adapted here as group-wise techniques for attaining such basic satisfactions as fellowship, recognition, security, intellectual growth and recreation. These included temperance societies, workers' educational associations, trade unionism, socialism and the Finnish church. In one way or another, each of these social instruments contributed to the development of consumers' cooperation. The temperance societies and workers' associations served as propaganda agencies as well as excellent training schools in the art of democratic discussion. The socialist movement among the Finns, in particular, exerted a tremendous influence. It diffused a liberal ideology of working class welfare and urged the development of cooperatives as a phase of an aggressive labor movement. It supplied much of the early leadership in the cooperatives. Moreover, the Finnish socialist clubs, supported by the Finnish socialist press, played a major role in publicizing the Old World cooperative movement and the principles underlying it among Finnish workers in the area. This oft-repeated story of Rochdale cooperation in Finland and England acted as a potent stimulus to the development of cooperatives among these workers and also provided the basic principles underlying their organization.

The movement under study clearly had its roots in American soil in that it was an adjustment response to conditions in the Upper Lake region. On the other hand, it also had nourishing roots in the Old World since its sponsors shared and profited by the experience of co-operators abroad. In brief summary, the following factors in the total situation out of which the Finnish-initiated cooperative movement developed stand out in relief.

1. The geographical, economic and ecological situations were characterized by limited resources, a specialized, unstable economy, and a selective migration and settlement of diverse foreign-born peoples that tended to encourage social cohesion and self-sufficiency within homogeneous groups while producing social distance and conflict in intergroup relations as well as insecurity and frustration in the lives of individuals.

2. The large number of Finnish immigrants concentrated in the region were forced into unfamiliar and undesired occupations. Changes in the economy of the region increased the occupational hazards and produced as well much group and individual insecurity.

3. The social situation among Finnish immigrants made it virtually impossible earlier for individual satisfactions to be obtained except through close adherence to their own nationality group. This put a premium upon group isolation, group solidarity and the techniques of group-wise adjustment.

4. Finnish immigrants brought to America a workingman's culture that included a liberal social philosophy and a group of related associations and institutions which fostered socialism in politics, trade

unionism in production and eventually consumers' cooperation in consumption.

Variable conditions in different cooperatives influence the success of the enterprises. Space is too limited here, however, to deal with these individual situations. As an alternative the author proposes to appraise the present elements of strength and of weakness in the movement as a whole.

A vital and enduring need. It is virtually a sociological axiom that a vital and enduring need for it, is a basic element of strength in any social institution. The geographical and occupational circumstances that in the past gave rise to the severe handicaps of urban and agricultural workers in the region remain, with no prospects of significant permanent improvement in the near future. It is likely, therefore, that economic need will continue to provide a strong incentive to cooperative development in the area.

The circumstances underlying the felt needs for recognition and self-realization are, however, in gradual transition. Formerly these needs were intensified by the social isolation and the inferior occupational status of the Finnish immigrant group. The Finn is now becoming more of a participating member of the community as a whole. Here in a larger social setting he will find individual sources of recognition and expression that were denied him in former days. This may reduce the feeling of need for group solidarity and for group-wise attainment of goals through cooperative effort.

Community setting. It has been in the intimate neighborly social setting of the hamlet, village or small town community that the cooperatives in this movement have, as a rule, had their firmest roots. Here occupational and other class differences are minor, and as a consequence economic wants are sufficiently commonplace and uniform to be served by a relatively simple institutional structure. Furthermore the face-to-face contacts of everyday life provide the ideal social experience for the development of common understanding and the formation of attitudes of group solidarity so essential to voluntary cooperative effort. In antithesis, the typical city situation has not proven congenial to the growth of strong cooperatives in the movement. The social groupings and the cultural standards of the city are more heterogeneous, individual interests and wants are more diversified and social contacts are more secondary and impersonal. Cooperators nurtured in such a situation are likely to feel no deep need for cooperative enterprise, nor do they form a conscious consumers' group equipped with common understanding, attitudes and habits necessary for the pursuit of long-time objectives of consumers' cooperation. Experience seems to show that if the movement is to expand into larger urban centers it must adopt the most improved merchandising methods and develop effective techniques of organizing city consumers.

In-group solidarity and democratic organization and control. An outstanding element of strength in the movement has been the unusual solidarity of the cooperative group, based largely on its social and cultural homogeneity. As noted later, the growth of a more diversified membership and the consequent weakening of the earlier cultural ties must be counteracted by a more effective educational and merchandising program.

An aspect of internal solidarity which is of growing importance concerns the harmonizing of the producer and the consumer interests of the members. The main element of strength to be observed in the situation is that through a process of democratic discussion a basis of voluntary cooperation between these two diverging interests has been evolved, whereby adjustment of prices, standardization of quality and allocation of earnings can be achieved with greater justice and satisfaction to both.

The Finns built their cooperative structure in the most orthodox Rochdale fashion—from the bottom up. By erecting their cooperatives on a foundation of local interest, local ownership and local control, Finnish cooperators strongly believed that they could obtain the understanding, the sense of responsibility and the loyalty of the membership necessary for an enduring movement. The growth of federation, both regional and district, has remained democratic and flexible. On the commercial side, and more recently on the service side as well, it is centered in the Central Cooperative Wholesale. This regional federation has coordinated the business strength of the local societies, developed expert regional leadership and forged technical and economic weapons to fight growing competition. In addition its educational department is a major factor in diffusing cooperative sentiment throughout the area and in fostering social solidarity in the movement. Nothing would seem so likely to reduce the movement to the status of local shopkeeping as the neglect or abuse of its federated regional strength.

Outside support. Its early tie-up with the Finnish liberal labor movement made the cooperative movement sectarian. To a certain extent this resulted both in internal conflict and in outside antagonisms. During the early years, the cooperative movement to the politically conservative, represented radical socialist intrigue; to nationalistic elements it was a Finnish monopoly; to the religious-minded it was chiefly the work of atheists; and to the middle class consumer it was merely a common laborer's store.

The bitter factional struggle for control in the late twenties liquidated the influence of the radical socialist in the movement, strongly reaffirmed the Rochdale principles of open membership and democratic control and fostered an independent philosophy of cooperation. This transition has largely removed the sectarian barriers to expansion, and, together with the general liberal reaction which swept the country this past decade, has led to an increasing support of cooperatives by non-Finnish people and by certain elements in powerful American institutions.

The growing number of church people among the cooperatives' members and patrons, and the increasingly sympathetic attitude of many ministers in the area are indications of growing church support locally. The public schools have manifested a growing interest in the study of cooperation in all its phases. Under the pressure of public opinion legislative action has been taken in the states of Wisconsin, Minnesota and North Dakota leading to the inclusion of "Cooperation" as a definite subject in the school curriculum. During the past eight years, several officials and agencies of the federal government, from the President down, have given effective support to the cooperative idea. The governors of some states, particularly those of Wisconsin and Minnesota, have openly fostered it. What support or opposition from these sources may be forthcoming in the future is hard to judge. There is a hostile press and, of course, there are unfriendly political, religious, educational and business leaders.

Loyal and informed adherents. No institution or movement can grow, or in the long run survive, that does not produce successive generations of loyal and informed adherents, both leaders and followers. This movement has a special problem of this nature in the transition of its controlling leadership from the older Finnish immigrant generation to the younger Finnish and non-Finnish generation. The older leaders and a large proportion of their followers have been extremely loyal and have possessed a deep understanding of cooperative principles and a religious-like determination to put them into practice. Whether or not the movement can replace these leaders and followers with others of the oncoming generations who have a sufficient amount of understanding, loyalty and determination to insure its perpetuation, is a major problem. It is, in part, a critical test of the whole educational and promotional nexus developed by the movement or allied to it.

The educational activity of the movement, designed both to develop cooperative sentiment and train personnel, has been greatly accelerated in the past four years. A variety of agencies and techniques, suited to a many-sided approach to the problem have been developed. As yet, however, only scattered and intangible evidence of the success of this educational program in meeting the problem is available.

Loyal and competent personnel. The ability to attract a loyal and competent personnel is a vital element of strength in this as in other co-operative movements. In general the movement has not lacked for loyal employees, but due to increasing competition it has a perennial need for better trained ones. The organized employee-training program, which is now primarily a responsibility of the Central Cooperative Wholesale, includes at present regional and district managers' meetings, resident employee training schools, and since 1938, circuit employee training schools for employees in service. These are functioning with considerable success.

Wage scales, hour schedules, opportunities for promotion and general economic security are normally factors that greatly influence the ordinary individual in his choice of an occupation and in the quality of his performance in it. In their religious-like zeal to further cooperation, the immigrant generation of employees tended to minimize these factors, but the younger generation is inclined to be much more strongly influenced by them. Indications are that several of the cooperatives, in order to attract and hold desirable personnel in the future, will find it necessary to make more favorable adjustments in these working conditions. Particularly, greater remuneration for responsible administrative positions seems indicated. While there is a need for the working out of well-reasoned policies of consumer-employee relationships, a strengthening element in the labor situation, if handled properly, is that the consumer-employee relationships in the movement as a whole seem favorable for progressive adjustments of all potential differences.

Ideological and philosophical foundations. An important element of strength in the movement is to be found in its deeply ingrained ideological and philosophical foundations. It is guided by sound consumers' cooperative principles, is supported by a liberal social philosophy and is rooted in realistic needs of human nature and society.

While it is true that Finnish socialist influence distorted for a time the principles of open membership and democratic control in the movement, these and other Rochdale principles have provided a reliable basis for the organization and functioning of the cooperatives from the beginning.

Although retaining the labor sympathies and strong liberal emphasis of its origin, in recent years consumers' cooperation has emerged more clearly in cooperators' minds as a transforming social movement in its own right. Although to most cooperators this philosophy is vague in its details, it nevertheless exists as a compelling general idea and as a persistent inspiration to many. It adds strength to the movement by transforming it from a mere program of collective shopkeeping to something of a social crusade.

The men and women who sponsored the Finnish-initiated cooperative movement were well acquainted with physical hardship, economic exploitation, poverty, social isolation and personal frustration. In developing cooperatives they were not hazy sentimentalists toying with an intriguing idea of a social utopia, but were hard-pressed working people who desperately sought an effective social instrument to aid them in a struggle against economic and social handicaps. The claims of individual self-realization, therefore, underlie the movement and provide it with realistic support in basic human needs and values. The pursuit of personal realization, however, has not been narrowly self-seeking or socially destructive. On the contrary, through the cooperative process the individual's interest has been best served by promoting the common good. The movement has gained strength from the realistic character and fundamental harmony of its individual and social purposes.

Conclusion. The object of the study upon which this article is based was to understand from a sociological point of view a significant adventure in consumers' cooperation in the United States. An effort was made to observe and analyze first hand the actual cooperative experiences of specific human groups in a concrete social and cultural setting. The results clearly indicate that a nexus of sociological factors conditions the genesis, development and functioning of the cooperatives in question. These factors represent several major areas of sociological interest—regional economic and ecological organization, population migration and settlement, cultural heritage and change, social aspects of personality, group organization and interaction, community structure, and institutional organization and functioning.

In general the elements of weakness in the Finnish-initiated consumers' cooperative movement in the North Central states spring from the uncertainties of its incomplete adaptation to the American community. It is still somewhat of a marginal institution with receding roots in a Finnish workingmen's culture on the one hand and with increasing social, psychological and cultural foundations in the American community on the other.

The principal elements of strength in the institution, on the other hand, lie partly in the successful adaptations that it has already made to the American scene, but even more in the sound ideological foundations and well-intrenched democratic techniques that make continued transition possible.

There is evidently a close interrelation of the main features of a specific cooperative enterprise or movement with the geographical setting, the historical background and principal socio-economic and cultural patterns of the cooperating group. For this reason conclusions and generalizations drawn from a study of one specific cooperative situation must be applied to others with understanding and insight.

❧⸱❧⸱❧❧⸱❧⸱

87. The Changing Structure of the Detroit Mexican Family: An Index of Acculturation *

WE LIVE in a period of extensive human migration—sometimes voluntary, sometimes not. This mobility often exposes people to cultural patterns other than those in which they were reared. The process of modification undergone by the immigrant as he gradually discards his native cultural garb and re-clothes himself in that of his adopted society is known as *acculturation*. Drawing upon materials with which he is intimately acquainted, Norman D. Humphrey, in this selection, illustrates this process by reporting on changes in one set of institutional patterns of relationship, the family, within a particular immigrant group, Mexicans in Detroit.

THE PEASANT FAMILY in Mexico often has been characterized as "patriarchal." The roles of members are rather strictly defined by the pervasive folk culture. The father occupies a position in which he exercises considerable authority over his wife and children, and some of this power is extended to his grown sons who function partly to control their sisters' activities. The concepts of acceptable family behavior

* Norman D. Humphrey, *American Sociological Review*, 9, No. 6 (December, 1944), 622-626. Reprinted by permission of the publisher and the author.

The author (b. 1911) is Associate Professor of Sociology and Anthropology, Wayne University. Visiting professor, Escuela Nor. Superior, Bogota, Colombia, and Consultant, Institute Nac. de Antropol. Social, auspices U. S. Dept. of State and Colombian Ministry of Education. Areas of interest: people and cultures of Middle and South America, peasants (Mexican and Colombian), American race relations, community organization. Co-author, *Race Riot* and *The New Outline of the Principles of Sociology*.

are at first retained when Mexican migrants settle in Detroit. There, however, like those of other immigrants, these concepts and the behavior correlative to them undergo transformation. It is the contention of this paper that the changes in the structure of the family, under the impact of a new social and cultural environment, constitute a highly sensitized index of the process of acculturation.

The family is a *social structure*. A social structure is regarded here as a system of culturally defined status roles which form a relatively stable nexus of subordinate and superordinate selves. The significance of the social structure is the point of juncture of society and culture, and changes in the structure will index what happens in the merging of cultures. However, adjustments of social structures to changes in the total culture do not occur automatically. When there is agreement as to the definitions of status roles in a culture a social structure is stable, since duties and obligations accord with the roles which individuals must act out. New conceptions of self arise as the individual takes on new duties and obligations under the new cultural pressures. These new selves do not fit the old roles and immediately the stability of the social structure is threatened; eventually the structure changes. This is true for any structure. But since we regard the family as the one in which the self-conceptions of those who occupy roles are most intimately related to one another, we believe it will reflect most truly the changing meanings generated by the larger culture. All immigrant families obviously do not undergo simultaneous and equivalent changes. The roles portrayed, although empirically determined, will be synthesized into idealized types. Each of the several roles in the family will now be examined, at first, separately, later in combination.

The role of the father and head of the family has two major aspects: food provider, and family judge and protector.

The vicissitudes of employment, the seasonal character of work, and the long periods of unemployment, all have affected the status and role of the breadwinner, both in his own eyes and in those of other members of his family. Ill at ease when out of work, cognizant of violating a major obligation as head of the family, yet concerned with maintaining the respect from his wife and children which he considered his right, he might desert them to seek work and thus to re-establish his position. "Now I ask you," one breadwinner wrote his case worker, "for a chance to look for work in another place like I used to and as soon as I find one [a job] I will let you know as soon as possible." Refused by his case worker, he deserted, returned briefly to his family, and then left permanently for Mexico, leaving his family behind. More temporary desertions often followed flare-ups engendered by the husband's lack of employment and his accompanying loss of status in the home. This is indicated by an excerpt from a public welfare case record.

Mr. V explained to the worker that he had not deliberately deserted his family. He had gotten "mad," he said, because he wasn't working. He thought it was better to try to earn a little money on a sugar beet farm than to stay at home and do nothing.

The loss of status attendant on lack of financial support was further accentuated if the family head demanded complete subordination from his wife and grown sons. This is illustrated by Mr. P.

Mr. P admitted that on several occasions he struck his wife, but felt himself quite justified in having done so. His wife, he said, was continually accusing him of taking small sums of money which she had hidden in the house. It was beneath him, he said, to take money which did not belong to him, and when he was accused of such behavior he was enraged to the point where he struck his wife. He said that all women are fools and that he would like to be arrested so as to show the people in the United States how to treat women.

In general, however, the decline in status of the father, due to his failure to provide adequately for the family, was so gradual, both in the eyes of the wife and the children, that a lessening of respect was not accompanied by overt family conflict. The extent to which the father has continued to command respect is largely determined by the degree of assimilation of the non-patriarchal American culture by the wife and children.

A second facet of the father's role which has undergone change in Detroit is that concerned with the exercise of moral protection over the wife and female children. The protection of girls is a function the father shares with his wife, but he alone must see that no conceivable advances are made toward his mate. No man can talk to another's wife in what passes for a suspicious manner without invoking wrath on the part of her husband. This is seen in the case of Mrs. G.

Mrs. G was beaten by Mr. G because he found her talking to a former boarder in front of the G residence. She was beaten so severely that a city physician was called and he ordered her taken to Receiving Hospital where she was later released to her mother. She refused to swear out a warrant against Mr. G. Mr. G does not drink. He was reported to have become angered when his son Harold, aged four, told "lies" about the relation between Mrs. G and the boarder, which tales he preferred to believe to those of Mrs. G.

Protection of the wife extended into the area of pregnancy and child-birth.

Mr. M refused to go to his W.P.A. job during the period immediately pre-ceding his wife's labor, for, as he insisted, he had to "watch his wife." He did this despite the fact that his landlady volunteered to call the ambulance to take her to Herman Kiefer Hospital as soon as the child was coming.

The protective function was invoked to prevent a wife from in any way "Americanizing" herself or her home.

Mr. P complained to the worker that Mrs. P wished to Americanize their home and to disregard all of the customs of the old country that they had been used to. Mrs. P in turn said that Mr. P was so concerned with pro-tecting herself and the girl children that he did such absurd things as to hide behind cars in the vicinity of the children's school to see if they spoke or walked home with any of the boys in their classes.

Such protection even extended to a husband quarreling with a woman who unwittingly aided in Americanizing his wife.

Mr. S called Mrs. T a bad name because Mrs. T had taken Mrs. S to a theater one afternoon. Mr. S said that he did not approve of his wife going to a show either by herself or with another woman.

Girls must be vigilantly protected from situations which would allow personal contact with men.

Joseph, a widower, and his sister Mary, a deserted woman, kept house to-gether. Joseph brought home a friend, but the friend acted toward his sister in such a way as to displease Joseph, and he ordered the erstwhile friend from his home. Joseph said that he believed his sister better off with no friends than with "any kind of people."

Women, in general, are not in a position to oppose the exercise of these protection compulsions and are thereby bound to accept them.

The affectional role of the father toward his offspring contrasts with their unwillingness to accept his authority and protection. Mexican fathers show a genuine concern for their own children, and they easily extend this love to foster children.

When Marie's real father came and took her from Mr. O he was sincerely disappointed, for Mr. O wished always to keep the little girl.

No distinct pattern is evident in a man's treatment of his wife's illegitimate children for, while in some cases, they are readily accepted by the husband, in others they are not, and in some instances are raised by the grandparents. The duty to care for aged relatives, so strong in Mexico, in some cases is maintained and in some cases breaks down in Detroit. When it breaks down, it is largely a consequence of the wage system in the urban environment which precludes carrying such burdens.

The role of father is given a culturally sanctioned extension in the form of the *compadre* or godparent. This role involves duties and obligations of the same general sort as does the real parental relationship. The less the assimilation of American culture, the greater the probability of the maintenance of this role.

Mexican men in Detroit generally expect their wives to behave in much the same fashion that they did in Mexico, and in order to obtain wives who will conduct themselves in traditional ways some immigrants return to Mexico to marry. Most Mexican women in Detroit have remained subordinate, home-centered creatures.

Mr. M complimented his wife by saying that he has noticed no change in her in the twenty years that she has lived in Detroit. She stays at home and "keeps the old ways." While the interview with Mr. M went on, Mrs. M sat quietly nearby with her hands folded in her lap. She spoke only when he asked her a question, answering in Spanish since she knew no English.

The woman's role is that of a homemaker, an inculcator of religious precepts, a protector of her girl children. While most women accept the restraints imposed on them by the culture of the homeland, a small proportion of Detroit Mexican women come to take advantage of the greater freedom possible there. If the wife has assimilated American culture more rapidly than has her husband, she may use her knowledge to effect a reversal, from subordination to superordination, in family roles. Regarding one wife a case record reports:

Woman is a very dominant person, quite excitable in her manner . . . very loud. . . . Mrs. A seems to be spokesman for the family.

Such transformation of roles was most possible when the wife was considerably younger than the husband, or in cases, as was true in several instances, where the wife was American-born but of Mexican derivation.

As a result of the differing degrees to which they have acquired American culture and retained Mexican culture, the members of the Mexican family have changed positions relative to one another within that unit.   More abstractly, changed levels of status appear in the social structure of the family.

In general, the structure of the peon family in Detroit has changed in three ways: the status role and corresponding conception of self of the father has declined relative to that of the women and children; the wife has tended to retain her previous status role position through the greater retention of Mexican meanings and understandings, although in some instances the wife has come to occupy a position of social superordination; the status role of the children has largely reversed itself, and this is particularly true for the oldest boy, who plays an entirely new role.

The oldest child acts as mentor to later born siblings.   He has paved the way.   His experiences and directions in regard to Mexican and American cultural meanings and understandings serve as a framework for their later definitions.   As mentor in American ways, as one who knows the rights and wrongs of American culture, the oldest child may assume parental functions.   He becomes protector, orderer, and forbidder; in short, a foster parent, schooled in American ways.   His ordering and forbidding, his age, may make him socially a hostile competitor, a family member exercising authority over the whole family which he could exercise only over his sister in the homeland.   Young men have assumed positions either of dominance or of equality to their fathers, while in general girls have acquiesced to a subordinate, home-centered position; yet even the conformers possess more freedom for outside activities than do their mothers, and hence have somewhat higher status than their mothers.

The second generation, and particularly the boys of this generation, have been so broadly exposed to the dominant American culture that they have come to possess meanings which are at times in direct opposition to those of their parents.   Thus, for a working youth to contribute his whole earnings to family support is in addition to its utility for the family, a social value (an emotionally charged meaning) to the immigrant; countrariwise, some male children, who follow American norms in this regard, do not recognize, or choose to ignore, the value elements in surrendering their pay checks.   They see only a practice lacking utility for themselves and therefore to be opposed.   It is clear that many things which for the parental generation were values of peasant Mexico, as for example regular church attendance or respect for the inexorable authority of the father, lie for the children in the realm of utilitarian symbols (closely empirically grounded meanings), concerning which choice may be exercised.

It is evident that the dissimilar symbols and values possessed by each member of the family is largely a consequence of differential association of family members with Americans, of unlike participation in American culture, and of the dissimilar store of meanings originally carried by these individuals. These factors have given rise to discordant conceptions of self. Conceptions of self get out of harmony with previously defined status roles. The father has tried unsuccessfully to maintain his conception of himself and of his role, particularly in the eyes of his children, whose own conceptions of themselves and definitions of their roles clash with those of their parents.

In Mexico, the status hierarchy in the family runs father, mother, son, and daughter, in that order, from high to low position. Four fairly distinct levels are apparent, and there is a large gap between the father on the topmost rung, and the daughter on the lowest.

In Detroit the positioning is decisively altered. The son has assumed a position about equal with the father, and above the mother; while the daughter has climbed at least onto the same level with the mother. Also it appears that the possible overall range of status has been distinctly narrowed: only two of the former four planes now accommodate all four positions. This may be interpreted as a phenomenon of leveling out, or democratizing within the family.

The assimilation indicated herein has been one of process, rather than that of a completed readjustment. Reorganization on a new level has not sufficiently advanced in the second generation to allow for the empiric construction of emergent and stabilized status roles. Some conditions of the "typical" immigrant family can be indicated, however, and following this some features of the second generation family may be noted.

The immigrant family's aspirations do not as yet include the conventional middle class American ones of a better home, travel, and education for the children. The children range in age from those in grammar school to the oldest who has completed the tenth grade in school, and who is now employed in an unskilled factory job. The younger children plan to complete the twelfth grade, and then train for a trade.

The children attend, as much as they are able, the Mexican club dances, and together with the rest of the family go to the club picnics in the summer months. The main occupation of the woman is housewife; that of the man intermittent provider. The girls complain that their parents don't want them to go out with boys, although occasionally they disobey. The boys disregard parental restraint as much as possible.

The family somewhat irregularly attends the Catholic church, though the children go largely to please their parents. The children speak English among themselves, and Spanish to their parents. The children do not belong to any Mexican clubs, and although the father once belonged to clubs, he no longer attends their regular meetings. He has accepted the concept of individuality and recognizes the necessity of competition. He knows that the Mexican concept, "brother helps brother," is supplanted in Detroit by the slogan, "every man for himself."

When the children leave home after marriage (although they may remain at home for a time), they virtually stop speaking Spanish, and in their own homes give up the holiday celebrations their parents enjoyed. The young husband still expects his wife to be subordinate to him, although he allows her much more freedom than his father gave his mother. His wife remains a quiet, "sweet" person, who is aware of the vicissitudes of American economic life, and tries to save some of his income for the future. Their home, however, is better furnished than that of their parents, and Mexican objects are largely absent. Their main recreational outlet is the movies, and their main goal the husband's regular employment in the "shop." In short, they have become functionally a young American working class family.

CHAPTER X

SOCIAL AND CULTURAL CHANGE: DISORGANIZATION, PLANNING AND VALUES

88. The Process of Adjustment to New Inventions *

WE ACCEPT many miracles of modern scientific technology as commonplace: airplanes that span oceans and continents almost as fast as the sun; navigational aids that permit safe airplane travel regardless of local visibility; on-the-spot and up-to-the-minute reports and interpretations of significant recent events in foreign capitals around the globe by means of short-wave radio; the atom-splitting technology of nuclear physics that overnight makes necessary a re-examination of the geography of crucial natural resources. The list could be extended almost indefinitely. William F. Ogburn, who has in the past twenty-five years made outstanding contributions on cultural and social change, is the author of the present selection. In this excerpt his primary concern is "with how invention and science affect international relations," a subject of overwhelming importance. Incidental to this discussion, the principle of multiple causation—almost always operative in social and cultural phenomena —is also clearly illustrated.

* William Fielding Ogburn, Technology and International Relations (Chicago: The University of Chicago Press, 1949), pp. 16-27. Reprinted by permission of the author and the publisher.

The author (b. 1886) is Professor Emeritus, Sociology, University of Chicago. Sewell L. Avery Distinguished Service Professor at Chicago since 1933. From 1930-43, Director of Research, Social Trends, President's Research Committee; Consumers Advisory Board, National Recovery Administration; Consultant, National Resources Planning Board. Coined the term "cultural lag." Among his works are Social Change, American Marriage and Family Relationships, You and Machines, The Social Effects of Aviation, Technology and International Relations.

THE SUBJECT OF INTERNATIONAL RELATIONS is often presented in terms of policies. These policies are generally seen in terms of choice, will, and action by leaders. Bismarck's policy was one of moderation as compared to that of Kaiser Wilhelm. Or Bismarck chose to wage war. Stories of alliances, of national commitments, and of diplomatic strategy are dramatic accounts of human behavior. Then, too, the explanations of international action are frequently in terms of principles. The enemy wants to enslave the world; or we wish to make it safe for democracy.

Into such an atmosphere technology appears as a strange intrusion. Against the mighty force of morals it seems incidental rather than a determining force to be reckoned with seriously. For is not an invention an instrument to do man's bidding for such ends as he chooses?

Yet few would doubt that the early acquisition of steam power by the British before other states acquired it helped them to become the leading world power of the nineteenth century and thereby made the task of British diplomacy much easier. Britain's steel mills, with their products for peace and for war, enabled her to spread much more effectively the ways of European civilization into Africa and southern and southeastern Asia. Yet we are disposed to give credit to Gladstone, or even to Queen Victoria. Another illustration is the praise we extend to Columbus for the discovery of America. Yet without the new large boats and their equipment, this continent would not have been discovered from Europe; and with such boats, if Columbus had not lived, some other adventurous navigator would have made the discovery. No one thinks of attributing the discovery of America to a boat, though.

We may say, then, that technology makes possible certain human achievements, and we may also admit that without such material aids these achievements would not be possible. But there are other ways in which invention affects human action. The purpose of this chapter is to inquire into these processes.

SOME BASIC CONCEPTIONS

We begin by pointing out a restriction of the subject. We are concerned here only with how invention and science affect international relations and not with how international relations affects science and invention. Though we recognize that international relations, to wit, war, was a factor in developing the submarine, for instance, a more proper concern under this limitation would be with how the submarine affected international relations, to wit, Germany's relations with Britain, whose ships could, without the submarine, blockade the Baltic Sea.

Furthermore, when it is found that technology affects international relations, it is not to be implied that no other factor is of any influence. Several causes often exist, of which only one is a new invention. Thus the development of heavy industry, driven with mechanical power, in the Soviet Union will increase her might as a state. But so will the growth of her population of military age, which will occur at the same time that her factory production will be increased. The problem here, however, is to trace out the processes of one factor, technology, and not to appraise the relative strength of each of the many factors involved.

Quite a problem in analysis is what to do with the factor that does not change. For instance, shall we credit Britain's increase as a power in the nineteenth century to her coal mines? But the island had coal when it was not a power, as when the Romans or the Normans occupied it. Coal only becomes useful when there are steam engines in which to burn it. The coming of the steam engine, not coal, is the variable which explains the increase of Britain as a power in the nineteenth century.

The phenomenon we seek to explain is a variable, namely, a change in Britain's position as a power. A change must be explained in terms of a change. Thus the reader is reading this page not because there is oxygen in the air but for some other reason. The necessity of the oxygen in reading is apparent, but it is useless as an explanation of why a reader is reading this page instead of attending a theater, say, or reading something else.

Returning to the illustration of coal, while it has been a constant over time in Britain and hence could not explain a change in her position, coal is not a constant between two nations. Thus, France has little coal and Germany has much; hence coal is a factor in explaining why Germany is a greater power than France. In these illustrations coal is a variable over space but not over time.

An interesting question is whether human nature should be considered a constant. Sometimes it is and sometimes it is not. Between individuals there is great variation in some traits—desire for power, for instance. But between large populations, perhaps, the percentage of the population that desire power may be about the same.

If a new invention calls forth the same response from human beings in the societies being compared which use it, we think of the new invention, a variable, as a causative factor and not human behavior, which is in this situation a constant. Thus, in all cities, automobiles have developed suburbs. Human beings in all cities want more space in which to live. The desire for more space is a constant, then, from one large city to another. Hence we do not say that the desire for space caused the suburbs. The desire for space is a variable, though, between the open country and the city. Ranchers do not desire more space in which to live and do not use the automobile for that purpose.

Inventions are made relatively suddenly and are dropped, so to speak, into a social situation. Often this social situation is the same as to basic human attitudes before the invention occurs and after the invention is adopted. So we do not say that the attitude is a factor in explaining a change following the invention, because the attitude is a constant. These social situations may vary, though, from one country to another. Thus, the appearance of contraceptives in China may not lead to the same results as did their appearance in Protestant western Europe, for attitudes on the Chinese desire for children is different, with their ancestor worship and their familial institutions. So also the effect of the airplane on international relations would be quite different in a world situation which is not warlike from what it is in a world in which a power struggle is going on.

In international relations the variables often stressed are leaders, personalities, social movements, and organizations. These are important variables in explaining particular actions and specific achievements. But because of their significance the variations of the technological factors should not be obscured. . . .

One reason technological factors are obscured is that causes appear in a sequence like the links of a chain, and the link signifying the factor of technology is often somewhat removed and not so close to the change being explained as is the leader of a movement or the head of an organization. Thus, we observed the prime minister of the United Kingdom, as World War II came to a close, repeatedly advancing the interests of France in international conferences. But back of this British policy we note the invention of the rocket carrying an explosive and the airplane, both of which have rendered water barriers to Britain less effective and have increased the value of defense in depth. Britain becomes increasingly eager for a strong and a friendly France. Thus, the inclusion of France in many postwar actions is caused first by the political leaders, but also a cause back of that is the changed nature of war occasioned by new transportation inventions. This is not to say that there were not other factors or that Britain has not wanted the support of France long before these inventions of the airplane. It is rather that the increased need of Britain for France is caused by a change in technology.

One final observation should be made on the idea of inevitability, often implied in speaking of the influence of an invention. It is as though men had no choice in the matter. Thus, we think of the invention of gunpowder as inevitably changing the course of feudalism. But, it may be argued, men had the "choice" of using the explosive to propel missiles. The Chinese did not so use it. In the past, where the effect of invention in history has already occurred, we more readily admit inevitability than we do in looking to the future, where we seem to have choice, for instance, as to what we shall do about using the atomic bomb. We are using the word "choice" as it is popularly used and shall here not go beyond this conception. It may be preferable in referring to the future to speak of "adjustment to technology" rather than to the "effect of technology."

Inevitability and choice are a dichotomy of extremes. A more realistic approach is to think in terms of degrees of a continuum rather than of two extreme categories. Hence, it is preferable to think of the influences of invention in terms of probabilities. A good way of visualizing probabilities of a relationship of two variables is in terms of a correlation table, in which the coefficient may vary from zero to one, and, when it does, there are other factors involved which if unknown may carry the idea of chance or choice. It does not appear necessary that ideas of free will complicate the analysis in the paragraphs which follow.

THE FIRST EFFECTS OF AN INVENTION

Let us start our inquiry with the fact of an invention. A new invention is made. It is here. In what ways will civilization be different because of it?

The first stage of inventional influence is in its use. It should be observed, however, that not every invention is used. Probably more than 90 per cent of them are not used. There appears to be a "choice" as to whether we shall make use of a scientific discovery or not. We did not choose to use poison gas in World War II. In other cases, where the demand is strong, continuous, and widely spread, the use is assured, as in the case of the discovery of anesthetics. All of us, except a few eccentrics, want to avoid pain.

Once a significant invention is widely used, there follow changes in the habits of the users. Steamships change the habits of sailors. So an early stage in the social effects of an invention is changes in the habits of users.

For an invention to be used, it must be produced. So, parallel with these changes due to use, there occur changes due to production. If we decide to use the atom bomb, new types of factors are set up. Using an invention makes changes due to its production inevitable, though there are some choices, as in the location of factories or in the materials to be used. The impact of an invention upon consumers and producers is generally recognized.

DERIVATIVE INFLUENCES

That the impact of inventions upon society extends beyond their influence upon consumers and producers is not generally appreciated. The influence of the long-range air bomber does not cease with its changes in the usages of warfare. It extends beyond and affects the foreign policies of states during peacetime. This influence on foreign policies is derived from its use and is therefore called a "derivative influence."

Derivative influences of science flow not only from users but also from producers. For instance, the changes in the production of explosives due to atomic fission have a derivative influence upon the relation of small states or outlying areas, with possible or actual uranium deposits, to great powers making atomic bombs. The competition for atomic bombs thus leads through the first stage of production to rivalries in the search for raw materials—a derivative effect from the production of the invention.

WHY THERE ARE DERIVATIVE EFFECTS

The reason derivative influences spread from users and producers to social institutions is the existence of interconnections between the parts of civilization. Our modern culture is put together more like a clock, with its interrelationships of parts, than it is, let us say, like a chain, where some links may be changed without greatly affecting the whole. In a total war today almost every institution, every organization, is affected, so closely interconnected are the different parts of modern civilization.

Hence, if an invention through its use changes one part of our social organization, its influence does not stop there but extends toward the other parts of our social order which are connected with it. For instance, in societies, travel is interconnected with a system of lodgings. When one travels a long distance, one must have a place to spend the night away from home. If the method of travel which depends upon time schedules and afew fixed tracks is changed by the addition of the private automobile, independent of schedules and for which there are many different highways, a change in the system of lodging is inevitable, whether it be tourist camps, motels, or guest homes. Once we decide to use private automobiles for traveling long distances, the derivative change in the hotel system follows.

Sometimes the linkages between the parts of the social order are not so strong as that between travel and inns, in which case the derivative effect is not so certain. A rather weak linkage exists, for instance, between the transportation system and resettlement—not so strong as between transportation and temporary lodgings. The addition to overseas transportation of fast and large steamships with regular schedules was accompanied by an increase in emigration from Europe to America; but such a derivative effect as migration does not appear to follow inevitably solely because of the new invention of the steamboat. For, later, this immigration was stopped while the steamboats continued to run; nor did immigration occur in transportation across the Pacific Ocean. Thus it is not at all certain that resettlement will be a derivative influence of transportation changes.

The reason resettlement is not always a derivative effect of a new transportation invention is that transportation is only one of many factors in peoples' determining to change their home. Other factors are economic opportunity, population pressure, the fluctuations of the business cycle, and political barriers. Most social phenomena, like immigration, are the products of many different variables.

CONVERGENCE

Often several of these variables which operate to produce a social change are influences from several different inventions. The influences of these inventions are said to converge to bring about a result. A good illustration is the widening differential between the small powers and the large ones since the second World War. This is one of the effects of the air bomber. Small countries with few heavy industries cannot well provide the necessary defenses in fighter planes and antiaircraft guns to stop a great power's large destructive fleet of bombers. Furthermore, the development of the airplane is achieved much better in states with a great expanse of territory, which a small state does not have. With the ability of the airbomber to hit military objectives anywhere, the resistance of a small state is greatly weakened.

The invention of the armored tank has the same general effect on widening the comparative military strengths of small and large states. So also do rockets and guided projectiles, especially if there are many cities in the small state. A great power can have more scientific laboratories and greater use of mass production. There then is the convergence of the influence of many different inventions to make the great power stronger and the little power weaker. In this case the influences of these different converging inventions is additive. In convergence the contribution of any invention to a social change is a fraction.

SUCCESSIVE DERIVATIVES

We have shown that the effect of an invention does not stop with its uses. Nor does it stop with its first derivative influence. It proceeds to still other linked institutions. The process of successive derivative influences is much like the game of billiards when the cue ball strikes another, which in turn hits still another, and so on.

The invention of the cotton gin, for example, by removing a bottle-neck to cotton utilization, led to increased production of cotton in the southern states by an expansion of slave labor, since the world demand for cotton cloth from the mills of England was very great. There followed a struggle for new slave territory in the western states about ready to be admitted to the Union as states. This struggle for political power between the northern and southern states accentuated the issue of a high tariff versus free trade, since the South could export more cotton with free trade and since the industries of the North could grow faster under the protection of a tariff. This struggle reached a climax in the War between the States. There were, then, a succession of derivative influences following the invention of the cotton gin.

It seems absurd to imply that the invention of the cotton gin caused the war of 1860-64. But such is not the implication. The cotton gin was only one factor, large or small, in a series of successive convergences of derivative influences, such as the expanding market for textiles from British factories, the opening of new lands for settlement, the development of new factories in northern states, etc.

The proportional influence of the cotton gin becomes smaller as new influences are added in successive convergences. If an inventional influence is one in three other influences on convergence No. 1, and the influence of convergence No. 1 is one in four other influences on convergence No. 2, then the invention's influence is only one in seven on the second convergence. So the proportional influence of an invention diminishes through a succession of derivatives.

It is not customary to think of an invention like the cotton gin of the 1800's as having an influence on the tariff of the 1850's, for the invention of the gin is far removed not only in time but in successive convergences. Nevertheless, we may ask the pertinent question: "If the cotton gin had never been invented, would the tensions between the northern and southern states have reached an intensity great enough to start a conflagration of war?" The removal of an invention from society, if no substitute is provided, would show how far-reaching are its derivative influences.

RESISTANCES TO TECHNOLOGICAL INFLUENCES

Convergence is a phenomenon of social change. In a stationary society its analogue would be a pattern of linked parts of society. The family as an institution is linked to education, to production, to protection, etc. The appearance of a new invention in a system of linked material objects, institutions, and habits may modify the system, that is, the system adjusts to the invention.

These adjustments do not take place easily. Sometimes the pattern of a culture cannot assimilate a new invention. An area without coal and iron cannot assimilate the blast furnace, though it could buy the products of the Industrial Revolution. Japan could incorporate into its system the steam and steel complex, but the Australian aborigine could not. In other cases assimilation may be readily accomplished. To adopt the jet fighter plane by a country engaged in the war production of planes was not difficult.

An invention is, then, like a seed which may fall on different kinds of soil. The soils that are too sandy, too wet, too dry, or too rocky may be said to offer resistances to the growth from the seed. So there are obstacles to the adoption of inventions. A law was passed in Hungary in 1523 to prevent the use of four-wheeled coaches, since there was fear that the training of cavalry would be less effective. It should be observed that eventually the people of Hungary did use coaches.

There are also resistances to the derivative influences, as in the case of inventions of local transportation which have spread the economic city beyond the boundaries of the political city. There is great resistance to extending outward the political boundaries of an expanding city.

Similarly, the influence of various transportation, communication, and military inventions is to spread the influence of a state, which is a great center of dispersal, outward to the small border states, sometimes called a "zone of influence." But the influence of large states over the small neighboring political units is resisted. Any loss of sovereignty or change of boundary lines particularly is expected to be resisted. There are many linkages of different parts of a state with its political structure.

LAGS

This resistance, which inventions and their influences meet, means delays in time in the spread of technological effects on society. One such delay is that of straightening highways and rail tracks to permit the speeds which new engines yield. The linkage is close, but the adjustment to the new speeds lags.

Some of these lags are very long indeed. The uniting of the European states economically or politically has lagged a long time after the inventions of production and transportation have made it possible and desirable and long after the disadvantage of this lack of union is evident in comparison with large united areas like the United States and the U.S.S.R.

The long lag in yielding to the influence of technological developments has made the correlation between technological change and social change more difficult to see. An illustration is the counties in the United States. The political units were laid out in the days of horse-drawn transportation and when the technology of production was on farms fairly equably distributed. Now the administration of counties would probably be better and cheaper per capita if a state had five or ten counties instead of a hundred. If the county lines are not changed, they will become less and less functional, and the adjustments to the new technological developments will be made by grants-in-aid, new taxation procedures, and the shifting of functions to states and cities. The long delays in adjustments obscure the correlation.

THE WEIGHT OF THE TECHNOLOGICAL FACTOR

We have now traced the main steps in the process of social changes flowing from inventions and scientific discoveries. But an analysis of the process is not an assessment of the importance of technology as compared with other factors. An analysis of ideational innovations would probably have shown somewhat similar processes. Regarding the relative importance of technological forces, a few remarks in the nature of theory will be made.

THE VARIABILITY OF MODERN TECHNOLOGY

One reason we think technology is important in international relations is its great variability. There are many new and important inventions occurring every decade: fascimile transmission, radio telephone, jet propulsion, rockets, helicopters, radar, television, photography, lithoprinting, plant hormones, alloys, atomic fission, and many others. Indeed, the number of inventions tends to grow exponentially.

The significance of the variability of invention lies in the fact that we do not consider a constant as a causal factor in change. It must be a variable that explains a variation. Thus a variation from sailing ships to steamships led to changes in British foreign policy. National interest is, of course, a factor in British foreign policy, but that is a constant, which was present both before and after the appearance of the steamship, and does not explain the changes.

Another constant in international relations, at least for a time, is the desire for national security. The new inventions of war give emphasis to the policy of the Soviet Union to obtain a zone of security around it. The ideological constant is the desire for security. The new inventions lead to policies regarding particular countries.

THE VARIATION IN IDEOLOGIES

Ideologies vary, too; and, in so far as they do, they must be given weight. We have no conclusive answer as to whether in modern times as many important ideological factors vary as do important technological factors. We have recently seen the rise of fascism and communism, important ideological developments. It should not be assumed, however, that fascism and communism originated independently of technological changes. In some cases the technological factor in the origin of ideologies or their variation is clear. The safety-first movement, incorporating the social invention of workmen's compensation, was occasioned by the invention of fast-moving metal machines and vehicles. It may also be argued that the idea of the federation of the Western nations arises in part because of the variation in the transportation and military inventions. The ideology of "isolationism," so prominent in the United States, is being eliminated, by the airplane.

On the other side, ideologies cause changes in technology. The atom bomb, jet propulsion, and radar were creations of the war ideas. The influence of war on creating inventions is more the influence of demand arising from a social condition than the force of an ideology.

War is an illustration of a nontechnological factor that is not always a constant, not so much so as national interest and national security. The prospects of war vary from decade to decade and from one continent to another. Indeed, one foreign policy in which the people of the United States are deeply interested is to produce a more marked variation in this factor of war, that is, to eliminate it.

The foregoing discussion does not settle the question of the relative importance of technology but is rather an exploration of some aspects of the problem. In any case, the purpose of this paper is rather to describe the processes whereby technological change influences society.

SUMMARY

We may now summarize the processes of change instituted by the appearance of an invention in our culture. Society is different, first, because of the new habits of users and producers of the invention, assuming the invention meets a demand and is not rejected. This first step in the impact of technology upon civilization is common knowledge. But the effect of an invention is not restricted solely to its direct influence on its users and its producers. Institutions and ideologies may also make adjustments to the new habits of users and consumers. Thus an invention has a derivative influence upon social institutions indirectly through its users or producers. This derivative influence is often not recognized by casual observers because it is once removed from the invention. This observation is most commonly left unmade in the case of a chain of successive derivative influences. The phenomenon of derivative influences arises because of the intercorrelation of the parts of culture.

The derivative influence of any particular invention is often not appreciated because it is only one of many converging influences, many of which flow from other inventions, mechanical or social. In the case of successive derivative convergences of inventions, the influence of one early invention may be comparatively small.

Because of the intercorrelation of the parts of culture and the fact that many social phenomena exist because of the presence of many factors, the effects of inventions are resisted or delayed until a favorable situation develops. Sometimes the derivative influence of an invention requires for an adjustment an ideational or social invention.

All these processes may be observed in the influence of the inventions of steam and steel, aviation, and other means of transportation, the atom bomb and the mass-communications inventions, upon the ranking of powers, the federation of nations, spheres of influence, and diplomatic procedure.

89. Descent to Anomy *

To MOST OF US our social ties, the values by which we live, and our
sense of "belonging" are so much a part of us that we have little
conception of their deep significance to us and to our society.
Hence, we are inclined to take social cohesion for granted. But this
social cohesion through which the unity of our personalities is secured and maintained always rests in delicate balance. In a complex society, even under the most favorable conditions, there are
individuals who fall into anomy (sometimes spelled *anomie*)—a condition where the sense of "belonging" to the group is lost and the
norms or values of society are rejected. In times of crisis such as
these, "whole groups are exposed to the malady." In this selection, MacIver describes the anomic person, and shows how the
presence of anomy is evidenced in a modern society. He suggests,
in addition, the conditions we must guard against, and what we must
do if the growth of anomy is to be checked.

LET US LOOK next at *anomy*, the other malady of democratic man that
becomes most virulent in times of crisis and turbulent change, the
breakdown of the individual's sense of attachment to society, to all
society. Anomy is not simply lawlessness. A gangster or a pirate or a
mere law-evading rogue is not as such, indeed is not likely to be, anomic.
He has his own code of law against law and is under strong sanctions
to obey it. He need not be the victim of that inner detachment, of
that cleavage between the real self and the projected self, of that total
rejection of indoctrinated values that characterizes the anomic person.
Anomy signifies the state of mind of one who has been pulled up from
his moral roots, who has no longer any standards but only disconnected
urges, who has no longer any sense of continuity, of folk, of obligation.
The anomic man has become spiritually sterile, responsive only to himself, responsible to no one. He derides the values of other men. His
only faith is the philosophy of denial. He lives on the thin line of sensation between no future and no past.

In any times particular individuals may fall into anomy. It happens
when sensitive temperaments suffer without respite a succession of
shocks that disrupt their faith. And not a few men have temporary
moods that resemble anomy, periods when the spirit of denial rules

---

* Robert M. MacIver, *The Ramparts We Guard* (New York: The Macmillan
Company, 1950), pp. 84-92. Reprinted by permission of the publisher and the
author.
For a biographical sketch of the author see selection 77, p. 671.

them, after they have experienced some grave bafflement. But there are times of profound disturbance when whole groups are exposed to the malady. The soldiers in Mailer's novel, *The Naked and the Dead*, talk the language of anomy. They have been torn in youth from their environments, their careers, their dreams, their hopes, to face laborious tedium and the ugliest forms of death. They have been bereft of the sustaining ways of their culture. They are thrust back on the immediate needs and demands of each perilous hour. The present offers nothing but sensations; there are periods of boredom and drudgery, and then they are alone with nature and sudden death. So they use the language of sensation—there is nothing else to express. It means little but there is nothing else to mean. The livid, gory, sexy words they utter soon convey precisely nothing, nothing but the denudation they feel. For them, however, for those who survive, there is a return to nearly all the things they have lost. For most of them anomy wears away in their restoration to their society. But there are others, the hopelessly displaced, the totally uprooted, the permanently insecure, those who need the support of authority and have lost it without hope of recovery, the over-sophisticated who find that the challenges of life cannot be met by sophistication—among such people anomy takes full command.

Anomy is a state of mind in which the individual's sense of social cohesion—the mainspring of his morale—is broken or fatally weakened. In this detachment of the anomic person from social obligation his whole personality is injured. He has lost the *dynamic unity* of personality. The anomic fall into various types, though we do not have so far the psychological researches necessary for the adequate classification of these types. We can, however, broadly distinguish the following.

First, there are those who, having lost altogether, or in great measure, any system of values that might give purpose or direction to their lives, having lost the compass that points their course into the future, abandon themselves to the present, but a present emptied of significance. They resort, in other words, to a sophisticated cynicism, by aid of which they rationalize their loss. They live by the hour, seeking immediate gratification on whatever level it is available. They tend to be sensationalists and materialists. It is their defense against the ghosts of perished values.

Second, there are those who, having lost their ethical goals, having no longer any intrinsic and socialized values to which they can harness their drive to action, transfer this drive to extrinsic values instead, to the pursuit of means instead of to the pursuit of ends beyond them, and particularly to the pursuit of power, so far as that lies within their reach. It has been claimed that there is a "strain toward anomy" in modern capitalistic society, with its emphasis on competitive success measured by the purely extrinsic standard of money-making. There can be little doubt that engrossment in the competitive struggle, especially when it is carried on under the aegis of the "soul-less body-less" corporation, diverts men from the search for intrinsic satisfactions and erodes their recognition of the common interests of their society, the inclusive more abiding interests that bind men in the responsible fellowship of their community. At the same time, the experience of the past two generations suggests that it requires the violence of change, the deeper perturbations that disorient and displace men from their former ways, their former goals, their former faiths, to bring anomy to its full being, and in particular this second type of anomy. Those who exhibit it tend to be domineering, sadistic, ruthless, irascible, vain, inherently destructive. Unlike the first type, they live for a future, they have objectives that bind today to the further tomorrow, but these objectives are self-centered, ego-glorifying, bereft of social obligation. Often they profess adherence to some intrinsic faith or value, but primarily because that profession enhances their private designs. They are then like Machiavelli's prince, who must appear to be religious and high-minded if he is to retain his prestige and power. Moreover, they make the creeds of other men the instruments of their own aggrandisement, the utilitarian myths of their authority. On another level they are racketeers, buccaneers of industry or finance, unprincipled exploiters of whatever position, privilege, or power they acquire. All men or nearly all men cherish their private interest and frequently enough they allow it to overcome their public obligation. But they are restrained within certain limits set by loyalties of one kind or another, and when they transgress they are conscious of dereliction. But the truly anomic man has no limit short of necessity and no conscience that is more than expediency.

Third, we may distinguish a type of anomy that is characterized above all by a fundamental and tragic insecurity, something that cuts deeper than the anxieties and dreads that beset other men. It is the insecurity of the hopelessly disoriented. They have lost the ground on which they stood, the ground of their former values. Usually it happens when they have lost also their former environment, their former connections, their social place, their economic support. In the profoundest sense they are "displaced persons." The displacement, however, may not be physical. There is, for example, the social alienation of those who feel themselves rejected and become the victims of a persecution complex. This is perhaps the bitterest of all forms of anomy. There is a crushing sense of indignity, of exclusion, of injustice, of defeat, arousing feelings of intense hate, counter-aggressiveness, total revulsion from things as they are, sometimes accompanied by unquiet introspection and self-torture.

This cursory review is intended to suggest types, not to classify them. In any event there is a considerable overlapping of attributes between our types. We should also remember that many people approach the full bent of anomy in various degrees. As we have already suggested, the conditions of our civilization create some predisposition to it and when our kind of civilization is racked by abrupt and violent change anomy grows rampant. Anomy is a disease of the civilized, not of the simpler peoples. As Durkheim pointed out, one index of anomy is the number of suicides, and suicide is much more frequent among the civilized.

It is noteworthy that modern doctrines of violent social change are initiated by those who have at least a tendency to anomy. Let us take for example the case of Karl Marx. He was from his early youth subjected to some of the conditions that breed anomy. His family belonged to the rabbinical elite in Germany. While he was still an infant his father, to the general surprise, announced his conversion to the Protestant Evangelical Church. This was the cause of a bitter dispute between his father and his mother. In the end, when Karl was six years old, his father had his way, and Karl, along with the six other children of the family, was baptized into the new faith. We know from modern studies how deeply disturbing it is to the mind of a child to have his first indoctrinations shattered by a "culture clash" on the hearth. The secret churning of the young boy's mind was the first preparation of the revolutionist-to-be, greatly heightening that sense of aloofness and disorientation that is the lot of many a Jewish boy in a society that stupidly clings to its hoary prejudices. The first obvious effect on Karl Marx was his loathing of all religions.

He grew into an impetuous, irascible, opinionated, and still idealistic youth. Then his ambitions suffered a series of reverses and frustrations. At this stage he fell in with the "communist rabbi," Moses Hess. He was ripe for the new gospel. He embraced it avidly, inclining at first toward the French socialists but soon repudiating and scorning them to assert his own truly scientific brand. It was the culmination of a process that began in the disorientation of childhood. Marx had become completely alienated from the society in which he lived, not its economic order particularly but its whole being and all the culture it nourished. In the background of his mind there flickered visions of an ideal society. But his love of the ideal was pale and distant compared with his hatred of the actual. He turned early to dreams of power, of lonely mastery. He was at enmity with the world. He denounced with incredible bitterness his own best friends the moment they ventured to question in any way his authority.

A man may condemn the society in which he lives without being himself anomic. But only if he is sustained by the engrossing vision of a better society, only if he is working to hasten the coming of some "new Jerusalem," only if he lives in fellowship with some brotherhood of the faithful who share his vision, only, in the last resort, if he is already, prophetically, a member of the society for which he yearns. There are those who believe the main inspiration of Marx was just some such redemption of mankind, that he was filled with the vision of a world in which men would be liberated from exploitation and injustice, from the gross oppression of every form of power. To the present writer that seems a mistaken interpretation. In the voluminous writings of Marx there are only one or two most fleeting references to "the good society." There is no evidence that he really cared for his fellowmen. He never uses kindly language except for those who looked upon him as their infallible leader. He hated those of his own party who showed any independence of thought. He was venomous toward all whom he could not dominate.

Marx focused his sharp intelligence on the worst sore of the society he hated. A new industrial system had been growing up. It was being exploited with callous disregard for the welfare of the workers. In the "dark Satanic mills," as the poet Blake called them, men, women, and young children labored endlessly long days, under the worst conditions, for subsistence wages or less. There were riots and threats of revolution. The French Revolution had shown how a class system could be overthrown. Here Marx found his opportunity. With immense vigor and remarkable propagandistic skill he proclaimed the inevitable victory of the proletariat. Marx had never mixed with any proletarians. He was himself a bourgeois. He never showed any interest in proletarians as human beings—only as a class. As he himself said, he found in the proletariat the "material weapon of philosophy," of his philosophy, of his revenge on society, of his triumph. He was the wrathful divider. The "bourgeoisie" became the fixed objective of his hate, the source of all evil. He identified it with the society that had rejected him. It was anathema. He devoted his being to its destruction.

The presence of anomy in modern society is evidenced by the spread of violently divisive doctrines, doctrines of all-or-nothing, doctrines that loudly preach a reactionary or a revolutionary authoritarianism, doctrines that appeal to men not as human beings but as de-individualized masses in motion. The anomic and near-anomic persons of the second and third types are particularly prone to such doctrines. For they offer a congenial release from anomy, a drastic remedy for its bitterness and frustration, a refuge from its insecurity, a means of reconciling its destructive tendencies with its secret need for social reintegration.

All these doctrines are enemies of democracy. They reject its tolerance, its acceptance of difference, its respect for the individual, its faith in the healing processes of free opinion. The anomic man has lost the balance of social health, mostly through no fault of his own. In his alienation he seeks a quick and false prescription. The anomic who cannot be masters are often ready to be slaves. They cry out for the superman to save them, for some equivalent of a Providence, a God, the ineluctable authority who will end their alienation by saying, "I command you to follow," making his command ring with the magic of a lost obligation.

What then can democracy do to meet these two perils that threaten it in this age of violent change—group anarchy and individual anomy? We remarked in passing that we should not blame the anomic for their plight; they are suffering from a disease incident to our civilization. The remark may seem at best a truism—of what other social ailment might not the same be said? But it was said to call attention to the proper ways in which democracy can safeguard itself against these dangers. When we seek to heal a social ailment—or a physical one— we should always treat it as a disease and not as a sin. Unfortunately we often proceed on the latter assumption, as we have been doing, for example, in our "denazification" policies, with mostly unhappy consequences. To protect democracy against anomy or against group anarchy we must endeavor to get at and to remove their causes.

In the first place we should realise that all our efforts to protect democracy against these and other dangers are wholly futile unless we can protect it first against the catastrophe of war. For war has now become so immeasurably ruinous that the shaken and impoverished survivors would be driven to desperate measures that might be fatal to the very existence of democracy. Therefore while we still possess the inestimable spiritual heritage of democracy we must assure it against the very possibility of war, showing an alertness and a forethought that in the past two generations the democratic world most deplorably failed to show.

To achieve this end democracy must be strong in its quality as democracy, not only in its arms. The spiritual weakness of democracy is the strength of its enemies. In some respects we still make only a pretence at democracy. Ask the Mexican-Americans within our borders, whom we do not permit to sit at the same table with our noble Nordics.

Ask the Negroes, whom we segregate as pariahs, so that we may not be contaminated by the social presence of a lower caste. Ask the Jewish people, who cannot live in the same hotels, sometimes cannot even be treated in the same hospitals as their democracy-loving fellow-Americans. Ask the Eastern Europeans, who are still frequently treated as second-class citizens, especially if their names have a Slavic sound. Ask the Chinese among us, the Japanese, the Filipinos, the Hindus—and remember that by our treatment of these people we are betraying our democracy before the greater part of the human race; remember also that the Orient is now stirring to new political life and that its decision between democracy and dictatorship will profoundly affect our future and the future of all mankind. Ask these questions, remember these things, and you must see that our failure to be true to our democracy is in the last resort the main reason why democracy is in danger.

The diseases of group anarchy and of personal anomy are peculiarly incident to modern democracies. The unfree systems are authoritarian; by authority and by sheer compulsion they suppress such manifestations. Democracy places responsibility in the individual and in the group—it asks their free allegiance, their free cooperation. But it must on that account assure its citizens the conditions in which they can exercise their freedom. It must guard them from haunting economic insecurity or their civic freedom becomes a mockery. It must guard them against the rank prejudice that cuts them off from the equal partnership of democratic society. Otherwise democracy will breed the seeds of its own destruction.

Lastly, it must make its own meaning, its own philosophy, its own spirit, positive and vital. It cannot rest in the outworn liberalism that never rose above the negative of non-intervention. No vague negative faith can meet men's needs in this age where dogmatic authoritarian creeds deride the democratic ideal, and promise men, however falsely, a greater security and a greater reward. Democracy must become self-conscious of its own worth. Here we reach a theme that needs our most earnest attention.

&5&5&5&

90. The American Way of Life *

To SEE THE COLOR of your own eyes unaided is clearly impossible. To see one's own culture with true objectivity is equally unattainable without help. Any course in introductory sociology has as one of its purposes the development in the student of a more objective perspective regarding the culture in which he lives. This *Fortune* article was chosen not so much *in spite of* certain biases it contains as *because of* them. The same is true of the selection immediately following this one (91). These provide two opposing treatments of the diverse unity that is our American culture. This one is sympathetic; the next is critical, written from the point of view of a visiting Communist intellectual. Taken together each throws light on the other. They should raise questions, provoke observation, critical reflection, and educational experience generally, leading toward greater objectivity regarding "the color of your own eyes"— one's own culture.

WHEN A FRENCHMAN wants to explain his country he speaks simply of "*la belle France*." The Britisher says, "There'll always be an England." These and other nations of the earth explain a lot about themselves just by the use of their proper names. But the citizen of the U.S. has a different problem. There lives in him a kind of unspoken assumption that his nation is something more than a nation; that it is an experiment, perpetually evolving into something new; that it embodies an ideal. In referring to his country, therefore, he feels the need of including an abstraction or a general principle; and this leads him on a quest for words.

The best he has ever found is "Liberty"; but for reasons explained in "Individualism Comes of Age," the rise of the social problem has somewhat tarnished the sheen of this greatest of all American abstractions. In the last century there was something called "Manifest Destiny." From time to time someone always comes up with "the American Dream." But these phrases do violence to another favorite Americanism, common sense. As a result, when Americans of the mid-twentieth century want to refer in an inclusive way to all that vast complex of manners, customs, techniques, ideas, laws, and principles that they know as the U.S., they take refuge in a vague but tantalizing abstraction that they call "the American way of life."

Precise thinkers detest this phrase. It is used by every orator on

* Reprinted from the February, 1951, issue of *Fortune* by Special Permission of the Editors; Copyright 1951 Time, Inc.

every side of every issue; by the labor leader haranguing his local, the businessman squeezed into an elevator on his way up to a metropolitan luncheon club, the dentist flourishing his drill at a patient who is trying not to think. It is used beyond our shores by pundits and intellectuals —and there, indeed, lies the rub. For "the American way of life," besides being a vague phrase, is an ambiguous one. It seems to imply that those who advocate it wish to impose on the rest of the world all that which goes to make up a "way of life," all the customs and manners, the economic practices and the governmental forms—all the *particulars*— that make America what it is. But this is as far from the truth as anything could be. Americans never have advocated, and so long as they faithfully practice their "way of life" never will advocate, the imposition on other peoples of the American particulars.

The phrase gets the American into other difficulties, too. In a way, it sets him apart from the rest of the human race, as if he had taken up residence on another planet. This aspect of the matter worries him deeply. In the first place, he likes to be liked—indeed, he carries his craving for popularity and human "acceptance" to extremes that are sometimes pathetic. Besides, he really likes people. Then there is this ideal of his, which is a human ideal, not a national or a racial ideal. All these factors combine to make the American feel that he is very much a part of *this* planet. He is proud that his country is populated by so many races and national origins. He welcomes into his midst their various cultures and traditions. He cherishes a liking for many distant peoples—the Chinese, for instance, have always been favorites of his (and the fact that he is fighting them now is a tragic incongruity). Finally, he is taking very seriously his new role of leadership in the Western world, whose culture and spiritual traditions form the basis of his own, and whose civilization he is prepared to defend. The idea that he, of all people, wants to be set apart from the rest of humanity is a mockery of the way he really feels.

Thus this phrase, "the American way of life," however useful for certain purposes, has become productive of a great deal of misunderstanding and friction. But on the other hand, it would not be practical to abandon it, because it does mean something important—indeed, to the American, something indispensable. So the only way to proceed is to try to clear up the misunderstanding. And this in turn involves an understanding of what the American way of life is really like.

THE MATERIALISTIC SOCIETY

To the foreign visitor the most disturbing thing about the American way of life is its unabashed "materialism." The visitor is drenched with sights and sounds and smells emanating from a man-made environment to which almost all Americans appear to give almost all their energies. Pervading these sensory experiences there are the psychological ones— the insouciant way in which the radio combines "entertainment" with the most humiliating requirements of the human organism—the ubiquitous advertising, seeking to identify human happiness with bright teeth —the infantile movie heroes—the wasteful "abundance" protruding from every store. The visitor sees all this, and is impelled to somber speculations concerning the fate of humanity. What price "the American way of life"?

The somber speculations lead to two forms of criticism. The first, fanned by Mr. Vishinsky, runs to the effect that American capital exists for the purpose of exploiting the people, who have thereby been degraded. This attack, however, is an easy one to meet. It may be a halfway adequate picture of what capitalism in America used to be like, or of what it is still like in some places today. But it no more fits modern America than a description of the living habits of Caesar.

The U.S. Bureau of Labor Statistics maintains a Consumers' Price Index, which is intended to show changes in the current cost of living, and which is therefore composed of the index levels of all articles that enter into the cost of living in an important way. This index, which is compiled specifically for "moderate income families," has for years included radios, electric sewing machines, electric refrigerators, vacuum cleaners, automobiles, tires, gasoline, and insurance; medical, dental, surgical, and hospital care; drugs and beauty-shop services—all this, that is to say, over and above necessities like food, clothing, and shelter. But the BLS has felt for some time that this index was deficient; certain items, important enough materially to affect the cost of living, were not included. These, therefore, have been added. They include television sets, electric toasters, frozen foods, canned baby foods, home permanent-wave lotions, and group hospitalization contracts. As the New York *Herald Tribune* wryly remarked, "What, no caviar?"

Now to talk of the exploitation of human needs, in an economy where all these items have become so important to the standard of living that they must be figured into the cost of living, is to talk nonsense. The American capitalistic system still works injustices; but to think of it in terms of exploitation is to think in terms of a past century. It is perfectly evident from the above list that it is not the capitalists who are using the people, but the people who are using the capitalists. Capital has become, not the master of this society, but its servant. No better evidence could be adduced than the figures recently made public

by the Federal Reserve Board, which show that four out of ten American families possess at least $5,000 of assets over liabilities; and that
nearly one family in ten has net assets of $25,000 or more. It is not
just a capitalistic system. It is a capitalistic people.

But this raises the second form of criticism. If the trouble isn't
with the capitalists, then it must be with the people. Men and women
who insist on such a high standard of living, and are willing to expend
so much energy to get it, must be hopeless materialists. Is it not true
that the curse of this majestic continent is the drab uniformity of its
products and the discouraging conformity of its mores? The itinerant
lecturer is especially exposed to this dreary prospect. On his way from
town to town he sees the same ads for the same products; he hears the
same clichés; he is asked the same questions by people who look and act
and dress and entertain themselves, apparently, in exactly the same way
as the people in the town he thought he had left behind him—the name
of whose central thoroughfare, incidentally, was also Main Street. If
this is "freedom," thinks the itinerant lecturer, then what is all the
shouting and ballyhoo about? There are quicker ways to build an
anthill.

INFINITE DIVERSITY

Now the American admits that his society is materialistic; that standardization is an essential of the "way of life"; that conformity is a danger
he must watch and learn to counteract. Nevertheless, this criticism
from the itinerant lecturer baffles him on the whole, because it seems
to overlook more than it takes into account. For example, it overlooks
the great American love of diversity.

The American responds to diversity as to something good, absolutely.
The presence in his society of a bewildering number of races and national
origins, creeds and shibboleths, economic interests and explosive ideas,
is to him no problem at all. On the contrary, it is a great asset. In
his labyrinthine political system the same idea is carried out. The
forty-eight states, each with its separate constitution and different
set of laws, each requiring special examinations or licenses for its
lawyers, its doctors, its civil servants, even its automobile drivers, confront the foreigner as an irrationally complicated structure calculated
to produce nothing but chaos. But the American thinks it is good,
he can even prove that it is good. If there is only one of something,
he is suspicious of it—as for example his federal government. This is
only partly because he dreads the power of monopoly, whether political
or economic. It is also because he sees diversity as the expression of

freedom, the living proof that men and women are given the opportunity to be true to themselves.

There is a practical side to this also, as there is to everything American. The tendency of industrial enterprise is to wind up into big units; but industrial managers are increasingly discovering that another kind of efficiency, a more creative kind, can be achieved through decentralization—that is to say, through a diversity of operations.   Outsiders often boggle at the idea of competition.   But they should remember that competition in America is not the dog-eat-dog affair that social planners and Russian propaganda have made it out to be.   Competition has caused suffering in America; it still does hurt when your company is thrown out of business and your job is lost.   And yet the essence of American competition is far less desperate than that.   It involves primarily the releasing of energies for the development of new ideas, new modifications, new "slants," any one of which may end up by revolutionizing some segment of human affairs.   That is what diversity means to an American.   And that is why he welcomes the existence in his society of people, of beliefs, of ideas that are difficult if not impossible to reconcile.

Thus it will be found upon closer inspection that there is not just one American way of life.   There are American ways of life, almost without number.   For example, there are the great regional differentiations, where nature herself has conspired with American institutions to create ways of life as different from each other as those of two nations might be.   It is true that these American "sub-nations" are bound together by many common ties, including the important tie of language; yet their temperamental characteristics, their customs, their values and views, their personal objectives differ so greatly that a man who is happy and effective in one might be miserable and frustrated in another.

THE FAR WEST

Take the Far West.   This vast area, which begins, roughly speaking, just east of Colorado, has of course many important things in common with the rest of the U.S.   Yet the ways of those people are very different from the ways of the Easterner.   Nature herself has made sure of that, for the Far West is a region of majestic drama, of mountains and buttes and deserts, beside which the woods and streams of the east coast look puny.   The western people, generally speaking, are more outspoken than the Easterners, more cordial, more generous of their time and money; they speak slower, and they have a way of cutting through a lot of argument to reach a quick conclusion on which they are willing to stand or fall. The Easterner is endlessly fascinated by them; but he considers them naive, unsophisticated, lacking in perspective in the ways of the world. In fact, the West is to the East as the East is to Europe.

And yet, as anyone knows who has lived out there, these generalizations misrepresent the realities. The Far West itself includes many ways of life. Take, for example, the differences between the Pacific Northwest and California. In the Pacific Northwest the great rivers rise in snow-capped mountains and wind down through gorges to the sea. The cities are incredibly young—Seattle has not yet celebrated its centenary. It is trade-union country and the standard of living is high. But happiness is pursued in the Northwest with a certain calm simplicity that is rare in America. For all the youth of his region, the Northwesterner is something of a philosopher; he expects a lot out of life, but he doesn't aim to get very rich. He attends to his business all right, but he is more interested in his mountains and his waters; he would rather pack up with his wife and kids, with about $200 worth of camping gear in the back of his car, and push off for a ten-day tour of his magnificent state parks; or go cruising in a small boat, or salmon fishing in the foaming streams of the Columbia River watershed, or skiing on the mighty slopes of Mount Rainier.

In the eyes of the Northwesterner, the Californian, therefore, is a noisy fellow. The Californian goes about in bright informal clothing of many colors and lolls on bright beaches along the shores of the bright-blue Pacific and grows oranges that shine brightly from the dark-green foliage of the orange trees. That is to say, the southern Californian does; the northern Californian is altogether different. Northern California merges with the Pacific Northwest and has its roots firmly planted in San Francisco, the westernmost metropolis of Western civilization. San Francisco has become a place where a man can find anything he wants to find, which is perhaps the best definition of metropolitanism.

But Los Angeles, which is the headquarters of the southern Californian, is not like that. Los Angeles is big and boastful and overrun with Easterners and movie actors and cultists of infinite variety. It is also the mecca of the retired couple who took the life-insurance ads seriously and have come out here to enjoy "beauty" and "leisure" and watch the sun set westwardly over the Pacific. But the Northwesterner has the feeling, as he passes the innumerable little "bungalows" that sprawl out into what was only a few decades ago a near desert, that the beauty is wasted here, that it is not appreciated as in the Northwest, that it has not been absorbed. Somehow, like the movie industry that it houses, southern California seems to be removed one step from the real, to live in a world that nature never made—or, for that matter, man. That is the big difference between southern California and the Northwest.

THE MIDWEST

Then there is that other vast region of the U.S., lying between the Rocky Mountains and the Appalachians, where a river may be a thousand miles long, and where everything drains into the Mississippi. Here all lines are horizontal, life is intensely practical and "real," and the quarter sections and the fields and the towns duplicate themselves, league after league, in seemingly endless repetition. It is here in this great "valley" that the itinerant lecturer has his worst time and reaches his most pessimistic conclusions; for unless these people are studied community by community, they appear to vanish into sociological generalizations.

But actually when you come to know Kansas you find it very different from Minnesota, for example, with its high percentage of Swedes and Germans and a better-balanced economy than Kansas has ever had. Kansas, Nebraska, and the Dakotas are heavy agricultural exporters; their way of life is based upon the soil, and even their towns exist for the farmers, not the townspeople. This makes town life quite different from that of an eastern town, or even of a town in a manufacturing area of the Midwest (such as Chicago or St. Louis, for example), where the town exists, so to speak, for itself, and lives on its own exports. The Midwest farmer is fat with the world's riches—and safe from its depredations. But he is not in the least soft. On the contrary, he has time after time challenged the power of the East, which he regards with a congenital suspicion that is much more marked in the Midwest than in the Far West.

The Midwest merges into the South, and as it does the standard of living declines. The South is problem country. It grew up differently from the rest of the nation, with an economy based on big landholdings and slave labor. It still has with it the problem of the Negro; in many towns of Mississippi and Alabama the Negroes outnumber the whites, who cling to their political power by any means, fair or foul. The southern way of life differs radically from other American ways of life. The pace is slower. The extremes of poverty and riches are greater. The traditions are better preserved. The storied southern "aristocracy" is becoming something of a myth; but it has left behind it the tradition of southern cooking, which is supposed to be the best in the U.S. (though no vestige of it is to be found in the hotels and public eating places); of hospitality, which makes the New Yorker look like a boor; of flirtatious women; and of peaceful ways whose like is to be found nowhere else in the U.S.

And then there is Texas, the independent nation that became a state in 1845. Geographically Texas belongs to both the Midwest and the South, but in terms of its way of life it belongs to neither. Maybe California has outstripped Texas in population growth, but Texas has got richer faster than any comparable region of the U.S. ever has. Oil derricks, skyscrapers, flamboyant hotels, oil and gas pipelines, canals, piers, and great industrial shapes have sprung like mushrooms from a landscape that the Northwesterner would consider quite drab. It is the land of the big rich; the making of wealth dominates the way of life. And yet wealth is really only a symbol for the Texan; he likes to spend it just as wildly as he makes it; he loves the "feel" of struggle, the exhilaration of victory, of "getting ahead." Everything here is on a big scale, as if the gods had lifted the curtain for a drama on Valhalla. The young folks associate in droves—one of their barbecues will be attended by a hundred or more. As an Easterner once complained, he wished that Texans could be friendly on a neighborhood basis instead of on a state basis. The ordinary Texan thinks nothing of driving two or three hundred miles just to see a "local" football game.

The Texan way of life, indeed, represents an extension into the twentieth century of certain ideas that animated all Americans up to the first world war. Here is the land of opportunity, where anybody can rise to the "top," where tomorrow is unpredictable and yesterday unnecessary. Here the intrepid individual, the risk, the adventure, the fabulous reward, have somehow come to fruition in a world largely occupied with the less romantic problems of social "security" and social "science." It is possible for the modern American to feel somewhat nostalgic about Texas, however he may smile—or cringe—at its excesses.

THE INDUSTRIAL EAST

But in the East the way of life is crowded. In the winter the Easterner takes to the trains and planes if he wants to go anywhere; in the summer he chugs despondently along obsolete highways, breathing carbon monoxide from the car ahead, snarled in the traffic of his innumerable cities. He lives in an industrial jungle. His most awe-inspiring sights are not the works of nature but the works of man. He is caught in a maze of brick walls and steel shapes, communications lines and enormous switchboards, six-lane clover-leaf highways and railroad switchyards of such complexity that the eye cannot predict the path that a train will follow through them. The island of Manhattan consists of only twenty-two square miles of rocky land; but two million people live on it, tier above tier, with the subways and three trunkline railroads underneath them, and tunnels under the subways, and tunnels under the rivers, and eighteen bridges gripping Long Island and the mainland. And all around them are clustered miles on miles of houses, and highways extending outward to the "dormitory towns." The Westerner could not endure it.

Yet the East is exciting, too. It generates ideas—big, continental ideas that have had enormous influence in the development of America. The ideas radiate outward and merge with native ideas in the different regions, to bring forth new ventures and new shapes. Thus from the Manhattan apex there extends westward an enormous triangle, one side 900 miles to Chicago, the other 1,000 miles to St. Louis. This is the "industrial triangle," the jugular vein of Western civilization. If an enemy could knock it out, or any substantial part of it, the U.S. would be unable to fight. For it contains more than half of all the capital investment of American industry and employs more than half of the industrial workers. Yet even within the triangle the ways of life differ. The people of Pittsburgh, who live among the ruddy fires of the steel mills, are "Westerners" to the New Yorker, who works or lives several hundred feet above the earth, has two martinis for lunch, and charges the rest of the country exorbitant sums for the use of his fertile imagination. And the people of Chicago really belong to the Midwest.

Nor is the way of life in New York City the same as the way of life in Boston, the hub of another industrial complex, composed chiefly of textiles, machine tools, high skills, and industrial specialties. Perhaps New England contains more incongruities than any region. The "elite" —for here, at any rate, there are such—still cling to a great cultural tradition that reached its climax with Ralph Waldo Emerson and shed a mellow light into the twentieth century through the pen of Henry Adams. Boston still has in the Athenaeum the nation's most notable private library, whose shelves are accessible only to "proprietors"; and it also has in the Widener at Harvard the biggest university library in the world. Yet the casual visitor to New England, including the American tourist who goes there for his summer vacation, has increasing difficulty in finding vestiges of the cultural tradition; for a large part of New England is encased like one of its famous clams in a shell of modern industrialization, in all of its ugliest aspects, including a plethora of billboards and hot-dog stands, together with an ex-Governor recently released from jail.

Up in Vermont and New Hampshire you will find a stubborn folk

who have never yielded to the most "advanced" versions of the industrialized life—on a number of instances they have even refused to
accept federal aid. And it is commonly said that this ruggedness, for
which New England was once famed, is on the wane. Yet this is not
really the case, as anyone who tries to live there will soon discover.
Within its industrialized shell the New England clam still flourishes—
sober, hard-working, inventive, prudent, much more reserved than the
Westerner, and downright unsympathetic to the flashy airs of the
California goldfish.

Which one of these ways of life does the American mean by "the
American way of life"? The answer is none of them. New England
is no more "American" than the Northwest, nor Denver more so than
Atlanta. This diversity itself is the way of life—nations within nations.

Nor can the way of life be defined by the life of any one particular
community—the late Sinclair Lewis notwithstanding. For it is at the
community level that America really begins to get diverse, because
American life is not regional but local. The life of one town is influenced by a newspaper editor who wrote a history of his county and
is a specialist on Indian warfare; the life of another, by a doctor interested in psychology. Here is a town addicted to schottisches, another
whose social life centers around a Norwegian Harmony Club, another
that features Czech gymnastic festivals. Here is a town with a Chinese
restaurant, over there a town with German *verein*; over there a town,
redolent of frijoles, that speaks mostly Spanish. All cultures are
cherished—interwoven—modified. Here there are no memories and
the town is flat and everyone eats out of cans. But there the memories
of the old country are strong; the housewives treasure old Finnish recipes
handed down from grandmothers who never saw America; or creole
dishes, or Irish remedies for the gout.

And all this is accented by the extremists, the individualists, the eccentrics: the man with a thousand canaries; the man who keeps five
buffalo in Connecticut; the electrician with odd working hours who
spends his mornings in the town library in blue jeans reading Shakespeare; the nudists, the vegetarians, the Indian fortunetellers, the
perpetual-motion inventors; the Amish who won't wear buttons; the old
lady who writes poetry in the manner of Sara Teasdale. And then
there are the hobbyists—the carpenters and gardeners—the man in the
Great Plains who builds model ships—the amateur painters—the man
who plays the flute in the morning, and the expert on Japanese prints,
and the collector of chess sets. The way of life is none of these ways
of life. And as for "standardization," it is lost in a forest of human
foibles.

And yet, also, the way of life is *all* of these. For there is an extraordinary unity in this diversity, a coherence that resists all eccentricities, all power concentrations even. And this unity, which is not merely national in the ordinary sense of the word, pertains to quite another level of existence, another level of values from that which manifests itself with such diversity. It has to do with ideals, with a complex of principles and beliefs, to which all American life has reference. The truth, which has thus far been difficult for the rest of the world to grasp, is that Americans live on two planes at once—the practical and the ideal. The conflicts created by this ambivalent existence, which worry other people so much that they often feel constrained to reject one plane or the other, bother the American scarcely at all. Take for example one of his leading national characteristics.

THE STRENUOUS LIFE

"I wish to preach," said Theodore Roosevelt at the turn of the century, "not the doctrine of ignoble ease, but the doctrine of the strenuous life." And when he said that he said something profoundly American. The strenuosity of American life simply appalls the European. Why go at things so hard? Why take these interminable gambles, follow these restive hunches, constantly uproot that which has been successfully established? Why not be content with that which is good enough?

Of course, lots of things have happened since T. R. made that remark. In terms of physical work—of *toil*—American life is far less strenuous. The forty-hour week is almost universal; Saturdays are for the most part holidays; the lunch break is getting longer. The ECA productivity teams that visited this country observed that Americans did not seem to work any harder than Europeans. However, they got more done, and that is perhaps the key to the matter. Increasingly, Americans are emphasizing *mind*. They have discovered that through the use of the mind, especially in the development of technology, life can be made strenuous in a different and pleasanter way. To the visitor, whose technology may not be so advanced, or whose powers of invention may be less well developed, the distinction may seem somewhat academic; American life remains too strenuous to emulate. But to the American the distinction is a real one. He has discovered ways to keep up the pace without the physical punishment that old T. R. very likely had in mind. What makes his modern life strenuous, therefore, is simply that he insists *that the pace be kept up.*

The outsider, to be sure, may wonder to what purpose. For Americans not only work hard, they play hard; simple gaiety, as the Italians

know it, for example, seems not to be in their make-up.   All the energy
that the American saves from toil by the smart application of technology
is freely expended on his most conspicuous passion, the great American
outdoors.   In every section of the country, even the industrial East,
Americans pour out an incredible amount of energy whacking golf balls,
playing tennis, baseball, hiking, camping, sailing, fishing, hunting—
everything but just "walking."   Most foreigners fail to understand—let
alone enjoy—all this dashing around.   The strenuous life is bad enough
at the factory: why double it during leisure time?   This reaction is a
matter of temperament, and Americans must be prepared to accept the
criticism that they are just too damn energetic.

However, there is a principle involved which foreigners ought not to
overlook.   In the view of the American, life is not just a matter of the
conservation of energy.   On the contrary, in his experience, energy
creates energy; a good hard game of tennis, or a hike in the hills, will
actually improve your mental faculties the next morning.   Thus the
pace of technological life is maintained, not through the cultivation
of repose, but by building up a kind of counterforce through physical
exertions—supported to be sure, by abundant vitamins.   Here is *mens
sana in corpore sano*, but raised to a higher power—to the great advantage, incidentally, of the $7-billion sports and vacation industries.

THE DEMOCRATIC VIRTUES

The strenuous life, then, is an American characteristic.   But it is
interesting, not merely as a characteristic but because it illustrates so
aptly the ambivalent nature of the American.   The strenuous life derives, on the one hand, from the practical necessities of a virginal
continent on which there was much work to do.   But it derives, on
the other, from an *ideal*: the ideal of the perfectibility of man, of human
improvement.   Where this ideal came from is a matter for scholars to
debate; it has in any case been accepted in one form or another by
Americans from the very beginning.   It has given rise to many American
faults, such as overoptimism and a superficial concept of "progress."
But above all, it has kept Americans working, risking, venturing, striving; it has sparked the strenuous life.

This same ambivalence manifests itself in many other American
characteristics.   For instance, take those characteristics having to do
with the great ideal of Equality, the fundamental "tendency" of American life, as shown in "The American System."   The confidence that
he is the equal of any man gives the American a certain ease of manner,
even a brashness, which can be extremely irritating to those who have

not been bred to "equality." On the other hand, it helps the American to be a friendly fellow, a trait that almost every foreigner notices upon arriving on our shores—despite the seemingly deliberate inhospitality of the immigration service and the customs officials. The American does not recognize many social barriers. This is especially true of the West, where the man who is painting your house will probably call you by your first name before you have decided how to address him. One of the little shockers for American labor leaders who went to England some while ago to help with productivity was the sight of English workers tipping their hats to the boss. American workers consider themselves the equals of the boss in everything except the externals, so they don't tip their hats. In fact—and this is key to an understanding of Americans—the boss wouldn't like it if they did; it would make him feel uncomfortable: for he too has the ideal of equality.

Equality thus has its positive side: it does not merely equate privileges, it asserts obligations. There is the other fellow, and he has just the same rights as you. This doesn't mean that Americans go around thinking of the "other fellow" all the time; in fact, they may be planning some competitive scheme to put him out of business. But they are oriented from their childhood to the idea of the rights of other people. The civil liberties are not merely constraining laws. They, too, are ideals, imperfectly realized, but entering into the life of every American in such a way as to encourage qualities or virtues, the best word for which is "democratic."

The American has an ideal of generosity, also. He doesn't live up to this one any better than—or even as well as—he lives up to the related ideals of the civil liberties; but generosity is bred into him, neverthless, as a great democratic virtue. Sometimes the American's generosity is no more than an openhanded way of doing things, which at its worst leads to sheer waste. At its best, however, no other national characteristic exhibits more clearly the way the American can combine the ideal and the practical. For, aside from its ethical status, generosity appeals to the American as an eminently practical trait to encourage. Wouldn't it be a much better world if everybody were generous? Then nobody, including you yourself, would have to worry so much. That is the practical side of the matter. But, he would add, you should never carry it so far as to look like a "sucker."

Still another ideal related to the general ideal of equality is that of kindness. This too the American regards as a democratic virtue. The American is capable of being brutish and some people think of him as ruthless. He himself likes to parade as a "tough guy." But his armor is usually paper-thin, and there are apt to be vulnerable spots—for example, children. Americans love children to the point of being silly about them, as almost everyone who has known the G.I.'s has observed. In fact, they universally spoil their own.

Whether Americans have more or less of these democratic virtues, whether they are friendlier than other people, or more generous, or kinder, is not at all the point. Such generalizations can never be proved and only lead to resentful arguments. The point is that Americans, practical and pragmatic by temperament, have nevertheless taken very seriously certain ideals having to do in a general way with the ideal of democratic equality.

And perhaps, next to their Proposition itself, this is the most valuable contribution that Americans have to offer the world. It is wrong, at the present stage of our evolution, to expect some great "cultural" development in America, equivalent to the culture of Europe that extends back for twenty or twenty-five creative centuries. The intellectuals who castigate Americans on this score miss the point. In the first place, they overlook the fact that there is a great activity in the creative arts throughout the country, especially at the community level; and second, they too easily forget that American culture is of necessity a *popular* culture, and hence inherently different from that which we inherit from Europe. Yet even after these modifications have been made, the fact remains that high culture is not what Americans have primarily to give. The big American contribution to Western civilization has to do, rather, with certain qualities of the heart deriving from democratic ideals. These ideals, in the form of recognized democratic virtues, are constantly at work in American society, and have a great deal to do with what is meant by "the American way of life." In fact, if this were not so, if the ideals were to vanish, or if the American were to abandon the hope that people would someday learn to practice them, then the American way of life, as he construes it today, would also disappear. It would become something quite different. It survives as it is only on the presumption that most of the people will try to realize the democratic virtues most of the time.

THE INDIVIDUAL HUMAN BEING

Yet these ideals that the American cherishes are not just hung up in the air. They have a reference point that walks and talks and is "real"— the individual human being. Everything in America, be it national, regional, subregional, or local, comes back somehow to the individual. And the American can live his life on two planes at once in such a strenuous way precisely because he recognizes that the human individual may have—must have—ideals. That is the inner secret of the American way of life. It is a way of life to permit and encourage the development of the human individual, by his own free will, toward his own ideals.

This fact is nowhere better illustrated than in the American attitude toward "standardization." To see "standardization" as the American sees it, one must bring it back to the individual. The intelligent American will agree that standardization represents a certain danger. But on the other hand he will point out that in his society—in the American way of life—the individual does have opportunity, does develop and grow. And in the light of this great, essential truth he can put standardization in a certain perspective, which Europeans have not yet learned. For what is being standardized in America? Not the individual human spirit, which the American way of life intends to hold inviolately free. But the things that the human spirit uses—these are being standardized: the houses and vehicles, the tools and machines, to some extent the clothing and even the food. But these are, after all, the shell. They are not the human being himself, and so long as American institutions are careful to distinguish between human beings and things, why not standardize the things? Nature herself, after all, has in a certain sense standardized the human body. We don't expect to find people with five arms or with eyes in the backs of their heads. But we don't say for that reason that the human spirit cannot be free. The body is just a vehicle.

Indeed, to say that standardization must be the death of freedom is to express a far more materialistic attitude than the American attitude. It is to define man in terms of things—in terms of his body. To the American, his machines and gadgets are *extensions* of man. They are extensions of his faculties and powers—wings to enable him to fly, wheels to enable him to run, antennae to enable him to hear and see at great distances. Americans, indeed, have taken on the task of extending man in this way with a certain positive attitude, as if it were their special cosmic assignment. They really believe and really feel that they are doing something important, not to enchain the human soul, but to increase its power and scope, and thus to help emancipate it from the merely physical, from the earth. That is the positive side of American "materialism."

As for "conformity," the danger here may be greater, because one is not dealing with things but with the standardization of people themselves. Yet here too the same principle can be applied to a certain extent. Much American conformity may be due to a kind of social compulsion that is highly undesirable; but much of it also is simply a matter

of convenience. The reason why garden clubs are more or less alike
is not that anyone compels them to be alike, but just that it is easier to
organize them that way. Anyone who might try to enforce conformity
upon the American would find out soon enough that where his convictions are concerned he is capable of non-conformity to the point of
bloodshed. Here, too, the American feels, a little perspective is in
order. Conformity has not yet engulfed him. And he doubts that it
ever really will.

THE CHRISTIAN IMPULSE

This central focus of the American way of life—the human individual
—was born politically in the Age of Reason and implemented by the
announcement of the American Proposition. But spiritually it
goes back to the founding of Christianity, whence the American derives his basic concept of the individual. Christianity has had many
versions in America, many strange and eccentric variants. Yet it has
always been inherent in the American way of life, binding it together in
subtle ways, even for Americans who do not actually profess it. The
idea of the perfectibility of man, for example, which gives Americans
so much drive, is a Christian ideal. And the democratic virtues, which
have to do with the relation of one man to another, are essentially
Christian virtues. The American's Christianity is, to be sure, somewhat
one-sided; his idea of "perfectibility," for example, is theologically naive;
his optimism leads him to overlook some of the profounder, more tragic
depths of the human soul; he is apt to translate spiritual truths too
facilely into practical terms. Nevertheless, his tremendous faith in the
human spirit saves him, most of the time, from the consequences of his
own errors—and may yet save the free world.

For the forces released by this faith are dynamic, in the sense that
there is no point at which their action may be calculated to cease. It
is impossible to talk about the American way of life without talking
about change. Twenty-one years ago, when FORTUNE was founded, the
present issue could not have been written: for the face of America
twenty-one years ago, and during the stormy period of the thirties, was
the face of a society that could not solve, did not know how to solve,
internal problems that threatened to destroy it. To take the matter
of industrial relations alone, violence, espionage, and coercion were commonplace. The right to organize and bargain, which in an industrial
society is the minimum economic right, was recognized in theory but
was little practiced. Bloodshed and hate stalked the streets of Gadsden,
Toledo, Detroit, Aliquippa. Looking back, indeed, these memories

seem almost incredible: not because we have solved all of our internal problems, but because industrial violence, at least, is now recognized as a social crime.   There is growing up in our society, as pointed out in "Individualism Comes of Age," a sense of social partnership that only the craziest optimist could have predicted from the social data of the thirties.

In his speeches before the United Nations, Mr. Vishinsky has sought to portray Americans in terms of their own past—blacker than their past ever was, to be sure, but nevertheless reminiscent of problems they used to have.   That is deliberate misrepresentation and it makes the American mad.   But what makes him even madder is that this constitutes an attempt to *fix him in time*, to arrest him in the image, however caricatured, of what he used to be.   And, on top of his anger, the American is then chagrined to find that other people, people whom he considers to be his friends and allies, half believe what Mr. Vishinsky says; are indeed so blind to the native dynamism within the American way of life, released by the energies of free individuals, that they fail to take into account the constant change, the constant correction of errors, the constant reappraisal, the constant evolution of American aims.   Americans wish that other people could see their country as it really is: not as an achievement, but as a *process*—a process of becoming.

What the purpose of the "becoming" is, and where it leads to, are not yet questions for the American way of life.   Perhaps the day will come when this kind of question will occupy Americans, but thus far their mission has been the mission of action—the mission of the will. Metaphysical speculation is hardly yet a national specialty.   In the American's eyes the individual is, in the end, an enigma.   Therefore, America is an enigma.

Anyone inclined to doubt that America is an enigma should study the Great Seal, reproduced on every dollar bill: an Egyptian pyramid rising from a mysterious plain; a mystic eye blazing light from the pyramid's tip; and an occult inscription, "*Annuit Coeptis . . . Novus ordo seclorum.*"   Practically no American can tell you what that seal means. But that is not the point.   The point is that the American way of life embodies a mystery, which no one has yet solved, but which is common to all men: the mystery of the human spirit.

91. Ilya Ehrenburg's America *

TRANSLATIONS OF SIX ARTICLES PUBLISHED IN IZVESTIA

OUR JOURNALISTS give us as much information as they can gather
about life in Russia. Here is some information about us given to
the Russian people by Ilya Ehrenburg, recently characterized as
"the foremost Soviet journalist." It is enlightening to see ourselves
and our institutions through the eyes of someone from a different
social milieu, especially from a social system so much at variance
with ours that its proponents show positive hostility to much that
we value. We may wince at the ridicule and resent the distortions
that at times amount to misrepresentation more monstrous than
out-and-out lies. But though the picture as a whole is out of focus,
to the extent that some of these unpleasant statements have a basis
in fact, we cannot do otherwise than acknowledge the criticisms as
valid.

CONTEMPORARY COLUMBUSES have little time and a Constellation takes
less than twenty-four hours to cross the Atlantic. It is a beautiful and
comfortable machine: the air is conditioned and there is no pain in the
ears even at great heights. We were given a sheet of instructions which
declared that in the event of a forced landing in the ocean it was best to
take off one's shoes and jump into a small rubber boat. This advice did
not seem very tempting to me. I was confused by the behavior of the
hour hand of my watch. It showed seven o'clock in the morning; yet
we had arrived at midnight and had been flying all night. We were
still drinking morning tea in European fashion, and the Americans were
going to bed.

When I climbed out of the plane excited reporters at once began
cross-questioning me as to how I liked America. What could I talk
about then? The perspicacity of the customs officials? Or the blindness of the reporters? I know certain American journalists have come
to Russia with a prepared book on Russia (sometimes in their heads,
sometimes in their portfolios). I didn't want to be like them; I looked
around attentively and tried to understand what I saw.

---

* Ilya Ehrenburg, *Harper's Magazine*, 193 (December, 1946), 562-576. Reprinted
by permission of the publisher.

The author (b. 1891) is a Russian novelist, poet, short story writer; war correspondent, U.S.S.R.; broadcasts from Moscow Radio. Translations of his works
made in several languages. His books include *Out of Chaos*, *Moscow Does Not
Believe in Tears*, *The Love of Jeanne Ney*, *Russia at War*.

In my time I have traveled a good deal and have been all over Europe. I sometimes thought I had lost the ability to be amazed. Upon arriving in America I realized that there was much of which I had no conception. Everything here is different—the cities, the trees, and the customs. The summer here is very hot, but the heat is not European; the air is damp, as in a hothouse. The olives here are larger than plums and devoid of taste. People gesticulate more often with their legs than with their arms, and in the theaters spectators who wish to show approval whistle deafeningly.

Modernity cannot be understood without understanding America. Hundreds of odes and pamphlets have been dedicated to her; she can be exalted or ridiculed with ease. But this is not merely a peculiar country, but also a diverse one, difficult to understand. It is hard to set forth vivid, often contradictory, impressions in brief notes. Behind the complexity of technology there is sometimes concealed spiritual simplicity, and behind this simplicity—unexpected complexity.

I rate American literature very highly. It is not easy now to find writers in Western Europe equal to Hemingway, Faulkner, Steinbeck, or Caldwell. I might venture to add two or three more names. Right behind them is a vacuum—stories in illustrated weeklies which are so cheap and stupid that even the most unexacting readers in Europe would recoil from them. There is no intermediate literature here, just as there are no four- or five-story houses. The skyscrapers of New York are justified by geography: this is a huge city built on small islands. But in any provincial city one may see several skyscrapers surrounded by thousands of single-story houses.

At the railway station in Atlanta I was amazed by the automatic checking booths which have replaced the cloakroom. You insert a coin, receive a key, and can lock up your luggage yourself. I was about to say to my American companion, "You know how to make human existence easier," but before I could speak I noticed a dark, noisome room marked "For non-Whites" in which Negroes and mulattoes were dozing. In the state of Mississippi I saw the home of a plantation owner. It had a refrigerator, a washing machine, a marvelous radio, and wonderful ventilators. The planter calmly explained to me that black-skinned people aren't people at all. Neither the radio nor the ventilators had any reflection on the mental development of this slave-owner.

I stayed in several university towns. In America a great deal is done to elevate knowledge to its proper height. I saw superb libraries and laboratories: I saw scientists surrounded with attention. But in Tennessee professors told me they were not allowed the right to expound the theory of evolution in the schools: the law forbids any departure from the biblical myth of Adam and Eve.

In all American cities there are "lions' " clubs: I was fortunate enough to attend a luncheon at such a club in one town. Respectable business men assembled there, each one wearing a tag indicating the place and nature of his business; luncheons are closely associated with business. Before those present at the luncheon began to eat their compotes and mayonnaise and ham with raisins, the chairman banged the table with a wooden hammer and exclaimed: "Greetings, lions!" The middle-aged business men at once rose and chorused: "Woo-woo-woo-woo." I quailed, but they explained that they were imitating the lion's roar.

Naturally, the sound-imitations of dealers in suspenders are an innocent affair. There are worse ideas. A parade of the Ku Klux Klan recently took place in Georgia. The members of this supposedly secret society donned fools' hoods and took an oath of loyalty to the local fascist führer, whom they call the "Grand Dragon." They then swore to hang several Negroes and kill several freethinkers.

Everyone knows that in America money is surrounded with respect. Apart from many hundreds of registered churches and sects there is still another cult—the dollar. An art critic, after introducing a young artist to me, reeled off his surname and then, enunciating precisely, said, "Three thousand dollars." A master of ceremonies at a cabaret announced that eminent visitors were present: an actress, a senator, and a business man "who has tripled his capital turnover since the war." I attended many dinner meetings with a program much like this one: first, everybody quickly chews the chicken, then orators give lengthy speeches; then a female singer renders a sentimental ballad; and finally a pastor takes a collection for charity. He recites the names of the liberal donors: "Mr. Smith gave five hundred dollars." Everyone applauds and Mr. Smith rises and bows.

It is not well known that, along with brisk business men, there are also many naïve day-dreamers and noble idealists in America. I met a prominent inventor who renounced a fortune, fearing that the machine he invented would deprive hundreds of thousands of workers of their bread. I spoke to provincial Utopians who go without food and sleep, devoting their money and energy to the fantastic project of creating a "world government." In one town I found a circle of eccentrics who were convinced that they could render the atomic bomb harmless with the aid of Esperanto. Everywhere there are societies to protect the rights of Negroes. Every year innocent Negroes are condemned and put to death in the electric chair, and every year the best people in America protest against racial barbarism. Yes, the cult of the dollar does exist in America, but in America there are also people who deny themselves a pair of shoes and tickets to the cinema in order to send gifts to Yugoslav children.

There is much that is childish in Americans. They are not artificial; they are frank, curious, and noisy. The oldest part of America is called New England. Everything in America is new; everything is young. In New Orleans, however, houses built in the seventeenth and eighteenth centuries have been preserved in the French Quarter. Such houses are legion in Europe and are ignored by even the most painstaking tourists. But the "Old Quarter" of New Orleans is like Pompeii—a real center of pilgrimage. There is either an antique shop or a stylized tavern in almost every house. I was in New Orleans on a very sultry day (the tropics are not far off), and a fire was burning in the grate of one house —to re-create the atmosphere of a bygone epoch. Perspiring Americans were sitting by the fire drinking iced water; they wanted to spend several minutes in an old house. One must remember the age of the country to understand Americans.

People here like to wander about. If they are sitting in a room, they jump up from time to time and change seats; they move readily from city to city and from state to state. They regard a person who lives in the place where he was born as a rarity.

There is nothing more the reverse of the British character and customs than the character and customs of the average American. The Englishman is polite and phlegmatic; he loves to live out his life in the home of his grandfather; he orders his suit of first-quality material, expecting to wear it, if not until he dies, at least until the next elections. The American likes only new clothes. Hardly has he furnished his apartment than he is looking for another. He never has a suit made to order; why should he? In any shop he can find a cheap, well-made suit; can wear it a little and then throw it out. He will buy a shirt that is not worth washing. He respects old stones, but loves flashy new ties— and noise.

The history of the United States is indeed a new history. I might say, incidentally, that history studied by school children appears to vary in different states: in the North the Southerners are called "defenders of slavery," and in the South the Northerners are called "oppressors." Vexed issues here frequently hide the feeling of history. For the average American nearly a whole epoch passes between the morning and evening papers; he doesn't always remember in the evening exactly what disturbed him in the morning. One lady told me: "Don't read this novel. It's not a new one; it came out two years ago."

•   •   •   •   •   •   •

II

Anti-Soviet ideologists like to depict our country as a sort of barracks in which everyone is deprived of individuality. The Soviet reader will be amused by the surprise of some American editors who, on seeing us three visitors, said in amazement: "Why, they don't look much like one another."

As a matter of fact, I don't know of any country which has achieved such perfection in standardization as the United States. I was in dozens of American cities which were impossible to distinguish from each other. Every city has its Main Street—the principal street—with fashion shops, a cinema, and lighted signs advertising cigarettes or Coca-Cola. Not a single American can distinguish Main Street in one town from Main Street in one of a hundred others from a photograph. Naturally, New York has its own distinctive character, yet Americans usually complain that "New York is not America." For the inhabitant of Birmingham or St. Louis, gigantic New York, with its many different races, is like a headquarters or a den of freethinkers. The visitor is shaken by the external appearance of New York. The architect Le Corbusier called this city "a catastrophic fairyland." It seems to me that it can also be called "a fairy-like catastrophe." It has grown exclusively upward and has become a tall forest of reinforced concrete. At night it resembles mountains with lighted huts. It is multi-colored, noisy, and fatiguing. It contains dozens of separate towns—Negro, Jewish, Italian, Puerto Rican, German, and others. In Chinatown barbers promise on their placards to remove bruises from the face without trace. In Negro Harlem there are "shirt hospitals" and private pawnshops where torn trousers may be pawned. On 57th Street dealers sell masterpieces of European art. The wives of millionaires wander down Fifth Avenue in beaver coats. New York is the center of political thought and art. Officially it is not even the capital of a state but only an insignificant town. It is, however, the real capital of America. Two or three other towns—San Francisco, New Orleans and Boston—have preserved their individual aspects. But the remaining towns are without personality; they are simply aggregations of a given number of Americans.

Trousers, percolators, and armchairs are standardized, too. I do not say this reproachfully, for Americans have succeeded in raising the material level of life, thanks to mass production. I think we can learn something from the Americans: how to turn out shoes or saucepans quickly and well. However, almost all luxury articles in America are imported and a salesman who wishes to explain why this or that is expensive says, "But this is *imported*."

There is a certain depression in such uniformity: the same houses, the same furniture, the same crockery; men in identical suits, women in identical dresses. But still I do not agree with the European aesthetes who have ridiculed the standardization in America. Perhaps all the suits are alike; on the other hand, they are accessible to all.

Much more deplorable is a certain spiritual standardization. Americans are fond of speaking about their liberty; but their views, tastes, emotions, and consequent behavior are regulated from outside. The cinema, for instance, lays down the standard for beauty, and the papers supply all the details of the "ideally shaped" woman. This is the standard of desire. All American women are guided by these references in their efforts to resemble some film star, while men fall in love according to the same references without noticing it. There are no books with average circulation. Even the most remarkable book will not be circulated in more than several thousand copies unless it has been pronounced worth reading by some "book club," in which case it will be published in hundreds of thousands of copies. Since the average American does not like to choose, he entrusts the right to choose to his "club." The press and cinema de-personalize the ideas of people who stroll along thousands of Main Streets in the evening. This forms the key to the sense of depression which is linked with leisure in America.

Americans know very well how to earn money, but they have not yet learned to spend it. I do not mean that they are mean; they spend money swiftly and energetically—but without originality. They work with much greater talent than they amuse themselves. I would say that the gayest times in America are when townspeople meet nature; on the seashore, for instance, youth is full of *joie-de-vivre*. But in the cinema one is struck by their drowsiness and torpor, the rare laughter in response to the most humorous, or apparently humorous, situations.

There are many drunks, despite the fact that the sale of strong drink is restricted in one way or another in the majority of states. There are "dry" states, those in which whiskey is rationed, those in which liquor sales cannot be made on Sunday, and those in which one may drink sitting but not standing.

Automobiles in America are wonderful and numerous, and the average American loves a car. He used to change his car once every two or three years. Now he can buy a car but will not be able to receive it for six months—an unpleasant reminder that a terrible war has been raging somewhere in the world. I understand the love of Americans for cars.

But I do not understand why some of them turn their car into a home. There are restaurants which one is not allowed to enter; dinner is brought out on a tray and people eat in their cars. There are cinemas outside towns where people can draw up their cars in the yard in front of the screen and watch the films without getting out. Finally, it is sufficient to take a walk through Central Park, New York, in the evening to see yet another purpose of the automobile: it replaces the nuptial bed for lovers. Such habits make life somewhat mournful, not because people wear fashionable jackets, but because underneath these fashionable jackets there are at times fashionable feelings.

The average American in the average American city will tell you with certainty that he is the freest man in the world. Why does he pay dearly for electricity? His answer is ready: electricity belongs to private firms and the state has no right to interfere in the affairs of private firms—this is liberty. In America there are private bridges, private roads, and private aqueducts. In order to cross the bridge linking the state of Mississippi with Louisiana, one has to pay the owner of the bridge a dollar and a half. However, the government and the state do interfere in the private lives of citizens, and Americans regard this as quite compatible with their conception of personal freedom. The police may break into a room in any New York hotel and, if they find a couple, can check as to whether they have a marriage certificate. In order to be married as quickly as possible, one has to get from the state of Tennessee to the state of Alabama. Near the boundary line in Alabama there are alluring placards—"Get Married Here Quickly and Cheaply"—posted by private people who have acquired the right to perform the marriage ceremony. In order to get a divorce without unpleasant procedure, the inhabitants of New State state go to the state of Nevada, where hotel owners have become quite wealthy. In order to obtain a quiet glass of whiskey, an inhabitant of Mississippi must go to Louisiana. Just across the border of this state I saw several drinking establishments called "Last Chance."

In a relatively short time the Americans have created an astonishing technology. I saw how swiftly they build skyscrapers, how well and with what precision they produce automobiles in Detroit, and how many inventions they possess which ease the daily life of man. How can one not praise American roads, with their cheap and comfortable roadhouses for motorists who decide to spend a night on the road? Some Americans, glancing at the factories, the excellent bridges of New York, the automatic restaurants, and the electric razors, are prepared to believe that the whole of human culture is concentrated in America. One journalist in Jackson said to me: "Rome is a dirty and ugly city; there is nothing to look at in it—not a single skyscraper or a good drug store. After Rome, Jackson seemed to me more like a capital." How is one to explain to such a man that the ancient basilicas and palaces of the Renaissance are worth the skyscrapers of Jackson, or that, besides drug stores where cigars, fountain pens, chewing gum, and even sausages may be bought, there also exist the mosaics of Byzantium and the frescoes of Raphael?

The Americans are inadequately acquainted with the rest of the world. They do not know the history and geography of the Old World. One group of school children was not able to name to me a single city in the Soviet Union. Their political level is just as low. People know the intimate side of the lives of different senators, but in many states the word "Socialist" (let alone "Communist") is considered offensive. American papers frequently write that the existence of two parties is a guarantee of genuine democracy. One might note that no one is capable of explaining where the ideological demarcation line runs between the two parties, and in what way the Northern Republicans differ from the Southern Democrats.

Some Europeans have ridiculed America for her cult of technology. Now the same Europeans look to their ridiculed cousins with servility in the hope of obtaining from them an old car or an out-dated suit. There is nothing to laugh at here and nothing to flatter. American development has proceeded along a different path from the ways of old Europe. France started almost from the Gothic cathedral and the troubadours. America started with automobiles, drug store feeding houses, and gold fever. She swiftly reached a high level of material culture, but her spiritual culture is only awakening. Knowing the intelligence, liveliness, and energy of the Americans, we have the right to say that the spiritual culture of this great people will be great and independent.

Certain changes have taken place in the political consciousness of the average American; he is gradually moving away from the abyss. Roosevelt was surrounded by people who were honest thinkers, capable of realizing the trend of history. Even if these people have now been removed (or have removed themselves), there is still a trace of the late President's activity. I observed a beginning of independent thought, genuine solidarity, and a consciousness of their national mission among many workers. The era in which they were led only by demagogues and adventurers is coming to an end. We see the contributions made to the world by American scientists. The American writers are not renegades or salon aesthetes; they are people connected with the nation, even though the reading masses don't read them. In contrast to French

writers, American writers seem to me organic, like huge trees with
tenacious roots. The American cinema has already created genuine,
universal humor; apart from the genius Chaplin, I will name the
Brothers Marx. The cinema has also created the multiplicity of Disney,
real poetry capable of stirring a man devoid of all lyricism. Finally,
there is beauty—uneasy, but indisputable—in the architecture of New
York.

The American intelligentsia has been born. It is still weak and lacks
self-confidence; it hides from the illuminated advertisements, from the
deafening juke-boxes in the bars, from ecclesiastical sermons with references to business firms, and advertisements with quotations from the
Bible. It hides itself in a melancholy which I will call Chekhovian,
sometimes in cynicism and sometimes in Utopianism. But among the
intelligentsia more and more bold people are appearing. They understand that salvation does not lie in flight or repulsion or solitude. The
spiritual world of the average American must be raised to the level of
the technology which surrounds him from the maternity home to the
crematorium.

III

* * * * * *

It would seem that in this country of diverse races united by patriotism, national equality would prevail. However, America, which never
knew feudalism, has established a racial hierarchy. The aristocracy are
the English, Scotch, and Irish. After them come the Scandinavians
and Germans, then the French and Slavs; much lower are the Italians,
even lower still the Jews and Chinese; lower still the Puerto Ricans, and
finally, at the bottom of the scale, the Negroes.

In the war against Hitlerism America played a prominent part; yet
racialism here has a legal standing. When I entered America I had to
fill out a questionnaire which contained the question: "Race—White or
Colored?" If a person has a "colored" great-grandfather he is designated as "colored" and is subject to various restrictions. We were the
guests of the government, and I was often amused by the thought of
the reaction the representatives of the State Department might have had
if Pushkin had come to America. I met a lawyer in Nashville who
spent a long time trying to persuade me that there are "inferior and
superior races." He reiterated the theories of Rosenberg and other
ideologists of the Third Reich. Then he showed me the portrait of
his brother who was killed on the Rhine; he was proud of his brother,
who had perished in the struggle against racialists.

Anti-Semitism is an ordinary phenomenon to most Americans; it seems quite natural to them that some institutions accept only Aryans and that certain hotels do not admit Jews. On the West Coast the Chinese are the pariahs. There are organizations in which Italians are not accepted as members. The fate of the Negroes is especially tragic. There are twelve million of them in the United States, and it may be said that one out of every ten Americans is deprived of all human rights.

Natives of New York like to emphasize the liberalism of the North— "Our grandfathers fought against slavery." In any Southern town, on the other hand, you may see a monument to the soldiers of the Southern Army. This is a monument to the vanquished, because in the war which shook America the Southerners were defeated. However, it seemed to me more than once that these were monuments, not to the vanquished, but to the victors; since the South not only preserved the principles of slavery but was able, in some degree, to inject them into the North. Certainly equal rights among the races exist *theoretically* in New York. A Negro may not be ejected from a restaurant because he is a Negro, but not a single well-ordered American restaurant will admit a Negro. If it occurs to him to persist, he is told that the empty tables are reserved. A Negro cannot rent a room anywhere except in a Negro "ghetto." He may work in the most different sort of quarters, but he is obliged to live in Harlem, a Negro city within a city—dirty and impoverished, unhappy but still gay. New Yorkers amuse themselves in the cabarets in Harlem. The Negroes are the best dancers and musicians in America; they are gifted with a high sense of rhythm and are not as inherently mechanical as other Americans. In the center of New York there are theaters where Negro troupes perform excellently and are willingly applauded by the whites. But if a Negro wants to have a snack in a restaurant near the theater in which he is playing, he is calmly evicted.

Real estate speculators have a favorite trick; they buy a house in a good residential district and settle a Negro in it. The quarter then becomes taboo immediately, and all the whites depart. The speculator then buys the neighboring houses for a song, moves out the single Negro, and the section again becomes respectable—and the houses rise in price.

Still, in order to understand the place of the Negro in America, it is essential to see the South. When we were asked which part of America we wanted to see, my fellow-travelers chose California and Chicago. I wanted to see the Southern states. Remembering stories I had read —the novels of Steinbeck and Faulkner—I wanted to find out if reality resembled literature. Thus, after the skyscrapers of New York I saw

Uncle Tom's Cabin, and I can say that this cabin has changed little.

In all the Southern states there is a "segregation of the races" law. Negroes are not forbidden to use railroads, but they must travel in special cars (always over-crowded). In streetcars, seats are set aside for Negroes in the rear. A car frequently leaves almost empty while Negroes stand and wait for the next one, as the seats for them are occupied. Negroes may not attend meetings of whites, they dare not enter a church where white people are praying, and of course they must not even dream of entering theaters or cinemas for whites.

The Constitution of the United States guarantees that all citizens, male and female, have the right to take part in elections. However, the Negroes in the Southern states do not possess the right to vote. In the state of Alabama there are three million inhabitants, of whom 1,100,000 are Negroes. Among the voters of the state are 496,000 whites and 4,000 Negroes. In Birmingham, Alabama, there are 130,000 Negroes who have reached the age of twenty-one, but the total number of Negro voters is only 1,400. How do the Southern states get around the federal Constitution? There are several ways: one, the poll tax; another, examinations. The qualified voter must know and "be able to interpret" the Constitution. Clearly the examiners can cut out many Negroes. Finally, if the Negroes pay their poll tax, pass the examination, and go to the voting places, the guardians of slavery frighten away the unwanted voters with sturdy clubs. Obviously they do indeed know how to "interpret" the Constitution in the Southern states! In the state of Mississippi, Negroes form half of the population; half the inhabitants of the state are deprived of the right to vote. All this is done cynically and is well-known to all Americans both in the North and the South.

When I was in Mississippi I remembered how certain American journalists had been indignant when the Yugoslav National Front government had deprived about 200,000 people who had aided the Germans of the right to vote. These same American journalists consider it quite natural, however, that millions of American Negroes (among them soldiers who took part in the war for the freedom of America) are not allowed to vote. I would ask a question of my American readers: which is more fair—to take away the right to vote from people with black consciences or with black skins?

The Northerners know that Negroes in the South are deprived of political rights, but they cannot imagine the fearful life of Southern Negroes. When Sam Grafton, one of New York's brilliant journalists, saw the hovel in which two or three Negro families made their home, he lost his self-control. "Is this really possible?" he gasped. Uncle Sam had met Uncle Tom.

The delta of the Mississippi is made up of many cotton plantations. The land is owned by the whites and rented to the blacks. The tenants must deliver half their cotton to the landowners; they are also bound to sell the other half to the same owners. The sum which the Negroes receive may be spent only in the shops of the same landlords. This may be legally close to tenantry, but in reality it is slavery. The land-owner, who is also the purchaser of the cotton and dealer in shoes, kerosene, and salt, goes around his plantation shouting at the Negroes, issuing orders, and behaving like a king and a god.

I saw a family which earned $300 in a year and another which earned $200. The owner of the plantation on which they lived said to me that last year had been "unsuccessful," and that he had earned only $25,000. I saw one house in which twenty-three people lived, sleeping side by side on the floor. How far this is from the renowned American comfort, the refrigerators, elevators, and chewing gum! The Mississippi, a broad and bright yellow river, sees grief—the black grief of the blacks.

I was often told in New York that all American children under sixteen must go to school. An illusion. In the South I saw youths who cannot read, who have not seen schools, and since early youth have known only one thing—hard labor. In super-hygienic America, people are living in stalls. When births are difficult women cannot have medi-cal assistance; a visit from the doctor costs $60, and the yearly income is only $200. But the slaveowners smile: "You don't know the Negroes. They are living in paradise. Of course they don't need anything more."

IV

•   •   •   •   •   •

Racialism has penetrated into the thick of American labor. Many union leaders tell the white workers that the trouble does not lie in the greed of white owners, but in the black skin of famished "competitors." Only in recent years have progressive unions been formed which include both white and black workers. Other chauvinistic—or rather, racialist —organizations do not want to admit Negroes to skilled jobs, and there have been strikes and pogroms because of this. In the South Negro workers live separately and in greater poverty. Solitude hangs over them; they are the rejected ones. The chairman of one progressive trade union—a bold and cultured Negro—told me, with the sagacity which comes from long consciousness of grief, that never once had a white comrade visited him or asked him to his home.

The slaveowners of the South assure you that it is impossible to grant rights to the Negroes, because they are "devoid of culture." Personally, I met many educated Negro scholars in the South—writers, doctors, teachers, lawyers. These Negro members of the intelligentsia form unexpectedly bright spots against the background of the South, where there are many whites who, although supplied with varying diplomas, are by nature uncivilized. But it is worth noting that the slaveowners who talk hypocritically about the cultural backwardness of the Negroes make every effort to prevent "colored" people from obtaining knowledge. This does not mean, however, that the owners wish to add to the knowledge of whites. The "Democrats" of the South prefer the knout to the primer. In the state of Mississippi a teacher receives six hundred dollars a year—a truly miserable salary. But the situation of black people is even worse. They are not only deprived of tolerable living conditions but also of human dignity. When an inspector (who is, of course, white) visits a Negro school, he calls the teacher by his first name as he would a boy, even if the teacher is an old, gray-haired Negro—"Sam," or "Bill." The teacher must address the white inspector with respect, even if he is a callow youth—"Mr. Smith," or "Mr. Davis."

In the state of Alabama all the money set aside for education has somehow been released to the whites. To clear their consciences a group of school administrators summoned a Negro professor and began to explain to him that the budget was limited, the money had all been spent, and so on. The Negro answered: "You are right. The whites need education even more."

I was in a Negro university where there are about seven hundred students of both sexes. They will become doctors, teachers, and lawyers; but they will only be able to help Negroes and teach Negro children. "Colored" professors and students have no access to the public library. Professor Brady, a chemist of high reputation, told me that he did not have the right to work in a state university laboratory.

In Fisk University there is a Russian girl student whose father is from Odessa and whose mother is a Negro. She speaks Russian and does not have negroid features. But her passport declares her "colored," and she comes under the law on the "segregation of the races." In New Orleans I knew an architect—a ginger-haired man with freckles—who was one of the best educated persons in the city. I wanted him to go with me to a café, but he declined. Afterward friends explained to me that this light-skinned man was a Negro and consequently did not have the right to go into a café.

There are also unwritten laws in the South. A white man may rape a Negro woman but is not punishable for this. On the other hand, if a Negro cohabits with a white woman, he is accused of rape and condemned to the electric chair. Justice in the South is close to "lynch law." Not long ago six whites in Albeville raped a Negro girl. The court found "no case of crime." In Pessemor a Negro traveling in a streetcar stepped over the permitted "border" several inches. The driver wounded him. What happened then? The police arrested not the white driver but the Negro and killed him as a precaution. In the city of Columbia thirty Negroes were brought up for trial. Why? The whites, in organizing a pogrom, which is called a "racial disorder" in the South, killed two Negroes and injured twelve. It is not the murderers who have to answer, but the fathers, brothers, and sons of those murdered. A lawyer in Jackson who was trying to save the life of an innocent Negro told me that no one really doubted the innocence of the Negro, but that white people had given evidence against him; the court could not believe black men's testimony contrary to the evidence of whites, even if the latter were false witnesses. There are no Negro jurors in the South, and the courts do not acquit Negroes. On the other hand, if by any chance the people who have lynched a Negro land on the prisoner's bench, their acquittal is guaranteed.

At the head of the slaveowners stands Senator Bilbo, a red-haired demagogue who attracts hearers with stormy appeals to "bridle the blacks." Bilbo has proposed removing all American Negroes to Liberia. The slaveowners would look well without slaves! However, everyone knows that this was only said by the Senator in jest. He is a Senator of the state of Mississippi, where Negroes are no fewer than whites, and where the whites often shiver when they think of the mass of destitute, embittered people who may someday become fed up with singing hallelujah in expectation of the regular hanging.

Not a few Negroes have been in Europe; many fought for America against racialist Germany. They saw that in Paris or Rome no one looked at them as though they were plagued, and they returned home with even greater bitterness. The South is on the eve of a decisive event: either the owners will yield, or the Negroes—yesterday's men of the front line—will open the struggle for equality.

I am convinced that in the end racialism will be overthrown in America; but it must be understood that this disease has penetrated deeply into the mind of the average American. I did not meet a single

white in the South who was not contaminated with racialism. One of
the most fervent opponents of the slaveowners admitted to me in a
frank and intimate conversation: "Yes, I defend the Negroes, but just
the same, for me these are not people. I was playing yesterday with
our Negro maid's child and found myself thinking that I was playing,
not with a child, but with a nice puppy." Racialism has infected even
the persecuted; I met Negro anti-Semites and Jews convinced of the
superiority of whites over blacks.

Americans love to drink mixtures of different liquors. Among the
multitude of cocktails there is one which resembles the rainbow—yellow,
emerald, and red liquors which do not mix in the glass but lie in multi-
colored layers. They are mixed only in the mouth of the drinker. I
could compare this drink with the racial layers of America. How
strange it is that the idea of racial "purity" finds fervent supporters in
a country which is strong through the mixture of different races! Cocktails may be liked or disliked, but it is difficult to imagine a bartender
preparing a mixture for a customer who will insist on purity, organic
nature, and maturity in his drink. I have seen racialists in America
defending the idea of the racial superiority of Americans over other
peoples. For what did the American soldiers die in Normandy and on
the Rhine?

The famous journalist, Walter Lippmann, said that in my article on
America I was criticizing what was easy to criticize—racial intolerance;
Americans themselves know about this vice and are happy to be able to
criticize their own vices. Lippmann says that when we Soviet people
are capable of appreciating the merits of America and criticizing our own
faults, then he, Lippmann, will agree to accept us as "real people."
Yes, I know that the best people are ashamed of their attitude toward
the Negro. But in my opinion doctors are good, not because they treat,
but because they heal. It is no easier for Negroes because Lippmann
recognizes Senator Bilbo as an evil and writes articles in New York,
while Bilbo and others like him are oppressing Negroes in Mississippi.
As for ourselves, we have never denied the merits of America, nor have
ever hidden from ourselves or others our own faults. In America, for
instance, there are wonderful telephones; from New York it is easier to
speak by telephone to San Francisco than from Moscow to Tula. In
America there are good passenger planes which fly from city to city every
hour day and night. Perhaps Lippmann will say that I am limiting
myself to praising technology. No, I have already written that I like
American literature. I think we can learn much from American writers,
American architects, and even (despite the shattering cheapness of the
average production) from American cinema producers. We know our

own faults—we criticize our own bureaucracy, our rudeness, and at times our technical backwardness—but we do not criticize just to criticize, but to improve. We have no slaveowners, and it is not a question of whether Lippmann recognizes us as a people, but of whether we recognize racialists and slaveowners as people. I believe in the great future of America, and I am convinced that the American nation will soon be healed of its most bitter and shameful ailment.

V

• • • • • •

The press, radio, and cinema are in the hands of various reliable and unreliable firms. The editor of a large provincial newspaper said to me with a sigh: "Our independent paper depends entirely on advertise‧ ments. If we were to lose our advertising, we would not last a week." The wireless stations are owned by private firms and also depend upon advertising for their existence.

I was reminded again of the book I wrote many years ago about the cinema "dream factory." The American's desire to forget and divert himself by day-dreaming in the evening has given birth to a vast in‧ dustry; in Hollywood mass dreams are turned out just as skillfully and quickly as tinned meat in Chicago. However, the dream factory is more dangerous than the hash factory; film producers organize the spiritual world of the average American, inculcating him with portable morals and guiding his thoughts and feelings. The producers may compete with each other over directors and actresses, but they are all subordinate to their own internal censorship, the Hays Office, which ruthlessly cuts out everything that may resemble free thinking.

Hollywood is a dangerous den for Quakers and slaveowners. Indeed, art claims its own and scores of talented people work in Hollywood; but they are surrounded by a wall. Chaplin himself found out what going against the wall of money means. The average American is convinced that he is inwardly independent, and he is terrified by "propa‧ ganda." In actual fact he repeats what he has read in the paper, heard on the radio, and seen on the screen. I often had occasion to meet representatives of the press; I inspected the offices of large papers, and I learned how public opinion is formed in them.

How do the huge trusts organize public opinion? Not by articles, because few people read them and the readers are incredulous. The majority of American newspapers wrote against Roosevelt, but the readers preferred Roosevelt to Dewey. The President's activity was

apparent for all to see, and every American was a competent judge—
all the more so as Roosevelt and his supporters spoke at thousands of
meetings refuting the distortions of the newspapers. When I said to
my American friends that the press poisoned readers they usually
answered: "You over-emphasize the importance of newspapers. We do
not submit to propaganda; we know how to think independently."

However, in order to think independently, one must know of what
one is thinking. The average American knew Roosevelt's tax policy,
but can he know exactly what is going on in Iran, Germany, or Bulgaria? He thinks "independently" about the distortions which are
brought to him by the first page of the newspaper. He asks himself
whether the Russians are doing right or wrong in moving their tanks
on Teheran and whether or not the Bulgarians are right in striving to
retain the Greek Rhodopes; he does not know the data of the problem
which he is attempting to solve. He does not suspect that Soviet tanks
were never moved to Teheran; nor that there is not a single Greek in
the Bulgarian Rhodopes.

The papers controlled by the trusts or by individual magnates of the
printed word occupy themselves in misinforming people under an appearance of information. They are crafty and pretend to be objective:
for every ten anti-Soviet articles showing that our country allegedly
wishes to swallow the whole world right up to Guatemala and the
Honduras, a small article is invariably published praising the works of
a Soviet botanist or the skill of Soviet sportswomen. Many papers
publishing monstrous fables about our country requested me to write
something for them. The misled reader repeats: "Whatever you may
say, our press is the most objective in the world."

•   •   •   •   •   •

Reporters in general are energetic people but not overeducated. I
noted down several questions which one reporter put to me and here-
with quote them in order: "Are you wearing an American or a Russian
suit? Do the Russian people know that America helped them in the
war? How do people in Moscow find out the latest trends on the stock
market? Have you been married long? Why do you have only one
political party in Russia and not two? Do you get up late? Why do
you want to take possession of Albania?"

I will stipulate, however, that misconceptions occur not only among
reporters. In New Orleans a lady professor of sociology who sat next
to me at an official dinner asked me: "Are you a Red or a White
Russian?"

I am convinced that the American reader is usually more intelligent than the newspaper which he reads, but involuntarily he yields to a lot of nonsense. The day before yesterday he was frightened to death by the atom bomb tests. Yesterday, disillusioned, he was saying that "Gilda" (the nickname for the bomb) had made a laughing-stock of herself. Today he is struck with emotion by the death of the goats and pigs which perished in the tests, since the paper told him in detail that a memorial would be erected in honor of the dead animals. He does not even think that perhaps his children are threatened with death from some sort of "Gilda."

VI

I talked to a farmer in Tennessee—a peaceful man entirely absorbed in his cows, which he was milking with the aid of electric milkers. He told me that the Americans would evidently have to fight the Russians. The farmer now has infinitely more free time, and it is not surprising that he reads the local newspaper from cover to cover. But this paper, the *Knoxville Journal*, each week reports fresh machinations on the part of Soviet Russia. In the words of this paper, the Russians are now "swallowing" Trieste, then "invading" Iran, and then "conquering" Korea. The poor farmer knows a great deal more about the milk yield of cows than he does about geography. Reading the newspaper, he is amazed—what wicked people these "Reds" are! I don't doubt that he read the appeal of a certain "brotherhood" in the *Knoxville Journal* last May. The appeal stated that Moscow was not Moscow at all, but Mesech, mentioned in Psalm 120; that Magog of whom the prophet Ezekiel speaks is nothing other than Soviet Russia; and that "it is essential to destroy the country of the Communist Magog." All this resembles delirium, but it is printed in the paper. I recalled the old Spanish song:

> "Some sing of what they know,
> Others know of what they sing."

The farmers sing what they know, and the "brotherhood," the publisher of the Knoxville paper, various trusts (Hearst and others), the Southern Democrats, and the Northern Republicans—these gentlemen know well just exactly what they are singing.

Americans frequently talk of the "iron curtain" which is said to fence off the Soviet Union from the world. I have to admit that the iron curtain really does exist and prevents the average American from seeing what is going on in our country. This curtain is fabricated in America, in the editorial offices of the newspapers, in the radio broadcasting stations, and in the offices of film producers and film distributors.

Many American newspapers daily deceive their readers with "private correspondence." How can the average American test the truth of information about Hungary or Bulgaria? He does not even know just exactly where these countries are. They are far away. I was on the spot in America, and a great deal of nonsense was written about me. They wrote, for example, that I was not traveling alone in America. A "representative of the GPU" accompanied me. As a matter of fact, I was accompanied by a representative of the State Department (the name for the Ministry of Foreign Affairs here) whom the newspapers transformed into a "secret Soviet agent." Speaking of my visit to America the magazine *Time* exclaims: "He enjoyed a freedom about which American correspondents in Moscow frequently but vainly dream." This is printed on page 70 of Volume 23 of the magazine; in the same issue on page 30 I read that the American newspaperman, John Fischer, had been traveling around alone through the Ukraine for three months. It is hard to say just exactly what freedom Mr. John Fischer dreamt of when he was in the Soviet Union. Perhaps he was regretting that nobody accompanied him. I, personally, am greatly indebted to the State Department for the attention shown me, the more so as Mr. Nelson, who accompanied me, is a man of great culture and tact. But how am I to understand the tirades of *Time* magazine? If a representative of the Soviet Ministry of Foreign Affairs accompanies an American newspaperman, the American journalists scream that they are being deprived of freedom. If a representative of the State Department accompanies a Soviet journalist, *Time* magazine writes that American newspapermen in Moscow do not dare even to dream of such liberty. I do not understand such logic, or I fear that I understand it too well.

When American friends asked me what should be done to improve our mutual relations, I replied: "Set up a single standard." The reader must not think that I am proposing that the Americans introduce the metric system; I have no wish to interfere in their affairs. If they like having water freeze at 32 degrees Fahrenheit, that is their business. But a single standard should be set up in evaluating behavior. Too frequently I saw two standards here: one for the virtuous Anglo-Saxons and another for the dishonorable "Reds." If the Americans consider Iceland their base, it is called a "guarantee of security for the entire world"; but if the Soviet Union does not wish to have states which neighbor upon it becomes bases for an attack upon Russia, this is "Red imperialism." When the Americans are engaged in manufacturing atom bombs, this is an innocent game like football; but when Red Army men play football in the suburbs of Moscow, this is "preparation for conquering the world."

The American people are kind-hearted and industrious; they do not want war. At present the country is rich, particularly as compared with a Europe ravaged by war. In Detroit the automobile plants are working at top speed and still cannot satisfy all the would-be customers. People "sign up" for refrigerators, vacuum cleaners, and radios. America did not feel the iron boot of war; inconveniences which are trifling to a European seem to be great deprivations here. You will hear amusing complaints here: "There is little butter . . . poultry or mutton instead of beefsteak . . . the line for nylon stockings . . . it is hard to get white shirts, only colored ones." Here and there strikes are breaking out; the workers are seeking an increase in wages to match the rising cost of living. Demobilized servicemen have returned. The country reminds one of a housewarming or of the beginning of the school year. The people are thinking with pleasure about tomorrow, which will certainly be better than today. They have long since forgotten yesterday, and they are little concerned with the day after tomorrow. If occasionally someone stops to think that suddenly a depression and unemployment may be upon him, he at once drives away these gloomy thoughts. These are people who do not want to look into the future. Many of them have more than once lived through the transitions from wealth to poverty and from poverty to wealth. They have adopted a peculiar fatalism and take things in their stride. They do not want a depression and they do not want war. Newspaper articles about a "Third World War" make them justly indignant. But such articles, talks, and sermons repeated too often are designed to accustom the average American to the idea that a Third World War is inevitable.

* * * * * *

I left many sincere friends in America—not only personal friends, but friends of the Soviet people, friends of thought and conscience. Americans are fond of directness. I stated frankly what I liked and did not like in America. Only the sick and impotent should have their feelings spared. Americans have a super-abundance of youth and health. Besides, they now have many European flatterers, eager for loans, trousers, and canned goods. And the Americans themselves love to judge—to judge and condemn. I know that they will receive my words as the words of a friend. This great people has great strength and great will. Its history must be worthy of it.

꧁ ꧂ ꧁ ꧂

92. Encounters Between Civilizations *

A CERTAIN PROFESSOR of sociology sometimes takes his classes on an airplane ride over Chicago, so they may see the general ecological pattern of the city. From such a vantage point one gets an enlarged perspective. Details become smaller and often obscured, but relationships between details are revealed. In this article, historian Arnold Toynbee takes us up above the confining horizon of our own time and culture and reveals to us a great panorama of societal interaction. We see civilizations growing, blending, and dying. We see our own culture as it is related to this larger pattern. Some aspects of our civilization take on greater significance while others shrink in proportion. Ethnocentric attitudes and interpretations seem less reasonable. Cultural variability, diffusion, and borrowing become more meaningful concepts.

WHAT WILL BE SINGLED OUT as the salient event of our time by future historians, centuries hence, looking back on the first half of the twentieth century and trying to see its activities and experiences in that just proportion which the time-perspective sometimes reveals? Not, I fancy, any of those sensational or tragic or catastrophic political and economic events which occupy the headlines of our newspapers and the foregrounds of our minds; not wars, revolutions, massacres, deportations, famines, gluts, slumps, or booms, but something of which we are only half-conscious, and out of which it would be difficult to make a headline. The things that make good headlines attract our attention because they are on the surface of the stream of life, and they distract our attention from the slower, impalpable, imponderable movements that work below the surface and penetrate to the depths. But of course it is really these deeper, slower movements that, in the end, make history, and it is they that stand out huge in retrospect, when the sensational passing events have dwindled, in perspective, to their true proportions.

Mental perspective, like optical perspective, comes into focus only when the observer has put a certain distance between himself and his

* Arnold J. Toynbee, Harper's Magazine, 194 (April, 1947), 289-294. Reprinted by permission of the author.

The author (b. 1889) is a British historian and economist. Director of Studies, Royal Institute of International Affairs; Research Professor of International History, University of London; Editor, British Commonwealth Relations. Director of Research Department, Foreign Office, 1943-46. Delivered lecture series in America (with V. M. Boulter), A Journey to China, Study of History (6 vols.), and Civilizaton several occasions. Among his writings are A Survey of International Affairs tion on Trial.

object. When, for example, you are traveling by air from Salt Lake City to Denver, the nearest view of the Rockies is not the best one. While you are actually over the mountains, you see nothing but a maze of peaks, ridges, gullies, and crags. It is not until you have left the mountains behind you and are looking back at them as you fly over the plains that they rise up before you in their magnificent order, range behind range. It is only then that you have a vision of the Rockies themselves.

With this vision in my mind, I believe that future historians will be able to see our age in better proportion than we can. What are they likely to say about it?

Future historians will say, I think, that the great event of the twentieth century was the impact of the Western Civilization upon all the other living societies of the world of that day. They will say of this impact that it was so powerful and so pervasive that it turned the lives of all its victims upside down and inside out—affecting the behavior, outlook, feelings, and beliefs of individual men, women, and children in an intimate way, touching chords in human souls that are not touched by mere external material forces—however ponderous and terrifying. This will be said, I feel sure, by historians looking back on our times even from as short a time hence as A.D. 2047.

What will the historians of A.D. 3047 say? If we had been living a century ago, I should have had to apologize for the fantastic conceit of pretending to speculate about anything that might be said or done at so immensely remote a date. Eleven hundred years was a very long time for people who believed that the world had been created in 4004 B.C. But I need not apologize today; for, since our great-grandfathers' time, there has been so great a revolution in our time scale that, if I were to try to plot out to scale, on one of these pages, a chart of the history of this planet since its birth, I should not be able to make so short a period as eleven hundred years visible to the naked eye.

The historians of A.D. 3047, then, may have something far more interesting than those of A.D. 2047 to say, because they, by their time, may know much more of the story of which we, today, are perhaps in a rather early chapter. The historians of A.D. 3047 will, I believe, be chiefly interested in the tremendous countereffects which, by that time, the victims will have produced in the life of the aggressor. By A.D. 3047, our Western Civilization, as we and our Western predecessors have known it, say, for the last twelve or thirteen hundred years, since its emergence out of the Dark Ages, may have been transformed, almost out of all recognition, by a counterradiation of influences from the foreign worlds which we, in our day, are in the act of engulfing in ours—influences from Orthodox Christendom, from Islam, from Hinduism, from the Far East.

By A.D. 4047 the distinction—which looms large today—between the Western Civilization, as an aggressor, and the other civilizations, as its victims, will probably seem unimportant. When radiation has been followed by counterradiation of influences, what will stand out will be a single great experience, common to the whole of mankind: the experience of having one's parochial social heritage battered to bits by collision with the parochial heritages of other civilizations, and then finding a new life—a new common life—springing up out of the wreckage. The historians of A.D. 4047 will say that the impact of the Western Civilization on its contemporaries, in the second half of the second millennium of the Christian Era, was the epoch-making event of that age because it was the first step toward the unification of mankind into one single society. By their time, the unity of mankind will perhaps have come to seem one of the fundamental conditions of human life—just part of the order of nature—and it may need quite an effort of imagination on their part to recall the parochial outlook of the pioneers of civilization during the first six thousand years or so of its existence. Those Athenians, whose capital city was no more than a day's walk from the farthest frontiers of their country, and those American contemporaries—or virtual contemporaries—of theirs, whose country you could fly across from sea to sea in sixteen hours—how could they behave (as we know they did behave) as if their own little country were the universe?

And the historians of A.D. 5047? The historians of A.D. 5047 will say, I fancy, that the importance of this social unification of mankind was not to be found in the field of technics and economics, and not in the field of war and politics, but in the field of religion.

II

Why do I venture on these prophecies about how the history of our own time will appear to people looking back at it several thousand years hence? Because we have about six thousand years of past history to judge by, since the first emergence of human societies of the species we call "civilizations."

Six thousand years is an almost infinitesimally short time compared to the age of the human race, of mammals, of life on earth, of the planetary system round our sun, of the sun itself, and of the star-cluster of which our sun is a not particularly conspicuous member. Still, for our present purpose, these last six thousand years—brief though they are—do provide us with other examples of the phenomenon we are studying—examples of encounters between different civilizations. In relation to some of these cases, we ourselves, in our day, are already enjoying the advantage —which the historians living in A.D. 3047 or 4047 are going to have in looking back at us—of knowing the whole story. It is with some of these past encounters in mind that I have been speculating on how our own encounter with our own contemporaries is likely to turn out.

Take the history of one of our predecessors, the Græco-Roman civilization, and consider how this looks to us in the fairly distant perspective in which we are now able to see it:

As a result of the conquests of Alexander the Great and of the Romans, the Græco-Roman civilization radiated over most of the old world—into India, into the British Isles, and even as far as China and Scandinavia. The only civilizations of that day which remained untouched by its influence were those of Mexico and Peru, so that its expansion was not incomparable to our own in extent and vigor. When we look back on the history of the Græco-Roman World during the last four centuries B.C., it is this great movement of expansion and penetration that stands out now. The wars, revolutions, and economic crises that ruffled the surface of Græco-Roman history during those centuries, and occupied so much of the attention of the men and women who were struggling to live through them, do not mean much to us now compared with that great tide of Greek cultural influence invading Asia Minor, Syria, Egypt, Babylonia, Persia, India, China.

But why does the Græco-Roman impact on these other civilizations matter to us now? Because of the counterattack of these other civilizations on the Græco-Roman World.

This counterattack was partly delivered in the same style as the original Græco-Roman attack: that is, by force of arms. But we are not much interested today in the forlorn hope of Jewish armed resistence to Greek and Roman imperialism in Palestine; or in the successful counterattack of the Parthians and their Persian successors under the Sassanian Dynasty east of the Euphrates; or in the sensational victories of the early Muslim Arabs, who in the seventh century of the Christian era liberated the Middle East from Græco-Roman rule in as short a number of years as it had taken Alexander the Great to conquer it a thousand years earlier.

But there was another counterattack, a non-violent one, a spiritual one, which attacked and conquered, not fortresses and provinces, but hearts and minds. This attack was delivered by the missionaries of new religions which had arisen in the worlds which the Græco-Roman civilization had attacked by force and submerged. The prince of these missionaries was Saint Paul, who, starting from Antioch, made the audacious march on Macedonia, Greece, and Rome which King Antiochus the Great had once attempted unsuccessfully. These religions were different in kind from the native religion of the Græco-Roman World. The gods of Græco-Roman paganism had been rooted in the soil of particular communities; they had been parochial and political: Athene Polias, Fortuna Praenestina, Dea Roma. The gods of the new religions that were making this non-violent counterattack on Greek and Roman hearts and minds had risen above their original local origins. They had become universal gods, with a message of salvation for all mankind, Jew and Gentile, Scythian and Greek. Or, to put this great historical event in religious terms, one might say that the One True God had taken this opportunity of the opening of men's minds through the collision and collapse of their old local traditions; He had taken advantage of this excruciating experience in order to illuminate these momentarily open minds with a fuller and truer vision of His nature and purpose than they had been capable of receiving before.

Take the two words "Jesus Christ," which are so very important for us, and which, we may venture to prophesy, will still be important for mankind two or three thousand years hence. These very words are witnesses to the encounter between a Græco-Roman civilization and a Syrian civilization out of which Christianity came to birth. "Jesus" is the third person singular of a Semitic verb; "Christ" is the passive participle of a Greek verb. The double name testifies that Christianity was born into this world from a marriage between those two cultures.

Consider the four higher religions, with a world-wide mission, which exist in the world today: Christianity, Islam, Hinduism, and the Mahayana form of Buddhism which prevails in the Far East. All four are, historically, products of the encounter between the Græco-Roman civilization and its contemporaries. Christianity and Islam arose as alternative responses of the Syrian World to Græco-Roman penetration: Christianity a non-violent response, Islam a violent one. Mahayanian Buddhism and Hinduism are the gentle and the violent responses of the Hindu World to the same Græco-Roman challenge.

Looking back on Græco-Roman history today, about thirteen hundred years after the date when the Græco-Roman civilization became extinct, we can see that, in this perspective, the most important thing in the history of the Græco-Roman World is its meeting with other civilizations; and these encounters are important, not for their immediate political and economic consequences, but for their long-term religious consequences. This Græco-Roman illustration, of which we know the whole story, also gives us some idea of the time-span of encounters between civilizations. The Græco-Roman World's impact upon other contemporary civilizations, which corresponds to the modern Western World's impact on its own contemporaries since the turn of the fifteenth and sixteenth centuries, started with the conquests of Alexander the Great in the fourth century B.C.; and the Middle Eastern World was still translating the classical works of Greek philosophy and science some five or six centuries after the liberation of the Middle East from Græco-Roman rule by the early Muslim Arabs in the seventh century of the Christian era. From the fourth century B.C. to the thirteenth century of the Christian era, it took the best part of sixteen hundred years for the encounter between the Græco-Roman civilization and its contemporaries to work itself out.

Now measure against that span of sixteen hundred years the duration, to date, of the encounter between our modern Western Civilization and its contemporaries. One may say that this encounter began with the Ottoman attack on the homelands of the Western Civilization and with the great Western voyages of discovery at the turn of the fifteenth and sixteenth centuries of our era. That makes only four-and-a-half centuries to the present.

Let us assume, if you like, that people's hearts and minds move rather faster nowadays (though I know of no evidence that the unconscious part of the human psyche ever greatly varies its pace)—even so, it looks as if we were still only in an early chapter of the story of our encounter with the civilizations of Mexico and Peru and Orthodox Christendom and Islam and the Hindu World and the Far East. We are just beginning to see some of the effects of our action on them, but we have hardly begun to see the effects—which will certainly be tremendous—of their coming counteraction upon us.

It is only in our generation that we have seen one of the first moves in this counteroffensive, and we have found it very disturbing; whether we have liked it or not, we have felt it to be momentous. I mean, of course, the move made by the offshoot of Orthodox Christendom in Russia. It is momentous and disturbing not because of the material power behind it. The Russians . . . have already shown (and this is the point) the power to convert Western souls to a non-Western "ideology."

The Russians have taken up a Western secular social philosophy, Marxism; you might equally well call Marxism a Christian heresy, a leaf torn out of the book of Christianity and treated as if it were the whole gospel. The Russians have taken up this Western heretical religion, transformed it into something of their own, and are now shooting it back at us. This is the first shot in the anti-Western counteroffensive; but this Russian counterdischarge in the form of Communism may come to seem a small affair when the probably far more potent civilizations of India and China respond in their turn to our Western challenge. In the long run India and China seem likely to produce much deeper effects on our Western life than Russia can ever hope to produce with her Communism. But even the comparatively feeble native civilization of Mexico is beginning to react. The revolution through which Mexico has been passing since A.D. 1910 may be interpreted as a first move to shake off the top-dressing of Western Civilization which we imposed on Mexico in the sixteenth century; and what is happening today in Mexico may happen tomorrow in the seats of the native civilization of South America: in Peru, Bolivia, Ecuador, and Colombia.

III

Before leaving off, I must say a word about one question which I have begged up to this point, and that is: what do we mean by a "civilization"? Clearly, we do mean something, for even before we have tried to define what our meaning is, this classification of human societies— the Western Civilization, the Islamic, the Far Eastern, the Hindu, and so on—does seem to make sense. These names do call up distinct pictures in our minds in terms of religion, architecture, painting, manners, and customs. Still, it is better to try to get closer to what we mean by a term which we have already been working so hard. I believe I do know what I mean by a civilization; at least, I am sure I know how I have arrived at my own idea of it.

I mean, by a civilization, the smallest unit of historical study at which one arrives when one tries to understand the history of one's own country: the United States, say, or the United Kingdom. If you were to try to understand the history of the United States by itself, it would be unintelligible: you could not understand the part played in American life by federal government, representative government, democracy, industrialism, monogamy, Christianity, unless you looked beyond the bounds of the United States—out beyond her frontiers to Western Europe and the other overseas countries founded by West Europeans, and back beyond her local origins to the history of Western Europe in centuries before Columbus or Cabot had crossed the Atlantic. But, to make American history and institutions intelligible for practical purposes, you need not look beyond Western Europe into Eastern Europe or the Islamic World, nor behind the origins of our Western European civilization to the decline and fall of the Græco-Roman civilization. These limits of time and space give us the intelligible unit of social life of which the United States or Great Britain or France or Holland is a part: call it Western Christendom, Western Civilization, Western Society, the Western World.   Similarly, if you start from Greece or Serbia or Russia, and try to understand their histories, you arrive at an Orthodox Christendom or Byzantine World.   If you start from Morocco or Afghanistan, and try to understand their histories, you arrive at an Islamic World.   Start from Bengal or Mysore or Rajputana, and you find a Hindu World.   Start from China or Japan and you find a Far Eastern World.

While the state of which we happen to be citizens makes more concrete and more imperious claims on our allegiance, especially in the present age, the civilization of which we are members really counts for more in our lives.   And this civilization of which we are members includes—at most stages in its history—the citizens of other states besides our own.   It is older than our own state: the Western Civilization is about thirteen hundred years old, whereas the Kingdom of England is only one thousand years old, the United Kingdom of England and Scotland less than two hundred and fifty, the United States not more than one hundred and fifty.   States are apt to have short lives and sudden deaths: the Western Civilization of which you and I are members may be alive centuries after the United Kingdom and the United States have disappeared from the political map of the world like their late contemporaries, the Republic of Venice and the Dual Monarchy of Austria-Hungary.   This is one of the reasons why I have been asking you to look at history in terms of civilizations, and not in terms of states, and to think of states as rather subordinate and ephemeral political phenomena in the lives of the civilizations in whose bosoms they appear and disappear.

<hr/>

93. *Ignorance Is Strength* *

LIGHTENED in part though it is by the inevitable boy-meets-girl theme, the novel *1984* from which this selection is taken is a deadly serious, satirical exposition of life in the totalitarian society of the future.   Its author, George Orwell, develops to their ostensibly logi-

* George Orwell.   From *Nineteen Eighty-Four*, pp. 202-218.   Copyright 1949 by Harcourt, Brace and Company, Inc.
George Orwell was the pseudonym of Eric Blair (1903-1951), a British writer. Born in Motihari, Bengal, of Anglo-Indian parents.   After being badly wounded in

cal limits the institutions that characterize all modern authoritarian cultures. By the device of a book within a book he presents, in this selection, the core of the theory of his 1984 society. The central problem in the theory seems to be this: Modern science, mass production, and technology offer the possibility of practically eliminating the great class differences in material and mental well-being that, up to now, have always characterized the major societies of the world. Under these conditions, how can a hierarchical society, with all the tangible and intangible differential benefits this implies, be indefinitely maintained by the "ruling class"?

THROUGHOUT RECORDED TIME, and probably since the end of the Neolithic Age, there have been three kinds of people in the world, the High, the Middle, and the Low. They have been subdivided in many ways, they have borne countless different names, and their relative numbers, as well as their attitude toward one another, have varied from age to age; but the essential structure of society has never altered. Even after enormous upheavals and seemingly irrevocable changes, the same pattern has always reasserted itself, just as a gyroscope will always return to equilibrium, however far it is pushed one way or the other. . . .

The aims of these groups are entirely irreconcilable. The aim of the High is to remain where they are. The aim of the Middle is to change places with the High. The aim of the Low, when they have an aim— for it is an abiding characteristic of the Low that they are too much crushed by drudgery to be more than intermittently conscious of anything outside their daily lives—is to abolish all distinctions and create a society in which all men shall be equal. Thus throughout history a struggle which is the same in its main outlines recurs over and over again. For long periods the High seem to be securely in power, but sooner or later there always comes a moment when they lose either their belief in themselves, or their capacity to govern efficiently, or both. They are then overthrown by the Middle, who enlist the Low on their side by pretending to them that they are fighting for liberty and justice. As soon as they have reached their objective, the Middle thrust the Low back into their old position of servitude, and themselves become the High. Presently a new Middle group splits off from one of the other groups, or from both of them, and the struggle begins over again. Of the three groups, only the Low are never even temporarily successful in achieving their aims. It would be an exaggeration to say that through-

Spain, he settled down in England to write. His books include *Down and Out in Paris and London, Burmese Days, The Lion and the Unicorn, Animal Farm, Shooting an Elephant,* and *Critical Essays.*

out history there had been no progress of a material kind. Even today, in a period of decline, the average human being is physically better off than he was a few centuries ago. But no advance in wealth, no softening of manners, no reform or revolution has ever brought human equality a millimeter nearer. From the point of view of the Low, no historic change has ever meant much more than a change in the name of their masters.

By the late nineteenth century the recurrences of this pattern had become obvious to many observers. There then arose schools of thinkers who interpreted history as a cyclical process and claimed to show that inequality was the unalterable law of human life. This doctrine, of course, had always had its adherents, but in the manner in which it was now put forward there was a significant change. In the past the need for a hierarchical form of society had been the doctrine specifically of the High. It had been preached by kings and aristocrats and by the priests, lawyers, and the like who were parasitical upon them, and it had generally been softened by promises of compensation in an imaginary world beyond the grave. The Middle, so long as it was struggling for power, had always made use of such terms as freedom, justice, and fraternity. Now, however, the concept of human brotherhood began to be assailed by people who were not yet in positions of command, but merely hoped to be so before long. In the past the Middle had made revolutions under the banner of equality, and then had established a fresh tyranny as soon as the old one was overthrown. The new Middle groups in effect proclaimed their tyranny beforehand. Socialism, a theory which appeared in the early nineteenth century and was the last link in a chain of thought stretching back to the slave rebellions of antiquity, was still deeply infected by the Utopianism of past ages. But in each variant of Socialism that appeared from about 1900 onwards the aim of establishing liberty and equality was more and more openly abandoned. The new movements which appeared in the middle years of the century, Ingsoc in Oceania, Neo-Bolshevism in Eurasia, Death-worship, as it is commonly called, in Eastasia, had the conscious aim of perpetuating unfreedom and inequality. These new movements, of course, grew out of the old ones and tended to keep their names and pay lipservice to their ideology. But the purpose of all of them was to arrest progress and freeze history at a chosen moment. The familiar pendulum swing was to happen once more, and then stop. As usual, the High were to be turned out by the Middle, who would then become the High; but this time, by conscious strategy, the High would be able to maintain their position permanently.

The new doctrines arose partly because of the accumulation of historical knowledge, and the growth of the historical sense, which had hardly existed before the nineteenth century. The cyclical movement of history was now intelligible, or appeared to be so; and if it was intelligible, then it was alterable. But the principal, underlying cause was that, as early as the beginning of the twentieth century, human equality had become technically possible. It was still true that men were not equal in their native talents and that functions had to be specialized in ways that favored some individuals against others; but there was no longer any real need for class distinctions or for large differences of wealth. In earlier ages, class distinctions had been not only inevitable but desirable. Inequality was the price of civilization. With the development of machine production, however, the case was altered. Even if it was still necessary for human beings to do different kinds of work, it was no longer necessary for them to live at different social or economic levels. Therefore, from the point of view of the new groups who were on the point of seizing power, human equality was no longer an ideal to be striven after, but a danger to be averted. In more primitive ages, when a just and peaceful society was in fact not possible, it had been fairly easy to believe in it. The idea of an earthly paradise in which men should live together in a state of brotherhood, without laws and without brute labor, had haunted the human imagination for thousands of years. And this vision had had a certain hold even on the groups who actually profited by each historic change. The heirs of the French, English, and American revolutions had partly believed in their own phrases about the rights of man, freedom of speech, equality before the law, and the like, and had even allowed their conduct to be influenced by them to some extent. But by the fourth decade of the twentieth century all the main currents of political thought were authoritarian. The earthly paradise had been discredited at exactly the moment when it became realizable. Every new political theory, by whatever name it called itself, led back to hierarchy and regimentation. And in the general hardening of outlook that set in round about 1930, practices which had been long abandoned, in some cases for hundreds of years— imprisonment without trial, the use of war prisoners as slaves, public executions, torture to extract confessions, the use of hostages and the deportation of whole populations—not only became common again, but were tolerated and even defended by people who considered themselves enlightened and progressive.

It was only after a decade of national wars, civil wars, revolutions and counterrevolutions in all parts of the world that Ingsoc and its rivals emerged as fully worked-out political theories. But they had been foreshadowed by the various systems, generally called totalitarian, which had appeared earlier in the century, and the main outlines of the world which would emerge from the prevailing chaos had long been obvious. What kind of people would control this world had been equally obvious. The new aristocracy was made up for the most part of bureaucrats, scientists, technicians, trade-union organizers, publicity experts, sociologists, teachers, journalists, and professional politicians. These people, whose origins lay in the salaried middle class and the upper grades of the working class, had been shaped and brought together by the barren world of monopoly industry and centralized government. As compared with their opposite numbers in past ages, they were less avaricious, less tempted by luxury, hungrier for pure power, and, above all, more conscious of what they were doing and more intent on crushing opposition. This last difference was cardinal. By comparison with that existing today, all the tyrannies of the past were half-hearted and inefficient. The ruling groups were always infected to some extent by liberal ideas, and were content to leave loose ends everywhere, to regard only the overt act, and to be uninterested in what their subjects were thinking. Even the Catholic Church of the Middle Ages was tolerant by modern standards. Part of the reason for this was that in the past no government had the power to keep its citizens under constant surveillance. The invention of print, however, made it easier to manipulate public opinion, and the film and the radio carried the process further. With the development of television, and the technical advance which made it possible to receive and transmit simultaneously on the same instrument, private life came to an end. Every citizen, or at least every citizen important enough to be worth watching, could be kept for twenty-four hours a day under the eyes of the police and in the sound of official propaganda, with all other channels of communication closed. The possibility of enforcing not only complete obedience to the will of the State, but complete uniformity of opinion on all subjects, now existed for the first time.

After the revolutionary period of the Fifties and Sixties, society regrouped itself, as always, into High, Middle, and Low. But the new High group, unlike all its forerunners, did not act upon instinct but knew what was needed to safeguard its position. It had long been realized that the only secure basis for oligarchy is collectivism. Wealth and privilege are most easily defended when they are possessed jointly. The so-called "abolition of private property" which took place in the middle years of the century meant, in effect, the concentration of property in far fewer hands than before; but with this difference, that the new owners were a group instead of a mass of individuals. Individually, no member of the Party owns anything, except petty personal

belongings.   Collectively, the Party owns everything in Oceania, because
it controls everything and disposes of the products as it thinks fit.   In
the years following the Revolution it was able to step into this commanding position almost unopposed, because the whole process was
represented as an act of collectivization.   It had always been assumed
that if the capitalist class were expropriated, Socialism must follow; and
unquestionably the capitalists had been expropriated.   Factories, mines,
land, houses, transport—everything had been taken away from them;
and since these things were no longer private property, it followed that
they must be public property.   Ingsoc, which grew out of the earlier
Socialist movement and inherited its phraseology, has in fact carried
out the main item in the Socialist program, with the result, foreseen and
intended beforehand, that economic inequality has been made permanent.

But the problems of perpetuating a hierarchical society go deeper than
this.   There are only four ways in which a ruling group can fall from
power.   Either it is conquered from without, or it governs so inefficiently
that the masses are stirred to revolt, or it allows a strong and discontented Middle Group to come into being, or it loses its own self-
confidence and willingness to govern.   These causes do not operate
singly, and as a rule all four of them are present in some degree.   A
ruling class which could guard against all of them would remain in power
permanently.   Ultimately the determining factor is the mental attitude
of the ruling class itself.

After the middle of the present century, the first danger had in reality
disappeared.   Each of the three powers which now divide the world is
in fact unconquerable, and could only become conquerable through slow
demographic changes which a government with wide powers can easily
avert.   The second danger, also, is only a theoretical one.   The masses
never revolt of their own accord, and they never revolt merely because
they are oppressed.   Indeed, so long as they are not permitted to have
standards of comparison they never even become aware that they are
oppressed.   The recurrent economic crises of past times were totally
unnecessary and are not now permitted to happen, but other and equally
large dislocations can and do happen without having political results,
because there is no way in which discontent can become articulate.
As for the problem of overproduction, which has been latent in our
society since the development of machine technique, it is solved by the
device of continuous warfare, which is also useful in keying up public
morale to the necessary pitch.   From the point of view of our present
rulers, therefore, the only genuine dangers are the splitting-off of a new
group of able, underemployed, power-hungry people, and the growth of

liberalism and skepticism in their own ranks. The problem, that is to say, is educational. It is a problem of continuously molding the consciousness both of the directing group and of the larger executive group that lies immediately below it. The consciousness of the masses needs only to be influenced in a negative way.

Given this background, one could infer, if one did not know it already, the general structure of Oceanic society. At the apex of the pyramid comes Big Brother. Big Brother is infallible and all-powerful. Every success, every achievement, every victory, every scientific discovery, all knowledge, all wisdom, all happiness, all virtue, are held to issue directly from his leadership and inspiration. Nobody has ever seen Big Brother. He is a face on the hoardings, a voice on the telescreen. We may be reasonably sure that he will never die, and there is already considerable uncertainty as to when he was born. Big Brother is the guise in which the Party chooses to exhibit itself to the world. His function is to act as a focusing point for love, fear, and reverence, emotions which are more easily felt toward an individual than toward an organization. Below Big Brother comes the Inner Party, its numbers limited to six million, or something less than two per cent of the population of Oceania. Below the Inner Party comes the Outer Party, which, if the Inner Party is described as the brain of the State, may be justly likened to the hands. Below that come the dumb masses whom we habitually refer to as "the proles," numbering perhaps eighty-five per cent of the population. In the terms of our earlier classification, the proles are the Low, for the slave populations of the equatorial lands, who pass constantly from conqueror to conqueror, are not a permanent or necessary part of the structure.

In principle, membership in these three groups is not hereditary. The child of Inner Party parents is in theory not born into the Inner Party. Admission to either branch of the Party is by examination, taken at the age of sixteen. Nor is there any racial discrimination, or any marked domination of one province by another. Jews, Negroes, South Americans of pure Indian blood are to be found in the highest ranks of the Party, and the administrators of any area are always drawn from the inhabitants of that area. In no part of Oceania do the inhabitants have the feeling that they are a colonial population ruled from a distant capital. Oceania has no capital, and its titular head is a person whose whereabouts nobody knows. Except that English is its chief lingua franca and Newspeak its official language, it is not centralized in any way. Its rulers are not held together by blood ties but by adherence to a common doctrine. It is true that our society is stratified, and very rigidly stratified, on what at first sight appear to be hereditary lines.

There is far less to-and-fro movement between the different groups than happened under capitalism or even in the pre-industrial ages. Between the two branches of the Party there is a certain amount of interchange, but only so much as will ensure that weaklings are excluded from the Inner Party and that ambitious members of the Outer Party are made harmless by allowing them to rise. Proletarians, in practice, are not allowed to graduate into the Party. The most gifted among them, who might possibly become nuclei of discontent, are simply marked down by the Thought Police and eliminated. But this state of affairs is not necessarily permanent, nor is it a matter of principle. The Party is not a class in the old sense of the word. It does not aim at transmitting power to its own children, as such; and if there were no other way of keeping the ablest people at the top, it would be perfectly prepared to recruit an entire new generation from the ranks of the proletariat. In the crucial years, the fact that the Party was not a hereditary body did a great deal to neutralize opposition. The older kind of Socialist, who had been trained to fight against something called "class privilege," assumed that what is not hereditary cannot be permanent. He did not see that the continuity of an oligarchy need not be physical, nor did he pause to reflect that hereditary aristocracies have always been shortlived, whereas adoptive organizations such as the Catholic Church have sometimes lasted for hundreds or thousands of years. The essence of oligarchical rule is not father-to-son inheritance, but the persistence of a certain world-view and a certain way of life, imposed by the dead upon the living. A ruling group is a ruling group so long as it can nominate its successors. The Party is not concerned with perpetuating its blood but with perpetuating itself. Who wields power is not important, provided that the hierarchical structure remains always the same.

All the beliefs, habits, tastes, emotions, mental attitudes that characterize our time are really designed to sustain the mystique of the Party and prevent the true nature of present-day society from being perceived. Physical rebellion, or any preliminary move toward rebellion, is at present not possible. From the proletarians nothing is to be feared. Left to themselves, they will continue from generation to generation and from century to century, working, breeding, and dying, not only without any impulse to rebel, but without the power of grasping that the world could be other than it is. They could only become dangerous if the advance of industrial technique made it necessary to educate them more highly; but, since military and commercial rivalry are no longer important, the level of popular education is actually declining. What opinions the masses hold, or do not hold, is looked on as a matter of indifference. They can be granted intellectual liberty because they have no intellect. In a Party member, on the other hand, not even the smallest deviation of opinion on the most unimportant subject can be tolerated.

A Party member lives from birth to death under the eye of the Thought Police. Even when he is alone he can never be sure that he is alone. Wherever he may be, asleep or awake, working or resting, in his bath or in bed, he can be inspected without warning and without knowing that he is being inspected. Nothing that he does is indifferent. His friendships, his relaxations, his behavior toward his wife and children, the expression of his face when he is alone, the words he mutters in sleep, even the characteristic movements of his body, are all jealously scrutinized. Not only any actual misdemeanor, but any eccentricity, however small, any change of habits, any nervous mannerism that could possibly be the symptom of an inner struggle, is certain to be detected. He has no freedom of choice in any direction whatever. On the other hand, his actions are not regulated by law or by any clearly formulated code of behavior. In Oceania there is no law. Thoughts and actions which, when detected, mean certain death are not formally forbidden, and the endless purges, arrests, tortures, imprisonments, and vaporizations are not inflicted as punishment for crimes which have actually been committed, but are merely the wiping-out of persons who might perhaps commit a crime at some time in the future. A Party member is required to have not only the right opinions, but the right instincts. Many of the beliefs and attitudes demanded of him are never plainly stated, and could not be stated without laying bare the contradictions inherent in Ingsoc. If he is a person naturally orthodox (in Newspeak, a *goodthinker*), he will in all circumstances know, without taking thought, what is the true belief or the desirable emotion. But in any case an elaborate mental training, undergone in childhood and grouping itself round the Newspeak words *crimestop*, *blackwhite*, and *doublethink*, makes him unwilling and unable to think too deeply on any subject whatever.

A Party member is expected to have no private emotions and no respites from enthusiasm. He is supposed to live in a continuous frenzy of hatred of foreign enemies and internal traitors, triumph over victories, and self-abasement before the power and wisdom of the Party. The discontents produced by his bare, unsatisfying life are deliberately turned outwards and dissipated by such devices as the Two Minutes Hate, and the speculations which might possibly induce a skeptical or rebellious attitude are killed in advance by his early acquired inner discipline. The first and simplest stage in the discipline, which can be taught even to young children, is called, in Newspeak, *crimestop*. *Crimestop* means the faculty of stopping short, as though by instinct, at the threshold of any dangerous thought.   It includes the power of not grasping analogies, of failing to perceive logical errors, of misunderstanding the simplest arguments if they are inimical to Ingsoc, and of being bored or repelled by any train of thought which is capable of leading in a heretical direction.   *Crimestop*, in short, means protective stupidity.   But stupidity is not enough.   On the contrary, orthodoxy in the full sense demands a control over one's own mental processes as complete as that of a contortionist over his body.   Oceanic society rests ultimately on the belief that Big Brother is omnipotent and that the Party is infallible.   But since in reality Big Brother is not omnipotent and the Party is not infallible, there is need for an unwearying, moment-to-moment flexibility in the treatment of facts.   The key word here is *blackwhite*.   Like so many Newspeak words, this word has two mutually contradictory meanings.   Applied to an opponent, it means the habit of impudently claiming that black is white, in contradiction of the plain facts.   Applied to a Party member, it means a loyal willingness to say that black is white when Party discipline demands this.   But it means also the ability to *believe* that black is white, and more, to *know* that black is white, and to forget that one has ever believed the contrary.   This demands a continuous alteration of the past, made possible by the system of thought which really embraces all the rest, and which is known in Newspeak as *doublethink*.

The alteration of the past is necessary for two reasons, one of which is subsidiary and, so to speak, precautionary.   The subsidiary reason is that the Party member, like the proletarian, tolerates present-day conditions partly because he has no standards of comparison.   He must be cut off from the past, just as he must be cut off from foreign countries, because it is necessary for him to believe that he is better off than his ancestors and that the average level of material comfort is constantly rising.   But by far the more important reason for the readjustment of the past is the need to safeguard the infallibility of the Party.   It is not merely that speeches, statistics, and records of every kind must be constantly brought up to date in order to show that the predictions of the Party were in all cases right.   It is also that no change of doctrine or in political alignment can ever be admitted.   For to change one's mind, or even one's policy, is a confession of weakness.   If, for example, Eurasia or Eastasia (whichever it may be) is the enemy today, then that country must always have been the enemy.   And if the facts say otherwise, then the facts must be altered.   Thus history is continuously rewritten.   This day-to-day falsification of the past, carried out by the Ministry of

Truth, is as necessary to the stability of the regime as the work of repression and espionage carried out by the Ministry of Love.

The mutability of the past is the central tenet of Ingsoc. Past events, it is argued, have no objective existence, but survive only in written records and in human memories. The past is whatever the records and the memories agree upon. And since the Party is in full control of all records, and in equally full control of the minds of its members, it follows that the past is whatever the Party chooses to make it. It also follows that though the past is alterable, it never has been altered in any specific instance. For when it has been recreated in whatever shape is needed at the moment, then this new version *is* the past, and no different past can ever have existed. This holds good even when, as often happens, the same event has to be altered out of recognition several times in the course of a year. At all times the Party is in possession of absolute truth, and clearly the absolute can never have been different from what it is now. It will be seen that the control of the past depends above all on the training of memory. To make sure that all written records agree with the orthodoxy of the moment is merely a mechanical act. But it is also necessary to *remember* that events happened in the desired manner. And if it is necessary to rearrange one's memories or to tamper with written records, then it is necessary to *forget* that one has done so. The trick of doing this can be learned like any other mental technique. It *is* learned by the majority of Party members, and certainly by all who are intelligent as well as orthodox. In Oldspeak it is called, quite frankly, "reality control." In Newspeak it is called *doublethink*, although *doublethink* comprises much else as well.

Doublethink means the power of holding two contradictory beliefs in one's mind simultaneously, and accepting both of them. The Party intellectual knows in which direction his memories must be altered; he therefore knows that he is playing tricks with reality; but by the exercise of *doublethink* he also satisfies himself that reality is not violated. The process has to be conscious, or it would not be carried out with sufficient precision, but it also has to be unconscious, or it would bring with it a feeling of falsity and hence of guilt. *Doublethink* lies at the very heart of Ingsoc, since the essential act of the Party is to use conscious deception while retaining the firmness of purpose that goes with complete honesty. To tell deliberate lies while genuinely believing in them, to forget any fact that has become inconvenient, and then, when it becomes necessary again, to draw it back from oblivion for just so long as it is needed, to deny the existence of objective reality and all the while to take account of the reality which one denies—all this is indispensably necessary. Even in using the word *doublethink* it is necessary to exercise *doublethink*. For by using the word one admits that one is tampering with reality; by a fresh act of *doublethink* one erases this knowledge; and so on indefinitely, with the lie always one leap ahead of the truth. Ultimately it is by means of *doublethink* that the Party has been able—and may, for all we know, continue to be able for thousands of years—to arrest the course of history.

All past oligarchies have fallen from power either because they ossified or because they grew soft. Either they became stupid and arrogant, failed to adjust themselves to changing circumstances, and were overthrown, or they became liberal and cowardly, made concessions when they should have used force, and once again were overthrown. They fell, that is to say, either through consciousness or through unconsciousness. It is the achievement of the Party to have produced a system of thought in which both conditions can exist simultaneously. And upon no other intellectual basis could the dominion of the Party be made permanent. If one is to rule, and to continue ruling, one must be able to dislocate the sense of reality. For the secret of rulership is to combine a belief in one's own infallibility with the power to learn from past mistakes.

It need hardly be said that the subtlest practitioners of *doublethink* are those who invented *doublethink* and know that it is a vast system of mental cheating. In our society, those who have the best knowledge of what is happening are also those who are furthest from seeing the world as it is. In general, the greater the understanding, the greater the delusion: the more intelligent, the less sane. One clear illustration of this is the fact that war hysteria increases in intensity as one rises in the social scale. Those whose attitude toward the war is most nearly rational are the subject peoples of the disputed territories. To these people the war is simply a continuous calamity which sweeps to and fro over their bodies like a tidal wave. Which side is winning is a matter of complete indifference to them. They are aware that a change of overlordship means simply that they will be doing the same work as before for new masters who treat them in the same manner as the old ones. The slightly more favored workers whom we call "the proles" are only intermittently conscious of the war. When it is necessary they can be prodded into frenzies of fear and hatred, but when left to themselves they are capable of forgetting for long periods that the war is happening. It is in the ranks of the Party, and above all of the Inner Party, that the true war enthusiasm is found. World-conquest is believed in most firmly by those who know it to be impossible. This peculiar linking-together of opposites—knowledge with ignorance, cynicism with fanaticism—is one of the chief distinguishing marks of Oceanic society. The official ideology abounds with contradictions even where there is no practical reason for them. Thus, the Party rejects and vilifies every principle for which the Socialist movement originally stood, and it chooses to do this in the name of Socialism. It preaches a contempt for the working class unexampled for centuries past, and it dresses its members in a uniform which was at one time peculiar to manual workers and was adopted for that reason. It systematically undermines the solidarity of the family, and it calls its leader by a name which is a direct appeal to the sentiments of family loyalty. Even the names of the four Ministries by which we are governed exhibit a sort of impudence in their deliberate reversal of the facts. The Ministry of Peace concerns itself with war, the Ministry of Truth with lies, the Ministry of Love with torture, and the Ministry of Plenty with starvation. These contradictions are not accidental, nor do they result from ordinary hypocrisy: they are deliberate exercises in *doublethink*. For it is only by reconciling contradictions that power can be retained indefinitely. In no other way could the ancient cycle be broken. If human equality is to be forever averted—if the High, as we have called them, are to keep their places permanently—then the prevailing mental condition must be controlled insanity.

But there is one question which until this moment we have almost ignored: It is: why should human equality be averted? Supposing that the mechanics of the process have been rightly described, what is the motive for this huge, accurately planned effort to freeze history at a particular moment of time?

Here we reach the central secret. As we have seen, the mystique of the Party, and above all of the Inner Party, depends upon *doublethink*. But deeper than this lies the original motive, the never-questioned instinct that first led to the seizure of power and brought *doublethink*, the Thought Police, continuous warfare, and all the other necessary paraphernalia into existence afterwards. This motive really consists. . . .

⋙⋘⋙⋘⋙⋘

94. Human Welfare *

CULTURAL AND SOCIAL CHANGE cannot be rationally planned or efficiently developed without clearly defined objectives. Basic to the formulation of goals, however, is explicit recognition of the fundamental or ultimate values toward which these are aimed. According to the United States Constitution one of the purposes of the federal government is to "promote the general welfare." Frequently this phrase appears as one of the ends to be accomplished by specific federal laws. Such an all-inclusive objective, however, is subject to many interpretations regarding both ends and means. The Study Committee of the Ford Foundation, in the present selection has prepared one of the best recent statements on the meaning of "human welfare." It may be regarded as a formulation of the basic value system in which enlightened Americans at mid-twentieth century believe.

THE AIM OF THE FORD FOUNDATION is to advance human welfare. The Study Committee's conception of the basic elements of human welfare is presented below.

Fundamental to any consideration of human welfare is human survival. All efforts to prolong life, to eradicate disease, to prevent malnutrition and famine, to remove the causes of violent accidents, and, above all, to prevent war, are efforts to forward the welfare of man.

The improvement of physical standards of living is clearly a basic part of human welfare. Living standards can be considered high enough only when the inhabitants of this country and the entire world have been freed from undue anxiety about the physical conditions of survival and from inordinate preoccupation with obtaining those conditions. Of course, the goals of human welfare are not merely survival and the improvement of physical standards of living. Not until the physical requirements of life and good health are well met may men progress toward the fullest realization of their mental, emotional, and spiritual capacities. All are essential to the achievement of human welfare.

Human dignity. Basic to human welfare is the idea of the dignity of man—the conviction that man must be regarded as an end in himself, not as a mere cog in the mechanisms of society. At heart, this is a belief in the inherent worth of the individual, in the intrinsic value of

* Ford Foundation, Report of the Study for the Ford Foundation on Policy and Program (Detroit: Ford Foundation, 1949), pp. 17-22. Reprinted by permission of the publisher.

human life. Implicit in it is the conviction that society must accord all men equal rights and equal opportunity to develop their capabilities and must, in addition, encourage individuality and inventive and creative talent.

Personal freedom and rights. Also basic to human welfare is the right of each person to enjoy the largest measure of liberty consistent with the equal claims of other persons. Freedom cannot, of course, be absolute but must be enjoyed under a rule of law so that all may share equally in its benefits and opportunities.

Human welfare requires tolerance and respect for individual, social, religious, and cultural differences and for the varying needs and aspirations to which these differences give rise. Within wide limits, every person has the right to go his own way and to be free from interference or harassment on grounds of nonconformity.

Political freedom and rights. The Committee believes that inherent in the concept of human welfare are freedom of worship, freedom of speech, and freedom of association; self-government; justice; and the right and opportunity of every citizen to play a real and effective part in his government.

Social responsibility and the duty of service. Human welfare also requires that power at all levels and in all forms—political, economic, or social—be exercised by those who possess it with a full sense of social responsibility; further, that every person recognize a moral obligation to use his capabilities, whatever they may be, so as not merely to avoid being a burden on society, if he can help it, but to contribute positively to the welfare of society.

HUMAN WELFARE AND DEMOCRATIC IDEALS

The Committee's concept of human welfare is closely related to the ideals of democratic peoples—belief in human dignity; in personal freedom; in equality of rights, justice, and opportunity; in freedom of speech, religion, and association; and in self-government as the best form of government. Through the fuller realization of these ideals the life of the individual would become more productive, purposeful, gracious, and secure. In the belief that any successful attempt to improve the lot of mankind must be made on terms compatible with these fundamental principles, the Committee used them as a base in estimating the gravity of human welfare's problems and as a standard in considering programs for their solution.

Democracy does not, of course, consist of the numerical aggregate of these principles or in the exaltation of one at the expense of another.

It consists rather in a meaningful relationship among them, resting always on the fundamental conviction of the dignity of man.

These democratic ideals represent for the Committee a particularly significant expression of human welfare since they emphasize man's most crucial problems—the intricate relationships among human beings and social organizations, now so heavily marked by tension and disorder.

While our ultimate concern is with the individual, it is clear that only in society can his full development take place. Modern man cannot forsake society in search of freedom; freedom, for him, exists only within and by means of the social order. Men are no freer than the arrangements and conditions of society enable them to be. In the complex modern world large-scale and complicated arrangements are necessary to provide the social and economic conditions under which freedom can be assured. One of the primary functions of government is to ensure the presence of such conditions, guarding continuously, however, against the danger that in the process it may take over too many of the individual's activities or decisions, and thereby undermine his moral energy and initiative.

Recent developments have brought increasing general awareness of how dependent men are on one another. No longer can individuals, or nations, retreat into self-sufficiency. Men live together whether they want to or not; all are thrust, from birth, into an immense network of political, economic, and social relationships. This interdependence can be the most abasing of conditions in societies where men are enslaved as tools of other men or of a state machine; it can be the source of greatest satisfaction if it means the enrichment of personal life by the sharing of the best by the most—through a realization of common interests, common efforts, common humanity, and common fate.

Our political institutions do not themselves constitute democracy. They can only establish a climate in which democracy may flourish. Majority rule and peaceful concurrence by the minority, which are terms of democracy, have validity only when the majority exercises its power both with restraint and with concern for the problems and attitudes of the minority. Both sides must have that essential respect for themselves and for each other which makes them unwilling to be either masters or slaves.

Our political institutions will, then, have real meaning and a good chance of survival only if they reflect a way of life in which all the myriad nonpolitical associations and relationships between people and organizations breathe the spirit of democracy. When the democratic spirit is deep and strong in a society it animates every phase of living: economic, social, and political relations among groups and nations, as well as personal relations among men. This integration of democratic ideals with the life of individuals and with society can be realized only when it is lived—when it has become an established attitude and custom, a way by which men work and live each day of their lives—not just an abstract theory. Only then will democracy permeate the entire structure of our society, bringing with it a wide diffusion of contentment and confidence.

The real meaning of democracy for the people of this or any generation lies in how it is interpreted in action, how it is applied in their daily lives, in the means it uses, and in the character of its institutions and practices. No one pretends that democracy here or elsewhere is now perfect or that it will ever become perfect. For this is the essence of democracy, that it is a system of principles and not of rigid rules, that these principles must be reinterpreted as times and conditions change, and that the need for new interpretation and application will always exist.

Clearly, therefore, in speaking of democracy, the Committee is not thinking merely of the form of our institutions and organizations, which are but means or instruments for men's requirements. To identify present forms too closely with democratic ideals is to make idols of the forms, thereby hindering their improvement for the service of mankind.

In times of uncertainty many people tend to resist change, in the illusion that democracy and its institutions are made more secure by an unchanging order. This, we believe, strikes at the very heart of democracy by denying to it the right to grow. For democracy's greatest strength lies in its ability to move constantly forward in action toward the increasing fulfillment of people's needs and the greater achievement of its goals. It is man's faith in this ability which assures the survival of democracy.

DEMOCRACY ON CHALLENGE

During its investigation the Committee was constantly reminded that democracy is on challenge in the world today. A great new foundation can thus most appropriately make its entrance into human affairs with a reaffirmation of democratic ideals and with the expressed intention of assisting democracy to meet that challenge and to realize its ideals.

The crisis in the world today requires that democracy do more than restate its principles and ideals; they must be translated into action. We must take affirmative action toward the elimination of the basic causes of war, the advancement of democracy on a broad front, and the strengthening of its institutions and processes. National conduct based solely upon fear of communism, upon reaction to totalitarian tactics, or upon the immediate exigencies of avoiding war, is defensive and negative. If such a defensive attitude is allowed to control our planning and thinking, our national effort will be diverted unduly to expedient and temporary measures from the more important tasks ahead, and we may grow like the thing we fight.

When democracy is threatened by war we must be prepared to defend it by military action. But military strength is not enough. We must at the same time press democracy forward by reaffirming its principles in action. Without the resulting internal vitality and stability, national security in the long run is unattainable.

APPENDIX

CAREER OPPORTUNITIES FOR PERSONS TRAINED IN SOCIOLOGY

A. Careers in Sociology *

THE EDITORS of this book recognize that most students who take a course in introductory sociology are not planning to become sociology "majors." Nevertheless, we believe that sociology will increasingly be recognized as providing a focus for a pre-professional or a liberal arts education. Moreover, even today sociology is being chosen as a major field of study by large numbers of undergraduates at many institutions. With these thoughts in mind we have sought in this final section to give information about two of the many vocations that these students may later enter.

In some colleges the undergraduate sociology curriculum is strongly oriented toward preparation for careers in social work. In other cases undergraduate work in sociology is primarily considered as a foundation for the graduate training of the professional sociologist. The nature of these two careers and the specialized training required for each are described in these two selections.

THE PRACTICE OF SOCIOLOGY as a profession is a distinctively American development. While its roots are as old in history as speculations about the nature of human society, it is only during the last thirty years

---

* Myron F. Lewis, School and College Placement, 12, No. 1 (October, 1951), 48-53. Reprinted by permission of the Association of School and College Placement and the author.

The author (b. 1913) is staff assistant in charge of sociological and demographic studies, President's Commission on the Health Needs of the Nation. Formerly professor of sociology at various universities. Has held several other government positions. Special field of interest the professional practice of sociology.

that the idea of a social technology based on theory and tested by empirical investigation has become acceptable. The field is still a small one—there are today less than 5000 sociologists—and is at present especially short of persons trained to act as practicing professionals. Indeed, there is reason to think that some of the important social conflicts of our time remain unresolved because of the absence of competent social technologists.

Sociology is one of the social sciences, closely related academically to anthropology, education, psychology and social administration. It is not easy to draw clearcut boundaries which divide sociology from the other behavior sciences. If it is assumed that it is worthwhile to study and investigate the nature of personality, culture, and society, one may then conveniently identify sociology with the study of society, psychology with the study of personality and anthropology with the study of culture. In actual fact it is becoming increasingly difficult to distinguish among the three, for they are in process of merging into a unified science of social relations to which each contributes essentially complementary theory and finding.

More specifically, sociology is the study of situations in which human beings are in relationship with one another. It analyzes the forms of group organization of which a vast number are found in any modern society: communities, families, clubs, fraternal orders, labor unions, business associations, professions, etc. Sociology seeks to explain social institutions, standards, cultures, and the forces that operate in social change such as leadership and invention. In combination with psychology, sociology becomes social psychology, which is concerned with the mental processes and reactions of men in groups or masses. This part of sociology especially has contributed to the treatment of problems of human behavior under stress, as in time of war, defense mobilization or inter-group conflict of any kind.

The study of American society and its culture is carried on at all school levels, beginning with the elementary social studies of the grammar school. The social studies are often developed in the high schools in terms of social problems and the inadequacy of social institutions. In the first half of a college course, many students are required to take introductory courses in social science as a part of the program of general education, and these courses often include subject matter from anthropology and sociology. It is usually not until the senior college level that a student encounters sociology as a distinct discipline or major course of study. Most American colleges and universities have the resources for a major in sociology, either as an independent department or as a part of a social science major.

WHY STUDENTS MAJOR IN SOCIOLOGY

Students select a major in sociology at the undergraduate level for one of three reasons. Probably the most important is the selection of this field as an area of undergraduate concentration for the sake of a general liberal arts education on the same basis as other students major in biology or literature. In such cases students feel that study of the structure, functions and changes in modern society contributes meaningfully to their standing as educated individuals.

Many other students choose an undergraduate major in sociology as preprofessional training. The majority of persons accepted into graduate schools of social work have had prior training in sociology, and the relationship between sociology and social work is about the same as that between biology and medicine. Sociology courses, with or without a major in the subject, can also be an important part of preprofessional training for careers in law, business, industrial relations, personnel work and public administration. The idea is to provide the student with some basic ideas about human society and human relations. The more complex our culture becomes, the more necessary it is to obtain adequate background training for any sort of managerial or administrative work. To some extent the skills basic to organization and administration are obtained through formal instruction in sociology, psychology and the other social sciences.

The third group of students who select an undergraduate major in sociology consists of those who wish to plan for careers as professional social scientists. For these the bachelor's degree program, allowing for about 36 semester hours in the field, is necessarily only an introduction to further university study. Only in very few cases, and these more rarely than formerly, can the bachelor's program of studies be used as a basis for a professional career in the social sciences. The period of university (graduate) study is required not only to master the discipline but also to provide maturity necessary to a scientist working with behaving human beings. Accordingly, the prospective sociologist should plan to spend four years in advanced study and to obtain the doctorate. The minimum professional preparation is four semesters of full-time graduate work and the master's degree.

SELECTING THE UNIVERSITY

One of the chief decisions facing the graduate student is the choice of a university at which to pursue his studies. Approximately half of the 100 or more American universities which offer the doctorate provide higher training in sociology, but of these some ten or twelve institutions train about 90 per cent of the active professionals in this field. One of the best ways for a student to judge the merit of a given institution is to determine how many graduate students it had in a given year and how many doctorates were granted in that same year. It is rarely wise to attend any university where the ratio of students to degrees granted is higher than ten to one; a better ratio would be five to one. Graduate students are a valuable asset to a large university, especially after they have successfully completed their first year of advanced study. They are frequently assigned to work as instructors, readers and research assistants. The majority of advanced students in sociology, particularly those in the last two years of graduate work, may expect to obtain part-time professional duties which will serve to finance in part the lengthy period of advanced study.

The areas of specialization within a university sociology curriculum vary considerably from one institution to another. Often the first graduate year will consist of a group of basic courses, several of which may be required of all students. The entire four-year study program must necessarily have several objectives and sometimes these are not entirely compatible. Instruction must be organized so as to continue to provide information on a level much more advanced than in the undergraduate course. The student must be provided with instruction in research methods and techniques to prepare him for his doctoral research study. The curriculum must also take into account the fact that many sociologists make permanent careers in teaching, and most of them teach at the college level at one time or another, while relatively few earn a living as research investigators alone. Finally, an increasing number of sociologists enter some form of professional practice, although not ordinarily of a type involving the person-to-person relationship which characterizes the physician and his patient.

Training in research, which some universities announce as the sole function of their graduate schools, is often not the best way to prepare for careers in social technology. While some universities have modified their doctoral study programs to permit preparation for other types of careers, the majority have not yet done so. This may account in part for the scarcity of competent social administrators, and the reluctance of some sociologists to forego teaching for careers as practitioners and technologists.

During his last two years of graduate study each student is required to master general and theoretical sociology and methods of research, but to some extent the choice of other areas of study is his own. He may elect industrial relations, social psychology, correctional administra-

tion, demography, marriage and family counseling, communications research, public opinion management, group dynamics or other specialties.
He is guided in his choice not only by his own interests and preference,
but by the resources of the department in which he is working.

In every doctoral program the student must undertake an extensive
research project, usually in the area in which he intends to specialize.
Ordinarily he cannot complete such a study by the use of library facilities
alone. This means that the young sociologist is faced with the problem
of acquiring funds, time, contacts, and field-work facilities in order to
bring his dissertation to a successful conclusion. While some universities plan the administration of the student's research program,
others refuse to assist in any way with part of the degree requirements.
Every effort should be made to determine departmental policy in this
matter well in advance since it can make an appreciable difference in
the cost of and time required to complete the degree. The student
needs to have, if possible, a definite commitment regarding what he may
expect from the faculty and department in this respect.

In June, 1950, the Social Science Research Council published a directory of 281 organizations conducting or financing research in the
social sciences in 104 colleges and universities. While only a fraction
of these conducted research in sociology, it is probably wise for the
prospective graduate student to consider no university not listed in
this directory. In general the large private universities have a better
record for training sociologists than do the publicly supported institutions, many of which must of necessity concentrate their facilities on
undergraduates.

The young sociologist who has obtained the doctorate or its equivalent
possesses certain skills, knowledge and information not available to
anyone who has not completed the same training. It is customary to
point out that he is trained to conduct certain types of research, but
since little basic sociological research is carried on in the world of work
outside the academic environment, it is possibly more accurate to say
that the trained sociologist is able to comprehend, analyze and interpret
certain kinds of situations and the data relating thereto, and to solve
or assist in solving certain kinds of problems. In every case the data
and problems are those of human beings in action situations, either
past, present or planned or anticipated in the future. There is literally
no limit to the vast variety of social situations which may be so studied
and interpreted, and over which controls may be established on the
basis of the knowledge obtained. Sociologists at work today have
analyzed a great variety of these social situations and their patterns of
inter-personal relations. The range and scope of social analysis extends

from international warfare to the interaction of a seven-year-old youngster with his playmates. The focus of such analysis is not the occurrences themselves in their unique or particular characteristics, but rather the regular patterns of behavior repeatedly found in the series of events under observation. This broad scope of interest which the trained sociologist has means that his professional preparation is adaptable to a variety of specific jobs.

HOW SOCIOLOGISTS ARE EMPLOYED

Actually very few individuals are at work today under the job title of sociologist, although their number is larger than ten or even five years ago. By far the largest number of the members of the profession are college teachers and some teach sociology and other social sciences in high schools. By and large, those who carry on basic theoretical research in sociology are also members of university teaching staffs. It should not be supposed, however, that these academic sociologists have no other professional activities. From time to time a sociology professor will be found acting as a consultant to a city or state planning board, serving as advisor to a citizens' housing commission, taking part as a professional on a mayor's committee for intergroup relations, serving on a board of probation and parole or helping to solve the problem of juvenile delinquency in a given locality.

More and more frequently the sociologist is leaving his teaching job and going to work as a staff professional for public and private institutions and agencies. Sometimes he finds employment with a business organization, perhaps in the field of labor relations or personnel administration or as an industrial research specialist. Market analysis, public opinion polling, radio research and other fact-finding services have sociologists as staff members and occasionally as directors of research. Utilization of sociologists and other social scientists in connection with the management of men is on the increase. Such work depends for its future expansion upon a recognition of the need for facts about social situations as the bases for making policy and for solving all sorts of social-conflict problems. Inter-racial, industrial, labor, personnel and even familial relations, if productive of conflict and social disorganization, can be diagnosed and treated by the sociologist working as a professional practitioner.

The results which can be achieved along these lines were amply demonstrated during World War II. In a time of national crisis answers to problems in human relations must be obtained, especially when these exist within the armed forces, in civilian morale or in defense plants producing goods for war. If a race riot breaks out in a war plant, a team of social science experts is likely to be consulted in order to avert future outbreaks of social tension. The work performed may be called social research or social administration. In any case, expert diagnosis and some form of skilled therapy will be called for. If excessive absenteeism exists in another plant, the cure will require an analysis of the action-patterns of the workers. Sociologists took part in propaganda analysis, in ˚psychological warfare campaigns, in the selection of personnel, in intelligence work, in area studies and in the many attitude and opinion surveys conducted as evaluations or checks on the efficiency of both civilian and military operations. In all of these important wartime projects sociologists worked alongside other behavior scientists —psychiatrists, anthropologists, educationists and psychologists.

Not only during the war years, but since the early 1930's, there has been a growing recognition that sociology and the allied social sciences could contribute to policy formation and to the conduct of public administration in government at the national level. In the beginning, during the depression years, sociology furnished some of the criteria which served as bench-marks of national welfare. Very gradually, and especially during the last decade, individual sociologists have begun to find employment in the federal service and to make a contribution in specific jobs as trained scientists. All students of sociology and those planning to make careers in the field as professional workers should read the pamphlet published in 1950 by the Russell Sage Foundation, "Effective Use of Social Science Research in the Federal Service." The purpose of the publication is to describe what the social scientist can do as well as to promote the greater utilization of social research within the government service.

GOVERNMENT OPPORTUNITIES

There are at present four "series" or classes of positions defined by the U.S. Civil Service Commission which contain positions for which sociologists may qualify by means of the regularly scheduled examinations. These are the social science series, the social administration series, the intelligence research series and the military intelligence research series. For each of the last three of these several different examinations were kept open during 1950 and 1951 in order to recruit qualified personnel for defense mobilization work in Washington. Examinations opened for new workers (entry federal jobs) were junior management assistant, junior professional assistant, and junior social science analyst.

Two units of government—the Population Division of the Census Bureau and the Division of Farm Population of the Bureau of Agricultural Economics—have for some years employed a few sociologists, although under other job titles. Several other agencies each have a few professionals, often selected as much for their knowledge of an allied field (economics, statistics, housing, demography, etc.) as for their professional competence as sociologists.

Leading sociologists are occasionally asked to provide specialist consultant services to government agencies and to supervise operating research projects on a temporary basis. Although there are no federal jobs bearing the job title of sociologist, a rather large number of individuals numbering perhaps several thousands are performing successful and responsible work in the federal service because of prior training in sociology which fitted them for these careers. In some cases the formal education in sociology is used rather specifically; in other cases it has served these workers as a background for technical or administrative work. Occasionally the trained sociologist has been able to create his own professional job and in doing so to improve some aspect of government operations.

The whole field of government work is still very much open for sociologists who can pay especial attention to its needs and requirements. In the summer of 1951 there were less than 50 persons with the doctorate in sociology at work in Washington. The government's needs for trained social scientists has increased as a result of the Korean conflict and sociologists with the doctor's degree were locating positions without difficulty.

The long-run outlook for social scientists in government service is expected to be excellent. While there is little prospect that the federal government will undertake any work in sociology as such, the nation's need for trained social technologists in many areas of operating research and administrative work will increase. Whether sociologists or other social scientists obtain these positions will depend in part on whether the traditional graduate sociology curriculum is modified so as to train competent social technologists at the highest level.

The American Sociological Society is the national professional organization for sociologists. It publishes the official *American Sociological Review*, provides employment information, and holds an annual meeting of its members. Several regional societies affiliated with the national group hold meetings somewhat more frequently and each makes provision for student memberships. This year the American Sociological Society began publication of a series of bulletins, the first of which was issued in April and reports on employment opportunities in the federal service, describes civil service procedures relevant to making application for such positions, and discusses salaries paid in government work at the time the bulletin was issued. The Society has about 2500 members, most of whom are engaged in teaching. Many sociologists not in academic work do not as yet belong to the Society. Membership classes are student, associate and active. The requirements are set by the members themselves, and the minimum amount of graduate training specified for active membership is, in effect, the official definition of the professional sociologist. The executive secretary of the American Sociological Society maintains permanent headquarters at the Washington Square Campus of New York University.

◦◦◦

B. Social Work as a Profession *

PERSONAL REQUIREMENTS AND REWARDS

THE SELECTION OF A VOCATION is a matter of individual preference and choice—no more important choice is made in a lifetime. Because it is so important it is essential to know beforehand what one should have to give to the job to make it a good job. What are the personal qualifications that make for success in social work? And what has the job to give to the individual? What are the financial and other rewards that ensue? If there is reciprocity, then both sides know satisfaction and a person may find a profession of which he can be genuinely a part, and to which he responds from "an inner summons."

There are two things that one gives to a job—one's innate qualities and capacities and one's acquired knowledge and skills. Anyone interested in entering a school of social work for professional education should ask himself what he will bring with him in terms of native ability. A keen, flexible mind and common sense are important. With these qualities should be combined a sense of humor and a sense of responsibility. An interest in people, a faith that human beings have within themselves the power to change—these are indispensable. Dealing with people who may not be behaving normally or desirably requires patience, tolerance, adaptability, resourcefulness, and sound

---

* Reprinted with permission from "Social Work as a Profession," revised edition, 1947, published by the American Association of Social Workers.

judgment. It means too, that the social worker himself must be mentally and emotionally well balanced, in good health with a zest for living.

In the realm of the acquired, that which is basic to all kinds of social work is an understanding of the world in which one lives. Economics, sociology, political science, biology, history, psychology, literature—these are the raw materials of which that understanding is formed. The rest of acquired learning that should be brought to the job is the special knowledge and technical skill that is learned in professional schools. Some of it is basic to all kinds of social work, some of it is peculiar to specialized jobs. All of it is the body of known truth that is the nucleus of social work as a profession.

But what about the rewards of social work—its contribution to the lives of those who are dedicated to it?

Social work is not a profession to be selected by those who are ambitious for large financial returns. Nevertheless, the salaries compare favorably with those in teaching and public health nursing; their trend is upward, particularly in the public services; and for those with professional education, a reasonable standard of living is assured.

· · · · · · ·

But it is not the economic advantages, such as they are, that should be the determining factor in leading a person to choose social work as a profession. There are others that will appeal still more strongly to young people of intelligence, vigor, and some insight into the social problems that now beset our modern world. Social work offers an opportunity of rendering a service to the community that is clearly constructive. It is a profession that is still comparatively undeveloped, with much pioneering and working on social frontiers to be done. It gives to those who become proficient in it a broad understanding of the stream of human life about them. It offers rich rewards in warm human associations for those who "like people" and can associate freely and happily with their fellowmen in all walks of life. It is not an easy profession, one to be entered into casually as a means of making a living. But for those who are concerned with a way of life as well as with a vocation it can be challenging and vital in the extreme and can offer great satisfaction in experience and in accomplishment.

EMPLOYMENT OPPORTUNITIES IN SOCIAL WORK

Since social work deals with a wide range of human needs, social workers are employed in many different types of programs and agencies.

Sometimes these are primarily social work agencies, such as county or state public welfare departments or private family and child welfare societies. Sometimes they are other types—schools, hospitals, or courts —to which social workers are attached as specialists. Since ninety per cent of social work is public, many of the opportunities lie with governmental agencies.

Expansion of the public social services has been so rapid that schools of social work have been able to supply only a portion of their personnel needs. Furthermore, the personnel required is increasing because the public social services are still expanding, and new ones are constantly being added. They include all governmental social services, whether local, state, or federal. And since they cover all the major fields of social work, they employ all types of workers—family and child welfare workers, medical and psychiatric workers, as well as those trained in group work, community organizations, and social research. All grades of maturity and experience are needed, from the beginning case worker to the widely experienced executive and administrator. The challenge and opportunity are great, not only because trained leadership in pro-gram-planning and skillful practice may influence the whole develop-ment of public welfare, but because many of the programs are new and policies are still in the making.

The greatest number of social workers is probably employed by county or state welfare departments in the administration of public assistance. But other programs, too, use thousands of workers—child welfare, recreation, and the newer programs like social insurance and housing.

There is increasing recognition of the importance of the quality of service in these far-flung programs that reach from our most congested cities to our most remote rural counties. It is recognized, for instance, that the giving of financial relief is not a mechanical process but a service demanding knowledge, judgment, and skill in understanding the needs of each applicant as a person, and in helping him to deal with the social difficulties that are associated with his economic distress. The social worker who understands the complex psychological problems involved in sickness and dependency can do much to prevent more serious incapacity. Treatment of each applicant as an individual shifts the emphasis from palliative service toward a more vigorous goal, aiming at the greatest possible degree of rehabilitation to active, social life.

In recognition of these truths, the public services for the most part require that those who work in them demonstrate their competence in civil service examinations. Furthermore, training for social work is regarded as an essential for the public assistance and child welfare programs and as having a potential contribution for other programs like the employment services and unemployment insurance.

In reviewing the major social work fields, it becomes evident that for the most part they fall into—Social Case Work, Social Group Work, Community Organization, and Social Research. Social Case Work involves direct service to individuals and families. Social Group Work deals primarily with persons in their group relationships and Community Organization is the method of furthering inter-group relationships toward social ends.

SOCIAL CASE WORK

Some of the areas in which social case workers are most frequently found are family social work, child welfare, medical social work, and psychiatric social work.

Family social work is one of the oldest and most basic types of service. Here the social worker gives assistance in relation to situations where family friction, broken homes, economic distress, personality maladjustments, and similar difficulties are affecting individuals within a family group or the family as a whole. The aim is to build up the strengths of individual personality and family life. Family social work is of special importance because it is here that most of the fundamental case work processes were first defined and that present practice has reached a high level of skilled performance.

Child welfare deals with problems similar to those in family welfare work but focuses upon the needs of the child. Many children live in families that lack the economic security, healthful environment, and affection that every child needs. When the deficiencies are so great that remedial work cannot be done, effort is made to supply a substitute through a foster-home or institutional plan of living. Many agencies and institutions, public and private, have been established for the care and protection of children who are dependent, neglected, delinquent, physically handicapped, and mentally defective, and for children whose physical and moral welfare is endangered by conditions in the home or in the community. Under the leadership of the United States Children's Bureau a child welfare program has in recent years been successfully established to meet the needs of children in rural areas throughout the country. Often the problem is first manifested when the child develops some type of behavior that creates difficulty in the home, the school, or the community. Social workers prepared to deal with these particularly complex problems are employed on the staffs of child guidance clinics, schools, and juvenile courts. School social work, in particular, is a field of interest to social case workers who wish an opportunity to help individual children make creative use of their school experience. It involves counseling with children who are having difficulty in school and with their parents and teachers. Whatever its type, however, child welfare work has strong appeal. The need of the child is great, and it is in childhood that the best preventive work can be done.

Medical social work is practiced under the auspices of a hospital or program of medical care. Medical social workers collaborate with doctors and nurses in meeting social problems related to illness and medical care. Through their efforts, the doctor is helped toward a better understanding of the patient's needs while the patient and his family are aided to solve the difficulties that stand in the way of successful medical treatment and a return to normal living. The medical social worker may be a member of the hospital staff or attached to an agency with a health program covering a whole county or state. Rapid developments in scientific medicine and public health have made medical social work a stimulating field. Before the war there was already a shortage of qualified workers because of the spread of medical social work from the hospital into broader community programs. Now the demands of military medical institutions have increased that shortage.

Psychiatric social work resembles medical social work in that it is always practiced in association with another profession—in this instance, that of psychiatry. Both medical and psychiatric social workers work so closely and continuously with physicians, psychiatrists, nurses, dietitians, psychologists, occupational therapists, and others, that they must be particularly successful at teamwork. While medical social work deals primarily with problems of physical illness, psychiatric social work is concerned with mental illness and defects and the more serious emotional difficulties. From its earliest beginnings in the last war, psychiatric social work has been making a continuous contribution to the rest of social work through a deepening of the understanding of personality and of methods of working with emotionally disturbed persons. Psychiatric social workers have therefore been employed not only in the characteristic environment of the child guidance clinic and mental hospital but also in all types of social case work. War needs now create a special demand for their services in military institutions.

Such, then, are some of the kinds of case work that social workers do. It is impossible to describe them all. Mention should be made, however, of positions of this sort associated with courts and other agencies set up to deal with problems of delinquency. In the formal court setting, the social worker may be a probation officer; in the less formal setting of a children's agency or child guidance clinic he may work with pre-delinquent children. It is a challenging area that is not as yet clearly organized, and those interested in pioneer work will feel its appeal. It is a good field for men since boys and young men predominate among delinquents.

SOCIAL GROUP WORK

Social group work deals primarily with persons in their group relationships. Its greatest development has been in recreational and informal educational activities where the trained social worker functions chiefly as a supervisor of volunteer and paid leaders of groups.[1] Through the use of group work methods, these activities become a potent means for making democratic principles meaningful in daily life. Social workers who have had professional preparation in group work find positions in such organizations as social settlements, community centers, churches, camps, housing projects, and a wide variety of projects sponsored by both public and private agencies and receiving both local and national support. Group workers are employed by the federal government in about sixteen different federal departments or bureaus. They are employed by state and local governments in supervisory positions related to recreational and educational work in parks, playgrounds, and indoor activities. They are also employed by such well-known private organizations as the Boy and Girl Scouts, Y.M.C.A., Y.W.C.A., and Jewish centers. Agencies serving special sections of the population, like foreign-born groups, farm groups, and industrial-worker groups, likewise need workers with this training. New programs that have developed in response to war needs, such as the recreational activities of the United Service Organizations, also need them. In addition, they are wanted by the Red Cross in its extensive recreational programs in Army and Navy hospitals and in mobile field units that go overseas with the armed forces. Both men and women are in demand for group work posts, and promotion is rapid for the well-qualified.

COMMUNITY ORGANIZATION

Some types of social work programs have to do with larger aggregations than those commonly known as "groups"—several groups for

---

[1] Ed. note: In recent years there has been increasing use of the group medium and the group work method in the treatment of socially and emotionally maladjusted children and adults. This is seen as complementary to the individual method of treating such problems.

instance, or a whole community. The social worker who works with these inter-group processes works in the field of community organization. Its method is the furthering of inter-group relationships toward social ends. While all social workers are naturally to some degree working in this area, it is essential that some should be especially trained for it. Such agencies as councils of social agencies, coordinating councils, and councils of defense, have community organization as their primary function. By bringing together representatives of all kinds of agencies, the social worker helps organize for the purpose of welfare planning and of coordination of efforts within a given neighborhood or community. For mature, experienced persons, this is a fascinating and remunerative field.

SOCIAL RESEARCH

Another type of social work, in addition to case work, group work, and community organizations, also deserves mention. That is social research—which offers positions to those who have obtained education and experience in both social work practice and statistical and research methods. While all social workers are continually in touch with social data, it is the primary function of research personnel to bring together facts for purposes of social planning. All types of social agencies, public and private, engage in research. Sometimes this is undertaken as a special survey or study project for the analysis of community needs or for the evaluation of an agency program. Sometimes there is a permanent research department, continually engaged in carrying on various types of investigation. In still other instances, there are social agencies whose primary activity is research. Many social research positions are to be found in national and federal agencies, universities, councils of social agencies, and similar organizations. For the person who combines interest in scientific methods with the wish to keep in touch with vital human problems, social research is stimulating work.

SOCIAL ADMINISTRATION

Still another angle from which the field of social work must be approached in order to appreciate its many opportunities is that of the various grades of responsibility assigned to the personnel within any social agency or program. Education in a school of social work prepares a younger worker to begin usually in giving direct service to persons with one or another kind of need. As the worker becomes more experienced, additional responsibilities are assigned to him. These may be supervision of other workers, teaching, consultant service, or administration. For the latter, because of the complexity of the problems involved in operating an agency or program, special education and experience are needed; and while only the most highly qualified and capable persons may expect to function as administrators, all social workers need to understand the principles of administration and may have opportunity to participate in program-planning and administrative activities.

Whatever the setting within which they work, however, social workers have the same basic purposes and methods. On the one hand, they endeavor to develop the community's resources and programs toward a healthier, more satisfying, and more meaningful way of life for all persons, with a special emphasis upon underprivileged sections of the population. On the other hand, they work directly with individuals and groups in relation to their particular needs and problems, helping them to make more effective use of their own capacities and the community's resources.

Their purpose is to serve both the individual and the community It is an inspiring task whichever field, whichever agency is chosen.

•   •   •   •   •   •

GENERAL EDUCATION

The best foundation for social work is completion of an undergraduate course of study in liberal arts with a group major in the social sciences. Since the social worker is concerned with the whole range and complex of social, economic, and psychological factors which affect the welfare and happiness of individuals, groups, and communities, whatever contributes to the growth of understanding and the broadening and deepening of sympathies is pertinent. Thus, any study of art, literature, science, social science, and philosophy is germane. Some courses relating to the field of social work may also be given at the college level, but experience in schools of social work and in social agencies during the past two decades shows that they should be general and non-technical.

Most of the member schools of the American Association of Schools of Social Work require that applicants for admission show that they have completed a certain amount of study in the social sciences. Some schools also require that a minimum amount of work in the biological sciences has been completed. Economics, political science, psychology, and sociology, including social anthropology, are usually considered the pre-professional subjects most closely related to the social service curriculum. While it is desirable that the student know something about each of these, no one has been designated as more important than the other.

This policy with reference to the social sciences is supported by the membership requirements of the American Association of Social Workers, which specify, in addition to certain minimum professional education, that the applicant must have completed fifteen semester hours of social and biological sciences for junior membership, and twenty semester hours of social and biological sciences for full membership. Sociology, economics, political science, psychology, and anthropology may be offered to meet these social science requirements although certain other courses are acceptable substitutes.

⋙⋙⋙⋙

CORRELATION OF THIS BOOK WITH ELEMENTARY SOCIOLOGY TEXTS

Text chapters	Bennett and Tumin *Social Life* Knopf 1948	Bogardus *Sociology* 3rd ed. Macmillan 1949	Cuber *Sociology* 2nd ed. Appleton-Century-Crofts 1951	Davis *Human Society* Macmillan 1949	Dawson and Gettys *An Introduction to Sociology* 3rd ed. Ronald, 1948
		Related Articles in Outside Readings in Sociology			
1	37, 45, 46	9, 23, 25, 26, 28	1-7	1-4, 7	23-28, 31, 47
2	1, 8, 9, 12-14, 47, 51	10, 11, 19, 35, 44, 58, 90, 91	" "	10	10, 11, 18, 19, 28, 66-72, 87, 90-92 " " " "
3	14, 23, 24	9, 13, 15, 18, 19, 25, 34, 41, 66-68, 73-75, 87	1, 3, 7	11, 24, 35, 36, 47	" " " " " "
4	4, 47, 52, 89, 94	24, 25, 27, 31, 69-77	1, 3, 6, 7	16-22	" " " " " "
5	1-4, 7, 18, 28, 36	20, 21, 29, 33, 34, 41-44, 47, 48, 54-59, 66, 82, 86, Appendix	10	6, 14, 25, 27, 32, 43, 89	13-22
6	11, 15, 17, 19-23	22, 32, 38, 65, 81	8, 44, 67, 70	53, 55-57, 81-84	15, 16, 18, 19, 31, 52, 68, 89
7	11, 15, 17, 19-23, 33, 40, 45	9, 19, 21, 63, 64, 78, 79	10, 20, 67, 87, 90, 91	18, 19, 68	8, 12, 69-77, 87
8	3, 11, 14-20, 48, 53, 83	39, 50-53, 85	35, 36	9, 10, 13, 14, 25, 30, 64	" " " " " "
9	16, 17, 29-33, 50, 54	12, 44-46, 58, 67, 75, 76, 87	10, 20	6, 11, 14, 16, 33, 40, 67	" " " " " "
10	13, 20, 23-28	12, 28, 77, 88, 90-93	8, 10	15, 16, 18, 31, 89, 93	31, 69, 77, 81, 83, 84
11	20, 23-28, 37-39	2, 3, 12, 37, 51, 59-63, 70, 71, 76, 84, 86, 92-94	9, 11, 13	23-26, 28, 29, 31, 32, 77	28, 47, 77

12	35, 36, 49, 51-59, 76, 77	15, 19, 31, 32, 37-39, 59-62, 71, 84, 89	13, 14	66, 67, 69-77	19, 47-68
13	2, 7, 48-50, 53-61, 66, 81, 90	10, 24-26, 29-40, 44-46, 53, 80, 81, 84, 93	9, 20-22, 32, 43	37-39, 65, 81	29, 78-87
14	10, 11, 15, 18, 19, 24	3, 16, 21, 30, 32, 33, 39, 40, 49, 80, 85	16, 22, 34, 38	41-46, 52	12, 88, 90-93
15	34, 35, 44	1, 13, 20, 73, 78-87, 92	15, 16, 89	18, 19, 44, 58, 66-68, 87	44-46, 67, 87
16	8, 10, 15, 18, 19, 28, 35, 44	2-7, 13, 23, 27, 28, 33, 40, 41, 47, 73, Appendix	11, 14, 15, 17, 19, 21, 22, 33, 68	54, 56, 63, 78, 88, 94	" " "
17	5, 6, 9, 13, 14, 16, 40, 67		13, 15, 31	36, 54-59, 61, 62, 82, 86	11, 17-22, 33, 41-43, 80
18	9, 13, 14		23-26, 28, 31, 32	40, 44, 48, 49, 53, 62, 77, 79	24, 25, 31, 32, 52, 53, 84
19	5, 9, 30, 40		19, 27, 45, 46	50-53	69-75, 81-83
20	9, 15, 24, 31, 33, 34		12, 27, 44, 69	8, 12, 24, 59-62	63, 64, 85, 92-94
21	10, 15, 19, 24, 31, 59, 68		12, 27, 66, 69, 75	12, 27, 28, 44, 92	12, 24, 73
22	12, 44, 62, 64-69		66, 71-74	88-94	27, 35, 36, 59-62, 88
23	66, 69, 74, 92		15, 17, 29, 41-45		33, 34, 37-40
24	27, 28, 54, 56, 65, 90-92		15, 18, 19, 68, 87		11, 35, 36, 57, 85, 93, 94
25	37, 44-46, 49		33, 43, 51, 54-58		33, 52, 59-62, 86
26	41-43, 58, 75, 76		49, 53, 57, 79		1-7
27	1-3, 7, 28, 36, 51, 55		38, 63, 64		
28	10, 27, 50, 53, 55, 84, 93		50-53		
29	18, 58, 66-68, 87		20, 28, 30, 39, 40, 78, 79, 81, 92		
30	41-46, 70, 90, 91		26, 36, 61, 65, 89		
31	10, 16, 32-34, 38, 40		39, 43, 79-81, 85-87		
32	10, 39, 40, 63, 76, 79, 80		26, 37, 79-81, 83, 87		
33	5, 7, 15, 25, 26, 32, 35		36, 51, 53, 54, 59, 62, 68-70		

CORRELATION OF THIS BOOK WITH ELEMENTARY SOCIOLOGY TEXTS (Continued)

Related Articles in Outside Readings in Sociology

Text chapters	Eldridge and Associates Fundamentals of Sociology Crowell 1950	Gillin and Gillin Cultural Sociology Macmillan 1948	Jones Basic Sociological Principles Ginn 1949	Landis Man in Environment Crowell 1949	MacIver and Page Society Rinehart 1949
1	4-6	1-7	2-10, 13	2, 3, 7, 95, 96, Appendix	1-4, 20, 24, 27, 35, 47, 77
2	9, 28	90-93	3, 5-7	—	5, 6, 14-16, 24, 32
3	2, 3, 7, 59-62	45, 46	2, 7, 10, 56, 82, 92, Appendix	13	9, 10, 13, 14, 37, 44, 52, 83-85
4	11, 24	8, 9, 13	13, 23, 25, 26, 28, 77	1, 9, 78-80	9, 13, 14
5	10	12	8, 9, 13, 27, 71, 93	11	9, 12, 28, 71, 88
6	10, 88, 92	10, 11, 44, 94	10, 11, 17, 21, 24, 35, 36, 64, 87, 88, 90-92	8	4, 8, 10, 28, 36, 44
7	88	" " " "	12, 27, 43, 49, 56, 69, 72, 74, 87	23, 25, 26, 28	6, 10, 11, 15, 16, 25, 26, 29-31, 35, 36
8	31, 88, 89, 92-94	23, 26, 28, 29, 32	11, 37, 43-46, 58, 67, 75, 87	5, 6, 24, 37-39	17, 25, 26, 30, 37, 39, 50-54
9	8	13, 25, 66-68, 87	9, 13-22, 25, 32, 33	27, 44, 69, 70, 72-75, 77	5, 11, 14, 18, 25, 26, 34, 79, 89
10	—	18, 19	23-36, 41, 54, 70, 77, 93	15	20, 23-26, 28, 77, 92
11	27, 54, 69, 70, 77	27, 37, 39, 69-75	—	45, 46	11, 17, 18, 25, 60, 66-68, 87

12	71-75	9, 11, 13, 15, 18, 19, 25, 41, 58, 66-68	14, 17, 21, 22	20, 27, 31, 44, 69-71, 74, 75
13	70, 71, 76	33, 39, 41-45, 54-58, 86, 90, 91, 93	16, 18, 19	39, 44, 65, 69-75
14	12	3, 11, 39, 50-53, 85	66-68	5, 11, 15, 37, 41-45
15	58	19, 21, 63, 64, 78, 79	63, 64	15, 44-46, 87
16	24	29-31, 40, 47-49, 53, 57, 84, 93	47-49	32, 37, 52, 63, 78, 81, 93
17	49	5, 37, 41-45, 54, 57, 82-84, 89, 93	50-53	28, 31, 57, 60, 62, 77, 86
18	58	" " " " " "	54, 55, 57, 58, 65	40, 53, 77, 88, 90, 91, 93
19	1, 78-80	43, 46, 85-87	59-62	33, 34, 54-58, 73, 86
20	82-86	3, 28, 71, 88, 90, 91, 94	93	44, 50-53, 63, 64
21	46, 87	31, 37, 47, 53, 84	41, 42, 56	4, 10, 51, 53, 55, 76, 79, 92
22	30, 32, 33, 37-40	" " " " "	43, 46	4, 12, 25, 35, 36, 64, 88, 89
23	5, 6, 81	15, 16, 39, 45, 55, 59-62, 71, 75, 89, 93 — 87, Appendix B	82-87	18, 28, 34, 36, 42, 54, 61
24	34-36	2, 3, 12, 71, 94	32, 34, 35, 81	12, 21, 44, 49, 60, 62
25	66-68		29, 31, 36, 40, 76	34, 36, 42, 54, 57, 71, 88
26	55-58		10	4, 10, 26, 36, 79
27	63, 64		88	50, 51
28	50-53		91, 92	25, 28, 72, 93
29	47-49		20, 95	7, 18, 29, 51, 90, 94
30	13, 14, 17		12	
31	16, 20-22		30, 33	
32	15, 18, 19, 23, 25, 26, 41-46		89	
33	65, 90, 91			
34	90, 94		71, 94	

CORRELATION OF THIS BOOK WITH ELEMENTARY SOCIOLOGY TEXTS (Continued)

Text chapters	McCormick Sociology Ronald 1950	Merrill and Eldredge Culture and Society Prentice-Hall 1952	Ogburn and Nimkoff Sociology 2nd ed. Houghton Mifflin 1950	Sutherland, Woodward, and Maxwell Introductory Sociology 4th ed. Lippincott, 1952	Young Sociology American Book Co. 1949
			Related Articles in Outside Readings in Sociology		
1	9, 13	1-3, 4, 7	1-3, 5-7, 13	1-7, Appendix	1-7
2	14-22, 25, 26	13, 23, 25, 26, 28, 31, 35	" " " "	4, 10, 11, 35, 36	8, 10, 11, 18, 19, 35
3		8, 10, 34, 39	4, 10, 11, 35, 36	" " " " "	8, 11, 19, 20, 30, 35, 44, 66-72
4	23, 24, 34-36, 81	35, 90-92	9	11, 44, 50, 58, 66, 67	14, 17, 21, 22, 37, 40, 41, 44, 46, 57, 80-83
5	28, 29, 31	8, 11, 18, 19, 36, 68	8	" " " "	" " " " "
6	5, 6, 47, 48, 57, 83-86, 89	19, 24, 50, 61, 88	23-33, 80, 81	9, 13	9, 13
7	41, 42, 44	5, 6, 13-15, 20, 22, 33	37-40, 52, 78, 79, 84	14, 25, 26	5, 9, 11, 13-22, 26, 35,
8	44	11, 16, 17, 19, 21, 29, 32	41-46, 56	17-22	85, 89, " " " "
9	20, 24, 43, 46, 49	13, 15, 30, 40, 42, 46, 52, 85	27, 30, 37, 56, 57, 59-62, 82-86, 93	" "	" " " " "
10	45	9, 15, 32, 89, 93	29, 31, 32, 46, 87	15, 16	8, 10, 12
11	32	12, 70-72	9	78-82, 85, 86	45, 46
12	10, 11, 68	45, 46, 91	14, 16, 17, 20-22	29, 31, 37, 46, 83, 84, 87, 93	8, 12, 73, 94
13	8, 12	44-46	11, 15, 17-19, 34	23-34	18, 19, 41, 44, 45, 72

14	10, 11, 44, 58, 87, 90, 91	41-43, 52	15, 68, 89	32, 37-39, 84	25-27, 58, 66-70, 81
15	87, 88, 92	78-81, 83	27, 69-77, 81	12, 41-44, 56, 77, 90-92	65, 71-75, 77, 94
16	58, 66, 68	33, 37-39, 63, 84	12	45, 46	12, 27, 28, 73, 76, 90, 91
17	" " "	57, 59, 60, 79, 93	"	12, 73-75	11, 15-19, 24, 25, 43, 46, 66-68, 73, 87
18	27, 69, 70, 73, 74	30, 33, 40, 49, 51, 62	4, 47, 48	24, 27, 69-72, 76, 90	" " " " "
19	71, 72, 75	36, 47-49, 77	34, 43, 48, 54-58, 80	47-49, 54-58	21, 25, 30, 33, 41, 63, 64, 79, 83
20	50-53	66, 69-72	47-49, 53, 57, 77, 84	30, 63, 64	50-53, 55, 85, 92
21	21, 65, 66, 78-80	65, 73-75	12, 77, 90-92	50-53	22, 35, 47, 56, 63, 65, 92
22	90, 91, 93	18, 19, 25, 53, 60, 67, 68, 87	50-53	59-62, 65	24, 33, 34, 43, 48, 54-58, 78, 80, 82, 86, 90, 94
23	" " "	" " " " "	11, 15, 18, 19, 66-68	11, 15, 18, 19, 66-68	40, 47-49, 57-62, 79, 81, 84, 88, 90, 93
24	54, 59-62	48-58, 63-65, 76, 77	64, 65, 88	8, 12, 88	27, 28, 88, 90-94
25	37-40, 62, 81, 84, 86	43, 53, 55, 57, 82-86	92	" " "	11, 13-15, 17-24, 33, 43, 66-68
26	30, 32, 33	89, 92, 93	88	33, 78, 79, 89 "	" " " " "
27		56, 69, 76, 79, 88, 90, 94	89		30-34, 37, 40, 54, 56, 63, 84
28		71-74	2, 59-62, 93-94	81, 93, 94	41-46, 49, 52, 56, 58, 80, 83
29		3, 90, 92, 94			11, 20, 21, 25, 26, 30, 34, 35, 40, 47, 48, 53, 57, 79-81, 89, 93
30					10, 24, 59-62, 74, 76, 87, 88, 92-94
31					2, 12, 73, 88, 90-94
32					2, 3, 40, 92-94

INDEX